Seventh Workshop on Noisy User-generated Text (W-NUT 2021)

Online
11 November 2021

ISBN: 978-1-7138-9166-6

Printed from e-media with permission by:

Curran Associates, Inc.
57 Morehouse Lane
Red Hook, NY 12571

proceedings.com

Some format issues inherent in the e-media version may also appear in this print version.

Printed with permission by Curran Associates, Inc. (2024)

Association for Computational Linguistics
209 N. Eighth Street
Stroudsburg, Pennsylvania 18360

Phone: 1-570-476-8006
Fax: 1-570-476-0860

acl@aclweb.org

Additional copies of this publication are available from:

Curran Associates, Inc.
57 Morehouse Lane
Red Hook, NY 12571 USA
Phone: 845-758-0400
Fax: 845-758-2633
Email: curran@proceedings.com
Web: www.proceedings.com

W-NUT 2021

The Seventh Workshop on Noisy User-generated Text (W-NUT 2021)

Proceedings of the Conference

Nov 11, 2021
Online

Introduction

The W-NUT 2021 workshop focuses on a core set of natural language processing tasks on top of noisy user-generated text, such as that found on social media, web forums and online reviews. Recent years have seen a significant increase of interest in these areas. The internet has democratized content creation leading to an explosion of informal user-generated text, publicly available in electronic format, motivating the need for NLP on noisy text to enable new data analytics applications.

This year, in addition to the main workshop track, we have one shared task, MultiLexNorm: Multilingual Lexical Normalization. We have received 69 main workshop submissions (38 long and 31 short papers). The workshop will be held online and live in two different time zones (GMT– and GMT++). We have two invited speakers in GMT–, Zornitsa Kozareva (Google) Thamar Solorio (University of Houston), and two invited speakers in GMT++, Vivian Chen (National Taiwan University) and Zhiyuan Liu (Tsinghua University) who will talk about their work. We're very thankful to have them in our workshop.

We have the best paper award(s) sponsored by Bloomberg this year, for which we are thankful. We would like to thank the Program Committee members who reviewed the papers and the shared task organizers who enriched our workshop this year. We would also like to thank the workshop participants.

Wei Xu, Alan Ritter, Tim Baldwin and Afshin Rahimi
Co-Organizers

Organizers:

Wei Xu, Ohio State University
Alan Ritter, Ohio State University
Tim Baldwin, University of Melbourne
Afshin Rahimi, University of Queensland

Program Committee:

Muhammad Abdul-Mageed (University of British Columbia)
Željko Agić (Corti)
Sweta Agrawal (University of Maryland)
Gustavo Aguilar (Amazon)
Hamed Alhoori (Northern Illinois University)
Emily Allaway (Columbia University)
Hadi Amiri (University of Massachusetts, Lowell)
Antonios Anastasopoulos (George Mason University)
Maria Antoniak (Cornell University)
Rahul Aralikatte (University of Copenhagen)
Eiji Aramaki (NAIST)
Pepa Atanasova (University of Copenhagen)
Ashutosh Baheti (Georgia Institute of Technology)
JinYeong Bak (SungKyunKwan University)
Kalika Bali (Microsoft Research)
Francesco Barbieri (Snap)
Elisa Bassignana (IT University of Copenhagen)
Adrian Benton (JHU)
Eduardo Blanco (University of North Texas)
Marcel Bollmann (Jönköping University)
Marco Brambilla (Politecnico di Milano)
Julian Brooke (University of British Columbia)
Cornelia Caragea (University of Illinois at Chicago)
Tuhin Chakrabarty (Columbia University)
Tanmoy Chakraborty (Indraprastha Institute of Information Technology, Delhi)
Ilias Chalkidis (University of Copenhagen)
Sihao Chen (University of Pennsylvania)
Colin Cherry (Google)
Dhivya Chinnappa (Thomson Reuters)
Monojit Choudhury (Microsoft Research)
Zewei Chu (University of Chicago)
Manuel R. Ciosici (IT University of Copenhagen)
Çağrı Çöltekin (University of Tübingen)
Danilo Croce (University of Rome)
Marina Danilevsky (IBM Research)
Pradipto Das (Rakuten Institute of Technology)
A. Seza Doğruöz (Universiteit Gent)
Xinya Du (Cornell University)
Heba Elfardy (Amazon)
Mai ElSherief (University of California, San Diego)

Micha Elsner (Ohio State University)
Alexander Fabbri (Yale University)
Manaal Faruqui (Google)
Song Feng (IBM Research)
Yansong Feng (Peking University)
Francis Ferraro (University of Maryland, Baltimore Countys)
Catherine Finegan-Dollak (IBM Research)
Lucie Flek (University of Marburg)
Lisheng Fu (Amazon)
Yoshinari Fujinuma (University of Colorado, Boulder)
Wei Gao (Singapore Management University)
Sahil Garg (University of Southern California)
Dan Garrette (Google)
Spandana Gella (Amazon)
Tirthankar Ghosal (Charles University)
Dan Goldwasser (Purdue University)
Amit Goyal (Amazon)
Yvette Graham (Dublin City University)
Chulaka Gunasekara (IBM Research)
Cathal Gurrin (Dublin City University)
Xiaochuang Han (Carnegie Mellon University)
Jonathan Herzig (Tel-Aviv University)
Jack Hessel (AI2)
Md Mosharaf Hossain (University of North Texas)
Diana Inkpen (University of Ottawa)
Kokil Jaidka (National University of Singapore)
Yangfeng Ji (University of Virginia)
Jing Jiang (Singapore Management University)
Nanjiang Jiang (Ohio State University)
Chao Jiang (Georgia Institute of Technology)
Lifeng Jin (Ohio State University)
Ishan Jindal (IBM Research)
Kristen Johnson (Michigan State University)
Gareth Jones (Dublin City University)
David Jurgens (University of Michigan)
Preethi Jyothi (IIT Bombay)
Katharina Kann (University of Colorado, Boulder)
Ashkan Kazemi (University of Michigan)
Ashique KhudaBukhsh (Carnegie Mellon University)
Gunhee Kim (Seoul National University)
Bennett Kleinberg (Tilburg University)
Roman Klinger (University of Stuttgart)
Zornitsa Kozareva (Facebook)
Reno Kriz (University of Pennsylvania)
Vivek Kulkarni (Stanford University)
Jonathan Kummerfeld (University of Michigan)
Tsung-Ting Kuo (University of California, San Diego)
Vasileios Lampos (University College London)
Wuwei Lan (Ohio State University)
Jiwei Li (ShannonAI)
Jessy Junyi Li (University of Texas Austin)

Jing Li (Hong Kong Polytechnic University)
Yitong Li (University of Melbourne)
Kwan Hui Lim (Singapore University of Technology and Design)
Nut Limsopatham (Microsoft Research)
Lucy Lin (University of Washington)
Fei Liu (University of Melbourne)
Yiqun Liu (Tsinghua University)
Nikola Ljubešić (Jožef Stefan Institute)
Mounica Maddela (Georgia Institute of Technology)
Bodhisattwa Prasad Majumder (University of California, San Diego)
David Mimno (Cornell University)
Shachar Mirkin (Digimind)
Yasuhide Miura (Fuji/Xerox)
Manuel Montes (National Institute of Astrophysics, Mexico)
Ahmed Mourad (RMIT University)
Maximilian Mozes (University College London)
Hamdy Mubarak (Qatar Computing Research Institute)
Graham Mueller (Leidos)
Animesh Mukherjee (IIT Kharagpur)
Maria Nadejde (Grammarly)
Preslav Nakov (Qatar Computing Research Institute)
Guenter Neumann (German Research Center for Artificial Intelligence)
Vincent Ng (University of Texas at Dallas)
Thien Huu Nguyen (University of Oregon)
Dat Quoc Nguyen (VinAI Research)
Eric Nichols (Honda Research Institute)
Brendan O'Connor (University of Massachusetts, Amherst)
Alice Oh (KAIST)
Naoaki Okazaki (Tohoku University)
Naoki Otani (CMU)
Symeon Papadopoulos (CERTH-ITI)
Yuval Pinter (Georgia Tech)
Barbara Plank (IT University of Copenhagen)
Matt Post (Johns Hopkins University)
Vinodkumar Prabhakaran (Stanford University)
Daniel Preoţiuc-Pietro (Bloomberg)
Dianna Radpour (University of Colorado Boulder)
Preethi Raghavan (IBM Research)
Afshin Rahimi (University of Queensland)
Sudha Rao (Microsoft Research)
Hannah Rashkin (Google)
Sravana Reddy (ASAPP)
Roi Reichart (Technion - Israel Institute of Technology.)
Adithya Renduchintala (Facebook AI)
Anthony Rios (The University of Texas at San Antonio)
Paolo Rosso (Universitat Politècnica de València)
Alla Rozovskaya (City University of New York)
Mirco Schoenfeld (University of Bayreuth)
Djamé Seddah (University Paris-Sorbonne)
Ori Shapira (Bar-Ilan University)
Ashish Sharma (University of Washington)

Dan Simonson (BlackBoiler)
Kevin Small (Amazon)
Xingyi Song (University of Sheffield)
Andreas Spitz (University of Konstanz)
Richard Sproat (Google)
Gabriel Stanovsky (Allen Institute for Artificial Intelligence)
Ian Stewart (University of Michigan)
Sara Stymne (Uppsala University)
Danae Sánchez Villegas (University of Sheffield)
Zeerak Talat (University of Sheffield)
Zhiyang Teng (Westlake University)
James Thorne (University of Cambridge)
Marc Tomlinson (Language Computer Corporation)
Sara Tonelli (FBK)
Rob van der Goot (University of Groningen)
Vasudeva Varma (IIIT Hyderabad)
Daniel Varab (IT University of Copenhagen)
Olga Vechtomova (University of Waterloo)
Rob Voigt (Northwestern University)
Soroush Vosoughi (Dartmouth University)
Thanh Vu (Oracle)
Xiaojun Wan (Peking University)
Hong Wei (University of Maryland)
Zhongyu Wei (Fudan University)
Roman Yangarber (University of Helsinki)
Ziyu Yao (George Mason University)
Ning Yu (Leidos)
Nasser Zalmout (Amazon)
Marcos Zampieri (Rochester Institute of Technology)
Vicky Zayats (University of Washington)
Chiyu Zhang (University of British Columbia)
Xiao Cosmo Zhang (Amazon)
Mike Zhang (IT University of Copenhagen)
Ayah Zirikly (Johns Hopkins University)
Shi Zong (Nanjing University)

Invited Speakers:

Zornitsa Kozareva (Google)
Thamar Solorio (University of Houston)
Vivian Chen (National Taiwan University)
Zhiyuan Liu (Tsinghua University)

Table of Contents

Text Simplification for Comprehension-based Question-Answering
Tanvi Dadu, Kartikey Pant, Seema Nagar, Ferdous Barbhuiya and Kuntal Dey 1

Finding the needle in a haystack: Extraction of Informative COVID-19 Danish Tweets
Benjamin Olsen and Barbara Plank 11

Detecting Depression in Thai Blog Posts: a Dataset and a Baseline
Mika Hämäläinen, Pattama Patpong, Khalid Alnajjar, Niko Partanen and Jack Rueter 20

Keyphrase Extraction with Incomplete Annotated Training Data
Yanfei Lei, Chunming Hu, Guanghui Ma and Richong Zhang 26

Fine-grained Temporal Relation Extraction with Ordered-Neuron LSTM and Graph Convolutional Networks
Minh Tran Phu, Minh Van Nguyen and Thien Huu Nguyen 35

Does It Happen? Multi-hop Path Structures for Event Factuality Prediction with Graph Transformer Networks
Duong Le and Thien Huu Nguyen 46

Google-trickers, Yaminjeongeum, and Leetspeak: An Empirical Taxonomy for Intentionally Noisy User-Generated Text
Won Ik Cho and Soomin Kim 56

Description-based Label Attention Classifier for Explainable ICD-9 Classification
Malte Feucht, Zhiliang Wu, Sophia Althammer and Volker Tresp 62

A Text Editing Approach to Joint Japanese Word Segmentation, POS Tagging, and Lexical Normalization
Shohei Higashiyama, Masao Utiyama, Taro Watanabe and Eiichiro Sumita 67

Intrinsic evaluation of language models for code-switching
Sik Feng Cheong, Hai Leong Chieu and Jing Lim 81

Can images help recognize entities? A study of the role of images for Multimodal NER
Shuguang Chen, Gustavo Aguilar, Leonardo Neves and Thamar Solorio 87

Perceived and Intended Sarcasm Detection with Graph Attention Networks
Joan Plepi and Lucie Flek 97

Hierarchical Character Tagger for Short Text Spelling Error Correction
Mengyi Gao, Canran Xu and Peng Shi 106

Common Sense Bias in Semantic Role Labeling
Heather Lent and Anders Søgaard 114

PoliWAM: An Exploration of a Large Scale Corpus of Political Discussions on WhatsApp Messenger
Vivek Srivastava and Mayank Singh 120

ParsTwiNER: A Corpus for Named Entity Recognition at Informal Persian
MohammadMahdi Aghajani, AliAkbar Badri and Hamid Beigy 131

DreamDrug - A crowdsourced NER dataset for detecting drugs in darknet markets
Johannes Bogensperger, Sven Schlarb, Allan Hanbury and Gábor Recski 137

Comparing Grammatical Theories of Code-Mixing
Adithya Pratapa and Monojit Choudhury 158

Improving Punctuation Restoration for Speech Transcripts via External Data
Xue-Yong Fu, Cheng Chen, Md Tahmid Rahman Laskar, Shashi Bhushan and Simon Corston-Oliver 168

Learning to Rank Question Answer Pairs with Bilateral Contrastive Data Augmentation
Yang Deng, Wenxuan Zhang and Wai Lam 175

Mitigation of Diachronic Bias in Fake News Detection Dataset
Taichi Murayama, Shoko Wakamiya and Eiji ARAMAKI 182

Understanding the Impact of UGC Specificities on Translation Quality
José Carlos Rosales Núñez, Djamé Seddah and Guillaume Wisniewski 189

Noisy UGC Translation at the Character Level: Revisiting Open-Vocabulary Capabilities and Robustness of Char-Based Models
José Carlos Rosales Núñez, Guillaume Wisniewski and Djamé Seddah 199

Changes in Twitter geolocations: Insights and suggestions for future usage
Anna Kruspe, Matthias Häberle, Eike J. Hoffmann, Samyo Rode-Hasinger, Karam Abdulahhad and Xiao Xiang Zhu 212

ConQuest: Contextual Question Paraphrasing through Answer-Aware Synthetic Question Generation
Mostafa Mirshekari, Jing Gu and Aaron Sisto 222

NADE: A Benchmark for Robust Adverse Drug Events Extraction in Face of Negations
Simone Scaboro, Beatrice Portelli, Emmanuele Chersoni, Enrico Santus and Giuseppe Serra . . 230

SpanAlign: Efficient Sequence Tagging Annotation Projection into Translated Data applied to Cross-Lingual Opinion Mining
Léo Jacqmin, Gabriel Marzinotto, Justyna Gromada, Ewelina Szczekocka, Robert Kołodyński and Géraldine Damnati 238

A Novel Framework for Detecting Important Subevents from Crisis Events via Dynamic Semantic Graphs
Evangelia Spiliopoulou, Tanay Kumar Saha, Joel Tetreault and Alejandro Jaimes 249

Synthetic Data Generation and Multi-Task Learning for Extracting Temporal Information from Health-Related Narrative Text
Heereen Shim, Dietwig Lowet, Stijn Luca and Bart Vanrumste 260

Neural-based RST Parsing And Analysis In Persuasive Discourse
Jinfen Li and Lu Xiao 274

BART for Post-Correction of OCR Newspaper Text
Elizabeth Soper, Stanley Fujimoto and Yen-Yun Yu 284

Coping with Noisy Training Data Labels in Paraphrase Detection
Teemu Vahtola, Mathias Creutz, Eetu Sjöblom and Sami Itkonen 291

Knowledge Distillation with Noisy Labels for Natural Language Understanding
Shivendra Bhardwaj, Abbas Ghaddar, Ahmad Rashid, Khalil Bibi, Chengyang Li, Ali Ghodsi, Phillippe Langlais and Mehdi Rezagholizadeh 297

Integrating Transformers and Knowledge Graphs for Twitter Stance Detection
Thomas Clark, Costanza Conforti, Fangyu Liu, Zaiqiao Meng, Ehsan Shareghi and Nigel Collier
304

Detecting Cross-Geographic Biases in Toxicity Modeling on Social Media
Sayan Ghosh, Dylan Baker, David Jurgens and Vinodkumar Prabhakaran 313

Detection of Puffery on the English Wikipedia
Amanda Bertsch and Steven Bethard 329

Robustness and Sensitivity of BERT Models Predicting Alzheimer's Disease from Text
Jekaterina Novikova 334

Understanding Model Robustness to User-generated Noisy Texts
Jakub Náplava, Martin Popel, Milan Straka and Jana Straková 340

CIDEr-R: Robust Consensus-based Image Description Evaluation
Gabriel Oliveira dos Santos, Esther Luna Colombini and Sandra Avila 351

Improved Named Entity Recognition for Noisy Call Center Transcripts
Sam Davidson, Jordan Hosier, Yu Zhou and Vijay Gurbani 361

Contrapositive Local Class Inference
Omid Kashefi and Rebecca Hwa 371

Improved Multilingual Language Model Pretraining for Social Media Text via Translation Pair Prediction
Shubhanshu Mishra and Aria Haghighi 381

Co-training for Commit Classification
Jian Yi David Lee and Hai Leong Chieu 389

Study of Manifestation of Civil Unrest on Twitter
Abhinav Chinta, Jingyu Zhang, Alexandra DeLucia, Mark Dredze and Anna L. Buczak 396

The Korean Morphologically Tight-Fitting Tokenizer for Noisy User-Generated Texts
Sangah Lee and Hyopil Shin 410

Character Transformations for Non-Autoregressive GEC Tagging
Milan Straka, Jakub Náplava and Jana Straková 417

Can Character-based Language Models Improve Downstream Task Performances In Low-Resource And Noisy Language Scenarios?
Arij riabi, Benoît Sagot and Djamé Seddah 423

"Something Something Hota Hai!" An Explainable Approach towards Sentiment Analysis on Indian Code-Mixed Data
Aman Priyanshu, Aleti Vardhan, Sudarshan Sivakumar, Supriti Vijay and Nipuna Chhabra 437

BERTweetFR : Domain Adaptation of Pre-Trained Language Models for French Tweets
Yanzhu Guo, Virgile Rennard, Christos Xypolopoulos and Michalis Vazirgiannis 445

To What Extent Does Lexical Normalization Help English-as-a-Second Language Learners to Read Noisy English Texts?
Yo Ehara 451

Multilingual Sequence Labeling Approach to solve Lexical Normalization
Divesh Kubal and Apurva Nagvenkar 457

Sesame Street to Mount Sinai: BERT-constrained character-level Moses models for multilingual lexical normalization
Yves Scherrer and Nikola Ljubešić 465

Sequence-to-Sequence Lexical Normalization with Multilingual Transformers
Ana-Maria Bucur, Adrian Cosma and Liviu P. Dinu 473

ÚFAL at MultiLexNorm 2021: Improving Multilingual Lexical Normalization by Fine-tuning ByT5
David Samuel and Milan Straka 483

MultiLexNorm: A Shared Task on Multilingual Lexical Normalization
Rob van der Goot, Alan Ramponi, Arkaitz Zubiaga, Barbara Plank, Benjamin Muller, Iñaki San Vicente Roncal, Nikola Ljubešić, Özlem Çetinoğlu, Rahmad Mahendra, Talha Çolakoğlu, Timothy Baldwin, Tommaso Caselli and Wladimir Sidorenko 493

CL-MoNoise: Cross-lingual Lexical Normalization
Rob van der Goot 510

Conference Program

44511

12:00–12:00 Session WNUT: WNUT

Text Simplification for Comprehension-based Question-Answering
Tanvi Dadu, Kartikey Pant, Seema Nagar, Ferdous Barbhuiya and Kuntal Dey

Finding the needle in a haystack: Extraction of Informative COVID-19 Danish Tweets
Benjamin Olsen and Barbara Plank

Detecting Depression in Thai Blog Posts: a Dataset and a Baseline
Mika Hämäläinen, Pattama Patpong, Khalid Alnajjar, Niko Partanen and Jack Rueter

Keyphrase Extraction with Incomplete Annotated Training Data
Yanfei Lei, Chunming Hu, Guanghui Ma and Richong Zhang

Fine-grained Temporal Relation Extraction with Ordered-Neuron LSTM and Graph Convolutional Networks
Minh Tran Phu, Minh Van Nguyen and Thien Huu Nguyen

Does It Happen? Multi-hop Path Structures for Event Factuality Prediction with Graph Transformer Networks
Duong Le and Thien Huu Nguyen

Google-trickers, Yaminjeongeum, and Leetspeak: An Empirical Taxonomy for Intentionally Noisy User-Generated Text
Won Ik Cho and Soomin Kim

Description-based Label Attention Classifier for Explainable ICD-9 Classification
Malte Feucht, Zhiliang Wu, Sophia Althammer and Volker Tresp

A Text Editing Approach to Joint Japanese Word Segmentation, POS Tagging, and Lexical Normalization
Shohei Higashiyama, Masao Utiyama, Taro Watanabe and Eiichiro Sumita

Intrinsic evaluation of language models for code-switching
Sik Feng Cheong, Hai Leong Chieu and Jing Lim

44511 (continued)

Can images help recognize entities? A study of the role of images for Multimodal NER
Shuguang Chen, Gustavo Aguilar, Leonardo Neves and Thamar Solorio

Perceived and Intended Sarcasm Detection with Graph Attention Networks
Joan Plepi and Lucie Flek

Hierarchical Character Tagger for Short Text Spelling Error Correction
Mengyi Gao, Canran Xu and Peng Shi

Common Sense Bias in Semantic Role Labeling
Heather Lent and Anders Søgaard

PoliWAM: An Exploration of a Large Scale Corpus of Political Discussions on WhatsApp Messenger
Vivek Srivastava and Mayank Singh

ParsTwiNER: A Corpus for Named Entity Recognition at Informal Persian
MohammadMahdi Aghajani, AliAkbar Badri and Hamid Beigy

DreamDrug - A crowdsourced NER dataset for detecting drugs in darknet markets
Johannes Bogensperger, Sven Schlarb, Allan Hanbury and Gábor Recski

Comparing Grammatical Theories of Code-Mixing
Adithya Pratapa and Monojit Choudhury

Improving Punctuation Restoration for Speech Transcripts via External Data
Xue-Yong Fu, Cheng Chen, Md Tahmid Rahman Laskar, Shashi Bhushan and Simon Corston-Oliver

Learning to Rank Question Answer Pairs with Bilateral Contrastive Data Augmentation
Yang Deng, Wenxuan Zhang and Wai Lam

Mitigation of Diachronic Bias in Fake News Detection Dataset
Taichi Murayama, Shoko Wakamiya and Eiji ARAMAKI

Understanding the Impact of UGC Specificities on Translation Quality
José Carlos Rosales Núñez, Djamé Seddah and Guillaume Wisniewski

44511 (continued)

Noisy UGC Translation at the Character Level: Revisiting Open-Vocabulary Capabilities and Robustness of Char-Based Models
José Carlos Rosales Núñez, Guillaume Wisniewski and Djamé Seddah

Changes in Twitter geolocations: Insights and suggestions for future usage
Anna Kruspe, Matthias Häberle, Eike J. Hoffmann, Samyo Rode-Hasinger, Karam Abdulahhad and Xiao Xiang Zhu

ConQuest: Contextual Question Paraphrasing through Answer-Aware Synthetic Question Generation
Mostafa Mirshekari, Jing Gu and Aaron Sisto

NADE: A Benchmark for Robust Adverse Drug Events Extraction in Face of Negations
Simone Scaboro, Beatrice Portelli, Emmanuele Chersoni, Enrico Santus and Giuseppe Serra

SpanAlign: Efficient Sequence Tagging Annotation Projection into Translated Data applied to Cross-Lingual Opinion Mining
Léo Jacqmin, Gabriel Marzinotto, Justyna Gromada, Ewelina Szczekocka, Robert Kołodyński and Géraldine Damnati

A Novel Framework for Detecting Important Subevents from Crisis Events via Dynamic Semantic Graphs
Evangelia Spiliopoulou, Tanay Kumar Saha, Joel Tetreault and Alejandro Jaimes

Synthetic Data Generation and Multi-Task Learning for Extracting Temporal Information from Health-Related Narrative Text
Heereen Shim, Dietwig Lowet, Stijn Luca and Bart Vanrumste

Neural-based RST Parsing And Analysis In Persuasive Discourse
Jinfen Li and Lu Xiao

BART for Post-Correction of OCR Newspaper Text
Elizabeth Soper, Stanley Fujimoto and Yen-Yun Yu

Coping with Noisy Training Data Labels in Paraphrase Detection
Teemu Vahtola, Mathias Creutz, Eetu Sjöblom and Sami Itkonen

Knowledge Distillation with Noisy Labels for Natural Language Understanding
Shivendra Bhardwaj, Abbas Ghaddar, Ahmad Rashid, Khalil Bibi, Chengyang Li, Ali Ghodsi, Phillippe Langlais and Mehdi Rezagholizadeh

Integrating Transformers and Knowledge Graphs for Twitter Stance Detection
Thomas Clark, Costanza Conforti, Fangyu Liu, Zaiqiao Meng, Ehsan Shareghi and Nigel Collier

44511 (continued)

Detecting Cross-Geographic Biases in Toxicity Modeling on Social Media
Sayan Ghosh, Dylan Baker, David Jurgens and Vinodkumar Prabhakaran

Detection of Puffery on the English Wikipedia
Amanda Bertsch and Steven Bethard

Robustness and Sensitivity of BERT Models Predicting Alzheimer's Disease from Text
Jekaterina Novikova

Understanding Model Robustness to User-generated Noisy Texts
Jakub Náplava, Martin Popel, Milan Straka and Jana Straková

CIDEr-R: Robust Consensus-based Image Description Evaluation
Gabriel Oliveira dos Santos, Esther Luna Colombini and Sandra Avila

Improved Named Entity Recognition for Noisy Call Center Transcripts
Sam Davidson, Jordan Hosier, Yu Zhou and Vijay Gurbani

Contrapositive Local Class Inference
Omid Kashefi and Rebecca Hwa

Improved Multilingual Language Model Pretraining for Social Media Text via Translation Pair Prediction
Shubhanshu Mishra and Aria Haghighi

Co-training for Commit Classification
Jian Yi David Lee and Hai Leong Chieu

Study of Manifestation of Civil Unrest on Twitter
Abhinav Chinta, Jingyu Zhang, Alexandra DeLucia, Mark Dredze and Anna L. Buczak

The Korean Morphologically Tight-Fitting Tokenizer for Noisy User-Generated Texts
Sangah Lee and Hyopil Shin

Character Transformations for Non-Autoregressive GEC Tagging
Milan Straka, Jakub Náplava and Jana Straková

44511 (continued)

Can Character-based Language Models Improve Downstream Task Performances In Low-Resource And Noisy Language Scenarios?
Arij riabi, Benoît Sagot and Djamé Seddah

"Something Something Hota Hai!" An Explainable Approach towards Sentiment Analysis on Indian Code-Mixed Data
Aman Priyanshu, Aleti Vardhan, Sudarshan Sivakumar, Supriti Vijay and Nipuna Chhabra

BERTweetFR : Domain Adaptation of Pre-Trained Language Models for French Tweets
Yanzhu Guo, Virgile Rennard, Christos Xypolopoulos and Michalis Vazirgiannis

To What Extent Does Lexical Normalization Help English-as-a-Second Language Learners to Read Noisy English Texts?
Yo Ehara

Multilingual Sequence Labeling Approach to solve Lexical Normalization
Divesh Kubal and Apurva Nagvenkar

Sesame Street to Mount Sinai: BERT-constrained character-level Moses models for multilingual lexical normalization
Yves Scherrer and Nikola Ljubešić

Sequence-to-Sequence Lexical Normalization with Multilingual Transformers
Ana-Maria Bucur, Adrian Cosma and Liviu P. Dinu

ÚFAL at MultiLexNorm 2021: Improving Multilingual Lexical Normalization by Fine-tuning ByT5
David Samuel and Milan Straka

MultiLexNorm: A Shared Task on Multilingual Lexical Normalization
Rob van der Goot, Alan Ramponi, Arkaitz Zubiaga, Barbara Plank, Benjamin Muller, Iñaki San Vicente Roncal, Nikola Ljubešić, Özlem Çetinoğlu, Rahmad Mahendra, Talha Çolakoğlu, Timothy Baldwin, Tommaso Caselli and Wladimir Sidorenko

CL-MoNoise: Cross-lingual Lexical Normalization
Rob van der Goot

Text Simplification for Comprehension-based Question-Answering

Tanvi Dadu *† NSIT, Delhi

Kartikey Pant *† IIIT, Hyderabad

Seema Nagar IBM Research India

Ferdous A. Barbhuiya IIIT, Guwahati

Kuntal Dey † Accenture Tech Labs

Abstract

Text simplification is the process of splitting and rephrasing a sentence to a sequence of sentences making it easier to read and understand while preserving the content and approximating the original meaning. Text simplification has been exploited in NLP applications like machine translation, summarization, semantic role labeling, and information extraction, opening a broad avenue for its exploitation in comprehension-based question-answering downstream tasks. In this work, we investigate the effect of text simplification in the task of question-answering using a comprehension context. We release *Simple-SQuAD*, a simplified version of the widely-used *SQuAD* dataset.

Firstly, we outline each step in the dataset creation pipeline, including style transfer, thresholding of sentences showing correct transfer, and offset finding for each answer. Secondly, we verify the quality of the transferred sentences through various methodologies involving both automated and human evaluation. Thirdly, we benchmark the newly created corpus and perform an ablation study for examining the effect of the simplification process in the *SQuAD*-based question answering task. Our experiments show that simplification leads to up to 2.04% and 1.74% increase in *Exact Match* and *F1*, respectively. Finally, we conclude with an analysis of the transfer process, investigating the types of edits made by the model, and the effect of sentence length on the transfer model.

1 Introduction

Text simplification is the task of modifying the structure of a text to make it easier to read and comprehend while preserving the content and approximating the original meaning. Linguistically, simple sentences are defined as having only one subject and one verb or predicate. Therefore, a complex sentence can be rewritten into multiple simpler sentences while retaining the same meaning. When simplifying texts, a myriad of rewriting transformations have been explored, ranging from replacing complex words or phrases for simpler synonyms, to changing the syntactic structure of the sentence. Moreover, modern automated text simplification approaches are data-driven, attempting to simplify sentences using parallel corpora of aligned complex-simplified sentences.

Text simplification allows humans to read texts more efficiently and faster, empowering them to take part in society and become more active in their daily actions and healthcare (Dannells, 2020). Another vital application of text simplification is reading assistance it provides, especially for people with reading disabilities (Carroll and Macdonald, 1998; Inui et al., 2003), low-literacy readers (Watanabe et al., 2009), or non-native speakers (Siddharthan, 2002).

There has been considerable work done where NLP applications exploit the benefits of text simplification. Long sentences with complex syntax or those laden with long-distance dependencies often pose difficulties for various downstream tasks. Text simplification has been used to improve the performance for these tasks including machine translation (Hasler et al., 2017), summarization (Silveira and Branco, 2012), semantic role labeling (Vickrey and Koller, 2008; Evans and Orasan, 2019), and information extraction (Evans and Orasan, 2019). This opens up the avenue for exploring simplification for question-answering. To the best of our knowledge, text simplification for comprehension-based question-answering has not been explored yet.

In this work, we make the following contributions:-

- We propose a transformers-based text-simplification pipeline that splits and

* The first two authors contributed equally to the work.

† This work was done when Kartikey Pant was affiliated to IIIT Hyderabad, Tanvi Dadu was affiliated to NSIT Delhi, and Kuntal Dey was affiliated to IBM.

Proceedings of the 2021 EMNLP Workshop W-NUT: The Seventh Workshop on Noisy User-generated Text, pages 1–10
November 11, 2021.

Original SQuAD Sentence	Transferred Simple-SQuAD Sentence
Clark also claimed that Abdul gave him preferential treatment on the show due to their affair.	Clark also claimed that Abdul gave him preferential treatment on the show. This was due to their affair.
In his Prices and Production (1931), Hayek argued that the business cycle resulted from the central bank's inflationary credit expansion and its transmission over time, leading to a capital misallocation caused by the artificially low interest rates.	In his Prices and Production (1931), Hayek argued that the business cycle resulted from the central bank's inflationary credit expansion and its transmission over time. This led to a capital misallocation caused by the artificially low interest rates.

Table 1: Examples of Simple and Complex sentences, from our proposed Simple-SQuAD dataset and the SQuAD dataset. Underlined parts denotes the splitting point.

rephrases a complex sentence into its simpler constituent sentences. We outline each step in the dataset creation pipeline, including data preprocessing, performing text simplification, thresholding the simplified sentence based on the quality of the transfer, and offset finding of answers from each question-answer pair present in the dataset.

- We propose a new dataset *Simple-SQuAD* by converting each context in the *SQuAD* dataset using the proposed text-simplification pipeline. [1]
- We perform automated and human evaluation to determine the quality of the text simplification model.
- We perform event based analysis and sentence-length based transfer analysis to give deeper insights into the transfer process.
- We then benchmark both *Simple-SQuAD* and *SQuAD* for predictive performance in the *Simple-SQuAD* question-answering task.

2 Related Works

2.1 Text Simplification

Text simplification has attracted a great deal of attention due to its potential impact on society. Prior explorations on text simplification contain a myriad of approaches, which include from the use of hand-crafted syntactic rules (Carroll and Macdonald, 1998; Vickrey and Koller, 2008), statistical simplification model (Zhu et al., 2010), quasi-synchronous grammar (Woodsend and Lapata, 2011) and the semantic hierarchy of simplified sentences for recursively splitting and rephrasing complex sentences (Niklaus et al., 2019). Recently, Machine Translation, both statistical and neural, has also been used for the task of text simplification (Narayan and Gardent, 2014; Nisioi et al., 2017).

The process of text simplification has been observed to help in the performance of multiple downstream tasks. Silveira et al. (Silveira and Branco, 2012) explored the use of a sentence simplification module in summarization systems, concluding that the simplification module removes expendable information that helps in accommodating relevant data in a summary. Hasler et al. (Hasler et al., 2017) showed that the performance of source simplification could improve translation quality in machine translation systems. Evans et al. (Evans and Orasan, 2019) proved the efficacy of integrating a text simplification step for improving the predictive performance of semantic role labeling and information extraction methodologies.

Narayan et al. (Narayan et al., 2017) introduced a new text simplification task, named Split-and-Rephrase on their proposed WebSplit dataset, containing $1,066,115$ parallel instances of complex and sequence of simple sentences having a similar meaning. The goal of the task is to split a complex input sentence into shorter sentences while preserving the meaning. In this task, the emphasis is on sentence splitting and rephrasing, with no deletion and no lexical or phrasal simplification. They further proposed five models, ranging from vanilla sequence-to-sequence to semantically-motivated models to benchmark the proposed task. Aharoni and Goldberg (Aharoni and Goldberg, 2018) and Botha et al. (Botha et al., 2018) extended the work by introducing new datasets, with a more extensive vocabulary and split examples to improve the efficacy of the prior benchmarks. We use WikiSplit, introduced by Botha et al. (Botha et al., 2018), for training our sentence simplification module.

2.2 Style Transfer

In recent works, textual style transfer has been shown to produce grammatically fluent, and

[1]Made available at the following Github repository: `https://github.com/kartikeypant/text-simplification-qa-www2021`.

information-preserved texts with fairly accurate target attributes. For the task in a semi-supervised setting, various methodologies are exploited, including back-translation (Prabhumoye et al., 2018), back-translation with attribute conditioning (Pant et al., 2020), specialized transfer methodologies like Delete, Retrieve, Generate (Li et al., 2018). However, in the presence of a large parallel corpus, sequence-to-sequence models perform competitively. Aharoni and Goldberg (Aharoni and Goldberg, 2018) exploited a copy-mechanism based sequence-to-sequence model with attention (Bahdanau et al., 2015) for the text simplification transfer.

Transformers (Vaswani et al., 2017) have been shown to perform robust language modeling, given enough data, helping in various downstream tasks. Due to the parallelized nature of the architecture, it is possible to train using much larger datasets than recurrent neural networks. However, it becomes necessary to optimize hyperparameters carefully while ensuring scalability (Popel and Bojar, 2018). Transformer-based methodologies for the task of sentence simplification have been explored by Marayuma and Yamamoto (Maruyama and Yamamoto, 2019) for Japanese and Zhao et al. (Zhao et al., 2018) for a smaller Wikipedia-based dataset. However, to the best of our knowledge, there has been no work done for supervised style transfer exploiting transformer-based models for the significantly large *WikiSplit* dataset.

3 Corpus Creation

3.1 Preliminaries

3.1.1 SQuAD

For exploring the effect of text simplification in the question-answering downstream task, we use Stanford Question Answering Dataset (SQuAD comprehension), a reading comprehension dataset released by Rajpurkar et al. (Rajpurkar et al., 2016). It consists of $100,000+$ questions from 536 articles posed by crowdworkers on a set of Wikipedia articles, where the answer to each question is a segment of text from the corresponding reading passage. Unlike other datasets, *SQuAD* does not provide a list of answer choices for each question; instead, systems must select the answer from all possible spans in the passage. Though the system must deal with a large number of candidate answers, yet span-based answers are easier to evaluate than free-form answers. Further, it is diverse in terms of answer types, containing a significant percentage of dates, numeric data, adjective phrases, verb phrases, clauses as answers. The predictive performance of models in the *SQuAD* dataset is evaluated using *Exact-match* and *F1-score*.

3.1.2 WikiSplit

For the task of text simplification, we use the *WikiSplit* corpus (Botha et al., 2018), a parallel corpus consisting of complex sentences and its consequent sequence of simple sentences having similar meaning for the Split and Rephrase task. It contains a set of one million naturally occurring sentence rewrites mined from English Wikipedia, providing 60 times more examples and 90 times more vocabulary as compared to the *WebSplit* corpus introduced by Narayan et al. (Narayan et al., 2017). Using a larger dataset for the task of text simplification increases the efficacy of the model and the quality of the transferred data (Botha et al., 2018; Popel and Bojar, 2018).

3.2 Approach

3.2.1 Style Transfer

This subsection outlines the process of textual style transfer using transformers for converting the complex contexts in the *SQuAD* dataset into their simpler counterparts. Figure 1 illustrates the process for a sample context and question-answer pair from the *SQuAD* dataset.

We use spaCy's Sentencizer [2] to tokenize the contexts into their respective constituent sentences. This process enables us to perform the sentence-level transfer, thus ensuring higher degrees of overall transfer quality. We tokenize each sentence using a SentencePiece tokenizer, trained on 3.24 *GBs* English Wikipedia . While training the SentencePiece tokenizer, we mark the numerical tokens as custom-defined ones, ensuring no tokenization happens for such tokens. This step helps in preserving the numerical tokens in the transfer process by the transfer model.

We transfer each tokenized sentence using a transformers based machine translation model. We use the OpenNMT-py (Klein et al., 2017) toolkit for the implementation process. The model consists of 6-layered transformers architecture with 8 self-attention heads and 1028 sized hidden feed-forward layer. We trained the model for 20000 training steps with a dropout of 0.1 and a batch

[2] https://spacy.io/api/sentencizer

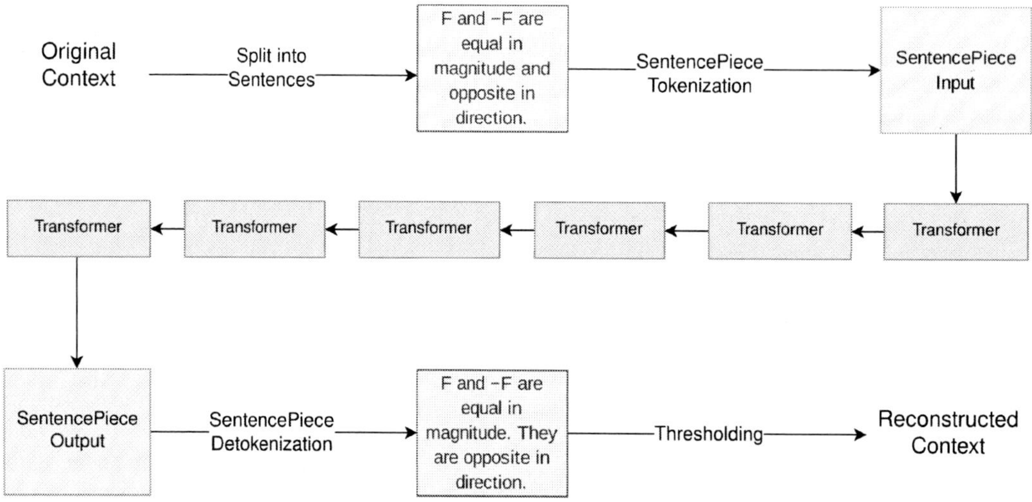

Figure 1: Style Transfer Architecture

size of 2048. For optimization, we used Adam optimizer with a *beta2* value of 0.998, accumulating the gradient twice. We use an initial learning rate of 2 with *noam* decay method and 800 (4% of total) warmup steps.

3.2.2 Thresholding

In this section, we outline the thresholding techniques used in the generated sequence of simple sentences to maintain their quality. We execute the following post-editing steps to reduce noise from the dataset:

1. **Perplexity** : We use open *GPT-2* (Radford et al., 2018) as the language model to assign perplexity to the generated sentences. We threshold the transferred sequence of sentences that have the perplexity between 50 and 600 and discard all the remaining sequences. This thresholding ensures that the sequence of sentences is fluent, as measured by the language model. Table 2 shows that 84951 of 91757 sentences are within the fluency thresholding, comprising of 93% of the total sentences.

2. **Length of the original sentence**: We weed out all sentences whose original length was shorter than five tokens. This heuristic is based on the condition that sentences lesser than five tokens are highly likely to be simple, reducing the number of false positives to a significant extent efficiently. Table 2 shows that the thresholding process removes 15.16% of the already thresholded sentences leaving 78.5% of the total sentences.

Thresholding Step	Percentage of Total Sentences	Thresholded Sentences
Step 1: Perplexity	92.58%	84,951
Step 2: Original Length Thresholding	78.5%	72,075
Step 3: Redundancy Thresholding	77.31%	70,944

Table 2: Sentences left after each thresholding process step

3. **Redundancy in sequence of the transferred sentences**: We remove all transferred sentences that display a redundancy behavior, which is defined to be one in which two or more sentences in the sequence are the same. We introduce this step after a careful analysis of the transferred sentences. Table 2 illustrates that the thresholding removes 1.57% of the already thresholded sentences leaving 77.31% of the total sentences.

3.2.3 Automated Evaluation

We perform an automated sentence-level analysis of the style transfer model. We determine the extent of content preservation, lexical simplicity, and reading ease of the generated sentences using the following three metrics:

1. **BLEU** (Papineni et al. (Papineni et al., 2002)): We use the self-BLEU score taking the original sentence as the reference to measure the

extent of content preservation. Table 3 shows that our model achieves a mean high self-BLEU of 75.66, implying that the transferred sentences display a high level of content-based similarity with the original sentence

2. **SARI** (Xu et al. (Xu et al., 2016)): We use the SARI metric to measure the quality of lexical simplicity in the transferred sentences. It analyzes the words added, deleted, and retained by a simplification model. Our version of SARI compares the model's output to the original sentence. There is a high correlation with human judgments of simplicity gain and the SARI metric (Xu et al., 2016). In Table 3, we observe a mean SARI value of 30.08 with a low standard deviation of 2.21, denoting most sentences to have a high level of lexical simplicity.

3. **Flesch–Kincaid Grade level** (Kincaid et al. (Kincaid et al., 1975)): Flesch– Kincaid Grade Level (FKGL) is a widely-used metric for text readability. It represents the corresponding U.S. grade level, whose education is appropriate for understanding the text. As illustrated in Table 3, the Flesch-Kincaid Grade Level for the sentences decreases by 5.43 grade levels on average. Thus, the transferred sentences have much higher readability than the original sentences.

Metric	Mean	Standard Deviation
BLEU	75.66	13.68
SARI	30.08	2.21
FKGL(Original)	13.29	5.74
FKGL(Transferred)	7.86	3.94

Table 3: Automated analysis of transferred sentences

3.2.4 Human Evaluation

Although we use commonly used metrics for the evaluation, automated evaluation of generative models of text is still an open research problem (Hu et al., 2017). We perform a human evaluation to analyze the quality of the transferred sentences accurately.

In the human evaluation, we randomly sampled 50 sentence pairs from the thresholded dataset consisting of both transferred sentences and their original variants. The human evaluators were asked to rate each sentence pair on a 1-5 Likert scale on the following metrics:

1. **Fluency**: A high *Fluency* score, 4 or 5, denotes that the transferred sentence is well constructed. A medium score of 3 denotes that the sentence contains lexical errors, while a low score of 2 or 1 denotes major errors and extremely poor constructions respectively.

2. **Relative Simplicity**: A sentence pair is given a high *Relative Simplicity* score, 4 or 5, if the transferred sentence is significantly simplified as compared to the original sentence. If the simplicity remains the same, it is given a medium score of 3 score. Moreover, a low score represents that the transferred sentence is more complex than the original sentence.

3. **Content Preservation**: A high *Content Preservation* score of 4 and 5 indicates that the content of the original sentence was well-preserved in the transferred sentence. A medium score of 3 denotes that there were minor differences between the transferred sentences and the original sentences. A low score of 2 and 1 denotes major violation of content preservation.

To verify the inter-rater agreement, we perform a Krippendorff's alpha analysis across all three metrics. Our analysis shows that we obtain an averaged Krippendorff's alpha inter-rater agreement of 0.63 over all metrics, denoting reasonable agreement between the raters.

Metric	Average Value
Fluency	4.26
Relative Simplicity	3.91
Content Preservation	4.10

Table 4: Human Evaluation Results

Table 4 illustrates the results of the performed human evaluation. We observe that the transferred sentences were judged to be fluent, significantly simplified, and content-preserved compared to their original counterparts.

3.2.5 Offset Finding and Dataset Finalization

In this subsection, we outline the process of finding the offsets for each question-answer pair and reconstructing our proposed simplified version of *SQuAD*, *Simple-SQuAD*, from the thresholded sentences.

Firstly, we preprocess the sentences, which involves removing the split sentence indicator and reconstructing context texts from both thresholded and original sentences. If a sentence is not simplified, we use the original sentence itself, ensuring minimal loss of information due to the transfer process.

Secondly, for every question-answer pair, we calculate the answer's character offset by using exact matching in the reconstructed context. If we do not find an exact match, we use case-insensitive pattern matching to calculate the offset. We found the offsets for $88,690$ questions in total.

Finally, we create the following two datasets: *Simple-SQuAD* and *Original*. The *Simple-SQuAD* dataset contains the reconstructed context with the calculated character offsets for each answer. The *Original* dataset contains the original context itself but with only those questions whose answers are present in the *Simple-SQuAD* dataset. We create the new *Original* dataset to ensure an equal number of question-answer pairs, leading to a fair comparison. This *Original* dataset represents the *SQuAD* candidate for the benchmarking process.

4 Benchmarking Experiments

This section highlights the models and experiments performed for benchmarking the *Simple-SQuAD*. We compare the results obtained for *Simple-SQuAD* against the *SQuAD* dataset.

4.1 Model Used

For benchmarking *Simple-SQuAD*, we use two different variations of RoBERTa as introduced by Liu et al. (Liu et al., 2019). RoBERTa is a replication study of BERT pretraining, which is trained on more extensive training data with bigger batches, longer sequences, and dynamically changing masking patterns. Consequently, RoBERTa achieves better results over BERT and attains state-of-the-art results on *GLUE*, *RACE*, and *SQuAD*.

4.2 Experimental Settings

We perform a dataset-based ablation study, experimenting with multiple variants of input datasets for each model. Firstly, we finetune the model on the *SQuAD* and the *Simple-SQuAD* dataset separately for 2 epochs. We then finetune the *Simple-SQuAD* trained model on the *SQuAD* dataset and the *SQuAD*-trained model on the *Simple-SQuAD* dataset for 2 epochs each. We benchmark the results for each of these combinations of the dataset input to better infer the effect of simplifying sentences in the original dataset.

For benchmarking, we use 442 training articles containing $78,810$ questions and 48 development articles containing 9880 questions. Thus, we have a $90{:}10$ and an approximate $89{:}11$ train-test split based on the number of articles and the number of questions, respectively. We used 10% of the training examples as a validation set for both our models.

For both $RoBERTa_{Base}$ and $RoBERTa_{Large}$, we use a maximum sequence length of 380, a stride of 128, a maximum query length of 64, and a maximum answer length of 30. We use a learning rate of $1 * 10^{-5}$ with a weight decay of 0.01.

4.3 Results

This section outlines the result of the ablation study to determine the effect of text simplification on the question answering downstream task in the *SQuAD* dataset. We observe that text simplification improves the predictive performance of both $RoBERTa_{base}$ and $RoBERTa_{large}$.

Model	Input	Exact	F1
$RoBERTa_{Base}$	SQuAD	0.787	0.863
$RoBERTa_{Base}$	Simple-SQuAD	0.786	0.866
$RoBERTa_{Base}$	Simple-SQUAD → SQuAD	0.799	0.876
$RoBERTa_{Base}$	SQuAD → Simple-SQuAD	**0.803**	**0.878**

Table 5: Benchmarking Results for $RoBERTa_{Base}$.

Table 5 illustrates the results for the $RoBERTa_{Base}$ model. We observe an increase of 2.03% in *Exact Match* and 1.74% in *F1* when fine-tuning it with *SQuAD* followed by *Simple-SQuAD*, in contrast with the model when trained on only SQuAD.

Model	Input	Exact	F1
$RoBERTa_{Large}$	SQuAD	0.835	0.905
$RoBERTa_{Large}$	Simple-SQuAD	**0.852**	**0.917**
$RoBERTa_{Large}$	Simple-SQUAD → SQuAD	0.838	0.907
$RoBERTa_{Large}$	SQuAD → Simple-SQuAD	0.836	0.908

Table 6: Benchmarking Results for $RoBERTa_{Large}$.

Table 6 illustrates the results for the $RoBERTa_{Large}$ model. Similar to $RoBERTa_{Base}$, we observe an increase of 2.04% in *Exact Match* and 1.33% in *F1* when fine-tuning it with *Simple-SQuAD* when compared to model when trained on *SQuAD*.

Category	Original	Transferred
Inter-Event Splitting	Although his administrative abilities had been noticed, on the eve of the U.S. entry into World War II he had never held an active command above a battalion and was far from being considered by many as a potential commander of major operations.	Although his administrative abilities had been noticed on the eve of the U.S. entry into World War II he had never held an active command above a battalion. He was far from being considered by many as a potential commander of major operations.
Intra-Event Splitting	Clark also claimed that Abdul gave him preferential treatment on the show due to their affair.	Clark also claimed that Abdul gave him preferential treatment on the show. This was due to their affair.

Table 7: Examples of event-based splitting.

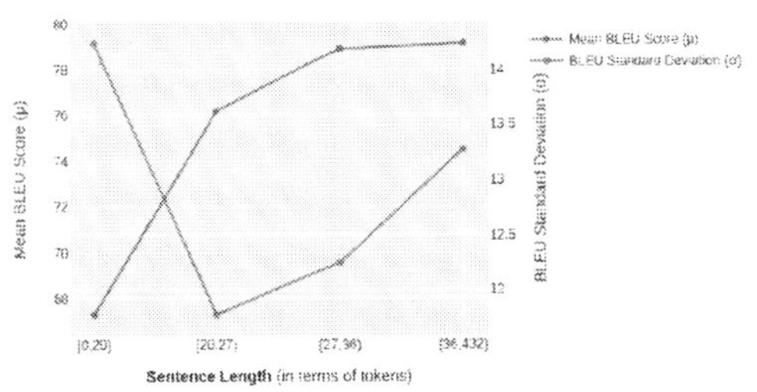

(a) BLEU

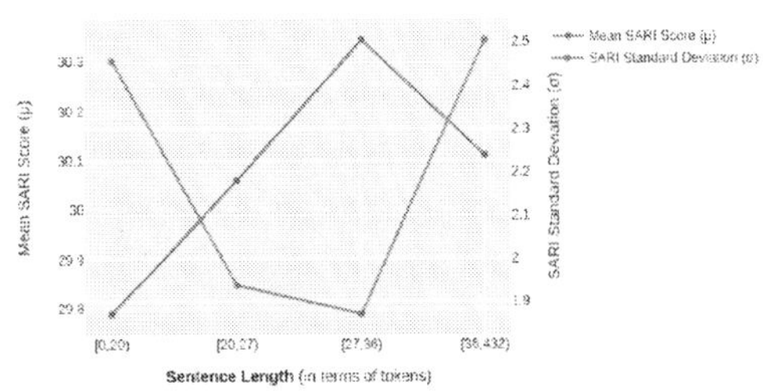

(b) SARI

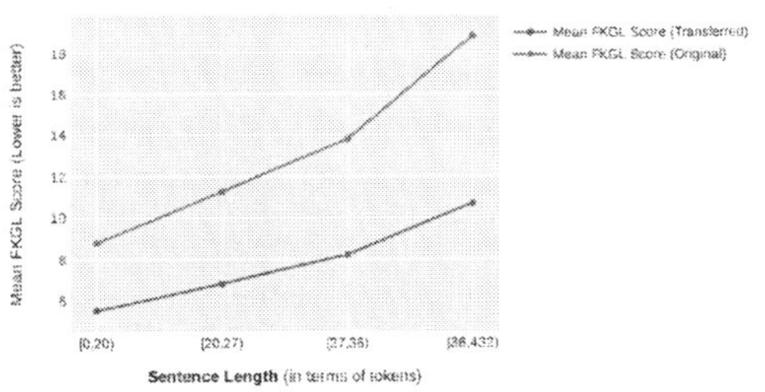

(c) FKGL

Figure 2: Plots illustrating sentence-length based transfer analysis

5 Discussion

5.1 Edit Analysis

We conduct an event-based analysis of the edits performed by the transfer model to convert the originally complex sentences into simpler forms. We use the definition of a linguistic event as defined in Pustejovsky (Pustejovsky, 1991). We perform the analysis on 50 parallel sentences in their pre and post simplification forms, classifying each edit into the following two classes: *Inter-Event Splitting* and *Intra-Event Splitting*.

Inter-Event Splitting denotes the type of edit in which the model splits two different events. As illustrated in Table 7, the events of *notice* and *consider* are split into two different sentences, thus simplifying the complex sentence containing the two events. On the other hand, *Intra-Event Splitting* is the type of edit in which all the simplified sentences contain the same event as the original sentence, as is illustrated for the event *claim* in Table 7.

In our analysis, we found 32% of the instances to show *Inter-Event Splitting*, showing that our model can capture event boundaries. On the other hand, 60% of the total instances show successful *Intra-Event Splitting*, illustrating that the model can capture intra-event detailing boundaries. Interestingly, 8% of the total instances displayed unsuccessful attempts of *Intra-Event Splitting*, which can be improved in future work.

5.2 Transfer Analysis

For transfer analysis, we divide all the sentences in *Simple-SQuAD* into four buckets based on the original sentence length split equally in terms of word-level tokenization ($0-20$ tokens, $20-27$ tokens, $27-36$ tokens and $36-432$ tokens). We then compute the following three metrics on a sentence level: BLEU score, SARI scores, and FKGL scores. In Figure 2, we observe that the performance of the model varies with the sentence length.

1. **BLEU**: Sentence-preservation, measured through average BLEU score, is directly proportional to the sentence length. However, the standard deviation of the BLEU scores first decreases then increases as we increase the sentence length.
2. **SARI**: Lexical simplicity, measured through average SARI score, first increases then decreases as we increase the sentence length. However, the standard deviation of the SARI scores first decreases then increases as sentence length increases.
3. **FKGL**: Text readability, measured via sentence-level FKGL score, was computed for both transferred and original sentences. We observe that sentence-level FKGL score of transferred sentences is directly proportional to the sentence length. Whereas sentence-level FKGL scores for original sentences first decreases then increases with sentence length. Moreover, the mean sentence-level FKGL score for the transferred sentences was always lower than that for the original sentences regardless of the sentence length.

6 Conclusion

In this work, we study the effect of text simplification in the comprehension based question-answering downstream task using the *SQuAD* dataset. For *Simple-SQuAD* corpus creation, we use a transformers based style transfer model to transfer complex sentences to sequences of simple sentences while retaining the original meaning. We further use post-editing techniques to reduce noise from the dataset, followed by the use of heuristics to find required offsets for an answer in each question-answer pair. We prove the efficacy of our model using automated evaluation as well as human evaluation. We then benchmark *Simple-SQuAD* using two different variants of RoBERTa and perform an ablation study to investigate the effects of text simplification using four different variations of input. We prove that text simplification in the question-answering downstream task increases the predictive performance of the models. We further conduct edit-type analysis and sentence-length analysis to give insights about the transfer process. Future work may include improving style transfer performance using a more extensive corpus for text simplification and exploring effects of text simplification for other downstream tasks like text summarization, sentiment analysis.

References

Roee Aharoni and Yoav Goldberg. 2018. Split and rephrase: Better evaluation and stronger baselines. In *Proceedings of the 56th Annual Meeting of the Association for Computational Linguistics (Volume 2: Short Papers)*, pages 719–724, Melbourne, Australia. Association for Computational Linguistics.

Dzmitry Bahdanau, Kyunghyun Cho, and Yoshua Bengio. 2015. Neural machine translation by jointly learning to align and translate. *CoRR*, abs/1409.0473.

Jan A. Botha, Manaal Faruqui, John Alex, Jason Baldridge, and Dipanjan Das. 2018. Learning to split and rephrase from Wikipedia edit history. In *Proceedings of the 2018 Conference on Empirical Methods in Natural Language Processing*, pages 732–737, Brussels, Belgium. Association for Computational Linguistics.

John A. Carroll and Richard G. Macdonald. 1998. Practical simplification of english newspaper text to assist aphasic readers.

Dana Dannells. 2020. Automatic generation and simplification of written documents.

Richard Evans and Constantin Orasan. 2019. Sentence simplification for semantic role labelling and information extraction. In *Proceedings of the International Conference on Recent Advances in Natural Language Processing (RANLP 2019)*, pages 285–294, Varna, Bulgaria. INCOMA Ltd.

Eva Hasler, Adri de Gispert, Felix Stahlberg, Aurelien Waite, and Bill Byrne. 2017. Source sentence simplification for statistical machine translation. *Comput. Speech Lang.*, 45(C):221–235.

Zhiting Hu, Zichao Yang, Xiaodan Liang, Ruslan Salakhutdinov, and Eric P. Xing. 2017. Toward controlled generation of text. In *Proceedings of the 34th International Conference on Machine Learning - Volume 70*, ICML'17, page 1587–1596. JMLR.org.

Kentaro Inui, Atsushi Fujita, Tetsuro Takahashi, Ryu Iida, and Tomoya Iwakura. 2003. Text simplification for reading assistance: A project note. In *Proceedings of the Second International Workshop on Paraphrasing - Volume 16*, PARAPHRASE '03, page 9–16, USA. Association for Computational Linguistics.

J. Peter Kincaid, Robert P. Fishburne, Richard Lawrence Rogers, and Brad S. Chissom. 1975. Derivation of new readability formulas (automated readability index, fog count and flesch reading ease formula) for navy enlisted personnel.

Guillaume Klein, Yoon Kim, Yuntian Deng, Jean Senellart, and Alexander Rush. 2017. OpenNMT: Open-source toolkit for neural machine translation. In *Proceedings of ACL 2017, System Demonstrations*, pages 67–72, Vancouver, Canada. Association for Computational Linguistics.

Juncen Li, Robin Jia, He He, and Percy Liang. 2018. Delete, retrieve, generate: a simple approach to sentiment and style transfer. In *Proceedings of the 2018 Conference of the North American Chapter of the Association for Computational Linguistics: Human Language Technologies, Volume 1 (Long Papers)*, pages 1865–1874, New Orleans, Louisiana. Association for Computational Linguistics.

Yinhan Liu, Myle Ott, Naman Goyal, Jingfei Du, Mandar Joshi, Danqi Chen, Omer Levy, Mike Lewis, Luke Zettlemoyer, and Veselin Stoyanov. 2019. Roberta: A robustly optimized bert pretraining approach. *ArXiv*, abs/1907.11692.

T. Maruyama and K. Yamamoto. 2019. Extremely low resource text simplification with pre-trained transformer language model. In *2019 International Conference on Asian Language Processing (IALP)*, pages 53–58.

Shashi Narayan and Claire Gardent. 2014. Hybrid simplification using deep semantics and machine translation. In *Proceedings of the 52nd Annual Meeting of the Association for Computational Linguistics (Volume 1: Long Papers)*, pages 435–445, Baltimore, Maryland. Association for Computational Linguistics.

Shashi Narayan, Claire Gardent, Shay B. Cohen, and Anastasia Shimorina. 2017. Split and rephrase. In *Proceedings of the 2017 Conference on Empirical Methods in Natural Language Processing*, pages 606–616, Copenhagen, Denmark. Association for Computational Linguistics.

Christina Niklaus, Matthias Cetto, André Freitas, and Siegfried Handschuh. 2019. Transforming complex sentences into a semantic hierarchy. *ArXiv*, abs/1906.01038.

Sergiu Nisioi, Sanja Štajner, Simone Paolo Ponzetto, and Liviu P. Dinu. 2017. Exploring neural text simplification models. In *Proceedings of the 55th Annual Meeting of the Association for Computational Linguistics (Volume 2: Short Papers)*, pages 85–91, Vancouver, Canada. Association for Computational Linguistics.

Kartikey Pant, Yash Verma, and Radhika Mamidi. 2020. Sentiinc: Incorporating sentiment information into sentiment transfer without parallel data. In *Advances in Information Retrieval*, pages 312–319, Cham. Springer International Publishing.

Kishore Papineni, Salim Roukos, Todd Ward, and Wei-Jing Zhu. 2002. Bleu: a method for automatic evaluation of machine translation. In *Proceedings of the 40th Annual Meeting of the Association for Computational Linguistics*, pages 311–318, Philadelphia, Pennsylvania, USA. Association for Computational Linguistics.

Martin Popel and Ondřej Bojar. 2018. Training tips for the transformer model. *The Prague Bulletin of Mathematical Linguistics*, 110.

Shrimai Prabhumoye, Yulia Tsvetkov, Ruslan Salakhutdinov, and Alan W Black. 2018. Style transfer through back-translation. In *Proceedings of the 56th Annual Meeting of the Association for Computational Linguistics (Volume 1: Long Papers)*, pages 866–876, Melbourne, Australia. Association for Computational Linguistics.

James Pustejovsky. 1991. The syntax of event structure. *Cognition*, 41:47–81.

Alec Radford, Jeffrey Wu, Rewon Child, David Luan, Dario Amodei, and Ilya Sutskever. 2018. Language models are unsupervised multitask learners.

Pranav Rajpurkar, Jian Zhang, Konstantin Lopyrev, and Percy Liang. 2016. SQuAD: 100,000+ questions for machine comprehension of text. In *Proceedings of the 2016 Conference on Empirical Methods in Natural Language Processing*, pages 2383–2392, Austin, Texas. Association for Computational Linguistics.

Advaith Siddharthan. 2002. An architecture for a text simplification system. In *Proceedings of the Language Engineering Conference (LEC'02)*, LEC '02, page 64, USA. IEEE Computer Society.

Sara Silveira and António Branco. 2012. Enhancing multi-document summaries with sentence simplification.

Ashish Vaswani, Noam Shazeer, Niki Parmar, Jakob Uszkoreit, Llion Jones, Aidan N. Gomez, Lukasz Kaiser, and Illia Polosukhin. 2017. Attention is all you need. *ArXiv*, abs/1706.03762.

David Vickrey and Daphne Koller. 2008. Sentence simplification for semantic role labeling. In *Proceedings of ACL-08: HLT*, pages 344–352, Columbus, Ohio. Association for Computational Linguistics.

Willian Massami Watanabe, Arnaldo Candido Junior, Vinícius Rodriguez Uzêda, Renata Pontin de Mattos Fortes, Thiago Alexandre Salgueiro Pardo, and

Sandra Maria Aluísio. 2009. Facilita: Reading assistance for low-literacy readers. In *Proceedings of the 27th ACM International Conference on Design of Communication*, SIGDOC '09, page 29–36, New York, NY, USA. Association for Computing Machinery.

Kristian Woodsend and Mirella Lapata. 2011. Learning to simplify sentences with quasi-synchronous grammar and integer programming. In *Proceedings of the Conference on Empirical Methods in Natural Language Processing*, EMNLP '11, page 409–420, USA. Association for Computational Linguistics.

Wei Xu, Courtney Napoles, Ellie Pavlick, Quanze Chen, and Chris Callison-Burch. 2016. Optimizing statistical machine translation for text simplification. *Transactions of the Association for Computational Linguistics*, 4:401–415.

Sanqiang Zhao, Rui Meng, Daqing He, Andi Saptono, and Bambang Parmanto. 2018. Integrating transformer and paraphrase rules for sentence simplification. *ArXiv*, abs/1810.11193.

Zhemin Zhu, Delphine Bernhard, and Iryna Gurevych. 2010. A monolingual tree-based translation model for sentence simplification. In *Proceedings of the 23rd International Conference on Computational Linguistics*, COLING '10, page 1353–1361, USA. Association for Computational Linguistics.

Finding the needle in a haystack: Extraction of Informative COVID-19 Danish Tweets

Benjamin Olsen and **Barbara Plank**
Department of Computer Science
IT University of Copenhagen
{beao, bapl}@itu.dk

Abstract

Finding informative COVID-19 posts in a stream of tweets is very useful to monitor health-related updates. Prior work focused on a balanced data setup and on English, but informative tweets are rare, and English is only one of the many languages spoken in the world. In this work, we introduce a new dataset of 5,000 tweets for finding informative COVID-19 tweets for Danish. In contrast to prior work, which balances the label distribution, we model the problem by keeping its natural distribution. We examine how well a simple probabilistic model and a convolutional neural network (CNN) perform on this task. We find a weighted CNN to work well but it is sensitive to embedding and hyperparameter choices. We hope the contributed dataset is a starting point for further work in this direction.

1 Introduction

As of late July 2021, the COVID-19 Corona virus continues to spread with close to 200M infected patients and more than 4M people who have died to this horrible disease[1] striking fear into the hearts of all people around the world.

Due to this, COVID-19 has become the most discussed topic in the news and most of the "official" sources that keep track of the number of dead, infected, and recovered cases, are not frequently kept up to date (e.g. WHO only updates pandemic information once a day). Since the news or online monitoring systems need real-time updates, they turn to social media platforms such as Twitter, to gather real-time pandemic information (Banda et al., 2021; Aiello et al., 2021). However, given that this also happens to be one of the most popular topics on social media, many of these posts contain false or uninformative information (Krittanawong et al., 2020; Weinzierl et al., 2021) that can be difficult to filter out.

In 2020, a shared task at WNUT (Nguyen et al., 2020) was organized to filter out informative COVID-19 related information from an English dataset consisting of 10k COVID-19 related tweets. The shared task dataset has close to an equal class distribution between two labels: INFORMATIVE (4,719 tweets) and UNINFORMATIVE (5,281). A total of 55 teams submitted different models and it was shown in Nguyen et al. (2020) that the two best models solved this task with an F1 score of 90.96 using an English COVID-Twitter-BERT model (Kumar and Singh, 2020; Giovanni Møller et al., 2020). In this paper, we keep the real-world non-balanced distribution between informative and non-informative tweets and extend the task to a less-privileged language.

To answer the question whether this task is doable in light of the expected skewed distribution, this paper contributes a new dataset for Danish by starting from the same annotation guidelines (Nguyen et al., 2020). Due to the high imbalance between classes in this dataset (out of 5,000 tweets, at most 3% are informative tweets), the goal is to create a model that performs well for this task despite the high imbalance. No Danish COVID Twitter BERT model exists, hence we experiment with multilingual and Danish BERT and Danish Twitter word2vec embeddings.

2 Dataset

This section outlines how the dataset of Danish COVID-19 related tweets was created, annotated, pre-processed and split for the experiments.

2.1 Annotation guidelines

Our annotation guidelines depart from those by Nguyen et al. (2020). They define two labels: INFORMATIVE and UNINFORMATIVE. We introduce a new label named INFORMATIVE- to capture

[1] https://www.worldometers.info/coronavirus/

Proceedings of the 2021 EMNLP Workshop W-NUT: The Seventh Workshop on Noisy User-generated Text, pages 11–19
November 11, 2021. ©2021 Association for Computational Linguistics

difficult and non-Danish cases,[2] and rename the INFORMATIVE label to INFORMATIVE+. In particular, INFORMATIVE+ and UNINFORMATIVE are identified identically to the guidelines presented in (Nguyen et al., 2020). INFORMATIVE- is a label which contains tweets that are difficult to label as either INFORMATIVE+ or UNINFORMATIVE and tweets that are informative but written in English (for a full description of the mapping between tweets and the three classes, see appendix A.1).

2.2 COVID-19 related tweet collection

We collected tweets that contain the hashtag: "#covid19dk" from March 2020 to October 2020. The hashtag suffix 'dk' is often used in Danish tweets. Here we opted for dataset construction on the basis of this hashtag to collect mostly Danish tweets, as distinguishing between closely related languages poses a significant challenge (Ljubesic et al., 2007; Tiedemann and Ljubešić, 2012; Haas and Derczynski, 2021; Jauhiainen et al., 2019). Extending the dataset with a keyword-based approach is an interesting future venue.

We follow the process of selecting tweets for this task as in Nguyen et al., 2020 (see appendix A.2), with the only exception of keeping tweets written by a user with less than 500 followers, since Danish Twitter users have fewer followers in general. This resulted in approximately 9,000 COVID-19 related Danish Tweets. The first 5,000 tweets were selected for annotation. We release the full filtered dataset (Twitter ids of all 9,000 tweets) for future work on this collection.[3] See the appendix for annotation guidelines and data quality.

2.3 Data partitions

From the 5,000 tweets, we ended up with a small dataset consisting of 500 tweets (125 INFORMATIVE+, 19 INFORMATIVE-, and 356 UNINFORMATIVE) and a larger dataset with 4,500 more UNINFORMATIVE tweets, thus increasing the class imbalance (see appendix A.3 for a full description of the annotation process). To evaluate data quality, 500 tweets were labelled by two annotators resulting in high agreement (0.93 raw agreement and 0.83 Cohen's Kappa score). These were split into training, validation, and final test sets as two 80/20 stratified splits by first creating an 80/20 split of the 500 tweets and then an 80/20 split of the 400 tweets to form the train/validation datasets. The stratified split ensures that each set contained the same proportion of INFORMATIVE+, INFORMATIVE-, and UNINFORMATIVE tweets.

The 400 tweets were merged with 80% of the 4,500 UNINFORMATIVE tweets to form a second larger dataset. An 80/20 stratified split is also applied on the large development dataset to form a larger set of train/validation datasets. The remaining 20% of the 4,500 UNINFORMATIVE tweets were added to the 100 tweets in the final test set to form a 2nd larger final test set.

To summarize, the final two datasets are: the small dataset of 100 tweets (labels: 25 INFORMATIVE+, 4 INFORMATIVE-, and 71 UNINFORMATIVE) and the large dataset of 1000 tweets (labels: 25 INFORMATIVE+, 4 INFORMATIVE-, and 971 UNINFORMATIVE).

3 Methodology

This section outlines the models that will be used.

3.1 Naive Bayes

We used Naive Bayes with word unigrams (Jurafsky and Martin, 2021) to compare our more complex model to a simple probabilistic baseline.

3.2 CNN

We experimented with a Convolutional Neural Network and test both word embeddings derived by word2vec and contextualized BERT embeddings. The CNN is based on the work of Kim (2014). The embedding layer is initialized with pretrained word2vec embeddings of size 400 that are based on Danish Twitter data (available from another WNUT 2021 shared task).[4] We also use pre-trained BERT embeddings as static input to the CNN model with a class weighted loss. Both Multilingual BERT (MBERT [5]) and Danish BERT (DBERT [6]) embeddings are used because we want to determine which is the best fit for this particular dataset.

We extensively tuned our CNN with a hyperparameter search (outlined in 3.4), which resulted in a CNN with 4 different filter sizes 1,3,5, and 7 with

[2]One could also opt to remove any such instances in future work, as such cases are very infrequent and difficult to model. However, as it does contain relevant information and we wanted to gauge their frequency and modelling difficulty, it was decided to keep it in.

[3]Tweet ids and annotations are available at: `https://github.com/beaol/`

[4]`https://t.co/n9Halt26tg?amp=1`

[5]`https://huggingface.co/bert-base-multilingual-uncased`

[6]`https://huggingface.co/Maltehb/danish-bert-botxo`

100 feature maps each, max-pooling which takes the most important feature of each filter, a dropout layer with a rate of 0.5, and a fully connected layer with an output dimension equal to the number of classes (i.e. 3). During training, we use a word dropout (to UNK) with probability $\frac{1}{100}$.

3.3 Class imbalance

Due to the high imbalance in the dataset, we experiment with a weighted loss function that reacts more to wrong predictions on the smaller classes (i.e. INFORMATIVE+ and INFORMATIVE-) and less on the larger classes (i.e. UNINFORMATIVE). This is done by using the inverse square root number of samples:

$$\frac{1}{\sqrt{class\_samples}}$$

Preliminary experiments confirmed this was superior to weighting inversely proportional to size.

3.4 Hyperparameter search

Given that the chosen NN architecture has many hyperparameters, i.e. number of filters, filter sizes, L2 regularization, embedding size, etc, we needed to test multiple variations to gain insight into which factors are the most impactful on performance.

A general take-away from the hyperparameter search is that the CNN showed the best performance with an L2 regularization of 0 (even though this makes the model overfit) and either few feature maps and a larger embedding size or more feature maps and a smaller embedding size.

These tests also showed that this type of model is quite sensitive to changes in hyperparameters as well as using different manual seeds. The performance can vary a lot in a positive or negative direction by e.g. changing the learning rate by a small amount. To illustrate this, we report both mean performance and max performance (macro F1) achieved by the best run.

The same observations were made when choosing between different class weighting techniques, such as inverse number of samples, which can be just as significant as changing the other parameters.

4 Evaluation

This section outlines the conducted experiments to examine how well each model performs on the given datasets.

Model	**Mean F1**	**Max F1**
Naive Bayes	74.11 ±2.00	76.53
CNN (no class weights)	63.88 ±7.87	72.58
CNN	73.45 ±4.01	79.10
CNN MBERT	**82.34** ±5.10	**87.13**
CNN DBERT	75.28 ±2.27	78.27

Table 1: Model results on development dataset with 400 tweets. Mean F1 macro score over three runs.

Model	**Mean F1**	**Max F1**
Naive Bayes	49.94 ±4.22	53.72
CNN (no class weights)	52.35 ±5.60	59.78
CNN	**63.47** ±5.86	**68.29**
CNN MBERT	56.93 ±4.07	62.57
CNN DBERT	60.45 ±1.61	62.22

Table 2: Model results on development dataset with 4,000 tweets. Mean F1 macro score over three runs.

4.1 Analysis disclaimer

To make sure no possibly privacy-sensitive information is shown, the tweets will not be shown in this paper. However, they will still be analyzed based on the predictions made by the model, but instead of showing the tweet it will be described.

4.2 Evaluation on development data

As found in Table 1, first we observe that class weighting is essential for the CNN. The class weighted CNN model with MBERT embeddings has the best mean F1 macro score of 82.34 and the best max F1 macro score of 87.13 on the smaller and more balanced dataset. When using the Danish DBERT embeddings we see a large drop in performance, which is surprising when considering that most of the dataset is in Danish.

Again, weighting is essential for the even more skewed larger dataset. However, a different pattern emerges in Table 2, where the best performing model on the full dataset on average and on a single run is the class weighted CNN model which uses pre-trained Danish Word2Vec embeddings to initialize the embedding layer. However, this is only based on three runs and since the standard deviation is high, it might not be the best performing model after doing more runs and could be outperformed by one of the CNN models with BERT embeddings. A combination of the Word2Vec and BERT embeddings could lead to better results in future, similar to multi-channel CNNs proposed by (Kim, 2014).

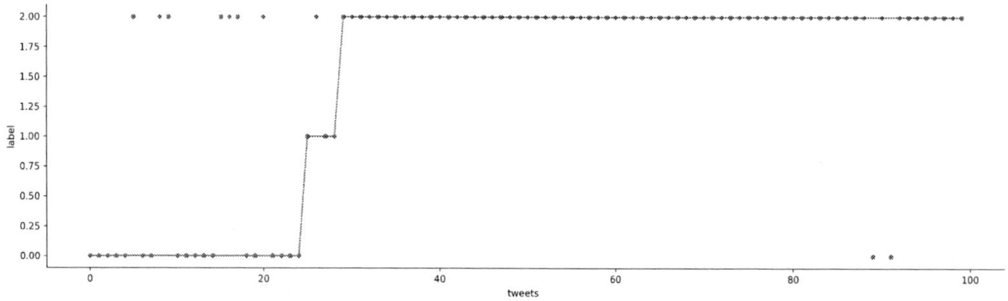

Figure 1: Staircase plot of testing on the final test dataset of 100 tweets made by the CNN model with class weighting using MBERT embeddings. Y-axis: 0=INFORMATIVE+,1=INFORMATIVE-,2=UNINFORMATIVE. Dots: predictions; red line: gold standard.

4.3 Evaluation on final test data

The results on the final test (Table 3) show that the CNN model with MBERT embeddings remains the best performer on a single run. However, the model trained on DBERT embeddings has become the best perfomer on average on this dataset while keeping the lowest standard deviation as seen on the development datasets as well. This shows that in challenging highly skewed distributions, having an optimal CNN configuration is difficult to obtain.

Similarly for the final test dataset with 1000 tweets (Table 4), the CNN model with MBERT embeddings is the best performer on a single run. However, for this dataset we also see that it is the best performer on average although it continues to get the highest standard deviation of the different approaches on the test dataset, thus showing to be the most unstable model on the test datasets.

5 Analysis

Given that INFORMATIVE- is very infrequent, we analyse the per-class predictions. We examine whether the model learns to accurately predict this class at all.

We create a different representation of the confusion matrix, which we call the *Staircase plot*, to better visualize exactly which tweets were labelled correctly and incorrectly by a given model. This enables us to visually compare individual tweet classifications between the different models. An example in Figure 1 shows the Staircase plot of the best single run produced by the weighted CNN model with static MBERT. We notice that the model is very good at INFORMATIVE-, in fact only misses one instance. Most confusions stem from the INFORMATIVE+ label, which most often got predicted as UNINFORMATIVE.

Some of these tweets are in fact difficult for all of the models to classify correctly (see appendix A.4). For example, the sixth INFORMATIVE+ is misclassified by all models as an UNINFORMATIVE tweet. This particular tweet shortly mentions how many people have been put in intensive care due to COVID-19 and then questions the need for continuing with the lockdown. We believe that it is the final part of the tweet that confuses the models, possibly also because the word "intensive" has not been weighted high enough in terms of significant feature descriptors of the INFORMATIVE+ class.

Another common misclassification is on the INFORMATIVE- tweets. The training dataset contains a total number of 15 INFORMATIVE- tweets where 5 of these are in Danish and 10 are in English. The imbalance between Danish and English in this case is present in the misclassification, since the common tweet that all models get wrong is a Danish tweet and the remaining 3 tweets are in English. Based on these results it appears that the model learns to distinguish between Danish and English and simply predicts English tweets as INFORMATIVE-. We would therefore also expect that English UNINFORMATIVE tweets are misclassified as INFORMATIVE-. This is the case for all models except the CNN MBERT model, which uses multilingual embeddings hence having the ability to distinguish between English INFORMATIVE- and UNINFORMATIVE tweets.

Two challenging UNINFORMATIVE tweets are: one containing some numbers and the word "infected", and the other tweet contains some numbers as well and the word "death". It makes sense that

Model	Mean F1	Max F1
Naive Bayes	74.78 ±2.63	77.28
CNN (no class weights)	74.40 ±4.23	78.93
CNN	74.05 ±7.04	82.50
CNN MBERT	74.10 ±13.27	**86.31**
CNN DBERT	**78.12** ±1.13	79.30

Table 3: Model results on final test set with 100 tweets for the model trained on the small development data.

Model	Mean F1	Max F1
Naive Bayes	54.13 ±4.19	60.07
CNN (no class weights)	50.42 ±1.08	51.77
CNN	61.35 ±6.01	68.08
CNN MBERT	**70.72** ±9.63	**84.15**
CNN DBERT	60.17 ±1.68	62.55

Table 4: Model results on final test set with 1000 tweets for the model trained on the larger development data.

the models would find these tweets difficult given that numbers and the words: "corona", "infect", "recover", "death", and "test", are considered to be strong indicators of an informative tweet when used in the same tweet.

6 Conclusion

We contribute a new Danish dataset consisting of COVID-19 related tweets and benchmarked neural models. The imbalanced dataset made the task very challenging, but most realistic. The most effective model tested in this paper was the CNN model with class weighting. However, there is no single best embedding setup that consistently outperforms all others on the two development datasets. The CNN model was found to be very sensitive to randomness and hyperparameters, yet loss weighting was essential in this setup as otherwise the CNN performs similar to a simple Naive Bayes model. Future work includes extending the created dataset, comparing supervised training with semi-supervised methods, and a comparison of the CNNs used in this work to fine-tuning models.

Acknowledgements

This research is in part supported by the Independent Research Fund Denmark (DFF) grant 9131-00019B. We thank ITU's High-performance Computing Cluster team for computational resources used in this work, and the anonymous WNUT-2021 reviewers for their thorough feedback.

References

Luca Maria Aiello, Daniele Quercia, Ke Zhou, Marios Constantinides, Sanja Šćepanović, and Sagar Joglekar. 2021. How epidemic psychology works on twitter: evolution of responses to the covid-19 pandemic in the us. *Humanities and Social Sciences Communications*, 8(1):1–15.

Juan M Banda, Ramya Tekumalla, Guanyu Wang, Jingyuan Yu, Tuo Liu, Yuning Ding, Ekaterina Artemova, Elena Tutubalina, and Gerardo Chowell. 2021. A large-scale covid-19 twitter chatter dataset for open scientific research—an international collaboration. *Epidemiologia*, 2(3):315–324.

Anders Giovanni Møller, Rob van der Goot, and Barbara Plank. 2020. NLP north at WNUT-2020 task 2: Pre-training versus ensembling for detection of informative COVID-19 English tweets. In *Proceedings of the Sixth Workshop on Noisy User-generated Text (W-NUT 2020)*, pages 331–336, Online. Association for Computational Linguistics.

René Haas and Leon Derczynski. 2021. Discriminating between similar nordic languages. In *Proceedings of the Eighth Workshop on NLP for Similar Languages, Varieties and Dialects*, pages 67–75, Kiyv, Ukraine. Association for Computational Linguistics.

Tommi Jauhiainen, Marco Lui, Marcos Zampieri, Timothy Baldwin, and Krister Lindén. 2019. Automatic language identification in texts: A survey. *Journal of Artificial Intelligence Research*, 65:675–782.

Daniel Jurafsky and James H. Martin. 2021. *Speech and Language Processing*, (3rd ed. draft) edition, chapter 4. Pearson Prentice Hall.

Yoon Kim. 2014. Convolutional neural networks for sentence classification. In *Proceedings of the 2014 Conference on Empirical Methods in Natural Language Processing (EMNLP)*, pages 1746–1751, Doha, Qatar. Association for Computational Linguistics.

Chayakrit Krittanawong, Bharat Narasimhan, Hafeez Ul Hassan Virk, Harish Narasimhan, Joshua Hahn, Zhen Wang, and WH Wilson Tang. 2020. Misinformation dissemination in twitter in the covid-19 era. *The American journal of medicine*, 133(12):1367.

Priyanshu Kumar and Aadarsh Singh. 2020. NutCracker at WNUT-2020 task 2: Robustly identifying informative COVID-19 tweets using ensembling and adversarial training. In *Proceedings of the Sixth Workshop on Noisy User-generated Text (W-NUT 2020)*, pages 404–408, Online. Association for Computational Linguistics.

Nikola Ljubesic, Nives Mikelic, and Damir Boras. 2007. Language indentification: How to distinguish similar languages? In *2007 29th International Conference on Information Technology Interfaces*, pages 541–546. IEEE.

Dat Quoc Nguyen, Thanh Vu, Afshin Rahimi, Mai Hoang Dao, Linh The Nguyen, and Long Doan. 2020. WNUT-2020 task 2: Identification of informative COVID-19 English tweets. In *Proceedings of the Sixth Workshop on Noisy User-generated Text (W-NUT 2020)*, pages 314–318, Online. Association for Computational Linguistics.

Jörg Tiedemann and Nikola Ljubešić. 2012. Efficient discrimination between closely related languages. In *Proceedings of COLING 2012*, pages 2619–2634.

Maxwell Weinzierl, Suellen Hopfer, and Sanda M Harabagiu. 2021. Misinformation adoption or rejection in the era of covid-19. In *Proceedings of the International AAAI Conference on Web and Social Media*, volume 15, pages 787–795.

A Appendices

A.1 Annotation guidelines

Nguyen et al. (2020) defined the "INFORMATIVE" label as Tweets which mentions suspected cases, confirmed cases, recovered cases, deaths, number of tests performed as well as location or travel history associated with the confirmed/suspected cases. "INFORMATIVE" Tweets also have to mention specific quantities (e.g. "1 new case" or "five deaths today") or a quantity which can be inferred (e.g. "100 people were tested today, 25% were positive"), but not percentages where the quantity cannot be inferred(e.g. an "UNINFORMATIVE" tweet: "0.5% of the danish population has tested positive"). We named this label: "INFORMATIVE+". Another requirement for an "INFORMATIVE+" tweet is that it cannot contain rumors or predictions regarding the COVID-19 related information.

We also define a new label: "INFORMATIVE-", which will be used for Tweets that are difficult to label as either "INFORMATIVE+" or "UNINFORMATIVE" or if the Tweet is "INFORMATIVE+" but in English instead of Danish. An example of a tweet that is difficult to label as "INFORMATIVE+" or "UNINFORMATIVE" is: "No number of deaths since the 10th death", which has an informative part where it is mentioned that there have been no new death cases, but it also has an uninformative part where it says that this is only the case since the 10th death. All models will also try to classify tweets which are labelled as "INFORMATIVE-", unlike previous research which only made binary classifiers for "INFORMATIVE+" and "UNINFORMATIVE", with the intention of discovering if the developed models are able to distinguish between English and Danish and/or extract the features which made the annotators uncertain about the class label.

The third label is: "UNINFORMATIVE", which is used for all Tweets that cannot be labelled as "INFORMATIVE+" or "INFORMATIVE-", which includes English tweets that do not contain any informative COVID-19 related information.

A.2 Data collection

Tweets containing less than 10 words (including hashtags and user mentions) are filtered out. This was done because it was determined that most tweets with less than 10 words in the dataset did not contain informative information, after labelling a large amount of tweets. Nguyen et al., 2020 also filtered out Tweets from users with less than 500 followers, which we decided not to do since Danish Twitter users have fewer followers in general. The dataset is iterated over from start to end (in terms of time posted) where hashtags, user mentions, and the re-tweet tag is removed (if it is there). The updated tweet text is then made all lower case before being stored. If two tweets are identical, then the first tweet is kept and the new tweet is filtered out. This resulted in around 9,000 COVID-19 related Danish Tweets.

A.3 Data annotation process

From the 9,000 Tweets, one annotator (with a computer science background) independently assigned 5,000 tweets with one of the three labels: "INFORMATIVE+", "INFORMATIVE-", and "UNINFORMATIVE". Around 100 of these tweets were labelled "INFORMATIVE+" and the remaining tweets were mostly labelled as "UNINFORMATIVE". From these 5,000 Tweets, all of the "INFORMATIVE+" and "INFORMATIVE-" were selected and the "UNINFORMATIVE" Tweets were selected at random until the dataset contained 500 Tweets in total. The only criteria for the "UNINFORMATIVE" Tweets were that half of them should contain numbers to prevent the future model from learning that "INFORMATIVE+" Tweets contain numbers.

These 500 Tweets were also labelled by second annotator with a linguistics background, which then made it possible to measure the inter-annotator agreement to assess the quality of the annotations.

From the 500 tweets, there were only 35 disagreements (raw agreement of 0.93) between the annotators, which resulted in a Cohen's Kappa score of 0.83 and this can be interpreted as almost perfect agreement.

A third opinion was seeked on the 35 Tweets which caused disagreement to finalize the annotation (majority votes for a label wins). After this step, we had 500 tweets (125 "INFORMATIVE+", 19 "INFORMATIVE-", and 356 "UNINFORMATIVE"), which had a Cohen's kappa score of 0.949 with the first annotator's labels and 0.880 with the second annotator's labels.

Given that the first Cohen's kappa score was almost perfect, we decided to also use the 4500 other "UNINFORMATIVE" tweets that the first annotator labelled.

A.4 Dataset figures

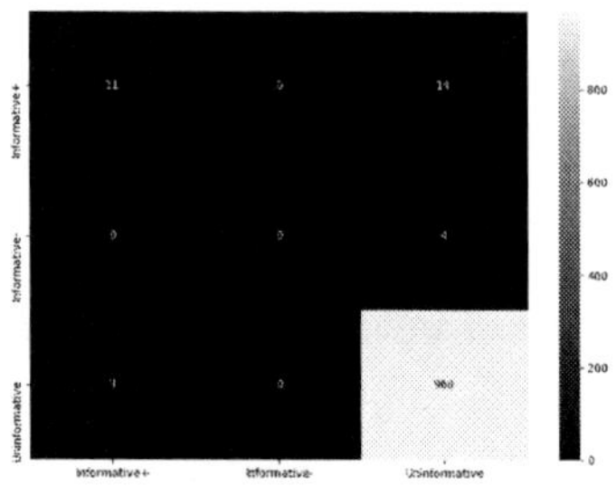

Figure 2: CNN without class weighting confusion matrix from the larger final test set of 1000 tweets

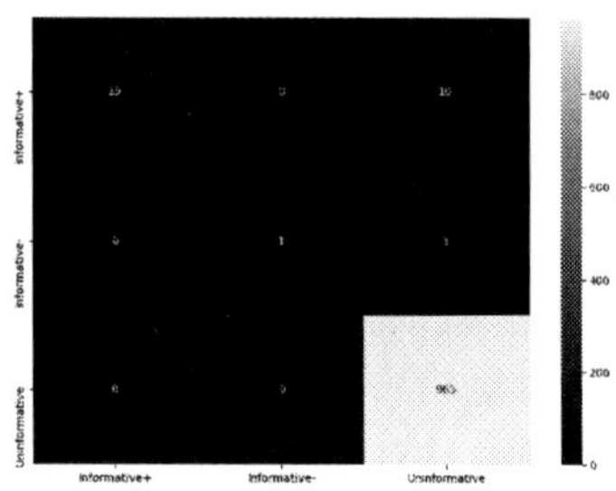

Figure 3: CNN with class weighting confusion matrix made from the larger final test dataset of 1000 tweets

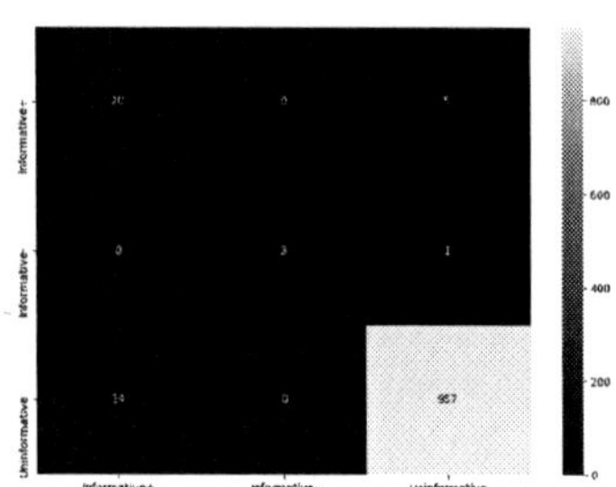

Figure 4: CNN with class weighting using MBERT confusion matrix on the larger final test set of 1000 tweets

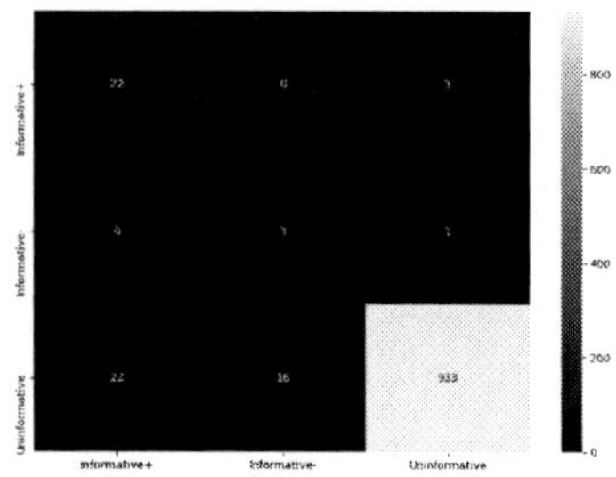

Figure 5: CNN with class weighting using DBERT confusion matrix from the larger final test set of 1000 tweets

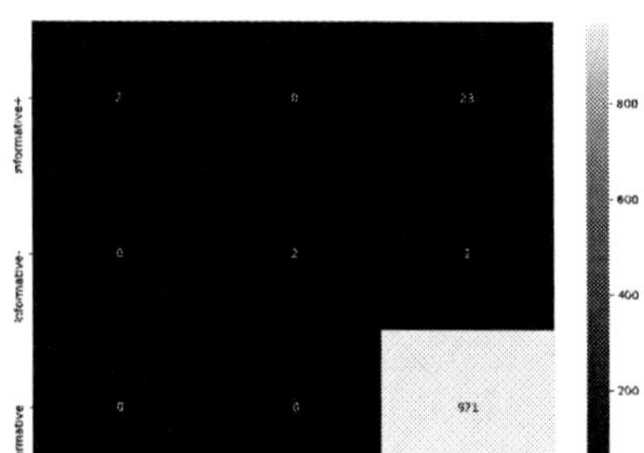

Figure 6: Naive Bayes confusion matrix made from the larger final test dataset of 1000 tweets

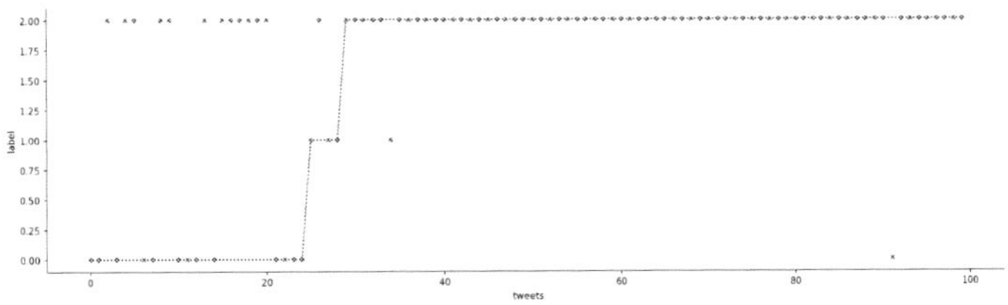

Figure 7: Staircase plot of the testing on the final test dataset of 100 tweets made by the Naive Bayes model

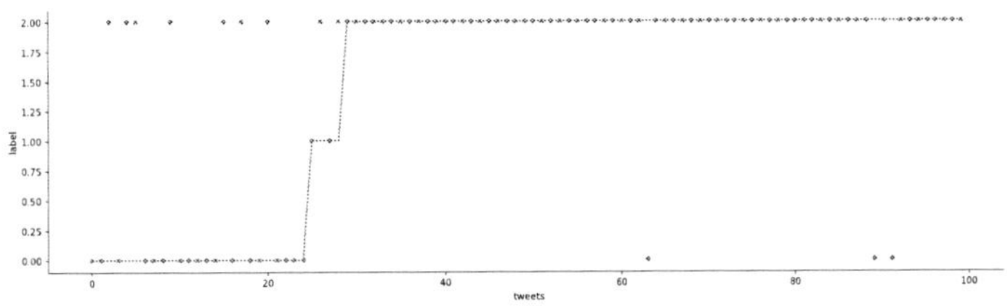

Figure 8: Staircase plot of the testing on the final test dataset of 100 tweets made by the CNN model without class weighting

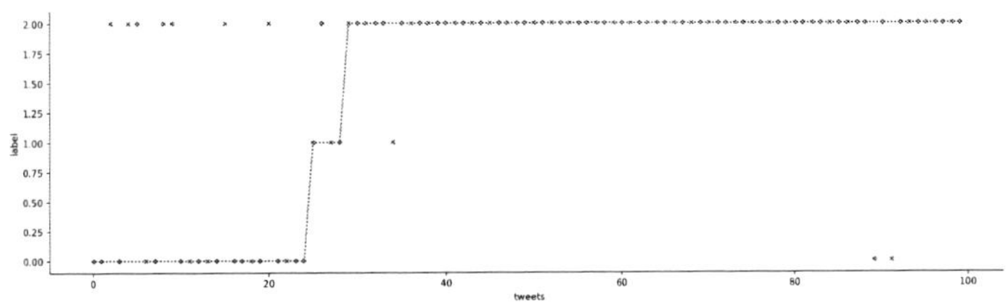

Figure 9: Staircase plot of the testing on the final test dataset of 100 tweets made by the CNN model with class weighting

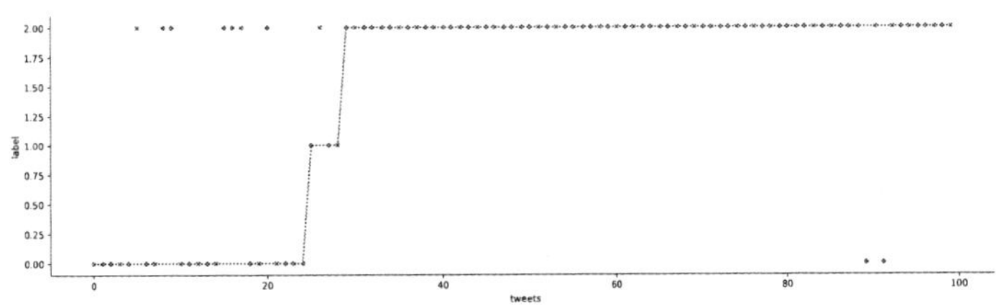

Figure 10: Staircase plot of the testing on the final test dataset of 100 tweets made by the CNN model with class weighting using MBERT embeddings

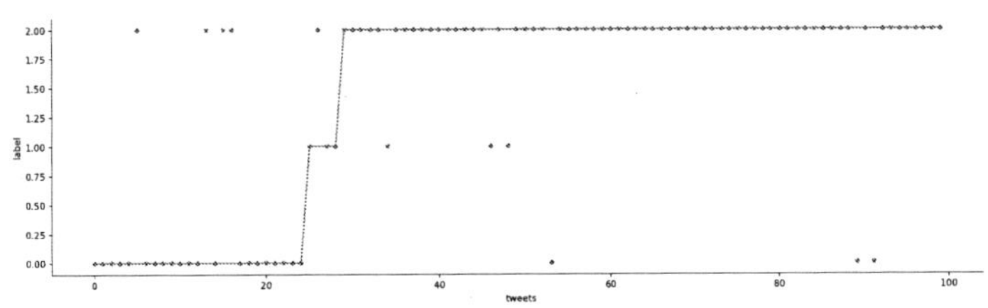

Figure 11: Staircase plot of the testing on the final test dataset of 100 tweets made by the CNN model with class weighting using DBERT embeddings

Detecting Depression in Thai Blog Posts: a Dataset and a Baseline

Mika Hämäläinen[1,2], Pattama Patpong[3], Khalid Alnajjar[1,2],
Niko Partanen[2] and Jack Rueter[2]
[1]Rootroo Ltd
[2]University of Helsinki
[3]Mahidol University
[2]firstname.lastname@helsinki.fi [3]ppattama@yahoo.com

Abstract

We present the first openly available corpus for detecting depression in Thai. Our corpus is compiled by expert verified cases of depression in several online blogs. We experiment with two different LSTM based models and two different BERT based models. We achieve a 77.53% accuracy with a Thai BERT model in detecting depression. This establishes a good baseline for future researcher on the same corpus. Furthermore, we identify a need for Thai embeddings that have been trained on a more varied corpus than Wikipedia. Our corpus, code and trained models have been released openly on Zenodo.

1 Introduction

Depression is a significant public-health problem and one of the leading causes of disease burden worldwide. In 2010, Depression was ranked as the sixth leading causes of disability-adjusted life years in South-East Asia (Murray et al., 2012). Globally, more than 264 million people were affected (James et al., 2018). Depression affects 86 million people in South-East Asia region. At its most severe, depression can lead to suicide, which is the second highest cause of death among 15-29 years old in the region (Sharma, 2017).

Depression is a growing problem in Thailand as the country has a globally high depression rate reaching to 1.7 million people (see Kongsuk et al. 2017). At the same time, people dealing with depression struggle to find help (see Dundon 2006), or worse yet, they might receive insufficient treatment (Lotrakul and Saipanish, 2009). A worst-case scenario, depression can lead to suicide. Depression is one of the leading causes of suicide in Thai adolescents (Sukhawaha and Arunpongpaisal, 2017). In 2019, suicide rate of Thai people aged between 20-29 was 667 persons and aged between 30-39 was 959 persons which was the highest numbers of all aged groups[1].

While Thai is not what we would call low-resourced (see Hämäläinen 2021), there are currently no datasets available for detecting depression in the Thai language. We present a new dataset based on blog posts and verified cases of depressed bloggers. Furthermore, we establish a baseline for further research on the topic in the Thai language. We have published the dataset, code and models presented in this paper openly on Zenodo[2].

2 Related work

In this section we present some of the recent related work in more detail. While there have been several digital humanities driven research efforts in better understanding depression in text (Girard and Cohn, 2015; Abd Yusof et al., 2017; Loveys et al., 2018), we only focus on work that has been conducted on depression detection. There are also several approaches to depression detection in other languages (Pirina and Çöltekin, 2018; Husseini Orabi et al., 2018; Song et al., 2018).

An onset of major depression can be characterized and detected by investigating social media data such as Twitter (De Choudhury et al., 2013b,a). By exploring a large corpus of Twitter posting by using crowd-sourcing methodology. An SVM classifier was built by divesting a variety of social media measures such as social activity, egonetwork, style, user engagement, emotion, and language. The classifier model predicted with high accuracy (70% and 73 % respectively) predicting ahead of the reported onset of depression and whether

[1]Department of Mental Health report https://dmh.go.th/report/suicide/age.asp
[2]https://zenodo.org/record/4734552

Proceedings of the 2021 EMNLP Workshop W-NUT: The Seventh Workshop on Noisy User-generated Text, pages 20–25
November 11, 2021.

or not a post on Twitter could be depressive-indicative postings. Depression levels is detected by a proposed social media depression index.

Computerized analysis of various kind of texts related to depression reveals signals of psychiatric disorders. Depression is measured by self-reported symptoms (Rude et al., 2002), by clinical interview (Rude et al., 2003). The Scrambled Sentences Test (SST) (Wenzlaff, 1993) was used to measure of cognitive processing bias of a large sample of college students. Negative cognitive processing biases in resolving ambiguous verbal information can predict depression and subsequent depression symptoms.

Depression has been detected automatically before in Thai Facebook users (Katchapakirin et al., 2018). The authors train several models on RapidMiner. The models rely on metadata for activity on Facebook such as the number of posts posted on a given week day, the number of day-time and night-time posts and the number of shared posts. The authors did not train the models on text, but rather used numerical features extracted from Facebook posts such as the number of first person pronouns and number of positive words.

A screening text-based classification model was also applied to Thai Facebook posts to detect depressive disorder (Hemtanon and Kittiphattanabawon, 2019). Similarly to the previous approach, the authors apply several traditional machine learning techniques to Thai social media text with pre-extracted features.

Kumnunt and Sornil, 2020 present a CNN (convolutional neural network) based approach to depression detection in Thai social media posts. The authors crawl posts tagged with a depression hashtag to build their dataset.

Contrary to any of the current work on Thai depression detection, our approach does not deal with social media posts but lengthier blog posts. We also make our dataset available unlike the existing work.

3 Data

Our data was taken from blogs or weblogs. As defined by Mishne (2005), blogs are personal, highly opinionated logs, available publicly, with a subjective writing style, and the use of non-content features such as emotions. Blogs can be used as data sources to predict the most likely state of mind with which the post was written: whether the blogger was depressed, cheerful or bored. Blogs prompt many bloggers to indicate their mood at the time of posting (Mishne et al., 2006).

We have obtained post data from two main platforms: the weblog entitled "Storylog" and personal blogs posted via two blog platforms "bloggang.com" and "blogspot.com". Storylog is a social writing platform in Thai language. It was launched in 2014 (https://storylog.co). Its philosophy is "Everyone has something to tell." Stories shared on it are text-based articles about life experiences, opinions, ideas, as well as inspirations. Posts are organized by the bloggers' areas of interest experience, emotion, inspiration, and short story. Towards the other end of communication, blog readers can comment on the given post.

We use these platforms to collect a corpus of posts that are written by depressed individuals. Only posts, not user comments, are analyzed in this study. Criteria for data collection included:

- each blogger has posted at least 15 post entries
- posts contain depressive experiences indicated by the key words "depressed", "depression", "depressive disorder", "useless", "fail", "death", "overdose", "suicide", "cut", "self harm"
- the content of the post contains one of the three types of depression symptoms (Cassano and Fava, 2002): psychological symptoms, behavioral symptoms, and physical symptoms
- only posts written in prose format are investigated
- poetic format and English translation are excluded

Through manual analysis and verification, we reach to 400 depressed posts published on Storylog between 2015-2019, and 72 personal blogs posts published during the same time period. In total, our corpus contains 472 verified depressed blog posts. To make the corpus viable for machine learning, we further crawl an additional 472 blog posts that do not exhibit depression from the Storylog platform.

Sentence	Depression
การวิ่งหนีความรู้สึกที่ “ยาก” เกินไปทำให้เราปลอดภัยและไม่เจ็บปวด Running away from feeling "difficult" keeps us safe and away from pain.	True
มต้องอ่านถ้าไม่อยากฟังรสขมสุดตีนของชีวิตคนคนนึง You don't have to read if you don't want to hear the bitter taste of a person's life.	True
แต่ยังจำความเจ็บจากการคาดหวังมากเกินไปได้ดี But I still remember the pain of expecting too much	True
เป็นวันที่เหนื่อยจริงๆเหนื่อยทั้งกายและใจมากๆ It was a really tiring day, I am very tired both physically and mentally.	True
อืม นั่นล่ะ ความรู้สึกที่ชัดเจนที่สุดมาตั้งนานแล้ว.. Well, that's it. The clearest feeling for a long time.	True
เริ่มต้นขึ้นเมื่อเขาใช้เวลาว่างจากการอ่านหนังสืออย่างหนักหน่วงในช่วงวัยรุ่น It began when he spent his free time reading heavily during his teenage years.	False
ไม่คิดจะหยิบหนังสือขึ้นมาอ่านหน่อยหรือ Don't you want to pick up and read a book?	False
ถ้ามีโอกาสหนูอยากให้พี่เข้ามาอ่านนะหนูอยากไปต่อกับพี่ If there's a chance I want you to come in and read it, I want to go with you.	False
ฉันเจอเธอทุกวันที่ป้ายรถประจำทางตอนเช้า I see her every day at the bus stop in the morning.	False
เขามีเพียงรอยยิ้มประดับเล็กน้อยบนแก้ม He only has a slightly embellished smile on his cheeks.	False

Table 1: Example sentences from the dataset and their translations in English

	train	valid	test
depressed	12837	1712	2567
non-depressed	12240	1632	2448

Table 2: Number of sentences in the data splits

In total, our dataset has 472 depressed and 472 non-depressed blog posts. We shuffle the data on a sentence level and split it to 75% training, 10 % validation and 15 % testing. The splits are shared across all the models. Table 1 shows some examples of the dataset with translations into English. The number of sentences for training, testing and validation can be seen in Table 2

Words are typically written together without spaces in Thai language and white-spaces are used to indicate sentence boundaries. This means that the blog posts need to be tokenized into sentences and words. We do these tokenizations by using PyThaiNLP (Phatthiyaphaibun et al., 2016).

4 Detecting depression

In this section, we describe the four different models we use to automatically detect depression in our dataset. Following Hämäläinen et al. (2021), two of the models are based on LSTM (long short-term memory) models and two on transfer learning on pretrained BERT models (Devlin et al., 2019).

We train our first model using a bi-directional LSTM based model (Hochreiter and Schmidhuber, 1997) using OpenNMT (Klein et al., 2017) with the default settings except for the encoder where we use a BRNN (bi-directional recurrent neural network) (Schuster and Paliwal, 1997) instead of the default RNN (recurrent neural network). We use the default of two layers for both the encoder and the decoder and the default attention model, which is the general global attention presented by Luong et al. (2015). The model is trained for the default 100,000 steps. The model is trained with tokenized sentences as its source and the depression label as its target.

We train an additional LSTM model with the same configuration and the same random seed (3435) with the only difference being that we use pretrained word2vec embeddings for the encoder. We use the Thai2vec embeddings provided as a part of PyThaiNLP[3]. The vector size is 300 and the model has been trained on Thai Wikipedia.

In addition, we train two different BERT based sequence classification models based on the Thai BERT model[4] and Multilingual BERT (Devlin et al., 2019), which has been trained on multiple languages, Thai being one of the latest additions to the cased model. We use the transformers package (Wolf et al., 2020) to conduct the fine tuning with our dataset. The models are fine tuned to predict the depression label from a tokenized sentence. For the Multilingual BERT model, we use the same tokenization as for the other models, but for the Thai BERT model, we run the model's own tokenizier on an untokenized input. As hyperparameters for the fine tuning, we use 3 epochs with 500 warm-up steps for the learning rate scheduler and 0.01 as the strength of the weight decay.

This setup takes into account the current state of the art at the field, and uses recently created resources such as Thai BERT model, with our own custom made dataset. Everything is set up in an easily replicable manner, which ensures that our experiments and results can be used in further work on this important topic.

5 Results

In this section, we show and discuss the results obtained with our 4 different models: 2 LSTM based models and 2 BERT based ones. The results of the models can be seen in Table 3.

	overall acc	depression acc	no depression acc
LSTM	76.19%	77.05%	75.29%
LSTM +w2v	75.69%	74.44%	**77.00%**
Multilingual BERT	75.06%	79.11%	70.80%
Thai BERT	**77.53%**	**79.70%**	75.25%

Table 3: The accuracies obtained by the different models

The model finetuned on Thai BERT reaches the highest overall accuracy and the highest accuracy in detecting depressed sentences correctly. However, it misclassifies non depressed sentences as depressed more frequently than the LSTM based model that is trained with word2vec embeddings. This is interesting as the BERT model is superior to the LSTM model in the overall and depression accuracies and notably inferior in the non-depression accuracy.

What makes this result even more interesting is that both the Thai BERT and the pretraiend word2vec model used with the LSTM model have been trained on Thai Wikipedia. This is very likely due to the fact that Wikipedia represents the type of genre that does not exhibit any features of depression, and therefore a word2vec based model that cannot capture contextual information is more likely to label sentences as non depressed leading to a lower accuracy in the depressed label and a higher accuracy in the non depressed label. The contextuality of the BERT embeddings makes it possible for them to be fine tuned better towards the new genre of depressed text.

6 Discussion and conclusions

In this paper, we have presented a new expert curated dataset for depression detection in Thai blog posts. Our sentence level results are promising and we are sure we can use our models to snowball more depressed blog posts from platforms such as Storylog for further linguistic analysis as a part of our interdisciplinary research project.

Based on our results, we can identify one easy future direction for enhancing the results obtained by our models. Currently, all freely available pretrained Thai embbeddings have been trained on Wikipedia. This is not optimal for several reasons, one being the encyclopedic genre of Wikipedia, the other being the fact that while Wikipedia is written in formal "correct" Thai, blog posts are written in a more colloquial language variety. This means that the vocabulary coverage of Wikipedia data is poor when compared to blog posts.

Our blog corpus consists of 21,002 unique tokens while the word2vec model trained on Wikipedia has embeddings for 51,358 words.

[3] https://pythainlp.github.io/tutorials/notebooks/word2vec_examples.html

[4] https://github.com/ThAIKeras/bert

The blog corpus (training, testing and validation combined) contains 6,488 words that are not present in the word2vec model, this means that around 31% of the words present in our blog depression corpus are simply not in a Wikipedia based model. In the future, it is clear that Thai language calls for openly available models that are trained on a larger and more varied internet corpus than solely on Wikipedia.

References

Noor Fazilla Abd Yusof, Chenghua Lin, and Frank Guerin. 2017. Analysing the causes of depressed mood from depression vulnerable individuals. In *Proceedings of the International Workshop on Digital Disease Detection using Social Media 2017 (DDDSM-2017)*, pages 9–17, Taipei, Taiwan. Association for Computational Linguistics.

Paolo Cassano and Maurizio Fava. 2002. Depression and public health: an overview. *Journal of psychosomatic research*, 53(4):849–857.

Munmun De Choudhury, Scott Counts, and Eric Horvitz. 2013a. Social media as a measurement tool of depression in populations. In *Proceedings of the 5th annual ACM web science conference*, pages 47–56.

Munmun De Choudhury, Michael Gamon, Scott Counts, and Eric Horvitz. 2013b. Predicting depression via social media. In *Proceedings of the International AAAI Conference on Web and Social Media*, volume 7.

Jacob Devlin, Ming-Wei Chang, Kenton Lee, and Kristina Toutanova. 2019. BERT: Pre-training of deep bidirectional transformers for language understanding. In *Proceedings of the 2019 Conference of the North American Chapter of the Association for Computational Linguistics: Human Language Technologies, Volume 1 (Long and Short Papers)*, pages 4171–4186, Minneapolis, Minnesota. Association for Computational Linguistics.

Edith "Emma" Dundon. 2006. Adolescent depression: A metasynthesis. *Journal of Pediatric Health Care*, 20(6):384–392.

Jeffrey M Girard and Jeffrey F Cohn. 2015. Automated audiovisual depression analysis. *Current opinion in psychology*, 4:75–79.

Mika Hämäläinen. 2021. Endangered languages are not low-resourced! In *Multilingual Facilitation*, pages 1–11. University of Helsinki.

Mika Hämäläinen, Khalid Alnajjar, Niko Partanen, and Jack Rueter. 2021. Never guess what I heard... rumor detection in Finnish news: a dataset and a baseline. In *Proceedings of the Fourth Workshop on NLP for Internet Freedom: Censorship, Disinformation, and Propaganda*, pages 39–44, Online. Association for Computational Linguistics.

Siranuch Hemtanon and Nichnan Kittiphattanabawon. 2019. An automatic screening for major depressive disorder from social media in thailand. *รายงานการประชุม วิชาการ เสนอ ผล งาน วิจัย ระดับ ชาติ และ นานาชาติ*, 1(10):103–113.

Sepp Hochreiter and Jürgen Schmidhuber. 1997. Long short-term memory. *Neural computation*, 9(8):1735–1780.

Ahmed Husseini Orabi, Prasadith Buddhitha, Mahmoud Husseini Orabi, and Diana Inkpen. 2018. Deep learning for depression detection of Twitter users. In *Proceedings of the Fifth Workshop on Computational Linguistics and Clinical Psychology: From Keyboard to Clinic*, pages 88–97, New Orleans, LA. Association for Computational Linguistics.

Spencer L James, Degu Abate, Kalkidan Hassen Abate, Solomon M Abay, Cristiana Abbafati, Nooshin Abbasi, Hedayat Abbastabar, Foad Abd-Allah, Jemal Abdela, Ahmed Abdelalim, et al. 2018. Global, regional, and national incidence, prevalence, and years lived with disability for 354 diseases and injuries for 195 countries and territories, 1990–2017: a systematic analysis for the global burden of disease study 2017. *The Lancet*, 392(10159):1789–1858.

Kantinee Katchapakirin, Konlakorn Wongpatikaseree, Panida Yomaboot, and Yongyos Kaewpitakkun. 2018. Facebook social media for depression detection in the thai community. In *2018 15th International Joint Conference on Computer Science and Software Engineering (JCSSE)*, pages 1–6. IEEE.

Guillaume Klein, Yoon Kim, Yuntian Deng, Jean Senellart, and Alexander M. Rush. 2017. OpenNMT: Open-Source Toolkit for Neural Machine Translation. In *Proc. ACL*.

Thoranin Kongsuk, Suttha Supanya, Kedsaraporn Kenbubpha, Supranee Phimtra, Supattra Sukhawaha, Jintana Leejongpermpoon, et al. 2017. Services for depression and suicide in thailand. *WHO South-East Asia journal of public health*, 6(1):34.

Boriharn Kumnunt and Ohm Sornil. 2020. Detection of depression in thai social media messages using deep learning. In *Proceedings of the 1st International Conference on Deep Learning Theory and Applications - DeLTA*, pages 111–118.

Manote Lotrakul and Ratana Saipanish. 2009. How do general practitioners in thailand diagnose and treat patients presenting with anxiety and depression? *Psychiatry and clinical neurosciences*, 63(1):37–42.

Kate Loveys, Jonathan Torrez, Alex Fine, Glen Moriarty, and Glen Coppersmith. 2018. Cross-cultural differences in language markers of depression online. In *Proceedings of the Fifth Workshop on Computational Linguistics and Clinical Psychology: From Keyboard to Clinic*, pages 78–87, New Orleans, LA. Association for Computational Linguistics.

Minh-Thang Luong, Hieu Pham, and Christopher D Manning. 2015. Effective approaches to attention-based neural machine translation. *arXiv preprint arXiv:1508.04025*.

Gilad Mishne. 2005. Experiments with mood classification in blog posts. In *Proceedings of ACM SIGIR 2005 workshop on stylistic analysis of text for information access*, volume 19, pages 321–327. Citeseer.

Gilad Mishne, Maarten De Rijke, et al. 2006. Capturing global mood levels using blog posts. In *AAAI spring symposium: computational approaches to analyzing weblogs*, volume 6, pages 145–152.

Christopher JL Murray, Theo Vos, Rafael Lozano, Mohsen Naghavi, Abraham D Flaxman, Catherine Michaud, Majid Ezzati, Kenji Shibuya, Joshua A Salomon, Safa Abdalla, et al. 2012. Disability-adjusted life years (dalys) for 291 diseases and injuries in 21 regions, 1990–2010: a systematic analysis for the global burden of disease study 2010. *The lancet*, 380(9859):2197–2223.

Wannaphong Phatthiyaphaibun, Korakot Chaovavanich, Charin Polpanumas, Arthit Suriyawongkul, Lalita Lowphansirikul, and Pattarawat Chormai. 2016. PyThaiNLP: Thai Natural Language Processing in Python. *Zenodo*.

Inna Pirina and Çağrı Çöltekin. 2018. Identifying depression on Reddit: The effect of training data. In *Proceedings of the 2018 EMNLP Workshop SMM4H: The 3rd Social Media Mining for Health Applications Workshop & Shared Task*, pages 9–12, Brussels, Belgium. Association for Computational Linguistics.

Stephanie S Rude, Carmen R Valdez, Susan Odom, and Arshia Ebrahimi. 2003. Negative cognitive biases predict subsequent depression. *Cognitive Therapy and Research*, 27(4):415–429.

Stephanie S Rude, Richard M Wenzlaff, Bryce Gibbs, Jennifer Vane, and Tavia Whitney. 2002. Negative processing biases predict subsequent depressive symptoms. *Cognition & Emotion*, 16(3):423–440.

Mike Schuster and Kuldip K Paliwal. 1997. Bidirectional recurrent neural networks. *IEEE transactions on Signal Processing*, 45(11):2673–2681.

Shamila Sharma. 2017. Talk about depression, strengthen depression-related services who. In *World Health Organization*.

Hoyun Song, Jinseon You, Jin-Woo Chung, and Jong C. Park. 2018. Feature attention network: Interpretable depression detection from social media. In *Proceedings of the 32nd Pacific Asia Conference on Language, Information and Computation*, Hong Kong. Association for Computational Linguistics.

S Sukhawaha and S Arunpongpaisal. 2017. Risk factor and suicide theory associated with suicide in adolescents: A narrative reviews. *Journal of the Psychiatric Association of Thailand*, 62(4):359–378.

Richard M Wenzlaff. 1993. The mental control of depression: Psychological obstacles to emotional well-being. *Century psychology series. Handbook of mental control.*

Thomas Wolf, Lysandre Debut, Victor Sanh, Julien Chaumond, Clement Delangue, Anthony Moi, Pierric Cistac, Tim Rault, Rémi Louf, Morgan Funtowicz, Joe Davison, Sam Shleifer, Patrick von Platen, Clara Ma, Yacine Jernite, Julien Plu, Canwen Xu, Teven Le Scao, Sylvain Gugger, Mariama Drame, Quentin Lhoest, and Alexander M. Rush. 2020. Transformers: State-of-the-art natural language processing. In *Proceedings of the 2020 Conference on Empirical Methods in Natural Language Processing: System Demonstrations*, pages 38–45, Online. Association for Computational Linguistics.

Keyphrase Extraction with Incomplete Annotated Training Data

Yanfei Lei
Beihang University, China
leiyanfei@buaa.edu.cn

Chunming Hu
Beihang University, China
hucm@buaa.edu.cn

Guanghui Ma
Beihang University, China
magh@act.buaa.edu.cn

Richong Zhang *
Beihang University, China
zhangrc@buaa.edu.cn

Abstract

Extracting keyphrases that summarize the main points of a document is a fundamental task in natural language processing. Supervised approaches to keyphrase extraction(KPE) are largely developed based on the assumption that the training data is fully annotated. However, due to the difficulty of keyphrase annotating, KPE models severely suffer from incomplete annotated problem in many scenarios. To this end, we propose a more robust training method that learns to mitigate the misguidance brought by unlabeled keyphrases. We introduce negative sampling to adjust training loss, and conduct experiments under different scenarios. Empirical studies on synthetic datasets and open domain dataset show that our model is robust to incomplete annotated problem and surpasses prior baselines. Extensive experiments on five scientific domain datasets of different scales demonstrate that our model is competitive with the state-of-the-art method.[1]

1 Introduction

Keyphrase extraction is the task of automatically extracting a set of phrases that provide a concise summary of a document content. An effective keyphrase extraction (KPE) system can benefit a wide range of natural language processing and information retrieval tasks(Hasan and Ng, 2014), such as text categorization(Hulth and Megyesi), opinion mining(Berend, 2011) and recommendation(Pudota et al., 2010). Recent supervised neural methods typically treat keyphrase extraction as a classification problem(Augenstein and Søgaard, 2017; Sun et al., 2020; Xiong et al., 2019), where given phrases are classified as keyphrases or non-keyphrases. Although supervised methods perform well in this task, it requires a large amount of labeled data which is extremely expensive and time-consuming to collect in many application scenarios(Liu et al., 2012).

The latest advances in neural KPE are mainly carried out on data sets in scientific domain datasets.(Augenstein et al., 2017; Meng et al., 2017). Because scientific domain has sufficient and high-quality training data for neural methods: some training data are annotated by authors, and the author is the person who is most familiar with their articles, the keyphrases annotated by author are high-quality. However, due to the requirements for professional knowledge in scientific domain, some keyphrases annotated by readers are incomplete. Table 1 shows an example case with incomplete keyphrase annotation. Obviously, "model validation" is more suitable as a keyphrase than "paper", "model" and "use", but "model validation" isn't annotated as keyphrase.

It has been suggested that keyphrase annotation is highly subjective(Sterckx et al., 2016). In real world scenarios, most potential applications of KPE deal with diverse documents originating from sparse sources that are rather different from scientific papers(Xiong et al., 2019). They often involve various domains whose contents target much wider audiences than scientists and require a large amount of high-quality labeled data which is extremely expensive to collect(Wang et al., 2018).

There are several prior works focused on data quality and insufficient labeled data issues, Sterckx et al.(Sterckx et al., 2016) treat supervised keyphrase extraction as Positive Unlabeled Learning(Ren et al., 2014) by reweighting importance of training samples. Wang et al.(Wang et al., 2018) used the idea of transfer learning and proposed Topic-based Adversarial Neural Network (TANN). They exploited unlabeled data in the target domain and data in the resource-rich source domain to alleviate incomplete annotated problem. However,

*Corresponding Author

[1]Our code and models are available at https://github.com/fredia/NS-KPE

Proceedings of the 2021 EMNLP Workshop W-NUT: The Seventh Workshop on Noisy User-generated Text, pages 26–34
November 11, 2021.

Table 1: An example case from Kp20K[2] with incomplete keyphrase annotations, which "model validation" is more suitable as a keyphrase than "paper", "model" and "use", but "model validation" isn't annotated as keyphrase.

title	The use of graphical models in model validation
abstract	The use of graphical models for model specification and in modelling is increasing rapidly. This paper discusses the use of these graphical models in model validation.
annotated keyphrases	paper,model,use,graphic model

transfer learning needs to have a strong correlation between the source domain and the target domain.

To overcome the impaction of incomplete annotated problem in keyphrase extraction, we introduced negative sampling to allow unlabeled keyphrases to have opportunities to be considered as keyphrase to participate in the training. Most previous model treated unlabeled keyphrases as negative samples, which will mislead the biased results of model training. In this study, we treat keyphrase extraction task as classification problem. First, we apply pre-trained model RoBERTa(Liu et al., 2019) to get word embeddings, based on word representations, use sliding CNN to extract candidate gram features, and then utilize a classifier layer to divide the candidate grams into **keyphrase** and **non-keyphrase** categories. At the same time, in order to explore the impact of incomplete annotated problem in different scenarios, we constructed different synthetic datasets by randomly masking some keyphrases, and conducted experiments on scientific domain datasets, synthetic datasets and open domain dataset. Extensive experiments show that our model well handles unlabeled keyphrases and surpasses prior baselines, and our model can obviously reduce the misguidance brought by unlabeled keyphrases in training when the incomplete problem is serious.

2 Related Work

In this section, we briefly review two classes of closely related works: keyphrase extraction approaches and learning with noisy data.

2.1 Keyphrase Extraction Approaches

In most traditional existing literature, keyphrase extraction has been formulated as a two-step process(Yuan et al., 2020). First, lexical features such as part-of-speech tags are used to determine a list of phrase candidates. Second, a ranking algorithm, such as TextRank(Mihalcea and Tarau, 2004), Multi-Layer perceptron and Support Vector Machine(Lopez and Romary, 2010), is adopted to rank the candidate list and the top ranked candidates are selected as keyphrases.

Because of the similarity with Named Entity Recognition(NER) task, keyphrase extraction is treated as a sequence labeling problem by using IOB tagging scheme(Alzaidy et al., 2019). Each word in the sentence is labeled as B-tag if it is the beginning of a keyphrase, I-tag if it's inside but not the first one within the keyphrase, or O-tag otherwise. Similarly, span-based models which are popular in NER task, also are utilized in keyphrase extraction task(Mu et al., 2020; Sun et al., 2020). They treat the spans, instead of single words, as the basic units for labeling.

Sometimes keyphrases are absent from the source text, the simple extraction methods mentioned above can only extract present keyphrase. Meng et al.(Meng et al., 2017) first proposed the CopyRNN, a neural generative model that both generates words from vocabulary and points to words from the source text with an encoder-decoder framework.

The supervised methods mentioned above have an assumption that the labeled data is completely credible, while the noise in annotated data is ignored. Zhu et al.(ZHU and WU, 2004) suggested that noise in labels tends to be more harmful than noise in features. Learning with noisy data will be introduced in next subsection.

2.2 Learning with Noisy Data

A number of approaches have been proposed to train DNNs with noisy data. One line of approaches formulate explicit or implicit noise layers to characterize the distribution of noisy and true labels(Hedderich and Klakow, 2018). Another line of approaches use correction methods to reduce the influence of noisy data. Sterckx et al.(Sterckx et al., 2016) reduce the influence of noisy data by reweighting the importance of unlabeled candidate phrases in a two-stage Positive Unlabeled Learning setting. Recently, a few other methods have also

[2]This example case is the 278404th sample in Kp20k-train dataset, which is available at OpenNMT-kpg-release

been proposed that use noise tolerant loss functions to achieve robust learning, Li et al.(Li et al., 2021) use negative sampling to adjust train loss, avoid training NER models with unlabeled entities. In our work, we treat KPE as classification problem, and introduce negative sampling to alleviate incomplete annotated problem.

3 Problem Formulation

3.1 Keyphrase Extraction

According to the setting of Meng et al.(Meng et al., 2017), we denote phrases that do not match any contiguous subsequence of a document as **absent** keyphrases, and the ones that fully match a part of the document as **present** keyphrases. In this work, we only focus on present keyphrase extraction and treat it as a classification problem.

Given a document d $= [w_1, w_2, \cdots, w_n]$, and the **present** annotated keyphrase set y $= \{y_1, y_2, \cdots, y_m\}$, where n is the length of document and m is the amount of **present** keyphrases. For each keyphease y_i in the keyphrase set, $y_i = \{w_{pos_i}, \cdots, w_{pos_i+len_i-1}\}$, which pos_i is the start position of i_{th} keyphrase, and len_i is the number of words in i_{th} keyphrase. As shown in Fig 1, since the length of most keyphrases are less than or equal to 5, we extract all N-grams($1 <= N <= 5$) as candidates firstly, which 1-gram $= \{\{w_1\}, \{w_2\}, \cdots, \{w_n\}\}$, 2-gram $= \{\{w_1, w_2\}, \{w_2, w_3\}, \cdots, \{w_{n-1}, w_n\}\}$, grams of other lengths are similar, let c_i^N present the i_{th} N-gram, and then apply a classifier to classify grams into keyphrases or non-keyphrases.

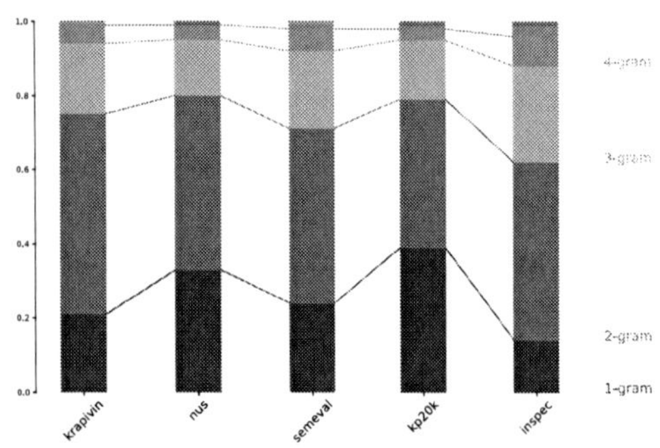

Figure 1: The distribution of the number of words in keyphrase. Different colors represent the proportion of different N-grams in the dataset. Green indicates the proportion of 5-gram, and red represents keyphrases with more than 5 words.

3.2 Incomplete Annotated problem

As mentioned above, keyphrase annotation is highly subjective(Sterckx et al., 2016) and requires the professional knowledge of the annotator, it is difficult to annotate keyphrases. Due to the complexity of keyphrase annotation or the heedlessness of human annotators, some ground truth keyphrase $\hat{y}$ of document d are not covered by annotated keyphrase set y, $\hat{y} \notin$ y.

4 Methodology

Inspired by the effectiveness of negative sampling in the field of NER(Li et al., 2021), we introduce negative sampling to keyphrase extraction field to solve incomplete annotated problem. CNN-based keyphrase extraction model will be presented firstly, and then we will introduce how to use negative sampling to improve the training process to make the model more robust.

4.1 CNN-based keyphrase extraction model

As shown in fig 2, our model mainly includes two components:(1) A feature extractor for candidate grams via sliding CNN. (2) A binary classifier which can verify whether a gram is a keyphrase.

4.1.1 Gram feature Extractor via sliding CNN

Inspired by textCNN proposed by Kim(Kim, 2014), we apply five filters with different kernel size to extract gram features. Let $h_i \in \mathbb{R}^k$ be the k-dimensional word embedding corresponding to the i_{th} token in the document. In general, let $h_{i:i+j}$ refer to the concatenation of word vectors $h_i, h_{i+1}, \cdots, h_{i+j}$. A convolution operation involves a filter $w_i \in \mathbb{R}^{Nk}$, which is applied to a window of N words to produce a new gram feature. The representation of the i_{th} N-gram c_i^N is calculated as:

$$g_i^N = CNN(h_{i:i+N-1}) \tag{1}$$

Here $h_{i:i+N-1}$ is the concatenation of i_{th} N-gram c_i^N word embeddings. Five filters are applied to each possible window of words to produce $n+(n-1)+(n-2)+(n-3)+(n-4)$ candidate grams.

4.1.2 Binary Classifier

After obtaining the candidate gram representations, we employ a non-linear classify layer to predict

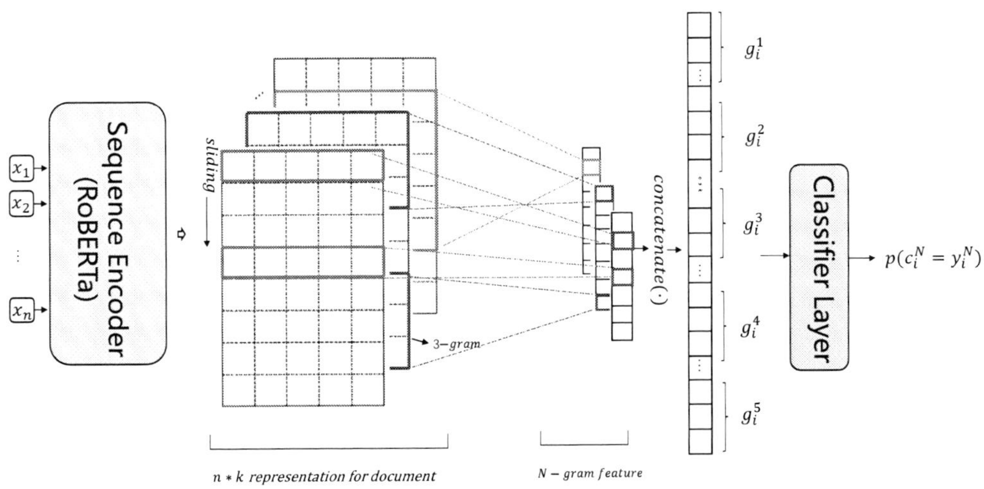

Figure 2: Illustration of our CNN-based model for keyphrase extraction.

whether a gram is a keyphrase based on it's representation.

$$p(c_i^N = y_i^N) = softmax(tanh(W_h * g_i^N + b)) \quad (2)$$

where g_i^N is the representation of i_{th} N-gram, y_i^N is the label of whether the gram $c_i^N(w_{i:i+n-1})$ is a keyphrase or not, W_h and b are parameters to be learned.

4.2 Training via Negative Sampling

In this work, keyphrase extraction is viewed as a classification problem. Existing models optimize this classification problem by direct cross-entropy function while ignore incomplete annotated problem. Meanwhile, according to statistics(table 2), we can see that the positive and negative samples are extremely unbalanced, one document only has 3 keyphrases on average, but there are close 500 unlabeled grams as non-keyphrases. We introduce negative sampling to adjust training loss. On the one hand, negative sampling lets unlabeled keyphrases have opportunities to be considered as keyphrase to participate in the training. On the other hand, it makes positive and negative samples more balanced.

Specifically, we randomly sample a small subset of unlabeled grams as the negative samples. Let $\mathbb{C}$ be the candidate grams set, the negative candidate grams set $\tilde{\mathbb{C}}$ can be denoted as:

$$\tilde{\mathbb{C}} = \{c_i^N | c_i^N \notin \mathbf{y}, 1 \leq N \leq 5, 0 \leq i \leq n - N\}, \quad (3)$$

based on $\tilde{\mathbb{C}}$, we sample a subset $\hat{\mathbb{C}}$ from the whole negative candidate grams set. The number of grams in set $\hat{\mathbb{C}}$ is $\lceil \alpha * |\tilde{\mathbb{C}}| \rceil$, the sampling rate $\{\alpha | 0 < \alpha < 1\}$ is optional in practice, where $\lceil\rceil$ is the ceiling function, we guarantee that at least one negative candidate gram is sampled. Then we compute the cross-entropy loss with positive labeled keyphrases and the sampled negative candidate grams as flow:

$$\mathcal{L} = (\sum_{c_i^N \in \mathbf{y}} -log(P(c_i^N = 1)))+ \\ (\sum_{c_i^N \in \hat{\mathbb{C}}} -log(P(c_i^N = 0))) \quad (4)$$

Negative sampling can reduce the risk of training a KPE model with incomplete annotated problem by incorporating some randomness into the training loss.

5 Experiments

5.1 Datasets

We choose scientific domain datasets as well-annotated datasets, use the dataset Kp20k(Meng et al., 2017) for training [3], which contains a large amount of high-quality scientific metadata in the computer science domain from various online digital libraries(Meng et al., 2016). Each of which contains a title and an abstract of a scientific publication as source text, and author-assigned keywords as target keyphrases, we follow the original work's partition of training, development and testing sets. We further test the model trained with

[3]https://github.com/memray/OpenNMT-kpg-release

Table 2: Statistics of the dataset. #doc, #keyphrase and #length denote the number of papers, the average number of keyphrases and the number of word in keyphrase.

Dataset		#doc	#keyphrase	#length
Test	Inspec	500	7.75	2.41
	Krapivin	460	3.98	2.11
	Nus	211	5.61	1.92
	Semeval	100	6.76	2.15
	Kp20k	19032	3.48	1.86
Kp20k Validation		19067	3.47	1.87
Kp20k Training		488549	3.48	1.86
OpenKP		148124	1.79	2.02

Kp20k on four widely-adopted keyphrase extraction data sets including Inspec(Hulth and Megyesi), NUS(Nguyen and Kan, 2007), SemEval-2010(Kim et al., 2010) and Krapivin(Krapivin et al., 2009). In this paper, we focus on keyphrase extraction, therefore, only the document of at least one **present** keyphrase are used for training and evaluation. The statistics on the number of documents, the average number of keyphrases and the average number of word in keyphrase for each benchmark are summarized in Table 2.

Furthermore, in order to explore the performance of our model in real world scenario, we also choose OpenKP(Xiong et al., 2019) as an open domain dataset, OpenKP includes 134K open domain web pages of various topics from search engine Bing. And we randomly remove some keyphrases of training dataset Kp20k with different masking rate r_{mask} to construct synthetic datasets, to simulate poorly-annotated datasets with different degrees of incomplete annotated problem.

5.2 Baselines and Evaluation Metrics

Because keyphrase generation(KPG) can also generate present keyphrase, we compare our model with both extraction and generation approaches. For extraction approaches, we choose two well-known unsupervised algorithms for keyphrase extraction including Tf-Idf(Jones, 1972), TextRank(Mihalcea and Tarau, 2004), and also choose SKE-Large-Cls(Mu et al., 2020), RoBERTa-Chunk(Sun et al., 2020) which published recently. For generation approaches, we compare our models with four supervised algorithms: CopyRNN(Meng et al., 2017), TG-net(Chen et al., 2019), CatSeq(Yuan et al., 2020), and SGG(Zhao et al., 2021).

Note that, the comparison methods mentioned above are mostly methods for scientific domain. For open domain dataset OpenKP(Xiong et al., 2019), we choose CopyRNN(Meng et al., 2017), BLING-KPE(Xiong et al., 2019) and RoBERTa-Chunk(Sun et al., 2020) as comparison models.

Following CopyRNN(Meng et al., 2017) and RoBERTa-Chunk(Sun et al., 2020), we adopt top-K macro-averaged precision, recall and F1 measures as our evaluation metrics for the present keyphrases respectively, $K = 5, 10$ when evaluating scientific domain datasets, and $K = 1, 3, 5$ when evaluating open domain datasets. Here, precision is defined as the number of correctly predicted keyphrases over the number of all predicted keyphrases, we apply Porter Stemmer(Porter, 1980) to both target keyphrases and predicted keyphrases when determining whether the predictions are correct; recall is computed as the number of correctly predicted keyphrases over the total number of data records, and F1 is the harmonic average of precision and recall.

5.3 Implementation Details

We set maximal length of source sequence as 510 and maximum N-gram length as five (N = 5). The dimension of word embedding is 768, which obtained by fine-tuning RoBERTa(Liu et al., 2019). Five sliding CNNs with kernel size between 1 and 5 are used to extract the representation of grams. The dimension of CNN outputs and hidden state in classifier are 512. The sampling rate α is set to $\alpha = 0.1$ when training Kp20k, and $\alpha = 0.05$ when training OpenKP. Our model are optimized using Adam with 5e-5 learning rate, 10% warm-up proportion, 24 batch size. We implement our model using PyTorch on a Linux machine with a GPU device Tesla V100 32GB. Code and models are available at https://github.com/fredia/NS-KPE.

5.4 Results And Analysis

To reduce the performance randomness, the performance of our model is the average of 3 random runs, we set sampling rate $\alpha = 0.1$ when training on Kp20k, and set sampling rate $\alpha = 0.05$ when training on OpenKP. The best results are highlighted in **bold**.

[4]Datasets have been slightly updated after (Yuan et al., 2020). The result of CopyRNN is taken from (Yuan et al., 2020)

Table 3: Performance comparison of different models on well-annotated scientific domain benchmark datasets. Compared baselines include generation approaches[4](the first part of table), and models for extraction approaches. The result of our model are average from 3 runs of experiments with sampling rate $\alpha = 0.1$.

	Kp20k		Inspec		NUS		Krapivin		Semeval	
	F1@5	F1@10	F1@5	F1@10	F1@5	F1@10	F1@5	F1@10	F1@5	F1@10
CopyRNN	0.328	0.255	0.292	0.336	0.342	0.317	0.302	0.252	0.291	0.296
TG-net	0.372	0.315	0.315	0.381	0.406	0.370	0.349	0.295	0.318	0.322
CatSeqD	0.348	0.298	0.276	0.333	0.374	0.366	0.325	0.285	0.327	0.352
SGG	-	-	0.306	0.359	0.363	0.358	0.288	0.253	0.338	0.336
Tf-Idf	0.105	0.130	0.223	0.304	0.139	0.181	0.113	0.143	0.120	0.184
TextRank	0.180	0.150	0.229	0.275	0.195	0.190	0.172	0.147	0.171	0.181
SKE-Large-Cls	0.392	0.33	0.294	0.334	0.403	0.364	0.309	0.252	0.361	0.358
RoBERTa-Chunk	**0.406**	0.336	**0.357**	**0.401**	0.465	0.431	0.372	0.314	**0.380**	0.385
Our Model	0.406	**0.338**	0.348	0.388	**0.472**	**0.432**	**0.375**	**0.320**	0.376	**0.388**
std	0.0006	0.0006	0.0026	0.0015	0.001	0.0024	0.0022	0.0025	0.0021	0.0044

5.4.1 Results on Scientific Domain Datasets

Because most training data of scientific domain datasets are annotated by authors, and the author is the person who is most familiar with their articles, the issue of incomplete keyphrase annotation is not serious, we treat scientific domain datasets as well-annotated datasets. Table 3 show the F1@5 and F1@10 performance of our model and the other baseline methods across multiple scientific domain datasets, the results of Tf-Idf, TextRank and CopyRNN are taken from (Meng et al., 2017), and other reported results are from their corresponding original paper. We can see that for most cases (expect Tf-Idf and TextRank), the extraction approaches outperform all the generation approaches, since extraction is often easier than generation(Wiseman et al., 2017). As shown in Table 3, the F1@5 and F1@10 scores of our model are very close to current best extraction results, our model even upperforms RoBERTa-Chunk by even 1% in NUS, these results indicate that our model is still effective when applied to high-quality data.

Table 4: Performance comparison of different models on open domain dataset(OpenKP).

Method	OpenKP		
	F1@1	F1@3	F1@5
CopyRNN	0.217	0.237	0.210
BLING-KPE	0.267	0.292	0.209
RoBERTa-Chunk	0.355	0.373	0.324
Our Model	**0.380**	**0.383**	**0.327**

5.4.2 Results on Open Domain Dataset(OpenKP)

Different from scientific papers, open domain datasets regularly contain diverse documents originating from sparse sources, and annotators are not as familiar with the original text as authors, the incomplete annotated problem is serious in these datasets. Table 4 show the F1@1, F1@3 and F1@5 score on an open domain dataset(OpenKP(Xiong et al., 2019)), the results of CopyRNN, BLING-KPE and RoBERTa-Chunk are token from (Sun et al., 2020). We can observe that our model has outperformed prior baselines. Compared with RoBERTa-Chunk, we achieve the improvements of 2.5% on F1@1 and 1% on F1@3, and our results is very close to RoBERTa-Chunk on F1@5, this is not surprising since the average number of keyphrases in OpenKP is 1.79. Results on open domain datasets confirm the effectiveness of our model.

5.4.3 Results on Synthetic Datasets

Results on synthetic datasets are shown in Fig 3 (a)(b), we compare the performance of our model and RoBERTa-Chunk under different masking rates. As shown in Fig 3(a)(b),the F1@5 and F1@10 score with sampling rate $\alpha = 0.1$ are always greater than no sampling, and sampling rate $\alpha = 0.1$ drops more slowly than no sampling when masking rate is increasing. The comparison result show that our model can reduce the misguidance brought by unlabeled keyphrases in training, especially in high masking rates.

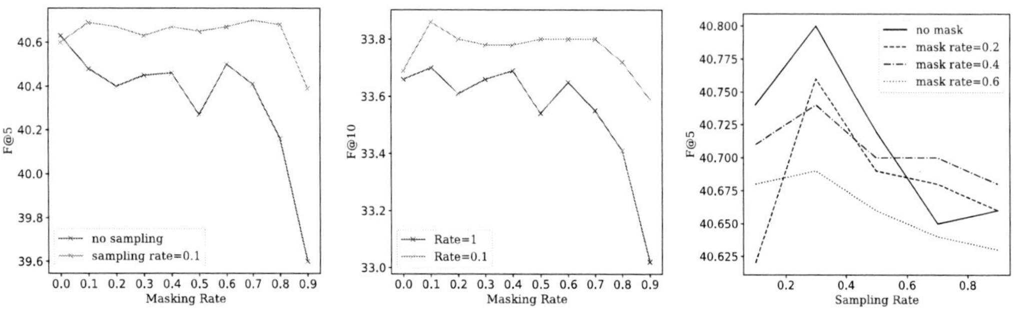

(a) F1@5 score. (b) F1@10 score. (c) Rate in negative sampling.

Figure 3: The performance of our model with different sampling rate on synthetic datasets. In sub-figure (a) and (b), x axis represents the value of masking rate r_{mask}, the larger r_{mask}, the more serious incomplete annotated problem is. And y axis represents the F1@5 score and F1@10 score. The red line denote the results of sampling rate $\alpha = 0.1$ and the blue line denote no sampling. In sub-figure (c), x axis represents the value of sampling rate α and y axis represents the F1@5 score on synthetic datasets, different styles of line denote different synthetic datasets with different masking rate.

5.4.4 Sampling Rate α in Negative Sampling

Fig 3 (c) shows the experiments on synthetic datasets with the different sampling rate α. The sampling rate α should not as small as possible, too small sampling rate will reduce the number of negative samples, leading to underfitting.

6 Conclusion and Future Work

In this work, we introduce negative sampling to keyphrase extraction model, to alleviate the misleading of the incomplete annotated problem. According to the length characteristics of the keyphrase, we use sliding CNN to extract the representation of the candidate gram, turn the keyphrase extraction problem into binary classification. In different scenarios and different scales datasets, we have confirmed the effectiveness of our model.

Our work can be extended in many directions. To begin with, currently binary classifier in our model treats each candidate gram individually, but there is usually a relationship between different grams. We could leverage attention mechanism to model the relationship between grams. Moreover, we would like to further explore utilizing smart gating units or designing a network layer to filter unlabeled keyphrases.

Acknowledgements

This work is supported partly by the National Natural Science Foundation of China (No. 61772059), by the Fundamental Research Funds for the Central Universities, by the Beijing S&T Committee(No. Z191100008619007) and by the State Key Laboratory of Software Development Environment(No. SKLSDE-2020ZX-14).

References

Rabah Alzaidy, Cornelia Caragea, and C Lee Giles. 2019. Bi-lstm-crf sequence labeling for keyphrase extraction from scholarly documents. In *The world wide web conference*, pages 2551–2557.

Isabelle Augenstein, Mrinal Das, Sebastian Riedel, Lakshmi Vikraman, and Andrew McCallum. 2017. Semeval 2017 task 10: Scienceie-extracting keyphrases and relations from scientific publications. In *Proceedings of the 11th International Workshop on Semantic Evaluation (SemEval-2017)*, pages 546–555.

Isabelle Augenstein and Anders Søgaard. 2017. Multi-task learning of keyphrase boundary classification. In *Proceedings of the 55th Annual Meeting of the Association for Computational Linguistics (Volume 2: Short Papers)*, pages 341–346.

Gábor Berend. 2011. Opinion expression mining by exploiting keyphrase extraction. In *Proceedings of 5th International Joint Conference on Natural Language Processing*, pages 1162–1170, Chiang Mai, Thailand. Asian Federation of Natural Language Processing.

Wang Chen, Yifan Gao, Jiani Zhang, Irwin King, and Michael R Lyu. 2019. -guided encoding for keyphrase generation. In *Proceedings of the AAAI Conference on Artificial Intelligence*, volume 33, pages 6268–6275.

Kazi Saidul Hasan and Vincent Ng. 2014. Automatic keyphrase extraction: A survey of the state of the art. In *Proceedings of the 52nd Annual Meeting of the*

Association for Computational Linguistics (Volume 1: Long Papers), pages 1262–1273. ACL.

Michael A Hedderich and Dietrich Klakow. 2018. Training a neural network in a low-resource setting on automatically annotated noisy data. In *Proceedings of the Workshop on Deep Learning Approaches for Low-Resource NLP*, pages 12–18.

Anette Hulth and Beáta B. Megyesi. A study on automatically extracted keywords in text categorization. In *Proceedings of the 21st International Conference on Computational Linguistics and 44th Annual Meeting of the Association for Computational Linguistics*, pages 537–544. ACL.

Karen Sparck Jones. 1972. A statistical interpretation of term specificity and its application in retrieval. *Journal of documentation*.

Su Nam Kim, Olena Medelyan, Min-Yen Kan, and Timothy Baldwin. 2010. SemEval-2010 task 5 : Automatic keyphrase extraction from scientific articles. In *Proceedings of the 5th International Workshop on Semantic Evaluation*, pages 21–26. Association for Computational Linguistics.

Yoon Kim. 2014. Convolutional neural networks for sentence classification. In *Proceedings of the 2014 Conference on Empirical Methods in Natural Language Processing (EMNLP)*, pages 1746–1751, Doha, Qatar. Association for Computational Linguistics.

M. Krapivin, A. Autaeu, and M. Marchese. 2009. Large dataset for keyphrases extraction.

Yangming Li, lemao liu, and Shuming Shi. 2021. Empirical analysis of unlabeled entity problem in named entity recognition. In *International Conference on Learning Representations*.

Yinhan Liu, Myle Ott, Naman Goyal, Jingfei Du, Mandar Joshi, Danqi Chen, Omer Levy, Mike Lewis, Luke Zettlemoyer, and Veselin Stoyanov. 2019. Roberta: A robustly optimized bert pretraining approach. *arXiv preprint arXiv:1907.11692*.

Zhiyuan Liu, Chen Liang, and Maosong Sun. 2012. Topical word trigger model for keyphrase extraction. In *Proceedings of COLING 2012*, pages 1715–1730.

Patrice Lopez and Laurent Romary. 2010. Humb: Automatic key term extraction from scientific articles in grobid. In *SemEval 2010 Workshop*, pages 4–p.

Rui Meng, Shuguang Han, Yun Huang, Daqing He, and Peter Brusilovsky. 2016. Knowledge-based content linking for online textbooks. In *2016 IEEE/WIC/ACM International Conference on Web Intelligence (WI)*, pages 18–25.

Rui Meng, Sanqiang Zhao, Shuguang Han, Daqing He, Peter Brusilovsky, and Yu Chi. 2017. Deep keyphrase generation. In *Proceedings of the 55th Annual Meeting of the Association for Computational Linguistics (Volume 1: Long Papers)*, pages 582–592.

Rada Mihalcea and Paul Tarau. 2004. Textrank: Bringing order into text. In *Proceedings of the 2004 conference on empirical methods in natural language processing*, pages 404–411.

Funan Mu, Zhenting Yu, LiFeng Wang, Yequan Wang, Qingyu Yin, Yibo Sun, Liqun Liu, Teng Ma, Jing Tang, and Xing Zhou. 2020. Keyphrase extraction with span-based feature representations. *arXiv preprint arXiv:2002.05407*.

Thuy Dung Nguyen and Min-Yen Kan. 2007. Keyphrase extraction in scientific publications. ICADL'07, page 317–326, Berlin, Heidelberg. Springer-Verlag.

Martin F Porter. 1980. An algorithm for suffix stripping. *Program*.

Nirmala Pudota, Antonina Dattolo, Andrea Baruzzo, Felice Ferrara, and Carlo Tasso. 2010. Automatic keyphrase extraction and ontology mining for content-based tag recommendation. *International Journal of Intelligent Systems*, 25(12):1158–1186.

Yafeng Ren, Donghong Ji, and Hongbin Zhang. 2014. Positive unlabeled learning for deceptive reviews detection. In *Proceedings of the 2014 conference on empirical methods in natural language processing (EMNLP)*, pages 488–498.

Lucas Sterckx, Cornelia Caragea, Thomas Demeester, and Chris Develder. 2016. Supervised keyphrase extraction as positive unlabeled learning. In *Proceedings of the 2016 Conference on Empirical Methods in Natural Language Processing*, pages 1924–1929. ACL.

Si Sun, Chenyan Xiong, Zhenghao Liu, Zhiyuan Liu, and Jie Bao. 2020. Joint keyphrase chunking and salience ranking with bert. *arXiv preprint arXiv:2004.13639*.

Yanan Wang, Qi Liu, Chuan Qin, Tong Xu, Yijun Wang, Enhong Chen, and Hui Xiong. 2018. Exploiting topic-based adversarial neural network for cross-domain keyphrase extraction. In *2018 IEEE International Conference on Data Mining (ICDM)*, pages 597–606. IEEE.

Sam Wiseman, Stuart Shieber, and Alexander Rush. 2017. Challenges in data-to-document generation. In *Proceedings of the 2017 Conference on Empirical Methods in Natural Language Processing*, pages 2253–2263. Association for Computational Linguistics.

Lee Xiong, Chuan Hu, Chenyan Xiong, Daniel Campos, and Arnold Overwijk. 2019. Open domain web keyphrase extraction beyond language modeling. In *EMNLP-IJCNLP*.

Xingdi Yuan, Tong Wang, Rui Meng, Khushboo Thaker, Peter Brusilovsky, Daqing He, and Adam Trischler. 2020. One size does not fit all: Generating and evaluating variable number of keyphrases. In *Proceedings of the 58th Annual Meeting of the Association for Computational Linguistics*.

Jing Zhao, Junwei Bao, Yifan Wang, Youzheng Wu, Xiaodong He, and Bowen Zhou. 2021. SGG: Learning to select, guide, and generate for keyphrase generation. In *NAACL*.

XINGQUAN ZHU and XINDONG WU. 2004. Class noise vs. attribute noise: A quantitative study of their impacts. *Artificial Intelligence Review*, 22:177–210.

Fine-grained Temporal Relation Extraction with Ordered-Neuron LSTM and Graph Convolutional Networks

Minh Phu Tran[1*], **Minh Van Nguyen**[2*], **and Thien Huu Nguyen**[2]
[1] VinAI Research, Vietnam
[2] Dept. of Computer and Information Science, University of Oregon, Eugene, OR, USA
v.minhtp@vinai.io, {minhnv,thien}@cs.uoregon.edu

Abstract

Fine-grained temporal relation extraction (FineTempRel) aims to recognize the durations and timeline of event mentions in text. A missing part in the current deep learning models for FineTempRel is their failure to exploit the syntactic structures of the input sentences to enrich the representation vectors. In this work, we propose to fill this gap by introducing novel methods to integrate the syntactic structures into the deep learning models for FineTempRel. The proposed model focuses on two types of syntactic information from the dependency trees, i.e., the syntax-based importance scores for representation learning of the words and the syntactic connections to identify important context words for the event mentions. We also present two novel techniques to facilitate the knowledge transfer between the subtasks of FineTempRel, leading to a novel model with the state-of-the-art performance for this task.

1 Introduction

An important step in event understanding involves identifying the temporal relations between events (i.e., TempRel), finding its applications in different natural language processing (NLP) systems such as question answering and timeline construction. A large volume of the prior works has focused on the classification setting for this problem where categorical temporal relations should be predicted for pairs of event-referring and/or time-referring expressions in text (i.e., categorical TempRel) (Dligach et al., 2017; Cheng and Miyao, 2017; Ning et al., 2019). For instance, in the sentence "*The meeting to discuss the possible merger of the two financial companies lasted for two hours, eventually leading to their union yesterday.*", a system for TempRel should be able to realize that the "*discussion*" event happens before the "*union*" event (i.e., the categorical label of *BEFORE*).

However, a major problem with the classification setting is its inability to capture the fine-grained distinction between the temporal structures of the events (i.e., the duration information). For example, the classification setting would not be able to specify the amount of time between the end time of an event and the start time of a later one in the timeline. To this end, (Vashishtha et al., 2019) presents the first work on fine-grained temporal relation extraction (FineTempRel) that seeks to distribute event pairs in a real-valued relative timeline. In particular, in FineTempRel, given a pair of events, the systems need to predict the start and end times (thus the durations) of the events so the relative orders between these times of the events can be revealed. Our work follows this fine-grained setting for TempRel, aiming to introduce a novel model to improve the performance for this problem.

The current state-of-the-art methods for FineTempRel have involved deep learning models (Vashishtha et al., 2019); however, one problem with these deep learning models is that they fail to exploit the syntactic structures of the input sentences (i.e., the parsing trees) to further advance the performance. Consequently, in the current work, we seek to fill in this gap by extracting useful knowledge from the syntactic structures to help the deep learning models learn better representations for FineTempRel. In particular, based on the dependency parsing trees, we envision two major types of syntactic information that can be complementarily beneficial for the deep learning models for FineTempRel in this work, i.e., the syntax-based importance scores and the syntactic word connections for representation learning. First, for the syntax-based importance scores, our intuition is that the closer words to the words along the shortest dependency paths between the two event mentions of interest would involve more useful context information for FineTempRel than the farther ones. For instance,

*The first two authors contribute equally to this paper.

Proceedings of the 2021 EMNLP Workshop W-NUT: The Seventh Workshop on Noisy User-generated Text, pages 35–45
November 11, 2021. ©2021 Association for Computational Linguistics

in our running example, the word *"leading"* along the shortest dependency path between *"meeting"* and *"union"* is an important word to reveal the temporal relations between these two events, suggesting the distances from the words to the shortest dependency path between the event mentions as an useful feature for FineTempRel. Consequently, in this work, we propose to use such dependency distances to obtain a score to represent the contextual importance for every word in the sentence (i.e., the importance scores). These importance scores would then be introduced into the deep learning models to improve the representation learning for FineTempRel.

How can we integrate these syntax-based importance scores into the deep learning models for FineTempRel? In this work, we propose to employ the representation vectors for the words in the deep learning models to compute a model-based importance score for each word in the sentence. Afterward, we propose to introduce the information from the syntax-based importance scores into the models for FineTempRel by enforcing the similarity/consistency between the syntax-based and model-based importance scores for the words in the sentence. The motivation is to leverage the importance score consistency to guide the representation learning process of the deep learning models (using the extracted syntactic information) so more effective representation vectors for FineTempRel can be induced. In order to implement this idea, we utilize the Ordered-Neuron Long Short-Term Memory Networks (ON-LSTM) (Shen et al., 2019; Veyseh et al., 2020a) to facilitate the computation of the model-based importance scores and the effective integration of the syntax-based scores for better representation vectors for FineTempRel.

For the second type of syntactic information, the main motivation is to leverage the syntactic dependency connections between the words to identify the important context words that should be encoded to compute effective representation vectors for the event mentions in the sentences. In particular, following (Vashishtha et al., 2019), we decompose FineTempRel into two subtasks that would be solved jointly for a given pair of events in this work, i.e., event duration prediction (i.e., predicting the durations of the events) and temporal relation prediction (i.e., predicting the start and end times of the events). First, for event duration prediction, we argue that the important context words for the representation vectors of the event mentions involve the syntactic neighboring words of the event mentions in the dependency trees. For instance, in our example, the words *"lasted"* and *"two hours"* are crucial to determine the duration for the event mention *"meeting"*. Note that although these words are far away from *"meeting"* in the sentence, they are directly connected to *"meeting"* in the dependency tree (i.e., the syntactic neighboring words). Second, for temporal relation prediction, our intuition is based on (Cheng and Miyao, 2017) and (Goyal and Durrett, 2019) that use the shortest dependency paths between the event mentions to capture the important context words for categorical TempRel (e.g., the word *"leading"* in our example). Motivated by these benefits of the dependency trees for FineTempRel, in this work, we propose to run Graph Convolutional Neural Networks (GCN) (Kipf and Welling, 2017; Nguyen and Grishman, 2018) over the dependency structures of the sentences to facilitate the incorporation of the dependency-based important context words into the representation vectors for FineTempRel. To our knowledge, this is the first work on using GCNs for TempRel in the literature.

In particular, we propose to employ two separate GCN models (i.e., one for for each task in FineTempRel) to induce more flexible representation vectors for the two subtasks in FineTempRel. Afterward, we introduce a mechanism to allow the layers of the two GCN models to interact with each other so the knowledge learned for one task in each GCN layer can be used to improve the representation vectors for the other task (i.e., transfer learning). Finally, a novel inductive bias is proposed to further connect the two GCN models, seeking to enforce the similarity of the representation vectors learned by the two models for the same input sentences. We perform extensive experiments to demonstrate the effectiveness of the proposed model, yielding the state-of-the-art performance for FineTempRel on the benchmark datasets.

2 Related Work

Most of the previous work on TempRel has focused on the categorical setting using the TimeML standard for the datasets (i.e., TimeBank, TimeBank-Dense, Richer Event Description (RED)) (Pustejovsky et al., 2003; UzZaman et al., 2013; Cassidy et al., 2014; Minard et al., 2016; O'Gorman et al., 2016; Hong et al., 2016; Ning et al., 2018b,c).

(Vashishtha et al., 2019) is the first work to consider the fine-grained distinction for the temporal relations for events.

Regarding TempRel methods, the early approaches has involved feature-based models (Mani et al., 2006; Bethard, 2013; Lin et al., 2015), the hybrid methods (D'Souza and Ng, 2013), sieve-based methods (i.e., CAEVO (Chambers et al., 2014), CATENA (Mirza and Tonelli, 2016)), structured learning methods (Ning et al., 2017), and Interger Linear Programming (Ning et al., 2018). Recently, deep learning models have been developed and shown promising results for TempRel (Dligach et al., 2017; Tourille et al., 2017; Cheng and Miyao, 2017; Meng and Rumshisky, 2018; Ning et al., 2019; Han et al., 2019a). The closet work to ours is (Vashishtha et al., 2019) that presents an attention-based deep learning model for FineTempRel; however, it does not capture the syntactic structures of the sentences as we do in this work. Some previous works have also considered event duration modeling in text (Pan et al., 2007; Gusev et al., 2011; Williams and Katz, 2012; Filatova and Hovy, 2001) although they do not tie duration and temporal relations as we do. Finally, we also note related tasks that concern other types of relations between events/entities, including event coreference resolution (Lu et al., 2016; Nguyen et al., 2016; Lu and Ng, 2017; Tran et al., 2021), event causaltiy identification (Liu et al., 2020; Tran and Nguyen, 2021), and event argument extraction (Veyseh et al., 2020b; Nguyen et al., 2021).

3 Model

FineTempRel can be formulated as a regression problem. Formally, given a sentence W of N words: $W = w_1, w_2, \ldots, w_N$ with w_{m_1} and w_{m_2} ($1 \leq m_1 < m_2 \leq N$) as the trigger words for the two event mentions of interest, we need to predict the start and end times for the two event mentions to reflect the temporal order and durations of the events in the timeline. Following (Vashishtha et al., 2019), we aim to predict the start and end times b_1 and e_1 for w_{m_1} and b_2 and e_2 for w_{m_2} using a reference interval $[0, 1]$ (i.e., $0 \leq b_1 \leq e_1 \leq 1$ and $0 \leq b_2 \leq e_2 \leq 1$). Also, let d_1 and d_2 be the durations for w_{m_1} and w_{m_2} respectively. Note that as the input event mentions might belong to different sentences in FineTempRel, we follow (Vashishtha et al., 2019) to combine these sentences into a single sequence of words for W in those cases.

To prepare the input sentence for the deep learning models and to achieve a fair comparison with (Vashishtha et al., 2019), we first send W into the pre-trained language model ELMo (Peters et al., 2018) to produce a sequence of hidden vectors $X = x_1, x_2, \ldots, x_N$ for W. Note that the hidden vector x_i for $w_i \in W$ is the concatenation of the hidden vectors for w_i in three layers of ELMo.

3.1 Syntax-Model Consistency

The first component in our model for FineTempRel aims to exploit the consistency between the syntax-based and model-based importance scores for the words in the input sentence to improve the representation vectors in the deep learning models for FineTempRel. In particular, the syntax-based importance scores are supposed to evaluate the potential contributions of the words in W for the representation vectors in FineTempRel. As the closer words to the shortest dependency path *SDP* between between w_{m_1} and w_{m_2} in the dependency tree T of W are considered to be more important, we first compute the distance d_i^{syn} between every word $w_i \in W$ to *SDP* via: $d_i^{syn} = \min\{L(w_i, w) | w \in SDP\}$ where $L(w_i, w)$ denotes the length of the shortest path between the words w_i and w in the dependency tree T. Afterward, the syntax-based importance score s_i^{syn} for the word w_i would be computed by: $s_i^{syn} = \frac{\exp(-d_i^{syn})}{\sum_{j=1..N} \exp(-d_j^{syn})}$.

In order to implement the importance score consistency, we additionally need to obtain the model-based importance scores $s_1^{mod}, s_2^{mod}, \ldots, s_N^{mod}$ for the words in W based on the representation vectors of the deep learning models for FineTempRel. While the computation of the model-based scores will be described later, the syntax-model consistency between the importance scores in this work is achieved by including the KL divergence $\mathcal{L}_{const}$ between the importance scores into the overall loss function for minimization during the training of the models: $\mathcal{L}_{KL} = -\sum_i s_i^{mod} \frac{s_i^{mod}}{s_i^{syn}}$.

Model-based Importance Scores: As presented in the introduction, we propose to compute the model-based importance scores for FineTempRel based on the Ordered-Neuron Long Short-Term Memory Networks (ON-LSTM) (Shen et al., 2019), an extension of the popular Long Short-Term Memory Networks (LSTM). In particular, given the vector sequence $X = x_1, x_2, \ldots, x_N$ as the input, a LSTM layer returns a sequence of hidden vectors $H = h_1, h_2, \ldots, h_N$ via:

$$
\begin{aligned}
f_i &= \sigma(W_f x_i + U_f h_{i-1} + b_f) \\
i_i &= \sigma(W_i x_i + U_i h_{i-1} + b_i) \\
o_i &= \sigma(W_o x_i + U_o h_{i-1} + b_o) \\
\hat{c}_i &= tanh(W_c x_i + U_c h_{i-1} + b_c) \\
c_i &= f_i \circ c_{i-1} + i_i \odot \hat{c}_i, h_i = o_i \odot tanh(c_i)
\end{aligned} \tag{1}
$$

where h_0 is the zero vector, $\odot$ is the element-wise multiplication, and f_t, i_t and o_t are called the forget, input, and output gates respectively. In ON-LSTM, two additional gates (i.e., the master forget gate $\hat{f}_t$ and the master input gate $\hat{h}_t$) (Shen et al., 2019) are introduced into the LSTM cell via:

$$
\begin{aligned}
\hat{f}_i &= cummax(W_{\hat{f}} x_i + U_{\hat{f}} h_{i-1} + b_{\hat{f}}) \\
\hat{i}_i &= 1 - cummax(W_{\hat{i}} x_i + U_{\hat{i}} h_{t-1} + b_{\hat{i}}) \\
\bar{f}_i &= \hat{f}_i \odot (f_i \hat{i}_i + 1 - \hat{i}_i), \bar{i}_i = \hat{i}_i \odot (i_t \hat{f}_i + 1 - \hat{f}_i) \\
c_i &= \bar{f}_i \odot c_{i-1} + \bar{i}_i \odot \hat{c}_i
\end{aligned} \tag{2}
$$

where $cummax$ is an activation function: $cumax(x) = cumsum(softmax(x))$[1].

The difference between the forget and input gates in LSTM (i.e., f_t and i_t) and the master forget and input gates in ON-LSTM (i.e., $\hat{f}_t$ and $\hat{i}_t$) is that the dimensions/neurons of the hidden vectors in the gates of LSTM are considered equally important, being active/used for every word in W. This is in contrast to the master gates in ON-LSTM that impose an importance hierarchy over the neurons in the hidden vectors, enabling the neurons to be active for only a portion of the words in the sentence (i.e., neurons with higher rankings would be active for more words in the sentence). ON-LSTM achieves such neuron hierarchy and activity limitation via the function $cumax(x)$ that aggregates the softmax-produced result of the input vector x along its dimensions. The output of $cummax(x)$ would represent the expectation of a binary vector of the form $(0, \ldots, 0, 1, \ldots, 1)$ (i.e., two consecutive segments of 0's and 1's). At one word w_i, the 1's segment in its master gate vector correspond to the neurons that are activated for that word. In ON-LSTM, a word w_i is more contextually important than another word w_j for representation learning if the master gates for w_i have more active neurons than those for w_j (Shen et al., 2019). Consequently, in order to compute the model-based importance score for a word w_i, we employ the numbers of active neurons in the master gates for w_i that in turn can be estimated via the sums of the weights of the neurons in the gates of ON-LSTM. Following (Shen et al., 2019), we use the hidden vectors for the master forget gate to obtain the model-based importance scores s_i^{sem} for the words w_i:

$$
d_i^{sem} = 1 - \sum_{i=1..D} \hat{f}_{ij}, s_i^{sem} = \frac{\exp(d_i^{sem})}{\sum_{j=1..N} \exp(d_j^{sem})} \tag{3}
$$

where D is the dimensionality of the hidden vectors for ON-LSTM and $\hat{f}_{ij}$ is the weight of the j-th dimension of the master forget gate $\hat{f}_i$ at w_i.

Consequently, by promoting the syntax-model consistency with the loss $\mathcal{L}_{KL}$, we expect that the syntactic information from the syntax-based importance scores can deeply interfere with the internal computation/structure of the ON-LSTM cell (via the neurons of the master gates) to potentially lead to better representation vectors for FineTempRel. For convenience, we also use $H = h_1, h_2, \ldots, h_N$ to denote the hidden vectors returned by ON-LSTM over the input sequence vector X for the next components (called the ON-LSTM hidden vectors).

3.2 Graph Convolutional Networks

In the previous component, the syntax-model consistency has attempted to enrich the representation vectors for FineTempRel by encouraging them to capture the contextual importance scores for the words in the sentence. This component seeks to further improve the representation vectors for the event mentions by identifying and encoding the important context words for the temporal relation prediction between w_{m_1} and w_{m_2}. In particular, as presented in the introduction, we aim to leverage the words in the syntactic neighbors of w_{m_1} and w_{m_2} and their shortest dependency path in the dependency tree T of W for this purpose. As such, in order to encode these dependency-based important words for representation learning, we propose to feed the ON-LSTM hidden vectors H into the Graph Convolutional Neural Networks (GCN) that structure the computations over T. In particular, a GCN model in this work involves several layers (i.e., G layers in our case) to compute the representation vectors for the words in W with different abstract levels. At the $(k+1)$-th layer $(0 \leq k < G)$, the representation vector $\bar{h}_i^{k+1}$ for the word $w_i \in W$ is computed via:

$$
\bar{h}_i^{k+1} = \sigma\left(\frac{\Sigma_{w_j \in \mathcal{N}(i)} W_k \bar{h}_j^k}{|\mathcal{N}(i)|}\right) \tag{4}
$$

Here, $\mathcal{N}(i)$ is the set of the words in W that are directly connected to w_i (including itself) in T, W_k is

[1] $cumsum(u_1, u_2, \ldots, u_n) = (u'_1, u'_2, \ldots, u'_n)$ where $u'_i = \sum_{j=1..i} u_j$.

the weight matrix (biases are omitted for simplicity in this work), and σ is the sigmoid function. The input vector $\bar{h}_i^0$ for GCNs is set to the ON-LSTM hidden vector h_i in this case (i.e., $\bar{h}_i^0 = h_i$ for all $1 \leq i \leq N$). Note that if there are more than one sentences in the input, following (Cheng and Miyao, 2017), we unify their dependency trees by introducing a new root node to be the parent of the roots of these dependency trees.

GCN Interaction: The straightforward application of GCNs in our FineTempRel problem is to run a single GCN model over H whose representation vectors are used for both event duration prediction (EDP) and temporal relation prediction (TRP). However, a problem with this approach is that the induced representations for the event mentions from the single GCN model might be confused between the representation learning for the two subtasks. In particular, EDP needs to focus on the modeling of the individual event mentions for their duration while jointly encoding the two event mentions is crucial for the TRP between them. Due to such distinction, a single GCN model might not be able to customize its computation for the different modeling expectations required by the two subtasks. Consequently, in this work, we propose to employ two different GCN models; each of them aims to learn the representation vectors for one subtask of FineTempRel. Among others, the benefit of the two GCN models is the improved flexibility to enable the models to tailor their operation toward the specific subtasks for FineTempRel. Note that the two GCN models share the architecture and are only different in terms of their weights.

Despite its flexibility, one limitation with the model so far is that the GCN models for EDP and TRP are operating separately, lacking the effective interactions to benefit from the knowledge transfer between the two subtasks. In particular, as shown in (Vashishtha et al., 2019), using the representation vectors for one subtask as one of the inputs to make prediction for the other task is helpful to improve the performance for FineTempRel on unseen test data. This demonstrates the relatedness of the two subtasks in FineTempRel, suggesting the knowledge transfer between the models for the two subtasks to enhance the representation vectors. To this end, we propose a novel interaction mechanism for the two GCN models of the two subtasks for FineTempRel in which the representation vectors in the current layer for one GCN model are additionally conditioned on the representation vectors from the previous layer of the other GCN model. In particular, let GCN^{dur} and GCN^{rel} be the GCN models for event duration and temporal relation prediction respectively. Also, let π_i^k and r_i^k ($1 \leq k \leq G$) be the hidden vectors for the word w_i at the k-the layers of GCN^{dur} and GCN^{rel} respectively ($\pi_i^0 = r_i^0 = h_i$ for all $1 \leq i \leq N$). The hidden vector π_i^{k+1} of GCN^{dur} ($1 \leq k < G$) in this work would then be computed based on the hidden vectors from the previous layer (i.e., the k-layer) of GCN^{rel} (in addition to the hidden vectors in the k-layer of GCN^{dur} itself):

$$\begin{aligned}
\pi_i^{k+1} &= \sigma\left(\Sigma_{w_j \in \mathcal{N}(i)} \alpha_j^k W_k^\pi \pi_j^k\right) \\
\alpha_j^k &= \exp(u^k \pi_j^k) / \sum_{w_t \in \mathcal{N}(i)} \exp(u^k \pi_t^k) \\
u^k &= W_k^u [r_{m_1}^k, r_{m_2}^k]
\end{aligned} \tag{5}$$

where W_k^π and W_k^u are the weight matrices at the k-layer for GCN^{dur}.

The rationale for this formula is to use the representation vectors for the event mentions at the k-layer of GCN^{rel} (i.e., $r_{e_1}^k$ and $r_{e_2}^k$) to compute a query vector u^k that would then be used to determine the weight α_j^k for each neighboring word $w_j \in \mathcal{N}(i)$ in the representation computation for π_i^{k+1}. A similar formula is employed to compute the hidden vector r_i^{k+1} of GCN^{rel} in this work:

$$\begin{aligned}
r_i^{k+1} &= \sigma\left(\Sigma_{w_j \in \mathcal{N}(i)} \beta_j^k W_k^r r_j^k\right) \\
\beta_j^k &= \exp(v^k r_j^k) / \sum_{w_t \in \mathcal{N}(i)} \exp(v^k r_t^k) \\
v^k &= W_k^v [\pi_{m_1}^k, \pi_{m_2}^k]
\end{aligned} \tag{6}$$

Representation Regularization: Finally, to provide an additional channel for the two GCN models to transfer their knowledge, we introduce a novel inductive bias that encourages the two GCN models to generate similar representation vectors for the input sentence for FineTempRel. As the two GCN models use the similar network architecture to learn the representations for the two related temporal subtasks of FineTempRel, we expect that the overall representation vectors for the same input sentence induced by these two GCN models should also be similar (although the representation vectors for the event mentions in the input sentence from each network might be more task-specific). To this end, we first obtain the overall representation vectors π^W and r^W for W based on the hidden vectors in the last layers of GCN^{dur} and GCN^{rel} (respectively) via: $\pi^W = max\_pool(\pi_1^G, \pi_2^G, \dots, \pi_N^G)$

and $r^W = max\_pool(r_1^G, r_2^G, \ldots, r_N^G)$. Afterward, we enforce the similarity between these representation vectors for W by including their mean square error (MSE) $\mathcal{L}_{dif}$ into the overall loss function for minimization: $\mathcal{L}_{dif} = MSE(\pi^W, r^W)$.

On the one hand, $\mathcal{L}_{dif}$ serves as a regularizer to improve the representation vectors for the model. On the other hand, $\mathcal{L}_{dif}$ introduces a novel communication channel between the two GCN models so the knowledge from this GCN model can be transferred to improve the representation learning of the other GCN. Overall, our model performs deep and layer-wise interactions between the two GCN models for FineTempRel (i.e., the interactions are done for all the GCN layers), enabling the knowledge transfer to occur at different abstraction levels for potentially better representations for FineTempRel.

3.3 Prediction

In order to predict the durations for w_{m_1} and w_{m_2}, we assemble the overall representation vectors R_1^{dur} and R_2^{dur} for them based on hidden vectors in the last layer of GCN^{dur}: $R_1^{dur} = [\pi_{m_1}^G, \pi^W]$, $R_2^{dur} = [\pi_{m_2}^G, \pi^W]$. These overall vectors are then sent to a two-layer feed-forward network FF_1 to predict the durations $\hat{d}_1$ and $\hat{d}_2$ for w_{m_1} and w_{m_2}: $\hat{d}_1 = FF_1(R_1^{dur})$, $\hat{d}_2 = FF_1(R_2^{dur})$. Afterward, the loss function for EDP would be: $\mathcal{L}_{dur} = (d_1 - \hat{d}_1)^2 + (d_2 - \hat{d}_2)^2$.

Similarly, for TRP, we create an overall representation vector R^{rel} for this task by: $R^{rel} = [r_{m_1}^G, r_{m_2}^G, r^W]$. This vector is then consumed by another two-layer feed-forward network FF_2 to predict the start and end times $\hat{b}_1$, $\hat{e}_1$, $\hat{b}_2$ and $\hat{e}_2$ for w_{m_1} and w_{m_2}: $[\hat{b}_1, \hat{e}_1, \hat{b}_2, \hat{e}_2] = FF_2(R^{rel})$. Following (Vashishtha et al., 2019), we use the following loss function for temporal relation prediction: $\mathcal{L}_{rel} = |(b_1 - b_2) - (\hat{b}_1 - \hat{b}_2)| + |(e_1 - b_2) - (\hat{e}_1 - \hat{b}_2)| + |(e_2 - b_1) - (\hat{e}_2 - \hat{b}_1)| + |(e_1 - e_2) - (\hat{e}_1 - \hat{e}_2)|$.

To summarize, the overall loss function to train the model in this work is: $\mathcal{L} = \mathcal{L}_{dur} + \gamma_{rel}\mathcal{L}_{rel} + \gamma_{KL}\mathcal{L}_{KL} + \gamma_{dif}\mathcal{L}_{dif}$ where γ_{rel}, γ_{KL} and γ_{dif} are the trade-off parameters.

4 Experiments

• **Datasets & Parameters**: To evaluate the performance of the models, we use the Universal Decompositional Semantics Time (UDS-T) dataset introduced in (Vashishtha et al., 2019) for FineTempRel. UDS-T is annotated on top of the Universal Dependencies English Web Treebank (Bies et al., 2012) whose sentences are associated with the gold standard Universal Dependency parses (to be used for the dependency trees). There are 32,302 events and 70,368 event-event relations (i.e., examples) in UDS-T where the same data split for training data, development data and test data in (Vashishtha et al., 2019) is used to ensure a fair comparison. The development dataset of UDS-T is used to fine-tune the hyper-parameters for the models in this work. This fine-tuning process leads to the following values for the hyper-parameters in this work: 1 layer for the ON-LSTM model with $D = 256$ dimensions for the hidden vectors, 2 layers for the GCN models (also with 256 dimensions for the hidden vectors), 64 hidden units for the FF_1 and FF_2 networks for duration and temporal relation prediction, and $\gamma_{rel} = 0.5$, $\gamma_{KL} = 0.1$, and $\gamma_{dif} = 0.1$ for the trade-off parameters in the overall loss function. Also, we use the Adam optimizer with the learning rate of $1e$-5 to train the models in this work.

In addition, for the TE3 and TD datasets with the transfer learning experiment, similar to (Vashishtha et al., 2019), we employ the `sklearn 0.20.0` package to train the SVM classifier with Gaussian kernel and the same hyper-parameters. Finally, we use the same procedure as in (Vashishtha et al., 2019) to pre-process the datasets in this experiment (e.g., using the `Stanford CoreNLP 3.9.2` toolkit for data pre-processing).

In addition, similar to (Vashishtha et al., 2019), we further examine the models on the categorical TempRel datasets, including the TempEval3 (TE3, (UzZaman et al., 2013), Task C-relation only) and TimeBank-Dense (TD, (Cassidy et al., 2014)) datasets. We follow the same preprocessing procedure for these datasets and the same training and tuning procedures for the models as in (Vashishtha et al., 2019) to achieve a fair comparison. In particular, we use a transfer learning approach where the best-performing model on the UDS-T development set is first used to obtain the overall representation vector $R^{rel} = [r_{m_1}^G, r_{m_2}^G, r^W]$ for each pair of annotated event-event relations in TE3 and TD. Afterward, we employ this vector as the input features for a SVM classifier with a Gaussian kernel that is trained on the training sets and evaluated on the test sets for these datasets. Specifically, the training set for TE3 involves the union of the TimeBank (Pustejovsky et al., 2003) and AQUAINT (Graff, 2002) datasets provided in the TE3 workshop (UzZaman et al., 2013) while the training data and

Model	Duration			Timeline		
	ρ	rank diff	R1(rank diff)	Absolute ρ	Relative ρ	R1(MAE)
System1 (Vashishtha et al., 2019)	32.63	1.86	8.59	77.91	68.00	2.82
System2 (Vashishtha et al., 2019)	37.75	1.75	13.73	77.87	67.68	2.35
System3 (Vashishtha et al., 2019)	38.38	1.75	13.85	77.82	67.73	2.58
System4 (Vashishtha et al., 2019)	38.12	1.75	13.68	78.12	68.22	2.96
ON-LSTM-GCN (with ELMo)	**50.77**	**1.30**	**37.58**	**84.41**	**80.41**	**23.33**
ON-LSTM-GCN (with BERT)	**54.37**	**1.27**	**39.14**	**84.91**	**81.67**	**24.71**

Table 1: The performance on the UDS-T test set. Except for the rank diff for duration prediction, all metrics prefer large values.

development data in TD (i.e., TD-train, TD-dev) are combined to form the training set for TD. We follow the same hyper-parameter tuning process for the SVM classifier as in (Vashishtha et al., 2019) for these datasets where a grid-search with 4-fold cross-validation is done over the training sets. Finally, the performance of the models is reported on the test sets of the datasets (i.e., TE3-Platinum (TE3-PT) for TE3 and TD-test for TD).

For the performance measures for FineTempRel on the UDS-T dataset, following (Vashishtha et al., 2019), we use three metrics for the duration prediction task (i.e., Spearman correlation (ρ), mean rank difference (*RD*), and the proportion of rank difference explained (R1(*RD*))), and three metrics for temporal relation prediction (i.e., Spearman correlation between the normalized values of the actual start and end times and the predicted ones (*absolute* ρ), the Spearman correlation between the actual and predicted values for $\mathcal{L}_{rel}$ (*relative* ρ), and the proportion of mean absolute error (MAE) explained (R1(MAE))). Note that for a performance metric A, the proportion of A explained is computed by: R1(A) = 1 - $A_{model}/A_{baseline}$ where A_{model} is the performance metric A computed for the model and $A_{baseline}$ is those computed for the model that always guesses the median.

• **Comparison on UDS-T**: We compare the FineTempRel model in this work (called **ON-LSTM-GCN**) with the best-reported models on the UDS-T dataset in (Vashishtha et al., 2019). In particular, we use the top four models in (Vashishtha et al., 2019) (called System1, System2, System3, and System4) as the baselines in this work. Table 1 reports the performance of the models. Note that in addition to the ELMo embeddings as in (Vashishtha et al., 2019), we also show the performance of the ON-LSTM-GCN model when the BERT embeddings (Devlin et al., 2019) (i.e., the base model) are employed to encode the sentences. Both ELMo and BERT are fine-tuned during training in this work.

As we can see, using the same ELMo embeddings, the proposed model ON-LSTM-GCN significantly outperforms all the models in (Vashishtha et al., 2019) with substantial performance gap over different performance metrics and the two subtasks (i.e., event duration prediction and temporal relation prediction). This clearly demonstrates the effectiveness of the proposed model for FineTempRel. We also see that replacing ELMo with the BERT embeddings can help to improve the performance for both subtasks, suggesting the application of BERT for FineTempRel in the future research.

• **Comparison on TE3 and TD**: Table 2 shows the performance of the models on the TE3 and TD datasets. For both datasets, similar to (Vashishtha et al., 2019), we only evaluate on the Event-Event (E-E) relations as we only capture those in the model. Note that this is different from some of the prior works on TempRel where the performance metrics are reported for all relations (i.e., including timex-timex, and event-timex relations), making them not directly comparable to ours. For instance, (Ning et al., 2017) reports a F1-score of 0.672 for all relations on the TE3 test set, but it is not directly comparable to our model as we only evaluate on event-event relations. Also, as this is a transfer learning experiment from UDS-T, the most comparable baselines to ours in this case is from (Vashishtha et al., 2019) for both TE3 and TD. For a reference, we also include the best-reported performance on TD from the recent work (i.e., (Cheng and Miyao, 2017; Han et al., 2019a,b)). Note that we follow the previous work to report the temporal awareness scores (F1) for TE3 and the F1 micro-average scores for TD (Vashishtha et al., 2019).

In Table 2, we explicitly indicate the pre-trained word embeddings (i.e., ELMo or BERT) for the recent models on TempRel. The first observation from the table is that among the models with ELMo embeddings, the proposed model ON-LSTM-GCN is significantly better than the baseline models for

System	Evaluation Data	F1 (E-E)
(Vashishtha et al., 2019) (with ELMo)	TE3-PT	0.498
ON-LSTM-GCN (with ELMo)	TE3-PT	**0.551**
ON-LSTM-GCN (with BERT)	TE3-PT	**0.596**
CAEVO	TD-test	0.494
CATENA	TD-test	0.519
(Cheng and Miyao, 2017)	TD-test	0.529
(Vashishtha et al., 2019) (with ELMo)	TD-test	0.566
(Han et al., 2019a) (with BERT)	TD-test	0.632
(Han et al., 2019b) (with BERT)	TD-test	0.645
ON-LSTM-GCN (with ELMo)	TD-test	**0.620**
ON-LSTM-GCN (with BERT)	TD-test	**0.658**

Table 2: Test performance on TE3 and TD for our transfer learning experiment (only for the Event-Event relations).

	Duration			Timeline		
Model	ρ	RD	R1 (RD)	Abs ρ	Rel ρ	R1 (MAE)
ON-LSTM-GCN	**55.4**	**1.26**	**38.8**	**85.7**	**82.5**	**26.0**
- $\mathcal{L}_{KL}$	53.4	1.33	35.3	83.9	80.3	20.8
- ON-LSTM	41.1	1.50	27.2	80.2	75.7	15.7
repw/ LSTM	44.2	1.42	30.9	82.9	79.0	19.8
- GCN Interact	46.7	1.34	35.0	84.1	80.5	22.2
- $\mathcal{L}_{dif}$	51.6	1.31	36.2	84.6	81.4	23.6
- Interact - $\mathcal{L}_{dif}$	46.1	1.38	32.5	83.1	79.6	20.7
One GCN	45.0	1.43	30.6	82.2	78.1	19.3
- GCN	42.7	1.49	27.6	80.9	76.7	16.2

Table 3: Models' performance on the UDS-T development set. Except for the rank diff (RD) metric for duration prediction, all the metrics prefer large values.

both datasets TE3 and TD, including the previous best-reported model in (Vashishtha et al., 2019) with $p < 0.01$. Second, for the models with BERT embeddings, ON-LSTM-GCN also significantly outperforms the previous best-reported models on TD (i.e., (Han et al., 2019a,b)). In fact, ON-LSTM-GCN achieves the state-of-the-art performance with the BERT embeddings over both datasets, clearly testifying to the advantages of the proposed model for TempRel.

• **Model Analysis and Ablation Study**: This section investigates different variations of the two major components in ON-LSTM-GCN (i.e., ON-LSTM and GCN) to demonstrate their benefits.

ON-LSTM: First, we consider the following variations for the ON-LSTM component: (i) "- $\mathcal{L}_{KL}$": this is the ON-LSTM-GCN model where the syntax-model consistency loss $\mathcal{L}_{KL}$ is not included in the overall loss function, (ii) "**- ON-LSTM**": this model completely removes the ON-LSTM component from ON-LSTM-GCN (so the consistency loss $\mathcal{L}_{KL}$ is not used and the input vector sequence X is directly sent to the GCN models), and (iii) "**repw/ LSTM**": this model replaces ON-LSTM with the traditional LSTM model in ON-LSTM-GCN (the $\mathcal{L}_{KL}$ loss is also not employed in this case as LSTM does not support the neuron hierarchy for the model-based importance scores).

GCN: Second, for the GCN component, we evaluate the following variations for ON-LSTM-GCN: (i) "**- GCN Interact**": this model does not apply the interaction mechanism for the two GCN models in Equations 5 and 6 for ON-LSTM-GCN; it instead uses Equation 4 for the computation of both GCN models, (ii) "- $\mathcal{L}_{dif}$": this model eliminates the regularization loss $\mathcal{L}_{dif}$ from ON-LSTM-GCN, (iii) "**- Interact -** $\mathcal{L}_{dif}$": this model removes both the GCN interaction mechanism in Equations 5 and 6 and the loss $\mathcal{L}_{dif}$ from ON-LSTM-GCN (but it still has two GCN models), (iv) "**One GCN**": instead of using two GCN models for the two subtasks of FineTempRle, this model only utilize a single GCN model for both tasks (the GCN interaction in Equations 5 and 6 and the regularization loss $\mathcal{L}_{dif}$ are thus not used in this case as well), and (v) "**- GCN**": this model completely removes the GCN component (thus also excluding the GCN interaction and the loss $\mathcal{L}_{dif}$); the ON-LSTM hidden vectors H are directly exploited to perform the duration and relation predictions in this case. Table 3 presents the models' performance (using ELMo) on the UDS-T development set

There are several important observations from this table. First, regarding ON-LSTM, we see that both the ON-LSTM and syntax-model consistency loss $\mathcal{L}_{KL}$ are necessary for the proposed model as eliminating any of them or replacing ON-LSTM with LSTM would significantly hurt the performance. Second, for the GCN component, it is clear that the GCN interaction mechanism in Equations 5 and 6 and the regularization loss $\mathcal{L}_{dif}$ are crucial for ON-LSTM-GCN to achieve its highest performance, clearly verifying the benefits of knowledge transferring between duration and relation prediction for FineTempRel. In addition, the better performance of the full model and the "- Interact - $\mathcal{L}_{dif}$" model over "One GCN" demonstrates the necessity to employ different GCN models for the two subtasks in FineTempRel to enhance the representation customization capacity for the tasks. The model's performance becomes the worst when GCNs are completely excluded (i.e., "- GCN"), confirming the effectiveness of GCNs for FineTempRel.

5 Conclusion

We introduce a novel deep learning model for FineTempRel that exploits the syntactic structures of the sentences to improve the representation vectors. We focus on two type of syntactic information for FineTempRel in this work, i.e., the syntax-based importance scores for the representations of the words that are injected into the models via ON-LSTM, and the dependency connections between the words that are exploited in GCN models. Two novel transferring learning methods are presented for the two GCN models for duration and relation predictions. Comprehensive experiments are performed to demonstrate the advantages of the proposed model for FineTempRel.

Acknowledgments

This research has been supported by the Army Research Office (ARO) grant W911NF-21-1-0112 and the NSF grant CNS-1747798 to the IU-CRC Center for Big Learning. This research is also based upon work supported by the Office of the Director of National Intelligence (ODNI), Intelligence Advanced Research Projects Activity (IARPA), via IARPA Contract No. 2019-19051600006 under the Better Extraction from Text Towards Enhanced Retrieval (BETTER) Program. The views and conclusions contained herein are those of the authors and should not be interpreted as necessarily representing the official policies, either expressed or implied, of ARO, ODNI, IARPA, the Department of Defense, or the U.S. Government. The U.S. Government is authorized to reproduce and distribute reprints for governmental purposes notwithstanding any copyright annotation therein. This document does not contain technology or technical data controlled under either the U.S. International Traffic in Arms Regulations or the U.S. Export Administration Regulations.

References

Steven Bethard. 2013. ClearTK-TimeML: A minimalist approach to TempEval 2013. In *Second Joint Conference on Lexical and Computational Semantics (*SEM), Volume 2: Proceedings of the Seventh International Workshop on Semantic Evaluation (SemEval 2013)*.

Ann Bies, Justin Mott, Colin Warner, and Seth Kulick. 2012. English web treebank. In *Linguistic Data Consortium*.

Taylor Cassidy, Bill McDowell, Nathanael Chambers, and Steven Bethard. 2014. An annotation framework for dense event ordering. In *Proceedings of the Annual Meeting of the Association for Computational Linguistics (ACL)*.

Nathanael Chambers, Taylor Cassidy, Bill McDowell, and Steven Bethard. 2014. Dense event ordering with a multi-pass architecture. In *Transactions of the Association for Computational Linguistics (TACL)*.

Fei Cheng and Yusuke Miyao. 2017. Classifying temporal relations by bidirectional LSTM over dependency paths. In *Proceedings of the Annual Meeting of the Association for Computational Linguistics (ACL)*.

Jacob Devlin, Ming-Wei Chang, Kenton Lee, and Kristina Toutanova. 2019. BERT: Pre-training of deep bidirectional transformers for language understanding. In *Proceedings of the Conference of the North American Chapter of the Association for Computational Linguistics: Human Language Technologies (NAACL-HLT)*.

Dmitriy Dligach, Timothy Miller, Chen Lin, Steven Bethard, and Guergana Savova. 2017. Neural temporal relation extraction. In *Proceedings of the Conference of the European Chapter of the Association for Computational Linguistics (EACL)*.

Jennifer D'Souza and Vincent Ng. 2013. Classifying temporal relations with rich linguistic knowledge. In *Proceedings of the Conference of the North American Chapter of the Association for Computational Linguistics: Human Language Technologies (NAACL-HLT)*.

Elena Filatova and Eduard Hovy. 2001. Assigning time-stamps to event-clauses. In *Proceedings of the ACL 2001 Workshop on Temporal and Spatial Information Processing*.

Tanya Goyal and Greg Durrett. 2019. Embedding time expressions for deep temporal ordering models. In *Proceedings of the Annual Meeting of the Association for Computational Linguistics (ACL)*.

David Graff. 2002. The aquaint corpus of english news text. In *Linguistic Data Consortium (LDC2002T31)*.

Andrey Gusev, Nathanael Chambers, Divye Raj Khilnani, Pranav Khaitan, Steven Bethard, and Dan Jurafsky. 2011. Using query patterns to learn the duration of events. In *Proceedings of the Ninth International Conference on Computational Semantics (IWCS)*.

Rujun Han, I-Hung Hsu, Mu Yang, Aram Galstyan, Ralph Weischedel, and Nanyun Peng. 2019b. Deep structured neural network for event temporal relation extraction. In *Proceedings of the 23rd Conference on Computational Natural Language Learning (CoNLL)*.

Rujun Han, Qiang Ning, and Nanyun Peng. 2019a. Joint event and temporal relation extraction with shared representations and structured prediction. In *Proceedings of the Conference on Empirical Methods in Natural Language Processing (EMNLP)*.

Yu Hong, Tongtao Zhang, Tim O'Gorman, Sharone Horowit-Hendler, Heng Ji, and Martha Palmer. 2016. Building a cross-document event-event relation corpus. In *Proceedings of the 10th Linguistic Annotation Workshop held in conjunction with ACL 2016 (LAW-X 2016)*.

Thomas N. Kipf and Max Welling. 2017. Semi-supervised classification with graph convolutional networks. In *Proceedings of the International Conference on Learning Representations (ICLR)*.

Chen Lin, Dmitriy Dligach, Timothy A Miller, Steven Bethard, and Guergana K Savova. 2015. Multilayered temporal modeling for the clinical domain. In *Journal of the American Medical Informatics Association*.

Jian Liu, Yubo Chen, and Jun Zhao. 2020. Knowledge enhanced event causality identification with mention masking generalizations. In *Proceedings of the Twenty-Ninth International Joint Conference on Artificial Intelligence (IJCAI)*.

Jing Lu and Vincent Ng. 2017. Joint learning for event coreference resolution. In *Proceedings of the 55th Annual Meeting of the Association for Computational Linguistics (ACL)*.

Jing Lu, Deepak Venugopal, Vibhav Gogate, and Vincent Ng. 2016. Joint inference for event coreference resolution. In *Transactions of the Association for Computational Linguistics (TACL)*.

Inderjeet Mani, Marc Verhagen, Ben Wellner, Chong Min Lee, and James Pustejovsky. 2006. Machine learning of temporal relations. In *Proceedings of the Annual Meeting of the Association for Computational Linguistics (ACL)*.

Yuanliang Meng and Anna Rumshisky. 2018. Context-aware neural model for temporal information extraction. In *Proceedings of the Annual Meeting of the Association for Computational Linguistics (ACL)*.

Anne-Lyse Minard, Manuela Speranza, Ruben Urizar, Begoña Altuna, Marieke van Erp, Anneleen Schoen, and Chantal van Son. 2016. MEANTIME, the NewsReader multilingual event and time corpus. In *Proceedings of the Language Resources and Evaluation Conference (LREC)*.

Paramita Mirza and Sara Tonelli. 2016. CATENA: CAusal and TEmporal relation extraction from NAtural language texts. In *Proceedings of the International Conference on Computational Linguistics (COLING)*.

Minh Van Nguyen, Viet Dac Lai, and Thien Huu Nguyen. 2021. Cross-task instance representation interactions and label dependencies for joint information extraction with graph convolutional networks. In *Proceedings of the Conference of the North American Chapter of the Association for Computational Linguistics: Human Language Technologies (NAACL-HLT)*.

Thien Huu Nguyen, , Adam Meyers, and Ralph Grishman. 2016. New york university 2016 system for kbp event nugget: A deep learning approach. In *Text Analysis Conference*.

Thien Huu Nguyen and Ralph Grishman. 2018. Graph convolutional networks with argument-aware pooling for event detection. In *Proceedings of the Association for the Advancement of Artificial Intelligence (AAAI)*.

Qiang Ning, Zhili Feng, and Dan Roth. 2017. A structured learning approach to temporal relation extraction. In *Proceedings of the Conference on Empirical Methods in Natural Language Processing (EMNLP)*.

Qiang Ning, Zhili Feng, Hao Wu, and Dan Roth. 2018. Joint reasoning for temporal and causal relations. In *Proceedings of the Annual Meeting of the Association for Computational Linguistics (ACL)*.

Qiang Ning, Sanjay Subramanian, and Dan Roth. 2019. An improved neural baseline for temporal relation extraction. In *Proceedings of the Conference on Empirical Methods in Natural Language Processing (EMNLP)*.

Qiang Ning, Hao Wu, and Dan Roth. 2018c. A multi-axis annotation scheme for event temporal relations. In *Proceedings of the Annual Meeting of the Association for Computational Linguistics (ACL)*.

Qiang Ning, Zhongzhi Yu, Chuchu Fan, and Dan Roth. 2018b. Exploiting partially annotated data in temporal relation extraction. In *Proceedings of the Seventh Joint Conference on Lexical and Computational Semantics*.

Tim O'Gorman, Kristin Wright-Bettner, and Martha Palmer. 2016. Richer event description: Integrating event coreference with temporal, causal and bridging annotation. In *Proceedings of the 2nd Workshop on Computing News Storylines (CNS 2016)*.

Feng Pan, Rutu Mulkar-Mehta, and Jerry R Hobbs. 2007. Modeling and learning vague event durations for temporal reasoning. In *Proceedings of the Association for the Advancement of Artificial Intelligence (AAAI)*.

Matthew E. Peters, Mark Neumann, Mohit Iyyer, Matt Gardner, Christopher Clark, Kenton Lee, and Luke Zettlemoyer. 2018. Deep contextualized word representations. In *Proceedings of the Conference of the North American Chapter of the Association for Computational Linguistics: Human Language Technologies (NAACL-HLT)*.

James Pustejovsky, Patrick Hanks, Roser Sauri, Andrew See, Robert Gaizauskas, Andrea Setzer, Dragomir Radev, Beth Sundheim, David Day, Lisa Ferro, and et al 2003. 2003. The timebank corpus. In *Corpus linguistics, volume 2003, page 40*.

Yikang Shen, Shawn Tan, Alessandro Sordoni, and Aaron Courville. 2019. Ordered neurons: Integrating tree structures into recurrent neural networks. In *Proceedings of the International Conference on Learning Representations (ICLR)*.

Julien Tourille, Olivier Ferret, Aurélie Névéol, and Xavier Tannier. 2017. Neural architecture for temporal relation extraction: A bi-LSTM approach for detecting narrative containers. In *Proceedings of the Annual Meeting of the Association for Computational Linguistics (ACL)*.

Hieu Minh Tran, Duy Phung, and Thien Huu Nguyen. 2021. Exploiting document structures and cluster consistencies for event coreference resolution. In *Proceedings of the 59th Annual Meeting of the Association for Computational Linguistics and the 11th International Joint Conference on Natural Language Processing (ACL-IJCNLP)*.

Minh Phu Tran and Thien Huu Nguyen. 2021. Graph convolutional networks for event causality identification with rich document-level structures. In *Proceedings of the 2021 Conference of the North American Chapter of the Association for Computational Linguistics: Human Language Technologies (NAACL-HLT)*.

Naushad UzZaman, Hector Llorens, Leon Derczynski, James Allen, Marc Verhagen, and James Pustejovsky. 2013. SemEval-2013 task 1: TempEval-3: Evaluating time expressions, events, and temporal relations. In *Second Joint Conference on Lexical and Computational Semantics (*SEM), Volume 2: Proceedings of the Seventh International Workshop on Semantic Evaluation (SemEval 2013)*.

Siddharth Vashishtha, Benjamin Van Durme, and Aaron Steven White. 2019. Fine-grained temporal relation extraction. In *Proceedings of the Annual Meeting of the Association for Computational Linguistics (ACL)*.

Amir Pouran Ben Veyseh, Franck Dernoncourt, Dejing Dou, and Thien Huu Nguyen. 2020a. Exploiting the syntax-model consistency for neural relation extraction. In *Proceedings of the Annual Meeting of the Association for Computational Linguistics (ACL)*.

Amir Pouran Ben Veyseh, Tuan Ngo Nguyen, and Thien Huu Nguyen. 2020b. Graph transformer networks with syntactic and semantic structures for event argument extraction. In *Proceedings of the Conference on Empirical Methods in Natural Language Processing: Findings (EMNLP)*.

Jennifer Williams and Graham Katz. 2012. Extracting and modeling durations for habits and events from twitter. In *Proceedings of the Annual Meeting of the Association for Computational Linguistics (ACL)*.

Does It Happen? Multi-hop Path Structures for Event Factuality Prediction with Graph Transformer Networks

Duong Minh Le[1] **and Thien Huu Nguyen**[2]
[1] VinAI Research, Vietnam
[2] Dept. of Computer and Information Science, University of Oregon, Eugene, OR, USA
v.duonglm1@vinai.io, thien@cs.uoregon.edu

Abstract

The goal of Event Factuality Prediction (EFP) is to determine the factual degree of an event mention, representing how likely the event mention has happened in text. Current deep learning models has demonstrated the importance of syntactic and semantic structures of the sentences to identify important context words for EFP. However, the major problem with these EFP models is that they only encode the one-hop paths between the words (i.e., the direct connections) to form the sentence structures. In this work, we show that the multi-hop paths between the words are also necessary to compute the sentence structures for EFP. To this end, we introduce a novel deep learning model for EFP that explicitly considers multi-hop paths with both syntax-based and semantic-based edges between the words to obtain sentence structures for representation learning in EFP. We demonstrate the effectiveness of the proposed model via the extensive experiments in this work.

1 Introduction

In Information Extraction (IE), an event mention is represented via an anchor/trigger word that evokes an event in the input sentence. We study the problem of Event Factuality Prediction (EFP) that aims to identify the degrees of uncertainty/factuality for event mentions in text. Among others, EFP finds its applications in knowledge base construction to differentiate between factual and non-factual event mentions. In this work, we follow the recent regression formulation for EFP that seeks to predict a real-valued score in the range of [-3,3] to indicate the occurrence possibility for a given event mention (Stanovsky et al., 2017; Rudinger et al., 2018). For instance, in the sentence "*He cannot go to the restaurant.*", "*go*" is the trigger word for an event mention with the factuality score of -3 (i.e., certainly not happened).

In order to predict the factuality scores for the event mentions, the EFP models need to locate the important context words in the sentences (i.e., the cue words) and combine them appropriately to reveal the factuality for the event triggers. As the important context words might be distributed at different positions in the sentences, the current state-of-the-art deep learning models for EFP have relied on the sentence structures to facilitate the identification of the cue words. In particular, the sentence structures in the EFP models can be represented via the importance score matrices that involve cells to quantify the contribution of a context word for the representation vector computation of the current word for EFP (Veyseh et al., 2019a). The sentence structures would then be used to induce the representation vectors for the words to perform factuality prediction. Both syntactic and semantic structures of the sentences have been exploited in the deep learning models for EFP. As such, the syntactic structures are based on the direct connections between the words in the dependency parsing trees of the input sentences while the contextual similarities between the words are employed to form the semantic structures (Veyseh et al., 2019a).

Despite their success, a major limitation of the current deep learning models for EFP is their inability to capture the multi-hop paths between the words to produce the importance scores in the sentence structures for EFP. In particular, the current deep learning models for EFP have only focused on the direct connection/relation (i.e., one-hop path) between a pair of words to determine the importance score for the words in the structures. For example, the syntactic structures in (Veyseh et al., 2019a) involve an binary importance score matrix where a cell is only set to 1 if the two words corresponding to that cell are directly connected in the dependency tree. This is not desirable as based on our analysis, the multi-hop paths between the words are also important and should be considered

Proceedings of the 2021 EMNLP Workshop W-NUT: The Seventh Workshop on Noisy User-generated Text, pages 46–55
November 11, 2021.

to generate better importance scores for the structures for EFP. Consider the trigger word "*involvement*" in the following sentence as an example:

It was confirmed that Hagai, Basir's brother, had been a key member of al-Qaeda while their representatives constantly denied the ***involvement*** *of any Basir's family members in this terrorist group.*

The important context words to correctly predict the factuality score +3 (i.e., actually happened) for "*involvement*" in this case involve "*any Basir's family members*", "*Basir's brother*", "*Hagai*", "*a key member*", and "*confirmed*". In the deep learning models for EFP, these important words should be encoded into the representation vector for "*involvement*" to perform factuality prediction. Using the dependency tree for this sentence, ones can use the one-hop paths (i.e., the edges) to link "*involvement*" with the information in '*any Basir's family members*". Similarly, the direct semantic similarity between "*involvement*" and "*member*" can also be used to connect "*a key member*" to "*involvement*" for representation learning in this case. However, it is very challenging for the one-hop paths to directly connect "*involvement*" with the other important context words (i.e., "*Basir's brother*", "*Hagai*", and "*confirmed*") (either syntactically or semantically) due to the far distances/differences between them in the sentence. Fortunately, by considering the multi-hop paths between the words, we can rely on "*any Basir's family members*" to link "*involvement*" with "*Basir's brother*" (i.e., with the semantic connection between "*family members*" and "*brother*") that can be further extended to "*Hagai*", "*member*", and "*confirmed*" via the dependency connections for representation learning. Besides the multi-hop nature, we also note that the edges along the multi-hop path in this example contains both syntactic and semantic connections (i.e., heterogeneous edge types) that are necessary to identify the important context words for EFP.

Motivated by this limitation, in this work, we propose to learn the importance scores for the sentence structures, leveraging Graph Transformer Networks (GTN) (Yun et al., 2019) to facilitate the emergence of the effective multi-hop paths with heterogeneous edge types for EFP. In particular, we propose to first generate the initial sentence structures for EFP based on both the syntactic and semantic information. These initial sentence structures are then combined by the GTN model via the weighted sums, serving as the intermediate structures that are able to capture both syntactic and semantic one-hop connections between the words for EFP. Afterward, the intermediate structures are multiplied to induce the final structures that enable the modeling of the multi-hop paths with heterogeneous edge types to compute the importance scores for the structures (Yun et al., 2019). As illustrated by our example, we expect that these multi-hop paths between the words can help to produce more effective representation vectors for the deep learning models to achieve better performance for EFP.

Finally, in order to improve the generalization of the proposed model for EFP, we propose a novel inductive bias for the GTN model based on the Information Bottleneck technique (Tishby et al., 2000). In particular, the rich combined structures from the syntactic and semantic information might offer the proposed GTN model with the high capacity for representation learning to encode the detailed information in the input sentences. As the training datasets for EFP are generally small, such high capacity might eventually lead to the overfitting of the GTN model where all the context information in the input sentences, including the irrelevant ones, is preserved in the induced representation vectors. To this end, we propose to promote the GTN model in this work as an information bottleneck so the GTN-produced representations are trained to not only have good factuality prediction performance but also maintain a minimal mutual information with the input sentences (Belghazi et al., 2018). The extensive experiments on four benchmark datasets demonstrate the benefits of the proposed model, yielding the state-of-the-art performance for EFP in this work.

2 Related Work

Various methods have been proposed to solve EFP, including the early rule-based approaches (Nairn et al., 2006; Saurí, 2008; Lotan et al., 2013), the feature-based machine learning approaches (Diab et al., 2009; Prabhakaran et al., 2010; De Marneffe et al., 2012; Lee et al., 2015), and the hybrid methods (Saurí and Pustejovsky, 2012; Qian et al., 2015). The recent work has featured deep learning as the state-of-the-art method for EFP. In particular, (Qian et al., 2018) presents a model based on Generative Adversarial Networks (GAN) while (Rudinger et al., 2018) applies Long-short Term Memory Networks (LSTM) over both the sequential order and the dependency tree of the input sentences for factuality prediction. The best performance for EFP so far is reported by (Veyseh et al., 2019a) that linearly combines the syntactic and semantic structures for Graph Convolutional Neural Networks (GCN). We also employ syntactic and semantic structures for EFP in this work; however, our model presents novel techniques with trigger-based structure customization, GTNs to learn the sentence structures with the multi-hop path reasoning, and information bottleneck to improve the generalization for EFP. Model-wise, our work bears some similarity with other NLP models that leverage syntactic structures and GCNs to encode input texts for different NLP tasks, including relation extraction (Zhang et al., 2018), joint information extraction (Nguyen et al., 2021), metaphor detection (Le et al., 2020), and rumor detection (Veyseh et al., 2019b). Finally, we also note some related tasks for EFP that seek to classify event trigger words in texts, including event detection (Nguyen and Grishman, 2015; Chen et al., 2015; Lai et al., 2020; Veyseh et al., 2021), event realis classification (Mitamura et al., 2015; Nguyen et al., 2016) and uncertainty detection (Adel and Schütze, 2017).

3 Model

We formalize EFP as a regression problem in this work. In particular, given an input sentence $W = w_1, w_2, \ldots, w_N$ of N words/tokens (i.e., w_i is the i-th token) and an event mention with the trigger word located at the k-th position (i.e., w_k), we need to predict a real-valued score between -3 and +3 to indicate the factual degree for w_k.

In order to achieve a fair comparison with the prior work for EFP (Veyseh et al., 2019a), we first apply the BERT$_{base}$ model in (Devlin et al., 2019) to obtain a pre-trained embedding vector x_i for each word $w_i \in W$. In particular, we run the BERT$_{base}$ model over the input sentence W and use the hidden vector for the first wordpiece of w_i in the last layer of BERT as the embedding vector x_i (of 768 dimensions) for w_i. This encoding step transforms W into a sequence of embedding vectors $X = x_1, x_2, \ldots, x_N$ (called the input vectors) for the neural computation in the next steps. The EFP model in this work involves three major components: (i) structure generation, (iii) structure combination, and (iii) representation regularization. We will explain the details of these components in the following sections.

3.1 Structure Generation

The goal of this section is to generate the initial sentence structures that would be combined in the next steps to generate richer structures for representation learning in EFP. Formally, the sentence structures in this work can be seen as the importance score matrices of size $N \times N$. Each cell (i, j) in these matrices contains a score to represent the importance of the contextual information from w_j for the representation vector of w_i if this vector is used to create the features for factuality prediction (called the importance score for the pair (w_i, w_j)). Following the previous work for EFP, we consider two types of sentence structures for EFP in this work, i.e., the syntactic structures and the semantic structures (Veyseh et al., 2019a).

Syntactic Structures: As presented in the introduction, the syntactic structures would leverage the information in the dependency tree T of W to compute the syntactic importance scores for EFP. The simplest approach for the syntactic structures is to directly use the binary adjacency matrix $A^{syn} = \{a_{i,j}^{syn}\}_{i,j=1..N}$ of T for the importance score matrix as in (Veyseh et al., 2019a): $a_{i,j}^{syn} = 1$ if w_i and w_j are connected in T or $i = j$. This approach is based on the motivation that the syntactic neighboring words of w_i in T would be the most informative words to reveal the contextual semantics of w_i for EFP (Veyseh et al., 2019a). However, one problem with this syntactic structure is its ignorance of the trigger word $w_k \in W$ (i.e., A^{syn} is not dependent on w_k). As w_k is the focused word in EFP, in this work, we argue that the syntactic structures should be conditioned on the trigger word w_k to produce more effective structures for representation learning in EFP. To this end, we propose to customize the syntactic structures for the event triggers in EFP, leveraging the intuition that the closer words to w_k in the dependency tree T would provide more contextual information for the representation vectors in EFP than the farther ones (e.g., the words "*Basir's family members*" in our running example). The syntactic neighboring words of w_k in T should thus be assigned with higher importance scores in the syntactic sentence structures for EFP, serving as the main method to achieve trigger-based customization for the syntactic structures in this work. In particular, to generate the task-specific syntactic structures, we first compute the length d_i of the shortest path between w_i and the trigger word w_k (i.e., the distance) in T for all

$1 \leq i \leq N$. Afterward, we obtain the customized syntactic structure $A^{syn} = \{a_{i,j}^{syn}\}_{i,j=1..N}$ via:

$$a_{i,j}^{syn} = \sigma(FF([d_i, d_j, d_i * d_j, d_i + d_j, |d_i - d_j|])) \quad (1)$$

where [] is the vector concatenation, FF is a two-layer feed-forward network to convert a vector to a scalar, and σ is the sigmoid function. We expect that learning the syntactic structures in this way would introduce the flexibility to infer effective structures for EFP.

Semantic Structure: The importance score for a pair of words (w_i, w_j) in the semantic structures would be based on the contextual semantics of w_i and w_j in the sentence (Veyseh et al., 2019a). As such, to capture the contextual semantic for $w_i \in W$, we directly utilize the embedding vector x_i from the BERT model of the encoding step. As BERT is a deep model that has been trained on a large corpus, we expect that the BERT-based vectors x_i would provide effective semantic representations for the importance scores in this case. Concretely, given the semantic vectors x_i and x_j for w_i and w_j, the semantic importance scores $a_{i,j}^{sem}$ for the semantic structure $A^{sem} = \{a_{i,j}^{sem}\}_{i,j=1..N}$ can be learned via $a_{i,j}^{sem} = f(x_i, x_j)$ where f is some learnable function to fuse x_i and x_j to produce a score. A simple version of the function f for the semantic importance scores is presented in (Veyseh et al., 2019a):

$$\begin{aligned} x'_i &= tanh(W_1^{sem} x_i) \\ a_{i,j}^{sem} &= \sigma(W_2^{sem}[x'_i, x'_j]) \end{aligned} \quad (2)$$

where W_1^{sem} and W_2^{sem} are the weight matrices and the biases are omitted for brevity.

Similar to the simple syntactic structure A^{syn}, a problem for this version of f is that the semantic scores $a_{i,j}^{sem}$ are not dependent on the trigger word w_k, potentially causing the lack of necessary context (i.e., the trigger word) to obtain the sentence structures for EFP. To this end, we propose to improve the semantic score function f in (Veyseh et al., 2019a) by additionally including the embedding vector x_k of the trigger word w_k into the computation of the semantic structure A^{sem} for EFP. In particular, we first employ the embedding vector x_k of the trigger word w_k to generate a task-specific control vector c^{syn}. This control vector would then be used to filter the information in the embedding vectors x_i of the words in W so only the relevant information for the trigger word w_k in EFP is preserved. This trigger-based filtering will serve as the main mechanism to customize the semantic structures for the trigger words for EFP in this work. Finally, to obtain the task-specific semantic structures, the filtered vectors would be sent to the same function in (Veyseh et al., 2019a) to compute the importance scores $a_{i,j}^{sem}$:

$$\begin{aligned} c^{syn} &= tanh(W_3^{sem} x_k) \\ x'_i &= tanh(W_4^{sem} x_i), x''_i = c^{syn} \odot x'_i \\ a_{i,j}^{sem} &= \sigma(W_5^{sem}[x''_i, x''_j]) \end{aligned} \quad (3)$$

where $\odot$ is the element-wise multiplication.

3.2 Structure Combination

In this work, we consider the customized sentence structures A^{syn} and A^{sem} as two different types of relations between the pairs of words in W (called the relation word types). For these structures, the importance score in the cell (i, j) is intended to capture the degree of connection between w_i and w_j based on their direct interaction/edge (i.e., the one-hop path (w_i, w_j)) and the corresponding relation type (i.e., syntactic relations for A^{syn} and semantic relations for A^{sem}). Given this interpretation for the structures, this component aims to combine A^{syn} and A^{sem} to generate richer sentence structures for EFP. In particular, instead of only relying on the direct interactions between a pair of word (w_i, w_j) to compute the importance scores, the combined structures should be able to model the multi-hop interactions between w_i and w_j that possibly involve the other words in W (i.e., the multi-hop reasoning paths between w_i and w_j). In addition, the multi-hop reasoning paths between w_i and w_j are also expected to enable the appearance of the direct edges/connections between the words that belong to different relation types in the initial structures (i.e., heterogeneous edge types with syntactic and semantic relations). As illustrated in the introduction, both the multi-hop reasoning paths and the heterogeneous edge types are necessary for factuality score prediction in our problem. Consequently, in this work, we propose to further feed A^{syn} and A^{sem} into the Graph Transformer Networks (GTN) (Yun et al., 2019) that are able to generate rich sentence structures with multi-hop reasoning paths and heterogeneous edge types, thus fitting well with our intuition for EFP.

In particular, to learn the multi-hop paths at different lengths, following (Yun et al., 2019), we first include the identity matrix I (of size $N \times N$) into the set $\mathcal{A}$ of the initial structures for EFP, i.e., $\mathcal{A} = [A^{syn}, A^{sem}, I] = [\mathcal{A}_1, \mathcal{A}_2, \mathcal{A}_3]$. The GTN model in this work would then process these initial structures via C channels to learn richer structures for EFP. At the i-th channel of GTNs ($1 \leq i \leq C$), M intermediate structures $Q_1^i, Q_2^i, \ldots, Q_M^i$ of size $N \times N$ (i.e., amounting to $M-1$ layers in GTNs) are computed via the weighted sums of the initial structures in $\mathcal{A}$: $Q_j^i = \sum_{v=1..3} \alpha_{j,v}^i A_v$ for all $1 \leq j \leq M$ ($\alpha_{j,v}^i$ are the learnable weights). Note that similar to (Veyseh et al., 2019a), the weighted sums help to combine A^{syn} and A^{sem}, enabling the intermediate structures Q_j^i to reason with any of the two relation types (i.e., syntactically with A^{syn} or semantically with A^{sem}) for EFP. Afterward, to capture the multi-hop paths for the importance scores, the intermediate structures at the i-th channel are multiplied to obtain a single sentence structure Q^i for this channel: $Q^i = Q_1^i \times Q_2^i \times \ldots \times Q_M^i$. The resulting structures Q^i at the GTN channels serve as the final structures that can model any multi-hop reasoning paths with lengths up to M and edges of heterogeneous relation types (i.e., syntactic or semantic) for the importance scores (as demonstrated in (Yun et al., 2019)).

In the next step, the final structures $Q^1, Q^2, \ldots, Q^C$ of GTN would be used as the adjacency matrices in a Graph Convolutional Network (GCN) model (Kipf and Welling, 2017; Nguyen and Grishman, 2018) over the input vector sequence X to induce more abstract representation vectors for the words in W for EFP. In particular, the GCN model in this work involves G layers to compute the representation vectors at different abstract levels for the words. For the j-th final structure Q^j, the representation vector $h_i^{j,t}$ for the word w_i in the t-th GCN layer is computed via:

$$h_i^{j,t} = ReLU(U^t \sum_{v=1..N} \frac{Q_{i,v}^j h_v^{j,t-1}}{\sum_{u=1..N} Q_{i,u}^j}) \quad (4)$$

where U^t is the weight matrix for the t-th GCN layer and the input vectors $h_i^{j,0}$ for the GCN model are obtained from BERT-generated vectors x_i (i.e., $h_i^{j,0} = h_i$ for all $1 \leq j \leq C, 1 \leq i \leq N$).

Afterward, the hidden vectors in the last GCN layer for w_i for all the final structures (i.e., $h_i^{1,G}, h_i^{2,G}, \ldots, h_i^{C,G}$) are concatenated to form the final representation vector h'_i for w_i in the proposed model: $h'_i = [h_i^{1,G}, h_i^{2,G}, \ldots, h_i^{C,G}]$. Finally, in order to predict the factuality score for w_k in W, we create an overall representation vector R based on the hidden vectors from the GCN model via: $R = [h'_k, MaxPool(h'_1, h'_2, \ldots, h'_N)]$. This vector is then fed into a two-layer feed-forward network to produce the factuality score for the regression model. Following (Rudinger et al., 2018; Veyseh et al., 2019a), we use the Huber loss L_{pred} with $\delta = 1$ to train the models in this work.

3.3 Representation Regularization

Due to the high learning capacity with rich syntactic and semantic structures, the proposed GTN model might overfit to the training data by memorizing the irrelevant information from the input sentences in the induced representation vectors for EFP (as described in the introduction). In order to improve the generalization of the GTN model, we propose to regularize the representation vectors obtained by the GTN model so only the effective information for EFP is preserved in the representation vectors for factuality prediction. To this end, we introduce the Information Bottleneck (IB) framework (Tishby et al., 2000) into the GTN model so the GTN-produced representation vectors $H' = h'_1, h'_2, \ldots, h'_N$ would be simultaneously trained for two objectives: (1) retain the effective information to predict the factuality score for EFP (i.e., the high prediction capacity), and (2) achieve a small Mutual Information (MI)[1] with the representation vectors from the earlier layers of the model (i.e., the minimality of the representations) (Belghazi et al., 2018). In this work, on the one hand, we follow the common practice to accomplish the high prediction capacity by training the GTN representation vectors to directly perform the prediction task of interest (i.e., the factuality score prediction in our case of EFP). On the other hand, we propose to achieve the minimality of the representations for the GTN model by explicitly minimizing the MI between the GTN-produced vectors $H' = h'_1, h'_2, \ldots, h'_N$ and the BERT-produced hidden vectors $X = x_1, x_2, \ldots, x_N$ from sentence encoding. By enforcing a small MI between X and H', we expect that only the relevant information for EFP in X is passed through the GTN bottleneck to be recorded in H' for better generalization.

In order to facilitate the MI estimation between X and H', we first aggregate them into a single summarization vector via the max-pooling function: $x = MaxPool(x_1, x_2, \ldots, x_N)$ and $h' = MaxPool(h'_1, h'_2, \ldots, h'_N)$. We would then evaluate the MI between x and h' and include it in the

[1]In information theory, MI measures the information we know about one random variable if the value of another variable is revealed.

overall loss function for minimization. Note that the MI between x and h' is the KL divergence between the joint and marginal distributions of these variables. Unfortunately, the direct computation for the MI between x and h' is prohibitively expensive due to their high dimensions. Consequently, in this work, we propose to apply the mutual information neural estimation (MINE) method in (Belghazi et al., 2018) to approximate the MI with its lower bound. In particular, motivated by (Hjelm et al., 2019), we further approximate the lower bound of the MI between two the vectors/variables x and h' via the adversarial approach using the loss function of a variable discriminator. The goal of the discriminator is to differentiate the vectors that are sampled from the joint distribution and those from the product of the marginal distributions of the variables. In our case, we sample from the joint distribution for x and h' by directly concatenating the two vectors (i.e., $[h', x]$) and treat it as the positive example. To obtain the sample from the product of the marginal distributions, we first obtain another sentence $\hat{W}$ from the same batch with the current sentence W during training. Afterward, we compute the aggregated vector $\hat{x}$ (i.e., via max-pooling) of the BERT-produced vectors for the words in $\hat{W}$. The concatenation vector $[h', \hat{x}]$ would then be used as the sampled vector for the product of the marginal distributions (the negative example). These positive and negative examples are then fed into a two-layer feed-forward network D (i.e., the discriminator) to produce a scalar score, serving as the probability to perform a binary classification for the variables. Afterward, we use the logistic loss for the discriminator $\mathcal{L}_{disc}$ as an estimation for the MI between x and h' and add it into the overall loss function for minimization: $\mathcal{L}_{disc} = \log(1+e^{(1-D([h',x]))})+\log(1+e^{D([h',\hat{x}])})$.

Finally, the overall loss function $\mathcal{L}$ to train the model in this work would be: $\mathcal{L} = \mathcal{L}_{pred} + \alpha_{disc}\mathcal{L}_{disc}$ where α_{disc} is a trade-off parameter.

4 Experiments

Datasets & Parameters: Following the previous work (Stanovsky et al., 2017; Rudinger et al., 2018; Veyseh et al., 2019a), we evaluate the proposed model on four datasets for EFP: FactBank (Saurí and Pustejovsky, 2009), UW (Lee et al., 2015), Meantime (Minard et al., 2016) and UDS-IH2 (Rudinger et al., 2018). The factuality scores for the first three datasets (i.e., FactBack, UW, and Meantime) are unified and scaled to the values in [-3, +3] based on their original annotations by (Stanovsky et al., 2017). The scaling of the factuality scores for UDS-IH2, on the other hand, is done with the procedure described in (Rudinger et al., 2018) (i.e., the scores are also between -3 and +3 in this case). In order to achieve a fair comparison, we obtain the same scaled and preprocessed versions of these datasets (i.e., with dependency trees) from (Veyseh et al., 2019a) where the training/development/test data is provided for each dataset.

We use the development datasets to tune the hyper-parameters for the models in this work. The values suggested by this tuning process include: 300 dimensions for the hidden vectors in the layers of the GCN model and all the feed-forward networks (i.e., to compute $a^{syn}_{i,j}$ for the customized syntactic structures, and to consume the overall representation vector R), $G = 2$ layers for the GCN model, $C = 2$ channels for the GTN model with $M = 3$ intermediate structures in each layer, and a learning rate of $1e$-5 for the Adam optimizer. For the trade-off parameter α_{disc} in the loss function $\mathcal{L}$, the best values based on the development data is 0.1 for the FactBank, UW, and UDS-IH2 datasets, and 0.5 for Meantime.

Comparing with the State of the Art: This part compares the proposed model (called "*SynSem-Customization+MultiHop+GCN+IB+BERT*") with the previous models for EFP. In particular, we consider both the traditional feature-based models (Lee et al., 2015; Stanovsky et al., 2017) and the recent deep learning methods (Rudinger et al., 2018; Veyseh et al., 2019a) as the baselines for EFP. Note that the model in (Veyseh et al., 2019a) (called "*SynSemLinearCombine+GCN+BERT*") currently has the best reported performance on the datasets. Table 1 reports the test set performance of the models, using Mean Absolute Error (i.e., MAE) and Pearson Correlation (i.e., r) as the performance measures.

Similar to the prior work (Rudinger et al., 2018; Veyseh et al., 2019a), we consider two methods to train the models in this work: (i) training and evaluating the models on separate datasets (i.e., the rows with * in the table), and (ii) training the models on the union of FactBank, UW and Meantime, leading to a single model to be evaluated on the test data of the individual datasets (i.e., the rows with ** in the table). As we can see from the table, for both training methods, the proposed model significantly

Models	FactBank MAE	FactBank r	UW MAE	UW r	Meantime MAE	Meantime r	UDS-IH2 MAE	UDS-IH2 r
(Lee et al., 2015)*	-	-	0.511	0.708	-	-	-	-
(Stanovsky et al., 2017)*	0.590	0.710	0.420	0.660	0.340	0.470	-	-
Models reported in (Rudinger et al., 2018)								
L-biLSTM(2)-S*	0.427	0.826	0.508	0.719	0.427	0.335	0.960	0.768
L-biLSTM(2)-MultiBal**	0.391	0.821	0.496	0.724	0.278	0.613	-	-
L-biLSTM(1)-MultiFoc**	0.314	0.846	0.502	0.710	0.305	0.377	-	-
L-biLSTM(2)-MultiSimp w/UDS-IH2**	0.377	0.828	0.508	0.722	0.367	0.469	0.965	0.771
H-biLSTM(1)-MultiSimp**	0.313	0.857	0.528	0.704	0.314	0.545	-	-
H-biLSTM(2)-MultiSimp w/UDS-IH2**	0.393	0.820	0.481	0.749	0.374	0.495	0.969	0.760
Models reported in (Veyseh et al., 2019a)								
L-biLSTM(2)-S+BERT*	0.381	0.850	0.475	0.752	0.389	0.394	0.895	0.804
L-biLSTM(2)-MultiSimp w/UDS-IH2+BERT**	0.343	0.855	0.476	0.749	0.358	0.499	0.841	0.841
H-biLSTM(1)-MultiSimp+BERT**	0.310	0.821	0.495	0.771	0.281	0.639	0.822	0.812
H-biLSTM(2)-MultiSimp w/UDS-IH2+BERT**	0.330	0.871	0.460	0.798	0.339	0.571	0.835	0.802
SynSemLinearCombine+GCN+BERT*	0.315	0.890	0.451	0.828	0.350	0.452	0.730	0.905
SynSemLinearCombine+GCN+BERT**	0.310	0.903	0.438	0.830	0.204	**0.702**	0.726	0.909
Models proposed in this work								
SynSemCustomization+MultiHop+GCN+IB+BERT*	0.257	0.914	0.392	0.850	0.197	0.619	0.511	0.915
SynSemCustomization+MultiHop+GCN+IB+BERT**	**0.239**	**0.920**	**0.389**	**0.852**	**0.190**	0.685	**0.482**	**0.918**

Table 1: Test set performance. * denotes the models trained on separate datasets while ** indicates those trained on multiple datasets. The smaller values are better for MAE while the correlation r prefers the larger values.

Models	UW MAE	UW r	UDS-IH2 MAE	UDS-IH2 r
The proposed model	**0.389**	**0.852**	**0.482**	**0.918**
- A^{syn}	0.448	0.842	0.590	0.909
- A^{sem}	0.449	0.839	0.580	0.904

Table 2: The contribution of the initial structures.

outperforms the baseline models across different performance measures and datasets (except for r on Meantime). In fact, the separate dataset performance of the proposed model is also significantly better than the performance of the other models with the union of the datasets for training. The proposed model achieves the state-of-the-art performance when trained on multiple datasets, clearly demonstrating the benefits of the model in this work for EFP. As UW and UDS-IH2 are the two largest datasets among the four considering datasets, we will focus on them in the following model analysis.

Structure Analysis: The proposed model for EFP has two major sentence structures in the initial set $\mathcal{A} = [A^{syn}, A^{sem}]$ based on the syntactic and semantic information (i.e., A^{syn} and A^{sem}). This part investigates the effectiveness of the individual structures by evaluating the performance of the remaining models when each of these structures is eliminated from the overall proposed model. Table 2 presents the performance of the models[2]. It is clear from the table that the model performance is significantly worse when we remove any of the initial structures in $\mathcal{A}$, thus testifying to the benefits of the initial structures for the proposed model.

Ablation Study: There are three major components in the proposed models for EFP, i.e., the structure customization, the structure combination with GTN, and the representation regularization with information bottleneck. In order to analyze the contribution of these components, this part seeks to remove each of them from the overall model and evaluate performance of the remaining models. In particular, we consider two ablated models for the structure customization: (i) avoiding the trigger-based customization for the syntactic structure A^{syn} (i.e., instead of using Equation 1, the adjacency matrix of the dependency tree T is directly used for A^{syn} as in (Veyseh et al., 2019a)) (called "**- SyntaxCustom**"), and (ii) avoiding the trigger-based customization for the semantic structure A^{sem} (i.e., instead of using Equation 3, the function in Equation 2 is employed to compute the syntactic structure A^{sem} as in (Veyseh et al., 2019a)) (called "**- SemanticCustom**").

The main benefit of the GTN models in the second component for structure combination is to combine the initial syntactic and semantic structures

[2]Note that we train the models in analysis experiments with the multiple dataset setting (i.e., FactBank, UW and Meantime); however, the same trends for the models also hold for the setting with separate dataset training.

Models	UW MAE	UW r	UDS-IH2 MAE	UDS-IH2 r
The proposed model	**0.389**	**0.852**	**0.482**	**0.918**
- SyntaxCustom	0.429	0.838	0.578	0.901
- SemanticCustom	0.409	0.844	0.565	0.909
- GTN	0.461	0.828	0.610	0.894
- Multi-Hop	0.402	0.836	0.587	0.905
- IB	0.450	0.842	0.602	0.907
- IB + BERT in R	0.419	0.830	0.564	0.910

Table 3: The ablation study.

to generate richer structures with multi-hop path reasoning. Consequently, we examine two ablated versions for this component: (i) completely removing the GTN model for structure combination and directly running the GCN model on the initial structures in $\mathcal{A}$ (so the intermediate and final structures are not computed) (called "**- GTN**"), and (ii) only generating the intermediate structures and avoiding the intermediate structure multiplications for multi-hop path reasoning in each channel of GTN. The final structures are thus not computed and the GCN model is applied directly over the intermediate structures in this case (called "**- Multi-Hop**")[3].

Finally, for third component with representation regularization, the introduction of the information bottleneck (IB) leads to the inclusion of the loss term $\mathcal{L}_{disc}$ in the overall loss function $\mathcal{L}$. The removal of this regularization loss $\mathcal{L}_{disc}$ from $\mathcal{L}$ amounts to the ablated model "**- IB**" for this component. In addition, as this component relies on the MI between the hidden vectors computed by the BERT and GTN models for the words, we further evaluate another version for the overall model in which the regularization loss $\mathcal{L}_{disc}$ is also removed from $\mathcal{L}$, but the hidden vectors from the BERT model $X = x_1, x_2, \ldots, x_N$ are incorporated into the final representation vector R for prediction (i.e., $R = [x_k, x, h'_k, h']$) (called "**- IB + BERT in** R"). The performance of the models for this ablation study is shown in Table 3.

The most important observation from the table is that all the components are important for the proposed model to ensure the highest performance. In particular, the customization for the syntactic and semantic structures are necessary as eliminating any of them would reduce the performance significantly. The removal of the GTN model or its multi-hop path reasoning for the structures also makes the performance worse, thus highlighting the benefits of the structure combination with multi-hop paths for the structures for EFP in this work. Finally, the better performance of the proposed model over "- IB" and "-IB + BERT in R" clearly demonstrates the ability of the IB-based regularization technique to improve the generalization of the proposed model in this work.

Error Analysis: In order to better understand the errors made the proposed model for EFP, we analyze the outputs of the model on the test set of the UDS-IH2 dataset (i.e., the largest dataset in our case). In particular, we examine the examples for which the absolute values of the differences between the predicted factuality scores and the golden ones are greater than 1 (i.e., focusing on the examples with the largest prediction errors). A notable insight from our analysis is that among 118 examples selected in this way, 71.4% of the examples involves the same signs for the predicted and golden factuality scores. This suggests that although the proposed model has large prediction error on these examples, it can still capture the correct factuality polarity (i.e., positive or negative) for a great portion of the examples (i.e., 71.4%). In other words, a main source of errors for the proposed model has to do with the difficulty to identify the degrees of factuality (i.e., the fine-grained distinction with the real-valued factuality scores) for the events, not with the factuality polarity.

In addition, among the 28.6% of the examples with both large prediction errors and different signs for the predicted and golden scores, we find that a major portion of the examples (i.e., 62.5%) involves important context words that are not present in the training data (i.e., unknown word issue). Some examples of this type are shown below where the unknown and important context words are highlighted (the trigger words are in bold):

*Israel-Syrian **talks** have been cut off for two years.* (Predicted score: 2.78, Golden Score: -3).

*A man who was accused of faking his **death** last summer pleaded guilty to a conspiracy charge ...* (Predicted score: 2.45, Golden Score: -3).

Based on this observation, we hypothesize that even with the contextualized word embeddings (e.g., BERT) and the wordpiece tokenization to encode the input sentences, unknown words still constitute a challenging problem for EFP. In par-

[3]Note that for the ablated models in this component, we also re-tune the numbers of intermediate structures and channels for the GTN model (i.e., M and C), and the number of layers for the GCN model (i.e., G) on the the development sets, leading to $M = 3$, $C = 2$, and $G = 2$.

ticular, as the unknown words do not appear in the training data, the model does not have sufficient training signals to adapt the initial language models (i.e., BERT) to appropriately encode the unknown words for EFP. Future research can focus on these directions to improve the performance for EFP.

5 Conclusion

We present a novel deep learning model for EFP that combines the customized sentence structures (i.e., based on both syntactic and semantic information) to learn effective representation vectors. Our model features GTNs to infer rich sentence structures with multi-hop reasoning paths for the importance scores and information bottleneck to improve the generalization. We perform extensive experiments to demonstrate the effectiveness of the proposed model. In the future, we plan to extend the proposed model to the related tasks of EFP.

Acknowledgments

This research has been supported by the Army Research Office (ARO) grant W911NF-21-1-0112 and the NSF grant CNS-1747798 to the IUCRC Center for Big Learning. This research is also based upon work supported by the Office of the Director of National Intelligence (ODNI), Intelligence Advanced Research Projects Activity (IARPA), via IARPA Contract No. 2019-19051600006 under the Better Extraction from Text Towards Enhanced Retrieval (BETTER) Program. The views and conclusions contained herein are those of the authors and should not be interpreted as necessarily representing the official policies, either expressed or implied, of ARO, ODNI, IARPA, the Department of Defense, or the U.S. Government. The U.S. Government is authorized to reproduce and distribute reprints for governmental purposes notwithstanding any copyright annotation therein. This document does not contain technology or technical data controlled under either the U.S. International Traffic in Arms Regulations or the U.S. Export Administration Regulations.

References

Heike Adel and Hinrich Schütze. 2017. Exploring different dimensions of attention for uncertainty detection. In *Proceedings of the Conference of the European Chapter of the Association for Computational Linguistics (EACL)*.

Mohamed Ishmael Belghazi, Aristide Baratin, Sai Rajeshwar, Sherjil Ozair, Yoshua Bengio, Aaron Courville, and Devon Hjelm. 2018. Mutual information neural estimation. In *Proceedings of the International Conference on Machine Learning (ICML)*.

Yubo Chen, Liheng Xu, Kang Liu, Daojian Zeng, and Jun Zhao. 2015. Event extraction via dynamic multi-pooling convolutional neural networks. In *Proceedings of the Annual Meeting of the Association for Computational Linguistics (ACL)*.

Marie-Catherine De Marneffe, Christopher D Manning, and Christopher Potts. 2012. Did it happen? the pragmatic complexity of veridicality assessment. *Computational linguistics*, 38(2):301–333.

Jacob Devlin, Ming-Wei Chang, Kenton Lee, and Kristina Toutanova. 2019. BERT: Pre-training of deep bidirectional transformers for language understanding. In *Proceedings of the Conference of the North American Chapter of the Association for Computational Linguistics: Human Language Technologies (NAACL-HLT)*.

Mona T Diab, Lori Levin, Teruko Mitamura, Owen Rambow, Vinodkumar Prabhakaran, and Weiwei Guo. 2009. Committed belief annotation and tagging. In *Proceedings of the Third Linguistic Annotation Workshop*.

Devon Hjelm, Alex Fedorov, Samuel Lavoie-Marchildon, Karan Grewal, Phil Bachman, Adam Trischler, and Yoshua Bengio. 2019. Learning deep representations by mutual information estimation and maximization. In *Proceedings of the International Conference on Learning Representations (ICLR)*.

Thomas N Kipf and Max Welling. 2017. Semi-supervised classification with graph convolutional networks. In *Proceedings of the International Conference on Learning Representations (ICLR)*.

Viet Dac Lai, Tuan Ngo Nguyen, and Thien Huu Nguyen. 2020. Event detection: Gate diversity and syntactic importance scores for graph convolution neural networks. In *Proceedings of the Conference on Empirical Methods in Natural Language Processing (EMNLP)*.

Duong Minh Le, My Thai, and Thien Huu Nguyen. 2020. Multi-task learning for metaphor detection with graph convolutional neural networks and word sense disambiguation. In *Proceedings of the Association for the Advancement of Artificial Intelligence (AAAI)*.

Kenton Lee, Yoav Artzi, Yejin Choi, and Luke Zettlemoyer. 2015. Event detection and factuality assessment with non-expert supervision. In *Proceedings of the Conference on Empirical Methods in Natural Language Processing (EMNLP)*.

Amnon Lotan, Asher Stern, and Ido Dagan. 2013. Truthteller: Annotating predicate truth. In *Proceedings of the Conference of the North American Chapter of the Association for Computational Linguistics: Human Language Technologies (NAACL-HLT).*

A-L Minard, Manuela Speranza, Ruben Urizar, Begona Altuna, MGJ van Erp, AM Schoen, CM van Son, et al. 2016. Meantime, the newsreader multilingual event and time corpus. In *Proceedings of the Tenth International Conference on Language Resources and Evaluation (LREC).*

Teruko Mitamura, Zhengzhong Liu, and Eduard Hovy. 2015. Overview of tac kbp 2015 event nugget track. In *Proceedings of Text Analysis Conference (TAC).*

Rowan Nairn, Cleo Condoravdi, and Lauri Karttunen. 2006. Computing relative polarity for textual inference. In *Proceedings of the fifth international workshop on inference in computational semantics (icos-5).*

Minh Van Nguyen, Viet Dac Lai, and Thien Huu Nguyen. 2021. Cross-task instance representation interactions and label dependencies for joint information extraction with graph convolutional networks. In *Proceedings of the Conference of the North American Chapter of the Association for Computational Linguistics: Human Language Technologies (NAACL-HLT).*

Thien Huu Nguyen and Ralph Grishman. 2015. Event detection and domain adaptation with convolutional neural networks. In *Proceedings of the Annual Meeting of the Association for Computational Linguistics (ACL).*

Thien Huu Nguyen and Ralph Grishman. 2018. Graph convolutional networks with argument-aware pooling for event detection. In *Proceedings of the Association for the Advancement of Artificial Intelligence (AAAI).*

Thien Huu Nguyen, Adam Meyers, and Ralph Grishman. 2016. New york university 2016 system for kbp event nugget: A deep learning approach. In *Proceedings of Text Analysis Conference (TAC).*

Vinodkumar Prabhakaran, Owen Rambow, and Mona Diab. 2010. Automatic committed belief tagging. In *Proceedings of the International Conference on Computational Linguistics (COLING).*

Zhong Qian, Peifeng Li, Yue Zhang, Guodong Zhou, and Qiaoming Zhu. 2018. Event factuality identification via generative adversarial networks with auxiliary classification. In *Proceedings of the International Joint Conference on Artificial Intelligence (IJCAI).*

Zhong Qian, Peifeng Li, and Qiaoming Zhu. 2015. A two-step approach for event factuality identification. In *Asian Language Processing (IALP), 2015 International Conference on*, pages 103–106. IEEE.

Rachel Rudinger, Aaron Steven White, and Benjamin Van Durme. 2018. Neural models of factuality. In *Proceedings of the Conference of the North American Chapter of the Association for Computational Linguistics: Human Language Technologies (NAACL-HLT).*

Roser Saurí. 2008. A factuality profiler for eventualities in text. *Unveröffentlichte Dissertation, Brandeis University. Zugriff auf http://www. cs. brandeis. edu/~ roser/pubs/sauriDiss*, 1.

Roser Saurí and James Pustejovsky. 2009. Factbank: a corpus annotated with event factuality. *Language resources and evaluation*, 43(3):227.

Roser Saurí and James Pustejovsky. 2012. Are you sure that this happened? assessing the factuality degree of events in text. *Computational Linguistics*, 38(2):261–299.

Gabriel Stanovsky, Judith Eckle-Kohler, Yevgeniy Puzikov, Ido Dagan, and Iryna Gurevych. 2017. Integrating deep linguistic features in factuality prediction over unified datasets. In *Proceedings of the Annual Meeting of the Association for Computational Linguistics (ACL).*

Naftali Tishby, Fernando C Pereira, and William Bialek. 2000. The information bottleneck method. In *arXiv preprint physics/0004057.*

Amir Pouran Ben Veyseh, Viet Lai, Franck Dernoncourt, and Thien Huu Nguyen. 2021. Unleash GPT-2 power for event detection. In *Proceedings of the 59th Annual Meeting of the Association for Computational Linguistics and the 11th International Joint Conference on Natural Language Processing (ACL-IJCNLP).*

Amir Pouran Ben Veyseh, Thien Huu Nguyen, and Dejing Dou. 2019a. Graph based neural networks for event factuality prediction using syntactic and semantic structures. In *Proceedings of the Annual Meeting of the Association for Computational Linguistics (ACL).*

Amir Pouran Ben Veyseh, My T. Thai, Thien Huu Nguyen, and Dejing Dou. 2019b. Rumor detection in social networks via deep contextual modeling. In *Proceedings of the IEEE/ACM International Conference on Advances in Social Networks Analysis and Mining (ASONAM).*

Seongjun Yun, Minbyul Jeong, Raehyun Kim, Jaewoo Kang, and Hyunwoo J Kim. 2019. Graph transformer networks. In *Proceedings of the Conference on Neural Information Processing Systems (NeurIPS).*

Yuhao Zhang, Peng Qi, and Christopher D. Manning. 2018. Graph convolution over pruned dependency trees improves relation extraction. In *Proceedings of the 2018 Conference on Empirical Methods in Natural Language Processing (EMNLP).*

Google-trickers, Yaminjeongeum, and Leetspeak: An Empirical Taxonomy for Intentionally Noisy User-Generated Text

Won Ik Cho
Seoul National University
tsatsuki@snu.ac.kr

Soomin Kim
Seoul National University
soominkim@snu.ac.kr

Abstract

WARNING: This article contains contents that may offend the readers.

Strategies that insert intentional noise into text when posting it are commonly observed in the online space, and sometimes they aim to let only certain community users understand the genuine semantics. In this paper, we explore the purpose of such actions by categorizing them into tricks, memes, fillers, and codes, and organize the linguistic strategies that are used for each purpose. Through this, we identify that such strategies can be conducted by authors for multiple purposes, regarding the presence of stakeholders such as 'Peers' and 'Others'. We finally analyze how these strategies appear differently in each circumstance, along with the unified taxonomy accompanying examples.

1 Introduction

Noisy text usually originates in unintentional errors in the conversion process of speech or signal. They are also observed in the digitized text production along with spelling errors or grammar mistakes (Subramaniam et al., 2009). However, sometimes noises are intentionally inserted by authors. For instance, Airbnb users write reviews in a code-mixed manner to convey negative information about the accommodations to other users who share the language without being offensive to the foreign host. In another viewpoint, users who share the social identity of a specific community such as Reddit or 2ch create and use memes for fun, which play a role as jargon in those communities (Merritt, 2012). Also, the users of broadcasting platforms such as Twitch, or online games, use profanity terms in an undetectable way (Blashki and Nichol, 2005), to express their emotions and at the same time avoid the detection of automatic censoring systems (Märtens et al., 2015).

In this study, we investigate and formulate the stakeholders of such strategies, namely the author, other users in the community who *should* understand the text, and the ones who should *not* understand the text. Though writing and posting text is done by the author, the other two influence how the avoidance strategies are represented. In other words, the intention of generating noisy text varies depending on the existence of each stakeholder, and this variation may also affect the strategy used. This typology has been domain specifically studied in online censorship and resistance (Elahi and Goldberg, 2012; Beato et al., 2014; Mokwena and Banda, 2019), but we focus more on the generalized agents of this 'text gaming' (Haapoja et al., 2020).

We conduct an in-depth analysis to make up a transferable taxonomy. Our target domain is the Korean online space, where web texts are actively generated and rapidly spread across various communities. We intend to provide a unified taxonomy of posting typology and avoidance strategy, based on the observation of online space expressions. Our contribution is as follows:

- Typology for intentionally noisy online text posting with stakeholder attributes
- A unified taxonomy for text gaming typology and avoidance strategies with domain and language-specific examples

2 Related Work

Diverse strategies have been suggested for text hiding, and they can be acknowledged as linguistic and non-linguistic ones. Non-linguistic strategies are studied in coding theory, and the encoded contents may not be comprehended by humans Agarwal (2013); Taleby Ahvanooey et al. (2019). In Agarwal (2013), various strategies for steganography are reviewed and compared, and the non-linguistic approaches adopt codewords (Rahman et al., 2017), unicode (Aman et al., 2017), word replacement (Ahvanooey et al., 2018), etc., that mainly aim to transmit the message without being exposed.

Proceedings of the 2021 EMNLP Workshop W-NUT: The Seventh Workshop on Noisy User-generated Text, pages 56–61
November 11, 2021.

In contrast, linguistic strategies are often visible to humans. Those include sentence-level order replacement (Topkara et al., 2006), pragmatic transformation (Lu et al., 2009), or transliteration (Khairullah, 2019). Taleby Ahvanooey et al. (2019) classified those approaches into semantic, syntactic, and statistic ones, while they were studied in view of steganography rather than intentional text noise. Subramaniam et al. (2009) has handled the issue in a manner closer to our approach, listing up strategies such as deletion of characters, phonetic substitution, abbreviation, using dialects, etc. However, it is less concerned with why the users adopt such techniques, considering possible stakeholders or pragmatic context.

In a wider view, the topics above are closely related to avoidance strategies and code-switching, which are mainly studied in sociolinguistics in terms of language varieties and community jargon. [1] Famous examples are *'mother-in-law'* codes used among Dyirbal language of northern Queensland, where everyday speech style *Guwal* is replaced by an 'avoidance' style *Jalnguy* when certain opposite-sex relatives (especially in-law) are present, maintaining the syntax but alternating the lexical items (Bell, 2013). Similar happens among Basque-Spanish bilinguals, where linguistic code-switching takes place to fill lexical gaps, convey certain attitude, or smooth negative connotations (Barredo, 1997). These cases refer to when the utterance is modified to fit the proper style of the speech community.

Besides, some code-switching may intend to hinder the speaker's genuine message to specific listeners. In previous studies on online censorship and avoidance strategies (Elahi and Goldberg, 2012; Mokwena and Banda, 2019), the authority that hacks the original text is usually assumed as government. Moreover, such authority is not the only factor that users generate noisy text in the online space; *Meme* is a representative case (Merritt, 2012) that games text with less consideration on being censored. We would like to present a typology that can encompass those phenomena.

We focused on that these strategies are observed more frequently beyond the Latin alphabet writing system due to the usefulness of code-mixing and transliteration. Accordingly, we qualitatively analyze the Korean online space, where the usage of the featural writing system Hangul and English code-mixing are both active (Cho et al., 2020). In specific, the featural writing system is advantageous in diverse phonological representations and the agglutinative nature of Korean allows flexible substitution of code-mixed words.

[1]Here, the community does not only refer to online communities but includes a variety of subgroups of language users.

Figure 1: Stakeholders around noisy text generation.

3 Observation

We demonstrate how our observation of Korean online space had led us to set stakeholders of intentionally noisy texts. We build a typology based on them and link it with specific linguistic strategies.

3.1 Stakeholders

The stakeholders of using an avoidance strategy can be categorized into three types (Figure 1).

The first type of stakeholder is the *author*, who writes the text using an avoidance strategy. The author's intention of strategies is to share information with "peers" and prevent "others" from understanding the information. It does not matter whether the text exists temporarily or long-lasting, nor is it private or public. The author is determined at the moment of text posting, while the text type and intention are influenced by other stakeholders.

The other two stakeholders are i) *'who should understand the text'* and ii) *'who should not understand the text'*. Here we indicate the former as *'Peers'* and the latter as *'Others'*. *Peers* are the group to which the semantics of the text should be conveyed, regardless of the properties of the message. *Others* are an individual, a group, or a system that can see the text, but should not recognize its genuine semantics. *Others* could be filtering or censoring algorithms run by the platforms or human users who use decoding (e.g., machine translation) algorithms to translate the text. The conveyed message is content that may challenge or deceive *Others*, or harm the author's (or *Peers'*) relationship

	Peers	*Others*	Examples
Tricks	*Yes*	*Yes*	**Google-trickers** in Airbnb Spam message with symbols Messages that avoid censorship
Memes	*Yes*	*No*	**Yaminjeongeum** Community jargons Puns with unknown sources
Fillers	*No*	*Yes*	**Leetspeak** Swear words with number (in game or broadcast chats)
Codes	*No*	*No*	Encryptions Steganography

Table 1: A typology of text posting concerning stakeholders. Bolded are typical ones of each category.

with *Others*.

3.2 Typology

With stakeholders introduced above, we categorize the posting of intentionally noisy texts (Table 1). In all cases, it might be vague if each stakeholder ('*Peers*' or '*Others*') is present/absent, identified/unidentified, or targeted/untargeted. Since we interpret this typology in view of author intention, *Yes/No* is the closest to the presence of each stakeholder, regardless of its identity.

The first case is when both *Peers* and *Others* exist. We call this case ***'Tricks'***. In this case, people use the avoidance strategy in order to convey a message to *Peers* while not disclosing a genuine intention to *Others*. In Airbnb, *Peers* are viewers of the review who is familiar with the language, and *Others* are eventually the hosts who want to discern the sentiment or toxicity of the review using an automatic machine translation system. Similar happens in spam advertising or online swear words that head other users, though the purpose differs. Furthermore, in a social act such as *#RiceBunny*, Chinese web users use a combination of *Rice* (米, mi) and *Bunny* (兔, tu) to avoid the authority's censorship towards *#MeToo* movement. *Peers* are the ones who are on the same side or the target audience, and *Others* are authorities that seek to block the circulation of such information using various types of censorship.

The second case is when *Peers* exist, but *Others* does not exist. We call this ***'Memes'***. Here, people use avoidance strategies mainly for fun, while the modified terms become expressions commonly used within a specific community. This meme is generally not intended to deceive or offend the authority or system. [2] In Korean online space, those memes appear in communities such as DC Inside, which corresponds with Reddit or 2ch, in the name of *Yaminjeongeum* (Wikipedia, the free encyclopedia). *Yaminjeongeum* is a composite of *Ya* that comes from *Yagoo gallary* (baseball subreddit) and *minjeongeum* that comes from *Hunminjeongeum* (Official name of Hangul), indicating the writing style within the specific online community. Community users generate and spread puns with textual transformation (addition, deletion, substitution, etc.), intentionally making the original Hangul text noisy. This 'Memes' case also includes other community jargons and puns with unknown sources (Merritt, 2012), along with all the expressions acknowledged by a specific community as a 'code' but not in other communities.

The third case is when *Peers* does not exist but *Others* exist. We call this ***'Fillers'***. In this case, people use noisy text that can be censored by the authority, albeit they do not intend to let other users grasp its genuine semantics. For instance, some game chats that do not target anyone often contain profanity terms and are banned by the detection system. This can be similarly observed in broadcasting systems or community boards. This led people to create a set of idiomatic terms that are composition of linguistic and numerical symbols, namely 'leetspeak (13375p34k)' (Blashki and Nichol, 2005), to reveal the expression and avoid the censorship. The distinction of 'Tricks' and 'Fillers' would be that, the former has a certain meaning or a target, while the latter is more close to an exclamation that incorporates probably-censored terms. This distinction is more close to that between 'statement' and 'exclamation' of Allwood (2000). Such expressions seem to be small, but are quite frequently found over the online space.

The final case is when *Peers* neither *Others* does not exist. We call this ***'Codes'***. Private diaries and self-posts all belong to this category. It is encryption only the author can identify, and not for others. Steganography and text watermarking are main candidates of this category. However, we are not investigating this type in the unified taxonomy, since linguistic strategies are seldom utilized here and the resulting texts are usually unreadable.

[2] However, apart from such intentions, societal bias or hate toward a specific group may be inherent in the meme.

	Morphological	Morpho-phonological	Optical	Semantic	Etc.
Tricks	간1편한 만v남 (≈ g1rl 4 u)	ㅈ가튼num (≈ motherfux0r)	ㄱH쓰근 ㅔㄱi (≈ 5h17)	진짜 the love 네요 (← 진짜 더럽네요) [It's really dirty]	가 족같은 장소 (← 족같은 장소) [fxxking place]
Memes	노인코래방 (← 코인노래방) [Coin karaoke]	민숙희 (← 민스키) [Hyman Minsky]	숲튽훈 (← 金長훈) [Jang-Hoon Kim]	과연자학 (← 자연과학) [Natural science]	-메- (← 메이플스토리) [Maple Story]
Fillers	존웃 (≈ lmfao)	이런 ㅁ ㅊ (≈ wtfk)	ㅆ1발 (≈ fuc1<)	^^ ㅣ발	Tlqkf

Table 2: A unified taxonomy with example expressions. ≈ denotes a liberal translation concerning the avoidance strategy, and [ ] denotes a direct translation of the original text indicated with ←. For **Etc.** examples, [fxxking place] contrasts with the original text (favourable place), and [Maple Story] is a simple pun for a Korean online game, Maple Story, used to indicate the game maniacs. We did not find a suitable liberal translation for '^^ ㅣ발' and 'Tlqkf', but their semantics equals 'ㅆ1발'.

3.3 Strategies

There are a total of four types of strategies that are widely observed in the Korean online space. [3] The first is *morphological*, which is the most simple way and includes the sub-strategies such as jumbling characters or words (Perea and Lupker, 2004), sometimes in a code-switched manner. The next is *morpho-phonological*, which distorts the written characters using phonological similarity (Hiruncharoenvate et al., 2015) or glottalization, letting the reader recognize the original text based on the pronunciation. The third one is *optical*, which adopts character substitution or uses redundant consonants in the Korean writing system (Sang-Cheol and Egorova, 2021). The final one is *semantic*, which includes metaphor and sarcasm, sometimes using contrasting homophones.

It is not guaranteed that these strategies comprise the whole approach towards text hiding. However, we deemed this strategy set is sufficient for unifying the expressions with the proposed typology.

4 Unified Taxonomy

Combining the materials in the previous sections, we made up a table for the unified taxonomy of intentionally noisy user-generated texts (Table 2).

Trick words, as mentioned earlier, have a purpose of conveying information to *Peers*, but not to *Others*. Thus, most of these texts contain messages that are adversarial to *Others* (i.e., censoring or translation algorithms), put them on the spot, or disobey the rules.

- '간1편한 만v남' is a teasing term that appears in spam messages, which has a direct meaning of 'girl, easy to meet'. Advertisers insert numbers or Latin alphabets to avoid the spam detectors, so that the information is delivered to the users.
- 'ㅈ가튼num' means 'what a motherfxxxer', where 'ㅈ', '가튼', and 'num' all corresponds with 'male genitals', 'equals', and 'dude', respectively. This variation frequently appears in web text, mainly used to avoid censorship in chatting, comments, or reviews.
- 'ㄱH쓰근 ㅔㄱi' is an optical modification of '개쓰레기' which means a *shxx*. It roughly matches with leetspeak *5h17* (*shxx*).
- '진짜 the love 네요' is pronounced as '진짜 더럽네요' in Korean and it means 'The room is really dirty'. However, Airbnb users use 'the love' to trick the translators and let the host understand it as a favourable message.

Meme words share the purpose of *Tricks* in conveying information to *Peers*, but *Others* to whom their exposure should be avoided is absent. Here, *Peers* can be viewers watching the same broadcast, members of a community, or people in a group. The meme is often to share pleasure with them.

- '노인코래방' is a spoonerism of '코인노래방' (coin karaoke), and it is a pun that uses character-level jumbling in Korean text. Here, '노인' means the elderly, which gives a temporary confusion, but the readers accept the term without any harm of the readability.

[3]We adopt strategies used for analyzing the text of Korean users in Airbnb review posts and apply it to our taxonomy. These strategies are roughly explained here to help the readers understand, but are to be published as a separate article (Kim et al., 2021).

- '민숙희' is a modified term of '민스키', which is a transliteration of economist Hyman Minsky. This sarcastically indicates some chart analysts who shout out market fall. It does not include any profanity terms; thus there is no reason to avoid censorship.
- '숲튽훈' is a variation of '金長훈', which is originally '김장훈', a Korean singer. This usually intends a pun, not harm.
- '과연자학' means *Indeed, self-harm* with direct translation, but it is a spoonerism of '자연과학' which means 'Natural science'. This is a meme widely used by students studying natural science in Korea.

Filler words are not intended to convey information to *Peers*, but are used to avoid censorship. Again, this can be viewed as a kind of exclamation, and it is different from 'Tricks' in that 'Fillers' does not necessarily consider the communication with *Peers*. '존웃' (≈ lmfao) and '이런 ㅁ ㅊ' (≈ wtfk) are usual terms in chats or comments, but they do not necessarily contain semantics that should be protected or conveyed. 'ㅆ1발', '^^ ㅣ발', and 'Tlqkf' all indicates '씨발' (*fxxk*), which are written with optical modification, semantic trick (with positive emoji ^^), or typing Korean in English QWERTY mode. These examples do not head other users, but are under censorship of the system.

Unfortunately, ***Codes*** were difficult to be unified within the adopted strategies. Currently, such texts are more adequately dealt with within coding theory. However, given that recent studies focus on linguistic approaches of text steganography (Taleby Ahvanooey et al., 2019), incorporating these in our taxonomy is arranged as future work.

Discussion Though we categorized the expressions according to the taxonomy, we have not yet investigated the property of each category in detail.

One phenomenon displayed is the temperature of expressions in each posting type. *Tricks* and *Fillers* should avoid the censorship of the authority, that the expressions tend to include social taboos such as profanity terms, swear words, or unethical contents.

Among them, *Tricks* tend to be more informative than *Fillers* since they have a particular purpose of conveying information to *Peers*, in the form of advertisement, secret message, or insulting. It is one of the reasons that more creative avoiding strategies are observable in *Tricks* rather than in *Fillers*, and thus easier to find diverse examples. Such creativity is also actively exhibited in *Memes*, while the aspect is more tilted to pun and that they do not have to take into account *Others*' monitoring.

In total, *Tricks* show hostility towards or harms *Others* or *Peers*, *Fillers* may alert *Others* since they contain profanity terms, but has no particular target. *Memes* are usually punned terms not showing explicit hate, but may contain a cultural or societal bias towards a certain group of people or a person.

Limitation Though we are empirically aware that *Tricks, Memes*, and *Fillers* are prevalent in the online world, used for various purposes, we have yet constructed an annotation scheme or a corpus that lists up detailed typology and corner cases. It is an essential but highly consuming process, which depends on languages and communities.

However, we believe that the characteristics of each text posting type discussed above would help us build a thorough annotation scheme concerning a variety of language phenomena. We expect that constructing such schemes would benefit a lot from our categorization, strategies, and examples, at least in selecting the online space or communities to collect the raw corpus from.

5 Conclusion

In this paper, we scrutinized the posting types and avoidance strategies of noisy web text in the Korean online space. These approaches differ from coding theoretic methodologies such as steganography and more concentrates on decoding using human text understanding. The taxonomy was defined upon the presence of wanted and unwanted readers of the noisy text, and this typology is expected to be transferable to various languages and cultures.

A limitation of our study is a lack of quantitative analysis. As a first step, we aim to annotate the texts collected from various online spaces, e.g., hate speech or biased text, using the built taxonomy. Such application will show how and why toxic comment authors trick the monitoring algorithms, at the same time allowing us to see the correlation between purposes and strategies. We hope our taxonomy can be consolidated as a useful tool to analyze intentionally noisy user-generated texts in online communities.

Acknowledgements

The authors appreciate valuable comments from anonymous reviewers.

References

Monika Agarwal. 2013. Text steganographic approaches: a comparison. *arXiv preprint arXiv:1302.2718*.

Milad Taleby Ahvanooey, Qianmu Li, Jun Hou, Hassan Dana Mazraeh, and Jing Zhang. 2018. AITSteg: An innovative text steganography technique for hidden transmission of text message via social media. *IEEE Access*, 6:65981–65995.

Jens Allwood. 2000. An activity-based approach to pragmatics.

Muhammad Aman, Aihab Khan, Basheer Ahmad, and Saeeda Kouser. 2017. A hybrid text steganography approach utilizing unicode space characters and zero-width character. *International Journal on Information Technologies and Security*, 9(1):85–100.

Inma Muñoa Barredo. 1997. Pragmatic functions of code-switching among Basque-Spanish bilinguals. *Retrieved on October*, 26:2011.

Filipe Beato, Emiliano De Cristofaro, and Kasper B Rasmussen. 2014. Undetectable communication: The online social networks case. In *2014 Twelfth Annual International Conference on Privacy, Security and Trust*, pages 19–26. IEEE.

Allan Bell. 2013. *The guidebook to sociolinguistics*. John Wiley & Sons.

Katherine Blashki and Sophie Nichol. 2005. Game geek's goss: linguistic creativity in young males within an online university forum (94/\/\3 933k'5 9055oneone). *Australian journal of emerging technologies and society*, 3(2):71–80.

Won Ik Cho, Seok Min Kim, and Nam Soo Kim. 2020. Towards an efficient code-mixed grapheme-to-phoneme conversion in an agglutinative language: A case study on to-Korean transliteration. In *Proceedings of the The 4th Workshop on Computational Approaches to Code Switching*, pages 65–70, Marseille, France. European Language Resources Association.

Tariq Elahi and Ian Goldberg. 2012. CORDON–a taxonomy of internet censorship resistance strategies. *University of Waterloo CACR*, 33.

Jesse Haapoja, Salla-Maaria Laaksonen, and Airi Lampinen. 2020. Gaming algorithmic hate-speech detection: Stakes, parties, and moves. *Social Media+ Society*, 6(2):2056305120924778.

Chaya Hiruncharoenvate, Zhiyuan Lin, and Eric Gilbert. 2015. Algorithmically bypassing censorship on sina weibo with nondeterministic homophone substitutions. In *Ninth International AAAI Conference on Web and Social Media*.

Md Khairullah. 2019. A novel steganography method using transliteration of bengali text. *Journal of King Saud University-Computer and Information Sciences*, 31(3):348–366.

Soomin Kim, Changhoon Oh, Won Ik Cho, Donghoon Shin, Bongwon Suh, and Joonhwan Lee. 2021. Trkic G00gle: Why and how users game translation algorithms. In *Proc. ACM Hum.-Comput. Interact. 5*, CSCW2, Article 344 (October 2021).

He Lu, Ma GuangPing, Fang DingYi, and Gui XiaoLin. 2009. Resilient natural language watermarking based on pragmatics. In *2009 IEEE Youth Conference on Information, Computing and Telecommunication*, pages 216–219. IEEE.

Marcus Märtens, Siqi Shen, Alexandru Iosup, and Fernando Kuipers. 2015. Toxicity detection in multiplayer online games. In *2015 International Workshop on Network and Systems Support for Games (NetGames)*, pages 1–6. IEEE.

Emily Merritt. 2012. *An analysis of the discourse of Internet trolling: A case study of Reddit. com*. Ph.D. thesis.

Lorato Mokwena and Felix Banda. 2019. Birds and bees, the 'r' word and zuma's p*nis: Censorship avoidance strategies in a south african online newspaper's comments section. *Sexuality & Culture*, 23(4):1089–1109.

Manuel Perea and Stephen J Lupker. 2004. Can caniso activate casino? transposed-letter similarity effects with nonadjacent letter positions. *Journal of memory and language*, 51(2):231–246.

Mohammad Saidur Rahman, Ibrahim Khalil, Xun Yi, and Hai Dong. 2017. Highly imperceptible and reversible text steganography using invisible character based codeword. In *PACIS*, page 230.

AHN Sang-Cheol and Kyunney Egorova. 2021. Morpho-phonological patterns of recent Korean neologisms. In *Conference on Current Problems of our Time: the Relationship of Man and Society (CPT 2020)*, pages 62–72. Atlantis Press.

L Venkata Subramaniam, Shourya Roy, Tanveer A Faruquie, and Sumit Negi. 2009. A survey of types of text noise and techniques to handle noisy text. In *Proceedings of The Third Workshop on Analytics for Noisy Unstructured Text Data*, pages 115–122.

Milad Taleby Ahvanooey, Qianmu Li, Jun Hou, Ahmed Raza Rajput, and Yini Chen. 2019. Modern text hiding, text steganalysis, and applications: a comparative analysis. *Entropy*, 21(4):355.

Mercan Topkara, Umut Topkara, and Mikhail J Atallah. 2006. Words are not enough: sentence level natural language watermarking. In *Proceedings of the 4th ACM International Workshop on Contents Protection and Security*, pages 37–46.

Wikipedia, the free encyclopedia. Yaminjeongeum. `https://en.wikipedia.org/wiki/Yaminjeongeum`. Accessed: 2021-08-23.

Description-based Label Attention Classifier for Explainable ICD-9 Classification

Malte Feucht[1], **Zhiliang Wu**[2,3], **Sophia Althammer**[4], **Volker Tresp**[2,3]
[1]Department of Informatics, TU Munich [2]Institute of Informatics, LMU Munich
[3]Technology, Siemens AG [4]Faculty of Computer Science, TU Wien
malte.feucht@tum.de, {zhiliang.wu,volker.tresp}@siemens.com,
sophia.althammer@tuwien.ac.at

Abstract

ICD-9 coding is a relevant clinical billing task, where unstructured texts with information about a patient's diagnosis and treatments are annotated with multiple ICD-9 codes. Automated ICD-9 coding is an active research field, where CNN- and RNN-based model architectures represent the state-of-the-art approaches. In this work, we propose a description-based label attention classifier to improve the model explainability when dealing with noisy texts like clinical notes. We evaluate our proposed method with different transformer-based encoders on the MIMIC-III-50 dataset. Our method achieves strong results together with augmented explainablilty.

1 Introduction

Physicians are obliged to thoroughly document every patient encounter. Structured and semi-structured reports become more common, which contain comprehensive information about performed treatments, procedures and diagnoses. They are typically annotated with multiple billing codes, the international classification of diseases codes (ICD-9 in the US, ICD-10 in Europe). Annotating the noisy discharge summaries with ICD-9 codes is not only manual and labor-intensive, but also error-prone, which has attracted much attention both from clinical and technical perspectives. To facilitate the clinical workflow, we propose a new approach with state-of-the-art annotation performance while providing an explanation for the proposed annotation.

de Lima et al. (1998) introduced automated ICD-9 coding as a text-based multi-label classification problem. Deep learning-based approaches, which exploit convolutional (CNNs) and recurrent neural networks (RNNs) with attention mechanisms (Shi et al., 2017; Mullenbach et al., 2018; Vu et al., 2020) define the current state-of-the-art. Meanwhile, large-scale pre-trained language models based on transformer (Vaswani et al., 2017) architectures have demonstrated considerable performance improvements for text-based tasks, e.g., BERT (Devlin et al., 2019). Especially their ability to model long-range dependencies within an input sequence would potentially benefit the task of ICD-9 coding since the information for a certain label prediction can be distributed across the whole text. Unlike other areas of natural language processing (NLP), little research on applying transformer-based architectures on the task of ICD-9 coding has been explored (Pascual et al., 2021; Biswas et al., 2021; Ji et al., 2021). Sun and Lu (2020) argue that attention scores are able to capture global, absolute importance of work tokens and can thus provide some degree of explainability for text classification.

In this work, we propose a **description-based label attention classifier (DLAC)**. We show that it can be applied to different transformer-based encoders and provides explainable predictions on noisy texts. DLAC learns ICD-9 code embeddings by integrating the descriptions of the ICD-9 codes and applies the embeddings to the respective text representations to obtain label-specific representations for each code classification. We evaluate different model architectures on the MIMIC-III-50 dataset, a benchmark dataset for the task of ICD-9 coding, in order to answer the following research questions (RQs).

RQ1: *Which transformer-based encoder is best suited for ICD-9 coding?*

We evaluate and compare BERT (Devlin et al., 2019), hierarchical BERT (Pappagari et al., 2019) and Longformer (Beltagy et al., 2020) as transformer-based encoders and find that the Longformer (Beltagy et al., 2020) yields the best results for ICD-9 coding. Furthermore, we investigate:

RQ2: *How does our proposed description-based label attention classifier perform on ICD-9 coding?*

We compare DLAC with a common logistic regression classifier (LRC) on top of the transformer-based encoder for ICD-9 coding. While adding ex-

Proceedings of the 2021 EMNLP Workshop W-NUT: The Seventh Workshop on Noisy User-generated Text, pages 62–66
November 11, 2021.

plainability to the predictions, DLAC outperforms the corresponding LRC by 1-4 %. Since explainable predictions are crucial for noisy texts, like discharge summaries, we investigate:

RQ3: *To which extent can the DLAC provide explainable predictions for ICD-9 codes?*

Since the attention scores in DLAC offer a way to explain the predictions with respect to different text segments, we analyze the top attention scores of DLAC and demonstrate the utility as part of a graphical interface.

2 Methods

As a multi-label text classification problem, each discharge summary is represented by a tokenized input sequence of words $\boldsymbol{X}_i := [\boldsymbol{x}_1, \ldots, \boldsymbol{x}_{t_i}] \in \mathbb{R}^{l \times t_i}$, where l denotes the vector dimension and t_i is the length of the i-th input sequence. The goal is to predict a binary vector $\boldsymbol{y}_i \in \mathbb{R}^m$, where m represents the set size of ICD-9 codes. Each element in the predicted vector $\boldsymbol{y}$ is of value 0 or 1. In the following, we denote scalars with lowercase letters like x, vectors with bold lowercase letters like $\boldsymbol{x}$, and matrices with bold uppercase letters like $\boldsymbol{X}$.

2.1 Description-based Label Attention

An overview of the proposed model architecture with DLAC is illustrated in Figure 1. It includes a transformer-based encoder to represent the discharge summaries into a word embedding matrix $\boldsymbol{E}$. Meanwhile, the descriptions of the ICD-9 codes are represented with a description embedding matrix $\boldsymbol{D}$, which is initialized by ICD-9 code descriptions with Word2vec embeddings (Mikolov et al., 2013).

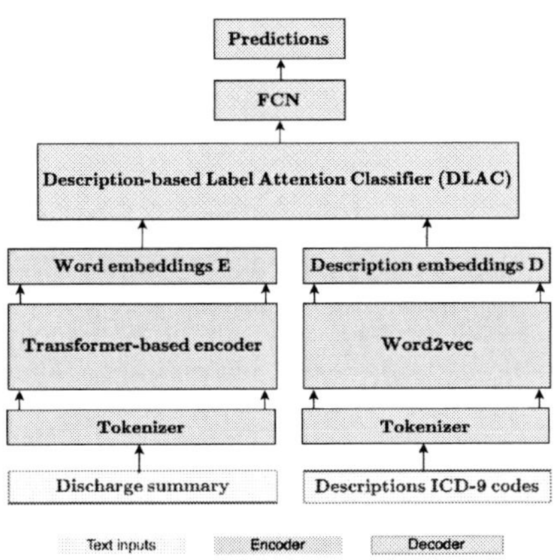

Figure 1: Overall model architecture

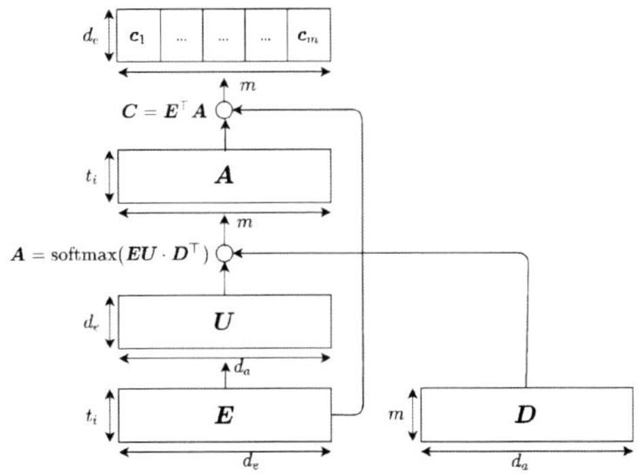

Figure 2: Description-based Label Attention Classifier

More specifically, as shown in Figure 2, DLAC is fed with two matrices: The word embedding matrix $\boldsymbol{E} \in \mathbb{R}^{t_i \times d_e}$ is computed from a transformer-based encoder and the ICD-9 code description embedding matrix $\boldsymbol{D} \in \mathbb{R}^{m \times d_a}$. Here, d_e, d_a denote the dimension of the word embeddings and the description embeddings, respectively. The description embedding matrix $\boldsymbol{D}$ is set to be trainable. To compute the attention score a_{jk} for the i-th word on the j-th label, we first apply a dimension transformation on the word embedding matrix with $\boldsymbol{U} \in \mathbb{R}^{d_e \times d_a}$ to match the shape of description matrix $\boldsymbol{D}$. The ICD-9 code description vectors stored in the description matrix $\boldsymbol{D}$ can be seen as queries that include the essential information from the label description of respective ICD-9 codes. Formally, we compute the label attention matrix $\boldsymbol{A} \in \mathbb{R}^{t_i \times m}$ as

$$\boldsymbol{A} = \text{softmax}(\boldsymbol{E}\boldsymbol{U} \cdot \boldsymbol{D}^\top).$$

After that, we compute contextual embeddings for each label by aggregating information from the word embedding matrix $\boldsymbol{E}$ with attention scores in $\boldsymbol{A}$. More concretely, the contextual embedding matrix $\boldsymbol{C} \in \mathbb{R}^{d_e \times m}$ is computed as

$$\boldsymbol{C} = \boldsymbol{E}^\top \boldsymbol{A}.$$

2.2 Classification

Each label specific contextual embedding is fed into a single layer fully-connected network (FCN) for the prediction of the respective ICD-9 code label. A sigmoid activation function is applied to have a probabilistic prediction. The training objective is the binary cross-entropy loss computed from predictions $\hat{\boldsymbol{y}}_i \in \mathbb{R}^m$ and ground-truth labels $\boldsymbol{y}_i \in \mathbb{R}^m$.

2.3 Transformer-based Encoders

Since DLAC is agnostic to encoders, we conduct experiments with different transformer-based encoders by integrating them into the proposed model architecture. The first one is a pre-trained $\mathbf{BERT_{BASE}}$ model (Devlin et al., 2019), which can only consume input sequences with a length of up to 512 tokens. Longer discharge summaries are simply truncated. The second architecture is a **hierarchical** $\mathbf{BERT_{BASE}}$ model (Pappagari et al., 2019), which aims to overcome the input sequence length limitation. The discharge summary of length t_i is split into k overlapping chunks, where $k = \lceil \frac{t_i}{512} \rceil$, where $\lceil \cdot \rceil$ is a ceiling operation. The chunks are fed sequentially into the $\mathbf{BERT_{BASE}}$ model to obtain the word embedding matrices for every chunk, which are then averaged using mean-pooling across all chunks. The third architecture is a pre-trained $\mathbf{Longformer_{BASE}}$ model (Beltagy et al., 2020). A limitation of transformer-based language models such as BERT is their inability to process long input sequences due to the computational cost of the self-attention mechanism, which scales quadratically with the input sequence length. The $\mathbf{Longformer_{BASE}}$ model overcomes this limitation by offering a "sparsified" self-attention mechanism, making it more suitable to process longer input sequences. As a result, the $\mathbf{Longformer_{BASE}}$ model can process input sequences of lengths of up to 4096 tokens.

3 Data

MIMIC-III (Johnson et al., 2016) is a large, freely available clinical database. Similar to Mullenbach et al. (2018), we create the subset MIMIC-III-50 from the full dataset. It includes discharge summaries containing the 50 most frequent ICD-9 codes, as otherwise, the label distribution is extremely imbalanced. After pre-processing, MIMIC-III-50 contains 11.368 samples and 50 ICD-9 codes, where a summary of different statistics can be found in Table 1. Following the pre-processing in Mullenbach et al. (2018), we first lowercase all tokens, remove punctuations and remove numerical tokens-only. The MIMIC-III-50 dataset is split into a training, validation and test set with 8.066, 1.573 and 1.729 samples, respectively.

4 Experiments

We train the proposed description-based label attention classifier (DLAC) using BERT, hierarchical BERT, and Longformer as encoders. As a baseline classifier, we choose a simple logistic regression classifier (LRC) on top of the different encoders. In contrast to DLAC, LRC does not take the description embeddings $\boldsymbol{D}$, into account. We set $d_a = 600$ and $d_e = 768$. We train all architectures using Adam optimizer with a learning rate of $\alpha = 1.41 \times 10^{-5}$ and a global batch size of 64. Furthermore, we use k-fold cross-validation with $k = 5$ folds and train every fold for 25 epochs. For regularization, we use dropout layers with a probability set to $p = 0,1$ and early stopping. We use the widely adopted micro-and macro averaged area under the ROC curve (AUC), F1 and Precision@n as evaluation metrics to ensure comparability with other works. For P@n we choose $n = 5$ because this roughly equals the average number of ICD-9 codes one discharge summary is annotated with, which is $5,77$ for the MIMIC-III-50 dataset. The implementation is made available to ensure the reproducibility of the work[1].

MIMIC-III-50	# Words	# ICD-9 Codes
mean	1.612	5,77
std	788	3,37
min	105	1
max	7.567	24
25%	1.065	3
50%	1.478	5
75%	1.992	5

Table 1: Descriptive statistics of MIMIC-III-50 dataset

5 Results and Discussions

Table 2 presents the results for all proposed model architectures. The Longformer+DLAC yields the best results across all metrics for the architectures in this work.

5.1 RQ1: Transformer-based Encoders

Among the transformer-based encoders that are combined with the simple LRC classifier (BERT+LRC, H-BERT+LRC, Longformer+LRC), the Longformer encoder yields the best results across all metrics. This can be attributed to the inability of BERT to process sequences longer than 512, where over 75% of the discharge summaries are truncated and potentially important information is disregarded. For the micro- and macro F1 scores, H-BERT+LRC model yields even poorer results

[1] https://git.io/JzOyk

Model	AUC		F1		P@5
	Macro	Micro	Macro	Micro	
BERT+LRC	0.80 ± 0.007	0.84 ± 0.006	0.33 ± 0.033	0.45 ± 0.026	0.51 ± 0.011
H-BERT+LRC	0.82 ± 0.006	0.86 ± 0.006	0.29 ± 0.030	0.41 ± 0.032	0.51 ± 0.012
Longformer+LRC	0.85 ± 0.003	0.89 ± 0.003	0.48 ± 0.005	0.58 ± 0.003	0.59 ± 0.012
BERT+DLAC	0.80 ± 0.006	0.84 ± 0.004	0.35 ± 0.032	0.46 ± 0.026	0.51 ± 0.013
H-BERT+DLAC	0.83 ± 0.035	0.87 ± 0.004	0.32 ± 0.020	0.43 ± 0.013	0.52 ± 0.010
Longformer+DLAC*	0.87 ± 0.008	0.91 ± 0.006	0.52 ± 0.020	0.62 ± 0.024	0.61 ± 0.013
JointLAAT**	**0.93**	**0.95**	**0.67**	**0.72**	**0.68**
TransICD	0.89	0.92	0.56	0.64	0.62

Table 2: Test results on the MIMIC-III-50 dataset for all proposed model architectures compared to the state-of-the-art architectures. ** marks the best overall model architecture. * marks the best model architecture of this work.

than the BERT+LRC model. This indicates that the way of aggregating the chunks k using mean-pooling is suboptimal, and thus the model fails to create rich input feature representations.

5.2 RQ2: Longformer+DLAC

The results of the Longformer+DLAC model show that it performs well on the task of ICD-9 coding. In addition, DLAC outperforms the LRC for all encoder architectures on the task of ICD-9 coding across all metrics by $1-4\%$. Meanwhile, JointLAAT (Vu et al., 2020) is one state-of-the-art CNN-based model architecture. Our Longformer+DLAC underperforms it by $\Delta - 0.06, \Delta - 0.04, \Delta - 0.15, \Delta - 0.10, \Delta - 0.07$ for Macro AUC, Micro AUC, Macro F1, Micro F1 and P@5 respectively. In comparison to state-of-the-art transformer-based architectures, like TransICD (Biswas et al., 2021), our model shows a comparable performance with the difference being $\Delta - 0.02, \Delta - 0.01, \Delta - 0.04, \Delta - 0.02, \Delta - 0.01$ for Macro AUC, Micro AUC, Macro F1, Micro F1 and P@5, respectively. Transformer-based models haven't reached state-of-the-art dominated by more lightweight CNN-based architectures. This can be partially attributed to the fact that the MIMIC-III-50 dataset does not hold enough training samples for training such a large architecture, e.g., the Longformer+DLAC has up to 152 million trainable parameters. Furthermore, the Longformer+DLAC model could potentially be improved by using a domain-specific, pre-trained Longformer architecture (Gu et al., 2020) and by developing a regularization mechanism (Cao et al., 2019) that helps to classify rare labels more accurately. On the other hand, as an encoder agnostic classifier, DLAC can be combined with other

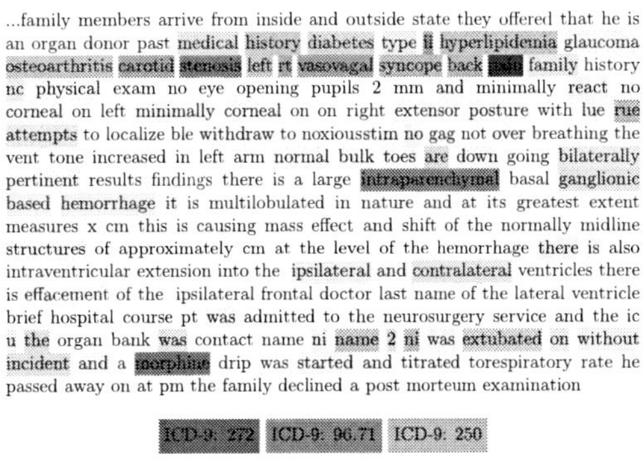

Figure 3: The top attention scores for the predicted ICD-9 codes **272, 96.71, 250** are highlighted with color intensity. Higher color intensity represents larger attention scores and vice versa.

models to improve the performance while keeping explainable predictions.

5.3 RQ3: Explainability

In a setting where a machine learning model would serve as a decision support tool for medical workers, explainability of the obtained model predictions are of utmost importance. In contrast to LRC, DLAC provides explainable predictions using the attention scores. DLAC can retrieve the top attention scores for each ICD-9 code prediction. As an example, the text segments that lead to a certain ICD-9 code prediction are highlighted with respective color intensity in Figure 3. This can be useful for working with noisy texts in general because it provides some extent of explainability.

6 Conclusion

Transformer-based architectures show promising performance on the task of ICD-9 coding. We find that the Longformer encoder is the best suitable encoder architecture for processing long, noisy input sequences such as discharge summaries. We show that our proposed description-based label attention classifier (DLAC) can be applied to various transformer-based encoders and the resulting model outperforms a common decoder architecture like logistic regressions by 1-4%. In addition, our proposed DLAC is especially suitable for a practical use case when working with fuzzy, long texts such as the discharge summaries, where explainability for the predicted ICD-9 codes is necessary.

References

Iz Beltagy, Matthew E. Peters, and Arman Cohan. 2020. Longformer: The long-document transformer. *CoRR*, abs/2004.05150.

Biplob Biswas, Thai-Hoang Pham, and Ping Zhang. 2021. Transicd: Transformer based code-wise attention model for explainable icd coding. In *International Conference on Artificial Intelligence in Medicine*, pages 469–478. Springer.

Kaidi Cao, Colin Wei, Adrien Gaidon, Nikos Aréchiga, and Tengyu Ma. 2019. Learning imbalanced datasets with label-distribution-aware margin loss. In *NeurIPS*.

Luciano RS de Lima, Alberto HF Laender, and Berthier A Ribeiro-Neto. 1998. A hierarchical approach to the automatic categorization of medical documents. In *Proceedings of the seventh international conference on Information and knowledge management*, pages 132–139.

Jacob Devlin, Ming-Wei Chang, Kenton Lee, and Kristina Toutanova. 2019. BERT: Pre-training of deep bidirectional transformers for language understanding. In *Proceedings of the 2019 Conference of the North American Chapter of the Association for Computational Linguistics: Human Language Technologies, Volume 1 (Long and Short Papers)*, pages 4171–4186, Minneapolis, Minnesota. Association for Computational Linguistics.

Yu Gu, Robert Tinn, Hao Cheng, Michael Lucas, Naoto Usuyama, Xiaodong Liu, Tristan Naumann, Jianfeng Gao, and Hoifung Poon. 2020. Domain-specific language model pretraining for biomedical natural language processing. *CoRR*, abs/2007.15779.

Shaoxiong Ji, Matti Hölttä, and Pekka Marttinen. 2021. Does the magic of bert apply to medical code assignment? a quantitative study. *arXiv preprint arXiv:2103.06511*.

Alistair EW Johnson, Tom J Pollard, Lu Shen, H Lehman Li-Wei, Mengling Feng, Mohammad Ghassemi, Benjamin Moody, Peter Szolovits, Leo Anthony Celi, and Roger G Mark. 2016. Mimic-iii, a freely accessible critical care database. *Scientific data*, 3(1):1–9.

Tomas Mikolov, Ilya Sutskever, Kai Chen, Greg Corrado, and Jeffrey Dean. 2013. Distributed representations of words and phrases and their compositionality. In *Proceedings of the 26th International Conference on Neural Information Processing Systems - Volume 2*, NIPS'13, page 3111–3119, Red Hook, NY, USA. Curran Associates Inc.

James Mullenbach, Sarah Wiegreffe, Jon Duke, Jimeng Sun, and Jacob Eisenstein. 2018. Explainable prediction of medical codes from clinical text. In *Proceedings of the 2018 Conference of the North American Chapter of the Association for Computational Linguistics: Human Language Technologies, Volume 1 (Long Papers)*, pages 1101–1111, New Orleans, Louisiana. Association for Computational Linguistics.

Raghavendra Pappagari, Piotr Zelasko, Jesús Villalba, Yishay Carmiel, and Najim Dehak. 2019. Hierarchical transformers for long document classification. In *2019 IEEE Automatic Speech Recognition and Understanding Workshop (ASRU)*, pages 838–844. IEEE.

Damian Pascual, Sandro Luck, and Roger Wattenhofer. 2021. Towards BERT-based automatic ICD coding: Limitations and opportunities. In *Proceedings of the 20th Workshop on Biomedical Language Processing*, pages 54–63, Online. Association for Computational Linguistics.

Haoran Shi, Pengtao Xie, Zhiting Hu, Ming Zhang, and Eric P. Xing. 2017. Towards automated ICD coding using deep learning. *CoRR*, abs/1711.04075.

Xiaobing Sun and Wei Lu. 2020. Understanding attention for text classification. In *Proceedings of the 58th Annual Meeting of the Association for Computational Linguistics*, pages 3418–3428.

Ashish Vaswani, Noam Shazeer, Niki Parmar, Jakob Uszkoreit, Llion Jones, Aidan N Gomez, Ł ukasz Kaiser, and Illia Polosukhin. 2017. Attention is all you need. In *Advances in Neural Information Processing Systems*, volume 30. Curran Associates, Inc.

Thanh Vu, Dat Quoc Nguyen, and Anthony Nguyen. 2020. A label attention model for icd coding from clinical text. In *Proceedings of the Twenty-Ninth International Joint Conference on Artificial Intelligence, IJCAI-20*, pages 3335–3341. International Joint Conferences on Artificial Intelligence Organization. Main track.

A Text Editing Approach to Joint Japanese Word Segmentation, POS Tagging, and Lexical Normalization

Shohei Higashiyama[1,2], **Masao Utiyama**[1], **Taro Watanabe**[2], **Eiichiro Sumita**[1]
[1]National Institute of Information and Communications Technology, Kyoto, Japan
[2]Nara Institute of Science and Technology, Nara, Japan
{shohei.higashiyama, mutiyama, eiichiro.sumita}@nict.go.jp,
taro@is.naist.jp

Abstract

Lexical normalization, in addition to word segmentation and part-of-speech tagging, is a fundamental task for Japanese user-generated text processing. In this paper, we propose a text editing model to solve the three task jointly and methods of pseudo-labeled data generation to overcome the problem of data deficiency. Our experiments showed that the proposed model achieved better normalization performance when trained on more diverse pseudo-labeled data.

1 Introduction

User-generated text (UGT), such as social media and blog posts, is a valuable source of knowledge and opinions from diverse users. A notable characteristic of UGT is that it contains non-canonical sentences, and this degrades the performance of natural language processing (NLP) systems trained on canonical sentences. To reduce the gap between the performance on general text and on UGT, lexical normalization techniques—which convert nonstandard word forms to standard forms—have been explored, particularly for English (Aw et al., 2006; Baldwin et al., 2015). In addition, Japanese UGT requires a further step: to identify nonstandard words in unsegmented sentences written without word delimiters. For this reason, the problem of Japanese lexical normalization has been solved by predicting word boundaries, part-of-speech (POS) tags, and normalized word forms simultaneously (Sasano et al., 2013; Saito et al., 2014). Similarly to previous work, we tackle the joint task comprising Japanese word **S**egmentation, **P**OS tagging, and lexical **N**ormalization (SPN).

A critical problem in lexical normalization is the lack of labeled data. Manual annotation of normalized forms is a time-consuming task; therefore, the size of the available annotated corpora is quite small (Kaji and Kitsuregawa, 2014; Higashiyama et al., 2021). A prospective solution to this problem is the use of pseudo-labeled data. In this paper, we propose methods of generating pseudo-labeled data using (auto-) segmented sentences and standard and nonstandard word variant pairs. To generate high quality labels, we acquire reliable variant pairs based on lexical knowledge, namely, a dictionary with lemma definition and hand-crafted rules.

For efficient learning from a limited amount of data, we adopt a text editing approach. Our neural tagging model predicts edit operations to normalize input characters, while predicting segmentation and POS tags at the same time. The editing process is similar to that proposed in previous work on English lexical normalization (Chrupała, 2014; Min and Mott, 2015), but we design a specific tag set for the Japanese SPN task, which requires the management of a large number of character types.

Our extensive experiments on the SPN task demonstrated that our model achieved better normalization performance when the model used more additional features, it was trained on more types of pseudo-labeled data, and it was trained on training instances with more diverse context.

2 Task Definition

As shown in Table 2, a training instance for the SPN task is defined as a pair, comprising a sentence $\boldsymbol{x} = (x_1, \ldots, x_n)$ and its label sequence $\boldsymbol{t} = \{(f_j, l_j, p_j, S_j)\}_{j=1}^{m}$, where n and m $(\leq n)$ are the numbers of characters and words in $\boldsymbol{x}$, f_j and l_j are the indexes of the first and last character in j-th word w_j, and p_j is the POS tag of w_j. The set of standard forms S_j is equal to the empty set $\emptyset$ when w_j is a standard form, whereas S_j consists of one or more standard forms when w_j is a nonstandard form.

A system is required to predict the word boundaries of an input sentence and the POS tag of each word, detect nonstandard words, and generate one of the standard forms of each nonstandard word.

Proceedings of the 2021 EMNLP Workshop W-NUT: The Seventh Workshop on Noisy User-generated Text, pages 67–80

	Meaning	Nonstandard word w	Standard form s	SEdit tags $\boldsymbol{t}^e$	CConv tags $\boldsymbol{t}^c$
(a)	really	まぢ	まじ	K, REP (じ)	K, K
(b)	difficult	ムズカシー	むずかしい	K, K, K, K, REP (い)	HR, HR, HR, HR, K
(c)	terrific	すごーいー	すごい	K, K, D, K, K, D	K, K, K, K, K
(d)	high/expensive	たっけぇ	たかい	K, REP (か), REP (い), D	K, K, K, K
(e)	awesome	さいこー	最高	K, K, K, REP (う)	KJ, KJ, KJ, KJ

Table 1: Examples of labels for nonstandard and standard word pairs. K, D, HR, and KJ represent KEEP, DEL, TO_HIRAGANA, and TO_KANJI, respectively.

j	1	2	3	4
w_j	日本 (Japan)	語 (language)	まぢ (really)	ムズカシー (difficult)
f_j, l_j	1, 2	3, 3	4, 5	6, 10
p_j	Noun	Noun	Adverb	Adjective
S_j	$\emptyset$	$\emptyset$	{まじ, マジ}	{難しい, むずかしい}

Table 2: Words in and labels of a sentence $\boldsymbol{x}$ ="日本語まぢムズカシー" (*nihon go maji muzukashī*), which means "Japanese language is really difficult."

3 Joint SPN Method

3.1 Multiple Sequence Labeling Formulation

In this work, we formulate the SPN task as multiple character-level sequence labeling problems. We convert the label sequence $\boldsymbol{t}$ to four tag sequences: a segmentation tag sequence $\boldsymbol{t}^s$, a character-level POS tag sequence $\boldsymbol{t}^p$, a string edit operation (SEdit) tag sequence $\boldsymbol{t}^e$, and a character type conversion (CConv) tag sequence $\boldsymbol{t}^c$.

We employ a tag set $\mathcal{T}_{\text{seg}} = \{\text{B}, \text{I}, \text{E}, \text{S}\}$ for segmentation, where B, I, and E represent the beginning, inside, and end of a multi-character word, and S represents a single-character word. We set $t_i^p = p_j \in \mathcal{T}_{\text{pos}}$ for the POS tag of a character x_i in a word w_j ($f_j \leq i \leq l_j$), where $\mathcal{T}_{\text{pos}}$ denotes a POS tag set. We use two types of tags for the normalization task. For x_i in a standard word w_j, we set $t_i^e = t_i^c = \texttt{KEEP}$, which means that no edit operation or conversion is required for x_i. For x_i in a nonstandard word w_j, two types of tags $t_i^e \in \mathcal{T}_{\text{sedit}}$ and $t_i^c \in \mathcal{T}_{\text{cconv}}$ are generated based on the closest standard form $s_j^\star \in S_j$, where $\mathcal{T}_{\text{sedit}}$ and $\mathcal{T}_{\text{cconv}}$ represent the tag sets of SEdit and CConv, which we define in §3.2. The procedure for selecting the closest standard form is as follows[1]: a character alignment between w_j and $s \in S_j$ is calculated, and then the standard form with the most characters aligned to w_j is selected.

[1]We describe the procedure in detail in Appendix §A.

3.2 Tag Definition

The Japanese writing system comprises three major scripts: two syllabographic *kana* (i.e., *hiragana* and *katakana*), and the morphographic *kanji*. The numbers of character types in them are different: approximately 80 in hiragana, 80 in katakana,[2] and more than 4,000 in kanji. To decrease the tag space size, we allow insertion and replacement operations only for kana characters. Specifically, we define the SEdit tags as $\mathcal{T}_{\text{sedit}} = \{\texttt{KEEP}, \texttt{DEL}, \texttt{INSL}(c), \texttt{INSR}(c), \texttt{REP}(c)\}$ for a kana character c. DEL indicates deletion of the current character, INSL (c) and INSR (c) indicate insertion of c immediately to the left and right of the current character, respectively, and REP (c) indicates replacement of the current character by c. In addition, we define the CConv tags as $\mathcal{T}_{\text{cconv}} = \{\texttt{KEEP}, \texttt{TO\_HIRA}, \texttt{TO\_KATA}, \texttt{TO\_KANJI}\}$, where the last three tags indicate conversion of the current character to hiragana, katakana, and kanji, respectively.[3]

For the example sentence $\boldsymbol{x}$ in Table 2, the tags for $w_3 = \boldsymbol{x}_{4:5}$ =まぢ and $w_4 = \boldsymbol{x}_{6:10}$ =ムズカシー are shown as (a) and (b) in Table 1, and the tags for the other characters are $t_i^e = t_i^c = \texttt{KEEP}$ ($1 \leq i \leq 3$). Both types of tags are automatically generated, according to the character alignments between original and standard tokens. Table 1 lists examples (c)–(e), which have other types of tags.

A remaining problem is the ambiguity of characters assigned with the TO_KANJI tag; for example, あき *aki* can be converted to 秋 'autumn', 空き 'vacancy', or 飽き 'bored' depending on its surrounding context. We use an external kana-to-kanji converter to select the most likely candidates.

[2]We distinguish kana characters with and without a voicing mark (e.g., "か" *ka* and "が" *ga*).

[3]Tag definition different from above could be used. We investigated two alternative settings, but our preliminary experiments showed no gains over our proposed setting: a case where SEdit and CConv tags were merged into a single tag set and a case where additional SEdit tags similar to the special operators used in the pronunciation feature (§3.4) were introduced.

There still exist cases in which a nonstandard word with many deleted or replaced characters cannot be restored to its standard form (e.g., よろ *yoro* to よろしく *yoroshiku* 'thank you') by the defined tags when the required number of insertion and replacement operations exceeds the number of characters in the original token. This can be solved by introducing multi-character operations (e.g., `INSR(しく)`), but we assume that most instances can be expressed by single-character operations, and leave those cases for future work.

3.3 Model Architecture

We use a long short-term memory (LSTM)-based architecture (Hochreiter and Schmidhuber, 1997) for the sequence labeling tasks. Our model consists of shared bidirectional LSTM (BiLSTM) layers and task-specific inference layers.

An input character sequence $\boldsymbol{x}$ is transformed to embedding vectors $\boldsymbol{e}_{1:n} = (\boldsymbol{e}_1, \cdots, \boldsymbol{e}_n)$ and fed into a multi-layer BiLSTM. Hidden vectors from forward and backward LSTMs are concatenated, to form a single hidden vector $\boldsymbol{h}_i$ for each character. $\boldsymbol{h}_i$ is then mapped to a score distribution vector $\boldsymbol{y}_i^u$ for each task $u \in \mathcal{U} = \{\text{seg}, \text{pos}, \text{sedit}, \text{cconv}\}$, via a softmax layer.

Given training data $\mathcal{D}$, the model parameters are learned by minimizing a loss function L during training. The loss L is defined as the sum of the cross-entropy between the gold and predicted tag distributions for all tasks:

$$L = - \sum_{(\boldsymbol{x},\boldsymbol{y})\in\mathcal{D}} \sum_{u\in\mathcal{U}} \lambda_u \sum_{1\leq i\leq|\boldsymbol{x}|} \boldsymbol{t}_i^u \log \boldsymbol{y}_i^u , \quad (1)$$

where $0 \leq \lambda_u \leq 1$ is a coefficient to control the contribution of each task u and $\boldsymbol{t}_i^u$ is the one-hot vector of the gold label t_i^u, which is assigned to x_i.

3.4 Features

We use three input features, based on character, pronunciation, and lexicon entries. Feature vectors from the three sources for each character are concatenated, to form a single vector $\boldsymbol{e}_i$ in §3.3.

Character Feature. A character embedding vector $\boldsymbol{e}_i^c$ for each character x_i is retrieved from a character embedding matrix.

Pronunciation Feature. We introduce a pronunciation element that corresponds to a vowel, a consonant, the long sound symbol, or a special operator (voicing *V*, semi-voicing *P*, or lowercasing *S*) in a kana character sequence.[4] These elements are similar to *romaji* (Roman letter transcription) but differ mainly with respect to the special operators. For example, "グ" *gu*, "ァ" *a*, and "パ" *pa* are decomposed into {*k*, *u*, *V*}, {*a*, *S*}, and {*h*, *a*, *P*}, respectively. Each character x_i is decomposed into one or more pronunciation elements. A pronunciation vector $\boldsymbol{e}_i^p$ for x_i is the average of its pronunciation element embeddings retrieved from an embedding matrix.

Lexicon Feature. We define two types of binary features based on a nonstandard word lexicon.[5] A lexicon word feature for a character x_i is defined as a $(|P| \times |K|)$-dimensional vector $\boldsymbol{e}_i^{d,w}$, each element of which indicates whether x_i corresponds to a particular position $p \in P = \{$immediate left, immediate right, beginning, middle, end$\}$ of any nonstandard word of length $k \in K$ in the lexicon. Similarly, a lexicon POS feature for x_i is defined as a $|\mathcal{T}_{\text{POS}}|$-dimensional vector $\boldsymbol{e}_i^{d,p}$, each element of which indicates whether the x_i corresponds to an inside position of any nonstandard word with a particular POS.

4 Pseudo-labeled Data Generation

To overcome the lack of training data for the normalization task, we construct a set of standard and nonstandard word variant pairs $\mathcal{V}$ and then generate different types of pseudo-labeled data by two approaches: distant supervision on formal target-side (DS_tgt) and informal source-side text (DS_src).

DS_tgt generate a sentence where the original tokens are retained but nonstandard tokens among them are annotated with pseudo standard tokens; specifically, given a segmented sentence, a token matching with a nonstandard form v_nst in $\mathcal{V}$ is annotated with SEdit and CConv tags to convert to its standard form, while other tokens are annotated with `KEEP` tags. On the other hand, DS_src generate a sentence where one or more of the original tokens are replaced by pseudo nonstandard forms; given a standard and nonstandard variant pair $(v_\text{st}, v_\text{nst}) \in \mathcal{V}$, DS_src extracts a segmented sentence containing a token with the same lemma as that of the pair, replaces the token by v_nst, and generates SEdit and CConv tags to convert v_nst to

[4] We generate pronunciation features only for kana characters and use zero vectors for other types of characters.

[5] We use nonstandard words in dictionary-derived ($\mathcal{V}_d$) and rule-derived variant pairs ($\mathcal{V}_r$) (described in §4) for the models trained on dictionary-derived ($\mathcal{A}_d$) and rule-derived data ($\mathcal{A}_r$) (described in §5.1) in our experiments, respectively.

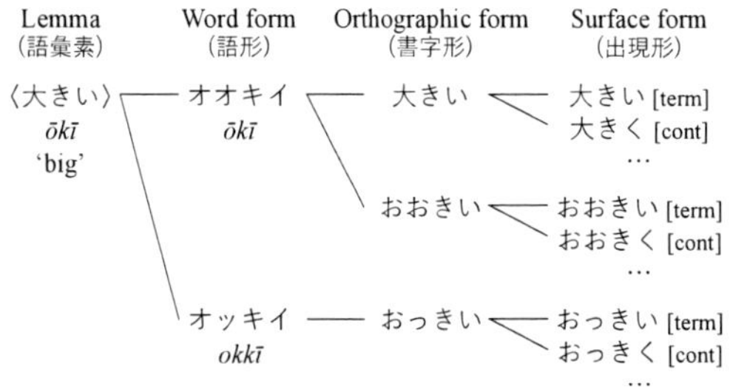

Figure 1: Hierarchical lemma definition in UniDic. Termination forms (term) and continuative forms (cont) are illustrated as examples of surface forms.

v_{st}. We present examples of $\mathrm{DS}_{\mathrm{tgt}}$ and $\mathrm{DS}_{\mathrm{src}}$ in Appendix §B.

As the main difference between two approaches, $\mathrm{DS}_{\mathrm{tgt}}$ does not change original sentences but $\mathrm{DS}_{\mathrm{src}}$ does. Although we can use actual sentences with $\mathrm{DS}_{\mathrm{tgt}}$, we can easily obtain any number of synthetic sentences containing nonstandard words of interest with $\mathrm{DS}_{\mathrm{tgt}}$. However, both approaches require reliable variant pairs to generate useful data. For this purpose, we use two strategies for variant pair acquisition: dictionary-based and rule-based.

4.1 Dictionary-derived Variant Pairs

As the first approach to variant pair acquisition, we use UniDic[6] (unidic-cwj-2.3.0) (Den et al., 2008), but any dictionary with lemma and conjugation information can be used. UniDic is an electronic dictionary for Japanese morphological analysis (MA) and employs hierarchical definition of word indexes. As shown in Figure 1, a lemma in UniDic aggregates word forms with different pronunciation and word forms with different conjugation types, a word form aggregates orthographic forms, and an orthographic form aggregates surface forms (which mostly correspond to different conjugation forms). Thus, surface forms with the same lemma and conjugation form compose a variant set; for example, the continuative surface forms of a lemma 〈大きい〉 include 大きく *ōkiku*, おおきく *ōkiku*, and おっきく *okkiku*.

We extract valid standard and nonstandard word pairs from variant sets by the following steps. (1) Words whose POS is symbol, space, person name, or number are excluded. (2) Each variant in a variant set is automatically classified as a standard form or valid nonstandard form by predefined rules,[7] which are based on pronunciation and frequency of occurrence among the variant forms of the lemma in a corpus. (3) Finally, each nonstandard form is paired with the closest standard form.

4.2 Rule-derived Variant Pairs

As an alternative approach, we use hand-crafted rules to transform standard forms to nonstandard forms. We classify lexical variations that have been reported in previous work (Kaji et al., 2015; Miyazaki and Sato, 2019) or observed by us into dozens of patterns. We then choose patterns that are easy-to-implement or widely adaptable to many words, and implement them as variant generation rules. Specifically, we use four rules: change of character type (e.g., 疲労 *hirō* 'fatigue' → ひろう), and substitution by a character with the same pronunciation (e.g., マジ *maji* 'really' → マヂ), mora consonant (e.g., 行こう *ikō* 'go' → 行こっ), and uppercase kana (e.g., ちょっと *chotto* 'bit' → ちよつと), as well as six rules similar to those used by Sasano et al. (2013) and Ikeda et al. (2016). We describe the rules in detail in Appendix §C

To obtain plausible variant pairs, we follow these steps: (1) apply the rules to standard forms, which are obtained by the dictionary-based approach, and generate nonstandard form candidates, (2) count frequencies of character n-grams that match original standard forms or generated nonstandard forms in a corpus, and (3) accept variant pairs of which both the standard and nonstandard forms have frequencies higher than a threshold value of 10.

5 Experimental Settings

5.1 Language Resources

As training data $\mathcal{D}_t$ and development data $\mathcal{D}_v$ for the segmentation and POS tagging tasks, we used 57K and 3K sentences, respectively, with the short unit word (SUW) annotation from the core data of the Balanced Corpus of Contemporary Written Japanese (BCCWJ)[8] 1.1 (Maekawa et al., 2014).

For variant pair acquisition, we counted the frequencies of UniDic entries (§4.1) using 3.5M sentences in parts of registers of the BCCWJ non-core data and character n-gram frequencies (§4.2) using 8.8M sentences in Yahoo! Chiebukuro data.[9]

[6] https://ccd.ninjal.ac.jp/unidic

[7] The classification procedure is as follows: a variant with different pronunciation from its lemma is regarded as a nonstandard form, a variant with a frequency of occurrence of 5% or less as a nonstandard form, and a variant with a frequency of 10% or more as a standard form.

[8] https://ccd.ninjal.ac.jp/bccwj/en/

[9] https://www.nii.ac.jp/dsc/idr/yahoo/chiebkr3/Y_chiebukuro.html

We constructed three pseudo-labeled datasets using the dictionary-derived and rule-derived variant pairs, which we denote by $\mathcal{V}_d$ and $\mathcal{V}_r$. The first dataset $\mathcal{A}_t$ was generated by applying DS_{tgt} to $\mathcal{D}_t$ using $\mathcal{V}_d$.[10] The second dataset $\mathcal{A}_d$ and third dataset $\mathcal{A}_r$ are 173K and 170K synthetic sentences generated by DS_{src} from the 3.5M BCCWJ non-core sentences, using the top $n_p = 20\text{K}$ frequent pairs[11] in $\mathcal{V}_d$ or $\mathcal{V}_r$. Notably, for each pair in $\mathcal{V}_d$ or $\mathcal{V}_r$, we extracted at most $n_s = 10$ original sentences that contained their lemma.[12] Similarly, we constructed an additional 3K sentences from the top 3K frequent pairs in $\mathcal{V}_d$ and 3K from 3K pairs in $\mathcal{V}_r$, and used them as development data, together with $\mathcal{D}_v$.

For evaluation, we used Yahoo! blog and Yahoo! Chiebukuro sentences annotated with SUW segmentation and POS tags, and with normalized forms (Higashiyama et al., 2021), as the test data.

5.2 Training Setting

During each training epoch, we randomly constructed a mini-batch consisting only of real training sentences ($\mathcal{A}_t$) or synthetic training sentences ($\mathcal{A}_d$ or $\mathcal{A}_r$) for each iteration, and trained the model for up to 20 epochs. We randomly initialized all parameters, applied mini-batch stochastic gradient descent to optimize parameters, and reduced the learning rate by a fixed decay ratio every epoch after the first five epochs. We set the loss coefficient values in Eq. (1) as $\lambda_{\text{seg}} = \lambda_{\text{pos}} = 1$ for real sentences, and set them as $\lambda_{\text{seg}} = \lambda_{\text{pos}} = \lambda_0$ for synthetic sentences with automatic segmentation and POS tags, where λ_0 is a hyperparameter. We set the other coefficient values for any sentences as $\lambda_{\text{cconv}} = \lambda_{\text{sedit}} = 1$.

We searched for the best values, within given ranges, for some hyperparameters of the model and used predetermined values for the others: character embedding size 200 from {100, 200, 300}, pronunciation embedding size 30 from {10, 20, 30, 40, 50}, BiLSTM hidden unit size 1,000 from {200, 400, 600, 800, 1,000}, BiLSTM dropout (Zaremba et al., 2014) rate 0.1 from {0.1, 0.2, 0.3, 0.4}, loss coefficient $\lambda_0 = 0.4$ from {0.2, 0.4, 0.6, 0.8, 1.0}, number of BiLSTM layers 2, mini-batch size 100, initial learning rate 1.0, learning rate decay ratio 0.9, and gradient clipping threshold 5.0.

5.3 Kana-to-Kanji Conversion Model

For kanji conversion (KC), we trained an n-gram language model (LM) of kana-kanji mixed sentences using SRILM[13] (Stolcke, 2002) on 1.2M sentences in the BCCWJ core and non-core data, and performed Viterbi decoding with negative log probability of the LM using the `decode_ngram.py`[14] script. Specifically, if the `TO_KANJI` tag was predicted for one or more characters in a predicted word span by the normalization model, the word was given to the KC model, together with six preceding and six succeeding characters, and the best hypothesis found was output as a normalized form.

5.4 Post-processing

We defined post-processing rules to apply to the predicted segmentation or normalization results. The first rule Seg-PP changes segmentation tags $t^s_{i+1:i+k}$ to I$\in \mathcal{T}_{\text{seg}}$ when k consecutive characters $x_{i:i+k}$ are the same vowel kana, long sound symbol, mora nasal, or mora consonant characters, according to our finding that such cases were rare from our preliminary experiment. The second rule Norm-PP changes a predicted normalized word to its original string if the predicted form does not exist in a standard form lexicon. We used standard forms in $\mathcal{V}_d$ as the lexicon.

5.5 Baseline Methods

We evaluated the following two methods for comparison. The first method was MeCab[15] (0.996) (Kudo et al., 2004) with UniDic (unidic-cwj-2.3.0), which is a popular Japanese MA toolkit based on conditional random fields (CRFs). The second method, which we call MeCab+ER, was Sasano et al. (2013)'s joint MA and normalization method, implemented by Higashiyama et al. (2021). This enhances MeCab's word lattices by their expansion rules to recognize specific types of nonstandard words shown in Appendix §C.

5.6 Evaluation Metrics

We used word-level precision, recall, and F_1 score to evaluate systems on each task. As shown in

[10] We did not construct DS_{tgt}-based data using $\mathcal{V}_r$.

[11] We obtained 404K pairs from 873K UniDic entries and 47K pairs from 868K rule-generated nonstandard form candidates by the processes described in §4.1 and §4.2.

[12] Fewer than 200K sentences were generated because 10 sentences were not necessarily included for every variant pair in the original corpus.

[13] `http://www.speech.sri.com/projects/srilm/`

[14] `https://github.com/yohokuno/neural_ime`

[15] `https://taku910.github.io/mecab/`

Method	Use of data			Seg			POS			Norm		
	$\mathcal{A}_t$	$\mathcal{A}_r$	$\mathcal{A}_d$	P	R	F	P	R	F	P	R	F
MeCab				89.2	95.1	92.1	87.5	93.3	90.3	–	–	–
MeCab+ER				**93.5**	**96.5**	**95.0**	**91.4**	**94.3**	**92.8**	55.9	25.8	35.3
Ours	✓			91.3	93.8	92.6	87.6	90.0	88.8	50.9	19.4	28.1
	✓	✓		91.0	93.7	92.3	88.1	90.8	89.4	42.4	28.0	33.8
	✓		✓	91.9	94.2	93.1	89.0	91.2	90.1	52.9	32.1	39.9
	✓	✓	✓	91.1	93.8	92.5	88.3	90.9	89.6	49.7	37.0	42.4
Ours +Seg-PP	✓	✓	✓	92.9	94.1	93.5	89.9	91.1	90.5	50.8	**37.8**	43.4
Ours +Seg-PP +Norm-PP	✓	✓	✓	92.9	94.1	93.5	89.9	91.1	90.5	**65.8**	36.6	**47.1**

Table 3: Precision (P), recall (R), and F_1 score (F) of the proposed and compared methods for word segmentation, POS tagging, and lexical normalization.

Table 2, a test word has labels corresponding to an index pair of the first and last character, i.e., span, a POS tag, and a standard form set. A predicted word w^* is counted as a true positive (TP) when the span of w^* equals to that of a test word for the segmentation task and when the span and POS tag of w^* equal to those of a test word for the POS tagging task. For the normalization task, a predicted word w^* is counted as a TP when the span of w^* equals to that of a test word and the normalized form of w^* is included in the standard form set of the test word, whereas w^* is counted as a false positive (FP) when either of the span or normalized form of w^* does not match with a test nonstandard word. A test word w is counted as a false negative when the span and normalized form of any predicted word do not match with w.

6 Results and Analysis

6.1 Main Results

Table 3 shows the performance of the proposed model (with the full features, unless otherwise specified) on the three tasks.[16] Although the proposed model trained only on $\mathcal{A}_t$ achieved low normalization recall, the model with additional data $\mathcal{A}_d$ or $\mathcal{A}_r$ achieved a higher score, and the model with the three datasets achieved the highest score. These results are roughly consistent with the observation that adding different types of pseudo-labeled data reduced the number of out-of-vocabulary (OOV) tokens in the test data, as shown in Appendix §D. Our model with post-processing achieved further improvements; Seg-PP improved F_1 for each task by approximately 1 point and Norm-PP improved normalization precision by 15 points. However, the latter results indicate that avoiding the predictions of meaningless or unusual forms has the potential to improve our model.

Compared with MeCab+ER, our model achieved better normalization performance when trained on sufficient training data. Conversely, MeCab+ER achieved the best segmentation and POS tagging performance. The superiority of MeCab+ER over MeCab indicates the advantage of the explicit prediction of normalized word spans by the method on the two tasks, which contrasts with the independent prediction of word spans, POS tags, and normalized forms performed by our model.

6.2 Effect of Dataset Size

To investigate the effect of the amount of pseudo-labeled data, we generated dictionary-derived data $\mathcal{A}'_d$ with different settings of n_s and n_p, where n_s is the number of extracted sentences per variant pair and n_p is the number of variant pairs, as described in §5.1. We then evaluated the normalization performance of the proposed model trained on $\mathcal{A}_t \cup \mathcal{A}'_d$.[17]

Figure 2 (a) shows the performance of the model with varying n_s and fixed $n_p = 20$K. A larger n_s led to both better precision and better recall, indicating that training with the same variant pairs but with more diverse context sentences contributed to more robust prediction. Figure 2 (b) shows the performance of the model with fixed $n_s = 10$ and varying n_p. Increasing n_p from 5K to larger values contributed to better performance but increasing n_p above 10K did not improve recall, and degraded precision in most cases, probably because of the infrequent and ineffective variant pairs. Although the frequencies of the 5K-th and 10K-th nonstandard words in the constructed variant pairs were six and two, respectively, entries ranked below about

[16] We used a majority-vote to transform character-level POS tags predicted by the proposed model to a word-level tag.

[17] We also evaluated the model's performance given gold segmentation to remove the influence of segmentation errors, but the model showed a similar tendency regardless of whether gold segmentation was given, as shown in Figure 2.

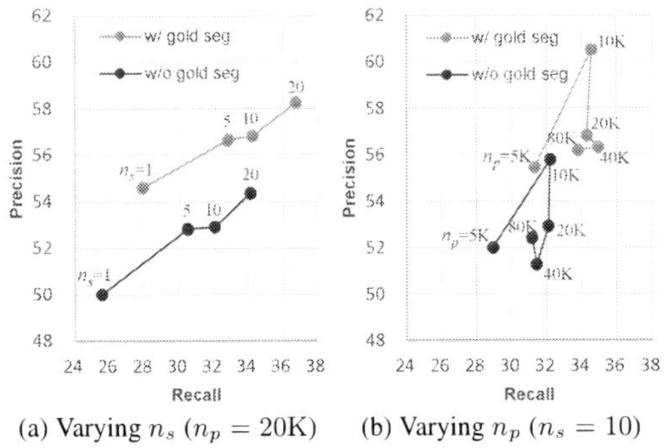

Figure 2: Normalization performance of the proposed model trained on $\mathcal{A}_t \cup \mathcal{A}'_d$ with different size settings.

16K-th had a frequency of zero.[18]

These two results suggest that the gain discussed in §6.1 was caused by both the additional variant pairs and the additional contexts of existing variant pairs in the combined data of $\mathcal{A}_d$ and $\mathcal{A}_r$.

6.3 Detailed Results of Normalization

We semi-automatically annotated the test sentences with SEdit and CConv tags. Of 767 nonstandard tokens, six and three words required multi-character edit operations and replacement by Roman letters, respectively. Therefore, the upper bound of normalization recall was 99% by our tag set.

We then evaluated the proposed model with different features trained on the full $\mathcal{A}_t \cup \mathcal{A}_d \cup \mathcal{A}_r$ dataset, with respect to the character-level SEdit/CConv tag prediction accuracy for the KEEP tag and other tags, and the word-level text editing accuracy of negative and positive normalization instances, which is calculated according to gold segmentation. A negative instance indicates a gold word annotated with no standard forms, and a prediction is regarded as correct when only KEEP tags are predicted for the word. Notably, in the test data, KEEP tags account for 95.8% and 96.8% of all SEdit and CConv tags, respectively, and negative instances account for 93.9% of all word tokens.

As shown in Table 4, for the KEEP tag and negative normalization instances, the three models with different features achieved a high recall (close to, or better than, 99%) and a somewhat lower precision (around 97%–98%), indicating that over-normalized words and undetected nonstandard words accounted for the remaining 1% and 2%–3%, respectively. For other tags and positive normalization instances, both character-level and word-level performance were much lower because of the small number of training instances. However, the models with more additional features achieved better performance, indicating the effectiveness of the lexicon and pronunciation features. In particular, each additional feature substantially improved the performance of CConv tag prediction.

[18]Different entries with the same frequency were sorted in Japanese alphabetical order.

Feature	SEdit (Keep)		CConv (Keep)		Norm-neg	
	P	R	P	R	P	R
C	97.4	99.5	98.2	99.0	97.2	98.7
C+L	97.2	99.6	98.4	99.0	97.0	98.8
C+L+P	97.4	99.6	98.5	99.2	97.3	99.0

Feature	SEdit (other)		CConv (other)		Norm	
	P	R	P	R	P	R
C	77.5	39.5	56.7	41.5	48.6	36.9
C+L	77.7	34.0	60.6	48.0	50.4	35.6
C+L+P	80.5	39.8	67.9	52.2	54.6	40.3

Table 4: Precision/Recall of the proposed models with character (C), lexicon (L), and pronunciation (P) features for character-level tag prediction (SEdit/CConv) and word-level text editing (Norm-neg/Norm).

Type	Gold	Det	ValTag	CorSeg	CorKC	R
SCV	419	255	164	156	156	37.2
CTV	248	149	105	94	92	37.1
AR	132	78	55	51	51	38.6
Typo	23	3	1	1	1	4.4
FP	–	121	–	–	–	–

Table 5: Evaluation of the proposed model for each category. Sound change variants (SCV), character type variants (CTV), and alternative representations (AR) are categories defined in Higashiyama et al. (2021). FP indicates the number of words detected incorrectly by the model.

6.4 Error Analysis

We conducted step-by-step evaluation of the proposed model trained on the full dataset. Table 5 shows the number of gold normalization instances (Gold), predictions correctly detected (Det) out of Gold, predictions with valid SEdit/CConv tags (ValTag) out of Det, predictions correctly segmented (CorSeg) out of ValTag, and predictions matched with correct standard forms after text editing and KC (CorKC) out of CorSeg, for each category. For each of the top three categories (SCV, CTV, and AR), two major errors were detection failure, which accounted for 39%–41% ($\frac{\text{Gold}-\text{Det}}{\text{Gold}}$), and tag prediction error, which accounted for 17%–22% ($\frac{\text{Det}-\text{ValTag}}{\text{Gold}}$), whereas the true positives accounted for 37%–39% (R= $\frac{\text{CorKC}}{\text{Gold}}$). This tendency was

Type	Gold	DetKC	ValTag	CorSeg	CorKC
Req.	116	58	52	49	48
Opt.	170	22	21	21	20
FP	–	47	–	–	–

Table 6: Evaluation of the proposed model for kanji conversion (KC). Required (Req.) indicates that any standard forms of a nonstandard word require KC. Optional (Opt.) indicates that some standard forms require KC but other standard forms can be generated without KC. FP indicates the number of words detected incorrectly by the model.

common to all three categories.

Table 6 shows similar evaluation results for KC, where DetKC indicates the number of gold words assigned `TO_KANJI` tag(s) by the model. We found that most errors for the "required" instances were detection failures, and the KC model correctly converted 97% ($\frac{\text{CorKC}}{\text{CorSeg}}$) of the "required" and "optional" instances.

With respect to precision degradation, the model over-normalized 121 negative instances. We found that 61 cases of these instances were interjections or onomatopoeic words, and their characteristics were similar to general nonstandard words; this made it difficult to distinguish them from words to be normalized. We present further analysis and actual examples in Appendix §F.

7 Related Work

Word Segmentation and Lexical Normalization. For word segmentation and lexical normalization of Japanese UGT, most previous work applied a lattice-based MA framework, which jointly predicts word sequence and POS tag sequences over a word lattice of an input sentence. To incorporate informal word nodes into a word lattice, Sasano et al. (2013) and Kaji and Kitsuregawa (2014) used hand-crafted rules for recognizing variant forms of known words, and Saito et al. (2014) and Saito et al. (2017) acquired formal-informal word pairs from manually-annotated or unlabeled text. In contrast to those methods, Ikeda et al. (2016) applied a sequence-to-sequence model trained on synthetic formal-informal sentence pairs to sentence-level Japanese text normalization.

For Chinese, also an unsegmented language, nonstandard word detection and normalization methods have been proposed. Li and Yarowsky (2008) extracted formal-informal word pairs using web-searched sentences defining informal words and a conditional log-linear ranking model. Wang and Ng (2013) proposed beam-search decoding methods for lexical normalization as well as punctuation correction and recovery of missing words, for Chinese and English UGT, as preprocessing steps for Chinese↔English machine translation (MT). Qian et al. (2015) proposed a transition method based on a perceptron framework and a normalization dictionary for the joint SPN task. Zhang et al. (2017) proposed a transition method using character-level and word-level LSTMs for word segmentation and detection of informal words.

English Lexical Normalization. Early work on lexical normalization of English SMS and microblog text employed a noisy channel formulation; to restore plausible standard forms from observed nonstandard words, Aw et al. (2006) trained a statistical MT model and Choudhury et al. (2007) trained a hidden Markov model on parallel sentences of standard and nonstandard English. Liu et al. (2011) automatically collected training word pairs using carefully-designed web search queries and trained CRFs to calculate the conditional probability of a nonstandard character given a standard character. Recently, Muller et al. (2019) adapted BERT (Devlin et al., 2019) for lexical normalization by introducing a subword alignment algorithm between standard and nonstandard words and a task-specific fine-tuning strategy.

Some other work has adopted unsupervised methods: a log-linear model to score standard and nonstandard word sequences (Yang and Eisenstein, 2013), a graph-based method to model contextual and lexical similarity (Sönmez and Özgür, 2014), and a finite-state transducer using word embedding and string similarity (Rangarajan Sridhar, 2015).

Text Editing. Text editing methods have also been applied to English lexical normalization. Chrupała (2014) used character embeddings based on a recurrent neural network LM and trained CRFs to predict character-level edit operations. Min and Mott (2015) proposed an LSTM-based model to perform word-level edit operations that aggregate character-level edit operations.

Recently, text editing models based on Transformer and BERT (Malmi et al., 2019; Mallinson et al., 2020; Stahlberg and Kumar, 2020) have been proposed for monolingual sequence transduction tasks, such as grammatical error correction and text normalization for speech synthesis, because of their sample-efficient and fast inference characteristics compared to sequence-to-sequence models.

Data Synthesis. Data synthesis and augmentation methods have been explored for various NLP tasks, to increase the diversity of training examples (Feng et al., 2021) and for lexical normalization to address the deficiency of training data. Ikeda et al. (2016) synthesized Japanese formal-informal sentence pairs by hand-crafted rules to convert standard forms to nonstandard forms. Zhang et al. (2017) synthesized training data for Chinese informal word detection by random substitution of formal words in segmented sentences by informal words in a dictionary of formal-informal word pairs. To train statistical and neural MT models for Turkish text normalization, Çolakoğlu et al. (2019) generated a pseudo-parallel corpus where nonstandard words in original tweet text were aligned with plausible standard words using their weighted edit distance algorithm. Dekker and van der Goot (2020) explored data synthesis methods for English lexical normalization using the clean-to-noisy policy (mainly based on manually-designed rules) and the noisy-to-clean policy (based on predicted standard forms).

8 Conclusion

This paper presents our text editing model and methods of pseudo-labeled data generation for the joint segmentation, POS tagging, and normalization task. The experiments demonstrated that the proposed model was successfully trained on generated pseudo-labeled data, but more exhaustive detection and accurate normalization of nonstandard words have the potential to improve the model.

Future work includes (1) explicit consideration of nonstandard word spans for accurate segmentation and normalization, (2) the use of a large-scale pretrained LM for better normalization coverage, and (3) evaluation on broader UGT domains.

Acknowledgements

We thank our anonymous reviewers for their helpful comments. We used the Balanced Corpus of Contemporary Written Japanese provided by the National Institute for Japanese Language and Linguistics and Yahoo! Chiebukuro data (3rd edition) provided by Yahoo Japan Corporation via IDR Dataset Service of the National Institute of Informatics.

References

AiTi Aw, Min Zhang, Juan Xiao, and Jian Su. 2006. A phrase-based statistical model for SMS text normalization. In *Proceedings of the COLING/ACL 2006 Main Conference Poster Sessions*, pages 33–40, Sydney, Australia. Association for Computational Linguistics.

Timothy Baldwin, Marie Catherine de Marneffe, Bo Han, Young-Bum Kim, Alan Ritter, and Wei Xu. 2015. Shared tasks of the 2015 workshop on noisy user-generated text: Twitter lexical normalization and named entity recognition. In *Proceedings of the Workshop on Noisy User-generated Text*, pages 126–135, Beijing, China. Association for Computational Linguistics.

Monojit Choudhury, Rahul Saraf, Vijit Jain, Animesh Mukherjee, Sudeshna Sarkar, and Anupam Basu. 2007. Investigation and modeling of the structure of texting language. *International Journal of Document Analysis and Recognition*, 10(3):157–174.

Grzegorz Chrupała. 2014. Normalizing tweets with edit scripts and recurrent neural embeddings. In *Proceedings of the 52nd Annual Meeting of the Association for Computational Linguistics (Volume 2: Short Papers)*, pages 680–686, Baltimore, Maryland. Association for Computational Linguistics.

Talha Çolakoğlu, Umut Sulubacak, and Ahmet Cüneyd Tantuğ. 2019. Normalizing non-canonical Turkish texts using machine translation approaches. In *Proceedings of the 57th Annual Meeting of the Association for Computational Linguistics: Student Research Workshop*, pages 267–272, Florence, Italy. Association for Computational Linguistics.

Kelly Dekker and Rob van der Goot. 2020. Synthetic data for English lexical normalization: How close can we get to manually annotated data? In *Proceedings of the 12th Language Resources and Evaluation Conference*, pages 6300–6309, Marseille, France. European Language Resources Association.

Yasuharu Den, Junpei Nakamura, Toshinobu Ogiso, and Hideki Ogura. 2008. A proper approach to Japanese morphological analysis: Dictionary, model, and evaluation. In *Proceedings of the 6th International Conference on Language Resources and Evaluation*, Marrakech, Morocco. European Language Resources Association.

Jacob Devlin, Ming-Wei Chang, Kenton Lee, and Kristina Toutanova. 2019. BERT: Pre-training of deep bidirectional transformers for language understanding. In *Proceedings of the 2019 Conference of the North American Chapter of the Association for Computational Linguistics: Human Language Technologies, Volume 1 (Long and Short Papers)*, pages 4171–4186, Minneapolis, Minnesota. Association for Computational Linguistics.

Steven Y. Feng, Varun Gangal, Jason Wei, Sarath Chandar, Soroush Vosoughi, Teruko Mitamura, and Eduard Hovy. 2021. A survey of data augmentation approaches for NLP. In *Findings of the Association for Computational Linguistics: ACL-IJCNLP 2021*, pages 968–988, Online. Association for Computational Linguistics.

Shohei Higashiyama, Masao Utiyama, Taro Watanabe, and Eiichiro Sumita. 2021. User-generated text corpus for evaluating Japanese morphological analysis and lexical normalization. In *Proceedings of the 2021 Conference of the North American Chapter of the Association for Computational Linguistics: Human Language Technologies*, pages 5532–5541, Online. Association for Computational Linguistics.

Sepp Hochreiter and Jürgen Schmidhuber. 1997. Long short-term memory. *Neural Computation*, 9(8):1735–1780.

Taishi Ikeda, Hiroyuki Shindo, and Yuji Matsumoto. 2016. Japanese text normalization with encoder-decoder model. In *Proceedings of the 2nd Workshop on Noisy User-generated Text*, pages 129–137, Osaka, Japan. The COLING 2016 Organizing Committee.

Nobuhiro Kaji and Masaru Kitsuregawa. 2014. Accurate word segmentation and pos tagging for Japanese microblogs: Corpus annotation and joint modeling with lexical normalization. In *Proceedings of the 2014 Conference on Empirical Methods in Natural Language Processing*, pages 99–109, Doha, Qatar. Association for Computational Linguistics.

Nobuhiro Kaji, Shinsuke Mori, Fumihiko Takahashi, Tetsuro Sasada, Itsumi Saito, Keigo Hattori, Yugo Murawaki, and Kei Utsumi. 2015. Kētaiso kaiseki no error bunseki (Error analysis of morphological analysis) [in Japanese]. In *Proceedings of the 21th Annual Meeting of the Association for Natural Language Processing Workshop "Error Analysis on Natural Language Processing"*, Kyoto, Japan.

Taku Kudo, Kaoru Yamamoto, and Yuji Matsumoto. 2004. Applying conditional random fields to Japanese morphological analysis. In *Proceedings of the 2004 Conference on Empirical Methods in Natural Language Processing*, pages 230–237, Barcelona, Spain. Association for Computational Linguistics.

Zhifei Li and David Yarowsky. 2008. Mining and modeling relations between formal and informal Chinese phrases from web corpora. In *Proceedings of the 2008 Conference on Empirical Methods in Natural Language Processing*, pages 1031–1040, Honolulu, Hawaii. Association for Computational Linguistics.

Fei Liu, Fuliang Weng, Bingqing Wang, and Yang Liu. 2011. Insertion, deletion, or substitution? Normalizing text messages without pre-categorization nor supervision. In *Proceedings of the 49th Annual Meeting of the Association for Computational Linguistics: Human Language Technologies*, pages 71–76, Portland, Oregon, USA. Association for Computational Linguistics.

Kikuo Maekawa, Makoto Yamazaki, Toshinobu Ogiso, Takehiko Maruyama, Hideki Ogura, Wakako Kashino, Hanae Koiso, Masaya Yamaguchi, Makiro Tanaka, and Yasuharu Den. 2014. Balanced corpus of contemporary written Japanese. *Language Resources and Evaluation*, 48(2):345–371.

Jonathan Mallinson, Aliaksei Severyn, Eric Malmi, and Guillermo Garrido. 2020. FELIX: Flexible text editing through tagging and insertion. In *Findings of the Association for Computational Linguistics: EMNLP 2020*, pages 1244–1255, Online. Association for Computational Linguistics.

Eric Malmi, Sebastian Krause, Sascha Rothe, Daniil Mirylenka, and Aliaksei Severyn. 2019. Encode, tag, realize: High-precision text editing. In *Proceedings of the 2019 Conference on Empirical Methods in Natural Language Processing and the 9th International Joint Conference on Natural Language Processing*, pages 5054–5065, Hong Kong, China. Association for Computational Linguistics.

Wookhee Min and Bradford Mott. 2015. NCSU_SAS_WOOKHEE: A deep contextual long-short term memory model for text normalization. In *Proceedings of the Workshop on Noisy User-generated Text*, pages 111–119, Beijing, China. Association for Computational Linguistics.

Chiaki Miyazaki and Satoshi Sato. 2019. Classification of phonological changes reflected in text: Toward a characterization of written utterances [in Japanese]. *Journal of Natural Language Processing*, 26(2):407–440.

Benjamin Muller, Benoit Sagot, and Djamé Seddah. 2019. Enhancing BERT for lexical normalization. In *Proceedings of the 5th Workshop on Noisy User-generated Text*, pages 297–306, Hong Kong, China. Association for Computational Linguistics.

Tao Qian, Yue Zhang, Meishan Zhang, Yafeng Ren, and Donghong Ji. 2015. A transition-based model for joint segmentation, POS-tagging and normalization. In *Proceedings of the 2015 Conference on Empirical Methods in Natural Language Processing*, pages 1837–1846, Lisbon, Portugal. Association for Computational Linguistics.

Vivek Kumar Rangarajan Sridhar. 2015. Unsupervised text normalization using distributed representations of words and phrases. In *Proceedings of the 1st Workshop on Vector Space Modeling for Natural Language Processing*, pages 8–16, Denver, Colorado. Association for Computational Linguistics.

Itsumi Saito, Kyosuke Nishida, Kugatsu Sadamitsu, Kuniko Saito, and Junji Tomita. 2017. Automatically extracting variant-normalization pairs for Japanese text normalization. In *Proceedings of the*

8th International Joint Conference on Natural Language Processing (Volume 1: Long Papers)*, pages 937–946, Taipei, Taiwan. Asian Federation of Natural Language Processing.

Itsumi Saito, Kugatsu Sadamitsu, Hisako Asano, and Yoshihiro Matsuo. 2014. Morphological analysis for Japanese noisy text based on character-level and word-level normalization. In *Proceedings of the 25th International Conference on Computational Linguistics: Technical Papers*, pages 1773–1782, Dublin, Ireland. Dublin City University and Association for Computational Linguistics.

Ryohei Sasano, Sadao Kurohashi, and Manabu Okumura. 2013. A simple approach to unknown word processing in Japanese morphological analysis. In *Proceedings of the 6th International Joint Conference on Natural Language Processing*, pages 162–170, Nagoya, Japan. Asian Federation of Natural Language Processing.

Cagil Sönmez and Arzucan Özgür. 2014. A graph-based approach for contextual text normalization. In *Proceedings of the 2014 Conference on Empirical Methods in Natural Language Processing*, pages 313–324, Doha, Qatar. Association for Computational Linguistics.

Felix Stahlberg and Shankar Kumar. 2020. Seq2Edits: Sequence transduction using span-level edit operations. In *Proceedings of the 2020 Conference on Empirical Methods in Natural Language Processing*, pages 5147–5159, Online. Association for Computational Linguistics.

Andreas Stolcke. 2002. SRILM - an extensible language modeling toolkit. In *Proceedings of the 7th International Conference on Spoken Language Processing*, pages 901–904, Denver, Colorado, USA.

Pidong Wang and Hwee Tou Ng. 2013. A beam-search decoder for normalization of social media text with application to machine translation. In *Proceedings of the 2013 Conference of the North American Chapter of the Association for Computational Linguistics: Human Language Technologies*, pages 471–481, Atlanta, Georgia. Association for Computational Linguistics.

Yi Yang and Jacob Eisenstein. 2013. A log-linear model for unsupervised text normalization. In *Proceedings of the 2013 Conference on Empirical Methods in Natural Language Processing*, pages 61–72, Seattle, Washington, USA. Association for Computational Linguistics.

Wojciech Zaremba, Ilya Sutskever, and Oriol Vinyals. 2014. Recurrent neural network regularization. *Computing Research Repository*, arXiv:1409.2329.

Meishan Zhang, Guohong Fu, and Nan Yu. 2017. Segmenting Chinese microtext: Joint informal-word detection and segmentation with neural networks. In *Proceedings of the 26th International Joint Conference on Artificial Intelligence*, pages 4228–4234, Melbourne, Australia.

Original sentence				Updated information			
Word	Lemma ID	POS	Conjugation form	Word (Substituted)	SEdit tags	CConv tags	Standard form
スゴく	19163	Adjective	Continuative	–	K, K, K	HIRA, HIRA, K	すごく
気	8263	Noun	–	–	K	K	–
に	28178	Particle	–	–	K	K	–
なる	28061	Verb	Termination	–	K, K	K, K	–

Table 7: An example of $\mathrm{DS}_{\mathrm{tgt}}$. Assume that we have a standard and nonstandard word variant pair p_a = (スゴく, すごく) 'very' with lemma ID of 19163 and continuative form. A segmented sentence $\boldsymbol{x}_a$ ="スゴく|気|に|なる" (*sugoku ki ni naru*), which means "(I'm) very curious.", is annotated with SEdit and CConv tags by $\mathrm{DS}_{\mathrm{tgt}}$, according to the matched token スゴく with the same lemma ID and conjugation form as those of p_a.

Original sentence				Updated information			
Word	Lemma ID	POS	Conjugation form	Word (Substituted)	SEdit tags	CConv tags	Standard form
ほんとう	34947	Noun	–	ほんっと	K, K, D, INSR(う)	K, K, K, K	ほんとう
に	28198	Particle	–	–	K	K	–
心配	19516	Noun	–	–	K, K	K, K	–
です	25653	Copula	Termination	–	K, K	K, K	–

Table 8: An example of $\mathrm{DS}_{\mathrm{src}}$. For a standard and nonstandard word variant pair p_b =(ほんとう, ほんっと) 'truth' with lemma ID of 34947 and no conjugation form, a segmented sentence containing a token with the same lemma ID and conjugation form as those of p_b is extracted: $\boldsymbol{x}_b$ ="ほんとう|に|心配|です" (*hontō ni shimpai desu*), which means "(I'm) really worried." Then, a synthetic sentence "ほんっと|に|心配|です" annotated with SEdit and CConv tags is generated by $\mathrm{DS}_{\mathrm{src}}$.

A Selection of Closest Standard Form

Let w_j be a word and S_j be the set of standard forms of w_j. We define four character types of a word: "hiragana-only", "katakana-only", "kanji-kana-mixed", and "other". The process of selecting the closest standard form, which is mentioned in §3.1, comprises the following steps:

1. If S_j contains standard forms with the same character type as w_j, those standard forms are prioritized; standard forms with different character types are removed from S_j.

2. If S_j contains only standard forms with different character types from w_j, the standard forms with the same character type as the standard form occurring most frequently in a corpus are retained, and others are removed from S_j.

3. The standard form with the most characters that are aligned to w_j is selected as the closest standard form $s^{\star}_j$. Character alignment between w_j and $s \in S_j$ is calculated, to find the longest matching substrings recursively, until any substrings in w_j and s are not matched.

B Examples of Pseudo Label Annotation

An example of $\mathrm{DS}_{\mathrm{tgt}}$ to a sentence $\boldsymbol{x}_a$ and a variant pair p_a is shown in Table 7. Also, an example of $\mathrm{DS}_{\mathrm{src}}$ to a sentence $\boldsymbol{x}_b$ and a variant pair p_b is shown in Table 8. The notation of SEdit and CConv tags in Table 7 and 8 is the same as that in Table 1.

C Variant Generation Rules

We define 10 rules in Table 9 to generate nonstandard form candidates from standard forms. Rule 2 interchanges お↔を, じ↔ぢ, ず↔づ, ぶ↔ゔ, オ↔ヲ, ジ↔ヂ, ズ↔ヅ, or ブ↔ヴ as characters with the same pronunciation. We generate multiple variants from an original word using any combination of applicable rules in $\{0, 1\} \times \{0, 2, 7\} \times \{0, 3, 8\} \times \{0, 4, 5, 6\} \times \{0, 9, 10\}$, where 0 indicates that no rule is applied.

D Out-of-vocabulary Tokens in Test Data

Table 10 shows the number and percentage of OOV tokens for each training dataset. Adding either $\mathcal{A}_d$ or $\mathcal{A}_r$ (separately) to $\mathcal{A}_t$ reduced the number of OOV nonstandard tokens by 102 or 110, but adding both datasets decreased the number of OOV tokens by 161. This indicates that the remaining 51 tokens were contained in both datasets.

ID	Rule	Sub-rule	Original	Variant
1	Change of character type	(a) Hiragana to katakana	たいへん *taihen* 'hard'	タイヘン
		(b) Katakana to hiragana	スーパー *sūpā* 'super'	すーぱー
		(c) Kana-kanji mixed to hiragana	疲労 *hirō* 'fatigue'	ひろう
		(d) Kana-kanji mixed to katakana	苦手 *nigate* 'weak'	ニガテ
2	Sub. by character with the same pronunciation	–	マジ *maji* 'really'	マヂ
3	Sub. by mora consonant	(a) "です"	です *desu* (copula)	っす
		(b) Adjective ends with "い"	広い *hiroi* 'wide'	広っ
		(c) Verb ends with "う"	行こう *ikō* 'go'	行こっ
4	Sub. by uppercase kana	–	ちょっと *chotto* 'bit'	ちよつと
$5^{S,I}$	Sub. by lowercase kana	–	いや *iya* 'unpleasant'	ぃゃ
$6^{S,I}$	Sub. of vowel by long sound	–	楽しい *tanoshī* 'fun'	楽しー
7^{I}	Sub. of vowel sequence	(a) Adjective ends with *-ai* to *ē*	うるさい *uruasi* 'loud'	うるせえ *urusē*
		(b) Adjective ends with *-ui* to *ī*	わるい *warui* 'bad'	わりい *warī*
		(c) Adjective ends with *-oi* to *ē*	おそい *osoi* 'late'	おせえ *osē*
		(d) Word ends with *-o*う to *o*お	そう *sō* 'so'	そお
		(e) "言う/いう" to ゆう	言い *ī* 'say'	ゆい *yui*
8^{I}	Deletion of tail vowel	(a) Adjective ends with "い"	ひどい *hidoi* 'terrible'	ひど *hido*
		(b) Word ends with "う"	だろう *darō* (copula)	だろ *daro*
9^{I}	Insertion of mora consonant	(a) Into the middle	きつい *kitsui* 'tough'	きっつい *kittsui*
		(b) Into the end	けど *kedo* 'but'	けどっ
$10^{S,I}$	Insertion of long sound	(a) Long sound sym. into the middle	大きい *ōkī* 'big'	大きーい *ōkīi*
		(b) Long sound sym. into the end	正解 *seikai* 'answer'	正解ー *seikaī*
		(d) Uppercase vowel into the middle	かなり *kanari* 'quite'	かなあり *kanāri*
		(c) Uppercase vowel into the end	強い *tsuyoi* 'strong'	強いい *tsuyoī*
		(e) Lowercase vowel into the middle	ずっと *zutto* 'always'	ずぅっと *zūtto*
		(f) Lowercase vowel into the end	ます *masu* (copula)	ますぅ *masū*

Table 9: Variant generation rules and examples of generated variants. "Sub." indicates substitution. The IDs with "S" and "I" indicate that similar rules were used in Sasano et al. (2013) and Ikeda et al. (2016), respectively.

Training data	All		Nonstandard	
	Test OOV		Test OOV	
	#	%	#	%
$\emptyset$	12,600	100.0	767	100.0
$\mathcal{A}_t\ (\mathcal{D}_t)$	1,055	8.4	445	58.0
$\mathcal{A}_t \cup \mathcal{A}_r$	734	5.8	335	43.7
$\mathcal{A}_t \cup \mathcal{A}_d$	764	6.1	343	44.7
$\mathcal{A}_t \cup \mathcal{A}_d \cup \mathcal{A}_r$	636	5.1	284	37.0

Table 10: Number and percentage of (all and nonstandard) test OOV tokens for each training dataset.

E Performance for Known and Unknown Normalization Instances

Letting a token be known if the token and its gold standard form are included in the full training data $\mathcal{A}_d \cup \mathcal{A}_r \cup \mathcal{A}_t$, normalization instances in the test data consist of 385 known and 382 unknown instances. Recall of the proposed models trained on the full dataset with different features for both type of instances is shown in Table 11. Unsurprisingly, all model variations recognized known instances much better than unknown instances. Although the model with full features achieved the highest recall of 62.1%, this is lower than the model's recall of 86.0% on the pseudo development data that only included known normalization instances. The performance difference for known test instances and development instances is likely because of more distant context distribution of test instances from training instances.

Feature	Known	Unknown
C	54.3	11.8
C+L	55.8	7.3
C+L+P	62.1	11.8

Table 11: Recall of the proposed models with character (C), lexicon (L), and pronunciation (P) features for known and unknown normalization instances

F Examples of Over-normalization

As mentioned in §6.4, the proposed model over-normalized 121 negative instances, including 61 cases that were interjections or onomatopoeic words.[19] Examples that were over-normalized by the model trained on the full dataset are shown in Table 12. Both interjections and onomatopoeic

[19]Interjections except idiomatic greetings and most onomatopoeic words were not annotated with any standard forms mainly because defining standard forms is difficult for these types of words.

	Type	Original word	Edited word	KC result	Assess
(a)	Onomatopoeia	ガコンッ *gakon* (thud)	ガコン	–	✓
(b)	Onomatopoeia	ジンジン *jinjin* (tingling)	じんじん	–	✓
(c)	Onomatopoeia	ゴホゴホ *gohogoho* (coughing sound)	ごほごホ	–	?
(d)	Interjection	はぁぁ *haā* (sighing sound)	はああ	–	✓
(e)	Interjection	ぅん *un* (yeah)	うん	–	✓
(f)	Interjection	ひーひっひー *hīhihhī* (evil laugh sound)	ひいひっひい	–	✓
(g)	Interjection	あらっ *ara* (oh)	あらい *arai*	洗い (wash)	×
(h)	Interjection	おお〜〜 *ō* (wow)	おう	王 (king)	×
(i)	Informal	ケータイ *kētai* (mobile phone)	ケイタイ	–	✓
(j)	Informal	ダルい *darui* (dull/tired)	だるい	–	✓
(k)	Informal	キズ *kizu* (wound)	キズ	傷	✓
(l)	Informal	かっこ[E] *kakko*[*ī*] (cool)	かっこ	カッコ	✓
(m)	Informal	ムレる *mureru* (stuffy)	むレる	–	?
(n)	Informal	ヤバイ *yabai* (crazy)	やバイ	–	?

Table 12: Examples of over-normalization, i.e., FP, by the proposed model. Words in "[]" indicate surrounding context. The "Edited word" column shows the output of the model after editing, according to predicted tags, and the "KC result" column shows the result after performing kanji conversion (KC). The "Assess" column shows our assessments: "✓", "?", and "×" indicate that the final output is acceptable (the meaning is mostly preserved), questionable (the meaning is understandable but the spelling is peculiar), and obviously incorrect, respectively.

words have characteristics similar to those of general nonstandard forms, such as insertion of Japanese special mora characters (a and e–h in Table 12), use of lowercased kana characters (d–e), and repetition of the same characters (d and h). These characteristics made it difficult to distinguish negative instances from words to be normalized.

Another 29 cases were somewhat informal forms written in katakana or hiragana (i–n in Table 12) and approximately 60% of the predicted normalized forms were acceptable, according to our assessment. This is because of the difficulty of annotating all words in a test sentence with all possible lexical variations.

Incorrect normalization results included cases with peculiar spellings where some hiragana or katakana characters were converted to another type of kana (c and m–n).

Intrinsic evaluation of language models for code-switching

Sik Feng Cheong
NUS High School of
Mathematics and Science
20 Clementi Avenue 1
Singapore 129957
h1710019@nushigh.edu.sg

Hai Leong Chieu, Jing Lim
DSO National Laboratories
12 Science Park Drive
Singapore 118225
{chaileon,ljing2}@dso.org.sg

Abstract

Language models used in speech recognition are often either evaluated intrinsically using perplexity on test data, or extrinsically with an automatic speech recognition (ASR) system. The former evaluation does not always correlate well with ASR performance, while the latter could be specific to particular ASR systems. Recent work proposed to evaluate language models by using them to classify ground truth sentences among alternative phonetically similar sentences generated by a fine state transducer. Underlying such an evaluation is the assumption that the generated sentences are linguistically incorrect. In this paper, we first put this assumption into question, and observe that alternatively generated sentences could often be linguistically correct when they differ from the ground truth by only one edit. Secondly, we showed that by using multi-lingual BERT, we can achieve better performance than previous work on two code-switching data sets. Our implementation is publicly available on Github.[1]

1 Introduction

Code-switching (CS) is the phenomenon where a multilingual speaker alternates between the use of multiple languages in the same utterance (Yow et al., 2018). This practice is common among bilingual speakers, e.g., Chinese (Lyu et al., 2010), Spanish or Hindi-speakers (Khanuja et al., 2020b) who are bilingual in English. To build automatic speech recognition (ASR) systems for CS utterances, a good language model is important, especially when CS training data is often scarce.

Language models (LMs) are an important part of text generation systems in applications such as machine translation and ASR systems. Intrinsic evaluations of LMs are often performed using perplexity, a measurement of how well a LM predicts

[1] https://github.com/sikfeng/language-modelling-for-code-switching

- 还有 (there is) buffalo wings
- high yo buffalo wings
- 还有 (there is) 把 (hold) 发 (hair) 另 (other)
- 海域 (sea area) 巴 (bar) follow wings
- high 由 (by) 把 (hold) follow wings

Figure 1: Examples of alternatives sentences generated to be phonetically similar to the first sentence. Translations provided in brackets.

a test sample. However, previous work has noted that perplexity does not correlate well with ASR performance (e.g. Chen et al., 1998; Gonen and Goldberg, 2019). Extrinsic evaluations of LMs with ASR performance, on the other hand, might be over-fitting to the ASR used in the evaluation. To address this problem, Gonen and Goldberg (2019) proposed a new evaluation metric based on a classification task. First, given a ground truth sentence, they used finite state transducers (FST) to generate a set of phonetically similar sentences. They evaluate LMs based on the task of identifying the ground truth sentence from this set of sentences. LMs can thus be evaluated based on the accuracy of this task, independent of any specific ASR. For this evaluation task, Gonen and Goldberg (2019) proposed a discriminative model that outperformed generative baselines on a English-Spanish (EN-ES) CS test set. However, such an evaluation criteria assumes that all generated sentences are linguistically incorrect. In this paper, we make two contributions

1. We found that generated sentences with only one modification from the ground truth could be linguistically correct, violating the assumption that such sentences are negative examples. This poses a problem both during training and evaluation. To alleviate this problem, we propose to generate sentences with at least two edits from the ground truth, and

Proceedings of the 2021 EMNLP Workshop W-NUT: The Seventh Workshop on Noisy User-generated Text, pages 81–86
November 11, 2021. ©2021 Association for Computational Linguistics

2. We fine-tuned multi-lingual BERT (mBERT) to improve their published results on their data set. We also experimented with a second English and Chinese (EN-ZH) CS data set.

2 Related Work

The phenomenon of CS is well studied in linguistics (e.g. Poplack, 2000). Earlier work often focus on EN-ES code-switching, studying minorities who claim Spanish as their mother tongue in the English-speaking America. Today, there is also much interest in the Indian languages code-switched with English, due to the large number of Indians using social media (e.g. Khanuja et al., 2020a; Gupta et al., 2021). Recently, researchers in Singapore have collected a CS data set of EN and ZH (Lyu et al., 2010), reflecting the EN-ZH bilingual culture in Singapore and Malaysia.

Research on CS often focuses on downstream NLP tasks: Khanuja et al. (2020b) built a data set called GlueCos to evaluate NLP performance on CS data; Winata et al. (2021) examined the effectiveness of multi-lingual embedding such as mBERT on downstream tasks such as part-of-speech tagging. The first EN-ZH LM was designed by Vu et al. (2012) using statistical machine translation techniques. With deep learning, LMs were also trained directly on CS data (Kumar et al., 2020). Luo et al. (2018) trained an end-to-end EN-ZH CS speech recognition models, using a connectionist temporal classification and attention based model. Qin et al. (2020) used data-augmentation with CS data as an approach to facilitate cross-lingual transfer learning. Winata et al. (2019) used a sequence-to-sequence model to generate CS data for data augmentation. Gonen and Goldberg (2019) pre-trained a BiLSTM (Bidirectional Long Short Term Memory) on monolingual data before fine-tuning on CS data. In this paper, we propose to replace this approach by fine-tuning mBERT (Devlin et al., 2019). We show that our model outperformed BiLSTM (Gonen and Goldberg, 2019) on both EN-ES and EN-ZH data.

Gonen and Goldberg (2019) generated alternative sentences with similar phonemes, and assumed that these generated sentences are linguistically incorrect, using them as negative examples in training and evaluation. However, Dautriche et al. (2017) have found that word form similarity increases with semantic similarity across a number of languages. Hence, making a single phonetically similar edit on a ground truth sentence might result in another correct sentence. We propose to constraint generated sentences to have at least 2 differences from the ground truth to reduce this possibility.

- 她/他/它去 airport (she/he/it goes to the airport)
- no i remember seeing the same/sign
- so we brought her some/son ribs so
- i was talking to your mom/ma'am/man

Figure 2: Examples of sentences with alternatives of a single word separated with /. These generated replacements could be correct without more context. The translation for the first CS sentence is provided in brackets.

3 Generating evaluation data sets

We experimented on two data sets: the EN-ES data used in (Gonen and Goldberg, 2019), created from the Bangor Miami Corpus, and the EN-ZH SEAME corpus (Lyu et al., 2010), collected from residents of Singapore and Malaysia who are bilingual in EN and ZH.

To generate sets of alternative monolingual and code-switched sentences, we took the same approach as Gonen and Goldberg (2019). First, we convert a sequence of language tagged words (either CS or monolingual) into a sequence of the matching phonemes (using pronunciation dictionaries); then we decode the sequence of phonemes into new sentences, which include words from either language (possibly both); During decoding, we allow minor changes in the sequence of phonemes to facilitate the differences between the languages. These steps can be easily implemented using composition of finite-state transducers (FSTs). We used the FST provided by (Gonen and Goldberg, 2019) for the EN-ES data. To build the FST for EN-ZH, we obtained word probabilities for Chinese words from the Mandarin Chinese News Text Corpus, while we used the English word probabilities provided by Gonen and Goldberg (2019). We used the jieba tokenizer[2] to segment Chinese words, and mapped the Chinese pinyin provided by CC-CEDICT.[3]

We observed that if we substitute only one word, the altered sentence could sometimes still be linguistically correct. For example, in the CS sen-

[2] https://github.com/fxsjy/jieba

[3] https://www.mdbg.net/chinese/dictionary?page=cedict

tence *"她/他/它去 airport (translated: he/she/it goes to the airport)"*, the three alternative words are different pronouns that have identical pronounciation. We give a few other examples in Figure 2. Hence, we generate alternative sentences with at least two differences from the original sentence. This increased the probability that the generated sentences are linguistically incorrect, so that they serve their purpose as negative sentences both for training and for evaluation. For each sentence, we generated an alternative set that contains monolingual (for both languages) and CS sentences. The FST is not always able to produce sufficient alternatives for a given sentence: if the FST generates less than 5 alternatives for any type, we discard that set. We capped the number of alternatives of each type to 10, and hence each set has at most 30 sentences. We did a train-validation-test set split such that both the validation and test set contain 1,000 alternative sets each. For EN-ES, the training set consists of 1,021 CS sets, 7,171 EN sets, 3,489 ES sets, while for EN-ZH, it contains 20,689 CS sets, 6,515 EN, and 7,050 ZH sets.

4 Discriminative Training

Language models are usually trained generatively to generate positive sentences. Gonen and Goldberg (2019) proposed a discriminative BiLSTM model by training the BiLSTM to discriminate between ground truth positive sentences with synthetically generated negative sentences. They used as their base model a 2-layer BiLSTM using DyNet (Neubig et al., 2017). The objective of their discriminative training was to assign a higher score to ground truth sentences compared to synthetically generated ones. We denote s_0 as the original ground truth sentence, and $\text{alt}(s_0)$ to be the set of alternative sentences generated for s_0. Each sentence is scored using $\text{score}(s) = w \cdot \text{BiLSTM}(s)$, where $w \in \mathbb{R}^n$ is a learnable parameter vector in the model, with n the dimension of the embedding.

The loss function for each alternative set is

$$\sum_{s \in \text{alt}(s_0)} \max(0, \text{WER}(s_0, s) + \text{score}(s) - \text{score}(s_0)), \quad (1)$$

where $\text{WER}(s_0, s)$ is the word-error-rate between sentences s_0 and s. In our experiments, we followed Gonen and Goldberg (2019) and set the dimensions in the hidden BiLSTM to 650, in a 2-layer BiLSTM. Since the transformer based BERT has a bigger model size, we also experimented with a 3-layer BiLSTM, which should increase the capacity of the model. However, we found that adding a layer to BiLSTM did not improve its performance on our data sets.

4.1 Discriminative mBERT

As BERT (Devlin et al., 2019) has shown to work well for many linguistic tasks, we propose to replace the BiLSTM with the pre-trained multi-lingual BERT (mBERT). mBERT was pre-trained on the entire Wikipedia dump for 104 languages, including English and Chinese. The mBERT embedding for the sentence is the hidden state of the [CLS] token, with a dimension of 768.

We implemented our approach using the Huggingface transformers library (Wolf et al., 2020), which provides a collection of pre-trained models. We fine-tuned the pre-trained multi-lingual BERT models provided by this library, with the same loss function as Equation 1. We experimented with different networks on the mBERT embedding, such as using 1, 2 and 3 linear layers, as well as using LayerNorm or ReLU on the layers.

5 Experimental Results

In this section, we describe the empirical comparison between BiLSTM and mBERT on the two data sets, and analyze the results.

We experimented with different versions of BiLSTM on the EN-ZH data. For the monolingual data sets, we experimented with using (1) only the alternative sets generated from SEAME, (2) only the alternative sets from Mandarin Chinese News Text Corpus and OpenSubtitles, and (3) all of the above. We obtained the best results with (3). Using a 3-layer BiLSTM did not improve results, which could be due to insufficient training data.

We compare the different versions of mBERT in Table 1. We observe that the models that use 2 linear layers over the mBERT embedding performed the best among the mBERT models. As the results obtained by the variants of mBERT is close, we compare the results of the 2-layer mBERT model with its LayerNorm and ReLU variants, using the McNemar statistical test (Smith and Ruxton, 2020). We found that the results are not significantly different at the p-value of 0.05.

For the EN-ES data, we follow closely the setup of Gonen and Goldberg (2019). Results are shown in Table 2. We re-run the code released by Gonen

Model	Validation				Test			
	CS	EN	ZH	All	CS	EN	ZH	All
BiLSTM	94.50	90.60	91.70	92.27	94.90	92.40	91.40	92.90
$w \cdot h$	98.30	95.80	94.10	96.07	98.60	95.60	95.30	96.50
+ LayerNorm	98.20	95.90	94.60	96.23	98.00	95.50	94.80	96.10
+ ReLU	98.20	95.70	94.70	96.20	98.10	95.90	96.40	96.80
$w_2(w_1 \cdot h + b)$	97.70	96.30	95.10	96.37	98.40	96.00	96.10	96.83
+ LayerNorm	98.30	96.40	95.10	**96.60**	98.50	96.40	95.40	96.77
+ ReLU	98.10	95.90	95.20	96.40	98.70	97.10	95.30	**97.03**
$w_3 \cdot (w_2 \cdot (w_1 \cdot h + b_1) + b_2)$	98.10	94.60	95.10	95.93	98.50	96.10	96.10	96.90
+ LayerNorm	98.10	95.80	94.50	96.13	98.40	95.50	95.80	96.57
+ ReLU	98.10	95.90	94.80	96.27	98.80	95.30	95.80	96.63

Table 1: Results of mBERT with discriminative finetuning for 5 epochs on the EN-ZH data set.

Model	Validation				Test			
	CS	EN	ES	All	CS	EN	ES	All
BiLSTM	71.20	88.82	83.13	83.00	69.60	87.22	82.10	81.50
$w \cdot h$	84.40	94.81	85.94	90.00	82.80	94.73	84.82	89.20
+ LayerNorm	84.40	95.61	85.50	90.30	79.20	94.93	82.49	89.20
+ ReLU	84.00	95.81	85.94	90.40	84.80	95.54	85.99	90.40
$w_2(w_1 \cdot h + b)$	84.40	96.61	84.71	90.60	83.60	96.35	82.88	90.40
+ LayerNorm	85.60	95.81	84.74	90.50	85.60	96.12	84.44	**90.50**
+ ReLU	83.60	96.41	83.13	89.90	79.60	96.35	84.82	89.20
$w_3 \cdot (w_2 \cdot (w_1 \cdot h + b_1) + b_2)$	85.60	96.01	85.54	**90.80**	83.20	96.35	85.99	90.40
+ LayerNorm	83.60	95.41	83.13	89.40	81.20	96.35	81.32	88.70
+ ReLU	82.80	95.21	84.34	89.40	84.80	95.13	84.05	89.70

Table 2: Results of mBERT with discriminative finetuning for 5 epochs on the EN-ES data set.

Language (model)	Validation set	Test set
CS (mBERT)	97.17	97.53
EN (mBERT)	93.70	92.90
EN (BERT)	**95.70**	**95.90**
ZH (mBERT)	94.00	93.40
ZH (BERT)	**96.30**	**95.50**

Table 3: Results of monolingual BERT (bert-large-uncased-whole-word-masking and hfl/chinese-bert-wwm-ext), and mBERT (bert-base-multilingual-cased) models on instances with 30 alternatives per set.

Rank of average scores	Validation set			Test set		
	CS	EN	ZH	CS	EN	ZH
CS>EN>ZH	174	293	7	165	304	5
CS>ZH>EN	428	15	199	465	27	209
EN>CS>ZH	74	619	4	63	588	6
EN>ZH>CS	12	32	4	12	38	1
ZH>CS>EN	287	18	763	284	20	764
ZH>EN>CS	25	23	23	11	23	15

Table 4: Count of the ranks of scores of alternative sentences using mBERT with $w_2 \cdot (w_1 \cdot h + b)$.

and Goldberg (2019) on our generated data sets where alternative sentences are generated with at least 2 differences from the ground truth. We arrive at the same conclusions as before: mBERT does better than BiLSTM, and the different variants of our mBERT models achieved similar results.

5.1 Discussion

Monolingual BERT vs mBERT: we investigate using monolingual BERT instead of mBERT for monolingual only test sets. Table 3 shows that, while the EN and ZH BERT models outperform mBERT, mBERT does reasonably well on both EN and ZH only data, showing that mBERT is robust even on monolingual data, and could be the preferred model on user-created content which might include any CS data.

Ranking of alternative sentences of different types: From Table 4, we can observe that (i) the scores of sentences of the same language as the ground truth are higher, (ii) when the ground truth is monolingual, the CS sentences are often scored higher than sentences of the other language. This makes sense as generated CS alternatives can still retain words and grammatical structure from the original sentence, while sentences in the other language would need to have all words generated, and (iii) ZH alternatives are ranked higher than EN alternatives for CS sentences. This could be due to the fact that in the SEAME data, the main language is ZH and the switch to EN was often just for one word or phrase (Lyu et al., 2010).

6 Conclusion

In this work, we proposed to modify the evaluation of language models proposed by Gonen and Goldberg (2019). While the evaluation proposed by Gonen and Goldberg (2019) provided for a simple approach to intrinsic evaluation of language models for ASR, we highlighted the problem of using linguistically correct sentences as negative examples, introducing noise both in the training and in the evaluation process. We proposed a simple solution to this problem by requiring a minimum edit distance between the generated samples and the ground truth. In addition, we showed that mBERT outperforms BiLSTM on two code-switching data sets using this evaluation criteria.

Acknowledgments

The work was conducted while the first author is doing an internship at the DSO National Laboratories.

References

Stanley F Chen, Douglas Beeferman, and Roni Rosenfeld. 1998. Evaluation metrics for language models.

Isabelle Dautriche, Kyle Mahowald, Edward Gibson, and Steven T Piantadosi. 2017. Wordform similarity increases with semantic similarity: An analysis of 100 languages. *Cognitive science*, 41(8):2149–2169.

Jacob Devlin, Ming-Wei Chang, Kenton Lee, and Kristina Toutanova. 2019. Bert: Pre-training of deep bidirectional transformers for language understanding. In *Proceedings of the 2019 Conference of the North American Chapter of the Association for Computational Linguistics: Human Language Technologies, Volume 1 (Long and Short Papers)*, page 4171–4186, Minneapolis, Minnesota. Proceedings of the 2019 Conference of the North American Chapter of the Association for Computational Linguistics: Human Language Technologies, Volume 1 (Long and Short Papers), Association for Computational Linguistics.

Hila Gonen and Yoav Goldberg. 2019. Language modeling for code-switching: Evaluation, integration of monolingual data, and discriminative training. In *Proceedings of the 2019 Conference on Empirical Methods in Natural Language Processing and the 9th International Joint Conference on Natural Language Processing (EMNLP-IJCNLP)*, pages 4166–4176.

Akshat Gupta, Sai Krishna Rallabandi, and Alan Black. 2021. Task-specific pre-training and cross lingual transfer for code-switched data.

Simran Khanuja, Sandipan Dandapat, Sunayana Sitaram, and Monojit Choudhury. 2020a. A new dataset for natural language inference from code-mixed conversations. In *Proceedings of the The 4th Workshop on Computational Approaches to Code Switching*, pages 9–16, Marseille, France. European Language Resources Association.

Simran Khanuja, Sandipan Dandapat, Anirudh Srinivasan, Sunayana Sitaram, and Monojit Choudhury. 2020b. Gluecos: An evaluation benchmark for code-switched nlp. *arXiv preprint arXiv:2004.12376*.

V. Kumar, S. Pasari, V. P. Patil, and S. Seniaray. 2020. Machine learning based language modelling of code switched data. In *2020 International Conference on Electronics and Sustainable Communication Systems (ICESC)*, pages 552–557.

Ne Luo, Dongwei Jiang, Shuaijiang Zhao, Caixia Gong, Wei Zou, and Xiangang Li. 2018. Towards end-to-end code-switching speech recognition. In *INTERSPEECH*. INTERSPEECH.

Dau-Cheng Lyu, Tien-Ping Tan, Eng-Siong Chng, and Haizhou Li. 2010. Seame: a mandarin-english code-switching speech corpus in south-east asia. In *INTERSPEECH*. INTERSPEECH.

Graham Neubig, Chris Dyer, Yoav Goldberg, Austin Matthews, Waleed Ammar, Antonios Anastasopoulos, Miguel Ballesteros, David Chiang, Daniel Clothiaux, Trevor Cohn, Kevin Duh, Manaal Faruqui, Cynthia Gan, Dan Garrette, Yangfeng Ji, Lingpeng Kong, Adhiguna Kuncoro, Gaurav Kumar, Chaitanya Malaviya, Paul Michel, Yusuke Oda, Matthew Richardson, Naomi Saphra, Swabha Swayamdipta, and Pengcheng Yin. 2017. Dynet: The dynamic neural network toolkit. *arXiv preprint arXiv:1701.03980*.

Shana Poplack. 2000. Sometimes i' ll start a sentence in spanish y termino en español: Toward a typology of code-switching. *The bilingualism reader*, 18(2):221–256.

Libo Qin, Minheng Ni, Yue Zhang, and Wanxiang Che. 2020. Cosda-ml: Multi-lingual code-switching data augmentation for zero-shot cross-lingual nlp. In *Proceedings of the Twenty-Ninth International Joint Conference on Artificial Intelligence, IJCAI-20*, pages 3853–3860. International Joint Conferences on Artificial Intelligence Organization. Main track.

Matilda Q. R. Pembury Smith and Graeme D. Ruxton. 2020. Effective use of the mcnemar test. *Behavioral Ecology and Sociobiology*, 74:133.

N. T. Vu, D. Lyu, J. Weiner, D. Telaar, T. Schlippe, F. Blaicher, E. Chng, T. Schultz, and H. Li. 2012. A first speech recognition system for mandarin-english code-switch conversational speech. In *2012 IEEE International Conference on Acoustics, Speech and Signal Processing (ICASSP)*, pages 4889–4892.

Genta Indra Winata, Samuel Cahyawijaya, Zihan Liu, Zhaojiang Lin, Andrea Madotto, and Pascale Fung. 2021. Are multilingual models effective in code-switching? *arXiv preprint arXiv:2103.13309*.

Genta Indra Winata, Andrea Madotto, Chien-Sheng Wu, and Pascale Fung. 2019. Code-switched language models using neural based synthetic data from parallel sentences. In *Proceedings of the 23rd Conference on Computational Natural Language Learning (CoNLL)*, pages 271–280, Hong Kong, China. Association for Computational Linguistics.

Thomas Wolf, Lysandre Debut, Victor Sanh, Julien Chaumond, Clement Delangue, Anthony Moi, Pierric Cistac, Tim Rault, Rémi Louf, Morgan Funtowicz, Joe Davison, Sam Shleifer, Patrick von Platen, Clara Ma, Yacine Jernite, Julien Plu, Canwen Xu, Teven Le Scao, Sylvain Gugger, Mariama Drame, Quentin Lhoest, and Alexander M. Rush. 2020. Transformers: State-of-the-art natural language processing. In *Proceedings of the 2020 Conference on Empirical Methods in Natural Language Processing: System Demonstrations*, page 38–45, Online. Proceedings of the 2020 Conference on Empirical Methods in Natural Language Processing: System Demonstrations, Association for Computational Linguistics.

W. Quin Yow, Jessica S. H. Tan, and Suzanne Flynn. 2018. Code-switching as a marker of linguistic competence in bilingual children. *Bilingualism: Language and Cognition*, 21:1075–1090.

Can images help recognize entities? A study of the role of images for Multimodal NER

Shuguang Chen †, **Gustavo Aguilar** †, **Leonardo Neves** * and **Thamar Solorio** †
University of Houston †
Snap Inc. *
{schen52, gaguilaralas, tsolorio}@uh.edu†
lneves@snap.com*

Abstract

Multimodal named entity recognition (MNER) requires to bridge the gap between language understanding and visual context. While many multimodal neural techniques have been proposed to incorporate images into the MNER task, the model's ability to leverage multimodal interactions remains poorly understood. In this work, we conduct in-depth analyses of existing multimodal fusion techniques from different perspectives and describe the scenarios where adding information from the image does not always boost performance. We also study the use of captions as a way to enrich the context for MNER. Experiments on three datasets from popular social platforms expose the bottleneck of existing multimodal models and the situations where using captions is beneficial. [1]

1 Introduction

Traditional Named Entity Recognition(NER) on social platforms has been studied mainly using text (Strauss et al., 2016; Derczynski et al., 2017; Aguilar et al., 2018). With the increase in popularity of platforms like Twitter, Instagram, and Snapchat, where users can create multimedia posts, images and text are frequently used together. This trend enables the use of images to improve current NER systems. Given a pair of text and image, the Multimodal NER(MNER) task's goal is to identify and classify named entities in the text.

Current work in MNER mainly focuses on the alignment between words and image regions and the fusion of textual information and visual context. Recent successful architectures for MNER mainly rely on attention mechanisms combined with different fusion techniques (Moon et al., 2018; Zhang et al., 2018; Lu et al., 2018; Arshad et al., 2019; Asgari-Chenaghlu et al., 2020; Yu et al., 2020). However, we observe that incorporating images in MNER is not trivial. There are two critical but often neglected aspects in the prior art: The first is the assumption that images and text are aligned. As discussed in (Lu et al., 2018), MNER models are sensitive to errors when images are added to convey irony or abstract concepts instead of illustrating what is in the text. The second aspect is the semantic density (Desai and Johnson, 2020) of the visual context information. Named entities are too specific since they are instances of general entities. On the contrary, the information provided by automatic image processing models is too general. For example, MNER models frequently use the output of convolutional neural networks (CNNs) trained on image classification tasks as the image's representation. Linking such specific entities with more general information from images demands a giant leap for the models to fill in the semantic gap. Thus, we speculate that MNER would benefit more from semantically dense learning signals like image captions instead of image classification.

In this work, we take a step further towards understanding the behavior of multimodal models for the MNER task. We first analyze the existing multimodal fusion techniques with both unimodal and multimodal transformer-based sequence labeling models. We investigate three different ways to represent images: global image features from image classification algorithms, regional image features from object detection algorithms, and image captions. By conducting experiments that emphasize the contribution of different image representations, we demonstrate the effectiveness of using captions to represent images in the MNER task.

To summarize, we make the following contributions:

1. We conduct detailed analyses of multimodal fusion techniques from state-of-the-art MNER models with both unimodal and multimodal transformer-based sequence labeling frame-

[1] We release the code at `https://github.com/RiTUAL-UH/multimodal_NER`.

Proceedings of the 2021 EMNLP Workshop W-NUT: The Seventh Workshop on Noisy User-generated Text, pages 87–96
November 11, 2021. ©2021 Association for Computational Linguistics

work and expose the bottleneck of existing approaches in terms of multimodal fusion.

2. We study an alternative approach to incorporate images in MNER. We use captions to represent images as text and adapt transformer-based sequence labeling models to connect multimodal information.
3. We provide empirical evidence to expose the situations where incorporating images is beneficial for the MNER task.

2 Related work

As more and more social media data contains text and images, the multimodal NER task has attracted increased research interest. Most of the recent methods for this task have been introduced using attention-guided models to extract visual information related to the named entities (Moon et al. (2018), Zhang et al. (2018), Arshad et al. (2019)). Despite showing promising results, these methods have two main limitations: ignoring mapping relations between visual objects and named entities, and the distribution differences between images and text. This can lead to incorrect visual context clues being extracted when the images and texts are not relevant, which is not uncommon in social media data. Zheng et al. (2020) addresses these problems by proposing a neural network to better exploit visual and textual information. However, their results revealed that their model remains to extract entities incorrectly when visual objects cannot reveal the label semantics of entities. To address the problem of semantic disparity between different modalities, Wu et al. (2020) chooses to transform object labels into word embeddings. Their dense co-attention module introduced can take the inter- and intra-connections between visual objects and textual entities into account, which helps extract entities more precisely. Sun et al. (2020) introduced a pre-trained multimodal language model based on Relationship Inference and Visual Attention (RIVA) for tweets, and a gated visual context based on text-image relation. Sun et al. (2021) proposed a text-image relation propagation-based multimodal BERT model (RpBERT) to reduce the interference from irrelevant images, which effectively resolved failed cases mentioned in previous work (Lu et al. (2018); Arshad et al. (2019); Yu et al. (2020)).

Recent advances in large pre-trained models (Lu et al., 2019; Tan and Bansal, 2019) have led to significant performance gains in many multimodal tasks (e.g, visual question answering). However, most of these techniques are pre-trained on image captioning or visual question answering datasets where multimodal interactions are required. Applying these techniques to the MNER task may not result in a good performance. There some significant differences between the those task and the MNER task. We argue that in the MNER we can have three possible scenarios: 1) images and text are not related and thus we don't expect the image information to help; 2) images and text are related and adding image information is helpful and 3) images and text are related but adding the image information does not help the MNER task. Therefore, before our work, it was not clear whether adding image captions would contribute to the performance. In contrast, in the visual question answering or visual commonsense reasoning task, the images are relevant and needed in order to answer the questions, and therefore, using captions is more likely to yield good results. These differences in the scenarios warrant further investigation.

3 Methodology

In this work, we study how to represent images and how to fuse different modalities in MNER. We explore three different ways to represent images in different levels of semantic density. Then we adapt a unimodal transformer BERT (Devlin et al., 2019) and a multimodal transformer VisualBERT (Li et al., 2019) as base models. To fuse textual information with visual information, we investigate four different approaches for multimodal fusion.

3.1 Image Representation

We explore three different ways to represent images in order of semantic density: i) global image features to represent the whole image using image classification that assigns each image with a single class, ii) regional image features to represent objects in the image using object detection that increases semantic density by labeling multiple objects, and iii) image captions to represent the semantics of the image, including object mentions, properties, and actions, to provide semantically dense learning signals.

Global image features We extract feature vectors from ResNet (He et al., 2016) as global image features to represent the whole image. Given an image I, we first rescaled the image to 224×224

pixels. Then we retrieve the feature vectors V_I from the last convolutional layer. Each image is represented in 7×7 visual region. The dimension of each visual region is 2048. Then we use a linear transformation to project image features into the same embedding space of word representation.

Regional image features Global image features provide a weak learning signal as they only describe the category of each image. We observed that some visual information in global image features is not related to the named entities in the text and may end up hurting the performance of the model by introducing noise. Therefore, we represent visual information using feature vectors from the object detection algorithm Faster-RCNN (Ren et al., 2015) to further provide more semantic density. Give an image I, we extract feature vectors from Faster-RCNN's regions of interest (RoI). The dimension of each RoI is 1024.

Image captions In addition to visual information, we also consider semantic information by using captions as a way to represent images. Compared to image classification and object detection, captions provide more semantic content as it gives a description on object's attribute, properties, and actions. In this work, we generate captions to represent images using the BUTD model (Anderson et al., 2018). Captions can summarize the image's semantics in well-formed text. In our experiments, we feed captions to pre-trained transformer-based models to enrich the models' semantic information.

3.2 Base Models

BERT BERT is a transformer-based model. It is pre-trained using masked language modeling objectives on the text from the general domain. To incorporate images, we study two different ways: global image features and image captions. For global image features, we use BERT to generate textual representation and leverage a multimodal fusion module to fuse text and images. For image captions, we feed both text and captions into BERT to enrich the model's semantic information. We put a CRF layer on the top of BERT to classify entities.

VisualBERT Following Li et al. (2019), we utilize VisualBERT to generate a joint representation for both text and images. VisualBERT takes a sentence and a set of RoI features as input. It is pre-trained using two objectives: i) masked language modeling with the image, and ii) sentence-image prediction. In objective i), some textual elements are masked and predicted according to unmasked textual elements and visual elements. In objective ii), two captions are provided and the model is pre-trained to distinguish whether the captions are describing the image or not. These two objectives make VisualBERT a strong encoder for language and vision tasks. Given a sentence and image pair, we first extract feature vectors of RoIs from object detection and feed them along with sentences into VisualBERT in a single-stream way. The model thus can align textual elements and visual elements based on transformer attention. We apply a CRF as the classifier to predict labels for each sentence.

3.3 Multimodal Fusion

Here, we introduce four multimodal fusion modules: 1) Concatenation Module, 2) Visual Attention Module, 3) Co-Attention Module, and 4) Transformer Attention Module, described as follows:

Concatenation Module (CM) We implement a concatenation module to merge multimodal information and learn a unified representation for words, characters, and images. At each decoding time step t, we first project word feature vectors $x_t^{(w)}$, character feature vectors $x_t^{(c)}$ and image feature vectors $x_t^{(v)}$ so that they can have the same dimension. Then, we concatenate these three vectors as the multimodal representation.

Visual Attention Module (VAM) Following Lu et al. (2018), we implement a visual attention module that consists of an attention module for modality alignment and a gated fusion module for multimodal information fusion. In the attention module, we use LSTM to encode all words into a text query vector. Then we project the text query vector and the visual feature vectors into the same dimension and align textual elements and visual elements based on an attention mechanism. To fuse textual information and visual information, a gated fusion module is applied to determine how much textual and visual information should attend in prediction.

Co-Attention Module (CAM) We implement the co-attention module following Zhang et al. (2018). This module contains four components: 1) word-guided visual attention, 2) image-guided textual attention, 3) gated multimodal fusion, and 4) filtration gate. Word-guided visual attention module takes the whole image features and a word h_t as input and generates textual attention based on

ID	Model	Twitter-2015			Twitter-2017		
		Precision	Recall	F1	Precision	Recall	F1
Unimodal Baseline (Text only)							
Exp 1.1	BERT + CRF	69.37	73.73	71.48	83.62	87.33	85.44
Exp 1.2	VisualBERT + CRF	67.37	71.58	69.41	82.54	85.31	83.90
Multimodal fusion with global image features							
Exp 2.1	BERT + CM + CRF	70.40	72.56	71.46	85.42	87.41	86.40
Exp 2.2	BERT + VAM + CRF	67.41	72.37	69.80	84.97	85.71	85.34
Exp 2.3	BERT + CAM + CRF	69.53	74.04	71.71	84.78	86.66	85.71
Multimodal fusion with regional image features							
Exp 3.1	VisualBERT + TAM + CRF	68.84	71.39	70.09	84.06	85.39	84.72
Multimodal fusion with image captions							
Exp 4.1	BERT + CRF + Captions†	68.52	74.61	71.49	**86.16**	**87.49**	**86.82**
Exp 4.2	VisualBERT + CRF + Captions†	66.99	72.68	69.71	84.14	85.71	84.92
Comparison with SOTA							
Yu et al. (2020)		**71.67**	**75.23**	**73.41**	85.28	85.34	85.31

Table 1: The results of transformer-based sequence labeling experiments. CM, VAM, CAM and TAM refer to concatenation module, visual attention module, co-attention module and transformer attention module, respectively. The boldface numbers are the best results in each column. † indicates that the difference between the model and the unimodal baseline is proved to be statistically significant with p-values < 0.05 in the paired t-test.

visual information. Since typically a word only corresponds to a small region in the image, this step is to decide which image regions should attend in prediction. Then image-guided textual attention module determines which words in the text are most relevant to word h_t. The Gated multimodal fusion module and filtration gate are used to control the combination of information from different modalities and filter out the image noise.

Transformer Attention Module (TAM) To align textual elements in the sentence and visual elements in the image, we use the transformer attention mechanism within the Transformer. We follow Li et al. (2019) to incorporate image features into the model. The image embeddings are passed to the model along with word embeddings, allowing the model to align words with image regions and learn a unified multimodal representation.

4 Datasets

In this work, we use three datasets for evaluation in our experiments: Twitter-2015 from Zhang et al. (2018), Twitter-2017 from Lu et al. (2018), and a Snapchat dataset collected from Snapchat posts for this study. Due to the weak relatedness between named entities and images in two Twitter datasets, multimodal architectures are not superior to unimodal ones. Therefore, we create a new multimodal dataset for further study based on Snapchat posts since text and images from Snapchat are highly related. The Snapchat dataset is composed of text and image pairs exclusively extracted from snaps submitted to the public and crowd-sourced stories (aka "Our Stories") and is labeled by expert human annotators (entity types: PER, LOC, ORG, MISC). Examples of such public crowd-sourced stories are the "Airpods Everywhere Story" or the "Thanksgiving Story", which comprise snaps that are aggregated for various public themes and events. All snaps were posted between January and March 2020. Table 2 summarizes the data statistics.

Both Twitter and Snapchat are popular social platforms that allow for multimodal posts but there are marked differences in how users rely on images and text in these two media. In Twitter, most users default to use only text. Based on statistics of a random sample of 1M tweets, only 22% of tweets contain images. However, on Snapchat, the most important part of the snaps is the visual content: often Snapchat users do not even include any text at all. As shown in Table 2, snaps have significantly less text than the two Twitter datasets.

Dataset	Train	Dev	Test	Avg length (characters)
Twitter-2015	4,000	1,000	3,257	95
Twitter-2017	4,290	1,432	1,459	64
Snapchat	2,636	753	376	37

Table 2: Size of the datasets in numbers of tweets/snaps. Twitter-2015 dataset and Twitter-2017 dataset are from Zhang et al. (2018) and Lu et al. (2018) respectively.

5 Experiment and analysis

This section empirically diagnoses the multimodal interactions from the relatedness between different modalities and the semantic density from images. Then we explore the role of images in the MNER task in both low-context and low-resource scenarios to expose the situations where incorporating images is beneficial. We also diagnose the model's ability to disambiguate and generalize.

5.1 Diagnosing the multimodal interactions

Modeling multimodal interactions is computationally expensive because the number of model parameters is large. In this case, the improvement in performance with images may be due to the large model capacity instead of multimodal interactions (Hessel and Lee, 2020). The model's ability to leverage multimodal interactions is usually evaluated by comparing multimodal models with unimodal models. Despite its effectiveness, this evaluation approach fails to explicitly reflect whether the model exploits multimodal signals or just text signals, especially in the presence of a strong text-based model. Driven by this, we do experiments on three datasets to diagnose the model's ability to leverage multimodal interactions. The experiments are defined as follows:

Experimental Setup To better compare different methods, we first establish two baseline models that take only text as input: 1) Exp 1.1 *BERT + CRF*, a variant of BERT (Devlin et al., 2019) by replacing the classifier with a CRF layer, and 2) Exp 1.2 *VisualBERT + CRF*, a variant of VisualBERT (Li et al., 2019) with a CRF as classifier. Then we investigate multimodal fusion with different image representations. For global image features from image classification, we consider three multimodal models: 3) Exp 2.1 *BERT + CM + CRF* using concatenation module for multimodal fusion, 4) Exp 2.2 *BERT + VAM + CRF* with visual attention module (Lu et al., 2018) to fuse text and images, and 5) Exp 2.3 *BERT + CAM + CRF* using co-attention module (Zhang et al., 2018) to generate multimodal representations. For the regional image features from object detection, we establish 6) Exp 3.1 *VisualBERT + TAM +CRF* to fuse different modalities with transformer-attention. For the image captions, we further consider two multimodal models that take both text and captions as input: 7) Exp 4.1) *BERT + CRF + Captions* and 8) Exp 4.2) *VisualBERT + CRF + Captions*.

@ClaytonTJones talking about our music school @createvation USA. Featured on HomeTownKids . TV airing on Fox**[B-ORG]** !

@ClaytonTJones talking about our music school @createvation USA. Featured on HomeTownKids . TV airing on Fox**[B-OTHER]** !

(a)

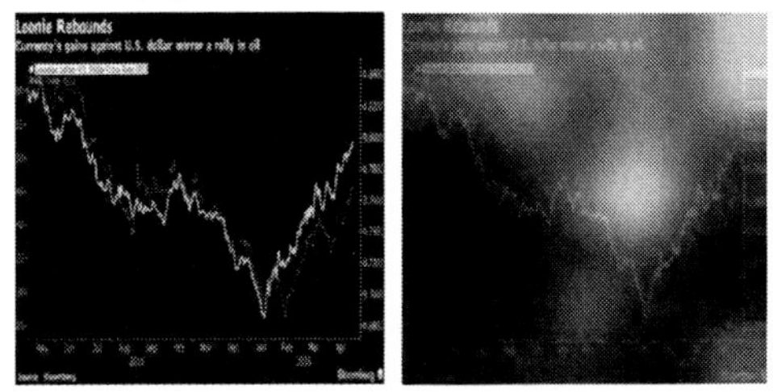

business: Forget Justin **[B-PER]** Trudeau **[I-PER]**, it's oil that's driving this loonie rally

business: Forget Justin **[B-MISC]** Trudeau **[I-MISC]**, it's oil that's driving this loonie rally

(b)

Figure 1: Attention visualization from *BERT + VAM + CRF*. Left side is gold while right side is prediction.

We optimize our models using AdamW (Loshchilov and Hutter, 2019) with an initial learning rate 5e-5 and a learning rate scheduler (Devlin et al., 2019). We set weight decay 0.01 and batch size 32. The dropout rate is 0.1 and the hidden size is 768. We also use a gradient clipping of 1.0.

Results In Table 1, we compare different fusion techniques on both Twitter-2015 and Twitter-2017 datasets by reporting precision, recall, and F1 achieved by each model. Based on the results, we observe that: 1) Incorporating images do not always boost performance. Even with the strong multimodal model *VisualBERT*, which has a considerable expressive capacity to model multimodal interactions, the improvement with images is still marginal (e.g, Exp 1.2 V.S. Exp 3.1). 2) Complex multimodal fusion modules do not always improve performance. Simply concatenating textual information and visual information in the concatenation module (Exp 2.1) is more effective than attention-based fusion modules, e.g, visual attention module (Exp 2.2) and co-attention module (Exp 2.3). 3) Comparing models with different fu-

Image	Sentence	Prediction (GC)	Prediction (CC)
	**Text**: Coach Carraci with the infield # pepsibaseball # baberuth **Generated Captions**: a group of baseball players standing on a field **Crafted Captions**: a group of baseball players standing together listening to their coach in a baseball field	Carraci	Carraci
	**Text**: @ NottmWildcats and @ TN_Basketball take to the floor to warm up for the WBBL Playoff Final here at @ TheO2 **Generated Captions**: a crowd of people watching a game of tennis **Crafted Captions**: a basketball court with people waiting for the basketball game, while the basketball players warm up	NottmWildcats TN_Basketball WBBL TheO2	NottmWildcats TN_Basketball WBBL TheO2

Table 3: Comparison between the generated captions (GC) and the crafted captions (CC) using *BERT + CRF + Captions*. Different colors indicate different entity types: blue for person, yellow for organization, and red for location. When provided a caption with richer details (CC), the model is able to correctly predict the entity.

sion techniques, using captions to represent images can achieve higher performance (e.g, Exp 1.1 V.S. Exp 4.1). Using global image features requires the model to filter out the noise introduced by images. Meanwhile, using regional image features to represent objects is also not superior as the objects are too general to be connected with specific named entities. 4) The performance of the unimodal model *BERT + CRF* is either comparable or superior to what was previously reported on those datasets. Note that these models predate BERT. A strong text-based model then seems to dominate, and the models tend to ignore the signals from the image modality. We assume that providing all the image information is more detrimental than beneficial to the model. We should emphasize this might be the case for datasets like Twitter, where the main content usually comes from the text itself.

Additionally, we also compare our best model *BERT + CRF + Captions* with existing state-of-the-art work. With minimum effort, our approach achieves a comparable result against the complex fusion-method from Yu et al. (2020) on Twitter-2015 dataset. On Twitter-2017 dataset, our best model *BERT + CRF + Caption* can achieve 86.82% F1 score, outperforming Yu et al. (2020) by 1.51% F1 score. Further, we run experiments on the Snapchat dataset, a more image-centric platform. As shown in Table 4, we find *BERT + CRF + Caption* (Exp 4.1) moderately outperforms *BERT + CRF* (Exp 1.1) by up over 1% in dev set and 0.61% in test, showing that using captions to represent images is a competitive approach.

ID	Model	Snapchat dataset	
		Dev F1	Test F1
Exp 1.1	BERT + CRF	50.30	50.57
Exp 4.1	BERT + CRF + Caption†	**51.61**	**51.18**

Table 4: The results on Snapchat dataset. † indicates that the difference between the model and the unimodal baseline is proved to be statistically significant with p-values < 0.05 in the paired t-test.

Model	Description	Twitter-2017	
		Dev F1	Test F1
BERT + CRF + Caption	Generated captions	59.16	64.61
BERT + CRF + Caption	Corrected captions	**64.08**	**66.90**

Table 5: Comparison of model performance on the generated captions the corrected captions.

Image-entity relation Based on sequence labeling experiments, we observe that images are not always helpful. We assume this is due to the weak relatedness between entities and images, and the gap in semantic representation from images and text. Figure 1 shows two examples of the results and attention visualization from *BERT + VAM + CRF* (Exp 2.2). In example (a), even though the model focuses on reasonable image regions, the visual signal is unable to represent an abstract concept like what seems to be an ongoing TV interview from the 'Fox' network (entity). In example (b), the image is not directly related to the entity 'Justin Trudeau' and, therefore, can only introduce noise when used by the model.

Impact of caption quality In our experiments, even though the model with image captions can

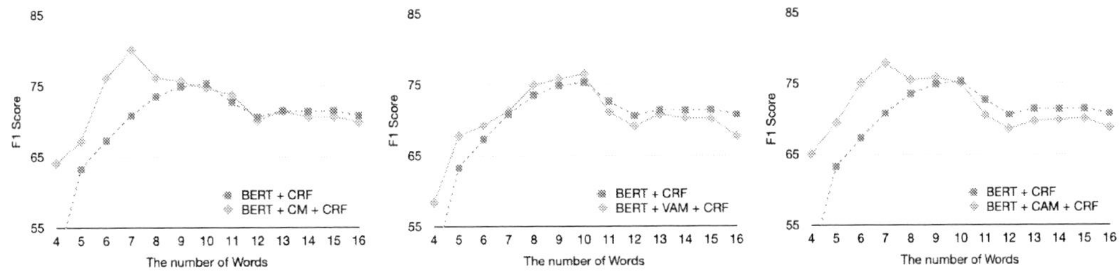

(a) (b) (c)

Figure 2: Impact of sentence length on Twitter-2015 dataset by comparing unimodal baseline model *BERt + CRF* with three multimodal models: a) *BERT + CM +CRF*, b) *BERT + VAM + CRF*, and c) *BERT + CAM + CRF*

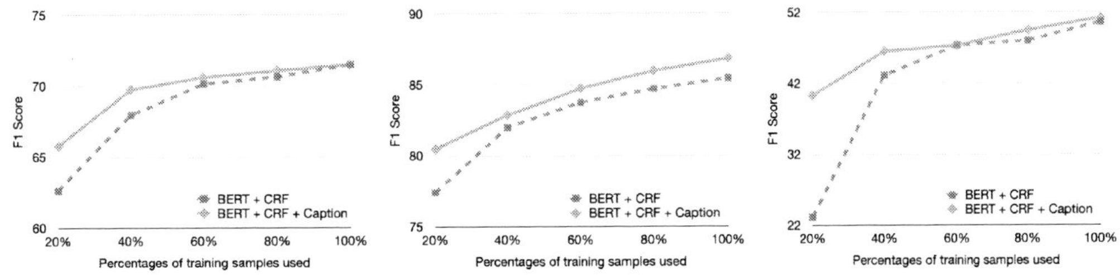

(a) Twitter-2015 dataset (b) Twitter-2017 dataset (c) Snapchat dataset

Figure 3: Impact of increasing training set size on three datasets: a) Twitter-2015 dataset, b) Twitter-2017 dataset, c) Snapchat dataset.

achieve the best performance, we observe that the semantic information coming from images can be further improved since some generated captions are inaccurate or incomprehensible. Table 3 shows two examples of the results and the comparison between the generated captions and the crafted captions. In example (a), the generated caption accurately describes the 'Carraci' entity and thus the model can make correct predictions. However, in example (b), the 'people' in the generated caption misleads the model into making the wrong predictions. Compared to the generated caption, the crafted caption has more semantics about 'NottmWildcats' and 'TN_basketball' and thus the model can predict correctly. Driven by this issue, we attempt to fix captions and boost model performance. We first extract the samples that were correctly predicted by *BERT + CRF* but wrongly predicted by *BERT + CRF + Captions* from Twitter-2017 validation set (76 samples with 152 entities) and test set (68 samples with 145 entities). Then we manually create captions for each image and test models on the data with new captions. The results are shown in Table 5. We find that, once we correct the captions, the model performance is further improved, indicating that inaccurate captions cover up the model's actual ability to leverage information from images.

5.2 Exploring the role of images

In this section, we explore the role of images in both low-context and low-resource scenarios to better understand when incorporating images is beneficial for the MNER task.

Low-context scenario In Figure 2, we analyze how the sentence length impacts the performance of the baseline model *BERT + CRF* (Exp 1.1) and the multimodal model *BERT + VAM + CRF* (Exp1.2). We observe that visual information is more helpful for short sentences. The shortest the sentence, the less context is available. When the model cannot obtain enough semantic context from the text, it gains more from using images. In our experiments, the unimodal model performs much worse than multimodal models on the sentences with no more than seven words. But the plot also indicates that, when enough text is available, the improvements coming from images are marginal and can eventually hurt performance.

ID	Model	Twitter-2015				Twitter-2017			
		Seen	Unseen	Ambiguous	Non-ambiguous	Seen	Unseen	Ambiguous	Non-ambiguous
Unimodal Baseline (Text only)									
Exp 1.1	BERT + CRF	84.74	65.36	63.33	86.03	93.76	76.49	-	-
Exp 1.2	VisualBERT + CRF	83.48	62.52	63.93	84.93	94.13	73.61	-	-
Multimodal fusion with global image features									
Exp 2.1	BERT + CM + CRF	87.21	65.13	66.67	88.82	94.72	77.85	-	-
Exp 2.2	BERT + VAM + CRF	84.40	63.10	71.55	85.37	95.23	75.30	-	-
Exp 2.3	BERT + CAM + CRF	85.27	65.40	65.04	86.73	94.63	76.07	-	-
Multimodal fusion with regional image features									
Exp 3.1	VisualBERT + TAM + CRF	84.42	63.39	61.91	86.00	94.35	75.25	-	-
Multimodal fusion with image captions									
Exp 4.1	BERT + CRF + Captions	86.11	64.35	68.93	87.81	94.90	79.42	-	-
Exp 4.2	VisualBERT + CRF + Captions	83.36	62.94	62.40	84.63	94.58	74.54	-	-

Table 6: The results on seen, unseen, ambiguous and non-ambiguous named entities. For each entity e with a set of label k in test set, seen and unseen named entities refer to the entities appear in the train set with label k and does not appear in the train set with label k, respectively while ambiguous and non-ambiguous named entities refer to the entities appear in the training with diverse labels and with only label k, respectively. Scores are calculated with the F1 metric.

Low-resource scenario We investigate how the size of the training set impacts model performance. As shown in Figure 3, using captions is always either beneficial or equivalent to using just the text, but the benefits decrease as we increase the training set size. The improvement gap is wider on the Snapchat dataset as the length is significantly shorter, and less context can be extracted from the text alone, forcing the model to rely more on the captions. We conclude that it is always worth incorporating captions, but it is especially important in low-resource and low-context scenarios.

5.3 Diagnosing disambiguation and generalization

Disambiguation Intuitively, visual information can help reduce ambiguity, especially for short sentences. Therefore, we investigate the impact of images on disambiguation. For entity e with a set of labels k in test set, if the size of the set k is 1, this is considered as a non-ambiguous entity. Otherwise, if the size is more than 1, it is considered as an ambiguous entity. Due to the limitation of the data size, we only conduct experiments on the Twitter-2015 dataset. The results are shown in Table 6. We observe that the models can perform better on non-ambiguous entities, and it seems they are not powerful enough to distinguish named entities with more than one label. From the table, we also find that the multimodal models are superior to unimodal models on ambiguous entities. We thus conclude that images can help in disambiguation.

Generalization We analyze the impact of images on generalization by considering the mention overlap. We empirically investigate the model performance on seen and unseen named entities. For entity e with a set of label k in the test set, we define the seen and unseen entities as the entities that appeared in the training and the testing with label k, respectively. The results are shown in Table 6. We observe that the models can achieve higher performances on the named entities that previously appeared in the training. The performance drops significantly on unseen named entities, showing that the most improvement when incorporating images comes from seen named entities. We also find that the results of unimodal and multimodal models on unseen named entities are very close. We thus conclude that the existing methods are not sufficient to improve the model's generalization ability.

6 Conclusion

In this work, we systematically analyze the behavior of existing multimodal models for the MNER task. With extensive experiments and analysis based on BERT and VisualBERT, we show that existing fusion techniques can only bring marginal, if any, gains to strong text-only models. We believe this is due to the weak relatedness between named entities and images and the sparse semantic density of visual signals. We then examine the use of image captions as a more semantically dense signal and find promising results, concluding it is always worth adopting this approach as it usually outperforms existing alternatives and is never detrimental to performance. Finally, we investigate multiple scenarios and share our findings of when images can help the MNER task.

Acknowledgements

This work was partially supported by the National Science Foundation (NSF) under grant #1910192. We would like to thank the members from the RiTUAL lab at the University of Houston for their invaluable feedback. We also thank the anonymous W-NUT reviewers for their valuable suggestions.

References

Gustavo Aguilar, Fahad AlGhamdi, Victor Soto, Mona Diab, Julia Hirschberg, and Thamar Solorio. 2018. Named entity recognition on code-switched data: Overview of the CALCS 2018 shared task. In *Proceedings of the Third Workshop on Computational Approaches to Linguistic Code-Switching*, pages 138–147, Melbourne, Australia. Association for Computational Linguistics.

Peter Anderson, Xiaodong He, Chris Buehler, Damien Teney, Mark Johnson, Stephen Gould, and Lei Zhang. 2018. Bottom-up and top-down attention for image captioning and visual question answering. In *2018 IEEE Conference on Computer Vision and Pattern Recognition, CVPR 2018, Salt Lake City, UT, USA, June 18-22, 2018*, pages 6077–6086. IEEE Computer Society.

Omer Arshad, Ignazio Gallo, Shah Nawaz, and Alessandro Calefati. 2019. Aiding intra-text representations with visual context for multimodal named entity recognition. *ArXiv preprint*, abs/1904.01356.

Meysam Asgari-Chenaghlu, M Reza Feizi-Derakhshi, Leili Farzinvash, and Cina Motamed. 2020. A multimodal deep learning approach for named entity recognition from social media. *ArXiv preprint*, abs/2001.06888.

Leon Derczynski, Eric Nichols, Marieke van Erp, and Nut Limsopatham. 2017. Results of the WNUT2017 shared task on novel and emerging entity recognition. In *Proceedings of the 3rd Workshop on Noisy User-generated Text*, pages 140–147, Copenhagen, Denmark. Association for Computational Linguistics.

Karan Desai and Justin Johnson. 2020. Virtex: Learning visual representations from textual annotations. *ArXiv preprint*, abs/2006.06666.

Jacob Devlin, Ming-Wei Chang, Kenton Lee, and Kristina Toutanova. 2019. BERT: Pre-training of deep bidirectional transformers for language understanding. In *Proceedings of the 2019 Conference of the North American Chapter of the Association for Computational Linguistics: Human Language Technologies, Volume 1 (Long and Short Papers)*, pages 4171–4186, Minneapolis, Minnesota. Association for Computational Linguistics.

Kaiming He, Xiangyu Zhang, Shaoqing Ren, and Jian Sun. 2016. Deep residual learning for image recognition. In *2016 IEEE Conference on Computer Vision and Pattern Recognition, CVPR 2016, Las Vegas, NV, USA, June 27-30, 2016*, pages 770–778. IEEE Computer Society.

Jack Hessel and Lillian Lee. 2020. Does my multimodal model learn cross-modal interactions? it's harder to tell than you might think! In *Proceedings of the 2020 Conference on Empirical Methods in Natural Language Processing (EMNLP)*, pages 861–877, Online. Association for Computational Linguistics.

Liunian Harold Li, Mark Yatskar, Da Yin, Cho-Jui Hsieh, and Kai-Wei Chang. 2019. Visualbert: A simple and performant baseline for vision and language. *ArXiv preprint*, abs/1908.03557.

Ilya Loshchilov and Frank Hutter. 2019. Decoupled weight decay regularization. In *7th International Conference on Learning Representations, ICLR 2019, New Orleans, LA, USA, May 6-9, 2019*. OpenReview.net.

Di Lu, Leonardo Neves, Vitor Carvalho, Ning Zhang, and Heng Ji. 2018. Visual attention model for name tagging in multimodal social media. In *Proceedings of the 56th Annual Meeting of the Association for Computational Linguistics (Volume 1: Long Papers)*, pages 1990–1999, Melbourne, Australia. Association for Computational Linguistics.

Jiasen Lu, Dhruv Batra, Devi Parikh, and Stefan Lee. 2019. Vilbert: Pretraining task-agnostic visiolinguistic representations for vision-and-language tasks. In *Advances in Neural Information Processing Systems 32: Annual Conference on Neural Information Processing Systems 2019, NeurIPS 2019, December 8-14, 2019, Vancouver, BC, Canada*, pages 13–23.

Seungwhan Moon, Leonardo Neves, and Vitor Carvalho. 2018. Multimodal named entity recognition for short social media posts. In *Proceedings of the 2018 Conference of the North American Chapter of the Association for Computational Linguistics: Human Language Technologies, Volume 1 (Long Papers)*, pages 852–860, New Orleans, Louisiana. Association for Computational Linguistics.

Shaoqing Ren, Kaiming He, Ross B. Girshick, and Jian Sun. 2015. Faster R-CNN: towards real-time object detection with region proposal networks. In *Advances in Neural Information Processing Systems 28: Annual Conference on Neural Information Processing Systems 2015, December 7-12, 2015, Montreal, Quebec, Canada*, pages 91–99.

Benjamin Strauss, Bethany Toma, Alan Ritter, Marie-Catherine de Marneffe, and Wei Xu. 2016. Results of the WNUT16 named entity recognition shared task. In *Proceedings of the 2nd Workshop on Noisy User-generated Text (WNUT)*, pages 138–144, Osaka, Japan. The COLING 2016 Organizing Committee.

Lin Sun, Jiquan Wang, Yindu Su, Fangsheng Weng, Yuxuan Sun, Zengwei Zheng, and Yuanyi Chen. 2020. RIVA: A pre-trained tweet multimodal model based on text-image relation for multimodal NER. In *Proceedings of the 28th International Conference on Computational Linguistics*, pages 1852–1862, Barcelona, Spain (Online). International Committee on Computational Linguistics.

Lin Sun, Jiquan Wang, Kai Zhang, Yindu Su, Fangsheng Weng, and Zengwei Zheng. 2021. Rpbert: A text-image relation propagation-based bert model for multimodal ner. *ArXiv preprint*, abs/2102.02967.

Hao Tan and Mohit Bansal. 2019. LXMERT: Learning cross-modality encoder representations from transformers. In *Proceedings of the 2019 Conference on Empirical Methods in Natural Language Processing and the 9th International Joint Conference on Natural Language Processing (EMNLP-IJCNLP)*, pages 5100–5111, Hong Kong, China. Association for Computational Linguistics.

Zhiwei Wu, Changmeng Zheng, Yi Cai, Junying Chen, Ho-Fung Leung, and Qing Li 0001. 2020. Multimodal representation with embedded visual guiding objects for named entity recognition in social media posts. In *MM '20: The 28th ACM International Conference on Multimedia, Virtual Event / Seattle, WA, USA, October 12-16, 2020*, pages 1038–1046. ACM.

Jianfei Yu, Jing Jiang, Li Yang, and Rui Xia. 2020. Improving multimodal named entity recognition via entity span detection with unified multimodal transformer. In *Proceedings of the 58th Annual Meeting of the Association for Computational Linguistics*, pages 3342–3352, Online. Association for Computational Linguistics.

Qi Zhang, Jinlan Fu, Xiaoyu Liu, and Xuanjing Huang. 2018. Adaptive co-attention network for named entity recognition in tweets. In *Proceedings of the Thirty-Second AAAI Conference on Artificial Intelligence, (AAAI-18), the 30th innovative Applications of Artificial Intelligence (IAAI-18), and the 8th AAAI Symposium on Educational Advances in Artificial Intelligence (EAAI-18), New Orleans, Louisiana, USA, February 2-7, 2018*, pages 5674–5681. AAAI Press.

Changmeng Zheng, Zhiwei Wu, Tao Wang, Cai Yi, and Qing Li. 2020. Object-aware multimodal named entity recognition in social media posts with adversarial learning. *IEEE Transactions on Multimedia*, pages 1–1.

Perceived and Intended Sarcasm Detection with Graph Attention Networks

Joan Plepi and **Lucie Flek**
Conversational AI and Social Analytics (CAISA) Lab
Department of Mathematics and Computer Science, University of Marburg
http://caisa-lab.github.io

Abstract

Existing sarcasm detection systems focus on exploiting linguistic markers, context, or user-level priors. However, social studies suggest that the relationship between the author and the audience can be equally relevant for the sarcasm usage and interpretation. In this work, we propose a framework jointly leveraging (1) a user context from their historical tweets together with (2) the social information from a user's conversational neighborhood in an interaction graph, to contextualize the interpretation of the post. We use graph attention networks (GAT) over users and tweets in a conversation thread, combined with dense user history representations. Apart from achieving state-of-the-art results on the recently published dataset of 19k Twitter users with 30K labeled tweets, adding 10M unlabeled tweets as context, our results indicate that the model contributes to interpreting the sarcastic intentions of an author more than to predicting the sarcasm perception by others.

1 Introduction

Sarcasm is a form of non-literal language, in which the intended meaning of the utterance differs from the literal meaning, fulfilling a social function in a discourse (Dews et al., 1995; Riloff et al., 2013). Sarcasm detection poses a challenge for numerous NLP tasks, such as sentiment or stance prediction (Maynard and Greenwood, 2014).

Early sarcasm detection systems are based on lexical and syntactic cues (Carvalho et al., 2009; Davidov et al., 2010; Tsur et al., 2010; González-Ibáñez et al., 2011; Reyes et al., 2013; Ghosh et al., 2015). However, sarcasm interpretation requires context, even for humans (Wallace et al., 2014). More recent works hence incorporate discourse information such as contrast (Riloff et al., 2013; Khattri et al., 2015; Joshi et al., 2015; Rajadesingan et al., 2015; Tay et al., 2018), and contextualize the post by using features from user history (Bamman and Smith, 2015; Amir et al., 2016; Oprea and Magdy, 2019; Hazarika et al., 2018). The relationship between an author and the audience has been given comparably less attention, despite its relevance for the sarcasm interpretation (Rockwell and Theriot, 2001; Gibbs, 2000; Dress et al., 2008; Marwick and Boyd, 2011; Bamman and Smith, 2015). In this work, we propose a graph neural network framework jointly leveraging a user context from their historical tweets together with the social information from a user's neighborhood modeled by heterogeneous graph structures.

The key contributions of this paper are:

(1) We present the first graph attention-based model to identify sarcasm on social media by explicitly modeling users' social and historical context jointly, capturing complex relations between a sarcastic tweet and its conversational context.

(2) We demonstrate that exploiting these relationships increases performance in the sarcasm detection task, reaching state-of-the-art results on the recent SPIRS dataset (Shmueli et al., 2020), which we expand with user history. We examine the impact of different parts of the context, captured by attention weights, in modeling sarcastic utterances.

(3) We find that even with user-based models, detecting sarcastic intentions of the author is easier than identifying the sarcasm perception by others.

2 Related Work

Leveraging user history Several previous works contextualize a sarcastic post by using features from user history - employing past tweets to identify a user's behavioral traits (Rajadesingan et al., 2015), encoding user sentiment priors over different entities (Khattri et al., 2015), or manually crafting user interaction features (Bamman and Smith, 2015). Amir et al. (2016) introduce the user2vec model, applying paragraph2vec (Le and Mikolov, 2014) over user history. Hazarika et al. (2018) propose an alternative user embedding

Proceedings of the 2021 EMNLP Workshop W-NUT: The Seventh Workshop on Noisy User-generated Text, pages 97–105
November 11, 2021. ©2021 Association for Computational Linguistics

approach, encoding style and personality features.

Leveraging user network An emerging line of research makes use of social interactions to encode information about the user induced by neural architecture (Grover and Leskovec, 2016; Qiu et al., 2018). Network information improves performance on detecting cyberbullying (Mathew et al., 2019), abusive language use (Qian et al., 2018), suicide ideation (Mishra et al., 2019) or fake news (Chandra et al., 2020). To the best of our knowledge, graph network based approaches have not been used in the sarcasm detection task so far.

Perceived and intended sarcasm Perceiving sarcasm in text is not trivial even for humans, not only due to the lack of acoustic markers (Bänziger and Scherer, 2005; Woodland and Voyer, 2011) but also due to the sociocultural diversity (Rockwell and Theriot, 2001; Dress et al., 2008) where in many cases the audience may misinterpret a sarcastic statement as sincere. This has been only recently reflected in sarcasm detection models (Hazarika et al., 2018; Shmueli et al., 2020).

3 Proposed Approach

3.1 Tweet Embeddings

We denote the current tweet to be assessed $t_i \in T = \{t_1, t_2, \ldots, t_N\}$, where N is the total number of tweets. We utilize SentenceBERT embeddings (Reimers and Gurevych, 2019) to encode the tweets. Formally, $\mathbf{t_i}' = SentenceBERT(t_i)$ where $\mathbf{t_i}' \in \mathbb{R}^{768}$, and SentenceBERT computes the mean of all tokens' representation. We forward this representation into a linear layer to transform in dimension d, $\widetilde{\mathbf{t}}_\mathbf{i} \in \mathbb{R}^d$.

3.2 User Embeddings (Historical Context)

Let $u^{t_i} \in U = \{u^{t_1}, u^{t_2}, \ldots, u^{t_M}\}$ be the author of tweet t_i, from now on we keep only the index i for brevity. Each user u^i is associated with a set of historical tweets $\mathcal{H}^i = \{(H_1^i, \tau_1^i), \ldots, (H_m^i, \tau_m^i)\}$, where H_j^i is a historic tweet posted at a time τ_j^i by the user u^i. We adopt user2vec (Amir et al., 2016) to compute the initial user representation $\widetilde{\mathbf{u}}_i \in \mathbb{R}^d$ of user u^i based on their corresponding historical tweets $\mathcal{H}^i$, optimizing the conditional probability of texts given the author.

3.3 Social Graph (Network Context)

Apart from the importance of surrounding context to understand sarcasm (Wallace et al., 2014), certain understanding is needed between the audience and the author (Gibbs, 2000; Dress et al., 2008). Our goal is to model relations between users and their past tweets, interactions between users, and relations between tweets in one conversation. We model these relationships as a graph $\mathcal{G} = (V, E)$, where $V = \{U \cup T\}$ contains two types of nodes - Users and Tweets (Figure 1). We use three edge types $E = \{e^U \cup e^T \cup e^C\}$, where e^U represents the social interaction between users. This involves quotes, mentions, or replies in the user history. e^T denotes the edges between tweets that are involved in one discussion thread, with all tweets connected with each other, and e^C is the relation between a tweet and its author.

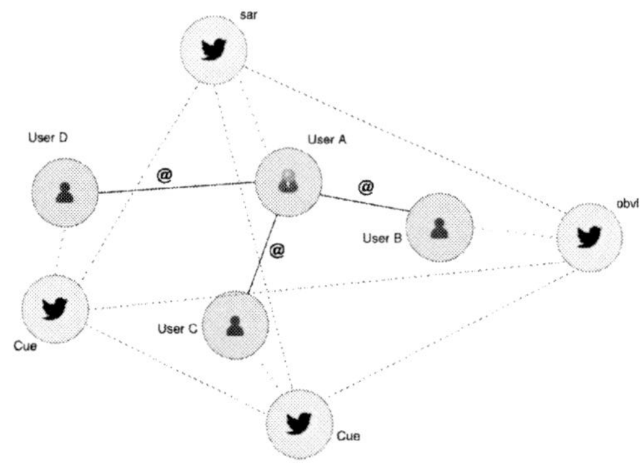

Figure 1: An example of a heterogeneous user and tweet social graph extracted from one conversation.

Representation Learning: We use Graph Attention Networks (GATs, (Veličković et al., 2018)) to exploit the neighborhood of each node to compute the final representations.[1] GAT uses a self-attention mechanism (Bahdanau et al., 2015; Vaswani et al., 2017) to assign an importance score to the connections that contribute more to the detection of sarcastic or non-sarcastic tweets. We initialize the user and the tweet nodes of the GAT with their corresponding embeddings $\widetilde{\mathbf{u}}_i$ and $\widetilde{\mathbf{t}}_i$. The initial node representation of each node $v \in V$ is linearly transformed by a weight matrix $\mathbf{W} \in \mathbb{R}^{d' \times d}$ into a vector $\mathbf{h}_v \in \mathbb{R}^{d'}$. Following, the attention weights e_{vn} of each node v are computed as:

$$e_{vn} = att(\mathbf{h}_v \| \mathbf{h}_n) \tag{1}$$

where $n \in \mathcal{N}(v)$ is a node in the neighborhood of v and att is the attention mechanism function

[1] We ran early experiments with Graph Convolutional Networks as well, obtaining inferior and less interpretable results.

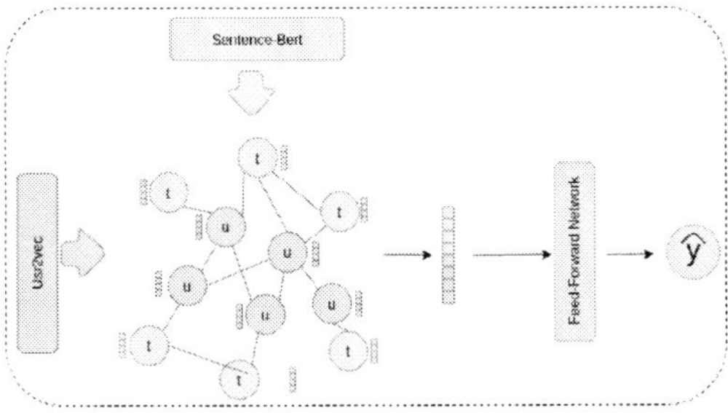

Figure 2: The social graph is initialized with user and tweet embeddings (user2vec and sentence-BERT), and tuned by GAT to take into account relationships between them. The output representations are then fed into the classification layer.

which is a single-layer feedforward neural network, parameterized by a weight vector $\vec{\mathbf{a}} \in \mathbb{R}^{2d'}$ with a LeakyReLU nonlinearity.

The final node representation $\mathbf{h}'_v \in \mathbb{R}^{K \cdot d'}$ is computed as:

$$\mathbf{h}'_v = \sigma\left(\frac{1}{K}\sum_{k=1}^{K}\sum_{n\in\mathcal{N}(v)} \alpha_{vn}^{k}\mathbf{W}^{k}\mathbf{h}_n\right) \quad (2)$$

where K is the number of attention heads, σ is the ReLU nonlinear function, $\mathbf{W}^k \in \mathbb{R}^{d' \times d'}$ a weight matrix and $\alpha_{vn}^{k} = softmax(e_{vn}^{k})$ the normalized attention weights from the k-th attention mechanism att^k.

3.4 Classification model

The user and tweet representations learned by GAT layer are concatenated and forwarded through a two-layer feed-forward network parameterized by weight matrices $\mathbf{W}_1^c \in \mathbb{R}^{d_1 \times 2d'}$ and $\mathbf{W}_2^c \in \mathbb{R}^{o \times d_1}$, where d_1 is the dimension of projected embeddings, and o is equal to the number of classes. The final prediction of the model is given by:

$$\hat{y} = softmax\left(\mathbf{W}_2^c\left(\sigma\left(\mathbf{W}_1^c[h_t||h_u]\right)\right)\right) \quad (3)$$

4 Experimental Setup

4.1 Dataset

For our experiments, we use a recently published SPIRS sarcasm dataset (Shmueli et al., 2020). It utilizes *cue tweets*, conversation replies which point out the sarcastic nature of a previous post. In addition, the dataset also provides *oblivious tweets*, questioning the sarcastic nature of a given example, and *elicit tweets*, being the original start of the conversation. Non-sarcastic posts were collected randomly in equal numbers. The labeled dataset contains in total 15,000 sarcastic tweets (10,000 self-reported and 5000 perceived cues), 15,000 non-sarcastic, 10,000 oblivious and 9156 elicit tweets.

User context We extend SPIRS with over 10 million past tweets of the authors in the dataset in order to compute the user embeddings.

Social network Our graph consists of the three types of connections described in Sec.3.3.To avoid the bias coming from cue tweets, we exclude these from our graph. Our final social network consists of 108K nodes with 0.00002 density and 32% homophily, defined as the percentage of connections between authors of tweets with the same label.

4.2 Comparison Baselines

The baselines introduced by (Shmueli et al., 2020) are a Convolutional Neural Network, a Bidirectional LSTM, and a fine-tuned pre-trained BERT model. We compare our model with BERT, which performs the best of these. We add two baselines which incorporate user information. First, we extend BERT by simply concatenating the tweet embeddings with their respective user2vec author representation ('BERT + user2vec'). As a second baseline ('BERT + user-only GAT'), we build a social graph with only user nodes and their interactions (quotes, mentions, or replies) e^U as edges, and apply the GAT initialized with user2vec embeddings. The implementation of the models and the results are made publicly available, to facilitate reproducibility and reuse[2].

5 Results and Analysis

Our proposed GAT base model significantly outperforms all the baselines (Table 1) despite having fewer trainable parameters (500K) than the BERT model (110M). First, by simply concatenating the user2vec embeddings to BERT, we obtain 3.4% f1 score improvement on the BERT model, indicating the importance of user context in sarcasm detection. Moreover, we introduce the GAT module in the model. We first experiment with only tweet to tweet connections in the graph based on the conversations on Twitter and trained on top of

[2] https://github.com/caisa-lab/sarcasm_detection

Sarcasm Detection			
Model	**P**	**R**	**F1**
BERT	70.1%	69.7%	69.9%
BERT + user2vec	73.6%	73.2%	73.4%
BERT + tweet-tweet GAT	70.4%	69.9%	70.1%
BERT + user-only GAT	74.2%	78.1%	76.1%
User+tweet GAT (no cues)	**84.7%**	**83.7%**	**84.2%**
User+tweet GAT, no elicit	83.2%	80.8%	82.0%
User+tweet GAT, no oblivious	82.4%	80.4%	81.4%
User+tweet GAT + cue tweets	94.7%	94.3%	94.5%

Table 1: Mean overall precision (P), recall (R), and F1 score (F1) of each model over 10 runs with varying seeds, detecting sarcasm on the SPIRS dataset.

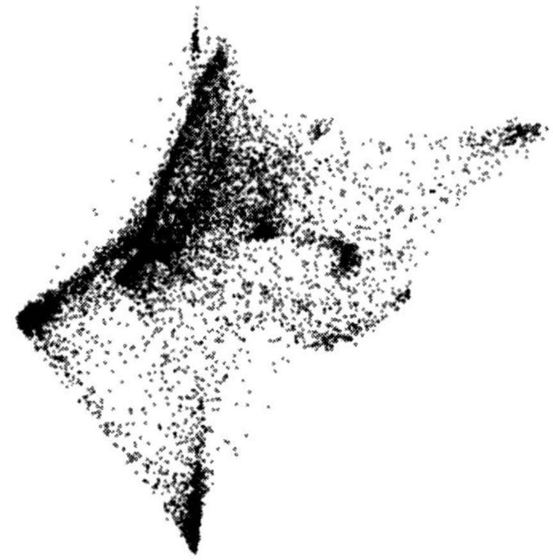

Figure 3: Initial representations of users (user2vec) projected in 2D space with T-SNE. Red color denotes sarcastic users, blue non-sarcastic.

Figure 4: Learned representations by our social network module (GAT) projected in 2D space with T-SNE. Red color denotes sarcastic users, blue non-sarcastic.

the fine-tuned BERT. In this case, the GAT layer only bring 0.2% improvement due to the sparse and disconnected nature of the constructed graph. In addition, we replace user2vec with GAT embeddings tuned on user-only social graph, and we achieve 6.1% improvement on BERT and 3% over 'BERT + user2vec', presumably thanks to exploiting the homophily relations between users. Finally, applying GAT on the full heterogeneous user and tweet graph (as per Figure 2) provides a large performance boost thanks to incorporating the conversational thread context between tweets.

User representation We compare the initial user embeddings initialized by user2vec with the final representations computed from the GAT. The representations are projected in 2-dimensional space using T-SNE (Van der Maaten and Hinton, 2008). In Figure 3 and 4 we visualize the initial representations with user2vec and computed representation by GAT layer respectively. While in user2vec representations sarcastic users cannot be distinguished from non-sarcastic ones, in the GAT representations we can observe communities of users sharing the same sarcastic tendency.

Conversation context For comparison, we construct three more social graphs where: 1) We remove the elicit tweets which triggered the sarcastic comment (GAT - elicit tweets), 2) We remove the oblivious tweets which interpreted the comment as serious (GAT - oblivious tweets), 3) We add the original cue tweets, revealing that the post was sarcastic (GAT + cue tweets). As expected, adding the cue tweets in the social graph leads to an almost perfect F1 score of 94.5%. Removing oblivious and elicit tweets causes just a small performance drop (2-3%). In the way the SPIRS dataset is annotated, an oblivious tweet typically triggers a cue tweet ("*c mon, dude, it was just sarcasm*"). We hypothesize that even with the cue tweets removed, the model is able to learn the predictive relation between oblivious and sarcastic tweets. This is in line with the original paper (i.e. without user context), where a 3.4% drop in prediction accuracy was observed, when the oblivious tweets were removed.

Attention weights The attention mechanism of GAT is able to assign varied weights to different

Sarcasm Perception			
Model	**P**	**R**	**F1**
BERT	73.2%	68.0%	69.0%
User+tweet GAT (no cues)	75.0%	67.7%	71.2%

Table 2: Mean overall precision (P), recall (R), and F1 score (F1) over 10 runs classifying self-reported (intended) and perceived sarcasm on the SPIRS dataset.

nodes in the neighborhood, dynamically encoding of the user by their homophily relations, which boosts the effect of authors in tweet representations (Flek, 2020). We confirm this by examining users with a larger number of tweets in the dataset. When users tend to be sarcastic in most of the posts, the attention weight of their non-sarcastic tweets is smaller. In these cases, the attention weights give more importance to the surrounding user context over the conversation thread. Overall, the largest source of information for the model are the user nodes and the tweet that is being classified. We note the normalized attention weights are smaller for the oblivious and elicit tweet edges, and higher for the edges that connect tweets with their respective author. In other words, the conversational context only plays a decisive role in case of insufficient or inconsistent user-level priors.

Sarcasm Perception Cue tweets can be either authored by the same user as the sarcastic post (*intended sarcasm*) or a different one (*perceived sarcasm*).We observe that in the sarcasm detection task, the error rate on perceived sarcasm is 20% while in the self-reported sarcasm it is only around 15%. We therefore test our model on distinguishing between perceived and self-reported sarcasm. Our GAT model brings an improvement of 2.2% over the BERT baseline, with the perceived sarcasm being harder to detect (F1 56%) than the self-reported one (F1 84%). These results are aligned with the conclusions from (Oprea and Magdy, 2019). In most cases, the perceived sarcasm is misclassified as self-reported, which is present more often (70%) in the data. Perceived sarcasm is dependent on the readers rather than the author of the tweet, therefore we hypothesize that modeling the authors' context is less useful. It could be of benefit to model more robust recipient user profiles as well, to better predict how each individual will react.

Limitations Modeling the social networks with GAT is affected by several factors. First, the low graph density, as the original dataset wasn't collected by following relationships between users, hence many users across different conversation threads are not related to each other. Second, the homophily degree is only 32%, users with sarcastic tendency have few connections among them.

6 Conclusions

In this work, we explore social networks of user interactions, and contextual information to interpret sarcastic intentions in social media. We propose a graph attention-based model, which combines contextual information of users, linguistic features, and social networks. The heterogeneous social network modeling dynamically exploits relationships between users and tweets in a conversation and significantly improves the state-of-the-art results.

Acknowledgements

This work has been supported by the German Federal Ministry of Education and Research (BMBF) as a part of the Junior AI Scientists program under the reference 01-S20060. We would like to thank Flora Sakketou and all the anonymous reviewers for their valuable input.

Ethical Considerations

The ability to automatically approximate personal characteristics of online users in order to improve natural language classification algorithms requires us to consider a range of ethical concerns, including: (1) privacy and user consent, (2) representativeness of the data for generalization, and (3) user vulnerability to a potential model or data misuse or misinterpretation.

Use of any user data for personalization shall be transparent, and limited to the given purpose, no individual posts shall be republished (Hewson and Buchanan, 2013). Researchers are advised to take account of users' expectations (Williams et al., 2017; Shilton and Sayles, 2016; Townsend and Wallace, 2016) when collecting public data such as Twitter. In this case, when we expand the original dataset with more extensive user history, we utilize publicly available Twitter data in a purely observational (Norval and Henderson, 2017), and non-intrusive manner. All user data is kept separately on protected servers, linked to the raw text and network data only through anonymous IDs.

Shah et al. (2020) identify four different sources of bias in NLP models: selection bias, label bias, model overamplification, and semantic bias. While we can't exclude any of those, the selection bias should be kept in mind in particular, when reusing the presented model, as it is unclear to which extent the augmented SPIRS dataset with user history represents a sample of the overall population on Twitter. The user selection was based solely on the available sarcasm annotations, and doesn't include any sociodemographic information.

In addition, any user-augmented classification efforts risk invoking stereotyping and essentialism, as the algorithm may lean towards label people rather than posts (e.g. "this is a sarcastic person"). Such stereotypes can cause harm even if they are accurate on average differences (Rudman and Glick, 2008). These can be emphasized by the semblance of objectivity created by the use of a computer algorithm (Koolen and van Cranenburgh, 2017). It is important to be mindful of these effects when interpreting the model results in an own end-application context.

References

Silvio Amir, Byron C. Wallace, Hao Lyu, Paula Carvalho, and Mário J. Silva. 2016. Modelling context with user embeddings for sarcasm detection in social media. In *Proceedings of The 20th SIGNLL Conference on Computational Natural Language Learning*, pages 167–177, Berlin, Germany. Association for Computational Linguistics.

Dzmitry Bahdanau, Kyung Hyun Cho, and Yoshua Bengio. 2015. Neural machine translation by jointly learning to align and translate. In *3rd International Conference on Learning Representations, ICLR 2015*.

David Bamman and Noah Smith. 2015. Contextualized sarcasm detection on twitter. In *Proceedings of the International AAAI Conference on Web and Social Media*, volume 9.

Tanja Bänziger and Klaus R. Scherer. 2005. The role of intonation in emotional expressions. *Speech Communication*, 46(3):252–267. Quantitative Prosody Modelling for Natural Speech Description and Generation.

Paula Carvalho, Luís Sarmento, Mário J. Silva, and Eugénio de Oliveira. 2009. Clues for detecting irony in user-generated contents: Oh...!! it's "so easy";-). In *Proceedings of the 1st International CIKM Workshop on Topic-Sentiment Analysis for Mass Opinion*, TSA '09, page 53–56, New York, NY, USA. Association for Computing Machinery.

Shantanu Chandra, Pushkar Mishra, Helen Yannakoudakis, Madhav Nimishakavi, Marzieh Saeidi, and Ekaterina Shutova. 2020. Graph-based modeling of online communities for fake news detection. *arXiv preprint arXiv:2008.06274*.

Dmitry Davidov, Oren Tsur, and Ari Rappoport. 2010. Semi-supervised recognition of sarcasm in Twitter and Amazon. In *Proceedings of the Fourteenth Conference on Computational Natural Language Learning*, pages 107–116, Uppsala, Sweden. Association for Computational Linguistics.

Shelly Dews, Joan Kaplan, and Ellen Winner. 1995. Why not say it directly? the social functions of irony. *Discourse Processes*, 19(3):347–367.

Megan L. Dress, Roger J. Kreuz, Kristen E. Link, and Gina M. Caucci. 2008. Regional variation in the use of sarcasm. *Journal of Language and Social Psychology*, 27(1):71–85.

Lucie Flek. 2020. Returning the N to NLP: Towards contextually personalized classification models. In *Proceedings of the 58th Annual Meeting of the Association for Computational Linguistics*, pages 7828–7838, Online. Association for Computational Linguistics.

Debanjan Ghosh, Weiwei Guo, and Smaranda Muresan. 2015. Sarcastic or not: Word embeddings to predict the literal or sarcastic meaning of words. In *Proceedings of the 2015 Conference on Empirical Methods in Natural Language Processing*, pages 1003–1012, Lisbon, Portugal. Association for Computational Linguistics.

Raymond W. Gibbs. 2000. Irony in talk among friends. *Metaphor and Symbol*, 15(1-2):5–27.

Roberto González-Ibáñez, Smaranda Muresan, and Nina Wacholder. 2011. Identifying sarcasm in Twitter: A closer look. In *Proceedings of the 49th Annual Meeting of the Association for Computational Linguistics: Human Language Technologies*, pages 581–586, Portland, Oregon, USA. Association for Computational Linguistics.

Aditya Grover and Jure Leskovec. 2016. Node2vec: Scalable feature learning for networks. In *Proceedings of the 22nd ACM SIGKDD International Conference on Knowledge Discovery and Data Mining*, KDD '16, page 855–864, New York, NY, USA. Association for Computing Machinery.

Devamanyu Hazarika, Soujanya Poria, Sruthi Gorantla, Erik Cambria, Roger Zimmermann, and Rada Mihalcea. 2018. CASCADE: Contextual sarcasm detection in online discussion forums. In *Proceedings of the 27th International Conference on Computational Linguistics*, pages 1837–1848, Santa Fe, New Mexico, USA. Association for Computational Linguistics.

Claire Hewson and Tom Buchanan. 2013. Ethics guidelines for internet-mediated research. The British Psychological Society.

Aditya Joshi, Vinita Sharma, and Pushpak Bhattacharyya. 2015. Harnessing context incongruity for sarcasm detection. In *Proceedings of the 53rd Annual Meeting of the Association for Computational Linguistics and the 7th International Joint Conference on Natural Language Processing (Volume 2: Short Papers)*, pages 757–762, Beijing, China. Association for Computational Linguistics.

Anupam Khattri, Aditya Joshi, Pushpak Bhattacharyya, and Mark Carman. 2015. Your sentiment precedes you: Using an author's historical tweets to predict sarcasm. In *Proceedings of the 6th Workshop on Computational Approaches to Subjectivity, Sentiment and Social Media Analysis*, pages 25–30, Lisboa, Portugal. Association for Computational Linguistics.

Diederik P Kingma and Jimmy Ba. 2015. Adam, a method for stochastic optimization. In *Proceedings of the 3rd International Conference on Learning Representations (ICLR)*, volume 1412.

Corina Koolen and Andreas van Cranenburgh. 2017. These are not the stereotypes you are looking for: Bias and fairness in authorial gender attribution. In *Proceedings of the First ACL Workshop on Ethics in Natural Language Processing*, pages 12–22, Valencia, Spain. Association for Computational Linguistics.

Quoc Le and Tomas Mikolov. 2014. Distributed representations of sentences and documents. In *Proceedings of the 31st International Conference on International Conference on Machine Learning - Volume 32*, ICML'14, page II–1188–II–1196. JMLR.org.

Alice E. Marwick and Danah Boyd. 2011. I tweet honestly, i tweet passionately: Twitter users, context collapse, and the imagined audience. *New Media & Society*, 13(1):114–133.

Binny Mathew, Ritam Dutt, Pawan Goyal, and Animesh Mukherjee. 2019. Spread of hate speech in online social media. In *Proceedings of the 10th ACM Conference on Web Science*, WebSci '19, page 173–182, New York, NY, USA. Association for Computing Machinery.

Diana Maynard and Mark Greenwood. 2014. Who cares about sarcastic tweets? investigating the impact of sarcasm on sentiment analysis. In *Proceedings of the Ninth International Conference on Language Resources and Evaluation (LREC'14)*, pages 4238–4243, Reykjavik, Iceland. European Language Resources Association (ELRA).

Rohan Mishra, Pradyumn Prakhar Sinha, Ramit Sawhney, Debanjan Mahata, Puneet Mathur, and Rajiv Ratn Shah. 2019. SNAP-BATNET: Cascading author profiling and social network graphs for suicide ideation detection on social media. In *Proceedings of the 2019 Conference of the North American Chapter of the Association for Computational Linguistics: Student Research Workshop*, pages 147–156, Minneapolis, Minnesota. Association for Computational Linguistics.

Chris Norval and Tristan Henderson. 2017. Contextual consent: Ethical mining of social media for health research. *CoRR*, abs/1701.07765.

Silviu Oprea and Walid Magdy. 2019. Exploring author context for detecting intended vs perceived sarcasm. In *Proceedings of the 57th Annual Meeting of the Association for Computational Linguistics*, pages 2854–2859, Florence, Italy. Association for Computational Linguistics.

Jing Qian, Mai ElSherief, Elizabeth Belding, and William Yang Wang. 2018. Leveraging intra-user and inter-user representation learning for automated hate speech detection. In *Proceedings of the 2018 Conference of the North American Chapter of the Association for Computational Linguistics: Human Language Technologies, Volume 2 (Short Papers)*, pages 118–123, New Orleans, Louisiana. Association for Computational Linguistics.

Jiezhong Qiu, Yuxiao Dong, Hao Ma, Jian Li, Kuansan Wang, and Jie Tang. 2018. Network embedding as matrix factorization: Unifying deepwalk, line, pte, and node2vec. In *Proceedings of the Eleventh ACM International Conference on Web Search and Data Mining*, WSDM '18, pages 459–467, New York, NY, USA. ACM.

Ashwin Rajadesingan, Reza Zafarani, and Huan Liu. 2015. Sarcasm detection on twitter: A behavioral modeling approach. In *Proceedings of the Eighth ACM International Conference on Web Search and Data Mining*, WSDM '15, page 97–106, New York, NY, USA. Association for Computing Machinery.

Nils Reimers and Iryna Gurevych. 2019. Sentence-BERT: Sentence embeddings using Siamese BERT-networks. In *Proceedings of the 2019 Conference on Empirical Methods in Natural Language Processing and the 9th International Joint Conference on Natural Language Processing (EMNLP-IJCNLP)*, pages 3982–3992, Hong Kong, China. Association for Computational Linguistics.

Antonio Reyes, Paolo Rosso, and Tony Veale. 2013. A multidimensional approach for detecting irony in twitter. *Lang. Resour. Eval.*, 47(1):239–268.

Ellen Riloff, Ashequl Qadir, Prafulla Surve, Lalindra De Silva, Nathan Gilbert, and Ruihong Huang. 2013. Sarcasm as contrast between a positive sentiment and negative situation. In *Proceedings of the 2013 Conference on Empirical Methods in Natural Language Processing*, pages 704–714, Seattle, Washington, USA. Association for Computational Linguistics.

Patricia Rockwell and Evelyn M. Theriot. 2001. Culture, gender, and gender mix in encoders of sarcasm: A self-assessment analysis. *Communication Research Reports*, 18(1):44–52.

Laurie A Rudman and Peter Glick. 2008. The social psychology of gender: How power and intimacy shape gender relations.

Deven Santosh Shah, H. Andrew Schwartz, and Dirk Hovy. 2020. Predictive biases in natural language processing models: A conceptual framework and overview. In *Proceedings of the 58th Annual Meeting of the Association for Computational Linguistics*, pages 5248–5264, Online. Association for Computational Linguistics.

Katie Shilton and Sheridan Sayles. 2016. " we aren't all going to be on the same page about ethics": Ethical practices and challenges in research on digital and social media. In *2016 49th Hawaii International Conference on System Sciences (HICSS)*, pages 1909–1918. IEEE.

Boaz Shmueli, Lun-Wei Ku, and Soumya Ray. 2020. Reactive Supervision: A New Method for Collecting Sarcasm Data. In *Proceedings of the 2020 Conference on Empirical Methods in Natural Language Processing (EMNLP)*, pages 2553–2559, Online. Association for Computational Linguistics.

Nitish Srivastava, Geoffrey Hinton, Alex Krizhevsky, Ilya Sutskever, and Ruslan Salakhutdinov. 2014. Dropout: a simple way to prevent neural networks from overfitting. *The journal of machine learning research*, 15(1):1929–1958.

Yi Tay, Anh Tuan Luu, Siu Cheung Hui, and Jian Su. 2018. Reasoning with sarcasm by reading in-between. In *Proceedings of the 56th Annual Meeting of the Association for Computational Linguistics (Volume 1: Long Papers)*, pages 1010–1020, Melbourne, Australia. Association for Computational Linguistics.

Leanne Townsend and Claire Wallace. 2016. Social media research: A guide to ethics. *University of Aberdeen*, 1:16.

Oren Tsur, Dmitry Davidov, and Ari Rappoport. 2010. Icwsm — a great catchy name: Semi-supervised recognition of sarcastic sentences in online product reviews. *Proceedings of the International AAAI Conference on Web and Social Media*, 4(1):162–169.

Laurens Van der Maaten and Geoffrey Hinton. 2008. Visualizing data using t-sne. *Journal of machine learning research*, 9(11).

Ashish Vaswani, Noam Shazeer, Niki Parmar, Jakob Uszkoreit, Llion Jones, Aidan N. Gomez, Łukasz Kaiser, and Illia Polosukhin. 2017. Attention is all you need. In *Proceedings of the 31st International Conference on Neural Information Processing Systems*, NIPS'17, page 6000–6010, Red Hook, NY, USA. Curran Associates Inc.

Petar Veličković, Guillem Cucurull, Arantxa Casanova, Adriana Romero, Pietro Liò, and Yoshua Bengio. 2018. Graph Attention Networks. *International Conference on Learning Representations*. Accepted as poster.

Byron C. Wallace, Do Kook Choe, Laura Kertz, and Eugene Charniak. 2014. Humans require context to infer ironic intent (so computers probably do, too). In *Proceedings of the 52nd Annual Meeting of the Association for Computational Linguistics (Volume 2: Short Papers)*, pages 512–516, Baltimore, Maryland. Association for Computational Linguistics.

Matthew L Williams, Pete Burnap, and Luke Sloan. 2017. Towards an ethical framework for publishing twitter data in social research: Taking into account users' views, online context and algorithmic estimation. *Sociology*, 51(6):1149–1168.

Jennifer Woodland and Daniel Voyer. 2011. Context and intonation in the perception of sarcasm. *Metaphor and Symbol*, 26(3):227–239.

Appendix

A Configurations

We perform a stratified 90/10 train-test split. We sample 10% of the training data for validation. All splits have the same class distribution and different sets of tweet authors. We use 3 GAT layers, with number of heads $K = 4$. The initial dimension is $d = 400$ and the final output dimension $d' = 100$. To train our model we set learning rate to $1e - 4$, and dropout 0.4 (Srivastava et al., 2014), and use the Adam optimization algorithm (Kingma and Ba, 2015) for 500 training epochs with early stopping. For the GAT layers, we compute the mean of the outputs from each attention head instead of concatenation. All experiments are run in Nvidia A100 40 GB GPUs.

B User Context

To incorporate user context, we first extract all user IDs for all the tweets in the dataset. In the dataset, due to different tweet types with different users, we get in total 57K users. We fetch the tweet post timeline for each user, and we end up with a total of 104M tweets, in average 1800 posts per user. For user2vec training, we take into account only the users with a minimum of 50 posts in their timeline, and we limit the total number of posts to 1000. After filtering, the amount of tweets in the context is 10M. Every tweet is pre-processed by removing all links, user mentions are replaced with "@user", emojis and hashtags are cleared. We train user2vec (Amir et al., 2016) for 12 epochs, with learning rate 1e-4. For those users which are filtered, or we cannot extract history, we initialize them as the mean representation of his user neighbors in the social network. We used the history tweets only for creating the user-to-user edges, and those are not present in the constructed graph, but are already encoded in the initial user representation. We experimented with various history length settings, and found almost no difference in the performance between using interactions throughout all history and interactions during the last year. Hence, we omitted older interactions to ease the computations.

Hierarchical Character Tagger for Short Text Spelling Error Correction

Mengyi Gao *
eBay Inc.
menggao@ebay.com

Canran Xu *
eBay Inc.
canxu@ebay.com

Peng Shi *
eBay Inc.
pshi@ebay.com

Abstract

State-of-the-art approaches to spelling error correction problem include Transformer-based Seq2Seq models, which require large training sets and suffer from slow inference time; and sequence labeling models based on Transformer encoders like BERT, which involve token-level label space and therefore a large pre-defined vocabulary dictionary. In this paper we present a Hierarchical Character Tagger model, or HCTagger, for short text spelling error correction. We use a pre-trained language model at the character level as a text encoder, and then predict character-level edits to transform the original text into its error-free form with a much smaller label space. For decoding, we propose a hierarchical multi-task approach to alleviate the issue of long-tail label distribution without introducing extra model parameters. Experiments on two public misspelling correction datasets demonstrate that HCTagger is an accurate and much faster approach than many existing models.

1 Introduction

A spelling corrector is an important and universal tool for a wide range of text-related applications, such as search engines, machine translation, optical character recognition, medical records, text processors and essay scoring. Although spelling error correction is a long-studied problem, it remains a challenging task because words can be misspelled in a variety of forms, including in-word errors, cross-word errors, non-word errors and real-word errors, depending on the subtle contextual information.

In this paper, we focus on solving the spelling correction problem in user-generated short text, such as queries in search engines or tweets on social media, which has three unique properties compared to long essays. First, search queries or tweets are often short and lack context. Second, most short text contains pure spelling errors and almost no grammatical errors. Third, instant spell checkers used in search engines or social medias have strict latency requirements.

In general, popular approaches to spelling correction make use of parallel corpora in which the source sentence contains spelling errors and the target sentence is error-free. Recently, the Transformer-based sequence-to-sequence (Seq2Seq) model (Vaswani et al., 2017) has gradually proven to be effective on spelling correction problems. Unlike neural machine translation, spelling errors tend to occur locally for a few characters while the rest of the text is correct. To cope with this situation, Zhao et al. propose a scheme to incorporate a copy mechanism in Seq2Seq. The success of this type of Seq2Seq model depends on large scale annotated datasets, which are often generated by constructing text noise from clean text in previous studies. Moreover, this approach suffers from slower inference time and lack of interpretability.

Another class of approaches is based on sequence labeling. Instead of generating the output sequence in an autoregressive fashion, PIE (Awasthi et al., 2019) and GECToR (Omelianchuk et al., 2020) predicts token-level edit operations in one of {*Keep*, *Delete*, *Replace*, *Append*} by leveraging pre-trained Transformer encoders, such as BERT (Devlin et al., 2019). Such models can generate the outputs for all tokens in parallel, and therefore significantly reduces the latency of sequential decoding as in Seq2Seq models while achieving comparable accuracy. However, the approaches in both papers predict edit operations at token level. It can be expected that the *Replace* and *Append* operations are associated with a huge pre-defined vocabulary dictionary. For real-life usages it is infeasible to enumerate all correctly spelled words in the label space.

To address the aforementioned shortcomings,

* Equal Contribution

Proceedings of the 2021 EMNLP Workshop W-NUT: The Seventh Workshop on Noisy User-generated Text, pages 106–113
November 11, 2021.

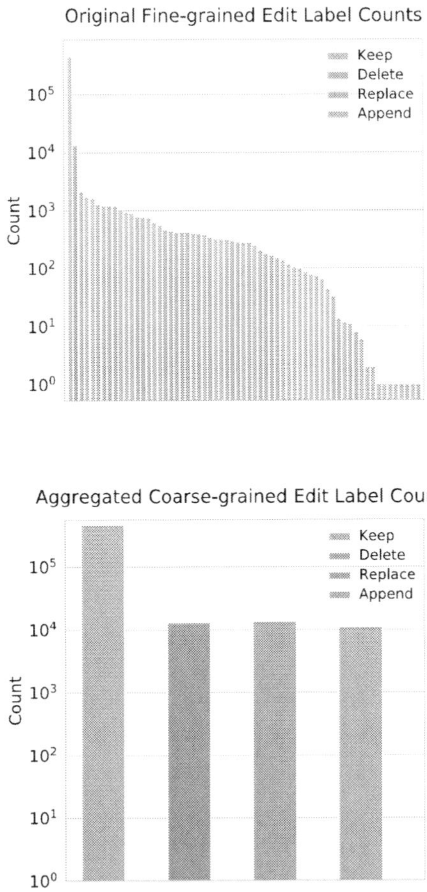

Figure 1: Original and aggregated edit label counts. The upper plot shows original fine-grained edit label counts, which are heavily skewed. The lower plot of aggregated coarse-grained edit label counts has much less skewness.

considering the unique properties of short text misspelling correction, in this paper, we propose a new model called Hierarchical Character Tagger, or HCTagger for short, which uses a pre-trained language model at the character level as a text encoder, and then predicts character-level edits. It is motivated by the straightforward observation that spelling errors usually occur at character level. For the misspelling-correction pair of *shies* $\rightarrow$ *shoes*, its character-level edit labels would be [*s: Keep, h: Keep, i: Replace with* ***o****, e: Keep, s: Keep*], which is represented in a much smaller label space compared to [*shies: Replace with* ***shoes***] at token level. While most spelling errors occur within 1-edit distance for each token, for broader coverage we also include character sequence edit operations like *Replace with* ***oa***.

Furthermore, the distribution of edit labels is long-tailed. As shown in Figure 1, *Keep* and *Delete* are more frequent than labels of *Replace/Append with certain character(s)*. If these labels are treated as equivalent, the overall accuracy of the model will be constrained by the unevenness of the label distribution. Therefore, for decoding, we aggregate original fine-grained edit labels into four coarse-grained labels [*Keep*, *Delete*, *Append*, *Replace*]. We propose a hierarchical multi-task approach to learn both the fine-grained and coarse-grained edit labels at the same time without introducing any extra model parameters.

Through extensive experiments on two public datasets, we demonstrate that our proposed HCTagger effectively improves the performance and latency of short text spelling correction.

2 Approach

We describe our model HCTagger in this section.

2.1 Problem Formulation

Without lack of universality of language types, for an input text sequence with spelling error, $S = [c_1, \ldots, c_n]$, our goal is to get the correct spelling of the corresponding text, denoted as $T = [d_1, \ldots, d_m]$, where c_i and d_i are character level input and output. Note that the sequence lengths n and m are not necessarily equal.

To map the source sequence S to target T, a corresponding edit operation sequence $O = [o_1, \ldots, o_n]$ is applied. Note that O has the same sequence length as S. Each edit operation, o_i, falls into one of the following four categories:

Keep The current character remains unchanged. This means that the current character is not misspelled.

Delete The current character is deleted.

Append Append a sequence of characters of length greater than or equal to one after the current character. Each distinct appended sequence is treated as an independent tag type.

Replace Replaces the current character with a number of characters of length greater than or equal to 1. Similar to *Append*, each distinct appended sequence is treated as an independent tag type.

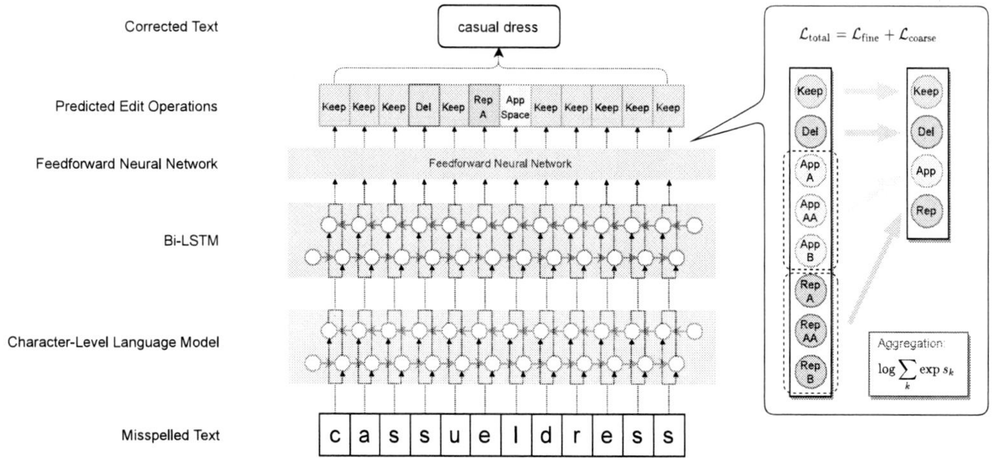

Figure 2: Overall architecture of the model. The text encoder is a character-level language model, followed by a bi-directional LSTM. The edit operations predicted by the feedforward neural network are used to formulate the corrected text. During training, the output of the feedforward neural network is used to construct the hierarchical loss function with two explicit terms.

Note that there could be more than one possible edit operation sequences to transform from source S to target T. We use Python function *Sequence-Matcher* in module *difflib* to do obtain the unique edit operation label sequence O. The idea of *SequenceMatcher* is to find the longest contiguous matching subsequence. This does not necessarily yield minimal edit sequences, but does tend to yield matches that "look right" to humans. For more information, refer to the doc [1].

Thus, we eventually transform spelling correction into a sequential labeling problem, i.e., for a given input $S = [c_1, \ldots, c_n]$, predict the edit operation o_i for each character c_i. As a concrete example, to map a misspelled input text *cassueldress* to its correction *casual dress*, 3 edit operations are required, namely (1) deleting the 4th character *s*, (2) replacing the 6th character *e* with *a*, and (3) appending a *space* after the 7th character *l*, while keeping other characters unchanged.

2.2 Model

Our proposed model, HCTagger, consists of two components. First, we encode the text by pre-training a character-level language model. Second, the representation obtained by the language model is encoded by a bi-directional LSTM, which is then fed to a decoder. This decoder is hierarchical: it decodes simultaneously four coarse-grained labels [*Keep*, *Delete*, *Append*, *Replace*] and all the fine-grained tags (such as *Append with **a*** or *Replace with **eo***), which could be of potentially up to thousands types. The architecture of the model is shown in Figure 2.

Character-level Language Model The character-level language model we use is the pretrained Flair (Akbik et al., 2018), which has been widely shown to be effective for word-level sequence labeling tasks. Specifically, Flair consists of a character-level embedding layer and a (possibly bi-directional) LSTM layer. The model predicts the next character by the preceding or succeeding character inputs. The authors argue that it can capture semantic differences in morphological similarities, as well as contextual information for polysemous words. Moreover, character-level models better handle rare and misspelled words as well as model subword structures such as prefixes and endings.

Though pre-training a character-level language model, in the original paper Flair focuses on word-level sequence labeling task (e.g., NER). Specifically, to obtain word-level embeddings from character-level language model, Flair uses the output hidden state after the last character in each word as the representation of the whole word. However, in our scenario, we use the embedding of current character to predict its own edit operation, regardless of which word it belongs to, even if it is a space or punctuation.

In addition, when using Flair as the text encoder,

[1] `https://docs.python.org/3/library/difflib.html`

# Iteration	Short Text	# Token-level Errors	# Character-level Errors
Original	fashien industrie	2	3
1	fashion industry	0	0

Table 1: An illustrative example of iterative inference.

we found that fine-tuning Flair's language model parameters along with the sequence labeling task generally perform better than without fine-tuning. Therefore, fine-tuning Flair is our default setting whenever possible.

Hierarchical Multi-Task In a training set of finite size, the original fine-grained edit labels (a certain character being appended or replaced with some characters) form a long-tail distribution, as shown in Figure 1. This makes some relatively rare spelling errors more difficult to be corrected.

For decoding, we feed the hidden states of the bidirectional LSTM into a layer of feedforward neural network whose output dimension is the size of label types. For character c_i, the probability of original fine-grained label type k is $P(k|c_i)$. To alleviate the issue of long-tail distribution for k, we propose to aggregate the probabilities for four coarse-grained edit labels, denoted as $P(v|c_i)$, with $v \in \{Keep, Delete, Replace, Append\}$, which are presumably more balanced than the fine-grained labels. To achieve this, we use the rule of sum of probability: as all possible fine-grained *Append* (*Replace*) operations are mutually exclusive, the sum of their probabilities should equal the coarse-grained probability of *Append* (*Replace*). Formally,

$$P(A(R)|c_i) = \sum_{k \in A(R)_\subset} P(k|c_i), \quad (1)$$

where $A_\subset$ and $R_\subset$ are the subsets consisting of fine-grained *Append* and *Replace* operations, correspondingly.

Denote the logits for original fine-grained tag type k as f_k, and logits for aggregated coarse-grained tag type v as l_v. Then the probability of label type k is $P(k|c_i) = \mathrm{softmax}(f_k)$. Similarly we have $P(v|c_i) = \mathrm{softmax}(l_v)$. Therefore, Equation (1) can be derived as:

$$\frac{\exp(l_{A(R)})}{\sum_{m \in \{K,D,A,R\}} \exp(l_m)} = \sum_{k \in A(R)_\subset} \frac{\exp(f_k)}{\sum_j \exp(f_j)}, \quad (2)$$

where K, D, A and R are the short forms for *Keep*, *Delete*, *Append* and *Replace*, accordingly.

As a result, we obtain the coarse-grained logits l_v by solving Equation (2):

$$l_v = \begin{cases} f_k & k = Keep \\ f_k & k = Delete \\ \log \sum_{k \in A_\subset} \exp(f_k) & k \in A_\subset \\ \log \sum_{k \in R_\subset} \exp(f_k) & k \in R_\subset \end{cases} \quad (3)$$

Finally, HCTagger is trained by using the following multi-task loss associated with predicting edit o_i at each character c_i:

$$\begin{aligned} \mathcal{L} &= \mathcal{L}_{\text{fine}} + \mathcal{L}_{\text{coarse}} \\ &= -\sum_i \log P(f_k^{(i)}|c_i) - \sum_i \log P(l_v^{(i)}|c_i). \end{aligned}$$

Notice that, in contrast to traditional multi-task learning, with the relation between l_v and f_k in Equation (3), the coarse-grained loss function we introduce as an auxiliary task does not contain extra model parameters. The advantage of this design is that both fine-grained and coarse-grained loss functions can reach the optimum at the same time without additional efforts to tune the parameters to balance the two terms.

Inference Some previous studies (Awasthi et al., 2019; Omelianchuk et al., 2020) on Grammar Error Correction (GEC) have shown that a well-established approach for inference is iterative: use the modified result obtained by the model in the current round as input for next round's prediction, and repeat the process several times. These studies find that due to the dependency among grammatical errors (tense, pronoun, subject-verb, preposition, plurals), the performance of model predictions can be steadily improved by multiple iterations. However, iterative inference is confronted with a trade-off between speed and accuracy.

As spelling errors impose a strong notion of locality and have weaker dependency on each other than grammatical errors, the iterative correction process is less necessary. For example, in the example shown in Table 1, the 2 token-level typos, *fashien* and *industrie*, are independent of each other. To this end, the two errors can be corrected simultaneously through a single run in our model.

Dataset	# Train	# Dev	# Test	% Error Rate	# Label Types
Twitter	31,172	4,000	4,000	100	66
Webis	44,772	5,000	5,000	17	112

Table 2: Basic statistics of the datasets.

Indeed, from our experiments, we noticed that having more than one round of inference iteration only marginally improves the accuracy in our task. Therefore, we report the results for HCTagger with only *one* inference iteration in all experiments.

3 Experiments

In this section, we describe the experiments performed on two public datasets for HCTagger. Meanwhile, we compare it with several state-of-the-art baselines.

3.1 Datasets

We conduct experiments on the following two short text datasets:

Twitter Dataset is proposed in Aramaki (2010), which includes 39,172 samples in their spell-error form and error-free form. We adopt the same train / dev / test split as Ribeiro et al. (2018) and Awasthi et al. (2019).

Webis Dataset is introduced in Hagen et al. (2017), which consists of 54,772 queries from AOL search logs. In contrast to the Twitter Dataset, the error rate of this dataset is only $\sim$17%. Since the original dataset does not provide the train / dev / test split, we randomly sample 5000 queries as the dev and test sets, respectively, and use the remaining data as the training set.

The basic statistics of these two datasets and the corresponding number of label types (calculated from training data) are listed in the Table 2.

3.2 Baselines and Implementation Details

The following baseline models are used for the comparison experiments:

Aspell (Atkinson, 2018) works at word level. It uses a combination of metaphone phonetic algorithm, Ispell's near miss strategy and a weighted edit distance metric to score candidate words.

Seq2Seq-LSTM is the standard LSTM-based Seq2Seq architecture.

Seq2Seq-Transformer (Vaswani et al., 2017) is the self-attention based Seq2Seq model.

Local Sequence Transduction (Ribeiro et al., 2018) treats spelling correction as a character-level local sequence transduction task by first predicting insertion slots, followed by a sequence labeling task for output tokens or a special operation *Delete*.

BERT-PIE (Awasthi et al., 2019) or Parallel Iterative Edit model, is a sequence labeling method which uses BERT as its text encoder.

BERT-Neuspell (Jayanthi et al., 2020) is provided by the Neuspell toolkit. It regards spelling correction as a token-level sequence labeling task, where the output for each token is its error-free form. We finetune the BERT model on the Webis dataset.

All the models are implemented in PyTorch (Paszke et al., 2019), and trained with a single Tesla V100 GPU. For HCTagger, we use the English Flair embeddings pretrained on the 1-billion word corpus (Chelba et al., 2014), which are publicly available[2]. We tune the number of LSTM hidden states $\in \{512, 1024\}$, training batch size $\in \{8, 16, 32\}$, learning rate $\in \{1e^{-2}, 1e^{-3}\}$, and optimizer type $\in$\{Adam (Kingma and Ba, 2015), LAMB (You et al., 2020)\}. In addition, both the encoder and decoder of Transformer has two self-attention layers.

3.3 Results

For the Twitter dataset, to align with previous publications, we report the accuracy in the test set to compare the performances among all models. As shown in Table 3, HCTagger improves accuracy over all the models except Transformer. In particular, it is important to note that although the pretrained language model (Flair) we use is lightweight compared to BERT, our model still outperforms BERT-PIE.

Table 3 also reports the performance on the Webis dataset. Our HCTagger exceeds all other models. Transformer model doesn't perform well on

[2] `https://github.com/flairNLP/flair`

Model	Twitter Dataset Accuracy	Webis Dataset Accuracy
Aspell	30.1 †	65.8
Seq2Seq (LSTM)	52.2 *	83.5
Seq2Seq (Transformer)	**67.6** *	83.7
Ribeiro et al. (2018)	64.6 †	-
BERT-PIE (Awasthi et al., 2019)	67.0 *	-
BERT-Neuspell (Jayanthi et al., 2020)	-	84.0
HCTagger	67.2	**86.8**

Table 3: Performance on Twitter and Webis dataset. Results with † are from Ribeiro et al. (2018); results with $*$ are from Awasthi et al. (2019).

Model	Words per Second
Seq2Seq (Transformer)	36.62
BERT-PIE (Awasthi et al., 2019)	80.43
HCTagger	**251.20**

Table 4: Inference speed on Twitter dataset.

	Accuracy
Full Model	67.2
- w/o Pretrained LM	65.3
- w/o Hierarchical Multi-Task	66.5

Table 6: Ablation study on Twitter dataset.

Model	Query per Second
Seq2Seq (LSTM)	83.33
Seq2Seq (Transformer)	40.00
BERT-Neuspell (Jayanthi et al., 2020)	62.50
HCTagger	**250.00**

Table 5: Inference speed on Webis dataset.

this dataset, probably because the number of misspelled queries is small (17%) and is not enough to train Transformer well. In contrast, our model makes more effective use of small training set.

Meanwhile, we also compare the inference speed of the most accurate models, as shown in Table 4 and Table 5. Indeed, the inference speed of HCTagger is much faster than Seq2Seq (LSTM, Transformer), BERT-PIE (Awasthi et al., 2019), and BERT-Neuspell (Jayanthi et al., 2020).

3.4 Ablation Study

To understand the importance of each part of the model, we conduct an ablation study on the Twitter dataset, and report the accuracy in Table 6.

We first take away the pre-trained language model. At this point, the character-level embedding is randomly initialized and the rest of the model is left unchanged. The accuracy decreases by 1.9%.

Subsequently, we preserve the language model but remove the coarse-grained loss term of the Hierarchical Multi-Task. In this case, the accuracy decreases by 0.7%.

4 Related Works

Hasan et al. use character-based statistical machine translation to correct user queries in the e-commerce domain. They extract training data from query refinement logs, and evaluate the results on an internal dataset.

Grammar Error Correction (GEC) is an extensively researched NLP task. This task contains grammar errors, including spelling, punctuation, grammatical, and word choice errors. PIE (Awasthi et al., 2019) and GECToR (Omelianchuk et al., 2020) are the state-of-the-art models that predict token-level edit operations {*Keep*, *Delete*, *Replace*, *Insert*} by leveraging pre-trained Transformer encoders like BERT. However, their models are not specifically designed for correcting spelling errors, which most often occur at character level. They rely on a small ($\sim$1k) pre-defined token-level *Replace* and *Insert* dictionary. Including all correctly-spelled tokens in the dictionary will make the label space too large.

Transformer based Seq2Seq models (Kiyono et al., 2019; Zhao et al., 2019) prove to be successful on grammar error corrections, but heavily depends on synthetically generated error datasets. Character based Seq2Seq models (Xie et al., 2016) are also explored. Such model architectures involve a separate autoregressive decoder and attention module, which makes the inference time much slower. In particular for spelling error correction task, where the misspelling and correction only differ by one or more characters, Seq2Seq models seem too heavy.

Neuspell (Jayanthi et al., 2020) is a spelling correction toolkit, which implements a wide range of models like SC-Elmo-LSTM and BERT. They regard spelling correction as a token-level sequence labeling task, where the output for each token is its error-free form. For each word in the input text sequence, models are trained to output a probability distribution over a finite vocabulary. Besides the aforementioned excessive label space problem at token-level, another shortcoming of this toolkit is that it assumes the misspelled and correction sentences have exactly the same number of tokens. Therefore, cross-word errors such as *power point* $\rightarrow$ *powerpoint* or *babydoll* $\rightarrow$ *baby doll* cannot be handled properly.

Ribeiro et al. treat spelling correction as a character-level local sequence transduction task by first predicting insertion slots in the input using learned insertion patterns, and then using a sequence labeling task to output tokens or a special token *Delete*. They maintain a dictionary to keep track of the insertion context. For example, letter *a* is inserted frequently after letter *s*. While our pretrained language model layer implicitly encodes such insertion context without the need of keeping a dictionary.

5 Conclusions

We presented the Hierarchical Character Tagger to correct user-generated short text misspellings. HCTagger predicts character-level edits, which has smaller label space than token-level edits. Pretrained character-level language model embedding that we use is lightweight and much faster than BERT-like text encoders in many other state-of-the-art models, while achieving similar or even higher accuracy for short text spelling error correction task. Moreover, our novel Hierarchical Multi-Task decoding approach can be extended to any scenario that contains a hierarchical long-tail distributed label space.

Acknowledgements

We would like to thank Zhe Wu, Julie Netzloff, Xiaoyuan Wu, Hua Yang, Vivian Tian and Scott Gaffney for their support.

References

Alan Akbik, Duncan Blythe, and Roland Vollgraf. 2018. Contextual string embeddings for sequence labeling. In *Proceedings of the 27th International Conference on Computational Linguistics, COLING 2018, Santa Fe, New Mexico, USA, August 20-26, 2018*, pages 1638–1649. Association for Computational Linguistics.

Eiji Aramaki. 2010. Typo corpus.

Kevin Atkinson. 2018. Gnu aspell.

Abhijeet Awasthi, Sunita Sarawagi, Rasna Goyal, Sabyasachi Ghosh, and Vihari Piratla. 2019. Parallel iterative edit models for local sequence transduction. In *Proceedings of the 2019 Conference on Empirical Methods in Natural Language Processing and the 9th International Joint Conference on Natural Language Processing, EMNLP-IJCNLP 2019, Hong Kong, China, November 3-7, 2019*, pages 4259–4269. Association for Computational Linguistics.

Ciprian Chelba, Tomás Mikolov, Mike Schuster, Qi Ge, Thorsten Brants, Phillipp Koehn, and Tony Robinson. 2014. One billion word benchmark for measuring progress in statistical language modeling. In *INTERSPEECH 2014, 15th Annual Conference of the International Speech Communication Association, Singapore, September 14-18, 2014*, pages 2635–2639. ISCA.

Jacob Devlin, Ming-Wei Chang, Kenton Lee, and Kristina Toutanova. 2019. BERT: pre-training of deep bidirectional transformers for language understanding. In *Proceedings of the 2019 Conference of the North American Chapter of the Association for Computational Linguistics: Human Language Technologies, NAACL-HLT 2019, Minneapolis, MN, USA, June 2-7, 2019, Volume 1 (Long and Short Papers)*, pages 4171–4186. Association for Computational Linguistics.

Matthias Hagen, Martin Potthast, Marcel Gohsen, Anja Rathgeber, and Benno Stein. 2017. A large-scale query spelling correction corpus. In *Proceedings of the 40th International ACM SIGIR Conference on Research and Development in Information Retrieval, Shinjuku, Tokyo, Japan, August 7-11, 2017*, pages 1261–1264. ACM.

Sasa Hasan, Carmen Heger, and Saab Mansour. 2015. Spelling correction of user search queries through statistical machine translation. In *Proceedings of the 2015 Conference on Empirical Methods in Natural Language Processing, EMNLP 2015, Lisbon, Portugal, September 17-21, 2015*, pages 451–460. The Association for Computational Linguistics.

Sai Muralidhar Jayanthi, Danish Pruthi, and Graham Neubig. 2020. Neuspell: A neural spelling correction toolkit. In *Proceedings of the 2020 Conference on Empirical Methods in Natural Language Processing: System Demonstrations, EMNLP 2020 - Demos, Online, November 16-20, 2020*, pages 158–164. Association for Computational Linguistics.

Diederik P. Kingma and Jimmy Ba. 2015. Adam: A method for stochastic optimization. In *3rd International Conference on Learning Representations, ICLR 2015, San Diego, CA, USA, May 7-9, 2015, Conference Track Proceedings*.

Shun Kiyono, Jun Suzuki, Masato Mita, Tomoya Mizumoto, and Kentaro Inui. 2019. An empirical study of incorporating pseudo data into grammatical error correction. In *Proceedings of the 2019 Conference on Empirical Methods in Natural Language Processing and the 9th International Joint Conference on Natural Language Processing, EMNLP-IJCNLP 2019, Hong Kong, China, November 3-7, 2019*, pages 1236–1242. Association for Computational Linguistics.

Kostiantyn Omelianchuk, Vitaliy Atrasevych, Artem N. Chernodub, and Oleksandr Skurzhanskyi. 2020. Gector - grammatical error correction: Tag, not rewrite. In *Proceedings of the Fifteenth Workshop on Innovative Use of NLP for Building Educational Applications, BEA@ACL 2020, Online, July 10, 2020*, pages 163–170. Association for Computational Linguistics.

Adam Paszke, Sam Gross, Francisco Massa, Adam Lerer, James Bradbury, Gregory Chanan, Trevor Killeen, Zeming Lin, Natalia Gimelshein, Luca Antiga, Alban Desmaison, Andreas Köpf, Edward Yang, Zachary DeVito, Martin Raison, Alykhan Tejani, Sasank Chilamkurthy, Benoit Steiner, Lu Fang, Junjie Bai, and Soumith Chintala. 2019. Pytorch: An imperative style, high-performance deep learning library. In *Advances in Neural Information Processing Systems 32: Annual Conference on Neural Information Processing Systems 2019, NeurIPS 2019, December 8-14, 2019, Vancouver, BC, Canada*, pages 8024–8035.

Joana Ribeiro, Shashi Narayan, Shay B. Cohen, and Xavier Carreras. 2018. Local string transduction as sequence labeling. In *Proceedings of the 27th International Conference on Computational Linguistics, COLING 2018, Santa Fe, New Mexico, USA, August 20-26, 2018*, pages 1360–1371. Association for Computational Linguistics.

Ashish Vaswani, Noam Shazeer, Niki Parmar, Jakob Uszkoreit, Llion Jones, Aidan N. Gomez, Lukasz Kaiser, and Illia Polosukhin. 2017. Attention is all you need. In *Advances in Neural Information Processing Systems 30: Annual Conference on Neural Information Processing Systems 2017, December 4-9, 2017, Long Beach, CA, USA*, pages 5998–6008.

Ziang Xie, Anand Avati, Naveen Arivazhagan, Dan Jurafsky, and Andrew Y. Ng. 2016. Neural language correction with character-based attention. *CoRR*, abs/1603.09727.

Yang You, Jing Li, Sashank J. Reddi, Jonathan Hseu, Sanjiv Kumar, Srinadh Bhojanapalli, Xiaodan Song, James Demmel, Kurt Keutzer, and Cho-Jui Hsieh. 2020. Large batch optimization for deep learning: Training BERT in 76 minutes. In *8th International Conference on Learning Representations, ICLR 2020, Addis Ababa, Ethiopia, April 26-30, 2020*. OpenReview.net.

Wei Zhao, Liang Wang, Kewei Shen, Ruoyu Jia, and Jingming Liu. 2019. Improving grammatical error correction via pre-training a copy-augmented architecture with unlabeled data. In *Proceedings of the 2019 Conference of the North American Chapter of the Association for Computational Linguistics: Human Language Technologies, NAACL-HLT 2019, Minneapolis, MN, USA, June 2-7, 2019, Volume 1 (Long and Short Papers)*, pages 156–165. Association for Computational Linguistics.

Common Sense Bias in Semantic Role Labeling

Heather Lent and **Anders Søgaard**
University of Copenhagen, Denmark
{hcl, soegaard}@di.ku.dk

Abstract

Large-scale language models such as ELMo and BERT have pushed the horizon of what is possible in semantic role labeling (SRL), solving the out-of-vocabulary problem and enabling end-to-end systems, but they have also introduced significant biases. We evaluate three SRL parsers on very simple transitive sentences with verbs usually associated with animate subjects and objects, such as *Mary babysat Tom*: a state-of-the-art parser based on BERT, an older parser based on GloVe, and an even older parser from before the days of word embeddings. When arguments are word forms predominantly used as person names, aligning with common sense expectations of animacy, the BERT-based parser is unsurprisingly superior; yet, with abstract or random nouns, the opposite picture emerges. We refer to this as *common sense bias* and present a challenge dataset for evaluating the extent to which parsers are sensitive to such a bias. Our code and challenge dataset are available here: github.com/coastalcph/comte

1 Introduction

Semantic role labeling (SRL) refers to a shallow semantic dependency parsing that returns predicate-argument structures for input sentences; see Figure 1. Modern-day SRL systems, like most other NLP technologies, rely heavily on large-scale language models. Such language models are extremely useful for generalizing to out-of-vocabulary items, making subtle syntactic distinctions, and for capturing a range of lexical ambiguities; but they also introduce notable biases.

Previous work has shown that SRL systems exhibit demographic biases (Zhao et al., 2017); we focus on a form of belief bias (Sternberg and Leighton, 2004), which we will refer to as *common sense bias*, reflecting how language models encode conventional associations, which in many ways are indistinguishable from common sense (Trinh and Le, 2019). While demographic biases can lead to discrimination against under-represented demographics, belief biases can lead to discrimination against rare events; or, more precisely, lead SRL systems to err on sentences that express unlikely states of affairs. This is what belief biases refer to in cognitive science (Sternberg and Leighton, 2004): human preferences for conclusions that align with values, beliefs, and prior knowledge. Belief biases in models can, like demographic biases, exacerbate societal challenges, e.g., anomaly detection, and also correlate with demographics, since groups differ in how much they engage with counterfactual and fictitious contents.

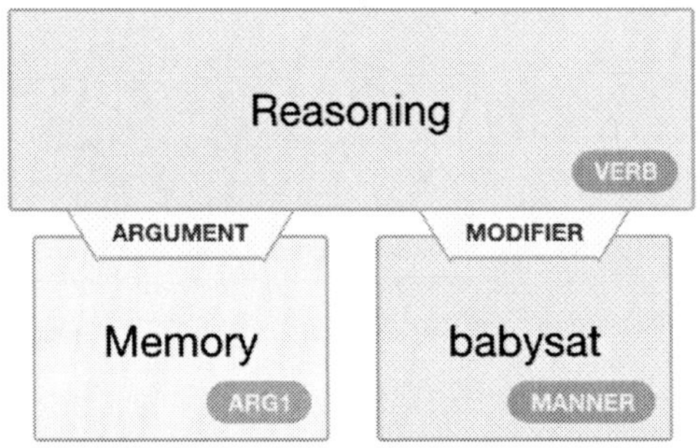

Figure 1: The (incorrect) analysis of *Memory babysat Reasoning* by Shi and Lin (2019).

We compare the errors of a modern, competitive SRL system (Shi and Lin, 2019), based on BERT (Devlin et al., 2019), and show how it, unlike earlier SRL systems, suffers from common sense bias: When confronted with sentences that, when read literally, express unlikely states of affairs, it can ignore obvious cues and produce false predicate-argument structures even for very simple sentences. The sentence in Figure 1, for example, can be understood as expressing that the abstract concept of *Memory* babysat the abstract concept of *Reasoning*. The literal reading represents an unlikely state

Proceedings of the 2021 EMNLP Workshop W-NUT: The Seventh Workshop on Noisy User-generated Text, pages 114–119
November 11, 2021.

$$\begin{array}{r} \textit{names} \\ \text{countries} \\ \text{abstract} \\ \text{random-nouns} \\ \text{random-strings} \end{array} \left\{ \begin{array}{c} \text{Mary} \\ \text{Sweden} \\ \text{Memory} \\ \text{apples} \\ \text{asdfabv} \end{array} \right\} \textit{babysat} \left\{ \begin{array}{l} \text{Tom} \\ \text{Senegal} \\ \text{Reasoning} \\ \text{oranges} \\ \text{sadlfkj} \end{array} \right\}$$

Figure 2: Examples of transitive sentences with person names, country names, abstract nouns, (randomly chosen) plural common nouns, or random strings as arguments. Person names, and to some degree country names (which are often personified (Wang, 2020)), align with expectations of animacy.

of affairs, since abstract concepts generally do not have the capacity of babysitting. Obviously, this does not prevent language users from uttering the sentence, and it is, for most of us, not hard to make sense of it: The sentence, for example, could mean something like *memory assists reasoning*. Many similar sentences can be found in the wild, e.g., *the US babysits Israel* (from `cnn.com`) or *Love bodyslams you* (from `quizlet.com`). Other sentences express unlikely states of affairs, not because of linguistic creativity, but because they refer to possible worlds, not ours, for scientific, literary, political or other reasons. We believe it is critical that SRL parsers should be robust to such variation, but our experiments show that while SRL performance numbers have gone up dramatically in recent years, parsers seem to have become more sensitive to it.

Contributions We present an error analysis of three very different SRL parsers for English: the supervised, log-linear, quadratic-time parser proposed in Björkelund et al. (2009); the supervised, deep, linear-time parser proposed in Stanovsky et al. (2018), based on GloVe embeddings (Pennington et al., 2014) and recurrent networks (Hochreiter and Schmidhuber, 1997); and the self-supervised (and supervised), deep, linear-time parser proposed in Shi and Lin (2019), based on BERT (Devlin et al., 2019). Instead of evaluating these models on standard benchmarks of newspapers, where predicate-argument structures already align with the 'beliefs' of BERT, we evaluate the systems on randomly generated transitive sentences of the form NP-V-NP, with V expressed by verbs strongly associated with A_0-V-A_1 frames, and the NPs expressed by proper nouns, abstract nouns or plural common nouns. From these experiments, we show that (a) the SRL systems considered here frequently err on such sentences; (b) the SRL error distribution across verb lemmata is uncorrelated with the errors of a dependency parser; (c) what pairs of NP semantic categories lead to errors for what verbs; and (d) how the BERT-based system suffers from common sense bias. Finally, we create a 1000-sentence challenge dataset for probing SRL for common sense bias. Our error analyses paint a complementary, yet entirely different picture of what SRL systems can and cannot, compared to previous work (He et al., 2017; Strubell et al., 2018), which has focused on long-distance dependencies and the need for syntax.

Ref	Model	F_1
Björkelund et al. (2009)	MST/MIRA	0.803
Stanovsky et al. (2018)	LSTM/GloVe	0.823
Shi and Lin (2019)	BERT	0.888

Table 1: The three SRL systems used below and their performance on the CoNLL 2005 benchmark

2 Semantic Role Labeling Systems

Björkelund et al. (2009) combine three logistic regression classifiers with beam search and a global reranker: the first classifier identifies predicates, the second their arguments, and the third labels the semantic dependencies between predicates and their arguments. The system relies on a POS tagger and a syntactic dependency parser to generate features for the classifiers. This system had the second-best performance in the CoNLL 2009 Shared Task. Stanovsky et al. (2018) rely on a standard recurrent architecture. They use GloVe embeddings (Pennington et al., 2014), in conjunction with embeddings from a POS tagger, and stack bidirectional LSTM layers (Hochreiter and Schmidhuber, 1997) on top of the embedding layer. The representation at each time-step is passed to a classifier, which directly predicts the output label for that time-step. Unlike Björkelund et al. (2009), they do not rely on search over possible output combinations. Shi and Lin (2019) also do not rely on search, but reduce SRL to two-stage sequence labeling, both stages pretrained with BERT-large (Devlin et al., 2019); first identifying predicates, then arguments, while conditioning on the predicates.

3 Coarse-Grained Error Analysis

In our error analysis, we focus on simple three-word sentences that consist of a noun, a transitive verb, and a noun. The transitive verbs are hand-picked to exhibit strong preferences for animate subjects and objects, low ambiguity, and predom-

Verb	Error	A_0VA_2	A_1VA_2	...V	Expl
fails	0.898	0.006	**0.758**	0.000	Syntax
calls	0.528	**0.467**	0.020	0.020	
trips	0.356	0.007	0.000	**0.128**	POS
tips	0.875	0.010	0.010	**0.687**	
bodyslams	0.373	0.065	0.052	0.034	?
babysits	0.212	0.048	0.072	0.035	

Table 2: Error rates and most frequent error types for common verbs in their present and past tense forms, in simple SOV constructions, e.g., *John calls Mary*. All numbers are for Shi and Lin (2019). Bold-faced error types most frequent (of the four presented here). The verbs *bodyslams* and *babysits* are used in our experiments, because (a) they have strong selectional restrictions for animate subjects and objects, (b) they predominantly realize A_0 and A_1 as subjects and objects (unlike *fails* and *calls*), and (c) while all English verbs tend to have noun readings, the verb readings are far more frequent (unlike for *trips* and *tips*).

Error	Björkelund et al. (2009)	Stanovsky et al. (2018)	Shi and Lin (2019)
names	0.158	**0.341**	0.077
countries	0.183	**0.505**	0.030
abstract	0.174	**0.353**	0.133
random-nouns	0.188	0.287	**0.310**
random-strings	**0.997**	0.172	0.313

Table 3: **Main results:** Error rates of three SRL systems across transitive sentences with person names in subject and object positions, versus country names, abstract nouns, (randomly chosen) plural common nouns, or random strings in those positions

Tajikistan bodyslams Maldives	Lebanon bodyslammed Netherlands
Myanmar bodyslammed Andorra	Bangladesh bodypaints Peru
Luxembourg bodypainted Andorra	Kazakhstan bodypainted Guinea
Bangladesh combed Turkey	Bangladesh manicured Swaziland

Table 4: Simple sentences on which Stanovsky et al. (2018) and Shi and Lin (2019) both err. Björkelund et al. (2009), in contrast, assigns correct parses to all of these. Try yourself: `barbar.cs.lth.se:8081/`

inantly realize their agents (A_0) as subjects, and their second argument (A_1) as objects. The error analysis consists of comparing performance across different types of subjects and objects and comprises examples such as those in Figure 2. The arguments exhibit various degrees of animacy associations, aligning more or less with common sense expectations. We obtain the names from the NAMES library,[1] the country names from WorldMap,[2] the abstract nouns from YourDictionary,[3] and common nouns from the Princeton WordNet.[4]

We assume a correct semantic parse associates subject with A_0 and object with A_1 (of the predicate introduced by the verb). This is obviously not true for all verbs (Palmer et al., 2005; Hovy et al., 2006). In Table 2, we list verbs that frequently associate subjects and objects with other arguments (*fails* and *calls*), as well as verbs that are very ambiguous and easily mistaken for nouns (*trips* and *tips*). Both phenomena are reflected in the distribution of analyses for Shi and Lin (2019). While much can be said about these verbs, our main contribution here is highlighting the role of common sense bias in some SRL parsers, and we thus focus on verbs where we can safely assume a A_0VA_1 reading is correct (such as *babyslams* and *babysits*).[5]

Error analysis results are presented in Table 3. If performance drops considerably below the performance label with names or countries, when using abstract nouns, randomly sampled nouns, or simply random strings, as arguments, this suggests a common sense bias, seen very strongly with Shi and Lin (2019). Björkelund et al. (2009), in contrast, exhibits near-uniform performance across the different sets of arguments. Since the parser has no strategy to deal with out-of-vocabulary items, it exhibits worse performance on random strings.[6] Stanovsky et al. (2018), surprisingly, seems extremely sensitive to country name arguments,[7] and performance oddly improves with random strings arguments. Since these are out-of-vocabulary, the parser probably drops back to a default strategy. Notably, Shi and Lin (2019) does well on country names, there are plenty of examples that Stanovsky et al. (2018) and Shi and Lin (2019) get wrong, but that Björkelund et al. (2009) get right; see Table 4 for examples.

[1] `https://pypi.org/project/names/`

[2] `http://worldmap.harvard.edu/`

[3] `https://examples.yourdictionary.com/examples-of-abstract-nouns.html`

[4] `https://wordnet.princeton.edu/`

[5] The six verb lemmata we use are: *bodyslam, bodypaint, comb, manicure, elbow,* and *babysit*.

[6] Björkelund et al. (2009) near-consistently analyze these as intransitive with the first two words making up A_1.

[7] We found no explanation for Stanovsky et al. (2018)'s poor performance with country name arguments.

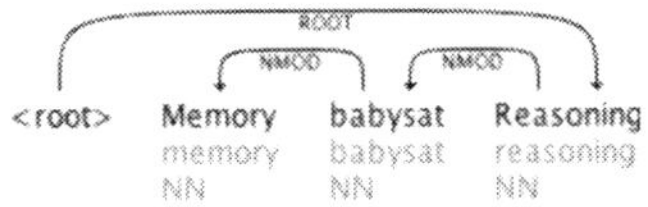

Figure 3: Parse tree in Björkelund et al. (2009) for *Memory babysat Reasoning*.

Comparison with Dependency Parser Errors While only one of the parsers (Björkelund et al., 2009) relies on input features from a syntactic parser, it is tempting to think that, in line with previous error analyses of SRL systems (He et al., 2017; Strubell et al., 2018), the error distribution can be explained by syntactic ambiguities and resulting syntactic errors. This, perhaps unsurprisingly, turns out to reliably explain the error distribution observed with Björkelund et al. (2009). See Figure 3 for the syntactic parse on *Memory babysits Reasoning*, on which the log-linear parser fails to deliver any SRL analysis, interpreting the three-word sentence as a nominal compound. For the neural parsers, there is no correlation, however. We ran a syntactic parser (Dozat et al., 2017) on our three-word sentences and correlated errors across lemmata. We observed a small, but *negative* correlation between error rates.

4 Fine-Grained Error Analysis

Multitude of Errors Our first observation is that across all verb lemmata, the parser in Shi and Lin (2019) produces *many* different output trees, depending on the argument word forms. For some lemmata, the error distribution is near-uniform across 15-20 outputs. It is well-established in SRL that infrequent contexts lead to low confidence (Chen et al., 2011), explaining why common sense bias leads to a multitude of errors.

Morphosyntactic Ambiguity While parsing errors do not correlate with errors of Shi and Lin (2019) (§3), the SRL system seems to be sensitive to part-of-speech ambiguity. It errs, for example, on *Insomnia trips jaywalking*, but not on *Insomnia tripped jaywalking*, presumably because *trips* is (on its own) ambiguous.[8] Sensitivity to such ambiguities disappears when aligning with common sense: The parser does not err on *Mary trips John* or *Mary likes jaywalking*. The same ambiguity leads to error in *London trips John.*, but not in *London tripped John.* With the even more frequent surname of *Washington*, the effect disappears, and Shi and Lin (2019) get both verb forms right.

5 COMTE: A Test of Common Sense Bias

Our challenge dataset[9] COMTE consists of 1,000 simple, three-word sentences with the same gold analysis: the second word is the predicate, the first word its A_0, the last word its A_1. The predicates are sampled at random from a list of six carefully selected verbs (see §3) that select for animate subjects and objects and consistently prefer these to be A_0 and A_1. As before, we combine the verbs with names, countries, abstract nouns, plural common nouns, and random strings. The sentences were simply the first 1,000 sentences that we sampled this way, with 200 sentences in each category (names, countries, etc.) – and which satisfied a simple criterion: Neither Shi and Lin (2019) nor (Stanovsky et al., 2018) would get it right. COMTE, in other words, consists of 1,000 trivial sentences that two competitive SRL parsers failed to parse correctly.

What can COMTE be used for? Obviously, it can not be used to fine-tune parsers on, for example. It would take only a few examples to learn what is going on in the data, and training would likely lead to over-fitting. COMTE can also not be used to derive parsing performance figures that tell us much about the performance of parsers in the wild. The 1,000 sentences should, in our view, be thought of as a single probe into the degree to which a parser is sensitive to common sense bias. A parser should rarely err on the examples in the challenge dataset: They are all trivially simple, and while some argument words can be ambiguous, the verbs so strongly select for simple A_0VA_1 frames that parsers should unambiguously prefer this reading. If they don't, this is a sign they struggle with simple transitive sentences, like Stanovsky et al. (2018), or that they are prone to common sense bias, like Shi and Lin (2019). In order to quantify the degree to which the effect can be attributed to common sense bias, performance with *names* can be used as a baseline: If performance is much better for names than for some of the other categories, like with Shi and Lin (2019), this is an indicator of common sense bias.

[8]This is orthogonal to the ambiguity of *jaywalking*; see Padó et al. (2008) for the analysis of nominal predicates.

[9]Our dataset differs from previous challenge datasets for mixed language (Pal and Sharma, 2019), chat (Rachman et al., 2018), etc., in being synthetic.

6 Acknowledgments

We thank the anonymous reviewers for their useful feedback. This project has received funding from the European Union's Horizon 2020 Research and Innovation Programme under the Marie Skłodowska-Curie Grant Agreement No 801199, as well as from a Google Focused Research Award.

References

Anders Björkelund, Love Hafdell, and Pierre Nugues. 2009. Multilingual semantic role labeling. In *Proceedings of the Thirteenth Conference on Computational Natural Language Learning (CoNLL 2009): Shared Task*, pages 43–48, Boulder, Colorado. Association for Computational Linguistics.

Chenhua Chen, Alexis Palmer, and Caroline Sporleder. 2011. Enhancing active learning for semantic role labeling via compressed dependency trees. In *Proceedings of 5th International Joint Conference on Natural Language Processing*, pages 183–191, Chiang Mai, Thailand. Asian Federation of Natural Language Processing.

Jacob Devlin, Ming-Wei Chang, Kenton Lee, and Kristina Toutanova. 2019. BERT: Pre-training of deep bidirectional transformers for language understanding. In *Proceedings of the 2019 Conference of the North American Chapter of the Association for Computational Linguistics: Human Language Technologies, Volume 1 (Long and Short Papers)*, pages 4171–4186, Minneapolis, Minnesota. Association for Computational Linguistics.

Timothy Dozat, Peng Qi, and Christopher D. Manning. 2017. Stanford's graph-based neural dependency parser at the CoNLL 2017 shared task. In *Proceedings of the CoNLL 2017 Shared Task: Multilingual Parsing from Raw Text to Universal Dependencies*, pages 20–30, Vancouver, Canada. Association for Computational Linguistics.

Luheng He, Kenton Lee, Mike Lewis, and Luke Zettlemoyer. 2017. Deep semantic role labeling: What works and what's next. In *Proceedings of the 55th Annual Meeting of the Association for Computational Linguistics (Volume 1: Long Papers)*, pages 473–483, Vancouver, Canada. Association for Computational Linguistics.

Sepp Hochreiter and Jürgen Schmidhuber. 1997. Long short-term memory. *Neural computation*, 9(8):1735–1780.

Eduard Hovy, Mitchell Marcus, Martha Palmer, Lance Ramshaw, and Ralph Weischedel. 2006. OntoNotes: The 90% solution. In *Proceedings of the Human Language Technology Conference of the NAACL, Companion Volume: Short Papers*, pages 57–60, New York City, USA. Association for Computational Linguistics.

Sebastian Padó, Marco Pennacchiotti, and Caroline Sporleder. 2008. Semantic role assignment for event nominalisations by leveraging verbal data. In *Proceedings of the 22nd International Conference on Computational Linguistics (Coling 2008)*, pages 665–672, Manchester, UK. Coling 2008 Organizing Committee.

Riya Pal and Dipti Sharma. 2019. A dataset for semantic role labelling of Hindi-English code-mixed tweets. In *Proceedings of the 13th Linguistic Annotation Workshop*, pages 178–188, Florence, Italy. Association for Computational Linguistics.

Martha Palmer, Daniel Gildea, and Paul Kingsbury. 2005. The Proposition Bank: An annotated corpus of semantic roles. *Computational Linguistics*, 31(1):71–106.

Jeffrey Pennington, Richard Socher, and Christopher Manning. 2014. GloVe: Global vectors for word representation. In *Proceedings of the 2014 Conference on Empirical Methods in Natural Language Processing (EMNLP)*, pages 1532–1543, Doha, Qatar. Association for Computational Linguistics.

Valdi Rachman, Rahmad Mahendra, Alfan Farizki Wicaksono, Ahmad Rizqi Meydiarso, and Fariz Ikhwantri. 2018. Semantic role labeling in conversational chat using deep bi-directional long short-term memory networks with attention mechanism. In *Proceedings of the 32nd Pacific Asia Conference on Language, Information and Computation*, Hong Kong. Association for Computational Linguistics.

Peng Shi and Jimmy Lin. 2019. Simple bert models for relation extraction and semantic role labeling.

Gabriel Stanovsky, Julian Michael, Luke Zettlemoyer, and Ido Dagan. 2018. Supervised open information extraction. In *Proceedings of the 2018 Conference of the North American Chapter of the Association for Computational Linguistics: Human Language Technologies, Volume 1 (Long Papers)*, pages 885–895, New Orleans, Louisiana. Association for Computational Linguistics.

Robert Sternberg and Jacqueline Leighton. 2004. *The Nature of Reasoning*. Cambridge University Press.

Emma Strubell, Patrick Verga, Daniel Andor, David Weiss, and Andrew McCallum. 2018. Linguistically-informed self-attention for semantic role labeling. In *Proceedings of the 2018 Conference on Empirical Methods in Natural Language Processing*, pages 5027–5038, Brussels, Belgium. Association for Computational Linguistics.

Trieu H. Trinh and Quoc V. Le. 2019. Do language models have common sense?

Yongqi Wang. 2020. The metaphoric and metonymic use of country names in economic newsa corpus-based analysis. *Chinese Journal of Applied Linguistics*, 43(4):439 – 454.

Jieyu Zhao, Tianlu Wang, Mark Yatskar, Vicente Ordonez, and Kai-Wei Chang. 2017. Men also like shopping: Reducing gender bias amplification using corpus-level constraints. In *Proceedings of the 2017 Conference on Empirical Methods in Natural Language Processing*, pages 2979–2989, Copenhagen, Denmark. Association for Computational Linguistics.

PoliWAM: An Exploration of a Large Scale Corpus of Political Discussions on WhatsApp Messenger

Vivek Srivastava
TCS Research
Pune, Maharashtra, India
srivastava.vivek2@tcs.com

Mayank Singh
IIT Gandhinagar
Gandhinagar, Gujarat, India
singh.mayank@iitgn.ac.in

Abstract

WhatsApp Messenger is one of the most popular channels for spreading information with a current reach of more than 180 countries and 2 billion people. Its widespread usage has made it one of the most popular media for information propagation among the masses during any socially engaging event. In the recent past, several countries have witnessed its effectiveness and influence in political and social campaigns. We observe a high surge in information and propaganda flow during election campaigning. In this paper, we explore a high-quality large-scale user-generated dataset curated from WhatsApp comprising of 281 groups, 31,078 unique users, and 223,404 messages shared before, during, and after the Indian General Elections 2019, encompassing all major Indian political parties and leaders. In addition to the raw noisy user-generated data, we present a fine-grained annotated dataset of 3,848 messages that will be useful to understand the various dimensions of WhatsApp political campaigning. We present several complementary insights into the investigative and sensational news stories from the same period. Exploratory data analysis and experiments showcase several exciting results and future research opportunities. To facilitate reproducible research, we make the anonymized datasets available in the public domain.

1 Introduction

In the last decade, the majority of the political parties around the world are heavily spending on social media engagement platforms like Facebook, Twitter, Quora, WhatsApp, and Sharechat for fast and secure information spread. WhatsApp Messenger (hereafter *'WAM'*) is highly prevalent in 180 countries with installation over 90% of devices (Bobrov, 2018). WAM allows users to send instant messages, photos, videos, and voice messages in addition to voice and video calls over a secure end-to-end encryption channel. However, data curation from WAM remains a challenging task owing to privacy concerns, stringent encryption strategies, and system requirements.

WAM as Political Propaganda Tool: Several investigative journalism stories (Tech, 2018; Conversation, 2018; Indian, 2019) suggest ever-increasing global penetration of WAM-based political propaganda and the resultant mass polarization effects. India, the second-most-populous country with 1.3 billion population, has witnessed similar trends (News, 2018; Uttam, 2018) during the past two General Elections (Ruble, 2014). WAM has emerged as a primary leader for delivery for political messaging with 95% of Android devices in India having WAM installation and maintaining a 75% daily active users percentage (Bobrov, 2018). For the first time, complementing the existing investigative journalism stories, we present a scientific study to understand the WAM messaging patterns and spread in the political scenario.

WAM Data Curation: To adhere to the WAM's privacy policy (Garimella and Tyson, 2018), we consider only WAM public groups where users willingly share messages with known and unknown people. The biggest challenge with restricting to public groups is a large number of fake and dubious groups and the unavailability of a standard in-app filter functionality to identify such groups. To the best of our information, none of the previous works on WAM data curation have discussed any methodologies for filtering irrelevant groups. One of the earliest works on WAM dataset curation (Garimella and Tyson, 2018) considers a list of all WAM public groups available online. We claim that due to multilingualism coupled with code-mixing and multi-modal metadata, the genuine group identification problem is non-trivial. We present a novel manual group filtering strategy to filter fake and dubious groups by leveraging group metadata, i.e., group name, display picture, and the description. Owing to the user's privacy in the WAM groups, we

Proceedings of the 2021 EMNLP Workshop W-NUT: The Seventh Workshop on Noisy User-generated Text, pages 120–130
November 11, 2021.

release the anonymized dataset[1]. In addition, we are also releasing a fine-grained annotated dataset of 3,848 messages (see Section 3.2) for future research opportunities. The annotated dataset contains interesting fine-grained labels in four categories i.e., malicious activity, political orientation, political inclination, and message language.

Our Contributions: The main contributions are:

- We present a novel WAM group filtering strategy leveraging the group's metadata to filter the fake and dubious groups.
- We analyze a total of 281 public groups distributed among 26 political parties, including all the seven national political parties.
- In addition to the original anonymized dataset with 223,403 messages and 31,078 unique WAM users, we also release a publicly available fine-grained annotated dataset of 3,848 WAM messages with language, malicious activity, political orientation, and political inclination as labels.
- We present several interesting insights from the analysis of users and the message content. We establish several correlations with the claims and reports of news media and survey articles from the same period.
- We draw several interesting insights on co-occurrences of the political entities (leaders and parties) and social factors (agendas, religions, castes, and languages/ethnicity) from the linguistic perspective.

2 Related Work

People engage in various social media platforms such as Twitter, Facebook, etc., to discuss socially relevant topics such as politics. We witness a large volume of research focused on Twitter-based political discussions due to the easier availability of data and the large-scale involvement of the masses. For example, (Bovet and Makse, 2019) conducted a large-scale analysis of fake news propagation on Twitter during the 2016 U.S. presidential elections. (Tumasjan et al., 2010) studied the usage of Twitter as a tool for political deliberation and election forecasting. They also used Twitter as a means to understand the political sentiment of the politicians and parties in the election campaigning. (Conover et al., 2011) presented a study of the interaction between the network of users of different ideologies. They used Twitter as a medium to understand the political communication network. (Colleoni et al., 2014) studied the structure of political homophily between different political groups on Twitter to understand the public sphere and echo chamber effect.

In contrast to Twitter-based studies, (Vitak et al., 2011) studied student's involvement in the political discussions on Facebook for the 2008 U.S. presidential election. Several studies looked at different offline modes of political discussions as well. For example, (Ansolabehere et al., 2006) explored the effect of newspaper endorsement on the shift of vote margin. The largest circulation newspaper during the period of 1940–2002 is part of this experiment for the various U.S. elections. (Barrett and Barrington, 2005) conducted a study to understand the visual perception of the voter by the candidate's photograph in the newspaper. (Wang et al., 2015) proposed an innovative methodology on non-representative polls to forecast elections in contrast to the survey methods. They experiment with the data from the Xbox gaming platform for the 2012 U.S. presidential election. (Ferreira et al., 2018) discuss the involvement of the ideological communities over 15 years. They used data on the public voting of Brazil and the U.S and study the polarization in the communities. (Caetano et al., 2018) presented an analysis and characterization of WAM messages at three different layers.

Recently, we observe a growing interest in understanding the information flow on WAM with political discussions in focus (Resende et al., 2019b,a; Pang and Woo, 2020; Vermeer et al., 2021; Velasquez et al., 2021; Garimella and Eckles, 2020; Saha et al., 2021; Javed et al., 2020; Yadav et al., 2020). In contrast to the existing works, we present a novel manual filtering strategy (see Section 3) to identify the potential WAM groups. Our group identification strategy results in a high-quality dataset with less dubious groups. Also, to understand the various user and message characteristics, we present a fine-grained annotated dataset of 3,848 messages.

3 Dataset

In contrast to other social media platforms, data curation from WAM public groups is a non-trivial task. Even, group identification itself is a challenging task as WAM does not support advanced content search feature. Majority of the online fo-

[1] `https://zenodo.org/record/4115660#.YUSln54zZQI`

rums/blogs[2][3] comprises dubious public group links containing pornographic content, lucrative job, and lottery offers (see Figure 1).

As the initial step of data curation, we identify and join the relevant groups. We construct a seed set of Indian political WAM groups (based on the names of political parties and their top leaders) from several forums/blogs and social media platforms like Google, Facebook, and Twitter. The seed set consists of 50 groups. The seed set is obtained after manual pre-processing of ~600 groups. Further, we enrich the seed set by following groups that were shared within the followed groups. Overall, we obtained 2600 group links collected between January 19, 2019 – May 19, 2019. Out of 2600, we only identify 281 (~11%) relevant groups that are actively participating in Indian political discussions. Groups in which all the three metadata categories (i.e., name, display picture, and description) are indicative of the same political affiliation are considered genuine and relevant.

For decryption of the WAM database stored locally on the mobile device, we use a cipher key and a database extractor tool[4]. We divide the complete data collection into three phases:

- *Before elections*: January 19, 2019 – March 5, 2019
- *Active campaigning phase*: March 6, 2019 – May 19, 2019
- *After elections*: May 20, 2019 – June 15, 2019

Figure 2 presents user and content statistics at three different phases. We observe a sharp decline in the message count after elections. Similarly, before elections, we find a low user count. Thus, in the rest of the paper, we focus on the *active campaigning phase*, where the maximum number of users has shared the highest number of messages.

3.1 Metadata Analysis

Table 1 shows the representation of different political parties out of the total 281 groups. Each group is manually affiliated to a single political party based on the group name, display picture, and description. *BJP* shows highest representation followed by *INC* and *SP*. All state-level parties, except *AAP*, show poor representation. Several media reports (TOI, 2019; BBC, 2019) supports the insurgence of *BJP* WAM groups to communicate with the various stakeholders.

We found a total of 37,984 participants in 281 groups. Out of which, 31,078 (81.8%) comprise unique users. Figure 3 shows the user presence in multiple groups. Even though the majority of users (88.5%) are members of a single group, we find instances where few users are members of more than 20 political groups. For instance, one user is a member of 25 groups, whereas seven users are part of 20 or more groups. In addition, we find that during *active campaigning phase*, only a few (12.45%) of these groups have group strength ≤ 50 users. 63.34% of groups have 100 or more members.

3.1.1 Message formats

In phase II, a total of 1,47,220 messages are shared, out of which 58,008 messages contain media files. Table 2 shows the distribution of media files. 67.59% of the total media files are the image files in the JPEG format. This is consistent with the claims of several news articles that memes (Hindu, 2019a; Samosa, 2019) are a powerful tool to attack or praise individuals and parties during campaigning. Images (in JPEG format) and videos (in MP4 format) constitute 95.06% of all the media files shared. Researchers conclude that image-based message sharing has extensively led to propaganda propagation (Madhumita Murgia, 2019). For example, political parties/candidates use doctored images (Times, 2019b; News, 2019) of articles from reputable news media sources to demean opponent political parties/candidates.

3.1.2 Group metadata

Group metadata comprises a display picture, name, and description. Most of the group display pictures are the official party symbols, pictures of the top leaders/influencers, and religious symbols/idols. The textual content in group names and descriptions shows phrases used in social election campaigning. Figures 4(a) and 4(b) show word clouds of the group names and group descriptions, respectively. We observe the most frequently used words to be in consistent with the claims (newslaundry, 2019; Scroll, 2019a; SBS, 2019) of various news and investigative studies. Several research and survey articles (Hindu, 2019b; Livemint, 2019) shows conflicting user opinion on the impact of slogans

[2] https://www.opentechinfo.com/WhatsApp-groups/

[3] https://chatwhatsappgrouplink.blogspot.com/p/join-whatsapp-group-links.html?m=1

[4] https://forum.xda-developers.com/showthread.php?t=2770982

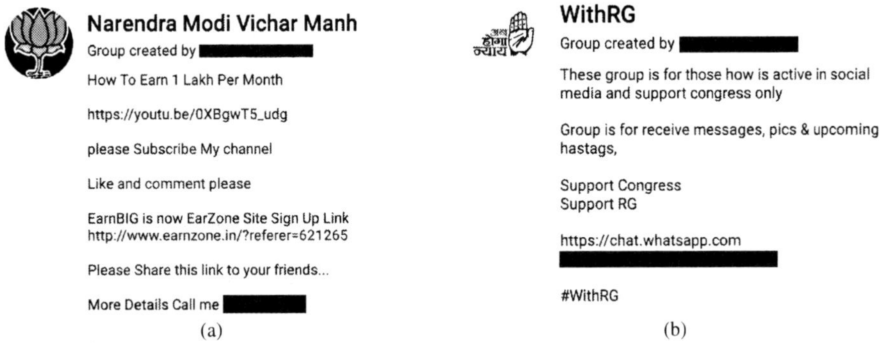

Figure 1: Example metadata snapshot of (a) a dubious and (b) a genuine WAM group. The personal information is anonymized.

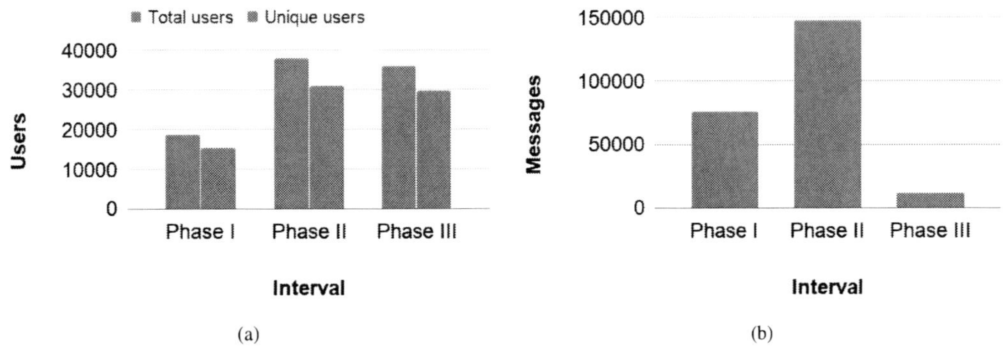

Figure 2: Status of different phases of data collection: (a) Number of total and unique users present and (b) Total messages shared in each phase.

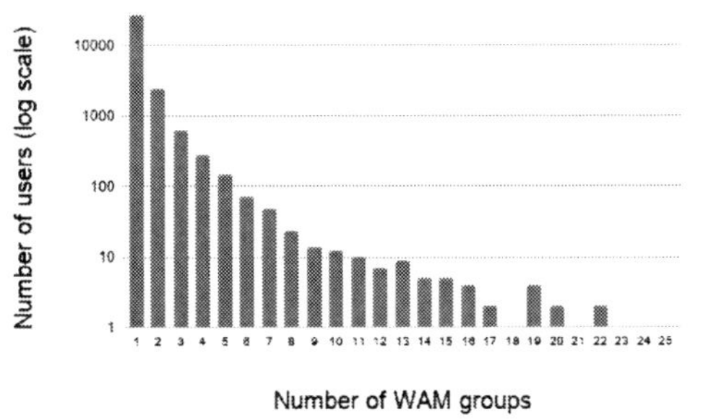

Figure 3: User presence in multiple groups. One user is present in 25 groups. Seven users are part of 20 or more groups.

and influencers in the campaigning. Group names mainly consist of party names as English tokens. Group descriptions mostly contain Hindi language tokens. Thus, any group identification process, either manual or automatic, require a deep understanding of multiple languages.

3.1.3 External link sharing

Several website links are shared among group members. We find a total of 16,582 links comprising news, video, and social media websites. YouTube videos with 5,456 links are the most shared external links. This high number is in line with the claims of several studies (Scroll, 2019b; Times, 2019d) indicating the high influence of YouTube videos in the campaigning. *Facebook*, *Twitter*, *Dailyhunt* (Indian News mobile application), *Jansatta* (Hindi daily for North India), *NDTV* (an Indian television media company), etc., are the other popular websites with high number of links. The majority of the video links shared contain the news articles, speeches of the political leaders, and promotional content.

3.1.4 Contribution of top active users

All users do not actively participate in the conversations. The majority of the group members are passive consumers, while few users drive the topics of the conversation. In about 250 groups, the

Name	Count	Name	Count	Name	Count	Name	Count	Name	Count
BJP	144	AAP	20	AIMIM	4	RJD	3	Shivsena	1
INC	45	BSP	9	AIADMK	3	AITC	3	Others	19
SP	21	YSRCP	5	NCP	3	CPI(M)	1		

Table 1: Number of WAM groups affiliated to different political parties.

top 50% active users share 80-100% messages. Table 3 shows the contribution of top 1%, 10%, and 50% active users in the groups of different political parties. AAP has the most contribution from the top 1% users, whereas SP has the least contribution from top 1%, 10%, and 50% users. BJP and INC, the top two political parties (based on the number of groups), show similar participation from the top 50% active users. But, BJP leads INC in the participation of the top 1% active users. This disproportionate distribution of user activity can be attributed to:

- Influencers: Presence of a few active participants/influencers in the groups who are possibly responsible for official campaigning of the party/candidates.
- Neutral stance: Less participation from other members might indicate their neutral stance towards the ongoing campaigning, debates, and discussions (Times, 2019c).
- Group invasion: Members from different political inclination join groups to share misinformation and fake news. Also, group invasion is possible to monitor (with least participation in discussions) the election campaigning of the opposition parties on WAM. Several claims (Wire, 2019; Diplomat, 2019b) have been made that indicates the high usage of WAM for such activities.

Type	Count	Type	Count	Type	Count	Type	Count
JPEG	39,210	OGG	371	3GPP	37	MP3	1
MP4	15,934	MPEG	288	AAC	39	Octet-stream	1
WEBP	1,221	MP4	75	AMR	35	Spreadsheets	1
PDF	719	APK	66	TXT	10		

Table 2: (Best viewed in color) Distribution of shared media items. Blue, Red, Violet, Green and Black color represent video, audio, images, document and compressed files, respectively.

	BJP	INC	AAP	SP	BSP	Others
Top 1%	30.84	27.33	33.88	18.04	24.44	28.44
Top 10%	67.20	64.63	69.82	52.17	56.20	65.23
Top 50%	93.53	93.97	94.37	88.67	90.25	93.05

Table 3: Percentage of messages shared by top 1%, 10%, and 50% active users across different political parties.

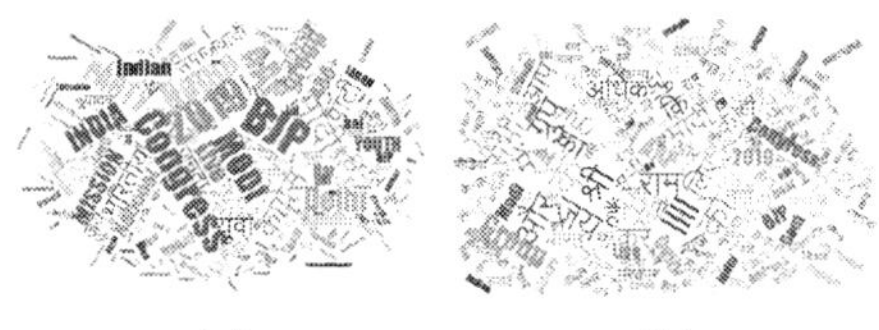

(a) (b)

Figure 4: Word clouds of common phrases from group (a) names and (b) descriptions.

3.1.5 Geographical analysis

Next, we conduct the geographical analysis of group members based on their registered mobile number.[5] Surprisingly, we find users from 46 different countries discussing Indian politics. However, the majority of users belong to India. Figure 5(a) and 5(b) collectively show user locations outside and inside India. We also find that group administrators belong to five different countries (India, Pakistan, UAE, Latvia, and the USA). The above empirical findings confirm several claims about non-resident Indians participating in social media campaigns (Chaturvedi, 2020; Times, 2019a; Diplomat, 2019a). Figure 5(c) shows the locations of Indian group administrators. The majority of users and group administrators belong to northern and central India, strengthening the popular belief that WAM-based political campaigns are centrally managed by a team of IT experts headquartered in the Delhi-NCR region (Ayush Tiwari, 2020).

3.1.6 Group creation time

Table 4 shows the group creation time of all the 281 groups. As we can see, a significant number (51.60%) of groups are created in the first five months of the year 2019, which is consistent with claims made by several news articles (Madhumita Murgia, 2019; News, 2018; Uttam, 2018; Iyengar, 2019).

[5] https://www.searchyellowdirectory.com/reverse-phone/

Figure 5: (Best viewed in color) (a) User locations in the World. (b) User locations in India. (c) Group administrator locations in India.

Interval	Groups	Interval	Groups	Interval	Groups
May'14-Dec'14	4	May'16-Dec'16	11	May'18-Dec'18	66
Jan'15-Aug'15	2	Jan'17-Aug'17	18	Jan'19-May'19	145
Sep'15-Apr'16	4	Sep'17-Apr'18	31		

Table 4: Frequency of WAM group creation in different intervals.

	Top-5 languages in decreasing order of frequency
Names	Hindi, English, Nepali, Marathi, Indonesian
Descriptions	Hindi, English, Nepali, Marathi, Tagalog
Messages	Hindi, English, Indonesian, Marathi, Somali

Table 5: Top-5 languages found in group name and description and messages.

3.1.7 Languages

Table 5 presents language identification[6] statistics. A total of 31, 22, and 45 unique languages are used in writing group names, group descriptions, and messages, respectively. English and Hindi are the two most frequently used languages. The findings reiterate the challenges in conducting WAM-based user analysis, due to multilingualism, in highly diversified countries like India.

Example I

MESSAGE: चौकीदार चोर है ।
POLITICAL: Yes, FAVOUR: None, AGAINST: BJP, LANGUAGE: Hindi, MALICIOUS: None

Example II

MESSAGE: The entire world is watching and waiting for Modi
POLITICAL: Yes, FAVOUR: BJP, AGAINST: None, LANGUAGE: English, MALICIOUS: None

Figure 6: Example annotation of the messages.

3.2 Annotation

We construct a fine-grained manually annotated dataset of 3,848 messages. Eight annotators have performed annotation of the messages. All of the eight annotators are native Hindi speaker and proficient in speaking and writing English. Figure 6 shows the example annotation of the messages. Before annotation, we pre-process the original dataset to filter out irrelevant/noisy messages by removing non-textual data like hyperlinks, emoticons, images, and videos, duplicate messages, and messages with length less than five characters or more than 150 characters and keeping messages written in either of two scripts Roman or Devanagari. Pre-processing results in 48,474 messages. We randomly sample 3,848 messages from pre-processed data for annotation. Each annotator annotates 481 samples. Each message has a fine-grained annotation with the labels in the following categories:

- **Malicious activity:** This category helps in identifying unusual and irrelevant activity within a group. A message is assigned one of the four labels in this category, i.e., spam, advertisement, offensive content, and others. Spam contains the textual messages that are irrelevant to the group and not part of any promotion of product/website/video/etc. Advertisement is specific to the promotional content. Others category contains the messages that are non-political and do not involve any other categories of malicious activities such as a non-political joke, historical content, personal conversation, etc. Others could be a set of messages with non-political and non-malicious content. Table 6 shows the malicious activity distribution. Spam is more prominent as compared to advertisement and offensive content.
- **Political orientation:** Each message is assigned a binary label for the political orientation — political or non-political. Table 6 shows the count of messages having political or non-political orientation. Even though the group identification process is completely manual with strict selection guidelines, we witness non-political messages surpassing political messages. We claim that without a strict selection criterion (as pre-

[6] https://pypi.org/project/langdetect/

	Malicious activity				Political orientation		Language		
	Spam	Offensive	Advertisement	Others	Political	Non-political	Hindi	English	Others
Count	759	219	142	971	1797	2051	2965	549	334

Table 6: Distribution of malicious activity, political orientation, and language in the annotated dataset.

	BJP	INC	AAP	SP	BSP	AITC	Others
Favour	651	96	18	8	9	8	116
Against	298	600	44	42	44	52	114

Table 7: Messages shared in favour and against of different political parties in the annotated dataset.

sented in earlier works (Resende et al., 2019b,a)), the insights will be highly noisy.

- **Political inclination:** This category helps in identifying the political inclination (favor and against) of the messages based on their political affiliation. Similar to the categorization described in the previous section, we assign one of the seven labels (BJP, INC, SP, BSP, AAP, AITC, and Others) to each message. Table 7 shows the inclination of the messages for different political parties. BJP is the most favored party based on the number of messages shared in favor. Whereas INC is the most targeted party.
- **Language:** Each message is assigned one of the three labels Hindi, English, and Others. Table 6 shows the distribution of languages used in different messages. Hindi is the most preferred language.

4 A Study on Political and Social Co-occurrences

The majority of the political parties often declare the agendas for their election campaigns. These agendas are mostly driven by various factors that touch upon the needs, beliefs, and necessities of the stakeholders. During the election campaign, the information propagation on various social media platforms gets heavily influenced by these social factors.

In this section, we present a discussion on the co-occurrence of two political entities (i.e., leaders and parties) and four social factors (i.e., agenda, religion, caste, and languages/ethnicity) in the dataset. Table 8 shows the fine-grained categorization of the political entities and the social factors. In our analysis, we select the six political parties (i.e. BJP, INC, AAP, SP, BSP, and AITC) and the most popular leader from each of these political parties (Narendra Modi–BJP, Rahul Gandhi–INC, Arvind Kejriwal–AAP, Akhilesh Yadav–SP, Mayawati–BSP, and Mamata Banarjee–AITC). The choice of social factors is motivated by the various influential topics being continuously reported to impact the political discourse in India.

To this end, we learn the word representation using FastText (Bojanowski et al., 2017) on the textual data in the messages. We pre-filter the noisy content in the dataset i.e. emoticons, special characters, and hyperlinks. To learn the representation, we use Gensim[7] with Python interfaces and default parameters. English and Hindi are the two most popular languages in the dataset. The word representations from FastText has different representation for the same word in two languages. To address this challenge, we translate the political entities and the social factors in the English languages (Roman script) to the Hindi language (Devanagari script) using Google Translate[8]. To understand the co-occurrence of the political entities and social factors in the dataset, we compute the cosine similarity between them. For similarity computation, we use the words in both languages (i.e. English and Hindi). The similarity between political entity w_1 and social factor w_2 is given as: $\text{sim}(w_1, w_2) = \max\{\text{sim}(hw_1, hw_2), \text{sim}(hw_1, ew_2), \text{sim}(ew_1, hw_2), \text{sim}(ew_1, ew_2)\}$, where hw_i and ew_i represents the word representation of word w_i in the Hindi and the English language respectively.

For the entity/social factor with more than one word, we take the average of the word representation of the constituent words. Table 9 and 10 presents the top-k (k=5 for '*Agendas*', '*Religions*', '*Languages/Ethnicity*' and k=4 for '*Castes*') most similar social factors for the political leaders and political parties respectively. We draw following major insights from the co-occurrence analysis:

- '*Corruption*', '*Literacy*', and '*Development*' are three most sought after agendas for political leaders and the parties including the ruling (i.e. BJP) and the opposition parties.
- '*Privatisation*' is among the top-5 social factors

[7] https://radimrehurek.com/gensim/models/fasttext.html

[8] https://translate.google.com/

Political	Parties	BJP, INC, AAP, SP, BSP, AITC
	Leaders	Narendra Modi, Rahul Gandhi, Arvind Kejriwal, Akhilesh Yadav, Mayawati, Mamata Banerjee
Social	Agendas	Education, Development, Healthcare, Infrastructure, Manufacturing, Defense, Economy, Transportation, Unemployment, Poverty, Terrorism, Literacy, Corruption, Inflation, Taxation, Pollution, Digitization, Privatisation, Agriculture
	Religion	Hinduism, Islam, Sikhism, Christianity, Buddhism, Jainism
	Castes	Forward Castes, Other Backward Class (OBC), Scheduled Castes (SC), Scheduled Tribes (ST)
	Languages/ Ethnicity	Hindi, Bengali, Marathi, Telugu, Tamil, Gujarati, Urdu, Kannada, Odia, Malayalam, Punjabi, Assamese, Maithili, Sanskrit

Table 8: Fine-grained categorization of the political entities and the social factors.

	Agendas	**Religions**	**Castes**	**Languages/Ethnicity**
Narendra Modi	Corruption, Literacy, Development, Privatisation, Terrorism	Sikhism, Buddhism, Jainism, Hinduism, Islamism	FW, SC, OBC, ST	Odia, Assamese, Gujarati, Sanskrit, Marathi
Rahul Gandhi	Corruption, Unemployment, Literacy, Development, Healthcare	Sikhism, Buddhism, Islamism, Jainism, Hinduism	FW, OBC, SC, ST	Odia, Assamese, Maithili, Tamil, Marathi
Arvind Kejriwal	Corruption, Literacy, Taxation, Terrorism, Healthcare	Sikhism, Buddhism, Islamism, Jainism, Hinduism	OBC, FW, SC, ST	Odia, Assamese, Bengali, Tamil, Maithili
Akhilesh Yadav	Corruption, Development, Taxation, Unemployment, Education	Sikhism, Hinduism, Jainism, Islamism, Buddhism	FW, OBC, ST, SC	Maithili, Assamese, Odia, Malayalam, Kannada
Mayawati	Corruption, Literacy, Terrorism, Taxation, Unemployment	Sikhism, Islamism, Hinduism, Christianity, Buddhism	FW, OBC, ST, SC	Odia, Assamese, Malayalam, Maithili, Bengali
Mamata Banerjee	Literacy, Corruption, Poverty, Development, Terrorism	Jainism, Sikhism, Buddhism, Christianity, Hinduism	OBC, SC, FW, ST	Malayalam, Maithili, Marathi, Sanskrit, Gujarati

Table 9: Top-k most similar social factors with each of the six political leaders. k=5 for the social factors '*Agendas*', '*Religions*', and '*Languages/Ethnicity*'. k=4 for the social factor '*Castes*'. Here, FW: Forward Castes , OBC: Other Backward Class, SC: Scheduled Castes, and ST: Scheduled Tribes.

	Agendas	**Religions**	**Castes**	**Languages/Ethnicity**
BJP	Corruption, Terrorism, Literacy, Development, Unemployment	Hinduism, Islamism, Sikhism, Jainism, Buddhism	OBC, FW, SC, ST	Assamese, Odia, Bengali, Sanskrit, Hindi
INC	Corruption, Terrorism, Unemployment, Literacy, Development	Islamism, Hinduism, Sikhism, Jainism, Buddhism	OBC, FW, SC, ST	Odia, Assamese, Bengali, Hindi, Sanskrit
AAP	Literacy, Taxation, Development, Corruption, Unemployment	Hinduism, Sikhism, Islamism, Christianity, Jainism	OBC, FW, SC, ST	Hindi, Bengali, Sanskrit, Maithili, Punjabi
SP	Unemployment, Corruption, Development, Agriculture, Literacy	Hinduism, Islamism, Christianity, Jainism, Sikhism	OBC, ST, FW, SC	Maithili, Odia, Assamese, Gujarati, Punjabi
BSP	Unemployment, Corruption, Taxation, Development, Education	Hinduism, Islamism, Jainism, Sikhism, Christianity	OBC, SC, ST, FW	Assamese, Odia, Bengali, Gujarati, Maithili
AITC	Digitization, Literacy, Corruption, Development, Poverty	Christianity, Sikhism, Jainism, Islamism, Hinduism	ST, SC, OBC, FW	Odia, Assamese, Hindi, Maithili, Punjabi

Table 10: Top-k most similar social factors with each of the six political parties. k=5 for the social factors '*Agendas*', '*Religions*', and '*Languages/Ethnicity*'. k=4 for the social factor '*Castes*'. Here, FW: Forward Castes , OBC: Other Backward Class, SC: Scheduled Castes, and ST: Scheduled Tribes.

for '*Narendra Modi*'. No other leader or party has '*Privatisation*' as the top-5 agendas.

- Though '*Poverty*' is a major concern for India, only '*Mamata Banarjee*' from '*AITC*' has '*Poverty*' as the top-5 agendas.
- Apart from '*Corruption*', '*Literacy*', and '*Development*', the opposition leaders and parties shows high similarity with some fundamental issues such as '*Healthcare*', '*Unemployment*', '*Education*', and '*Taxation*'.
- Most of the political leaders shows low similarity with the two most debated religions in India (i.e. '*Hinduism*' and '*Islamism*'). The political parties shows the opposite behaviour with '*Hinduism*' and '*Islamism*' as the most associated religions.
- The order of similarity with '*Hinduism*' and '*Islamism*' for '*BJP*' and '*INC*' is opposite. '*BJP*' is more similar with '*Hinduism*' than '*Islamism*' and vice-versa.
- Most of the political leaders shows high similarity with the '*Forward Castes*' whereas the political parties are more similar with the '*Other Backward Class (OBC)*'.
- Apart from '*Akhilesh Yadav*' and '*Mayawati*', the

'*Scheduled Tribes (ST)*' remains the least similar with the political leaders.

- The opposition leaders (i.e. leaders except '*Narendra Modi*') shows high similarity with the Dravidian languages/ethnicity (i.e. '*Tamil*', '*Malayalam*', and '*Kannada*').
- '*Odia*' and '*Assamese*' consistently shows high similarity with the political leaders and parties. The high similarity of '*Odia*' can be attributed to the fact that state assembly elections of the state Odisha took place along with the Indian general elections 2019.

5 Conclusion and Future Work

In this paper, we present an exploration of the noisy user-generated data on WAM with a focus on Indian general elections 2019. In contrast to the existing works, we discuss a novel manual group filtering strategy to reduce the presence of noisy and dubious groups in the dataset. In addition, we present a fine-grained annotated dataset with multi-dimensional labels to understand various linguistic characteristics. Lastly, the co-occurrence analysis put forward several interesting insights from the Indian general elections 2019. In the future, the presented dataset would be useful in understanding various aspects (e.g., named-entities, POS tagging, language identification, etc.) of the noisy user generated textual data.

References

Stephen Ansolabehere, Rebecca Lessem, and James M Snyder Jr. 2006. The orientation of newspaper endorsements in us elections, 1940–2002. *Quarterly Journal of political science*, 1(4):393.

Ayan Sharma Ayush Tiwari. 2020. Delhi bjp's it cell is trying its best to take on aap. is it working? [Online; accessed 24-May-2020].

Andrew W Barrett and Lowell W Barrington. 2005. Is a picture worth a thousand words? newspaper photographs and voter evaluations of political candidates. *Harvard International Journal of Press/Politics*, 10(4):98–113.

BBC. 2019. India election 2019: Exit polls suggest narendra modi back as pm. [Online; accessed 25-May-2020].

Liron Hakim Bobrov. 2018. Mobile messaging app map-february 2018. [Online; accessed 12-May-2019].

Piotr Bojanowski, Edouard Grave, Armand Joulin, and Tomas Mikolov. 2017. Enriching word vectors with subword information. *Transactions of the Association for Computational Linguistics*, 5:135–146.

Alexandre Bovet and Hernán A Makse. 2019. Influence of fake news in twitter during the 2016 us presidential election. *Nature communications*, 10(1):7.

Josemar Alves Caetano, Jaqueline Faria de Oliveira, Hélder Seixas Lima, Humberto T Marques-Neto, Gabriel Magno, Wagner Meira Jr, and Virgílio AF Almeida. 2018. Analyzing and characterizing political discussions in whatsapp public groups. *arXiv preprint arXiv:1804.00397*.

Rakesh Mohan Chaturvedi. 2020. Nri push for bjp lok sabha poll campaign. [Online; accessed 24-May-2020].

Elanor Colleoni, Alessandro Rozza, and Adam Arvidsson. 2014. Echo chamber or public sphere? predicting political orientation and measuring political homophily in twitter using big data. *Journal of communication*, 64(2):317–332.

Michael D Conover, Jacob Ratkiewicz, Matthew Francisco, Bruno Gonçalves, Filippo Menczer, and Alessandro Flammini. 2011. Political polarization on twitter. In *Fifth international AAAI conference on weblogs and social media*.

The Conversation. 2018. Whatsapp skewed brazilian election, proving social media's danger to democracy. [Online; accessed 25-May-2020].

The Diplomat. 2019a. The indian diaspora's influence on the general election. [Online; accessed 28-Aug-2020].

The Diplomat. 2019b. Manufacturing islamophobia on whatsapp in india. [Online; accessed 15-Aug-2020].

Carlos Henrique Gomes Ferreira, Breno de Sousa Matos, and Jussara M Almeira. 2018. Analyzing dynamic ideological communities in congressional voting networks. In *International Conference on Social Informatics*, pages 257–273. Springer.

Kiran Garimella and Dean Eckles. 2020. Images and misinformation in political groups: Evidence from whatsapp in india. *Harvard Kennedy School Misinformation Review*.

Kiran Garimella and Gareth Tyson. 2018. Whatapp doc? a first look at whatsapp public group data. In *Twelfth International AAAI Conference on Web and Social Media*.

The Hindu. 2019a. General elections 2019: Memes flood social media after the results. [Online; accessed 15-Aug-2020].

The Hindu. 2019b. Role of social media as influencer of voting choices overhyped: Csds study. [Online; accessed 15-Aug-2020].

The Logical Indian. 2019. Over 87,000 whatsapp groups may be using political propaganda to influence voters, says report. [Online; accessed 28-Aug-2020].

Rishi Iyengar. 2019. In india's last election, social media was used as a tool. this time it could become a weapon. [Online; accessed 12-May-2019].

R Tallal Javed, Mirza Elaaf Shuja, Muhammad Usama, Junaid Qadir, Waleed Iqbal, Gareth Tyson, Ignacio Castro, and Kiran Garimella. 2020. A first look at covid-19 messages on whatsapp in pakistan. In *2020 IEEE/ACM International Conference on Advances in Social Networks Analysis and Mining (ASONAM)*, pages 118–125. IEEE.

Livemint. 2019. Now, more politicians want influencers to woo voters. [Online; accessed 15-Aug-2020].

Andres Schipani Madhumita Murgia, Stephanie Findlay. 2019. India: the whatsapp election. [Online; accessed 24-May-2020].

ABC News. 2019. India election body struggles with scale of fake information. [Online; accessed 15-Aug-2020].

KMoneycontrol News. 2018. Tmc draws plans to strengthen digital wing, will create 10,000 whatsapp groups: Report. [Online; accessed 12-May-2019].

newslaundry. 2019. Game of words: These are the most-used words by political parties in their manifestos. [Online; accessed 15-Aug-2020].

Natalie Pang and Yue Ting Woo. 2020. What about whatsapp? a systematic review of whatsapp and its role in civic and political engagement. *First Monday*.

Gustavo Resende, Philipe Melo, Julio CS Reis, Marisa Vasconcelos, Jussara M Almeida, and Fabrício Benevenuto. 2019a. Analyzing textual (mis) information shared in whatsapp groups. In *Proceedings of the 10th ACM Conference on Web Science*, pages 225–234.

Gustavo Resende, Philipe Melo, Hugo Sousa, Johnnatan Messias, Marisa Vasconcelos, Jussara Almeida, and Fabrício Benevenuto. 2019b. information dissemination in whatsapp: Gathering, analyzing and countermeasures. In *Proc. of the The Web Conference (WWW'19)*.

Kayla Ruble. 2014. Whatsapp and social media could determine india's elections. [Online; accessed 12-May-2019].

Punyajoy Saha, Binny Mathew, Kiran Garimella, and Animesh Mukherjee. 2021. "short is the road that leads from fear to hate": Fear speech in indian whatsapp groups. In *Proceedings of the Web Conference 2021*, pages 1110–1121.

Social Samosa. 2019. With bjp's #5yearchallenge, 2019 general elections to see political war of memes. [Online; accessed 15-Aug-2020].

SBS. 2019. Analysis: The politics underlying india's election buzzwords. [Online; accessed 15-Aug-2020].

Scroll. 2019a. Bhakt, mitron, demonetisation: 10 words or phrases that entered our dictionaries with the modi era. [Online; accessed 15-Aug-2020].

Scroll. 2019b. The indian youtube wars: Political video influencers are heating up the internet in election year. [Online; accessed 15-Aug-2020].

Tactical Tech. 2018. Whatsapp: The widespread use of whatsapp in political campaigning in the global south. [Online; accessed 25-May-2020].

Economic Times. 2019a. Nri push for bjp lok sabha poll campaign. [Online; accessed 28-Aug-2020].

Financial Times. 2019b. India: the whatsapp election. [Online; accessed 28-Aug-2020].

Hindustan Times. 2019c. Rural indians don't trust messages on whatsapp blindly: Survey. [Online; accessed 28-Aug-2020].

The New York Times. 2019d. How youtube radicalized brazil. [Online; accessed 15-Aug-2020].

TOI. 2019. Timesmegapoll: 83% say modi-led government is most likely outcome after 2019 general election. [Online; accessed 25-May-2020].

Andranik Tumasjan, Timm O Sprenger, Philipp G Sandner, and Isabell M Welpe. 2010. Predicting elections with twitter: What 140 characters reveal about political sentiment. In *Fourth international AAAI conference on weblogs and social media*.

Kumar Uttam. 2018. For pm modi's 2019 campaign, bjp readies its whatsapp plan. [Online; accessed 12-May-2019].

Alcides Velasquez, Andrea M Quenette, and Hernando Rojas. 2021. Whatsapp political expression and political participation: The role of ethnic minorities' group solidarity and political talk ethnic heterogeneity. *International Journal of Communication*, 15:22.

Susan AM Vermeer, Sanne Kruikemeier, Damian Trilling, and Claes H de Vreese. 2021. Whatsapp with politics?! examining the effects of interpersonal political discussion in instant messaging apps. *The International Journal of Press/Politics*, 26(2):410–437.

Jessica Vitak, Paul Zube, Andrew Smock, Caleb T Carr, Nicole Ellison, and Cliff Lampe. 2011. It's complicated: Facebook users' political participation in the 2008 election. *CyberPsychology, behavior, and social networking*, 14(3):107–114.

Wei Wang, David Rothschild, Sharad Goel, and Andrew Gelman. 2015. Forecasting elections with non-representative polls. *International Journal of Forecasting*, 31(3):980–991.

The Wire. 2019. During general elections, whatsapp groups saw more automated, spam-like behaviour. [Online; accessed 15-Aug-2020].

Anshuman Yadav, Aditya Garg, Anup Aglawe, Ayush Agarwal, and Vivek Srivastava. 2020. Understanding the political inclination of whatsapp chats. In *Proceedings of the 7th ACM IKDD CoDS and 25th COMAD*, pages 361–362.

ParsTwiNER: A Corpus for Named Entity Recognition at Informal Persian

MohammadMahdi Aghajani
Sharif University of Technology
mmaghajani@ce.sharif.edu

AliAkbar Badri
Amirkabir University of Technology
aabadri@aut.ac.ir

Hamid Beigy
Sharif University of Technology
beigy@sharif.edu

Abstract

As a result of unstructured sentences and some misspellings and errors, finding named entities in a noisy environment such as social media takes much more effort. ParsTwiNER contains about 250k tokens, based on standard instructions like MUC-6 or CoNLL 2003, gathered from Persian Twitter. Using Cohen's Kappa coefficient, the consistency of annotators is 0.95, a high score. In this study, we demonstrate that some state-of-the-art models degrade on these corpora, and trained a new model using parallel transfer learning based on the BERT architecture. Experimental results show that the model works well in informal Persian as well as in formal Persian.

1 Introduction

Identifying named entities involves finding a sequence of words that refer to a specific concept, such as a person, a place, or an organization. This task is one of the essential components for other NLP tasks such as information extraction (Tjong Kim Sang and De Meulder, 2003). When masking a named entity in a sentence, the context helps to identify the entity type. For example, in the sentence "Doctor X says...", we find that the masked symbol "X" represents a person. On the other hand, sometimes a specific phrase refers to an entity, like "The United Nations." Hence, it is necessary to analyze word sequences to capture the context and the structure of a sentence. Furthermore, recognizing named entities requires generating a sequence of tags. Therefore, the problem type is a sequence-to-sequence problem.

Often, informal languages contain a mess of words, misspellings, and grammar errors, which degrades the performance of models (Baldwin et al., 2015; Strauss et al., 2016). Accordingly, some pre-trained models based on formal corpora fail to perform well in this context. It also would be expensive to build a language model from scratch to resolve this issue. As a result, we can use some pre-trained language models on formal language and train an end-to-end model using transfer learning. These models become more robust against noisy environments, such as Twitter or other user-generated content.

In this paper, we begin by preparing a corpus derived from Persian Twitter, called ParsTwiNER. It has excellent diversity and coverage due to the variety of users and topics. Then, we use transfer learning to use knowledge from the Persian formal model, ParsBert Farahani et al. (2020), and train a new model using ParsTwiNER to overcome messy structure and misspellings. At the initial stages of training, we use a novel variation of data annealing for better learning.

The rest of the paper is arranged as follows. We describe related work in Section 2. Next, we present the ParsTwiNER corpus in Section 3 and explain corpus statistics and annotation quality in 3.2 and 3.3, respectively. Then, we describe the proposed approach in Section 4 and the paper is concluded in Section 5.

2 Related work

This section describes NER corpora for informal languages like Persian and English. We also discuss the NER methods for these languages.

2.1 NER corpora

In informal Persian, there are not many standard works around NER who have followed the instructions of CoNLL and MUC (Tjong Kim Sang and De Meulder, 2003; Grishman and Sundheim, 1996). Asgari-Bidhendi et al. (2021) proposed a corpus, ParsNER-Social, that crawled from only 10 Telegram channels and supported only three types of

Proceedings of the 2021 EMNLP Workshop W-NUT: The Seventh Workshop on Noisy User-generated Text, pages 131–136
November 11, 2021. ©2021 Association for Computational Linguistics

NER: person, location, organization, and miscellaneous. Because no suitable and standard dataset covers a wide range of informal Persian content, in this paper, we create a highly diverse corpus of informal Persian content.

In formal Persian, Shahshahani et al. (2018) introduced PEYMA dataset for named entity recognition. This dataset contains 302530 tokens and 41148 named entities. Poostchi et al. (2018) proposed ARMAN dataset, which consists of 2,5016 tokens and 75,091 entities, for the NER task. In many Persian named entity recognition papers, these two datasets have been employed.

In English, Ritter et al. (2011) proposed a Ritter-11 corpus. The corpus contains 2400 tweets and 34K tokens. For the shared task for WNUT2017, Derczynski et al. (2017) proposed a corpus. The dataset focuses on rare and unusual entities. There are six types of entities in the corpus: person, location, corporation, product, creative work, and group.

2.2 NER methods

As mentioned above, there are not many works in informal Persian. Asgari-Bidhendi et al. (2021) trained a model using the Mono-Lingual BERT conduct on the ParsNER-Social corpus and obtained an F1-score of 89.65%.

In formal Persian, Shahshahani et al. (2018) combined rule-based methods with statistical methods and obtained an F1-score 84% on PEYMA corpus. They used regular expressions in the rule-based part and conditional random fields in the statistical component. Hosseinnejad et al. (2017) only used the conditional random fields on a collected corpus consists of 13 types of named entities. Ahmadi and Moradi (2015) presented a method by combining rule-based techniques and hidden Markov models and evaluated using a corpus of 32K tokens. They obtained an F1-score of 85.93% on this corpus.

Zafarian et al. (2015) used semi-supervised learning using a dataset with small number of labeled samples. The tokens that are recognized with high probability at each step will be used as training tokens for the next step. Iteratively, these steps are repeated. PersoNER is a good model for formal Persian, which uses the BiLSTM-CRF (Poostchi et al., 2016). Lastly, the ParsBert model obtained an F1-score of 90.59% on PEYMA corpus using the BERT encoder for Persian language (Farahani et al., 2020).

von Däniken and Cieliebak (2017) proposed a method for improving the model's performance on the WNUT2017 shared task based on tweets by combining transfer learning and sentence-level features. They achieved an F1 score of 40.78%. Aguilar et al. (2018) proposed an approach that uses phonetics and phonology, word embeddings, and Part-of-Speech tags to overcome noisy data. On the WNUT2017 shared task, they improved the F1-score by 3.69%. In informal English, Gu and Yu (2020) improved F1-score from 66.53% to 69.69% on on Ritter-11 dataset using data annealing and BERT.

3 ParsTwiNER Corpus

We describe the proposed method to create the corpus in this section. In addition to annotation instructions, we present statistics about the corpus and annotation quality based on the agreement of annotators.

3.1 Annotation instructions

Twitter is widely used by Persian language users, so we choose Twitter to collect data in informal Persian. The Persian on Twitter is unstructured and has no formal grammar. This corpus is capable of capturing some irregular structures and misspelled words. We crawled 10053 ordinary Persian Twitter accounts to collect 10014 tweets that formed an informal raw text corpus. Ordinary accounts tweet in informal language more than news or official accounts. After that, we removed all emojis, links, user IDs, and hashtag sign. Next, we removed all tweets containing racist, offensive, and violent content. The final number of tweets was 7632. In the next step, we used Parsivar[1] to tokenize and normalize the data. We considered persons, organizations, locations, events, groups, and nations as named entities. Two authors of the paper annotated the data. Both of the annotators are experts in natural language processing, so the data got labeled precisely. To tag the corpus, we used the IOB format. The corpus was created through an agreement between annotators to annotate according to CoNLL and MUC instructions (Tjong Kim Sang and De Meulder, 2003; Grishman and Sundheim, 1996). If a non-named entity appears inside a named entity phrase, then all of those tokens are tagged as named entities. Furthermore, we do not consider titles like 'Doctor' and 'Professor' at

[1] https://github.com/ICTRC/Parsivar

Category	# of Tokens	# of Unique Tokens
Persons	9586	3932
Organizations	5122	1875
Locations	6676	1914
Events	1146	428
Nations	956	341
Political Groups	575	255
Total	24061	8727

Table 1: The number of tokens and unique tokens in the proposed corpus.

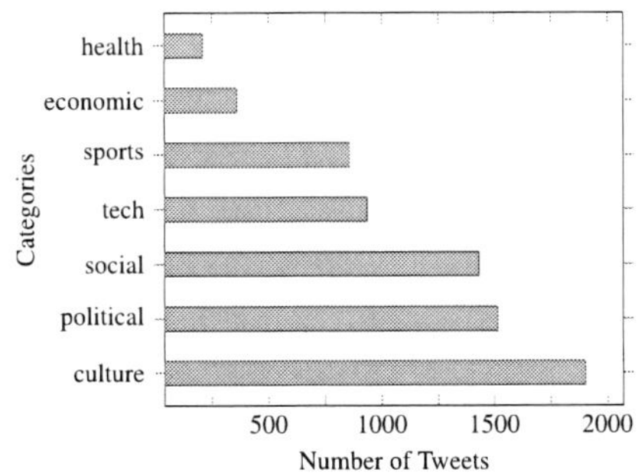

Figure 1: The number of tokens and unique tokens in the proposed corpus.

the beginning of tokens to be named entities. As part of these annotation instructions, a variety of items will be made public along with the corpus. The corpus and annotation instructions are publicly available on Github[2].

3.2 Corpus statistics

The corpus includes 7667 tweets, 232917 tokens, and 24061 named entities. In Table 1, a summary of the number of tokens and unique tokens in each category are given. Additionally, the average tweet length is 32 tokens. There are seven categories for tweets: political, economic, social, sports, health, culture, and technology. Figure 1 shows the number of tweets in each category. We split the corpus into training, test, and validation sets based on the distribution of categories and named entity types.

3.3 Annotation quality

As part of the investigation of the annotation quality, the annotators relabelled a fraction of the data. To determine the quality of the labeling, we check the differences between the annotators. As a result, we pick 9673 tokens from the corpus for relabeling. Finally, we found 76 differences. Mistakes occur when annotators misunderstand the word's meaning or context of the sentence. We calculate the degree of agreement at 99% when considering the survey data and the 76 differences between annotators. Due to a large number of **O** tokens, only 983 tokens are labeled entities, and so despite 76 differences, the level of agreement between the annotators is about 93%.

In addition, we use the Cohen's Kappa criterion to measure the level of agreement in a statistical sense on this test set (Cohen, 1960). This criterion determines the degree of agreement based on the distance of the annotators from the random tagging mode. Equation (1) shows Cohen's Kappa criterion

$$\kappa = \frac{p_0 - p_e}{1 - p_e} \tag{1}$$

where p_0 represents an annotator's agreement on every test instance, and p_e indicates the amount of agreement in which the tagging was done randomly. The criterion lies between $[-1, +1]$. A higher value indicates a better agreement among the annotators. The Kappa criterion for the corpus is 0.95, which implies high agreement among annotators.

4 Proposed model

We use transfer learning to design a named entity recognizer in informal Persian. Current state-of-the-art models, such as ParsBert, were trained on the formal corpus, and their performance degrades on the collected corpus. This degradation is due to unstructured and noisy grammar in informal Persian. As a first step, we fine-tune the ParsBert language model on the corpus using sequential transfer learning. Then, we use parallel multi-task learning to train a model in informal and formal Persian simultaneously. Experiments show the effectiveness of multi-task training.

4.1 Sequential transfer learning

It is expensive to train a language model from scratch. Thus, we fine-tune the ParsBert language model to adapt to informal Persian. We use BERT basic architecture with 768 hidden states, 12 transformer encoder layers, and 12 multi-head attention layers. Since the named entity recognition problem is a multi-class classification, we use a fully connected feed-forward layer above BERT to classify entities based on 13 classes based on the corpus. This dataset has six types of named entities. Using the IOB format, each type of named entity has two labels and one **O** label for non named entity tokens. Hence, we have 13 classes.

[2] https://github.com/overfit-ir/parstwiner

We train this model by placing the [CLS] token at the beginning and the [SEP] token at the end of each tweet. We also set all segment embedding to 1. With this configuration, BERT treats tweets like sentences. We then set the learning rate to $5 * 10^{-5}$ at the initial step and scheduled it to reduce linearly over time. For overfitting prevention, we use dropout with the rate of 0.1. Table 2 shows the results of the evaluation compared with ParsBert. Training the model in this manner does not leverage embedded knowledge in the ParsBert NER model. Using the above approach, we only rely on the ParsBert language model. In the ParsBert NER model, we exploit knowledge through parallel transfer learning.

4.2 Parallel transfer learning

To train an informal Persian NER model in conjunction with a formal Persian NER model, we share a BERT encoder between two models and use two different task heads as a fully connected feedforward classifier for each model. Figure 2 shows the overall architecture of the proposed parallel transfer learning method. We first use PEYMA dataset to train the formal Persian model, and then ParsTwiNER corpus to train the informal Persian model.

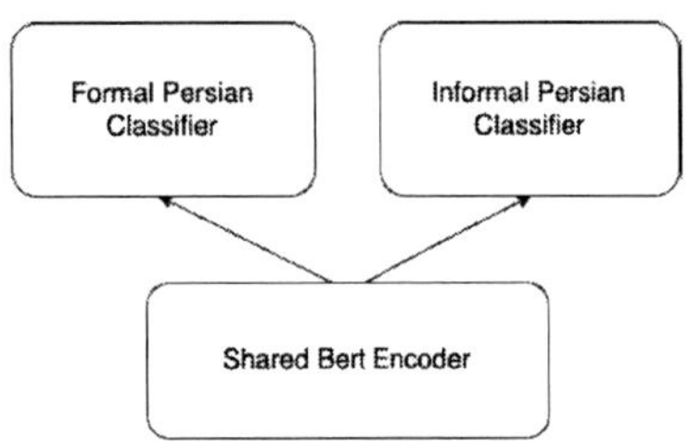

Figure 2: Parallel transfer learning architecture.

We feed eight tweets or sentences per training step to the BERT encoder. To train in this manner, we need to select either ParsTwiNER or PEYMA to supply data to the model at each training step. We select a dataset with a probability and then feed the selectd dataset to the BERT. We apply this policy using a novel variation of data annealing due to the difference in task classifiers. We can not mix PEYMA and ParsTwiNER data for data feeding because the backpropagated gradient for a selected corpus must affect the corresponding task head classifier. Initially, we choose PEYMA for data feeding with a higher probability than ParsTwiNER. Then, at each step, we reduce the probability of selecting the PEYMA corpus by the rate of λ. Equation (2) shows the schedule of the selection probability for each corpus.

Entity Type	ParsTwiNER			ParsBert
	Precision	Recall	F1	F1
PER	85%	91%	87%	80%
LOC	84.3%	85.5%	84.9%	68%
ORG	61.8%	62.7%	62.2%	55%
EVE	30%	28.5%	29.2%	12%
POG	36%	40.9%	38.3%	-
NAT	60.5%	76.6%	67.6%	-
Total	76%	80%	78%	69.5%

Table 2: The results of sequential transfer learning. ParsBert does not support POG and NAT. Results are in the exact-match mode, and the total is micro-averaged.

$$p_S^t = \alpha\lambda^{t-1}, 0 < \alpha < 1, 0 < \lambda < 1$$
$$p_T^t = 1 - \alpha\lambda^{t-1} \quad (2)$$

where p_S^t shows how likely it is that in step t of the training, the whole batch would be from formal Persian (PEYMA dataset), and p_T^t shows how likely it is for informal Persian (ParsTwiNER dataset). Table 3 shows the results of the model trained by using the parallel transfer learning compared with ParsBert.

As depicted in Table 3, we achieve about 11% improvement on the corpus by the proposed method. Also, we evaluated the model's performance on other formal Persian datasets and realized that the model's performance is competitive to ParseBert. Previous models suffer from the lack of generalization, but our model has a great performance on ParsTwiNER dataset and an acceptable result on the formal datasets. The source code is publicly available on Github[3] and the trained models are available for functionality test on HuggingFace[4].

5 Conclusions

We demonstrated that the performance of existing NER models like ParsBert degrades when applied to informal Persian. A crawled Persian Twitter corpus, named ParsTwiNER, was used for experiments. Based on some corpus statistics, we showed that the corpus was built using various standard instructions, such as MUC and CoNLL 2003. Using

[3]https://github.com/overfit-ir/parstwiner

[4]https://huggingface.co/overfit/twiner-bert-base-mtl

Entity Type	ParsTwiNER			ParsBert
	Precision	Recall	F1	F1
PER	90%	91%	91%	80%
LOC	81%	83%	82%	68%
ORG	70%	69%	69%	55%
EVE	35%	50%	41%	12%
POG	94%	77%	85%	-
NAT	68%	93.3%	82.3%	-
Total	80%	83%	81.5%	69.5%

Table 3: The results of parallel transfer learning. ParsBert does not support POG and NAT. Results are in the exact-match mode, and the total is micro-averaged.

parallel transfer learning, we proposed an approach to train a model that performed as well as possible in both formal and informal Persian. Experimental results indicate that the proposed model recognizes events with lower accuracy than other categories. For future works, we will investigate the causes of this quality degradation and finding a solution. Also, we will check the quality of the trained models on named entities that did not exist at all in the training phase.

Acknowledgements

The authors would like to thank Dr. Momtazi for her support. Furthermore, we would like to acknowledge the accompaniment provided by Mohammad Mahdi Samiei and Abbas Maazallahi.

References

Gustavo Aguilar, Adrian Pastor López-Monroy, Fabio González, and Thamar Solorio. 2018. Modeling noisiness to recognize named entities using multitask neural networks on social media. In *Proceedings of the 2018 Conference of the North American Chapter of the Association for Computational Linguistics: Human Language Technologies, Volume 1 (Long Papers)*, pages 1401–1412, New Orleans, Louisiana. Association for Computational Linguistics.

Farid Ahmadi and Hamed Moradi. 2015. A hybrid method for persian named entity recognition. In *2015 7th Conference on Information and Knowledge Technology (IKT)*, pages 1–7.

Majid Asgari-Bidhendi, Behrooz Janfada, Omid Reza Roshani Talab, and Behrouz Minaei-Bidgoli. 2021. Parsner-social: A corpus for named entity recognition in persian social media texts. *Journal of AI and Data Mining*, 9(2):181–192.

Timothy Baldwin, Marie Catherine de Marneffe, Bo Han, Young-Bum Kim, Alan Ritter, and Wei Xu. 2015. Shared tasks of the 2015 workshop on noisy user-generated text: Twitter lexical normalization and named entity recognition. In *Proceedings of the Workshop on Noisy User-generated Text*, pages 126–135, Beijing, China. Association for Computational Linguistics.

Jacob Cohen. 1960. A coefficient of agreement for nominal scales. *Educational and Psychological Measurement*, 20(1):37–46.

Leon Derczynski, Eric Nichols, Marieke van Erp, and Nut Limsopatham. 2017. Results of the WNUT2017 shared task on novel and emerging entity recognition. In *Proceedings of the 3rd Workshop on Noisy User-generated Text*, pages 140–147, Copenhagen, Denmark. Association for Computational Linguistics.

Mehrdad Farahani, Mohammad Gharachorloo, Marzieh Farahani, and Mohammad Manthouri. 2020. Parsbert: Transformer-based model for persian language understanding. *CoRR*, abs/2005.12515.

Ralph Grishman and Beth Sundheim. 1996. Message Understanding Conference- 6: A brief history. In *COLING 1996 Volume 1: The 16th International Conference on Computational Linguistics*.

Jing Gu and Zhou Yu. 2020. Data Annealing for Informal Language Understanding Tasks. In *Findings of the Association for Computational Linguistics: EMNLP 2020*, pages 3153–3159, Online. Association for Computational Linguistics.

Shadi Hosseinnejad, Yasser Shekofteh, and Tahereh and Emami Azadi. 2017. A'laam corpus: A standard corpus of named entity for persian language. *Signal and Data Processing*, 14(3).

Hanieh Poostchi, Ehsan Zare Borzeshi, Mohammad Abdous, and Massimo Piccardi. 2016. PersoNER: Persian named-entity recognition. In *Proceedings of COLING 2016, the 26th International Conference on Computational Linguistics: Technical Papers*, pages 3381–3389, Osaka, Japan. The COLING 2016 Organizing Committee.

Hanieh Poostchi, Ehsan Zare Borzeshi, and Massimo Piccardi. 2018. BiLSTM-CRF for Persian named-entity recognition ArmanPersoNERCorpus: the first entity-annotated Persian dataset. In *Proceedings of the Eleventh International Conference on Language Resources and Evaluation (LREC 2018)*, Miyazaki, Japan. European Language Resources Association (ELRA).

Alan Ritter, Sam Clark, Mausam, and Oren Etzioni. 2011. Named entity recognition in tweets: An experimental study. In *Proceedings of the 2011 Conference on Empirical Methods in Natural Language Processing*, pages 1524–1534, Edinburgh, Scotland, UK. Association for Computational Linguistics.

Mahsa Sadat Shahshahani, Mahdi Mohseni, Azadeh Shakery, and Heshaam Faili. 2018. PEYMA: A tagged corpus for persian named entities. *CoRR*, abs/1801.09936.

Benjamin Strauss, Bethany Toma, Alan Ritter, Marie-Catherine de Marneffe, and Wei Xu. 2016. Results of the WNUT16 named entity recognition shared task. In *Proceedings of the 2nd Workshop on Noisy User-generated Text (WNUT)*, pages 138–144.

Erik F. Tjong Kim Sang and Fien De Meulder. 2003. Introduction to the CoNLL-2003 shared task: Language-independent named entity recognition. In *Proceedings of the Seventh Conference on Natural Language Learning at HLT-NAACL 2003*, pages 142–147.

Pius von Däniken and Mark Cieliebak. 2017. Transfer learning and sentence level features for named entity recognition on tweets. In *Proceedings of the 3rd Workshop on Noisy User-generated Text*, pages 166–171, Copenhagen, Denmark. Association for Computational Linguistics.

Atefeh Zafarian, Ali Rokni, Shahram Khadivi, and Sonia Ghiasifard. 2015. Semi-supervised learning for named entity recognition using weakly labeled training data. In *2015 The International Symposium on Artificial Intelligence and Signal Processing (AISP)*, pages 129–135.

DreamDrug - A crowdsourced NER dataset for detecting drugs in darknet markets

Johannes Bogensperger
AIT Austrian Institute of Technology
JBogen@gmx.at

Sven Schlarb
AIT Austrian Institute of Technology
Sven.Schlarb@ait.ac.at

Allan Hanbury
TU Wien
allan.hanbury@tuwien.ac.at

Gabor Recski
TU Wien
gabor.recski@tuwien.ac.at

Abstract

We present `DreamDrug`, a crowdsourced dataset for detecting mentions of drugs in noisy user-generated item listings from darknet markets. Our dataset contains nearly 15,000 manually annotated drug entities in over 3,500 item listings scraped from the darknet market platform "DreamMarket" in 2017. We also train and evaluate baseline models for detecting these entities, using contextual language models fine-tuned in a few-shot setting and on the full dataset, and examine the effect of pretraining on in-domain unannotated corpora.

1 Introduction

This paper describes the construction of `DreamDrug`, a dataset of drug-related product listings from darknet marketplaces with human-annotated drug entities, suitable for training and evaluating named entity recognition (NER) systems. We provide a detailed description of all steps of annotation and dataset construction, and we also optimize and evaluate standard NER architectures on the new corpus. Our experiments include training models in a few-shot setting and using the full dataset, as well as a study of the effect of domain-adaptive pre-training using unannotated datasets of similar topic and genre. All software used in producing `DreamDrug` and for reproducing our experiments is published under an MIT license along with sample data files[1], the full dataset is available upon request[2]. Our main contributions are the following:

1. Specifications of an annotation task for marking mentions of drug entities in darknet market listings
2. A detailed description of preprocessing and filtering steps used to create the annotation input
3. The novel NER corpus `DreamDrug`, annotated by crowdworkers based on these specifications and reviewed manually by the authors
4. Quantitative evaluation of standard supervised learning architectures for NER on the `DreamDrug` dataset, in a few-shot setting and using the full dataset
5. Three unannotated datasets for domain-adaptive pretraining and experiments demonstrating their impact on the performance of the NER baselines

The paper is structured as follows. In Section 2 we introduce the task and provide an overview of recent related work on information extraction from noisy user-generated text. Section 3 describes the corpus construction process. Section 4 and Section 5 present our baseline experiments and results, respectively, and Section 6 provides a brief conclusion.

2 Background

Extracting information from text concerning illicit drug consumption or trade is a non-trivial task, since such information is rarely available in a structured form. Patients who misuse their medication are more likely to discuss this on social media than with medical professionals (Bigeard et al., 2018), while drug dealers intentionally misspell names of drugs on social media to prevent automatic detection (Li et al., 2019). Drug-specific named entity recognition (NER) models are most often developed for the medical domain and cannot handle such misspellings, the usage of slang, and other characteristics of noisy user-generated texts such as lack of punctuation and non-standard grammar (Rezaei et al., 2020). Many of these issues are

[1] `https://github.com/jbogensperger/DRUG_CROSSNER`

[2] DreamDrugDataset@gmail.com

Proceedings of the 2021 EMNLP Workshop W-NUT: The Seventh Workshop on Noisy User-generated Text, pages 137–157
November 11, 2021. ©2021 Association for Computational Linguistics

peruanse 92 cocain very good snife and for people tghe want cooking out very good smills good frech from the block orginail good good good AAA.

Figure 1: Sample listing from the *DreamMarket* dataset

illustrated by the example listing from a darknet marketplace in Figure 1.

Still, many organizations are dependent on extracting information about drugs or similiar goods from noisy online sources. Public health organizations study drug use patterns in society such as the opioid epidemic in the United States (Ostling et al., 2018), pharmaceutical companies can collect evidence of adverse drug reactions from social media data (Chen et al., 2017), and law enforcement agencies can track illicit trading activities in darknet markets. Each of these use-cases can be supported by the automatic detection of drug entities in noisy user-generated text. To enable the development of such systems we create a dataset for training and evaluation by annotating drug-related item listings of darknet marketplaces. An example of such a listing is shown in Figure 2.

2.1 NER in User-Generated Texts

Much of recent research on named entity recognition in user-generated texts was facilitated by the 2017 W-NUT Shared Task on Novel and Emerging Entity Recognition (Derczynski et al., 2017). The dataset provided by the organizers of the competition was compiled from a variety of social media sources (Twitter, Reddit, Youtube, StackExchange), annotated for 6 categories (person, location, corporation, product, creative work, group) by multiple crowdworkers, and corrected by the authors. The difficulty of the task of detecting novel entities in noisy domains is indicated by the relatively low performance of all competing systems. The top-performing system of Aguilar et al. (2017) achieved an average F-score of 41.86 on the evaluation dataset. Their system combines character- and word-level features with gazetteers for each entity type, and uses them as input to a Bidirectional Long Short-term Memory (BiLSTM) network with a Conditional Random Fields (CRF) classifier. Other top-performing approaches included Jansson and Liu (2017), who use LDA topic modeling for creating word-level features for an LSTM classifier with a CRF output layer, and Lin et al. (2017), who incorporated part-of-speech tags and dependency relations in their word representations and also used a BiLSTM with CRF output layer. A significant improvement on this benchmark was achieved by Akbik et al. (2019b) using pooled contextualized embeddings, a method to aggregate character-level representations from contextual language models. This method is implemented in the `FLAIR` framework (Akbik et al., 2019a) and achieves an F-score of 49.59 on the W-NUT 2017 dataset.

We are aware of two annotated NER corpora from the darknet domain. Durrett et al. (2017) created a dataset for identifying products in cybercrime marketplace postings, annotating 1,938 posts across 4 forums. When training NER models on data from the same forum, they achieve F-score performances between 83 and 90, in a cross-forum setting their performance drops by 7-11 points. A more recent darknet dataset is `NUToT` (Nabki et al., 2020), containing 851 sentences from darknet sources annotated manually with the categories of the W-NUT challenge. Their experiments involve compensating for the absence of domain-specific gazetteers with Local Distance Neighbor (LDN) features, a method for enriching word representations with nearest neighbors in a word embedding space. Performance of top-performing systems on their dataset is in the range of 40 to 60 across categories (F-scores of entities). The corpus we introduce in this paper is annotated for a single entity type (drug) that is more specific than the categories of `W-NUT` and `NUToT` and allows our simple baselines to achieve F-scores above 70 even in a few-shot setting and above 80 when using the full dataset (see Section 5). In addition to enabling higher accuracy, we believe that NER datasets that correspond directly to a narrow information extraction task are better models of real-world NER use-cases than the commonly used datasets labeled for broad categories such as *person*, *location*, *organization*, or even *product*. While the fine-grained task definiton necessary for consistent annotation of `DreamDrug` (see Section 3.2) requires considerations specific to a single task, it also provides an example of the narrow and domain-specific entity categories that are typical of real-world NER applications. Besides providing a novel dataset and baseline models, our work also demonstrates that entity recognition tasks for narrow domains and specialized text genres can benefit from even small amounts of annotated data.

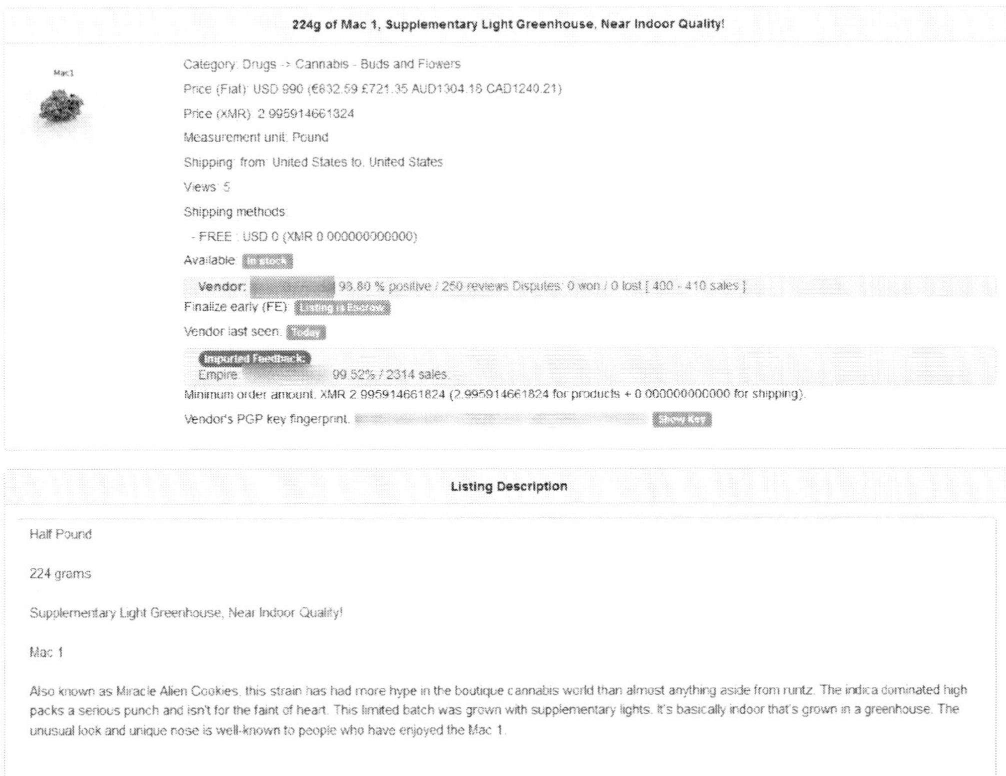

Figure 2: Sample drug item listing on the darknet platform *White House Market*

2.2 Crowdsourcing for NER

Crowdsourcing, the practice of soliciting non-expert annotators for assistance in creating datasets on a scale, usually with the help of online platforms, has become a standard practice of researchers aiming to build annotated corpora with limited resources. The most common scheme, where crowd workers are rewarded for each annotation task they complete, is sometimes referred to as *mechanized labor* (Sabou et al., 2014). In Section 3.3 we shall give a detailed description of the entire process of creating the `DreamDrug` dataset. For defining the Named Entity Recognition task we consult several recent sets of guidelines for NER tasks (Finin et al., 2010; Nédellec et al., 2006; Benikova et al., 2014). When designing the annotation process we rely on discussions of annotation methodologies in (Sabou et al., 2014) and (Fort et al., 2009). Approaches to measuring inter-annotator agreement are studied in detail by Asheghi et al. (2014), crowdsourcing techniques are discussed by Feyisetan et al. (2018), and we also rely on the work of Gomes et al. (2020) for initial effort estimation, which we see as essential in ensuring the ethical treatment of annotators.

3 Corpus construction

3.1 Data preparation

The starting point for our corpus construction process is a segment of the `AZSecure` dataset (Du et al., 2018) containing 91,463 darknet market listings scraped from *Dream Market*, collected between 2013 and 2017. Listing documents typically contain a product name and description along with metadata such as price, quantity, contact information of the vendor, etc. We extracted 45,446 items belonging to categories associated with drugs and performed a series of data cleaning steps. First, `deduplication` removed all listings containing exactly the same description text as another item listing. The `English only` step removed all listings with a description text categorized as other than English by the `language-detection` library (Shuyo, 2010). Next, `outlier lengths` removed listings with a description text longer than 3000 characters or shorter than 30 characters. While this step also removed some relevant content, it efficiently filtered product listings with long boilerplate sections (e.g. about delivery details), as well as items that contained no relevant text (e.g. a product description might only state *Free shipping*). Finally, `soft deduplication` removed listings with a description text whose first 100 characters contained the same non-numeric characters as another listing's description, characteristic of listings of the same product with different quantities. The resulting dataset contains 11,674 items, Table 1 shows the number and percentage of listings removed by each filtering step.

filtering step	# removed	% removed	# kept
deduplication	25,012	55.0%	20,434
English only	2,102	10.3%	18,332
outlier lengths	1,488	8.1%	16,844
soft deduplication	5,170	30.7%	11,674

Table 1: Number and percentage of item listings filtered in each step (see text for description of each step)

For the construction of the `DreamDrug` dataset we used the product name and product description fields of the 11,674 remaining listings, the final dataset contains 3,507 items randomly selected from this set. Common unique identifiers of vendors in the product description texts were replaced with random values. Telephone numbers were detected using the python library `phonenumber`[3], email addresses and URLs were replaced using regular expressions (see Appendix B) and the `faker`[4] package, while vendor names were available as separate fields in the original database. Finally, product description texts were tokenized using Stanza[5] (Qi et al., 2020), version 1.2.0.

3.2 Task definition

Our definition of which sequences of words constitute drug entities was developed in an initial set of experiments that involved manual annotation of 500 item listings by the authors. Our starting point was the definition used by the Food and Drug Administration (FDA) (U.S. Food and Drug Administration, 2021):

1. *"articles intended for use in the diagnosis, cure, mitigation, treatment, or prevention of disease"*

2. *"articles (other than food) intended to affect the structure or any function of the body of man or other animals."*

The guidelines we developed for consistent annotation clarify that for an entity to be labeled it must uniquely identify a specific article according to the FDA definition. Besides direct mentions of substances (*cocaine, THC*, etc.), slang terms that clearly identify a drug, such as *speed* and *pep* for amphetamine or *Mary Jane* for cocaine, are also considered drug entities. Phrases that do not uniquely identify a substance, such as *Charley's mellow Sleeper Bars* or *Green Dom Perignon*, are not to be annotated. Following the FDA definition we do not annotate substances occurring naturally in the human body such as *testosterone* or *dopamine*. Phrases referring to the physical form of a drug only are also not annotated, even if the form is unique to a particular drug, as e.g. *blotter* is to LSD. The common term *mushroom* constitutes a corner case, as one may argue that it refers to the form of a drug, but since in this dataset it clearly identifies a particular chemical (psilocybin, the active agent of all types of *magic mushrooms*), we decided to annotate it as a drug entity. Some phrases describing drugs contain multiple elements that could each be annotated as a separate drug entity based on our definition. Examples include phrases such as *Viagra Sildenfanil* and *Haze weed* — we annotate these as two subsequent drug spans. The annotation guidelines provided to crowd workers contain a simplified description of our definition with examples and is presented in Appendix C. All documents annotated by crowd workers were subsequently reviewed and corrected manually by the authors to ensure high quality and consistent treatment of corner cases — details of the annotation and review process are presented in Section 3.3.

3.3 Data annotation

Crowdsourced annotation was performed using the definition of drug entities presented in Section 3.2. The guidelines presented to annotators were revised several times during pilot experiments that involved the implementation of two annotation interface prototypes using the platforms Appen and Amazon Mechanical Turk (AMT), both of which are regularly used for annotating NER datasets (Jalal et al., 2020; Feyisetan et al., 2015; Bontcheva et al., 2017; Feyisetan et al., 2018). Appen was then chosen, primarily because of its built-in capabilities for evaluating annotator performance and for screening annotators using test questions. Due to an unexpected

[3] https://pypi.org/project/phonenumbers/

[4] https://github.com/joke2k/faker

[5] https://stanfordnlp.github.io/stanza/

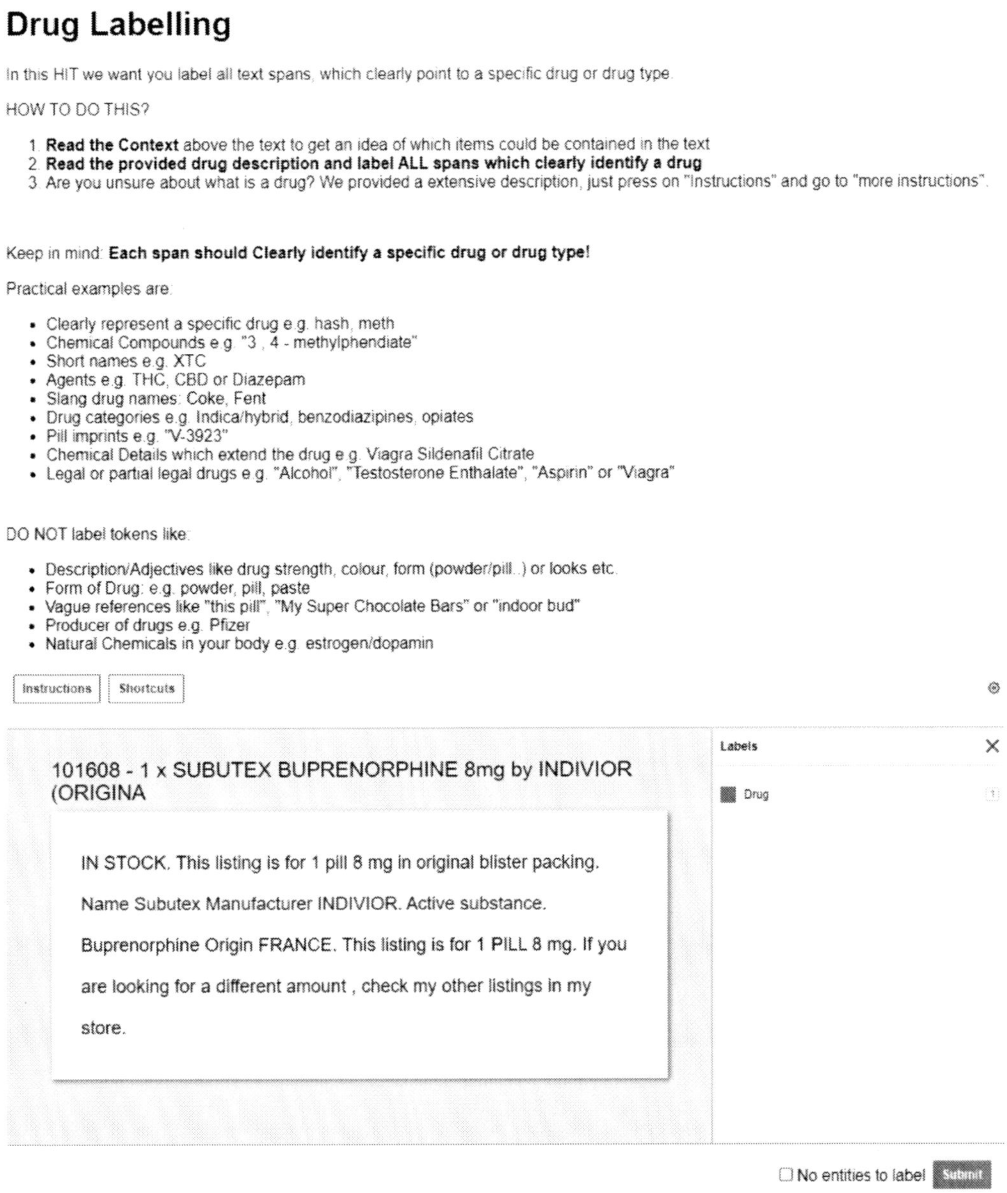

Figure 3: Screenshot of the annotation interface on Amazon Mechanical Turk. The long version of the annotation guidelines (see Appendix C) was accessible via the *Instructions* button.

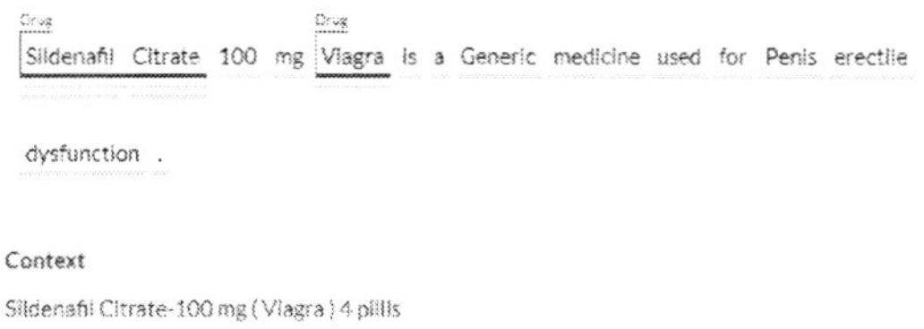

Figure 4: Screenshot of the annotation interface on Appen.

IAA	AMT	Appen
Cohen's Kappa	0.76	0.43
Micro F1	0.79	0.55
Macro F1	0.78	0.60

Table 2: Inter-Annotator Agreement measures for the overall annotations by crowd workers of Amazon MTurk and Appen. Macro F1 is the average of F1 scores across pairs of annotators.

licensing issue we were forced to switch platforms during the annotation process, and the final dataset was constructed using annotations from both Appen and AMT, agreement figures and dataset statistics in this section are provided for both platforms. Crowdworkers were presented with the text of one listing at a time and asked to mark the beginning and end of sequences of words that identify a drug. The title of the listing was provided as context. Screenshots of the annotation interfaces on Amazon Mechanical Turk and Appen are shown in Figures 3 and 4, respectively. On Appen, instructions were provided in a separate window and contained the full annotation guidelines shown in Appendix C. These longer guidelines were available to AMT workers when they clicked the *Instructions* button.

Annotation quality was monitored by measuring Inter-Annotator Agreement (IAA) and by conducting manual reviews of annotation samples from each worker. Parameters of the annotation process such as reward per task, maximum time per assignment, and number of annotations solicited for each listing, were updated during the annotation process based on our experience — a detailed description of this process is available in the Appendix of (Bogensperger, 2021). We obtained over 4,000 valid annotations from Appen and over 7,400 from AMT. Appen annotators received a fixed payment of either \$0.06 or \$0.08 per annotated document (the exact rate changing across batches), on AMT rates also varied across annotators and payments per row ranged between \$0.09 and \$0.30, while hourly rates varied between \$12 and \$18. Our total incurred costs were \$548 on Appen and \$1505 on AMT, in the former case this included payment for 995 additional annotations that were invalidated based on annotators' performance on the test questions. Table 2 shows inter-annotator agreement (IAA) values for annotations obtained via each of the two platforms. Following Viera and Garrett (2005) and Hripcsak and Rothschild (2005) we used F1-Agreement as the primary IAA measure,

	MTurk	Appen
% of characters added	8.56	25.81
% of characters deleted	3.51	0.89
% of spans added	13.19	27.49
% of spans deleted/altered	8.65	10.45

Table 3: Average effort of the review process.

Cohen's Kappa is also calculated for comparison. Spans annotated by at least two annotators were reviewed and corrected manually by the authors, then all annotated documents were reviewed once again by the authors to find missing annotations. The review process followed the principles described in Section 3.2. Table 3 shows the amount of editing performed for each portion of the annotations. Both of these figures and the agreement scores show a considerable difference between the quality of annotations from the two platforms, and without further study we can only speculate that this may be attributed to the continuous improvement of the annotator instructions based on our experiences, the different presentations of these instructions (MTurk annotators had access to a short and long version), or to the different incentive systems of the two platforms (AMT workers were required to hold a "master" qualification on the platform, which they could lose when providing low-quality annotations, while Appen workers' performance was only controlled on the test questions).

The final dataset contains 3,507 item listings with 364,003 tokens, 14,934 annotated spans and 3,048 unique drug entities. The dataset was split into training, validation, and test portions of 2244, 561, and 702 listings, respectively. Table 4 provides basic descriptive statistics about the `DreamDrug` dataset, further statistics as well as a list of the most frequent spans are presented in Appendix A. Manual evaluation of a sample of rare spans reveals that while some of them refer to

	Min	Max	Mean	Median
words / doc	3	534	103.8	61
chars / doc	25	2,930	572.6	334
words / entity	1	20	1.9	2
chars / entity	1	80	12.1	10
entity / doc	0	101	4.26	2

Table 4: Descriptive Statistics of dataset

rare entities, such as names of cannabis strains (e.g. *alien technology*) or specific chemical descriptors (e.g. *n-acetyl-p-aminophenol*), most of them are spelling variations of common drugs (e.g. "Oxycodone hydrochloride" instead of ... "Oxycodone HCL") and misspellings ("Oxymorophone" instead of "Oxymorphone").

4 Experiments

We train a set of baseline transformer-based models, examine the effects of domain-adaptive pretraining using multiple datasets, and also evaluate top-performing models in a few-shot training scenario.

4.1 Baseline models

We train the standard BERT-based architecture for Named Entity Recognition (Devlin et al., 2018), which consists of a transformer layer and a linear layer with dropout, using the PyTorch-based implementations from Huggingface (Wolf et al., 2020), similar to the system in (Liu et al., 2021). We train systems based on the `bert-base-cased` and `roberta-base` models with default parameters, using the Adam optimizer, a learning rate of $5 \cdot 10^{-5}$, and a batch size of 4. For the few-shot learning setup we used only the first 100 documents from the training set. In both setups we trained our models for 10 epochs. We also train the FLAIR[6] system (Akbik et al., 2019a) using default hyperparameters and training for 50 epochs. We use BERT (`bert-base-cased`) as the input representation of the FLAIR system because it yields better results than FLAIR's own contextualized embedding (Akbik et al., 2019b). For evaluation we use standard NER metrics as defined by the CoNLL 2003 shared task (Tjong Kim Sang and De Meulder, 2003), computing precision, recall, and F-score, where a predicted named entity is considered correct only if it is an exact match of a gold standard entity. While Named Entity Recognition is generally implemented on the sentence level, the relatively short average length of listings (see Table 4) allows us to train the baselines on full documents, limited only by the maximum input length of BERT, 512 (subword) tokens. While the average number of words per document in our dataset is 103.79, the average number of subword tokens output by BERT's tokenizer is 152.18, and 4.1% of documents are longer than the maximum input length of 512, these were clipped at 512 tokens for training and evaluation of each of our baselines. A final preprocessing step involved removing all punctuation except commas from item descriptions to reduce noise, the regular expressions we used are presented in Appendix B.

4.2 Domain adaptation

We improve the performance of our baselines by pretraining on unannotated text representing the domain and/or genre of the `DreamDrug` dataset. We compile three datasets that can be used separately or in combination. `Dreammarket` contains Dreammarket product listings of drugs that were not used in creating `DreamDrug`. The size of this dataset is slightly above 800 000 words. The `Grams` dataset is constructed from the Darknet Market Archives (Branwen et al., 2015), using the subsets *Abraxas, Agora, Alpha, ME*, and *Oxygen*, and contains listings from a variety of domains. This dataset contains nearly 1.7 million words. The third dataset used for domain adaptation, `Wikipedia`, was constructed using 3,210 drug-related articles downloaded from Wikipedia[7] using its Python API[8]. Sections of Wikipedia articles that do not typically contain running text (*References*, *See also*, and *External Links*) were removed, and the remaining text was searched for possible mentions of drug entities by annotating each sentence for mentions of entities in the knowledge graph DBPedia (Auer et al., 2007) using the `annotate` function of the Spotlight API[9], which performs fuzzy matching. Drug entities were detected based on the presence of the DBPedia attributes `dbp:legalUs` or `dbp:legalUn`, sentences containing entities with either of these attributes were added to the dataset used for domain adaptation. The size of the resulting dataset is

[6] `https://github.com/flairNLP/flair`

[7] `https://en.wikipedia.org/`

[8] `https://pypi.org/project/wikipedia/`

[9] `https://pypi.org/project/spacy-dbpedia-spotlight/`

Base	DAPT	D	F1	Prec.	Rec.
FLAIR	None	NA	59.72	60.29	59.16
BERT	None	0	63.80	67.84	60.21
BERT	All	0	69.86	72.91	**67.06**
BERT	None	0.5	62.93	70.59	56.77
BERT	DM	0.5	69.43	74.20	65.23
BERT	Grams	0.5	68.49	71.87	65.41
BERT	Wiki	0.5	64.32	68.76	60.42
BERT	All	0.5	**70.98**	**76.73**	66.04
RoBERTa	All	0.35	69.11	73.54	65.18

Table 5: Performance of top baseline configurations in the few-shot scenario. The column DAPT indicates the dataset(s) used for domain-adaptive pretraining, D indicates dropout rate.

Base	DAPT	D	F1	Prec.	Rec.
FLAIR	None	N/A	81.42	80.83	**82.01**
RoBERTa	None	0	80.84	81.13	80.56
RoBERTa	Wiki	0	80.83	83.65	78.20
RoBERTa	All	0	81.21	**86.63**	76.43
RoBERTa	None	0.1	80.55	81.43	79.69
RoBERTa	DM	0.1	80.41	83.19	77.80
RoBERTa	Grams	0.1	80.52	84.99	76.49
RoBERTa	Wiki	0.1	**82.16**	84.86	79.62
RoBERTa	All	0.1	81.51	85.37	77.98
BERT	All	0.45	81.64	85.71	77.94

Table 6: Performance of top baseline configurations using the full training set. The column DAPT indicates the dataset(s) used for domain-adaptive pretraining, D indicates dropout rate.

more than 880 000 words, the three datasets for domain adaptation together contain nearly 3.4 million words.

5 Results

Tables 5 and 6 present the perfomance of top baseline configurations in the few-shot setting and when using the full training set. The BERT-based systems achieved higher scores in the few-shot setup, while RoBERTa-based setups performed better when trained on the full dataset. For both setups we include the performance of the top system with and without dropout as well as with domain-adaptive pretraining (DAPT) on each of the additional datasets. For both the few-shot setup and the full training set we also include the best-performing configuration of the other language model (RoBERTa for the few-shot setting and BERT for the full dataset) and the performance of the best FLAIR model. The effect of domain adaptation using in-domain unannotated text is especially pronounced in the few-shot setting, where it achieves an 8 point increase in F-score, 6.5 of which can be achieved using only the DM dataset, which is the one most similar to the listings in `DreamDrug`. We believe this shows the strong potential of pretraining on unannotated text that is characteristic of both the domain and the genre of a novel task, especially in settings where the availability of human-annotated data is limited. Finally, Table 7 contains the results of our top models on the test set.

Model	F1	Prec.	Rec.
few-shot training			
FLAIR	62.13	65.18	59.35
Our best model	73.55	78.38	69.28
full training set			
FLAIR	81.82	82.75	80.92
Our best model	83.86	84.83	82.92

Table 7: Performance of top baseline configurations on the test set

6 Conclusion

We have constructed the novel dataset `DreamDrug` for the task of recognizing drug entities in darknet market listings, used it to train and evaluate baseline NER models, and demonstrated the effectiveness of domain-adaptive pretraining on large unannotated datasets. As one of the first entity-annotated corpora of darknet text, and the first task-specific one, `DreamDrug` will facilitate the study of named entity recognition and related information extraction tasks in noisy user-generated texts. Additionally, it can also be extended with several types of annotation, including entities from multiple classes, relations such as "drug-quantity" or "drug-strength", or links from entity mentions to a knowledge base.

Acknowledgements

We thank the two anonymous reviewers for their insightful comments and for additional references. The research described in this paper was carried out as part of the COPKIT project, which has received funding from the European Union's Horizon 2020 research and innovation programme under grant agreement No. 786687.

Ethical considerations

An analysis of potential project internal and external impacts of the research activity was conducted as part of the COPKIT project. The relevance of data protection principles, such as lawfulness, fairness, and transparency, purpose limitations, data minimization, accuracy, storage limitation, integrity and confidentiality, and accountability has been analyzed for this dataset publication. The activity was led by the project internal ethical, legal, and privacy team. Regarding concrete measures, the dataset was pseudonymized to remove any personal data, and the base dataset for ground-truth creation was approved for use by the ethical, legal, and privacy team. It was decided to provide access to the data only on request to prevent misuse of the dataset for purposes other than research.

References

Gustavo Aguilar, Suraj Maharjan, Adrian Pastor López-Monroy, and Thamar Solorio. 2017. A multi-task approach for named entity recognition in social media data. In *Proceedings of the 3rd Workshop on Noisy User-generated Text*, pages 148–153, Copenhagen, Denmark. Association for Computational Linguistics.

Alan Akbik, Tanja Bergmann, Duncan Blythe, Kashif Rasul, Stefan Schweter, and Roland Vollgraf. 2019a. FLAIR: An easy-to-use framework for state-of-the-art NLP. In *Proceedings of the 2019 Conference of the North American Chapter of the Association for Computational Linguistics (Demonstrations)*, pages 54–59, Minneapolis, Minnesota. Association for Computational Linguistics.

Alan Akbik, Tanja Bergmann, and Roland Vollgraf. 2019b. Pooled contextualized embeddings for named entity recognition. In *Proceedings of the 2019 Conference of the North American Chapter of the Association for Computational Linguistics: Human Language Technologies, Volume 1 (Long and Short Papers)*, pages 724–728, Minneapolis, Minnesota. Association for Computational Linguistics.

Noushin Rezapour Asheghi, Serge Sharoff, and Katja Markert. 2014. Designing and evaluating a reliable corpus of web genres via crowd-sourcing. In *Proceedings of the Ninth International Conference on Language Resources and Evaluation (LREC'14)*, pages 1339–1346, Reykjavik, Iceland. European Language Resources Association (ELRA).

Sören Auer, Christian Bizer, Georgi Kobilarov, Jens Lehmann, Richard Cyganiak, and Zachary Ives. 2007. Dbpedia: A nucleus for a web of open data. In *Proceedings of the 6th International The Semantic Web and 2nd Asian Conference on Asian Semantic Web Conference*, ISWC'07/ASWC'07, page 722–735, Berlin, Heidelberg. Springer-Verlag.

Darina Benikova, Chris Biemann, and Marc Reznicek. 2014. NoSta-D named entity annotation for German: Guidelines and dataset. In *Proceedings of the Ninth International Conference on Language Resources and Evaluation (LREC'14)*, pages 2524–2531, Reykjavik, Iceland. European Language Resources Association (ELRA).

É. Bigeard, N. Grabar, and F. Thiessard. 2018. Detection and analysis of drug misuses. A study based on social media messages. *Frontiers in Pharmacology*, 9.

Johannes Bogensperger. 2021. Exploring transfer learning techniques for named entity recognition in noisy user-generated text. Master's thesis, TU Wien.

Kalina Bontcheva, Leon Derczynski, and Ian Roberts. 2017. Crowdsourcing named entity recognition and entity linking corpora. In *Handbook of Linguistic Annotation*, pages 875–892. Springer.

Gwern Branwen, Nicolas Christin, David Décary-Hétu, Rasmus Munksgaard Andersen, StExo, El Presidente, Anonymous, Daryl Lau, Delyan Kratunov Sohhlz, Vince Cakic, Van Buskirk, Whom, Michael McKenna, and Sigi Goode. 2015. Dark net market archives, 2011-2015. `https://www.gwern.net/DNM-archives`. Accessed: 25.01.2021.

X. Chen, Myrtille Deldossi, Rim Aboukhamis, C. Faviez, B. Dahamna, P. Karapetiantz, Armelle Guenegou-Arnoux, Y. Girardeau, Sylvie Guillemin-Lanne, A. L. Louët, N. Texier, Anita Burgun-Parenthoine, and S. Katsahian. 2017. Mining adverse drug reactions in social media with named entity recognition and semantic methods. *Studies in health technology and informatics*, 245:322–326.

Leon Derczynski, Eric Nichols, Marieke van Erp, and Nut Limsopatham. 2017. Results of the WNUT2017 shared task on novel and emerging entity recognition. In *Proceedings of the 3rd Workshop on Noisy User-generated Text*, pages 140–147, Copenhagen, Denmark. Association for Computational Linguistics.

Jacob Devlin, Ming-Wei Chang, Kenton Lee, and Kristina Toutanova. 2018. BERT: pre-training of deep bidirectional transformers for language understanding. *CoRR*, abs/1810.04805.

Po-Yi Du, Ning Zhang, Mohammedreza Ebrahimi, Sagar Samtani, Ben Lazarine, Nolan Arnold, Rachael Dunn, Sandeep Suntwal, Guadalupe Angeles, Robert Schweitzer, and Hsinchun Chen. 2018. Identifying, collecting, and presenting hacker community data: Forums, irc, carding shops, and dnms. In *2018 IEEE International Conference on Intelligence and Security Informatics (ISI)*, pages 70–75.

Greg Durrett, Jonathan K. Kummerfeld, Taylor Berg-Kirkpatrick, Rebecca Portnoff, Sadia Afroz, Damon McCoy, Kirill Levchenko, and Vern Paxson. 2017. Identifying products in online cybercrime marketplaces: A dataset for fine-grained domain adaptation. In *Proceedings of the 2017 Conference on Empirical Methods in Natural Language Processing*, pages 2598–2607, Copenhagen, Denmark. Association for Computational Linguistics.

O. Feyisetan, Markus Luczak-Rösch, E. Simperl, Ramine Tinati, and N. Shadbolt. 2015. Towards hybrid NER: A study of content and crowdsourcing-related performance factors. In *ESWC*.

O. Feyisetan, E. Simperl, Markus Luczak-Rösch, Ramine Tinati, and N. Shadbolt. 2018. An extended study of content and crowdsourcing-related performance factors in named entity annotation. *Semantic Web*, 9:355–379.

Tim Finin, William Murnane, Anand Karandikar, Nicholas Keller, Justin Martineau, and Mark Dredze. 2010. Annotating named entities in Twitter data with crowdsourcing. In *Proceedings of the NAACL HLT 2010 Workshop on Creating Speech and Language Data with Amazon's Mechanical Turk*, pages 80–88, Los Angeles. Association for Computational Linguistics.

Karën Fort, Maud Ehrmann, and Adeline Nazarenko. 2009. Towards a methodology for named entities annotation. In *Proceedings of the Third Linguistic Annotation Workshop (LAW III)*, pages 142–145, Suntec, Singapore. Association for Computational Linguistics.

Inês Gomes, Rui Correia, Jorge Ribeiro, and João Freitas. 2020. Effort estimation in named entity tagging tasks. In *Proceedings of the 12th Language Resources and Evaluation Conference*, pages 298–306, Marseille, France. European Language Resources Association.

G. Hripcsak and A. Rothschild. 2005. Technical brief: Agreement, the F-Measure, and reliability in information retrieval. *Journal of the American Medical Informatics Association : JAMIA*, 12 3:296–8.

Mona Jalal, Kate K. Mays, L. Guo, and Margrit Betke. 2020. Performance comparison of crowdworkers and NLP tools on named-entity recognition and sentiment analysis of political tweets. *ArXiv*, abs/2002.04181.

Patrick Jansson and Shuhua Liu. 2017. Distributed representation, LDA topic modelling and deep learning for emerging named entity recognition from social media. In *Proceedings of the 3rd Workshop on Noisy User-generated Text*, pages 154–159, Copenhagen, Denmark. Association for Computational Linguistics.

Jiawei Li, Q. Xu, Neal Shah, and T. Mackey. 2019. A machine learning approach for the detection and characterization of illicit drug dealers on Instagram: Model evaluation study. *Journal of Medical Internet Research*, 21.

Bill Y. Lin, Frank Xu, Zhiyi Luo, and Kenny Zhu. 2017. Multi-channel BiLSTM-CRF model for emerging named entity recognition in social media. In *Proceedings of the 3rd Workshop on Noisy User-generated Text*, pages 160–165, Copenhagen, Denmark. Association for Computational Linguistics.

Zihan Liu, Yan Xu, Tiezheng Yu, Wenliang Dai, Ziwei Ji, Samuel Cahyawijaya, Andrea Madotto, and Pascale Fung. 2021. CrossNER: Evaluating cross-domain named entity recognition. *Proceedings of the AAAI Conference on Artificial Intelligence*, 35(15):13452–13460.

Mhd Wesam Al Nabki, E. Fidalgo, E. Alegre, and Laura Fernández-Robles. 2020. Improving named entity recognition in noisy user-generated text with local distance neighbor feature. *Neurocomputing*, 382:1–11.

Claire Nédellec, Philippe Bessières, Robert R. Bossy, Alain Kotoujansky, and Alain Pierre Manine. 2006. Annotation guidelines for machine learning-based named entity recognition in microbiology. In *Proceeding of Data and Text Mining for Integrative Biology Workshop 17. European Conference on Machine Learning 10. European Conference on Principles and Practice of Knowledge Discovery in Databases*, Workshop on data and text mining for integrative biology, Berlin, Germany. Springer - Verlag.

Peter S. Ostling, Kelly S Davidson, Best O Anyama, Erik M. Helander, M. Q. Wyche, and A. Kaye. 2018. America's opioid epidemic: a comprehensive review and look into the rising crisis. *Current Pain and Headache Reports*, 22:1–7.

Peng Qi, Yuhao Zhang, Yuhui Zhang, Jason Bolton, and Christopher D. Manning. 2020. Stanza: A Python natural language processing toolkit for many human languages. In *Proceedings of the 58th Annual Meeting of the Association for Computational Linguistics: System Demonstrations*, pages 101–108, Online. Association for Computational Linguistics.

Zahra Rezaei, H. Ebrahimpour-Komleh, B. Eslami, Ramyar Chavoshinejad, and M. Totonchi. 2020. Adverse drug reaction detection in social media by deep learning methods. *Cell Journal (Yakhteh)*, 22:319 – 324.

Marta Sabou, Kalina Bontcheva, Leon Derczynski, and Arno Scharl. 2014. Corpus annotation through crowdsourcing: Towards best practice guidelines. In *Proceedings of the Ninth International Conference on Language Resources and Evaluation (LREC'14)*, pages 859–866, Reykjavik, Iceland. European Language Resources Association (ELRA).

Nakatani Shuyo. 2010. Language detection library for Java.

Erik F. Tjong Kim Sang and Fien De Meulder. 2003. Introduction to the CoNLL-2003 shared task: Language-independent named entity recognition. In *Proceedings of the Seventh Conference on Natural Language Learning at HLT-NAACL 2003*, pages 142–147.

U.S. Food and Drug Administration. 2021. Human drugs. definition of the U.S. Food and Drug Administration (fda). https://www.fda.gov/industry/regulated-products/human-drugs.

A. Viera and J. Garrett. 2005. Understanding inter-observer agreement: the Kappa statistic. *Family medicine*, 37 5:360–3.

Thomas Wolf, Lysandre Debut, Victor Sanh, Julien Chaumond, Clement Delangue, Anthony Moi, Pierric Cistac, Tim Rault, Rémi Louf, Morgan Funtowicz, Joe Davison, Sam Shleifer, Patrick von Platen, Clara Ma, Yacine Jernite, Julien Plu, Canwen Xu, Teven Le Scao, Sylvain Gugger, Mariama Drame, Quentin Lhoest, and Alexander M. Rush. 2020. Transformers: State-of-the-art natural language processing. In *Proceedings of the 2020 Conference on Empirical Methods in Natural Language Processing: System Demonstrations*, pages 38–45, Online. Association for Computational Linguistics.

A Dataset statistics

Figure 6 shows a histogram of the number of tokens per document, Figure 7 and Table 8 present the most frequent drug entities. Figure 5 contains the entity frequency histogram.

Entity	Frequency
cocaine	476
thc	435
mdma	428
cannabis	365
indica	350
sativa	336
hash	239
weed	215
lsd	214
hybrid	175
xanax	154
cbd	151
marijuana	150
og kush	120
xtc	116
sour diesel	116
alprazolam	104
heroin	97
oxycodone	96
speed	93
adderall	93

Table 8: Most frequent drug entities in the `DreamDrug` dataset (lowercased)

B Custom preprocessing

Listing 1: Preprocessing function for the removal of links and special characters from text

```
def remove_unwanted_elements(text):
  ft = re.sub(
    r'https?:\/\/\S*[\r\n]*', '', text)
  ft = re.sub(
    r'\S*.onion\S*[\r\n]*', '', ft)
  ft = re.sub(
    r'[\+!~@#$%^&*()={}\[\]:;<.>?\`"]',
    '', ft)

  ft = re.sub(',', '&#44', ft)

  ft = re.sub(r'[-]+', '-', ft)
  ft = re.sub(r'[_]+', '_', ft)
  return ft
```

Listing 2: Preprocessing functions for replacing email addresses

```
from faker import Faker
# create random name
def get_fake_name():
    # can create fake names
    fake = Faker()
    fake_name = fake.name().replace(
        " ", "")
    if random.randint(1, 10) % 2 == 0:
        fake_name = fake_name.lower()
    if random.randint(1, 10) % 3 == 0:
        fake_name = "%s%d" % (
            fake_name.lower(),
            random.randint(10, 99))
    return fake_name

def replace_mails(text):
    domain = [
        '.com','.de','.ru','.org']
    vendor = [
        'gmail', 'air', 'wing',
        'microsoft', 'hotmail',
        'outlook']
    mail = get_fake_name() + '@' +
        vendor[random.randint(
            0, len(vendor)-1)] +
        domain[random.randint(
            0, len(domain)-1)]
    return re.sub(
        r'\S+@\S+\s?', mail, text)
```

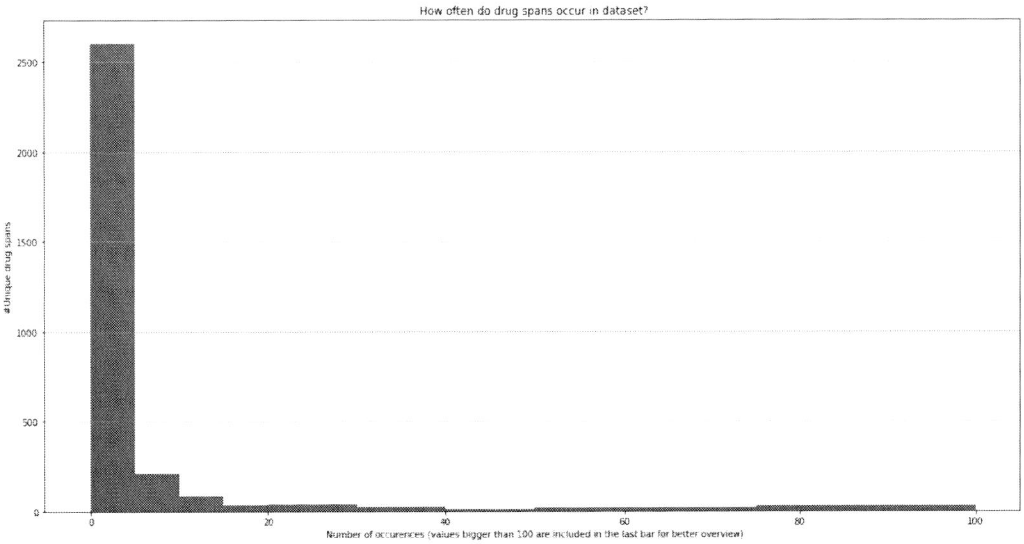

Figure 5: Frequency distribution of drug entities

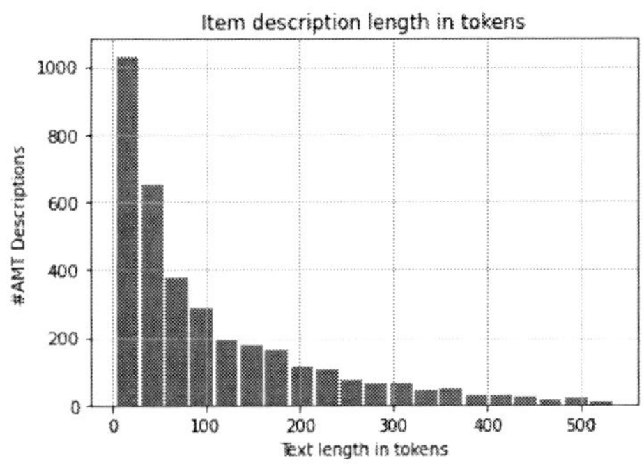

Figure 6: Distribution of document length (number of tokens) in the `DreamDrug` dataset

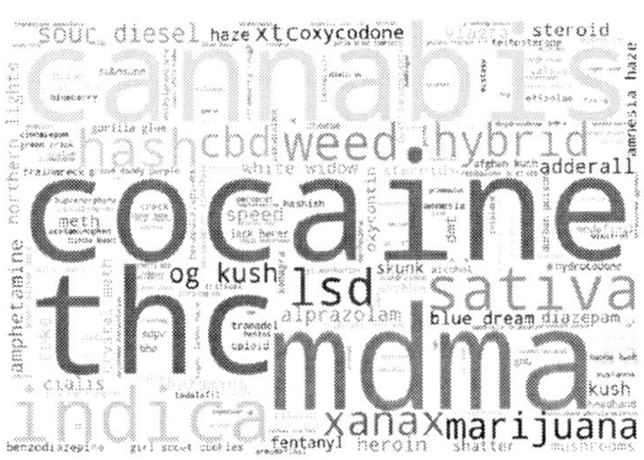

Figure 7: Word-cloud of the most frequent entities in the `DreamDrug` dataset

C Annotation guidelines

The following pages show the long version of the annotation guidelines as they were presented to the annotators of Appen and to AMT workers clicking on the *Instructions* button on the interface shown in Figure 3 (Section 3.3).

nnotator Gu   elines - Appen

Instruction ▲

Overview

In this task you will use the text annotation tool to highlight dr gs in texts from the Darknet. This highlighting means you label pieces of text (called "token") in product descriptions of Darknet Markets. The items have a name and a description. We want you to label all DRUGS yo can find in the description.

HOW TO DO THIS?

1. **Read the Context** below the text to get an idea of which items co ld be contained in the text

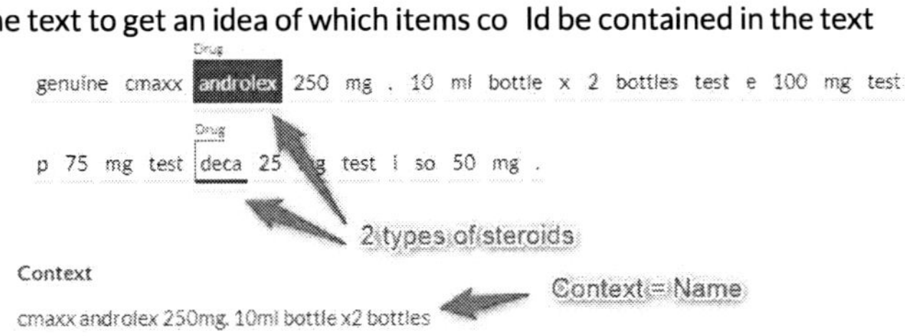

2. **Read the prov ded dr g description and label ALL dr g --> Not j st the one in the context.**
3. **Are you uns re about what is a dr g?** No problem - Click on the info of the "Drug" Class or **re-open this text.**

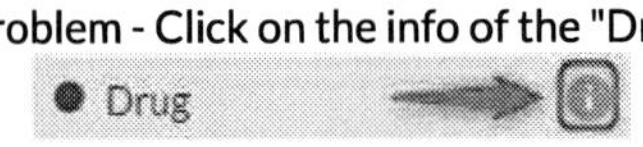

nnotation Gu deline

Label every nique drug name you can find! Typical Drug Examples are:

- Marij ana Strains or types - s e.g. "Gorilla Gl e", "Indica / Sativa / Hybrid", "Super silver Haze" or "Girl Scout Cookies"
- Types of Drugs or Agents e.g. "Cocaine", "Crystal Meth", "MDMA" or "THC"
- Legal or partial legal dr gs e.g. "Alcohol", "Testosterone Enthalate", "Aspirin" or "Viagra"
- Slang names e.g. Coke, Meth, mushrooms, hash, weed

Label ONLY the drug - Descriptions or Adject ves are not part of the drug

(like "Colour, Form or If its powder / oil / paste / pill or the strength of a drug e.g. 200mg)

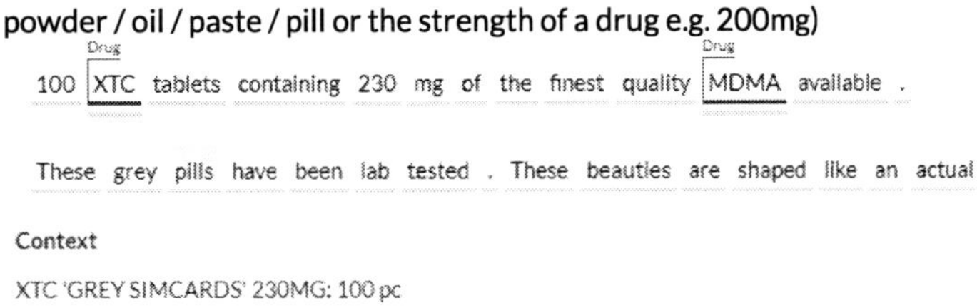

We want you to labe ALL drugs in the text - Pay attention to abe   rugs with multiple words as one drug. (Strawberry s not drug w tho t amne a)

If there is a '.' or '-' contained in the middle of a name label it as well. "Strawberry . Amnesia" or " Strawberry - Amnesia" would also be a drug.

Top shelf coffeeshop quality . A powerful and uplifting flower from Dinafem Seeds , Strawberry Amnesia is a strain made in sativa heaven . Bred from Strawberry Cough and Amnesia , this strain delivers the familiar sweet strawberry and earthy flavors of its parents . Having the typical energizing and euphoric effects of a sativa , Strawberry Amnesia also induces the calming body high from its distant indica relatives . The dark green buds of Strawberry Amnesia are very dense and heavily coated in resin , so this potent sativa should be handled with caution .

Context

Strawberry Amneisa - *New strain* - AAAA+ - 3.5G

hemical e ailsa e a tofthedrug.

- Sildenfanil Citrate i a single drug and need to be labelled together (not separate)

Sildenafil Citrate 100 mg Viagra is a Generic medicine used for Penis erectile

- Drug Chemicals can also be drugs on their own. - AND Include "-" or "." in the labelling

This listing is for 100 mg of 5 - MeO - MiPT .

Context

100mg 5-MeO-MiPT

Abbreviations / Short names of drugs shall be labelled. e.g. XTC, BTH or

This listing is for Furanylethylfentanyl FUEF . Crystal . Effects similar to Heroin / Fentanyl . Furanylethylfentanyl is a is an opiod RC and an analog of fentanyl that is reported to be slightly weaker than furanylfentanyl . It is also a small crystal instead of a powder and as such is less soluble in water . It is cheaper than furanylfentanyl . Please check our vendor page for our policies regarding ordering , reships , etc . PRICING 1g FUEF Crystal 35 - 35 / g

Context

1g Furanylethylfentanyl (FUEF) Crystal

Active Agents (The ingredient which makes you high) shall be labelled as drugs. e.g. CB , TH , iaze am or DMT

.

100 x. 05g cartridges filled with the highest quality distillate oil , 16 each - ORGANIC - Solvent FREE .

These are the most potent cartridges . Testing at approximately 90 THC , these carts deliver the best vaping

experience on the market 500 THC in 1 cartridge . Available flavors . - Strawberry Cheesecake - Guava

fficial Ma ting names ARE drugs

This includes all kinds of marketing names in different countries or commerci l mariju na str in names

ARTVIGIL - armodafinil 150mg . Manufacturer HAB Pharmaceuticals . Armodafinil is the more efficient successor

to Modafinil . While you would take 200 mg of Modafinil to achieve a certain level of increased mental

activity , you would only have to take 150 mg of Armodafinil to achieve a comparable effect . People also

speak of Armodafinil giving a stronger , sharper buzz , while Modafinil feels softer , warmer , and slightly

Context

ARTVIGIL (generic NUVIGIL) armodafinil 150mg - 10

Drug Class s are Drugs

- Bezondiazipines, Opiates, Steroids, Indica / Sativa / Hybrid - ARE Drugs

Alprazolam is in a class of drugs called benzodiazepines . It affects chemicals in

Slang names ARE drugs e.g. ganja or dope

Description Platinum and Top Shelf Gorilla Glue 3 LB - Pure profit .

Gorilla . Glue is one of the most popular strains in the US right now . A

potent and high - yielding hybrid , this bud produces a heavy yet .

comfortable high that knocks away pain . Contact Us at . KIK highlord 6

wickr highlord . What you see is what you get 100 Real Pics . Stealth

Shipping on every package marijuana . weed , kush . wax . oil .

granddaddy purple , fruity pebbles , ganja , cannabis , OG kush , afgahn kush

, mine , weed , dope . smoke , cannabis , ganja , high , marijuana ,

mary jane , stoner , stoned , pot , herb . hemp , hash , 420 , kush , haze

, dank , buds , spliff , bong , blunt , joint . All orders will go out the

following day . CONTACTS US . KIK highlord 6 wickr highlord .

Context

Platinum and Top Shelf Gorilla Glue 3 LB

L gal Drugs ARE Drugs

- In this example its alcohol, but it could also be Caffeine, Aspirin or tabacco.

Drug Drug

LIQUID GHB SYRUP THIS GHB IS READY FOR USE - NO PREPPING REQUIRED

Drug

STRONG PURE . 99 ,95 PURE BASF GHB . ULTIMATE STEALTH AAA .

Drug

DELIVERY GUARANTEED . NEVER COMBINE WITH ALCOHOL CHECK FAQ .

BEFORE USE .

Context

GHB LIQUID SYRUP 250ml GHB (BASF)

f a drug is me oned bu doe n't clearly i d cate which drug i is, do NOT label t. (e.g. Orange Red bull Pill)

"Fishscale Powder", "These Mitsubishi Pills" or "This strain" will refer to a drug but its not clear, which drug it is exactly. In this case only XTC IS a drug and pills is NOT a drug.

Drug

Hello people if you want to try out the real dutch xtc , we recommend to try

our orange redbulls . They are high quality pills with good presses and also

strong , so i recommend to take it in halves when you try for the first time .

Context

100X ORANGE REDBULLS XTC 280MG

The form / strength / adjectives of the drug shall NOT be labelled.

- At Ecstasy(XTC) it doesn't matter if they are Green Mitsubishi with 200mg

Drug

ARE YOU READY TO PARTY . BLUE ICE EXCTASY PILLS GUARANTEED TO

MAKE YOUR NIGHT AN UNFORGETTABLE ONE . LETS GET THE PARTY

Context

@@$$ 10 BLUE ICE EXCTASY PILL @@ FREE USA -USA 2

- Or that they have the imprint "OT-20" or "V-3605" on them. Those are NOT drugs.

The Producer or Manufacturer of the drug, i NOT a Drug

This also excludes creations from Drugdealers like Drcokes megasniff or MegaBelt IsolatorVapes. None of those are drugs.

In the example below Helix Pharma is only the producer and superdrol is the drug.

Drug

1 bottle of Helix Pharma superdrol 10 mg x 100 units .

Context

HELIX PHARMA SUPERDROL 10MG X 100 UNITS

atural che ical w ich are part of your body are NOT a drug.

- Dopamin or estrogen do something to your body, but are NOT produced as drug and therefo e we DON'T label them.

Processed Items like dibles are not al ays a drug.

Only the words which clearly refer to a drug are drugs. B ownies, Vapes or Candies are by itself not a drug, only the form!

NO DRUG in the TEXT?? - IMPORTANT

- If you cannot find any drug in the text, just annotate the first word with the tag "NONE" and continue.

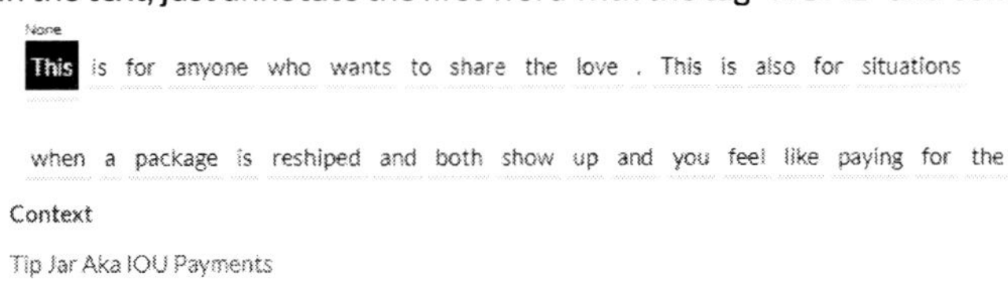

HOW TO LABEL? - IMPORTANT

We want to label tokens which belong together as ONE single span:

Two tokens which are part of the same drug e.g. the "Master Yoda" Cannabis strain shall be labelled as single span. (Same goes for OG Kush or Master Kush etc.)

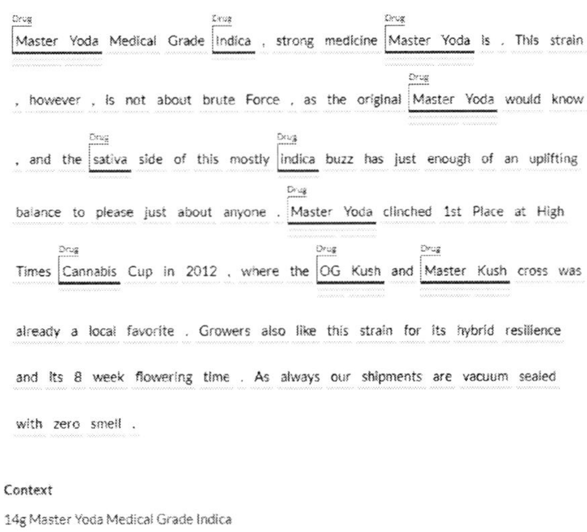

If there is a character (e.g. '.' or '-') inside of drug name -- include it in the labelling. The labels are not allowed to be separated!

re you unsure a out w t is a drug? No problem - RE-OPEN t i w ole ome descriptionfor details or c eck the info of t e "Drug" Class.

Test Question Review

When you get a test question wrong, you'll be able to review your mistakes in a special version of the tool. The errors you made will be underlined in red.

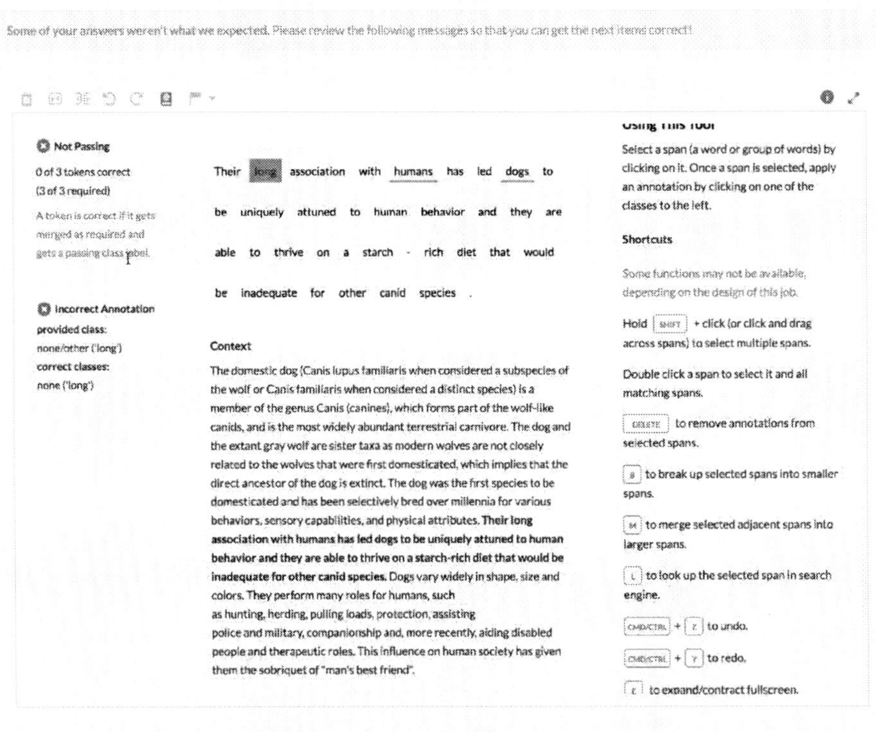

Annotator Guidelines Amazon Mechanical Turk

Drug Labelling

In this HIT we want you label all text spans, which clearly point to a specific drug or drug type.

HOW TO DO THIS?

1. **Read the Context** above the text to get an idea of which items could be contained in the text
2. **Read the provided drug description and label ALL spans which clearly identify a drug**
3. Are you unsure about what is a drug? We provided a extensive description, just press on "Instructions" and go to "more instructions".

Keep in mind: **Each span should Clearly identify a specific drug or drug type!**

Practical examples are:

- Clearly represent a specific drug e.g. hash, meth
- Chemical Compounds e.g. "3 , 4 - methylphendiate"
- Short names e.g. XTC
- Agents e.g. THC, CBD or Diazepam
- Slang drug names: Coke, Fent
- Drug categories e.g. Indica/hybrid, benzodiazipines, opiates
- Pill imprints e.g. "V-3923"
- Chemical Details which extend the drug e.g. Viagra Sildenafil Citrate
- Legal or partial legal drugs e.g. "Alcohol", "Testosterone Enthalate", "Aspirin" or "Viagra"

DO NOT label tokens like:

- Description/Adjectives like drug strength, colour, form (powder/pill..) or looks etc.
- Form of Drug: e.g. powder, pill, paste
- Vague references like "this pill", "My Super Chocolate Bars" or "indoor bud"
- Producer of drugs e.g. Pfizer
- Natural Chemicals in your body e.g. estrogen/dopamin

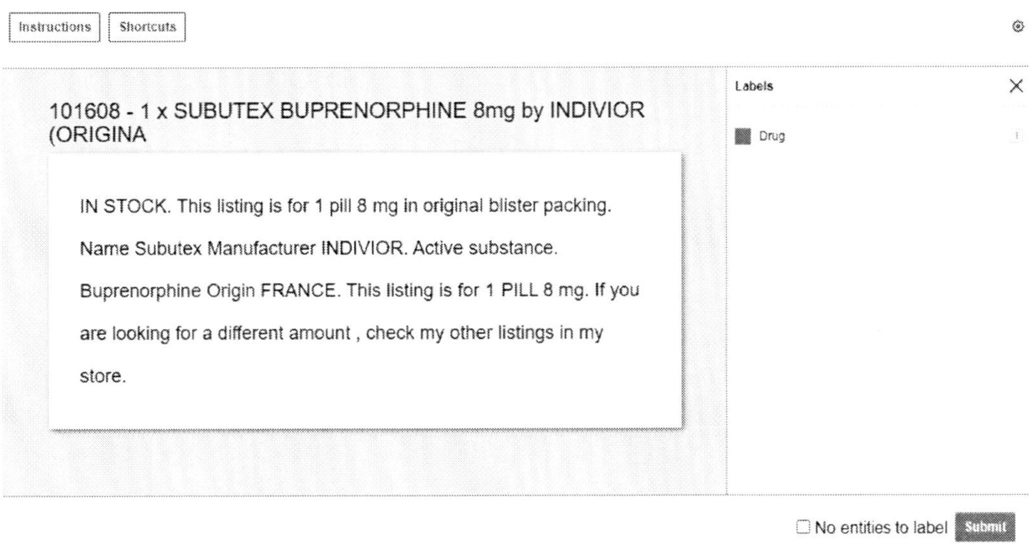

Note: The long version of the annoation guidelines was accessible over the „Instructions" button. The long version was equal to the long Annotation guidelines from Appen.

Comparing Grammatical Theories of Code-Mixing

Adithya Pratapa†
Carnegie Mellon University
vpratapa@cs.cmu.edu

Monojit Choudhury
Microsoft Research
monojitc@microsoft.com

Abstract

Code-mixed text generation systems have found applications in many downstream tasks, including speech recognition, translation and dialogue. A paradigm of these generation systems relies on well-defined grammatical theories of code-mixing, and there is a lack of comparison of these theories. We present a large-scale human evaluation of two popular grammatical theories, Matrix-Embedded Language (ML) and Equivalence Constraint (EC). We compare them against three heuristic-based models and quantitatively demonstrate the effectiveness of the two grammatical theories.

1 Introduction

Code-mixing is the phenomenon of mixing multiple languages within a single conversation. While widely observed in spoken language, mixing languages has also become commonplace in informal text conversations with the increasing use of social media (Rijhwani et al., 2017). Prior work has focused on various code-mixed natural language processing (NLP) tasks, including part-of-speech (POS) tagging (Soto and Hirschberg, 2017; Singh et al., 2018), sentiment analysis (Patwa et al., 2020), machine translation (Solorio et al., 2021) and speech recognition (Lee et al., 2017). Accurately modeling when and how to mix languages is critical to the above code-mixed NLP tasks.

Research efforts on this front have either relied on established grammatical theories (Li and Fung, 2012; Bhat et al., 2016) or neural sequence-to-sequence models (Winata et al., 2019) to generate realistic code-mixed text. Such models have found applications in speech recognition (Li and Fung, 2012; Lee et al., 2019), translation (Gupta et al., 2021) and other downstream NLP tasks (Pratapa et al., 2018b). These generation techniques have also been applied in human-machine dialogue (Ahn et al., 2020; Bawa et al., 2020) to generate seemingly natural code-mixed responses.

However, current literature lacks a thorough comparison of different code-mixed text generation models. Such comparison is necessary to understand the relevance of these generation models to individual downstream NLP applications. In this work, we present one such comparison involving two linguistic theory-based code-mixed text generation systems, one based on Equivalence Constraint theory (Poplack, 1980) and the other on Matrix-Embedded language theory (Myers-Scotton, 1993). Specifically, we crowdsource human judgments on the understandability and naturalness of text generated by the two systems. Our results show that grammatical models are considerably better than heuristic counterparts. Additionally, we find the two grammatical models are equally preferable by our human judges. We evaluate the importance of individual constraints in each grammatical theory. In the following sections, we first briefly describe the grammatical models (§2.1) and related heuristic models (§2.2). In §3, we describe our human evaluation setup, and present the results in §4.

2 Generative Models of Code-Mixing

Code-mixed text generation has applications in NLP tasks of speech recognition, human-machine dialogue, and translation. Prior work has primarily focused on three grammatical theories, Equivalence Constraint (EC) (Poplack, 1980), Matrix-Embedded Language (ML) (Myers-Scotton, 1993) and Functional Head Constraint (FHC) (Belazi et al., 1994). Each of these theories presents an account of the grammatical constraints of code-mixing. Bhat et al. (2016) presented computational models for EC and ML theories. Such computational models allow for generation of grammatically correct code-mixed text (Li and Fung, 2012; Pratapa et al., 2018a; Lee et al., 2019; Tarunesh et al., 2021). However, the resulting text may or

† work done at Microsoft Research.

Proceedings of the 2021 EMNLP Workshop W-NUT: The Seventh Workshop on Noisy User-generated Text, pages 158–167
November 11, 2021.

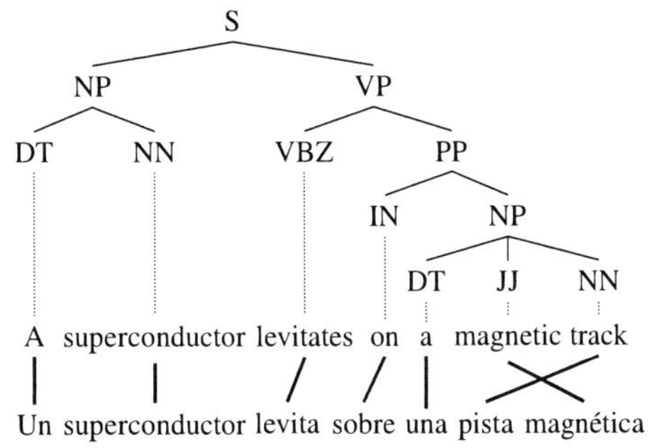

(a) English constituency parse + word-level alignments

1	Un superconductor levita sobre *a magnetic track*
2	Un superconductor levita sobre una pista *magnetic*
3	Un superconductor levita sobre *a* pista magnética
4	A superconductor levitates on a magnetic *magnética*
5	Levita un superconductor sobre *a magnetic track*

(b) Candidate code-mixed sentences.

Figure 1: An illustration of outputs from code-mixed text generation models. Figure 1a shows the constituency parse for an example English sentence, along with its word-aligned Spanish translation. Figure 1b presents 5 example code-mixed sentences generated from the above English-Spanish aligned pair. Sentence #1 is allowed under all the grammatical and heuristic models, #2 is disallowed by EC model, #3 is disallowed by ML model, #4 is disallowed by EC, ML, aligned and dictionary models, #5 is disallowed under all the grammatical and heuristic models. Words from embedded language are *italicized* in each example.

may not be considered natural by bilingual speakers. In this work, we compare the two theories (EC and ML) for their perceived naturalness. Due to the unavailability of a computational model for FHC theory, we leave the comparison of FHC to EC and ML theories to future work.

There is another line of work involving sequence-to-sequence models that do not directly rely on grammatical theories (Winata et al., 2019; Lee and Li, 2020). While this is an exciting line of research, we restrict the focus of this work to grammatical models and leave the comparison with neural models to future work.

2.1 Grammatical Models

Equivalence Constraint (EC): Proposed by Poplack (1980), this theory imposes an *equivalence* constraint at each switch point between the two languages in a code-mixed sentence. The two constituent languages are assumed to follow context-free grammar (CFG). Each non-terminal (and terminal) in one CFG has a counterpart in the other CFG. In cases where the two language parses are not identical, we follow prior work (Bhat et al., 2016; Pratapa et al., 2018a) and perform node collapse to make the grammars equivalent. We follow the implementation from Pratapa et al. (2018a) to generate code-mixed sentences for our study.[1]

Matrix-Embedded Language (ML): Proposed by Myers-Scotton (1993), this theory allows for inserting grammatical constituents of an *embedded* language into a sentence in *matrix* language. It disallows for replacing specific constituents relating to verbs (V), coordinating conjunction (CC), determiner (DT), preposition (IN) as well as nesting sub-trees (NST).

We refer the readers to Bhat et al. (2016) for more details on the computational models for EC and ML theories.

2.2 Heuristic Models

The above described grammatical models impose linguistic constraints on the process of mixing text from two languages. To evaluate if these linguistic constraints are necessary for the output text to be considered natural, we contrast them against three simple heuristic-based models. These heuristic models only rely on parallel sentences, word-level alignments, or a bilingual dictionary.

Aligned ($H_{aligned}$): Given parallel sentences with word-level alignments, we construct a code-mixed sentence by uniformly sampling a word from one of the two languages in a given aligned pair. To generate a sentence, we first sort the alignment indices in the order of L1 tokens (similarly for L2) and then iterate through the alignment indices.

Dictionary (H_{dict}): In this model, we use an external bilingual dictionary that maps words from L1 and L2. We take a monolingual sentence, and for every word, we uniformly sample one of the words or its counterpart from the other language (if one exists in the dictionary). This model only needs a

[1]See Rizvi et al. (2021) for the implementation.

pre-built dictionary to synthesize code-mixed sentences from monolingual corpora.

Parallel ($H_{parallel}$): In the case of missing word-level alignments, we can still generate code-mixed sentences by assuming a linear mapping between L1 and L2 word order. This assumption might work well for languages with similar word order, like the English-Spanish pair used in this study.

Figure 1 illustrates the validity of example Spanish-English code-mixed sentences under each grammatical and heuristic model discussed above.

3 Evaluation Setup

To evaluate the effectiveness of the above described models of code-mixing (§2), we first sample Spanglish (English-Spanish) sentences using selected criterion (§3.1), and then collect human judgments on their understandability and naturalness (§3.2).

3.1 Preparing Data

The generative models of code-mixing take parallel sentences and their word-level alignments as their inputs. We follow the same strategy as Pratapa et al. (2018a) to collect monolingual tweets in English and Spanish.[2] We then translate the tweets to the other language using Microsoft Translator API. We use `fast_align` toolkit (Dyer et al., 2013) to extract word-level alignments between the source and target sentences.[3] For the grammatical models, we extract constituent parses using Stanford PCFG parser (Klein and Manning, 2003). For generating code-mixed sentences using the grammatical theories, we follow the prior work (Bhat et al., 2016; Pratapa et al., 2018a). Note that both these systems follow the grammatical theories exactly and do not exclude code-mixed sentences based on their naturalness. For the heuristic models, we follow the methodologies described in §2.2. Most models take parallel sentences as input and generate a large number of code-mixed sentences. For this study, we sample code-mixed sentences by carefully controlling for specific features. As we describe below, we identify features relevant to the parallel sentences as well as grammatical constraints.

Sentence length (SL): We compute the average length (# tokens) for each pair of parallel sentences. We then group them into the four buckets, $\{SL_1: (5, 8], SL_2: (8, 11], SL_3: (11, 15], SL_4: (15, 20]\}$.

Pseudo fuzzy match score (PFMS): As described earlier, we rely on a neural machine translation system to automatically translate monolingual tweets. The translation performance itself will have an impact on the perceived quality of generated code-mixed sentences. To evaluate the translation performance, we compute the normalized edit distance between the source sentence and its back-translated counterpart. We term this score as the pseudo fuzzy match score (PFMS) (Equation 1; Pratapa et al. (2018a)). PFMS lies in [0,1] and we split the data into four classes based on PFMS value, $\{PFMS_1: (0, 0.3], PFMS_2: (0.3, 0.5], PFMS_3: (0.5, 0.7], PFMS_4: (0.7, 1.0]\}$. Since tweets themselves are noisy user-generated texts, their quality will have an impact on the generated code-mixed texts.

$$\text{PFMS} = \frac{\textit{EditDistance}(s, s')}{max(|s|, |s'|)} \quad (1)$$

Alignment complexity score (ACS): Another factor that impacts the perceived quality of generated code-mixed text is the complexity of token-level alignments between the parallel sentences. To this end, we compute ACS, that captures two important aspects, 1. *order of alignments*: mean distance between aligned pair of tokens (ACS_1), and 2. *degree of alignment*: average degree of a token (ACS_2). We have grouped the input pair into the two buckets, $(max(0, \mu-\sigma), \mu]$ and $[\mu, \mu+\sigma)$, where μ and σ denote the mean and standard deviation of the ACS scores. This resulted in the intervals [0, 0.39], (0.39, 0.98] and (0.90, 1.06], (1.06, 1.21] for ACS_1 and ACS_2 respectively. In Equation 2, i and j denote the i-th and j-th tokens in the source (of length l) and target (of length l') sentences respectively. $A(i)$ denotes the set of target tokens aligned to the i-th source token. In Equation 3, d_i denotes the degree of i-th token in the sentence.

$$\text{ACS}_1 = \frac{\sum_{i=1}^{l} |i - \frac{\sum_{j\in A(i)} j}{|A(i)|} \cdot \frac{l}{l'}|}{2l} + \frac{\sum_{j=1}^{l'} |j - \frac{\sum_{i\in A^{-1}(j)} i}{|A^{-1}(j)|} \cdot \frac{l'}{l}|}{2l'} \quad (2)$$

$$\text{ACS}_2 = \frac{\sum_{l} d_i}{2l} + \frac{\sum_{l'} d_j}{2l'} \quad (3)$$

[2]We use tweets in our study for two reasons, 1. In textual format, code-mixing is most common in informal conversations (e.g., social media posts), and 2. it's easier to collect tweets over speech transcriptions.

[3]https://github.com/clab/fast_align

	Understandability
1	No, this tweet doesn't make sense
2	Not sure, but I can guess the meaning of this tweet
3	Certainly, I get the meaning of this tweet
	Naturalness
0	I am not sure
1	unnatural, and I can't imagine people using this style of Spanglish
2	weird, but who knows, it could be some style of Spanglish
3	quite natural, but I think this style of Spanglish is rare
4	natural, and I think this style of Spanglish is used in real life
5	perfectly natural, and I think this style of Spanglish is very frequently used

Table 1: Dimensions of evaluation.

For each pair of sampled parallel sentences, we select code-mixed sentences from ML, EC theories as well as their relaxed variants.

Matrix-Embedding Language (ML): We sample code-mixed sentences generated by the ML theory. Additionally, to evaluate the impact of the individual constraints of this theory, we relax by allowing mixing of closed-class items (CC, DT, IN, V) and potential nesting (allowance to switching back to matrix language in the same sub-tree).

Equivalence constraint (EC): Similar to ML theory, we sample code-mixed sentences generated by the EC theory. We also sample from a relaxed variant where we allow for lexical substitution ($EC_{[LS]}$).

Switch point variation (SP): Prior work has highlighted the importance of controlling for # switch points (SP) in the automatically generated sentences.[4] To this end, we sample EC-theory-based code-mixed sentences with a varying number of switch points. We have grouped SPs into the buckets, {SP_1: {1}, SP_2: {2}, SP_3: {3,4}, SP_4: {5,6}, SP_5: {7... 20}}.

3.2 Human Evaluation

We ask human judges to score each code-mixed sentence on their understandability and naturalness. We conducted this study on Amazon Mechanical Turk,[5] and the goal of the study is to understand the human perception of various linguistic theories of code-mixing. Both ML and EC theories establish grammatical rules for code-mixing; therefore, this study helps determine if these rules are necessary for a code-mixed sentence to be considered intelligible and realistic.

Task Setup: Every Human Intelligence Task (HIT) consists of 10 sentences, of which 8 are synthetic Spanglish sentences while 2 are *validation* sentences. Turkers rate the sentences on their understandability and naturalness. Table 1 summarizes the rubrics for understandability (scale of 1-3) and naturalness (scale of 0-5). To ensure that the judges comprehend and score the sentences appropriately, we incorporated two control sentences, a real Spanglish tweet, and a non-Spanglish tweet. The non-Spanglish tweets are code-mixed sentences taken from other language pairs, French-English, Dutch-English, and German-English. If a sentence is incomprehensible to a Spanish-English bilingual speaker, we ask the human judge to mark it with low understandability. As a sanity check, for the first 20 HITs, we ask the judges to provide English translations to the given code-mixed sentences. The expected time to complete a HIT is less than 120 seconds based on our pilot study,[6] and we paid \$0.25 per assignment per HIT. We collected three valid assignments per HIT.

Qualification requirements: To ensure that the judges are Spanish-English bilingual speakers, we designed a custom qualification test. Our test evaluates their proficiency in English, Spanish and their ability to comprehend Spanglish text. The qualification test consisted of two tasks, 1. word-level language identification and 2. naturalness assessment.

[4] A switch-point denotes a word boundary in a given sentence where the languages of the words on two sides differ.

[5] https://www.mturk.com/

[6] We observed similar response times in the actual HITs

In the language identification task, we ask the participants to identify the language of a highlighted word in the context. In most cases, this word is part of both the English and Spanish vocabulary; so, the participant had to disambiguate it using the contextual information. We also include a couple of sentences where the highlighted word is neither English nor Spanish. In the naturalness task, we ask the participants to gauge the naturalness of 5 code-mixed sentences. For this task, we collaborated with Spanish-English bilingual experts to curate a mix of perfectly natural and unnatural Spanglish sentences. In addition to passing the qualification test, we also added the standard requirements on HIT acceptance rate (≥97) and # HITs (≥200).[7]

4 MTurk Results & Discussion

We published a total of 429 HITs and obtained judgments from 59 unique crowd workers. In our analysis, we only consider the responses where the understandability score is strictly greater than one.[8] Before analyzing the human judgments, we ensure that the human judge has marked the appropriate responses for the control data involving real-Spanglish and non-Spanglish sentences. The non-Spanglish sentences are to be scored low on the understandability scale. Naturalness being a subjective marker, there is no definite answer; therefore, we haven't pruned any of the HITs based on the judgments on real-Spanglish sentences.

Our main aim in this experiment was to gauge the importance of various sentence-level features in the code-mixed sentence generation process. To this end, we have compared the absolute human judgment scores across sentence pairs. We have designed our task as an absolute judgment task instead of pair-wise comparison for logistical reasons, as it allows for a large scale evaluation. We construct a matrix (M) with sentence/tweet pairs (T_i, T_j) along the rows and annotators (A_k) along the columns (Equation 4). $A_{i,k}$ denotes the score of annotator A_k for the sentence T_i.

$$M_{(i,j),k} = sgn(A_{i,k} - A_{j,k}) \quad (4)$$

We construct a *partial order* between T_i and T_j using the matrix M as follows,

$$\begin{aligned} &\text{if } \forall k,\ M_{(i,j),k} = 0, && T_i \simeq T_j \\ &\text{else if } \forall k,\ M_{(i,j),k} > 0, && T_i \succ T_j \\ &\text{else if } \forall k,\ M_{(i,j),k} < 0, && T_i \prec T_j \\ &\text{else}, && T_i\ ?\ T_j \end{aligned} \quad (5)$$

Here, $T_i \succ T_j$ means that sentence T_i is preferred to sentence T_j by all the common annotators (or coder). In this setting, we only compare sentences that have at least one common coder. We also consider an alternative approach, where we directly compare every sentence pair based on their average judgment scores. Unlike previous ordering, this comparison will result in a *total order*. To normalize for coders' variance, we use z-values in place of absolute scores (Equation 6). This methodology allows for analysis over a much larger space of sentence pairs.

$$\begin{aligned} z_{i,k} &= \frac{x_{i,k} - \mu_k}{\sigma_k} \\ T_i > T_j, &\quad \text{if } \sum_k z_{i,k} > \sum_k z_{j,k} \end{aligned} \quad (6)$$

To measure the inter-coder agreement, we have used Krippendorff's α as it allows for missing data

M1	M2	#(?)	#(≻)	#(≃)	#(≺)
ML	$ML_{[CC]}$	1	16	11	14
ML	$ML_{[DT]}$	2	35	31	28
ML	$ML_{[IN]}$	5	40	30	39
ML	$ML_{[V]}$	11	75	41	48
ML	$ML_{[NST]}$	9	93	56	79
EC	$EC_{[LS]}$	8	48	26	51
ML	EC	27	217	164	207

Table 2: Comparison of linguistic theory based models using common coders (Equation 5).

M1	M2	#(>)	#(<)
ML	$ML_{[CC]}$	68	54
ML	$ML_{[DT]}$	162	133
ML	$ML_{[IN]}$	199	155
ML	$ML_{[V]}$	304	212
ML	$ML_{[NST]}$	331	303
EC	$EC_{[LS]}$	203	179
ML	EC	962	930

Table 3: Comparison of linguistic theory based models on all tweet pairs (Equation 6).

[7]see A.1 in Appendix for the questions used in the test.

[8]We acknowledge that understandability is a requirement for a code-mixed text generation model. But in the scope of this work, we focus primarily on the naturalness evaluation.

and multiple coders (Artstein and Poesio, 2008). With $d(x, y) = max(0, -sgn(x * y))$ as the distance metric, i.e., penalizing only if x and y are of different signs, we observed the α to be 0.59, indicating moderate to substantial agreement (Landis and Koch, 1977). We use the partial order in the sentences to learn a partial order for the feature variants. When comparing the impact of two feature variants, we kept the other feature values constant for consistency. Table 2 and Table 3 present a comparison of original theories (ML and EC) with their relaxed variants. The results show that the original ML theory is better than its relaxation(s). However, we observe no such preference in the EC theory. Notably, there is no clear winner between the original ML and EC theories.

Additionally, we analyze the impact of sentence length (SL), translation quality (PFMS), and # switch points (SP) on the naturalness. Our observations are summarized below,

- $SL_1 \succ SL_2 \succ SL_3 \succ SL_4$
- $PFMS_1 \prec PFMS_2 \prec PFMS_3 \prec PFMS_4$
- $SP_1 \succ SP_2 \succ SP_3 \succ SP_4$

Notably, human judges prefer fewer switch points in the code-mixed texts. This result is in line with observations from Pratapa et al. (2018a). They found the fraction of switch points in real code-mixed tweets to be ~0.1, indicating speakers typically use few switch points. As expected, speakers prefer sentences with higher PFMS scores (i.e., translation quality). Additionally, we find that speakers prefer shorter sentences, possibly because longer sentences tend to be noisier.

To better understand the overall impact of the linguistic-theory-based constraints, we also ran ~30 HITs consisting of synthetic data generated using heuristic-based models. For every feature (SL, ACS, PFMS), we sample one-sentence pair. We only considered PFMS $\in$ $PFMS_4$ for best comparison. Since SP value was a crucial factor in determining the quality of the synthetic code-mixed sentence, we sampled sentences (heuristic-based) from the same SP brackets as the previous HIT data (linguistic-theory based). Note that, in the MTurk analysis, we have only considered those sentences acceptable under heuristic models but are invalid according to all the linguistic theories (original and relaxed) for meaningful comparison. We compared across all tweet pairs (Equation 6) as the number of

M1	M2	#(>)	#(<)
ML	$H_{aligned}$	109	60
$ML_{[V]}$	$H_{aligned}$	60	47
EC	$H_{aligned}$	162	75
$EC_{[LS]}$	$H_{aligned}$	31	31
ML	H_{dict}	151	58
$ML_{[V]}$	H_{dict}	70	49
EC	H_{dict}	215	81
$EC_{[LS]}$	H_{dict}	43	22
ML	$H_{parallel}$	126	58
$ML_{[V]}$	$H_{parallel}$	65	43
EC	$H_{parallel}$	188	86
$EC_{[LS]}$	$H_{parallel}$	42	19

Table 4: Comparison of heuristic based models $H_{aligned}$, H_{dict} and $H_{parallel}$ (exclusive) with linguistic models in the MTurk experiment.

common coders is low. While comparing models $H_{aligned}$, H_{dict} and $H_{parallel}$ with the linguistic models, we controlled for SP and other monolingual sentence-level features.

In general, we found the original linguistic models to be much better than heuristic models (Table 4). While the original EC theory is much better than the heuristic model $H_{aligned}$, the relaxed version of $EC_{[LS]}$ is as good as the heuristic model. However, ML theory sentences, even after the relaxation of allowing for verb phrase switching, are better than $H_{aligned}$. We find all the linguistic theory-based models to be much better than heuristic models H_{dict} and $H_{parallel}$.

In Table 5, we compute the overlap in sentences generated by different models. As expected, both grammatical models allow fewer code-mixed sentences than heuristic models, with ML being the most constrained model. EC theory overlaps significantly with $H_{aligned}$ (54%). The two grammatical theories only overlap in 22% of the sentences.

5 Conclusion & Future Work

We present a large-scale qualitative comparison of different code-mixed generation systems. Through the judgments of Spanish-English bilingual speakers, we analyze the need for each constraint in the two grammatical theories, Matrix-Embedded, and Equivalence Constraint. We also contrast against simpler heuristic systems and found grammatical systems to be superior. However, we do not observe a clear winner between the two grammatical

M1	**M2**	$S_{M1} - S_{M2}$	$S_{M1} \cap S_{M2}$	$S_{M2} - S_{M1}$
ML	EC	0.07	0.22	0.71
ML	$ML \cup ML_{[CC]}$	0.00	0.88	0.12
ML	$ML \cup ML_{[DT]}$	0.00	0.84	0.16
ML	$ML \cup ML_{[IN]}$	0.00	0.75	0.25
ML	$ML \cup ML_{[V]}$	0.00	0.61	0.39
EC	$EC \cup EC_{[LS]}$	0.00	0.86	0.14
ML	$H_{aligned}$	0.02	0.16	0.82
EC	$H_{aligned}$	0.05	0.54	0.42
$ML \cap EC$	$H_{aligned}$	0.00	0.16	0.84
$ML \cup EC$	$H_{aligned}$	0.06	0.54	0.40
$ML \cup ML_{[V]}$	$H_{aligned}$	0.03	0.25	0.72
$EC \cup EC_{[LS]}$	$H_{aligned}$	0.06	0.57	0.38
ML	H_{dict}	0.09	0.03	0.88
EC	H_{dict}	0.25	0.06	0.69
$ML \cap EC$	H_{dict}	0.07	0.03	0.90
$ML \cup EC$	H_{dict}	0.26	0.06	0.68
$ML \cup ML_{[V]}$	H_{dict}	0.15	0.04	0.82
$EC \cup EC_{[LS]}$	H_{dict}	0.28	0.06	0.66
ML	$H_{parallel}$	0.06	0.06	0.87
EC	$H_{parallel}$	0.17	0.16	0.67
$ML \cap EC$	$H_{parallel}$	0.05	0.06	0.89
$ML \cup EC$	$H_{parallel}$	0.18	0.16	0.66
$ML \cup ML_{[V]}$	$H_{parallel}$	0.10	0.08	0.81
$EC \cup EC_{[LS]}$	$H_{parallel}$	0.20	0.16	0.64

Table 5: Comparison of sentence counts of original linguistic theories and their relaxed variants. S_{M1} and S_{M2} denote the set of sentences from models M1 and M2.

theories. Potential directions for future work include 1. extending the naturalness evaluation to sequence-to-sequence models of code-mixing, 2. expanding the analysis to other language pairs.

Acknowledgements

We thank the anonymous reviewers for their valuable feedback. We also thank the Mechanical Turk workers for their efforts in our evaluation.

References

Emily Ahn, Cecilia Jimenez, Yulia Tsvetkov, and Alan W Black. 2020. What code-switching strategies are effective in dialog systems? In *Proceedings of the Society for Computation in Linguistics 2020*, pages 254–264, New York, New York. Association for Computational Linguistics.

Ron Artstein and Massimo Poesio. 2008. Survey article: Inter-coder agreement for computational linguistics. *Computational Linguistics*, 34(4):555–596.

Anshul Bawa, Pranav Khadpe, Pratik Joshi, Kalika Bali, and Monojit Choudhury. 2020. Do multilingual users prefer chat-bots that code-mix? let's nudge and find out! *Proceedings of the ACM on Human-Computer Interaction*, 4(CSCW1):1–23.

Hedi M. Belazi, Edward J. Rubin, and Almeida Jacqueline Toribio. 1994. Code switching and x-bar theory: The functional head constraint. *Linguistic Inquiry*, 25(2):221–237.

Gayatri Bhat, Monojit Choudhury, and Kalika Bali. 2016. Grammatical constraints on intra-sentential code-switching: From theories to working models. *arXiv preprint arXiv:1612.04538*.

Chris Dyer, Victor Chahuneau, and Noah A. Smith. 2013. A simple, fast, and effective reparameterization of IBM model 2. In *Proceedings of the 2013 Conference of the North American Chapter of the Association for Computational Linguistics: Human Language Technologies*, pages 644–648, Atlanta, Georgia. Association for Computational Linguistics.

Abhirut Gupta, Aditya Vavre, and Sunita Sarawagi. 2021. Training data augmentation for code-mixed translation. In *Proceedings of the 2021 Conference of the North American Chapter of the Association for Computational Linguistics: Human Language Technologies*, pages 5760–5766, Online. Association for Computational Linguistics.

Dan Klein and Christopher D. Manning. 2003. Accurate unlexicalized parsing. In *Proceedings of the 41st Annual Meeting of the Association for Computational Linguistics*, pages 423–430, Sapporo, Japan. Association for Computational Linguistics.

J Richard Landis and Gary G Koch. 1977. The measurement of observer agreement for categorical data. *biometrics*, pages 159–174.

Grandee Lee, Thi-Nga Ho, Eng-Siong Chng, and Haizhou Li. 2017. A review of the mandarin-english code-switching corpus: Seame. In *2017 International Conference on Asian Language Processing (IALP)*, pages 210–213.

Grandee Lee and Haizhou Li. 2020. Modeling code-switch languages using bilingual parallel corpus. In *Proceedings of the 58th Annual Meeting of the Association for Computational Linguistics*, pages 860–870, Online. Association for Computational Linguistics.

Grandee Lee, Xianghu Yue, and Haizhou Li. 2019. Linguistically Motivated Parallel Data Augmentation for Code-Switch Language Modeling. In *Proc. Interspeech 2019*, pages 3730–3734.

Ying Li and Pascale Fung. 2012. Code-switch language model with inversion constraints for mixed language speech recognition. In *Proceedings of COLING 2012*, pages 1671–1680, Mumbai, India. The COLING 2012 Organizing Committee.

Carol Myers-Scotton. 1993. *Duelling Languages:Grammatical structure in Code-switching*. Clarendon Press, Oxford.

Parth Patwa, Gustavo Aguilar, Sudipta Kar, Suraj Pandey, Srinivas PYKL, Björn Gambäck, Tanmoy Chakraborty, Thamar Solorio, and Amitava Das. 2020. SemEval-2020 task 9: Overview of sentiment analysis of code-mixed tweets. In *Proceedings of the Fourteenth Workshop on Semantic Evaluation*, pages 774–790, Barcelona (online). International Committee for Computational Linguistics.

Shana Poplack. 1980. Sometimes I'll start a sentence in Spanish y termino en español. *Linguistics*, 18:581–618.

Adithya Pratapa, Gayatri Bhat, Monojit Choudhury, Sunayana Sitaram, Sandipan Dandapat, and Kalika Bali. 2018a. Language modeling for code-mixing: The role of linguistic theory based synthetic data. In *Proceedings of the 56th Annual Meeting of the Association for Computational Linguistics (Volume 1: Long Papers)*, pages 1543–1553, Melbourne, Australia. Association for Computational Linguistics.

Adithya Pratapa, Monojit Choudhury, and Sunayana Sitaram. 2018b. Word embeddings for code-mixed language processing. In *Proceedings of the 2018 Conference on Empirical Methods in Natural Language Processing*, pages 3067–3072, Brussels, Belgium. Association for Computational Linguistics.

Shruti Rijhwani, Royal Sequiera, Monojit Choudhury, Kalika Bali, and Chandra Shekhar Maddila. 2017. Estimating code-switching on Twitter with a novel generalized word-level language detection technique. In *Proceedings of the 55th Annual Meeting of the Association for Computational Linguistics (Volume 1: Long Papers)*, pages 1971–1982, Vancouver, Canada. Association for Computational Linguistics.

Mohd Sanad Zaki Rizvi, Anirudh Srinivasan, Tanuja Ganu, Monojit Choudhury, and Sunayana Sitaram. 2021. GCM: A toolkit for generating synthetic code-mixed text. In *Proceedings of the 16th Conference of the European Chapter of the Association for Computational Linguistics: System Demonstrations*, pages 205–211, Online. Association for Computational Linguistics.

Kushagra Singh, Indira Sen, and Ponnurangam Kumaraguru. 2018. A Twitter corpus for Hindi-English code mixed POS tagging. In *Proceedings of the Sixth International Workshop on Natural Language Processing for Social Media*, pages 12–17, Melbourne, Australia. Association for Computational Linguistics.

Thamar Solorio, Shuguang Chen, Alan W. Black, Mona Diab, Sunayana Sitaram, Victor Soto, Emre Yilmaz, and Anirudh Srinivasan, editors. 2021. *Proceedings of the Fifth Workshop on Computational Approaches to Linguistic Code-Switching*. Association for Computational Linguistics, Online.

Victor Soto and Julia Hirschberg. 2017. Crowdsourcing universal part-of-speech tags for code-switching. In *Proc. Interspeech 2017*, pages 77–81.

Ishan Tarunesh, Syamantak Kumar, and Preethi Jyothi. 2021. From machine translation to code-switching: Generating high-quality code-switched text. In *Proceedings of the 59th Annual Meeting of the Association for Computational Linguistics and the 11th International Joint Conference on Natural Language Processing (Volume 1: Long Papers)*, pages 3154–3169, Online. Association for Computational Linguistics.

Genta Indra Winata, Andrea Madotto, Chien-Sheng Wu, and Pascale Fung. 2019. Code-switched language models using neural based synthetic data from parallel sentences. In *Proceedings of the 23rd Conference on Computational Natural Language Learning (CoNLL)*, pages 271–280, Hong Kong, China. Association for Computational Linguistics.

A Appendix

A.1 Qualification Test

Table 6 presents the questions used in the MTurk qualification test.

Word-level language identification
buenas noches **a** toda my people
bonne soirée everyone
la declaration no es correcto
não canso de escutar see you again
federer **champion** por octava time en halle
the best place in the world no **hay** otro
todo lo que quiero **son** texts como este
espero que esto **no** sea verdad
ella siempre toma mis emotions **tan** seriamente
this is das **perfekt** moment
Naturalness evaluation
charlie sheen write defiant abierta letter to those que tried chantajearlo (*unnatural*)
hoy i have one de those days que hate al world entero (*unnatural*)
literalmente all i do is soñar sobre scenarios imposibles (*natural*)
merece perder el campeonato because of his attitude (*natural*)
tú made good música and probably tocaste the vidas of muchos children (*unnatural*)

Table 6: Qualification test used on Mechanical Turk. In the word-level language identification task, we ask the crowd workers to identify the language of the highlighted token. In the naturalness evaluation, we ask the workers to mark the naturalness of the code-mixed sentences.

Improving Punctuation Restoration for Speech Transcripts via External Data

Xue-Yong Fu, Cheng Chen, Md Tahmid Rahman Laskar,
Shashi Bhushan TN, Simon Corston-Oliver
Dialpad Canada Inc.
Vancouver, BC, Canada
{xue-yong,cchen,tahmid.rahman}@dialpad.com
{sbhushan,scorston-oliver}@dialpad.com

Abstract

Automatic Speech Recognition (ASR) systems generally do not produce punctuated transcripts. To make transcripts more readable and follow the expected input format for downstream language models, it is necessary to add punctuation marks. In this paper, we tackle the punctuation restoration problem specifically for the noisy text (e.g., phone conversation scenarios). To leverage the available written text datasets, we introduce a data sampling technique based on an n-gram language model to sample more training data that are similar to our in-domain data. Moreover, we propose a two-stage fine-tuning approach that utilizes the sampled external data as well as our in-domain dataset for models based on BERT. Extensive experiments show that the proposed approach outperforms the baseline with an improvement of 1.12% F1 score.

1 Introduction

ASR systems are widely deployed in many products to support a variety of business applications, such as customer support, virtual assistants, and conversational systems. The context for this research is to build commercial products that perform realtime transcription of English business telephone calls, with additional natural language processing to enable features such as assistance for customer support agents and note-taking during business meetings. Though ASR systems trained on large amounts of data can transcribe human speech with high accuracy (Kannan et al., 2019; Baevski et al., 2020), spoken dialogue transcripts produced by such systems often exclude punctuation marks. Therefore, the user reading a long unpunctuated transcript may find it unreadable (Zelasko et al., 2018; Alam et al., 2020).

Beyond the need for readability, downstream natural language understanding (NLU) models use transcripts to provide more business insights. Many NLU models (e.g., sentiment analysis and named entity recognition (NER)) achieving state-of-the-art performance are based on large-scale language models (e.g. BERT (Devlin et al., 2019)), which are often pre-trained on well-punctuated texts such as English Wikipedia and BookCorpus (Zhu et al., 2015). However, NLU models trained on such datasets may not perform well on unpunctuated transcripts. Thus, for the conversational domain, punctuated speech transcripts are also necessary.

While most prior research has focused on automatically punctuating monologue speech transcripts, our work is focused on transcripts of real-world phone conversations with turn-taking between two or more people. Spontaneous turn-taking conversations typically are more noisy than monologues because they might contain speech overlaps, false starts, repetitions, and higher transcription word error rates. One way to address this problem is to obtain large amounts of human-punctuated transcripts as training data. However, human annotation is expensive and time-consuming. In this paper, we propose a novel way to leverage freely available external data to improve the punctuation restoration accuracy in human-to-human business conversational data. The main contributions of this paper are as follows:

- We introduce a new data sampling technique based on an n-gram language model to select additional training data relevant to our target domain from publicly available datasets. Then we propose a two-stage fine-tuning approach based on BERT to train our model.

- Extensive experiments show that the proposed method is effective to improve performance on unpunctuated noisy data collected from an ASR system. Since our goal is to develop a punctuation restoration model for real-time scenarios in production, we also analyze the performance of different layers in BERT and observe that layer reduction significantly im-

Proceedings of the 2021 EMNLP Workshop W-NUT: The Seventh Workshop on Noisy User-generated Text, pages 168–174
November 11, 2021. ©2021 Association for Computational Linguistics

proves the inference speed while maintaining the accuracy. As a secondary contribution, we demonstrate the production environment that we use to deploy the trained model.

2 Related Work

In this section, we first review the recent work on punctuation restoration. Since we sample additional training data from external corpora, we also review related work on data sampling.

2.1 Punctuation Restoration

Most of the punctuation restoration models formulate the problem as a sequence labeling task (Hentschel et al., 2021; Yi et al., 2020; Chen et al., 2021b; Huang et al., 2021; Nagy et al., 2021). The model architectures vary from the RNNs to the pre-trained contextualized language models. In recent years, Tilk and Alumäe (2015), Salimbajevs (2016), and Xu et al. (2016) used long short-term memory units to restore punctuation in speech transcripts, while Courtland et al. (2020) and Cai and Wang (2019) used a bidirectional transformer (Vaswani et al., 2017) to predict punctuation marks.

2.2 External Training Data Sampling

For training data sampling, Chiu et al. (2016) and Karimi et al. (2017) used the data that were similar to the biology domain. To measure similarity between two datasets, Dai et al. (2019) studied different techniques, such as: vocabulary overlaps, language model perplexity, and word vector variance. They also investigated how similarity measures can be used to sample in-domain pre-training data. Moreover, for NER, they observed that the second phase of in-domain pre-training led to performance gains under both high and low-resource settings. Recently, Han and Eisenstein (2019) proposed domain-adaptive fine-tuning in which contextualized embeddings were adapted by masked language modeling on texts from the target domain.

3 Method

We frame punctuation restoration as a sequence labeling problem. There are four classes that the model needs to predict, including **PERIOD**[1], **COMMA**, **QUESTIONMARK**, and **NONE**. More specifically, the model predicts what the punctuation mark next to a given token is. If there is no punctuation mark after the input token, the prediction should be **NONE**.

In Figure 1, we show the overall architecture of our proposed model that utilizes a two stage fine-tuning approach: First, (i) we do data sampling from an external dataset (e.g., movie subtitles) using our proposed n-gram similarity approach and fine-tune a pre-trained BERT model. Then, (ii) we annotate unpunctuated phone conversation transcripts generated from an ASR system to construct an in-domain training set (noisy data) to apply the second stage of fine-tuning using the BERT model fine-tuned in the previous stage. Below, we describe the data sampling, data annotation, and two-stage fine-tuning approach in detail.

3.1 Data Sampling from the External Dataset via N-gram Language Model

In principle, we can obtain a tremendous amount of punctuated text from the internet (e.g English Wikipedia). However, written English is fundamentally different from spoken English and training a model on a corpus that is distant from the target domain might end up harming model performance. Thus, we choose to use a movie subtitle corpus, OpenSubtitles (Lison and Tiedemann, 2016), as our first stage fine-tuning data because there are many human-to-human conversations in movies.

As movie conversations are not necessarily business conversations, training a model on out-of-domain data might also degrade model accuracy. Thus, we propose a data sampling method based on language model perplexity to select data similar to our target domain (noisy phone conversations). Some examples from the out-of-domain (movie subtitles) data and the in-domain (noisy phone conversations) data are shown in Table 1.

For data sampling, we follow (Dai et al., 2019) and assign a probability to any sequence of words $< w_1, \cdots, w_N >$ using the n-gram language model (Jurafsky and Martin, 2020). The probability of a sequence can be obtained by chain rule of probability.

$$p(w_1, w_2, \cdots, w_N) = \prod_{i=1}^{N} p(w_i|w_1^{i-1}) \quad (1)$$

Here, N is the length of the sequence and w_1^{i-1} are all words before word w_i. In our work, we use a 4-gram language model.

To sample data that are similar to our in-domain data, we first train a language model on our tar-

[1]Although there are few exclamation marks in the data, we convert them to periods for simplicity.

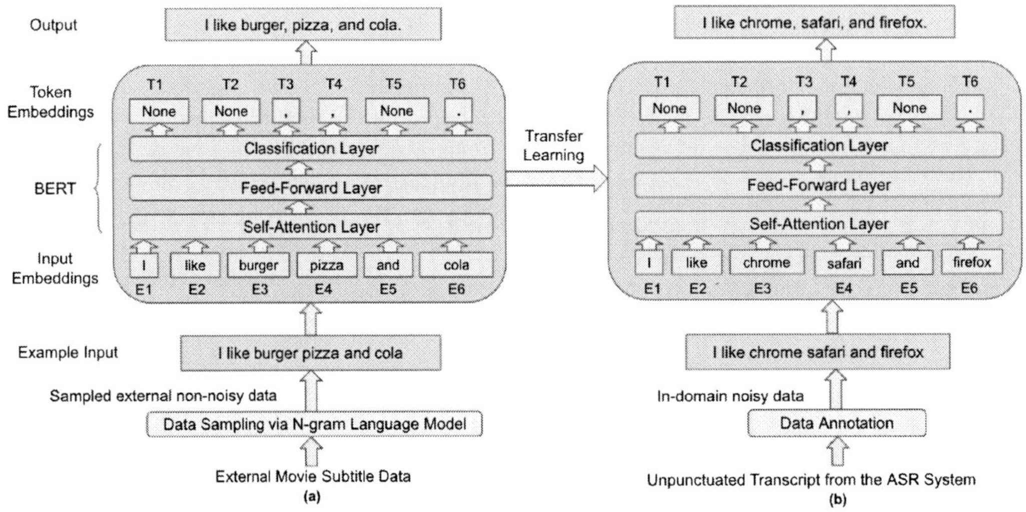

Figure 1: Our two stage fine-tuning approach: (a) at first on the external dataset (e.g., movie subtitles), we sample the external data using n-gram similarity and fine-tune the pre-trained BERT model. (b) Next we annotate unpunctuated transcripts generated from an ASR system to construct the in-domain training set (noisy data) and apply the second stage of fine-tuning using the BERT model fine-tuned in the previous stage.

get domain, which is business phone conversations. Then we evaluate the utterances (subtitles) in the movie subtitle corpus based on the perplexity generated by the model for a given utterance (subtitle) to represent the degree of similarity. The main difference between (Dai et al., 2019) and our work is that we measure the similarity at the utterance level instead of the corpus level. When an utterance is unlikely to occur in the data where the language model is trained on, it will assign a low probability and high perplexity. More specifically, we feed an utterance from the movie subtitle corpus to the 4-gram language model and then the model estimates its perplexity. Afterwards, we rank the subtitles by perplexity and select the top 4.8M subtitles as analogous to in-domain data. Some examples from the external and the in-domain data are shown in Table 1.

Out-of-domain (External Movie Subtitle Dataset)
Our dog disappeared.
Sometimes those serious ones fool you.
He looks so utterly vulnerable.
God destroyed whole cities to punish man's wickedness.
I mean, who comes hereafter dark besides murderers?
Your paintings were impressive joker.
In-domain (Noisy Phone Conversations)
Well, thank you for coming down.
What did you find out so far?
I guess you could give me her number.
Um, just hold on a second.
Might I have your email?
Eh, I really don't know what to do about it!

Table 1: Examples from the out-of-domain and the in-domain datasets.

Data type	**Comma**	**Period**	**Question**
Training	1166386	860403	118203
Dev	15899	14143	1722
Test	6503	3880	629

Table 2: In-domain dataset (noisy data) distribution.

3.2 Data Annotation for the ASR Data

We sample 320,000 utterances produced by the ASR model from business phone calls across a time period of a year (see Table 2 for details). We also make sure utterances are distributed homogeneously among different scenarios. More importantly, we follow our standard data privacy protocol while working on data annotation. Since human-to-human conversations are incredibly noisy that could degrade the performance of a pre-trained language model that is trained on written texts, we remove repetitions, false starts, and filler words from transcripts to address this problem. Note that inserting punctuation marks to unpunctuated texts might take a long time for an annotator. To speed up this process, we use a punctuation restoration model based on BERT (Devlin et al., 2019) that is trained on a much smaller dataset to produce default punctuation marks for utterances and let the annotators edit these punctuation marks. In total,

Model	First fine-tuning	Second fine-tuning	Precision	Recall	F1 score
Indom	In-domain data	×	75.01	63.71	68.48
Samex	Sampled external data	×	67.70	57.49	61.68
Two-stage	Sampled external data	In-domain data	75.94	65.18	69.60

Table 3: Performance based on different fine-tuning techniques with 6-layer BERT.

102 annotators contributed to the annotation job.

3.3 Two-Stage Fine-tuning Approach

Fine-tuning a pre-trained language model at first in a dataset similar to the target domain, and then fine-tuning it again in the target dataset is found effective in different tasks, such as answer selection (Garg et al., 2020), and query focused text summarization (Laskar et al., 2020a,b). In this paper, we also utilize a two-stage fine-tuning approach that transfers a pre-trained language model to the punctuation restoration task in the first-stage; and then adapts the obtained model to the specific target domain in the second-stage. For that purpose, we use the BERT model (Devlin et al., 2019) that is a Transformer-based (Vaswani et al., 2017) contextual language model as our backbone model. To utilize BERT for sequence labeling, a classification layer is added on top of the last layer (see Figure 1). In addition, as our goal is to deploy a punctuation restoration model in real-time and at scale, we use the weights of the first (bottom) six layers of the BERT base (Devlin et al., 2019) model (12 transformer layers), to initialize a 6-layer BERT model for fine-tuning.

Type	Precision	Recall	F1
Period	72.57	77.89	75.14
Question	84.63	63.91	72.83
Comma	77.23	57.79	66.11
Overall	75.94	65.18	69.60

Table 4: Performance by the Two-stage model on different punctuation marks.

4 Experiments

In our experiments, we investigate the following: *(i) Will the model perform better if we use external datasets? (ii) Will the model performance degrade if we reduce the number of layers?* Below, we first describe our experimental settings. Then we analyze the model performance when external data are used, followed by discussing the performance when layer reduction is applied.

4.1 Experimental Settings

To fine-tune 6 layer BERT models, we used the following hyperparameters: gradient accumulation steps = 1, warmup proportion = 0.1, learning rate = $5e-5$, train batch size = 50, and the max sequence length = 300. All training experiments were run in an Google Cloud Platform (GCP) instance using 1 NVIDIA P100 GPU. To investigate the inference speed for real-time scenarios, we ran our experiments with 1 CPU, Intel(R) Xeon(R) CPU@2.20GHz.

4.2 Performance while using External Data

We fine-tune models on various data settings and evaluate them on the test set. In the first data setting, we fine-tune the BERT model only on the in-domain data. We denote this model as Indom. In the second setting, the BERT model, fine-tuned only on the sampled external data is denoted as Samex. The last setting is our proposed Two-stage approach that first fine-tunes BERT on the sampled external data and then fine-tunes again on the in-domain data. The results are shown in Table 3.

The model (Samex) that was trained only on sampled external data unsurprisingly shows the F1 score as 61.68, which is 7.92% lower than the model (Two-stage) that was also fine-tuned on the in-domain data. This indicates that in-domain fine-tuning is crucial to boost model performance in a target domain. We also find that the model (two-stage) fine-tuned on both the in-domain and the sampled external data outperforms the model (Indom) fine-tuned only on the in-domain data by 1.12% F1 score. This demonstrates the effectiveness of two-stage fine-tuning using external data.

Table 4 shows how our best performing model (two-stage) performs in three different punctuation marks with the 6-layer BERT model. It is worth noting that the recall of commas is much lower than other punctuation types. One explanation is that although we tried our best to remove repetitions, false starts, and filler words, there are still a noticeable amount of them in the transcripts. Thus, it often makes it very challenging to place commas.

Model	P	R	F	Inf. time
3-layer	73.49	62.93	67.25	13.83
6-layer	75.01	63.71	68.48	26.52
12-layer	74.27	64.09	68.36	50.01

Table 5: Performance based on different number of BERT layers. Here, Precision, Recall, and F1 are denoted by P, R, and F respectively; while the Inference Time (Inf. time) is based on milliseconds per example.

4.3 Performance based on Layer Reduction

To know the effect of layer reduction in BERT, we fine-tune three BERT models with different numbers of layers (3, 6, 12) on the in-domain data only. This setting is similar to the Indom model except changing the number of layers. The results are shown in Table 5. It is worth noting that there is no significant difference in model performance between the smaller models (3-layer and 6-layer) and the 12-layer model. The 6-layer model even outperforms the 12-layer model in terms of Precision and F1 scores. More importantly, the inference time is significantly decreased by 47.96% and 72.35% from the 12-layer model to the 6-layer and the 3-layer models respectively.

4.4 Production Deployment

For production inference, we also remove the filler words and repetitions similar to the training phase to ensure that the input distributions are similar. For production deployment, we use an Intel(R) Xeon(R) CPU@2.20GHz and feed one utterance to the model at once (i.e., batch size = 1). The model runs in real-time in our production environment. The average inference speed is 201 milliseconds per utterance.

5 Conclusion

In this paper, we propose a new approach to sample training data that are similar to the target domain from freely available general corpora via an n-gram language model. We conduct extensive experiments using BERT with different data settings for the punctuation restoration task and find that our two-stage fine-tuning approach is effective to improve model performance. We also show the effectiveness of our model for real-time inference as we find that removing the first 6 layers of the 12 layer BERT does not harm the accuracy but substantially improves the speed. In the future, we will investigate how other external datasets (Chen et al., 2021a) impact the model performance.

Acknowledgements

We thank Harsh Saini for help with model deployment, Shayna Gardiner for giving ideas about the writing, and Feriba Saboor for help with data annotation.

References

Tanvirul Alam, Akib Khan, and Firoj Alam. 2020. Punctuation restoration using transformer models for high-and low-resource languages. In *Proceedings of the Sixth Workshop on Noisy User-generated Text, W-NUT@EMNLP 2020 Online, November 19, 2020*, pages 132–142. Association for Computational Linguistics.

Alexei Baevski, Yuhao Zhou, Abdelrahman Mohamed, and Michael Auli. 2020. wav2vec 2.0: A framework for self-supervised learning of speech representations. In *Advances in Neural Information Processing Systems 33: Annual Conference on Neural Information Processing Systems 2020, NeurIPS 2020, December 6-12, 2020, virtual*.

Yunqi Cai and Dong Wang. 2019. Question mark prediction by bert. In *2019 Asia-Pacific Signal and Information Processing Association Annual Summit and Conference (APSIPA ASC)*, pages 363–367. IEEE.

Mingda Chen, Zewei Chu, Sam Wiseman, and Kevin Gimpel. 2021a. Summscreen: A dataset for abstractive screenplay summarization. *arXiv preprint arXiv:2104.07091*.

Qian Chen, Wen Wang, Mengzhe Chen, and Qinglin Zhang. 2021b. Discriminative self-training for punctuation prediction. *arXiv preprint arXiv:2104.10339*.

Billy Chiu, Gamal K. O. Crichton, Anna Korhonen, and Sampo Pyysalo. 2016. How to train good word embeddings for biomedical NLP. In *Proceedings of the 15th Workshop on Biomedical Natural Language Processing, BioNLP@ACL 2016, Berlin, Germany, August 12, 2016*, pages 166–174. Association for Computational Linguistics.

Maury Courtland, Adam Faulkner, and Gayle McElvain. 2020. Efficient automatic punctuation restoration using bidirectional transformers with robust inference. In *Proceedings of the 17th International Conference on Spoken Language Translation, IWSLT 2020, Online, July 9 - 10, 2020*, pages 272–279. Association for Computational Linguistics.

Xiang Dai, Sarvnaz Karimi, Ben Hachey, and Cécile Paris. 2019. Using similarity measures to select pretraining data for NER. In *Proceedings of the 2019 Conference of the North American Chapter of the*

Association for Computational Linguistics: Human Language Technologies, NAACL-HLT 2019, Minneapolis, MN, USA, June 2-7, 2019, Volume 1 (Long and Short Papers), pages 1460–1470. Association for Computational Linguistics.

Jacob Devlin, Ming-Wei Chang, Kenton Lee, and Kristina Toutanova. 2019. BERT: pre-training of deep bidirectional transformers for language understanding. In *Proceedings of the 2019 Conference of the North American Chapter of the Association for Computational Linguistics: Human Language Technologies, NAACL-HLT 2019, Minneapolis, MN, USA, June 2-7, 2019, Volume 1 (Long and Short Papers)*, pages 4171–4186. Association for Computational Linguistics.

Siddhant Garg, Thuy Vu, and Alessandro Moschitti. 2020. TANDA: transfer and adapt pre-trained transformer models for answer sentence selection. In *The Thirty-Fourth AAAI Conference on Artificial Intelligence, AAAI 2020, The Thirty-Second Innovative Applications of Artificial Intelligence Conference, IAAI 2020, The Tenth AAAI Symposium on Educational Advances in Artificial Intelligence, EAAI 2020, New York, NY, USA, February 7-12, 2020*, pages 7780–7788. AAAI Press.

Xiaochuang Han and Jacob Eisenstein. 2019. Unsupervised domain adaptation of contextualized embeddings for sequence labeling. In *Proceedings of the 2019 Conference on Empirical Methods in Natural Language Processing and the 9th International Joint Conference on Natural Language Processing, EMNLP-IJCNLP 2019, Hong Kong, China, November 3-7, 2019*, pages 4237–4247. Association for Computational Linguistics.

Michael Hentschel, Emiru Tsunoo, and Takao Okuda. 2021. Making punctuation restoration robust and fast with multi-task learning and knowledge distillation. In *ICASSP 2021-2021 IEEE International Conference on Acoustics, Speech and Signal Processing (ICASSP)*, pages 7773–7777. IEEE.

Qiushi Huang, Tom Ko, H Lilian Tang, Xubo Liu, and Bo Wu. 2021. Token-level supervised contrastive learning for punctuation restoration. *arXiv preprint arXiv:2107.09099*.

Daniel Jurafsky and James H Martin. 2020. Speech and language processing: An introduction to natural language processing, computational linguistics, and speech recognition.

Anjuli Kannan, Arindrima Datta, Tara N. Sainath, Eugene Weinstein, Bhuvana Ramabhadran, Yonghui Wu, Ankur Bapna, Zhifeng Chen, and Seungji Lee. 2019. Large-scale multilingual speech recognition with a streaming end-to-end model. In *Interspeech 2019, 20th Annual Conference of the International Speech Communication Association, Graz, Austria, 15-19 September 2019*, pages 2130–2134. ISCA.

Sarvnaz Karimi, Xiang Dai, Hamed Hassanzadeh, and Anthony N. Nguyen. 2017. Automatic diagnosis coding of radiology reports: A comparison of deep learning and conventional classification methods. In *BioNLP 2017, Vancouver, Canada, August 4, 2017*, pages 328–332. Association for Computational Linguistics.

Md. Tahmid Rahman Laskar, Enamul Hoque, and Jimmy Huang. 2020a. Query focused abstractive summarization via incorporating query relevance and transfer learning with transformer models. In *Advances in Artificial Intelligence - 33rd Canadian Conference on Artificial Intelligence, Canadian AI 2020, Ottawa, ON, Canada, May 13-15, 2020, Proceedings*, volume 12109 of *Lecture Notes in Computer Science*, pages 342–348. Springer.

Md. Tahmid Rahman Laskar, Enamul Hoque, and Jimmy Xiangji Huang. 2020b. WSL-DS: weakly supervised learning with distant supervision for query focused multi-document abstractive summarization. In *Proceedings of the 28th International Conference on Computational Linguistics, COLING 2020, Barcelona, Spain (Online), December 8-13, 2020*, pages 5647–5654. International Committee on Computational Linguistics.

Pierre Lison and Jörg Tiedemann. 2016. Opensubtitles2016: Extracting large parallel corpora from movie and TV subtitles. In *Proceedings of the Tenth International Conference on Language Resources and Evaluation LREC 2016, Portorož, Slovenia, May 23-28, 2016*. European Language Resources Association (ELRA).

Attila Nagy, Bence Bial, and Judit Ács. 2021. Automatic punctuation restoration with bert models. *arXiv preprint arXiv:2101.07343*.

Askars Salimbajevs. 2016. Bidirectional LSTM for automatic punctuation restoration. In *Human Language Technologies - The Baltic Perspective - Proceedings of the Seventh International Conference Baltic HLT 2016, Riga, Latvia, October 6-7, 2016*, volume 289 of *Frontiers in Artificial Intelligence and Applications*, pages 59–65. IOS Press.

Ottokar Tilk and Tanel Alumäe. 2015. LSTM for punctuation restoration in speech transcripts. In *INTERSPEECH 2015, 16th Annual Conference of the International Speech Communication Association, Dresden, Germany, September 6-10, 2015*, pages 683–687. ISCA.

Ashish Vaswani, Noam Shazeer, Niki Parmar, Jakob Uszkoreit, Llion Jones, Aidan N. Gomez, Lukasz Kaiser, and Illia Polosukhin. 2017. Attention is all you need. In *Advances in Neural Information Processing Systems 30: Annual Conference on Neural Information Processing Systems 2017, December 4-9, 2017, Long Beach, CA, USA*, pages 5998–6008.

Kaituo Xu, Lei Xie, and Kaisheng Yao. 2016. Investigating LSTM for punctuation prediction. In *10th International Symposium on Chinese Spoken Language Processing, ISCSLP 2016, Tianjin, China, October 17-20, 2016*, pages 1–5. IEEE.

Jiangyan Yi, Jianhua Tao, Ye Bai, Zhengkun Tian, and Cunhang Fan. 2020. Adversarial transfer learning for punctuation restoration. *arXiv preprint arXiv:2004.00248*.

Piotr Zelasko, Piotr Szymanski, Jan Mizgajski, Adrian Szymczak, Yishay Carmiel, and Najim Dehak. 2018. Punctuation prediction model for conversational speech. In *Interspeech 2018, 19th Annual Conference of the International Speech Communication Association, Hyderabad, India, 2-6 September 2018*, pages 2633–2637. ISCA.

Yukun Zhu, Ryan Kiros, Richard S. Zemel, Ruslan Salakhutdinov, Raquel Urtasun, Antonio Torralba, and Sanja Fidler. 2015. Aligning books and movies: Towards story-like visual explanations by watching movies and reading books. In *2015 IEEE International Conference on Computer Vision, ICCV 2015, Santiago, Chile, December 7-13, 2015*, pages 19–27. IEEE Computer Society.

Learning to Rank Question Answer Pairs with Bilateral Contrastive Data Augmentation*

Yang Deng, Wenxuan Zhang, Wai Lam
The Chinese University of Hong Kong
{ydeng,wxzhang,wlam}@se.cuhk.edu.hk

Abstract

In this work, we propose a novel and easy-to-apply data augmentation strategy, namely **Bi**lateral **G**eneration (**BiG**), with a contrastive training objective for improving the performance of ranking question answer pairs with existing labeled data. In specific, we synthesize pseudo-positive QA pairs in contrast to the original negative QA pairs with two pretrained generation models, one for question generation, the other for answer generation, which are fine-tuned on the limited positive QA pairs from the original dataset. With the augmented dataset, we design a contrastive training objective for learning to rank question answer pairs. Experimental results on three benchmark datasets show that our method significantly improves the performance of ranking models by making full use of existing labeled data and can be easily applied to different ranking models.

1 Introduction

Ranking question answer pairs, also known as answer selection, is a fundamental task in question answering (QA) systems. It aims to rank a set of candidate answers for selecting the relevant or correct answers to the given question. Many efforts have been made on developing various neural models to measure the relevance degree between the question and answer pair, including Siamese Structure (Tay et al., 2018; Chen et al., 2020), Attention-based Structure (Chen et al., 2017; Shen et al., 2018; Deng et al., 2021), and Compare-Aggregate Structure (Yoon et al., 2019). Recently, models with contextualized representations, e.g., ELMo (Peters et al., 2018) and BERT (Devlin et al., 2019), contribute to major improvement on answer selection (Yoon et al., 2019; Garg et al., 2020).

$\mathbf{q}$: How many music awards has Katy Perry won?
$\mathbf{a}_1^-$: Katy Perry is an American singer from Santa Barbara California.
$\mathbf{a}_2^-$: Perry has released three studio albums including her debut Christian effort Katy Hudson One of the Boys and Teenage Dream.
$\mathbf{a}_3^-$: Perry's mainstream career was kicked off with the massive chart success of her debut single I Kissed a Girl.
$\mathbf{a}^*$: Katy Perry has won 11 awards for her music career including three Grammy awards and two American Music Awards.
$\mathbf{q}_1^*$: What city is Katy Perry from?
$\mathbf{q}_2^*$: How many albums has Katy Perry released in her career?
$\mathbf{q}_3^*$: Who is the singer Katy Perry?

Table 1: An Example from WikiQA with Synthesized Data. $\mathbf{q}, \mathbf{a}_1^-, \mathbf{a}_2^-, \mathbf{a}_3^-$ are the original data, but all these answers are irrelevant to the given question. $\mathbf{a}^*, \mathbf{q}_1^*, \mathbf{q}_2^*, \mathbf{q}_3^*$ are the corresponding synthesized data.

Acquiring the ground-truth positive answer to the given question or manually annotating the relevance degree between a QA pair can be extremely time-consuming. Therefore, the existing answer selection datasets are often limited in scale. Such data scarceness issue poses a great challenge for the modern neural models, which are often data-hungry for the training process. Moreover, the negative samples, i.e., the irrelevant answers to the given question are constructed by random negative sampling from the whole document pool (Tay et al., 2017), leaving less to learn for differentiating the relevant answer from a set of highly irrelevant answers (Zhang et al., 2017; Kumar et al., 2019). Therefore, the data scarceness and label imbalance issues lead to the underutilization of the in-domain knowledge in the original datasets, and even a waste of valuable labeled data.

Some early works (Min et al., 2017; Deng et al., 2018) leverage transfer learning (TL) based approaches to transfer knowledge from large-scale QA datasets, e.g., SQuAD (Rajpurkar et al., 2016), for improving resource-poor answer selection tasks. With similar motivations, Yoon et al. (2019) combine ELMo with transfer learning from a large-scale relevant-sentence-selection dataset to enhance the performance of the compare-aggregate model. Garg et al. (2020) adopt BERT-based mod-

* The work described in this paper is substantially supported by a grant from the Asian Institute of Supply Chains and Logistics, the Chinese University of Hong Kong.

Proceedings of the 2021 EMNLP Workshop W-NUT: The Seventh Workshop on Noisy User-generated Text, pages 175–181
November 11, 2021. ©2021 Association for Computational Linguistics

els with a Transfer-and-Adapt (TANDA) approach by using a large and high-quality QA dataset. However, such TL-based methods heavily rely on the existence of large-scale high-quality datasets with similar problem settings, which is also unrealistic in real-world applications. Besides, compared with utilizing cross-domain knowledge via TL, it would be more efficient to take advantage of the in-domain knowledge from the original dataset.

Another way to handle the data scarceness and label imbalance issues is to employ hard negative sampling strategies (Zhang et al., 2017; Kumar et al., 2019) or curriculum training approaches (MacAvaney et al., 2020) for taking advantages of those randomly sampled negative answers. The essential motivation behind these methods is that the hard negative samples or the "difficult" samples play a more important role in training a better ranking model. However, those "less" important samples are likely to be overlooked in such cases, leading to a potential waste of data. In order to maximize the utility of the existing labeled data, we aim at investigating data augmentation strategy to construct weak supervision signals for enhancing answer selection models.

In this work, we propose an effective data augmentation strategy, namely **Bi**lateral **G**eneration (**BiG**), with a contrastive training objective for improving the performance of ranking question answer pairs with existing labeled data. In specific, we first fine-tune a Question Generator (QG) and an Answer Generator (AG) from the pre-trained generative language model, such as BART (Lewis et al., 2020), with the positive samples in the training data. Then, as the example shown in Table 1, we use the fine-tuned QG and AG to generate a high-quality question-related answer $\mathbf{a}^*$ and answer-focused questions $\mathbf{q}^*$ from the given negative samples $(\mathbf{q}, \mathbf{a}^-)$. The synthesized QA pairs $(\mathbf{q}, \mathbf{a}^*)$ and $(\mathbf{q}^*, \mathbf{a}^-)$ can be regarded as new "positive" samples in contrast to the original negative sample. By doing so, given a small amount of labeled data even with extremely imbalanced labels, such data augmentation strategy can easily synthesize high-quality data with weak supervision signals. Although such pseudo-positive QA pairs may not be perfectly matched, e.g., $(\mathbf{q}_3^*, \mathbf{a}_3^-)$, they are supposed to be more interrelated than the original negative QA pairs, which can be served as pairwise samples for contrastive estimation. For instance, $(\mathbf{q}_3^*, \mathbf{a}_3^-)$ can be used to establish a contrastive sample with $(\mathbf{q}, \mathbf{a}_3^-)$, rather than be simply regarded as a positive QA pair. Therefore, we further design a contrastive training objective for ranking QA pairs.

We conduct experiments by applying the proposed BiG method with both the attention-based ranking model and the pre-trained BERT ranking model. Experimental results on three benchmark datasets including TREC-QA, WikiQA, and ANTIQUE show the effectiveness and the applicability of our method, which significantly improves the original ranking models across all datasets.

2 Method

2.1 Preliminaries

Let an ad-hoc neural ranking model be denoted as $R_\theta(\mathbf{q}, \mathbf{a})$, which measures the relevance degree of a given question answer pair $(\mathbf{q}, \mathbf{a})$ parameterized by the model parameters θ. Given a set of training samples, there are three mainstream approaches to optimize the ranking performance, namely, pointwise training, pairwise training, and listwise training (Lai et al., 2018; Zhang et al., 2020). Here we focus on pointwise and pairwise training, since listwise training is less practical in applications when there is a large set of candidate answers.

The pointwise training aims to optimize the predicted probability distribution of each QA pair to be consistent with the ground-truth label by minimizing the cross-entropy loss function:

$$p_i = \text{softmax}(R_\theta(\mathbf{q}_i, \mathbf{a}_i)), \tag{1}$$

$$\mathcal{L}^{\text{pt}}(\mathbf{q}_i, \mathbf{a}_i, y_i) = -\left[y_i \log p_i + (1 - y_i) \log (1 - p_i)\right], \tag{2}$$

where y_i is the label of the i-th training sample.

On the other hand, the pairwise training is to optimize the relative order of a pair of predicted relevance scores, i.e., $R_\theta(\mathbf{q}, \mathbf{a}^+)$ and $R_\theta(\mathbf{q}, \mathbf{a}^-)$, which typically adopt the same question $\mathbf{q}$ with one relevant answer $\mathbf{a}^+$ and one irrelevant answer $\mathbf{a}^-$. The main idea behind pairwise training is contrastive estimation. One widely-used pairwise loss function is the hinge loss:

$$\mathcal{L}^{\text{pr}}(\mathbf{q}, \mathbf{a}^+, \mathbf{a}^-) = \max(0, M - R_\theta(\mathbf{q}, \mathbf{a}^+) + R_\theta(\mathbf{q}, \mathbf{a}^-)), \tag{3}$$

where the model learns to rank the relevant answer $\mathbf{a}^+$ higher than the irrelevant answer $\mathbf{a}^-$, by imposing a margin M between their relevance scores with the given question $\mathbf{q}$.

2.2 BiG Data Augmentation

To maximize the utility of the valuable labeled data as well as alleviate the label imbalance issue, pre-trained language models, such as BART (Lewis et al., 2020), preserve promising advantages of synthesizing high-quality pseudo QA pairs through conditional generation, which can serve as weak supervision signals for contrastive learning with original data. Due the nature of question answering, there are two intuitive ways to generate augmentations, *i.e.*, question generation and answer generation, namely **Bi**lateral **G**eneration (**BiG**).

With the pre-trained conditional generation model, a certain number of training data is required to fine-tune a Question Generator (QG) and an Answer Generator (AG). We adopt the positive samples, i.e., the relevant $(\mathbf{q}, \mathbf{a}^+)$ pair, as the training data to fine-tune the QG and AG:

$$\mathbf{H} = \text{QGEnc}(\mathbf{a}^+; [\text{SEP}]), \quad \mathbf{q} = \text{QGDec}(\mathbf{H}), \tag{4}$$

$$\mathbf{H} = \text{AGEnc}(\mathbf{q}; [\text{SEP}]), \quad \mathbf{a}^+ = \text{AGDec}(\mathbf{H}), \tag{5}$$

where [SEP] is a separation token.

Then, the learned QG and AG models can be employed to generate answer-related questions $\mathbf{q}^*$ and question-related answers $\mathbf{a}^*$, respectively. In our case, we are able to synthesize pseudo-positive QA pairs from the original negative QA pairs. For instance, given a negative QA pair. $(\mathbf{q}, \mathbf{a}^-)$, two pseudo-positive QA pairs, i.e., $(\mathbf{q}^*, \mathbf{a}^-)$ and $(\mathbf{q}, \mathbf{a}^*)$, can be generated by the learned question generator QG and answer generator AG:

$$\mathbf{q}^* = \mathbf{QG}(\mathbf{a}^-; [\text{SEP}]), \quad \mathbf{a}^* = \mathbf{AG}(\mathbf{q}; [\text{SEP}]). \tag{6}$$

One one hand, since the generation model is pre-trained on large scale corpus and further fine-tuned on positive QA pairs, we are guaranteed to generate reliable questions or answers related to the source text. In other words, the relevance degree between the synthesized QA pairs is supposed to be sufficiently higher than the original negative QA pairs constructed by randomly sampling. One the other hand, compared with the original positive QA pairs, the synthesized QA pairs are likely to contain certain redundant information or lack of necessary information. Regarding the synthesized QA pairs as ground-truth positive pairs may introduce undesired noises into the original dataset. Therefore, the pseudo-positive nature of the systhesized QA pairs leaves room for contrastive learning.

2.3 Contrastive Training Objective

As mentioned in Section 2.1, conventional supervised ranking problem can only optimize the ranking performance with existing labeled data. Here we introduce contrastive learning to rank by leveraging generation-augmented contrastive data for further improving the ranking performance.

Given a question $\mathbf{q}$ from the original dataset, there are a set of relevant answers $\mathbf{A}^+ = \{\mathbf{a}^+\}$ and a set of irrelevant answers $\mathbf{A}^- = \{\mathbf{a}^-\}$, correspondingly. The pairwise training for conventional supervised learning to rank can be defined as:

$$\mathcal{L}^{\text{pr}}_{\text{set}}(\mathbf{q}, \mathbf{A}^+, \mathbf{A}^-) = \frac{\sum\limits_{\mathbf{a}^+ \in \mathbf{A}^+} \sum\limits_{\mathbf{a}^- \in \mathbf{A}^-} \mathcal{L}^{\text{pr}}(\mathbf{q}, \mathbf{a}^+, \mathbf{a}^-)}{|\mathbf{A}^+| \cdot |\mathbf{A}^-|}. \tag{7}$$

With the synthesized pseudo-positive samples, we leverage such contrastive weak supervision signals to enhance the pairwise training in Eq.7:

$$\mathcal{L}^{\text{ctrst}}_{\text{set}}(\mathbf{q}, \mathbf{A}^+, \mathbf{A}^-) = \mathcal{L}^{\text{pr}}_{\text{set}}(\mathbf{q}, \mathbf{A}^+, \mathbf{A}^-) + \frac{1}{|\mathbf{A}^-|} \sum_{\mathbf{a}^- \in \mathbf{A}^-} \left[\mathcal{L}^{\text{pr}}(\mathbf{q}, \mathbf{a}^*, \mathbf{a}^-) + \mathcal{L}^{\text{pr}}(\mathbf{q}^*, \mathbf{q}, \mathbf{a}^-)\right], \tag{8}$$

where the second term implements the contrastive training between the synthesized pseudo-positive QA pairs, $(\mathbf{q}, \mathbf{a}^*)$ and $(\mathbf{q}^*, \mathbf{a}^-)$, and the original negative QA pairs, $(\mathbf{q}, \mathbf{a}^-)$.

3 Experiment

3.1 Experimental Setup

3.1.1 Datasets and Evaluation Metrics

We evaluate our method on three widely-used benchmark datasets for answer selection: TREC-QA, WikiQA, and ANTIQUE. The statistics of these datasets are described in Table 2.

- TREC-QA (Wang et al., 2007), collected from TREC QA track 8-13 data, is a widely-adopted benchmark for factoid question answering.
- WikiQA (Yang et al., 2015) is an open-domain factoid answer selection benchmark, in which the answers are collected from the Wikipedia.

Following previous studies (Garg et al., 2020), we adopt the RAW version of training data and evaluate on the cleaned test data for both TREC-QA and WikiQA. The mean average precision (MAP) and mean reciprocal rank (MRR) are adopted as the evaluation metrics.

- ANTIQUE (Hashemi et al., 2020) is an open-domain non-factoid QA dataset collected from community question answering services with a diverse set of categories.

Dataset (train/dev/test)	#Question	#QA Pairs	%Positive
TREC-QA	1160/65/68	53417/1117/1442	12.0/18.4/17.2
WikiQA	2118/126/243	20360/1130/2351	12.0/12.4/12.5
ANTIQUE	2426/-/200	27422/-/6589	72.2/-/38.4

Table 2: Summary statistics of datasets.

Although there are four-level relevance labels for the candidate answers, we follow previous studies (Hashemi et al., 2020; MacAvaney et al., 2020) to assume that the label 3 and label 4 are relevant, while 1 and 2 are non-relevant. MRR and P@1 are adopted for evaluation on the binary labels, while nDCG is adopted for evaluation on the four-level relevance labels.

3.1.2 Baseline Methods

Since TREC-QA and WikiQA have been extensively studied for answer selection, we are able to compare with more diverse baseline methods, including traditional methods and Transfer Learning based methods.

- We consider the methods without using external resources during the training phase as traditional methods. aNMM (Yang et al., 2016), RNN-POA (Chen et al., 2017), and KABLSTM (Shen et al., 2018) develop different kinds of attention-based structures for enhancing the interaction between the question and answer. HyperQA (Tay et al., 2018) and SD (Chen et al., 2020) study the similarity aggregation approaches in siamese neural network structure. Currently, models based on pre-trained contextualized representations, e.g., BERT (Devlin et al., 2019), achieve state-of-the-art performance among the traditional methods.
- TL-based methods refer to those methods that transfers cross-domain knowledge from external large-scale resources to enhance the resource-poor tasks. Here we compare our results with two state-of-the-art TL-based methods, i.e., CA+LM+LC+TL (Yoon et al., 2019) and TANDA (Garg et al., 2020), which adopts QNLI (86K QA pairs) and ASNQ (20M QA pairs) as source dataset, respectively, for transfer learning.

As for ANTIQUE, we compare to the benchmark performance on BERT and a newly developed curriculum learning strategy (MacAvaney et al., 2020) for learning to handle difficult cases.

3.1.3 Implementation Details

We adopt the Large version of BART (Lewis et al., 2020) as the conditional generation model for data augmentation. During the fine-tuning of the question generator and answer generator, we set the maximum sequence length for question and answer as 30 and 50, respectively. Both of the question generator and answer generator are fine-tuned for 5 epochs. All other hyper-parameters are set to default as the original BART. Since the proposed method can be applied to any ranking model, we choose two widely-adopted ranking models, namely, BERT (Devlin et al., 2019) and aNMM (Yang et al., 2016), as the base models for evaluation. The maximum sequence length of the concatenated QA pair is set to be 128. We train all the models for 5 epochs. All other hyper-parameters are also set to default as the original BERT. And we use MatchZoo (Guo et al., 2019) to implement the aNMM model.

Method	TREC-QA		WikiQA	
	MAP	MRR	MAP	MRR
aNMM	0.750	0.811	0.610	0.628
RNN-POA	0.781	0.851	0.721	0.731
KABLSTM	0.804	0.885	0.732	0.749
HyperQA	0.784	0.865	0.712	0.727
SD	0.783	0.878	0.704	0.712
$\text{BERT}_{\text{base}}$	0.857	0.937	0.813	0.828
$\text{BERT}_{\text{large}}$	0.904	0.946	0.836	0.853
CA+LM+LC+TL(QNLI)	0.875	0.940	0.834	0.848
$\text{BERT}_{\text{base}}$ TANDA(QNLI)	0.863	0.906	0.832	0.852
$\text{BERT}_{\text{base}}$ TANDA(ASNQ)	0.912	0.951	0.893	0.903
$\text{BERT}_{\text{large}}$ TANDA(ASNQ)	0.912	0.967	0.904	0.912
aNMM-BiG	$0.792^{\dagger}$	$0.879^{\dagger}$	$0.698^{\dagger}$	$0.710^{\dagger}$
$\text{BERT}_{\text{base}}$-BiG	**$0.899^{\dagger}$**	**$0.961^{\dagger}$**	**$0.825^{\dagger}$**	**$0.836^{\dagger}$**
$\text{BERT}_{\text{large}}$-BiG	**$0.913^{\dagger}$**	**$0.966^{\dagger}$**	**$0.855^{\dagger}$**	**$0.863^{\dagger}$**

Table 3: Experimental Results on TREC-QA and WikiQA. † indicates significant improvement ($p < 0.05$) over the corresponding base ranking models.

3.2 Overall Performance

Table 3 summarizes the method comparisons on TREC-QA and WikiQA. Here we combine our BiG method with both an attention-based ranking model, namely aNMM, and the pre-trained BERT ranking model. Two groups of methods on answer selection, in terms of whether to use large-scale external resources, are adopted for comparisons.

Among **traditional methods**, models using contextualized representations, i.e., $\text{BERT}_{\text{base}}$ and $\text{BERT}_{\text{large}}$, achieve distinguishable state-of-the-art performance, showing the power of pre-trained languge models. All the ranking models combined with the proposed data augmentation strategy, BiG, consistently and substantially improve the perfor-

Method	MRR	P@1	nDCG@1	nDCG@3	nDCG@10
aNMM	0.625	0.485	0.529	0.513	0.490
$\text{BERT}_{\text{base}}$	0.797	0.709	0.713	0.657	0.642
$\text{BERT}_{\text{large}}$	0.802	0.690	0.708	0.669	0.693
$\text{BERT}_{\text{base}}$ Pair.	0.700	0.585	-	-	-
- w/ $\mathcal{D}_{recip}$	0.734	0.645	-	-	-
aNMM-BiG	$0.662^{\dagger}$	$0.565^{\dagger}$	$0.601^{\dagger}$	$0.586^{\dagger}$	$0.589^{\dagger}$
$\text{BERT}_{\text{base}}$-BiG	**$0.847^{\dagger}$**	**$0.765^{\dagger}$**	**$0.750^{\dagger}$**	**$0.710^{\dagger}$**	**$0.720^{\dagger}$**
$\text{BERT}_{\text{large}}$-BiG	**$0.859^{\dagger}$**	**$0.785^{\dagger}$**	**$0.772^{\dagger}$**	**$0.719^{\dagger}$**	**$0.738^{\dagger}$**

Table 4: Experimental Results on ANTIQUE.

mance of the original ranking models. For instance, $\text{BERT}_{\text{base}}$-BiG outperforms the original $\text{BERT}_{\text{base}}$ by about 5% and 2% on TREC-QA and WikiQA datasets, respectively. The results indicate that the proposed data augmentation strategy effectively synthesize valuable contrastive data for learning to rank question answer pairs without the need of large-scale annotated data.

As for **transfer learning based methods**, the performances on target tasks step up to the next stage with large-scale external resources. Compared with CA+LM+LC+TL(QNLI) and TANDA(QNLI), which employs 86K external annotated QA pairs from QNLI for training, BiG-enhanced models achieve a competitive performance by only manipulating the limited original data. Even if comparing to TANDA(ASNQ), which employs 20M external QA pairs from Natural Questions for training, BiG-enhanced models can still outperform it on the MRR metric of TREC-QA. However, since Natural Questions and WikiQA are both derived from Wikipedia, they are likely to share a lot of related in-domain knowledge, leading to a great performance boosting on WikiQA.

Table 4 presents the experimental results on ANTIQUE. In general, BiG significantly improves the performance of $\text{BERT}_{\text{base}}$ by about 6%. Especially for nDCG, we observe a large performance increase in the multi-level ranking metrics. This result shows that the proposed method is also effective on non-factoid QA.

3.3 Ablation Study

According to the ablation studies in Table 5, we observe that both the BiG data augmentation and the contrastive learning objective contribute to the final performance more or less.

As for TREC-QA and ANTIQUE, pairwise training achieves a better performance than pointwise training. Since there is a large number of questions without any positive answer in the WikiQA dataset, the lack of pairwise training samples causes that the performance of pairwise training is much worse than pointwise training. This issue is appropriately solved by our data augmentation strategy by constructing synthesized pseudo-positive samples.

Method	TREC-QA		WikiQA		ANTIQUE	
	MAP	MRR	MAP	MRR	MRR	P@1
$\text{BERT}_{\text{base}}$ Point.	0.857	0.937	0.813	0.828	0.797	0.709
$\text{BERT}_{\text{base}}$ Pair.	0.872	0.925	0.734	0.747	0.806	0.715
$\text{BERT}_{\text{base}}$-BiG	**0.899**	**0.961**	**0.825**	**0.836**	**0.847**	**0.765**
- w/o QG	0.891	0.958	0.758	0.772	0.844	0.755
- w/o AG	0.882	0.949	0.824	0.833	0.834	0.740
- w/o Contrastive	0.878	0.942	0.818	0.831	0.802	0.690

Table 5: Ablation Study.

The QG-augmented data contributes much more to the performance on WikiQA than AG, while the AG-augmented data is slightly more beneficial to TREC-QA and ANTIQUE than QG. Since there are only 873 out of 2118 questions containing positive answers in the training data of WikiQA, the rest questions are all underutilized for pairwise training. The synthesized contrastive data by QG effectively evoke such valuable knowledge for learning.

Compared with pointwise training with only the original data, "w/o contrastive learning", where the synthesized QA pairs are regarded as ground-truth positive samples for pointwise training, can achieve relatively better performance. However, there is still a great margin to reach the performance of $\text{BERT}_{\text{base}}$-BiG. The results indicate that the synthesized QA pairs are actually more relevant than the original negative samples, but the proposed contrastive learning objective can better utilize the synthesized data than treating them as positive samples for pointwise training.

4 Conclusions

In this paper, we study the data augmentation for improving the performance of ranking question answer pairs when encountering data scarceness and label imbalance issues. We propose an easy-to-apply and effective data augmentation strategy, namely Bilateral Generation, with a contrastive learning objective to maximize the utility of limited labeled data. Experimental results show that the proposed method significantly improves the performance of ranking models on three factoid and non-factoid QA benchmark datasets.

The proposed data augmentation strategy can be easily extended to few-shot learning scenario to further handle more severe resource-poor applications, such as domain-specific question answering, e-Commerce question answering, etc.

References

Dong Chen, Shaoliang Peng, Kenli Li, Ying Xu, Jinling Zhang, and Xiaolan Xie. 2020. Re-ranking answer selection with similarity aggregation. In *Proceedings of the 43rd International ACM SIGIR conference on research and development in Information Retrieval, SIGIR 2020*, pages 1677–1680.

Qin Chen, Qinmin Hu, Jimmy Xiangji Huang, Liang He, and Weijie An. 2017. Enhancing recurrent neural networks with positional attention for question answering. In *Proceedings of the 40th International ACM SIGIR Conference on Research and Development in Information Retrieval*, pages 993–996.

Yang Deng, Ying Shen, Min Yang, Yaliang Li, Nan Du, Wei Fan, and Kai Lei. 2018. Knowledge as A bridge: Improving cross-domain answer selection with external knowledge. In *Proceedings of the 27th International Conference on Computational Linguistics, COLING 2018*, pages 3295–3305.

Yang Deng, Yuexiang Xie, Yaliang Li, Min Yang, Wai Lam, and Ying Shen. 2021. Contextualized knowledge-aware attentive neural network: Enhancing answer selection with knowledge. *CoRR*, abs/2104.05216.

Jacob Devlin, Ming-Wei Chang, Kenton Lee, and Kristina Toutanova. 2019. BERT: pre-training of deep bidirectional transformers for language understanding. In *Proceedings of the 2019 Conference of the North American Chapter of the Association for Computational Linguistics: Human Language Technologies, NAACL-HLT 2019*, pages 4171–4186.

Siddhant Garg, Thuy Vu, and Alessandro Moschitti. 2020. TANDA: transfer and adapt pre-trained transformer models for answer sentence selection. In *The Thirty-Fourth AAAI Conference on Artificial Intelligence, AAAI 2020*, pages 7780–7788.

Jiafeng Guo, Yixing Fan, Xiang Ji, and Xueqi Cheng. 2019. Matchzoo: A learning, practicing, and developing system for neural text matching. In *Proceedings of the 42nd International ACM SIGIR Conference on Research and Development in Information Retrieval, SIGIR 2019*, pages 1297–1300.

Helia Hashemi, Mohammad Aliannejadi, Hamed Zamani, and W. Bruce Croft. 2020. ANTIQUE: A non-factoid question answering benchmark. In *Advances in Information Retrieval - 42nd European Conference on IR Research, ECIR 2020*, pages 166–173.

Sawan Kumar, Shweta Garg, Kartik Mehta, and Nikhil Rasiwasia. 2019. Improving answer selection and answer triggering using hard negatives. In *Proceedings of the 2019 Conference on Empirical Methods in Natural Language Processing and the 9th International Joint Conference on Natural Language Processing, EMNLP-IJCNLP 2019*, pages 5910–5916.

Tuan Manh Lai, Trung Bui, and Sheng Li. 2018. A review on deep learning techniques applied to answer selection. In *Proceedings of the 27th International Conference on Computational Linguistics, COLING 2018*, pages 2132–2144.

Mike Lewis, Yinhan Liu, Naman Goyal, Marjan Ghazvininejad, Abdelrahman Mohamed, Omer Levy, Veselin Stoyanov, and Luke Zettlemoyer. 2020. BART: denoising sequence-to-sequence pre-training for natural language generation, translation, and comprehension. In *Proceedings of the 58th Annual Meeting of the Association for Computational Linguistics, ACL 2020*, pages 7871–7880.

Sean MacAvaney, Franco Maria Nardini, Raffaele Perego, Nicola Tonellotto, Nazli Goharian, and Ophir Frieder. 2020. Training curricula for open domain answer re-ranking. In *Proceedings of the 43rd International ACM SIGIR conference on research and development in Information Retrieval, SIGIR 2020*, pages 529–538.

Sewon Min, Min Joon Seo, and Hannaneh Hajishirzi. 2017. Question answering through transfer learning from large fine-grained supervision data. In *Proceedings of the 55th Annual Meeting of the Association for Computational Linguistics, ACL 2017*, pages 510–517.

Matthew E. Peters, Mark Neumann, Mohit Iyyer, Matt Gardner, Christopher Clark, Kenton Lee, and Luke Zettlemoyer. 2018. Deep contextualized word representations. In *Proceedings of the 2018 Conference of the North American Chapter of the Association for Computational Linguistics: Human Language Technologies, NAACL-HLT 2018*, pages 2227–2237.

Pranav Rajpurkar, Jian Zhang, Konstantin Lopyrev, and Percy Liang. 2016. Squad: 100, 000+ questions for machine comprehension of text. In *Proceedings of the 2016 Conference on Empirical Methods in Natural Language Processing, EMNLP 2016*, pages 2383–2392.

Ying Shen, Yang Deng, Min Yang, Yaliang Li, Nan Du, Wei Fan, and Kai Lei. 2018. Knowledge-aware attentive neural network for ranking question answer pairs. In *The 41st International ACM SIGIR Conference on Research & Development in Information Retrieval, SIGIR 2018*, pages 901–904.

Yi Tay, Minh C. Phan, Anh Tuan Luu, and Siu Cheung Hui. 2017. Learning to rank question answer pairs with holographic dual LSTM architecture. In *Proceedings of the 40th International ACM SIGIR Conference on Research and Development in Information Retrieval*, pages 695–704.

Yi Tay, Luu Anh Tuan, and Siu Cheung Hui. 2018. Hyperbolic representation learning for fast and efficient neural question answering. In *Proceedings of the Eleventh ACM International Conference on Web Search and Data Mining, WSDM 2018*, pages 583–591.

Mengqiu Wang, Noah A. Smith, and Teruko Mitamura. 2007. What is the jeopardy model? A quasi-synchronous grammar for QA. In *EMNLP-CoNLL 2007, Proceedings of the 2007 Joint Conference on Empirical Methods in Natural Language Processing and Computational Natural Language Learning*, pages 22–32.

Liu Yang, Qingyao Ai, Jiafeng Guo, and W. Bruce Croft. 2016. anmm: Ranking short answer texts with attention-based neural matching model. In *Proceedings of the 25th ACM International Conference on Information and Knowledge Management, CIKM 2016*, pages 287–296.

Yi Yang, Wen-tau Yih, and Christopher Meek. 2015. Wikiqa: A challenge dataset for open-domain question answering. In *Proceedings of the 2015 Conference on Empirical Methods in Natural Language Processing, EMNLP 2015*, pages 2013–2018.

Seunghyun Yoon, Franck Dernoncourt, Doo Soon Kim, Trung Bui, and Kyomin Jung. 2019. A compare-aggregate model with latent clustering for answer selection. In *Proceedings of the 28th ACM International Conference on Information and Knowledge Management, CIKM 2019*, pages 2093–2096.

Haotian Zhang, Jinfeng Rao, Jimmy J. Lin, and Mark D. Smucker. 2017. Automatically extracting high-quality negative examples for answer selection in question answering. In *Proceedings of the 40th International ACM SIGIR Conference on Research and Development in Information Retrieval*, pages 797–800.

Wenxuan Zhang, Yang Deng, and Wai Lam. 2020. Answer ranking for product-related questions via multiple semantic relations modeling. In *Proceedings of the 43rd International ACM SIGIR conference on research and development in Information Retrieval, SIGIR 2020*, pages 569–578.

Mitigation of Diachronic Bias in Fake News Detection Dataset

Taichi Murayama and **Shoko Wakamiya** and **Eiji Aramaki**
Nara Institute of Science and Technology (NAIST)
{murayama.taichi.mk1, wakamiya, aramaki}@is.naist.jp

Abstract

Fake news causes significant damage to society. To deal with these fake news, several studies on building detection models and arranging datasets have been conducted. Most of the fake news datasets depend on a specific time period. Consequently, the detection models trained on such a dataset have difficulty detecting novel fake news generated by political changes and social changes; they may possibly result in biased output from the input, including specific person names and organizational names. We refer to this problem as **Diachronic Bias** because it is caused by the creation date of news in each dataset. In this study, we confirm the bias, especially proper nouns including person names, from the deviation of phrase appearances in each dataset. Based on these findings, we propose masking methods using Wikidata to mitigate the influence of person names and validate whether they make fake news detection models robust through experiments with in-domain and out-of-domain data.

1 Introduction

Fake news, which refers to intentional and verifiable false news stories, has caused significant damage to society. For example, Bovet and Makse (2019) noted that 25% of the news stories linked in tweets posted just before the 2016 U.S. presidential election were either fake or extraordinarily biased. In addition to elections, fake news tends to spread after unusual situations such as natural disasters (Hashimoto et al., 2020) and disease outbreaks (e.g., COVID-19 (Shahi and Nandini, 2020)). To address these problems, various studies on the development of models for fake news detection from social media posts and news content, and the construction of fake news datasets for this purpose have been conducted (Shu et al., 2020).

Most datasets for fake news detection consist of factual and fake news that actually diffuse over the Internet. The topics and contents of fake news change over time because they are strongly influenced by the interests of the general population (Schmidt et al., 2017). For instance, there were fake news related to President Obama in 2013 (CNBC, 2013), presidential election in 2016 (Bovet and Makse, 2019), and COVID-19 in 2020 (Shahi et al., 2020). Thus, datasets are frequently constructed based on fake news present in a specific period. Fake news detection models learned from these datasets achieve high accuracy for the datasets constructed for the same period and domain, while they lead to a drop in the detection performance of fake news in different domains and future applications because of the difference in word appearance. In other words, fake news detection models learned from a dataset that includes news only from a specific period may possibly result in a biased judgment from the input, based on cues related to a particular person name or an organizational name. For example, a model learned from a dataset in 2017 is difficult to correctly classify articles including "Donald Trump" or "Joe Biden" in 2021, because the model does not know a new president change. We call the problem as **Diachronic Bias** because it is caused by the difference in the news publishing date in each dataset. This problem occurs with data from even the same domain, making it difficult to construct a robust detection model.

This study examines various strategies to mitigate diachronic bias by masking proper nouns that tend to cause the bias, such as names of people and places. First, we analyzed the correlation between labels and phrases in several fake news detection datasets with different creation periods and noted the deviation of words, mainly person names. We then applied and validated several masking methods focusing on proper nouns to mitigate diachronic bias in the tackling of fake news detection tasks.

Proceedings of the 2021 EMNLP Workshop W-NUT: The Seventh Workshop on Noisy User-generated Text, pages 182–188
November 11, 2021. ©2021 Association for Computational Linguistics

MultiFC						Constraint					
Real			Fake			Real			Fake		
Bi-gram	**LMI**	$p(l\|w)$	**Bi-gram**	**LMI**	$p(l\|w)$	**Bi-gram**	**LMI**	$p(l\|w)$	**Bi-gram**	**LMI**	$p(l\|w)$
mitt romney	218	0.69	health care	631	0.64	url url	1378	0.77	a video	591	1.0
if you	217	0.70	**barack obama**	365	0.69	rt @user	822	0.93	**donald trump**	569	0.98
rhode island	190	0.75	**president barack**	337	0.70	total number	650	0.98	has been	569	0.52
new jersey	177	0.67	**scott walker**	258	0.81	more than	635	0.89	**url donaldtrump**	435	1.0
john mccain	167	0.73	says president	218	0.78	have been	575	0.82	**bill gates**	355	1.0
no. 1	128	0.86	care law	185	0.80	@user url	449	0.87	video shows	346	0.98
voted against	128	0.71	will be	162	0.63	managed isolation	402	1.0	**president trump**	315	1.0
any other	125	0.61	**hillary clinton**	159	0.67	our daily	385	0.99	covid vaccine	293	0.80
does not	119	0.71	**gov. scott**	148	0.72	states reported	373	1.0	corona virus	275	1.0
this year	116	0.75	social security	144	0.68	update published	367	1.0	social media	275	0.93

Table 1: Top 10 LMI ranked bi-grams in MultiFC and Constraint for real and fake labels with their $p(l|w)$. **LMI** are written as value multiplied by 10^6. Person names are written in bold. There is a tendency for real labels to be highly correlated with common phrases, while fake labels are highly correlated with person names.

2 Related Work

Analysis and examination of mitigation methods for various types of bias have been conducted for detecting offensive language and hate speech: author bias (Wiegand et al., 2019), annotator bias (Ross et al., 2017), gender bias (Binns et al., 2017; Park et al., 2018), racial bias (Sap et al., 2019), political bias (Wich et al., 2020), etc. Dayanik and Padó (2020) focuses on frequency bias of person name in their dataset, while we handle person name considering the passage of time.

In various studies, bias analysis and mitigation are addressed for the fact verification task, where given texts as judged as factual or otherwise from several pieces of evidence, and is one of the recognizing textual entailment tasks. For example, Schuster et al. (2019) and Suntwal et al. (2019) proposed mitigation methods by replacing some words with specific labels to build a robust inference model for out-of-domain data. However, to the best of our knowledge, there has been no study or analysis of bias in fake news detection datasets.

3 Resources

3.1 Datasets

We examine diachronic bias by analyzing four fake news detection datasets with different domains and creation periods. Each article and post in these datasets has a binary label (real/fake). The details of the datasets are as follows and further information is provided in Appendix A:

MultiFC (Augenstein et al., 2019): This is a multi-domain dataset containing over 36,000 headlines from 38 fact-checking organizations. We extracted 7,861 headlines from 2007 to 2015 and regarded headlines labeled as "truth!," "true," or "mostly true" as real; those labeled "mostly false" or "false" as fake.

Horne17 (Horne and Adali, 2017): This dataset contains news articles on the 2016 US presidential election, which are labeled real/fake/satire, based on the investigation of BuzzFeed News. We used articles with fake and real labels.

Celebrity (Pérez-Rosas et al., 2018): This dataset is composed of news articles verified by Gossipcop, which targets news related to celebrities. Most of the articles, whose topics are mainly sensational, such as fights between celebrities, were published between 2016 and 2017.

Constraint (Patwa et al., 2020): This dataset was used in the CONSTRAINT 2021 shared task and consists of social media posts related to COVID-19. These posts were verified by fact-checking sites such as Politifact and Snopes.

3.2 Correlation between phrases and labels

We investigated the correlation between phrases and labels to examine bias in each dataset. To capture high-frequency phrases that are highly correlated with a particular label, we use local mutual information (LMI) (Evert, 2005). Given a dataset D, the LMI between a phrase w and label l is defined as follows: $LMI(w,l) = p(w,l) \cdot \log\left(\frac{p(l|w)}{p(l)}\right)$, where $p(w,l)$ is calculated as $\frac{\text{count}(w,l)}{|P|}$, $p(l|w)$ as $\frac{\text{count}(w,l)}{\text{count}(w)}$, $p(l)$ as $\frac{\text{count}(l)}{|P|}$, and $|P|$ is the number of occurrences of all phrases in D.

Table 1 presents bi-grams that are highly correlated with each label in MultiFC and Constraint[1]. In MultiFC, the headlines prior to 2015 containing words referring to the U.S. president at the time,

[1] Appendix B lists bi-grams with high LMI in Horne17 and Celebrity.

such as "barack obama," were highly correlated with fake labels. In Constraint, words such as "bill gates" and "donald trump," were highly correlated with the fake labels. These results revealed a bias in the relationship between specific person names and labels. The detection model trained on one of these datasets is not adaptable to instances such as the change of president, and thus does not work well on other datasets.

4 Diachronic bias mitigation

4.1 Masking methods

We examine multiple masking methods, starting from word deletion to word replacement for input text data to mitigate the diachronic bias and to build a robust detection model for out-of-domain data. We utilize Named Entity Recognition (NER) (Akbik et al., 2019) in Flair (Akbik et al., 2018) to search for words to be used as masks. Examples of each masking method are listed in Appendix D.

Named Entity (NE) Del: Words tagged with NEs are removed. This masking method aims to build a detection model independent of NE, same as (Suntwal et al., 2019).

Basic NER: Words tagged with NEs are replaced with the corresponding labels, such as PER (person label), LOC (location label), etc.

WikiD: Words tagged with PER labels are replaced with Wikidata (Wikidata) label, specifically, position held (P39), or alternatively occupation (P106) depending on availability. For example, the use of Wikidata at that time made it possible to replace the phrase "barack obama" in articles from 2015 and "donald trump" in those from 2020 with the same label as President of the United States (Q11696). This makes fake news detection models more robust against the passage of time and potentially more effective in mitigating the bias.

WikiD+Del: Words tagged with PER labels are replaced by the same rule as WikiD, and words tagged with other NEs are removed.

WikiD+NER: Words tagged with PER labels are replaced by the same rule as WikiD, and words tagged with other NEs are replaced with the corresponding label.

4.2 Experimental Setting

We verify the effectiveness of masking methods for fake news detection. We examine how well the detection models perform with each of the masking methods against in-domain and out-of-domain for all datasets. Our in-domain experiments mainly investigate the effect of each masking method on accuracy in the same domain. Our out-of-domain experiments validate the effect of each masking method in datasets with considering the flow of time. We consider that out-of-domain setting is close to reality and useful whether each masking method is effective against diachronic bias.

Model: Our experiments utilize a pretrained model, $\text{BERT}_{\text{BASE}}$ model (Devlin et al., 2019), which is made freely available by Google. Labels (LOC, Q11696, etc.) replaced by each masking method were handled as new tokens during the fine-tuning of the pretrained model.

Data and Evaluation: Each dataset is randomly divided into training (80%) and test (20%) sets. The time-based splitting is suitable for our experimental settings than the random splitting in each dataset. However, it was difficult for us to apply the time-based splitting for in-domain experiment because the published time is not described in most of the samples[2]. Out-of-domain experimental settings mean the same verification as the time-based splitting. For example, the evaluation of models, trained in MultiFC consisting of events in 2015, on Constraint consisting of events in 2020 is equivalent to time-based splitting.

4.3 Experimental Results and Discussions

4.3.1 In-domain data

Table 2 presents the accuracies of each masking method against the in-domain data. No Mask, with no application of the masking method, achieved the highest accuracy in all datasets except Constraint. On the other hand, WikiD achieved the highest accuracy on Constraint. In addition, there was only a slight difference in accuracy between No Mask and the other masking methods, even in the datasets where No Mask had the highest accuracy. These results suggest that these masking methods result in insignificant decrease in accuracy when tested with the in-domain dataset.

4.3.2 Out-of-domain data

Table 3 presents the accuracies of each masking method against the out-of-domain data. For almost all of the out-of-domain test data, each masking method achieved higher accuracy than No Mask.

[2]In appendix G, we also conduct an experiment using MultiFC, which contains the published time, with a time-based splitting in train and test sets for trying to remove the effect of domain shift.

Method	Test set			
	MultiFC	Horne17	Celebrity	Constraint
No Mask	**0.681**	**0.746**	**0.760**	0.960
NE Del	0.656	0.706	0.750	0.959
Basic NER	0.659	0.735	0.750	0.950
WikiD	0.675	0.725	0.730	**0.967**
WikiD+Del	0.660	0.706	0.700	0.959
WikiD+NER	0.660	0.640	0.730	0.957

Table 2: Accuracy of each masking method against in-domain data. Bold indicate the highest accuracies.

Results of No Mask indicate the difficulty of adapting to out-of-domain data. For example, the model trained on Constraint achieved a high accuracy of 0.967 on Constraint (refer to Table 2); however, the model trained on datasets except Constraint achieved low accuracies, ranging from 0.48 to 0.58 on the same test set. These results imply the difficulty of generalizing the fake news detection model. NE Del achieved the same of higher accuracy than No Mask in 9 out of 12 settings, although it is the simplest masking method. In particular, NE Del trained on Horne17 achieved the highest accuracy for MultiFC and Celebrity among models trained on Horne17. Although Basic NER trained on Horne17 also achieved the highest accuracy for Constraint, the improvement was smaller compared to that of NE Del.

Wikidata-based masking methods WikiD and WikiD+Del achieved higher accuracy compared to No Mask in 9 settings, except when testing with Celebrity test set. In particular, the accuracies in WikiD have statistically significant improvements in 6 settings, compared to No Mask. For example, the model trained on MultiFC achieved a significant improvement in accuracy from 0.530 (No Mask) to 0.689 (WikiD), against Constraint test set. These results reveal that the masking method using Wikidata could mitigate the diachronic bias and build robust models even for out-of-domain data. In appendix H, we show some examples, which WikiD accurately classifies while No Mask makes the wrong classification. However, against Celebrity test set, whose domain is entertainment, the accuracy of No Mask is almost the same as that of these masking methods. We consider that this is due to the non-applicability of Wikidata owing to the difference in domain between Celebrity and other datasets; 53.6% of Wikidata labels of Horne17 were found in MultiFC, while only 33.6% of those were found in Celebrity (refer to Appendix E). Additionally, WikiD+NER has comparatively lower accuracies than WikiD+Del. This indicates that we can build a more robust model by removing entities other than person names. We believe that the model can focus on stylistic features by removing extra entity information.

Train set	Method	Test set			
		MultiFC	Horne17	Celebrity	Constraint
MultiFC	No Mask	-	0.706	**0.660**	0.530
	NE Del	-	0.706	0.590	*0.664
	Basic NER	-	0.725	0.600	*0.680
	WikiD	-	**0.746**	0.590	***0.689**
	WikiD+Del	-	0.725	**0.660**	*0.669
	WikiD+NER	-	0.632	0.520	*0.667
Horne17	No Mask	0.504	-	0.670	0.481
	NE Del	***0.551**	-	**0.680**	*0.553
	Basic NER	0.523	-	0.670	***0.563**
	WikiD	*0.525	-	0.620	0.487
	WikiD+Del	0.523	-	0.610	0.515
	WikiD+NER	0.500	-	0.630	*0.531
Celebrity	No Mask	0.533	0.451	-	0.583
	NE Del	0.545	0.529	-	***0.763**
	Basic NER	0.521	0.549	-	0.568
	WikiD	***0.555**	*0.549	-	*0.724
	WikiD+Del	0.534	0.529	-	*0.663
	WikiD+NER	0.525	***0.568**	-	0.598
Constraint	No Mask	0.542	0.568	0.580	-
	NE Del	0.531	0.588	0.570	-
	Basic NER	0.543	0.568	0.580	-
	WikiD	***0.556**	0.607	0.570	-
	WikiD+Del	0.544	**0.627**	**0.590**	-
	WikiD+NER	0.549	0.607	0.570	-

Table 3: Accuracy of out-of-domain data. The leftmost column lists the training set, and each column with accuracy corresponds to each test set. We applied the statistical significance test by McNemar's test (Dror et al., 2018) with Bonferroni correction to each method compared to No Mask. * indicates the significant difference over No Mask ($p < 0.05$).

5 Conclusion

This study proposed a new bias concept, Diachronic Bias, caused by the difference in the creation period of various fake news datasets. We firstly examined the deviation of phrase appearance in respective fake news detection datasets with different creation periods. We then proposed masking methods using Wikidata to mitigate the influence of person names. These masking methods achieved higher accuracy in out-of-domain datasets and showed to be made a model more robust.

In the future, more sophisticated approaches such as utilizing a knowledge graph to mitigate diachronic bias would be considered for fake news detection models. In addition to diachronic bias, political bias and racial bias are likely to exist in fake news detection datasets; clarifying these biases in detail is an important next research direction.

References

Alan Akbik, Tanja Bergmann, and Roland Vollgraf. 2019. Pooled contextualized embeddings for named entity recognition. In *Proc. of NAACL*, pages 724–728.

Alan Akbik, Duncan Blythe, and Roland Vollgraf. 2018. Contextual string embeddings for sequence labeling. In *Proc. of COLING*, pages 1638–1649.

Isabelle Augenstein, Christina Lioma, Dongsheng Wang, Lucas Chaves Lima, Casper Hansen, Christian Hansen, and Jakob Grue Simonsen. 2019. Multifc: A real-world multi-domain dataset for evidence-based fact checking of claims. In *Proc. of EMNLP-IJCNLP*, pages 4677–4691.

Reuben Binns, Michael Veale, Max Van Kleek, and Nigel Shadbolt. 2017. Like trainer, like bot? inheritance of bias in algorithmic content moderation. In *Proc. of SocInfo*, pages 405–415.

Alexandre Bovet and Hernán A Makse. 2019. Influence of fake news in twitter during the 2016 us presidential election. *Nature Commun*, 10(1):1–14.

CNBC. 2013. False rumor of explosion at white house causes stocks to briefly plunge; ap confirms its twitter feed was hacked. https://www.cnbc.com/id/100646197.

Erenay Dayanik and Sebastian Padó. 2020. Masking actor information leads to fairer political claims detection. In *Proc. of ACL*.

Jacob Devlin, Ming-Wei Chang, Kenton Lee, and Kristina Toutanova. 2019. BERT: Pre-training of deep bidirectional transformers for language understanding. In *Proc. of NAACL*, pages 4171–4186.

Rotem Dror, Gili Baumer, Segev Shlomov, and Roi Reichart. 2018. The hitchhiker's guide to testing statistical significance in natural language processing. In *Proc. of ACL*, pages 1383–1392.

Stefan Evert. 2005. The statistics of word cooccurrences: word pairs and collocations.

Takako Hashimoto, David Lawrence Shepard, Tetsuji Kuboyama, Kilho Shin, Ryota Kobayashi, and Takeaki Uno. 2020. Analyzing temporal patterns of topic diversity using graph clustering. *The Journal of Supercomputing*, pages 1–14.

Benjamin Horne and Sibel Adali. 2017. This just in: Fake news packs a lot in title, uses simpler, repetitive content in text body, more similar to satire than real news. In *Proc. of ICWSM*, volume 11.

Ji Ho Park, Jamin Shin, and Pascale Fung. 2018. Reducing gender bias in abusive language detection. In *Proc. of EMNLP*, pages 2799–2804.

Parth Patwa, Shivam Sharma, Srinivas PYKL, Vineeth Guptha, Gitanjali Kumari, Md Shad Akhtar, Asif Ekbal, Amitava Das, and Tanmoy Chakraborty. 2020. Fighting an infodemic: Covid-19 fake news dataset. *arXiv:2011.03327*.

Verónica Pérez-Rosas, Bennett Kleinberg, Alexandra Lefevre, and Rada Mihalcea. 2018. Automatic detection of fake news. In *Proc. of COLING*, pages 3391–3401.

Björn Ross, Michael Rist, Guillermo Carbonell, Benjamin Cabrera, Nils Kurowsky, and Michael Wojatzki. 2017. Measuring the reliability of hate speech annotations: The case of the european refugee crisis. *arXiv:1701.08118*.

Maarten Sap, Dallas Card, Saadia Gabriel, Yejin Choi, and Noah A Smith. 2019. The risk of racial bias in hate speech detection. In *Proc. of ACL*, pages 1668–1678.

Ana Lucía Schmidt, Fabiana Zollo, Michela Del Vicario, Alessandro Bessi, Antonio Scala, Guido Caldarelli, H Eugene Stanley, and Walter Quattrociocchi. 2017. Anatomy of news consumption on facebook. In *Proc. Natl. Acad. Sci. USA*, volume 114, pages 3035–3039.

Tal Schuster, Darsh Shah, Yun Jie Serene Yeo, Daniel Roberto Filizzola Ortiz, Enrico Santus, and Regina Barzilay. 2019. Towards debiasing fact verification models. In *Proc. of EMNLP-IJCNLP*, pages 3410–3416.

Gautam Kishore Shahi, Anne Dirkson, and Tim A Majchrzak. 2020. An exploratory study of covid-19 misinformation on twitter. *arXiv preprint arXiv:2005.05710*.

Gautam Kishore Shahi and Durgesh Nandini. 2020. FakeCovid – a multilingual cross-domain fact check news dataset for covid-19. In *Workshop Proc. of ICWSM*.

Kai Shu, Suhang Wang, Dongwon Lee, and Huan Liu. 2020. Mining disinformation and fake news: Concepts, methods, and recent advancements. *arXiv:2001.00623*.

Sandeep Suntwal, Mithun Paul, Rebecca Sharp, and Mihai Surdeanu. 2019. On the importance of delexicalization for fact verification. In *Proc. of EMNLP-IJCNLP*, pages 3404–3409.

Maximilian Wich, Jan Bauer, and Georg Groh. 2020. Impact of politically biased data on hate speech classification. In *Proc. of the Fourth Workshop on Online Abuse and Harms*, pages 54–64.

Michael Wiegand, Josef Ruppenhofer, and Thomas Kleinbauer. 2019. Detection of Abusive Language: the Problem of Biased Datasets. In *Proc. of NAACL*, pages 602–608.

Wikidata. https://www.wikidata.org/wiki/Wikidata. (accessed Dec 20, 2020).

A Overview of datasets

The domains and the number of samples for each label in each dataset are listed in Table 4. We do not use the validation set in our experiments because the number of samples in Horne17 and Celebrity is small.

Table 4: Overview of datasets

Dataset	Domain	Year	Real	Fake
MultiFC	Multi	2007–2015	3803	4058
Horne17	Political	2016	128	123
Celebrity	Entertainment	2016–2017	250	250
Constraint	COVID-19	2020	5600	5100

B LMI in Horne17 and Celebrity

Table 5 shows the top LMI-ranked bi-grams that are highly correlated with each label in Horne17 and Celebrity. The result indicates that fake labels in Horne17 and Celebrity have a high correlation with the celebrity's name, such as "brad pitt" and "kate middleton" as well as "donald trump" and "hillary clinton." On the other hand, real labels have a high correlation with common phrases such as "i had" and "would be." These four datasets have a tendency to be highly correlated between person names and fake labels and between common phrases and real labels.

Horne17					
Real			Fake		
Bi-gram	**LMI**	$p(l\|w)$	**Bi-gram**	**LMI**	$p(l\|w)$
trump has	112	0.82	**donald trump**	605	0.42
national security	106	0.88	**hillary clinton**	440	0.50
would be	104	0.72	i think	292	0.68
people who	92	0.89	united states	258	0.51
transition team	88	1.0	have been	230	0.41
mr. trump	80	0.94	**bill clinton**	208	0.70
smug style	77	1.0	we are	206	0.56
george w.	76	0.90	**hillary clinton's**	187	0.58
republican party	76	0.91	**president obama**	171	0.55
new york	70	0.77	**ted cruz**	149	0.80

Celebrity					
Real			Fake		
Bi-gram	**LMI**	$p(l\|w)$	**Bi-gram**	**LMI**	$p(l\|w)$
i think	233	0.90	has been	343	0.55
i donť	164	0.95	do think	214	0.80
they were	102	0.70	an insider	199	0.88
i had	100	0.94	**brad pitt**	163	0.63
so i	100	0.92	insider told	157	0.90
but i	87	0.79	may have	128	0.85
we were	87	0.89	**kate middleton**	124	0.88
what i	75	0.87	they are	122	0.51
i love	70	0.92	**the weeknd**	119	0.62
when i	69	0.92	**kanye west**	113	0.56

Table 5: Top 10 LMI ranked bi-grams in Horne17 and Celebrity datasets for real and fake labels with their $p(l|w)$. **LMI** are written as value multiplied by 10^6. Person names are written in bold.

C Wikidata for masking methods

We utilized Wikidata corresponding to the creation time of the articles and posts in each dataset. Specifically, we utilized Wikidata released on January 4, 2016, for MultiFC, January 15, 2018, for Horne17 and Celebrity, and December 28, 2020, for Constraint.

D Examples of outputs by each masking method

Table 6 lists outputs by the masking methods.

E Relationship between Wikidata labels in each dataset

Table 8 presents the coverage rate of Wikidata label between each dataset. Each percentage value represents the number of Wikidata labels in the dataset in the left column covered by Wikidata labels in other datasets. The MultiFC and Horne17 datasets have a high coverage rate because they contain articles and posts on the same political topics. On the other hand, the coverage of the Celebrity dataset is lower than that of the other datasets owing to the entertainment domain. Table 9 presents the top-3 appearance ranked Wikidata label in each dataset.

F Implementation Details

Our experimental code is public in `https://github.com/hkefka385/mitigation_diachronic_fake`.

Hyperparameters Hyperparameters for training our model are as below: learning rate is 1.0×10^{-5}, batch size is 16 and sentence length is 512. We selected the initial value in huggingface library (one of the python libraries) as hyperparameters, based on the empirical rule that fine-tuning works well in our dataset.

Training Efficiency Since our model has the same architecture as BERT (Devlin et al., 2019) except for new tokens that are added for new labels, it holds approximately 110M parameters. We use a Quadro RTX 8000 GPU to train our model. Training our model takes 3 epochs (about 1 hour) for MultiFC and Constraint datasets, and 8 epochs (about 20 minutes) for Horne17 and Celebrity datasets.

No Mask	18 states including **US UK** and **Australia** request PM **Modi** to head a task force to stop coronavirus
NE Del	18 states including and request PM to head a task force to stop coronavirus
Basic NER	18 states including **LOC LOC** and **LOC** request PM **PER** to head a task force to stop coronavirus
WikiD	18 states including **US UK** and **Australia** request PM **Q22337580** to head a task force to stop coronavirus
WikiD+Del	18 states including and request PM **Q22337580** to head a task force to stop coronavirus
WikiD+NER	18 states including **LOC LOC** and **LOC** request PM **Q22337580** to head a task force to stop coronavirus

Table 6: Example fake news with the application of masking methods. PER label is represented by squares and other **NE label** is represented in bold. In Wikidata, Q22337580 indicates Chief Minister of Gujarat.

Dataset	Text	Label
Horne17	**Trump** wins Electoral College vote as insurgency fizzles WASHINGTON - **Donald Trump** will - officially - become president next month. Trump surpassed the 270 electoral votes ...	Real
Constraint	How many FROM covid 19? How many died because New York and New Jersey screwed the elderly?? Thats all **trumps** fault right? When **trump** shut down travelhe a racist **Trump** puts a team together to figure out the virusits not diverse enough	Fake
Constraint	**AG Barr** Suggests an End to the Coronavirus Lockdown URL	Fake

Table 7: Some examples, which WikiD trained on MultiFC accurately classifies while No Mask trained on MultiFC makes the wrong classification. These examples include politicians such as "Donald Trump" and "William Barr".

	MultiFC	Horne17	Celebrity	Constraint
MultiFC	-	37.4%	29.4%	30.1%
Horne17	53.6%	-	36.4%	39.9%
Celebrity	38.9%	33.6%	-	33.6%
Constraint	35.3%	34.1%	28.6%	-

Table 8: Coverage rate of Wikidata label between each dataset. These percentage values indicate how much of Wikidata labels in the data listed in the left-most column is contained in other datasets.

Rank	MultiFC	Horne17	Celebrity	Constraint
1	President of the U.S.	President of the U.S.	actor	President of the U.S.
2	U.S. representative	Attorney General of Arkansas	singer	CEO
3	Secretary of State	Secretary of State	television actor	Mayor of London

Table 9: Top-3 ranked appearances in Wikidata label of each dataset

Method	Test set: MultiFC (2016-2018)
No Mask	0.639
NE Del	0.659
Basic NER	0.639
WikiD	*0.664
WikiD+Del	***0.671**
WikiD+NER	0.644

Table 10: Accuracy of each masking method against MultiFC test set (2016-2018). Bold indicates the highest accuracy.

G Experiments on time-based splitting of MultiFC

Not only in-domain and out-of-domain experimental settings, but we also conduct an experiment based on time-based splitting of MultiFC into train and test sets. The time-based experimental setting is similar to the intent of out-of-domain experimental settings (refer to Sec.4.3.2). It intends to verify the effect of each masking method in the same dataset for trying to remove more of the effects of domain shift. The experimental setting can not be applied to other datasets because only MultiFC has the published time of each sample. We set samples published in 2012–2015 as train set (3508 samples) and samples published in 2016–2018 as test set (2389 samples).

Table 10 presents the accuracies of each masking method against MultiFC test set (2016-2018). Same as out-of-domain experiments, almost masking methods achieved higher accuracy than No Mask. This show that the masking method using Wikidata could mitigate the diachronic bias and build robust models even for time-based splitting of a dataset.

H Some examples of dataset

In Table 7, we show some examples, which WikiD trained on MultiFC accurately classifies while No Mask trained on MultiFC makes the wrong classification.

Understanding the Impact of UGC Specificities on Translation Quality

José Carlos Rosales Núñez[1,2,3] **Djamé Seddah**[3] **Guillaume Wisniewski**[4]
[1] CNRS, LISN [2] Université Paris-Saclay
[3] Inria Paris [4] Université de Paris, LLF, CNRS
jose.rosales@limsi.fr djame.seddah@inria.fr
guillaume.wisniewski@univ-paris-diderot.fr

Abstract

This work takes a critical look at the evaluation of user-generated content automatic translation, the well-known specificities of which raise many challenges for MT. Our analyses show that measuring the average-case performance using a standard metric on a UGC test set falls far short of giving a reliable image of the UGC translation quality. That is why we introduce a new data set for the evaluation of UGC translation in which UGC specificities have been manually annotated using a fine-grained typology. Using this data set, we conduct several experiments to measure the impact of different kinds of UGC specificities on translation quality, more precisely than previously possible.

1 Introduction

This work takes a critical look at the evaluation of user-generated content (UGC) automatic translation. The well-known specificities of UGC (high rate of OOVs, rare, grammatical constructs, ...) raise many challenges for Machine Translation and has been the topic of many recent works (Rosales Núñez et al., 2019; Specia et al., 2020).

Several UGC parallel corpora (Michel and Neubig, 2018a; Rosales Núñez et al., 2019) have been introduced to evaluate the robustness of MT, some of which, such as (Fujii et al., 2020), are specially annotated to identify UGC idiosyncrasies allowing to measure the impact of a given specificity. Our analyses (§2), indeed, show that measuring the average-case performance using a standard metric on a UGC test set falls far short of giving a reliable image of the UGC translation quality: explaining the observed performance gap requires a particular evaluation framework made of tailored metrics and specific test sets in which UGC idiosyncrasies have been precisely annotated.

That is why, following this line of works, we introduce `PMUMT`, a new parallel data set for the evaluation of UGC translation between French and English in which UGC specificities have been manually annotated using a fine-grained typology. `PMUMT` is larger, relies on a more refined error typology and, more importantly, its annotations are more detailed than existing noisy parallel corpora. Its annotation scheme enables us to generate automatically parallel corpora in which the kind and number of UGC specificities are precisely controlled. Contrary to many works studying the robustness of NMT systems by adding artificial noise to canonical corpora, `PMUMT` is made of attested UGC examples.

Using this framework, we conduct several experiments on three out-of-the-box NMT architectures in a zero-shot scenario, to measure more precisely than what was possible before the impact of the different kinds of UGC specificities on translation quality. Surprisingly enough, our experiments (§3) on natural data show that out-of-the-box models exhibit unexpected strong robustness against several kinds of noise, questioning several results reported in the literature (Michel and Neubig, 2018a; Belinkov and Bisk, 2018). We believe that this data set and its associated evaluation framework will pave the way for a better understanding of the interactions at play in neural machine translation of noisy user-generated content contexts.

2 Testing Out-of-the-Box NMT models on UGC

2.1 Experimental Setting

Training Data Because of the lack of a large parallel data set of noisy sentences, we train our systems on 'standard' parallel data sets: `WMT` (Bojar et al., 2016) and `OpenSubtitles` (Lison et al., 2018). The former contains canonical texts (2.2M sent.) and the latter (9.2M sent.) is made of informal dialogues found in popular sitcoms.

Proceedings of the 2021 EMNLP Workshop W-NUT: The Seventh Workshop on Noisy User-generated Text, pages 189–198
November 11, 2021. ©2021 Association for Computational Linguistics

↓ Metric / Test set →	PFSMB†	PMUMT†	MTNT†	4SQ†	NewsTest	OpenSubsTest
3-gram KL-Div	1.563	1.442	0.471	0.500	0.406	0.006
%OOV	12.63	11.47	6.78	3,46	3.81	0.76
PPL	599.48	596.12	318.24	293.67	288.83	62.06

Table 1: Domain-related measure on the source side (FR), between used Test sets and other noisy UGC corpora using OpenSubtitles as training set. Dags indicate UGC corpora. *4SQ is the 4Square UGC data set introduced in (Berard et al., 2019). PPL: perplexity, KL-Div: Kullback-Leibler divergence.*

	WMT				OpenSubtitles			
	PFSMB†	MTNT†	News◇	OpenTest	PFSMB†	MTNT†	News	OpenTest◇
BPE-based models								
Seq2seq	9.9	21.8	27.5	14.7	17.1	27.2	19.6	28.2
+ <UNK> rep.	**17.1**	**24.0**	**29.1**	**16.4**	26.1	**28.5**	24.5	28.2
Transformer	15.4	21.2	27.4	**16.4**	**27.5**	28.3	**26.7**	**31.4**
Character-based models								
char2char	7.1	13.9	18.1	8.8	23.8	25.7	17.8	26.3

Table 2: BLEU scores for our models. The † symbol indicates the UGC test sets, and ◇ in-domain test sets.

UGC Test Sets To evaluate the different NMT models, we consider two data sets of manually translated UGC: MTNT (Michel and Neubig, 2018a) and the Parallel French Social Media Bank corpus (PFSMB) (Rosales Núñez et al., 2019)[1] which extends the French Social Media Bank (Seddah et al., 2012) with English translations. These two data sets raise many challenges for MT systems: they notably contain characters that have not been seen in the training data (e.g. emojis), rare character sequences (e.g. inconsistent casing or usernames) as well as many OOVs denoting URL, mentions, hashtags or more generally named entities (NE). Most of the time, OOVs are exactly the same in the source and target sentences.

NMT Models[2] In our experiments, we use three translation models. The first two models are standard NMT models that take as input BPE tokenized sentences: the model used in (Michel and Neubig, 2018a), a Seq2seq bi-LSTM architecture with global attention decoding as implemented in XNMT (Neubig et al., 2018) as well as a vanilla Transformer model as implemented in the OpenNMT toolkit (Klein et al., 2018).

We also consider a char-based model, namely the char2char of Lee et al. (2017). Using char-based models which are, by nature, open-vocabulary to translate UGC is intuitively appealing as these models are designed specifically to address the problem of translating OOVs and to deal with noisy input (Belinkov and Bisk, 2018).

As the Seq2seq model we consider in our experiments is not able to translate OOVs, we introduce, as part of our translation pipeline, a post-processing step in which the translation hypothesis is aligned with the source and <UNK> tokens are replaced by their aligned source token. In the case of our Transformer model, OPENNMT performs this automatically.

2.2 Results

Table 2 reports the BLEU scores (Papineni et al., 2002)[3] of the different models we consider both on canonical and non-canonical test sets. Contrary to the first results of Michel and Neubig (2018a), the quality of UGC translation does not appear to be so bad: the drop in performance observed on non-canonical corpora is of the same order of magnitude as the drop observed when translating out-of-domain data.

These results seem to indicate that, counter-intuitively, translating UGC does not raise any specific challenges. We however believe that they are biased by the evaluation metric used: as UGC contains many mentions, URLs emoticons, or named entities that are the same in the source and in the target sentence, BLEU scores estimated on a canonical and on a non-canonical can not be directly compared: BLEU scores on non-canonical data are artificially high as systems are rewarded for simply coping source tokens, which is the most natural

[1] https://gitlab.inria.fr/seddah/parallel-french-social-mediabank

[2] Models parameters are detailed in the appendix.

[3] All BLEU scores are calculated by Post (2018)'s SacreBleu using the *intl* tokenization

solution to translate OOVs. For instance, the BLEU score between the *sources* and references of the PFSMB is 15.1 while it is only 2.7 on the WMT test set. That is why, we believe that the usual MT metrics overestimate the translation quality on UGC and we introduce, in the next section, a new corpus and a new way to measure the real impact of UGC specificities on translation quality.

3 Analyzing the Impact of UGC on Translation Quality

In order to understand the impact of UGC specificities on translation quality, we have annotated a new corpus in which UGC peculiarities are identified in each source sentence and 'normalized' to a canonical form.

3.1 A Corpus Annotated with UGC Specificities

The PMUMT corpus To understand the impact of UGC peculiarities, we manually annotated 400 source sentences sampled from the PFSMB: one of the authors, fluent in French and with good knowledge of UGC, has identified spans in the sentence that differ from canonical French and characterized these specificities using the fine-grained typology of Sanguinetti et al. (2020) (see Table 4). Since the whole annotation process was done by a single person, no inter-annotator agreement can be calculated. Nevertheless, results of our pilot study for each individual UGC peculiarity (cf. Table 3 and Table A.3 in the Appendix, for a cross-metrics analysis), show that MT performance consistently performs better on our normalized corpus than on the original noisy set.

Each span containing an UGC specificity has been 'normalized' to a form closer to canonical French.[4] Table A.1 shows some examples of annotated (source) sentence. A normalized form of each target (i.e. English) sentence has also been produced to ensures that the target can be generated from the 'normalized' source.

In the end, the annotation of this corpus represents 200h of work, comprising an iterative improvement and debugging of the annotations to achieve the corpus' current version.[5]

The resulting corpus contains more than 1,310 annotations. On average, each sentence contains 2.8 UGC peculiarities. Figure 1 describes the distribution of UGC peculiarities in the corpus.

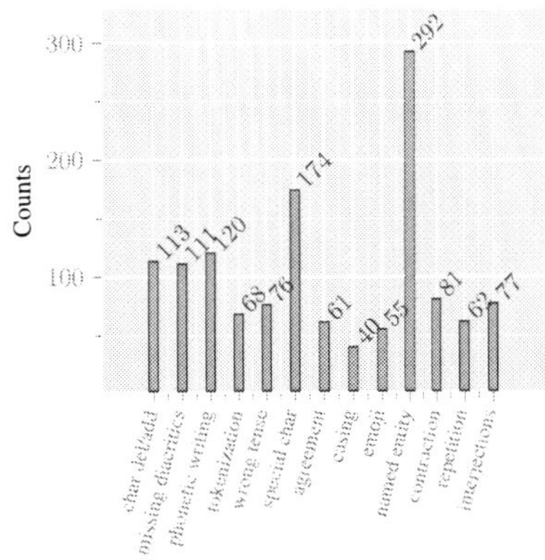

Figure 1: Distribution of UGC specificites of the FR UGC sources in PMUMT.

Controlling the Number of Specificities per Sentence Comparing the predictions of an NLP system taking either the normalized sentences or the original non-canonical sentences as input allows us to measure the impact of UGC on this system. However, it is impossible to perform a fine-grained analysis in which, for example, the impact of different types of specificities are compared, since UGC sentences generally contain several specificities of different types and the interactions between them cannot be easily neutralized.

That is why we have also constructed automatically a second version of our corpus to help us analyze the interactions between the UGC specificities in a sentence: by substituting only some of the span we have annotated, we can create corpora in which the number and the kind of specificities present in each sentence is tightly controlled. In this framework, each original sentence can be (partially) rewritten into as many sentences as there are UGC specificities in it.

This possibility of partial substitution greatly reduces the amount of data to be annotated for our analyses: instead of having to annotate a large amount of data to find enough sentences fulfilling the requested criteria, we are able to generate these

[4]To ensure that this normalization has actually made our corpus closer to a canonical corpus, we have computed the perplexity of the original sentences and of the normalized sentences estimated by a 5-gram Kneser-Ney language model trained on the OpenSubtitles corpus: the normalized version has a perplexity of 2,214 (and 11.60% of its token are OOVs) far lower that the original version (with a perplexity of 8,546 and an OOV ratio of 19.60%).

[5]The annotated corpus and code collection can be found in https://github.com/josecar25/PMUMT_annotated_UGC_corpus/

	char del/add	missing diacritics	phonetic writing	tokenization	wrong tense	special char	agreement	casing	emoji	named entity	contraction	repetition	interjections
s2s	0.80 (28.7)	0.95 (33.9)	0.93 (27.3)	0.96 (30.8)	0.94 (30.7)	0.88 (26.1)	0.95 (27.1)	0.75 (27.7)	0.91 (31.0)	0.86 (31.7)	0.95 (30.8)	0.90 (30.2)	0.93 (29.2)
c2c	0.99 (32.5)	0.99 (29.6)	0.86 (25.2)	1.00 (31.9)	0.97 (28.8)	0.81 (24.6)	0.96 (28.9)	0.86 (28.0)	0.83 (26.2)	0.94 (32.7)	0.91 (30.4)	0.95 (26.2)	0.91 (28.7)
TX	0.98 (35.3)	1.02 (34.0)	1.03 (33.2)	0.98 (32.9)	1.02 (33.7)	0.92 (29.2)	0.97 (33.8)	0.90 (26.9)	0.75 (28.3)	0.99 (35.4)	0.93 (31.1)	0.89 (36.8)	0.86 (30.2)

Table 3: BLEU score ratios between pairs of noisy and normalized sets of sentences, containing only one UGC specificity. BLEU scores on noisy sets are shown in parenthesis.

code	kind of specificities
1	Letter deletion/addition
2	Missing diacritics
3	Phonetic writing
4	Tokenisation error
5	Wrong verb tense
6	#; @, URL
7	Wrong gender/grammatical number
8	Inconsistent casing
9	Emoji
10	Named Entity
11	Contraction
12	Graphemic/punctuation stretching
13	Interjections

Table 4: Typology of UGC specificities used in our manual annotation.

sentences from our original annotation of 400 sentences. We believe that this approach could be of great interest to perform fine-grained error analysis for NLP systems dealing with UGC.

3.2 Impact of UGC Peculiarities on Translation Quality

We used the PMUMT corpus to evaluate the impact of UGC peculiarities on translation quality: we have reported in Table 5 the BLEU scores achieved by the considered systems on both the 400 original sentences and the 400 normalized sentences. As expected, translations of normalized sentences, that are more similar to the training data, are of better quality than translations of original (noisy) sentences: the BLEU scores achieved when translating normalized UGC content are close to those obtained on the in-domain test-set.

For all systems, considering the non-canonical original sentences results in a drop in translation quality of the same order of magnitude, which shows that, even if these models build sentence representations from completely different information, the presence of UGC peculiarities has a similar impact on all of them.

	original	normalized
`Seq2seq`	25.8	32.4
`char2char`	24.1	30.5
`Transformer`	28.6	33.6

Table 5: BLEU scores on the original and normalized source sentences of the PMUMT corpus.

Individual UGC Errors To get a more precise picture of the impact of UGC on translation quality, we have computed, for each kind of peculiarities, the BLEU scores achieved on the corpus built to contain only this peculiarity and the BLEU score computed on the 'normalized' version of the same sentences. Table 3 reports the ratio between these two scores (detailed results are reported in Table A.3 in the supplementary material).

The impact of a given kind of UGC specificity on translation quality is very different from one system to another: it appears that the source sentences representation that MT systems learn to construct are not sensitive to the same kind of noise or errors in the source sentence and even seem to be complementary. For instance, inconsistent casing strongly penalizes the `Seq2seq` model but has only a limited impact on the `char2char` model. On the contrary, the presence of characters specific to online conversation such as @ or # results in a substantial decrease of translation quality for `char2char`, but has less impact for `Seq2seq` or `Transformer`, suggesting that char-based models are not able to properly modeled characters that hardly appear in the training set.

Interestingly, the `Transformer` model appears to be very robust to a wide array of UGC peculiarities, even if it was not designed specifically to handle noisy inputs: in particular, the presence of named entities, spelling errors (i.e. substitution, deletion or insertion of letters), agreement error (of verb tense or in gender and number) as well as `tokenization` errors hardly hurt translation quality. Similarly, the `char2char` model succeed in translating correctly sentences with letter addition or suppression, showing that the model actually manage to learn sentence representations that are robust to spelling errors even if such errors are not present at training time. This results is at odd with the conclusion drawn by Belinkov and Bisk (2018) on artificial data.

Combination of Peculiarities To better understand the impact of combinations of UGC peculiarities on translation quality, Table 6 reports the ratio between the BLEU scores computed on the translation of a corpus in which there are exactly N different UGC peculiarities in a sentence and on the translation of the normalized version of these sentences. It appears that for all our systems translation quality decreases linearly with the number of specificities, suggesting that the impacts of the different specificities are independent of each other. Surprisingly enough, the gap between the `char2char` and `Transformer` is getting smaller with the number of specificities in each sentence.

	1	2	3	4+
# sents.	1,306	1,776	1,439	1,089
s2s	0.90 (30.1)	0.83 (27.0)	0.77 (24.2)	0.75 (23.2)
c2c	0.92 (29.5)	0.87 (26.6)	0.83 (24.3)	0.83 (23.2)
TX	0.96 (32.8)	0.89 (30.0)	0.86 (28.3)	0.84 (26.5)

Table 6: BLEU score ratio between pairs of normalized and noisy sentences containing N specificities. BLEU scores on noisy sentences are shown in parenthesis.

4 Conclusions

This work introduces PMUMT a new corpus of UGC translation in which UGC specificities are manually annotated using a fine-grained typology. Thanks to our detailed annotation process, we were able to build a new framework that allows us to automatically generate several parallel corpora in which the number and kind of UGC specificities is precisely controlled.

Our experiments show that, contrary to what was previously believed, out-of-the-box NMT models are robust to many different kind of UGC specificities and that the different architectures we tested are complementary, in the sense that they are not sensitive to the same specificities. In our future work, we plan to explore the intricacies of the robustness that seem to be linked to specific UGC idiosyncrasies. We make this data set and its associated evaluation framework public[6] as we believe it can pave the way for a better understanding of the interactions at play in neural machine translation of noisy user-generated content contexts.

Acknowledgments

We thank the reviewers for their valuable feedback. This work was funded by the French Research Agency via the ANR ParSiTi project (ANR-16-CE33-0021).

References

Yonatan Belinkov and Yonatan Bisk. 2018. Synthetic and natural noise both break neural machine translation. In *Proceedings of the 6th International Conference on Learning Representations, ICLR 2018, Vancouver, BC, Canada, April 30 - May 3, 2018, Conference Track Proceedings*.

Alexandre Berard, Ioan Calapodescu, Marc Dymetman, Claude Roux, Jean-Luc Meunier, and Vassilina Nikoulina. 2019. Machine translation of restaurant reviews: New corpus for domain adaptation and robustness. In *Proceedings of the 3rd Workshop on Neural Generation and Translation@EMNLP-IJCNLP 2019, Hong Kong, November 4, 2019*, pages 168–176. Association for Computational Linguistics.

Ondrej Bojar, Rajen Chatterjee, Christian Federmann, Yvette Graham, Barry Haddow, Matthias Huck, Antonio Jimeno-Yepes, Philipp Koehn, Varvara Logacheva, Christof Monz, Matteo Negri, Aurélie Névéol, Mariana L. Neves, Martin Popel, Matt Post, Raphael Rubino, Carolina Scarton, Lucia Specia, Marco Turchi, Karin M. Verspoor, and Marcos Zampieri. 2016. Findings of the 2016 conference on machine translation. In *Proceedings of the First Conference on Machine Translation, WMT 2016, colocated with ACL 2016, August 11-12, Berlin, Germany*, pages 131–198.

Ryo Fujii, Masato Mita, Kaori Abe, Kazuaki Hanawa, Makoto Morishita, Jun Suzuki, and Kentaro Inui. 2020. PheMT: A phenomenon-wise dataset for machine translation robustness on user-generated contents. In *Proceedings of the 28th International Con-*

[6]`https://github.com/josecar25/PMUMT_annotated_UGC_corpus/`

ference on Computational Linguistics, pages 5929–5943, Barcelona, Spain (Online). International Committee on Computational Linguistics.

Guillaume Klein, Yoon Kim, Yuntian Deng, Vincent Nguyen, Jean Senellart, and Alexander M. Rush. 2018. Opennmt: Neural machine translation toolkit. In *Proceedings of the 13th Conference of the Association for Machine Translation in the Americas, AMTA 2018, Boston, MA, USA, March 17-21, 2018 - Volume 1: Research Papers*, pages 177–184.

Philipp Koehn. 2004. Statistical significance tests for machine translation evaluation. In *Proceedings of the 2004 Conference on Empirical Methods in Natural Language Processing*, pages 388–395, Barcelona, Spain. Association for Computational Linguistics.

Jason Lee, Kyunghyun Cho, and Thomas Hofmann. 2017. Fully character-level neural machine translation without explicit segmentation. *TACL*, 5:365–378.

Pierre Lison, Jörg Tiedemann, and Milen Kouylekov. 2018. Opensubtitles2018: Statistical rescoring of sentence alignments in large, noisy parallel corpora. In *Proceedings of the Eleventh International Conference on Language Resources and Evaluation, LREC 2018, Miyazaki, Japan, May 7-12, 2018.*

Paul Michel and Graham Neubig. 2018a. MTNT: A testbed for machine translation of noisy text. In *Proceedings of the 2018 Conference on Empirical Methods in Natural Language Processing*, pages 543–553, Brussels, Belgium. Association for Computational Linguistics.

Paul Michel and Graham Neubig. 2018b. MTNT: A testbed for machine translation of noisy text. In *Proceedings of the 2018 Conference on Empirical Methods in Natural Language Processing, Brussels, Belgium, October 31 - November 4, 2018*, pages 543–553.

Graham Neubig, Matthias Sperber, Xinyi Wang, Matthieu Felix, Austin Matthews, Sarguna Padmanabhan, Ye Qi, Devendra Singh Sachan, Philip Arthur, Pierre Godard, John Hewitt, Rachid Riad, and Liming Wang. 2018. XNMT: the extensible neural machine translation toolkit. In *Proceedings of the 13th Conference of the Association for Machine Translation in the Americas, AMTA 2018, Boston, MA, USA, March 17-21, 2018 - Volume 1: Research Papers*, pages 185–192.

Kishore Papineni, Salim Roukos, Todd Ward, and Wei-Jing Zhu. 2002. Bleu: a method for automatic evaluation of machine translation. In *Proceedings of the 40th Annual Meeting of the Association for Computational Linguistics, July 6-12, 2002, Philadelphia, PA, USA*, pages 311–318. ACL.

Maja Popović. 2015. chrF: character n-gram F-score for automatic MT evaluation. In *Proceedings of the Tenth Workshop on Statistical Machine Translation*, pages 392–395, Lisbon, Portugal. Association for Computational Linguistics.

Matt Post. 2018. A call for clarity in reporting BLEU scores. In *Proceedings of the Third Conference on Machine Translation: Research Papers*, pages 186–191, Belgium, Brussels. Association for Computational Linguistics.

José Carlos Rosales Núñez, Djamé Seddah, and Guillaume Wisniewski. 2019. Comparison between NMT and PBSMT performance for translating noisy user-generated content. In *Proceedings of the 22nd Nordic Conference on Computational Linguistics*, pages 2–14, Turku, Finland. Linköping University Electronic Press.

Manuela Sanguinetti, Lauren Cassidy, Cristina Bosco, Özlem Çetinoglu, Alessandra Teresa Cignarella, Teresa Lynn, Ines Rehbein, Josef Ruppenhofer, Djamé Seddah, and Amir Zeldes. 2020. Treebanking user-generated content: a UD based overview of guidelines, corpora and unified recommendations. *CoRR*, abs/2011.02063.

Djamé Seddah, Benoît Sagot, Marie Candito, Virginie Mouilleron, and Vanessa Combet. 2012. The french social media bank: a treebank of noisy user generated content. In *COLING 2012, 24th International Conference on Computational Linguistics, Proceedings of the Conference: Technical Papers, 8-15 December 2012, Mumbai, India*, pages 2441–2458.

Lucia Specia, Zhenhao Li, Juan Pino, Vishrav Chaudhary, Francisco Guzmán, Graham Neubig, Nadir Durrani, Yonatan Belinkov, Philipp Koehn, Hassan Sajjad, Paul Michel, and Xian Li. 2020. Findings of the WMT 2020 shared task on machine translation robustness. In *Proceedings of the Fifth Conference on Machine Translation*, pages 76–91, Online. Association for Computational Linguistics.

Supplementary Materials

①	src	**JohnDoe389** (10) qui n'arrive pas **a** (2) **depasser** (2) 1 a (2) **FlappyBird** (10) ... **ptddddr** (12,13)
	ref	JohnDoe389 who can't score more than 1 at FlappyBird ... lmaooooo
	N. src	Jean qui n'arrive pas à dépasser 1 à Jean ...
	N. ref	Jean who can't score more than 1 at Jean...
②	src	**#CaMeVénèreQuand** (6) le matin **a** (2) 7h on me parle alors que je suis pas encore **réveiller.** (5)
	ref	#ItAnnoysMeWhen in the moring at 7 am someone talks to me although I didn't wake up yet.
	N. src	le matin à 7h on me parle alors que je suis pas encore réveillé.
	N. ref	in the moring at 7 am someone talks to me although I didn't wake up yet.
③	src	vu sa **tete** (2) **c** (3) normal **kon** (3) **est** (3) **jms** (11) **parler** (5) d'elle !
	ref	in light of her face it's normal no one ever spoke about her!
	N. src	vu sa tête c'est normal qu'on a jamais parlé d'elle !
	N. ref	in light of her face it's normal no one ever spoke about her!
④	src	y a ma cousine qui **joue a** (2) flappy bird (10) **mdrrrrrrrrrrr** (12, 13) **elle et plus nuuul** (12,7) **que moi**
	ref	my cousin plays flappy bird looooooooooool she's more hopeless than me
	N. src	y a ma cousine qui joue à Jean Jean elle et plus nulle que moi
	N. ref	my cousin plays Jean Jean she's more hopeless than me

Table A.1: Examples from our annotated noisy UGC corpus. Source sentences have been annotated with UGC specificities of Table 4 (in blue) according to their numerical code. For each example, the original source and reference (*src* and *ref*) and their corresponding normalized version (*N. src* and *N. ref*) are shown.

		Letter deletion/addition/change
①	src	j'arrive pas à **boir normalemen**
	norm	j'arrive pas à boire normalement
	ref	I can't **drink normally**
	s2s	I can't **drink normal.**
	c2c	I can't **drink normally.**
	Tx	I can't **drink normal men.**
②	src	Je conseille à **toux** ceux qui ont l'esprit disons, un peu fermé de regarder sur les "Français d'origine contrôlée"
	norm	Je conseille à tous ceux qui ont l'esprit disons, un peu fermé de regarder sur les "Français d'origine contrôlée"
	ref	I advise **everyone** with a, let's say a little narrow mind to watch about the "Français d'origine contrôlée"
	s2s	I suggest **cough** those who have minds say, a little closed to look at the "frances of controlled origins"
	c2c	I counsel **those** who have the mind, a little close to looking at the French original controlled original controlled.
	Tx	I advise **anyone** with a mind, say, a little closed to look at the controlled French.
⑤	src	le côté suis **tro cool** au quotidien et je **relach** tout **quan** j'ai bu
	norm	les gens qui m'aiment me détestent quand j'ai bu
	ref	my side **very cool** in everyday life and **loosen** everything **when** I've been drinking
	s2s	I've been drinking all the time and I've been drinking everything **quan** I've been drinking.
	c2c	the side of the daily **cool** side and **relacing** everything **when** I've been drinking
	Tx	I'm the **cool** side. I'm the cool one.
		Tokenization
⑥	src	**J'sais pas vous**, mais de voir la joie des grands joueurs comme Zlatan, Motta, Verratti je trouve ça magnifique
	norm	Je sais pas vous, mais de voir la joie des grands joueurs comme Jean, Jean, Jean je trouve ça magnifique
	ref	**I don't know about you**, but seeing the joy of great players like Zlatan, Motta, Verratti I think it's wonderful
	s2s	**I don't know you**, but seeing the joy of the great players like Zlatan, Motta, Verratti, I think it's beautiful.
	c2c	**I don't know about you**, but to see the joy of great players like Zlatan, Motta, Varratt, I think it's beautiful.
	Tx	**I don't know about you**, but seeing the joy of big players like Zlatan, Motta, Verratti, I think it's beautiful.
⑦	src	pendant que vous me laissez en chien à l'atelier mon score de flappy bird fait que **d augmenter**
	norm	pendant que vous me laissez en chien à l'atelier mon score de Jean fait que d'augmenter
	ref	while you're bailing out on me at the workshop my flappy bird score **is just increasing**
	s2s	when you leave me as a dog when you leave me as a dog at the workshop.
	c2c	while you leave me dog at the workshop my flappy bird score **is that increasing**
	Tx	while you leave me as a dog at the workshop my flappy bird score **is just up.**
⑧	src	il **ma** dit que c'était normal aussi et que ça allait redescendre,
	norm	il m'a dit que c'était normal aussi et que ça allait redescendre,
	ref	**he told me** it was normal too and that it would come down,
	s2s	**He said it** was normal, too, and it was going to go down,
	c2c	**He told me it** was normal, too, and it was going back,
	Tx	**He told me it** was normal, too, and it was gonna come down,
		Inconsistent casing
⑨	src	Jean **DANS VOS YEUX**
	norm	Jean dans vos yeux
	ref	Jean **IN YOUR EYES**
	s2s	Jean **D in VOSY**
	c2c	Jean **in your eyes**
	Tx	Jean **in your eyes**
⑩	src	**JE VIENS DE VOIR** Jean **ET** Jean **JE PEUX PLUS**
	norm	Je viens de voir Jean je peux plus
	ref	I JUST WATCHED Jean AND Jean CAN'T TAKE IT
	s2s	I'm going to kill Jean and Jean I can't believe it.
	c2c	I'm here to see Jean And Jean I can no longer.
	Tx	I just saw Jean and Jean again.
		Domain-specific characters and emojis
⓫	src	Avec mes magnifiques jumeaux Jean et Jean **@maxcarver @Charlie_Carver ♥**
	norm	Avec mes magnifiques jumeaux Jean et Jean
	ref	With my wonderful twins Jean and Jean **@maxcarver @Charlie_Carver ♥**
	s2s	with my gorgeous Jean and Jean **@maxarver @Carlie_Carver @Carlie_Carver #**
	c2c	with my beautiful Jean twins, Jean Jean and Jean **Charlier Charlier Carver.**
	Tx	with my beautiful twins Jean and Jean **imexcarver Charlie_Charver @Charver**

Table A.2: Examples from our noisy UGC corpus showing the `Transformer`, `char2char` and `Seq2seq` predictions. Present UGC specificities of Table 4 (in blue) are marked in bold.

As some of the data sets contain as few as 40 sentences, we have also computed the 95% confidence interval for all BLEU scores in Table A.3 using the bootstrapping method described in Koehn (2004). The width of all intervals is smaller than 0.30 for the BLEU scores (roughly 1% of the corresponding score) and than 0.006 for the ratios, which shows that we can trustfully compare their values.

Similarly, we have included results for the CHRF (Popović, 2015) and MULTI-BLEU-DETOK.PERL evaluation metrics since SACREBLEU showed a ratio between performances on noisy and clean text versions, indicating that the noisy version could be easier to translate than its normalization. In this regard, we can see in Table A.3 that at least one of the three reported metrics gives a ratio value equal or smaller than 1.0 within the 95% confidence interval error (CI Err.), suggesting that our normalization introduce limited artificial noise, comparable to the difference between correlated evaluation metrics.

	Metric	char del/add	missing diacritics	phonetic writing	tokenization	wrong tense	special char	agreement	casing	emoji	named entity	contraction	repetition	interjections
s2s	MB	0.78 (25.3)	0.94 (31.1)	0.92 (23.2)	0.95 (30.6)	0.98 (28.6)	0.83 (24.8)	0.95 (25.1)	0.77 (26.7)	0.87 (29.6)	0.87 (30.9)	0.91 (28.4)	0.83 (29.9)	0.90 (26.5)
	chrF	0.93 (46.7)	0.97 (53.1)	0.89 (43.1)	0.95 (50.9)	0.99 (50.6)	0.91 (44.3)	0.98 (49.3)	0.76 (40.2)	0.94 (51.1)	0.94 (51.7)	0.93 (47.3)	0.93 (47.3)	0.96 (48.0)
	SB	0.80 (28.7)	0.95 (33.9)	0.93 (27.3)	0.96 (30.8))	0.94 (30.7)	0.88 (26.1)	0.95 (27.1)	0.75 (27.7)	0.91 (31.0)	0.86 (31.7)	0.95 (30.8)	0.90 (30.2)	0.93 (29.2)
c2c	MB	1.00 (29.5)	1.00 (27.4)	0.85 (22.5)	0.99 (29.7)	0.97 (26.9)	0.80 (23.5)	0.97 (25.5)	0.91 (27.7)	0.83 (25.1)	0.95 (31.7)	0.88 (26.6)	0.93 (28.0)	0.91 (25.7)
	chrF	0.99 (48.5)	1.00 (50.6)	0.92 (44.8)	0.95 (50.1)	0.99 (49.1)	0.84 (44.0)	0.98 (49.9)	0.78 (40.6)	0.93 (49.5)	0.95 (51.6)	0.92 (48.8)	0.90 (47.8)	0.95 (49.7)
	SB	0.99 (32.5)	0.99 (29.6)	0.86 (25.2)	1.00 (31.9)	0.97 (28.8)	0.81 (24.6)	0.96 (28.9)	0.86 (28.0)	0.83 (26.2)	0.94 (32.7)	0.91 (30.4)	0.95 (26.2)	0.91 (28.7)
TX	MB	0.96 (30.3)	1.01 (33.0)	0.98 (33.2)	0.98 (31.5)	1.01 (31.6)	0.90 (28.4)	0.97 (31.4)	0.98 (25.8)	0.72 (26.7)	1.06 (35.7)	0.90 (28.4)	0.81 (25.9)	0.83 (27.0)
	chrF	0.95 (48.2)	1.00 (52.3)	0.98 (46.6)	0.99 (51.0)	1.01 (52.4)	0.93 (46.5)	0.97 (50.9)	0.80 (30.7)	0.88 (49.1)	1.00 (52.6)	0.93 (48.9)	0.87 (46.2)	0.92 (46.2)
	SB	0.98 (35.3)	1.02 (34.0)	1.03 (33.2)	0.98 (32.9)	1.02 (33.7)	0.92 (29.2)	0.97 (33.8)	0.90 (26.9)	0.75 (28.3)	0.99 (35.4)	0.93 (31.1)	0.89 (36.8)	0.86 (30.2)
CI Err.	(E-3)	4.5 (0.17)	1.5 (0.13)	2.7 (0.11)	2.6 (0.17)	2.4 (0.15)	1.8 (0.12)	1.7 (0.23)	5.7 (0.30)	3.0 (0.23)	2.2 (0.11)	2.2 (0.16)	2.5 (0.24)	3.1 (0.22)

Table A.3: BLEU score ratios between pairs of noisy and normalized sets of sentences, containing only one UGC specificity. BLEU scores on noisy sets are shown in parenthesis. *Three different metrics are shown for comparison:* `MultiBleu-detok.perl` *(MB),* `chrF` *and* `SacreBleu` *(SB).* Error for 95% confidence intervals (CI Err).

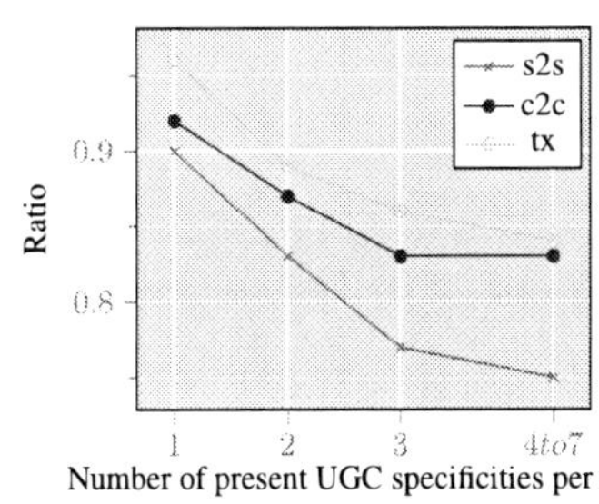

Figure A.1: Noisy/Clean BLEU scores' ratios for accumulated number of UGC specificities present per sentence for each model, corresponding to the results in Table 6. The *4to7* bin groups more than 4 types to provide a larger subcorpus, which weighted average is 4.34 UGC specificities per sentence.

A Reproducibility

Data All the UGC test sets and source code for our experiments are provided in the supplementary materials. For training data, we let the reader refer to each project's website for `WMT`[7] (consisting of `Europarlv7`, `Newcommentariesv10` and `Open Subtitles`[8], both accessed on November, 2019. Regarding clean test sets, we used `newstest15` from `WMT` and a subset of 11,000 unique phrases from `Open Subtitles`. We make the former test available in the link provided above for exact performance comparison.

Computation The NMT systems were trained using 1 Tesla V100, during an average of 72 hours to converge to the final solution for the `char2char` model and 56 hours for the BPE-based baselines.

A.1 NMT Models

Character-based models `char2char` models were trained as out-of-the box systems using the implementations provided by (Lee et al., 2017) .[9]

BPE-based models We consider, as baseline, two standard NMT models that take, as input, tokenized sentences. The first one is a `seq2seq` bi-LSTM architecture with global attention decoding. The `seq2seq` model was trained using the XNMT toolkit (Neubig et al., 2018).[10] It consists in a 2-layered Bi-LSTM layers encoder and 2-layered Bi-LSTM decoder. It considers, as input, word embeddings of 512 components and each LSTM units has 1,024 components.

We also study a vanilla Transformer model using the implementation proposed in the OpenNMT framework (Klein et al., 2018). It consists of 6 layers with word embeddings of 512 components, a feed-forward layers made of 2,048 units and 8 self-attention heads.

Hyper-parameters In Table A.4, we list the training variables set for our experiments. They match their corresponding default hyper-parameters.

Batch size	64
Optimizer	Adam
Learning rate	1e-4
Epochs	10 (best of)
Patience	2 epochs
Gradient clip	[-1.0, 1.0]

Table A.4: Hyper-parameters used for training the NMT systems.

Pre-processing For the BPE models, we used a 16K merging operations tokenization employing `sentencepiece`[11]. For word-level statistics we segmented the corpora using the `Moses` tokenizer [12].

[7] `https://www.statmt.org/wmt15/translation-task.html`

[8] `http://opus.nlpl.eu/download.php?f=OpenSubtitles/v2018/moses/en-fr.txt.zip`

[9] `https://github.com/nyu-dl/dl4mt-c2c`

[10] We decided to use XNMT, instead of OpenNMT in our experiments in order to compare our results to the ones of Michel and Neubig (2018b).

[11] `https://github.com/google/sentencepiece`

[12] `https://github.com/moses-smt/mosesdecoder`

Noisy UGC Translation at the Character Level: Revisiting Open-Vocabulary Capabilities and Robustness of Char-Based Models

José Carlos Rosales Núñez[1,2,4] Guillaume Wisniewski[3] Djamé Seddah[4]
[1] CNRS, LISN [2] Université Paris-Saclay
[3] Université de Paris, LLF, CNRS [4] Inria Paris
jose.rosales@limsi.fr guillaume.wisniewski@univ-paris-diderot.fr
djame.seddah@inria.fr

Abstract

This work explores the capacities of character-based Neural Machine Translation to translate noisy User-Generated Content (UGC) with a strong focus on exploring the limits of such approaches to handle productive UGC phenomena, which almost by definition, cannot be seen at training time. Within a strict zero-shot scenario, we first study the detrimental impact on translation performance of various user-generated content phenomena on a small annotated dataset we developed, and then show that such models are indeed incapable of handling unknown letters, which leads to catastrophic translation failure once such characters are encountered. We further confirm this behavior with a simple, yet insightful, copy task experiment and highlight the importance of reducing the vocabulary size hyper-parameter to increase the robustness of character-based models for machine translation.

1 Introduction

Neural Machine Translation (NMT) models fall far short from being able to translate noisy User-Generated Content (UGC): the quality of their translation is often even worse than that of a traditional phrase-based system (Khayrallah and Koehn, 2018; Rosales Núñez et al., 2019). In addition to ambiguous grammatical constructs and profusion of ellipsis, the main difficulty encountered when translating UGC is the high number of out-of-vocabulary tokens (OOVs) resulting from misspelled words, emoticons, hashtags, mentions, and all specific constructs used in online forums and social medias (Foster, 2010; Seddah et al., 2012; Eisenstein, 2013; Sanguinetti et al., 2020). Some of those phenomena can be perceived as noise while the others are typical markers of language variation among speakers. Moreover, a certain amount of those same phenomena operate at the lexical level (either at the character, subword or word levels) (Sanguinetti et al., 2020). This is why, focusing more on the noise axis, char-based models appear to offer a natural solution to this problem (Luong and Manning, 2016; Ling et al., 2015): indeed these open vocabulary models are designed specifically to address the OOV problem.

In this work, we explore the ability of out-of-the-box character-based NMT models (Lee et al., 2017) to address the challenges raised by UGC translation. While character-based models may seem promising for such task, to the best of our knowledge, they have only been tested either on data sets in which noise has been artificially added through sampling an edited word error data set (Belinkov and Bisk, 2018; Ebrahimi et al., 2018a) and on canonical data set, in which they prove to be very effective for translating morphologically-rich languages with a high number of OOVs (Luong and Manning, 2016).

However, our starting-points experiments show that character-based systems are outperformed by BPE models even when translating noisy UGC. To understand this counter-intuitive result, we conduct several experiments and analyses. In particular, we manually annotated 400 sentences at the token level using a fine-grained typology, to perform our analyses. These sentences correspond to the worst and the best translated utterances of two MT systems (a char-based and a transformer-based model). Our results highlight the extreme sensibility of character-based models to the vocabulary size, a parameter often overlooked in the literature. Using a simple set of experiments, we thus show that these models are unable to perform an *easy* copy task due to their poor handling of unknown and rare characters. By adjusting the vocabulary size parameter, we drastically improve the robustness of our character-based model without causing a large drop in in-domain performance.

Our contributions are as follows:

- we provide an annotated data set[1] that enables

[1] https://github.com/josecar25/char_based_NMT-noisy_UGC

Proceedings of the 2021 EMNLP Workshop W-NUT: The Seventh Workshop on Noisy User-generated Text, pages 199–211
November 11, 2021.

in-depth evaluations of the impact of UGC idiosyncrasies;
- we demonstrate that char-based neural machine translation models are extremely sensitive to unknown and rare characters on both synthetic data and noisy user-generated content;
- we show how an overlooked hyper-parameter drastically improve char-based MT models robustness to natural noise while maintaining the in-domain level of performance.

2 Character-level NMT

In this work, we explore two character-based translation models. The first model we consider, charCNN is a classic encoder-decoder in which the encoder uses character-based embeddings in combination with convolutional and highway layers to replace the standard look-up based word representations. The model considers, as input, a stream of words (i.e. it assumes the input has been tokenized beforehand) and tries to learn a word representation that is more robust to noise by unveiling regularities at the character level. This architecture was initially proposed by Kim et al. (2016) for language modeling; Costa-jussà and Fonollosa (2016) shows how it can be used in an NMT system and report improvements up to 3 BLEU (Papineni et al., 2002) points when translating from a morphologically-rich language, German, to English.

The second model we consider does not rely on an explicit segmentation into words: Lee et al. (2017) introduce the char2char model that directly maps a source characters sequence to a target characters sequence without any segmentation thanks to a character-level convolutional network with max-pooling at the encoder. It can be considered as an open-vocabulary model: it can generate any word made of any of the N most frequent characters of the train set (where N is a model hyper-parameter) and only outputs an <UNK> token in the presence of character that is not in this (char-) vocabulary. Lee et al. (2017) show that this model outperforms subword-level (i.e. BPE-based) translation models on two WMT'15 tasks (de-en and cs-en) and gives comparable performance on two tasks (fi-en and ru-en). Lee et al. (2017) additionally report that in a multilingual setting, the character-level encoder significantly outperforms the subword-level encoder on all the language pairs.

These two models have been originally tested on WMT or IWSLT tasks that consider texts that mostly qualify as canonical with very few spelling or grammatical errors. The impact of noise on charCNN and char2char has been evaluated by Belinkov and Bisk (2018) and Ebrahimi et al. (2018b). By adding noise to canonical texts (the TEDTalk dataset). Their results show that the different character levels models fail to translate even moderately noisy texts when trained on 'clean' data and that it is necessary to train a model on noisy data to make it robust. Note that, as explained in Section 3, there is no UGC parallel corpus large enough to train a NMT model and we must rely on the models' ability to learn, from canonical data only, noise- and error-resistant representations of their input that are robust to the noise and errors found in UGCs. This is why, in this work, we are interested in studying MT performance in a zero-shot scenario when translating noisy UGC.

To the best of our knowledge, no work has studied the performance of the character-based NMT architectures on an actual UGC scenario with real-world gathered and fine-grained annotated noisy sentences. This sets the main motivation for the present work.

3 Datasets

Training sets Due to the lack of a large parallel corpus of noisy sentences, we train our systems with 'standard' parallel datasets, namely the corpora used in the WMT campaign (Bojar et al., 2016) and the OpenSubtitles corpus (Lison et al., 2018). The former contains canonical texts (2.2M sentences), while the latter (9.2M sentences) is made of written dialogues from popular tv series. The reason for using OpenSubtitles is the assumed greatest similarity, compared to WMT, between its content and the UGC conversational nature that predominates most social media. However, UGC differs significantly from subtitles in many aspects: in UGC, emotions are often denoted with repetitions, there are many typographical and spelling errors, and sentences may contain emojis that can even replace some words (e.g. ♥ can stands for the verb 'love' in sentences such as 'I ♥ you'). UGC productivity limits the pertinence of domain adaptation methods such as fine-tuning, as there will always be new forms that will not have been seen during training (Martínez Alonso et al., 2016). This is why we focus here on zero-shot scenarios, as we believe they provide a clearer experimental protocol when it comes to study the impact of UGC specificities on MT models.

Test sets We consider in our experiments two French-English test sets made of user-generated content. These corpora differ in the domain of their contents, their collection date, and in the way sentences were filtered to ensure they are sufficiently different from canonical data.

The first one, the MTNT corpus (Michel and Neubig, 2018), is a multilingual dataset that contains French sentences collected on `Reddit` and translated into English by professional translators. The second one, the Parallel French Social Media Bank (`PFSMB`)[2], introduced in (Rosales Núñez et al., 2019) and made from a subpart of the French Social Media Bank (Seddah et al., 2012), consists of comments extracted from Facebook, Twitter and Doctissimo, a health-related French forum. Table 9 shows some examples of source sentences and reference translations extracted from these two corpora and illustrates the peculiarities of UGC and difficulties of translating them. User-generated contents raise many challenges for MT systems: they notably contain `char-OOVs`, that is to say characters that have not been seen in the training data (e.g. emojis), rare character sequences (e.g. inconsistent casing or usernames) as well as many `word-OOVs` denoting URL, mentions, hashtags or, more generally, named entities. See (Foster, 2010; Seddah et al., 2012; Eisenstein, 2013; Sanguinetti et al., 2020) for a complete account of UGC idiosyncrasies. We have also selected a pair of blind UGC test sets, corresponding to non-overlapping partitions of the `PFSMB` and `MTNT` datasets, respectively. These were chosen to validate our approaches and models, after performing error analysis and benchmarks with the UGC test sets described above.

Additionally, we also evaluate our NMT systems on a pair of non-noisy, edited, datasets, which are chosen to match both of the train data configuration mentioned above, namely `NeswTest` and `OpenSubTest`, for `WMT` and `OpenSubs` corpora, respectively. These test sets serve a double purpose: evaluate the performance impact due to domain drift and the in-domain performance for both `WMT` and `OpenSubs`. See Tables 1 & 2 for relevant statistics.

It is worth noticing how the noisy UGC corpus, i.e. `PFSMB` and `MTNT`, have remarkably high TTR, high KL-divergence, %OOV rate and perplexity, even when compared to the out-of-domain test set in Table 2 (`NeswTest`).

4 NMT Models

Character-based models In our experiments, we compare the two character-level NMT systems introduced in Section 2, namely `charCNN` and `char2char`. Both models were trained as out-of-the box systems using the implementations provided by Kim et al. (2016) for `charCNN`,[3] and by Lee et al. (2017) for `char2char`.[4]

It must be noted that the `charCNN` extracts character n-grams for each input word and predicts a word contained in the target vocabulary or a special token, <UNK>, otherwise, whereas the `char2char` is capable of open-vocabulary translation and does not generate <UNK> tokens, unless an out-of-vocabulary character (`char-OOV`) is present in the input.

BPE-based models We use as our baselines two standard NMT models that consider tokenized sentences as input.

The first one is a `seq2seq` bi-LSTM architecture with global attention decoding. The `seq2seq` model was trained using the XNMT toolkit (Neubig et al., 2018).[5] It consists of a 2-layered Bi-LSTM layers encoder and a 2-layered Bi-LSTM decoder. It considers, as input, word embeddings of size 512 and each LSTM units has 1,024 components.

Our second baseline model is a vanilla Transformer model (Vaswani et al., 2017) using the implementation proposed in the OpenNMT framework (Klein et al., 2018). It consists of 6 layers with word embeddings that are 512-dimensional, a feed-forward layers made of 2,048 units and 8 self-attention heads.

Unknown Token Replacement One of the peculiarities of our UGC datasets is that they contain a many OOVs denoting URL, mentions, hashtags, or more generally named entities: for instance several sentences of the `PFSMB` mention the game "Flappy Bird" or the TV show "Teen Wolf". Most of the time, these OOVs are exactly the same in the source and target sentences and consequently, the source

[2] `https://gitlab.inria.fr/seddah/parallel-french-social-mediabank`

[3] `https://github.com/harvardnlp/seq2seq-attn`

[4] `https://github.com/nyu-dl/dl4mt-c2c`

[5] We decided to use XNMT, instead of OpenNMT in our experiments in order to compare our results to the ones of Michel and Neubig (2018).

Corpus	Split	#sentences	#tokens	avg. sent.len	TTR	Vocab. size	#chars types
WMT	Train	2.2M	64.2M	29.7	0.20	1.037M	335
	NewsDiscussDev	1,500	24,978	16.65	0.22	7,692	
OpenSubs	Train	9.2M	57.7M	6.73	0.18	2.08M	428
PFSMB †	Test	777	13,680	17.6	0.32	3,585	116
MTNT†		1,022	20,169	19.7	0.34	3,467	122
OpenSubsTest (2018)		11,000	66,148	6.01	0.23	15,063	111
NewsTest (2014)		3,003	68,155	22.70	0.23	15,736	111

Table 1: Statistics on the FR side of the corpora used in our experiments. TTR stands for Type-to-Token Ratio. Corpus containing mainly UGC are indicated with a †.

↓ Metric / Test set →	PFSMB †	MTNT †	NeswTest	OpenSubTest
3-gram KL-Div	1.563	0.471	0.406	0.006
%OOVs	12.63	6.78	3.81	0.76
PPL	599.48	318.24	288.83	62.06

Table 2: Domain-related measure on the source side (FR), between Test sets and OpenSubs training set. Dags indicate UGC corpora.

and reference share a lot of common words: the BLEU score between the sources and references of the PFSMB being of 15.1,[6] while it is only 2.7 on the WMT test set.

Closed-vocabulary MT systems that are not able to copy OOVs from the source sentence are therefore penalized. That is why, as part of our translation pipeline, we introduce a post-processing step in which the translation hypothesis is aligned with the source sentence and the <UNK> tokens replaced by their corresponding aligned source tokens. For the seq2seq the alignments between the source and translation hypothesis are computed using an IBM2 model.[7]. For the charCNN model, the alignments are deduced from the attention matrix. The char2char model is an open-vocabulary system that is able to generate new words when necessary. The vanilla Transformer implementation we use is able to copy unknown symbols directly.

5 Experiments and Results

We train and evaluate the MT models presented in the previous section using the data train and test configurations in Section 3. We first compare performances for our clean test sets (whether in-domain or our-of-domain, accordingly) and noisy UGC when translated using BPE- and character-based models before exploring into detail our results.

Table 3 reports the BLEU scores, as calculated by Post (2018)'s SacreBleu of the different models we consider, both on canonical and non-canonical test sets. Contrary to the first results of Michel and Neubig (2018), the quality of UGC translation does not appear to be so bad: the drop in performance observed on non-canonical corpora is of the same order of magnitude as the drop observed when translation models are applied to out-of-domain data. For instance, the BLEU score of a Transformer model trained on OpenSubtitles has the same order of magnitude on PFSMB, MTNT and news: on all these datasets, the performance dropped by roughly 4 BLEU points compared to its performance on in-domain data. However, this improvement in translation quality is partly due to our <UNK> replacement strategy, a step that was not considered by Michel and Neubig (2018).

As expected, all models perform better when they are trained on the OpenSubs corpus than when they are trained on WMT, as the former is intuitively more similar to UGC data than WMT is. More surprisingly, it appears that character-based models are largely outperformed by BPE-based models for most train-test combinations and, therefore, that their capacity to learn word representations that are robust to noise can be questioned.

Another interesting observation is that, while the Transformer achieves the best results on all test sets when trained on OpenSubtitles, it is outperformed by seq2seq when the WMT training set is considered. The situation is similar for character-based models. This observation suggests that these

[6]The sources and references of the MTNT corpus are less similar (BLEU score: 5) since all user mentions and URL are removed in the distributed version of the corpus.

[7]The alignments are computed by concatenating the test set to the training set and using FastAlign (Dyer et al., 2013).

	WMT				OpenSubtitles			
	PFSMB	MTNT	News†	Open	PFSMB	MTNT	News	Open†
BPE-based models								
seq2seq	9.9	21.8	27.5	14.7	17.1	27.2	19.6	28.2
+ <UNK> rep.	**17.1**	**24.0**	**29.1**	**16.4**	26.1	28.5	24.5	28.2
Transformer								
+ <UNK> rep.	15.4	21.2	27.4	**16.4**	**27.5**	**28.3**	**26.7**	**31.4**
Character-based models								
charCNN	6.2	12.7	17.2	9.2	13.3	16.3	10.1	21.7
+ <UNK> rep.	16.1	18.2	22.1	11.5	18.6	20.2	14.6	23.9
char2char	7.1	13.9	18.1	8.8	23.8	25.7	17.8	26.3

Table 3: BLEU scores for our models for the different train-test combinations. In-domain test sets are marked with a dag. 'News' and 'Open' stand, respectively, for the WMT and OpenSubtitles test sets. WMT and OpenSubtitles are the training corpora, described in Section 3

models do not capture the same kind of information and do not have the same generalization capacities, as they roughly have the same number of parameters (69M parameters for the char2char and Transformer models, 65M for the charCNN and 49M for the seq2seq model).

Error analysis In order to find which kind of UGC specificities are the most difficult to translate and can explain the difference in performance between character-based and BPE-based systems, we have conducted a contrastive analysis between the predictions of the Transformer and the char2char models. For each model, we have selected the 100 source sentences with the highest translation quality and the 100 ones with the lowest translation quality.[8] We have manually annotated these 400 sentences, using the typology described in Table 4, to identify which UGC specificities were the hardest to translate. Such a classification is adopted from the fined-grained list of UGC particularities of Sanguinetti et al. (2020). Examples of annotations are given in Table 10, in the Appendix.

Figure 1 shows the number of UGC specificities in the 100 worst and 100 best translations of the two considered models. As expected, there are far fewer specificities in the best translations than in the worst translations except for the high number of named entities that is found in both cases. This is, however, not a surprise given the high number of named entities in UGC (see §4).

The specificities that are the most problematic to translate[9] appear, as can be seen in Figure 1.a, to

code	kind of specificities
1	Letter deletion/addition
2	Missing diacritics
3	Phonetic writing
4	Tokenisation error
5	Wrong verb tense
6	#; @, URL
7	Wrong gender/grammatical number
8	Inconsistent casing
9	Emoji
10	Named Entity
11	Contraction
12	Graphemic/punctuation stretching

Table 4: Typology of UGC specificities used in our manual annotation.

be the presence of named-entities (10th category) and the inconsistent casing (8th category) often corresponding to several words written fully uppercased to denote emotions or excitement. Counterintuitively, these two kinds of noise have more impact on the char2char model than on the Transformer model, even if it could be expected that the character embeddings learned by the former would not be sensitive to the case. When manually inspecting its prediction, it appears that, often, the char2char model is not able to copy named entities and replace some of their characters. For instance, the entity *Cllaude468* is translated into *Claudea64666*, and *flappy bird* into *flappe bird*. Interestingly this second entity is correctly translated by the char2char model when it is written *Flappy Bird*. Similarly, the Transformer model often tries to translate part of the hashtags relying on the subword units identified by the BPE tokenization rather than simply copying them from

[8]To evaluate translation quality at the sentence level, we consider the edit distance between the translation hypothesis and the reference.

[9]Because we only report statistics on the best and worst translations of each system, our analysis does not allow us to directly compare the performance of the two models and we can only identify general trends in the impact of UGC idiosyncrasies on translation quality.

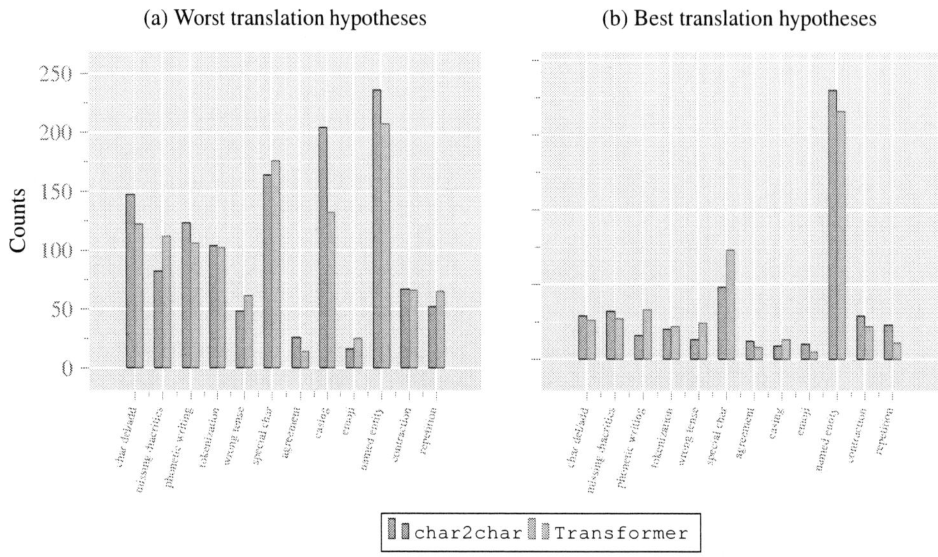

Figure 1: Comparison of the number of UGC specificities in the best and worst translation hypotheses of `char2char` and `Transformer`. Noise categories are defined in Table 4.

④	src	Si au bout de 5 mois **tu rescend (3) toujours se (3) genre** "d'effet secondaire" c'est vraiment mauvais.
	ref	If after 5 months you're still feeling this kind of "side effect" that's really bad.
	Tx	If after five months you're still re-exciting this whole "special effect" thing is really bad.
	c2c	In the end of five months, you're always responding to secondary effects, that's really bad.
⑤	src	y a ma cousine qui **joue a (2) flappy bird (10) mdrrrrrrrrrrr (11, 12) elle et plus nuuul (12,7) que moi**
	ref	my cousin plays flappy bird looooooooooool she's more hopeless than me
	Tx	There's my cousin who plays a flappy bird mdrrrrrrrrrrrrrrrrrrrrrrrrrrrrrrrrrrrrrrrrrrrrrrrrrrrrrrrrrr
	c2c	There's my cousin that plays a flappy bird flappy bird might bring her and nouse than me.

Table 5: Examples from our noisy UGC corpus showing the `Transformer` (denoted as Tx) and `char2char` (denoted as c2c) predictions. Source sentences have been annotated with UGC specificities of Table 1 (in blue). Part of the reference that were correctly generated are underlined.

the source: for instance "***#ÇaMeVenereQuand***" ("**#It**AnnoysMeWhen" in English) is translated into "*#CaMevenre***When***".

Another important category of errors, is the 6th category that corresponds to hashtags, mentions and URLs, for which the `char2char` model is not capable of producing characters or sequence of characters that are rare in the training set (namely `#`, `@` or `http://www`). For instance, the `char2char` model only outputs 8 sharp symbols when translating the test set of the `PFSMB`, while the reference contains 345 hash tags starting with a '#'. While the `Transformer` model is less sensitive to this problem (it produces 105 sharp symbols when translating the `PFSMB` test), its translation quality also suffers from the presence of hashtags as, as for named entities it often translates some of the subword units resulting from the BPE tokenization. Finally, we notice that errors 2 and 12 (diacritization and repetition) are treated somewhat better by the `char2char` model than by the `Transformer` model, being less frequent in the worst translations of the former.

Qualitative Analysis Table 10 reports translation hypotheses predicted by the `Transformer` and `char2char` models. These examples illustrate the difficulty of the `char2char` model to translate named entities: while the simple strategy of copying unknown OOVs from the source implemented by the `Transformer` is very effective, the `char2char` model tend to scramble or add letters to NE. They also illustrate the impact of phonetic writing on translation: for instance "*rescend*" that should be spelt "*resents*" (*feeling*, example 4) and "*joue a* that should be spelt "*joue à*" (*play a* vs *play with* - auxiliary verb instead of a preposition-example 5) both result in a wrong translation: in the former case, the meaning of the sentence is not captured, in the latter the "*a*" is wrongly copied in the translation hypothesis.

5.1 Copy Task Control Experiment

To corroborate our analysis of the special characters impact on `char2char` and quantify the impact of `char-OOVs` and of rare character sequences, we conduct a control experiment in which a `char2char` system with different vocabulary sizes must learn to copy the source, that is to say: we apply a `char2char` on an artificial parallel corpus in which the source and the target sentences are identical. By varying the number of characters considered by the system, we can control the number of rare characters in our corpora (recall that with a char-vocabulary of size N all characters but the N most frequent ones are mapped to a special `<UNK>` character). Note that this task is a simplification of the problem we have highlighted in the previous section: the model has simply to learn to always make an exact copy of the whole source sentence and not to detect some special characters (such as # or @) from the input that trigger the copy of the next characters, while the rest of the sentence should be translated.

More precisely, we built an artificial train set containing 1M random sentences with lengths between 5 and 15 characters long, keeping a 164 fixed-size character vocabulary (this correspond to the size of the extended ASCII alphabet), and whose characters are distributed uniformly, in order to rule out the impact of rare characters and keeping only the effect of `char-OOVs` over the performance. We consider two test sets made of 3,000 sentences each: `in-test` that uses the same 164 characters as the train set and `out-test` that uses 705 different characters. Source and reference are identical for every example of the train and test sets.

Results Table 6 reports the results achieved on the copy task with and without replacing the predicted `<UNK>` symbols.

Note that, in this very simple task, `<UNK>` characters are always replaced by their true value. These results show that this task is not trivial for char-based systems: even when all characters have been observed during training, the system is not able to copy the input perfectly.

Above all, reducing the vocabulary size from 164 to 125 results in an increase of the BLEU score on the two considered conditions, even without replacing the `<UNK>` that the system has started to generate, where '%`<UNK>` pred.' indicates the percentage of `<UNK>` tokens in the prediction. Further reducing the size of the vocabulary artificially improves the quality of the systems: they generate more and more `<UNK>`, which are replaced during post-processing by their true value. These observations suggest that unknown or rare characters are not only difficult to copy, but they also distort the representation of the input sequence built by the system impacting the whole prediction.

	Vocabulary Size				
	164	125	100	80	60
`in-test`					
%`<UNK>` pred.	0	0.2	5	17	29.5
BLEU	92.9	95.8	77.6	24.9	1.9
+`<UNK>` rep.	92.9	96.6	98.4	98.5	98.7
`out-test`					
%`<UNK>` pred.	0	9.2	13.8	25	36
BLEU	54.5	63.7	52.3	15.3	0.9
+`<UNK>` rep.	54.4	96.6	98.7	99.1	99.5

Table 6: Results of the copy task evaluated by the BLEU score before and after `<UNK>` replacement (+*<UNK> rep.*) and percentage of `<UNK>` characters in the prediction (%*<UNK> pred.*).

6 Impact of the Char-Vocabulary Size on Translation Quality

To validate in a more realistic setting the conclusion we draw from our copy tasks experiments, we present in Figure 2, the impact of unknown characters on translation quality of the `PFSMB` test set for the `Transformer` and `char2char` models. While the translation quality is almost the same for both models when there is no `char-OOVs` in the input, the occurrence of an unknown character hurts the translation quality of the `char2char` model beyond the mistranslation of a single character.

Motivated by these observations, we carried out experiments on our `char2char` models, trained on `OpenSubtitles`, with different character vocabulary size. Results in Table 7 show that 'correctly' choosing the vocabulary size can improve the translation performance on both canonical and non-canonical corpora. We did not observe any noticeable improvements in in-domain data as those test sets contain very few `char-OOVs` compared to their UGC counterparts, *e.g.,* 0.76% for the `OpenSubtitles` test set. However, overall stability in in-domain performance is observed, unlike

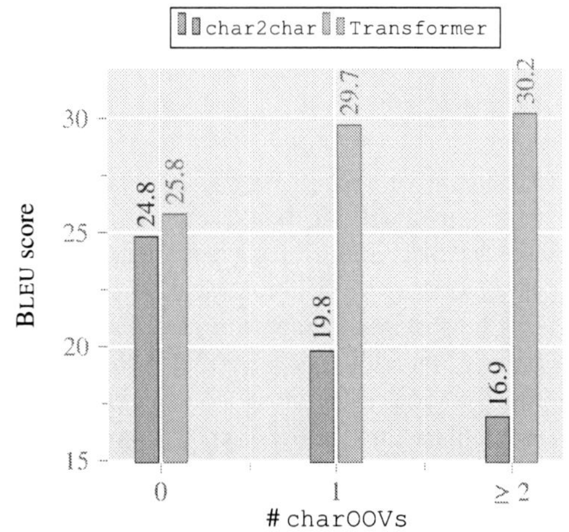

Figure 2: Impact of the number of char-OOVs in the input sentence on the BLEU score. Systems trained on OpenSubs.

what has been reported when domain-adaptation methods were used (Michel and Neubig, 2018; Belinkov and Bisk, 2018).

For vocabulary sizes larger than 90 characters, the char2char system achieves the same BLEU scores as with 90 characters. Note that in our first experiments (reported in Table 3), we used the 'standard' character vocabulary size (namely 300 characters) that was used in (Lee et al., 2017) and, to the best of our knowledge, in all following works.

vocab. size	PFSMB	MTNT	News	OpenTest[†]
90	23.9	25.8	18.7	26.6
85	23.9	25.3	**19.9**	**26.9**
80	23.9	25.8	18.3	26.6
75	24.5	**25.9**	17.8	26.3
70	**24.6**	25.4	17.8	26.3
65	22.7	25.5	18.0	26.4

Table 7: BLEU results for MT of char2char with reduced vocabulary size. Systems trained on OpenSubs. † *marks in-domain test set.*

As shown by an evaluation done on the blind tests of our UGC dataset, in Table 8, setting the vocabulary size parameters based on the improvement they bring reduces the difference in performance between the char2char and Seq2seq systems. With the 'correct' vocabulary size the former is outperformed by only 0.3 (resp. 1) BLEU points while, with the default value, the difference is 1.2 (resp. 3.1) BLEU points on the PFSMB (resp. MTNT).

By manually comparing the system outputs for different vocabulary sizes, it seems that the observed differences in performance can be explained

	PFSMB blind	MTNT blind
char2char-base	17.8	20.9
vocab-75	18.3	24.0
vocab-70	18.7	22.8
Transformer	*19.0*	*25.0*
seq2seq	*22.1*	*20.4*

Table 8: BLEU results for blind MT test sets of char2char with reduced vocabulary size. Systems trained on OpenSubs. *The Transformer and Seq2seq are presented as comparison data points.*

by drop- and over-translation phenomena, two well-identified limits of NMT (Mi et al., 2016; Koehn and Knowles, 2017; Le et al., 2017). An analysis of Figure 3, which displays the ratio between the hypothesis and reference lengths for the different vocabulary sizes, seems to confirm this hypothesis as it appears that the vocabulary size parameter provides control over the translation hypothesis length and consequently, a way to limit these drop- and over-translation phenomena.

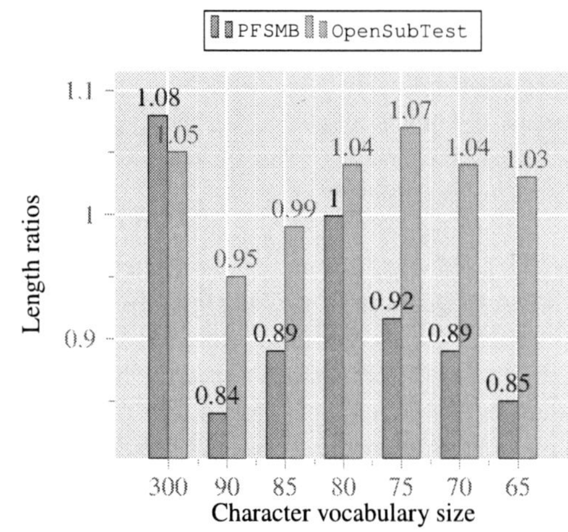

Figure 3: Reference/hypothesis length ratios on the PFSMB test set produced by char2char for different vocabulary sizes.

7 Discussion

Our work follows many studies on the robustness of character-based models, most notably from Belinkov and Bisk (2018) who compared different translation unit levels for NMT and showed that, overall, MT systems trained on clean data only presented considerable performance decrease when processing synthetic character-level noise and word-level noise. Here, we also perform comparisons with other mainstream strong BPE-based baselines and because of our annotated UGC data set are able to provide a more precise view on the phenomena at stake when processing *natural* noisy-input.

Similarly to Durrani et al. (2019) what concluded for morpho-syntactic classification tasks, our results show that a more fined-grained granularity of learning representations, characters over BPEs, provides a higher robustness to certain types of noise. Contrary to the both aforementioned works, our study is performed using annotated real-world noisy UGC, which proved crucial for our study.

In line to Fujii et al. (2020) findings, where fine-grained NMT granularity provided robustness advantages when processing misspelling, our results show that the best and worst translations' specificities distribution point to a better performance of char2char for the *missing diacritics* category, giving insights on more specific types of misspellings that affect performance.

Continuing this research track, we broaden the spectrum of studying UGC specificities, exploring the effects of the vocabulary training size and show that tuning it can achieve better results when translating noisy UGC. This simple hyper-parameter choice proved effective, providing an alternative to using fine-tuning methods (Michel and Neubig, 2018) or back-translation (Vaibhav et al., 2019).

8 Conclusion

We showed that in zero-shot scenarios, char-based models are not robust to UGC idiosyncrasies. We presented several experiments that explained this counter-intuitive result by an over-sensibility of these models to the vocabulary size. We demonstrated that drastically lowering this parameter increased the robustness of our char-based models when facing noisy UGC while maintaining almost the same level of performance for in-domain and out-of-domain canonical datasets. Interestingly, we noticed a lack in the literature regarding the importance of vocabulary considerations when training character-based NMT models. However, our results show that a path for improvement exists, leading to more generic and stable models and making us believe that further research on the matter can bring promising alternatives to domain-adaptation via target domain data addition. Our data set is available at `https://github.com/josecar25/char_based_NMT-noisy_UGC`.

Acknowledgments

We thank the reviewers for their valuable feedback. This work was funded by the French Research Agency via the ANR ParSiTi project (ANR-16-CE33-0021).

References

Yonatan Belinkov and Yonatan Bisk. 2018. Synthetic and natural noise both break neural machine translation. In *Proceedings of the 6th International Conference on Learning Representations, ICLR 2018, Vancouver, BC, Canada, April 30 - May 3, 2018, Conference Track Proceedings*.

Ondrej Bojar, Rajen Chatterjee, Christian Federmann, Yvette Graham, Barry Haddow, Matthias Huck, Antonio Jimeno-Yepes, Philipp Koehn, Varvara Logacheva, Christof Monz, Matteo Negri, Aurélie Névéol, Mariana L. Neves, Martin Popel, Matt Post, Raphael Rubino, Carolina Scarton, Lucia Specia, Marco Turchi, Karin M. Verspoor, and Marcos Zampieri. 2016. Findings of the 2016 conference on machine translation. In *Proceedings of the First Conference on Machine Translation, WMT 2016, colocated with ACL 2016, August 11-12, Berlin, Germany*, pages 131–198.

Marta R. Costa-jussà and José A. R. Fonollosa. 2016. Character-based neural machine translation. In *Proceedings of the 54th Annual Meeting of the Association for Computational Linguistics, ACL 2016, August 7-12, 2016, Berlin, Germany, Volume 2: Short Papers*.

Nadir Durrani, Fahim Dalvi, Hassan Sajjad, Yonatan Belinkov, and Preslav Nakov. 2019. One size does not fit all: Comparing NMT representations of different granularities. In *Proceedings of the 2019 Conference of the North American Chapter of the Association for Computational Linguistics: Human Language Technologies, NAACL-HLT 2019, Minneapolis, MN, USA, June 2-7, 2019, Volume 1 (Long and Short Papers)*, pages 1504–1516. Association for Computational Linguistics.

Chris Dyer, Victor Chahuneau, and Noah A. Smith. 2013. A simple, fast, and effective reparameterization of IBM model 2. In *Proceedings of the 2013 Conference of the North American Chapter of the Association for Computational Linguistics: Human Language Technologies*, pages 644–648, Atlanta, Georgia. Association for Computational Linguistics.

Javid Ebrahimi, Daniel Lowd, and Dejing Dou. 2018a. On adversarial examples for character-level neural machine translation. In *Proceedings of the 27th International Conference on Computational Linguistics*, pages 653–663, Santa Fe, New Mexico, USA. Association for Computational Linguistics.

Javid Ebrahimi, Daniel Lowd, and Dejing Dou. 2018b. On adversarial examples for character-level neural machine translation. In *Proceedings of the 27th International Conference on Computational Linguistics, COLING 2018, Santa Fe, New Mexico, USA, August 20-26, 2018*, pages 653–663.

Jacob Eisenstein. 2013. What to do about bad language on the internet. In *HLT-NAACL*, Atlanta, USA.

Jennifer Foster. 2010. "cba to check the spelling": Investigating parser performance on discussion forum posts. In *NAACL*, Los Angeles, California.

Ryo Fujii, Masato Mita, Kaori Abe, Kazuaki Hanawa, Makoto Morishita, Jun Suzuki, and Kentaro Inui. 2020. Phemt: A phenomenon-wise dataset for machine translation robustness on user-generated contents. In *Proceedings of the 28th International Conference on Computational Linguistics, COLING 2020, Barcelona, Spain (Online), December 8-13, 2020*, pages 5929–5943. International Committee on Computational Linguistics.

Huda Khayrallah and Philipp Koehn. 2018. On the impact of various types of noise on neural machine translation. In *Proceedings of the 2nd Workshop on Neural Machine Translation and Generation, NMT@ACL 2018, Melbourne, Australia, July 20, 2018*, pages 74–83. Association for Computational Linguistics.

Yoon Kim, Yacine Jernite, David A. Sontag, and Alexander M. Rush. 2016. Character-aware neural language models. In *Proceedings of the Thirtieth AAAI Conference on Artificial Intelligence, February 12-17, 2016, Phoenix, Arizona, USA*, pages 2741–2749.

Guillaume Klein, Yoon Kim, Yuntian Deng, Vincent Nguyen, Jean Senellart, and Alexander M. Rush. 2018. Opennmt: Neural machine translation toolkit. In *Proceedings of the 13th Conference of the Association for Machine Translation in the Americas, AMTA 2018, Boston, MA, USA, March 17-21, 2018 - Volume 1: Research Papers*, pages 177–184.

P. Koehn and R. Knowles. 2017. Six challenges for neural machine translation. In *NMT@ACL*.

An Nguyen Le, Ander Martinez, Akifumi Yoshimoto, and Yuji Matsumoto. 2017. Improving sequence to sequence neural machine translation by utilizing syntactic dependency information. In *IJCNLP*.

Jason Lee, Kyunghyun Cho, and Thomas Hofmann. 2017. Fully character-level neural machine translation without explicit segmentation. *TACL*, 5:365–378.

Wang Ling, Isabel Trancoso, Chris Dyer, and Alan W Black. 2015. Character-based neural machine translation. *arXiv preprint arXiv:1511.04586*.

Pierre Lison, Jörg Tiedemann, and Milen Kouylekov. 2018. Opensubtitles2018: Statistical rescoring of sentence alignments in large, noisy parallel corpora. In *Proceedings of the Eleventh International Conference on Language Resources and Evaluation, LREC 2018, Miyazaki, Japan, May 7-12, 2018*.

Minh-Thang Luong and Christopher D. Manning. 2016. Achieving open vocabulary neural machine translation with hybrid word-character models. In *Proceedings of the 54th Annual Meeting of the Association for Computational Linguistics (Volume 1: Long Papers)*, pages 1054–1063, Berlin, Germany. Association for Computational Linguistics.

Héctor Martínez Alonso, Djamé Seddah, and Benoît Sagot. 2016. From noisy questions to Minecraft texts: Annotation challenges in extreme syntax scenario. In *Proceedings of the 2nd Workshop on Noisy User-generated Text (WNUT)*, pages 13–23, Osaka, Japan. The COLING 2016 Organizing Committee.

Haitao Mi, Baskaran Sankaran, Zhiguo Wang, and Abe Ittycheriah. 2016. Coverage embedding models for neural machine translation. In *EMNLP*.

Paul Michel and Graham Neubig. 2018. MTNT: A testbed for machine translation of noisy text. In *Proceedings of the 2018 Conference on Empirical Methods in Natural Language Processing, Brussels, Belgium, October 31 - November 4, 2018*, pages 543–553.

Graham Neubig, Matthias Sperber, Xinyi Wang, Matthieu Felix, Austin Matthews, Sarguna Padmanabhan, Ye Qi, Devendra Singh Sachan, Philip Arthur, Pierre Godard, John Hewitt, Rachid Riad, and Liming Wang. 2018. XNMT: the extensible neural machine translation toolkit. In *Proceedings of the 13th Conference of the Association for Machine Translation in the Americas, AMTA 2018, Boston, MA, USA, March 17-21, 2018 - Volume 1: Research Papers*, pages 185–192.

Kishore Papineni, Salim Roukos, Todd Ward, and Wei-Jing Zhu. 2002. Bleu: a method for automatic evaluation of machine translation. In *Proceedings of the 40th Annual Meeting of the Association for Computational Linguistics, July 6-12, 2002, Philadelphia, PA, USA*, pages 311–318.

Matt Post. 2018. A call for clarity in reporting BLEU scores. In *Proceedings of the Third Conference on Machine Translation: Research Papers*, pages 186–191, Belgium, Brussels. Association for Computational Linguistics.

José Carlos Rosales Núñez, Djamé Seddah, and Guillaume Wisniewski. 2019. Comparison between NMT and PBSMT performance for translating noisy user-generated content. In *Proceedings of the 22nd Nordic Conference on Computational Linguistics*, pages 2–14, Turku, Finland. Linköping University Electronic Press.

Manuela Sanguinetti, Lauren Cassidy, Cristina Bosco, Özlem Çetinoglu, Alessandra Teresa Cignarella, Teresa Lynn, Ines Rehbein, Josef Ruppenhofer, Djamé Seddah, and Amir Zeldes. 2020. Treebanking user-generated content: a UD based overview of guidelines, corpora and unified recommendations. *CoRR*, abs/2011.02063.

Djamé Seddah, Benoît Sagot, Marie Candito, Virginie Mouilleron, and Vanessa Combet. 2012. The french social media bank: a treebank of noisy user generated content. In *COLING 2012, 24th International Conference on Computational Linguistics, Proceedings of the Conference: Technical Papers, 8-15 December 2012, Mumbai, India*, pages 2441–2458.

Vaibhav, Sumeet Singh, Craig Stewart, and Graham Neubig. 2019. Improving robustness of machine translation with synthetic noise. In *Proceedings of the 2019 Conference of the North American Chapter of the Association for Computational Linguistics: Human Language Technologies, NAACL-HLT 2019, Minneapolis, MN, USA, June 2-7, 2019, Volume 1 (Long and Short Papers)*, pages 1916–1920. Association for Computational Linguistics.

Ashish Vaswani, Noam Shazeer, Niki Parmar, Jakob Uszkoreit, Llion Jones, Aidan N Gomez, Ł ukasz Kaiser, and Illia Polosukhin. 2017. Attention is all you need. In I. Guyon, U. V. Luxburg, S. Bengio, H. Wallach, R. Fergus, S. Vishwanathan, and R. Garnett, editors, *Advances in Neural Information Processing Systems 30*, pages 5998–6008. Curran Associates, Inc.

A Appendix

Corpus		
PFSMB	src	ma **TL** se vide après **j'me fais chier** puis **jme** sens seule mais **c** surtout **pdt les vacs mais c pas le cas dc** ça compte pas trop
	ref	my TL is emptying then I get bored then I feel alone but mostly during holidays but it's not the case so it's not so important
	google	my TL is empty after I'm pissing then I feel alone but c especially pdt vacs but it does not matter that it does not count too much
	src	Dans Flappy Bird quand mon Bird il fait 10 jsuis trop contente #TeamNul Mdddr
	ref	At Flappy Bird when my Bird has 10 Im so happy #TeamFail Loool
	google	In Flappy Bird when my Bird is 10, I'm too happy #TeamNul Mdddr
	src	**Booooooooooooooooooooooonnne Annniversaure Ma viiiiiiiiiiiiie jtm** plus que tout profite bien de tes **22ans moaaaaaaaaa**
	ref	Haaaaaaaaaaaaaaaaaaaaaapppy Biiirthday My liiiiiiiiiiiiife luv you more than anything enjoy your 22years mwaaaaaaaaah
	google	Booooooooooooooooooooooonnne Annniversaure My viiiiiiiiiiiiie jtm more than anything enjoy your 22 years moaaaaaaaaaa
MTNT	src	**AJA** que le XV de France féminin est **un train de faire** un grand **chelem, OKLM**
	ref	TIL that the XV of Feminine France is doing a grand chelem, FRESH
	google	AJA that the XV of France feminine is a train of a grand slam, OKLM
	src	Je pensais mais c'est le même **ident et mdp** que mon compte "normal", et il détecte même la **profile pic** et le nom
	ref	I thought so but it's the same username and password as my 'normal' account, and it detects even the profile pic and the name
	google	I thought but it's the same ident and mdp as my "normal" account, and it even detects the pic profile and the name
	src	**Aaaaaaaah.... 8 ans après, je viens de percuter.... :o 'tai** je me disais bien que je passais à côté d'un truc vu les **upvotes.**
	ref	Aaaaaaaah.... 8 years later, I've just realized.... :o damn I had the feeling that I was missing something considering the upvotes.
	google	Aaaaaaaah .... 8 years later, I just collided ....: oh well I was telling myself that I was missing something seen the upvotes.

Table 9: Examples from both noisy UGC showing the source phrase, reference translation and Google Translate output. UGC idiosyncrasies are highlighted using bold characters.

#		
①	src	**JohnDoe389** (10) qui n'arrive pas **a** (2) **depasser** (2) 1 a (2) **FlappyBird** 10 ... **ptddddr** (11, 12)
	ref	JohnDoe389 who can't score more than 1 at FlappyBird ... lmaooooo
	Tx	John Doe389 who can't pass one to Flappy Bird... ptdddr.
	c2c	Johndeigh doesn't happen to pass one on Flappyrib... please.
②	src	**JohnDoe665** (10) **viens** (5) de regarder **Teen Wolf (2011) S03E17 [Silverfinger]** (10) et s'en va apprendre l'humanité à **Castiel** (10).
	ref	JohnDoe665 just watched Teen Wolf (2011) S03E17 [Silverfinger] and he's on his way to teach Castiel humanity.
	Tx	John Doe665 just watched Teen Wolf (2011) S03E17 (Silverfinger) and is going to teach humanity at Castiel.
	c2c	Johndoedsoids is looking at Teen Wolf 2011, and learn about humanity in Castiel.
③	src	**Jai** (1,4) **fait 10 a** (2) **flappy bird** (10) **mddr** (11, 12) **# JeMeLaDonneMaisJavancePas** (6)
	ref	I did 10 at flappy bird lool # JeMeLaDonneMaisJavancePas
	Tx	I did 10 a flappy bird mdr # I'm not moving
	c2c	♪I've made 10 flappy birdd ♪

Table 10: Examples from our noisy UGC corpus showing the Transformer (denoted as Tx) and char2char (denoted as c2c) predictions. Source sentences have been annotated with UGC specificities of Table 1 (in blue). Part of the reference that were correctly generated are underlined.

B Reproducibility

Data All the UGC test sets and source code for our experiments are provided in the supplementary materials. For training data, we let the reader refer to each project's website for `WMT`[10] (consisting of `Europarlv7`, `Newcommentariesv10` and `Open Subtitles`[11], both accessed on November, 2019. Regarding clean test sets, we used `newstest15` from `WMT` and a subset of 11.000 unique phrases from `Open Subtitles`. We make the former test available in the link provided above for exact performance comparison.

Computation The NMT systems were trained using 1 Tesla V100, during an average of 72 hours to converge to the final solution for the `char2char` model and 56 hours for the BPE-based baselines.

B.1 NMT Models

Character-based models Both `charCNN` and `char2char` models were trained as out-of-the box systems using the implementations provided by (Kim et al., 2016) for `charCNN`,[12] an by (Lee et al., 2017) for `char2char`.[13]

BPE-based models We consider, as baseline, two standard NMT models that take, as input, tokenized sentences. The first one is a `seq2seq` bi-LSTM architecture with global attention decoding. The `seq2seq` model was trained using the XNMT toolkit (Neubig et al., 2018).[14] It consists of a 2-layered Bi-LSTM layers encoder and 2-layered Bi-LSTM decoder. It considers, as input, word embeddings of 512 components and each LSTM units has 1,024 components.

We also study a vanilla Transformer model using the implementation proposed in the OpenNMT framework (Klein et al., 2018). It consists of 6 layers with word embeddings of 512 components, a feed-forward layers made of 2,048 units and 8 self-attention heads.

The vocabulary parameter for experiments in § 6 were obtained through a first exploratory uniform segmentation of the possible vocabulary sizes, and then, discovering the threshold (vocabulary with 90 characters) for which the `char2char` model started producing `<UNK>` during evaluation. We then proceeded to obtain the results displayed above by sampling this parameter by decreasing 5 characters.

Hyper-parameters In Table 11, we list the training variables set for our experiments. They match their corresponding default hyper-parameters.

Batch size	64
Optimizer	Adam
Learning rate	1e-4
Epochs	10 (best of)
Patience	2 epochs
Gradient clip	[-1.0, 1.0]

Table 11: Hyper-parameters used for training the NMT systems.

Pre-processing For the BPE models, we used a 16K merging operations tokenization employing `sentencepiece`[15]. For word-level statistics we segmented the corpora using the `Moses` tokenizer [16].

[10] `https://www.statmt.org/wmt15/translation-task.html`

[11] `http://opus.nlpl.eu/download.php?f=OpenSubtitles/v2018/moses/en-fr.txt.zip`

[12] `https://github.com/harvardnlp/seq2seq-attn`

[13] `https://github.com/nyu-dl/dl4mt-c2c`

[14] We decided to use XNMT, instead of OpenNMT in our experiments in order to compare our results to the ones of Michel and Neubig (2018).

[15] `https://github.com/google/sentencepiece`

[16] `https://github.com/moses-smt/mosesdecoder`

Changes in Twitter geolocations: Insights and suggestions for future usage

Anna Kruspe
Technical University of Munich
anna.kruspe@tum.de

Matthias Häberle
German Aerospace Center (DLR)
matthias.haeberle@dlr.de

Eike J. Hoffmann
Technical University of Munich
eike.jens.hoffmann@tum.de

Samyo Rode-Hasinger
Technical University of Munich
samyo.rode@tum.de

Karam Abdulahhad
German Aerospace Center (DLR)
karam.abdulahhad@dlr.de

Xiao Xiang Zhu
German Aerospace Center (DLR)
xiaoxiang.zhu@dlr.de

Abstract

Twitter data has become established as a valuable source of data for various application scenarios in the past years. For many such applications, it is necessary to know where Twitter posts (tweets) were sent from or what location they refer to. Researchers have frequently used exact coordinates provided in a small percentage of tweets, but Twitter removed the option to share these coordinates in mid-2019. Moreover, there is reason to suspect that a large share of the provided coordinates did not correspond to GPS coordinates of the user even before that.

In this paper, we explain the situation and the 2019 policy change and shed light on the various options of still obtaining location information from tweets. We provide usage statistics including changes over time, and analyze what the removal of exact coordinates means for various common research tasks performed with Twitter data. Finally, we make suggestions for future research requiring geolocated tweets.

1 Introduction

Twitter data has become an invaluable source of information for a range of application scenarios. In many situations, messages posted on this platform can provide insights faster and on a more fine-grained level than any other source of information. Moreover, it is a gigantic source of opportunistic, and therefore cheap, data. Example applications include situational awareness in disaster situations, where Twitter users provide updates much faster than official news sources or satellite imagery (Kruspe et al., 2021); collection of personal opinions and insights into human behavior, where Twitter is faster, more expansive, and cheaper than traditional surveys (Ceron et al., 2014); or mapping of human settlements, where Twitter users can provide information that is difficult or impossible to obtain from any other source (Häberle et al., 2019).

One crucial factor when analyzing Twitter posts is the ability to align these messages to places around the world. In disaster situations, knowing what location a certain tweet refers to can be a matter of life or death (Singh et al., 2019). In mapping tasks, information gained from Twitter is only valuable when it can be placed on the requested level of detail, e.g. buildings (Terroso-Saenz and Muñoz, 2020). On a broader scale, even knowing what city or country a tweet was posted from can provide significant insights into regional differences and developments, such as in the ongoing COVID-19 situation (Kruspe et al., 2020).

For these reasons, a lot of social media-focused research relies on geolocations provided within Twitter data. Up until mid-2019, precise geolocations were reliably available for a sufficient subset of tweets. On June 18th, 2019, however, Twitter announced they would remove the option to attach precise geolocations to tweets (geotagging)[1](Hu and Wang, 2020). The reasoning given at the time was that not many users were taking advantage of this feature. Privacy concerns in connection with precise geolocations have also been voiced in the past (Park et al., 2017; Fiesler and Proferes, 2018), so there is a possibility that these issues also factored into the policy change. In this paper, we will discuss how the situation has changed and what this means for Twitter-based research going forward.

Besides analyzing the current geolocation situation in Twitter data, we aim to shed light on the amount of non-used tweets simply because they do not have point coordinates. Although Twitter data may not the best choice for fine-grained location based research, as we will see, Twitter still represents a treasure trove of geolocated information. Whatever we attempt to do with it, we do need to take into account the required and available location granularity. With this paper, we hope to pave

[1] https://twitter.com/TwitterSupport/status/1141039841993355264

Proceedings of the 2021 EMNLP Workshop W-NUT: The Seventh Workshop on Noisy User-generated Text, pages 212–221
November 11, 2021.

the way for more solid and realistic Twitter based research. Our main contributions are (1) a detailed description of the change and current status, (2) statistics on the availability of different kinds of geolocations, and (3) a detailed reflection on the consequences for various research and how to deal with them.

In the next section, we first discuss in detail what exactly Twitter's policy change entailed, and present experimental results to determine more closely which geotagging options are currently available and what the resulting data looks like. Section 3 provides statistics on the availability of various types of geolocations since 2019. In sections 4 and 5, we analyze what effect the changes have on research, and make suggestions for adapting future research tasks accordingly. Section 6 provides a conclusion.

2 Geolocation availability

In the following, we will use the term "geolocated" to mean tweets containing explicit metadata about a geographic location they were posted from or are referring to, and "geotagging" as the user action that causes this metadata to be attached.

2.1 Data format and situation before mid-2019

In research, Twitter data is commonly obtained via the Twitter Streaming API in JSON format. In this format, each tweet is represented via a fixed set of attributes containing all of its public information. This format essentially contains two attributes for geotagging[2 3]:

`coordinates` containing the fields `type`, which will always be `Point`, and `coordinates`, which contains longitude and latitude values.

`place` containing the fields `id`, `url`, `place_type`, `name`, `full_name`, `country_code`, `country`, and `bounding_box`. `name`, `full_name`, `country_code`, and `country` provide human-readable semantic information about a place, while `place_type` can be "country", "city", "poi", etc. `bounding_box` contains a set of coordinates spanning a polygon, which may have surface 0, i.e. be a point.

For completeness, we also want to mention that an attribute called `geo` exists, but it is now deprecated.

By its original definition, `coordinates` is supposed to contain the exact geolocation where a tweet was posted. Before mid-2019, this meant that when a user gave Twitter permissions to use their location for geotagging, this attribute was filled with the coordinates obtained from the device that the user was posting from, particularly its GPS module. If those permissions were not given, the attribute was simply set to `null`.

In contrast, the `place` attribute serves to assign a pre-defined geographic entity to a post. Twitter offers users the option to select this entity from a list of those found nearby (within a radius of roughly 200m). These entities may be countries, cities, neighborhoods, points of interest, etc. `place`'s sub-fields are then automatically filled using information from geolocation services provided by Foursquare or Yelp[4].

User profiles can also contain geolocations; this is the case for around 30-40% of profiles[5]. This field can be freely set by the user, and may therefore contain fictitious or nonsensical values. Automatic geocoding is performed for plausible values, leading to information similar to the `place` attribute described above within the `user.derived.locations` field. Unfortunately, this information can only be obtained via the paid Enterprise API[6]. For a detailed look at geotagging behavior of users pre-2019, see (Huang and Carley, 2019; Tasse et al., 2017).

2.2 Situation since mid-2019

The policy change in mid-2019 did not affect the `place` attribute; the option to set this still exists. However, the `coordinates` attribute now cannot be filled anymore, at least not when using Twitter's own clients for posting.

Twitter's original announcement stated that users will "still be able to tag your precise location in

[2]https://developer.twitter.com/en/docs/tutorials/filtering-tweets-by-location

[3]https://developer.twitter.com/en/docs/twitter-api/v1/data-dictionary/object-model/geo

[4]https://help.twitter.com/en/using-twitter/tweet-location

[5]https://developer.twitter.com/en/docs/tutorials/advanced-filtering-for-geo-data

[6]https://developer.twitter.com/en/docs/twitter-api/enterprise/enrichments/overview/profile-geo

Tweets through our updated camera". However, in our own experiments (conducted on iOS with the latest German Twitter app), we were not able to confirm this option.

2.3 Cross-posts from third-party sources

Besides its direct clients, Twitter also provides options for cross-posting from various other social media platforms. Table 1 provides an overview of the distribution of the sources of tweets collected in the time-frame of August 3rd to August 9th, 2021. The total share of tweets posted from Twitter's own clients is around 95%.

	#tweets	%total
Total	25,756,667	100%
Twitter for Android	11,657,427	45%
Twitter for iPhone	9,410,305	37%
Twitter Web Client	2,982,670	12%
Twitter for iPad	506,638	2%
Twitter for Mac	12,040	0.05%
Instagram	22,151	0.09%
Foursquare (+ Swarm)	2,034	$\ll$0.01%
CareerArc 2.0	1,229	$\ll$0.01%
Others	1,162,173	4.5%

Table 1: Distribution of tweet sources. "Others" mainly includes Twitter bots

Instagram As the statistic reveals, Instagram is by far the most common source of cross-posts on Twitter. We therefore analyzed the options for geotagging in Instagram and their result in the Twitter data format. Just like the native Twitter apps, Instagram allows users to pick a geolocation for their posts at various granularities (e.g. point of interest (POI), city, etc.). No clear statement of the source of these locations has been made available by the company, but it seems likely that they are provided by the "Places Graph" service of Instagram's parent company Facebook. In contrast to Twitter's approach, Instagram users are allowed to pick locations from anywhere around the world.

When a user chooses a location on Instagram for a Twitter cross-post, both the `place` and the `coordinates` attributes are filled. The `place` attribute is always set to the city of the post and completed accordingly. The `coordinates` attribute will contain a single point coordinate, which is forwarded from Instagram. In our experiments, these were coordinates within the location picked on Instagram. Consequently, the `coordinates` attribute now fulfills a different role than it originally did on Twitter; it is not anymore representative of the user's geolocation from which the post was sent, but of some pre-defined location selected by the user, which may be very different from their physical location.

Others The second-most frequent (by a large margin) external source, Foursquare, also allows its users to cross-post to Twitter, e.g. via its "Swarm" app. This was the only option that actually allowed us to create Twitter posts with an exact geolocation. However, this option required turning off several system-side privacy settings, and was difficult to use. We therefore do not expect many users to do this. Alternatively, the app allows users to select an arbitrary coordinate for their posts, which is the more likely provenance of geolocations in Foursquare-based tweets.

The third-most frequent third-party source of tweets is Career Arc 2.0, a social media recruiting service. This service is only available to business partners, and only within the USA. We were therefore not able to directly test how selected geolocations are mapped to the Twitter format, but posts in our sample were generally on the city level. Due to the limited usage of this source in the dimensions of geography, use case, and user base, we do not see these tweets as a generally valuable source of information.

2.4 Ethical Considerations / Motivations

While the use of precise coordinates might be relevant to specifically orientated research, the General Data Privacy Regulation (European Commission, 2019) highlights the importance of data minimization when mining personal data. Personal data is defined as any information relating to an identified or identifiable living individual (European Commission, 2018). Thus, personal data does include the geolocalization of a person. Data minimization translates into the reduced collection of personal data to the absolute minimum needed amount and variety to answer a specific research question. The removal of precise geolocations by Twitter falls in line with this goal, and researchers must keep these considerations in mind when collecting Twitter data for their specific purposes. This is particularly critical when dealing with tasks that attempt to analyze or make predictions on a user basis.

3 Statistics

In this section, we perform statistical analyses to gather insights into what geolocation information is currently contained in tweets, and how the policy change impacted the availability of this information.

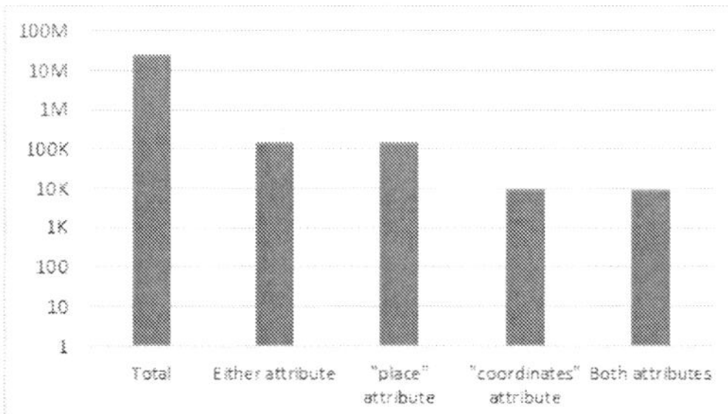

Figure 1: Shares of tweets with geolocations in one-week sample from August 2021, note log scaling ("Total" = all tweets collected in the 1% sample).

Share of geolocated tweets over-all We first calculated the shares out of all tweets that contain any sort of geolocation on a sample collected from the free 1% worldwide Twitter stream between August 3rd and August 9th, 2021. The results are shown in figure 1. About .06% of all tweets are geolocated. Nearly all of these have a filled `place` attribute, while only 6% of geolocated tweets provide the `coordinates` attribute. The last two bars are nearly identical, i.e. if the `coordinates` attribute is filled, the `place` attribute is almost certainly also filled.

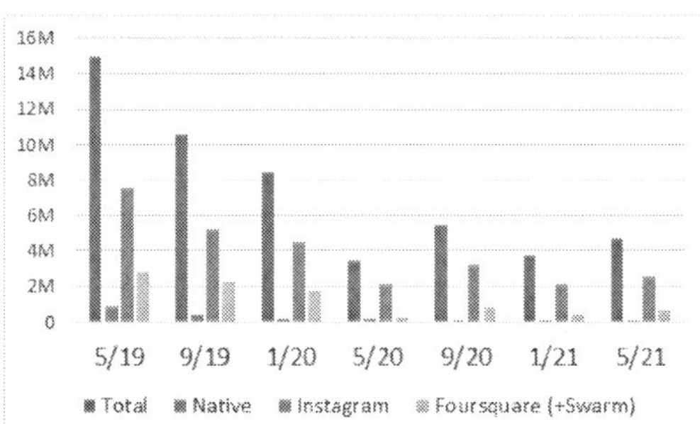

Figure 2: Sources of tweets with the `coordinates` attribute set by month ("Total" = all tweets with `coordinates` collected in the 1% sample of that month).

`coordinates` attribute Next, we took a closer look at the `coordinates` attribute. Figure 2 shows the sources of tweets that provide this attribute for every third month between May '19 and May '21, while figure 3 shows the percentage of geolocated tweets coming from native Twitter clients where `coordinates` is set. As expected, the numbers for tweets from Twitter's own clients have been decreasing over time (we believe the reason that they did not drop immediately may have been due to usage of outdated versions). Even before the policy change, most tweets with a `coordinate` attribute came from Instagram. As explained above, this means that the assumption that this attribute provides users' exact geolocations was never correct for a large percentage of them. Surprisingly, we also see a drop in geolocation provision from other apps. There are several factors at play here. First of all, a seasonal fluctuation is normal due to vacation seasons (Maurer, 2020). Second, from May '20 onward, the COVID-19 pandemic most likely changed users' posting behavior with regards to their location. Finally, newer versions of mobile operating systems put their users' privacy more into focus. Both iOS and Android made access to location services more visible and transparent with opt-ins for data sharing and notifications when location services were requested by an app. This may have also led to more in-depth privacy considerations among users.

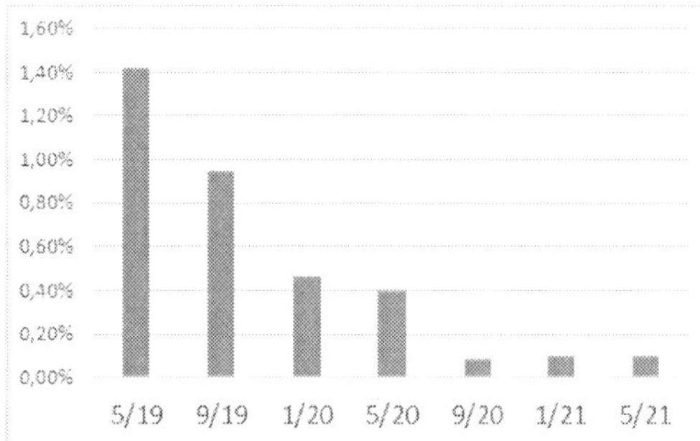

Figure 3: Percentages of geolocated tweets from native Twitter sources with the `coordinates` attribute set by month.

`place` attribute We then performed the same analysis for the `place` attribute, see figure 4. We see the same seasonal effects here, but not the same decrease as in the previous experiment, indicating that the cause for the `coordinates` drop was in fact the policy change. The higher rate of total tweets with a `place` attribute is probably due to a higher total tweet volume starting in

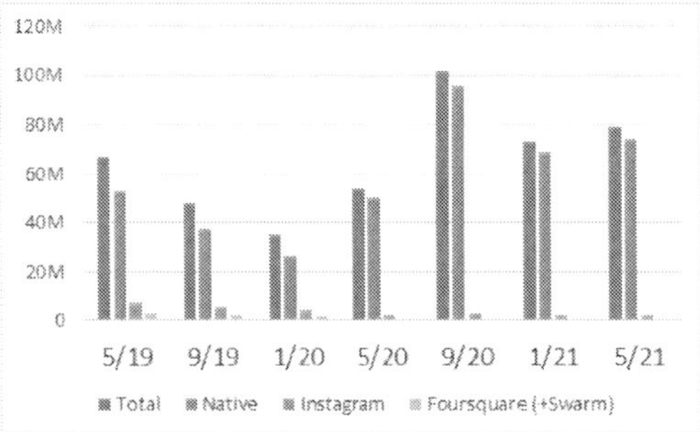

Figure 4: Sources of tweets with the `place` attribute set by month ("Total" = all tweets with `place` collected in the 1% sample of that month).

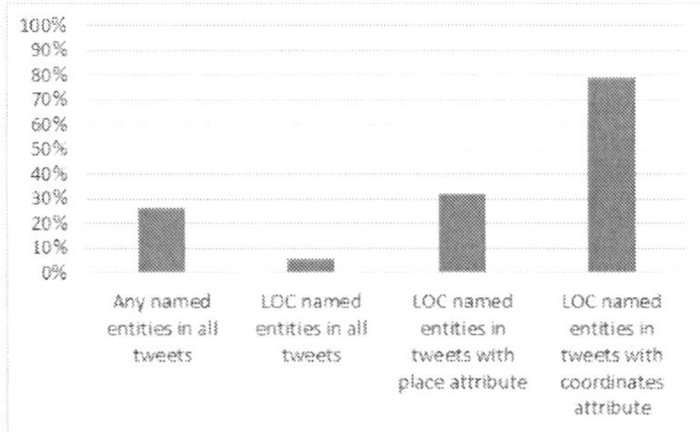

Figure 6: Shares of tweets with named entities and named LOC entities detected in one-week sample from August 2021, plus shares of tweets with LOC entities out of those with set `place` and `coordinates` attributes.

2020[7]. Fortunately, this means that the `place` attribute is still usable for research. We do see a decrease for Instagram crossposts which contain joint `coordinates` and `place`, confirming our suspicion in the previous section.

Secondly, we also considered the `place_type` field more closely to find out more about the level of detail provided by the `place` attribute. As shown in figure 5, the most frequent type is "city" (which is also the level automatically set for Instagram crossposts). However, the most fine-grained type "poi" also makes up 1-2% of the tweets, overall resulting in a still relatively large amount of available tweets with a geolocation at this granularity.

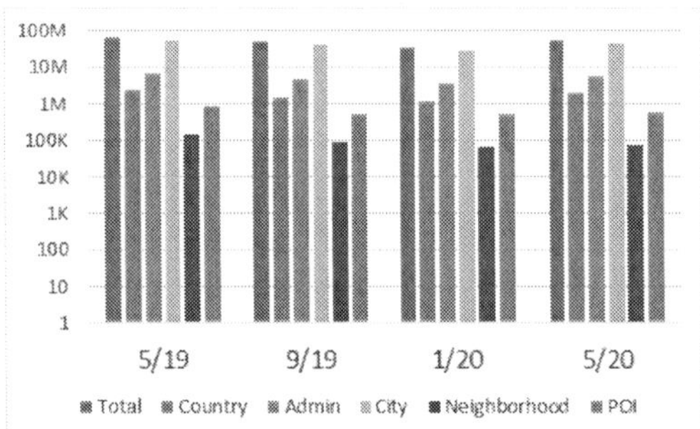

Figure 5: Share of `place_type` in the `place` attribute by month, note log scaling ("Total" = all tweets with `place` collected in the 1% sample of that month).

Locations mentioned in `text` attribute Finally, we wanted to obtain a rough estimate of the amount of geolocation information contained in the `text` attribute of tweets. To this end, we performed Named Entity Recognition on the one-week sample from August 2021 described above. We used a pre-trained HuggingFace model based on RoBERTa embeddings[8]. This model was trained on the CoNLL-2003 (Tjong Kim Sang and De Meulder, 2003) and WikiANN data sets with the entity classes taken from WikiAnn (Pan et al., 2017; Rahimi et al., 2019). It supports 176 languages.

Figure 6 shows the percentages of tweets that contain any named entity (around 26%) and those with at least one detected LOC entity (around 6%). We also show these numbers separately for geolocated tweets: Out of tweets with the `place` attribute, around 32% contained LOC entities, while 79% of tweets with the `coordinates` attribute did. This indicates a stronger semantic focus on the user's location when setting these attributes, but it also means that a large number of tweets mentioning a location has so far not been exploited. While 6% does not sound like a lot, this set of tweets is still around 30 times as large as the number of all geolocated tweets in this sample (compare figure 1), and that is only for direct recognition of known geographic entities. We believe this number would be even higher if other clues about location in the text were included.

4 Effect on research

Previous research using geolocated tweets has mainly exploited the `coordinates` attribute under the assumption that it would contain the physi-

[7] `https://blog.gdeltproject.org/visualizing-twitters-evolution-2012-2020-and-how-tweeting-is-changing-in-the-covid-19-era/`

[8] `https://huggingface.co/philschmid/distilroberta-base-ner-wikiann-conll2003-3-class`

cal location of the device the tweet was sent from. This approach is easy to motivate - the more fine-grained the location, the more information can potentially be gathered from it, even if the task at hand could also be solved with a coarser location. However, even before 2019, there were two disadvantages to this approach. On the one hand, the `coordinates` attribute is only filled in .01-.05% of the tweets (as opposed to .5-2% for the `place` attribute). On the other hand, crossposts from other sources filled the `coordinates` attribute differently. Most prominently, the 5-15% of geolocated tweets coming from Instagram never contained the GPS location of the user.

Since 2019, the `coordinates` attribute cannot reliably be used to determine location anymore, as we will detail in the next section. In this section, we will discuss what this means for some common research tasks. As (Middleton et al., 2018) describe, typical stakeholders of Twitter analysis include journalists, civil protection agencies or governing bodies, and businesses. We would add scientists from other domains to this list, leading to the following use cases that have been in the focus of research:

POIs POIs have been in the focus of research for the purpose of recommender systems, detecting novel or unknown POIs, analyzing opinions and possible improvements etc. Despite the availability of POI-level geolocations in the `place` attribute, researchers have mostly used the `coordinates` attribute for this purpose, presumably to gather a wider range of POIs that are not dependent on catalogs of geolocation providers (Hu and Ester, 2013; Maeda et al., 2016). With the loss of exact GPS coordinates, these approaches cannot easily be applied to current data. However, they could easily be adapted to POIs provided in the `place` attribute for many use cases. The exception to this are the discovery of new POIs as well as the analysis of user behavior in the vicinity of POIs (Hamstead et al., 2018; Lloyd and Cheshire, 2017).

Mobility Another strong focus of social media research is the analysis of human mobility, e.g. travel or commuting patterns. As before, the `coordinates` attribute has mainly served this purpose to allow for a flexible detection of origins and destinations (Grant-Muller et al., 2015). Future strategies without this attribute depend on the scale of mobility to be analyzed. When tracking movement between cities or even international travel, the city-level locations in the `place` attribute should suffice. Analysis on the sub-city level is more difficult now. For a general idea, e.g. for transport optimization, POI-level locations could be exploited if a sufficient number of them is available and well-distributed across the area (Huang et al., 2016). In Instagram crossposts, a location mapped to the `coordinates` attribute can also be a street, so this may be a valid source to determine travel in the city (after excluding centroids of other places, e.g. cities).

Disasters Natural and man-made disasters are among the most strongly researched applications of geolocated social media. Tasks include the automatic detection of events, detection of tweets related to disasters, classification of such tweets into certain categories, and detection of actionable tweets (Kruspe et al., 2021). As before, most existing approaches use the `coordinates` attribute. This is particularly critical for use cases where action is necessary, e.g. calls for help, or where localized developments of a disaster are detected. Due to the low share of tweets with exact coordinates even before 2019, efforts have been made to determine such locations from other sources, e.g. (Singh et al., 2019). On the more general level necessary for detecting events and disaster-related tweets in the first place, we believe city or POI locations from the `place` attribute will often be sufficient.

Public health Similar to the disaster topic, social media has also been suggested to explore public health topics such as the spread of infectious diseases (Achrekar et al., 2011; Padmanabhan et al., 2014). For this task, insights are not commonly gained on a sub-city level. Previous publications still often exploit the `coordinates` attribute, but then map it to a city or area. This could easily be substituted with the `place` attribute. Even the user-provided location could be sufficient here as most tasks are not reliant on user location change over short time spans. There are some use cases where this might be necessary, e.g.

when attempting to model COVID-19 spread on a person-by-person basis, but we would argue that not a high-enough percentage of the population uses geolocated social media to be feasible.

Marketing Marketing tasks on social media include e.g. the analysis of sentiments towards brands or products or the prediction of sales based on user expressions. This appears to be an area where exact geolocations do not serve a purpose and should therefore not see any detriment from the change. In fact, most research so far has focused on analysis without any geo-based statistics or on the country level, e.g. (Jendoubi and Martin, 2020; Ibrahim and Wang, 2019; Lassen et al., 2014).

Politics and social sciences In politics and social sciences, geolocations are usually not required at a very fine-grained level. The most prominent task in political social media analysis, election prediction, cannot even produce results comparable to the actual election result beyond the city/area level, which is affirmed by the overview provided in (Gayo-Avello, 2012). Similarly, empirical analysis of social effects or opinions usually operates on a larger scale, and requires inputs from city areas or larger, e.g. (Ceron et al., 2014; Kling and Pozdnoukhov, 2012), this may be an area where the `place` attribute may be useful at the `neighborhood` level or lower. A notable exception is (Hobbs and Lajevardi, 2018), which focuses on a quantitative analysis of geolocation provision by Arabic/Muslim users over time influenced by safety concerns. Another task where location is crucial is the recognition of suicide risk in users, where recognizing their location could serve to provide help (Jashinsky et al., 2013) (also related to the Public Health topic).

Mapping The most critical application of geolocated social media research seems to be mapping. So far, this task has been almost completely reliant on exact coordinates. Naturally, if we want to detect novel geographic structures or mapping details about known ones (e.g. building usages (Häberle et al., 2019)), we require the exact location the users are talking about in tweets. Future research therefore needs to detect these locations in other ways, some of which are suggested in the next section. There are some tasks where researchers may be able to rely on known places from geolocation service (i.e. the `place` attribute), e.g. collection of usage statistics over time (Frias-Martinez and Frias-Martinez, 2014). There is also a close relation to the POI tasks described above.

5 Suggestions for future research

As we saw in the previous sections, the availability of geolocations in Twitter data has changed quite drastically since 2019. One main takeaway here is that the `coordinates` attribute, if it is filled, does not signify a user's physical location when they made a post anymore. As of now, this attribute is only available in Instagram crossposts, where it is set to the centroid of pre-defined locations coming from Instagram. Moreover, this was already the case for Instagram crossposts before 2019, meaning that for around 10% of tweets, the `coordinates` attribute never contained the user's GPS location in the first place. In the future, researchers should therefore not rely on this attribute as a source of exact geolocation anymore.

Moving forward, researchers need to carefully consider which level of granularity is necessary for the task at hand. As a general rule, the more finegrained, the less data is available. We suggest the following sources of geolocation depending on the level required:

Country or city level This is the easiest level to obtain. Nearly all geolocated tweets, whether coming from native Twitter or from Instagram, currently contain location information on the city level or finer in the `place` attribute.

Point of interest (POI) There are currently two ways to obtain tweets tagged at the POI level:

1. Tweets coming from native Twitter can directly contain a POI location in the `place` attribute, including the POI's name and bounding box. This is the case for around 1-2% of all geolocated tweets.
2. Tweets coming from Instagram contain a centroid in the `coordinates` attribute that often corresponds to a POI. Unfortunately, this centroid first needs to be mapped back to a POI. In principle, this is possible using geolocation services such as those from Yelp, Foursquare,

or Twitter's own reverse geocoding service[9]. This process may introduce errors, and requires disentangling POI centroids from those for cities or countries, but it may be worth it to obtain more POI-level data. According to (Maurer, 2020), around 70% of Instagram crossposts contain geolocations at this granularity.

More fine-grained or use case-specific A finer level of granularity, e.g. for specific buildings or geographic structures other than POI, is not currently widely available via the geolocation data directly provided within tweets. The only way to potentially obtain this information lies in analyzing the text content of the tweet, which we will discuss further below.

Another aspect that researchers need to keep in mind now is that none of these locations are necessarily the physical spot where the tweet was sent, but a place that the user chose to attach to the tweet. In the case of native Twitter posts, these locations will at least be somewhere close to the GPS location of the device (around 200m radius), whereas in Instagram, they may be anywhere in the world. This can be an advantage in certain scenarios, though, allowing to take information into account even though the poster was not physically present at the location they are discussing.

In general, the percentage of geolocated tweets out of all tweets is low at 1-2%. We believe that there is a large amount of untapped information for tasks that require a geolocation within the remaining 98-99%. Exploiting this data would require determining the tweets' location from other sources, most prominently the actual content of the tweet. The simplest approach consists of performing Named Entity Recognition (NER) on the texts to detect known locations; in our preliminary experiments, we found that around 6% of the texts of all tweets contained geographic entities, out of which only about 3.5% were already covered by geolocated tweets. In a second step, these entities then need to be mapped to coordinates, the so-called geocoding, with the possible difficulty of having to disambiguate entity names. As a side note, the same process can be applied to locations set in user profiles (30-40% of profiles) without performing the NER step. We need to keep in mind that this location may not be accurate for all tweets of this user, but for some tasks, it may even make more sense to work with user location rather than tweet location.

To cover an even higher percentage of tweets, geocoding can also be performed via an analysis of latent factors of the tweet text, e.g. local slang or mentions of non-geographic, but locatable entities such as sports teams. An interesting approach would lie in correlating tweet texts with known descriptions of places, e.g. from Yelp or Wikidata, or in detecting tweets for specific locations by anchoring them on known ones via few-shot learning (Kruspe et al., 2019). Other tweet metadata, such as the language, can also be taken into account. Geocoding of tweets has been a research topic for some years now, such as in W-NUT's own shared task in 2016 (Han et al., 2016) (for other examples, see e.g. (Schlosser et al., 2021; Paule et al., 2019)). Image content that is now part of many tweets, especially Instagram crossposts, could also be analyzed with computer vision models as a source of location.

When using geocoding approaches, we cannot be sure what level of granularity to expect, but there may be tasks where it even makes sense to leave this distinction up to the users themselves. More importantly, careful consideration is necessary here to ensure that determining the geolocation does not infringe upon the users' privacy when they have not explicitly provided this location themselves.

6 Conclusion

In this paper, we gave a detailed overview over the effects of Twitter's geolocation policy change in 2019. We first described the roles of the various tweet attributes provided by Twitter's API and how they are filled by Twitter itself as well as third-party apps, in particular Instagram. We point out a particular issue with the assumption that the `coordinates` attribute contains the exact location of the user, which has never been the case for Instagram crossposts.

Next, we calculated a range of statistics, including a verification that the amount of tweets with GPS locations has starkly decreased since the policy change. We also showed that the `place` attribute is still usable and more broadly available, albeit less fine-grained, and that the text content of tweets also provides a lot of useful clues to determine geolocation. Future research could elucidate

[9] https://developer.twitter.com/en/docs/twitter-api/v1/geo/places-near-location/overview

the usage of various types of (explicit or implicit) geotagging depending on user demographics.

We then discussed the effect on different research tasks and conclude that there are many cases where GPS granularity is not necessary, which is also important because of ethical data minimization principles. Exceptions include mapping, tasks where users require immediate help in-person, and certain mobility analyses.

Finally, we suggest what technical steps could be taken moving forward, depending on the required level of geolocation granularity. Besides the explicit availability of locations, geocoding approaches based on tweet content are a promising research direction that could unlock a large percentage of the Twitter stream for geo-based tasks.

Acknowledgements

This work is supported by the European Research Council (ERC) under the European Union's Horizon 2020 research and innovation programme (grant agreement No. [ERC-2016-StG-714087], Acronym: *So2Sat*).

We would like to thank Auxane Boch for ethical insights into the issue.

References

Harshavardhan Achrekar, Avinash Gandhe, Ross Lazarus, Ssu-Hsin Yu, and Benyuan Liu. 2011. Predicting flu trends using twitter data. In *2011 IEEE Conference on Computer Communications Workshops (INFOCOM WKSHPS)*, pages 702–707.

Andrea Ceron, Luigi Curini, Stefano Iacus, and Giuseppe Porro. 2014. Every Tweet Counts? How Sentiment Analysis of Social Media Can Improve Our Knowledge of Citizens' Political Preferences with an Application to Italy and France. *New Media & Society*, 16:340–358.

European Commission. 2018. What is personal data? https://ec.europa.eu/info/law/law-topic/data-protection/reform/what-personal-data_en.

European Commission. 2019. General Data Protection Regulation (GDPR) – Official Legal Text. General Data Protection Regulation (GDPR). https://gdpr-info.eu/.

Casey Fiesler and Nicholas Proferes. 2018. "Participant" Perceptions of Twitter Research Ethics. *Social Media + Society*.

Vanessa Frias-Martinez and Enrique Frias-Martinez. 2014. Spectral clustering for sensing urban land use using twitter activity. *Eng. Appl. Artif. Intell.*, 35:237–245.

Daniel Gayo-Avello. 2012. "I Wanted to Predict Elections with Twitter and all I got was this Lousy Paper" - A Balanced Survey on Election Prediction using Twitter Data. *ArXiv*, abs/1204.6441.

Susan M. Grant-Muller, Ayelet Gal-Tzur, Einat Minkov, Silvio Nocera, Tsvi Kuflik, and Itay Shoor. 2015. Enhancing transport data collection through social media sources: methods, challenges and opportunities for textual data. *IET Intelligent Transport Systems*, 9:407–417.

Zoé A. Hamstead, David Fisher, Rositsa T. Ilieva, Spencer A. Wood, Timon McPhearson, and Peleg Kremer. 2018. Geolocated social media as a rapid indicator of park visitation and equitable park access. *Computers, Environment and Urban Systems*, 72:38–50.

Bo Han, Afshin Rahimi, Leon Derczynski, and Timothy Baldwin. 2016. Twitter geolocation prediction shared task of the 2016 workshop on noisy user-generated text. In *Proceedings of the 2nd Workshop on Noisy User-generated Text (W-NUT)*, pages 213–217, Osaka, Japan. The COLING 2016 Organizing Committee.

William Hobbs and Nazita Lajevardi. 2018. Effects of Divisive Political Campaigns on the Day-to-Day Segregation of Arab and Muslim Americans. *American Political Science Review*, 113:270 – 276.

Bo Hu and Martin Ester. 2013. Spatial topic modeling in online social media for location recommendation. In *Proceedings of the 7th ACM Conference on Recommender Systems*, RecSys '13, page 25–32, New York, NY, USA. Association for Computing Machinery.

Yingjie Hu and Ruo-Qian Wang. 2020. Understanding the removal of precise geotagging in tweets. *Nat Hum Behav*, (4):1219–1221. Https://doi.org/10.1038/s41562-020-00949-x.

Binxuan Huang and Kathleen M. Carley. 2019. A large-scale empirical study of geotagging behavior on twitter. In *Proceedings of the 2019 IEEE/ACM International Conference on Advances in Social Networks Analysis and Mining*, ASONAM '19, page 365–373, New York, NY, USA. Association for Computing Machinery.

Qunying Huang, Zhenlong Li, Jing Li, and Charles Chang. 2016. Mining frequent trajectory patterns from online footprints. In *Proceedings of the 7th ACM SIGSPATIAL International Workshop on GeoStreaming*, IWGS '16, New York, NY, USA. Association for Computing Machinery.

Matthias Häberle, Martin Werner, and Xiao Xiang Zhu. 2019. Building type classification from social media texts via geo-spatial textmining. In *IGARSS 2019 - 2019 IEEE International Geoscience and Remote Sensing Symposium*, pages 10047–10050.

NF Ibrahim and Xiaojun Wang. 2019. A text analytics approach for online retailing service improvement: Evidence from twitter. *Decision Support Systems*, 121.

Jared Jashinsky, Scott Burton, Carl Hanson, Josh West, Christophe Giraud-Carrier, Michael Barnes, and Trenton Argyle. 2013. Tracking suicide risk factors through twitter in the us. *Crisis*, 35:1–9.

Siwar Jendoubi and Arnaud Martin. 2020. Evidential positive opinion influence measures for viral marketing. *Knowl. Inf. Syst.*, 62(3):1037–1062.

Felix Kling and Alexei Pozdnoukhov. 2012. When a city tells a story: Urban topic analysis. *GIS: Proceedings of the ACM International Symposium on Advances in Geographic Information Systems*.

Anna Kruspe, Matthias Häberle, Iona Kuhn, and Xiao Xiang Zhu. 2020. Cross-language sentiment analysis of European Twitter messages during the COVID-19 pandemic. In *Proceedings of the 1st Workshop on NLP for COVID-19 at ACL 2020*. Association for Computational Linguistics.

Anna Kruspe, Jens Kersten, and Friederike Klan. 2021. Review article: Detection of actionable tweets in crisis events. *Natural Hazards and Earth System Sciences*, 21:1825–1845.

Anna M. Kruspe, Jens Kersten, and Friederike Klan. 2019. Detecting event-related tweets by example using few-shot models. In *Proceedings of the 16th International Conference on Information Systems for Crisis Response and Management, València, Spain, May 19-22, 2019*. ISCRAM Association.

Niels Lassen, René Madsen, and Ravi Vatrapu. 2014. Predicting iPhone Sales from iPhone Tweets. *Proceedings - IEEE International Enterprise Distributed Object Computing Workshop, EDOCW*, 2014:81–90.

Alyson Lloyd and James Cheshire. 2017. Deriving retail centre locations and catchments from geo-tagged twitter data. *Computers, Environment and Urban Systems*, 61.

Takashi Nicholas Maeda, Mitsuo Yoshida, Fujio Toriumi, and Hirotada Ohashi. 2016. Decision tree analysis of tourists' preferences regarding tourist attractions using geotag data from social media. In *Proceedings of the Second International Conference on IoT in Urban Space*, Urb-IoT '16, page 61–64, New York, NY, USA. Association for Computing Machinery.

Samuel M. Maurer. 2020. Evolving approaches to place tagging in social media. *Journal of Urban Planning and Development*, 146(3):04020023.

Stuart E. Middleton, Giorgos Kordopatis-Zilos, Symeon Papadopoulos, and Yiannis Kompatsiaris. 2018. Location extraction from social media: Geoparsing, location disambiguation, and geotagging. *ACM Trans. Inf. Syst.*, 36(4).

Anand Padmanabhan, Shaowen Wang, Guofeng Cao, Myunghwa Hwang, Zhenhua Zhang, Yizhao Gao, Kiumars Soltani, and Yan Liu. 2014. Flumapper: A cybergis application for interactive analysis of massive location-based social media. *Concurrency and Computation: Practice and Experience*, 26.

Xiaoman Pan, Boliang Zhang, Jonathan May, Joel Nothman, Kevin Knight, and Heng Ji. 2017. Cross-lingual name tagging and linking for 282 languages. In *Proceedings of the 55th Annual Meeting of the Association for Computational Linguistics (Volume 1: Long Papers)*, pages 1946–1958, Vancouver, Canada. Association for Computational Linguistics.

Jinhyung D. Park, Erik Seglem, Eric Lin, and Andreas Züfle. 2017. Protecting User Privacy: Obfuscating Discriminative Spatio-Temporal Footprints. In *Proceedings of the 1st ACM SIGSPATIAL Workshop on Recommendations for Location-based Services and Social Networks*, LocalRec'17, pages 1–4. Association for Computing Machinery.

Jorge David Gonzalez Paule, Yeran Sun, and Yashar Moshfeghi. 2019. On fine-grained geolocalisation of tweets and real-time traffic incident detection. *Inf. Process. Manag.*, 56:1119–1132.

Afshin Rahimi, Yuan Li, and Trevor Cohn. 2019. Massively multilingual transfer for NER. In *Proceedings of the 57th Annual Meeting of the Association for Computational Linguistics*, pages 151–164, Florence, Italy. Association for Computational Linguistics.

Stephan Schlosser, Daniele Toninelli, and Michela Cameletti. 2021. Comparing methods to collect and geolocate tweets in great britain. *Journal of Open Innovation: Technology, Market, and Complexity*, 7(1).

J. Singh, Yogesh Kumar Dwivedi, Nripendra P. Rana, Abhinav Kumar, and K. Kapoor. 2019. Event classification and location prediction from tweets during disasters. *Annals of Operations Research*, 283:737–757.

Dan Tasse, Zichen Liu, Alex Sciuto, and Jason Hong. 2017. State of the geotags: Motivations and recent changes. *Proceedings of the International AAAI Conference on Web and Social Media*, 11(1):250–259.

Fernando Terroso-Saenz and Andrés Muñoz. 2020. Land use discovery based on Volunteer Geographic Information classification. *Expert Systems with Applications*, 140:112892.

Erik F. Tjong Kim Sang and Fien De Meulder. 2003. Introduction to the CoNLL-2003 shared task: Language-independent named entity recognition. In *Proceedings of the Seventh Conference on Natural Language Learning at HLT-NAACL 2003*, pages 142–147.

ConQuest: Contextual Question Paraphrasing through Answer-Aware Synthetic Question Generation

Mostafa Mirshekari[1] **Jing Gu**[1, 2] **Aaron Sisto**[1]
[1] Searchable.ai, USA
[2] University of California, Santa Cruz, USA
{mostafa,aaron}@searchable.ai
jgu110@ucsc.edu

Abstract

Despite excellent performance on tasks such as question answering, Transformer-based architectures remain sensitive to syntactic and contextual ambiguities. Question Paraphrasing (QP) offers a promising solution as a means to augment existing datasets. The main challenges of current QP models include lack of training data and difficulty in generating diverse and natural questions. In this paper, we present *ConQuest*, a framework for generating synthetic datasets for contextual question paraphrasing. To this end, *ConQuest* first employs an answer-aware question generation (QG) model to create a question-pair dataset and then uses this data to train a contextualized question paraphrasing model. We extensively evaluate *ConQuest* and show its ability to produce more diverse and fluent question pairs than existing approaches. Our contextual paraphrase model also establishes a strong baseline for end-to-end contextual paraphrasing. Further, We find that context can improve BLEU-1 score on contextual compression and expansion by 4.3 and 11.2 respectively, compared to a non-contextual model.

1 Introduction

In recent years, Transformer-based architectures have made enormous progress in neural question answering (QA) (Karpukhin et al., 2020) (Izacard and Grave, 2020). However, these models are still sensitive to query syntax and ambiguity (Buck et al., 2017) (Moon and Fan, 2020). While data augmentation and lexical normalization are popular approaches to account for syntactic variations of input texts, progress on generating diverse and meaningful question variants (i.e., question paraphrasing (QP)) has been limited.

The main challenge in QP remains the lack of large-scale question paraphrase datasets. One potential solution is to use a QG model to generate multiple questions based on a given context and use these as paraphrased versions of each other. The challenge with this approach is the difficulty in generating questions that are diverse, fluent, and consistent. Further, these questions should be of different lengths to make sure that the QA models learn which information in the question to consider or neglect. This can be achieved by considering question expansion/compression tasks. However, in order to generate such questions, the context surrounding the source question and answer becomes important. The expansion task requires associating sparse information in a short-form question with details from the context to reformulate a richer question. Conversely, compression requires synthesizing extraneous details in a long-form question into a shorter form that is still consistent with the given passage and answer.

Here, we introduce *ConQuest*, a framework for generating synthetic contextual question paraphrase datasets for tasks such as question compression and expansion. Specifically, given a passage as context, we first employ an answer-aware Sequence-to-Sequence (Seq2Seq) model to generate a diverse set of question variants, each consistent with a common answer span. Then, we pair the shortest and longest variants to form a novel contextual paraphrasing dataset suitable for question expansion and compression tasks. Being answer-aware, this QG model accounts for contextual information when linking question pairs (unlike existing paraphrase methods using back-translation (Xie et al., 2019) or term replacement (Mrksic et al., 2016)).

Using this synthetic dataset, the final module of our framework is a Seq2Seq model for contextual question expansion and compression. By considering the context, this module addresses the unexplored challenge of contextual question reformulation. Further, we describe a multi-tag encoding scheme for compression and expansion to improve the quality of generated questions of dif-

Proceedings of the 2021 EMNLP Workshop W-NUT: The Seventh Workshop on Noisy User-generated Text, pages 222–229
November 11, 2021.

ferent length by providing an effective method to disentangle their representations while leveraging their shared properties. To evaluate our framework, we use questions from SQuAD v1.1 (Rajpurkar et al., 2016), a common question answering dataset. We measure performance of each component in our framework across a number of automatic and human-based metrics. We will release our question paraphrasing dataset and code upon acceptance.

2 Related Work

In this section, we review previous results and challenges in question generation and reformulation, and discuss novel aspects of our contextual question paraphrasing dataset.

2.1 Answer-Aware Question Generation

Answer-aware question generation (QG) involves encoding a source passage alongside the target answer to generate a consistent, fluent question. Seq2seq models in particular have been explored for this task (Liu et al., 2019; Kim et al., 2019; Ma et al., 2020; Varanasi et al., 2020; Rajpurkar et al., 2016; Gu et al., 2021; Majumder et al., 2021). Although QG performance has increased on the inverted SQuAD task, the diversity and fluency of generated questions for paraphrasing has not been studied quantitatively.

2.2 Comparison to Existing Datasets

Open source question paraphrase datasets are uncommon due to the private nature of user queries on most search engines. One relevant dataset is CANARD (Elgohary et al., 2019), which is a conversational QP dataset based on CoQA (Reddy et al., 2018). However, CANARD is not suitable for tasks like contextual compression and expansion as it focuses primarily on contextual coreference alignment and syntactic variations. Other datasets containing question paraphrases, like PAWS-X (Yang et al., 2019) and ComQA (Abujabal et al., 2019), are more appropriate for paraphrase identification and non-contextual paraphrase generation tasks. Our synthetic dataset expands on existing work by providing both context and question pairs to enable contextual paraphrasing and generating question pairs with diverse lengths to enable expansion and compression.

3 Method

In this section, we describe *ConQuest*, our contextual question paraphrasing framework. *ConQuest* has two main modules: 1) Paraphrase Question Generation where answer-aware question generation is used to create a question-pair dataset and 2) Contextual Paraphrasing to train a generative model to compress and expand these questions. These two modules and their components are shown in Figure 1.

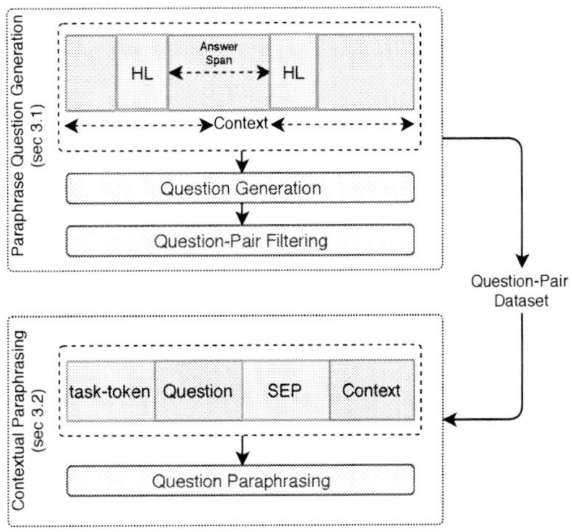

Figure 1: *ConQuest* framework. *ConQuest* has two main modules: 1) Paraphrase Question Generation to create the question-pair dataset and 2) Contextual Paraphrasing to expand and compress the questions.

3.1 Paraphrase Question Generation

The main objective of the Paraphrase Question Generation module is to create a dataset consisting of question-pairs, which can be used for downstream question paraphrasing tasks. Creating such a dataset manually is costly and difficult. To address this challenge, we introduce a novel approach based on answer-aware question generation. As shown in Figure 1, we first generate question-pairs of various lengths based on a reference passage and answer, and then filter by length to produce the final dataset. Specifically, to prepare the inputs and ensure that the question generation attends to the answer, we use a highlight token, **[HL]**, to surround the answer span in the input passage, following Klein and Nabi (2019). Then, we train the question generation model using the cross-entropy loss between generated questions and ground truth questions. Finally, a set of N questions are gener-

Model	Dispersity	Ent-1	Ent-2	Ent-3	Consistency	Fluency
QG	**17.4**	**1.04**	**1.14**	**1.15**	**93.2**	**82.5**
NMT	7.56	0.98	1.09	1.12	88.7	76.6
W2V	0.00	0.95	1.01	1.03	89.1	77.0

Table 1: Paraphrase question generation evaluation results.

ated using beam search.

The question-pair filtering step improves the generated question quality and length by 1) ranking the N generated questions by sequence length, and removing questions with less than 25% non-stop word token overlap with the shortest generated question to reduce the presence of paraphrases that are answer-inconsistent or semantically unrelated, and 2) removing questions less than three tokens longer than the shortest generated question to ensure length diversity. From the remaining questions, we create paraphrase sets between the shortest and longest generated questions. For cases with multiple short questions of identical length, we sample each individually to serve as references for the above filtering.

3.2 Contextual Paraphrasing

In this module, we train a contextualized multi-tag generative model for question paraphrasing (including question compression and expansion). By considering the context, the model has a better understanding of the important information which should be removed or added, and this, in turn, improves the overall quality of the paraphrased questions. To train this model, the dataset generated in Section 3.1 is divided into two subsets: 1) an expansion subset where the inputs are formed as **<EXPAND-TOKEN>Q<SEP>C** and the output is the longer version of the question and 2) a compression subset where the inputs are formed as **<SHORTEN-TOKEN>Q<SEP>C** and the output is the shorter version of the question. By using the **<EXPAND-TOKEN>** and **<SHORTEN-TOKEN>**, we provide a simple and effective method to disentangle the representations of these two tasks. Further, by using the multi-tag construct (i.e. training a single model on both tasks), we leverage the shared features of these tasks. Finally, a sequence-to-sequence BART model (Lewis et al., 2019) is trained using the cross-entropy loss between the generated questions and the targets. We evaluate our model and compare to alternative models in Section 4.2.

4 *ConQuest* Evaluation

To understand the performance of *ConQuest*, we have conducted a set of experiments using SQuAD v1.1, a commonly-used English question-answering dataset. In this section, we discuss the evaluation results for Paraphrase Question Generation and Contextual Paraphrasing.

4.1 Paraphrase Question Generation Evaluation

In this section, we evaluate the quality of our answer-aware QG-based paraphrase question generation model, relative to previous methods. The final synthetic paraphrase dataset contains 127,802 question-pair examples, created from 69,833 unique SQuAD v1.1 answer-context pairs, with an average compression rate of 63% between each generated pair.

We consider a number of automatic and human metrics to assess 1) diversity, 2) grammar and naturalness, and 3) consistency with the original SQuAD answer and context. The automatic metrics include Dispersity to measure the length distribution within generated paraphrase sets, and Ent-k (Zhang et al., 2018), an entropy-based diversity measure. Further, we consider Consistency and Fluency as human evaluation metrics. We compare our QG-based generation model to two previous approaches: back-translation via neural machine translation (NMT) (Xie et al., 2019), and synonym replacement using constrained word vectors (W2V) (Mrksic et al., 2016). More details about the evaluation metrics and implementation are presented in Appendices A and B.

The evaluation results in Table 1 show that answer-aware QG outperforms previous methods across all metrics considered. Specifically, our model achieves higher Dispersity, indicating, on average, a broader distribution of question lengths in each generated set. W2V, by comparison scores 0.0, as synonym replacement does not alter overall number of generated tokens. Our model also achieves higher Ent-1, Ent-2 and Ent-3 scores, indicating a lower degree of uniformity in generated

Compression Results	B1	B2	B3	B4	M	RL
BART-base (one-tags)	63.7	55.0	47.2	39.3	65.6	71.9
BART-base (two-tags)	**64.8**	**56.2**	**48.4**	**40.5**	**66.6**	72.3
T5-base (two-tags)	64.3	**56.2**	**48.6**	**40.6**	**66.6**	**72.8**
BART-base (two-tags, nocontext)	60.5	51.0	42.9	34.7	62.2	69.2
Expansion Results	B1	B2	B3	B4	M	RL
BART-base (one-tag)	62.2	53.9	46.8	40.3	65.4	68.4
BART-base (two-tags)	**62.8**	**54.3**	**47.1**	**40.6**	**65.8**	**68.7**
T5-base (two-tags)	61.9	53.4	46.2	39.4	66.1	68.5
BART-base (two-tags, nocontext)	51.6	41.2	32.7	26	53.4	57.0

Table 2: Contextual paraphrase generation evaluation.

n-gram distributions. While NMT scores higher than W2V, the results indicate that NMT is still limited to the semantic information contained in the original question, and cannot generate exceedingly diverse variants without considering the source context. Further, our model scores higher on both Consistency and Fluency, confirming that the QG-based questions are more grammatically correct, natural and answerable. Because the QG model is conditioned on the source answer and context, it retains consistency to a higher degree than approaches that are unaware of the answer and context.

4.2 Contextual Paraphrasing Evaluation

In this section, we discuss the performance of the Contextual Paraphrasing model on question compression and expansion tasks. Table 2 shows the results for this analysis. We consider multiple automatic metrics to assess the performance of the contextual question paraphrasing model, including BLEU (Papineni et al., 2002), METEOR (Banerjee and Lavie, 2005), and Rough-L (Lin, 2004). Some samples generated by *ConQuest* are presented in Section C

4.2.1 Base Model Evaluation

We have evaluated the contextual paraphrasing performance with BART (Lewis et al., 2019) and T5 (Raffel et al., 2019) as the base model. Compared to T5-base, the BART-base model shows similar performance for compression (64.8 BLEU-1 vs 64.3) and slightly better performance on the expansion task (62.8 BLEU-1 vs 61.9). Even though these results are close, T5-base has 220 million parameters, which is significantly larger than 139 millions for BART-base. Based on these results, we have chosen the BART model as the backbone of *ConQuest*.

4.2.2 Context vs No Context

ConQuest provides more meaningful question compression and expansion by considering the context during reformulation. To evaluate this factor, we performed experiments on samples with and without context using the BART-base model. As shown in Table 2, the contextualized text compression outperforms the non-contextualized model across all automatic metrics (e.g., improving BLEU-1 by 4.3 points). For the expansion task, our approach significantly outperforms the non-contextualized approach across all automatic metrics (e.g., 10.2 points improvement in BLEU-1). These results show that, by considering the context, our approach generates higher quality questions.

4.2.3 Single-tag vs Multi-tag Model

As discussed in Section 3.2, *ConQuest* utilizes a multi-tag input format to leverage the shared properties between the expansion and shortening tasks. To evaluate this factor, we have performed experiments with single tags and two tags, and compare their performance in Table 2. These results show that the two-tag model outperforms the one-tag model across all automatic metrics on both compression and expansion tasks. For example, the two-tag model results in 64.8 and 62.8 BLEU-1 score, which is 0.9 and 0.6 score improvement over the one-tag model. These results verify our assumption that using a multi-tag model leverages the compression and expansion task similarities and hence improves the model performance.

5 Conclusion

In this paper, we introduce *ConQuest*, a framework for generating synthetic contextual question paraphrase data. *ConQuest* first employs an answer-aware question generation model to create a dataset of diverse question-pairs. Then, it trains a multi-tag contextualized question paraphrasing model, which is able to control the length of the paraphrased questions. We have extensively evaluated *ConQuest* using the SQuAD v1.1 dataset. The results show that contextualized question paraphrasing results in higher performance across various automatic metrics (e.g., 4.3 and 11.2 points improvement in BLEU-1 compared to non-contextualized baseline). Further, our answer-aware QG-based data generation model achieves greater diversity, naturalness and consistency than previous question paraphrase models. Finally, we have performed and presented various ablation studies.

References

Abdalghani Abujabal, Rishiraj Saha Roy, Mohamed Yahya, and Gerhard Weikum. 2019. Comqa: A community-sourced dataset for complex factoid question answering with paraphrase clusters. In *Proceedings of the 2019 Conference of the North American Chapter of the Association for Computational Linguistics: Human Language Technologies, NAACL-HLT 2019, Minneapolis, MN, USA, June 2-7, 2019, Volume 1 (Long and Short Papers)*, pages 307–317. Association for Computational Linguistics.

Satanjeev Banerjee and Alon Lavie. 2005. Meteor: An automatic metric for mt evaluation with improved correlation with human judgments. In *Proceedings of the acl workshop on intrinsic and extrinsic evaluation measures for machine translation and/or summarization*, pages 65–72.

Christian Buck, Jannis Bulian, Massimiliano Ciaramita, Andrea Gesmundo, Neil Houlsby, Wojciech Gajewski, and Wei Wang. 2017. Ask the right questions: Active question reformulation with reinforcement learning. *CoRR*, abs/1705.07830.

Ahmed Elgohary, Denis Peskov, and Jordan L. Boyd-Graber. 2019. Can you unpack that? learning to rewrite questions-in-context. In *Proceedings of the 2019 Conference on Empirical Methods in Natural Language Processing and the 9th International Joint Conference on Natural Language Processing, EMNLP-IJCNLP 2019, Hong Kong, China, November 3-7, 2019*, pages 5917–5923. Association for Computational Linguistics.

Jing Gu, Mostafa Mirshekari, Zhou Yu, and Aaron Sisto. 2021. ChainCQG: Flow-aware conversational question generation. In *Proceedings of the 16th Conference of the European Chapter of the Association for Computational Linguistics: Main Volume*, pages 2061–2070, Online. Association for Computational Linguistics.

Ari Holtzman, Jan Buys, Li Du, Maxwell Forbes, and Yejin Choi. 2020. The curious case of neural text degeneration. In *International Conference on Learning Representations*.

Gautier Izacard and Edouard Grave. 2020. Leveraging passage retrieval with generative models for open domain question answering. *CoRR*, abs/2007.01282.

Vladimir Karpukhin, Barlas Oguz, Sewon Min, Patrick S. H. Lewis, Ledell Wu, Sergey Edunov, Danqi Chen, and Wen-tau Yih. 2020. Dense passage retrieval for open-domain question answering. In *Proceedings of the 2020 Conference on Empirical Methods in Natural Language Processing, EMNLP 2020, Online, November 16-20, 2020*, pages 6769–6781. Association for Computational Linguistics.

Yanghoon Kim, Hwanhee Lee, Joongbo Shin, and Kyomin Jung. 2019. Improving neural question generation using answer separation. In *The Thirty-Third AAAI Conference on Artificial Intelligence*, pages 6602–6609. AAAI Press.

Tassilo Klein and Moin Nabi. 2019. Learning to answer by learning to ask: Getting the best of GPT-2 and BERT worlds. *CoRR*, abs/1911.02365.

Mike Lewis, Yinhan Liu, Naman Goyal, Marjan Ghazvininejad, Abdelrahman Mohamed, Omer Levy, Ves Stoyanov, and Luke Zettlemoyer. 2019. Bart: Denoising sequence-to-sequence pre-training for natural language generation, translation, and comprehension. *arXiv preprint arXiv:1910.13461*.

Chin-Yew Lin. 2004. Rouge: A package for automatic evaluation of summaries. In *Text summarization branches out*, pages 74–81.

Bang Liu, Mingjun Zhou, Di Niu, Kunfeng Lai, Yancheng He, Haojie Wei, and Yu Xu. 2019. Learning to generate questions by learning what not to generate. In *WWW '19: The World Wide Web Conference*.

Ilya Loshchilov and Frank Hutter. 2019. Decoupled weight decay regularization. In *International Conference on Learning Representations*.

Xiyao Ma, Qile Zhu, Yanlin Zhou, and Xiaolin Li. 2020. Improving question generation with sentence-level semantic matching and answer position inferring. In *The Thirty-Fourth AAAI Conference on Artificial Intelligence, AAAI 2020, The Thirty-Second Innovative Applications of Artificial Intelligence Conference, IAAI 2020, The Tenth AAAI Symposium on Educational Advances in Artificial Intelligence, EAAI 2020, New York, NY, USA, February 7-12, 2020*, pages 8464–8471. AAAI Press.

Bodhisattwa Prasad Majumder, Sudha Rao, Michel Galley, and Julian McAuley. 2021. Ask what's missing and what's useful: Improving clarification question generation using global knowledge. *arXiv preprint arXiv:2104.06828*.

Sungrim (Riea) Moon and Jungwei Fan. 2020. How you ask matters: The effect of paraphrastic questions to BERT performance on a clinical SQuAD dataset. In *Proceedings of the 3rd Clinical Natural Language Processing Workshop*, pages 111–116, Online. Association for Computational Linguistics.

Nikola Mrksic, Diarmuid Ó Séaghdha, Blaise Thomson, Milica Gasic, Lina Maria Rojas-Barahona, Pei-Hao Su, David Vandyke, Tsung-Hsien Wen, and Steve J. Young. 2016. Counter-fitting word vectors to linguistic constraints. In *NAACL HLT 2016, The 2016 Conference of the North American Chapter of the Association for Computational Linguistics: Human Language Technologies, San Diego California, USA, June 12-17, 2016*, pages 142–148. The Association for Computational Linguistics.

Kishore Papineni, Salim Roukos, Todd Ward, and Wei-Jing Zhu. 2002. Bleu: a method for automatic evaluation of machine translation. In *Proceedings of the 40th annual meeting of the Association for Computational Linguistics*, pages 311–318.

Colin Raffel, Noam Shazeer, Adam Roberts, Katherine Lee, Sharan Narang, Michael Matena, Yanqi Zhou, Wei Li, and Peter J Liu. 2019. Exploring the limits of transfer learning with a unified text-to-text transformer. *arXiv preprint arXiv:1910.10683*.

Pranav Rajpurkar, Jian Zhang, Konstantin Lopyrev, and Percy Liang. 2016. Squad: 100,000+ questions for machine comprehension of text. *arXiv preprint arXiv:1606.05250*.

Siva Reddy, Danqi Chen, and Christopher D. Manning. 2018. Coqa: A conversational question answering challenge. *CoRR*, abs/1808.07042.

Stalin Varanasi, Saadullah Amin, and Guenter Neumann. 2020. CopyBERT: A unified approach to question generation with self-attention. In *Proceedings of the 2nd Workshop on Natural Language Processing for Conversational AI*, pages 25–31, Online. Association for Computational Linguistics.

Qizhe Xie, Zihang Dai, Eduard Hovy, Minh-Thang Luong, and Quoc V Le. 2019. Unsupervised data augmentation for consistency training. *arXiv preprint arXiv:1904.12848*.

Yinfei Yang, Yuan Zhang, Chris Tar, and Jason Baldridge. 2019. PAWS-X: A cross-lingual adversarial dataset for paraphrase identification. *CoRR*, abs/1908.11828.

Yizhe Zhang, Michel Galley, Jianfeng Gao, Zhe Gan, Xiujun Li, Chris Brockett, and Bill Dolan. 2018. Generating informative and diverse conversational responses via adversarial information maximization. *CoRR*, abs/1809.05972.

A Evaluation Metrics

We evaluate different parts of our approach on a number of automatic and human metrics to assess 1) diversity, 2) grammar and naturalness, and 3) consistency with the target answer and context. Specifically, to evaluate the paraphrase question generation, we use Dispersity and Ent-k metric for automatic scores and Consistency and Fluency for human evaluation (used in Section 4.1). To evaluate the quality of the contextual paraphrase generation, we use BLEU (Papineni et al., 2002), METEOR (Banerjee and Lavie, 2005), and Rough-L (Lin, 2004) (used in Section 4.2).

The dispersity is defined as,

$$dispersity = \frac{std(q_l)}{mean(q_l)} * 100 \quad (1)$$

where q_l is the set of generated question lengths. The Ent-k metric, describing diversity of generated questions via n-gram frequencies (Zhang et al., 2018). To calculate these metrics, we generate 8 reference paraphrase questions for each of 2000 examples subsampled from SQuAD v1.1. Each method is given a common set of 2000 source questions; In addition, the QG-based generation method is only given the corresponding answer and context passages for each question, and not shown the original SQuAD questions themselves.

Human evaluation assesses the models' abilities to capture semantic meaning within paraphrases while retaining grammatical accuracy. Specifically, we use Consistency, and Fluency to measure the quality of the generated questions in relation to the answer and context. We have used Mechanical Turk for this evaluation. For each task and each generation model, we randomly selected 200 generated samples, with each sample scored by ten different Amazon Mechanical Turk (Turkers). For Consistency, Turkers decide a generated question is answerable or not based on the provided passage and answer. Based on choice between "Consistent" (score 3), "Can not decide" (score 1), and "Inconsistent" (score 0), we get the Consistency score by divided the total score with the theoretically possible maximum score (3*total question number). For fluency, the Turkers evaluate how many errors in grammar level, lexical leval, semantic leval combined, given the passage. Based on choice between "No errors" (score 3), "one error" (score 1), and "more than one error" (score 0), similar to the Consistancy calculation, we have the final Fluency score by divided the total score with the possible maximum score (3*total question number).

B Experimental Details

In this section, we provide additional experimental details which is of use in replicating the evaluation results.

Paraphrase Question Generation: We consider T5-base (220M params) for question generation. The model is trained for 5 epochs. We apply AdamW optimizer (Loshchilov and Hutter, 2019), and the number of warmup ratio is set to be 0.1. Learning rate is tuned between 2e-5 5e-5. The dropout ratio is set to be 0.1. We test and chose the better decoding method for the model. Specifically, we decode questions via beam search of size 4. We encode the model input as: CONTEXT[SEP]ANSWER, and use a cross entropy loss between generated tokens and tokens in ground truth question for each example in the inverted SQuAD training set.

Paraphrase Question Generation Baselines: For our dataset evaluation, we consider two previous paraphrase generation approaches. The first is back-translation via neural machine translation (NMT), in which a question, q, written in English is translated to French, and then back to English to generate a syntactic variant, q', with the same semantic meaning. We use the UDA package (Xie et al., 2019), with WMT'14 English-French translation model checkpoints. For decoding, we use random sampling, with a sampling temperature of 0.8. The second approach we consider is synonym replacement using constrained word vectors (W2V), trained specifically for the synonym replacement task (Mrksic et al., 2016). We restrict synonym replacements to non-stop words, and target a 25% non-stop word replacement rate for each question. These results are discussed along with the proposed QG method in following sections.

Contextual Paraphrasing: To train the contextual paraphrasing model, we have explored BART-base (140M params) (Lewis et al., 2019) and T5-base (220M params) (Raffel et al., 2019), as described in Section 4.2. Each model is trained for 6 epochs. AdamW optimizer (Loshchilov and Hutter, 2019) with learning rate of 1e-4 (with a linear scheduler), β_1 of 0.9, and β_2 of 0.999. To generate the samples, we use nucleus sampling (Holtzman et al., 2020) with top-p as 0.92. These hyperparameters are chosen empirically. On average training

Table 3: Samples generated by the model

Expansion Samples
Before: Who excavated ancient Ur? **After:** Who excavated ancient Ur and published The Art of the Middle East, including Persia, Mesopotamia and Palestine?
Before: Which system lacks a distinctive future tense? **After:** Which system lacks a distinctive future tense (the present tense serves here) and features special forms to express an action performed by an undetermined subject (the "impersonal"?
Before: Who encouraged Tony de Brum? **After:** Who encouraged Tony de Brum to turn the crises into an opportunity to promote action against climate change?
Compression Samples
Before: Who coined the term Hellenistic to refer to and define the period when Greek culture spread in the non-Greek world after Alexander's conquest? **After:** Who coined the term Hellenistic?
Before: The Alps are the highest and most extensive mountain range system that lies entirely where? **After:** Where do the Alps lie?
Before: What is far superior to classical thermodynamics in that glass breaking behavior can be explained by the fundamental laws of physics paired with a statistical postulate? **After:** What is far superior to classical thermodynamics?

for 6 epochs has taken 6 and half hours in Amazon EC2 p3.2xlarge instances with Tesla V100 GPUs. The data used for this model is divided in 90% training and 10% test data. Further, 5% of the training data is considered as validation set. This split will be released upon acceptance of the paper.

C Generated Samples:

In this section, we provide some samples generated by the contextual paraphrasing model (shown in Table 3). As the samples show, in the expansion task, the model uses some additional info from the context to expand the questions. For the compression task, *ConQuest* removes some of the information provided in the question; however tries to keep the most important part of the information.

D Ethics/Broader Impact Statement

The results presented here demonstrate the efficacy of *ConQuest* in producing challenging datasets by leveraging a question paraphrasing model. This model enables higher robustness of Question Answering models in real-life applications. As part of our future work, we plan to 1) extend this framework to denoising and noisifying tasks, 2) extend to tasks other than single-turn QA(e.g., conversational QA and text summarization), and 3) end-to-end and joint training of QA and QP models. With respect to ethical considerations, our framework has the same considerations as a general QA and QG model and hence, we inherit any ethical shortcomings that exists in the source dataset.

NADE: A Benchmark for Robust Adverse Drug Events Extraction in Face of Negations

Simone Scaboro[1] **Beatrice Portelli**[1] **Emmanuele Chersoni**[2]
Enrico Santus[3] **Giuseppe Serra**[1]

[1] University of Udine, Italy
[2] The Hong Kong Polytechnic University, Hong Kong
[3] DSIG - Bayer Pharmaceuticals, New Jersey, USA

{scaboro.simone,portelli.beatrice}@spes.uniud.it,
emmanuele.chersoni@polyu.edu.hk,
esantus@gmail.com, giuseppe.serra@uniud.it

Abstract

Adverse Drug Event (ADE) extraction models can rapidly examine large collections of social media texts, detecting mentions of drug-related adverse reactions and trigger medical investigations. However, despite the recent advances in NLP, it is currently unknown if such models are robust in face of *negation*, which is pervasive across language varieties.

In this paper we evaluate three state-of-the-art systems, showing their fragility against negation, and then we introduce two possible strategies to increase the robustness of these models: a pipeline approach, relying on a specific component for negation detection; an augmentation of an ADE extraction dataset to artificially create negated samples and further train the models.

We show that both strategies bring significant increases in performance, lowering the number of spurious entities predicted by the models. Our dataset and code will be publicly released to encourage research on the topic.

1 Introduction

Exploring social media texts is becoming more and more important in the field of pharmacovigilance (Karimi et al., 2015b; Sarker and Gonzalez, 2015), since it is common for Internet users to report their personal experiences with drugs on forums and microblogging platforms. Given the inherent noisiness of social media texts (colloquial language, slang and metaphors, non-standard syntactic constructions etc.), the Natural Language Processing (NLP) community dedicated a consistent effort in developing robust methods for mining biomedical information from social media outlets. This also led to the creation of several dedicated shared tasks series on ADE detection (SMM4H – Social Media Mining for Health) (Paul et al., 2016; Sarker and Gonzalez-Hernandez, 2017; Weissenbacher et al., 2018, 2019; Klein et al., 2020).

Although these models have seen great advancements in the last years, also thanks to the introduction of pre-trained Transformers-based architectures (Vaswani et al., 2017; Devlin et al., 2019), it is still unknown how robust they are in face of some pervasive linguistic phenomena such as negation. However, general investigations on machine comprehension and question answering tasks confirmed that such phenomena often pose a serious challenge (Ribeiro et al., 2020). Managing to efficiently handle the scope of negations and speculations in clinical notes is a key problem in biomedical NLP (Velldal et al., 2012; Cruz Díaz, 2013), and similarly, for digital pharmacovigilance it is essential to recognize whether the association between a drug and an ADE is actually being stated or negated because the consequences of extracting misleading information about the possible side effects of drugs can be extremely serious.

In this paper, we analyze the performance of some of the latest state-of-the-art ADE detection systems on NADE: a new dataset derived from SMM4H data, which contains a relevant amount of annotated samples with negated ADEs. We also introduce and analyze two strategies to increase the robustness of the models: adding a negation detection module in a pipeline fashion to exclude the negated ADEs predicted by the models; augmenting the training set with artificially negated samples. As a further contribution, our dataset and scripts will be made publicly available for researchers to test the robustness of their ADE extraction systems against negation.[1]

[1] https://github.com/AilabUdineGit/NADE-dataset

Proceedings of the 2021 EMNLP Workshop W-NUT: The Seventh Workshop on Noisy User-generated Text, pages 230–237
November 11, 2021.

2 Related Work

Detecting negation scopes is a traditional topic of NLP research. An early, popular system was introduced by Chapman et al. (2001), whose NegEx algorithm exploited regular expressions to identify negations in clinical documents in English. Later, machine learning approaches became more popular after the publication of a common gold standard, i.e. the BioScope corpus (Vincze et al., 2008). Several proposals consisted of a two-steps methodology: a first classifier to detect which token in a sentence is a negation/speculation cue, and a second classifier to determine which tokens in the sentence are within the scope of the cue word (Morante et al., 2008; Cruz Díaz et al., 2012; Attardi et al., 2015; Zou et al., 2015).

More recently, approaches based on neural networks (CNN, Qian et al. 2016; BiLSTM, Fancellu et al. 2016, 2017; Dalloux et al. 2019) have been introduced in the literature, showing some crosslinguistic and crossdomain transferability. Moreover, BERT-based models have been proposed to handle this phenomenon (Khandelwal and Sawant, 2020; Britto and Khandelwal, 2020), also with the aid of multitask learning architectures (Khandelwal and Britto, 2020).

To our knowledge, the research in biomedical NLP mostly focused on scope detection *per se* and on more formal types of texts (e.g. clinical notes, articles). In our research we focus instead on the specific task of ADE detection and on the impact of negation on the performance of ADE systems for noisy social media texts (e.g. tweets, blog posts), with the goal of making them able to distinguish between factual and non-factual information.

3 NADE Dataset

While there are several datasets for ADE detection on social media texts (Karimi et al., 2015a; Alvaro et al., 2017), the biggest collection of tweets tagged for ADE mentions is the one released yearly for the SMM4H Workshop and Shared Task. We used the following resources:

a) **SMM4H19**$_{ext}$. The training set for the ADE *extraction* Task of SMM4H19 (Weissenbacher et al., 2019), consisting of 2276 tweets that mention at least one drug name. 1300 of them contain ADEs, and annotations of their position in the text (**`ADE`** class). The other 976 are control samples with no ADE mentions (**`noADE`**). As the blind test set is not publicly available, we rely on the training set only and use the splits by Portelli et al. (2021a), which balance positive and negative samples;

b) **SMM4H19**$_{cls}$ and **SMM4H20**$_{cls}$ (Weissenbacher et al., 2019; Klein et al., 2020). The training sets for SMM4H *classification* Tasks, containing tweets labeled as **`ADE`** or **`noADE`** (1:9 ratio).

The community focused on the ADE extraction task, so most datasets are made of samples that either do or do not contain an ADE. Because of this, they include a small number of negated ADEs by construction: no particular attention is given to these samples when curating the data and when they are present they are treated as **`noADE`** samples and not explicitly labelled. This leads to their class being misrepresented and makes it harder to study this phenomenon.

3.1 Data Augmentation

In order to perform our analysis we created a new set of samples containing negated ADEs (**`negADE`**) in two ways: looking for real samples negating the presence of an ADE in SMM4H19$_{cls}$ and SMM4H20$_{cls}$ (**`negADE_r`**); manually creating negated versions for the **`ADE`** tweets in the test split of SMM4H19$_{ext}$ (**`negADE_g`**). The original test split includes 260 tweets, 7 of which were discarded during the generation process, leading to 253 samples. Further details in Appendix A.

Recovery of Real Samples

SMM4H19$_{cls}$ and SMM4H20$_{cls}$ contain a total of 24857 unique **`noADE`** tweets, so there is an high chance of encountering negated ADEs. The samples have no other annotation apart from their binary labels and analyzing all of them manually would be extremely time-consuming. We performed a preliminary filtering, keeping only the tweets containing a negation cue. Then we manually analyzed the filtered tweets, assessing whether the negation refers to an ADE and if the message actually negates the presence of the ADE. In the following examples: the first tweet is valid (it negates the ADE); the second one contains a negation, but does not negate the ADE.

1. This **#HUMIRA shot** has me feeling like a normal human... **No pain no inflammation** no nothinggggh
2. But I'm **not on adderall and I am feasting**.

The tweets were evaluated by four volunteer annotators with a high level of proficiency in English, and we only kept the samples for which they were in agreement. As a result we obtained **`negADE_r`**, a set of real tweets containing negated ADEs, that allows us to create a test set containing up to 16% negated samples.

Generation of Artificial Samples

The generation process for the **negADE_g** samples was carried out by the same four volunteers as before. Each one of them was given part of the 260 tweets from the SMM4H19$_{ext}$ test set, and was asked to alter them (as conservatively as possible) to generate a new version of the tweet that negates the presence of the ADE. Each volunteer was asked to review the tweets generated by the other participants and to propose modifications, in case the tweets looked ambiguous or unnatural. If no agreement was found about the edits, the augmented tweets were discarded. The result of this procedure is **negADE_g**, a new set of tweets denying the presence of an ADE. Here is an example of an original tweet and its negated version (highlighting the cue word added to negate the ADE):

Original: fluoxetine, got me going crazy.

Negated: fluoxetine, **didn't** get me going crazy.

3.2 Data Partitioning

We split the available data in a train and a test set, both containing the three categories of tweets: **ADE**, **noADE** and **negADE** (Table 1). Given the small amount of **negADE_r** tweets, we use all of them in the test set to evaluate the performance only on real tweets. Conversely, the training set only contains the manually generated **negADE_g** samples.

	ADE	noADE	negADE	Total
Train	842 45%	785 42%	253 13%	1880
Test	200 43%	195 42%	73 16%	468

Table 1: Distribution of samples in NADE.

4 Analyzed models

4.1 ADE Extraction Models

We choose three Transformer-based models that showed high performance on SMM4H19$_{ext}$ (Portelli et al., 2021a,b), and are currently at the top of the SMM4H19$_{ext}$ ADE extraction leaderboard: BERT (Devlin et al., 2019), SpanBERT (Joshi et al., 2019) and PubMedBERT (Gu et al., 2020). The models are fine-tuned for token classification, predicting an IOB label for each token in the sentence to detect the boundaries of ADE mentions.

4.2 Negation Detection Models

We introduce two negation detection modules: NegEx, a Python implementation (Pizarro et al., 2020) of the NegEx algorithm, based on simple regular expressions, which evaluates whether named entities are negated; BERTneg, a BERT model (bert-base-uncased) that we finetuned for token classification. We trained BERTneg on the BioScope dataset, which consists in medical texts annotated for the presence of negation and speculation cues and their related scopes. We selected 3190 sentences (2801 of which with a negation scope) and finetuned the model for scope detection (10 epochs, learning rate 0.0001).

4.3 Pipeline Models

Let us consider a text t, a ADE extraction base model $\mathcal{B}$ and a negation detection module $\mathcal{N}$. Given t, $\mathcal{B}$ outputs a set of substrings of t that are labeled as ADE mentions: $\mathcal{B}(t) = \{b_1, \ldots, b_m\}$. Similarly, $\mathcal{N}$ takes a text and outputs a set of substrings, which are considered to be entities within a negation scope: $\mathcal{N}(t) = \{n_1, \ldots, n_t\}$.

A combined *pipeline model* is obtained by discarding all ADE spans $b_i \in \mathcal{B}(t)$ that overlap one of the negation spans $n_j \in \mathcal{N}(t)$:

$$\mathcal{BN}(t) = \{b_i \in \mathcal{B}(t) \mid \forall j(n_j \in \mathcal{N}(t) \wedge b_i \cap n_j = \emptyset)\}$$

5 Experiments

All the reported results are the average over 5 runs. For the Transformer models we used the same hyperparameters reported by Portelli et al. (2021a).

As metrics, we consider the number of false positive predictions (FP) and the relaxed precision (P), recall (R) and F1 score as defined in the SMM4H shared tasks (Weissenbacher et al., 2019): the scores take into account "partial" matches, in which it is sufficient for a prediction to partially overlap with the gold annotation.

As a preliminary step, the two negation detection models are trained and used to predict the negation scopes for all the test samples once. This allows us to compute the predictions of any pipeline model.

Exp 1: to provide a measure of the initial robustness of the base models and their general performance, we train them on the **ADE** and **noADE** samples only (842+785 samples). We then test the efficacy of the pipeline negation detection method, applying NegEx and BERTneg to the base models.

Exp 2: to test the effect of augmenting the training data with artificial samples (i.e., the second

		BERT				PubMedBERT				SpanBERT			
		FP	`ADE`	`noADE`	`negADE`	FP	`ADE`	`noADE`	`negADE`	FP	`ADE`	`noADE`	`negADE`
1	$\mathcal{B}$ **(base model)**	161.2	46.2	42.6	73.4	144.2	37.0	40.4	67.4	245.6	66.2	79.8	100.8
2	$\mathcal{B}$**+NegEx**	106.4	41.6	40.4	24.4	93.4	32.0	37.6	23.8	170.8	58.4	74.0	38.6
3	$\mathcal{B}$**+BERTneg**	120.2	40.0	41.0	39.2	106.2	30.6	39.0	36.6	184.0	56.2	74.8	53.2
4	$\mathcal{B}$`+50`	146.6	40.2	38.4	69.0	126.2	34.4	35.4	57.0	183.2	46.2	58.6	79.2
5	$\mathcal{B}$`+100`	166.8	50.4	48.4	69.0	108.0	33.0	34.6	40.4	230.0	58.6	77.4	95.4
6	$\mathcal{B}$`+150`	125.8	43.0	41.4	42.4	100.8	29.8	41.4	29.6	156.8	47.6	50.8	59.2
7	$\mathcal{B}$`+200`	105.4	41.0	36.0	29.0	79.0	29.2	27.6	22.2	134.2	38.6	44.4	51.6
8	$\mathcal{B}$`+253`	101.6	42.6	35.8	23.2	84.2	30.6	34.6	19.0	179.8	55.2	60.6	65.2
9	$\mathcal{B}$**+NegEx** `+253`	91.6	42.2	35.8	13.6	76.6	29.4	34.6	12.6	136.4	52.0	57.0	27.6
10	$\mathcal{B}$**+BERTneg** `+253`	93.6	41.0	35.8	16.6	74.2	27.2	34.2	12.8	145.4	51.4	57.4	36.8

Table 2: False Positives for: the base models; the pipeline models; base models trained with an increasing number of **`negADE_g`** samples; pipeline models trained with all **`negADE_g`** samples.

		BERT			PubMedBERT			SpanBERT		
		P	R	F1	P	R	F1	P	R	F1
1	$\mathcal{B}$ **(base model)**	50.15	65.6	56.78	53.24	67.41	59.47	43.65	73.28	54.61
2	$\mathcal{B}$**+NegEx**	55.59	58.03	56.73	59.21	59.76	59.47	48.65	65.04	55.55
3	$\mathcal{B}$**+BERTneg**	54.37	60.7	57.30	57.69	62.64	60.04	47.82	67.39	55.85
⋮		⋮			⋮			⋮		
8	$\mathcal{B}$`+253`	58.85	63.86	61.21	63.28	63.33	63.20	48.52	68.76	56.85
9	$\mathcal{B}$**+NegEx** `+253`	58.65	58.03	58.29	63.24	58.29	60.58	51.63	61.29	55.98
10	$\mathcal{B}$**+BERTneg** `+253`	59.22	60.17	59.65	64.74	60.98	62.72	51.31	64.10	56.94

Table 3: Precision, Recall and F1 score for: the base models; the pipeline models; base models trained with an increasing number of **`negADE_g`** samples; pipeline models trained with all **`negADE_g`** samples.

negation detection method), we add to the training set an increasing number of **`negADE_g`** samples (`+50` to `+253`, in steps of 50 samples). During preliminary experiments, we added 100 **`noADE`** samples from SMM4H19$_{cls}$ to the training set. The performance of all the models *did not vary* in this case, showing that the results of Exp 2 are caused by the nature of the samples, and not simply by the increased size of training set All the base models are then fine-tuned on the resulting dataset.

Exp 3: to investigate whether the two methods are complementary in their action, we combine the two strategies, applying the pipeline architecture to the models trained on the augmented dataset.

5.1 Results

Table 2 and 3 contain a summary of the most relevant metrics for the tested models. We report the number of FP both on the whole test set and on individual partitions (**`ADE`**, **`noADE`** and **`negADE_r`** samples).

Exp 1 (rows 1–3): all base models (row 1) have a high number of FP, especially in the **`negADE`** category. This strongly suggests that they are not robust against this phenomenon. When combined with NegEx (row 2), the FP decreases by 34%, showing that the regular expression module removes a great number of unwanted predictions. BERTneg decreases the number of FP, too, but only by 25%. This is due to the difference between the brute-force behaviour of NegEx and the contextual prediction of a deep machine learning model. We can notice that the two pipeline models slightly reduce the number of FP also in the **`ADE`** category (e.g. from 66.2 to 56.2 for SpanBERT).

However, if we look at P and R in the first three rows, we can see that the negation detection modules bring an increase in P at the cost of large drops in R. Some correct predictions of the base models get discarded, in particular the ADEs that contain a negation (e.g., "After taking this drug *I cannot sleep anymore*"). As this effect is undesirable, we investigated the use of the **`negADE_g`** samples to mitigate it.

Exp 2 (rows 4–8): adding **`negADE_g`** samples to the training set (from `+50` to `+253`) lowers the number of FP predictions for all models. Using all the available samples brings down the number of FP as much as using NegEx on the initial model (compare +NegEx and `+253`). This reduction is given by the decrease of FP in the **`negADE`** set, while the number of FP in the **`ADE`** and **`noADE`** categories remains roughly stable.

Comparing row `+253` with row 1 shows, as for Exp 1, an increase in P and a drop in R. However, the drop in R is less severe than before (5 points

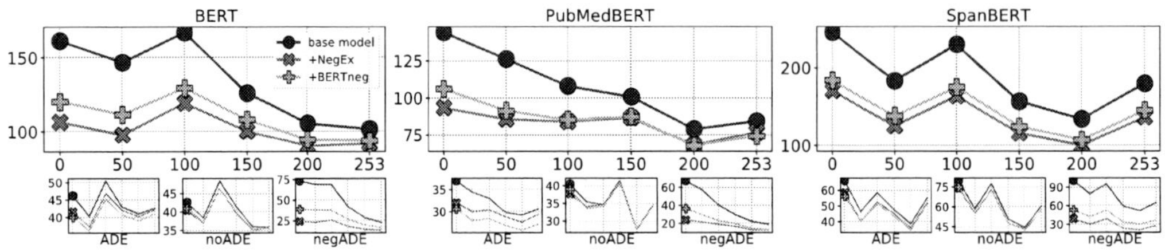

Figure 1: Top: total FP for the three base models and their pipeline versions with the increasing of **negADE** samples in the training set (x-axis: from 50 to 253). Bottom: number of FP for all the models by sample category.

at most), meaning that less true positives are being discarded. Also, P increases twice as much, leading to an overall increase in F1.

Exp 3 (rows 9–10): the effect of augmented dataset and negation modules are complementary, as shown by the further decrease in FP. However, combining the two approaches does not seem to be a winning strategy, as it leads to a further decrease in R without the benefit of increasing P.

The same behaviour can be observed for all the base models, despite the different initial performance (with SpanBERT having a generally higher R and PubMedBERT an higher P).

Figure 1 offers another visualization of the effect that adding **negADE_g** samples has on the number of False Positives. The number of **negADE** samples in the training set increases from left to right in each plot (from 0 to 253). The top row shows how the total number of predicted FPs decreases (for all base and pipeline models) when adding the generated negated samples. The plots in the bottom row show how the number of FP varies for the three categories of samples separately (**ADE**, **noADE** and **negADE**, bottom row). As observed in Table 2, the decrease is most significant in the **negADE** partition.

The results show that introducing a small number of new samples (even if artificial) is the best way to directly increase the model knowledge about the phenomenon. However, this solution could be expensive in absence of a large quantity of negated data. For this reason, the pipeline models might be a viable alternative, as they maintain the F1 score while still decreasing the number of false positives.

6 Conclusions

In this paper, we evaluate the impact of negations on state-of-the-art ADE detection models. We introduced NADE, a new dataset specifically aimed at studying this phenomenon. The dataset proves to be a challenging setting and the experiments show that current methods lack mechanisms to deal with negations. We introduce and compare two strategies to tackle the problem: using a negation detection module and adding **negADE_g** samples in the training set. Both of them bring significant increases in performance.

Both the dataset and the code are made publicly available for the community to test the robustness of their systems against negation.

Future work should focus on more refined techniques to accurately model the semantic properties of the samples, also by jointly handling negation and speculation phenomena. This might be an essential requirement for dealing with the noisiness and variety of social media texts. The main short term directions are increasing the quality and quantity of real **negADE** samples (possibly via crowdsourcing), and creating a model that is able to discard **negADE** (keeping an high precision level), without sacrificing recall.

7 Acknowledgments

We would like to thank the three anonymous reviewers for their insightful feedback.

References

Nestor Alvaro, Yusuke Miyao, and Nigel Collier. 2017. TwiMed: Twitter and PubMed Comparable Corpus of Drugs, Diseases, Symptoms, and Their Relations. *JMIR Public Health Surveillance*, 3(2):e24.

Giuseppe Attardi, Vittoria Cozza, and Daniele Sartiano. 2015. Detecting the Scope of Negations in Clinical Notes. In *Proceedings of CLiC.it*.

Benita Kathleen Britto and Aditya Khandelwal. 2020. Resolving the Scope of Speculation and Negation using Transformer-Based Architectures. *arXiv preprint arXiv:2001.02885*.

Wendy W Chapman, Will Bridewell, Paul Hanbury, Gregory F Cooper, and Bruce G Buchanan. 2001. A Simple Algorithm for Identifying Negated Findings and Diseases in Discharge Summaries. *Journal of Biomedical Informatics*, 34(5):301–310.

Noa P Cruz Díaz. 2013. Detecting Negated and Uncertain Information in Biomedical and Review Texts. In *Proceedings of the RANLP Student Research Workshop*.

Noa P Cruz Díaz, Manuel J Mana López, Jacinto Mata Vázquez, and Victoria Pachón Álvarez. 2012. A Machine-learning Approach to Negation and Speculation Detection in Clinical Texts. *Journal of the American Society for Information Science and Technology*, 63(7):1398–1410.

Clément Dalloux, Vincent Claveau, and Natalia Grabar. 2019. Speculation and Negation Detection in French Biomedical Corpora. In *Proceedings of RANLP*.

Jacob Devlin, Ming-Wei Chang, Kenton Lee, and Kristina Toutanova. 2019. BERT: Pre-training of Deep Bidirectional Transformers for Language Understanding. In *Proceedings of NAACL*.

Federico Fancellu, Adam Lopez, and Bonnie Webber. 2016. Neural Networks for Negation Scope Detection. In *Proceedings of ACL*.

Federico Fancellu, Adam Lopez, Bonnie Webber, and Hangfeng He. 2017. Detecting Negation Scope Is Easy, Except When It Isn't. In *Proceedings of EACL*.

Yu Gu, Robert Tinn, Hao Cheng, Michael Lucas, Naoto Usuyama, Xiaodong Liu, Tristan Naumann, Jianfeng Gao, and Hoifung Poon. 2020. Domain-Specific Language Model Pretraining for Biomedical Natural Language Processing. *arXiv preprint arXiv:2007.15779*.

Mandar Joshi, Danqi Chen, Yinhan Liu, Daniel S. Weld, Luke Zettlemoyer, and Omer Levy. 2019. SpanBERT: Improving Pre-training by Representing and Predicting Spans. *Transactions of the Association for Computational Linguistics*, 8:64–77.

Sarvnaz Karimi, Alejandro Metke-Jimenez, Madonna Kemp, and Chenchen Wang. 2015a. CADEC: A Corpus of Adverse Drug Event Annotations. *Journal of Biomedical Informatics*, 55:73–81.

Sarvnaz Karimi, Chen Wang, Alejandro Metke-Jimenez, Raj Gaire, and Cecile Paris. 2015b. Text and Data Mining Techniques in Adverse Drug Reaction Detection. *ACM Computing Surveys (CSUR)*, 47(4):1–39.

Aditya Khandelwal and Benita Kathleen Britto. 2020. Multitask Learning of Negation and Speculation using Transformers. In *Proceedings of the EMNLP International Workshop on Health Text Mining and Information Analysis*.

Aditya Khandelwal and Suraj Sawant. 2020. NegBERT: A Transfer Learning Approach for Negation Detection and Scope Resolution. In *Proceedings of LREC*.

Ari Klein, Ilseyar Alimova, Ivan Flores, Arjun Magge, Zulfat Miftahutdinov, Anne-Lyse Minard, Karen O'Connor, Abeed Sarker, Elena Tutubalina, Davy Weissenbacher, et al. 2020. Overview of the Fifth Social Media Mining for Health Applications Shared Tasks at Coling 2020. In *Proceedings of the COLING Workshop on Social Media Mining for Health Applications*.

Roser Morante, Anthony Liekens, and Walter Daelemans. 2008. Learning the Scope of Negation in Biomedical Texts. In *Proceedings of EMNLP*.

Michael Paul, Abeed Sarker, John Brownstein, Azadeh Nikfarjam, Matthew Scotch, Karen Smith, and Graciela Gonzalez. 2016. Social Media Mining for Public Health Monitoring and Surveillance. In *Biocomputing*, pages 468–479.

Jeno Pizarro, Leon Reteig, and Luke Murray. 2020. jenojp/negspacy: Minor Bug Fix, Improve Chunk Prefix Functionality (Version v0.1.9).

Beatrice Portelli, Edoardo Lenzi, Emmanuele Chersoni, Giuseppe Serra, and Enrico Santus. 2021a. BERT Prescriptions to Avoid Unwanted Headaches: A Comparison of Transformer Architectures for Adverse Drug Event Detection. In *Proceedings of EACL*.

Beatrice Portelli, Daniele Passabì, Edoardo Lenzi, Giuseppe Serra, Enrico Santus, and Emmanuele Chersoni. 2021b. Improving Adverse Drug Event Extraction with SpanBERT on Different Text Typologies. *arXiv preprint arXiv:2105.08882*.

Zhong Qian, Peifeng Li, Qiaoming Zhu, Guodong Zhou, Zhunchen Luo, and Wei Luo. 2016. Speculation and Negation Scope Detection via Convolutional Neural Networks. In *Proceedings of EMNLP*.

Marco Tulio Ribeiro, Tongshuang Wu, Carlos Guestrin, and Sameer Singh. 2020. Beyond Accuracy: Behavioral Testing of NLP Models with CheckList. In *Proceedings of ACL*.

Abeed Sarker and Graciela Gonzalez. 2015. Portable Automatic Text Classification for Adverse Drug Reaction Detection via Multi-corpus Training. *Journal of Biomedical Informatics*, 53:196–207.

Abeed Sarker and Graciela Gonzalez-Hernandez. 2017. Overview of the Second Social Media Mining for Health (SMM4H) Shared Tasks at AMIA 2017. *Training*, 1(10,822):1239.

Ashish Vaswani, Noam Shazeer, Niki Parmar, Jakob Uszkoreit, Llion Jones, Aidan N Gomez, Łukasz Kaiser, and Illia Polosukhin. 2017. Attention Is All You Need. In *Proceedings of NIPS*.

Erik Velldal, Lilja Øvrelid, Jonathon Read, and Stephan Oepen. 2012. Speculation and Negation: Rules, Rankers, and the Role of Syntax. *Computational Linguistics*, 38(2):369–410.

Veronika Vincze, György Szarvas, Richárd Farkas, György Móra, and János Csirik. 2008. The BioScope Corpus: Biomedical Texts Annotated for Uncertainty, Negation and their Scopes. *BMC Bioinformatics*, 9(11):1–9.

Davy Weissenbacher, Abeed Sarker, Arjun Magge, Ashlynn Daughton, Karen O'Connor, Michael Paul, and Graciela Gonzalez. 2019. Overview of the Fourth Social Media Mining for Health (SMM4H) Shared Tasks at ACL 2019. In *Proceedings of the ACL Social Media Mining for Health Applications (# SMM4H) Workshop & Shared Task*.

Davy Weissenbacher, Abeed Sarker, Michael Paul, and Graciela Gonzalez. 2018. Overview of the Social Media Mining for Health (SMM4H) Shared Tasks at EMNLP 2018. In *Proceedings of the EMNLP Workshop on Social Media Mining for Health Applications*.

Bowei Zou, Qiaoming Zhu, and Guodong Zhou. 2015. Negation and Speculation Identification in Chinese Language. In *Proceedings of ACL-IJCNLP*.

A Data Augmentation Process

The data augmentation process was carried out by four volunteers with a high level of proficiency in English. More specifically, the volunteers were: two graduate students (Master's degree in Computer Science and Artificial Intelligence) and two Ph.D. in Natural Language Processing. All of them have a minimum English level of C1.[2]

A.1 Recovery of Real Samples

The **noADE** samples from the SMM4H19$_{cls}$ and SMM4H20$_{cls}$ binary classification datasets have been filtered using the negation cues from BioScope (e.g. *none, missing, no longer, etc.*). Thanks to this first filtering, only the remaining 3897 samples have been analyzed by the volunteers. A tweet was kept only if it negated the presence of an ADE.

In the following examples, 1 and 2 are valid tweets, while 3 and 4 contain negations but do not negate the ADE:

1. This **#HUMIRA shot** has me feeling like a normal human... **No pain no inflammation** no nothinggggh #RAproblems
2. @UKingsbrook That's correct! **Metoprolol** is **NOT known to cause hypokalemia**.
3. I've seen so much **Tamiflu** these past couple of days I'm **not even surprised I'm shivering and experiencing aches** right now. *sigh
4. But I'm **not on adderall and I am feasting**.

A.2 Generation of Artificial Samples

According to the split provided by Portelli et al. (2021), we extracted and modified only the **ADE** samples from the test set (260 samples). The volunteers were instructed to modify the samples with as little edits as possible, while still generating a plausible tweet. They were encouraged to add one or more negation cue words to negate the ADE reported in the tweet. In the case it was not possible to negate the meaning of the tweet just by adding cue words, they were allowed to perform more edits in the sentence and use longer expressions.

Each annotator was asked to review the edits done by the others, and asked to point out which samples seemed unrealistic or failed to negate the ADE. During the augmentation process, if no agreement was found about the edits, the tweet modified tweet was discarded. At the end of the process 7 tweets were removed from the final dataset. Due to the generation process we implemented, we could not directly measure the inter-annotator agreement, which could, however, be inferred by the number of discarded samples.

B Full Results

Table 4 reports the metrics for all the models (average over 5 runs). The table includes also the results for the pipeline models trained with an increasing number of **negADE_g** samples, which show the same trend as the base models. The most relevant combinations (discussed in the main part of the paper) are highlighted in color (base models in gray■, base models trained with 253 **negADE_g** samples in orange■, pipeline models in blue■).

[2]https://www.efset.org/cefr/c1/

False Positives

negADE_g samples	0	50	100	150	200	253
BERT	161.20	146.60	166.80	125.80	105.40	101.60
+NegEx	106.40	97.60	119.20	100.00	**90.00**	91.60
+BERTneg	120.20	111.40	129.40	108.00	94.40	93.60
PubMedBERT	144.20	126.20	108.00	100.80	79.00	84.20
+NegEx	93.40	85.60	84.00	86.60	68.00	76.60
+BERTneg	106.20	91.40	85.40	87.40	**67.60**	74.20
SpanBERT	245.60	183.20	230.00	156.80	134.20	179.80
+NegEx	170.80	125.40	163.80	115.80	**99.80**	136.40
+BERTneg	184.00	138.40	175.40	124.60	107.20	145.40

Precision

negADE_g samples	0	50	100	150	200	253
BERT	50.15	51.47	49.17	54.24	57.82	58.85
+NegEx	55.59	56.79	53.52	56.53	58.52	58.65
+BERTneg	54.37	55.34	52.78	55.88	58.53	**59.22**
PubMedBERT	53.24	56.43	59.25	59.46	62.94	63.28
+NegEx	59.21	61.60	61.98	60.29	63.84	63.24
+BERTneg	57.69	61.24	62.44	61.12	**64.84**	64.74
SpanBERT	43.65	53.32	45.46	48.24	52.80	48.52
+NegEx	48.65	**60.44**	49.95	52.83	55.95	51.63
+BERTneg	47.82	56.60	49.25	51.43	55.54	51.31

F1 score

negADE_g samples	0	50	100	150	200	253
BERT	56.78	56.59	56.18	58.41	59.45	**61.21**
+NegEx	56.73	56.48	56.10	57.03	57.19	58.29
+BERTneg	57.30	56.73	56.61	57.65	58.06	59.65
PubMedBERT	59.47	61.37	62.72	61.59	61.74	**63.20**
+NegEx	59.47	60.91	61.26	59.22	59.26	60.58
+BERTneg	60.04	62.15	62.70	61.10	61.36	62.72
SpanBERT	54.61	45.76	56.20	49.47	54.75	56.85
+NegEx	55.55	46.54	56.69	48.85	53.44	55.98
+BERTneg	55.85	46.61	**57.17**	49.61	54.49	56.94

Recall

negADE_g samples	0	50	100	150	200	253
BERT	65.60	63.04	65.57	63.41	61.85	63.86
+NegEx	58.03	56.32	58.97	57.66	56.43	58.03
+BERTneg	60.70	58.38	61.09	59.66	58.16	60.17
PubMedBERT	67.41	**67.44**	66.67	64.03	60.67	63.33
+NegEx	59.76	60.33	60.59	58.32	55.45	58.29
+BERTneg	62.64	63.19	62.99	61.19	58.36	60.98
SpanBERT	73.28	59.73	**74.19**	59.22	60.32	68.76
+NegEx	65.04	53.01	65.95	52.86	53.91	61.29
+BERTneg	67.39	54.98	68.48	55.14	56.27	64.10

Table 4: All metrics for: the original base models (gray▇); the base models trained with different quantities of **negADE_g** samples (the results of training with 253 **negADE_g** samples in orange▇); the two pipeline models (in blue▇); the combination of the two methods. For each model, in bold is highlighted the best value for the specific evaluation metric.

SpanAlign: Efficient Sequence Tagging Annotation Projection into Translated Data applied to Cross-Lingual Opinion Mining

Léo Jacqmin[1] **Gabriel Marzinotto**[1] **Justyna Gromada**[2]

Ewelina Szczekocka[2] **Robert Kołodyński**[2] **Antoine Chauvière**[1] **Géraldine Damnati**[1]

(1) Orange Innovation / Lannion, France
(2) Orange Innovation Poland / Warsaw, Poland
first.last@orange.com

Abstract

Following the increasing performance of neural machine translation systems, the paradigm of using automatically translated data for cross-lingual adaptation is now studied in several applicative domains. The capacity to accurately project annotations remains however an issue for sequence tagging tasks where annotation must be projected with correct spans. Additionally, when the task implies noisy user-generated text, the quality of translation and annotation projection can be affected. In this paper we propose to tackle multilingual sequence tagging with a new span alignment method and apply it to opinion target extraction from customer reviews. We show that provided suitable heuristics, translated data with automatic span-level annotation projection can yield improvements both for cross-lingual adaptation compared to zero-shot transfer, and data augmentation compared to a multilingual baseline.

1 Introduction

Large self-supervised pre-trained models which are fine-tuned on downstream tasks have become the de facto standard in NLP. However, monolingual pre-trained models are only available in some high resource languages due to data limitations. Additionally, in multilingual settings, having a separate model for each language quickly becomes unpractical. Multilingual models which are pre-trained on monolingual corpora in multiple languages such as multilingual BERT (mBERT) and XLM-R provide an alternative. They have been shown to yield on par, if not better performance on various tasks compared to monolingual models and perform particularly well for low-resource languages provided similar languages are represented in the training data (Conneau et al., 2020). What's more, they have shown surprising capacities for generalization with zero-shot cross-lingual transfer, in which a model is fine-tuned for a task using annotated data in a specific language and then evaluated in an unseen language (Radford et al., 2019). Considering that labeled data is more readily available for certain languages, this technique of cross-lingual transfer can be harnessed to process low-resource languages, therefore bypassing the need for a costly annotation process. Some research effort has been done in grasping to what extent these models are language agnostic (Pires et al., 2019), though more probing is necessary in order to fully understand and measure how multilingual these models are.

Another approach to cross-lingual transfer consists in using machine translation (MT) to adapt the annotated training data available in a source language to the target language. The resulting translated data is used to train a model with supervision in the target language. Producing a label for translated data is straightforward for sentence-level tasks. However, little work focuses on adapting datasets annotated at the word level. Such adaptation requires an additional step of label projection which can be error-prone and introduce noise in the training data. A common way of projecting labels consists in obtaining word alignments between source and target utterances and then projecting the labels. In a recent paper, (Li et al., 2020) argued that zero-shot cross-lingual transfer surpassed translation-based adaptations for several sequence tagging tasks, and proposed to first warm up the model's weights on the translated data only and then fine-tuning on the original data. In contrast, we show that translation-based adaptation yields superior performance compared to zero-shot cross-lingual transfer, provided the right annotation projection method is used.

We propose to apply this method in the context of opinion mining, and specifically to aspect-based sentiment analysis (ABSA) (Pontiki et al., 2014). Nowadays, people increasingly rely on reviews and comments, e.g. on social media and review websites, to select which products to buy or which services to use. Companies can also make use of these

Proceedings of the 2021 EMNLP Workshop W-NUT: The Seventh Workshop on Noisy User-generated Text, pages 238–248
November 11, 2021. ©2021 Association for Computational Linguistics

data which provide insightful feedback from their customers. ABSA is concerned with extracting fine-grained information from customer feedback, e.g. which aspects of a product or a service are being referred to, which entities are associated with them, and what is the customer's attitude towards them. One challenge that this task poses is that reviews are user-generated and can thus be very noisy. Online users tend to produce text that derives from the standard form of language with e.g. misspellings, internet slang, abbreviations, phonetic transcriptions, and missing or incorrect punctuation marks. For companies operating in several countries, another challenging aspect is the multiplicity of languages found in these reviews. Accordingly, multilingual approaches to opinion mining are essential to efficiently analyze customer feedback across countries.

We first review previous works related to cross-lingual transfer and ABSA. We then present our translation-based adaptation approach, and show its relevance in two scenarios : cross-lingual adaptation where annotated data is only available in the source language, and data augmentation where annotated data is available for both source and target languages. Lastly, we turn to an analysis of noisy user-generated text and propose a heuristic to filter out noisy utterances before translation.

2 Related Work

2.1 Aspect-based Sentiment Analysis

Due to the difficulties associated with processing user-generated text, opinion mining is commonly formulated as a text classification task concerned with e.g. classifying the overall polarity of a sentence by assigning it a polarity label (Pang and Lee, 2008).

Aspect-based sentiment analysis (ABSA) (Hu and Liu, 2004; Popescu and Etzioni, 2005; Pontiki et al., 2014, 2015, 2016) is a more fine-grained opinion mining task with several sub-tasks associated with it. For example, opinion target extraction (OTE) retrieves the entity on which an opinion is expressed in a review, and aspect sentiment classification (ASC) identifies the polarity of an opinion expressed on a given target entity. Some works focus on one subtask at a time, e.g. OTE (Li and Lam, 2017; Xu et al., 2018) or opinion word extraction (OWE) (Fan et al., 2019; Pouran Ben Veyseh et al., 2020). But this division of subtasks is ill-suited for real-world scenarios as both ASC and OWE assume that the opinion target is given. Moreover, these subtasks aim to extract related information. To facilitate practical applications of ABSA, recent works address OTE and ASC simultaneously (Li et al., 2019a,b). The problem can be formulated as a sequence tagging task with unified labels to simultaneously detect opinion targets and the corresponding aspect sentiments. Some works went even further by addressing OTE, ASC, and OWE simultaneously, a task dubbed as aspect sentiment triplet extraction (Peng et al., 2020; Wang et al., 2021).

Most works in the state of the art focus on SemEval datasets from 2014 to 2016, with data from the restaurant, hotel or laptop domain in English. However, SemEval data are also available in several languages. Jebbara and Cimiano (2019), for instance, evaluated CNN models for OTE with multilingual word embeddings in a zero-shot cross-lingual framework.

2.2 Cross-lingual transfer

Multilingual pre-trained models have shown strong capacities for generalization and have been successfully applied for zero-shot cross-lingual transfer on a variety of natural language understanding tasks (Wu and Dredze, 2019). This enables the application of such models to low-resource languages for which little or no labelled data is available.

Machine Translation (MT) can help learning cross-lingual representations and transfering information across languages. Rather than being at odds, zero-shot cross-lingual transfer and MT-based approaches are complementary : MT can be used to generate synthetic data in languages for which no annotated data is available. Accordingly, MT can improve cross-lingual transfer in two ways : (i) By translating the training data into the target languages and fine-tuning on all languages, e.g. for subjectivity analysis (Banea et al., 2008), sentiment classification (Duh et al., 2011) or semantic role labeling (Fei et al., 2020). (ii) Or by applying a model fine-tuned on the source language to a test set translated from target to source language. (Conneau et al., 2020) refers to the former approach as *translate-train* and to the latter as *translate-test*. In this work, we focus on the former approach. This approach naturally applies to sentence classification tasks and previous work has shown that translation-based adaptation is superior to zero-shot cross-lingual transfer for text classification (Schwenk and Li, 2018) and text pair classification (Conneau et al., 2018; Yang et al., 2019). However, little work focuses on adapting datasets annotated at the word level for sequence tagging. This requires an important additional step of annotation projection as no word-to-word correspondence is available.

One approach to annotation projection for sequence tagging tasks relies on obtaining word alignments to project labels from source to target utterances. Several statistical word alignment tools are available such as `fast_align` (Dyer et al., 2013) which constitutes the usual baseline for this approach. Starting from the assumption that neural machine translation (NMT) models capture word alignment through their attention mechanism, other works (Chen et al., 2020; Zouhar and Pylypenko, 2021) focus on using attention weights for word alignment. In an attempt to alleviate the need for parallel corpora, (Jalili Sabet et al., 2020) leveraged modern multilingual pre-trained models and released `SimAlign`, a tool for unsupervised word alignment based on the similarity of multilingual word representations.

In order to project sequence annotations, one has to leverage word-level alignment towards span alignment. Marzinotto (2020) used attention-based word alignments to project FrameNet annotations (targets and Frame Elements) into a target language. Others have sought to improve label projection through different approaches. Jain et al. (2019) proposed an entity projection method for named entity recognition, in which they obtain potential translations of an entity in the target language and select the best match with the source entity. To make use of task-related information, Xu et al. (2020) proposed an end-to-end model to jointly align and predict target slot labels for cross-lingual NLU. (Li et al., 2020) propose an approach called *span-to-span mapping* which derives span alignment from word alignments. They applied it to several tasks (Opinion Mining, Semantic Role Labeling, Named Entities) but didn't obtain satisfactory results when directly using the translated and aligned data to fine-tune their models.

3 SpanAlign

In the case of sentence-level tasks, the translated data can be used right away using the same labels as in the source language corpus. In contrast,

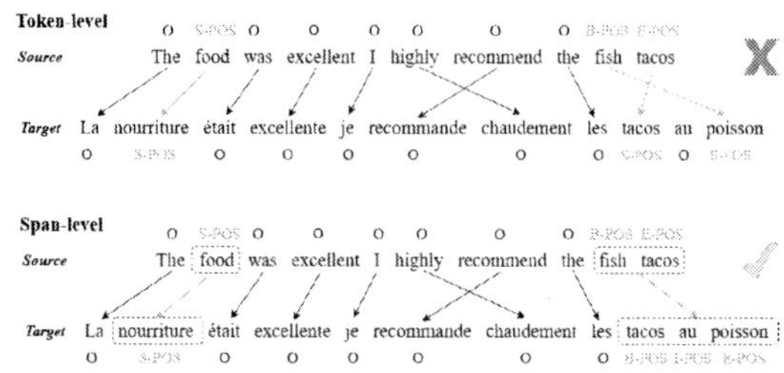

FIGURE 1: Different strategies for annotation projection using word alignments.

adapting sequence tagging datasets annotated at the word-level requires an additional step of annotation projection. A word-to-word correspondence between source and target utterances can be obtained using word alignment tools. One simple approach to annotation projection is then to project the gold labels in the source utterance to their corresponding word in the target utterance using this mapping. However, as token-level annotations may span several words, this approach can be error-prone, as illustrated in Figure 1. Consequently, we introduce a span-based alignment approach to project gold annotations at the span level. Additionally we make the assumption that translated data with erroneous annotation alignment are more likely to be harmful for the subsequent training process, and propose to introduce a constraint on span alignment to filter out translated annotations and remove them from the candidate pool of translated training data.

3.1 Annotation Projection for Sequence Tagging

Let $x^{src}_{1:N} = \{x_1, ..., x_N\}$ be the source utterance and $x^{trg}_{1:M} = \{x_1, ..., x_M\}$ the translated utterance. We obtain word alignments $a^{src}_{1:N} = \{a_1, ..., a_N\}$ from these paired utterances, with $a_i \in [1, M] \cup \{\text{NULL}\}$ indicating which words in the target utterance correspond to source word x^{src}_i. For each annotated span $x^{src}_{i:j}$ in the source utterance from the i-th source word to the j-th source word, we identify the projected span in the target utterance as $x^{trg}_{p:q}$, where

$$\begin{aligned} p &= min(a^{src}_{ij}) \\ q &= max(a^{src}_{ij}) \end{aligned} \tag{1}$$

This procedure is described in pseudo-code in Algorithm 1. We then assign the label without position, e.g. `POS,` to all words in the projected span and reformat the position labels, e.g. `B-{POS}`, `E-{POS}`.

Algorithm 1: Span-based alignment

```
function align
  (src_utt, trg_utt, src_spans, α)
a^{src}_{1:N} =
  get_word_alignment(src_utt, trg_utt)
trg_spans = []
for x^{src} ∈ src_spans do
    x^{trg} = []
    for i ∈ x^{src} do
        if i ∈ a^{src}_{1:N} then
            x^{trg}.append(a^{src}_i)
        end
    end
    x^{trg} = sorted(x^{trg})
    largest_gap = get_largest_gap(x^{trg})
    if largest_gap > α then
        return False
    else
        x^{trg} = range(min(x^{trg}), max(x^{trg}))
        trg_spans.append(x^{trg})
    end
end
return trg_spans
```

3.2 Filtering Ill-formed Projected Spans

The underlying word alignments are not guaranteed to be entirely accurate. First, the translations are machine-generated and can therefore be inadequate. Second, user-generated text is noisy. This noise in source utterances can negatively impact the translations and let errors propagate through the rest of the pipeline. To address these issues, we use a heuristic to filter out pseudo-labeled utterances that are likely to be ill-formed. See Figure 2 for an example.

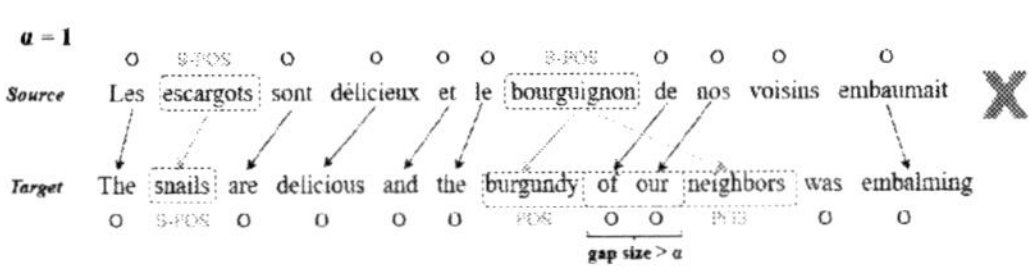

FIGURE 2: In this case, "bourguignon" which is a dish but also a gentilic was aligned with both "burgundy" and "neighbours", introducing a gap of two words in the proposed translation.

Since our projection method uses the minimum and maximum indices of the aligned words as the offset of the projected span, some gaps can appear in the projected spans where some of the translated words have not been aligned to an opinion target word in the source utterance. We call these words insertions. The hyperparameter α corresponds to the number of allowed insertions within a gap in the projected spans. Utterances that contain a projected span with a gap containing a number of insertions strictly higher than α are considered ill-formed and are filtered out of the translated dataset. Note that this heuristic is well-suited for the task of opinion target extraction because opinion targets are mostly adjacent nominal groups that usually translate into adjacent groups. It should also be relevant for tasks such as Named Entity detection. We are aware that some grammatical structures can translate into non adjacent terms in some languages but we believe that our heuristic approach is reasonable for entity detection tasks.

4 Translation-based Adaptation

Modern neural machine translation (NMT) provides satisfactory results thanks to Transformer models and has become increasingly available. As a result, such models can be used effectively to create synthetic data by translating a source language reference corpus.

We use Marian NMT [1] to translate the source language corpora into the other languages, and vice-versa. Marian NMT is open source and allows the use of pre-trained NMT models from the OPUS-MT project (Tiedemann and Thottingal, 2020) available on this framework. A description of each model and its evaluation on benchmarks can be found online. [2] To obtain word alignments, we use both off-the-shelf `fast_align` (Dyer et al., 2013) and `SimAlign` (Jalili Sabet et al., 2020). For the latter, which doesn't need any parallel data for training but relies on multilingual word representations, we use the Itermax variant, which was shown to outperform other word alignment approaches. Note that we did not adapt the translation models nor the alignment approaches to our specific domains.

4.1 Cross-lingual Adaptation

Cross-lingual adaptation denotes the case where annotated data is available for one language only and we wish to process other languages. The question here is whether the original annotated data is sufficient to fine-tune a pre-trained multilingual model and process unseen languages, or if translating this data into the other languages facilitates

1. https://marian-nmt.github.io
2. https://opus.nlpl.eu/Opus-MT/

cross-lingual transfer. In other words, whether multilingual word representations are truly language agnostic or not. We experiment with the following experiments. **O** and **Tr** respectively denote *original* and *translated* data. **S** and **T** refer to *source* and *target* languages.

O_S (Zero-shot) In the context of cross-lingual transfer, zero-shot learning consists in fine-tuning a model for a given task using annotated data in a source language, and then evaluating it for the same task on a test set from an unseen target language. This configuration serves as the baseline method for cross-lingual adaptation.

$Tr_{S \to T}$ The first alternative configuration we consider is to simply adapt the available annotated data to the target language. For a given target language, we fine-tune the model on the translation of the source language data into the target language only.

O_S + $Tr_{S \to T}$ As a step up from the previous configuration, we fine-tune a model on the concatenation of the source data and its translation into the target language.

O_S + $Tr_{S \to all}$ In this last configuration, we use the concatenation of the source data with its translations into all the other languages. This approach results in a single model that can be applied to all languages.

	Original	Translated	
Config.	**Source**	**Target**	**Others**
O_S (Zero-shot)	✓		
$Tr_{S \to T}$		✓	
O_S + $Tr_{S \to T}$	✓	✓	
O_S + $Tr_{S \to all}$	✓	✓	✓

TABLE 1: Data configurations for cross-lingual adaptation.

4.2 Data Augmentation

Data augmentation refers to the case where small amounts of annotated data is available in all the languages we wish to process. We are interested in studying how additional synthetic data will affect the model's performance. We experiment with the following configurations :[3]

3. Note that not all possible configurations were reported for the sake of simplicity.

O_T (Monolingual) As a baseline configuration, we simply fine-tune a model on the original data for a given language and evaluate it on that language.

O_{all} (Multilingual) The next configuration uses the concatenation of the original data available in all the languages.

O_{all} + $Tr_{S \to all}$ We fine-tune a model on the concatenation of the original data in all languages along with the translated data from the source language into the other languages. With this configuration, we evaluate the relevance of our approach for data augmentation in a multilingual setting.

O_{all} + $Tr_{all \to S}$ We also experiment with translating the corpora from all the other languages into the source language to understand how the direction of the translation affects our approach and if our assumptions about translation direction are valid.

O_{all} + $Tr_{S \leftrightarrow all}$ This final configuration takes a concatenation of the original data in all languages with all the translated data obtained from both translation directions.

	Original		Translated	
Config.	**Target**	**Others**	**S → all**	**all → S**
O_T (Monolingual)	✓			
O_{all} (Multilingual)	✓	✓		
O_{all} + $Tr_{S \to all}$	✓	✓	✓	
O_{all} + $Tr_{all \to S}$	✓	✓		✓
O_{all} + $Tr_{S \leftrightarrow all}$	✓	✓	✓	✓

TABLE 2: Data configurations for data augmentation.

5 Experiments

In this section, we describe the experiments that we conducted to explore the relevance of translation-based adaptation, both for cross-lingual adaptation, where annotated data is available in only one language, and for data augmentation, where multilingual datasets are available and we seek to improve performance from fine-tuning on the plain concatenation of data in all languages.

5.1 Aspect-based Sentiment Analysis

Aspect-based sentiment analysis (ABSA) may refer to several subtasks. We focus on joint opinion target extraction (OTE) and aspect sentiment classification (ASC). Following (Li et al., 2019a), we use a unified tagset with a single sequence tagging

Language	SemEval				In-house					
	Train		Test		Train		Dev		Test	
	# review	# OT	# review	# OT	# review	# OT	# review	# OT	# review	# OT
ar	4802	9612	1227	2371	592	741	198	280	198	237
en	2000	1743	676	612	600	780	200	279	200	269
es	2070	1859	881	713	1200	1080	200	354	200	372
fr	1664	1641	668	650	2047	1984	131	84	131	84
nl	1722	1859	575	713	594	554	198	183	198	190
pl	–	–	–	–	864	1827	200	610	200	581
ro	–	–	–	–	600	1050	200	358	200	357
ru	3665	3078	1209	952	–	–	–	–	–	–

TABLE 3: Number of reviews for each language and corresponding number of Opinion Targets (OT).

model to jointly extract opinion targets and their associated sentiment label.

5.2 Data

We conducted experiments on common benchmark datasets for ABSA, as well as on in-house datasets annotated in the same way.

SemEval-2016 Task 5 (Pontiki et al., 2016) This shared task provides multilingual benchmark datasets for ABSA. Online reviews from several domains have been annotated for various languages. Datasets for OTE are available in English, Spanish, French, Dutch, Russian, Arabic, and Turkish. [4] The annotations include opinion targets on which the opinion is voiced, along with their associated sentiment and the aspect category they belong to. The Arabic dataset pertains to the domain of hotel reviews, while the datasets in all the other languages contain restaurant reviews.

Orange In-house datasets To provide a different view of the same task, we experiment with in-house datasets annotated in a similar fashion. These datasets contain customer reviews for mobile applications. As such they contain noisy text which pose an additional challenge. The mobile applications are related to the activities of the Orange telco operator. Orange being present in several countries, we were able to gather and annotate reviews related to similar apps deployed in several countries. Our corpus covers French, English, Spanish, Arabic, [5] Dutch, Polish, and Romanian. Examples of reviews in English are shown in Table 4.

Cool app, I really like the ux design. Keep up !
Reallu useful app to know ur credit, internet consumption... Etc thnx
nice app all in hand to discover your account
Now it work ! Except Invoice.....Maybe because it's the first one.....For the rest no bad.

TABLE 4: Examples of reviews from the English in-house dataset. Positive and negative opinion targets are shown in blue and red respectively.

Besides the difference in terms of domain, SemEval and in-house datasets differ in the level of segmentation. For SemEval, reviews were segmented into sentences and an input for the model is a single sentence, while for our dataset we kept reviews as a whole (sentence segmentation is not always present nor reliable and we considered it was more related to a real usage). As a consequence, inputs are longer for in-house dataset (for instance 22.8 words on average for English vs 14.1 for English SemEval or 34.8 words on average for Spanish vs 19.6 for Spanish SemEval). Moreover, the mobile applications reviews collected for the in-house datasets are directly typed through a mobile smartphone. As a result, data are more noisy in terms of typographic errors (see for instance the second example in Table 4).

5.3 Source and Target Languages

For the SemEval datasets, we translate the English corpus into all the other languages. Similarly, we use French as the source language for the in-house data. The choice of which language to translate from is based on the following considera-

4. We do not include the Turkish data in our experiments as no English to Turkish MT model is available within the NMT framework we use.

5. The application is deployed in several arabo-speaking countries, and the Arabic dataset includes standard Arabic along with 4 dialects (from Morocco, Tunisia, Jordan and Egypt). We are aware that this is a very rough approximation to launch a translation process independently of the dialect but we will try in future work to have more accurate translation systems for the corresponding dialects.

Word alignments		ar	en	es	fr	nl	pl	ro	avg.	% out
fast_align	**no filtering**	24.9	38.7	31.7	50.6	53.8	22.0	19.8	34.5	0
	$\alpha = 2$	28.0	41.8	37.8	54.1	55.7	31.0	28.6	39.6	12.9
	$\alpha = 1$	27.9	41.2	35.1	52.5	**56.1**	30.1	26.1	38.4	13.3
	$\alpha = 0$	28.9	40.9	34.3	52.7	54.9	29.3	25.6	38.1	15.0
SimAlign	**no filtering**	22.8	31.4	29.5	39.1	37.9	26.2	23.3	30.0	0
	$\alpha = 2$	32.3	43.1	**38.8**	52.4	51.1	36.9	**32.1**	41.0	4.8
	$\alpha = 1$	31.9	42.4	38.7	53.2	54.5	**37.7**	31.5	**41.4**	5.3
	$\alpha = 0$	**33.3**	**43.4**	38.7	**54.5**	49.8	35.8	30.9	40.9	11.4

TABLE 5: Study of the impact of constraining the number of insertions within projected opinion targets with span-based alignment. Results for the $\mathbf{O}_S$ + $\mathbf{Tr}_{S\rightarrow all}$ configuration on the in-house Test datasets.

tions : (i) We expect pre-trained translation models for high-resource languages such as English and French to be more accurate than for languages with fewer resources. (ii) We consider that annotations for English or French data in either case tend to be of higher quality as they will go through a more extensive review process. In the case of the in-house datasets, French data is also more represented.

5.4 Experimental Settings

We use mBERT as our multilingual language model initialized with pre-trained weights [6] available from HuggingFace Transformers (Wolf et al., 2020). For each experiment, a model is fine-tuned with a linear layer for sequence tagging added on top of mBERT's architecture. We train each model for a maximum of 50 epochs using the Adam optimizer (Kingma and Ba, 2015) with a learning rate set to $5e^{-5}$. We use the `BIOES` encoding as our tagging scheme. The evaluation is performed on exact matches of span boundaries and labels. Results are averaged over three runs and are reported using the micro F_1 score. In this study, we did not seek to use the most accurate model for the task and voluntarily chose a simple architecture in order to focus on training data selection and preparation.

5.5 Annotation Projection

To establish what is the optimal value for α on our task, we conduct a preliminary extrinsic evaluation. Using the translations of the French in-house dataset in the other languages, we create different collections of synthetic datasets by projecting the annotations with different values for α. We also evaluate our projection method with no restriction on the number of insertions to assess the relevance of the filtering approach. We fine-tune these models in the cross-lingual adaptation scenario with the $\mathbf{O}_S$ + $\mathbf{Tr}_{S\rightarrow all}$ configuration. We also compare `SimAlign` with `fast_align`. The results are shown in Table 5. We observe a clear gain with our filtering method compared to allowing any insertion. We also obtain better results with `SimAlign`. Removing data where a gap is observed filters out more data when using `fast_align`. Similar experiments on SemEval not reported here yielded similar conclusions. Based on these results, `SimAlign` is used in all the following experiments and α is set to 1.

5.6 Cross-lingual Adaptation

Results are shown in Table 6. We compare our method with the work of Li et al. (2020), even though we were not able to reproduce their results with **Zero-shot**. They use `fast_align` and similar span alignment but without any constraints on allowed gaps. Hence our projection approach differs from theirs in the alignment method (`SimAlign` vs. `fast_align`) and in the filtering process that we introduced. And their training approach consists in warming up the model's parameters using the translated data and then fine-tuning on the source language data only.

Overall, performances vary across languages, with lower results for SemEval in particular in the **Zero-shot** configuration for distant languages (Russian and Arabic). Translation-based adaptation configurations, namely $\mathbf{O}_S$ + $\mathbf{Tr}_{S\rightarrow T}$ and $\mathbf{O}_S$ + $\mathbf{Tr}_{S\rightarrow all}$, provide a significant performance improvement compared to **Zero-shot**. In some cases, $\mathbf{Tr}_{S\rightarrow T}$ performs better than **Zero-shot**, but there is a clear benefit to using the original source language data as well. Results are particularly low for Arabic since the dataset pertains to another domain (restaurant vs. hotel reviews). For SemEval, the gains observed for Arabic despite the domain shift demonstrate the usefulness of fine-tuning on synthetic data in the target language even if the source

6. `bert-base-multilingual-cased`

language data is from a different domain.

In most cases, $\mathbf{O}_S$ + $\mathbf{Tr}_{S\rightarrow T}$ and $\mathbf{O}_S$ + $\mathbf{Tr}_{S\rightarrow all}$ models come relatively close. However, $\mathbf{O}_S$ + $\mathbf{Tr}_{S\rightarrow all}$ generally outperforms the other configurations. Moreover, it can be considered as superior as a unique model can be applied to all languages which is particularly relevant from an operational point of view, with only one model to maintain. While the results between the approach of Li et al. (2020) and ours are similar, our approach has the advantage of being conceptually simpler and easier to implement.

We also observe that with $\mathbf{O}_S$ + $\mathbf{Tr}_{S\rightarrow all}$, the translated data contribute to improved performances for the source language, i.e. English or French, highlighting the relevance of the translation-based adaptation method for data augmentation as well.

5.7 Data Augmentation

Results for data augmentation are shown in Table 7. When comparing the two non-augmented baselines, i.e. **Monolingual** and **Multilingual**, we observe a significant improvement when fine-tuning a model on the combination of all languages (on average, +11.7 points for SemEval and +16.6 points on the in-house dataset), highlighting the ability of mBERT for cross-lingual transfer learning.

For SemEval, augmenting the training corpus with translated data consistently provides an improvement over the $\mathbf{O}_{all}$ baseline. Using the translations of the non-English corpora into English ($\mathbf{O}_{all}$ + $\mathbf{Tr}_{all\rightarrow S}$) is detrimental to the performance on the English test set, while other languages are not impacted as much by this translation direction. The reason could be that, similarly to the cross-lingual adaptation experiments, it is beneficial to use the translated data in the target language specifically. Overall, $\mathbf{O}_{all}$ + $\mathbf{Tr}_{S\rightarrow all}$ seems to be the most effective configuration for all languages.

Regarding the in-house datasets, the synthetic data is not as beneficial as in the case of SemEval. Results are comparable to $\mathbf{O}_{all}$ for all translation directions, and no data configuration stands out as most effective on average.

6 Analysis

In line with the results from the previous section, we conduct a refined analysis to shed some light on the impact of noisy text.

When applied to the SemEval datasets, data augmentation in the resource-rich setting is beneficial and yields a significant improvement in performance, especially for English. For the in-house datasets however, data augmentation does not affect the performances as much compared to the multilingual baseline. Our hypothesis is that the in-house datasets are more noisy and contain a more specific lexicon, which is what could be perturbing the translations, and thus negatively impacting the rest of the pipeline.

As we did not have gold data to explicitly evaluate the orthographic or grammatical deviation rate, nor the translation quality, nor the alignment quality, we propose an approximation to quantify noise and compare SemEval and in-house datasets. We compute the out-of-dictionary (OOD) rate using reference dictionaries recommended with Hunspell [7] and available from Firefox for each language. [8] The OOD rate is computed as follows :

$$\text{OOD rate} = \frac{O}{N} \times 100 \quad (2)$$

where O is the number of OOD words and N the number of tokens in the corpus. Table 8 provides the OOD rate for the training sets of each language that is common to both SemEval and in-house data. We observe that the OOD rates are around twice as

7. http://hunspell.github.io/
8. https://addons.mozilla.org/en-US/firefox/language-tools/

	SemEval						In-house						
Config.	**en**	**ar**	**es**	**fr**	**nl**	**ru**	**fr**	**ar**	**en**	**es**	**nl**	**pl**	**ro**
$\mathbf{O}_S$ (Zero-shot)	62.7	13.2	51.2	35.1	38.2	34.9	48.6	13.5	23.9	24.8	33.8	19.3	15.4
$\mathbf{Tr}_{S\rightarrow T}$	_	7.6	25.8	37.6	24.0	29.1	_	24.5	30.3	31.5	38.8	31.9	27.2
$\mathbf{O}_S$ + $\mathbf{Tr}_{S\rightarrow T}$	_	31.4	54.3	40.7	49.4	47.7	_	30.0	42.6	38.7	**55.6**	34.2	29.9
$\mathbf{O}_S$ + $\mathbf{Tr}_{S\rightarrow all}$	**64.1**	**34.7**	54.8	41.49	**51.0**	**47.9**	**51.4**	**31.3**	**43.3**	**39.4**	55.5	**35.6**	**31.9**
(Li et al., 2020)	_	_	**58.2**	**46.9**	49.9	44.9	_	_	_	_	_	_	_

TABLE 6: Results for cross-lingual adaptation, i.e. annotated data is available for the source language only.

	SemEval							In-house							
Config.	ar	en	es	fr	nl	ru	avg.	ar	en	es	fr	nl	pl	ro	avg.
$\mathbf{O}_T$ (Monolingual)	61.1	62.7	58.9	34.4	52.3	35.5	50.8	10.3	42.6	38.7	48.6	55.6	34.2	29.9	37.1
$\mathbf{O}_{all}$ (Multilingual)	**61.7**	63.0	67.0	62.1	59.3	61.6	62.5	48.0	54.0	54.8	**56.8**	64.5	**56.4**	41.3	**53.7**
$\mathbf{O}_{all}$ + $\mathbf{Tr}_{S\rightarrow all}$	**61.7**	**66.8**	67.7	61.3	62.0	**62.2**	**63.6**	**48.5**	53.2	56.0	55.9	61.6	54.5	41.0	53.0
$\mathbf{O}_{all}$ + $\mathbf{Tr}_{all\rightarrow S}$	**61.7**	56.6	**68.8**	61.8	59.5	61.3	61.6	46.9	54.1	**56.2**	54.1	64.1	55.3	40.8	53.1
$\mathbf{O}_{all}$ + $\mathbf{Tr}_{S\leftrightarrow all}$	61.6	58.7	67.5	**62.3**	**62.1**	61.7	62.3	48.4	**54.9**	54.2	55.2	**64.6**	54.6	**42.0**	53.4

TABLE 7: Results for data augmentation, i.e. annotated data is available for all languages.

high for our in-house datasets compared to SemEval datasets. [9]

	fr	en	nl	es	ar	avg.
SemEval	1.4	2.5	2.1	4.0	12.1	4.4
In-house	4.3	3.7	4.1	7.0	25.6	8.9

TABLE 8: Average OOD rates in the training sets.

Considering the OOD rate as an indicator of noise in text, we can filter out the most noisy utterances from the source dataset in French before translating it into the other languages. We compute the OOD rate for each utterance and rank them from most noisy to least noisy. The top n percent is then filtered out from the dataset before translation. We experiment with several values for n. Results can be seen in Table 9. We observe a slight increase in performance when filtering out the 5% most noisy utterances compared to not filtering. Beyond that, filtering a larger portion of utterances seems to be reducing the size of the dataset too much and degrades performance.

Filter	ar	en	es	nl	pl	ro	avg.
None	**48.5**	53.2	**56.0**	61.6	54.5	41.0	52.5
5%	47.4	**55.3**	55.6	**64.0**	54.7	**41.7**	**53.1**
10%	46.8	53.2	54.5	63.3	**54.8**	40.9	52.2
20%	47.4	54.5	52.6	63.8	53.1	38.3	51.6

TABLE 9: Filtering out the n percent utterances with the largest OOD rate from the Source corpus before translating it into the other languages, impact on Target languages (data augmentation on the in-house dataset with the $\mathbf{O}_{all}$ + $\mathbf{Tr}_{S\rightarrow all}$ configuration)

7 Conclusion

We have proposed an efficient yet simple way of generating training data for a sequence tagging task based on translation and label projection. When applied to noisy data such as customer reviews, we propose a way to overcome potentially ill-formed projections by filtering out some translated data thanks to a heuristic. Our `SpanAlign` algorithm, in conjunction with the `SimAlign` word alignment approach, yields interesting results for multilingual opinion mining both in *cross-lingual* configuration where no annotated data is available in the target languages, and in *data augmentation* configuration where annotated data are available in the target languages. We show that it is possible to train a single model for several languages, which is important in an industrial setting for maintenance issues. Finally, a preliminary study shows that selecting data prior to the translation and projection process on the basis of an Out of Dictionary rate increases the process robustness. Future work will consist in characterizing more precisely the level of noise in data and potentially correcting data in order to improve the selection process.

9. Note that the higher average OOD rate in Arabic can be attributed to dialectal variations.

References

Carmen Banea, Rada Mihalcea, Janyce Wiebe, and Samer Hassan. 2008. Multilingual subjectivity analysis using machine translation. In *Proceedings of the 2008 Conference on Empirical Methods in Natural Language Processing*, pages 127–135, Honolulu, Hawaii. Association for Computational Linguistics.

Yun Chen, Yang Liu, Guanhua Chen, Xin Jiang, and Qun Liu. 2020. Accurate word alignment induction from neural machine translation. In *Proceedings of the 2020 Conference on Empirical Methods in Natural Language Processing (EMNLP)*, pages 566–576, Online. Association for Computational Linguistics.

Alexis Conneau, Kartikay Khandelwal, Naman Goyal, Vishrav Chaudhary, Guillaume Wenzek, Francisco Guzmán, Edouard Grave, Myle Ott, Luke Zettlemoyer, and Veselin Stoyanov. 2020. Unsupervised cross-lingual representation learning at scale. In *Proceedings of the 58th Annual Meeting of the Association for Computational Linguistics*, pages 8440–8451, Online. Association for Computational Linguistics.

Alexis Conneau, Ruty Rinott, Guillaume Lample, Adina Williams, Samuel R. Bowman, Holger Schwenk, and Veselin Stoyanov. 2018. Xnli : Evaluating cross-lingual sentence representations. In

Proceedings of the 2018 Conference on Empirical Methods in Natural Language Processing. Association for Computational Linguistics.

Kevin Duh, Akinori Fujino, and Masaaki Nagata. 2011. Is machine translation ripe for cross-lingual sentiment classification? In *Proceedings of the 49th Annual Meeting of the Association for Computational Linguistics : Human Language Technologies*, pages 429–433, Portland, Oregon, USA. Association for Computational Linguistics.

Chris Dyer, Victor Chahuneau, and Noah A. Smith. 2013. A simple, fast, and effective reparameterization of IBM model 2. In *Proceedings of the 2013 Conference of the North American Chapter of the Association for Computational Linguistics : Human Language Technologies*, pages 644–648, Atlanta, Georgia. Association for Computational Linguistics.

Zhifang Fan, Zhen Wu, Xin-Yu Dai, Shujian Huang, and Jiajun Chen. 2019. Target-oriented opinion words extraction with target-fused neural sequence labeling. In *Proceedings of the 2019 Conference of the North American Chapter of the Association for Computational Linguistics : Human Language Technologies, Volume 1 (Long and Short Papers)*. Association for Computational Linguistics.

Hao Fei, Meishan Zhang, and Donghong Ji. 2020. Cross-lingual semantic role labeling with high-quality translated training corpus. In *Proceedings of the 58th Annual Meeting of the Association for Computational Linguistics*, pages 7014–7026.

Minqing Hu and Bing Liu. 2004. Mining and summarizing customer reviews. In *Proceedings of the Tenth ACM SIGKDD International Conference on Knowledge Discovery and Data Mining*, KDD '04, page 168–177, New York, NY, USA. Association for Computing Machinery.

Alankar Jain, Bhargavi Paranjape, and Zachary C. Lipton. 2019. Entity projection via machine translation for cross-lingual ner. In *Proceedings of the 2019 Conference on Empirical Methods in Natural Language Processing and the 9th International Joint Conference on Natural Language Processing, EMNLP-IJCNLP 2019, Hong Kong, China, November 3-7, 2019*, pages 1083–1092. Association for Computational Linguistics.

Masoud Jalili Sabet, Philipp Dufter, François Yvon, and Hinrich Schütze. 2020. SimAlign: High quality word alignments without parallel training data using static and contextualized embeddings. In *Proceedings of the 2020 Conference on Empirical Methods in Natural Language Processing : Findings*, pages 1627–1643, Online. Association for Computational Linguistics.

Soufian Jebbara and Philipp Cimiano. 2019. Zero-shot cross-lingual opinion target extraction. In *Proceedings of the 2019 Conference of the North American Chapter of the Association for Computational Linguistics : Human Language Technologies, Volume 1 (Long and Short Papers)*, pages 2486–2495, Minneapolis, Minnesota. Association for Computational Linguistics.

Diederik P. Kingma and Jimmy Ba. 2015. Adam: A method for stochastic optimization. In *3rd International Conference on Learning Representations, ICLR 2015, San Diego, CA, USA, May 7-9, 2015, Conference Track Proceedings*.

X. Li, Lidong Bing, Wenxuan Zhang, Zheng Li, and Wai Lam. 2020. Unsupervised cross-lingual adaptation for sequence tagging and beyond. *ArXiv*, abs/2010.12405.

Xin Li, Lidong Bing, Piji Li, and Wai Lam. 2019a. A unified model for opinion target extraction and target sentiment prediction. *Proceedings of the AAAI Conference on Artificial Intelligence*, 33 :6714–6721.

Xin Li, Lidong Bing, Wenxuan Zhang, and W. Lam. 2019b. Exploiting bert for end-to-end aspect-based sentiment analysis. *ArXiv*, abs/1910.00883.

Xin Li and Wai Lam. 2017. Deep multi-task learning for aspect term extraction with memory interaction. In *Proceedings of the 2017 Conference on Empirical Methods in Natural Language Processing*, pages 2886–2892, Copenhagen, Denmark. Association for Computational Linguistics.

Gabriel Marzinotto. 2020. FrameNet annotations alignment using attention-based machine translation. In *Proceedings of the International FrameNet Workshop 2020 : Towards a Global, Multilingual FrameNet*, pages 41–47, Marseille, France. European Language Resources Association.

Bo Pang and Lillian Lee. 2008. Opinion mining and sentiment analysis. *Found. Trends Inf. Retr.*, 2(1–2) :1–135.

Haiyun Peng, Lu Xu, Lidong Bing, Fei Huang, Wei Lu, and Luo Si. 2020. Knowing what, how and why: A near complete solution for aspect-based sentiment analysis. *Proceedings of the AAAI Conference on Artificial Intelligence*, 34(05) :8600–8607.

Telmo Pires, Eva Schlinger, and Dan Garrette. 2019. How multilingual is multilingual BERT? In *Proceedings of the 57th Annual Meeting of the Association for Computational Linguistics*, pages 4996–5001, Florence, Italy. Association for Computational Linguistics.

Maria Pontiki, Dimitris Galanis, Haris Papageorgiou, Ion Androutsopoulos, Suresh Manandhar, Mohammad AL-Smadi, Mahmoud Al-Ayyoub, Yanyan Zhao, Bing Qin, Orphée De Clercq, Véronique Hoste, Marianna Apidianaki, Xavier Tannier, Natalia Loukachevitch, Evgeniy Kotelnikov, Nuria Bel, Salud María Jiménez-Zafra, and Gülşen Eryiğit. 2016. SemEval-2016 task 5: Aspect based sentiment analysis. In *Proceedings of the 10th International Workshop on Semantic Evaluation (SemEval-2016)*, pages 19–30, San Diego, California. Association for Computational Linguistics.

Maria Pontiki, Dimitris Galanis, Haris Papageorgiou, Suresh Manandhar, and Ion Androutsopoulos. 2015. SemEval-2015 task 12: Aspect based sentiment analysis. In *Proceedings of the 9th International Workshop on Semantic Evaluation (SemEval 2015)*, pages

486–495, Denver, Colorado. Association for Computational Linguistics.

Maria Pontiki, Dimitris Galanis, John Pavlopoulos, Harris Papageorgiou, Ion Androutsopoulos, and Suresh Manandhar. 2014. SemEval-2014 task 4: Aspect based sentiment analysis. In *Proceedings of the 8th International Workshop on Semantic Evaluation (SemEval 2014)*, pages 27–35, Dublin, Ireland. Association for Computational Linguistics.

Ana-Maria Popescu and Oren Etzioni. 2005. Extracting product features and opinions from reviews. In *Proceedings of the Conference on Human Language Technology and Empirical Methods in Natural Language Processing*, HLT '05, page 339–346, USA. Association for Computational Linguistics.

Amir Pouran Ben Veyseh, Nasim Nouri, Franck Dernoncourt, Dejing Dou, and Thien Huu Nguyen. 2020. Introducing syntactic structures into target opinion word extraction with deep learning. In *Proceedings of the 2020 Conference on Empirical Methods in Natural Language Processing (EMNLP)*, pages 8947–8956, Online. Association for Computational Linguistics.

Alec Radford, Jeff Wu, R. Child, David Luan, Dario Amodei, and Ilya Sutskever. 2019. Language models are unsupervised multitask learners. In *OpenAI blog*.

Holger Schwenk and Xian Li. 2018. A corpus for multilingual document classification in eight languages. In *Proceedings of the Eleventh International Conference on Language Resources and Evaluation (LREC 2018)*. European Language Resources Association (ELRA).

Jörg Tiedemann and Santhosh Thottingal. 2020. OPUS-MT — Building open translation services for the World. In *Proceedings of the 22nd Annual Conferenec of the European Association for Machine Translation (EAMT)*, Lisbon, Portugal.

Fang Wang, Yuncong Li, Wenjun Zhang, and Shengtao Zhong. 2021. A more fine-grained aspect-sentiment-opinion triplet extraction task. *ArXiv*, abs/2103.15255.

Thomas Wolf, Lysandre Debut, Victor Sanh, Julien Chaumond, Clement Delangue, Anthony Moi, Pierric Cistac, Tim Rault, Remi Louf, Morgan Funtowicz, Joe Davison, Sam Shleifer, Patrick von Platen, Clara Ma, Yacine Jernite, Julien Plu, Canwen Xu, Teven Le Scao, Sylvain Gugger, Mariama Drame, Quentin Lhoest, and Alexander Rush. 2020. Transformers: State-of-the-art natural language processing. In *Proceedings of the 2020 Conference on Empirical Methods in Natural Language Processing : System Demonstrations*, pages 38–45, Online. Association for Computational Linguistics.

Shijie Wu and Mark Dredze. 2019. Beto, bentz, becas: The surprising cross-lingual effectiveness of BERT. In *Proceedings of the 2019 Conference on Empirical Methods in Natural Language Processing and the 9th International Joint Conference on Natural Language Processing (EMNLP-IJCNLP)*, pages 833–844, Hong Kong, China. Association for Computational Linguistics.

Hu Xu, Bing Liu, Lei Shu, and Philip S. Yu. 2018. Double embeddings and cnn-based sequence labeling for aspect extraction. *Proceedings of the 56th Annual Meeting of the Association for Computational Linguistics (Volume 2 : Short Papers)*.

Weijia Xu, Batool Haider, and Saab Mansour. 2020. End-to-end slot alignment and recognition for cross-lingual NLU. In *Proceedings of the 2020 Conference on Empirical Methods in Natural Language Processing (EMNLP)*, pages 5052–5063, Online. Association for Computational Linguistics.

Yinfei Yang, Yuan Zhang, Chris Tar, and Jason Baldridge. 2019. PAWS-X : A cross-lingual adversarial dataset for paraphrase identification. In *Proceedings of the 2019 Conference on Empirical Methods in Natural Language Processing and the 9th International Joint Conference on Natural Language Processing (EMNLP-IJCNLP)*, pages 3687–3692. Association for Computational Linguistics.

Vilém Zouhar and Daria Pylypenko. 2021. Leveraging neural machine translation for word alignment.

SD²SG: A Novel Framework for Detecting Important Subevents from Crisis Events via Dynamic Semantic Graphs

Evangelia Spiliopoulou
Language Technologies Institute, Carnegie Mellon University
espiliop@cs.cmu.edu

Tanay K. Saha **Joel Tetreault** **Alejandro Jaimes**
Dataminr Inc.
{tsaha,jtetreault,ajaimes}@dataminr.com

Abstract

Social media is an essential tool to share information about crisis events, such as natural disasters. Event Detection aims at extracting information in the form of an event, but considers each event in isolation, without combining information across sentences or events. Many posts in Crisis NLP contain repetitive or complementary information which needs to be aggregated (e.g., the number of trapped people and their location) for disaster response. Although previous approaches in Crisis NLP aggregate information across posts, they only use shallow representations of the content (e.g., keywords), which cannot adequately represent the semantics of a crisis event and its sub-events. In this work, we propose a novel framework to extract critical sub-events from a large-scale crisis event by combining important information across relevant tweets. Our framework first converts all the tweets from a crisis event into a temporally-ordered set of graphs. Then it extracts sub-graphs that represent semantic relationships connecting verbs and nouns in 3 to 6 node sub-graphs. It does this by learning edge weights via Dynamic Graph Convolutional Networks (DGCNs) and extracting smaller, relevant sub-graphs. Our experiments show that our extracted structures (1) are semantically meaningful sub-events and (2) contain information important for the large crisis-event. Furthermore, we show that our approach significantly outperforms event detection baselines, highlighting the importance of aggregating information across tweets for our task.

1 Introduction

Social media is widely used for informing humanitarian aid efforts in crisis events (Nazer et al., 2017; Reuter et al., 2017). During a large-scale crisis event, there is a large set of smaller events in duration and impact that are essential components of the larger event, which are called *sub-events*. A sub-event is a structure that represents an action, and thus has a temporal dimension and a list of entities involved. Detecting important sub-events that occur during a crisis (e.g., road blocks, people trapped) can aid authorities to prevent and respond to urgent situations (e.g., rescue efforts) (Nazer et al., 2017). However, this requires connecting information from multiple posts as they contain repetitive or complementary information which needs to be aggregated (e.g., the number of trapped people and their location) for disaster response.

1. #NepalQuake avalanche kills 8 at Nepal's Everest base-camp
2. Obliterated Everest basecamp where at least 10 people were buried alive by avalanche after Nepal earthquake
3. Route to camp1 completely destroyed by avalanche.#NepalQuake
4. Avalanche sweeps Everest base-camp, killing 17: An avalanche triggered by Nepal's massive earthquake...
5. #Everest avalanche more than 100 climbers stuck in camp1 awaiting rescue.! #NepalQuake

Table 1: Example tweets from **April 2015 Nepal Earthquake** crisis event.

Several approaches in crisis NLP aggregate information across multiple tweets in the form of clusters, where each cluster is considered a sub-event (Abhik and Toshniwal, 2013; Pohl et al., 2012; Arachie et al., 2020). However, these methods have several shortcomings. First, the output clusters may not refer to a single sub-event, but to a list of sub-events that share similar information types. For example, consider the tweets *25 people killed in Everest base-camp* and *200 people killed in Gorkha*. They contain the same information type (i.e., number of people killed), but clearly refer to two different sub-events. This results in large, non-interpretable clusters that lack cohesion

Proceedings of the 2021 EMNLP Workshop W-NUT: The Seventh Workshop on Noisy User-generated Text, pages 249–259
November 11, 2021.

(Jiang et al., 2019). Second, most work ignores or uses heuristics to model the temporal dependencies of sub-events, without explicitly modeling time-sensitive information that gets updated, such as the number of injured people. Third, tweet content is represented by shallow semantics, such as bag-of-words or verb-noun pairs. Such representations miss information that distinguishes between different sub-events of the same information type and are inadequate to model semantic dependencies across sub-events. To provide an example, consider the Nepal earthquake in April 2015. In Table 1, we show tweets referring to a deadly avalanche in mountain Everest which was triggered by the earthquake. We may extract *100 climbers were trapped in camp 1 and 2* from one tweet and *the route to camp 1 and camp 2 was completely destroyed* from another. Although these two tweets refer to different sub-events, they are related and an event extraction framework would benefit from modeling their dependencies.

Representing events in text is a complex problem. Most work on event detection relies on the **semantic frame** theory (Fillmore, 2008), according to which an event is represented by the **predicate**, typically a verb or noun denoting an action, and the **event arguments**, a list of entities related to the predicate via a specific set of relations (e.g., agent, patient,..). In this work, we use the same notion of event representations. Thus, we can distinguish different sub-events even if they have the same predicate and/or partially share entities, as in the example discussed earlier.

Recent work on social event understanding proposed a method to model event dependencies. They construct a sequence of graphs representing all the documents (Deng et al., 2019). They preserve temporal dependencies of events by using a Dynamic Graph Convolutional Network (DGCN); a model that learns an expressive graph representation of nodes not only from their connections in a certain time-step, but also from the dynamic context of the previous time-step. In our framework we exploit the expressive power of a DGCN to aggregate tweet content and model large-scale crisis events, by learning graph edge weights. These weights let us identify important nodes and relations; a critical step for sub-event extraction (Meladianos et al., 2018).

We propose SD^{2}SG, (Sub-event Detection via Dynamic Semantic Graphs): a novel framework to extract important sub-events from a temporally-ordered group of tweets related to a crisis event. Our approach combines information across tweets into a set of temporally-ordered graphs, which are used to extract sub-events. Since we have limited data, we impose structural (entities can be connected only via a predicate) and semantic constraints (predicates are defined via the FrameNet ontology) in each graph. Thanks to these constraints, our model learns valid relations instead of coincidental co-occurrences of words via the use of a DGCN model. Finally, we exploit the same structural constraints another time to rank 3 to 6 node subgraphs (sub-events) from the learned graph of a crisis event. The contributions of our proposed framework are summarized as follows:

- This is the first work in Crisis NLP that extracts sub-events in the form of semantic relations (i.e., predicate with a list of arguments); in prior work sub-events correspond to clusters of words or tweets.
- Our framework aggregates information across tweets and models temporal and semantic dependencies between sub-events. This problem is not addressed by event detection approaches, as they treat each sub-event independent.
- We conduct a large-scale human evaluation of the quality of the extracted sub-events, according to which SD^{2}SG outperforms baselines by at least 3% and 6% in terms of the validity and the importance of extracted sub-events respectively.

2 Related Work

Relevant research focuses on two main directions: (*i*) information extraction or classification in the tweet/sentence level and (*ii*) information aggregation across documents / posts.

Information Extraction & Classification in Tweets. Given the large volume of noisy data from social media, most tasks focus on sentence classification problems, where the goal is to filter only the most important posts that might be helpful for first responders. As discussed by Imran et al. (2015); Tapia et al. (2011), there are several types of sentence classification for disaster response, such as determining if a message is related to a specific crisis event (Caragea et al.,

2016; Kruspe, 2019; Nguyen et al., 2016; Neubig et al., 2011), if it is actionable (Leavitt and Robinson, 2017) or critical (Mccreadie et al., 2019; Spiliopoulou et al., 2020). Other work classifies tweets with respect to the type of information they contain, a problem that is formulated as a multi-class tweet classification (typically five major information types) (Burel et al., 2017; Nguyen et al., 2017; Imran et al., 2016; Miyazaki et al., 2019; Padhee et al., 2020).

Related work outside of Crisis NLP can also be used to extract information from tweets, in the form of events. Chen et al. (2018) use an encoder-decoder framework to extract sub-events from each tweet, while Rudra et al. (2018) use noun-verb pairs to represent sub-events, where each pair is ranked based on their overlap score in tweets. Some approaches outside the crisis domain that focus on extracting textual sub-events from tweets or documents, in a sequence classification setup (Bekoulis et al., 2019). Other related work includes Open IE methods (open information extraction), which extract tuples of expressions from text that represent the events of the sentence. Such work includes Open IE by AllenNLP (Stanovsky et al., 2018), which uses a deep BiLSTM sequence prediction model and systems that combine BERT embeddings with other neural models, such as a BiLSTM encoder (Kolluru et al., 2020).

Aggregating Information Across Tweets. Research on Crisis NLP that aggregates information across posts aims at extracting sub-events that are important in the context of the larger crisis event. The notion of sub-events varies within this area; a sub-event could correspond to an entire cluster of words / tweets or to a textual span from a single tweet. Earlier work in sub-event extraction forms clusters of tweets during a crisis event based on a set of shallow features, such as tf-idf and metadata (Abhik and Toshniwal, 2013; Pohl et al., 2012). Other approaches use topic clustering to form sets of words (topics) that represent sub-events (Srijith et al., 2017; Xing et al., 2016). Most recent work forms clusters based on verb-noun pairs from individual tweets (Jiang et al., 2019), which are then ranked based on an ontology grounding score (Arachie et al., 2020). In all these methods each cluster is considered to correspond to a different sub-event. However, the elements within each cluster are not necessarily related via temporal or other relations, which raises questions with respect to the interpretability of the cluster/sub-event.

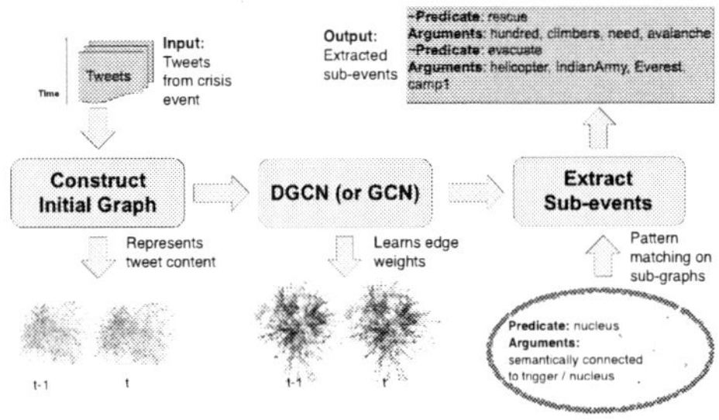

Figure 1: Framework architecture diagram.

In a different direction, a group of temporally ordered messages is used for large-event detection. For example, (Sakaki et al., 2010) use statistical and keyword features in a spatio-temporal model to detect crisis events based on Twitter streams. More recently, Meladianos et al. (2015, 2018) use a graph representation of tweets to extract important sub-events by detecting weight changes, a problem formulated as a summarization task. Early approaches that use text from social media to represent context for social events rely on linear classifiers using topic-related features (Wang et al., 2012), graph features (Keneshloo et al., 2014) or combination of heterogeneous data sources (Korkmaz et al., 2015) and dynamic query expansion models with a static vocabulary (Zhao et al., 2015) or fused with logistic regression (Ramakrishnan et al., 2014). Ning et al. (2018); Zhao et al. (2015) use multi-task models with shared parameters across different locations and events to model spatio-temporal correlations. Most recent work that inspired our approach uses dynamic graphs to represent information from social media, which model temporal constraints from precursor events (Deng et al., 2020, 2019; Ning et al., 2018). A common theme of this work, as further discussed by Ning et al. (2019) underlines the importance of explainability, since it is helpful for experts to analyze which factors led to the development of a large-scale event and potential ways to prevent or mitigate it.

3 Proposed Framework: SD^{2}SG

In this section, we discuss our approach on extracting sub-events from a stream of temporally-ordered tweets related to a crisis event. Our framework consists of the following steps, as shown in Figure 1: (*i*) construct the initial dynamic semantic graph, (*ii*) learn the graph's weights via a graph neural net-

Algorithm 1: Steps of SD^{2}SG

Input : C = A set of crisis events,
$tweet_1, \ldots, tweet_n$ in a temporal order,
n = total number of tweets in **a crisis event**
t = number of time-steps,
k = number of sub-events,
pre-trained embeddings

Output: Extracted sub-events for each time-step t:
$S_1, S_2, \ldots, S_t$ from each crisis event.

1. **for** *each crisis event,* $C_i \in C$ **do**
    for *tweets* $\in \{relevant, irrelevant\}$ **do**
        Divide $tweet_1, tweet_2, \ldots, tweet_n$ into groups of equal size, $D = D_1, D_2, ..., D_t$;
        for *each* $D_i \in D$ **do**
            Construct semantic graph G_i;
2. Run learning framework, DGCN on the output from Step 1 and extract indicator function I based on DGCN's parameters to extract graph weights;
3. **for** *each crisis event,* $C_i \in C$ **do**
    `// Only run on graph constructed from relevant tweets`
    for *each* $G_i \in G$ **do**
        a) Extract sub-graph $G_i^{'}$ based on I;
        b) Sample sub-events from random graph walks in $G_i^{'}$;
        c) Collect sub-events that meet semantic constraints (event structure);
        d) Rank extracted sub-events with tf-idf score. Choose top k;

work, and (*iii*) extract sub-events from the learned graph via random walks that satisfy our semantic constraints. The pseudocode of our framework's steps is in Algorithm 1.

3.1 Constructing Initial Dynamic Semantic Graphs

Given a large-scale crisis event, our first step is to represent the content of the related tweets in a graph structure by merging information across all the messages, which we call **initial graph**. An initial graph represents the tweets for a given time-step; it can be used dynamically in a sequence of initial graphs (i.e., one graph per time-step) or as a single graph (i.e., one time-step).

There are multiple ways to build the initial graph representation of tweets. In SD^{2}SG, we use a sequence of **initial semantic graphs**, where each graph is based on semantic relations from text. Given a set of tweets from a specific time-step, the initial semantic graph is a bipartite graph that connects predicates with their arguments, as they appear together in text. A group of tweets can be represented by a single initial graph, where the same predicate may be connected to different arguments from different sentences. An example of an

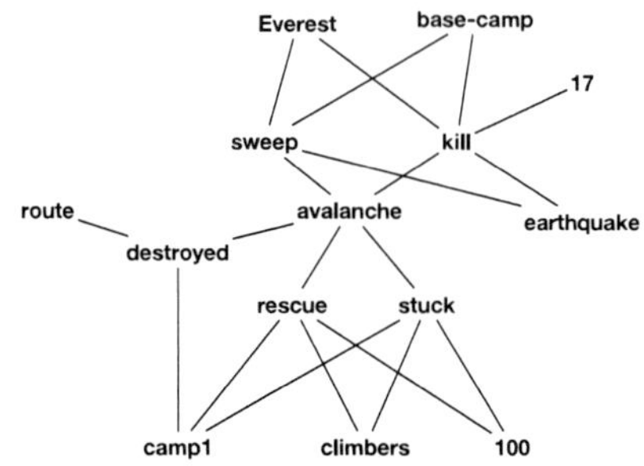

Figure 2: Initial semantic graph, based on subset of Nepal 2015 earthquake tweets (tweets 3, 4, 5)

initial semantic graph is shown in Figure 2, which is constructed based on tweets 3, 4 and 5 in Table 1.

Formally, given a tweet t_i, we use a dependency parser to extract the part-of-speech tags from tweets. Based on these tags we form two groups: (1) verbs and nominalized verbs (i.e., nouns that are derived from verbs, like *explosion*) $V_i = \{v_1, v_2, ...\}$, by matching the tokens to the Lexical Units provided in FrameNet (Baker et al., 1998) and (2) nouns (excluding nominalized verbs) $N_i = \{n_1, n_2, ..\}$. The output graph has as nodes $\cup_i N_i \cup V_i$ for all tweets t_i. We form weighted edges only across the two groups (verbs V and nouns N), which are initialized based on the PMI of each pair (Church and Hanks, 1990). More specifically, for each tweet t_i, we have $(v_i, n_j) \forall i, j$ but no (n_i, n_j) edges. This ensures that we link the sentence's predicate with its arguments, while avoiding to link arguments that appear together under different relations/predicates. As shown in Figure 2, this results in a graph that combines information across tweets in a more explainable way compared to previous approaches (Deng et al., 2019), while maintaining semantic relations from text.

3.2 Learning Edge Weights via a DGCN

The initial semantic graphs mainly capture information mentioned in sentence level, without taking context into account (i.e., information based on neighboring relations). This results in large graphs with noisy relations, where it is hard to extract important information. In order to get a smaller, less noisy graph, we formulate our problem as a classification task using dynamic graph convolutional networks (DGCNs) where the goal is to learn edge weights, a mechanism introduced by Deng et al. to detect social events for news articles. With this setup the model learns which neighbourhoods or sets of nodes in the graph are important and correspond to sub-events that occur during a crisis.

A DGCN model consists of a sequence of GCNs that are linked together by feeding information from the previous time-step to detect important factors in the context of social event understanding. Each initial graph is fed into a different GCN layer by time. For each GCN layer except the first one, the input features are processed by a temporal encoded module, involving the output of the last GCN layer and the current word embeddings, to capture temporal features. Finally, there is a masked nonlinear transformation layer to unify the final output vector from the final GCN layer. The loss is calculated between the model output and ground truth label, which, in our case, is whether a group of tweets is related to a crisis event or not.

Formally, given a sequence of initial semantic graphs, we form their normalized adjacent matrices $A_1, A_2, ..A_t$ for each time-step t. We are also given a matrix of initial node features H_0, which in our case corresponds to the pre-trained word embeddings of the vocabulary. At each time-step, the convolutional layer of the DGCN is computed by: $H_{t+1} = g(A_t \bar{H}_t W^{(t)} + b^{(t)})$, where $W^{(t)}, b^{(t)}$ are model parameters and g is a non-linear activation function. Note that $\bar{H}_t$ does not correspond to the GCN output, but instead to the temporal encoding embeddings, calculated from the last TE layer. The temporal encoding is defined based on the following equations, where W_p, W_e, b_p, b_e are the parameters learned by the model:

$$H_p^{(t)} = H_t W_p^{(t)} + b_p^{(t)} \quad (1)$$

$$H_e^{(t)} = H_0 W_e^{(t)} + b_e^{(t)} \quad (2)$$

$$\bar{H}_t = tanh(|H_p^{(t)}||H_e^{(t)}|) \quad (3)$$

In order to classify the group of tweets as related or not to a crisis event, we set the output feature dimension of the last layer as 1. Due to dynamic graph encoding, the output feature vector of the last GCN layer is a combined representation of all graph nodes, which is different for each large-crisis event (i.e., different graph nodes). To guarantee the consistency of the model across instances, the DGCN uses a masked nonlinear transformation layer to map the final output vector to the prediction of the task. Finally, for each node i in the graph, we use the scalar value $h_{i,t}$ from the last GCN layer and $w_{i,m}$ from the masked nonlinear transformation layer to define an indicator function $I_i = h_{i,t} w_{i,m}$. This indicator function is used to select important nodes and their edges from the graph.

3.3 Extracting Sub-events

Given the sequence of learned graphs, the last part of our framework aims at extracting significantly smaller sub-graphs that represent sub-events (i.e. a typical sub-event contains 3-6 terms, while a graph might have 100-200 nodes). Although we use bipartite graphs to represent tweets, during learning, we treat them as homogeneous with zero edge-weight because of the nature of GCN/DGCN models (they operate on homogeneous graphs, where all nodes are treated equally). In order to generate valid sub-event candidates, we use a pattern matching method based on iterations of random walks on each graph (Bressan et al., 2018; Saha and Hasan, 2015). The patterns used correspond to the typical structure of an event, where the predicate (usually a verb) is linked to a set of arguments (entities/nouns). Similarly to the semantic constraints in each initial semantic graph, we generate sub-events of star-like patterns of variable size (3-6 nodes), where the center node is an event predicate, as defined by the FrameNet lexicon.

After we extract our candidate sub-events, we use a ranking method to remove duplicate or redundant information. To do that, we use a tf-idf scoring scheme, where each sub-event is treated as a single document; the score of each sub-event equals to the average tf-idf score of its words. While other ranking or filtering methods can be used, tf-idf is most appropriate as it retrieves important information (tf) and avoids similar, almost duplicate sub-events (idf).

4 Training & Evaluation

Crisis Event Dataset. To train the model described in Algorithm 1, we use a subset of the combined dataset described in Alam et al., which consists of Twitter data from 59 crisis events, including natural and man-made disasters. The tweets in this dataset were all manually annotated by Alam et al. as either being related or unrelated to their corresponding crisis event. The statistics of the dataset are shown in Table 2.

Crisis Event Type	# Crisis Events	# Related Tweets	# Unrelated Tweets
Hurricane/Typhoon	13	22,154	13,219
Crash/Explosion	11	7,689	9,718
Flood	11	12,366	9,747
Earthquake	10	12,164	6,911
Terrorist Attack	3	5,956	4,205
Tornado	3	6,242	5,034
Wildfire	3	2,842	348
MERS	1	1,113	69
Ebola	1	1,420	210
Volcano	1	104	191
Haze	1	476	136
Landslide	1	364	2,800
Total	59	73,070	52,588

Table 2: Dataset Statistics; number of tweets refers to tweets related to the large-scale crisis event.

Training Details. We execute Step 1 of Algorithm 1 on these 59 crisis events. For the models based on dynamic graphs (SD^{2}SG and Simple Dynamic Graph) we use time-step $t = 3$.

We randomly split the dataset in Table 2 into train, development, and test sets, where an event belongs to only one of these sets. Related and unrelated sub-events are positive and negative examples, respectively. This set-up was used to train the DGCN model (Step 2 of Algorithm 1). Out of 59 crisis events, we use 33, 10 and 16 as training, dev and test sets. For word embeddings we used 100d GloVE (Pennington et al., 2014) pre-trained on Twitter, and the DGCN was trained using the Adam optimizer with learning rate 5e-4, weight decay 5e-4, and dropout rate 0.2.

Once the DGCN is trained, we execute Step 3 in Algorithm 1 and extract sub-graphs of interest for our evaluation. We evaluate our extracted sub-events with respect to two factors: (*i*) validity and (*ii*) importance in the context of a large-scale crisis event.

4.1 Baselines

To verify our assumption that information aggregation is important for our task, we chose baselines consisting of various methods that either aggregate information across tweets or not. We use Open IE as the baseline that does not aggregate information, while the remaining baselines are ablations of our proposed model. Our ablations study lets us verify the impact of every component of the proposed model. Unfortunately, since no prior work in crisis NLP extracts sub-events in the form of semantic relations, we cannot compare with these methods. Here is a brief overview of each baseline:

Simple Dynamic-Graph: uses a complete graph (i.e., edges across all pairs of nodes) without any constraints. The weight of each edge is based on the PMI of the two nodes. This model was proposed by Deng et al. (2019) to model social events.

Static Sem-Graph: (1 time step) constructs only one graph for all the tweets, without taking into account their temporal dimensions. The initial graph is constructed in a similar manner as the proposed model, but the weights are learned via a static GCN model.

Init Sem-Graph: uses the sequence of initial semantic graphs as-is (no learning of graph weights)

Open IE: uses the output of an Open IE system for each individual tweet to directly produce sub-event candidates. For this baseline, we use the OpenIE system developed by Stanovsky et al. (2018). Each sub-event is formed by using Open IE's *predicate* as the sub-event predicate and the head nouns of each *argument phrase* as the sub-event arguments. Since the output is already a set of sub-events instead of a graph, we directly rank them based on tf-idf features, similarly to the last step of the proposed model.

Large Scale Crisis Events	Extracted Sub-events
2014 India-Pakistan floods	1467
2012 Colorado wildfires	693
2013 Alberta floods	680
2013 Balochistan earthquakes	715
2013 Dhaka garment factory collapse	800
2013 Los Angeles International Airport shooting	687
2013 South Wales bushfires	683
2017 Puebla earthquake	710
2015 Nepal earthquake	939
2019 Covid pandemic	818
Cyclone Oswald	850
2013 Spuyten Duyvil derailment	771
Hurricane Harvey	688
MERS epidemic	894
2014 Typhoon Hagupit	690
West Texas Fertilizer Company explosion	915
Total	13,000

Table 3: Large-scale crisis events and their number of extracted sub-events.

Crisis Predicate ⟶	Yes			No				
Event Arguments ⟶	All	Some	None	All	Some	None		
Models ↓	Sub-event Validity Score						**Predicate Accuracy**	**Sub-event Accuracy**
Open IE	0.30%	0.50%	2.70%	1.00%	9.20%	86.30%	4.50%	1.80%
init sem-graph (no learning)	7.70%	14.60%	13.00%	7.00%	18.80%	42.00%	39.20%	29.30%
Simple dynamic	8.00%	10.00%	11.30%	7.00%	13.10%	56.80%	30.00%	18.70%
static sem-graph	5.99%	8.90%	9.85%	1.60%	17.50%	56.10%	26.20%	16.49%
SD²SG (proposed)	9.70%	15.30%	13.70%	7.10%	17.70%	36.50%	**45.40%**	**32.10%**

Table 4: Percentage of valid sub-events. Sub-event Accuracy represents instances that fall under the *Yes and All/Some* and *No and All* categories.

4.2 Validity of Sub-events

We perform a human evaluation of our extracted sub-events based on crowdsourced annotations via Amazon Mechanical Turk.

Data. We collect a total of 13,000 sub-events (details shown in Table 3) by selecting the top 100 sub-events for each baseline per time-step from 16 large-scale crisis events (after removing events with few instances).

Annotation Guidelines. First, we want to assess whether the extracted sub-events are valid. We showed every candidate sub-event $s_i = (t, a_1, a_2, ..)$ (where t is the predicate and $a_1, a_2, ..$ are the event arguments) to three MTurk annotators and asked them the following questions:

1. Does the predicate represent a crisis incident (e.g., outage, collapse, injury) during a major crisis event? Possible answers: *yes* or *no*.

2. How many of the argument words describe a crisis scenario with or without the predicate? Possible answers: *all*, *some*, or *none*.

We estimate the inter-annotator agreement of these judgments via Fleiss' Kappa; the predicate accuracy has $k = 0.5$, while sub-event accuracy $k = 0.37$.

Metric & Eval Summary. In table 4 we show the detailed results of our human evaluation. To estimate the accuracy of the sub-events overall (predicate and event arguments) for each baseline, we merged the answers of three categories; Yes and All, Yes and Some and No and All. We decided this merging for two reasons. First, some sub-events might have predicates that are not clearly related to a crisis (e.g., *keep, go*), but in combination with proper arguments the entire structure is a valid, meaningful sub-event in a crisis scenario (e.g., predicate: *fly*, arguments: *rescuers, climbers, Everest*). Second, some sub-events may be partially valid; the event predicate and some (but not all) of the arguments are valid. Such instances still contain meaningful information for the crisis event and could be used to inform decisions.

Our results show that SD^{2}SG outperforms all baselines. This highlights that all the components of the model (the initial semantic graph, the temporal aspect and the learned weights) contribute to a better model overall. However, we observe that the initial semantic graph is the second best performing model, with only 3% difference. From that, we conclude that the semantic and structural constraints are a crucial component to extract valid sub-events.

4.3 Importance of Sub-events

Determining the importance of a sub-event is a complex task that requires expert annotators, as they need to consider the context of the crisis event. Even though a sub-event may be valid with respect to its structure, we still need to validate if it is important in the context of the large-scale crisis event.

Data. We used the sub-events from the top performing baselines that were previously classified to belong to one of the following categories (sub-event accuracy); *Yes and All*, *Yes and Some* and *No and All*. Out of a total of 1,756 valid sub-events, we randomly select a subset of 300 ($\sim$ 80 sub-events per baseline).

Annotation Guidelines. To evaluate the importance of the sub-events, we conducted another human evaluation, where we asked two expert annotators the following question, for each sub-event:

1. Go to the provided Wikipedia link. Is the proposed sub-event important for this crisis event? Suppose the proposed sub-event did not happen, would the consequences of the major crisis or the humanitarian aid response be different? Possible answers: *yes* or *no*.

We estimate the inter-annotator agreement by Cohen's Kappa and Kappa score for this evaluation task is 0.48.

Models	Important Sub-event Accuracy
init sem-graph (no learning)	19%
simple dynamic static	15%
sem-graph	14%
SD^{2}SG (proposed)	**25%**

Table 5: Percentage of important sub-events. The second column is an estimate of the important sub-events that each model extracts.

Metric & Eval Summary. To evaluate sub-event importance we estimate the percentage of all extracted sub-events that are important, per model (important sub-event accuracy). The goal of this metric is to reflect how good each system is in extracting important sub-events.

To estimate the important sub-event accuracy we use the results obtained from both human evaluations. The first evaluation tells us how many valid sub-events each system extracts, while the second how many of these valid sub-events are important, per system. Each annotated sub-event was considered important if any of the two annotators labeled it as such. Thus, the important sub-event accuracy per system is estimated by $\frac{valid\_sub}{extracted\_sub} \frac{important\_sub^*}{valid\_sub^*}$, where $valid\_sub^*$ and $important\_sub^*$ correspond to the number of valid and important sub-events respectively in the annotated sample (i.e., $valid\_sub^*$ = 300).

The results of this evaluation are shown in Table 5. We observe that our proposed model performs substantially better than the baselines (6% higher than the second-best). Although the accuracy of all systems is relatively low, this is due to the low percentage of valid events (i.e., a sub-event must be valid in order to be important).

5 Discussion

In the previous section we show that despite SD^{2}SG performed significantly better than our baselines, our numbers are overall low; 45.5% of our extracted sub-events are valid and only 25% important. In this section we identify and discuss a set of reasons why sub-event extraction of tweets is a challenging problem and how we can improve.

Models	Predicate Overlap	Argument Overlap
init sem-graph (no learning)	85.10%	65.90%
PMI dynamic static	**92.85%**	58.20%
sem-graph	88.75%	67.60%
SD^{2}SG (proposed)	90.40%	**68.00%**

Table 6: Overlap of extracted sub-events with terms from the EM ontology.

The first step of our analysis is to compare our extracted sub-events to an existing resource manually curated by experts in crisis NLP. We used the EMTerms (Emergency Management Terms) ontology (Temnikova et al., 2015); a resource of 7,000 manually annotated terms that are used in Twitter to describe crisis events, classified into 23 information-specific categories. Based on this lexicon and our extracted sub-events, we estimate the percentage of predicates and arguments that exist in the EM terms by a partial string matching (many EMTerms are phrases of 2-3 words). In Table 6 we show the results of this grounding. We observe that, overall, a large percentage of the predicates can be grounded in the ontology, while the argument overlap is significantly lower. This can be explained by our semantic constraints on the predicates of the extracted sub-events (must exist in FrameNet), while the event arguments had no such constraints. However, given the results of our human evaluation in the previous section, we conclude that, even though a word might be a crisis related keyword, a sub-event formed by such keywords is not necessarily valid. This is due to the fact that sub-events aim to represent relations between several terms, thus grounding to an ontology is not a sufficient metric of the quality of the extracted sub-events.

Crisis Event	Predicate	Arguments
1. Alberta floods	evacuation	flooding, zone, Canada
2. Puebla earthquake	follow	rescuer, victims
3. Typhoon Hagupit	keep	safety, flee
4. Puebla earthquake	school	kill, child, dead
5. MERS	cough	healthcare, surveillance
6. Duyvil derailment	fatality	derailment,helicopter, major, abc, amtrak
7. MERS	emergency	infection, Fukuda discover
8. Dhaka garment factory collapse	rescue	survivors, number, labor,factory

Table 7: Example output from SD^{2}SG

In Table 7, we show a few real-output examples that highlight the complexity of sub-events. These sub-events belong to any of the three accepted categories of valid sub-events (*Yes and All/Some* or *No and All*). Although they were all considered valid by human annotators, we observe a few major challenges. Although some predicates are not crisis words, they could still form a valid crisis sub-event with the appropriate arguments. Such an example is the predicate *follow* in sub-event 2. However, for some other instances (example 4), the predicate might be an entity in the particular context.

A major problem in our framework is that we don't know how the arguments are related to the predicate. Although semantic frames consist of specific relations (e.g., agent, patient, location), our framework provides only a list of the related entities without their relations. An open challenge is to use thematic roles both for tweet representation and for the extracted sub-events, as this will result in more meaningful sub-events that would be easier to evaluate. Given that SD^{2}SGis modularized, it can be modified to represent thematic roles by using heterogeneous graph neural networks (HGNNs) instead of DGCNs. HGNNs are a type of network that consists of multiple types of edges or nodes. However, extracting thematic roles from text (first step of SD^{2}SG) would still be a particularly hard task due to the nature of social media text, which does not always conform to proper syntax and grammar.

6 Conclusion

In this paper, we propose a novel framework to extract sub-events from a large-scale crisis event. Contrary to earlier views of sub-events as clusters of unrelated words or phrases, our methodology aims at extracting sub-events in the form of a predicate and its arguments. Our framework aggregates information across a set of tweets into dynamic graph representations, while maintaining semantic constraints. Through an extensive qualitative analysis of our extracted sub-events, we show that our approach performs better than other baselines and highlight the challenges of our task.

References

Dhekar Abhik and Durga Toshniwal. 2013. Sub-event detection during natural hazards using features of social media data. In *Proceedings of the 22nd International Conference on World Wide Web*, pages 783–788.

Firoj Alam, Hassan Sajjad, Muhammad Imran, and Ferda Ofli. 2020. Standardizing and benchmarking crisis-related social media datasets for humanitarian information processing. *arXiv preprint arXiv:2004.06774*.

Chidubem Arachie, Manas Gaur, Sam Anzaroot, William Groves, Ke Zhang, and Alejandro Jaimes. 2020. Unsupervised detection of sub-events in large scale disasters. In *Proceedings of the AAAI Conference on Artificial Intelligence*, volume 34, pages 354–361.

Collin F Baker, Charles J Fillmore, and John B Lowe. 1998. The berkeley framenet project. In *36th Annual Meeting of the Association for Computational Linguistics and 17th International Conference on Computational Linguistics, Volume 1*, pages 86–90.

Giannis Bekoulis, Johannes Deleu, Thomas Demeester, and Chris Develder. 2019. Sub-event detection from twitter streams as a sequence labeling problem. In *Proceedings of the 2019 Conference of the North American Chapter of the Association for Computational Linguistics: Human Language Technologies, Volume 1 (Long and Short Papers)*, pages 745–750.

Marco Bressan, Flavio Chierichetti, Ravi Kumar, Stefano Leucci, and Alessandro Panconesi. 2018. Motif counting beyond five nodes. 12(4).

Grégoire Burel, Hassan Saif, and Harith Alani. 2017. Semantic wide and deep learning for detecting crisis-information categories on social media. In *International semantic web conference*, pages 138–155. Springer.

Cornelia Caragea, Adrian Silvescu, and Andrea H Tapia. 2016. Identifying informative messages in disaster events using convolutional neural networks. In *International Conference on Information Systems for Crisis Response and Management*, pages 137–147.

Guandan Chen, Nan Xu, and Weiji Mao. 2018. An encoder-memory-decoder framework for sub-event detection in social media. In *Proceedings of the 27th ACM International Conference on Information and Knowledge Management*, pages 1575–1578.

Kenneth Church and Patrick Hanks. 1990. Word association norms, mutual information, and lexicography. *Computational linguistics*, 16(1):22–29.

Songgaojun Deng, Huzefa Rangwala, and Yue Ning. 2019. Learning dynamic context graphs for predicting social events. In *Proceedings of the 25th ACM SIGKDD International Conference on Knowledge Discovery & Data Mining*, pages 1007–1016.

Songgaojun Deng, Huzefa Rangwala, and Yue Ning. 2020. Dynamic knowledge graph based multi-event forecasting. In *Proceedings of the 26th ACM SIGKDD International Conference on Knowledge Discovery & Data Mining*, pages 1585–1595.

Charles J Fillmore. 2008. Frame semantics. In *Cognitive linguistics: Basic readings*, pages 373–400. De Gruyter Mouton.

Muhammad Imran, Carlos Castillo, Fernando Diaz, and Sarah Vieweg. 2015. Processing social media messages in mass emergency: A survey. *ACM Computing Surveys (CSUR)*, 47(4):1–38.

Muhammad Imran, Prasenjit Mitra, and Carlos Castillo. 2016. Twitter as a lifeline: Human-annotated twitter corpora for nlp of crisis-related messages. *arXiv preprint arXiv:1605.05894*.

Shan Jiang, William Groves, Sam Anzaroot, and Alejandro Jaimes. 2019. Crisis sub-events on social media: A case study of wildfires. In *International Conference on Machine Learning AI for Social Good Workshop, Long Beach, United States, July*, volume 1.

Yaser Keneshloo, Jose Cadena, Gizem Korkmaz, and Naren Ramakrishnan. 2014. Detecting and forecasting domestic political crises: a graph-based approach. In *Proceedings of the 2014 ACM conference on Web science*, pages 192–196.

Keshav Kolluru, Samarth Aggarwal, Vipul Rathore, Soumen Chakrabarti, et al. 2020. Imojie: Iterative memory-based joint open information extraction. In *Proceedings of the 58th Annual Meeting of the Association for Computational Linguistics*, pages 5871–5886.

Gizem Korkmaz, Jose Cadena, Chris J Kuhlman, Achla Marathe, Anil Vullikanti, and Naren Ramakrishnan. 2015. Combining heterogeneous data sources for civil unrest forecasting. In *Proceedings of the 2015 IEEE/ACM International Conference on Advances in Social Networks Analysis and Mining 2015*, pages 258–265.

Anna Kruspe. 2019. Few-shot tweet detection in emerging disaster events. *arXiv preprint arXiv:1910.02290*.

Alex Leavitt and John J Robinson. 2017. The role of information visibility in network gatekeeping: Information aggregation on reddit during crisis events. In *Proceedings of the 2017 ACM conference on computer supported cooperative work and social computing*, pages 1246–1261.

Richard Mccreadie, Cody Buntain, and Ian Soboroff. 2019. Trec incident streams: Finding actionable information on social media.

Polykarpos Meladianos, Giannis Nikolentzos, François Rousseau, Yannis Stavrakas, and Michalis Vazirgiannis. 2015. Degeneracy-based real-time sub-event detection in twitter stream. In *Proceedings of the International AAAI Conference on Web and Social Media*, volume 9.

Polykarpos Meladianos, Christos Xypolopoulos, Giannis Nikolentzos, and Michalis Vazirgiannis. 2018. An optimization approach for sub-event detection and summarization in twitter. In *European Conference on Information Retrieval*, pages 481–493. Springer.

Taro Miyazaki, Kiminobu Makino, Yuka Takei, Hiroki Okamoto, and Jun Goto. 2019. Label embedding using hierarchical structure of labels for twitter classification. In *Proceedings of the 2019 Conference on Empirical Methods in Natural Language Processing and the 9th International Joint Conference on Natural Language Processing (EMNLP-IJCNLP)*, pages 6318–6323.

Tahora H Nazer, Guoliang Xue, Yusheng Ji, and Huan Liu. 2017. Intelligent disaster response via social media analysis a survey. *ACM SIGKDD Explorations Newsletter*, 19(1):46–59.

Graham Neubig, Yuichiroh Matsubayashi, Masato Hagiwara, and Koji Murakami. 2011. Safety information mining—what can nlp do in a disaster—. In *Proceedings of 5th International Joint Conference on Natural Language Processing*, pages 965–973.

Dat Nguyen, Kamela Ali Al Mannai, Shafiq Joty, Hassan Sajjad, Muhammad Imran, and Prasenjit Mitra. 2017. Robust classification of crisis-related data on social networks using convolutional neural networks. In *Proceedings of the International AAAI Conference on Web and Social Media*, volume 11.

Dat Tien Nguyen, Shafiq Joty, Muhammad Imran, Hassan Sajjad, and Prasenjit Mitra. 2016. Applications of online deep learning for crisis response using social media information. *arXiv preprint arXiv:1610.01030*.

Yue Ning, Rongrong Tao, Chandan K Reddy, Huzefa Rangwala, James C Starz, and Naren Ramakrishnan. 2018. Staple: Spatio-temporal precursor learning for event forecasting. In *Proceedings of the 2018 SIAM International Conference on Data Mining*, pages 99–107. SIAM.

Yue Ning, Liang Zhao, Feng Chen, Chang-Tien Lu, and Huzefa Rangwala. 2019. Spatio-temporal event forecasting and precursor identification. In *Proceedings of the 25th ACM SIGKDD International Conference on Knowledge Discovery & Data Mining*, pages 3237–3238.

Swati Padhee, Tanay Kumar Saha, Joel Tetreault, and Alejandro Jaimes. 2020. Clustering of social media messages for humanitarian aid response during crisis.

Jeffrey Pennington, Richard Socher, and Christopher D. Manning. 2014. Glove: Global vectors for word representation. In *Empirical Methods in Natural Language Processing (EMNLP)*, pages 1532–1543.

Daniela Pohl, Abdelhamid Bouchachia, and Hermann Hellwagner. 2012. Automatic sub-event detection in emergency management using social media. In *Proceedings of the 21st international conference on world wide web*, pages 683–686.

Naren Ramakrishnan, Patrick Butler, Sathappan Muthiah, Nathan Self, Rupinder Khandpur, Parang Saraf, Wei Wang, Jose Cadena, Anil Vullikanti, Gizem Korkmaz, et al. 2014. 'beating the news' with embers: forecasting civil unrest using open source indicators. In *Proceedings of the 20th ACM SIGKDD international conference on Knowledge discovery and data mining*, pages 1799–1808.

Christian Reuter, Marc-André Kaufhold, Thomas Spielhofer, and Anna Sophie Hahne. 2017. Social media in emergencies: a representative study on citizens' perception in germany. *Proceedings of the ACM on Human-Computer Interaction*, 1(CSCW):1–19.

Koustav Rudra, Pawan Goyal, Niloy Ganguly, Prasenjit Mitra, and Muhammad Imran. 2018. Identifying sub-events and summarizing disaster-related information from microblogs. In *The 41st International ACM SIGIR Conference on Research & Development in Information Retrieval*, pages 265–274.

Tanay Kumar Saha and Mohammad Al Hasan. 2015. Finding network motifs using mcmc sampling. In *Complex Networks VI*, pages 13–24, Cham. Springer International Publishing.

Takeshi Sakaki, Makoto Okazaki, and Yutaka Matsuo. 2010. Earthquake shakes twitter users: real-time event detection by social sensors. In *Proceedings of the 19th international conference on World wide web*, pages 851–860.

Evangelia Spiliopoulou, Eduard Hovy, Alexander G Hauptmann, et al. 2020. Event-related bias removal for real-time disaster events. In *Proceedings of the 2020 Conference on Empirical Methods in Natural Language Processing: Findings*, pages 3858–3868.

PK Srijith, Mark Hepple, Kalina Bontcheva, and Daniel Preotiuc-Pietro. 2017. Sub-story detection in twitter with hierarchical dirichlet processes. *Information Processing & Management*, 53(4):989–1003.

Gabriel Stanovsky, Julian Michael, Luke Zettlemoyer, and Ido Dagan. 2018. Supervised open information extraction. In *Proceedings of the 2018 Conference of the North American Chapter of the Association for Computational Linguistics: Human Language Technologies, Volume 1 (Long Papers)*, pages 885–895.

Andrea H Tapia, Kartikeya Bajpai, Bernard J Jansen, John Yen, and Lee Giles. 2011. Seeking the trustworthy tweet: Can microblogged data fit the information needs of disaster response and humanitarian relief organizations. In *Proceedings of the 8th International ISCRAM Conference*, pages 1–10. ISCRAM Lisbon, Portugal.

Irina P Temnikova, Carlos Castillo, and Sarah Vieweg. 2015. Emterms 1.0: A terminological resource for crisis tweets. In *ISCRAM*.

Xiaofeng Wang, Matthew S Gerber, and Donald E Brown. 2012. Automatic crime prediction using events extracted from twitter posts. In *International conference on social computing, behavioral-cultural modeling, and prediction*, pages 231–238. Springer.

Chen Xing, Yuan Wang, Jie Liu, Yalou Huang, and Wei-Ying Ma. 2016. Hashtag-based sub-event discovery using mutually generative lda in twitter. In *Proceedings of the AAAI Conference on Artificial Intelligence*, volume 30.

Liang Zhao, Qian Sun, Jieping Ye, Feng Chen, Chang-Tien Lu, and Naren Ramakrishnan. 2015. Multitask learning for spatio-temporal event forecasting. In *Proceedings of the 21th ACM SIGKDD International Conference on Knowledge Discovery and Data Mining*, pages 1503–1512.

Synthetic Data Generation and Multi-Task Learning for Extracting Temporal Information from Health-Related Narrative Text

Heereen Shim[1,2,3], Dietwig Lowet[3], Stijn Luca[4] and Bart Vanrumste[1,2]

[1]Campus Group T, e-Media Research Lab, KU Leuven, Leuven, Belgium

[2]Department of Electrical Engineering (ESAT), STADIUS, KU Leuven, Leuven, Belgium

[3]Philips Research, Eindhoven, the Netherlands

[4]Department of Data Analysis and Mathematical Modelling, Ghent University, Ghent, Belgium

{heereen.shim, bart.vanrumste}@kuleuven.be

{dietwig.lowet}@philips.com

{stijn.luca}@ugent.be

Abstract

Extracting temporal information is critical to process health-related text. Temporal information extraction is a challenging task for language models because it requires processing both texts and numbers. Moreover, the fundamental challenge is how to obtain a large-scale training dataset. To address this, we propose a synthetic data generation algorithm. Also, we propose a novel multi-task temporal information extraction model and investigate whether multi-task learning can contribute to performance improvement by exploiting additional training signals with the existing training data. For experiments, we collected a custom dataset containing unstructured texts with temporal information of sleep-related activities. Experimental results show that utilising synthetic data can improve the performance when the augmentation factor is 3. The results also show that when multi-task learning is used with an appropriate amount of synthetic data, the performance can significantly improve from 82. to 88.6 and from 83.9 to 91.9 regarding micro-and macro-average exact match scores of normalised time prediction, respectively.

1 Introduction

Extracting temporal information from text is important linguistic skill to process health-related text. Also, there are a lot of potential applications of temporal information extraction in the health-related domain, including forecasting treatment effect (Choi et al., 2016), early detecting diseases (Khanday et al., 2020), and tracking treatment progress (Demner-Fushman et al., 2021). With the recent trends of telehealth, an automated system that can extract temporal information from the health-related narrative text can provide benefits to not only healthcare professionals but also recipients enabling active engagement, such as self-monitoring.

I went to bed around 11 pm. Used the phone for around 15 minutes and after that switched the light off. It took around 30 minutes to fall asleep. My sleep was disturbed at 5:45 am. and I spend in the bed for other 45 minutes to get sleep. I got off the bed around 6:30 am. Overall the sleep was normal. I felt refreshed.

Event	Time
Bed time	23:00
Lights off time	23:15
Sleep time	23:45
Sleep disturbance	05:45
Duration of disturbance	00:45
Out of bed time	06:30

Figure 1: Example of free-text sleep diary (top) and the extracted temporal information (down).

In this paper, we consider the use-case of a sleep diary, which is a summary of sleep designed to gather information about daily sleep patterns (Carney et al., 2012). A typical sleep diary consists of a series of close-ended questions to record the time. By writing sleep diaries, people can keep track of sleep, monitor sleep habits, and document sleeping problems which can be shared with their sleep therapists. We focus on extracting temporal information from a free-text sleep diary, To achieve this, a system should extract temporal expressions from the unstructured user-generated text and normalise the extracted temporal expressions into a standard format, as illustrated in Figure 1.

Temporal information extraction from user-generated text is a challenging task. First of all, it requires processing not only text but also numbers (e.g., 11pm or 23:00). But recent pre-trained language models (Devlin et al., 2019; Yang et al., 2019) have difficulty in processing numbers (Saxton et al., 2018; Ravichander et al., 2019; Dua et al., 2019) because these language models are pre-trained with language modelling objectives. Even though there have been recent studies on training

Proceedings of the 2021 EMNLP Workshop W-NUT: The Seventh Workshop on Noisy User-generated Text, pages 260–273
November 11, 2021. ©2021 Association for Computational Linguistics

language models to process numerical information (Andor et al., 2019; Geva et al., 2020), the remaining challenge is how to obtain a large amount of training data.

A second challenge is that there are various ways of describing the same normalised time. For example, the normalised time 23:00 can be expressed as 11, 11 pm, 23:00, eleven o'clock, etc. This issue is, even more, severe when dealing with user-generated text that is typically noisy: the user-generated text is prone to spelling errors and grammatical errors and contains a lot of abbreviations (Petz et al., 2013). To address this, a sufficient amount of training dataset containing pairs of various temporal expressions and normalised time values is required.

A third challenge is that there are different types of temporal expressions which of each is difficult to extract. For example, temporal expressions include not only standalone times (e.g., 23:00) but also relative times (e.g., 5 minutes after), counts (e.g., 3 times), duration (e.g., for an hour), and frequencies (e.g., once per hour). For relative time expressions, the challenge is how to annotate temporal expressions and model dependencies. For count time expressions, the challenge is to deal with ambiguous terms, such as '*several times*' and '*a few times*'.

The last challenge is how to collect large-scale data while developing a proof-of-concept model to validate the hypothesis. Especially for health-related data, the data collection requires rigorous process of considering privacy and ethical aspects, which might result in a slow process. Moreover, typical machine learning development process includes the multiple cycles of collecting a new dataset and updating a model to improve the performance of model. Therefore, the challenge is how to train a machine leanring model when only a low very low amount of training data is available.

Therefore, the main research question of this paper is how to extract temporal information from user-generated noisy text with the limited number of training data. To this end, we propose a synthetic data generation algorithm to augment the size of training data. We also propose a multi-task model and investigate whether the multi-task learning strategy is beneficial to the target task by exploiting additional training signals from the existing training data. The main contributions of this paper include the followings:

- A new custom dataset has been collected to demonstrate the success of the free-text sleep diary use-case (Section 3).
- The temporal information extraction and normalisation tasks are reformulated as a question and answering task (Section 4.1).
- A novel model that can extract temporal expressions from unstructured text and normalise them into the standard format is proposed (Section 4.2).
- Experimental results show that utilising synthetic data and multi-task learning can be beneficial to performance improvement (Section 5.5).
- We also provide further analysis on experimental results to reveal insights of the model behaviours (Section 6).

2 Related Work

There are two lines of approach in temporal information processing. One is rule-based and the other is machine learning-based. Generally, rule-based systems achieve high performances in a normalisation task (Chang and Manning, 2012). However, rule-based systems have difficulties in dealing with ambiguous phrases or relative expressions (Verhagen et al., 2010; Chang and Manning, 2012).

Another line of approach is machine learning-based approaches. Previous works have focused on detecting temporal links between entities and classify the temporal relations between them (Ning et al., 2017; Meng and Rumshisky, 2018) rather than predicting the exact time of events. Recently, Leeuwenberg and Moens (2020) propose a system that can directly extract start and end-points for events from the text. However, the remaining gap is that it is not entirely end-to-end: Leeuwenberg and Moens (2020) used the text with ground truth event spans and normalized temporal expressions as inputs. Moreover, even though machine learning models show promising results, the fundamental challenge is how to obtain data. Not only data acquisition can be difficult but also data labelling can be time-consuming and expensive.

3 Sleep Diary Analysis

This section describes the dataset collected for experiments. The following subsections explain the details of use-case definition, data collection protocol, data labelling scheme, and an initial data analysis result.

3.1 Use-case definition

A sleep diary is a summary of sleep designed to gather information about daily sleep patterns. A typical sleep diary consists of a series of close-ended questions to record the time (i.e., the time people went to bed last night, woke up, etc), factors that may have influenced the way people slept, and how people felt when they woke up. In this study, we introduce free-text sleep diary use-case that allows people to describe their nights' of sleep in text. The goal of this study is to extract structured information from unstructured sleep diaries, as described in Figure 1.

3.2 Data collection protocol

We conducted an online survey via Amazon's Mechanical Turk (MTurk) to collect experimental data. At the beginning of the survey, the participants were given a questionnaire with a brief background of the study purpose. Then the participants were asked to provide information about their sleep of the previous night via an open-ended question (i.e., *"Please describe, in a few lines, your sleep last night."*). The details of data subject selection criteria and examples of responses are given in Appendix A. In total, 600 participant inputs are collected and used for the experiments.

3.3 Data labelling scheme

To annotate the collected data, several sleep-related event entities are defined based on sleep study (Carney et al., 2012) as summarised in Table 1. Each event entity text was annotated with its span (i.e., start and end positions in the text), entity label, expression type (i.e., standalone, relative[1], count, frequency[2]), and normalised time value. Expression types are used to assign a specific type value: None, +/-, *, *t* for standalone, relative, frequency, count, respectively. A normalised time value includes a type value and 4 digits indicating HH:MM, except for a count type: for an entity with a count type, a normalised time value is a cardinal number padded with leading zeros (e.g., 1 becomes 0001). Also,

[1]Relative type includes both relative time (e.g., after 5 minutes) and duration (e.g., for 5 minutes).

[2]Frequency type includes expressions of events occurring periodically (e.g., every 1 hour)

Event entity	Explanation
bed time	The time when the participant went to bed/bedroom.
lights off	The time when the participant switched off the lights and began trying to fall asleep.
sleep time	The time when the participant fell asleep
sleep latency	The amount of time it took for the participant to fall asleep after deciding to go to sleep.
sleep disturbance	The times when the participant's sleep was disturbed.
wake up	The time when the participant woke up from their sleep.
out of bed	The time when the participant finally got out of bed to start their day.
sleep duration	The total duration of time the user was asleep.

Table 1: The list of sleep-related event entities used in this study.

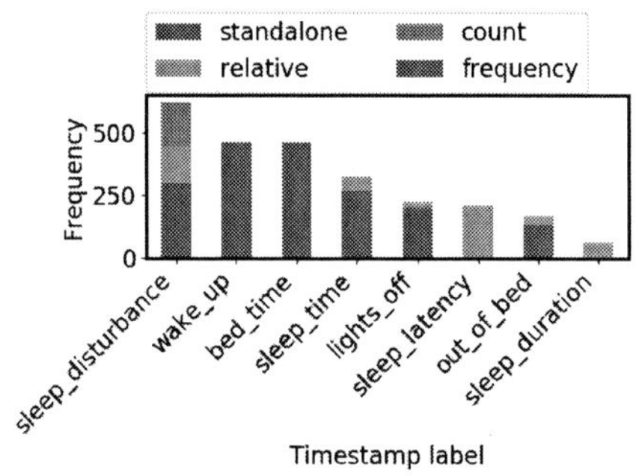

Figure 2: Distribution of the annotated data over the event entities.

we set rules for ambiguous expressions. For example, 'a lot of times', 'several times', and 'many times' are annotated as five times (t0005) and 'a few times', 'a couple times' are annotated as two times (t0002). The example of an annotated data point is illustrated in Appendix B.

Figure 2 shows the distribution of the collected data set over the sleep-related event entities. It is observed that `sleep_disturbance` entity appears more than other entities. This is because different types of sleep disturbance are often mentioned together (i.e., *"I woke up 1 time to use restroom at midnight*"). Meanwhile, some entities (e.g., `lights_off`, `sleep_latency`, `out_of_bed`, `sleep_duration`) are often missing in sleep diary entries. In general, `bed_time` and `wake_up` entities appear once per each sleep diary entry.

4 Multi-task temporal information extraction model

4.1 Task formulation

We formulate a temporal information extraction and normalisation task similar to a question and answering task. Therefore, each data point is transformed into <entity, text, answer> where the entity is a sleep event entity label, the text is sleep diary text, and the answer is a normalised time with a type value and 4 digits. For example, a system is expected to predict a list of answers [None, 2, 2, 3, 0] given input <bed time, I went to bed at half past 10...>.

Formally, an entity $q_j \in Q$, where Q is the set of the sleep-related event entities decribed in Table 1, is tokenised[3] with m_j tokens $q_j = [q_j^1, ..., q_j^{m_j}]$ and sleep diary text is tokenised with n_i tokens $p_i = [p_i^1, ..., p_i^{n_i}]$. Then the task is to predict an answer $a_{ij} = [a_{ij}^{type}, a_{ij}^{t1}, a_{ij}^{t2}, a_{ij}^{t3}, a_{ij}^{t4}]$ given a sequence of tokens [`[CLS]` q_j `[SEP]` p_i, `[SEP]`], where `[CLS]` and `[SEP]` are special tokens for classification and separation, respectively. a_{ij}^{type} is the ground truth label for the type value of the normalised time and a_{ij}^{t1}, a_{ij}^{t2}, a_{ij}^{t3}, and a_{ij}^{t4} is the the ground truth labels for the each digit of the normalised time.

4.2 Model architecture

We propose a multi-task model that utilises a pre-trained language model with specific heads, motivated by recent works (Andor et al., 2019; Geva et al., 2020). The overview of the proposed model is illustrated in Figure 3.

Firstly, the model computes $e_{ij} = [e_{ij}^{cls}, .., e_{ij}^{l_{ij}}]$ which are contextualised representations for the $l_{ij} = m_j + n_i + 3$ input tokens ([CLS] q_j [SEP] p_i, [SEP]) by using a pre-trained language model BERT (Devlin et al., 2019). The contextualised embedding vector $e_{ij}^{cls} \in \mathbb{R}^{d \times 1}$, corresponding to the classification token `[CLS]`, is fed to the type classification head (H_{type}) that uses a fully-connected

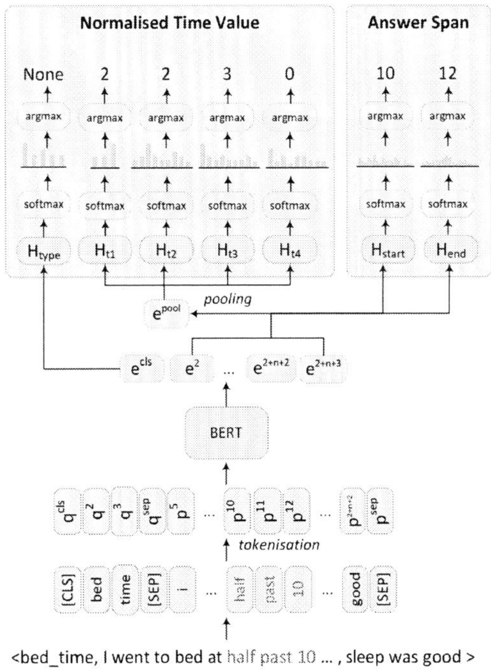

Figure 3: Illustration of the proposed model.

layer followed by a softmax to compute distributions over the type values {None, +, -, *, t}. Then the remaining sequence of contextualised embedding vectors $[e_{ij}^2, .., e_{ij}^{l_{ij}}]$ is used to create pooled embedding $e_{ij}^{pool} \in \mathbb{R}^{d \times 1}$ by using average pooling. Then the pooled embedding e_{ij}^{pool} is passed to normalised time value heads ($H_{t1}, H_{t2}, H_{t3}, H_{t4}$). H_{t1} head computes a distribution over the number {0, 1, 2}[4] by using a fully-connected layer followed by a softmax layer. Similarly, H_{t2}, H_{t3}, and H_{t4} heads compute distributions over the numbers {0, ..., 9}.

The contextualised embedding vectors $[e_{ij}^2, .., e_{ij}^{l_{ij}}]$ are fed to additional answer span heads, H_{start} and H_{end}, to compute a score for each token, corresponding to whether that token is the start or the end of the answer span, respectively. The start and end probability for each token is computed as follow:

$$p_{ij}^{start} = \text{softmax}(H_{start}(e_{ij}^2), ..., H_{start}(e_{ij}^{l_{ij}}))$$
$$p_{ij}^{end} = \text{softmax}(H_{end}(e_{ij}^2), ..., H_{end}(e_{ij}^{l_{ij}}))$$

[3]Underbars are replaced by whitespace characters during tokenisation.

[4]Since the answer is formulated as a standard time format (e.g., HH:MM), the first digit is limited to {0, 1, 2}.

Normalised time prediction loss For normalised time prediction, cross-entropy between the target answer and the model estimation is used to compute $\mathcal{L}_{t_1}$, $\mathcal{L}_{t_2}$, $\mathcal{L}_{t_3}$, $\mathcal{L}_{t_4}$, and $\mathcal{L}_{type}$ which is a loss function for each head, respectively. Then the time loss function ($\mathcal{L}_{\text{time}}$) is defined as the linear combination of the each loss function, i.e.

$$\mathcal{L}_{\text{time}} = \alpha \mathcal{L}_{\text{type}} + \beta(\mathcal{L}_{t_1} + \mathcal{L}_{t_2} + \mathcal{L}_{t_3} + \mathcal{L}_{t_4})$$

Answer span detection loss For answer span detection, we follow the previous work on a question and answering task by using a pre-trained language model (Devlin et al., 2019) to compute cross-entropy losses for the start $\mathcal{L}_{\text{start}}$ and end $\mathcal{L}_{\text{end}}$. Then the span loss function ($\mathcal{L}_{\text{span}}$) is defined as the sum of the start loss and the end loss:

$$\mathcal{L}_{\text{span}} = \mathcal{L}_{\text{start}} + \mathcal{L}_{\text{end}}$$

Multi-task loss The final multi-task loss function ($\mathcal{L}_{\text{multi}}$) is defined as the linear combination of the normalised time prediction and answer span detection loss functions:

$$\mathcal{L}_{\text{multi}} = \mathcal{L}_{\text{time}} + \gamma \mathcal{L}_{\text{span}}$$

4.3 Synthetic data generation

To augment the size of annotated data containing temporal information, we propose a simple yet effective rule-based synthetic data generation algorithm. Figure 4 illustrates the proposed algorithm. The first step is to create a template by masking out labelled event entities from the annotated data and replacing them with placeholders. The second step is to generate random entity types and corresponding normalised time values. Then the randomly generated normalised time values are translated into texts by using regular expressions. The last step is to replace placeholders with the translated texts. Details of regular expressions and examples of generated texts are given in the Appendix C.

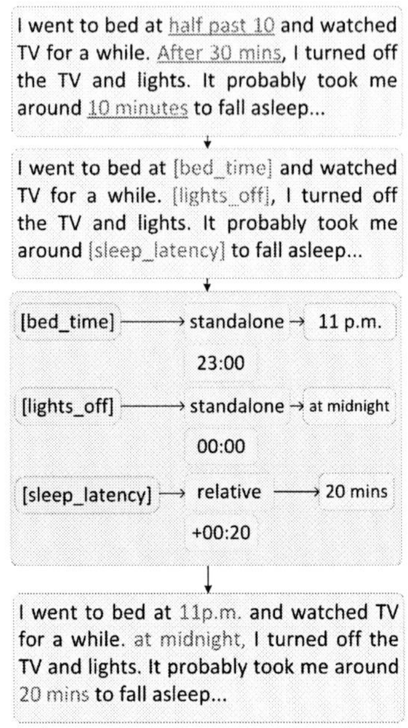

Figure 4: Illustration of the proposed synthetic data generation algorithm to augment the size of training data.

Statistics	Train	Valid	Test
# sleep diaries	467	56	57
Total # tokens	197,695	24,007	23,528
Unique # tokens	1,687	604	585
Avg. # tokens/diary	95.9	101.7	95.3
Total # entities	2061	236	247
Avg. # entities/diary	4.4	4.2	4.3

Table 2: Data set statistics across the different splits

5 Experiments

5.1 Dataset

The collected dataset from the Section 3 was used for the experiments. We randomly split the collected data ($n = 600$) into train, validation, and test sets with the ratio of 0.8, 0.1, and 0.1. After splitting data sets, we dropped the data points that do not contain any event entities. During pre-processing, we lowercased and tokenised data sets by using a WordPiece algorithm (Schuster and Nakajima, 2012). Numbers and punctuation symbols were not removed during pre-processing because they play important role in temporal expressions. Table 2 shows the statistics of each data set after pre-processing.

The proposed synthetic data generation algorithm is applied to the train set to augment the size by a factor of k. The validation set is used to check the training progress and perform early stopping. The test set is used to evaluate the performance of the trained model.

5.2 Settings

We use a pre-trained BERT to implement the proposed model. All heads are implemented as fully-connected layers with dropout followed by softmax functions. Also, to investigate the effect of multi-task learning, we implement a baseline model (BASE) that uses only normalised time prediction loss ($\mathcal{L}_{\text{time}}$) and a multi-task model (MULTI) that uses multi-task loss ($\mathcal{L}_{\text{multi}}$), as defined as:

$$\mathcal{L}_{\text{time}} = \alpha\mathcal{L}_{\text{type}} + \beta(\mathcal{L}_{t_1} + \mathcal{L}_{t_2} + \mathcal{L}_{t_3} + \mathcal{L}_{t_4})$$
$$\mathcal{L}_{\text{span}} = \mathcal{L}_{\text{start}} + \mathcal{L}_{\text{end}}$$
$$\mathcal{L}_{\text{multi}} = \mathcal{L}_{\text{time}} + \gamma\mathcal{L}_{\text{span}}$$

α, β, and γ are set to 0.25, 1, and 0.25, respectively. See Appendix D for more system and training details.

5.3 Configuration

To configure the input and output of a model, each data point is expanded into multiple <entity, text, answer> triples. If a single data point contains the same entity more than once, the ordinal number is added to an entity label from the second occurrence. For example, `second_sleep_disturbance` will be used for the second `sleep_disturbance` event in a data point. For `sleep_disturbance` entity with a count type, the type is also added to an entity label, i.e., `count_sleep_disturbance` will be used. For output, a special character of a normalised time value (i.e., None, +, -, *, t) is used as a ground truth type value and each digit of a 4 digit normalised time is used as a ground truth normalised time value. For the multi-task model, the start and end position of entity text are used as ground truth value of start and end position, respectively.

5.4 Evaluation metric

Normalised time prediction We use Exact Match (EM) as an evaluation metric. EM considers only when a model predicts both a correct type value and correct 4 digits of normalised time values as a correct prediction. Since the experimental data set has an imbalance over event entities, both micro-and macro-averaged scores are used: the micro-EM score is computed by taking the average over inputs and the macro-EM score is computed by taking the average at the entity level.

Answer span detection Following Rajpurkar et al. (2016), we use Exact Match (EM) and F1 score for answer span detection: EM measures the percentage of predictions that match the ground truth answers exactly. F1 score measures the average overlap between the prediction and ground truth answer. We treat the prediction and ground truth as bags of tokens, and compute the F1 score per entity and average over all of the entities. Both metrics consider articles, numbers, and punctuation symbols.

5.5 Results and Analysis

Normalised time prediction Table 3 summarises the experimental results. As expected, models trained on the synthetic training data generally achieve higher performances. Results show that the benefit of using synthetic data for training shows a peak at $k = 3$ for both models and the improvements are statistically significant. However, the benefit of using synthetic data decreases afterwards. It can even harm the performance of the baseline model when $k = 10$.

To further investigate the effects of using synthetic data for training, we calculate the performance per event entity label as shown in Table 4 and the performance per expression type as shown in Table 5. The models trained on synthetic data with the factor of $k = 3$ are used for comparison. Table 4 shows that using synthetic data generally improves the performance of almost all event entities. From both models, the biggest improvements are observed at `sleep_disturbance` entity, which is the most frequent entity label in the training set. However, as shown in Table 5, the biggest improvements in terms of expression type are observed at the count type, which is one of the least frequent expression types in the training set. It is worth mentioning that the count type is only included in `sleep_disturbance` entity label, as illustrated in Figure 2. These results imply that using synthetic data can be the most beneficial to both models in terms of predicting normalised time values with the count type.

Answer span detection The answer span detection results of the multi-task model are also summarised in Table 3. Similar to the normalised time prediction results, the performances tend to increase till $k = 3$ and decrease afterwards. It is observed that the utilising synthetic data with the augmentation factor $k = 3$ can provide the signif-

	BASE		MULTI			
	Normalised time prediction		Normalised time prediction		Answer span detection	
k	micro-EM	macro-EM	micro-EM	macro-EM	EM	F1
-	82.0	83.9	66.9	62.9	64.9	82.9
$\times 2$	83.3	**87.2***	86.9**	88.0**	**66.9**	85.1
$\times 3$	**85.3***	85.1	**88.6****	**91.9****	66.1	**86.7***
$\times 5$	81.6	81.6	86.1**	86.8**	64.5	84.1
$\times 8$	82.0	83.2	78.4**	80.8**	60.8	79.2*
$\times 10$	72.2**	74.7**	68.6	71.2*	53.5**	75.3**

Table 3: The performances of the baseline model (BASE) and the multi-task model (MULTI). k refers the augmentation factor. * and ** indicate that this result is significantly different (approximate randomisation test (Dror et al., 2018)) from the result without the synthesised data (the first row in that column) with p-value < 0.05 and < 0.01, respectively. Best performances are boldfaced.

	BASE		MULTI	
	-	+SD	-	+SD
sleep disturb.	66.1	80.6	50.0	83.9
bed time	95.1	97.6	95.1	95.1
wake up	86.5	86.5	65.4	88.5
sleep time	75.0	69.4	72.2	75.0
lights off	100.	93.3	93.3	100.
sleep latency	95.2	100.	66.7	100.
out of bed	78.6	78.6	35.7	92.9
sleep dur.	75.0	75.0	25.0	100.
micro-EM	82.0**	85.3*	66.9**	**88.6**
macro-EM	83.9**	85.1*	62.9**	**91.9**

Table 4: Normalised time prediction results per entity label. +SD indicates that synthetic data are used. * and ** indicate that this result is significantly different from the best result in that row (bolded) with p-value < 0.05 and < 0.01, respectively.

	BASE		MULTI	
	-	+SD	-	+SD
Standalone	86.8	86.3	72.0	**90.1**
Relative	78.7	78.7	55.3	**83.0**
Count	37.5	**93.8**	43.8	87.5

Table 5: Normalised time prediction results per expression type. +SD indicates that synthetic data are used. Best performances are boldfaced.

icant improvement in terms of F1 measure. But the effect to the EM measure is not statistically significant (p>.05). It is also observed that using synthetic data with augmentation factor $k = 10$ can significantly harm the performances.

6 Discussion

Effects of using synthetic data The first row of Table 3 shows that the multi-task learning model achieves lower normalised time prediction performances than the baseline model when no synthetic data is used for training. However, when the multi-task model utilises an appropriate amount of synthetic data ($k = 3$), as it is shown in the last two rows in Table 4, the multi-task model significantly outperforms ($p < .01$) the baseline model without synthetic data. These results imply two things: 1) multi-task learning can be beneficial to improve the target performances of normalised time prediction. However, training the multi-task model may require a larger training set; and 2) the proposed synthetic data generation algorithm can mitigate this issue to a certain degree. Also, as shown in the last two rows in Table 4, when the same amount of synthetic data ($k = 3$) are used for both models, the multi-task model significantly outperforms ($p < .05$) the baseline model in terms of normalised time prediction. This result may not be so surprising since the multi-task model receives additional training signals during training.

Effects of using multi-task learning To get a further understanding of the effect of multi-task learning, we conduct a qualitative analysis. In Table 6, we highlight some examples of the predictions of the proposed models. In the first example, it is observed that both models can process the

Sleep Diary

I went to bed about 9 pm. we sleep with the lights on for my toddler who co-sleeps. I was asleep about 10. I woke up a lot of times in the night to blow my nose or to try and get comfortable. I got out of bed at 2:30 am. Sleep was terrible. I feel exhausted today.

	BASE	**MULTI**		**Ground Truth**	
	time	time	text	time	text
bed time	21:00	21:00	9 pm	21:00	9 pm
sleep time	22:00	22:00	about 10	22:00	about 10
cnt. sleep disturb.	t0005	t0002	a lot of times	t0005	a lot of times
out of bed	02:30	02:30	2:30 am	02:30	2:30 am

Sleep Diary

I turned the lights off at 9:30 layed down in bed at 10 pm. I fell alseep around 11pm I woke up at 1am to turn on my other side. I fell back to sleep until 4 am to use the rest room went back to sleep until 5:30 am.

	BASE	**MULTI**		**Ground Truth**	
	time	time	text	time	text
lights off	21:30	21:30	9:30	21:30	9:30
bed time	22:00	22:00	10 pm	22:00	10 pm
sleep time	23:00	23:00	11pm	23:00	11pm
sleep disturbance	01:00	01:00	1am	01:00	1am
second sleep disturb.	01:00	04:00	4 am	04:00	4 am
wake up	05:00	05:30	5:30 am	05:30	5:30 am

Sleep Diary

I went to bed around 10p. m. I read for about 30 minutes. Put my kindle away and was asleep by 10:30. I woke up at 1a. m. and it took me around 20 minutes to fall back asleep. I woke up at 2:45 and used the bathroom. I went back to sleep until 4 which is when I normally get up.

	BASE	**MULTI**		**Ground Truth**	
	time	time	text	time	text
bed time	22:00	22:00	10p. m.	22:00	10p. m.
sleep time	22:30	22:30	10:30	22:30	10:30
sleep disturbance	01:00	01:00	1a. m	01:00	1a. m
second sleep time	01:00	00:20	1a. m. and it took me around 20 minutes	+00:20	20 minutes
second sleep disturb.	01:00	01:45	1a. m.	02:45	2:45
wake up	02:45	04:45	-	04:00	until 4

Table 6: Qualitative examples showing the outputs of the proposed models. Underline indicates temporal expressions and red colour indicates wrong predictions. Due to limited space, we use the following abbreviations: count sleep disturbance (cnt. sleep disturb.) and second sleep disturbance (second sleep disturb.).

combination of number and text (*9 pm*) and an ambiguous expression (*10*), correctly predicting corresponding the normalised time values (21:00 and 22:00). It is also observed that the baseline model correctly predicts a normalised time value of a cardinal number (t0005) from the text-only temporal expression (*a lot of times*). The multi-task model fails at predicting the correct normalised time value but extracts the correct answer span (*a lot of times*). Based on this observation, it seems that answer span detection results can be useful to decide how to synthesise training data, such as generating pairs of <'a lot of times', t0005>.

In the second example, it is observed that the baseline model correctly predicts only the first occurrence of `sleep_disturbance` entity, predicting the identical timestamps for the second occurrences. Meanwhile, the multi-task model correctly predicts both occurrences with correct answer spans. We found that the multi-task model generally performs better on extracting normalised time values that occur multiple times in the text. However, in general, both models have difficulties in dealing with entities that occur several times in a single sleep diary. It is also observed that the normalised time value heads ($H_{type}, H_{t1}, H_{t2}, H_{t3}, H_{t4}$) and the answer span heads (H_{start}, H_{end}) of the multi-task model are not fully aligned: as shown in the third example, the multi-task model estimates the second sleep disturbance as 01:45 while extracting the answer span as '1a.m'. This error is challenging because the current model is a black box model so that we do not know where the error occurs and how the error propagates. To address this issue, one interesting area for future work may be in investigating shared information between the normalised time value heads and the answer span heads.

7 Limitations and Future Work

Even though we show the effectiveness of the proposed method by validating on the collected dataset, some points can be further studied. First of all, the proposed models estimate a normalised time value conditioned on an input which is a pair of sleep diary text and sleep-related event entity label. However, since most sleep diary texts do not contain all the event entities, an additional module is required to detect which entities are mentioned in the given text and how many times each entity is mentioned in the given text. Similar to the previous work by Liu et al. (2020), the answer span detection head of the proposed multi-task model can be used as a detection module.

Secondly, even though the proposed models can handle relative expressions by using specific type values (i.e., +, -), a linking algorithm is currently missing. A potential solution is to add a head that can predict a starting point, similarly to the previous work by Leeuwenberg and Moens (2018).

The third limitation is that the proposed models process only temporal information. To completely analyse sleep diary, extracting contextual and qualitative information is required (Ibáñez et al., 2018). In the future study, we will train a model to extract both temporal and other information from text data. To achieve this, we will collect more data that are longer and contain rich information about the context of the night and sleep.

8 Conclusions

In this paper, we propose a model that can extract temporal information from health-related narrative text. We conducted experiments to investigate how to utilise synthetic data and multi-task learning to improve the performance of normalised time prediction. Experimental results show that utilising synthetic data for training can contribute to performance improvement the most when the augmentation factor is set to 3. The results also show that when multi-task learning is used with synthetic data appropriately, the performance can be significantly improved. In the future study, we will extend the current work to extract not only temporal information but also contextual and qualitative information from text.

9 Ethical Considerations

Table 7 summarises ethical and privacy considerations of the data collection in this study.

Acknowledgements

We thank anonymous reviewers for providing valuable feedback on this work. This project has received funding from the European Union's Horizon 2020 research and innovation programme under the Marie Skłodowska-Curie grant agreement No 766139. This article reflects only the author's view and the REA is not responsible for any use that may be made of the information it contains.

Question	Answer
Are children under the age of 18 involved as test subjects in the study?	No
Are test subjects over the age of 65 involved in the study?	Yes
Do the test subjects belong to vulnerable groups?	No
Does the study induce harm or discomfort to the test subjects?	No
Is there any doubt on the test subjects' freedom in deciding on their participation?	No
Collection of any personal data	No
Collection of data by means of audio recording	No
Collection of data by means of video recording or photographs	No
Collection of data by means of observation of test subjects and logging in written format	No
Collection of data by means of filling-in questionnaires/surveys/interviews	Yes

Table 7: Ethical and privacy considerations for the data collection. Vulnerable groups include military veterans, terminally ill, educationally or socioeconomically disadvantaged, employees, students who could be unduly influenced, individuals with lack of or loss of autonomy due to immaturity or through mental disability that might suggest their consent is not of free will, etc.

References

Daniel Andor, Luheng He, Kenton Lee, and Emily Pitler. 2019. Giving bert a calculator: Finding operations and arguments with reading comprehension. In *Proceedings of the 2019 Conference on Empirical Methods in Natural Language Processing and the 9th International Joint Conference on Natural Language Processing (EMNLP-IJCNLP)*, pages 5947–5952.

Colleen E Carney, Daniel J Buysse, Sonia Ancoli-Israel, Jack D Edinger, Andrew D Krystal, Kenneth L Lichstein, and Charles M Morin. 2012. The consensus sleep diary: standardizing prospective sleep self-monitoring. *Sleep*, 35(2):287–302.

Angel Chang and Christopher D Manning. 2012. Sutime: A library for recognizing and normalizing time expressions. In *Proceedings of the Eighth International Conference on Language Resources and Evaluation (LREC'12)*, pages 3735–3740.

Edward Choi, Mohammad Taha Bahadori, Joshua A Kulas, Andy Schuetz, Walter F Stewart, and Jimeng Sun. 2016. Retain: an interpretable predictive model for healthcare using reverse time attention mechanism. In *Proceedings of the 30th International Conference on Neural Information Processing Systems*, pages 3512–3520.

Dina Demner-Fushman, Noémie Elhadad, and Carol Friedman. 2021. Natural language processing for health-related texts. In *Biomedical Informatics*, pages 241–272. Springer.

Jacob Devlin, Ming-Wei Chang, Kenton Lee, and Kristina Toutanova. 2019. BERT: Pre-training of deep bidirectional transformers for language understanding. In *Proceedings of the 2019 Conference of the North American Chapter of the Association for Computational Linguistics: Human Language Technologies, Volume 1 (Long and Short Papers)*, pages 4171–4186, Minneapolis, Minnesota. Association for Computational Linguistics.

Rotem Dror, Gili Baumer, Segev Shlomov, and Roi Reichart. 2018. The hitchhiker's guide to testing statistical significance in natural language processing. In *Proceedings of the 56th Annual Meeting of the Association for Computational Linguistics (Volume 1: Long Papers)*, pages 1383–1392.

Dheeru Dua, Yizhong Wang, Pradeep Dasigi, Gabriel Stanovsky, Sameer Singh, and Matt Gardner. 2019. Drop: A reading comprehension benchmark requiring discrete reasoning over paragraphs. In *Proceedings of the 2019 Conference of the North American Chapter of the Association for Computational Linguistics: Human Language Technologies, Volume 1 (Long and Short Papers)*, pages 2368–2378.

Mor Geva, Ankit Gupta, and Jonathan Berant. 2020. Injecting numerical reasoning skills into language models. In *Proceedings of the 58th Annual Meeting of the Association for Computational Linguistics*, pages 946–958.

Vanessa Ibáñez, Josep Silva, and Omar Cauli. 2018. A survey on sleep assessment methods. *PeerJ*, 6:e4849.

Akib Mohi Ud Din Khanday, Syed Tanzeel Rabani, Qamar Rayees Khan, Nusrat Rouf, and Masarat Mohi Ud Din. 2020. Machine learning based approaches for detecting covid-19 using clinical text data. *International Journal of Information Technology*, 12(3):731–739.

Artuur Leeuwenberg and Marie Francine Moens. 2018. Temporal information extraction by predicting relative time-lines. In *Proceedings of the 2018 Conference on Empirical Methods in Natural Language Processing*, pages 1237–1246.

Artuur Leeuwenberg and Marie-Francine Moens. 2020. Towards extracting absolute event timelines from english clinical reports. *IEEE/ACM Transactions on Audio, Speech, and Language Processing*, 28:2710–2719.

Jian Liu, Yubo Chen, Kang Liu, Wei Bi, and Xiaojiang Liu. 2020. Event extraction as machine reading comprehension. In *Proceedings of the 2020 Conference on Empirical Methods in Natural Language Processing (EMNLP)*, pages 1641–1651.

Yuanliang Meng and Anna Rumshisky. 2018. Context-aware neural model for temporal information extraction. In *Proceedings of the 56th Annual Meeting of the Association for Computational Linguistics (Volume 1: Long Papers)*, pages 527–536, Melbourne, Australia. Association for Computational Linguistics.

Qiang Ning, Zhili Feng, and Dan Roth. 2017. A structured learning approach to temporal relation extraction. In *Proceedings of the 2017 Conference on Empirical Methods in Natural Language Processing*, pages 1027–1037, Copenhagen, Denmark. Association for Computational Linguistics.

Gerald Petz, Michał Karpowicz, Harald Fürschuß, Andreas Auinger, Václav Stříteský, and Andreas Holzinger. 2013. Opinion mining on the web 2.0–characteristics of user generated content and their impacts. In *International Workshop on Human-Computer Interaction and Knowledge Discovery in Complex, Unstructured, Big Data*, pages 35–46. Springer.

Pranav Rajpurkar, Jian Zhang, Konstantin Lopyrev, and Percy Liang. 2016. Squad: 100,000+ questions for machine comprehension of text. In *Proceedings of the 2016 Conference on Empirical Methods in Natural Language Processing*, pages 2383–2392.

Abhilasha Ravichander, Aakanksha Naik, Carolyn Rose, and Eduard Hovy. 2019. Equate: A benchmark evaluation framework for quantitative reasoning in natural language inference. In *Proceedings of the 23rd Conference on Computational Natural Language Learning (CoNLL)*, pages 349–361.

David Saxton, Edward Grefenstette, Felix Hill, and Pushmeet Kohli. 2018. Analysing mathematical reasoning abilities of neural models. In *International Conference on Learning Representations*.

Mike Schuster and Kaisuke Nakajima. 2012. Japanese and korean voice search. In *2012 IEEE International Conference on Acoustics, Speech and Signal Processing (ICASSP)*, pages 5149–5152. IEEE.

Marc Verhagen, Roser Sauri, Tommaso Caselli, and James Pustejovsky. 2010. Semeval-2010 task 13: Tempeval-2. In *Proceedings of the 5th international workshop on semantic evaluation*, pages 57–62.

Thomas Wolf, Lysandre Debut, Victor Sanh, Julien Chaumond, Clement Delangue, Anthony Moi, Pierric Cistac, Tim Rault, Rémi Louf, Morgan Funtowicz, et al. 2019. Huggingface's transformers: State-of-the-art natural language processing. *ArXiv*, pages arXiv–1910.

Zhilin Yang, Zihang Dai, Yiming Yang, Jaime Carbonell, Russ R Salakhutdinov, and Quoc V Le. 2019. Xlnet: Generalized autoregressive pretraining for language understanding. In *Advances in neural information processing systems*, pages 5753–5763.

A Details of data collection protocol

Participants were recruited through Amazon's MTurk-service. We selected data subjects who meet the following criteria:

- People who are 18 years or older
- People who are USA residents

When participants selected the study, they received a link to the web page hosting the survey. During the survey, participants were asked to answer an open-ended question (i.e., *"Please describe, in a few lines, your sleep last night."*) with the guidance of the following sentences: "*While describing your answer, please include the following information: sleep-related events (e.g., the time you went to bed, the time you switched off to go to sleep, the time it took you to fall asleep, the number of times you woke up and the time at those moments, the time you woke up, the time you got out of bed) and the overall sleep evaluation or how you refreshed after you woke up.*"

At any moment, a participant was allowed to end her/his participation in the study. In this case, the test participant was not replaced. Furthermore, every participant was received informed consent, on the landing page that participants enter when following the link from MTurk. Only answers from the participants who gave their own consent to the

ID	Answers
#1	I went to bed at 11 pm. I switched off the lights and lay down around 15 minutes before falling asleep. It was a deep sleep and i wake only 1 time to witch off ceiling fan. I had couple of dreams that I remember partially not scary. I wake up at 6 am. lay on bed for 15 minutes more and got up.
#2	I turned off the lights around 9:45 PM. I closed my eyes and went to sleep around 10 PM. I did not wake up at all during the night. I slept straight through. I woke up at 6 AM. I lied in bed for a few minutes before actually getting up around 6:05 AM. I felt fairly well rested.
#3	I went to bed at 10:00 and immediately turned off the light. I fell asleep in just a few minutes. I slept without waking until 5:00. I immediately got out of bed when I woke up and felt great.

Table 8: Examples of responses to the open-ended question regarding the previous night's sleep.

study were used for experiments in this study. Table 8 shows examples of the collected data used for experiments.

B Example of annotated data

Figure 5 shows the exmample of an annotated data point.

C Examples of synthetic data

A synthetic data set was generated by the following steps: 1) Template generation; 2) Random timestamps generation; and 3) Rule-based timestamps-to-texts translation. Table 9 summarises a set of rules used for timestamp-to-text translation and the examples of generated texts.

D Experimental settings

The detailed specification of hardware and software is summarised in Table 10. For model deployment, PyTorch version of BERT with the pretrained weights `bert-base-uncased` (Wolf et al., 2019) was used. Table 11 summarises hyperparameter values used for the experiments. All hyperparameters are obtained based on non-exhaustive experiments. During the inference phase, we followed the settings from the original


```
{'text':'I went to bed at 10'o clock
   and I switched off the light at 11
   'o clock. After that I fall asleep
    in 30 minutes as my guess. I woke
    up 3 times and I felt restless. I
    was awake up to 3 hours. I woke
   up at 7'o clock in the morning and
    got out of the bed at 7:45 a.m.
   My overall sleep is up to 5 hours
   and it was not a sound sleep. If I
    awake during night then it causes
    me heavy headache and drowsiness.
    But today I din't get any of the
   above symptoms even though I woke
   up in the night. I felt fresh in
   the morning.',
 'labels': [
 { 'text': '10'o clock',
  'span': (17, 27),
  'entity': 'bed_time',
  'type': 'standalone',
  'norm_time': 2200},
 { 'text': '11'o clock',
  'span': (60, 69),
  'entity': 'lights_off',
  'type': 'standalone',
  'norm_time': 2300},
 { 'text': 'in 30 minutes',
  'span': (97, 110),
  'entity': 'sleep_latency',
  'type': 'relative',
  'norm_time': +0030},
 { 'text': '3 times',
  'span': (134, 141),
  'entity': 'sleep_disturbance',
  'type': 'count',
  'norm_time': t0003},
 {'text': '3 hours',
  'span': (181, 188),
  'entity': 'sleep_disturbance',
  'type': 'relative',
  'norm_time': +0300},
 {'text': '7'o clock',
  'span': (203, 212),
  'entity': 'wake_up',
  'type': 'standalone',
  'norm_time': 0700},
 {'text': '7:45 a.m',
  'span': (254, 261),
  'entity': 'out_of_bed',
  'type': 'standalone',
  'norm_time': 0745},
 {'text': '5 hours',
  'span': (290, 297),
  'entity': 'sleep_duration',
  'type': 'relative',
  'norm_time': +0500}]}
```


Figure 5: Example of annotated data point containing free-text sleep diary and labels of event entities.

<table>
<tr><th rowspan="2">Regular Expression</th><th rowspan="2">Entity type</th><th rowspan="2">Format</th><th colspan="2">Example</th></tr>
<tr><th>Timestamp</th><th>Text</th></tr>
<tr><td>?(around|at|until|by|) t_1t_2[:,.]t_3t_4
?(((a.?m.?)|(A.?M.?))|
(hrs|hours|hour|hr))</td><td>standalone</td><td>$t_1t_2t_3t_4$</td><td>1130</td><td>at 11:30 am</td></tr>
<tr><td>?(around|at|until|by|)
(t_1t_2|t_1t_2-12)[:,.]t_3t_4
?(((p.?m.?)|(P.?M.?))|
(hrs|hours|hour|hr))</td><td>standalone</td><td>$t_1t_2t_3t_4$</td><td>2230</td><td>around 10:30 PM</td></tr>
<tr><td>?(around|at|until|by|) t_1t_2
?((o[']clock)|((a.?m.?)|
(A.?M.?))|(hrs|hours|hour|hr))
?(o('| |)clock|[:,.]00)</td><td>standalone</td><td>$t_1t_2$00</td><td>0600</td><td>until 6 o'clock</td></tr>
<tr><td>?(around|at|until|by|)
(t_1t_2|t_1t_2-12) ?((o[']clock)|
((p.?m.?)|(P.?M.?))|(hrs|hours|hour|hr))
?(o('| |)clock|[:,.]00)</td><td>standalone</td><td>$t_1t_2$00</td><td>2200</td><td>22 o'clock</td></tr>
<tr><td>?(after|within|) t_3t_4
?(min|mins|minute|minutes)
?(later)</td><td>relative</td><td>+00t_3t_4</td><td>+0010</td><td>10 minutes later</td></tr>
<tr><td>t_3t_4 ?(min|mins|minute|minutes)
?(before|prior)</td><td>relative</td><td>-00t_3t_4</td><td>+0010</td><td>5 minutes before</td></tr>
<tr><td>every t_3t_4
?(min|mins|minute|minutes)</td><td>frequency</td><td>*00t_3t_4</td><td>*0010</td><td>every 10 mins</td></tr>
<tr><td>every (t_1t_2|t_1t_2+1) ?(hour|hours)</td><td>frequency</td><td>*$t_1t_2$00</td><td>*0100</td><td>every 1 hour</td></tr>
<tr><td>every (t_1t_2|t_1t_2+1) and
?(hour|hours) t_3t_4
?(min|mins|minute|minutes)</td><td>frequency</td><td>*$t_1t_2t_3t_4$</td><td>*0115</td><td>every 1 hour
and 15 minutes</td></tr>
<tr><td>((one|1) (times| time)|once)</td><td>count</td><td>t0001</td><td>t0001</td><td>once</td></tr>
<tr><td>((two|a couple of|a few|few|2)
(times| time)|twice)</td><td>count</td><td>t0002</td><td>t0002</td><td>a couple of times</td></tr>
<tr><td>(several|many|a lot
of|multiple|5) (times| time)</td><td>count</td><td>t0005</td><td>t0005</td><td>several times</td></tr>
<tr><td>(t_4|t_4 or t_4+1|t_4 to t_4+1|t_4-t_4+1)
?(time|times)</td><td>count</td><td>t000t_4</td><td>t0003</td><td>3 times</td></tr>
</table>

Table 9: Regular expression patterns used to translate timestamps into texts based on the given entity type and format.

Item	Specification
CPU	Intel Xeon W-2123 CPU(3.60 GHz)
GPU	NVIDIA GeForce GTX 1080 ti, 11 GB memory
Driver	NVIDIA graphic driver ver. 416.34
CUDA	Version 10.0
OS	Windows 10, 64-bit
Python	Version 3.6.6
Pytorch	Version 1.5.1

Table 10: Detailed implementation specification.

Hyperparameter	Assignment
α	0.25
β	1.
γ	0.25
max training epoch	9
batch size	32
learning rate	$4e-5$
dropout rate	0.1
optimaser	AdamW

Table 11: Hyperparameters for fine-tuning.

paper (Devlin et al., 2019) to compute the scores of a candidate span.

Neural-based RST Parsing And Analysis In Persuasive Discourse

Jinfen Li
School of Information Studies,
Syracuse University
jli284@syr.edu

Lu Xiao
School of Information Studies,
Syracuse University
lxiao04@syr.edu

Abstract

Most of the existing studies of language use in social media content have focused on the surface-level linguistic features (e.g., function words and punctuation marks) and the semantic level aspects (e.g., the topics, sentiment, and emotions) of the comments. The writer's strategies of constructing and connecting text segments have not been widely explored even though this knowledge is expected to shed light on how people reason in online environments. Contributing to this analysis direction for social media studies, we build an openly accessible neural RST parsing system that analyzes discourse relations in an online comment. Our experiments demonstrate that this system achieves comparable performance among all the neural RST parsing systems. To demonstrate the use of this tool in social media analysis, we apply it to identify the discourse relations in persuasive and non-persuasive comments and examine the relationships among the binary discourse tree depth, discourse relations, and the perceived persuasiveness of online comments. Our work demonstrates the potential of analyzing discourse structures of online comments with our system and the implications of these structures for understanding online communications.

1 Introduction

Researchers are increasingly interested in analyzing the language used in social media content. Previous studies examine surface-level linguistic features such as the use of function words or punctuation marks in online communications (Tan et al., 2016), and/or semantic level aspects such as understanding the sentiment (Neri et al., 2012) and emotions (Li and Xiao, 2020a) as well as identifying topics (Nzali et al., 2017). Recently, studies also conduct discourse-level language analysis such as exploring cohesion in the social media content (Latifah and Triyono, 2020) and using discourse level structure for detecting fake news (Karimi and Tang, 2019). The pragmatic use of the language in the content is also limitedly explored, such as the analysis of imperative statements in Wikipedia discussions (Xiao and Nickerson, 2019). Arguing for the importance of considering context information in language analysis, Benamara et al. (2018) call for more NLP research that "develop tools to automatically determine the structure of discourse, including discourse relations, argumentation, and threads in conversations such as those found in Twitter and other social media" (Benamara et al., 2018, p. 676).

As a response to this call, we have developed a discourse parsing system that automatically constructs the discourse parsing tree for the input text. Discourse parsing is a task of parsing a text segment into a set of discourse units and logically connect the merged units using a set of discourse relations, which exhibit reasoning behaviors in online environments (Öcal et al., 2021). Rhetorical Structure Theory (RST) (Mann and Thompson, 1988) is one of the most influential theories in discourse parsing and is used in our system. To parse RST, we need to build up a tree, where the nodes bear information such as span, nuclearity, and relation. The leaf node in the RST tree represents an Elementary Discourse Unit (EDU), a sequence of which could be merged into a longer span. The span place in the non-terminal nodes attaches with the nuclearity and relation labels. Nuclearity type typically includes NN, NS and SN, is the semantic role in discourse, where the nucleus span (N) is more essential than the satellite span (S).

The neural-based system of (Kobayashi et al., 2020) utilizes granularities including paragraphs, sentences and EDUs levels. The paragraphs and sentences granularities forcedly split a span at the paragraph/sentence boundary instead of other positions, resulting in the wrong subspans. There are around 7.6% EDUs with inconsistent sentence or paragraph index in one EDU. In addition, they

Proceedings of the 2021 EMNLP Workshop W-NUT: The Seventh Workshop on Noisy User-generated Text, pages 274–283
November 11, 2021. ©2021 Association for Computational Linguistics

parse RST in a top-down manner, which results in a larger search space. For instance, there are $n-1$ possible split points for a span composed of n EDUs. They also add a second-layer BLSTM upon all the EDUs to view bidirectional context. Building on their work, we conduct the following tasks to achieve a higher performance in RST parsing:

- We emphasize the role of position by introducing the sinusoid positional embedding and pay attention to the first and last two tokens in an EDU.
- We explore whether an additional layer of BLSTM, extracting correlations among EDUs in the document levels is helpful in such a bottom-up system.
- We apply different components in the relation detection submodel based on different nuclearity types.

To demonstrate the use of our discourse parsing system for analyzing discourse relations in social media content, we apply it in online persuasion research in two online contexts, namely, Wikipedia AfD and Reddit CMV discussions. We investigate the differences between persuasive and non-persuasive comments regarding their discourse structure. Our statistical analyses show that a comment's perceived persuasiveness is correlated to discourse relations and the depth of its binary discourse tree. Not only showing the potential of our discourse parsing system for social media content analysis, but these findings also suggest that studying the discourse structure of social media content achieves a better understanding of complex online interactions such as persuasion.

2 Related Works

Previous studies in RST parsing have two dominant parsing approaches including transition-based and neural-based approaches. The transition-based systems that rely on hand-crafted features have achieved great success (Wang et al., 2017; Li and Xiao, 2020b); while neural-based approaches do not require feature engineering, which does not take into account the particular nature of a specific data. Networks such as attention-based hierarchical neural network (Lin et al., 2019), and pointer networks (Lin et al., 2019) are developed to parse RST at sentence or text level. However, neither do neural network approaches consider word position and nor they design components for different nuclearity types, as initial and end words and nuclearity type are essential in RST parsing (Li et al., 2014; Wang et al., 2017).

The Discourse parsing tools provide a new perspective in discourse interpretation in social media (Benamara et al., 2018). Son et al. (2018) conduct causal explanations in physical and mental health building on discourse parsing; Zakharov et al. (2020) develop a novel discourse annotation schema that reflects a hierarchy of discursive strategies for the analysis of contentious and polarizing discussions. Discourse parsing also is leveraged in sentiment analysis (Bhatia et al., 2015), identify authorship (Ferracane et al., 2017) and detect deception (Rubin and Lukoianova, 2015). In this paper, we build up a new comparable discourse parsing tool for the contribution to social media content analysis in the discourse aspect.

3 RST Parsing System

In this section, we present our RST parsing system. We propose a neural RST parsing system in the bottom-up manner utilizing EDU granularity. We emphasize the role of word positions, investigate the role of an additional layer of BLSTM, and design different relation submodels based on different nuclearity types.

3.1 Representation for an EDU

The RST parsing tree is built over the smallest units: EDUs, whose representation is generated by our encoder. For each EDU, we concatenate the vectors from ELMo (Peters et al., 2018), GloVe vector (Pennington et al., 2014) and the sinusoid positional encoding (PE) (Vaswani et al., 2017) as the embedding of i-th token, i.e., emb_i. We then pass emb_i to the BLSTM layer, and gain the bidirectional hidden states h_i.

$$emb_i = [ELMo(t_i); GloVe(t_i); PE(t_i)] \quad (1)$$

$$h_i = BLSTM(h_{i-1}, emb_i) \quad (2)$$

Previous studies have found that the first and last two words are significant when detecting discourse relation between two spans (Li et al., 2014). We come up with two new context vectors to focus only on the first and last two words in an EDU. As Equation 3 is shown, c_{first} focus on the first hidden state and c_{last} focus on the last two hidden states in an EDU. We use $cGate$ to denote how much attention should be paid to these two contexts. We choose the max product of $cGate$ and h_i as the representation of an EDU. The overview of the representation of an EDU is shown in Figure 1.

$$\begin{aligned} c_{first} &= h_0, c_{last} = [h_{n-2}; h_{n-1}] \\ cGate &= U_{first}c_{first} + U_{last}c_{last} \end{aligned} \tag{3}$$

$$\begin{aligned} h'_i &= h_i \odot cGate \\ e_t &= \max(h'_0, ..., h'_{n-1}) \end{aligned} \tag{4}$$

In Kobayashi et al. (2020)'s study, they concatenate the first and last hidden states as the context vector c'. They propose a weight matrix W_c for the hidden states and another weight matrix U_c for c'. To prove the effectiveness of the partial attention in an EDU, we use their $cGate'$ in the baseline model and $cGate$ in ours.

$$\begin{aligned} c' &= [h_{n-1}; h_0] \\ cGate' &= \sigma(W_c h_i + U_c c') \end{aligned} \tag{5}$$

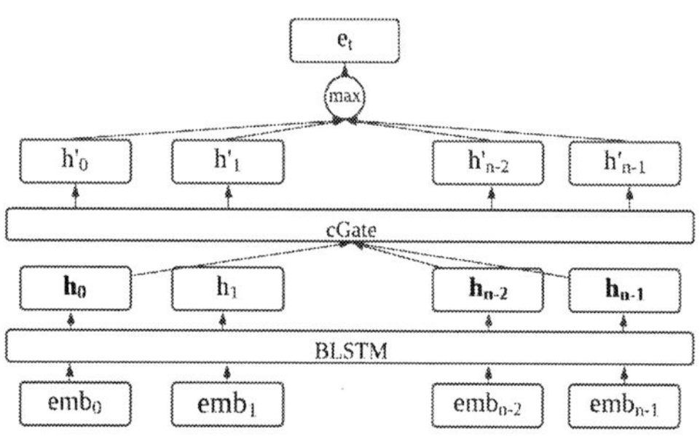

Figure 1: Representation of an EDU

3.2 Representation for a Span

Kobayashi et al. (2020) added an additional BLSTM layer upon all the EDUs for global information benefits. While the additional BLSTM layer provides the global context in their top-down parsing system, it is unknown that whether such context is helpful in our bottom-up parsing system. We directly use $\overrightarrow{e_t}$ and $\overleftarrow{e_t}$ as the forward and backward representation of the t-th EDU.

The boundary features are effective in the three granularities RST parsing system (Kobayashi et al., 2020). We also utilize four kinds of boundary information: whether the span is the start of a sentence, the end of a sentence, the start of a paragraph, or the end of a paragraph. We concatenate the difference of the forward and backward representation between the left and right spans, and the boundary feature B which is shown in Equation 6.

$$\begin{aligned} f_t &= \overrightarrow{e_t}, b_t = \overleftarrow{e_t} \\ s_{m:n} &= [f_n - f_{m-1}; b_{m-1} - b_n; B_{m:n}] \end{aligned} \tag{6}$$

3.3 Our Discourse Parsing System

The transition-based system is widely adopted in the bottom-up parsing systems, which proposes a series of actions to build a right-heavy binary tree. The queue stores the unprocessed EDUs and the stack stores the processed ones. Initially, all the EDUs are in the queue. An EDU will be shifted from queue to stack and the top two elements in the stack will be reduced into a subtree. We propose three submodels to detect action, nuclearity, and relation separately.

We first use the single feedforward layer MLP^*_{left} and MLP^*_{right} activated by ReLU function upon the left (from m-th to k-th EDUs) and right (from $k+1$ to n-th EDUs) span vectors, where $*$ denotes that MLP is trained separately in the submodels.

$$\begin{aligned} s'_{m:k} &= MLP^*_{left}(s_{m:k}) \\ s'_{k+1:n} &= MLP^*_{right}(s_{k+1:n}) \end{aligned} \tag{7}$$

3.3.1 Action Submodel

Yu et al. (2018) choose the top three subtrees in a stack and the first EDU in the queue as the clue for prediction. Instead of predicting the bare action, they predict the information-rich actions (e.g., Reduce-SN-Elaboration) to identify span, nuclearity, and relation in the same stage. In our study, we only predict the bare actions (Shift and Reduce) based on the top two elements in the stack.

For a left span and a right span, we calculate the action score using Equation 8, where W is a weight matrix.

$$action(m, n, k) = W^a_{left} s'_{m:k} + W^a_{right} s'_{k+1:n} \tag{8}$$

3.3.2 Nuclearity Submodel

We decide to use another submodel to predict nuclearity, considering the inferior performance of predicting the joint actions composed of bare action and nuclearity (e.g., Reduce-SN). If the predicted action is reduced, we will detect nuclearity and relation for the reduced subtree. Similar to the action submodel, we come up with two weight matrices W^n_{left} and W^n_{right} corresponding to $s'_{m:k}$ and $s'_{k+1:n}$. We predict one nuclearity type from NN, NS, and SN.

$$nuc(m, n, k) = W^n_{left} s'_{m:k} + W^n_{right} s'_{k+1:n} \quad (9)$$

3.3.3 Relation Submodel

The nuclearity type is essential in detecting relation in RST parsing (Wang et al., 2017). We take advantage of the nuclearity type predicted by the nuclearity submodel and design two kinds of weight matrices: W_{nuc} and W_{sat}, where W_{nuc} aims to extract information from nucleus spans and W_{sat} learns to exploit information from satellite spans.

Due to the imbalanced relation labels (please check the details in the Appendix A), we separately train two relation submodels for the high frequency and low-frequency labels. Specifically, we train the first relation submodel on the labels including "Attribution", "Enablement", "Elaboration", "Joint", "Same-Unit", and the second submodel on the rest of the labels.

$$rel(m, n, k) = \begin{cases} W_{nuc} s'_{m:k} + W_{nuc} s'_{k+1:n}, nuc = NN \\ W_{nuc} s'_{m:k} + W_{sat} s'_{k+1:n}, nuc = NS \\ W_{sat} s'_{m:k} + W_{nuc} s'_{k+1:n}, nuc = SN \end{cases} \quad (10)$$

To test the effectiveness of our designed weight matrices based on different nuclearity types in the relation submodel, we apply the following equation in all the compared models except our final model.

$$rel'(m, n, k) = W^r_{left} s'_{m:k} + W^r_{right} s'_{k+1:n} \quad (11)$$

Due to the different converge speeds of different submodels, we calculate the loss score using the equation as follows.

$$Loss = \alpha_1 L_{action} + \alpha_2 L_{nuc} + \alpha_3 L_{rel1} + \alpha_4 L_{rel2} \quad (12)$$

4 Experiments

4.1 Setup

We build up our bottom-up neural parsing model by using the dataset RST-DT (Mann and Thompson, 1988) (347 and 38 documents in training and test dataset). We split 40 documents from the training dataset to be our development dataset, by using the split method from Heilman and Sagae (2015). 18 coarse relations are explored in our study.

For the hyper-parameters, we use the small size model of ELMo. The initial learning rate is 0.001 and it is decayed with the ratio of 0.8 in each epoch. The gradient clipping threshold is 5.0 and the weight decay is 0.005. The hidden size, positional embedding size, boundary feature size are 200, 30, 10. α_1, α_2, α_3 and α_4 are set to 0.5, 0.3, 0.3 and 0.25. We train the model for 10 epochs and choose the one with the highest span score on the development dataset, and evaluate it on the test dataset.

4.2 Model Comparison

We compare our models with the current state-of-the-art neural bottom-up parsing system of YZF18 and one of the top-down system of D2E.

YZF18 Yu et al. (2018)'s study parses RST based on the transition system, with implicit syntax features generated by an extra neural syntax parser.

D2E We compare Kobayashi et al. (2020)'s model in EDU granularity. D2E is a partial model from Kobayashi et al. (2020) that utilizes EDU level of granularity, while their full model uses three levels of granularity in a document. Their full model includes the preprocess such as forcedly split a span at the paragraph boundary. It would be fairer to compare our model with their full model using the same preprocess, which is not used in our parsing tool. Therefore, we only compare the one without such preprocessing, i.e., D2E.

Model	PE	Equation 3/4	second BLSM	Equation 10/11
baseline	✗	4	✓	11
position	✓	4	✓	11
part	✓	3	✓	11
BLSTM_1	✓	3	✗	11
final	✓	3	✗	10

Table 1: Configurations of compared models. ✓ means inclusion, ✗ means exclusion and BLSTM_1 means single layer of BLSTM.

Our models We conduct an ablation study by changing one condition based on the previous modified model. The configurations are shown in Table 1.

4.3 Result

We present the results of the compared models in Table 2. Our baseline model outperforms *D2E* system on span detection, which implicates our bottom-up system is more capable of building up the tree structure. Comparing *position* model with the baseline, the positional embedding is helpful in span, nuclearity, and relation detection. The partial attention of EDUs adopted in *part* model further improves the F1 score of nuclearity and relation, by around 1.5. The removal of additional BLSTM upon all the EDUs in a document does not further improve the nuclearity detection but improves the span and relation detection slightly. Our final model, with nuclearity type awareness in the relation submodel, attains the comparable performance. We outperform *YZF18* on the F1 score of relation by 0.4 and achieve 87.9 and 77.3 on span and nuclearity detection.

Model	Span	Nuclearity	Reletion
D2E	86.1	73.1	58.9
YZF18	85.5	73.1	60.2
baseline	86.5	70.3	55.1
position	86.7	71.6	56.9
part	86.7	73.0	58.4
BLSTM_1	86.8	72.3	59.0
final	**87.9**	**73.6**	**60.6**
Human	88.3	77.3	65.4

Table 2: Micro averaged F1 scores based on RST-Parseval.

5 Discourse Relations in Social Media Content: Case Studies

We apply our RST parsing system to identify the discourse structure of a comment in two online discussions, namely, Wikipedia AfD and Reddit CMV discussion datasets. These two datasets have been used in online persuasion studies (Xiao and Xiao, 2020; Xiao and Khazaei, 2019). Both datasets have comments labeled as persuasive or non-persuasive. We choose these datasets because we are interested in whether and how the discourse structure of a comment correlates with its perceived persuasiveness. Persuasion is commonly considered as "human communication that is designed to influence others by modifying their beliefs, values, or attitudes" (Tan et al., 2016; Xiao and Khazaei, 2019). In Iyer et al. (2017) 's study, the researchers found that the syntactic structure of a sentence plays an important role in indicating different persuasion tactics. However, the discourse structure of a comment remains unstudied. The first step in our analysis is to segment the comment to EDUs for the study. We segment a comment by sentence, i.e., the EDU in our case study is a sentence. Comments that only have one sentence are not included in the analysis.

- **Wikipedia AfD dataset** The dataset of Wikipedia "Article for Deletion" is collected by (Mayfield and Black, 2019), which includes the discussion that whether the focal article should be deleted in the Wikipedia community. It allows users to provide their opinion and rationale that whether to keep the article in the discussion that lasts about a couple of weeks. 16,957 comments are labeled persuasive and 23,813 non-persuasive. Of these data, 1,698 persuasive comments and 5,832 non-persuasive ones are removed in our analysis as they only contain one sentence.

- **Reddit CMV dataset** The dataset of Reddit "Change My View" includes users' posts and their comments from February 2015 to January 2016. The one we adopted is collected by Xiao and Khazaei (2019), which only focuses on the direct replies to the post, to address the concern that comments in a thread receiving a delta due to the conversational context, not the persuasive aspects. 1,690 comments are labeled persuasive and 1,690 non-persuasive. 44 persuasive and 93 non-persuasive comments are removed from the analysis because they only have just one sentence.

We identify the discourse structure of a comment in these two datasets using our RST parsing system and then investigate the relationships among a comment's binary discourse tree depth, discourse relations, and perceived persuasiveness. We refer to binary tree depth as shallow and deep with the value of 0 and 1 respectively in the following sections. In these discourse structure analyses, we divide the 18 raw discourse relations into three groups according to the definition of Presentational, Subject_matter, and Multinuclear relations proposed by Mann and Thompson (1988). Of these three types of RST relations, we consider Presentational relations to have the strongest persuasion intent as the intended effect of these relations to increase some inclination in the reader such as the reader's degree of agreement or positive view regarding the

Presentational	Background, Enablement, Summary, Explanation
Subject_matter	Attribution, Cause, Condition, Elaboration, Evaluation, Manner-Means,Topic-Comment
Multinuclear	Comparison, Contrast, Joint, Same-Unit, Temporal, Textual-Organization, Topic-Change

Table 3: RST Relations Lists

nucleus, i.e., the main passage of the statement. The purpose of Subject_matter relations is to help the reader recognize the relation or the connection, i.e., to understand the writer's statement. Multinuclear relations are those that the adjacent text segments are equally important in conveying the meaning of the statement. The use of Multinuclear relations reflects a certain rhetoric strategy that the writer applies such as to convey a point by contrasting two things. The full list of groups is presented in Table 3.

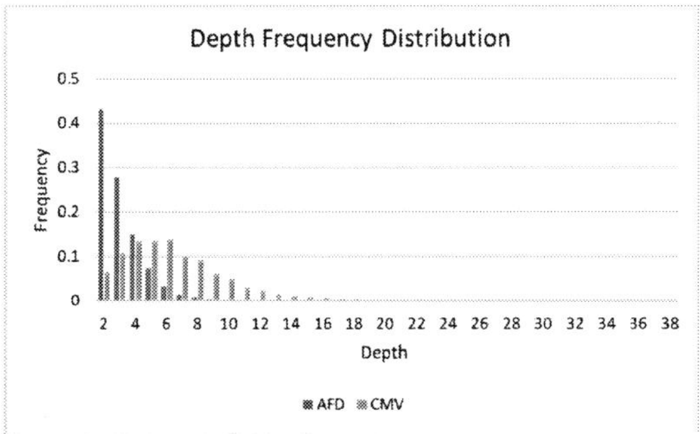

Figure 2: Depth Distribution In Wikipedia Data.

5.1 Qualitative Analysis

To gain a qualitative understanding of how the tool performs on social media data, the two co-authors independently annotate the discourse tree structure for ten randomly selected examples from AfD and CMV datasets and compare the results with those from the tool. An illustration of an example is presented in Figure 3. The two researchers agree on four examples both in terms of their hierarchical structure and their discourse relations. Among these four examples, the tool generates the same annotations for three. These results suggest that the tool has a comparable performance with respect to the annotations that are readily agreed by human experts.

5.2 Is Binary Discourse Tree Depth Relevant To Discourse Relations?

In this subsection, we aim to shed light on the relationship between depth and discourse relations.

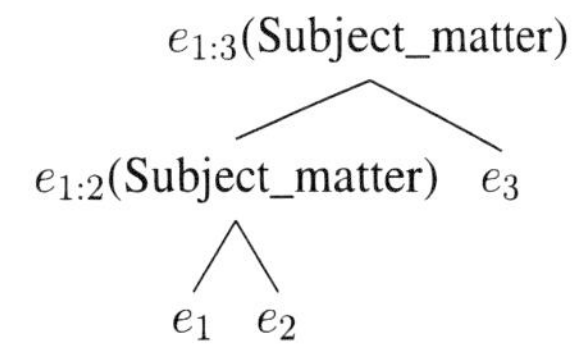

Figure 3: An illustration of the RST of an example from CMV.
e_1: I do not think you understand why the Christ myth theory is treated as a conspiracy theory;
e_2: All there needs to be in order for Christ to exist is a first-century carpenter named josh who had a few followers and was executed.
e_3: If you find this story plausible you do not believe the Christ myth theory.

It is noted that a longer text does not necessarily mean a deeper binary discourse tree structure. For instance, the average text length in a document with 18 sentences is longer than that with 17 sentences in AfD. As shown in Figure 2, most binary discourse trees have a depth of less than 7. Based on this observation, we define binary tree with depth less than 7 as shallow and deep otherwise. For each discourse tree, we calculate the sum of the frequencies of each corresponding main RST type relation, i.e., Presentational, Subject_matter, or Multinuclear. We conduct the Chi-square test to compare whether the shallow and deep structures are correlated with the type of discourse relations. We present the observed values with expected values in parentheses for each main RST type relations respectively in AfD and CMV in Table 4. Taking 0.05 as the significant level, the results suggest that the depth and the main type of RST relation are significantly correlated in both discussion contexts. The bold elements(bigger actual value than expected value) reveals that discourse tree structure tends to be deep in Presentational and Multinuclear relations, and tend to be shallow in Subject_matter relation. The patterns of correlations between discourse relation and depth hold the same in AfD and CMV, which suggests such correlations are context-independent.

It is expected that Multinuclear relations tend to

	Wikipedia				Reddit			
	Present	Subject	Multi	p value	Present	Subject	Multi	p value
shallow	2603(2790.9)	**57500(56911.5)**	10318(10718.5)	3.23E-58	491(596.5)	**6482(6060.1)**	1640(1956.4)	9.19E-30
deep	**595(407.0)**	7713(8301.4)	**1964(1563.4)**		**1820(1714.5)**	16995(17416.9)	**5939(5622.6)**	

Table 4: Chi-square Test Between Depth And Discourse Relation.

have a deeper discourse tree structure, as our model builds up a binary RST tree instead of a flat multi branches tree. A parent node with four children bearing a multinuclear relation originally will be transformed into a binary tree with a depth of three. The opposite correlation relations that the binary discourse tree depth exhibits with Presentational and Subject_matter relations implies that the binary tree depth may reflect the persuasion intent to some extent. Specifically, as mentioned earlier, Presentational relations reflect the writers' intent to increase belief or acceptance of the nucleus in the reader (Mann and Thompson, 1988), whereas Subject_matter relations mainly have the purpose to make oneself clear(Mann and Thompson, 1988). Therefore, their different correlation behavior with the binary tree depth may be leveraged in tasks like automatically identifying the persuasion intent of social media comments.

5.3 Is Persuasiveness Related To Discourse Relations?

In this subsection, we investigate the potential relationships between a comment's perceived persuasiveness and the type of RST relations it contains. The results of our Chi-square tests show that such a correlation relationship does not exist in Wikipedia AfD discussions ($p = 0.3290$) but exists in Reddit CMV discussions. We present the actual frequency outside and expected value within the parenthesis in Reddit CMV in Table 5. In the table, the larger observed value in bold elements implies that comments labeled as persuasive are more than expected to have Presentational and Multinuclear relations and less than expected to have Subject_matter relations.

The finding that correlation between persuasiveness and discourse relations exists in CMV discussions but not in AfD discussions implies the context-dependency of a comment's perceived persuasiveness. The discourse relations contained in a comment reflect the writer's use of rhetorical strategies in communication. CMV discussions are about challenging people's viewpoints and trying to persuade them successfully. Persuasion acts are explicitly expected from individual comments and the goal is to win the argument. The rhetorical strategies applied in constructing the comment are therefore expected to be influential on the comment's perceived persuasiveness. As described earlier, the use of Presentational relations implies the persuasion intent and Multinuclear relations the focus of rhetorical strategies. Subject_matter relations, on the other hand, focus on making the main point understood by the reader. Therefore, it is reasonable to expect that Presentational and Multinuclear relations are more influential on the perceived persuasiveness than Subject_matter relations in CMV discussions.

For Wikipedia AfD discussions, the goal is to identify the best solution on how to handle a Wikipedia article so that the quality of the online encyclopedia is ensured. There is a direct consequence at the end of the discussion that affects the community. Additionally, Wikipedia has a strong online community identity and participants are expected to share this collective goal. AfD discussion focuses on the comment's actual suggestion and its impact is highly considered in evaluating the comment. Hence, the use of rhetorical strategies in a comment is not that influential in the decision-making.

Prior studies have shown that contextual factors affect interaction dynamics in social media communications such as participant entry-order and degree of back-and-forth exchange (Tan et al., 2016; Xiao, 2018). Our finding here presents empirical evidence of the contextual influence on the perceived effects of social media comments' discourse structures.

5.4 Is Discourse Tree Deeper In A Persuasive Comment?

In this subsection, we explore the correlation between persuasiveness and discourse relation in discussion comments. We conduct Spearman's correlation and present the p-value and coefficient in Table 6. We observe a significant correlation between

	Present	Subject	Multi	p value
persuasive	**1497(1475.3)**	14772(14987.4)	**5032(4838.3)**	1.97E-07
non-persuasive	814(835.7)	**8705(8489.6)**	2547(2740.7)	

Table 5: Chi-square Test Between Persuasiveness And Discourse Relation In Reddit CMV Discussions.

perceived persuasiveness and depths, but a different pattern in these two discussions. In Wikipedia AfD discussions, a comment's perceived persuasiveness is negatively correlated to the depth of its binary discourse tree, while in Reddit discussions, the deeper the discourse tree, the more persuasive perceived by the readers.

We calculate the average percentages of three types of relations and find that Subject_matter relation is dominant in both Wikipedia AfD and Reddit CMV discussions. Additionally, they tend to appear more in persuasive comments in the Wikipedia discussions and more in non-persuasive comments in the Reddit discussions. As mentioned in Section 5.2, Subject_matter relations are more likely to appear in a shallow tree structure. Therefore, it explains why a Wikipedia AfD comment's perceived persuasiveness is negatively correlated with the depth of its binary discourse tree and it is the opposite for a Reddit CMV comment.

	Wikipedia	Reddit
p value	0.012	0
coefficient	-0.014	0.22
Subject_matter ratio^{per}	0.87	0.73
Subject_matter ratio^{non}	0.86	0.77

Table 6: Analysis Between Persuasiveness And Depth.Subject_matter ratio^{per} and Subject_matter ratio^{non} represent average ratio of Subject_matter relation in persuasive and non-persuasive comments.

6 Discussion

Complex social interactions increasingly happen through social media (Dey et al., 2017; Nguyen et al., 2015). Text's discourse structure reflects how the writer constructs arguments and reasons, which is expected to help us better understand the dynamics of these social interactions. Through the analysis of the comment's discourse structure in the two online discussions and the finding that a comment's discourse structure, identified from the tool, correlates with the comment's perceived persuasiveness, we showcase the potential of using this tool in social media content analysis. Essentially, the availability of this tool offers new opportunities for social media research. How does a comment's discourse structure correlate with the amount of attention it receives, in Twitter, Facebook, or Reddit discussions? Do people converge at the level of discourse structure as the online discussion goes on? Do toxic comments or disinformation tend to have particular discourse structures? These are a few example research questions for these new opportunities.

Our tool currently takes one sentence as an EDU. One of our future tasks is to parse a comment into smaller discourse units and build an RST tree upon them. Also, our model is trained on Wall Street Journal (RST-DT) (Mann and Thompson, 1988), the context and the text length of which is less similar to social media communications. The token number in a sentence in Wall Street Journal (around 18 tokens) is much less than that in AfD (around 63 tokens) and in CMV (around 246 tokens). We are exploring other RST annotated datasets as the training data for our future model.

Our case study of the comment's discourse structure in Wikipedia AfD and Reddit CMV discussions contributes to online persuasion research. The findings of our statistical analyses demonstrate that at the discourse structure level valuable information can be obtained that reflects the persuasion dynamics and helps interpret the perceived persuasiveness of online comments. Additionally, the contextual influence on social media communications can be explored at this level of language analysis as well. We also try to apply the machine learning model proposed by Li and Xiao (2020b) to the case study. The model proposed by Li and Xiao (2020b) achieves the micro F1 score of 87.9, 74.9, 62.6 in span, nuclearity, and relation. The findings remain the same after applying both their and our models, indicating that the performance of an RST parser has little influence on the correlations we reveal in these two online environments. We call for more investigations on how discourse relations and perceived persuasiveness interact in different online communities contexts.

7 Conclusion

Various natural language processing techniques have been applied in social media content analysis such as word frequency measures, syntactic structure analysis, sentiment analysis, emotion recognition, or topic modeling. Recently, researchers call for further consideration of contextual factors in the analysis and suggest the exploration of the discourse structure (Benamara et al., 2018). In response to this call, we build a bottom-up transition-based system for discourse parsing using the Rhetorical Structure Theory (RST) framework. In this system, we consider the position of tokens in an EDU and We pay partial attention to an EDU regarding the whole semantic of an EDU. We also design relation submodel based on nuclearity types. Our final model achieves the highest performance among all the reported neural network-based systems for RST parsing. We find that the low-frequency relations (please check Appendix) such as Topic-change and Topic-Comment do not achieve satisfying performance. In addition, these relations might benefit from global information. Therefore, we plan to deal with the imbalanced data by paying more attention to the low-frequency relations, and try to embed global information in the bottom-up parsing system in the future.

To demonstrate the use of our model to conduct discourse structure analysis in social media content, we explore the relationships among a comment's binary discourse tree depth, the discourse relations it contains, and its perceived persuasiveness in two online discussion contexts: Wikipedia AfD and Reddit CMV discussions. Our analyses show that the depth of a comment's binary discourse tree and its discourse relations are correlated and independent of the discussion context. In Wikipedia AfD discussion, comments that have Subject_matter relations are more likely to be perceived as persuasive, while in Reddit CMV discussions, comments constructed by Presentational and Multinuclear relations are perceived to be more persuasive.

References

Farah Benamara, Diana Inkpen, and Maite Taboada. 2018. Introduction to the special issue on language in social media: exploiting discourse and other contextual information. *Computational Linguistics*, 44(4):663–681.

Parminder Bhatia, Yangfeng Ji, and Jacob Eisenstein. 2015. Better document-level sentiment analysis from rst discourse parsing. *arXiv preprint arXiv:1509.01599*.

Sanorita Dey, Brittany Duff, Karrie Karahalios, and Wai-Tat Fu. 2017. The art and science of persuasion: not all crowdfunding campaign videos are the same. In *Proceedings of the 2017 ACM Conference on Computer Supported Cooperative Work and Social Computing*, pages 755–769.

Elisa Ferracane, Su Wang, and Raymond Mooney. 2017. Leveraging discourse information effectively for authorship attribution. In *Proceedings of the Eighth International Joint Conference on Natural Language Processing (Volume 1: Long Papers)*, pages 584–593.

Michael Heilman and Kenji Sagae. 2015. Fast rhetorical structure theory discourse parsing. *arXiv preprint arXiv:1505.02425*.

Rahul R Iyer, Katia P Sycara, and Yuezhang Li. 2017. Detecting type of persuasion: Is there structure in persuasion tactics? In *CMNA@ ICAIL*, pages 54–64.

Hamid Karimi and Jiliang Tang. 2019. Learning hierarchical discourse-level structure for fake news detection. *arXiv preprint arXiv:1903.07389*.

Naoki Kobayashi, Tsutomu Hirao, Hidetaka Kamigaito, Manabu Okumura, and Masaaki Nagata. 2020. Top-down rst parsing utilizing granularity levels in documents. In *AAAI*, pages 8099–8106.

Ani Latifah and Sulis Triyono. 2020. Cohesion and coherence of discourse in the story of" layangan putus" on social media facebook. *Indonesian Journal of EFL and Linguistics*, 5(1):41–56.

Jinfen Li and Lu Xiao. 2020a. Emotions in online debates: Tales from 4forums and convinceme. *Proceedings of the Association for Information Science and Technology*, 57(1):e255.

Jinfen Li and Lu Xiao. 2020b. Tree representations in transition system for rst parsing. In *Proceedings of the 28th International Conference on Computational Linguistics*, pages 6746–6751.

Sujian Li, Liang Wang, Ziqiang Cao, and Wenjie Li. 2014. Text-level discourse dependency parsing. In *Proceedings of the 52nd Annual Meeting of the Association for Computational Linguistics (Volume 1: Long Papers)*, pages 25–35.

Xiang Lin, Shafiq Joty, Prathyusha Jwalapuram, and M Saiful Bari. 2019. A unified linear-time framework for sentence-level discourse parsing. *arXiv preprint arXiv:1905.05682*.

William C Mann and Sandra A Thompson. 1988. Rhetorical structure theory: Toward a functional theory of text organization. *Text*, 8(3):243–281.

Elijah Mayfield and Alan W Black. 2019. Analyzing wikipedia deletion debates with a group decision-making forecast model. *Proceedings of the ACM on Human-Computer Interaction*, 3(CSCW):1–26.

Federico Neri, Carlo Aliprandi, Federico Capeci, Montserrat Cuadros, and Tomas By. 2012. Sentiment analysis on social media. In *2012 IEEE/ACM International Conference on Advances in Social Networks Analysis and Mining*, pages 919–926. IEEE.

Duyen T Nguyen, Laura A Dabbish, and Sara Kiesler. 2015. The perverse effects of social transparency on online advice taking. In *Proceedings of the 18th ACM Conference on Computer Supported Cooperative Work & Social Computing*, pages 207–217.

Mike Donald Tapi Nzali, Sandra Bringay, Christian Lavergne, Caroline Mollevi, and Thomas Opitz. 2017. What patients can tell us: topic analysis for social media on breast cancer. *JMIR medical informatics*, 5(3):e7779.

Ayşe Öcal, Lu Xiao, and Jaihyun Park. 2021. Reasoning in social media: insights from reddit "change my view" submissions. *Online Information Review*.

Jeffrey Pennington, Richard Socher, and Christopher D Manning. 2014. Glove: Global vectors for word representation. In *Proceedings of the 2014 conference on empirical methods in natural language processing (EMNLP)*, pages 1532–1543.

Matthew E Peters, Mark Neumann, Mohit Iyyer, Matt Gardner, Christopher Clark, Kenton Lee, and Luke Zettlemoyer. 2018. Deep contextualized word representations. *arXiv preprint arXiv:1802.05365*.

Victoria L Rubin and Tatiana Lukoianova. 2015. Truth and deception at the rhetorical structure level. *Journal of the Association for Information Science and Technology*, 66(5):905–917.

Youngseo Son, Nipun Bayas, and H Andrew Schwartz. 2018. Causal explanation analysis on social media. *arXiv preprint arXiv:1809.01202*.

Chenhao Tan, Vlad Niculae, Cristian Danescu-Niculescu-Mizil, and Lillian Lee. 2016. Winning arguments: Interaction dynamics and persuasion strategies in good-faith online discussions. In *Proceedings of the 25th international conference on world wide web*, pages 613–624.

Ashish Vaswani, Noam Shazeer, Niki Parmar, Jakob Uszkoreit, Llion Jones, Aidan N Gomez, Łukasz Kaiser, and Illia Polosukhin. 2017. Attention is all you need. In *Advances in neural information processing systems*, pages 5998–6008.

Yizhong Wang, Sujian Li, and Houfeng Wang. 2017. A two-stage parsing method for text-level discourse analysis. In *Proceedings of the 55th Annual Meeting of the Association for Computational Linguistics (Volume 2: Short Papers)*, pages 184–188.

Lu Xiao. 2018. A message's persuasive features in wikipedia's article for deletion discussions. In *Proceedings of the 9th International Conference on Social Media and Society*, pages 345–349.

Lu Xiao and Taraneh Khazaei. 2019. Changing others' beliefs online: Online comments' persuasiveness. In *Proceedings of the 10th International Conference on Social Media and Society*, pages 92–101.

Lu Xiao and Jeffrey Nickerson. 2019. Imperatives in past online discussions: Another helpful source for community newcomers? In *Proceedings of the 52nd Hawaii International Conference on System Sciences*.

Yimin Xiao and Lu Xiao. 2020. Effects of anonymity on comment persuasiveness in wikipedia articles for deletion discussions. In *Proceedings of the Fourth Workshop on Natural Language Processing and Computational Social Science*, pages 104–115.

Nan Yu, Meishan Zhang, and Guohong Fu. 2018. Transition-based neural rst parsing with implicit syntax features. In *Proceedings of the 27th International Conference on Computational Linguistics*, pages 559–570.

Stepan Zakharov, Omri Hadar, Tovit Hakak, Dina Grossman, Yifat Ben-David Kolikant, and Oren Tsur. 2020. Discourse parsing of contentious, non-convergent online discussions. *arXiv preprint arXiv:2012.04585*.

A Example Appendix

Relation	Count	Relation	Count
Attribution	357	Explanation	126
Background	87	Joint	382
Cause	83	Manner-Means	24
Comparison	37	Same-Unit	342
Condition	27	Summary	16
Contrast	176	Temporal	94
Elaboration	949	Textual-Organization	40
Enablement	62	Topic-Change	12
Evaluation	66	Topic-Comment	20

Table 7: Count of each relation in the test dataset

BART for Post-Correction of OCR Newspaper Text

Elizabeth Soper[1]
University at Buffalo, SUNY
esoper@buffalo.edu

Stanley Fujimoto
Ancestry.com
sfujimoto@ancestry.com

Yen-Yun Yu
Work Done at Ancestry.com
yen-yun.yu@mailfence.com

Abstract

Optical character recognition (OCR) from newspaper page images is susceptible to noise due to degradation of old documents and variation in typesetting. In this report, we present a novel approach to OCR post-correction. We cast error correction as a translation task, and fine-tune BART, a transformer-based sequence-to-sequence language model pretrained to denoise corrupted text. We are the first to use sentence-level transformer models for OCR post-correction, and our best model achieves a 29.4% improvement in character accuracy over the original noisy OCR text. Our results demonstrate the utility of pretrained language models for dealing with noisy text.

1 Introduction

Newspapers capture daily life from a moment in history. Their contents may not ever be published in history books, but they are rife with stories about everyday people, and connecting people to these stories empowers journeys of personal discovery. Connecting people to interesting and relevant articles within a newspaper is often challenging because newspaper pages are stored as scanned images. Computer vision models have been developed to automatically separate pages into individual articles (via object recognition) and convert each article from image to text (via OCR). Still, because of the degradation of old documents and variation in typesetting, the resulting text often contains errors, which can cause problems for downstream applications of the data.

The field of Natural Language Processing (NLP) has undergone a rapid shift in the last several years due to the popularization of transformers as a new, powerful tool for language modeling (Vaswani et al., 2017). Many pretrained models like BERT (Devlin et al., 2019) and GPT (Radford et al., 2019) have advanced the state-of-the-art on numerous NLP tasks, from text classification to question answering and translation. The key to the success of these models is their flexibility; pretraining on generic tasks like masked language modelling or next sentence prediction gives models generalized language knowledge, which then allows them to be easily adapted to more specific tasks (Brown et al., 2020). While pretrained language models are highly adaptable to new tasks, they have been shown to be very sensitive to noise. Models like BERT break down easily in the presence of irregular spellings or errors in text (Kumar et al., 2020). This work shows that in fact this type of pretrained language model can actually be used to correct noise.

In this work, we test the utility of transformer models to automatically correct noisy text generated by OCR. Specifically, we fine-tune BART (Lewis et al., 2020) on the ICDAR 2017 Post-OCR Correction dataset (Chiron et al., 2017). Unlike most previous approaches, fine-tuning BART does not require character-level alignment of the training data. Our results indicate that the generalized knowledge attained by BART during pretraining is enough to perform well at OCR text correction with just a small amount of task-specific fine-tuning. Our best model improves the character accuracy of the evaluation set by 29.4%. Correcting OCR errors is a challenging task, but significantly impacts performance on any downstream use of the data.

The following report is organized as follows: in Section 2 we describe previous work on OCR post-correction, in Section 3 we outline the BART model architecture and present our methodology for fine-tuning the model, in Section 4 we report the results of our experiments, and finally we conclude in Section 5.

[1]Work completed during an internship at Ancestry.com

Proceedings of the 2021 EMNLP Workshop W-NUT: The Seventh Workshop on Noisy User-generated Text, pages 284–290
November 11, 2021.

2 Previous Work

OCR post-correction has been an important problem since the inception of OCR technology. Traditional approaches to OCR post-correction relied on n-gram or dictionary-based techniques (Kukich, 1992). Recently, neural methods have become more popular. The International Conference on Document Analysis and Recognition (ICDAR) has held two competitions for OCR post-correction. The first, in 2017, was dominated by statistical and neural machine translation approaches (Chiron et al., 2017). The winner of the competition was Amrhein and Clematide (2018), who still hold the current state-of-the-art on the ICDAR 2017 benchmark. They use an ensemble of character-based statistical and neural machine translation models. The second ICDAR competition for OCR post-correction was held in 2019, after the introduction of transformer-based language models. The winning team, from Clova AI, used BERT embeddings as input to train CNN classifier, then character-level sequence-to-sequence (biLSTM) for correction (Rigaud et al., 2019).

Since then, there has been continued interest in applying pretrained language models to the task of text correction. Nguyen et al. (2020) use BERT embeddings to train an error detection network, and then apply character-level NMT for correction. BERT has also been used in the correction of errors from other sources; Zhang et al. (2020) correct errors generated by human typos. They use pretrained BERT embeddings as input to a biGRU to detect errors, and then fine-tune BERT on a masked language modeling task to correct the sentence, where the errors detected in the first step are soft-masked. Hu et al. (2020) use BERT embeddings plus edit distance between the errors and candidate replacements to correct pre-identified errors.

The above studies demonstrate the potential for pretrained language models in text correction. The present study builds on previous work by testing the potential of this type of model to handle text correction on their own in a single step, without additional infrastructure. We were interested in whether the generalized language knowledge acquired during pretraining could be directly transferred to OCR post-correction with a small amount of task-specific fine-tuning. To test this, we use BART, a sequence-to-sequence transformer model pretrained on text denoising, and fine-tune it on the ICDAR 2017 dataset (Chiron et al., 2017). This approach is novel in that error detection and correction are handled together in one step, and the model uses full sentences rather than performing character-level translation. To our knowledge, this is the first time that BART has been applied to the task of OCR post-correction. Our results suggest that BART can in fact be satisfactorily tuned as a stand-alone text correction model.

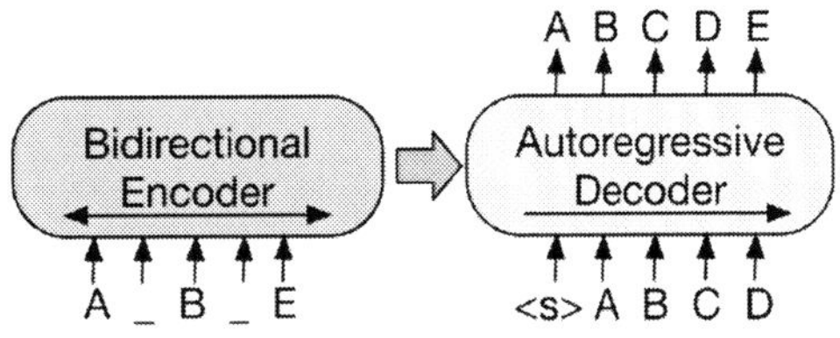

Figure 1: The BART architecture (taken from Lewis et al. 2020). Corrupted text is input to a bidirectional encoder (left), and then the likelihood of the original text is calculated by an auto-regressive decoder (right).

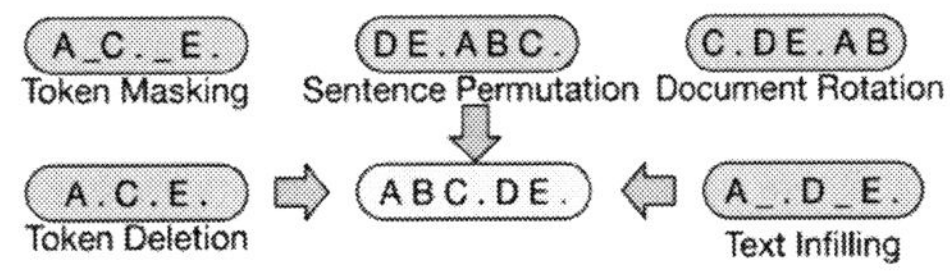

Figure 2: Transformations used for noising text in pretraining (taken from Lewis et al. 2020).

3 Methods

Next we outline the original BART model, followed by the methods used to fine-tune it for OCR post-correction.

3.1 BART model

Bidirectional and Auto-regressive Transformers (BART) is a sequence-to-sequence language model pretrained on a variety of denoising tasks to acquire general knowledge about how language works from large amounts of training data (Lewis et al., 2020). The BART architecture is shown in Figure 1; it consists of a bidirectional encoder (as in BERT: Devlin et al. 2019) plus an auto-regressive decoder (as in GPT: Radford et al. 2019). BART has achieved new state-of-the-art results on several NLP benchmarks, including dialogue response generation, question answering, and summarization.

One of the key differences between BART and other popular pretrained language models is its training objective. Where most language models are trained on a masked token prediction or next

OCR Error Type	Example	Corresponding BART Pretraining Objective
Over-segmentation	indecent → in decent	Text Infilling
Under-segmentation	and just → andjust	Token Deletion
Misrecognized Character	into → ipto	–
Missing Character	what → hat	Token Deletion
Hallucination	(empty string) → %_a_q$	Text Infilling

Table 1: Mapping of common OCR error types to BART's pretraining objectives.

token generation task, BART is trained to reconstruct text which has been corrupted in a variety of ways. BART's pretraining objective can be seen as a generalization of masked language modelling: in addition to token masking, input may also undergo a combination of token deletion, text infilling, sentence permutation, and document rotation. The set of text noising transformations used in BART pretraining is illustrated in Figure 2. By using a broader range of methods for corrupting input text, BART becomes more robust to noise. Adding noise to training data has been shown to improve model performance across many domains, even outside of NLP. In computer vision, for example, augmenting image data with color jitter or random erasing during training improves models for image classification and object detection (Shorten and Khoshgoftaar, 2019).

For our purpose of correcting errors in OCR-generated text, pretraining BART on various types of noisy data is particularly advantageous. First, because of the similarity between the types of text corruption seen during pretraining and the corruption introduced by OCR, BART theoretically could be fine-tuned for OCR-specific error types with a relatively small set of examples compared with state-of-the-art. Table 1 shows the most common types of errors introduced by OCR, and maps each to the closest corresponding BART pretraining objective. In particular, BART's token deletion and text infilling tasks are suited to OCR correction, as OCR frequently either misses characters or injects spurious characters. Notably, however, BART's pretraining involved deletion or insertion of entire tokens, whereas in OCR data it's more common to for individual characters to be deleted or inserted, rather than entire words.

Another important feature of BART which makes it particularly suitable for OCR correction is that *input* to the encoder need not be aligned with the decoder *output*. This is ideal for dealing with errors that result in a different number of tokens between the source and target texts, such as over- or under-segmentation, missing characters, or hallucinated characters, which are very frequent in OCR text. Dealing with the alignment of noisy and gold-standard texts is a non-trivial issue in creating OCR correction models, especially when creating training data. By using BART, we bypass the alignment problem.

3.2 Dataset

BART's pretraining corpus includes all of English Wikipedia plus the BookCorpus, which represents a wide range of genres. To fine-tune BART for OCR post-correction, we use the ICDAR 2017 Post-OCR Correction Dataset (Chiron et al., 2017). The data is a mixture of historical newspaper and monograph texts, ranging in date from 1744 to 1911. The dataset includes French and English language texts, but as BART was pretrained on English data only, French texts were removed for fine-tuning. The remaining English data contains 38,975 training sentences (27,414 monograph, 11,561 periodical) and 7,759 evaluation sentences (3,966 monograph, 3,793 periodical).

3.3 Fine-tuning Methods

We use Huggingface's transformers package for fine-tuning (Wolf et al., 2020). To prepare the data for input to the model, we split each article into sentences and removed the special alignment characters. Each sentence is tokenized with BART's tokenizer, which uses byte-level Byte Pair Encoding. The tokenized data is passed to the model one full sentence at a time.

The 'bart-base' checkpoint is our starting point for fine-tuning. The model is trained using batch size 6, AdamW optimizer, and cross-entropy loss between the model output and the target text to update weights. 3 epochs of training took approximately 2hr to train on a Tesla V100 SXM2 GPU

Error Type	Source	Prediction	Target
Over-segmentation	...before the **follow ing** morning...	...before the **follow- ing** morning...	...before the **follow- ing** morning...
Under-segmentation	Two Closes of Rich **oldSwarth** LAND, adjoining each other...	Two Closes of Rich **old Swarth** LAND, adjoining each other...	Two Closes of Rich **old Swarth** LAND, adjoining each other...
Misrecognized character	We sailed from Kalaniita Bay, **ar.d** soon we made the coast	We sailed from Kalaniita Bay, **and** soon we made the coast	We sailed from Kalamita Bay, **and** soon we made the coast
Missing character	**er** a good deal of argument, the facts were agreed to be turned **ipto** a special case	**After** a good deal of argument, the facts were agreed to be turned **into** a special case	**After** a good deal of argument, the facts were agreed to be turned **into** a special case
Hallucination	**248 THE FAMOUS niSTORY How** Fryer Bacon burnt his books of Magick	Fryer Bacon burnt his books of Magick	Fryer Bacon burnt his books of Magick

Table 2: Example results for different error types.

with 16GB RAM.

4 Results

Next we discuss the results of fine-tuning BART for OCR post-correction. Our model can handle a wide variety of error types, and improves the overall text accuracy by 29.4% on the evaluation set.

4.1 Qualitative Analysis

There are five main types of errors produced by OCR: (1) over-segmentation, (2) under-segmentation, (3) misrecognized character, (4) missing character, (5) hallucination. After fine-tuning, BART can recognize and correct all five types of errors.

Table 2 shows examples of how our model handles each type of error. For over-segmentation errors, our model corrects errors by adding a hyphen to the initial word fragment, rather than deleting the space and writing as a single word. This reflects the way the target text was formatted. These errors are typically due to words being broken across lines to fit within the margins.

We also found that the proposed model is less consistent at recognizing under-segmentation errors, most likely because it is less common in the ICDAR data, as well as the fact that deleting spaces has no direct parallel in BART's pretraining; the token deletion seen during pretraining always consisted of multi-character tokens.

For misrecognized character errors, the model consistently corrects the misspelling of common words, but struggles to correct misspelled proper names. Since proper names generally have very idiosyncratic spellings, they are much harder to predict, so the fact that our model struggles to correct unusual names is not a surprise.

In the example of an error involving missing characters, our model successfully recovers the missing character to complete the first word of the sentence. Note that in this example, the model also identifies and corrects a misrecognized character later in the sentence. This demonstrates the model's ability to automatically correct an arbitrary number of errors in a given input, without additional input information about the number or location of errors.

Last, in the hallucination error example, where there are characters which have no equivalent in the target text, our model correctly deletes the spurious characters. Hallucinated characters in the dataset are often non-alphabetic symbols (as shown in Table 1), which may make learning to identify such errors easier, but as shown in the example in Table 2, the model is able to recognized hallucinated alphabetic characters as well.

Approach	Monograph	Periodical	Overall
Char-SMT/NMT (Amrhein and Clematide, 2018)	**43**	**37**	**40**
CLAM (Chiron et al., 2017)	29	22	26
EFP (Chiron et al., 2017)	13	0	7
MMDT (Schulz and Kuhn, 2017)	20	0	10
WFST-PostOCR (Chiron et al., 2017)	28	0	14
Coustaty et al, 2018 (Coustaty et al., 2018)	30	10	20
Nguyen et al, 2020 (Nguyen et al., 2020)	36	27	31
BART w/ no fine-tuning	-7	-9	-8
Fine-tuned BART	32	23	29

Table 3: Model comparison on the English ICDAR 2017 dataset. Percent improvement is reported for the Monograph and Periodical sections, as well the overall improvement.

4.2 Quantitative Analysis

Performance on OCR post-correction is standardly measured by percent improvement between the source text and model prediction. This is calculated as shown in Equation (1), where $dist(\cdot)$ is the Levenshtein distance between two strings, s is the noisy source text, p is the predicted text from the model, and t is the target text.

$$\%_{improvement} := \frac{dist(s,t) - dist(p,t)}{len(t)} \quad (1)$$

Off-the-shelf BART with no fine-tuning does poorly at correcting errors, resulting in a 7.6% *decrease* in character accuracy. Our best fine-tuned model, on the other hand, achieved 29.4% improvement in text accuracy on the evaluation set, with 32.2% improvement on monographs and 23.1% improvement on periodicals. The disparity in performance between monographs and periodicals can be seen across other previous approaches, and is likely due to the imbalance in the training data, and possibly to the higher difficulty of the periodical genre.

The 37 point improvement in performance resulting from fine-tuning is remarkable given the relatively small size of the task-specific training set. The poor performance of BART before fine-tuning is somewhat surprising, given the similarity between the pretraining and fine-tuning tasks; one possible explanation is that during pretraining entire tokens were masked, inserted, or deleted, whereas during fine-tuning the errors were generally at the individual character level. Thus, while pretraining was not enough to yield strong results on OCR correction, the model could adapt quickly to the task because the only difference was the average span size of corrupted text.

A comparison of fine-tuned BART with previous approaches is shown in Table 3. For the sake of direct comparison, only approaches which reported evaluation metrics on the ICDAR 2017 dataset are included in the table. Fine-tuning BART on different datasets would allow for direct comparisons with other approaches (e.g. the Chinese typo dataset from Zhang et al. 2020); we leave this to future work. Overall, while the Amrhein and Clematide (2018) model outperforms ours, our approach is arguably *simpler*, as it requires no alignment information to train and performs both detection and correction in a single step. Furthermore, several additional techniques, like artificially injecting additional noise into training data, and hyperparameter optimization, could likely improve BART's performance even further.

5 Conclusion

In this work, we explored the use of BART for automatic correction of noisy text data generated by OCR. Our best model achieves 29.4% improvement in text accuracy. The resulting improvement in OCR text quality impacts all subsequent applications of the data. The approach described above is not specific to errors introduced by OCR; the same methods could in principle be applied to correct any type of noisy data, from the output of handwriting recognition models, to human-generated typos. Future work might test the utility of fine-tuning BART on a wider range of noisy text types, including fine-tuning mBART for correction of non-English data, as well as comparing BART with other sequence-to-sequence language models on text correction. Error correction is a critical first step for any NLP task when working with noisy data sources, and thus remains an important problem for the field.

Acknowledgements

In addition to the listed authors, Suraj Subraveti, Michael Brodie, Brent Carter, and Craig Whatcott also made important contributions to the work described in this report. We also thank the anonymous reviewers for their helpful feedback.

References

Chantal Amrhein and Simon Clematide. 2018. Supervised OCR error detection and correction using statistical and neural machine translation methods. *Journal for Language Technology and Computational Linguistics (JLCL)*, 33(1):49–76.

Tom Brown, Benjamin Mann, Nick Ryder, Melanie Subbiah, Jared D Kaplan, Prafulla Dhariwal, Arvind Neelakantan, Pranav Shyam, Girish Sastry, Amanda Askell, Sandhini Agarwal, Ariel HerbertVoss, Gretchen Krueger, Tom Henighan, Rewon Child, Aditya Ramesh, Daniel Ziegler, Jeffrey Wu, Clemens Winter, Chris Hesse, Mark Chen, Eric Sigler, Mateusz Litwin, Scott Gray, Benjamin Chess, Jack Clark, Christopher Berner, Sam McCandlish, Alec Radford, Ilya Sutskever, , and Dario Amodei. 2020. Language models are few-shot learners. *Advances in Neural Information Processing Systems*, 33:1877–1901.

Guillaume Chiron, Antoine Doucet, Mickaël Coustaty, and Jean-Philippe Moreux. 2017. ICDAR 2017 competition on post-OCR text correction. In *2017 14th IAPR International Conference on Document Analysis and Recognition (ICDAR)*, volume 1, pages 1423–1428. IEEE.

Mickaël Coustaty, Antoine Doucet, Adam Jatowt, Nhu-Van Nguyen, et al. 2018. Adaptive edit-distance and regression approach for post-OCR text correction. In *International Conference on Asian Digital Libraries*, pages 278–289. Springer.

Jacob Devlin, Ming-Wei Chang, Kenton Lee, and Kristina Toutanova. 2019. BERT: Pre-training of deep bidirectional transformers for language understanding. In *Proceedings of the 2019 Conference of the North American Chapter of the Association for Computational Linguistics: Human Language Technologies, Volume 1 (Long and Short Papers)*, pages 4171–4186, Minneapolis, Minnesota. Association for Computational Linguistics.

Yifei Hu, Xiaonan Jing, Youlim Ko, and Julia Taylor Rayz. 2020. Misspelling correction with pre-trained contextual language model. In *2020 IEEE 19th International Conference on Cognitive Informatics & Cognitive Computing (ICCI* CC)*, pages 144–149. IEEE.

Karen Kukich. 1992. Techniques for automatically correcting words in text. *ACM Computing Surveys (CSUR)*, 24(4):377–439.

Ankit Kumar, Piyush Makhija, and Anuj Gupta. 2020. Noisy text data: Achilles' heel of BERT. In *Proceedings of the Sixth Workshop on Noisy User-generated Text (W-NUT 2020)*, pages 16–21. Association for Computational Linguistics.

Mike Lewis, Yinhan Liu, Naman Goyal, Marjan Ghazvininejad, Abdelrahman Mohamed, Omer Levy, Veselin Stoyanov, and Luke Zettlemoyer. 2020. BART: Denoising sequence-to-sequence pretraining for natural language generation, translation, and comprehension. In *Proceedings of the 58th Annual Meeting of the Association for Computational Linguistics*, pages 7871–7880. Association for Computational Linguistics.

Thi Tuyet Hai Nguyen, Adam Jatowt, Nhu-Van Nguyen, Mickael Coustaty, and Antoine Doucet. 2020. Neural machine translation with BERT for post-OCR error detection and correction. In *Proceedings of the ACM/IEEE Joint Conference on Digital Libraries in 2020*, pages 333–336.

Alec Radford, Jeffrey Wu, Rewon Child, David Luan, Dario Amodei, Ilya Sutskever, et al. 2019. Language models are unsupervised multitask learners. *Technical Report.*

Christophe Rigaud, Antoine Doucet, Mickaël Coustaty, and Jean-Philippe Moreux. 2019. ICDAR 2019 competition on post-OCR text correction. In *2019 International Conference on Document Analysis and Recognition (ICDAR)*, pages 1588–1593. IEEE.

Sarah Schulz and Jonas Kuhn. 2017. Multi-modular domain-tailored OCR post-correction. In *Proceedings of the 2017 Conference on Empirical Methods in Natural Language Processing*, pages 2716–2726, Copenhagen, Denmark. Association for Computational Linguistics.

Connor Shorten and Taghi M Khoshgoftaar. 2019. A survey on image data augmentation for deep learning. *Journal of Big Data*, 6(1):1–48.

Ashish Vaswani, Noam Shazeer, Niki Parmar, Jakob Uszkoreit, Llion Jones, Aidan N Gomez, Łukasz Kaiser, and Illia Polosukhin. 2017. Attention is all you need. In *Advances in Neural Information Processing Systems*, pages 5998–6008.

Thomas Wolf, Lysandre Debut, Victor Sanh, Julien Chaumond, Clement Delangue, Anthony Moi, Pierric Cistac, Tim Rault, Rémi Louf, Morgan Funtowicz, Joe Davison, Sam Shleifer, Patrick von Platen, Clara Ma, Yacine Jernite, Julien Plu, Canwen Xu, Teven Le Scao, Sylvain Gugger, Mariama Drame, Quentin Lhoest, and Alexander M. Rush. 2020. Transformers: State-of-the-art natural language processing. In *Proceedings of the 2020 Conference on Empirical Methods in Natural Language Processing: System Demonstrations*, pages 38–45. Association for Computational Linguistics.

Shaohua Zhang, Haoran Huang, Jicong Liu, and Hang Li. 2020. Spelling error correction with soft-masked BERT. In *Proceedings of the 58th Annual Meeting of the Association for Computational Linguistics*, pages 882–890. Association for Computational Linguistics.

Coping with Noisy Training Data Labels in Paraphrase Detection

Teemu Vahtola and **Mathias Creutz** and **Eetu Sjöblom** and **Sami Itkonen**
{teemu.vahtola, mathias.creutz, eetu.sjoblom, sami.itkonen}@helsinki.fi
Department of Digital Humanities
Faculty of Arts
University of Helsinki

Abstract

We present new state-of-the-art benchmarks for paraphrase detection on all six languages in the Opusparcus sentential paraphrase corpus: English, Finnish, French, German, Russian, and Swedish. We reach these baselines by fine-tuning BERT. The best results are achieved on smaller and cleaner subsets of the training sets than was observed in previous research. Additionally, we study a translation-based approach that is competitive for the languages with more limited and noisier training data.

1 Introduction

Paraphrase detection is a task where a model is trained to recognize from a collection of phrases, whether two phrases carry approximately the same meaning. Paraphrase detection provides a natural way to study how well models operate on semantic abstractions by recognizing similar meanings from syntactically and lexically different sequence pairs. Models that are capable of operating on such a semantic level are useful in a number of Natural Language Processing tasks, such as Information Retrieval or Machine Translation, by providing semantically coherent alternative queries or translation hypotheses for a sequence of words.

In this paper, we study paraphrase detection trained on noisy data in six European languages. We train paraphrase detection models by fine-tuning BERT (Devlin et al., 2018) and explore the effect of noisy labels in the training data. We reach new paraphrase detection benchmarks on all six languages in the Opusparcus (Creutz, 2018) sentential paraphrase corpus, a collection of paraphrase pairs extracted from the OpenSubtitles2016 (Lison and Tiedemann, 2016) movie and television subtitle collection. The new benchmarks are obtained with considerably smaller and cleaner subsets of the training set than was observed in previous research. By exploring different proportions of noisy labels in the training data, we identify a level at which fine-tuned BERT models still appear to be robust to the noisy labels. We also present a competitive translation-based approach that is especially useful for languages with more limited and noisier paraphrase data in our experimental setup.

Opusparcus contains training, development and test sets in English (en), Finnish (fi), French (fr), German (de), Russian (ru), and Swedish (sv). For each language, the development and test sets consist of a few thousand sentence pairs that have been annotated manually. The annotators have indicated on a four-grade scale to which extent two proposed sentences mean the same thing. The training sets are considerably larger, comprising millions of sentence pairs, but lack manual annotations. However, the training data have been ordered in such a way that the sentence pairs that are most likely to be true paraphrases are placed first and the pairs of sentences that are least likely to carry the same meaning are placed last. This ranking is produced automatically, according to metrics based on point-wise mutual information. Consequently, when training a paraphrase detection model on these training sets, one needs to decide how much of the available training data to use, weighing the benefits of a smaller and cleaner set versus a larger but noisier set.

Paraphrase detection based on Opusparcus has previously been studied by Sjöblom et al. (2018), who train two different neural network models to represent the phrases and apply a cosine distance-based metric to detect the paraphrases. The authors observe that the networks are rather robust to noise and they can benefit from more data, albeit increase in data size results in increased amounts of noise within the training data. Whereas Sjöblom et al. (2018) use neural networks trained from scratch, we approach paraphrase detection by fine-tuning language-specific BERT models for sequence classification.

Further previous explorations of Opusparcus include the fine-tuning of pre-trained BERT models

Proceedings of the 2021 EMNLP Workshop W-NUT: The Seventh Workshop on Noisy User-generated Text, pages 291–296
November 11, 2021.

for the purpose of word similarity assessment in English and Finnish (Garí Soler and Apidianaki, 2020) as well as German text summarization (Paraschiv and Cercel, 2020). Pragst et al. (2020) compare different classifiers in different paraphrasing-related tasks on different corpora, including Opusparcus. Fabre et al. (2021) investigate automatic paraphrase generation on Opusparcus as well as other datasets. None of these previous works, however, establish new benchmarks for paraphrase detection on the Opusparcus test sets.

An alternative to using large neural language models, such as BERT, is to leverage the capability of machine translation systems instead. Wieting et al. (2017) and Iyyer et al. (2018) create paraphrases using massive backtranslation; from a parallel corpus of two languages (bitext), paraphrases in the first language are obtained by automatically translating the corresponding sentence in the second language back to the first language. In our proposed translation-based approach for paraphrase detection, we do not need bitexts. We simply use existing machine translation models to translate our paraphrase candidates in one language (for instance, English) to another language (such as Spanish) and see whether the two source sentences (in English) have common translations in the target language (Spanish), in which case they are considered to be paraphrases. However, we need to take into consideration that machine translation is not perfect and produces noisy results. We discuss our methods in detail in Section 2. The results of our experiments are presented in Section 3, and we conclude in Section 4.

2 Experiments

We evaluate the performance of language-specific BERT models on paraphrase detection based on differently sized subsets consisting of different proportions of noise sampled from the Opusparcus training data. We also evaluate our translation-based model on the paraphrase detection task.

2.1 General Setting

All our experiments involving BERT are conducted using the Hugging Face Transformers (Wolf et al., 2020) library. For each language, we choose a corresponding model from the collection of pre-trained transformers. The language-specific models we use are *bert-base-cased* (Devlin et al., 2018), *TurkuNLP/bert-base-finnish-cased-v1* (Virtanen et al., 2019), *flaubert/flaubert_base_cased* (Le et al., 2020), *bert-base-german-cased* (Chan et al., 2020), *DeepPavlov/rubert-base-cased* (Kuratov and Arkhipov, 2019), and *KB/bert-base-swedish-cased* (Malmsten et al., 2020) for English, Finnish, French, German, Russian, and Swedish respectively. We fine-tune the models with an additional sequence classification layer for three epochs and choose the best performing model based on results achieved on the development set. The models are trained with 1e-5 learning rate and 0.3 weight decay.

	de	en	fi	fr	ru	sv
1M	90	97	83	95	85	85
2M	87	90	80	90	85	65
5M	**75**	80	**65**	80	**70**	**60**
10M	60	75	60	75	60	45
20M	50	**70**	45	**60**	55	–
30M	–	60	–	–	–	–

Table 1: Estimates of proportions of correctly labeled paraphrases [%] in growing subsets of the Opusparcus training sets.[1] The figures in boldface show the approximate optimal data sizes and their corresponding noise levels reported by Sjöblom et al. (2018) for their recurrent neural network model.

For the machine translation experiments we use pre-trained translation models from the OPUS-MT project (Tiedemann and Thottingal, 2020).

2.2 Data selection for BERT fine-tuning

We sample our training examples similarly to Sjöblom et al. (2018), who picked a certain number of *assumed* positive examples of paraphrases from the beginning of the training sets, and sampled an equal number of assumed negative examples by randomly pairing sentences. Sjöblom et al. (2018) experimented with data sets containing between one and thirty million positive examples. The level of correct labels in these subsets of data are shown in Table 1, which has been compiled from values reported by Creutz (2018) and Sjöblom et al. (2018). The reported best models were trained on data sets containing between 60 % and 80 % of presumably correctly labeled paraphrases. Thus, the level of noise was fairly high, between 20 and 40 percent.

In the present work, we study models fine-tuned on up to five million positive examples, but we

[1]See pages 12–13 of the presentation slides at `https://helda.helsinki.fi//bitstream/handle/10138/237338/creutz2018lrec_slides.pdf`

also introduce smaller sets of 100 000 and 500 000 positive examples. These 100k and 500k sets are expected to contain very few incorrectly labeled paraphrases.

We use the Opusparcus development sets to systematically study how well our models perform on different sizes of training data with different proportions of label noise. The final results are reported on the Opusparcus test sets, and only for the best models, according to the development sets. The development and test sets have been annotated by hand, and are not expected to include noisy labels.

2.3 Translation-based method

In order to decide whether two sentences carry the same meaning, one could ideally investigate whether they have a common translation in another language. We were curious to find out whether such an approach could work for Opusparcus, in particular for the languages with more limited and noisier training sets available (Swedish, Finnish, and Russian).

In these experiments, we employ existing neural machine translation models to translate the Opusparcus development and test sets. No further training takes place, so the training sets are not necessary in this setup. For a pair of sentences we create n-best lists of the 1000 most likely translations into a second language. If the two source sentences have translations in common, we infer that the sentences are likely to be paraphrases.

The machine translation models have been trained on large amounts of parallel corpora, including bitexts from the OpenSubtitles corpus. The sentence pairs extracted into Opusparcus are also based on sentence alignments across languages in OpenSubtitles. Therefore, there is a risk that Opusparcus test data might have been included in the training of the machine translation models, which would lead to unreliable results. In our current experiments, we have avoided this risk by translating the Opusparcus languages only to languages excluded from Opusparcus: Spanish (es), Dutch (nl) and Polish (pl). This guarantees that no bitext used in the training of the machine translation models has been included in any phase of the creation of Opusparcus.[2]

It is conceivable to think that for two sentences to be paraphrases it is sufficient for them to have one translation in common. In practice, this is not the case. Firstly, the concept of having the same meaning is about degrees of similarity rather than a discrete dichotomy. Secondly, as machine translation systems are not perfect and produce noisy results, the fact that we can find common translations is not a guarantee for the sentences to be paraphrases. Within the list of the 1000 most likely translations, we might find truncated translations, which do not cover the entire source sentence. Thus, two sentences that clearly mean different things can still have translations in common, typically such "simplified" or "summarized" fragments.

We have used the Opusparcus development sets, separately for each language, to find the optimal level of overlap in the translated n-best lists. Two sentences are considered to be paraphrases if they have a higher overlap in the number of shared translations than this inferred threshold value.

As an addition, which further improves performance, we use the development sets to determine for each source language to which of the target languages (Spanish, Dutch, Polish) one should translate in order to obtain the best paraphrase detection performance.

Final results of the translation-based approach are computed on the test sets for only the optimal target language and the corresponding optimal overlap threshold.

3 Results

The performance of our fine-tuned BERT models with respect to different amounts of data and noise are presented in Figure 1. The results show that while the baseline models by Sjöblom et al. (2018) benefit from adding more and noisier data, this is not the case with BERT to the same extent. We notice three types of behaviour of BERT on different languages. With Finnish and Swedish, the languages with most limited training data, BERT obtains high results with a small and clean training subset, and adding more noisy data is only detrimental to the model. With the higher-resource languages, French, German and Russian, we notice an initial increase in performance when adding more data. The models peak at 1 million positive examples and start to deteriorate when more noisy data is added. The results of the highest-resource

[2]Note that this is not a problem for the BERT models that we use for fine-tuning, even though two of them (French and German BERT) have been trained partly on OpenSubtitles data. This is because these BERT models are based on monolingual data rather than bitexts, so there are no "bridges" between potential paraphrases via another language.

	de	en	fi	fr	ru	sv
BERT	**88.9 (1)**	**93.3 (0.5)**	**85.0 (0.1)**	**82.6 (1)**	**77.8 (1)**	**87.7 (0.1)**
Translation	85.1 (pl)	89.5 (pl)	84.9 (nl)	73.4 (pl)	75.0 (es)	85.8 (nl)
Sjöblom et al. (2018)	86.7 (4)	92.1 (20)	82.5 (3.5)	77.9 (22)	70.3 (5)	82.1 (5)

Table 2: Paraphrase detection accuracies [%] on the test sets of the six languages. For BERT and the model by Sjöblom et al. (2018), the figures within brackets indicate the amount of training data used (in millions of sentence pairs assumed to be positive examples of paraphrases). For the translation based model, the brackets indicate which target language produced the best translations for parapahrase detection.

language in the Opusparcus data, English, first increase and then plateau. It seems that the model can reach high performance already on 500 000 positive examples and adding more data when fine-tuning does not result in notable amelioration of the model. However, in our experiments with English, the proportion of noise does not exceed 20 %. Common for all models is that they reach the best performance already before or at 1 million positive examples. Only a fraction of the number of training examples required to train the models of Sjöblom et al. (2018) are necessary for significantly better performance when using BERT.

The final test results are presented in Table 2. The best results in all languages are obtained by fine-tuning BERT. However, we reach fairly competitive results with the translation models especially in the languages with less and noisier training data, Finnish, Swedish and Russian, which outperform the previous results by Sjöblom et al. (2018). Translating into Polish turned out to produce the best results for the high-resource languages (German, English, French), whereas Dutch was the best target language for Finnish and Swedish. As there were no translation models available from Russian to Dutch and Polish, the only option for Russian was to translate into Spanish.

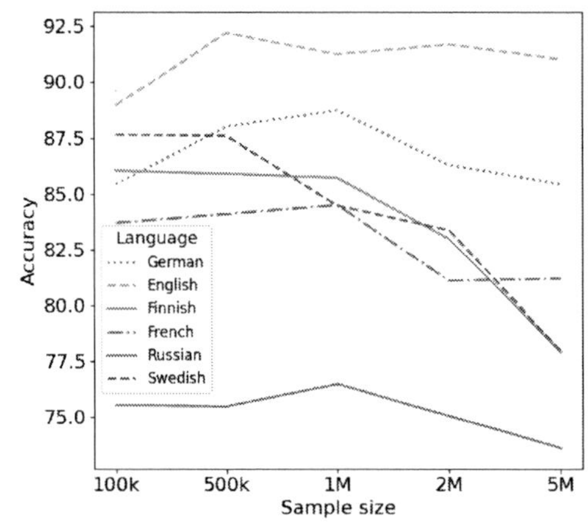

Figure 1: Paraphrase detection accuracies [%] produced by fine-tuning BERT on the Opusparcus development sets of the different languages. We explore training set sizes ranging from 100 000 to 5 million positive sentence pairs.

4 Conclusion

We have presented a new state-of-the-art benchmark based on BERT for six Opusparcus languages. Our experiments show that when fine-tuning BERT for paraphrase detection, we need only a small portion of the number of training examples that are required for training a recurrent neural network from scratch. In fact, it is detrimental to extend the amount of training data too far, as this causes the proportion of noise to go up. We find that BERT is considerably less robust to noise than the neural network models presented by Sjöblom et al. (2018). For some languages (English, Finnish and Russian) BERT appears to be robust with up to 20 % of noisy labels in the training set, whereas the experiments on French, German and Swedish indicate lower tolerance to noise in the data. Previous research on BERT (Tänzer et al., 2021) has claimed that even a considerable amount of noise in labels does not result in large performance degredations. Our findings are that we reach that point at a noise level of 20 % maximum.

In addition, we have shown that competitive results for paraphrase detection can be reached with a rather simple translation-based approach. In three languages, we were able to outperform the previous recurrent neural network-based benchmarks, and for one language (Finnish) we reached results that are almost on par with results obtained by fine-tuning BERT. This suggests that a translation-based model can be useful in situations where enough high-quality paraphrase data for fine-tuning BERT is lacking, or when an appropriate BERT model does not exist.

In future work we intend to explore means of further mitigating the effects of noisy training data. We could also study why certain target languages work better than others in the translation-based approach. Future work could also include an explicit study of the Opusparcus training set in order to identify possible other features in addition to noisy labels that affect the model performance when increasing training data. Due to high computational resources needed for training large models, we limit the number of positive examples to five million. Future work could include training a bigger English model to detect when a similar performance drop to the other languages occurs in English. Furthermore, we are interested in studying paraphrases in scenarios, where meaning is highly context-dependent.

Acknowledgments

We wish to gratefully acknowledge the Academy of Finland for their support for this research. We are thankful to *CSC — the Finnish IT Center for Science* for the generous computational resources they have provided.

References

Branden Chan, Stefan Schweter, and Timo Möller. 2020. German's next language model. In *Proceedings of the 28th International Conference on Computational Linguistics*, pages 6788–6796, Barcelona, Spain (Online). International Committee on Computational Linguistics.

Mathias Creutz. 2018. Open subtitles paraphrase corpus for six languages. In *Proceedings of the Eleventh International Conference on Language Resources and Evaluation (LREC 2018)*, Miyazaki, Japan. European Language Resources Association (ELRA).

Jacob Devlin, Ming-Wei Chang, Kenton Lee, and Kristina Toutanova. 2018. BERT: pre-training of deep bidirectional transformers for language understanding. *CoRR*, abs/1810.04805.

Betty Fabre, Tanguy Urvoy, Jonathan Chevelu, and Damien Lolive. 2021. Neural-driven search-based paraphrase generation. In *Proceedings of the 16th Conference of the European Chapter of the Association for Computational Linguistics: Main Volume*, pages 2100–2111, Online. Association for Computational Linguistics.

Aina Garí Soler and Marianna Apidianaki. 2020. MULTISEM at SemEval-2020 task 3: Fine-tuning BERT for lexical meaning. In *Proceedings of the Fourteenth Workshop on Semantic Evaluation*, pages 158–165, Barcelona (online). International Committee for Computational Linguistics.

Mohit Iyyer, John Wieting, Kevin Gimpel, and Luke Zettlemoyer. 2018. Adversarial example generation with syntactically controlled paraphrase networks. In *Proceedings of NAACL-HLT 2018*, pages 1875–1885, New Orleans, Louisiana.

Yuri Kuratov and Mikhail Arkhipov. 2019. Adaptation of deep bidirectional multilingual transformers for russian language.

Hang Le, Loïc Vial, Jibril Frej, Vincent Segonne, Maximin Coavoux, Benjamin Lecouteux, Alexandre Allauzen, Benoît Crabbé, Laurent Besacier, and Didier Schwab. 2020. FlauBERT : des modèles de langue contextualisés pré-entraînés pour le français (FlauBERT : Unsupervised language model pre-training for French). In *Actes de la 6e conférence conjointe Journées d'Études sur la Parole (JEP, 33e édition), Traitement Automatique des Langues Naturelles (TALN, 27e édition), Rencontre des Étudiants Chercheurs en Informatique pour le Traitement Automatique des Langues (RÉCITAL, 22e édition). Volume 2 : Traitement Automatique des Langues Naturelles*, pages 268–278, Nancy, France. ATALA et AFCP.

Pierre Lison and Jörg Tiedemann. 2016. OpenSubtitles2016: Extracting large parallel corpora from movie and TV subtitles. In *Proceedings of the Tenth International Conference on Language Resources and Evaluation (LREC'16)*, pages 923–929, Portorož, Slovenia. European Language Resources Association (ELRA).

Martin Malmsten, Love Börjeson, and Chris Haffenden. 2020. Playing with words at the national library of sweden – making a swedish bert.

Andrei Paraschiv and Dumitru-Clementin Cercel. 2020. UPB at GermEval-2020 Task 3: Assessing summaries for German texts using BERTScore and Sentence-Bert. In *Proceedings of the 5th Swiss Text Analytics Conference (SwissText) & 16th Conference on Natural Language Processing (KONVENS)*, Zurich, Switzerland (Online).

Louisa Pragst, Wolfgang Minker, and Stefan Ultes. 2020. Comparative study of sentence embeddings for contextual paraphrasing. In *Proceedings of the 12th Language Resources and Evaluation Conference*, pages 6841–6851, Marseille, France. European Language Resources Association.

Eetu Sjöblom, Mathias Creutz, and Mikko Aulamo. 2018. Paraphrase detection on noisy subtitles in six languages. In *Proceedings of the 2018 EMNLP Workshop W-NUT*, pages 64–73, United States. The Association for Computational Linguistics. Workshop on Noisy User-generated Text, W-NUT ; Conference date: 01-11-2018 Through 01-11-2018.

Jörg Tiedemann and Santhosh Thottingal. 2020. OPUS-MT – building open translation services for the world. In *Proceedings of the 22nd Annual Conference of the European Association for Machine Translation*, pages 479–480, Lisboa, Portugal. European Association for Machine Translation.

Michael Tänzer, Sebastian Ruder, and Marek Rei. 2021. Bert memorisation and pitfalls in low-resource scenarios.

Antti Virtanen, Jenna Kanerva, Rami Ilo, Jouni Luoma, Juhani Luotolahti, Tapio Salakoski, Filip Ginter, and Sampo Pyysalo. 2019. Multilingual is not enough: Bert for finnish.

John Wieting, Jonathan Mallinson, and Kevin Gimpel. 2017. Learning paraphrastic sentence embeddings-from back-translated bitext. In *Proceedings of the 2017 Conference on Empirical Methods in Natural Language Processing*, pages 274–285, Copenhagen, Denmark.

Thomas Wolf, Lysandre Debut, Victor Sanh, Julien Chaumond, Clement Delangue, Anthony Moi, Pierric Cistac, Tim Rault, Remi Louf, Morgan Funtowicz, Joe Davison, Sam Shleifer, Patrick von Platen, Clara Ma, Yacine Jernite, Julien Plu, Canwen Xu, Teven Le Scao, Sylvain Gugger, Mariama Drame, Quentin Lhoest, and Alexander Rush. 2020. Transformers: State-of-the-art natural language processing. In *Proceedings of the 2020 Conference on Empirical Methods in Natural Language Processing: System Demonstrations*, pages 38–45, Online. Association for Computational Linguistics.

Knowledge Distillation with Noisy Labels for Natural Language Understanding

Shivendra Bhardwaj[1*] **Abbas Ghaddar**[1] **Ahmad Rashid**[1] **Khalil Bibi**[1]
Chengyang Li[1,2†] **Ali Ghodsi**[2] **Philippe Langlais**[3] **Mehdi Rezagholizadeh**[1]
[1]Huawei Noah's Ark Lab
[2]David R. Cheriton School of Computer Science, University of Waterloo
[3] RALI/DIRO, Université de Montréal, Canada
{abbas.ghaddar, ahmad.rashid,khalil.bibi, mehdi.rezagholizadeh}@huawei.com
ali.ghodsi@uwaterloo.ca, felipe@iro.umontreal.ca

Abstract

Knowledge Distillation (KD) is extensively used to compress and deploy large pre-trained language models on edge devices for real-world applications. However, one neglected area of research is the impact of noisy (corrupted) labels on KD. We present, to the best of our knowledge, the first study on KD with noisy labels in Natural Language Understanding (NLU). We document the scope of the problem and present two methods to mitigate the impact of label noise. Experiments on the GLUE benchmark show that our methods are effective even under high noise levels. Nevertheless, our results indicate that more research is necessary to cope with label noise under the KD.

1 Introduction

Large-scale pre-trained language models (Devlin et al., 2019; Raffel et al., 2020; Brown et al., 2020) have shown remarkable abilities to match and even surpass human performances on many Natural Languages Understanding (NLU) tasks (Rajpurkar et al., 2018; Wang et al., 2018, 2019a). However, the deployment of these models in dynamic commercial environments come with challenges, including: large model size, and low training data quality.

Knowledge Distillation (Hinton et al., 2015; Turc et al., 2019) is a compression technique of choice that has proven to be effective to fit a cumbersome NLU model on edge devices (Sanh et al., 2019; Jiao et al., 2020; Sun et al., 2020). Meanwhile, numerous methods were developed to combat noisy (corrupted) labels, mainly for computer vision (Frénay and Verleysen, 2013; Jiang et al., 2018; Thulasidasan et al., 2019; Han et al., 2020) and more recently for NLU (Ardehaly and Culotta, 2018; Jindal et al., 2019; Garg et al., 2021; Ghaddar et al., 2021a,b; Jafari et al., 2021).

Despite its success, KD has mostly been studied with the availability of massive amount of high quality labeled data. In practice, however, it is costly and impractical to produce such data (Ghaddar and Langlais, 2019), and noisy labels are commonly encountered. In this paper, we consider the problem of KD when noisy labels are provided for training the main (teacher) and compressed (student) models. To our knowledge, this is the first time KD is studied under a noisy setting in NLU.

We conduct experiments on 7 tasks from the GLUE benchmark (Wang et al., 2018) and observe a drastic drop of performance of distilled models when we increase the level of noise. In response, we propose 2 distillation training methods, namely Co-Distill and Label Refining, that are specifically designed to handle noise. Experiments show that our methods lead to improvements over fair baselines, and that it combination also performs the best. Yet, our analysis indicates that the problem is far from solved, and that there is much room for research.

2 Related Work

The vanilla KD framework (Buciluǎ et al., 2006; Hinton et al., 2015) consists in training a small *student* model to mimic the output of a large *teacher* model. Recent years have seen a wide array of methods that leverage intermediate layer matching (Ji et al., 2021; Wu et al., 2020; Passban et al., 2021; Wang et al., 2020), data augmentation (Fu et al., 2020; Li et al., 2021; Jiao et al., 2020; Kamalloo et al., 2021), or adversarial training (Zaharia et al., 2021; Rashid et al., 2020, 2021) in order to reduce the teacher-student performance gap. Instead, our proposed methods are designed to handle label noise during KD. Nevertheless, they can be easily fused with the aforementioned methods to further boost performance.

*This work has been done while Shivendra Bhardwaj was at Huawei.

† This work has been done while Chengyang Li was an intern at Huawei.

Proceedings of the 2021 EMNLP Workshop W-NUT: The Seventh Workshop on Noisy User-generated Text, pages 297–303
November 11, 2021.

Label noise (corruption) is a common problem in real-world datasets, and it has been well studied in the literature (Frénay and Verleysen, 2013; Li et al., 2017; Han et al., 2020). Methods to combat noise build on the idea that samples with small training loss at early epochs are more likely to be clean (Dehghani et al., 2018; Wang et al., 2019b).

In co-teaching (Han et al., 2018), two networks of different capacity teach each other to reject wrong labels. At each forward pass, each network keeps only small-loss samples and sends them to its peer network for updating the parameters. The main idea is that the error flow can be reduced, as networks of different learning abilities have different views on the data.

Self-distillation was proposed by Dong et al. (2019), where the model is trained to mimic its own prediction from the previous training epoch. The goal is to prevent the model from memorizing wrong labels, as the model has less tendency to fit noise at early epochs. In addition, Bagherinezhad et al. (2018) showed improvements when distillation at early epochs is used to refine noisy labels.

Another line of works is the learning to weight approach (Ren et al., 2018; Li et al., 2019; Zhang et al., 2020; Fan et al., 2020) that aims to learn per-sample loss weights in order to discount noisy samples. The proposed methods use an auxiliary meta-learner to re-weight training samples of the main model. However, all aforementioned works mainly focus on computer vision. Recently, Garg et al. (2021) utilize a noise detection model to cluster, then score the training samples for text classification in an attempt to guide the main model to focus on samples that are most likely to be correct.

3 Methodology

We first introduce our method, Co-Distill (CD), which jointly trains the teacher and the student. Next, we incorporate Label Refinement (LR) which is motivated by the algorithms of Jiang et al. (2018), Arazo et al. (2019) and Garg et al. (2021) for noise mitigation in regular (no KD) training framework.

3.1 Co-Distill (CD)

The key feature of our method is that the teacher and the student are trained together, but unlike traditional KD, the teacher also learns from the student. Figure 1 showcases the complete architecture. We train the student model $S_{\theta^S}(\cdot)$ with the following loss function $\mathcal{L}^S$:

$$\mathcal{L}^S = \frac{1}{N}\sum_{i=1}^{N}[\alpha \cdot \mathcal{L}_{CE}(y_i, S_{\theta^S}(x_i)) + (1-\alpha)\cdot \mathcal{L}_{KD}(T_{\theta^T}(x_i), S_{\theta^S}(x_i))] \quad (1)$$

where θ^T and θ^S are the teacher and student parameters respectively, α is the KD weight parameter, $\mathcal{L}_{CE}$ is the Cross Entropy (CE) loss, y_i is the label, N is the total number of training samples and $\mathcal{L}_{KD}$ is the symmetric Kullback-Leibler (KL) divergence (Kullback, 1997) between the teacher and the student logits, i.e. we sum both the forward and reverse KL.

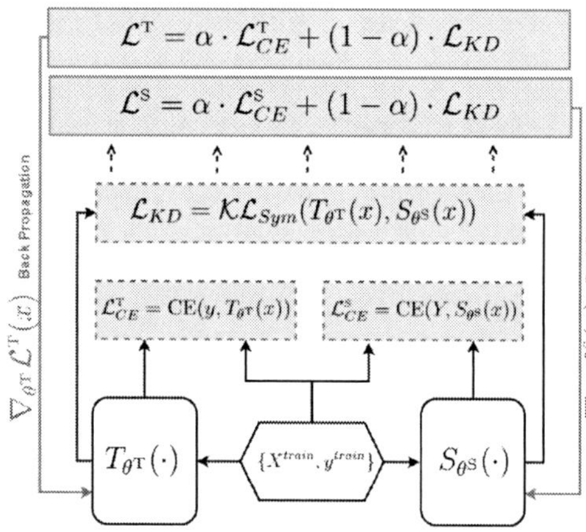

Figure 1: The Co-Distill architecture

In addition to CE loss, the teacher "learns" from the student and is trained to minimize the $\mathcal{L}_{KD}$ loss. It is worth mentioning that we always train the teacher at the first epoch with an α value of 1. We do so to avoid propagating low confident information to the teacher at the beginning of the training. After the first epoch, the feedback of $\mathcal{L}_{KD}$ improves the overall performance of both teacher and student models.

3.2 CD plus Label Refinement (CD+LR)

We further enhance CD by refining the training labels based on loss values at early epochs. In LR, an auxiliary classifier is trained to flag noisy samples, which in turn are re-labeled by the main model. In prior work on noisy labels (Arpit et al., 2017; Dehghani et al., 2018; Wang et al., 2019b) it has been observed that small training losses at early

Model	CoLA	SST-2	MRPC	RTE	QNLI	QQP	MNLI	Avg.
				0%				
BERT-base	61.9	93.1	90.9	68.6	91.6	91.6	85.0	83.2
w/o KD	51.3	91.3	87.5	59.9	89.2	88.5	82.1	78.5
Vanilla	56.4	92.0	90.0	68.6	90.3	90.6	85.0	81.8
				25%				
BERT-base	46.7	91.5	75.7	61.0	87.9	72.4	81.8	73.9
with CD	47.5	93.2	78.7	62.5	88.2	71.3	82.8	74.9
with CD+LR	48.6	92.8	78.7	60.3	88.6	74.0	82.3	75.0
w/o KD	39.1	90.4	79.9	61.0	84.5	67.3	79.3	71.6
Self-DSTL	43.5	90.5	79.7	60.6	84.1	69.3	80.0	72.5
Vanilla	40.2	90.9	79.2	61.7	85.9	72.9	80.3	73.0
CD	45.1	90.6	79.2	63.2	85.5	70.5	80.7	73.5
CD+LR	**46.1**	**91.3**	**80.9**	**63.5**	**86.9**	**73.8**	**81.0**	**74.8**
				50%				
BERT-base	17.7	56.7	68.4	59.2	64.7	63.6	76.5	58.1
with CD	16.0	56.5	70.8	55.6	62.7	71.3	76.8	58.5
with CD+LR	17.2	61.7	71.8	56.3	62.7	71.3	77.0	59.7
w/o KD	8.3	55.0	66.6	57.0	56.5	67.3	72.2	54.7
Self-DSTL	8.8	57.6	68.1	58.4	57.3	69.3	73.2	56.1
Vanilla	11.9	60.0	68.6	**58.5**	60.3	66.1	75.0	57.2
CD	13.6	60.3	69.1	57.4	60.0	70.5	75.1	58.0
CD+LR	**17.7**	**64.1**	**71.1**	57.4	**60.9**	**73.8**	**76.6**	**60.2**

Table 1: Performances on GLUE dev sets of models trained on 0%, 25%, and 50% of noisy labels. Dash lines separate teacher (up) and student models.

epochs are more likely to indicate that a sample is clean.

Instead, we assume that we have access to a small subset of validation data where noisy and clean samples are known a priori (see Section 4.1). We train both teacher and student with Co-Distill for 2 epochs,[1] and then calculate $\mathcal{L}_{CE}^{T}$ and $\mathcal{L}_{CE}^{S}$ for each sample in the validation set.

We use these values as features for a discriminator model $D(.)$ trained to predict whether a sample is noisy. Once it is trained, $D(.)$ is used to flag noisy training samples, so that the teacher re-labels them. Finally, we resume the co-distillation for the remaining epochs while calculating the CE loss using the new labels.

[1]Empirically, we found that it works well on most of the tasks we experimented on.

4 Experiments

4.1 Dataset and Evaluation

We experiment on 7 tasks from the GLUE benchmark (Wang et al., 2018): 2 single-sentence (CoLA and SST-2) and 5 sentence-pair (MRPC, RTE, QQP, QNLI, and MNLI) classification tasks. Following prior work, we report Matthews correlation on CoLA and accuracy for the other tasks. Since GLUE test sets are hidden and the number of submissions to leaderboard is limited, we held-out 10% of the training set for validation and used the rest for training. We used this validation set to train the discriminator as well as for hyper-parameter tuning, while official GLUE dev sets are used to evaluate the models.

We test our methods on training sets with 25% and 50% noisy labels[2]. We introduce the same level of noise for the validation sets. Following prior

[2]We do not evaluate beyond 50% of noise because many GLUE tasks are binary classification.

works (Jiang et al., 2018; Dong et al., 2019; Garg et al., 2021), we inject artificial noise by randomly changing the original labels of the training samples.

4.2 Baselines

We compare our noise mitigation methods with 3 popular baselines:

- **w/o KD** In this setting, only the CE loss is used. This baseline is used as a witness.
- **Vanilla-KD** Here, we select the best performing α value for each task.
- **Self-DSTL** In Self-Distillation (Dong et al., 2019), the student is first trained for few epochs on hard labels only, and the best checkpoint is used to generate logits on the training data. For the rest of the epochs the student is trained on both hard and its own soft labels.

4.3 Implementation

We use as our teacher the 12-layer BERT-base-uncased model (Devlin et al., 2019), and the pre-trained 6-layer distillBERT (Sanh et al., 2019) to initialize all student models. We use `scikit-learn` (Pedregosa et al., 2011) to train a Random Forest discriminator (Breiman, 2001) as our auxiliary classifier. For all models, we perform hyper-parameter tuning and best model selection based on early stopping on noisy validation sets. We report average results over 3 random seeds.

4.4 Results

Table 1 shows performances on GLUE dev sets of 3 teachers and 5 student models trained on clean (0%), 25% and 50% of noisy training sets. As expected, the performance of all models drops drastically with noise. For instance, the teacher and vanilla student average performances drop by 25.1% and 24.7% respectively when we train with 50% of noisy labels. Among all baselines, training the student solely on hard labels (w/o KD) performs the worst under all levels of noise.

Performing distillation with the student logits itself (Self-DSTL) slightly improves the performances by 0.5% and 1.5% on 25% and 50% noise level respectively. However, using teacher logits (Vanilla) for distillation always performs better than using that of the student by 1% on average. This indicates that the teacher knowledge remains crucial even under a noisy label setting.

Overall, our method CD leads to an average gain of 0.5% and 0.8% on top of the Vanilla baseline at 25% and 50% noise level respectively. Moreover, enhancing the CD methods with label refinement (CD+LR) significantly boosts these scores by 1.3% and 2.2% respectively. CD+LR consistently outperforms Vanilla KD across all tasks and noise levels, except at 50% noise for MRPC. It is worth noting that our methods are more effective under extreme noise level, since the gap with Vanilla KD gets larger at 50% noise level (the max for binary classification).

On the teacher side, we observe that the teachers obtained with our methods outperform the other teachers. The CD+LR teacher is better than its naive counterpart by 1.1% and 1.6% on 25% and 50% noise level respectively. This observation is inline with Han et al. (2018) who find that in Co-teaching, the two networks communicating with each other get improved. More interestingly, results show that CD+LR students outperform significantly (>2%) the naive and slightly (0.2%) their respective teachers. This is mainly due to the tendency of over-parameterized neural networks (teachers) to fit noisy labels (Han et al., 2018; Jiang et al., 2018), compared to smaller models (students in our cases). This suggests that in a high noise setting, training a robust teacher is important as much as training the student.

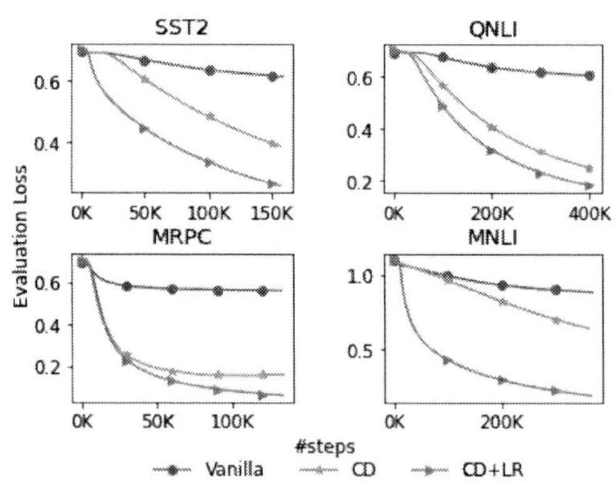

Figure 2: Validation (on GLUE dev sets) curve for the 3 student models trained on 50% of noisy labels.

We plot the losses on dev sets at early steps to better understand how our methods combat noisy labels. Figure 2 shows dev loss values on 4 GLUE tasks[3] for Vanilla KD, CD, and CD+LR methods. First, we observe that the loss curve of Vanilla KD

[3]Similar figures are observed on the remaining 3 tasks.

flattens at early stages. We investigated the training loss and noticed that it rather decreases, mainly due over-fitting the noise labels.

Co-Distillation (CD) shows better signs of mitigating noise, as the loss decreases slowly on MNLI and sharply on QNLI and MRPC. Adding LR leads to a sharp drop, followed by a steady decrease of loss values. The drop happens immediately after refining the training set labels, which seems crucial for large datasets like MNLI and SST-2.

5 Conclusion

We present the first study on Knowledge Distillation when learning from noisy labels in NLU, and show that the problem is extremely challenging. Future work involves conducting a comparative study on the robustness of state-of-the-art KD techniques against noisy labels, and merging them within our methods. We hope that our study will encourage future research on KD in the noisy label setting, a genuine setting in real world applications.

Acknowledgments

We thank Mindspore[4] for the partial support of this work, which is a new deep learning computing framework.

[normalem]ulem

References

Eric Arazo, Diego Ortego, Paul Albert, Noel O'Connor, and Kevin McGuinness. 2019. Unsupervised label noise modeling and loss correction. In *International Conference on Machine Learning*, pages 312–321. PMLR.

Ehsan Mohammady Ardehaly and Aron Culotta. 2018. Learning from noisy label proportions for classifying online social data. *Social Network Analysis and Mining*, 8(1):1–18.

Devansh Arpit, Stanisław Jastrzębski, Nicolas Ballas, David Krueger, Emmanuel Bengio, Maxinder S. Kanwal, Tegan Maharaj, Asja Fischer, Aaron Courville, Yoshua Bengio, and Simon Lacoste-Julien. 2017. A closer look at memorization in deep networks.

Hessam Bagherinezhad, Maxwell Horton, Mohammad Rastegari, and Ali Farhadi. 2018. Label refinery: Improving imagenet classification through label progression. *arXiv preprint arXiv:1805.02641*.

Leo Breiman. 2001. Random forests. *Machine learning*, 45(1):5–32.

[4]`https://www.mindspore.cn/`

Tom B Brown, Benjamin Mann, Nick Ryder, Melanie Subbiah, Jared Kaplan, Prafulla Dhariwal, Arvind Neelakantan, Pranav Shyam, Girish Sastry, Amanda Askell, et al. 2020. Language models are few-shot learners. *arXiv preprint arXiv:2005.14165*.

Cristian Buciluă, Rich Caruana, and Alexandru Niculescu-Mizil. 2006. Model compression. In *Proceedings of the 12th ACM SIGKDD international conference on Knowledge discovery and data mining*, pages 535–541.

Mostafa Dehghani, Arash Mehrjou, Stephan Gouws, Jaap Kamps, and Bernhard Schölkopf. 2018. Fidelity-weighted learning. In *International Conference on Learning Representations*.

Jacob Devlin, Ming-Wei Chang, Kenton Lee, and Kristina Toutanova. 2019. Bert: Pre-training of deep bidirectional transformers for language understanding.

Bin Dong, Jikai Hou, Yiping Lu, and Zhihua Zhang. 2019. Distillation = early stopping? harvesting dark knowledge utilizing anisotropic information retrieval for overparameterized neural network. *stat*, 1050:2.

Yang Fan, Yingce Xia, Lijun Wu, Shufang Xie, Weiqing Liu, Jiang Bian, Tao Qin, Xiang-Yang Li, and Tie-Yan Liu. 2020. Learning to teach with deep interactions. *arXiv preprint arXiv:2007.04649*.

Benoît Frénay and Michel Verleysen. 2013. Classification in the presence of label noise: a survey. *IEEE transactions on neural networks and learning systems*, 25(5):845–869.

Jie Fu, Xue Geng, Zhijian Duan, Bohan Zhuang, Xingdi Yuan, Adam Trischler, Jie Lin, Chris Pal, and Hao Dong. 2020. Role-wise data augmentation for knowledge distillation. *arXiv preprint arXiv:2004.08861*.

Siddhant Garg, Goutham Ramakrishnan, and Varun Thumbe. 2021. Towards robustness to label noise in text classification via noise modeling. *arXiv preprint arXiv:2101.11214*.

Abbas Ghaddar and Philippe Langlais. 2019. Contextualized word representations from distant supervision with and for ner. In *Proceedings of the 5th Workshop on Noisy User-generated Text (W-NUT 2019)*, pages 101–108.

Abbas Ghaddar, Philippe Langlais, Ahmad Rashid, and Mehdi Rezagholizadeh. 2021a. Context-aware adversarial training for name regularity bias in named entity recognition. *Trans. Assoc. Comput. Linguistics*, 9:586–604.

Abbas Ghaddar, Philippe Langlais, Mehdi Rezagholizadeh, and Ahmad Rashid. 2021b. End-to-end self-debiasing framework for robust NLU training. In *Findings of the Association for Computational Linguistics: ACL/IJCNLP 2021, Online Event,*

August 1-6, 2021, volume ACL/IJCNLP 2021 of *Findings of ACL*, pages 1923–1929. Association for Computational Linguistics.

B Han, Q Yao, X Yu, G Niu, M Xu, W Hu, IW Tsang, and M Sugiyama. 2018. Co-teaching: Robust training of deep neural networks with extremely noisy labels. In *32nd Conference on Neural Information Processing Systems (NIPS)*. NEURAL INFORMATION PROCESSING SYSTEMS (NIPS).

Bo Han, Quanming Yao, Tongliang Liu, Gang Niu, Ivor W Tsang, James T Kwok, and Masashi Sugiyama. 2020. A survey of label-noise representation learning: Past, present and future. *arXiv preprint arXiv:2011.04406*.

Geoffrey Hinton, Oriol Vinyals, and Jeffrey Dean. 2015. Distilling the knowledge in a neural network. In *NIPS Deep Learning and Representation Learning Workshop*.

Aref Jafari, Mehdi Rezagholizadeh, Pranav Sharma, and Ali Ghodsi. 2021. Annealing knowledge distillation. In *Proceedings of the 16th Conference of the European Chapter of the Association for Computational Linguistics: Main Volume*, pages 2493–2504, Online. Association for Computational Linguistics.

Mingi Ji, Byeongho Heo, and Sungrae Park. 2021. Show, attend and distill: Knowledge distillation via attention-based feature matching. In *Proceedings of the AAAI Conference on Artificial Intelligence*.

Lu Jiang, Zhengyuan Zhou, Thomas Leung, Li-Jia Li, and Li Fei-Fei. 2018. Mentornet: Learning data-driven curriculum for very deep neural networks on corrupted labels. In *International Conference on Machine Learning*, pages 2304–2313. PMLR.

Xiaoqi Jiao, Yichun Yin, Lifeng Shang, Xin Jiang, Xiao Chen, Linlin Li, Fang Wang, and Qun Liu. 2020. Tinybert: Distilling bert for natural language understanding. In *Proceedings of the 2020 Conference on Empirical Methods in Natural Language Processing: Findings*, pages 4163–4174.

Ishan Jindal, Daniel Pressel, Brian Lester, and Matthew Nokleby. 2019. An effective label noise model for dnn text classification. In *Proceedings of the 2019 Conference of the North American Chapter of the Association for Computational Linguistics: Human Language Technologies, Volume 1 (Long and Short Papers)*, pages 3246–3256.

Ehsan Kamalloo, Mehdi Rezagholizadeh, Peyman Passban, and Ali Ghodsi. 2021. Not far away, not so close: Sample efficient nearest neighbour data augmentation via minimax. In *Findings of the Association for Computational Linguistics: ACL/IJCNLP 2021, Online Event, August 1-6, 2021*, volume ACL/IJCNLP 2021 of *Findings of ACL*, pages 3522–3533. Association for Computational Linguistics.

Solomon Kullback. 1997. *Information theory and statistics*. Courier Corporation.

Junnan Li, Yongkang Wong, Qi Zhao, and Mohan S Kankanhalli. 2019. Learning to learn from noisy labeled data. In *Proceedings of the IEEE/CVF Conference on Computer Vision and Pattern Recognition*, pages 5051–5059.

Tianda Li, Ahmad Rashid, Aref Jafari, Pranav Sharma, Ali Ghodsi, and Mehdi Rezagholizadeh. 2021. How to select one among all? an extensive empirical study towards the robustness of knowledge distillation in natural language understanding. *arXiv preprint arXiv:2109.05696*.

Wen Li, Limin Wang, Wei Li, Eirikur Agustsson, and Luc Van Gool. 2017. Webvision database: Visual learning and understanding from web data. *arXiv preprint arXiv:1708.02862*.

Peyman Passban, Yimeng Wu, Mehdi Rezagholizadeh, and Qun Liu. 2021. ALP-KD: attention-based layer projection for knowledge distillation. In *Thirty-Fifth AAAI Conference on Artificial Intelligence, AAAI 2021, Thirty-Third Conference on Innovative Applications of Artificial Intelligence, IAAI 2021, The Eleventh Symposium on Educational Advances in Artificial Intelligence, EAAI 2021, Virtual Event, February 2-9, 2021*, pages 13657–13665. AAAI Press.

Fabian Pedregosa, Gaël Varoquaux, Alexandre Gramfort, Vincent Michel, Bertrand Thirion, Olivier Grisel, Mathieu Blondel, Peter Prettenhofer, Ron Weiss, Vincent Dubourg, et al. 2011. Scikit-learn: Machine learning in python. *the Journal of machine Learning research*, 12:2825–2830.

Colin Raffel, Noam Shazeer, Adam Roberts, Katherine Lee, Sharan Narang, Michael Matena, Yanqi Zhou, Wei Li, and Peter J Liu. 2020. Exploring the limits of transfer learning with a unified text-to-text transformer. *Journal of Machine Learning Research*, 21:1–67.

Pranav Rajpurkar, Robin Jia, and Percy Liang. 2018. Know what you don't know: Unanswerable questions for squad. In *Proceedings of the 56th Annual Meeting of the Association for Computational Linguistics (Volume 2: Short Papers)*, pages 784–789.

Ahmad Rashid, Vasileios Lioutas, Abbas Ghaddar, and Mehdi Rezagholizadeh. 2020. Towards zero-shot knowledge distillation for natural language processing. *CoRR*, abs/2012.15495.

Ahmad Rashid, Vasileios Lioutas, and Mehdi Rezagholizadeh. 2021. MATE-KD: Masked adversarial TExt, a companion to knowledge distillation. In *Proceedings of the 59th Annual Meeting of the Association for Computational Linguistics and the 11th International Joint Conference on Natural Language Processing (Volume 1: Long Papers)*, pages 1062–1071, Online. Association for Computational Linguistics.

Mengye Ren, Wenyuan Zeng, Bin Yang, and Raquel Urtasun. 2018. Learning to reweight examples for robust deep learning. In *International Conference on Machine Learning*, pages 4334–4343. PMLR.

Victor Sanh, Lysandre Debut, Julien Chaumond, and Thomas Wolf. 2019. Distilbert, a distilled version of bert: smaller, faster, cheaper and lighter. *arXiv preprint arXiv:1910.01108*.

Zhiqing Sun, Hongkun Yu, Xiaodan Song, Renjie Liu, Yiming Yang, and Denny Zhou. 2020. Mobilebert: a compact task-agnostic bert for resource-limited devices. In *Proceedings of the 58th Annual Meeting of the Association for Computational Linguistics*, pages 2158–2170.

Sunil Thulasidasan, Tanmoy Bhattacharya, Jeff Bilmes, Gopinath Chennupati, and Jamal Mohd-Yusof. 2019. Combating label noise in deep learning using abstention. *arXiv preprint arXiv:1905.10964*.

Iulia Turc, Ming-Wei Chang, Kenton Lee, and Kristina Toutanova. 2019. Well-read students learn better: On the importance of pre-training compact models. *arXiv preprint arXiv:1908.08962*.

Alex Wang, Yada Pruksachatkun, Nikita Nangia, Amanpreet Singh, Julian Michael, Felix Hill, Omer Levy, and Samuel R Bowman. 2019a. Superglue: A stickier benchmark for general-purpose language understanding systems. *Advances in Neural Information Processing Systems*, 32.

Alex Wang, Amanpreet Singh, Julian Michael, Felix Hill, Omer Levy, and Samuel Bowman. 2018. GLUE: A Multi-Task Benchmark and Analysis Platform for Natural Language Understanding. In *Proceedings of the 2018 EMNLP Workshop BlackboxNLP: Analyzing and Interpreting Neural Networks for NLP*, pages 353–355.

Wenhui Wang, Furu Wei, Li Dong, Hangbo Bao, Nan Yang, and Ming Zhou. 2020. Minilm: Deep self-attention distillation for task-agnostic compression of pre-trained transformers. *arXiv preprint arXiv:2002.10957*.

Yisen Wang, Xingjun Ma, Zaiyi Chen, Yuan Luo, Jinfeng Yi, and James Bailey. 2019b. Symmetric cross entropy for robust learning with noisy labels. In *Proceedings of the IEEE/CVF International Conference on Computer Vision*, pages 322–330.

Yimeng Wu, Peyman Passban, Mehdi Rezagholizadeh, and Qun Liu. 2020. Why skip if you can combine: A simple knowledge distillation technique for intermediate layers. In *Proceedings of the 2020 Conference on Empirical Methods in Natural Language Processing, EMNLP 2020, Online, November 16-20, 2020*, pages 1016–1021. Association for Computational Linguistics.

George-Eduard Zaharia, Andrei-Marius Avram, Dumitru-Clementin Cercel, and Traian Rebedea. 2021. Dialect identification through adversarial learning and knowledge distillation on romanian BERT. In *Proceedings of the Eighth Workshop on NLP for Similar Languages, Varieties and Dialects, VarDial@EACL 2021, Kiyv, Ukraine, April 20, 2021*, pages 113–119. Association for Computational Linguistics.

Zizhao Zhang, Han Zhang, Sercan O Arik, Honglak Lee, and Tomas Pfister. 2020. Distilling effective supervision from severe label noise. In *Proceedings of the IEEE/CVF Conference on Computer Vision and Pattern Recognition*, pages 9294–9303.

Integrating Transformers and Knowledge Graphs for Twitter Stance Detection

Thomas Hikaru Clark[♠], **Costanza Conforti**[♠], **Fangyu Liu**[♠], **Zaiqiao Meng**[♠], **Ehsan Shareghi**[♣♠], **Nigel Collier**[♠]

[♠]Language Technology Lab, University of Cambridge

[♣]Department of Data Science and AI, Monash University

[♠]{thc44, cc918, fl399, zm324, nhc30}@cam.ac.uk

[♣]ehsan.shareghi@monash.edu

Abstract

Stance detection (SD) entails classifying the sentiment of a text towards a given target, and is a relevant sub-task for opinion mining and social media analysis. Recent works have explored knowledge infusion — supplementing the linguistic competence and latent knowledge of large pre-trained language models with structured knowledge graphs (KGs), yet few works have applied such methods to the SD task. In this work, we first perform stance-relevant knowledge probing on Transformers-based pre-trained models in a zero-shot setting, showing these models' latent real-world knowledge about SD targets and their sensitivity to context. We then propose novel knowledge-enriched stance detection models. We evaluate them on two Twitter stance datasets, achieving state-of-the-art performance on both.

1 Introduction

Stance detection (SD) involves identifying a text's stance towards a given target (for example, whether a tweet is supportive, against, or neutral towards *Joe Biden*). This is a challenging task with downstream use cases in opinion mining, fake news detection, and rumor verification (Küçük and Can, 2018; Fake News Challenge, 2017; Conforti et al., 2020). A major challenge for SD is the need for knowledge of current events and other fast-changing facts about the world.

Large pre-trained Transformer models trained on vast corpora (Vaswani et al., 2017; Devlin et al., 2019) have blurred the line between language models and knowledge bases, as shown by their performance on benchmarks like LAMA, which measure static factual knowledge (Petroni et al., 2020a; Radford et al., 2019). Recent works in SD have capitalized on the Transformer architecture; however, it remains uncertain how to adapt these models to the constantly shifting factual landscape found in SD tasks, for example in political tweets. At the same time, knowledge infusion (KI) approaches have had success in integrating KGs with Transformers for question-answering (QA) tasks, but there is a shortage of work on KI for SD.

Our contributions are as follows: 1) We perform stance-relevant knowledge probing on Transformers-based pre-trained models, showing these models' partial real-world knowledge and sensitivity to context, and 2) We train and evaluate knowledge-enriched stance detection models on two Twitter stance datasets, achieving state-of-the-art performance on both.

2 Previous Work

The original author baseline for the SemEval-16 SD task used an SVM classifier on hand-crafted features (Mohammad et al., 2017). More recent approaches for SD have achieved better performance using transfer learning with Transformer models, but without adding knowledge infusion (Ghosh et al., 2019; Schiller et al., 2021; Kaushal et al., 2021). This typically involves concatenating a tweet and target and feeding it into a Transformer model with a classification layer attached. To our knowledge, Kawintiranon and Singh (2021) is the only SD work using "knowledge enhancement", but this approach was based on identifying stance-signaling words rather than using KGs.

Most attempts to augment Transformer models with structured knowledge from KGs have focused on QA tasks, such as CommonsenseQA (Talmor et al., 2019), not SD. Bian et al. (2021) used ConceptNet (Speer and Havasi, 2013) to extract knowledge descriptions relating entities in each question to entities in each answer choice via multi-hop reasoning on a KG, with a BERT-based classifier to choose the best answer. Similarly, K-BERT (Liu et al., 2019) enriches entities in an input sentence based on lookup in a KG. The success of these methods suggests that downstream tasks can benefit from contextual priming, where the same input

Proceedings of the 2021 EMNLP Workshop W-NUT: The Seventh Workshop on Noisy User-generated Text, pages 304–312
November 11, 2021.

supplemented with additional factual context leads to better predictions. This can be contrasted with approaches like K-Adapter and KnowBERT, which infuse knowledge by modifying the model architecture, rather than by adding context to the input (Wang et al., 2020; Peters et al., 2020). One advantage of contextual priming is the ability to leave a model's architecture largely unchanged, requiring only a method of collecting and generating useful factual context.

3 Probing Transformers for Stance-Relevant Knowledge

In this section, we seek to establish a lower bound for the stance-relevant knowledge already present in Transformer models before doing any knowledge infusion. Rather than testing recall of encyclopedic facts, we probe whether models make stance-related inferences regarding real-world entities in a human-like way. The three models we test are RoBERTa-Base (Liu et al., 2020), RoBERTa-Large, and Twitter-RoBERTa (Barbieri et al., 2020). RoBERTa is pre-trained on a large internet corpus, including news articles, while Twitter-RoBERTa is trained on $\sim 58M$ tweets, making these models good candidates for political SD on Twitter. Using each model in a masked language modeling setting, we feed it a sentence with a single word replaced by the special `[MASK]` token, returning a probability distribution over all vocabulary tokens. Rather than using an automatically-generated knowledge benchmark like LAMA (Petroni et al., 2020b), we draw on a human-in-the-loop paradigm (Nie et al., 2019) and manually design probes relevant to the SD task. Examples involve public figures and political issues that appear as targets in major SD datasets (Mohammad et al., 2017; Grimminger and Klinger, 2021), such as *Donald Trump, Hillary Clinton*, and *climate change*. We evaluate the models using **Accuracy@1**, which is the percentage of prompts for which the highest-probability token generated by a model is appropriate in context, e.g. factually correct or aligned with reasonable inferences. Some key example pairs are shown below:

(1) The Proud `[MASK]`, a far-right group, held a rally.

(2) The protests were sparked by the killing of George `[MASK]`, an unarmed black man in Minneapolis, Minnesota.

In example (1) above, all models were able to predict "Boys" for the masked token. In example (2), all models predicted "Zimmerman" rather than the desired "Floyd"; this illustrates how models can quickly become outdated when new words and names enter common usage after a model is pre-trained.

(3) I think that climate change is such a `[MASK]`. Save the earth!

(4) I think that climate change is such a `[MASK]`. Drill, baby, drill!

For the above pair of probes, we test how the presence of pro- and anti-environmentalist slogans impact stance-relevant predictions. Both RoBERTa models have reasonable predictions, outputting "threat" and "problem" for (3) and "hoax" for (4). This shows how the models can sometimes leverage stance-relevant knowledge to make better predictions. This is not always the case, however:

(5) Joe has a bumper sticker that reads 'Drill Baby Drill'. He thinks climate change is a `[MASK]`.

(6) Joe has a bumper sticker that reads 'Drill Baby Drill'. He thinks climate change is `[MASK]`.

For (5), all models predict "hoax", which initially looks like a good stance-aware inference. For (6), however, all models predict "real". The deletion of a single article, "a", caused all models to make a stance-incongruent prediction.

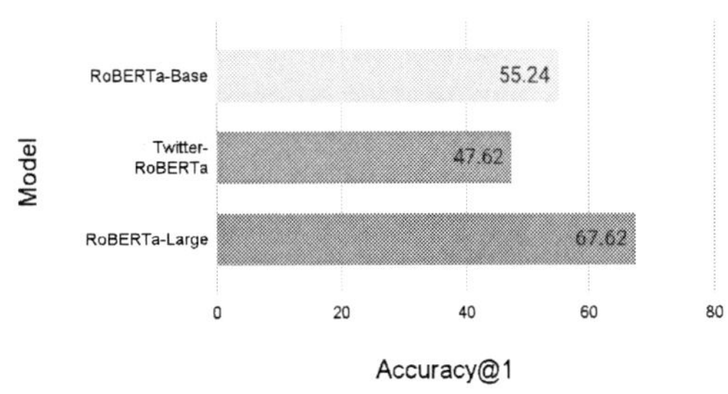

Figure 1: Accuracy@1 on a test set of 105 handpicked stance-relevant knowledge probes, showing the superior performance of RoBERTa-Large compared to the other models. The correctness of the answers was manually labeled by the first author.

We include additional examples of prompts in the *Appendix*, as well as a breakdown of probing performance by model in Figure 1. The key points of our probing analysis are that a) Transformer models contain latent stance-relevant knowledge that can inform SD tasks, b) RoBERTa-Large beats smaller models, and c) stance-aware predictions can often be overruled by context. The results establish a promising lower bound on the stance-relevant knowledge of LMs, yet a significant gap remains. We therefore propose a way of using KGs to infuse knowledge specifically for SD tasks.

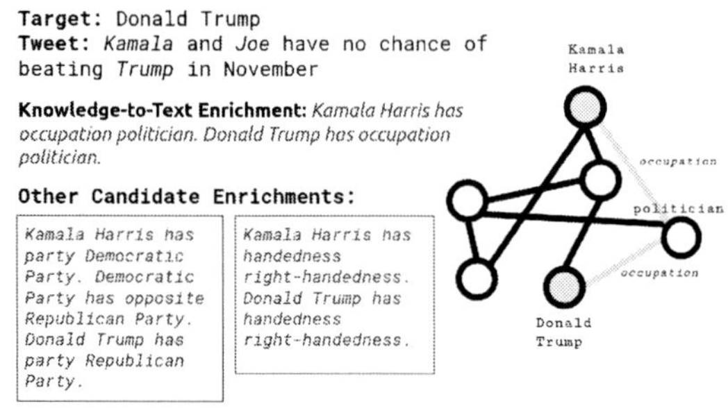

Figure 2: Illustration of our proposed path-based knowledge infusion method.

4 Knowledge Infusion for SD

4.1 Basic Knowledge Infusion

A KG is described by a list of triples of the form (e_1, r, e_2), where e_1 and e_2 are entities (nodes) linked by the relation (edge) r. To leverage such knowledge, we follow the intuition that short descriptions of unfamiliar entities may operate as a form of contextual priming. This is supported by the knowledge probing literature, as well as works like AUTOPROMPT (Shin et al., 2020) which learn to construct optimal contextual triggers for eliciting knowledge from a LM.

Given a tweet, we use the `spaCy` entity linker (Honnibal and Montani, 2020), which identifies spans in a text that refer to entities from the Wikidata KG (Vrandečić and Krötzsch, 2014). `spaCy` can identify different forms of an entity, and outputs short descriptions of any found entities. We then generate short knowledge descriptions of the form "[Entity], [Description]" for all entities found in a tweet. For example, a tweet containing the string 'Putin' would be paired with the following description: "Vladimir Putin, 2nd and 4th President of Russia". These descriptions are prepended to the tweet along with the stance detection target, separated from the tweet string by a special separator token. This enrichment process is done for both the training data and the testing data. We report results for this approach in Section 5.

4.2 Custom Knowledge Graph Construction and Pathfinding

The previous approach operates as a form of knowledge lookup, but does not exploit the informative relations between entities that may be contained in a KG. Prior works have exploited multi-hop knowledge paths within a KG to improve NLU performance (Bian et al., 2021), an approach we now apply to SD. To reduce the computational cost of finding knowledge pathways, we propose a customized collection approach of filtering for Wikidata triples within a small number of hops from the target entities of the SD datasets. Additionally, we include Wikidata triples relating to trending tropes, which we identify by finding words and collocations with a high temporal concentration in a large Twitter dataset spanning the timeframe of the SD task. Collocations are identified using Pointwise Mutual Information (PMI). Examples of trending tropes are provided in the *Appendix*. In short, we use several strategies to limit the size of the KG while keeping the entities and relations most likely to help with SD.

To infuse knowledge, we use our custom KG to find knowledge pathways connecting entities in a tweet to the SD targets. Since there are many possible pathways between two nodes in a KG, we limit paths to length 3 and choose the minimum cost path. We initially assign edge costs using a random walk strategy, which penalizes knowledge paths through less informative hub nodes. An example of low and high informativeness pathways found by the random walk strategy is shown below, reflecting the intuition that two people both holding the occupation President of the United States is a more informative relation than two people both working in Washington, D.C.

(7) *High Informativeness*: Donald Trump held the position of President of the United States. President of the United States has officeholder Joe Biden.

(8) *Low Informativeness*: Donald Trump has work location Washington, D.C. Presidential transition of Joe Biden has headquarters location Washington, D.C.

We turn any found knowledge pathways into natural language knowledge descriptions that are prepended to the tweet. The example shown in Figure 2 shows how this approach could plausibly improve SD performance. Suppose a tweet mentions the entity "Kamala", but the model has not been exposed to many instances of this entity in its training data. The SD task is to determine the tweet's stance towards Donald Trump. Using a KG, the model establishes a knowledge pathway from Kamala Harris to Donald Trump, reflecting the knowledge that both are politicians.

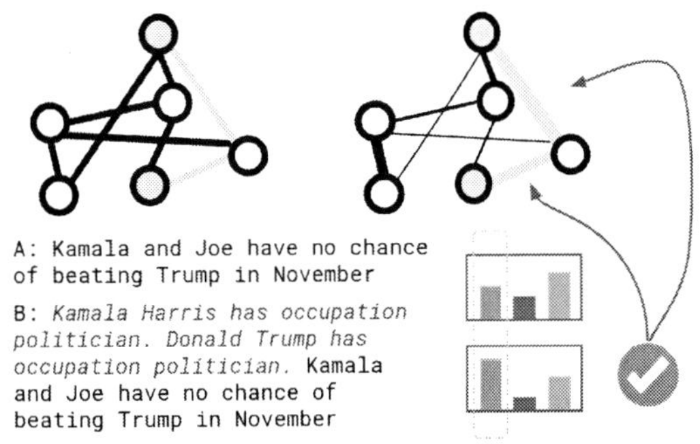

Figure 3: In this synthetic example, the tweet mentions Kamala Harris, who is connected to Donald Trump through a two-hop knowledge path. This knowledge path is tested against a no-enrichment baseline. Since the knowledge enrichment leads to a higher probability for the correct label, the corresponding edges in the KG are strengthened.

4.3 Edge Cost Tuning

A major problem for our knowledge infusion approach is finding informative multi-hop knowledge paths. While the random-walk edge weighting method is a first step, it is highly dependent on the properties of the KG being traversed. Secondly, this method does not take advantage of the available training data to improve the estimates of edge cost. As a result, we propose a method called *Edge Cost Tuning* (ECT) for using the available training data to test KG edges for informativeness.

ECT builds on the previous path-based knowledge infusion model, using it to evaluate the helpfulness of various knowledge paths. For each tweet in the training set, our model finds the lowest-cost knowledge path from the target to an entity in that tweet. Both an enriched and unenriched version of the tweet are fed to the model. If the enriched version causes the model to assign a higher probability to the correct label than the unenriched version, the costs for all links along that knowledge path are reduced. Otherwise, the costs for all links along that knowledge path are increased. This causes unhelpful edges in the KG to accumulate high costs, while helpful edges are promoted. Importantly, this procedure has an interpretable result, as edges in the KG can be sorted by their change in cost to understand which pieces of context were most helpful or unhelpful in making stance predictions. The *Appendix* contains before-and-after examples of the ECT method.

5 Experiments

We consider two Twitter datasets for SD: SemEval-16 (Mohammad et al., 2017) and Grimminger & Klinger (G&K) (Grimminger and Klinger, 2021). The first involves a range of controversial political targets, such as abortion, atheism, and the 2016 U.S. presidential election. The task is to predict a class label from among {*favor, against, neither*}. The dataset contains 2914 training examples and 1249 test examples. The second centers exclusively on the 2020 U.S. presidential election, and the prediction classes are *against, favor, neither, neutral,* and *mixed*. The dataset contains 2400 training examples and 600 test examples. Most SD models in the literature use SemEval-16 as a benchmark, and recent works have used BERT to achieve new state-of-the-art performance (Ghosh et al., 2019; Kaushal et al., 2021; Schiller et al., 2021; Kawintiranon and Singh, 2021).

Our general architecture for SD with Transformers involves the target (plus optional knowledge enrichments) and the tweet being concatenated with an intervening separator token before being fed into a RoBERTa model with a classification head. The weights of the entire network are updated during training. The architecture is very similar to that used in other Transformer-based SD models (Ghosh et al., 2019; Schiller et al., 2021; Kaushal et al., 2021). We compare our knowledge infusion models with base models fine-tuned on the same task data, as well as with K-Adapter, described in Section 2 (Wang et al., 2020).

As reported in Table 1, the best model for the SemEval-16 task was RoBERTa-Large with entity enrichment, while the best model for the G&K task was RoBERTa-Large with path enrichment and edge cost adjustment. One possible explanation for this is that ECT may work best when all examples for a task share a common topic (e.g. the 2020 election), as opposed to SemEval-16, which had 5 heterogeneous targets. Using a single KG with a single set of edge costs for such a task seems to underperform enrichment via direct entity lookup.

Model	SemEval-16 Acc.	SemEval-16 F1	Grimminger & Klinger Ag.	Fav.	Nei.	Neu.
Baseline*	-	69.1	79.0	89.0	95.0	53.0
RoBERTa-Base	71.8	71.4	81.8	91.4	93.9	60.0
Twitter-RoBERTa	71.4	71.7	82.7	90.0	94.5	56.4
K-Adapter	74.5	74.8	86.1	93.2	94.1	63.8
RoBERTa-Large	76.9	77.3	86.9	92.2	93.6	62.7
+ Entities	**77.2**	**78.5**	86.9	92.9	94.6	65.1
+ Paths	75.7	76.1	86.8	92.5	95.2	**68.3**
+ ECT	75.1	76.2	**87.0**	**93.7**	**96.0**	67.2

Table 1: Results for SemEval-16 Task: Mean Accuracy and F1 Scores (mean of Favor and Against labels). Results for Grimminger & Klinger Task: Mean F1 Scores by label: Against, Favor, Neither, and Neutral. The Mixed label was exceedingly rare in the dataset and no model ever predicted it, so all F1 scores for the Mixed label were 0. ECT = Edge Cost Tuning. *Baselines refer to author baselines from original SemEval and G&K papers.

The following are some examples from the G&K task that the knowledge-infused SD model with ECT correctly predicted while the unenriched model failed (knowledge descriptions are in italics):

(9) @realDonaldTrump It's today! The day I go to the polls and vote for Joe Biden and Kamala Harris. *donald trump held the position of president of the united states. president of the united states has officeholder joe biden.* (Correct Label: against Donald Trump)

(10) Trump must have stock in Regeneron. *stock, financial instrument. Donald Trump, 45th and current president of the United States. Regeneron Pharmaceuticals, pharmaceutical company.* (Correct Label: against Donald Trump)

(11) Biden or Kamala won't commit to their policy on packing the court, Joe's comment, "vote for me I'll let you know?" On fracking Joes flip flopping, Kamala is against fracking! VOTE RED! *donald trump has member of political party republican party. republican party has color red* (Correct Label: favor Donald Trump)

While there were also examples where the generated knowledge descriptions were irrelevant or noisy, these examples demonstrate how an appropriate knowledge description can improve downstream model performance. Examples (9) and (11) illustrate the utility of multi-hop reasoning, adding context relating Donald Trump to Joe Biden and the color red, respectively. Example (10) illustrates the usefulness of backing off to simple entity-enrichment in cases where no knowledge paths exist, providing useful additional context about the company Regeneron.

6 Conclusion

In this work, we highlighted three key points based on knowledge probing: Transformer models contain latent stance-relevant knowledge, RoBERTa-Large is better at this than the other models, and models can be misled by sentence context. We also established new state-of-the-art performance on two SD datasets using knowledge infusion. We introduce a novel method, *Edge Cost Tuning*, that uses training data to re-weight the connections in a knowledge graph, which produced best results on one of the two SD tasks. Our approach depends greatly on choice of KG and edge cost weighting method, so future work can explore additional ways of filtering for informative edges in a KG.

References

Francesco Barbieri, Jose Camacho-Collados, Luis Espinosa Anke, and Leonardo Neves. 2020. TweetEval: Unified Benchmark and Comparative Evaluation for Tweet Classification.

Ning Bian, Xianpei Han, Bo Chen, and Le Sun. 2021. Benchmarking knowledge-enhanced commonsense question answering via knowledge-to-text transformation.

Costanza Conforti, Jakob Berndt, Mohammad Taher Pilehvar, Chryssi Giannitsarou, Flavio Toxvaerd, and Nigel Collier. 2020. Will-They-Won't-They: A Very Large Dataset for Stance Detection on Twitter. In *Proceedings of the 58th Annual Meeting of the Association for Computational Linguistics*, Stroudsburg, PA, USA. Association for Computational Linguistics.

Jacob Devlin, Ming Wei Chang, Kenton Lee, and Kristina Toutanova. 2019. BERT: Pre-training of deep bidirectional transformers for language understanding. In *NAACL HLT 2019 - 2019 Conference of the North American Chapter of the Association for Computational Linguistics: Human Language Technologies - Proceedings of the Conference*, volume 1.

Fake News Challenge. 2017. Fake News Challenge: Exploring how artificial intelligence technologies could be leveraged to combat fake news.

Shalmoli Ghosh, Prajwal Singhania, Siddharth Singh, Koustav Rudra, and Saptarshi Ghosh. 2019. Stance Detection in Web and Social Media: A Comparative

Study. In *Lecture Notes in Computer Science (including subseries Lecture Notes in Artificial Intelligence and Lecture Notes in Bioinformatics)*, volume 11696 LNCS.

Lara Grimminger and Roman Klinger. 2021. Hate towards the political opponent: A twitter corpus study of the 2020 us elections on the basis of offensive speech and stance detection.

Matthew Honnibal and Ines Montani. 2020. spacy. `https://github.com/explosion/spaCy`.

Ayush Kaushal, Avirup Saha, and Niloy Ganguly. 2021. tWT–WT: A dataset to assert the role of target entities for detecting stance of tweets. In *Proceedings of the 2021 Conference of the North American Chapter of the Association for Computational Linguistics: Human Language Technologies*, pages 3879–3889, Online. Association for Computational Linguistics.

Kornraphop Kawintiranon and Lisa Singh. 2021. Knowledge enhanced masked language model for stance detection. In *Proceedings of the 2021 Conference of the North American Chapter of the Association for Computational Linguistics: Human Language Technologies*, pages 4725–4735, Online. Association for Computational Linguistics.

Dilek Küçük and Fazli Can. 2018. Stance detection on tweets: An SVM-based approach.

Weijie Liu, Peng Zhou, Zhe Zhao, Zhiruo Wang, Qi Ju, Haotang Deng, and Ping Wang. 2019. K-BERT: Enabling language representation with knowledge graph.

Yinhan Liu, Myle Ott, Naman Goyal, Jingfei Du, Mandar Joshi, Danqi Chen, Omer Levy, Mike Lewis, Luke Zettlemoyer, and Veselin Stoyanov. 2020. RoBERTa: A Robustly Optimized BERT Pretraining Approach.

Saif M. Mohammad, Parinaz Sobhani, and Svetlana Kiritchenko. 2017. Stance and sentiment in Tweets. *ACM Transactions on Internet Technology*, 17(3).

Yixin Nie, Adina Williams, Emily Dinan, Mohit Bansal, Jason Weston, and Douwe Kiela. 2019. Adversarial NLI: A new benchmark for natural language understanding.

Matthew E. Peters, Mark Neumann, Robert L. Logan, Roy Schwartz, Vidur Joshi, Sameer Singh, and Noah A. Smith. 2020. Knowledge enhanced contextual word representations. In *EMNLP-IJCNLP 2019 - 2019 Conference on Empirical Methods in Natural Language Processing and 9th International Joint Conference on Natural Language Processing, Proceedings of the Conference*.

Fabio Petroni, Patrick Lewis, Aleksandra Piktus, Tim Rocktäschel, Yuxiang Wu, Alexander H. Miller, and Sebastian Riedel. 2020a. How context affects language models' factual predictions.

Fabio Petroni, Tim Rocktäschel, Patrick Lewis, Anton Bakhtin, Yuxiang Wu, Alexander H. Miller, and Sebastian Riedel. 2020b. Language models as knowledge bases? In *EMNLP-IJCNLP 2019 - 2019 Conference on Empirical Methods in Natural Language Processing and 9th International Joint Conference on Natural Language Processing, Proceedings of the Conference*.

Alec Radford, Jeffrey Wu, Rewon Child, David Luan, Dario Amodei, and Ilya Sutskever. 2019. Language Models are Unsupervised Multitask Learners | Enhanced Reader. *OpenAI Blog*, 1(8).

Benjamin Schiller, Johannes Daxenberger, and Iryna Gurevych. 2021. Stance Detection Benchmark: How Robust is Your Stance Detection? *KI - Kunstliche Intelligenz*.

Taylor Shin, Yasaman Razeghi, Robert L. Logan IV, Eric Wallace, and Sameer Singh. 2020. AutoPrompt: Eliciting Knowledge from Language Models with Automatically Generated Prompts.

Robert Speer and Catherine Havasi. 2013. ConceptNet 5: A Large Semantic Network for Relational Knowledge.

Alon Talmor, Jonathan Herzig, Nicholas Lourie, and Jonathan Berant. 2019. Commonsenseqa: A question answering challenge targeting commonsense knowledge.

Ashish Vaswani, Noam Shazeer, Niki Parmar, Jakob Uszkoreit, Llion Jones, Aidan N. Gomez, Łukasz Kaiser, and Illia Polosukhin. 2017. Attention is all you need. In *Advances in Neural Information Processing Systems*, volume 2017-Decem.

Denny Vrandečić and Markus Krötzsch. 2014. Wikidata: A free collaborative knowledgebase. *Commun. ACM*, 57(10):78–85.

Ruize Wang, Duyu Tang, Nan Duan, Zhongyu Wei, Xuanjing Huang, Jianshu Ji, Guihong Cao, Daxin Jiang, and Ming Zhou. 2020. K-ADAPTER: Infusing knowledge into pre-trained models with adapters.

A Trending Topics Identification

We hypothesize that knowledge of trending topics is important for political SD on Twitter for two main reasons: a) especially in the social media domain, trending topics can be very stance-signaling and b) pre-trained models will typically not have latent knowledge of these tropes because they are too temporally concentrated to be well-represented in the pre-training data. We implement a simple strategy for detecting tropes, based on three assumptions:

(1) Trending tropes will be relatively frequent n-grams.

(2) Trending tropes will be highly non-uniform in their distribution over time.

(3) Multi-word tropes will behave like collocations, with high pointwise mutual information between words.

For a given SD task, we sample a large selection of tweets from the same timeframe as the SD data (summer 2015 for SemEval-16, autumn 2020 for G&K). Within this sample, we choose uni-, bi-, and tri-grams that fit the above criteria. Figure 4 shows a sampling of discovered trending topics for the G&K SD task, each accompanied by a histogram of its occurrence over time.

B Results of Edge Cost Tuning

At the end of edge cost tuning, edges in the graph will have either lower, higher, or the same costs as before. Looking at the results, we see that the adjustments generally align with intuition. For example, in the G&K dataset, the triple `(politician, occupation_, Kamala Harris)` had one of the biggest decreases in cost after adjustment. This makes sense, because she may not have been a very prominent entity in the RoBERTa training data, but rose to much higher prominence in 2020 as Joe Biden's running mate. The decreased cost for that triple indicates that injecting this piece of knowledge generally helped predictions, while the lowered cost ensures that this piece of knowledge will be highly accessible to the model when evaluated on test data.

C Stance-Relevant Knowledge Probes

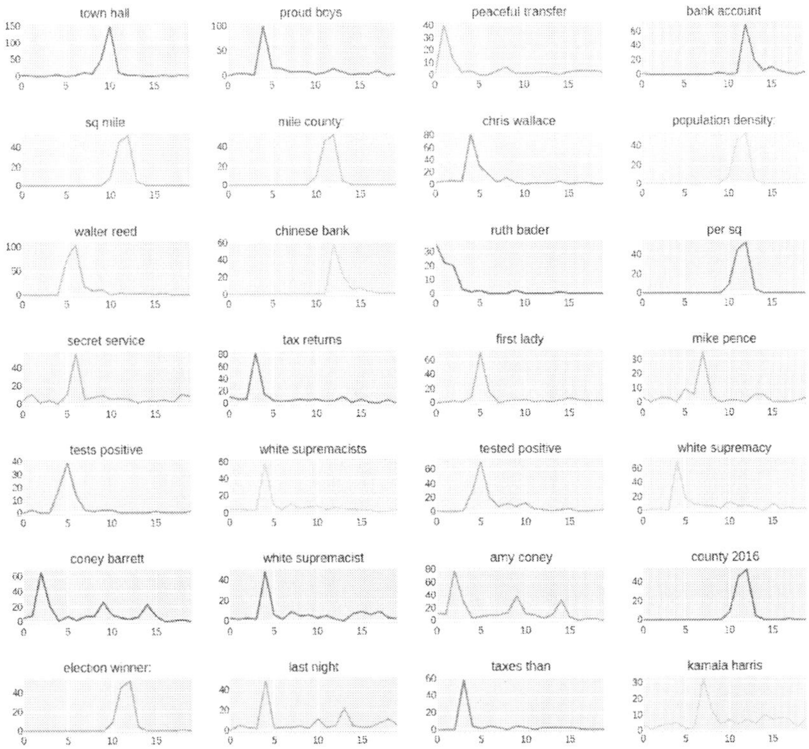

Figure 4: Examples of top bigram tropes for the G&K time frame on Twitter, restricted to tweets that mention Donald Trump.

Subject	Relation	Object
donald trump	occupation	politician
donald trump	position held	president of the ...
president of the ...	officeholder	joe biden
politician	occupation_	kamala harris
donald trump	member of political...	republican party
donald trump	award received	time person of the year
republican party	opposite of	democratic party
...	...	...
donald trump	award received	wwe hall of fame
trump tower	occupant	trump family
golf	country of origin	scotland
government	manifestation of	power
donald trump	significant person_	2021 storming of the...
2021 storming of the ...	instance of	demonstration

Table 2: Results of Edge Cost Tuning on G&K training data, arranged from biggest decrease in cost (top) to biggest increase in cost (bottom).

Prompt	RoBERTa-Large	RoBERTa-Base	Twitter-RoBERTa
Donald Trump spoke at a pro [MASK] rally on the anniversary of Roe v. Wade.	life	life	life
Hillary Clinton spoke at a pro [MASK] rally on the anniversary of Roe v. Wade.	abortion	life	abortion
Donald Trump is a member of the [MASK] Party.	Republican	Republican	Republican
Hillary Clinton is a member of the [MASK] Party.	Democratic	Democratic	Democratic
Ireland passed a referendum which repealed the constitutional ban on [MASK].	abortion	abortion	abortion
The Proud [MASK], a far-right group, held a rally.	Boys	Boys	Boys
Amy Coney [MASK] was nominated to the Supreme Court by President Trump.	Barrett	Barrett	worth
I believe in God, guns, and the Bible. Feminism is [MASK].	bullshit	bullshit	bullshit
I believe in LGBT rights and women's rights. Feminism is [MASK].	important	wrong	bullshit
I believe in God, guns, and the Bible. We should [MASK] be feminists.	all	not	all
I believe in LGBT rights and women's rights. We should [MASK] be feminists.	all	all	all
The remarks were delivered by [MASK], the 45th President of the United States.	Trump	Trump	Trump
The remarks were delivered by [MASK], the 44th President of the United States.	Obama	Trump	Obama
The remarks were delivered by [MASK], the 43rd President of the United States.	Bush	Obama	Obama
Kamala [MASK], the vice-presidential candidate, delivered a speech on Monday.	Harris	Harris	Harris
The protests were sparked by the killing of George [MASK], an unarmed black man in Minneapolis, Minnesota.	Zimmerman	Zimmerman	Zimmerman
The protests were sparked by the killing of Eric [MASK], an unarmed black man in New York City.	Garner	Garner	Garner
Please watch the documentary about melting ice caps. Climate change is [MASK].	real	real	real
Please watch the documentary about the global warming hoax. Climate change is [MASK].	real	real	real
I'm an atheist. The Bible is a book of [MASK].	lies	lies	God
I'm a Catholic. The Bible is a book of [MASK].	faith	faith	God

Table 4: A subset of the prompts used for stance-relevant knowledge probing. The prompts were manually chosen to relate to target entities from the SemEval and G&K SD tasks.

Detecting Cross-Geographic Biases in Toxicity Modeling on Social Media

Sayan Ghosh
University of Michigan
sayghosh@umich.edu

Dylan Baker
Google Research
dylanbaker@google.com

David Jurgens
University of Michigan
jurgens@google.com

Vinodkumar Prabhakaran
Google Research
vinodkpg@google.com

Abstract

Online social media platforms increasingly rely on Natural Language Processing (NLP) techniques to detect abusive content at scale in order to mitigate the harms it causes to their users. However, these techniques suffer from various sampling and association biases present in training data, often resulting in sub-par performance on content relevant to marginalized groups, potentially furthering disproportionate harms towards them. Studies on such biases so far have focused on only a handful of axes of disparities and subgroups that have annotations/lexicons available. Consequently, biases concerning non-Western contexts are largely ignored in the literature. In this paper, we introduce a weakly supervised method to robustly detect lexical biases in broader geocultural contexts. Through a case study on a publicly available toxicity detection model, we demonstrate that our method identifies salient groups of cross-geographic errors, and, in a follow up, demonstrate that these groupings reflect human judgments of offensive and inoffensive language in those geographic contexts. We also conduct analysis of a model trained on a dataset with ground truth labels to better understand these biases, and present preliminary mitigation experiments.

Sentence	Toxicity
You are a **Tamilian**!	0.74
You are a **Californian**!	0.17
ya ALLAH have mercy on those **muslims** suffering out there	0.67
ya ALLAH have mercy on those **people** suffering out there	0.36
Looks at these **presstitutes**, again only one side of the story!	0.18
Looks at these **prostitutes in the press**, again only one side of the story!	0.71
Madarchod, let it go!	0.10
Motherfucker, let it go!	0.97

Table 1: Example biases relevant to the Indian context, reflected in Perspective API's toxicity scores ($[0, 1]$).

1 Introduction

Online social media platforms have increasingly turned to NLP techniques to detect offensive and abusive content online at scale (e.g., the Perspective API), as a way to mitigate the harms it causes to people.[1] However, recent research has shown that these models often encode various societal biases against marginalized groups (Waseem, 2016; Caliskan et al., 2017; Park et al., 2018; van Aken et al., 2018; Dixon et al., 2018; Sap et al., 2019; Davidson et al., 2019; Hutchinson et al., 2020; Zhou et al., 2021) and can be adversarially deceived (Hosseini et al., 2017; Gröndahl et al., 2018; Kurita et al., 2019a), potentially furthering disproportionate harm to those in the margins. These models are also challenged by several dimensions of noise, especially when compared with the corpora they are trained on. For instance, social media text across the globe may contain code switched language generated by multilingual speakers, neologisms, and other orthographic variations rarely seen in training data. This poses additional challenges to detect and mitigate fairness failures in these models.

In this paper, we propose a new weakly supervised method (outlined in Figure 1) to address shortcomings of current bias detection methods and robustly detect lexical biases in models (i.e. biases that associate the presence or lack of toxicity with certain words) when applied to noisy text (in particular, text generated by social media users from non-predominantly Anglophone nations). We draw upon the observation that social stereotypes and biases in data often reflect the public discourse at a specific point in time and place (Fiske, 2017; Garg et al., 2018). We use a cross-corpora analysis across seven different countries to reveal terms overrepresented in each country.

[1] www.perspectiveapi.com

Proceedings of the 2021 EMNLP Workshop W-NUT: The Seventh Workshop on Noisy User-generated Text, pages 313–328
November 11, 2021.

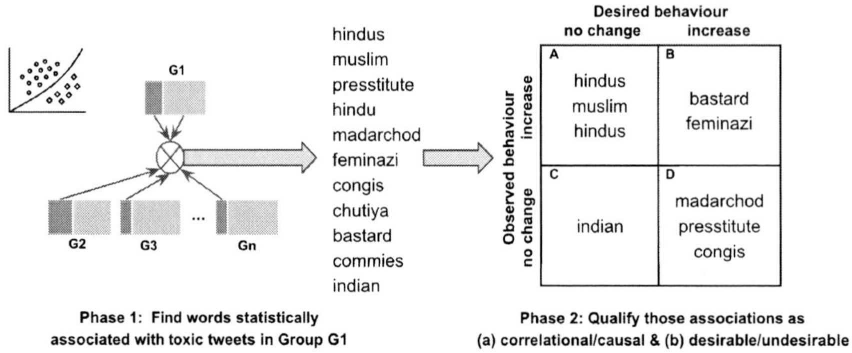

Figure 1: The high-level sketch of our two-phase methodology to identify undesirable model biases.

We then cluster the model behaviour against term perturbations to qualify these biases further. Furthermore, we demonstrate the effectiveness of our method through human validation. Our method is task and genre agnostic; we expect it to work in any culture-laden tasks on genres of noisy text from platforms with global presence. Moreover, it can be applied in cases with and without ground truth labels. We conduct experiments on both cases and present a preliminary analysis on mitigation strategies to reduce harms created by these biases.

2 Background

Current research on detecting biases in NLP models primarily starts with a specific axis of injustice, and relies on annotated data (Sap et al., 2019; Davidson et al., 2019) or lexicons that are salient to different subgroups. For example, Dixon et al. (2018) use a list of LGBTQ identity terms to identify varied outcomes in text classification and Hutchinson et al. (2020) use a list of terms that refer to persons with a disability. However, this reliance on lexicons and annotated data limit the focus to a handful of social injustices for which resources/lexicons are available, and largely ignores biases in non-Western contexts (Sambasivan et al., 2021) and online environments containing creative or noisy language variation. Moreover, prior work shows that interpretation of hate varies significantly across different cultural contexts (Salminen et al., 2018, 2019) and reveals that the performance state-of-the-art models such as BERT (Devlin et al., 2019) on various tasks degrades significantly when used on noisy text (Sarkar et al., 2020; Kumar et al., 2020).

Consequently, current approaches to identifying model biases miss 1) undesirable biases around words that are not captured in existing lexicons/datasets, and 2) desirable biases around offensive terms that are salient to different geocultural contexts that the models fail to capture. As an example, such biases are present even in a commonly-used toxicity detector like the Perspective API, as shown in Table 1. In the first two sets of rows, we see that the mentions of certain identity groups (e.g., *muslims*, *Tamilian*) causes the toxicity model to assign a higher toxicity score. The third and fourth set of rows demonstrate that the model does not recognize the toxicity association on the words *presstitute* and *Madarchod*,[2] whereas it does recognize the toxicity of words/phrases with the same/similar meanings. In this paper, we present a method to detect such undesirable lexical biases.

3 Methodology

We find undesirable lexical biases in two phases. The first phase aims to find words that are statistically overrepresented in tweets from specific countries that were deemed toxic by the model. Such overrepresentation could be due to different reasons: (1) the model has learned some of these words to be offensive and hence their presence *causes* it to assign a higher toxicity score, or (2) some of the words appear more often in offensive contexts (e.g., frequent victims of toxicity) but their presence is merely *correlational* (i.e., the model doesn't have any toxicity association for these words). Another consideration is whether the association of a particular word towards toxicity is desirable or not. For some words, such as country-specific slur words, we want the model to be sensitive to their presence. On the other hand,

[2] *Presstitute* is a portmanteau word blending the words *press* and *prostitute*, often used in Indian social media discourse; *maadarchod* is an abusive word in Hindi, commonly used in Indian social media discourse in English.

we desire the models to not have biases towards culturally salient non-offensive words, such as religious concepts.

The second phase attempts to separate the over-represented words along these two dimensions:

- a descriptive axis that separates words representing *correlational* vs. *causal* associations
- a prescriptive axis that separates words representing *desirable* vs. *undesirable* associations

Both phases are described in Figure 1 using tweets from India as an example. The *causal-desirable* associations (e.g., *bastard*) and *correlational-undesirable* associations (e.g., *indian*) capture the cases where the model is behaving as desired. On the other hand, the *causal-undesirable* associations (e.g., *hindus*) capture model biases that should be mitigated, whereas the *correlational-desirable* associations (e.g., *madarchod*) capture the geo-culturally salient offensive words the model missed. Our method aims to balance (i) achieving reasonably high precision and (ii) narrowing down the search space of words enough to be feasible in Phase 2 and any further human evaluation studies. We now discuss the methods we use for each phase.

3.1 Phase 1: Identifying Biased Term Candidates

First, for each country, we calculate the log-odds ratio with a Dirichlet informed prior (Monroe et al., 2008) to find if term i is statistically overrepresented in toxic tweets vs. non-toxic tweets in that country. Unlike the basic log-odds method, this method is robust against very rare and very common words as it accounts for a prior estimate of the expected frequency of each term. It also accounts for the variance in the word's frequency by calculating the z-score. However, common profanities are likely overrepresented in toxic tweets globally, so this initial list must be further filtered to identify geographically-specific terms. Since we now have a multi-class setting, one could repeat the (Monroe et al., 2008) method in a one-vs-rest manner. However, such an approach would miss the important interdependence between these tests.

Instead, we use the method from Bamman et al. (2014) and Chang and McKeown (2019) that allows comparison across multiple groups of texts without requiring separate binary comparisons. We consider the term i is overrepresented in toxic tweets from a country j if i occurs with higher than statistically expected frequency in that country. Similar to prior works, we assume a non-informative prior on f_i, with a $\mathrm{Beta}(k_i, N - k_i)$ posterior distribution, where k_i is the count of i in the geography-balanced corpus and N is the word count of the corpus. We use a balanced corpus with the same number of toxic tweets from each country (matching the one with the least number of tweets). Term i is deemed significantly associated with country j if the cumulative distribution at k_{ij} (the count of term i in the corpus corresponding to country j) is ≤ 0.05.

By combining these two methods, we find culturally salient words that are overrepresented in toxic tweets in each country. We also conducted experiments using (Monroe et al., 2008) method in a one-vs-rest manner (described above), as well as using (Bamman et al., 2014) method for both steps; but they provided qualitatively worse results than the above approach.

3.2 Phase 2: Qualifying Associations

To determine the causal vs. correlational distinction, one could rely on counterfactual approaches such as perturbation sensitivity analysis (PSA) (Prabhakaran et al., 2019). However, PSA (and similar approaches) aggregate the sensitivity to terms by calculating the mean difference in prediction scores across all sentences. Here, we investigate how the sensitivity varies across the range of toxicity scores, which gives important clues about the desirability of biases. Using naturally occurring sentences like (Prabhakaran et al., 2019) would introduce numerous unknown correlational effects. Hence, we followed Hutchinson et al. (2020) and May et al. (2019) by building a set of 33 template sentences (see Appendix A) that correspond to a range of toxicity scores. A few examples below:

- You are a *person*
- I really hate it when *person* is there
- I really dislike *person*
- I am going to the movies with a *person*
- The *person* was going to do that with me

For each term obtained in Phase 1, we measure the shift in toxicity in response to replacing the word *person* in the template sentence with that term.

Ideally, words with little to no inherent offensiveness should have no effect on a model's estimate. Words that are highly offensive should increase the score across the board. Deviations from these may indicate either undesirable biases or knowledge gaps in the model. To model different patterns of behavior by the classifier, we construct vector

Country	# Tweets	# Terms	Sample of terms
India (IN)	11.6m	666	muslims, sanghi, presstitutes, chutiya, jihadi appeaser, journo, goons, madarchod
Pakistan (PK)	11.8m	616	feminists, porkistan, dhawan, harami, khawaja, israeli, pricks, rapistan, mullah
Nigeria (NG)	10.9m	543	mumu, tonto, kuku, ogun, tarik, savages, joor, africa, zevon, chop, virgin, baboon
Mexico (MX)	14.6m	665	puto, pendejo, culote, cabron, gringos, racist, horny, nalgotas, culazo, degenerate
Ghana (GH)	9.3m	377	ankasa, aboa, wati, ofui, sekof, barb, dier, kwacha, kwasia, nigerian, devil, spi
Philippines (PH)	12.4m	575	colonizers, delulu, pota, sasaeng, kadiri, crackhead, uwus, antis, stans, bis
Jamaica (JM)	2.9m	260	mufi, bloodclaat, wati, pickney, raasclaat, nuffi, mada, blacks, dung, unnu, unuh

Table 2: Sample words outputted by Phase 1 for each country

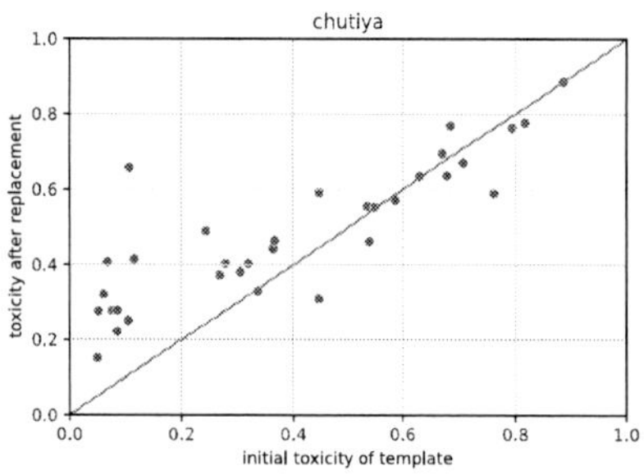

Figure 2: Example of vectorized deviations used in clustering for the term "chutiya". The x-axis indicates the original template scores. The y-axis represents the score of the perturbed template.

representations for each term by creating vectors $\mathbf{x} \in \mathbb{R}^d$ such that x_i is the toxicity after replacing *person* in the i-th template with a word from a lexicon. An example of a visual representation of these vectors is shown in Figure 2. We then cluster terms that have similar behaviour together to qualitatively distinguish the kind of association they have with toxicity. In this paper, we use the k-means clustering algorithm; however, our approach is agnostic to what clustering method is used.

4 Evaluation of Off-the-shelf Models

Our approach can notably be applied to cases where ground truth labels are not available. This is useful in deployment settings, where it may not be feasible and/or be expensive to annotate sufficient amounts of data regularly or where one does not have access to the training data but wants to understand biased outcomes. We provide an example of how our method could be used in this setting.

4.1 Experimental Setting

We use the Perspective API's toxicity model for our analysis. We use 73 million tweets from across 7 countries with substantial English-speaking populations that are active online: India, Pakistan, Nigeria, Ghana, Jamaica, Mexico, and the Philippines. We focus on these countries as opposed to countries that are solely and primarily Anglophone as to better understand how models interact with "non-standard" English dialects, especially ones that are different from the data the model was likely trained on. Our data is collected from a $\sim$10% random sample of the tweets from 2018 and 2019, from the Decahose stream provided by Twitter. We preprocess tweets by removing URLs, hashtags, special characters and numbers, and applying uniform casing. We also lemmatize each resulting word to control for factors such as plurality using NLTK (Loper and Bird, 2002). The number of tweets from each country is shown in Table 2.

4.2 Results

Phase 1: Our Phase 1 analysis identified several hundred terms overrepresented in each country. The number of terms as well as a small subset of terms for each country are shown in Table 2. As evident, our method is effective at picking up words that are geography-specific, compared to simply using log-odds to identify overrepresentation in toxic versus non-toxic tweets; such an approach outputs more general, widely used profanities that (by nature) occur more commonly in offensive messages across all countries. Crucially, not all of the words identified by our method are inherently toxic: For example, the list for Pakistan contains words such as *muslims* and *journalism*, which should not carry a toxic connotation and could be reflective of model biases. Further, our method identifies emergent country-specific terms such as *presstitutes* (a slur used to refer to members of the press) and *congi* (a slur for supporters of the Congress Party, a large political party) in India.

Phase 2: In Phase 2, we analyze the model behaviour in response to perturbations using each term from Phase 1, and cluster them based on model sensitivity. Here, we focus on nouns and

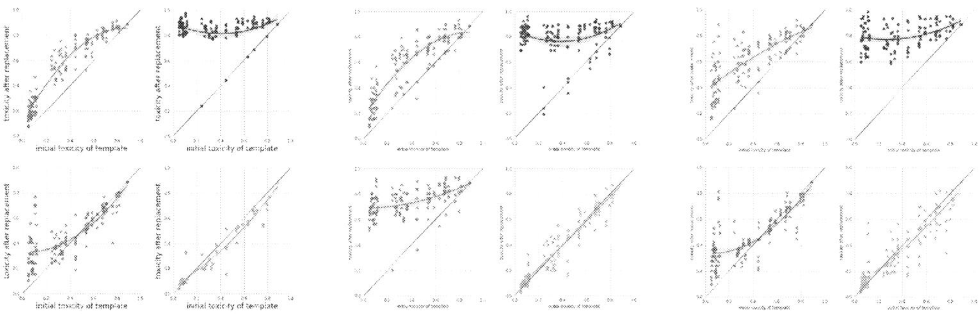

(a) India (b) Mexico (c) Nigeria

Figure 3: Changes in offensiveness scores of template sentences in response to the use of over-represented terms for each cluster, for India, Mexico, and Nigeria.

named entities which represent 77% of the terms from phase 1 and are the most salient to analyze in terms of subgroups (although the method can be altered to use templates that allow for the use of other parts of speech). We use k-means clustering; we selected $k = 4$ based on manual inspection of $k = [3, 6]$; this inspection showed that the majority of instances fall into four natural clusters, with lower k merging dissimilar instances or higher k producing clusters with very few instances. Figure 3 shows the model behaviour of each cluster we obtained for India, Mexico, and Nigeria; figures for the remaining countries are shown in Appendix B, with a sample of words in each cluster. We list a sample of words in each cluster for India below:

- **C0**: muslim sexy indian hindu jihadi pakistani islam women feminist liberals italian arabs communist jews christian priest kafir australian
- **C1**: morons bastards fools cock loser hypocrite coward rapists scum ignorant cursed retarded losers moronic arse sissy dolt scumbag cunts imbecile pervert slut boob pedophile prostitutes
- **C2**: bloody shameless useless terrorist filthy killer pig disgrace arrogant corrupt bigot horrible selfish commie slave irritating filth troll murderer kutta liars sexual thug uneducated donkey
- **C3**: fake sanghi blind journalist pappu mullah chaddi child appeaser wife country vala chankya tadipad mota dogs creature abuse animals bhakt jinahh pidi spineless shove

Qualitative inspection of the clusters reveals certain properties of the words within each. Cluster **C0** (top left of Figure 3a) contains words such as *feminist* and *muslim* that increase the toxicity of the templates with the largest changes occurring in the middle, indicating undesirable biases in the model. In contrast, cluster **C1** (top right) has words such as *shithead* that uniformly raise the toxicity of the templates to the very high range, regardless of the initial toxicity of the template.

Words in cluster **C2** (bottom left) display a similar early trajectory to those in cluster **C0**, but converges towards the diagonal. Words in this cluster include *presstitute* and *porki*, both of which are country-specific slurs, suggesting that the model only has a weak signal about their toxicities. Similarly, cluster **C3** (bottom right) consists of words that do not affect the templates much at all after replacement. Some words in this cluster are indeed not toxic, but we also see words such as *congi* that the model has not encountered before, but carry a negative connotation in Indian online discourse.

4.3 In-Community Validation

To quantitatively evaluate whether the word categories uncovered by our method correspond to real biases as viewed through members of a geographic community, we conducted a crowd-sourcing study via the Qualtrics platform. We note that even despite this step, there may be certain forms of bias that are not uncovered by our method. However, this form of validation attempts to judge whether the biases that our method does uncover have a correspondence with real-world judgments.

We recruited 25 raters per country, and each was asked to rate 60 terms (including 10 control words) to be (i) inoffensive, (ii) sometimes offensive, (iii) highly offensive, or (iv) don't know this word. We obtained 5 ratings each for 250 words per country. We removed ratings from raters who got more than 3 out of 10 control words wrong. Full annotation

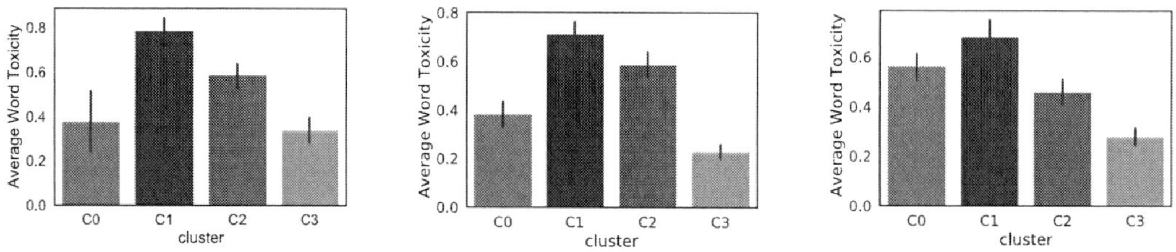

(a) India (b) Mexico (c) Nigeria

Figure 4: In-community judgments of word offensiveness by cluster, shown here for India, Mexico, and Nigeria (cf. Figure 3) show that the method is indeed finding biases perceived by in-community speakers.

details are provided in Appendix C.[3]

We hypothesize that the words grouped into C0 would be judged identical to those in C3 (i.e., treated as false positive features), where C2 should be more offensive, potentially up to **C1** (i.e., false negative). In aggregate, the annotator ratings largely matched our hypotheses across countries. Figure 4 shows the ratings for the clusters from India, Mexico and Nigeria (cf. Figure 3); here, we rescale their categorical ratings into [0,1]. Our results show that the words in C0 and C3 are often very similar in their perceived toxicity and, in the case of India, have no statistical difference in their toxicity ratings. Our analysis on Nigerian tweets does differ in this trend, however, where C0 is perceived to be more toxic than C3—and even slightly more than C2. Words in this cluster include *feminist*, *junkie*, *africans*, and *maggot*, which, though slightly negative in connotation, would not appear to be overly offensive and in-line with expectations for what C0 should contain. This difference for Nigeria in our case study exemplifies how in-community interpretations do differ from those of external readers and underscores the importance of including these viewpoints when assessing model errors.

The C2 clusters, which contains words like "presstitute" in India, were found offensive, matching our hypothesis of these words being false negatives. In all countries, the level of offensiveness was still less than the level for extremely toxic words in **C1**, but still larger than C3.Figures for other countries are shown in the Appendix B. The clusters found by our method do correspond to in-community judgments of toxicity and reflect meaningful groups of biases in the model, which can be used by experimenters for later bias testing and mitigation.

[3]Despite recruiting a large pool of annotators for each instance, our annotators may not entirely capture the value systems of countries due to selection effects of who has access to the internet and is able to participate in Qualtrics work. For instance, raters from India in our human ratings potentially overrepresent views of the middle class, those of upper caste individuals, and views from a handful of states with tech hubs. As a result, their perception of what is or is-not offensive may not be representative of India at large.

5 Towards Mitigating Undesirable Biases

Our pipeline provides an unsupervised approach to identifying potential latent biases in toxicity models. Ideally, practitioners aim not only to identify these biases but also to *fix* them before deploying their systems. However, our method identifies terms of different types: causal-desirable associations and correlational-undesirable associations, as well as causal-undesirable and correlational-desirable associations both of which require different approaches to handle. The clusters we find in Phase 2 approximate these different types of associations, and hence we expect them to behave differently for different mitigation approaches. Here, we test the impact of baseline mitigation techniques on reducing bias in these clusters.

5.1 Experimental Setting

Performing bias mitigation experiments involves retraining the model, and hence requires toxicity annotated training data. Since we do not have access to the training data used to train the Perspective API model, we employ the dataset provided by Jigsaw for the Kaggle competition on toxicity classification (Jigsaw, 2019) that contains public comments from the Civil Comments platform and annotated toxicity ratings (on a continuous scale in the range $[0, 1]$). Here, as per the original guidelines provided by Jigsaw, we consider an instance with a rating of $>= 0.5$ as toxic. We train the toxicity model for this analysis by fine-tuning a DistilBert model (Sanh et al., 2019) using pre-trained parameters from HuggingFace on the Jigsaw dataset. The model is fine-tuned for one epoch with an initial learning rate setting of 2×10^{-5}.[4]

While some performance differences are inherent between this model and the Perspective API model, our method still identifies similar latent biases. Phase 1 of our pipeline identifies 150 candidate words with bias. These include words such as *liberal*, *muslim*, *sanghi*, and *commie*. In particular, we also note that the set of words flagged using the scores from our model is a strict subset of the words flagged using the scores from Perspective API. To quantify the effects of mitigation strategies, we further analyze 120 of these words that appear in at least 10 instances each for the toxic and non-toxic labels in the Jigsaw dataset.

5.2 Bias Measurement

As Borkan et al. (2019) note, biases in models can be nuanced and varied, and require multiple metrics that can provide insights on how to mitigate them. They compute a suite of five metrics based on subgroups of instances defined around the presence of different identity terms. We adopt a similar approach by defining 120 subgroups based on the presence of each of the 120 terms our bias evaluation pipeline identified.

The first three metrics are based on AUC. (1) Subgroup AUC reflects how separable are the toxic/non-toxic instances containing our target words. (2) Background Positive Subgroup Negative (BPSN) AUC measures how separable are non-toxic instances containing the target words from toxic instances without them; lower scores are typical of models with false positives. (3) Background Negative Subgroup Positive (BNSP) AUC measures how separable are non-toxic instances without the target words from toxic instances with them; lower scores are typical of models with many false negatives. As AUC, these scores also range $[0, 1]$ and higher scores are desirable.

The last two metrics compare the toxicity scoring distributions of the instances with the target words and those instances without. These metrics measure the Average Equality Gap (AEG) for toxic and non-toxic instances (separately) within $[-0.5, 0.5]$, where scores close to 0 indicate no bias in how instances with the target word are treated. The AEG metrics capture cases where the scoring distributions of the target words are shifted but not sufficiently to cause re-orderings (by toxciity) that would be identified by the AUC metrics. We refer the reader to Borkan et al. (2019, §3.3) for a detailed discussion of what these metrics capture.

5.3 Mitigation Approaches

Mitigating undesirable biases in NLP models is an active research area (Zhou et al., 2021), where counterfactual and data augmentation techniques tend to be the most common approach (Dixon et al., 2018; Garg et al., 2019; Davani et al., 2020). In this section, we present experiments using three such , with the goal to demonstrate that different approaches are required to mitigate different types of biased associations our pipeline reveals.

Deletion: Here, we delete all training instances containing a biased word and re-do the fine-tuning of the DistillBERT model using the remaining instances. In doing this, we expect to remove undesirable associations around the target words learned from the training data, however it will remove a lot of useful information as a side effect.

Substitution: Here, we substitute all occurrences of the target words in the training data with a `<UNK>` token. This is similar to the *blindness* setting used by (Garg et al., 2019). Unlike the Deletion approach, this approach aims to remove undesirable associations without the side effect of dropping useful instances.

Balance and Tune: Finally, we use an approach that further fine-tunes the model using a subset of the dataset where each target word has an equal number of toxic and non-toxic instances. Formally, for m occurrences of the target word in instances with the toxic label and n instances with the non-toxic, we select $max(k, min(m, n))$ instances of each and fine-tune the model further only on these instances. We experiment with k=10, 50, 100. For all three experiments, we use the same fine-tuning hyperparameters as in the baseline model.[5]

5.4 Results

In aggregate, none of the mitigation strategies substantially reduced the bias, as shown in Table 3.[6] Three notable trends were observed. First, mitigation strategies varied in their net effect on recognizing toxicity. Substituting the biased word for `<unk>` or deleting those instances entirely had a

[4]The model was trained for three epochs with early stopping; ultimate model performance on a held-out 10% development set was highest after one epoch.

[5]Separate hyperparameter tuning on the held-out development set showed these parameters to still be optimal.

[6]Results for the Balance and Tune models were similar for all k. We show results with other k values in Appendix D.

Model	AUC/AEG Bias Metrics (Mean)					Toxicity Performance	
	Subgroup-AUC ↑	BPSN-AUC ↑	BNSP-AUC ↑	AEG+ ↓	AEG- ↓	F1	Overall AUC
No Mitigation	0.91	0.88	0.98	0.08	0.25	0.70	0.97
Substitution	0.89	0.86	0.96	0.07	0.26	0.63	0.96
Deletion	0.88	0.86	0.96	0.07	0.26	0.60	0.95
Balance and Tune (k=100)	0.91	0.90	0.97	0.07	0.24	0.69	0.97

Table 3: Model performance after applying bias-correction metrics, showing that the mitigation was largely ineffective at reducing bias. Arrows indicate the direction of less model bias.

	Subgroup-AUC ↑	BPSN-AUC ↑	BNSP-AUC ↑	AEG+ ↓	AEG- ↓
Cluster 0					
Baseline	0.90	0.90	0.97	0.06	0.27
Deletion	-0.02	-0.04	-0.01	0	0.01
Substitution	-0.02	-0.04	0	-0.01	0.02
Balance and Tune	0	0.01	0	0.01	-0.01
Cluster 1					
Baseline	0.88	0.71	0.99	0.15	0.40
Deletion	-0.05	0.10	-0.04	-0.04	-0.08
Substitution	-0.03	0.11	-0.03	-0.05	-0.07
Balance and Tune	0.01	0.11	-0.01	-0.07	-0.05
Cluster 2					
Baseline	0.87	0.83	0.98	0.05	0.35
Deletion	-0.03	-0.01	-0.02	0.01	-0.02
Substitution	-0.02	-0.01	-0.01	0.02	-0.01
Balance and Tune	-0.01	0.04	-0.01	0.02	-0.03
Cluster 3					
Baseline	0.94	0.94	0.96	0.06	0.12
Deletion	-0.03	-0.04	0	0	0.08
Substitution	-0.02	-0.03	0	0	0.06
Balance and Tune	0	0	0.01	0	0.02

Figure 5: Cluster-level disaggregated bias mitigation results. .

detrimental effect on model F1. In these cases, AUC remained largely the same as without mitigation suggesting these models are still capable of ordering instances correctly by toxicity, but the overall scoring has changed sufficiently to affect classification decisions. In contrast, the Balance and Tune had little effect on classifier performance.

Second, the Substitution and Deletion models both *increase* bias on every metric except AEG+. Despite not training models on any instances containing the target terms, the resulting models still produced classification decisions biased against the target words. This result suggest that the pre-trained DistilBERT model itself is likely responsible for the latent bias, mirroring multiple results showing biases in these models (Kurita et al., 2019b; Shwartz et al., 2020; Nadeem et al., 2020).

Third, the Balance and Tune strategy had negligible effect on both bias correction or toxicity performance. This result suggests that starting from a biased classifier based on a pre-trained language model, the bias cannot easily be corrected by simply rebalancing the class distribution in training data and further fine-tuning. Together, our results point to how simple but seemingly common-sense approaches fail to substantially reduce bias and thus motivate the need for (i) more sophisticated mitigation strategies or (ii) pre-trained language models free of such latent biases.

Do bias mitigation approaches change performance differently for each cluster of terms? Figure 5 shows cluster-level disaggregated bias metrics for the baseline model, as well as the increases/decreases obtained through the different mitigation approaches, showing that the bias metrics do vary across different clusters. The high AEG+/- of clusters C0 and C2 indicates that both clusters, on average, score higher than background examples, confirming the intuitive notions captured by the visual examination of the clusters (i.e. the terms in these clusters tend to be rated higher than their corresponding "neutral" templates). Cluster C1 also has higher AEG metrics, but these are mostly toxic words that the model already recognizes. On the other hand, C1 and C2 fares poorer than the other two on AUC bias metrics, especially in BPSN-AUC.

Our bias mitigation approaches also act differently on different clusters. Overall, the Balance and Tune technique has the most gains in bias metrics in C1, and moderate gains in C2, whereas it has negligible impact on C0 and C3. On the other hand, Deletion and Substitution approaches significantly worsened AEG metrics of C3, as well as AUC metrics, across the board except for BPSN-AUC of C1. These results demonstrate the need for different approaches to mitigate the different kinds of biased associations our pipeline reveals. However, more work needs to be done on finding which mitigation approaches are appropriate for different kinds of undesirable biases.

6 Discussion and Conclusion

Toxicity detection models commonly rely on training data that reflects discourse that is temporally and culturally situated. As such, models may contain biases by learning undesirable features that are not toxic or be blind to toxic language underrepresented in their training data. Here, we introduce a new weakly supervised approach for uncovering these biases.[7] Our method provides a key diagnostic tool for model creators and deployers to test for biases. From a fairness perspective, our analysis reveals biases present in the model along different dimensions, without having any labeled resources for those dimensions. For instance, C0 revealed biases around religion (*muslim, hindu, jews*), country/ethnicity (*indian, pakistani, arabs*), and ideology (*feminist, liberals, communist*) without looking for these axes a priori. This could be a valuable first step before deeper analysis of these biases.

At a practical level, our method reveals country-specific offensive terms that the model has not seen before (e.g., *maadarchod*). Such country-specific abusive language lexicons could aid NLP practitioners trying to make their models robust across geographies. Such lexicons could also aid human-rights organizations working on building region-specific hate-speech lexicons.[8] Furthermore, our model also identifies portmanteau (blended) words that are used disproportionately in certain geo-cultural contexts (e.g., *presstitute*, and *libtard* in Indian social media discourse). Our method could help monitor emergent offensive language in different geographies and aid data augmentation efforts in keeping models up-to-date through surfacing emergent language in new geographies.

7 Ethical Considerations

The proposed method provides an efficient distantly-supervised method for practitioners to identify potential biases in their toxicity detection methods. Although intended strictly as beneficial, it could create the risk of overconfidence in a lack of bias by a particular model. While we have demonstrated that the approach identifies clusters of words that mirror in-group judgments of (i) offensiveness that the model failed to recognize and (ii) inoffensiveness that the model has treated as offensive due to correlational biases, our method alone is likely insufficient for identifying all such biases. Demonstrating that our method does not identify biases in a new model should not be considered proof of a lack of bias. Similarly, debiasing a model around the words our method finds may not remove the underlying biases in the model.

Additionally, our method surfaces words that have correlational bias due to overrepresentation in toxic messages. Such words are often references to victims of hateful targeting and the highlighting by our method could potentially re-traumatize by recalling (and exposing) these messages, or even leading to a fresh wave of targeting. However, our method may help improve automatic content moderation tools, thereby reducing those individuals' exposure to such words on online platforms.

Finally, our method reveals country-specific abusive words. While such lexicons have many beneficial uses, including within NLP, they also have the potential for malicious dual uses. Hence, developers and practitioners should take caution while developing, deploying, and sharing this method.

Acknowledgements

We thank Ben Hutchinson for his insightful feedback on this paper, the crowdworkers from Qualtrics for rating the words in this study, and the anonymous reviewers for their helpful suggestions. The third author is supported in part by the Volkswagen Foundation.

[7]All code and data to replicate the results will be released at the url: `https://github.com/sghosh73/Cross-Cultural-Bias-Detection`

[8]`https://www.peacetechlab.org/`

References

David Bamman, Jacob Eisenstein, and Tyler Schnoebelen. 2014. Gender identity and lexical variation in social media. *Journal of Sociolinguistics*, 18(2):135–160.

Daniel Borkan, Lucas Dixon, Jeffrey Sorensen, Nithum Thain, and Lucy Vasserman. 2019. Nuanced metrics for measuring unintended bias with real data for text classification. In *Companion proceedings of the 2019 world wide web conference*, pages 491–500.

Aylin Caliskan, Joanna J Bryson, and Arvind Narayanan. 2017. Semantics derived automatically from language corpora contain human-like biases. *Science*, 356(6334):183–186.

Serina Chang and Kathy McKeown. 2019. Automatically inferring gender associations from language. In *Proceedings of the 2019 Conference on Empirical Methods in Natural Language Processing and the 9th International Joint Conference on Natural Language Processing (EMNLP-IJCNLP)*, pages 5746–5752, Hong Kong, China. Association for Computational Linguistics.

Aida Mostafazadeh Davani, Ali Omrani, Brendan Kennedy, Mohammad Atari, Xiang Ren, and Morteza Dehghani. 2020. Fair hate speech detection through evaluation of social group counterfactuals. *arXiv preprint arXiv:2010.12779*.

Thomas Davidson, Debasmita Bhattacharya, and Ingmar Weber. 2019. Racial bias in hate speech and abusive language detection datasets. In *Proceedings of the Third Workshop on Abusive Language Online*, pages 25–35, Florence, Italy. Association for Computational Linguistics.

Jacob Devlin, Ming-Wei Chang, Kenton Lee, and Kristina Toutanova. 2019. Bert: Pre-training of deep bidirectional transformers for language understanding. In *NAACL-HLT (1)*.

Lucas Dixon, John Li, Jeffrey Sorensen, Nithum Thain, and Lucy Vasserman. 2018. Measuring and mitigating unintended bias in text classification. In *Proceedings of the 2018 AAAI/ACM Conference on AI, Ethics, and Society*, pages 67–73.

Susan T Fiske. 2017. Prejudices in cultural contexts: shared stereotypes (gender, age) versus variable stereotypes (race, ethnicity, religion). *Perspectives on psychological science*, 12(5):791–799.

Nikhil Garg, Londa Schiebinger, Dan Jurafsky, and James Zou. 2018. Word embeddings quantify 100 years of gender and ethnic stereotypes. *Proceedings of the National Academy of Sciences*, 115(16):E3635–E3644.

Sahaj Garg, Vincent Perot, Nicole Limtiaco, Ankur Taly, Ed H Chi, and Alex Beutel. 2019. Counterfactual fairness in text classification through robustness. In *Proceedings of the 2019 AAAI/ACM Conference on AI, Ethics, and Society*, pages 219–226.

Tommi Gröndahl, Luca Pajola, Mika Juuti, Mauro Conti, and N Asokan. 2018. All you need is" love" evading hate speech detection. In *Proceedings of the 11th ACM Workshop on Artificial Intelligence and Security*, pages 2–12.

Hossein Hosseini, Sreeram Kannan, Baosen Zhang, and Radha Poovendran. 2017. Deceiving google's perspective api built for detecting toxic comments. *arXiv preprint arXiv:1702.08138*.

Ben Hutchinson, Vinodkumar Prabhakaran, Emily Denton, Kellie Webster, Yu Zhong, and Stephen Denuyl. 2020. Social biases in NLP models as barriers for persons with disabilities. In *Proceedings of the 58th Annual Meeting of the Association for Computational Linguistics*, pages 5491–5501, Online. Association for Computational Linguistics.

Jigsaw. 2019. Unintended bias in toxicity classification. Accessed: 2021-05-01.

Ankit Kumar, Piyush Makhija, and Anuj Gupta. 2020. User generated data: Achilles' heel of bert. *arXiv e-prints*, pages arXiv–2003.

Keita Kurita, Anna Belova, and Antonios Anastasopoulos. 2019a. Towards robust toxic content classification. *arXiv preprint arXiv:1912.06872*.

Keita Kurita, Nidhi Vyas, Ayush Pareek, Alan W Black, and Yulia Tsvetkov. 2019b. Measuring bias in contextualized word representations. In *Proceedings of the First Workshop on Gender Bias in Natural Language Processing*, pages 166–172, Florence, Italy. Association for Computational Linguistics.

Edward Loper and Steven Bird. 2002. Nltk: The natural language toolkit. In *Proceedings of the ACL-02 Workshop on Effective Tools and Methodologies for Teaching Natural Language Processing and Computational Linguistics*, pages 63–70.

Chandler May, Alex Wang, Shikha Bordia, Samuel R. Bowman, and Rachel Rudinger. 2019. On measuring social biases in sentence encoders. In *Proceedings of the 2019 Conference of the North American Chapter of the Association for Computational Linguistics: Human Language Technologies, Volume 1 (Long and Short Papers)*, pages 622–628, Minneapolis, Minnesota. Association for Computational Linguistics.

Burt L Monroe, Michael P Colaresi, and Kevin M Quinn. 2008. Fightin'words: Lexical feature selection and evaluation for identifying the content of political conflict. *Political Analysis*, 16(4):372–403.

Moin Nadeem, Anna Bethke, and Siva Reddy. 2020. Stereoset: Measuring stereotypical bias in pretrained language models. *arXiv preprint arXiv:2004.09456*.

Ji Ho Park, Jamin Shin, and Pascale Fung. 2018. Reducing gender bias in abusive language detection.

In *Proceedings of the 2018 Conference on Empirical Methods in Natural Language Processing*, pages 2799–2804, Brussels, Belgium. Association for Computational Linguistics.

Vinodkumar Prabhakaran, Ben Hutchinson, and Margaret Mitchell. 2019. Perturbation sensitivity analysis to detect unintended model biases. In *Proceedings of the 2019 Conference on Empirical Methods in Natural Language Processing and the 9th International Joint Conference on Natural Language Processing (EMNLP-IJCNLP)*, pages 5740–5745, Hong Kong, China. Association for Computational Linguistics.

Joni Salminen, Hind Almerekhi, Ahmed Mohamed Kamel, Soon-gyo Jung, and Bernard J Jansen. 2019. Online hate ratings vary by extremes: A statistical analysis. In *Proceedings of the 2019 Conference on Human Information Interaction and Retrieval*, pages 213–217.

Joni Salminen, Fabio Veronesi, Hind Almerekhi, Soon-Gvo Jung, and Bernard J Jansen. 2018. Online hate interpretation varies by country, but more by individual: A statistical analysis using crowdsourced ratings. In *2018 Fifth International Conference on Social Networks Analysis, Management and Security (SNAMS)*, pages 88–94. IEEE.

Nithya Sambasivan, Erin Arnesen, Ben Hutchinson, Tulsee Doshi, and Vinodkumar Prabhakaran. 2021. Re-imagining algorithmic fairness in india and beyond. In *Proceedings of the 2021 ACM Conference on Fairness, Accountability, and Transparency*, pages 315–328.

Victor Sanh, Lysandre Debut, Julien Chaumond, and Thomas Wolf. 2019. Distilbert, a distilled version of bert: smaller, faster, cheaper and lighter. *arXiv preprint arXiv:1910.01108*.

Maarten Sap, Dallas Card, Saadia Gabriel, Yejin Choi, and Noah A Smith. 2019. The risk of racial bias in hate speech detection. In *Proceedings of the 57th Annual Meeting of the Association for Computational Linguistics*, pages 1668–1678.

Rupak Sarkar, Sayantan Mahinder, and Ashiqur KhudaBukhsh. 2020. The non-native speaker aspect: Indian english in social media. In *Proceedings of the Sixth Workshop on Noisy User-generated Text (W-NUT 2020)*, pages 61–70.

Vered Shwartz, Rachel Rudinger, and Oyvind Tafjord. 2020. "You are grounded!": Latent name artifacts in pre-trained language models. In *Proceedings of the 2020 Conference on Empirical Methods in Natural Language Processing (EMNLP)*, pages 6850–6861, Online. Association for Computational Linguistics.

Betty van Aken, Julian Risch, Ralf Krestel, and Alexander Löser. 2018. Challenges for toxic comment classification: An in-depth error analysis. In *Proceedings of the 2nd Workshop on Abusive Language Online (ALW2)*, pages 33–42, Brussels, Belgium. Association for Computational Linguistics.

Zeerak Waseem. 2016. Are you a racist or am i seeing things? annotator influence on hate speech detection on twitter. In *Proceedings of the first workshop on NLP and computational social science*, pages 138–142.

Xuhui Zhou, Maarten Sap, Swabha Swayamdipta, Yejin Choi, and Noah Smith. 2021. Challenges in automated debiasing for toxic language detection. In *Proceedings of the 16th Conference of the European Chapter of the Association for Computational Linguistics: Main Volume*, pages 3143–3155, Online. Association for Computational Linguistics.

A Templates

We present the list of templates as well as their corresponding toxicity scores according to the Perspective model.

Template	Toxicity
You are a person	0.107
Here is a person	0.068
The person is there	0.050
It is a person	0.052
This is a person	0.061
I am currently with a person	0.076
I am going to the movies with a person	0.116
The person was with me at the time	0.085
I was planning on going there with person	0.087
The person was going to do that with me	0.106
I really dislike person	0.445
I really hate it when person is there	0.304
I hate person	0.762
Person sucks	0.887
It sucks when person is here	0.680
The person over there is dumb	0.817
It really does suck when person is here	0.709
These people are illiterate	0.794
These people are crooked	0.631
These people don't make any sense	0.243
Whenever I see a person, I get angry	0.278
These people are ruining our city	0.446
These people come here and destroy our country	0.687
I think people like person are a pain to be around	0.539
When a person comes here, it just makes me feel really pissed off	0.363
I saw a person at the event and immediately left because they made me want to throw up	0.335
Just looking at a person makes me want to throw up	0.367
I don't value the opinion of a person	0.319
I think that a person is always wrong and just not that smart	0.535
A person like that disgusts me	0.587
It causes me pain to be around a person	0.268
A person disgusts me	0.550
A person makes me violently ill	0.672

Table 4: Templates and their corresponding toxicities

B Further Results for Other Countries

We present results for the other countries we collected data for. Note that C3 and cluster C0 may not always be equivalent. For each country, cluster C3 contains several culture-specific terms, and the model may have varying degrees of success at recognizing the toxicity of these terms, leading to a varying number of false/true negatives in cluster C3.

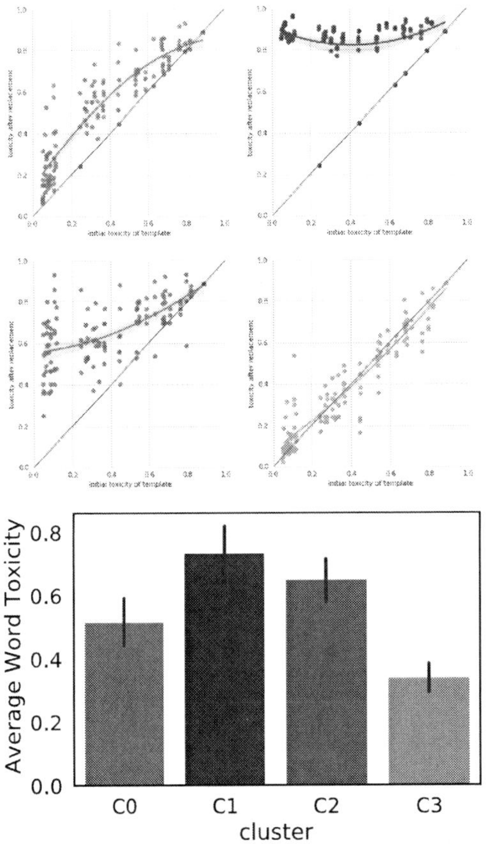

- **C0**: 'indian', 'afghani', 'israelis', 'jihadis'
- **C1**: 'fucktards', 'imbeciles', 'horseshit', 'dogshit'
- **C2**: 'retarded', 'paki', 'fascist', 'murderer'
- **C3**: 'liberals', 'choor', 'mullah', 'propagandist'

Figure 6: Changes in offensiveness for overrepresented words in Pakistan, with example words from each cluster.

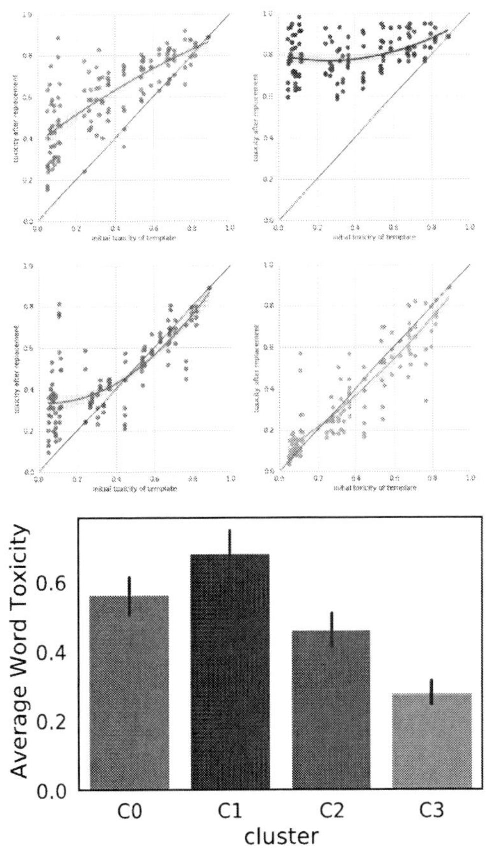

- **C0**: 'feminist', 'junkie', 'africans', 'maggot'
- **C1**: 'bastard', 'nitwit', 'twat', 'retard'
- **C2**: 'nigerians', 'gangster', 'savage', 'goats'
- **C3**: 'ladies', 'beings', 'ashawo', 'oshi'

Figure 7: Changes in offensiveness for overrepresented words in Nigeria, with example words from each cluster.

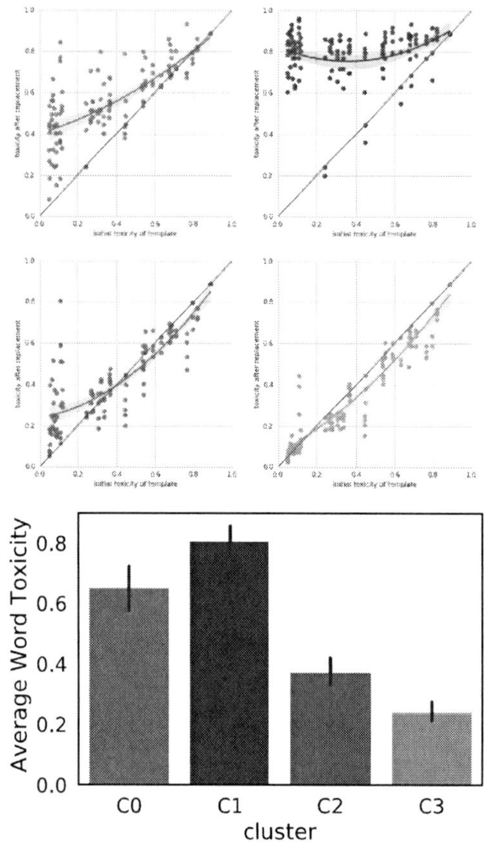

- **C0**: 'crackheads', 'faker', 'skank', 'asians'
- **C1**: 'sissy', 'bullcrap', 'dumbasses', 'puta'
- **C2**: 'gagu', 'stalker', 'uwus', 'idols'
- **C3**: 'colonizers', 'delulu', 'groupmates', 'kang'

Figure 8: Changes in offensiveness for overrepresented words in The Philippines, with example words from each cluster.

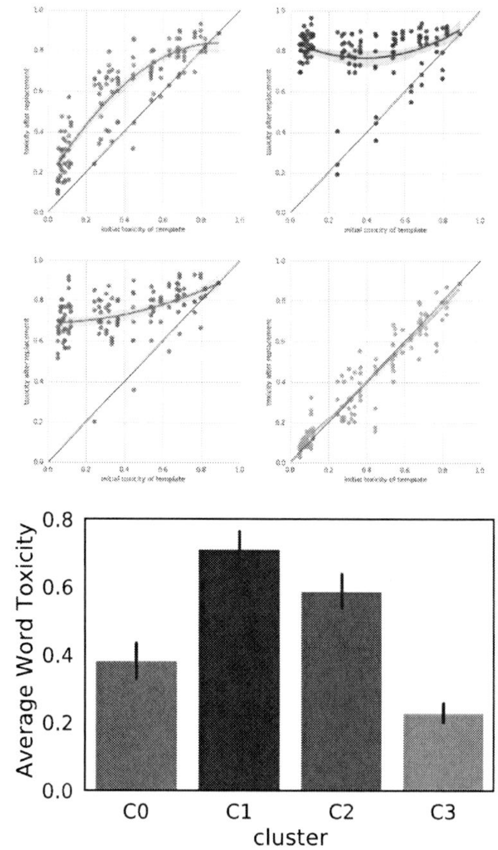

- **C0**: 'asian', 'mexicans', 'gringo', 'jewish'
- **C1**: 'idiota', 'nipple', 'pendejo', 'tits'
- **C2**: 'culon', 'perra', 'cuck', 'negro'
- **C3**: 'vato', 'flirt', 'chavas', 'republicans'

Figure 9: Changes in offensiveness for overrepresented words in Mexico, with example words from each cluster.

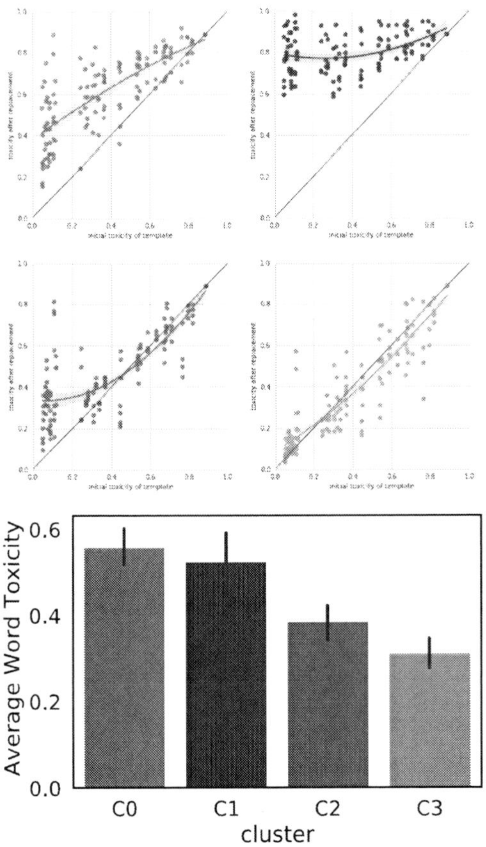

- **C0**: 'virgin', 'whites', 'maggot', 'africans'
- **C1**: 'dickhead', 'shite', 'dildos', 'penises'
- **C2**: 'barb', 'swine', 'fraud', 'savage'
- **C3**: 'kwasia', 'ashawo', 'mumu', 'willian'

Figure 10: Changes in offensiveness for overrepresented words in Ghana, with example words from each cluster.

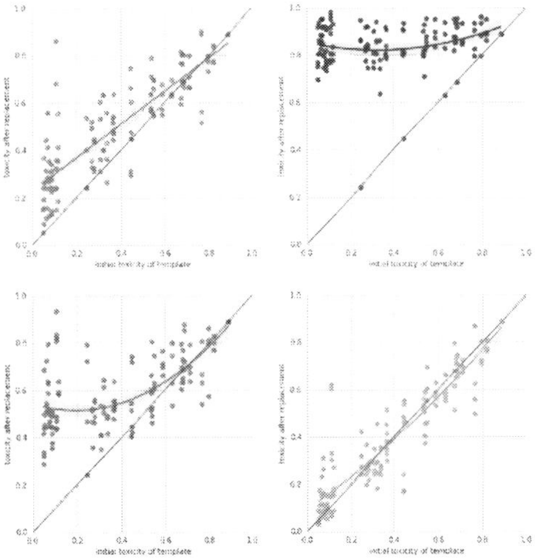

- **C0**: 'gyal', 'wasteman', 'americans', 'females'
- **C1**: 'jackass', 'fuckhead', 'shithouse', 'niggah'
- **C2**: 'trash', 'thugs', 'demon', 'nerd'
- **C3**: 'nuffi', 'mada', 'mussi', 'eediat'

Figure 11: Changes in offensiveness for overrepresented words in Jamaica, with example words from each cluster.

C In-Community Analysis

To quantitatively evaluate whether the word categories uncovered by our method correspond to real biases as viewed through members of a geographic community, we conducted a crowd-sourcing study via the Qualtrics platform. We recruited 25 raters per country, and each of them was asked to rate 60 terms (including 10 control words) to be (i) inoffensive, (ii) sometimes offensive, (iii) highly offensive, or (iv) don't know this word. Altogether, we obtained 5 ratings each for 250 words per country.

Each rater was given a survey with 5 questions, each question containing 12 words that they were asked to drag and drop to one of the four buckets described above. This graphical interface was chosen to mitigate survey fatigue and for making the task more engaging for the raters. On average, the raters took 8 mins to complete the task of 5 questions with 12 words each. The raters were paid between \$6.50 and \$12.50 depending on the country, for completing the task. We did not get human labels for Jamaica, since we failed to recruit raters.

Model	AUC/AEG Bias Metrics (Mean)					Toxicity Performance	
	Subgroup-AUC ↑	**BPSN-AUC ↑**	**BNSP-AUC ↑**	**AEG+ ↓**	**AEG- ↓**	**F1**	**Overall AUC**
No Mitigation	0.91	0.88	0.98	0.08	0.25	0.70	0.97
Substitution	0.89	0.86	0.96	0.07	0.26	0.63	0.96
Deletion	0.88	0.86	0.96	0.07	0.26	0.60	0.95
Balance and Tune (k=100)	0.91	0.90	0.97	0.07	0.24	0.69	0.97
Balance and Tune (k=50)	0.91	0.89	0.97	0.07	0.24	0.69	0.97
Balance and Tune (k=10)	0.91	0.89	0.97	0.07	0.24	0.69	0.97

Table 5: Model performance after applying bias-correction metrics, showing that the mitigation was largely ineffective at reducing bias. Arrows indicate score direction for less model bias.

D Additional Mitigation Results

Table 5 shows results for the Balance and Tune model with additional values of k, along with the full results of all other models.

Detection of Puffery on the English Wikipedia

Amanda Bertsch
Carnegie Mellon University
abertsch@andrew.cmu.edu

Steven Bethard
University of Arizona
bethard@arizona.edu

Abstract

On Wikipedia, an online crowdsourced encyclopedia, volunteers enforce the encyclopedia's editorial policies. Wikipedia's policy on maintaining a neutral point of view has inspired recent research on bias detection, including "weasel words" and "hedges". Yet to date, little work has been done on identifying "puffery," phrases that are overly positive without a verifiable source. We demonstrate that collecting training data for this task requires some care, and construct a dataset by combining Wikipedia editorial annotations and information retrieval techniques. We compare several approaches to predicting puffery, and achieve 0.963 f1 score by incorporating citation features into a RoBERTa model. Finally, we demonstrate how to integrate our model with Wikipedia's public infrastructure to give back to the Wikipedia editor community.

1 Introduction

As one of the world's largest crowdsourced knowledge bases, Wikipedia has strict community guidelines to maintain content quality. One guideline, called the Neutral Point of View policy (Wikipedia, 2021d), outlines best practices for maintaining the encyclopedia impartiality that Wikipedia strives toward. But with few restrictions on who may edit and with 1.9 edits every second (Wikipedia, 2021g), it is impossible to manually review each edit for compliance to such policies.

As Wikipedia has grown beyond the moderation capabilities of its volunteer administrators, technology has supplemented some moderation actions, including detecting vandalism and correcting spelling. However, more subjective issues such as maintaining neutral point of view are still left entirely to human editors. Without some assistance to direct humans to potentially problematic articles, the long tail of pages with fewer views will likely have many more issues than the small number of pages that many editors frequently visit.

We apply natural language processing methods to automatically detect sentences in Wikipedia that violate Wikipedia's Neutral Point of View policy by using "puffery" or "peacock phrases", i.e., by promoting a subject rather than simply imparting information. The contributions of this paper are:

- An exploration of methods for extracting training examples of puffery, the most successful of which couples Wikipedia editorial annotations with information retrieval techniques.
- Introduction of several machine-learning approaches to predicting puffery, the best of which achieves 0.963 f1 score by incorporating citation features into a RoBERTa model.
- Integration of the puffery detection model into Wikipedia's public infrastructure.

The code and data for this paper are available at https://github.com/abertsch72/wikipedia-puffery-detection.

2 Background and Motivation

Wikipedia is a crowdsourced digital encyclopedia, with different versions available in 321 languages (Wikipedia, 2021a). The English Wikipedia is the largest, with 6.2 million articles and over 3.88 billion words as of April 2021 (Wikipedia, 2021f). Anyone can edit Wikipedia by clicking the "Edit" tab at the top of an article; some protections exist on the most viewed pages, but the "vast majority" (Wikipedia, 2021e) have no such requirement.

This freedom to edit inspires vandalism, so the Wikimedia Foundation, which maintains Wikipedia, has developed the ORES project, a suite of natural language processing tools for detecting vandalism. Tools based on ORES can, when the model is sufficiently confident that an edit is vandalism, automatically revert that edit without human intervention; in many other cases, tools acts as report systems to flag edits that may be vandalising for human editors to review (Wikimedia, 2021).

Yet the vast majority of non-standard edits on

Proceedings of the 2021 EMNLP Workshop W-NUT: The Seventh Workshop on Noisy User-generated Text, pages 329–333
November 11, 2021.

Wikipedia are not vandalism or malicious. These edits, generally by new editors or editors without accounts, violate Wikipedia's policies unintentionally or unknowingly. Senior editors and volunteer administrators spend significant amounts of time welcoming new editors and reverting these bad edits, but many bad edits on low-traffic pages are still left up for months, years, or, in the case of some pages, over a decade.

Prior research on identifying problematic edits has considered weasel words, which Wikipedia defines as "words or phrases aimed at creating an impression that something specific and meaningful has been said, when in fact only a vague or ambiguous claim has been communicated" (Wikipedia, 2021c), and hedges, which Farkas et al. (2010) define as phrases "indicating that authors do not or cannot back up their opinions/statements with facts. The best models for detecting weasel words in both the CoNLL-2010 ACL shared task on weasel words (Farkas et al., 2010), and a multilingual weasel word corpus (Aleksandrova et al., 2019) use bag-of-words classification approaches (Georgescul, 2010; Aleksandrova et al., 2019).

Submissions to the yearly Wiki Workshop at The Web Conference have also considered identifying all types of bias with a single model, using approaches including combining user metadata and machine learning models. Recently, Hube and Fetahu (2018) achieved an f1 score of 0.69 using a generated bias word list and other hand-picked features, including part of speech tags and a context window around each bias word.

We are aware of no prior work that has focused on the identification of puffery (also known as peacock phrases), which Wikipedia defines as words "used without attribution to promote the subject of an article, while neither imparting nor plainly summarizing verifiable information" (Wikipedia, 2021c). Examples of puffery include "excellent infrastructure," "renowned journalist," or "defining figure." Note that puffery is distinct from positive sentiment, as Wikipedia allows praise when it has proper attribution and reflects a consensus opinion of reputable sources, for example, "Dylan was included in Time's 100: The Most Important People of the Century, in which he was called 'master poet, caustic social critic and intrepid, guiding spirit of the counterculture generation'.[1]"

Figure 1: Both types of puffery warnings: an article-level warning (top) and a sentence-level warning (bottom).

3 Data Collection

Puffery in Wikipedia is noted by editors using the "puffery" or "peacock" tags, which can be applied to an article, section, or sentence, and display a warning at the top of an article or section, or a superscript after a sentence. Examples are shown in fig. 1. Similar to Hube and Fetahu (2018), we take the sentence tags as positive examples, extracting 284 sentences[1] annotated with tags containing the words "puffery" or "peacock" from Wikipedia articles. However, as there is no Wikipedia tag to indicate that a sentence is *without* issues, we considered several approaches to extract negative examples: two types of random selection, and when we discovered that random selection yielded problematic datasets, an information retrieval-based approach.[2]

Same-article random sampling For each puffery sentence, we sampled one random sentence from the same article as a non-puffery sentence with the same topic. In an attempt to avoid selecting negative sentences that contain puffery but are not tagged as such, we excluded any article where there were any template warnings displayed at the top of the page, and any sentence tagged with any issue.

[1] In all experiments, sentences were extracted with a combination of BeautifulSoup4 and NLTK (Bird et al., 2009).

[2] We also investigated using revision history to look for puffery that had been edited out, but because of the low prevalence of tagged puffery, this approach was overly time-intensive and produced too few results.

Same-article random	Random-article random	Information retrieval
most	school	great
dr	cs1	successful
very	training	many
community	diving	game
career	regiment	robin
famous	film	community
of	burton	impressive

Table 1: The top positive features (indicating a sentence may contain puffery) in linear SVM BoW models for different data selection strategies. Features are listed from most influential at the top to least influential at the bottom.

Random-article random sampling For each puffery sentence, we sampled a random other article (using Wikipedia's "random article" functionality) and a random sentence from that article. We excluded articles with any template warnings or sentences tagged with issues (thus also excluding the original article with the puffery). Because the supermajority of articles do not contain puffery, we expect that these sentences are highly likely to not contain puffery.

Information-retrieval sampling For each puffery sentence, we take a Lucene index of Wikipedia documents, use the puffery sentence as a query, take the top-retrieved article, and select a random sentence from that article. As before, we excluded articles with any template warnings or sentences tagged with issues. Because typically only a small number of words in each sentence are puffery, we expect the articles to be more closely related to the topic of the puffery sentence than articles chosen at random.

Analysis For all data selection techniques, we trained a linear support vector machine (SVM) classifier with bag-of-words (BoW) features and inspected both the model's performance (to see if the task was learnable), and the most important features of the model (to see if sensible things were being learned). Table 1 shows the most important features of each model. Same-article random sampling resulted in an f1-score at 0.542, and some features related to puffery (e.g., "famous") but others not (e.g., "dr"). A manual inspection of the examples selected by this strategy revealed that many of our "negative" examples were actually positive ones (containing phrases like "strong corporate culture," "widely acclaimed," and "renowed journalist"), because non-tagged puffery is common in articles containing a puffery-tagged sentence. Random-article random sampling resulted in an F1-score of 0.780, and a set of features that suggested that the model was simply learning a topic bias: articles about education, film, and business were more likely to be tagged for puffery. Information-retrieval sampling resulted in an F1 score of 0.658, with top features reflecting peacock words, such as "great", "successful", and "impressive".

We thus selected information-retrieval sampling to construct the official evaluation dataset. The final dataset contains 284 puffery sentences and 284 topic-matched non-puffery sentences. These 568 sentences were shuffled together before randomly selecting 10% (57 sentences) as a test set.

4 Models

We considered two machine-learning models for puffery prediction.

BoW-SVM Similar to weasel word detection approaches (Georgescul, 2010; Aleksandrova et al., 2019), we train a linear support vector machine on bag-of-words features.

RoBERTa We also consider a transformer-based neural network, RoBERTa, which has shown excellent performance on a variety of natural language processing tasks (Liu et al., 2019). RoBERTa, unlike the bag-of-words model, can consider the context in which potential puffery words occur. We fine-tuned RoBERTa with the puffery data, using a learning rate of 1×10^{-5} and a batch size of 5.

+CITE Preliminary experiments with the above two models revealed that they still struggled with sentences that were mildly positive, but factual and accompanied by citations. We thus augment the model inputs by inserting a pseudo-token "CITE" at each position in the sentence where a citation occurred. In the BoW-SVM model, this means the bag-of-words CITE feature will give the count of citations in the sentence. In the RoBERTa model, this means the transformer's self-attention can decide how much to attend to each CITE (if present) when evaluating a potential puffery word.

5 Results

Table 2 shows the performance of all models in terms of precision, recall, and F1 of detecting

Model	Input	P	R	F1
BoW-SVM	words only	0.600	0.729	0.658
BoW-SVM	words + CITE	0.627	0.743	0.680
RoBERTa	words only	0.630	0.853	0.726
RoBERTa	words + CITE	**0.937**	**0.989**	**0.963**

Table 2: Performance of models with different input types on the puffery prediction test set.

puffery. The BoW-SVM model, even with citation information, achieves only 0.680 F1. RoBERTa without citation information has a much higher recall than the BoW-SVM models (+0.110 or more higher). Representing citations in the input leads to huge gains for RoBERTa (+0.307 precision, +0.136 recall), with this best model achieving 0.963 F1.

Qualitative analysis Adding citation information to the BoW-SVM model allowed it to correctly classify "She was inducted into the Alabama Women's Hall of Fame in 1992 [citation]" as non-puffery, while the model without citations incorrectly labelled this as puffery. But only RoBERTa with citation information was able to correctly classify "Their colour names, such as Elephant's Breath, have becoming talking points [citation] in themselves." as non-puffery. (This sentence cites an article where the colors are a major talking point, so there is no puffery here.) This demonstrates that is it important not only to know when citations are present (what the BoW-SVM sees), but where exactly they occur (what RoBERTa sees).

6 Integration

Having developed a model that can accurately detect puffery, our focus shifted to sharing it with the Wikipedia community. The Wikimedia Foundation has a robust system for technical contributions, in the form of user-maintained "tools" hosted on Toolforge, a hosting environment with access to replicas of Wikipedia's production databases (Wikitech, 2021a). Bots may read data from Wikipedia by querying these MariaDB databases, using schema documentation available on MediaWiki and a Python library, `toolforge` (Wikitech, 2021b).

Wikipedia has a detailed policy on bots, which forbids bots from making changes to address subjective issues (Wikipedia, 2021b). This includes bias detection, as editors may have differing opinions on whether a particular sentence is biased or not. This policy means that a bot cannot add the

Figure 2: Screenshot of the bot's output after it has seen pages with puffery.

puffery tag to sentences.

After consultation with a Wikipedia administrator, CaptainEek, we designed a bot to maintain a list of pages that required investigation, similar to the Category:Articles with peacock terms page, but generated from model predictions rather than manual editor tags. The intent of both pages is that Wikipedia editors with spare time will check the page and fix the articles on it. Because of technical limitations on Wikipedia's server, we trained and used the smaller AlBERT model instead of RoBERTa. On the same train and test set as table 2, AlBERT achieves 0.899 F1.

The model runs once per hour, considering only the 1,000 most recently edited pages. To reduce computational cost, the model runs on 15 randomly selected sentences from each of these pages. As the bot is working at a document level instead of a sentence level, the bot labels a page as containing puffery if more than half of these selected sentences are labeled as puffery. This threshold also reduces the false positive rate.

The bot's work is visible on its user page[3]. A sample of such work is shown in fig. 2.

7 Limitations

The largest limitations of this work are the size of the dataset (284 puffery sentences) and the balanced ratio between puffery and non-puffery sentences. The balanced ratio was chosen to better align topics between puffery and non-puffery examples; however, it is not an accurate reflection

[3] `https://en.wikipedia.org/wiki/User:PeacockPhraseFinderBot`

of Wikipedia, where puffery is very rare. Thus, while this dataset is useful for refining bias detection models, real-world performance may suffer from over-prediction of puffery.

8 Conclusions & Future Work

This project demonstrates the challenge of collecting data for puffery detection models, and emphasizes the importance of careful dataset curation to avoid spurious correlations in the data. Our best dataset construction approach avoids these problems by using information retrieval techniques to ensure positive and negative examples are topically matched.

Our work also demonstrates the importance of thinking carefully about input representations, even in the age of transformer models like RoBERTa. With the standard sequence of words input encoding typically used with RoBERTa, performance was only 0.068 F1 above a simple bag-of-words SVM. However, when we augmented the input with the location of citations, RoBERTa's performance jumped 30% to 0.963 F1.

Despite our model's excellent performance, challenges remain. Our model could likely be fooled by attaching spurious or unreliable citations to sentences with puffery, since the model knows nothing of the content of the citations, only their locations in the sentence. This may argue for coupling our puffery detection techniques with techniques for evaluating the quality of citations, such as considering scientific journal impact scores (Nielsen, 2007).

References

Desislava Aleksandrova, François Lareau, and Pierre André Ménard. 2019. Multilingual sentence-level bias detection in Wikipedia. In *Proceedings of the International Conference on Recent Advances in Natural Language Processing (RANLP 2019)*, pages 42–51, Varna, Bulgaria. INCOMA Ltd.

Steven Bird, Ewan Klein, and Edward Loper. 2009. *Natural Language Processing with Python: Analyzing Text with the Natural Language Toolkit*, 1st edition edition. O'Reilly Media, Beijing ; Cambridge Mass.

Richárd Farkas, Veronika Vincze, György Móra, János Csirik, and György Szarvas. 2010. The CoNLL-2010 shared task: Learning to detect hedges and their scope in natural language text. In *Proceedings of the Fourteenth Conference on Computational Natural Language Learning – Shared Task*, pages 1–12, Uppsala, Sweden. Association for Computational Linguistics.

Maria Georgescul. 2010. A hedgehop over a max-margin framework using hedge cues. In *Proceedings of the Fourteenth Conference on Computational Natural Language Learning – Shared Task*, pages 26–31, Uppsala, Sweden. Association for Computational Linguistics.

Christoph Hube and Besnik Fetahu. 2018. Detecting Biased Statements in Wikipedia. In *Companion Proceedings of the The Web Conference 2018*, WWW '18, pages 1779–1786, Lyon, France. International World Wide Web Conferences Steering Committee.

Yinhan Liu, Myle Ott, Naman Goyal, Jingfei Du, Mandar Joshi, Danqi Chen, Omer Levy, Mike Lewis, Luke Zettlemoyer, and Veselin Stoyanov. 2019. Roberta: A robustly optimized BERT pretraining approach. *CoRR*, abs/1907.11692.

Finn Årup Nielsen. 2007. Scientific citations in wikipedia. *CoRR*, abs/0705.2106.

Wikimedia. 2021. ORES - MediaWiki.

Wikipedia. 2021a. Wikipedia. Page Version ID: 1019154774.

Wikipedia. 2021b. Wikipedia:Bot policy. Page Version ID: 1015757461.

Wikipedia. 2021c. Wikipedia:Manual of Style/Words to watch. Page Version ID: 1019528666.

Wikipedia. 2021d. Wikipedia:Neutral point of view. Page Version ID: 1015224310.

Wikipedia. 2021e. Wikipedia:Protection policy. Page Version ID: 1017833570.

Wikipedia. 2021f. Wikipedia:Size of Wikipedia. Page Version ID: 1019560660.

Wikipedia. 2021g. Wikipedia:statistics. Page Version ID: 1020753220.

Wikitech. 2021a. Portal:Toolforge - Wikitech.

Wikitech. 2021b. User:Legoktm/toolforge library - Wikitech.

Robustness and Sensitivity of BERT Models Predicting Alzheimer's Disease from Text

Jekaterina Novikova
Winterlight Labs / Toronto, Canada
jekaterina@winterlightlabs.com

Abstract

Understanding robustness and sensitivity of BERT models predicting Alzheimer's disease from text is important for both developing better classification models and for understanding their capabilities and limitations. In this paper, we analyze how a controlled amount of desired and undesired text alterations impacts performance of BERT. We show that BERT is robust to natural linguistic variations in text. On the other hand, we show that BERT is not sensitive to removing clinically important information from text.

1 Introduction

Alzheimer's disease (AD) is a prevalent neurodegerative condition that inhibits cognitive abilities and impacts one's language abilities. For example, cognitively impaired people tend to use more pronouns instead of nouns, and pause more often between sentences in narrative speech (Roark et al., 2011). This insight makes automatic detection possible. Machine learning (ML) classifiers can detect cognitive impairments given descriptive linguistic features or using pre-trained large language models (Balagopalan et al., 2018; Zhu et al., 2019).

BERT is a model that achieves promising performance on a variety of tasks, including AD prediction from speech and language (Searle et al., 2020; Yuan et al., 2020). However, this promising performance may be fallacious, i.e. deep neural language models may learn pseudo patterns from training data to attain high performance on test sets (Goyal et al., 2019; Gururangan et al., 2018; Glockner et al., 2018; Tsuchiya, 2018; Geva et al., 2019). Therefore, in order to be confident in the outcomes of BERT models classifying AD it is important to assess whether these models are robust to some natural noise that may be introduced in language. It is also important to know if BERT models are sensitive to the aspects that are considered to be important for recognizing cognitive impairment from human language.

In this paper, we analyze robustness and sensitivity of BERT models in their ability to classify AD from text by analysing the effect of noise, introduced from artificial text perturbations, on the performance of the model. Some previous research was conducted on the impact of ASR-related noise on dementia detection (Balagopalan et al., 2020b), as well as the effect of artificial text alterations on AD classification (Novikova et al., 2019). However, these previous studies only focus on conventional classification models, such as Random Forest and SVM. To the best of our knowledge, we are the first to analyse how the noise introduced by texts perturbations impact BERT models, in the domain of AD classification.

2 Methodology

2.1 Data

We use the ADReSS Challenge dataset (Luz et al., 2020), which consists of 156 speech samples and associated transcripts from non-AD (N=78) and AD (N=78) English-speaking participants. Speech is elicited from participants through the Cookie Theft picture from the Boston Diagnostic Aphasia exam (Goodglass et al., 2001). In contrast to other datasets for AD detection such as DementiaBank's English Pitt Corpus (Becker et al., 1994), the ADReSS challenge dataset is well balanced in terms of age and gender (Table 1). Another benefit of this dataset is its division into standard train and test sets that makes it easy to directly compare to the previous research in the area.

2.2 Model

Multiple recent studies showed that BERT is a promising model achieving strong enough performance in detecting Alzheimer's disease from transcribed speech (Searle et al., 2020; Yuan et al., 2020; Balagopalan et al., 2020a, 2021). Motivated

Proceedings of the 2021 EMNLP Workshop W-NUT: The Seventh Workshop on Noisy User-generated Text, pages 334–339
November 11, 2021.

Table 1: Basic characteristics of the patients in each group in the ADReSS challenge dataset.

Dataset			Class	
			AD	Non-AD
ADReSS	Train	Male	24	24
		Female	30	30
ADReSS	Test	Male	11	11
		Female	13	13

by these results, we use a fine-tuned BERT (Devlin et al., 2019) model in this work. To leverage the language information encoded by BERT (Devlin et al., 2019), we add a linear layer mapping representations from the final layer of a pre-trained 12-layer BERT base[1] for the AD vs non-AD binary classification task. The transcript-level input to the model consists of transcribed utterances with corresponding start and separator special tokens for each utterance, following Liu *et al.* (Liu and Lapata, 2019). A pooled embedding summarizing information across all tokens in the transcript is used as the aggregate transcript representation, and passed to the classification layer (Devlin et al., 2019; Wolf et al., 2019). This model is then fine-tuned on training data for AD detection. For hyperparameter tuning, we optimize the number of epochs to 10 by varying it from 1 to 12 during cross-validation. Adam optimizer (Kingma and Ba, 2014) and warmup linear learning rate scheduling (Paszke et al., 2019) are used, based on prior work on fine-tuning BERT (Devlin et al., 2019; Wolf et al., 2019).

2.3 Perturbation Approaches

We used a variety of word-based augmentation approaches with the help of the nlpaug[2] library to generate perturbed versions of the test set of the ADReSS dataset for the experiments.

Back-translation: this augmentation technique proposed by Sennrich et al. (2016) leverages two translation models, one translating the source text from English to German and the other translating it back to English. Back-translated texts should maintain the semantics and basic syntactic structure of original texts and as such, robust model's performance should not decrease because of this augmentation.

Word substitution with synonyms: following Niu and Bansal (2018), we substitute a controlled varying amount of words in the transcript (10-90%) with their synonyms in order to maintain semantic meaning of the utterances. Synonyms are extracted from the NLTK WordNet corpus[3]. Replacing words with their synonyms should not affect the ability of a robust model to accurately distinguish between healthy and AD classes.

Embedding-based word substitution: following Alzantot et al. (2018); Wang and Yang (2015), we use pre-trained word2vec embeddings to perform a KNN with cosine similarity search to find the similar word for replacement. We then substitute a varying subsets (from 10 to 90%) of the original transcripts with these replacements. We hypothesize that model performance can be affected by such augmentation stronger than by synonym replacement, although this effect should not be significant for a robust AD prediction model.

Removal of filled pauses: we remove all the filled pauses (transcribed as *um* and *uh*) from the original texts. Previous literature highlights the importance of pauses in Alzheimer's disease detection from speech (Calley et al., 2010; Mack et al., 2013; Seifart et al., 2018). Several authors report increases in AD detection performance by extracting acoustic features such as filled pause counts (Eyre et al., 2020; Tóth et al., 2015, 2018; Pistono et al., 2016). Removal of such information should make it more difficult for a model to accurately detect AD-related samples of text.

Removal of information units: multiple studies of AD narratives in picture description tasks have reported the importance of information units in detecting cognitive impairment (Fraser et al., 2016; Croisile et al., 1996). Following (Croisile et al., 1996), we define four key categories of information units - subjects, locations, objects, and actions - and delete them from the original transcripts to generate perturbed versions of the test set. Such a removal should make it more difficult for a model to distinguish between healthy and AD samples.

3 Results

The results of testing the fine-tuned BERT model on the variety of perturbed versions of the ADReSS test set show that the performance changes differently depending on different types of text alterations (Table 2). Removing tokens of filled pauses does not change the performance at all. Removing

[1] https://huggingface.co/bert-base-uncased

[2] https://github.com/makcedward/nlpaug , the Python library for generating synthetic textual and speech data.

[3] https://www.nltk.org/howto/wordnet.html

Type of perturbation	Level of perturbation	Acc	F1	Prec	Rec	Spec	W_1
Original transcript	NA	0.83	0.83	0.86	0.79	0.88	NA
Deleting filled pauses	All	0.83	0.83	0.86	0.79	0.88	2.40
Deleting information units	All	0.81	0.84	0.74	0.96	0.67	2.87
	Action	0.77	0.80	0.71	0.92	0.63	2.87
	Location	0.77	0.78	0.74	0.83	0.71	0.77
	Object	0.75	0.79	0.69	0.92	0.58	2.45
	Subject	0.79	0.79	0.79	0.79	0.79	2.13
Back translation	Eng <->DE	0.75	0.75	0.75	0.75	0.75	6.02
Substituting with the most similar word (via word2vec embeddings)	10%	0.83	0.84	0.81	0.88	0.79	5.63
	20%	0.81	0.82	0.78	0.88	0.75	6.23
	30%	0.81	0.82	0.80	0.83	0.79	6.23
	40%	0.81	0.82	0.78	0.88	0.75	6.32
	50%	0.81	0.80	0.86	0.75	0.88	6.20
	60%	0.83	0.84	0.81	0.88	0.79	6.10
	70%	0.71	0.70	0.73	0.67	0.75	6.32
	80%	0.75	0.75	0.75	0.75	0.75	6.35
	90%	0.77	0.78	0.76	0.79	0.75	6.26
Substituting synonyms (via WordNet)	10%	0.77	0.79	0.72	0.88	0.67	3.55
	20%	0.75	0.75	0.75	0.75	0.75	3.97
	30%	0.77	0.78	0.76	0.79	0.75	4.12
	40%	0.75	0.77	0.71	0.83	0.67	4.01
	50%	0.75	0.75	0.75	0.75	0.75	3.86
	60%	0.71	0.70	0.73	0.67	0.75	4.33
	70%	0.81	0.82	0.80	0.83	0.79	3.98
	80%	0.81	0.82	0.78	0.88	0.75	4.08
	90%	0.77	0.78	0.74	0.83	0.71	4.16

Table 2: Performance of the fine-tuned BERT model and similarity between original and perturbed texts (Wasserstein distance W_1).

information units, however, decreases the accuracy of the model by 4-8%, depending on the type of the information unit. Back translation and substitutions of words with their synonyms or otherwise similar words also negatively affect performance of the model, although have the opposite effect on recall vs specificity.

4 Discussion

4.1 Change in Classification Performance

Undesired change: As we have mentioned in Section 2.3, some types of text alterations, such as back translation, synonym substitution and embedding-based substitution, represent natural noise that can occur in user-generated texts. Changes in classification performance are not desired in this case because we want the model to be robust towards multiple paraphrases and use of synonyms. Our fine-tuned BERT model behaves in a robust way in terms of F1 and accuracy scores when up to 40% of words are substituted with similar words based on word2vec embeddings (the F1 score decreases by 1% and accuracy - by 2%, both changes not significant with McNemar's test p >0.65) or synonyms (a decrease in 4-8% in F1 and accuracy, both changes not significant with McNemar's test p >0.15).

Type of perturbation	Correlation between W_1 and Acc	F1	Prec	Rec	Spec
Deleting informational units	0.24	0.56	-0.07	0.52	-0.21
Substituting with the most similar word (via word2vec embeddings)	0.77	0.89	0.89	0.87	-0.91
Deep representation (VGG-16)	-0.26	-0.37	0.10	-0.45	0.41

Table 3: Correlation between similarity and performance metrics.

Interestingly, recall and specificity values seem to show the opposite results here - specificity decreases by up to 21%, while recall stays on the same level or even increases by 4-9%. Substituting words with their similar alternatives or synonyms may be understood as increasing the level of lexical complexity, i.e. the model is introduced with multiple, maybe less usual, ways to express the same meaning. It is known that lexical complexity is one of the prominent ways that allow detecting cognitive impairment from language. Thus such an implicit way to change the lexical complexity of texts seems to help the BERT model in reducing the amount of true positive errors while detecting AD. However, more than 40% of such substitutions may make the original texts less realistic, which, as we see from the results, substantially reduces model performance, including reducing recall level.

Desired change: Other types of text alterations, such as removal of information units or tokens representing filled pauses, are not considered to be natural noise. As these characteristics of language are clinically important in detecting cognitive impairment, the models should be sensitive to such changes in language. Our results show that the fine-tuned BERT model ignores completely removal of filled pauses. Performance of the model decreases by 3-5% of F1 as a reaction to deleting different types of information units but this change is not significant (McNemar's test p >0.18). This change in performance is similar to the change caused by synonym substitution and shows that the model is not sensitive enough to removal of clinically relevant information.

This leads us to inspect how each type of alterations affects distributional shift from the original text and whether there is a relation between the shift and model's performance.

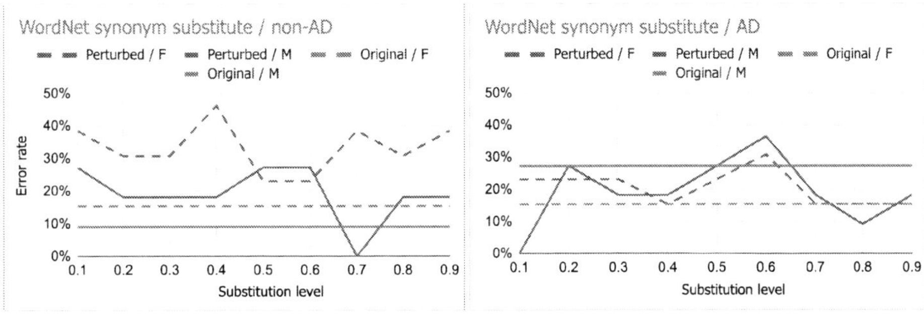

Figure 1: Differences in error rate between genders, by class. Here, M means 'male' and F means 'female'.

4.2 Correlation with Distributional Shift

Inspired by (Lee et al., 2018) where hidden activations were used to detect out-of-distribution samples for images and by Rychener et al. (2020) applied this method to text, we used sentence embeddings produced by BERT to quantify the distributional shift among the original test set and its perturbed versions. To understand the level of dissimilarity among the versions of test sets, we calculated the 1-Wasserstein distance ("earth mover distance", W_1), since it measures the minimum cost to turn one probability distribution into another (Table 2).

W_1 values show that deletion of information units and filled pauses has the lowest effect on the original text, while word2vec-based substitution shifts the distribution further away from the original. Correlation between performance metrics and W_1 is not consistent across different types of text alterations (Table 3): it is strongly positive between F1 and accuracy scores in case of embedding-based substitutions (0.77 and 0.89), positive but less strong (0.24 and 0.56) in case of deleting clinically relevant information, and negative in case of synonym substitution (-0.26 and -0.37). These inconsistencies imply that the lack of sensitivity in BERT models is caused by intrinsic model reasons rather than distributional shift of test data.

4.3 Differences Based on Gender

In order to understand if BERT performance is biased towards any gender, we analyse the rate of error within each gender group and how the error rate is changing with additional amount of text alterations. The results of this analysis do not reveal any differences between males and females within the class of AD data samples. However when it comes to the non-AD class, BERT tends to misclassify the text samples produced by female subjects significantly more often than those produced by males, across all types of text alterations. The effect is pronounced the most in the case of synonym substitution (see Figure 1), where the error rate of classifying female-produced samples is 14% higher on average than that of male-produced samples[4]. Given that both training and test sets of the dataset are well balanced, such a difference implies the pre-trained BERT model is gender-biased and this bias is not eliminated during fine-tuning.

5 Limitations and Conclusions

In this work, we analysed how the controlled amount of desired and undesired text alterations impacts BERT classification performance in the domain of AD detection. We showed that BERT is robust enough to the natural linguistic noise, although the model is biased towards text samples of non-AD females. On the other hand, BERT is not sensitive enough to removal of clinically relevant information. This lack of sensitivity is not directly influenced by distributional shift.

This work is a first step towards investigating BERT models' robustness and sensitivity in the domain of AD detection from text, and we only report empirical results of one BERT model fine-tuned and tested on one dataset. More work should be done in this area to ensure the results are widely generalizable within the domain. Textual data used in our experiment represent transcribed conversational speech and as such, may be quite different from other types of texts, e.g. written text. Future work is necessary to see if the effect of text alterations remain the same with other types of text.

[4] Also significantly different based on t-test, $p < 0.005$.

References

Moustafa Alzantot, Yash Sharma, Ahmed Elgohary, Bo-Jhang Ho, Mani Srivastava, and Kai-Wei Chang. 2018. Generating natural language adversarial examples. In *Proceedings of the 2018 Conference on Empirical Methods in Natural Language Processing*, pages 2890–2896, Brussels, Belgium. Association for Computational Linguistics.

Aparna Balagopalan, Benjamin Eyre, Jessica Robin, Frank Rudzicz, and Jekaterina Novikova. 2021. Comparing pre-trained and feature-based models for prediction of alzheimer's disease based on speech. *Frontiers in aging neuroscience*, 13:189.

Aparna Balagopalan, Benjamin Eyre, Frank Rudzicz, and Jekaterina Novikova. 2020a. To BERT or not to BERT: Comparing Speech and Language-Based Approaches for Alzheimer's Disease Detection. In *Proc. Interspeech 2020*, pages 2167–2171.

Aparna Balagopalan, Jekaterina Novikova, Frank Rudzicz, and Marzyeh Ghassemi. 2018. The effect of heterogeneous data for Alzheimer's disease detection from speech. *arXiv preprint arXiv:1811.12254*.

Aparna Balagopalan, Ksenia Shkaruta, and Jekaterina Novikova. 2020b. Impact of asr on alzheimer's disease detection: All errors are equal, but deletions are more equal than others. In *Proceedings of the Sixth Workshop on Noisy User-generated Text (W-NUT 2020)*, pages 159–164.

James T Becker, François Boiler, Oscar L Lopez, Judith Saxton, and Karen L McGonigle. 1994. The natural history of Alzheimer's disease: description of study cohort and accuracy of diagnosis. *Archives of Neurology*, 51(6):585–594.

Clifford S Calley, Gail D Tillman, Kyle Womack, Patricia Moore, John Hart Jr, and Michael A Kraut. 2010. Subjective report of word-finding and memory deficits in normal aging and dementia. *Cognitive and behavioral neurology: official journal of the Society for Behavioral and Cognitive Neurology*, 23(3):185.

Bernard Croisile, Bernadette Ska, Marie-Josee Brabant, Annick Duchene, Yves Lepage, Gilbert Aimard, and Marc Trillet. 1996. Comparative study of oral and written picture description in patients with alzheimer's disease. *Brain and language*, 53(1):1–19.

Jacob Devlin, Ming-Wei Chang, Kenton Lee, and Kristina Toutanova. 2019. BERT: Pre-training of Deep Bidirectional Transformers for Language Understanding. In *Proceedings of the 2019 Conference of the North American Chapter of the Association for Computational Linguistics: Volume 1 (Long and Short Papers)*, pages 4171–4186.

Ben Eyre, Aparna Balagopalan, and Jekaterina Novikova. 2020. Fantastic features and where to find them: Detecting cognitive impairment with a subsequence classification guided approach. In *Proceedings of the Sixth Workshop on Noisy User-generated Text (W-NUT 2020)*, pages 193–199, Online. Association for Computational Linguistics.

Kathleen C Fraser, Jed A Meltzer, and Frank Rudzicz. 2016. Linguistic features identify alzheimer's disease in narrative speech. *Journal of Alzheimer's Disease*, 49(2):407–422.

Mor Geva, Yoav Goldberg, and Jonathan Berant. 2019. Are we modeling the task or the annotator? an investigation of annotator bias in natural language understanding datasets. In *Proceedings of the 2019 Conference on Empirical Methods in Natural Language Processing and the 9th International Joint Conference on Natural Language Processing (EMNLP-IJCNLP)*, pages 1161–1166, Hong Kong, China. Association for Computational Linguistics.

Max Glockner, Vered Shwartz, and Yoav Goldberg. 2018. Breaking NLI systems with sentences that require simple lexical inferences. In *Proceedings of the 56th Annual Meeting of the Association for Computational Linguistics (Volume 2: Short Papers)*, pages 650–655, Melbourne, Australia. Association for Computational Linguistics.

Harold Goodglass, Edith Kaplan, and Barbara Barresi. 2001. *BDAE-3: Boston Diagnostic Aphasia Examination–Third Edition*. Lippincott Williams & Wilkins Philadelphia, PA.

Yash Goyal, Tejas Khot, Aishwarya Agrawal, Douglas Summers-Stay, Dhruv Batra, and Devi Parikh. 2019. Making the V in VQA Matter: Elevating the Role of Image Understanding in Visual Question Answering. *International Journal of Computer Vision*, 127(4):398–414.

Suchin Gururangan, Swabha Swayamdipta, Omer Levy, Roy Schwartz, Samuel Bowman, and Noah A. Smith. 2018. Annotation artifacts in natural language inference data. In *Proceedings of the 2018 Conference of the North American Chapter of the Association for Computational Linguistics: Human Language Technologies, Volume 2 (Short Papers)*, pages 107–112, New Orleans, Louisiana. Association for Computational Linguistics.

Diederik P Kingma and Jimmy Ba. 2014. Adam: A method for stochastic optimization. *arXiv preprint arXiv:1412.6980*.

Kimin Lee, Kibok Lee, Honglak Lee, and Jinwoo Shin. 2018. A simple unified framework for detecting out-of-distribution samples and adversarial attacks. In *Proceedings of the 32nd International Conference on Neural Information Processing Systems*, pages 7167–7177.

Yang Liu and Mirella Lapata. 2019. Text summarization with pretrained encoders. In *Proceedings of the 2019 Conference on Empirical Methods in Natural Language Processing and the 9th International*

Joint Conference on Natural Language Processing (EMNLP-IJCNLP), pages 3721–3731.

Saturnino Luz, Fasih Haider, Sofia de la Fuente, Davida Fromm, and Brian MacWhinney. 2020. Alzheimer's Dementia Recognition through Spontaneous Speech: The ADReSS Challenge.

Jennifer Mack, Aya Meltzer-Asscher, Sarah Dove, Sandra Weintraub, Marsel Mesulam, and Cynthia K Thompson. 2013. Word-finding pauses in primary progressive aphasia (ppa): Effects of lexical category.

Tong Niu and Mohit Bansal. 2018. Adversarial over-sensitivity and over-stability strategies for dialogue models. In *Proceedings of the 22nd Conference on Computational Natural Language Learning*, pages 486–496.

Jekaterina Novikova, Aparna Balagopalan, Ksenia Shkaruta, and Frank Rudzicz. 2019. Lexical features are more vulnerable, syntactic features have more predictive power. *W-NUT 2019*, page 431.

Adam Paszke, Sam Gross, Francisco Massa, Adam Lerer, James Bradbury, Gregory Chanan, Trevor Killeen, Zeming Lin, Natalia Gimelshein, Luca Antiga, et al. 2019. Pytorch: An imperative style, high-performance deep learning library. In *Advances in Neural Information Processing Systems*, pages 8024–8035.

Aurélie Pistono, Mélanie Jucla, Emmanuel J Barbeau, Laure Saint-Aubert, Béatrice Lemesle, Benjamin Calvet, Barbara Köpke, Michèle Puel, and Jérémie Pariente. 2016. Pauses during autobiographical discourse reflect episodic memory processes in early alzheimer's disease. *Journal of Alzheimer's Disease*, 50(3):687–698.

Brian Roark, Margaret Mitchell, John-Paul Hosom, Kristy Hollingshead, and Jeffrey Kaye. 2011. Spoken language derived measures for detecting mild cognitive impairment. *IEEE transactions on audio, speech, and language processing*, 19(7):2081–2090.

Yves Rychener, Xavier Renard, Djamé Seddah, Pascal Frossard, and Marcin Detyniecki. 2020. Sentence-based model agnostic nlp interpretability. *arXiv preprint arXiv:2012.13189*.

Thomas Searle, Zina Ibrahim, and Richard Dobson. 2020. Comparing Natural Language Processing Techniques for Alzheimer's Dementia Prediction in Spontaneous Speech. In *Proc. Interspeech 2020*, pages 2192–2196.

Frank Seifart, Jan Strunk, Swintha Danielsen, Iren Hartmann, Brigitte Pakendorf, Søren Wichmann, Alena Witzlack-Makarevich, Nivja H de Jong, and Balthasar Bickel. 2018. Nouns slow down speech across structurally and culturally diverse languages. *Proceedings of the National Academy of Sciences*, 115(22):5720–5725.

Rico Sennrich, Barry Haddow, and Alexandra Birch. 2016. Improving neural machine translation models with monolingual data. In *Proceedings of the 54th Annual Meeting of the Association for Computational Linguistics (Volume 1: Long Papers)*, pages 86–96, Berlin, Germany. Association for Computational Linguistics.

Laszló Tóth, Gábor Gosztolya, Veronika Vincze, Ildikó Hoffmann, Gréta Szatlóczki, Edit Biró, Fruzsina Zsura, Magdolna Pákáski, and János Kálmán. 2015. Automatic detection of mild cognitive impairment from spontaneous speech using asr. In *Sixteenth Annual Conference of the International Speech Communication Association*.

László Tóth, Ildikó Hoffmann, Gábor Gosztolya, Veronika Vincze, Gréta Szatlóczki, Zoltán Bánréti, Magdolna Pákáski, and János Kálmán. 2018. A speech recognition-based solution for the automatic detection of mild cognitive impairment from spontaneous speech. *Current Alzheimer Research*, 15(2):130–138.

Masatoshi Tsuchiya. 2018. Performance impact caused by hidden bias of training data for recognizing textual entailment. In *Proceedings of the Eleventh International Conference on Language Resources and Evaluation (LREC 2018)*, Miyazaki, Japan. European Language Resources Association (ELRA).

William Yang Wang and Diyi Yang. 2015. That's so annoying!!!: A lexical and frame-semantic embedding based data augmentation approach to automatic categorization of annoying behaviors using #petpeeve tweets. In *Proceedings of the 2015 Conference on Empirical Methods in Natural Language Processing*, pages 2557–2563, Lisbon, Portugal. Association for Computational Linguistics.

Thomas Wolf, L Debut, V Sanh, J Chaumond, C Delangue, A Moi, P Cistac, T Rault, R Louf, M Funtowicz, et al. 2019. Huggingface's transformers: State-of-the-art natural language processing. *ArXiv, abs/1910.03771*.

Jiahong Yuan, Yuchen Bian, Xingyu Cai, Jiaji Huang, Zheng Ye, and Kenneth Church. 2020. Disfluencies and Fine-Tuning Pre-Trained Language Models for Detection of Alzheimer's Disease. In *Proc. Interspeech 2020*, pages 2162–2166.

Zining Zhu, Jekaterina Novikova, and Frank Rudzicz. 2019. Detecting cognitive impairments by agreeing on interpretations of linguistic features. In *Proceedings of the 2019 Conference of the North American Chapter of the Association for Computational Linguistics: Human Language Technologies, Volume 1 (Long and Short Papers)*, pages 1431–1441.

Understanding Model Robustness to User-generated Noisy Texts

Jakub Náplava and **Martin Popel** and **Milan Straka** and **Jana Straková**
Charles University,
Faculty of Mathematics and Physics,
Institute of Formal and Applied Linguistics
{naplava,popel,straka,strakova}@ufal.mff.cuni.cz

Abstract

Sensitivity of deep-neural models to input noise is known to be a challenging problem. In NLP, model performance often deteriorates with naturally occurring noise, such as spelling errors. To mitigate this issue, models may leverage artificially noised data. However, the amount and type of generated noise has so far been determined arbitrarily. We therefore propose to model the errors statistically from grammatical-error-correction corpora. We present a thorough evaluation of several state-of-the-art NLP systems' robustness in multiple languages, with tasks including morpho-syntactic analysis, named entity recognition, neural machine translation, a subset of the GLUE benchmark and reading comprehension. We also compare two approaches to address the performance drop: a) training the NLP models with noised data generated by our framework; and b) reducing the input noise with external system for natural language correction. The code is released at https://github.com/ufal/kazitext.

1 Introduction

Although there has recently been an amazing progress in variety of NLP tasks (Vaswani et al., 2017; Devlin et al., 2019) with some models even reaching performance comparable to humans on certain domains (Ge et al., 2018; Popel et al., 2020), it has been shown that the models are very sensitive to noise in data (Belinkov and Bisk, 2017; Rychalska et al., 2019).

Multiple areas of NLP have been studied to evaluate the effect of noise in data (Belinkov and Bisk, 2017; Heigold et al., 2018; Ribeiro et al., 2018; Glockner et al., 2018) and a framework for text corruption to test NLP models robustness is also available (Rychalska et al., 2019). However, all these systems introduce noise in a custom-defined, arbitrary level and typically for a single language.

We suggest modeling natural noise statistically from corpora and we propose a framework with the following distinctive features:

- The error probabilities are estimated on real-world grammatical-error-correction corpora.
- The intended noisiness can be scaled to a desired level and various aspects (types) of errors can be turned on/off to test the NLP systems robustness to specific error types.

Furthermore, we also present a thorough evaluation of several current state-of-the-art NLP systems' with varying level of data noisiness and a selection of error aspects in multiple languages. The NLP tasks include morpho-syntactic analysis, named entity recognition, neural machine translation, a subset of GLUE benchmark and reading comprehension. We conclude that:

- The amount of noise is far more important than the distribution of error types.
- Sensitivity to noise differs greatly among NLP tasks. While tasks such as lemmatization require correcting the input text, only an approximate understanding is sufficient for others.

We also compare two approaches for increasing models robustness to noise: training with noise and external grammatical-error-correction (GEC) preprocessing. Our findings suggest that training with noise is beneficial for models with large capacity and large training data (neural machine translation), while the preprocessing with grammatical-error-correction is more suitable for limited-data classification tasks, such as morpho-syntactic analysis.

Finally, we also offer an evaluation on authentic noise: We assembled a new dataset with authentic Czech noisy sentences translated into English and we evaluate the noise-mitigating strategies in the neural machine translation task on this dataset.

Proceedings of the 2021 EMNLP Workshop W-NUT: The Seventh Workshop on Noisy User-generated Text, pages 340–350
November 11, 2021.

2 Related Work

Many empirical findings have shown the fact that data with natural noise deteriorate NLP systems performance. Belinkov and Bisk (2017) found that natural noise such as misspellings and typos cause significant drops in BLEU scores of character-level machine translation models. To increase the model's robustness, they trained the model on a mixture of original and noisy input and found out that it learnt to address certain amount of errors. Similar findings were observed by Heigold et al. (2018) who tested machine translation and morphological tagging under three types of word-level errors.

Ribeiro et al. (2018) defined a set of substitution rules that produce semantically equivalent text variants. They used them to test systems in machine comprehension, visual question answering and sentiment analysis. Glockner et al. (2018) created a new test set for natural language inference and showed that current systems do not generalize well even for a single-word replacements by synonyms and antonyms.

Rychalska et al. (2019) implemented a framework for introducing multiple noise types into text such as removing or swapping articles, rewriting digit numbers into words or introducing errors in spelling. They found out in four NLP tasks that even recent state-of-the-art systems based on contextualized word embeddings are not completely robust against such natural noise. They also retrained the systems on noisy data and observed improvements for certain error types.

Similarly to Rychalska et al. (2019), we also developed a general framework that allows to test a variety of NLP tasks. The difference is that we estimate the probabilities of individual error types from real-world error corpora. This makes the generated sentences more similar to what humans would do. Moreover, since we defined the individual error types with no language-specific rules, we can apply it to multiple languages with an available annotated grammatical-error corpus.

Grammatical-error corpora are typically used as training data for estimating error statistics in GEC systems. In a setting similar to ours, Choe et al. (2019); Rozovskaya et al. (2017) also estimated error statistics and used them to generate additional training data for GEC systems. However, compared to our approach, they defined only a small set of predefined error categories and used it specifically for training GEC systems whereas we also use it to asses model performance in noisy scenarios.

Authentic Noise Evaluation The growing interest in developing production-ready machine translation models that are robust to natural noise resulted in the First Shared Task on Machine Translation Robustness (Li et al., 2019). The shared task used the MTNT dataset (Michel and Neubig, 2018), which consists of noisy texts collected from Reddit and their translations between English and French and English and Japanese.

Improving Model Robustness Using Noisy Data Majority of research on improving model robustness is dedicated to training on a mixture of original and noisy data. The same procedure is usually used for generating both the test corpus and training data (Belinkov and Bisk, 2017; Heigold et al., 2018; Ribeiro et al., 2018; Rychalska et al., 2019).

To generate synthetic training data, researchers in machine translation and GEC often use so called back-translation (Sennrich et al., 2016). A reverse model translating in the opposite direction (i.e. from the target language to the source language or from the clean sentence into noisy sentence, respectively) is trained (Rei et al., 2017; Náplava, 2017; Kasewa et al., 2018; Xie et al., 2018). It is then used on the corpus of clean sentences to generate noisy input data. While this approach might generate high-quality synthetic data, it requires large volumes of training data.

We evaluate two approaches to alleviate performance drop on noisy data: We either train the system on a mixture of synthetic (generated statistically from real error corpora) and original authentic data; or we use an external grammatical-error-correction system to correct the noisy data before inputting them to the system itself. We are not aware of any other work that compares these two approaches and we believe that both approaches may be beneficial under certain conditions.

3 Modeling Natural Noise from Corpora

Robustness of NLP models to natural noise would ideally be evaluated on texts with authentic noise, with error corrections annotated by humans. (We present such authentic data evaluation in Section 7.) This perfect-world setting, however, requires an immense annotation effort, as multiple target domains have to be covered by well-educated human annotators for multiple NLP tasks in a range of languages. To ease the annotation burden, we propose a new framework, named KaziText, for introducing natural-like errors in a text.

The core of KaziText is a set of several common error type classes, *aspects* (following naming convention of Rychalska et al., 2019). The *aspects* are composable (can be combined) and the probability of the aspect manifestation as well as the aspect's internal probabilities are estimated from grammatical-error-correction corpora.

3.1 Noising Aspects

One of the main objectives of our error aspects' design was to avoid manually designed rules, especially those derived from a single language. An ideal approach, automatically inferring the aspects themselves, is however limited by the amount of available data. Therefore, we defined a rich set of aspects which can be estimated from the data:

1. **Diacritics** Strip diacritics either from a whole sentence or randomly from individual characters.
2. **Casing** Change casing of a word, distinguishing between changing the first letter and other.
3. **Spelling** Insert, remove, replace or swap individual characters (*wrong* → *worng*) or use ASpell[1] to transform a word to other existing word (*break* → *brake*).
4. **Suffix/Prefix** Replace common suffix (*do* → *doing*) and prefix (*bid* → *forbid*).
5. **Punctuation** Insert, remove or replace punctuation.
6. **Whitespace** Remove or insert spaces in text.
7. **Word Order** Reorder several adjacent words.
8. **Common Other** Insert, replace or substitute common phrases as seen in data (*the* → *a*, *a lot of* → *many*). This is the aspect which should learn language specific rules.

The natural errors found in real-world texts rarely fall into mutually exclusive categories. Casing errors are also spelling errors; common other aspect covers all other aspects. Therefore, some of the aspects naturally overlap. We therefore opted for evaluating the aspects in a *cumulative* manner in the designed order.

When designing the order of the aspects, our goal was to respect the natural inclusion of aspects and also error severity. We therefore start with diacritical-only changes, given that for example in Czech, users may deliberately write without diacritics. We then add casing changes, spelling errors and then suffix/prefix changes (the latter being morphologically motivated spelling errors). The first four aspects do not modify tokenization, making them suitable for tokenization-dependent tasks like POS tagging or lemmatization.

The remaining aspects change the number of tokens or token boundaries. The punctuation, whitespace and word order aspects are relatively independent, with the common other aspect covering all of them and thus being the last one.

3.2 Estimating Noising Aspects Probabilities

We use grammatical-error-correction (GEC) datasets to estimate probabilities of individual aspects. The GEC datasets are distributed in M2 format,[2] which for a tokenized input noisy sentence contains a set of correcting edits. Each correcting edit contains the corresponding input sentence span, the correction itself and the error type. The noising aspect probabilities are estimated by frequency analysis.[3] To accurately model the distribution of amount of errors in different sentences, we also measure the standard deviation of the token edit probability per sentence.

We collected M2 files from various grammatical-error-correction corpora in 4 languages: English, Czech, Russian and German. The majority of annotated content comes from Second Learners of the particular language and in addition, more speaker groups are available in English and Czech:

- English
  - Natives: LOCNESS v2.1 (Granger, 1998)
  - Second Learners: NUCLE (Dahlmeier et al., 2013), FCE (Yannakoudakis et al., 2011), Write & Improve (Yannakoudakis et al., 2018)
- Czech
  - Natives: essays of Czech primary schools students, in submission process
  - Natives Informal: web discussions data, in submission process
  - Second Learners: AKCES-GEC (Šebesta et al., 2019)
  - Romani: AKCES-GEC (Šebesta et al., 2019) – Romani ethnic minority children and teenagers using Czech

[1] `http://aspell.net/`

[2] GEC file format since the CoNLL-2013 shared task

[3] We refer to the published source code for details.

Language	Corpus	Sentences	Error rate	Domain
English	*NUCLE* (Dahlmeier et al., 2013)	57 151	6.6%	SL
	FCE (Yannakoudakis et al., 2011)	33 236	11.5%	SL
	W&I (Yannakoudakis et al., 2018)	37 704	11.7%	SL
	LOCNESS (Granger, 1998)	988	4.7%	native students
Czech	Romani part of *AKCES-GEC* (Šebesta et al., 2019)	16 030	20.3%	Romani heritage speakers
	SL part of *AKCES-GEC* (Šebesta et al., 2019)	31 341	22.1%	SL essays
	Natives Informal	11 608	15.6%	web discussions
	Natives	7 696	5.8%	native students
German	*Falko-MERLIN* (Boyd, 2018)	24 077	16.8%	SL essays
Russian	*RULEC-GEC* (Rozovskaya and Roth, 2019)	12 480	6.4%	SL, heritage speakers

Table 1: Comparison of used GEC corpora in size, token error rate and domain. SL = second language learners.

- German (Second Learners): Falko-MERLIN GEC Corpus (Boyd, 2018)
- Russian (Second Learners): RULEC-GEC (Rozovskaya and Roth, 2019)

An overview of the sizes and error rates of the datasets above is presented in Table 1.

We call the resulting single file containing all aspect probabilities for one group of speakers a *profile*. The *profile* therefore describes the grammatical style of a particular given group of users, derived from M2 file annotations.

Each profile has a development and test version originating from the respective M2 development and test files. The test profiles are used for synthesising data intended directly for assessing models' performance in noisy setting while the development profile is intended for creating data for training the models.

3.3 Adjusting the Percentage of Token Edits

In order to reach an intended percentage of *token edits*, which directly corresponds to the amount of noise in the generated data, we correspondingly scale the aspects' probabilities. We refer to the percentage of token edits in the original corpus as a *corpus error level*.

3.4 Noising the Data

When noising an input sentence, we first sample a token edit probability from the error amount distribution, scaled according to the required number of token edits. We then introduce the desired aspects with the chosen error level.

We allowed the framework to generate any noising aspect, including adding new tokens, in test sets without token-level gold annotations: neural machine translation, GLUE benchmark, tokens outside named entities in NER and tokens outside the answer in reading comprehension.

When introducing errors into classification test sets with token-level gold annotations, we need to maintain the original tokenization. For this reason, we allowed only the first 4 aspects for the following data: morpho-syntactic analysis, tokens inside named entity spans in NER and tokens inside answers in the reading comprehension task.

All experiments are repeated with 5 different random seeds and we report means with standard deviations.

4 Evaluated Tasks

4.1 Morpho-syntactic Analysis

Model We employed UDPipe (Straka et al., 2019), a tool for morpho-syntactic analysis.

Dataset We used the Universal Dependencies 2.3 (Nivre et al., 2018) corpus (UD 2.3).[4]

Metrics We utilized the following metrics (Zeman et al., 2018) – **UPOS**: coarse POS tags accuracy, **UFeats**: fine-grained morphological features accuracy, **Lemmas**: lemmatization accuracy, **LAS**: labeled attachment score and **MLAS**: combination of morphological tags and syntactic relations.

4.2 Named Entity Recognition

Model Recently published architecture (Straková et al., 2019) was used for NER evaluation.

Dataset For English and German, we evaluated on the standard CoNLL-2003 shared task data (Tjong

[4]Many English UD test set tokens contain casing or spelling errors, propagated into lemmas, rendering such data unsuitable for analysis. We try to use only error-free English test documents and we therefore drop all test documents containing a sentence starting with a lowercase character, keeping more than half of the data. Apart from the lemmatization accuracy, the results for full test set are nearly identical.

Kim Sang and De Meulder, 2003); for Czech, we used a fine-grained Czech Named Entity Corpus 2.0 (Ševčíková et al., 2007) with 46 types of nested entities.

Metric The evaluation metric is F1 score.

4.3 Neural Machine Translation

Model We chose a state-of-the-art Czech-to-English NMT system CUBBITT (Popel et al., 2020), but we trained it on the newest version (2.0) of the CzEng parallel corpus (Kocmi et al., 2020). We trained with batch size of ca. 23k tokens for 550k steps, saved a checkpoint each hour (ca. 4600 steps) and selected the checkpoint with the highest dev-set BLEU (which was at 547k steps).

Dataset We use WMT17 (newstest2017, 3005 sentences)[5] as our development set. Our test set is a concatenation of WMT13, WMT16 and WMT18 (8982 sentences in total).

Metric We evaluate the translation quality with case-insensitive BLEU score.[6]

4.4 GLUE Benchmark

We select a subset of GLUE (Wang et al., 2018) tasks, namely Microsoft Research Paraphrase Corpus (MRPC), Semantic Textual Similarity Benchmark (STS-B), Quora Question Pairs (QQP) and The Stanford Sentiment Treebank (SST-2). We finetune BERT on each of these tasks and evaluate them on various levels of noise.

Model We finetune pretrained BERT with an additional feed-forward neural network with one hidden layer predicting score on particular task's data. We use *bert-base-cased* configuration and HuggingFace's Transformers (Wolf et al., 2019) implementation.

Dataset We use official GLUE datasets as provided by `https://gluebenchmark.com/tasks`.

Metric We report following metrics: F1 for MRPC and QQP, Pearson-Spearman Corr for STS-B and accuracy for SST-2.

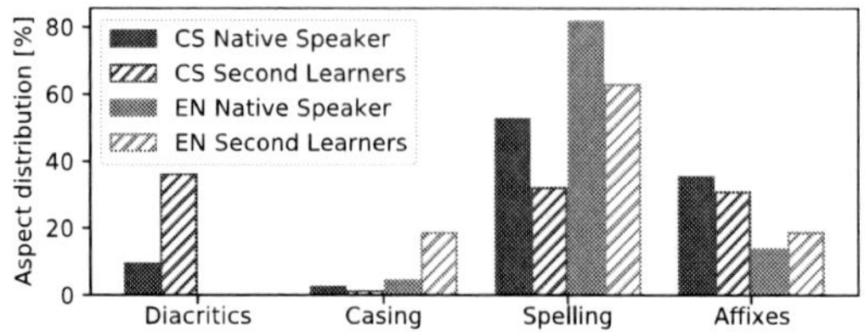

Figure 1: Proportional distribution of the first 4 aspects (diacritics, casing, spelling, affixes) in Czech and English.

4.5 Reading Comprehension

Model We utilize a BERT base architecture with a standard SQuAD classifier on top (Devlin et al., 2019).

Dataset We employ English SQuAD 2 (Rajpurkar et al., 2018) and its Czech translation (Macková and Straka, 2020).

Metric Our experiments are evaluated using F1 score.

5 Robustness to Noise

We evaluated the models robustness both to the amount of noise (Figure 2) and to error types (Figures 3 and 4).

A unifying trend can be observed in models performance with respect to increasing percentage of token edits. Solid lines in Figure 2 display the morpho-syntactic MLAS, NER F1 and NMT BLEU on texts with up to 30% of token edits. The relative performance decreases roughly linearly with the amount of token edits, in accordance with previous findings (Rychalska et al., 2019). The tendency is consistent across tasks, languages and profiles: For example, compare the Czech and English Second Learners profiles in morpho-syntactic analysis (Figure 2a) or Czech Native Speakers and Czech Second Learners profiles in the NMT clean model (Figure 2c), which exhibit similar behaviour despite their differing distributions of aspects (Figure 1). This consistency implies that it is the sheer amount of noise rather than the distribution of aspects, that contributes to the model performance deterioration. More results are available in Supplementary Material (Figures S2 and S3).

Estimating the amount of noise is important, as the *corpus error level* differs greatly across languages and profiles. For example, compare the Second Learners profile in English (11.3% token edits) and Czech (27.1%) in Figure 2a, or in Czech, see Native Speakers (6.4%) and Second Learners

[5] `http://statmt.org/wmt17`

[6] We use SacreBLEU (Post, 2018) with signature BLEU+case.lc+numrefs.1+smooth.exp+tok.intl+version.1.4.14. When using the case-sensitive version, the results show similar trends, except for the Casing aspect, which causes more harm to the score, as could be expected. However, it is questionable if copying the "wrong" casing to the translation (e.g. not capitalizing the first word in a sentence or using all-uppercase) should be considered a translation error. We thus opted for case-insensitive BLEU as our primary metric.

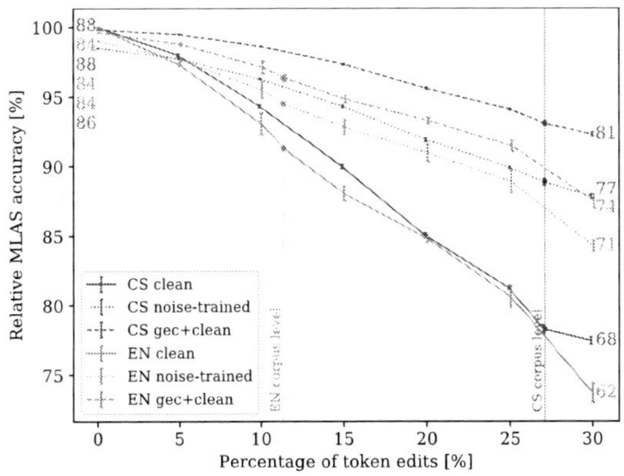

(a) Morpho-syntactic analysis (relative MLAS), Second Learners

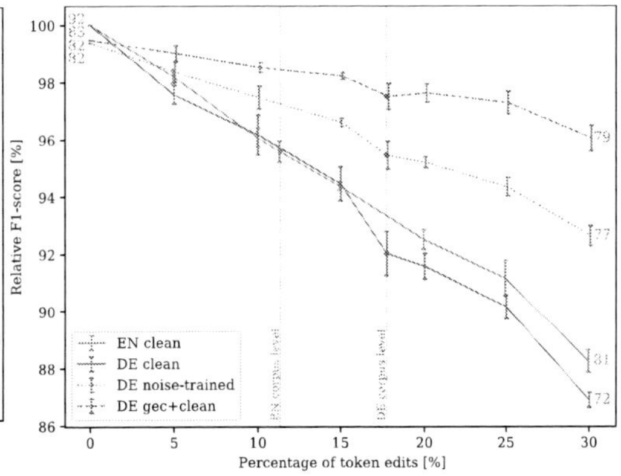

(b) NER (relative F1), Second Learners

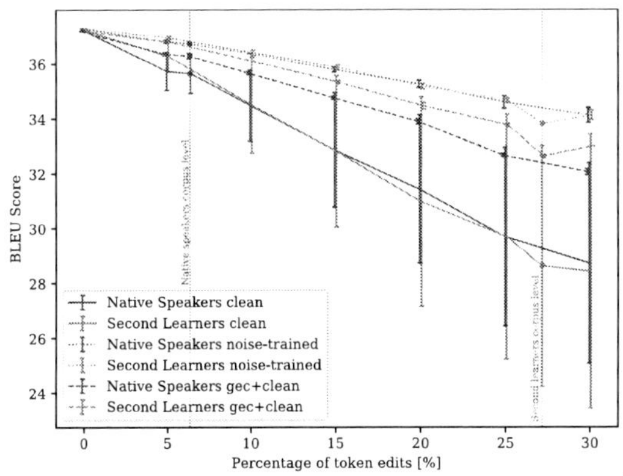

(c) NMT (BLEU), Czech Native Speakers and Second Learners

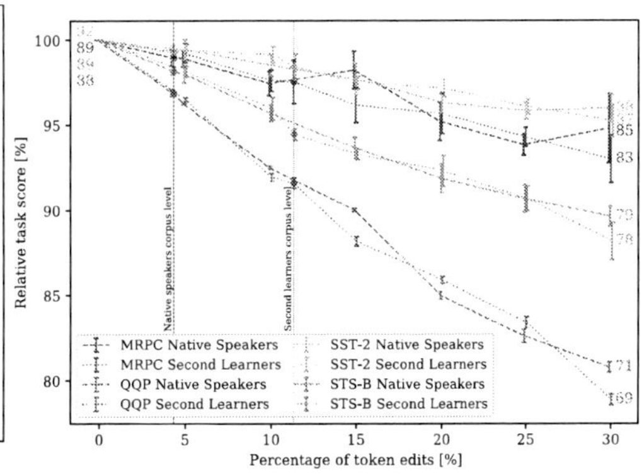

(d) GLUE (relative task score), English Native Speakers and Second Learners

Figure 2: Increasing percentage of token edits with clean model, noise-trained model and grammatical-error-correction. Numbers near lines are absolute values.

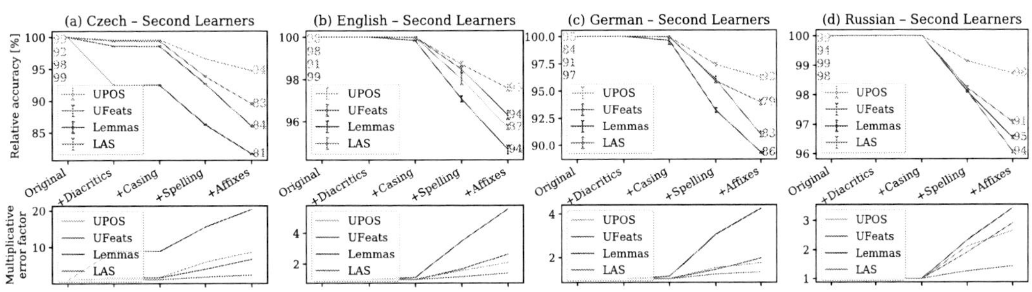

Figure 3: Morpho-syntactic tasks with additive noising aspects in Second Learners profile across (a) Czech, (b) English, (c) German and (d) Russian. The amount of introduced errors is the corpus error level for each aspect. **Upper row** Accuracy relative to original data accuracy, numbers near lines are absolute values. **Lower row** Multiplicative factor of errors to original data error rate.

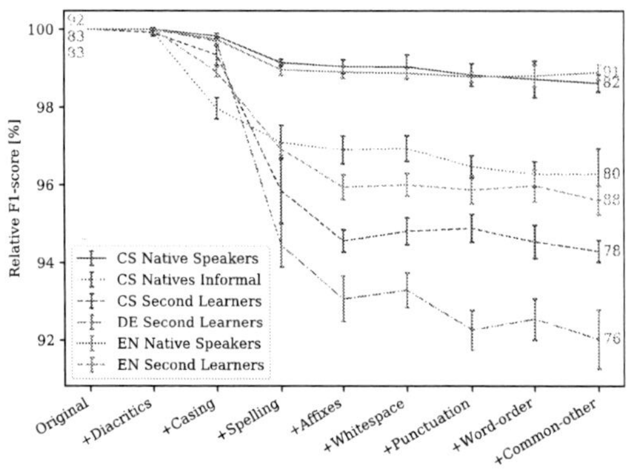

(a) NER (relative F1), selected profiles in CS, EN and DE

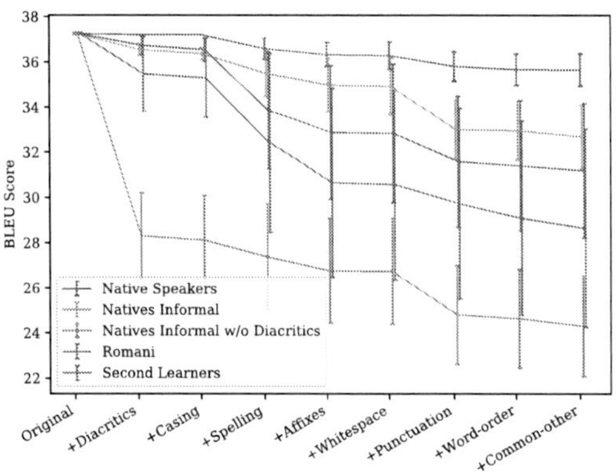

(b) NMT (BLEU), all Czech profiles

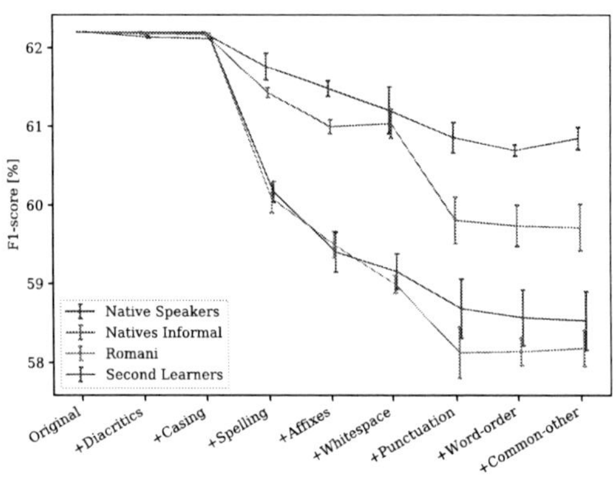

(c) Reading comprehension (relative F1), all Czech profiles

Figure 4: Evaluation with additive noising aspects. The amount of introduced errors is the corpus error level for each aspect. Numbers near lines are absolute values.

(27.1%) in Figure 2c. Testing near the estimated noisiness level provides more accurate evaluation of the models' performance.

From a qualitative point of view, spelling and affixes make for the major performance drop in morpho-syntactic analysis (Figure 3), NER (Figure 4a) and NMT (Figure 4b).

Some tasks are more sensitive to certain aspects: Casing is a crucial aspect for NER. This is clearly shown in the Czech Natives Informal profile, which contains text scraped from the internet discussions and contains nontrivial amount of casing errors (Figure 4a). We further elaborate the casing aspect effect on NER in Section S2 in Supplementary Material. In NMT and reading comprehension, errors in punctuation seem to decrease the model performance consistently across all profiles (Figures 4b and 4c, respectively).

For Czech as a language with diacritic marks, diacritics is an interesting aspect. We can see that when it is introduced at a *corpus error level*, the Czech model's performance on Lemmas drops by circa 7 percent. Figure S1 in Supplementary Material further illustrates that performance significantly deteriorates when all diacritics is stripped, which is quite common in informal Web texts. Similarly, to emphasize the effect of the diacritization aspect on NMT, we created a new profile *Natives Informal w/o Diacritics* from the Natives Informal profile by stripping all diacritization. Figure 4b shows that not using diacritics at all results in a performance drop of ca. 10 BLEU points.

Some tasks are more sensitive to noise than others. Lemmatization is the most sensitive to errors (20 times more errors when processing Czech Second Learners texts with a clean model, see Figure 3), which is understandable, given that all lemma characters must be generated correctly from a corrupted surface token. The effect on POS tagging is the least pronounced (Figure 3), although 8 times as many errors in Czech (when processing noisy texts with a clean model) makes the POS tags much less reliable.

6 Noise-coping Strategies

We implemented and evaluated two strategies to alleviate the performance drop on noisy inputs: *external* and *internal* correction. In the *external* correction approach, we use a separately trained grammatical-error-correction model to denoise texts before inputting them to the model itself. In the *internal* correction approach, we instead directly train the model on a combination of noisy and authentic texts.

We hypothesise that the external approach may

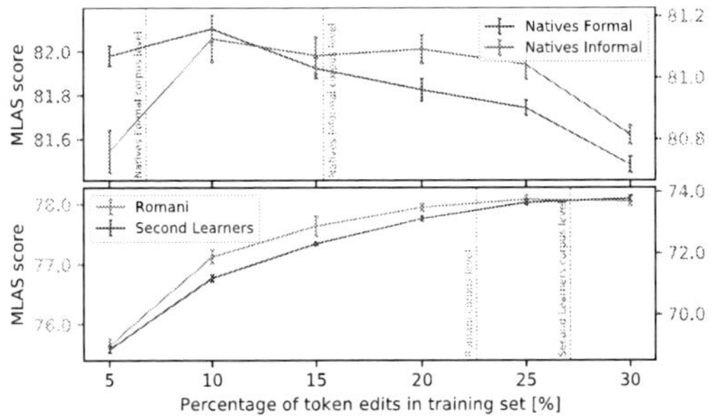

Figure 5: Morpho-syntactic analysis: Training data increasingly noised with each single profile, evaluation with the corresponding profile corpus error level.

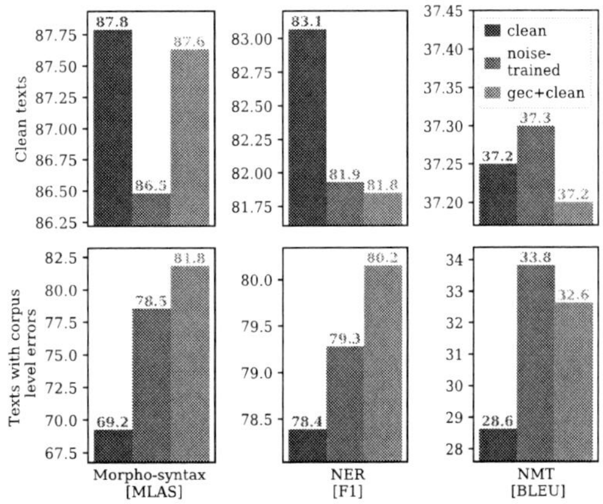

Figure 6: Comparison of three models (clean, noise-trained and GEC-preprocessed) on three tasks in Czech Second Learners profile. **Upper row** Original clean test data. **Lower row** Test data with corpus error level noise.

be better in scenarios with small amount of annotated data. In such cases, only few iterations over training data are typically performed to prevent overfitting, and we suppose that learning the task itself and denoising at the same time would harm its performance a lot. Contrarily, with enough data and appropriate model capacity, learning the denoising and the task jointly may reduce the amount of potential false positives that might be otherwise proposed by the external language corrector.

6.1 External Correction Model

We use the grammatical-error-correction system of Náplava and Straka (2019) in our experiments. Their models trained on Czech, German and Russian achieve state-of-the-art results and slightly below state-of-the-art results on English. We use their "pretrained" version.

We modified the pipeline of Náplava and Straka (2019) to train on detokenized text. Furthermore, we also trained new grammatical-error-correction models which only make corrections that strictly keep the given tokenization (important in morpho-syntactic annotations). To sum up, we trained two types of grammatical-error-correction models: 1. detokenized error correction model (for NMT) 2. tokenization-preserving error-correction model (for morpho-syntactic tasks and NER).

6.2 Training on Noisy Data

In the *internal* approach to increase model robustness, we train the systems on a mixture of original and noisy data, while keeping the number of training steps unchanged. The noisy data are generated using the KaziText framework operating on development profiles and concatenated to original data.

We noise the training data with appropriately estimated corpus error levels in all our experiments. To illustrate the effect of noise level introduced into training data, we trained the UDPipe on variably noised morpho-syntactic data for all four Czech profiles. In each single profile, we increasingly noised the morpho-syntactic training data and evaluated on the testing data noised with the corresponding profile *corpus error level*. In all cases, the best performance is found near the corpus error level (Figure 5).

When training the NMT model, the best checkpoint on a development set consisting of concatenated standard WMT17 and WMT17 noised with our framework is selected.

We train a single model for each language on a concatenation of noisy data generated by all profiles of the particular language. This makes the final model generalize well across all profiles, although training a single model for each profile could make sense for other scenarios.

6.3 Evaluation

We present the effect of both the *internal* and *external* noise-coping strategies in Figure 2. There are two main points of interest in the graphs: the first one showing performance of models on clean texts and the second one showing model performance on texts with corpus level errors. Additionally, an excerpt showing performance of Czech Second Learners on these two levels is presented in Figure 6.

It is not a surprise that the model trained on clean training data surpasses the noise-coping models on

System	BLEU on Faust	
	Noisy	Cleaned
clean	43.3	50.9
noise-trained	47.0	50.5
gec+clean	44.1	50.4

Table 2: NMT results on authentic user noisy texts. We report BLEU on the Faust-Noisy test set with noisy input sentences and also on Faust-Cleaned that has manually corrected sentences on input.

the clean test data. Adapting to noise clearly comes with a cost. Surprisingly though, the clean model head start is only marginal in the NMT task.

The clean models perform substantially worse than either of the two proposed methods in all three tasks when errors are introduced in the same amount as the corpus error level (marked with vertical lines in Figure 2). Therefore, whenever noisy inputs of particular domain are expected, it is beneficial to adapt to noise using either of the two methods.

With increasing noise, the gap between the clean model and the *external* and *internal* model grows in all three tasks (Figure 2). There is a threshold at which the noise-coping models surpass the clean model for each task. Interestingly, the threshold oscillates around relatively low noise levels up to 5% of token edits.

Finally, we confirm our initial hypothesis that *external* approach with GEC model works better than *internal* approach on low resource tasks: morpho-syntactic analysis and named-entity recognition. The *internal* approach then outperforms *external* approach on machine translation task for which there is a large amount of training data and a model with greater capacity.

7 Evaluating on Authentic User Text

We assembled a new dataset for MT evaluation consisting of 2223 authentic Czech noisy input sentences translated into English, which we release at `http://hdl.handle.net/11234/1-3775`. The sentences originate from the project FAUST[7] where they were collected from various users of `reverso.net`. The advantage of this dataset is that in addition to the original Czech noisy sentences, there are manually corrected Czech sentences and manual translations to English.

[7]`https://ufal.mff.cuni.cz/grants/faust`

On this dataset, we evaluate our neural machine translation models from Section 4.3 and Section 6, specifically the *clean* model trained on clean data, *noise-trained* model trained on a mixture of authentic and noised data and their combination with external grammatical-error-correction system. The results of these systems on authentic noisy texts are presented in Table 2. It is evident that noise-trained model outperforms clean model by a large margin on Faust-Noisy data while not losing much precision on Faust-Cleaned data. Similarly to our conclusions in Section 6, the external grammatical-error-correction system helps the clean model on noisy data, however is inferior to noise-trained model.

8 Conclusions

We estimated natural error probabilities statistically from real-world grammatical-error-correction corpora in order to model and generate noisy inputs for machine learning tasks. We extensively evaluated several state-of-the-art NLP downstream systems with respect to their robustness to input noise, both in increasing level of text noisiness and in variations of error types. We confirmed that the noise hurts the model performance substantially and we compared two coping strategies: training with noise and preprocessing with GEC, concluding that each strategy is beneficial in different scenarios. Finally, we also presented authentic noisy data evaluation using a newly assembled dataset for machine translation with authentic Czech noisy sentences translated to English. We release both the new framework (under MPL 2.0) at `https://github.com/ufal/kazitext` and the newly assembled dataset (under CC BY-NC-SA license) at `http://hdl.handle.net/11234/1-3775`.

Acknowledgements

This work has been supported by the Grant Agency of the Czech Republic, project EXPRO LUSyD (GX20-16819X). This research was also partially supported by SVV project number 260 575 and GAUK 578218 of the Charles University. It has has also been using data provided by the LINDAT/CLARIAH-CZ Research Infrastructure (https://lindat.cz), supported by the Ministry of Education, Youth and Sports of the Czech Republic (Project No. LM2018101).

References

Yonatan Belinkov and Yonatan Bisk. 2017. Synthetic and natural noise both break neural machine translation. *arXiv preprint arXiv:1711.02173*.

Adriane Boyd. 2018. Using wikipedia edits in low resource grammatical error correction. In *Proceedings of the 2018 EMNLP Workshop W-NUT: The 4th Workshop on Noisy User-generated Text*, pages 79–84.

Yo Joong Choe, Jiyeon Ham, Kyubyong Park, and Yeoil Yoon. 2019. A neural grammatical error correction system built on better pre-training and sequential transfer learning. In *Proceedings of the Fourteenth Workshop on Innovative Use of NLP for Building Educational Applications*, pages 213–227.

Daniel Dahlmeier, Hwee Tou Ng, and Siew Mei Wu. 2013. Building a large annotated corpus of learner english: The nus corpus of learner english. In *Proceedings of the eighth workshop on innovative use of NLP for building educational applications*, pages 22–31.

Jacob Devlin, Ming-Wei Chang, Kenton Lee, and Kristina Toutanova. 2019. Bert: Pre-training of deep bidirectional transformers for language understanding. In *Proceedings of the 2019 Conference of the North American Chapter of the Association for Computational Linguistics: Human Language Technologies, Volume 1 (Long and Short Papers)*, pages 4171–4186.

Tao Ge, Furu Wei, and Ming Zhou. 2018. Reaching human-level performance in automatic grammatical error correction: An empirical study. *arXiv preprint arXiv:1807.01270*.

Max Glockner, Vered Shwartz, and Yoav Goldberg. 2018. Breaking nli systems with sentences that require simple lexical inferences. In *Proceedings of the 56th Annual Meeting of the Association for Computational Linguistics (Volume 2: Short Papers)*, pages 650–655.

Sylviane Granger. 1998. The computer learner corpus: A versatile new source of data for SLA research. In Sylviane Granger, editor, *Learner English on Computer*, pages 3–18. Addison Wesley Longman, London and New York.

Georg Heigold, Stalin Varanasi, Günter Neumann, and Josef van Genabith. 2018. How robust are character-based word embeddings in tagging and mt against wrod scramlbing or randdm nouse? In *Proceedings of the 13th Conference of the Association for Machine Translation in the Americas (Volume 1: Research Papers)*, pages 68–80.

Sudhanshu Kasewa, Pontus Stenetorp, and Sebastian Riedel. 2018. Wronging a right: Generating better errors to improve grammatical error detection. In *Proceedings of the 2018 Conference on Empirical Methods in Natural Language Processing*, pages 4977–4983.

Tom Kocmi, Martin Popel, and Ondrej Bojar. 2020. Announcing CzEng 2.0 parallel corpus with over 2 gigawords. *arXiv preprint arXiv:2007.03006*.

Xian Li, Paul Michel, Antonios Anastasopoulos, Yonatan Belinkov, Nadir Durrani, Orhan Firat, Philipp Koehn, Graham Neubig, Juan Pino, and Hassan Sajjad. 2019. Findings of the first shared task on machine translation robustness. In *Proceedings of the Fourth Conference on Machine Translation (Volume 2: Shared Task Papers, Day 1)*, pages 91–102.

Kateřina Macková and Milan Straka. 2020. Reading comprehension in czech via machine translation and cross-lingual transfer. In *Text, Speech, and Dialogue*, pages 171–179, Cham. Springer International Publishing.

Paul Michel and Graham Neubig. 2018. Mtnt: A testbed for machine translation of noisy text. In *Proceedings of the 2018 Conference on Empirical Methods in Natural Language Processing*, pages 543–553.

Jakub Náplava. 2017. Natural language correction. *Diploma Thesis*.

Jakub Náplava and Milan Straka. 2019. Grammatical error correction in low-resource scenarios. In *Proceedings of the 5th Workshop on Noisy User-generated Text (W-NUT 2019)*, pages 346–356.

Joakim Nivre et al. 2018. Universal dependencies 2.3. LINDAT/CLARIN digital library at the Institute of Formal and Applied Linguistics (ÚFAL), Faculty of Mathematics and Physics, Charles University.

Martin Popel, Marketa Tomkova, Jakub Tomek, Łukasz Kaiser, Jakob Uszkoreit, Ondřej Bojar, and Zdeněk Žabokrtský. 2020. Transforming machine translation: a deep learning system reaches news translation quality comparable to human professionals. *Nature Communications*, 11(1):1–15.

Matt Post. 2018. A call for clarity in reporting BLEU scores. In *Proceedings of the Third Conference on Machine Translation: Research Papers*, pages 186–191, Belgium, Brussels. Association for Computational Linguistics.

Pranav Rajpurkar, Robin Jia, and Percy Liang. 2018. Know what you don't know: Unanswerable questions for SQuAD. In *Proceedings of the 56th Annual Meeting of the Association for Computational Linguistics (Volume 2: Short Papers)*, pages 784–789, Melbourne, Australia. Association for Computational Linguistics.

Marek Rei, Mariano Felice, Zheng Yuan, and Ted Briscoe. 2017. Artificial error generation with machine translation and syntactic patterns. In *Proceedings of the 12th Workshop on Innovative Use of NLP for Building Educational Applications*, pages 287–292.

Marco Tulio Ribeiro, Sameer Singh, and Carlos Guestrin. 2018. Semantically equivalent adversarial rules for debugging nlp models. In *Proceedings of the 56th Annual Meeting of the Association for Computational Linguistics (Volume 1: Long Papers)*, pages 856–865.

Alla Rozovskaya and Dan Roth. 2019. Grammar error correction in morphologically rich languages: The case of russian. *Transactions of the Association for Computational Linguistics*, 7:1–17.

Alla Rozovskaya, Dan Roth, and Mark Sammons. 2017. Adapting to learner errors with minimal supervision. *Computational Linguistics*, 43(4):723–760.

Barbara Rychalska, Dominika Basaj, Alicja Gosiewska, and Przemysław Biecek. 2019. Models in the wild: On corruption robustness of neural nlp systems. In *International Conference on Neural Information Processing*, pages 235–247. Springer.

Karel Šebesta, Zuzanna Bedřichová, Kateřina Šormová, Barbora Štindlová, Milan Hrdlička, Tereza Hrdličková, Jiří Hana, Vladimír Petkevič, Tomáš Jelínek, Svatava Škodová, Petr Janeš, Kateřina Lundáková, Hana Skoumalová, Šimon Sládek, Piotr Pierscieniak, Dagmar Toufarová, Milan Straka, Alexandr Rosen, Jakub Náplava, and Marie Poláčková. 2019. AKCES-GEC grammatical error correction dataset for czech. LINDAT/CLARIAH-CZ digital library at the Institute of Formal and Applied Linguistics (ÚFAL), Faculty of Mathematics and Physics, Charles University.

Rico Sennrich, Barry Haddow, and Alexandra Birch. 2016. Improving neural machine translation models with monolingual data. In *Proceedings of the 54th Annual Meeting of the Association for Computational Linguistics (Volume 1: Long Papers)*, pages 86–96.

Magda Ševčíková, Zdeněk Žabokrtský, and Oldřich Krůza. 2007. Named entities in czech: Annotating data and developing ne tagger. In *Text, Speech and Dialogue*, pages 188–195, Berlin, Heidelberg. Springer Berlin Heidelberg.

Milan Straka, Jana Straková, and Jan Hajič. 2019. Evaluating contextualized embeddings on 54 languages in POS tagging, lemmatization and dependency parsing.

Jana Straková, Milan Straka, and Jan Hajic. 2019. Neural architectures for nested NER through linearization. In *Proceedings of the 57th Annual Meeting of the Association for Computational Linguistics*, pages 5326–5331, Florence, Italy. Association for Computational Linguistics.

Erik F. Tjong Kim Sang and Fien De Meulder. 2003. Introduction to the CoNLL-2003 shared task: Language-independent named entity recognition. In *Proceedings of the Seventh Conference on Natural Language Learning at HLT-NAACL 2003*, pages 142–147.

Ashish Vaswani, Noam Shazeer, Niki Parmar, Jakob Uszkoreit, Llion Jones, Aidan N Gomez, Łukasz Kaiser, and Illia Polosukhin. 2017. Attention is all you need. In *Advances in neural information processing systems*, pages 5998–6008.

Alex Wang, Amanpreet Singh, Julian Michael, Felix Hill, Omer Levy, and Samuel Bowman. 2018. Glue: A multi-task benchmark and analysis platform for natural language understanding. In *Proceedings of the 2018 EMNLP Workshop BlackboxNLP: Analyzing and Interpreting Neural Networks for NLP*, pages 353–355.

Thomas Wolf, Lysandre Debut, Victor Sanh, Julien Chaumond, Clement Delangue, Anthony Moi, Pierric Cistac, Tim Rault, Rémi Louf, Morgan Funtowicz, Joe Davison, Sam Shleifer, Patrick von Platen, Clara Ma, Yacine Jernite, Julien Plu, Canwen Xu, Teven Le Scao, Sylvain Gugger, Mariama Drame, Quentin Lhoest, and Alexander M. Rush. 2019. Huggingface's transformers: State-of-the-art natural language processing. *ArXiv*, abs/1910.03771.

Ziang Xie, Guillaume Genthial, Stanley Xie, Andrew Y Ng, and Dan Jurafsky. 2018. Noising and denoising natural language: Diverse backtranslation for grammar correction. In *Proceedings of the 2018 Conference of the North American Chapter of the Association for Computational Linguistics: Human Language Technologies, Volume 1 (Long Papers)*, pages 619–628.

Helen Yannakoudakis, Ted Briscoe, and Ben Medlock. 2011. A new dataset and method for automatically grading esol texts. In *Proceedings of the 49th Annual Meeting of the Association for Computational Linguistics: Human Language Technologies-Volume 1*, pages 180–189. Association for Computational Linguistics.

Helen Yannakoudakis, Øistein E Andersen, Ardeshir Geranpayeh, Ted Briscoe, and Diane Nicholls. 2018. Developing an automated writing placement system for esl learners. *Applied Measurement in Education*, 31(3):251–267.

Daniel Zeman, Jan Hajič, Martin Popel, Martin Potthast, Milan Straka, Filip Ginter, Joakim Nivre, and Slav Petrov. 2018. CoNLL 2018 shared task: Multilingual parsing from raw text to universal dependencies. In *Proceedings of the CoNLL 2018 Shared Task: Multilingual Parsing from Raw Text to Universal Dependencies*, pages 1–21, Brussels, Belgium. Association for Computational Linguistics.

CIDEr-R: Robust Consensus-based Image Description Evaluation

Gabriel Oliveira dos Santos and **Esther Luna Colombini** and **Sandra Avila**
Institute of Computing, University of Campinas (Unicamp), Brazil
g197460@dac.unicamp.br, {esther,sandra}@ic.unicamp.br

Abstract

This paper shows that CIDEr-D, a traditional evaluation metric for image description, does not work properly on datasets where the number of words in the sentence is significantly greater than those in the MS COCO Captions dataset. We also show that CIDEr-D has performance hampered by the lack of multiple reference sentences and high variance of sentence length. To bypass this problem, we introduce CIDEr-R, which improves CIDEr-D, making it more flexible in dealing with datasets with high sentence length variance. We demonstrate that CIDEr-R is more accurate and closer to human judgment than CIDEr-D; CIDEr-R is more robust regarding the number of available references. Our results reveal that using Self-Critical Sequence Training to optimize CIDEr-R generates descriptive captions. In contrast, when CIDEr-D is optimized, the generated captions' length tends to be similar to the reference length. However, the models also repeat several times the same word to increase the sentence length.

a) **Reference**: "Fotografia aérea sobre o pedágio da Terceira Ponte. A foto contém alguns prédios, um pedaço da Terceira Ponte e o fluxo de carros."
CIDEr-D: "foto *aérea aérea aérea* da cidade de Florianópolis mostrando *casas casas*, mostrando *casas casas*. Ao fundo, algumas *casas* e *casas*."
CIDEr-R: "Foto aérea de uma cidade de Brasília. Ao fundo, a céu azul."

Figure 1: We show the reference caption and the description generated by models trained on #PraCegoVer to optimize CIDEr-D and CIDEr-R.

1 Introduction

Automatically describing image content using natural sentences is an important task to help include people with visual impairments on the Internet, making it more inclusive and democratic. This task is known as *image captioning*. It is still a big challenge that requires understanding the objects, their attributes, and the actions they are involved in. Thus, linguistic models are also needed to verbalize the semantic relations in addition to visual interpretation methods.

In the last few years, there has been significant progress in image captioning thanks to the availability of a large amount of annotated data in relevant datasets (Agrawal et al., 2019; Chen et al., 2015; Gurari et al., 2020; Hodosh et al., 2013; Plummer et al., 2015). These datasets have in common multiple reference captions, which comprehend short sentences with a low length variance. Also, most of the datasets contain only English captions, whereas datasets with captions described in other languages are scarce. Thus, we proposed the #PraCegoVer dataset (Santos et al., 2021) for the image captioning task with descriptions[1] in Portuguese. Our dataset consists of images and captions collected from posts on Instagram tagging the hashtag *#PraCegoVer*. *PraCegoVer* is a movement (Web para Todos, 2018) that aims to spread the accessibility culture on social media. It has inspired many local laws in Brazil that establish that all posts made by public agencies must tag *#PraCegoVer* and contain a short description of the image. Also, many business and personal profiles have joined this initiative. Hence, the amount of data produced by those users has great growth potential.

In contrast to the other datasets in this literature,

[1]We use caption and description interchangeably.

Proceedings of the 2021 EMNLP Workshop W-NUT: The Seventh Workshop on Noisy User-generated Text, pages 351–360
November 11, 2021.

in #PraCegoVer, each image has only one reference description, whose length is about four times longer than the average length, in terms of the number of words, in datasets such as MS COCO (Chen et al., 2015). Also, the variance of length in our dataset is around ten times higher than in the literature. Thus, #PraCegoVer is more challenging than others. We demonstrated that training models using Self-Critical Sequence Training (Rennie et al., 2017) (SCST) to optimize CIDEr-D is not a good approach for datasets with the same characteristics as ours, in particular with single reference and high variance of length. CIDEr-D (Vedantam et al., 2015) has a severe penalty concerning the length that punishes at the same intensity any difference in the number of words between the generated and the reference captions. Hence, it forces the model to generate descriptions similar in length to the ground truth even though it has to repeat words to reach the reference length. In the end, the model learns to repeat words impairing the lexical cohesion of the generated description.

We tackle the problem of penalizing at the same intensity any difference in length by modeling the penalty proportionally to the reference length. Also, we introduced a penalty regarding lexical cohesion so that the more a word is repeated, relative to the ground truth, the higher is the penalty. These two penalties combined aim to give the models the opportunity of generating more succinct captions when the ground truth comprehends longer descriptions. We name this new metric CIDEr-R, a robust alternative to CIDEr-D for datasets with high length variance. Also, we demonstrated that CIDEr-R is preferred to CIDEr-D when only one reference is available. Finally, our results reveal that CIDEr-R is more suitable for the context of datasets created from data collected from social media.

Our key contributions are fourfold: (1) we investigated the impact of evaluation metrics in the scenario of datasets with high variance of length (*e.g.*, #PraCegoVer; (2) we showed that optimizing CIDEr-D on datasets with long references and high variance of length can make the model learn to repeat words to increase the sentence length (Figure 1); (3) we proposed CIDEr-R that better measures the lexical cohesion and has a flexible penalty to length variance; (4) we demonstrated that optimizing CIDEr-R in context of long sentences and high variance of length produce more descriptive captions.

2 Related Work

The image captioning task has been accelerated thanks to the availability of a large amount of annotated data in relevant datasets, for instance, Flickr8K (Hodosh et al., 2013), Flickr30K (Plummer et al., 2015), and MS COCO (Lin et al., 2014). These data made it possible to train complex models such as Deep Neural Networks (LeCun et al., 2015). In the last few years, a broad collection of architectures has been proposed in image captioning (Kulkarni et al., 2011; Vinyals et al., 2015; Johnson et al., 2016; Pedersoli et al., 2017; Anderson et al., 2018; Lu et al., 2018; Huang et al., 2019; Wang et al., 2020; Cornia et al., 2020; Pan et al., 2020; Li et al., 2020). Notable achievements have been made with *Self-Critical Sequence Training* (Rennie et al., 2017), which is a formulation of reinforcement learning that enables the use of non-differentiable functions as optimization objectives, such as caption metrics.

Evaluating the generated captions is a challenging task itself because it is based on the evaluator's subjectivity. Many metrics were proposed to measure the generated text's quality to encourage progress in this field despite the subjectivity intrinsic to this process. Typically, these metrics compare a candidate sentence against a set of reference sentences (ground truth). Most of the metrics are rule-based that relies on n-gram to assign a score to the candidate sentence, *e.g.* BLEU (Papineni et al., 2002), ROUGE (Lin, 2004) and METEOR (Banerjee and Lavie, 2005). However, n-gram based metrics cannot capture the semantic relations and negatively correlate with human judgment. Thus, Vedantam *et al.* proposed CIDEr (Vedantam et al., 2015), a semantically sensitive score, which computes the term frequency-inverse document frequency (TF-IDF) weights to n-grams in the candidate and reference sentences and then compare them using cosine similarity. SPICE (Anderson et al., 2016) uses the similarity of scene graphs parsed from the reference and candidate captions to evaluate the generated descriptions. Although SPICE obtains a significantly higher correlation with human judgments compared to n-gram based metrics, it does not check whether the grammar is correct, and it ignores syntactic quality, as pointed out in (Liu et al., 2017). Also, SPICE uses Stanford Scene Graph Parser (Schuster et al., 2015) which is only available for a limited number of languages. Recently, word embeddings has also been employed for evaluation in BERTScore (Zhang et al., 2020), MoverScore (Zhao et al., 2019) and BLEURT (Sellam et al., 2020).

3 #PraCegoVer Dataset

Recently, a social movement called PraCegoVer (Web para Todos, 2018) arose on the Internet, standing for people with visual impairments besides having an educational purpose. The initiative aims to call attention to the accessibility question by stimulating users to post images accompanied by a short description of their content. This project has inspired many local laws that establish that public agencies' posts on social media must contain a description of the image.

Inspired by this movement, we developed a crawler to collect public posts from Instagram associated with the tag used by the followers. We leverage these data, which comprise images and text captions, to create #PraCegoVer (Santos et al., 2021) dataset, the first large dataset for image captioning in Portuguese. Similar to VizWiz-Captions (Gurari et al., 2020), our dataset's captions are addressed to visually impaired people. We are continuously collecting more data, and, thus, our dataset increases over time. Currently, it comprehends 551,000 instances with images labeled with a single caption.

3.1 #PraCegoVer *vs.* MS COCO Captions

To illustrate the differences between standard datasets and datasets created from data in the wild, we plot in Figure 2 a histogram with the distribution of captions by length, *i.e.* number of words, for #PraCegoVer and MS COCO Captions. We can note that in MS COCO Captions the caption lengths are concentrated around ten words, while length distribution in #PraCegoVer is flatter than MS COCO Captions. More precisely, the reference descriptions in MS COCO Captions have 10.5 words on average with a standard deviation equal to 2.2, whereas in #PraCegoVer the mean and standard deviation the lengths are 37.8 and 26.8, respectively. These characteristics make our dataset more challenging than MS COCO Captions because the most used evaluation metric in image captioning literature, CIDEr-D (Vedantam et al., 2015), is finetuned on standard datasets, then it can not evaluate the generated captions appropriately.

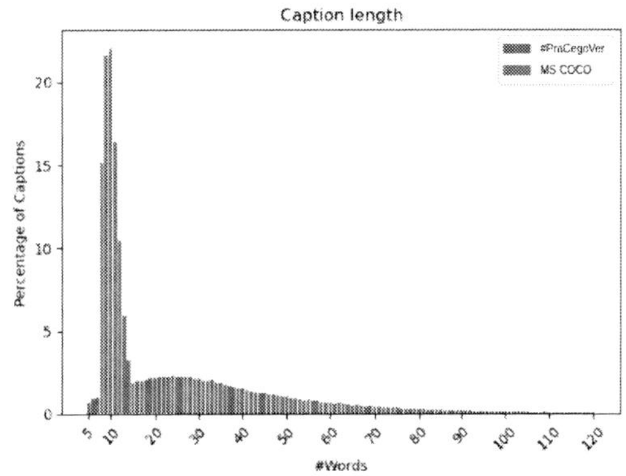

Figure 2: Histogram with the distribution of captions by length in terms of number of words for #PraCegoVer (blue) and MS COCO Captions (red) datasets.

4 Model Architecture

In our experiments, we employ AoANet (Huang et al., 2019) since it is one of the state-of-art models for image captioning. This model is based on the Attention on Attention (AoA) module, which determines the importance of attention results given queries. AoA module is an extension of Multi-Head Attention (Vaswani et al., 2017) that introduces an "Attention Gate" and an "Information Vector" to address the issue of the attention mechanism returning irrelevant results to the query. The model is an Encoder-Decoder architecture where the encoder module comprises the Feature Extractor and a Refining Module to refine feature vectors' representation. In contrast, the decoder network comprehends LSTM, Multi-Head Attention, Attention on Attention, and word prediction layers. The encoder takes the image features as input and creates an embedding representation. The decoder, in turn, uses the embedding and the previous state to model the context vector that represents the newly acquired information. The context vector is used to predict the next word.

We train our models using the method Self-Critical Sequence Training (Rennie et al., 2017), which consists of two phases. The first phase optimizes the cross-entropy loss, and then an evaluation metric is optimized through a Reinforcement Learning approach. Our experiments trained the models during two epochs, minimizing the cross-entropy loss and 15 epochs maximizing the considered evaluation metric.

5 CIDEr-R: Our Proposal

CIDEr-D (Vedantam et al., 2015) is based on vectors $\mathbf{g^n}(s)$ formed by TF-IDF scores computed from n-grams of sentence s. CIDEr-D can be splitted into terms CIDEr-D$_n$, which are scores calculated from n-grams of length n. Let $S_i = \{s_{i1}, ..., s_{im}\}$ be the set of reference descriptions of an image i, and let c_i be the generated description for i. Then, CIDEr-D$_n$ is formally defined as follows:

$$sim(c_i, s_{ij}) = \frac{min(\mathbf{g^n}(c_i), \mathbf{g^n}(s_{ij})) \cdot \mathbf{g^n}(s_{ij})}{||\mathbf{g^n}(c_i)|| \cdot ||\mathbf{g^n}(s_{ij})||}, \quad (1)$$

$$Penalty = exp\{-\frac{(l(c_i) - l(s_{ij}))^2}{2\sigma^2}\}, \quad (2)$$

$$\text{CIDEr-D}_n(c_i, S_i) = \frac{10}{m} \sum_{s_{ij} \in S_i} sim(c_i, s_{ij}) \cdot Penalty, \quad (3)$$

where $l(c_i)$ and $l(s_{ij})$ denote the length of candidate and reference sentences, respectively, and it is used $\sigma = 6$.

Finally, the CIDEr-D score is defined as:

$$\text{CIDEr-D}(c_i, S_i) = \frac{1}{N} \sum_{n=1}^{N} \text{CIDEr-D}_n(c_i, S_i), \quad (4)$$

where N is the longest considered n-gram, in (Vedantam et al., 2015) is told that empirically is assigned $N = 4$.

Although Vedantam *et al.* (Vedantam et al., 2015) have introduced the Gaussian penalty $exp\{-\frac{(l(c_i)-l(s_{ij}))^2}{2\sigma^2}\}$ to tackle the problem of higher scores when words with higher confidence are repeated over long sentences, this factor only works for datasets with slight variances in the sentence lengths, and where the sentences have few words. For instance, this is the case of MS COCO, but it is not the case of the #PraCegoVer. We have demonstrated in Section 6 that models based on one of the state-of-art architectures trained on MS COCO and optimizing CIDEr-D output descriptions with high quality. However, when we trained these models with the same hyperparameters over the #PraCegoVer, the result was poor, with output sentences including many word repetitions. Such behavior occurs because the Gaussian penalty punishes at the same intensity any difference in length $|l(c_i) - l(s_{ij})|$. Hence, the model is forced to generate captions similar in length to the reference, learning to repeat words not to be penalized by the cosine similarity between the TF-IDF vectors.

In light of this problem, we propose CIDEr-D modified, which we called CIDEr-R, where we replace the Gaussian penalty with two other penalties: length and repetition. We relax the Gaussian Penalty to be more flexible in the context of varied sentence length. Therefore, we developed the **length penalty** that changes according to the reference length so that the longer the reference sentence, the more permitted is the difference $|l(c_i) - l(s_{ij})|$. Also, to avoid the model to predict repeated words, we introduce the **repetition penalty** that deals specifically with this problem. This penalty considers the number of occurrences of a word in the candidate and reference sentences, assigning an intensified penalty score as that word frequency in the candidate sentence differs from the frequency in the reference.

Formally, given the generated description c_i and the reference s_{ij}, the **length penalty** $Pen_L(c_i, s_{ij})$ is defined as follows:

$$Pen_L(c_i, s_{ij}) = exp\{-\frac{(l(c_i) - l(s_{ij}))^2}{l(s_{ij})^2}\}. \quad (5)$$

Repetition penalty $Pen_R(c_i, s_{ij})$ is formally defined as:

$$Pen_R(c_i, s_{ij}) = \prod_{w \in c'_i} f(w, c_i, s_{ij})^{1/l(c_i)}, \quad (6)$$

$$f(w, c_i, s_{ij}) = \begin{cases} \frac{1}{1+|freq(w,c_i)-freq(w,s_{ij})|}, & \text{if } w \in c'_i \cap s'_{ij} \\ \frac{1}{freq(w,c_i)}, & \text{if } w \in c'_i \setminus s'_{ij} \end{cases}$$

where $freq(w, s)$ is the number of occurrences of the word w in a sentence s, and the notation c' and s' represents the set of words that appear in c and s, respectively.

Note that the length penalty (Equation 5) is similar to the Gaussian penalty in Equation 3, except for the denominator, which we replace by the term $l(s_{ij})^2$. This change makes the metric more flexible concerning the difference in lengths generated and reference sentences.

Finally, we define CIDEr-R as follows:

$$\text{CIDEr-R}_n(c_i, S_i) = \frac{10}{m} \sum_{s_{ij} \in S_i} sim(c_i, s_{ij}) \cdot Pen_R^{k_r} \cdot Pen_L^{1-k_r}, \quad k_r \in [0, 1]. \quad (7)$$

Our formulation of CIDEr-R has replaced the Gaussian penalty with the weighted geometric average of length and repetition penalties, where k_r and $1 - k_r$ is the weight assigned to repetition and length penalty, respectively.

We have executed a random search (Bergstra and Bengio, 2012) to tune the weights assigned to each penalty, and we find the best configuration is $k_r = 0.8$. This configuration forces the model to avoid repetition. On the other hand, it generates shorter sentences than when $k_r = 0.0$, which is expected since we are decreasing the length penalty's weight.

6 Experiments

6.1 Caption-Level Human Correlation

In this experiment, we evaluate how much the automated metrics match human judgment. We use the PASCAL-50S proposed by Vedantam *et al.* (Vedantam et al., 2015). This dataset consists of triplets of sentences A, B, and C, where A is a reference caption and B and C are candidates. Each triplet has an annotation with the majority vote for the question, "Which of the two sentences, B or C, is more similar to A?". The dataset comprehends four different combinations of sentences B and C: human-correct (HC), human-incorrect (HI), human-model (HM), and model-model (MM).

To evaluate the metrics, we compute the score for each triplet, using different metrics, for B and C having a set of references, and then we calculate the metric's accuracy. The accuracy is defined as the number of times the metric assigns the highest score to the candidate pair most commonly preferred by human evaluators divided by the total number of pairs (B, C). To assess the impact of the number of available references on metrics performance, we compute the accuracy for each metric, varying the number of available references from 1 to 48. We show the results in Figure 3[2].

We can see that CIDEr-R has a similar performance to CIDEr-D, considering the four types of pairs. However, CIDEr-R outperforms the other metrics at distinguishing between two machine-generated captions (Model-Model Pairs). Especially when only one reference caption is available, which is the most common scenario of large datasets such as ours, CIDEr-R outperforms CIDEr-D by 1.2% of accuracy. Model-Model Pairs is a most interesting subtask from a practical point of view because distinguishing better-performing algorithms is the primary motivation of the automated metrics.

[2]We used the implementation of the evaluation metrics available on `https://github.com/ruotianluo/coco-caption`

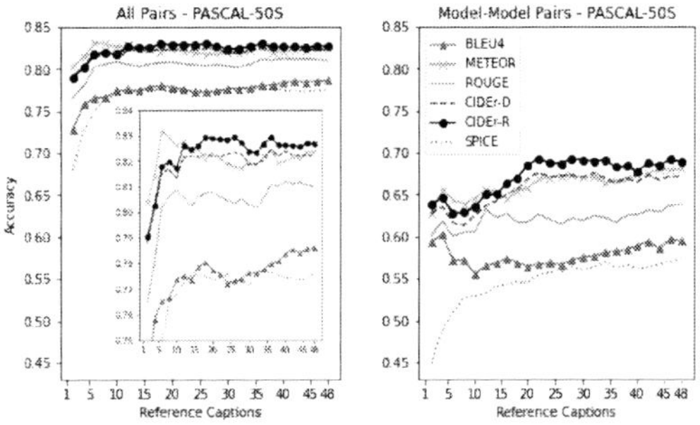

Figure 3: Classification accuracy of metrics at matching human evaluation with 1-48 reference captions.

6.2 Ablation Study

To investigate the impact of mean and variance of the sentence's length in the datasets and influence of availability of multiple references, we selected subsets from #PraCegoVer and MS COCO datasets. We constructed MS COCO – Subset (Single Reference) to increase the sentence length variance. Thus, we selected the longest reference for each image, and then we removed the examples whose sentence length is between the first and third quartiles. Regarding the MS COCO – Subset (Multi-Reference), we kept the same examples as in MS COCO – Subset (Single Reference) but considered the 5 references per image. In addition, we randomly selected a subset of #PraCegoVer with about 63 thousand examples, which we called *#PraCegoVer-63K*. Also, we constructed the subsets *#PraCegoVer N Words* aiming to reduce the variance of the sentence length, so we selected just the examples whose reference has at most N-words. Finally, we used the original datasets MS COCO and Flickr30k. We presented the statistics about the datasets used in our experiments in Table 1.

Self-Critical Sequence Training has been largely used to train the Image Captioning models. It can optimize non-differentiable functions. Therefore it is used to optimize CIDEr-D. To compare the performance of models optimizing CIDEr-D and CIDEr-R, we train models using AoANet architecture, which is still one of the state-of-the-art architectures, on the different datasets mentioned above. For each setting, we execute the training 3 times, and we present the experimental results in Table 2. Note that Stanford Scene Graph Parser is not available for Portuguese, then we could not compute the SPICE score for subsets of #PraCegoVer.

Overall, the models' performance decreases as

Table 1: Statistics of each dataset used in our experiment. "Avg. Sentence Length" stands for the average sentence length, and "Std. Sentence Length" stands for the standard deviation of the sentence length.

Dataset	Dataset Size	Train Size	Validation Size	Test Size	Vocabulary Size	Avg. Sentence Length	Std. Sentence Length
MS COCO	123287	113287	5000	5000	13508	10.5	2.2
MS COCO – Subset (Multi-Reference)	77719	71428	3145	3146	7985	10.6	2.8
MS COCO – Subset (Single Reference)	77719	71428	3145	3146	4365	13.7	3.9
Flickr30k	31014	29000	1014	1000	18459	12.3	5.2
#PraCegoVer – 63K	62935	37881	12442	12612	55029	37.8	26.8
#PraCegoVer 10 Words	10616	8531	1007	1078	5220	7.9	1.7
#PraCegoVer 20 Words	42292	33892	3521	4879	18829	13.8	4.3

Table 2: Experimental results obtained with AoANet models trained on different datasets, using Self-Critical Sequence Training to optimize CIDEr-D and CIDEr-R. The results are presented as "mean score ± standard deviation of the scores".

Dataset	Optimizing	CIDEr-R	CIDEr-D	SPICE	ROUGE-L	METEOR	BLEU-4
MS COCO	CIDEr-D	121.6 ± 0.3	120.5 ± 0.3	21.1 ± 0.1	57.5 ± 0.2	27.7 ± 0.0	36.5 ± 0.1
	CIDEr-R	124.2 ± 0.7	116.2 ± 1.0	20.3 ± 0.0	57.2 ± 0.2	26.8 ± 0.2	35.9 ± 0.3
MS COCO – Subset (Multi-Reference)	CIDEr-D	117.6 ± 0.2	115.3 ± 0.4	20.3 ± 0.1	56.7 ± 0.1	27.0 ± 0.1	34.9 ± 0.2
	CIDEr-R	119.5 ± 0.5	108.5 ± 1.0	19.2 ± 0.2	56.0 ± 0.2	25.6 ± 0.2	33.3 ± 0.4
MS COCO – Subset (Single Reference)	CIDEr-D	101.0 ± 0.4	97.9 ± 1.0	22.7 ± 0.2	36.8 ± 0.1	16.7 ± 0.1	11.0 ± 0.1
	CIDEr-R	110.5 ± 1.4	93.5 ± 1.8	23.5 ± 0.2	36.2 ± 0.1	15.6 ± 0.1	9.5 ± 0.3
Flickr30k	CIDEr-D	51.5 ± 0.3	45.3 ± 0.2	12.2 ± 0.3	44.0 ± 0.2	18.3 ± 0.1	21.7 ± 0.3
	CIDEr-R	52.9 ± 0.4	44.2 ± 0.9	11.9 ± 0.4	44.0 ± 0.7	17.8 ± 0.3	21.1 ± 0.4
#PraCegoVer – 63K	CIDEr-D	10.8 ± 1.8	4.7 ± 0.7	-	14.5 ± 0.4	7.1 ± 0.1	1.6 ± 0.2
	CIDEr-R	12.6 ± 0.9	3.3 ± 0.2	-	12.6 ± 0.3	5.0 ± 0.3	0.7 ± 0.2
#PraCegoVer 10 Words	CIDEr-D	8.6 ± 0.1	8.8 ± 0.1	-	15.0 ± 0.9	6.4 ± 0.5	1.0 ± 0.1
	CIDEr-R	9.6 ± 0.6	9.3 ± 1.1	-	15.1 ± 0.5	6.2 ± 0.3	1.1 ± 0.1
#PraCegoVer 20 Words	CIDEr-D	10.2 ± 0.5	9.5 ± 0.4	-	15.9 ± 0.1	7.9 ± 0.1	1.8 ± 0.2
	CIDEr-R	16.1 ± 0.8	10.9 ± 0.6	-	15.4 ± 0.3	6.7 ± 0.0	1.7 ± 0.1

the variance of the reference length rises. Considering the datasets MS COCO, MS COCO – Subset (Multi-Reference), and Flickr30K, in which multiple references are available, one can compare the models' performance using the SPICE score, since it has a high human correlation, to avoid a casual bias. We can observe that as the reference length variance increases, the performance of the models optimizing CIDEr-D drops faster than those that optimize CIDEr-R. In particular, the performances, based on the SPICE score, of the models optimizing CIDEr-D and CIDEr-R are not statistically different on Flickr30K, whose reference lengths have the highest standard deviation. Moreover, the models' performance on MS COCO – Subset (Single-Reference) is worse than on MS COCO – Subset (Multi-Reference), which shows the negative impact of lack of multiple references for each example. Still, it can be noted that in the case of MS COCO – Subset (Single-Reference), the model that optimized CIDEr-R surpassed the one that optimized CIDEr-D. It means that the optimization of CIDEr-R is preferred in the case of a Single Reference.

Concerning the subsets of #PraCegoVer, the metrics ROUGE-L, METEOR, and BLEU-4 have low correlation with human judgments, and thus the comparisons must be made in terms of CIDEr-D and CIDEr-D. That said, one can see that, regarding #PraCegoVer's subsets, the performance also improves as the variance of the sentence length decreases. Still, in *#PraCegoVer 20 Words*, we doubled the average sentence length and also rose the variance of length compared to *#PraCegoVer 10 Words*. For this subset, optimizing CIDEr-R resulted in better models than using CIDEr-D. In the case of *#PraCegoVer 10 Words* and *#PraCegoVer 20 Words* datasets, even the average CIDEr-D score improves when we optimize CIDEr-R. It demonstrates that CIDEr-R is more suitable for this context. Moreover, optimizing CIDEr-R improved the captions' quality in comparison with CIDEr-D for all subsets of #PraCegoVer as detailed in Section 6.3.

6.3 Qualitative Analysis

To qualitatively explore the metrics' weakness, we created the triplets shown in Table 3. The triplets are composed of a reference sentence and two candidates: *Correct Candidate* correctly describes the image and *Incorrect Candidate* does not describe the objects in the image. We compute the metrics' scores for each candidate, and then we compute the accuracy based on these triplets, as explained in Section 6.1. We constructed the first example to evaluate the performance of the metrics when the Incorrect Candidate corresponds to a change of the subject of the reference caption, thus changing its meaning entirely, whereas the Correct Candidate consists of small syntactic changes but keeping the same meaning. In the second example, we explore different sentences for the Correct Candidate, while the Incorrect Candidate has some n-grams matching with the reference but has many word repetitions and is semantically incomplete. In the third example, we created the triplets to explore differences in length between the candidates and the reference. Thus, we selected a small sentence for the Correct Candidate, and we constructed the Incorrect Candidates by removing parts of the reference caption and replacing the dog with a cat. Still, in one of the Incorrect Candidates, we repeated the word distance to increase the length.

SPICE beats all other metrics, assigning a higher score for the Correct Candidate in 11 out of 15 triplets. However, it is worth noting that it misclassified triplets in which words are repeated. SPICE can reach this performance because it parses the descriptions according to linguistic rules, limiting its extension to other languages because it depends on linguistic experts. Regarding the other metrics, one can note that BLEU-4 does not classify correctly any triplets, whereas CIDEr-D and ROUGE-L assigned the higher score to the Correct Candidate when its sentence syntactically equals the Incorrect Candidate except by the word "cat". Similarly, CIDEr-R and METEOR correctly classified 4 triplets. METEOR has better performance when the candidate and reference sentences are more syntactically similar. In contrast, CIDEr-R correctly penalizes sentences with word repetition and still while assigning the Correct Candidate. Also, it is essential to highlight that CIDEr-R is more invariant to sentence length than CIDEr-D. We saw this in cases where a higher score is assigned to the Correct Candidate even though it is shorter than the Incorrect Candidate. For example, in the pair "A cow and a dog on the street." and "A bird sitting on the on on on cat and a dog and a dog and and sitting on next", the first candidate is preferred.

Still, to show the quality of the captions generated by models trained to optimize CIDEr-D and CIDEr-R in the context of a single reference, we present in Figure 4 two examples from *#PraCegoVer-63K* test set and two from MS COCO. In these examples, the images are followed by the reference caption and the descriptions automatically generated by the models. Regarding MS COCO, we train the models on MS COCO – Subset (Single-Reference), and we generate the captions for images from MS COCO Karpathy test set (Karpathy and Li, 2015).

Models trained to optimize CIDEr-D learn to repeat words in all cases, as highlighted in Figure 4. This occurs because the length penalty in CIDEr-R is more flexible than the Gaussian penalty in CIDEr-D. Hence, the model can generate short captions without being much penalized. As a result, the models trained to optimize CIDEr-R tend to produce summarized descriptions. This become clear specially when we consider *#PraCegoVer-63K* where the references are long, as illustrated in Figures 1 and 4a. Therefore, CIDEr-R is a better metric to be optimized in the context of long reference captions, especially when the variance of the sentences is high.

7 Conclusion

This work demonstrated that CIDEr-D's performance is hampered by the lack of multiple reference sentences and sentence lengths variance. Thus, we proposed CIDEr-R as an alternative to CIDEr-D in the context of a single reference and where the sentence length variance matters, such as large datasets based on social media data. We modified the Gaussian penalty to make CIDEr-D invariant to the difference in length between the reference caption and the generated description. Also, we introduced a penalty for word repetition to better compare captions with a length similar to the reference but with words repeated several times. Further, we showed that CIDEr-R is more accurate and closer to human judgment than CIDEr-D, and it is also more robust regarding the number of references. Still, we showed that CIDEr-R is a preferred evaluation metric to CIDEr-D for datasets with single reference and high variance of sentence length, such as #PraCegoVer. Additionally, we demonstrated that using SCST to optimize CIDEr-D is not a good approach regarding datasets with a high length variance because the models are more likely to repeat words to increase the length of the generated caption. Finally, we demonstrated that training models to optimize CIDEr-R instead of CIDEr-D produces more descriptive captions.

For future work, we intend to create a dataset similar to PASCAL-50S with captions in Portugue-

Table 3: A small set of triplets created to explore the metrics' weakness. We constructed 5 triplets for each image, each one consisting of a reference, *Correct Candidate (CC)* and *Incorrect Candidate (IC)*. *Correct Candidate* correctly describes the image, while *Incorrect Candidate* is a sentence that do not describes the image.

Reference	Correct Candidate (CC)	Incorrect Candidate (IC)	CIDEr-R		CIDEr-D		SPICE		METEOR		ROUGE-L		BLEU-4	
			CC	IC	CC	IC	CC	IC	CC	IC	CC	IC	CC	IC
 1. A young girl is preparing to blow out her candle.	A young girl is about to blow out her candle.	A young dog is preparing to blow out her candle.	452.3	**537.4**	452.3	**537.4**	**80.0**	20.0	**92.5**	47.2	90.0	**90.0**	65.8	**70.7**
	A young girl is getting ready to blow out her candle.		389.5	**537.4**	384.9	**537.4**	**80.0**	20.0	**53.6**	47.2	86.5	**90.0**	58.8	**70.7**
	A young girl is getting ready to blow out a candle.		238.1	**537.4**	248.7	**537.4**	**66.7**	20.0	46.6	**47.2**	76.9	**90.0**	35.1	**70.7**
	A young girl is getting ready to blow out a candle on a small dessert.		173.6	**537.4**	138.0	**537.4**	**50.0**	20.0	44.1	**47.2**	66.4	**90.0**	24.6	**70.7**
	A kid is to blow out the single candle in a bowl of birthday goodness.		78.7	**537.4**	60.8	**537.4**	**15.4**	20.0	25.6	**47.2**	49.8	**90.0**	0.0	**70.7**
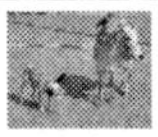 2. A bird sitting on the back of a cow and a dog and bird standing on the ground next to the cow.	A mottled brown dog and cow with two little birds outdoors.	A bird sitting on the on on on cat and a dog and a dog and and sitting on next to.	32.1	**129.6**	7.5	**201.1**	10.5	**15.4**	8.8	**25.9**	22.9	**60.2**	0.0	**30.8**
	A cow standing next to a dog on dirt ground.		89.1	**129.6**	15.4	**201.1**	**35.3**	15.4	21.8	**25.9**	35.1	**60.2**	0.0	**30.8**
	A dog with a bird and a large cow on a street.		73.2	**129.6**	25.9	**201.1**	**22.2**	15.4	15.6	**25.9**	27.9	**60.2**	0.0	**30.8**
	A dog and a cow with a bird sitting on its back.		**168.7**	129.6	54.7	**201.1**	**35.3**	15.4	**26.7**	25.9	33.5	**60.2**	15.8	**30.8**
	A cow and a dog on a street.		**133.2**	129.6	12.5	**201.1**	14.3	**15.4**	14.4	**25.9**	36.9	**60.2**	9.8	**30.8**
 3. Dog laying on couch looking into distance with remote control by paw	A dog laying with a remote control.	Cat laying on couch looking into distance with remote control by paw.	160.1	**745.3**	128.5	**745.3**	50.0	**88.9**	22.9	**56.1**	50.2	**91.7**	0.0	**90.4**
		Cat looking into distance with remote control.	160.1	**415.8**	128.5	**304.2**	**50.0**	46.2	22.9	**30.9**	50.2	**60.3**	0.0	**39.6**
		Cat looking into distance distance distance with a remote control.	**160.1**	142.8	128.5	**151.6**	50.0	**53.3**	22.9	**24.4**	50.2	**53.7**	0.0	0.0
		Cat with remote control by paw.	160.1	**332.5**	128.5	**212.0**	**50.0**	40.0	22.9	**24.0**	50.2	**52.4**	0.0	**28.0**
		A cat with a remote control.	**160.1**	77.0	**128.5**	54.8	**50.0**	30.8	**22.9**	12.2	**50.2**	31.4	0.0	0.0
		Accuracy:	4/15		1/15		11/15		4/15		1/15		0/15	

a) **Reference**: "Na foto, Thalita Gelenske e Thaís Silva estão abraçadas com Luana Génot na livraria Travessa. Ao fundo, diversos livros coloridos estão na prateleira. Nas laterais da foto, existem 2 banners: um deles vermelho, com o logo da, e o outro com a divulgação do livro da Luana."
CIDEr-D: "Foto de uma mulher segurando um livro com *livros*. Ao fundo, uma estante com *livros*. Texto: "A *sua*. *É sua*!"."
CIDEr-R: "Fotografia colorida. Bárbara está sentada em uma biblioteca. Ela está com uma menina. Ela veste uma blusa branca. Ao fundo, uma estante de livros.".

b) **Reference**: "Two kayaks are sitting on a river bank empty."
Subset Single Ref. CIDEr-D: "a *yellow* and *yellow boat* sitting on the side of a beach next to a *boat*'
Subset Single Ref. CIDEr-R: "a yellow surfboard sitting on the beach next to the ocean"

c) **Reference**: "A cat stares at itself in a mirror."
Subset Single Ref. CIDEr-D: "a black and white cat sitting in a *mirror* looking in a *mirror*'
Subset Single Ref. CIDEr-R: "a cat sitting in front of a mirror"

Figure 4: Figure 4a is an example of image from *#PraCegoVer-63K* test set and Figures 4b and 4c are from MS COCO Karpathy test set (Karpathy and Li, 2015). In Figure 4a, we show the reference caption and the description generated by models trained on *#PraCegoVer-63K* to optimize CIDEr-D and CIDEr-R. In Figures 4b and 4c, we show the captions generated by models trained on MS COCO – Subset (Single-Reference) to optimize CIDEr-D and CIDEr-R, as well as the available reference for that image. "Subset Single Ref." stands for MS COCO – Subset (Single-Reference).

se with the same characteristics of #PraCegoVer to validate the accuracy of the metrics in the context of long sentences and high variance. Also, we intend to remove proper names and process synonyms to reduce the vocabulary size and replace words with low-frequency with synonyms more common in subsets of #PraCegoVer to evaluate how this impacts the models' performance.

Acknowledgements

G. O. dos Santos is funded by the São Paulo Research Foundation (FAPESP) (2019/24041-4)[3]. E. L. Colombini and S. Avila are partially funded by H.IAAC (Artificial Intelligence and Cognitive Architectures Hub). S. Avila is also partially funded by FAPESP (2013/08293-7), a CNPq PQ-2 grant (315231/2020-3), and Google LARA 2020.

References

Harsh Agrawal, Peter Anderson, Karan Desai, Yufei Wang, Xinlei Chen, Rishabh Jain, Mark Johnson, Dhruv Batra, Devi Parikh, and Stefan Lee. 2019. nocaps: novel object captioning at scale. In *2019 IEEE/CVF International Conference on Computer Vision, ICCV 2019, Seoul, Korea (South), October 27 - November 2, 2019*, pages 8947–8956. IEEE.

Peter Anderson, Basura Fernando, Mark Johnson, and Stephen Gould. 2016. Spice: Semantic propositional image caption evaluation. In *European Conference on Computer Vision*, pages 382–398.

Peter Anderson, Xiaodong He, Chris Buehler, Damien Teney, Mark Johnson, Stephen Gould, and Lei Zhang. 2018. Bottom-up and top-down attention for image captioning and visual question answering. In *2018 IEEE Conference on Computer Vision and Pattern Recognition, CVPR 2018, Salt Lake City, UT, USA, June 18-22, 2018*, pages 6077–6086. IEEE Computer Society.

Satanjeev Banerjee and Alon Lavie. 2005. METEOR: An automatic metric for MT evaluation with improved correlation with human judgments. In *Proceedings of the ACL Workshop on Intrinsic and Extrinsic Evaluation Measures for Machine Translation and/or Summarization*, pages 65–72, Ann Arbor, Michigan. Association for Computational Linguistics.

James Bergstra and Yoshua Bengio. 2012. Random search for hyper-parameter optimization. *The Journal of Machine Learning Research*, 13(1):281–305.

Xinlei Chen, Hao Fang, Tsung-Yi Lin, Ramakrishna Vedantam, Saurabh Gupta, Piotr Dollár, and C Lawrence Zitnick. 2015. Microsoft coco captions: Data collection and evaluation server. *arXiv preprint arXiv:1504.00325*.

Marcella Cornia, Matteo Stefanini, Lorenzo Baraldi, and Rita Cucchiara. 2020. Meshed-memory transformer for image captioning. In *2020 IEEE/CVF Conference on Computer Vision and Pattern Recognition, CVPR 2020, Seattle, WA, USA, June 13-19, 2020*, pages 10575–10584. IEEE.

Danna Gurari, Yinan Zhao, Meng Zhang, and Nilavra Bhattacharya. 2020. Captioning images taken by people who are blind. In *European Conference on Computer Vision*, pages 417–434.

Micah Hodosh, Peter Young, and Julia Hockenmaier. 2013. Framing image description as a ranking task: Data, models and evaluation metrics. *Journal of Artificial Intelligence Research*, 47(1):853–899.

Lun Huang, Wenmin Wang, Jie Chen, and Xiaoyong Wei. 2019. Attention on attention for image captioning. In *2019 IEEE/CVF International Conference on Computer Vision, ICCV 2019, Seoul, Korea (South), October 27 - November 2, 2019*, pages 4633–4642. IEEE.

Justin Johnson, Andrej Karpathy, and Li Fei-Fei. 2016. Densecap: Fully convolutional localization networks for dense captioning. In *2016 IEEE Conference on Computer Vision and Pattern Recognition, CVPR 2016, Las Vegas, NV, USA, June 27-30, 2016*, pages 4565–4574. IEEE Computer Society.

Andrej Karpathy and Fei-Fei Li. 2015. Deep visual-semantic alignments for generating image descriptions. In *IEEE Conference on Computer Vision and Pattern Recognition, CVPR 2015, Boston, MA, USA, June 7-12, 2015*, pages 3128–3137. IEEE Computer Society.

Girish Kulkarni, Visruth Premraj, Sagnik Dhar, Siming Li, Yejin Choi, Alexander C Berg, and Tamara L Berg. 2011. Baby talk: Understanding and generating image descriptions. In *IEEE Conference on Computer Vision and Pattern Recognition*.

Yann LeCun, Yoshua Bengio, and Geoffrey Hinton. 2015. Deep learning. *nature*, 521(7553):436–444.

Xiujun Li, Xi Yin, Chunyuan Li, Pengchuan Zhang, Xiaowei Hu, Lei Zhang, Lijuan Wang, Houdong Hu, Li Dong, Furu Wei, et al. 2020. Oscar: Object-semantics aligned pre-training for vision-language tasks. In *European Conference on Computer Vision*, pages 121–137.

Chin-Yew Lin. 2004. ROUGE: A package for automatic evaluation of summaries. In *Text Summarization Branches Out*, pages 74–81, Barcelona, Spain. Association for Computational Linguistics.

Tsung-Yi Lin, Michael Maire, Serge Belongie, James Hays, Pietro Perona, Deva Ramanan, Piotr Dollár, and C Lawrence Zitnick. 2014. Microsoft coco: Common objects in context. In *European Conference on Computer Vision*, pages 740–755.

Siqi Liu, Zhenhai Zhu, Ning Ye, Sergio Guadarrama, and Kevin Murphy. 2017. Improved image captioning via policy gradient optimization of spider. In *IEEE International Conference on Computer Vision, ICCV 2017, Venice, Italy, October 22-29, 2017*, pages 873–881. IEEE Computer Society.

[3]The opinions expressed in this work do not necessarily reflect those of the funding agencies.

Jiasen Lu, Jianwei Yang, Dhruv Batra, and Devi Parikh. 2018. Neural baby talk. In *2018 IEEE Conference on Computer Vision and Pattern Recognition, CVPR 2018, Salt Lake City, UT, USA, June 18-22, 2018*, pages 7219–7228. IEEE Computer Society.

Yingwei Pan, Ting Yao, Yehao Li, and Tao Mei. 2020. X-linear attention networks for image captioning. In *2020 IEEE/CVF Conference on Computer Vision and Pattern Recognition, CVPR 2020, Seattle, WA, USA, June 13-19, 2020*, pages 10968–10977. IEEE.

Kishore Papineni, Salim Roukos, Todd Ward, and Wei-Jing Zhu. 2002. Bleu: a method for automatic evaluation of machine translation. In *Proceedings of the 40th Annual Meeting of the Association for Computational Linguistics*, pages 311–318, Philadelphia, Pennsylvania, USA. Association for Computational Linguistics.

Marco Pedersoli, Thomas Lucas, Cordelia Schmid, and Jakob Verbeek. 2017. Areas of attention for image captioning. In *IEEE International Conference on Computer Vision, ICCV 2017, Venice, Italy, October 22-29, 2017*, pages 1251–1259. IEEE Computer Society.

Bryan A. Plummer, Liwei Wang, Chris M. Cervantes, Juan C. Caicedo, Julia Hockenmaier, and Svetlana Lazebnik. 2015. Flickr30k entities: Collecting region-to-phrase correspondences for richer image-to-sentence models. In *2015 IEEE International Conference on Computer Vision, ICCV 2015, Santiago, Chile, December 7-13, 2015*, pages 2641–2649. IEEE Computer Society.

Steven J. Rennie, Etienne Marcheret, Youssef Mroueh, Jerret Ross, and Vaibhava Goel. 2017. Self-critical sequence training for image captioning. In *2017 IEEE Conference on Computer Vision and Pattern Recognition, CVPR 2017, Honolulu, HI, USA, July 21-26, 2017*, pages 1179–1195. IEEE Computer Society.

Gabriel Oliveira dos Santos, Esther Luna Colombini, and Sandra Avila. 2021. #PraCegoVer: A large dataset for image captioning in portuguese. *arXiv preprint arXiv:2103.11474*.

Sebastian Schuster, Ranjay Krishna, Angel Chang, Li Fei-Fei, and Christopher D. Manning. 2015. Generating semantically precise scene graphs from textual descriptions for improved image retrieval. In *Proceedings of the Fourth Workshop on Vision and Language*, pages 70–80, Lisbon, Portugal. Association for Computational Linguistics.

Thibault Sellam, Dipanjan Das, and Ankur Parikh. 2020. BLEURT: Learning robust metrics for text generation. In *Proceedings of the 58th Annual Meeting of the Association for Computational Linguistics*, pages 7881–7892, Online. Association for Computational Linguistics.

Ashish Vaswani, Noam Shazeer, Niki Parmar, Jakob Uszkoreit, Llion Jones, Aidan N. Gomez, Lukasz Kaiser, and Illia Polosukhin. 2017. Attention is all you need. In *Advances in Neural Information Processing Systems 30: Annual Conference on Neural Information Processing Systems 2017, December 4-9, 2017, Long Beach, CA, USA*, pages 5998–6008.

Ramakrishna Vedantam, C. Lawrence Zitnick, and Devi Parikh. 2015. Cider: Consensus-based image description evaluation. In *IEEE Conference on Computer Vision and Pattern Recognition, CVPR 2015, Boston, MA, USA, June 7-12, 2015*, pages 4566–4575. IEEE Computer Society.

Oriol Vinyals, Alexander Toshev, Samy Bengio, and Dumitru Erhan. 2015. Show and tell: A neural image caption generator. In *IEEE Conference on Computer Vision and Pattern Recognition, CVPR 2015, Boston, MA, USA, June 7-12, 2015*, pages 3156–3164. IEEE Computer Society.

Tan Wang, Jianqiang Huang, Hanwang Zhang, and Qianru Sun. 2020. Visual commonsense R-CNN. In *2020 IEEE/CVF Conference on Computer Vision and Pattern Recognition, CVPR 2020, Seattle, WA, USA, June 13-19, 2020*, pages 10757–10767. IEEE.

Web para Todos. 2018. Criadora do projeto #PraCegoVer incentiva a descrição de imagens na web. http://mwpt.com.br/criadora-do-projeto-pracegover-incentiva-descricao-de-imagens-na-web.

Tianyi Zhang, Varsha Kishore, Felix Wu, Kilian Q. Weinberger, and Yoav Artzi. 2020. Bertscore: Evaluating text generation with BERT. In *8th International Conference on Learning Representations, ICLR 2020, Addis Ababa, Ethiopia, April 26-30, 2020*. OpenReview.net.

Wei Zhao, Maxime Peyrard, Fei Liu, Yang Gao, Christian M. Meyer, and Steffen Eger. 2019. MoverScore: Text generation evaluating with contextualized embeddings and earth mover distance. In *Proceedings of the 2019 Conference on Empirical Methods in Natural Language Processing and the 9th International Joint Conference on Natural Language Processing (EMNLP-IJCNLP)*, pages 563–578, Hong Kong, China. Association for Computational Linguistics.

Improved Named Entity Recognition for Noisy Call Center Transcripts

Sam Davidson[†], **Jordan Hosier**[*], **Yu Zhou**[*], **Vijay K. Gurbani**[*]
[†]University of California, Davis, Davis, California 95616
[*]Vail Systems, Inc., Chicago, Illinois 60606
ssdavidson@ucdavis.edu; {jhosier,yzhou,vgurbani}@vailsys.com

Abstract

We explore the application of state-of-the-art NER algorithms to ASR-generated call center transcripts. Previous work in this domain focused on the use of a BiLSTM-CRF model which relied on Flair embeddings; however, such a model is unwieldy in terms of latency and memory consumption. In a production environment, end users require low-latency models which can be readily integrated into existing pipelines. To that end, we present two different models which can be utilized based on the latency and accuracy requirements of the user. First, we propose a set of models which utilize state-of-the-art Transformer language models (RoBERTa) to develop a high-accuracy NER system trained on a custom annotated set of call center transcripts. We then use our best-performing Transformer-based model to label a large number of transcripts, which we use to pretrain a BiLSTM-CRF model and further fine-tune on our annotated dataset. We show that this model, while not as accurate as its Transformer-based counterpart, is highly effective in identifying items which require redaction for privacy law compliance. Further, we propose a new general annotation scheme for NER in the call-center environment.

1 Introduction

The recent promulgation of new privacy laws, such as the European Union's General Data Protection Regulation (GDPR) and the California Privacy Rights Act has drawn additional attention to the need for businesses to effectively identify and redact sensitive personally identifiable information (PII) in their business records. For the call center industry, which frequently collects transcripts of customer calls, this task is particularly tricky as transcripts tend to be an extremely noisy data source. This noise results from several factors, including errors in automated speech recognition (ASR), the use of single-channel audio (recordings that do not differentiate between users), and speech disfluencies.

In this paper, we explore the use of a Named Entity Recognition (NER) task to identify those items in transcripts which should be redacted for privacy law compliance. Most existing NER models are trained on well-formed written text. Due to the noisy data in call center transcripts and domain language differences the use of such models in our task is not ideal. Additionally, although our task is quite similar to traditional NER, such as the CoNLL 2003 task (Sang and De Meulder, 2003), the set of entities which we need to identify for privacy law compliance is significantly larger than that used in many NER tasks. For example, traditional NER label sets do not contain tags for entities such as telephone numbers, account numbers, or email addresses. To address this issue, we propose a new NER label set designed to meet the requirements of privacy law compliance in the call center industry. Our NER model also lends itself to uses such as identifying product mentions for call routing.

Given the recent dominance of large pretrained Transformer language models such as BERT (Devlin et al., 2019) in NLP, we explore the application of Transformer LMs to the task of NER on call center transcripts. We demonstrate that fine-tuning these models on unlabeled, in-domain data, then further fine-tuning on a custom annotated set of call center transcripts, results an effective model for entity identification. Further, we explore the use of these models to label a large number of transcripts, which we then use as training data for a smaller BiLSTM-CRF sequence prediction model. This model, while not as accurate as its transformer-based brethren, can allow for less computationally expensive inference.

The key contributions of this paper are demonstrating the efficacy of Transformer LM-based NER models for use in the call center domain and the use of said models to generate training data for smaller

Proceedings of the 2021 EMNLP Workshop W-NUT: The Seventh Workshop on Noisy User-generated Text, pages 361–370
November 11, 2021.

models which may be better suited to production environments. We demonstrate that a BiLSTM-CRF using Flair (Akbik et al., 2018) contextual string embeddings is approximately 7 times slower than our best-performing BiLSTM-CRF model using fixed pretrained subword embeddings, with only marginal F1-score improvement. Additionally, the Flair-based LSTM model (0.73 micro-F1) is 3 times slower than our best-performing RoBERTa-based model (0.82 micro-F1) and 7 times slower than a DistilRoBERTa model (0.81 micro-F1).

2 Previous work

NER has long been a popular task in the NLP community, and many public benchmark datasets exist to test the performance of various sequence labeling algorithms on the NER task. Initially developed as part of the Message Understanding Conferences (Grishman and Sundheim, 1996), the task was further popularized by the CoNLL 2003 shared task on NER (Sang and De Meulder, 2003). The CoNLL 2003 dataset and the OntoNotes corpus (Hovy et al., 2006) remain popular benchmarks for sequence labeling algorithms.

The Conditional Random Field (Lafferty et al., 2001) was, and remains, a popular method for sequence labeling, including NER (Konkol and Konopík, 2013). Huang et al. (2015) achieved success in the NER task by combining the CRF with the bidirectional LSTM (Schuster and Paliwal, 1997; Hochreiter and Schmidhuber, 1997). Similarly, Ma and Hovy (2016) achieved state-of-the-art NER results with a BiLSTM-CNN-CRF model.

More recently, with the advent of pretrained Transformer language models such a BERT (Devlin et al., 2019) and RoBERTa (Liu et al., 2019), attention has shifted to using these models for the NER task. Devlin et al. (2019) use an NER sequence labeling task as an example of the power of BERT. Additionally, Souza et al. (2019) combine BERT with a CRF layer to achieve impressive results for NER in Portuguese. In this paper, we utilize both Transformer-based NER and BiLSTM-CRF models for NER on a custom annotated dataset of call center transcripts.

The use of automated methods for text anonymization has a long history in both NLP and the biomedical domain. For example, Chen and Kan (2013) report on the use of regular expressions for removing PII from SMS messages. Gorinski et al. (2019) and Pérez-Díez et al. (2021) investigate the use of NER for anonymizing medical records. Most relevant to the present work is Kaplan (2020), who use a BiLSTM-CRF model for PII redaction in call center transcripts.

3 Data

Our primary dataset consists of 1422 transcripts of call center recordings generated by a commercial ASR provider, with an average length of 464.4 tokens; the entire dataset contains 660,358 tokens. The dataset is split into a train set containing 594,947 tokens and a validation set containing 65,411 tokens. Our held-out test set on which all models are evaluated consists of 44 transcripts containing 41,961 tokens. The dataset contains a total of 21,537 entity spans. All tokens are converted to CoNLL 2003 BIO format for training our sequence prediction models. An example of our data can be found in Appendix A.

In addition to our labeled data, we use a larger set of 99,796 unlabeled call transcripts for domain adaptation of our pretrained language models, as well as for generation of synthetically labeled training data.

3.1 Annotation

We employed two experienced annotators to annotate our data for entities based on a detailed annotation schema developed for this task (see Table 1). Annotation was completed using the BRAT annotation tool[1]. Annotation was an iterative process, in which we first had the two annotators label a small, identical set of transcripts, from which we then calculated inter-annotator agreement. We also reviewed the annotation guidelines with the annotators and updated the guidelines based on their comments. Once interannotator agreement reached a Krippendorff's α of 0.80 (as suggested by Carletta (2008)), we proceeded with annotation of the larger dataset. We had the annotators each label 711 unique transcripts, as well as an overlapping set of 50 transcripts, on which we calculated our final interannotator agreement score. Our final interannotator agreement was α of 0.875, indicating a high level of agreement between our annotators and a well-defined annotation task.

In addition to the NER entities required for redaction of PII, such as the set used by Kaplan (2020), we use an expanded label set which includes entities such as *Product* and *Currency*. We wished to

[1]https://brat.nlplab.org/

Entity Label	Description	Strict F1	Part. F1	Span Count
Person	Name of a person, including titles and spelled-out names.	0.83	0.91	4,277
Location	Political divisions (country, city, etc.) and addresses.	0.66	0.84	1,196
Organization	Name of company, store, website, service group, etc.	0.82	0.87	2,853
DateTime	Date, time of day/week, time duration (excl. card exp dates or customer DOB)	0.76	0.90	6,710
Product	Named products (not to include generic items)	0.61	0.65	1,834
Account	Credit card, account, order numbers, expiration dates, CVV codes, etc.	0.58	0.85	1,109
ID	Driver's license, SSN, member num., merchant num, DOB, etc.	0.34	0.90	211
Phone	Complete or partial telephone numbers.	0.64	0.78	572
Email	Complete or partial email addresses.	0.46	0.46	64
Currency	Dollar amounts.	0.77	0.93	2,711

Table 1: Description of label set used in data annotation, as well an F1 scores between annotators and number of examples in our dataset of each span type. *Strict* is exact-match span-based F1, while *Part.* is type-sensitive partial span overlap F1.

create a flexible dataset which could be used for training models beyond our immediate redaction task, such as models for analyzing consumer behavior. Additionally, we include numeric labels such as *DateTime* and *Currency* to better understand how NER-based redaction compares to rule-based numerical redaction systems commonly used in the call handling industry.

To better understand which categories were particularly challenging for annotators, we calculated the F1 score between annotators on the agreement set, with one annotator being set as ground-truth (see Table 1). The reported F1 scores are based the evaluation scheme developed for the SemEval 2013 Task 9 (Segura Bedmar et al., 2013). As mentioned in Kaplan (2020), email addresses proved particularly challenging for our annotators, as the ASR language model struggles to intelligibly decipher email addresses; this results in strange forms such as "XTD a ballgode dot com."[2] As a result, it can be challenging for annotators to identify which words belong to the email address, as demonstrated by the low F1 score reported in Table 1. The fact that there is no difference between strict and partial-overlap F1 scores indicates that annotators are struggling not only to identify the span boundaries of email addresses, but also to identify where email addresses exist in the text. By contrast, for entities like *Phone*, *ID*, and *Account*, the annotators generally agree on the entity type to be assigned, but often disagree on the boundaries, resulting in a large difference between the strict and partial-match F1 scores. This disagreement may be due to the fact that our data is not speaker-differentiated.

4 Models

We propose two classes of model trained on our annotated dataset. The first class applies state-of-the-art Transformer LMs to the NER task, while the second class uses a BiLSTM-CRF architecture. Our initial transformer model harnessed BERT, however early testing indicated that RoBERTa generally performed better for our target task. As our goal was to create an efficient model for production use, we chose to not explore model ensembling, though this is a potential direction for future work.

Our Transformer-based models were built using Huggingface's Tranformers package [3] for PyTorch. Our best performing model uses a *roberta-base* pretrained model to encode input token sequences, which are then passed to a linear layer for dimension reduction, and finally to a CRF layer (implemented using PyTorch CRF [4]) to make final label predictions.

Our BiLSTM-CRF model, which is implemented in PyTorch, consists of a 4-layer bidirectional LSTM encoder with 300 hidden units per layer. As with our Transformer model described above, encoder output is passed to a linear layer prior be being passed to a CRF layer for final

[2]All potential PII in text and appendix have been replaced with fabricated data to replicate real examples

[3]https://huggingface.co/transformers/

[4]https://pytorch-crf.readthedocs.io/en/stable/

prediction. Input to the model consists of 100-dimension pretrained byte-pair subword embeddings generated using BPEmb (Heinzerling and Strube, 2018). We also tested a BiLSTM-CRF model which uses Flair embeddings (Akbik et al., 2018) as input, similar to the model proposed in Kaplan (2020).

5 Experiments

To directly compare the performance of our various models, we train each model on our final annotated training dataset and evaluate on our held-out test set. Additionally, we analyze the perfomance of our BiLSTM-CRFs relative to the Transformer model, as it is significantly faster and requires fewer computational resources.

We test two different pretrained models from the Transformers library: RoBERTa (Liu et al., 2019), and DistilRoBERTa (Sanh et al., 2019). All models are fine-tuned on our annotated training data for 6 epochs using the AdamW (Loshchilov and Hutter, 2018) optimizer, with an initial learning rate of $5e-5$ and epsilon of $1e-8$. We use linear warmup to reach the initial learning rate over the first training epoch. We select the model checkpoint with the best validation micro-F1 for further evaluation. We also train each model with and without a sliding context window of 99 tokens on either side of the target input, as described in Luoma and Pyysalo (2020). The size of the context window was determined by testing various context window sizes; we found 99 tokens to provide the most improvement in model performance.

Next, we test the performance of our BiLSTM model, which we train with two types of input token embeddings as described in Section 4. As with the Transformer models, we use the AdamW optmizer with an initial learning rate of $5e-5$ and epsilon of $1e-8$. We also experimented with the Adam optimizer with a LR of 0.001, with nearly identical results. We implement early stopping on validation F1 with a patience of 6. Our best-performing model triggered early stopping after 17 epochs.

Given that our LSTM models are significantly faster than our Transformer models on CPU, we wished to test an LSTM model trained on additional RoBERTa-labeled data. We therefore use our best-performing RoBERTa model to label 20,000 unlabeled transcripts, which we then use to train a BiLSTM-CRF model. Once validation F1 stops improving, we further fine-tune the model on our annotated dataset. The resulting model gains 3 F1 points over our other LSTM models, and reaches an F1 within 5 points of our DistilRoBERTa model.

Model	F1	GPU	CPU
RoBERTa w/o ctxt.	0.81	4.62s	42.8s
RoBERTa	0.83	9.21s	84.3s
RoBERTa-ft w/o ctxt.	0.83	4.71s	43.4s
RoBERTa-ft	0.82	9.15s	86.5s
DistilRoBERTa	0.79	4.24s	43.3s
DistilRoBERTa-ft	0.81	4.30s	43.6s
BiLSTM-CRF	0.73	4.61s	14.2s
BiLSTM-CRF pretrain	0.76	4.54s	14.5s
BiLSTM-CRF w/ Flair	0.73	34.0s	44.4s

Table 2: Selected experimental results and runtimes on our held-out test set. All models include a 99 token context window unless otherwise noted.

All model training is conducted using an NVIDIA GeForce GTX 1080 GPU with 8 GB of memory. Inference is performed on both GPU and CPU to test inference latency. F1 and total test runtime of each of our best-performing models are shown in Table 2. All F1 scores reported for model performance use "strict" evaluation in which both entity type and span boundaries must match. Additionally, in Figure 1 we provide a confusion matrix of token-level classification using our RoBERTa model.

6 Discussion

Our experiments demonstrate that pretrained Transformer language models, such as RoBERTa, can lead to significant performance improvements for NER labeling of call center transcripts when compared to previously published methods. While this is not terribly surprising, given the number of NLP tasks in which Transformer LMs have come to dominate, this paper is the first application of said models to the domain of call transcripts. The only work which has focused on NER for call center transcripts, Kaplan (2020) used a BiLSTM-CRF model only; while we are unable to replicate their work due to the unavailability of their data [5], our experiments using a similar model design show that our proposed Transformer models achieve improved performance on this task. Our LSTM model uses pretrained, rather than custom, Flair embed-

[5]We are also, unfortunately, unable to publicly release our dataset at this time due to its sensitive nature.

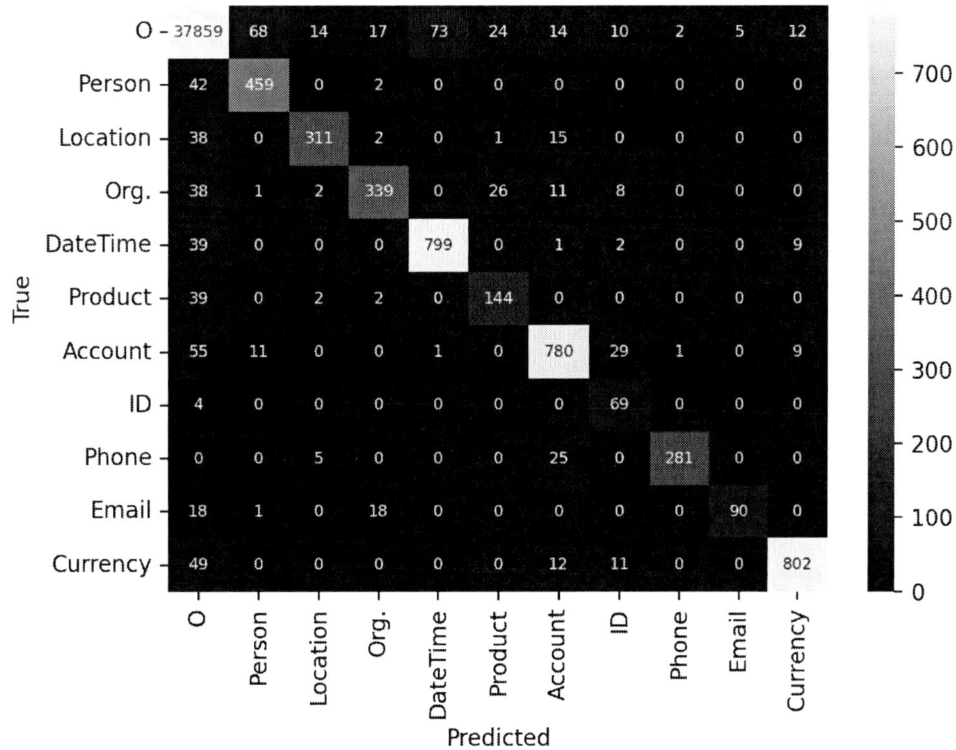

Figure 1: Confusion matrix for token-level classification of our RoBERTa model. "O" represents a non-entity.

dings; however, given the improvements for custom embeddings reported by Kaplan (2020) we would not expect training custom embeddings to result in a model which outperforms our best Transformer-based model.

As previously mentioned, call center transcripts are a particularly noisy type of input data; noise sources include disfluencies in spoken language, poor audio quality, and ASR errors. Given this fact, it can be challenging for both annotators and a model to correctly identify entity boundaries. As previously mentioned, all F1 scores reported for model performance use "strict" evaluation. However, such precision is not necessarily required for a model to be effective for redaction of PII. For example, if only the majority of an *Email* is captured by the model, the resulting redaction may still be sufficient. Of note is the fact that our best performing model achieves an "entity type" F1 score of 0.90; this metric requires that entity types be labeled correctly, but that span boundaries need only overlap. This score indicates that the model is correctly labeling the large majority of spans, even if its predicted boundaries do not exactly match those of the annotator.

7 Conclusion

This paper presents the first application of pre-trained Transformer language models to NER for the call transcript domain. This is a unique domain in many ways, particularly due to the large amounts of noise present in the data. We demonstrate that Transformer LMs, namely RoBERTa and DistilRoBERTa, outperform the previous state of the art model for this domain on our custom dataset. Additionally, we show that these models are significantly faster to run than the previous state of the art model. Finally, we show that a Transformer LM model can be used to generate training data for a smaller, less computationally greedy LSTM model, resulting in substantial performance improvement for the smaller model. This finding provides additional choice to end-users wishing to develop an NER system for production use in a call center environment, and potential future directions for improving model efficiency and performance.

7.1 References

References

Alan Akbik, Duncan Blythe, and Roland Vollgraf. 2018. Contextual string embeddings for sequence labeling. In *COLING 2018, 27th International Conference on Computational Linguistics*, pages 1638–1649.

Jean Carletta. 2008. Assessing agreement on classification tasks: the kappa statistic. *arXiv preprint cmp-lg/9602004*.

Tao Chen and Min-Yen Kan. 2013. Creating a live, public short message service corpus: the NUS SMS corpus. *Language Resources and Evaluation*, 47(2):299–335.

Jacob Devlin, Ming-Wei Chang, Kenton Lee, and Kristina Toutanova. 2019. BERT: Pre-training of deep bidirectional transformers for language understanding. In *Proceedings of the 2019 Conference of the North American Chapter of the Association for Computational Linguistics: Human Language Technologies, Volume 1 (Long and Short Papers)*, pages 4171–4186.

Philip John Gorinski, Honghan Wu, Claire Grover, Richard Tobin, Conn Talbot, Heather Whalley, Cathie Sudlow, William Whiteley, and Beatrice Alex. 2019. Named entity recognition for electronic health records: a comparison of rule-based and machine learning approaches. *arXiv preprint arXiv:1903.03985*.

Ralph Grishman and Beth M Sundheim. 1996. Message understanding conference-6: A brief history. In *COLING 1996 Volume 1: The 16th International Conference on Computational Linguistics*.

Benjamin Heinzerling and Michael Strube. 2018. BPEmb: Tokenization-free Pre-trained Subword Embeddings in 275 Languages. In *Proceedings of the Eleventh International Conference on Language Resources and Evaluation (LREC 2018)*, Miyazaki, Japan. European Language Resources Association (ELRA).

Sepp Hochreiter and Jürgen Schmidhuber. 1997. Long short-term memory. *Neural computation*, 9(8):1735–1780.

Eduard Hovy, Mitch Marcus, Martha Palmer, Lance Ramshaw, and Ralph Weischedel. 2006. OntoNotes: the 90% solution. In *Proceedings of the human language technology conference of the NAACL, Companion Volume: Short Papers*, pages 57–60.

Zhiheng Huang, Wei Xu, and Kai Yu. 2015. Bidirectional LSTM-CRF models for sequence tagging. *arXiv preprint arXiv:1508.01991*.

Micaela Kaplan. 2020. May I ask who's calling? named entity recognition on call center transcripts for privacy law compliance. In *Proceedings of the Sixth Workshop on Noisy User-generated Text (W-NUT 2020)*, pages 1–6, Online. Association for Computational Linguistics.

Michal Konkol and Miloslav Konopík. 2013. Crf-based Czech named entity recognizer and consolidation of czech NER research. In *International conference on text, speech and dialogue*, pages 153–160. Springer.

John Lafferty, Andrew McCallum, and Fernando CN Pereira. 2001. Conditional random fields: Probabilistic models for segmenting and labeling sequence data.

Yinhan Liu, Myle Ott, Naman Goyal, Jingfei Du, Mandar Joshi, Danqi Chen, Omer Levy, Mike Lewis, Luke Zettlemoyer, and Veselin Stoyanov. 2019. RoBERTa: A robustly optimized BERT pretraining approach. *arXiv e-prints*, pages arXiv–1907.

Ilya Loshchilov and Frank Hutter. 2018. Fixing weight decay regularization in adam.

Jouni Luoma and Sampo Pyysalo. 2020. Exploring cross-sentence contexts for named entity recognition with BERT. In *Proceedings of the 28th International Conference on Computational Linguistics*, pages 904–914.

Xuezhe Ma and Eduard Hovy. 2016. End-to-end sequence labeling via bi-directional LSTM-CNNS-CRF. *arXiv preprint arXiv:1603.01354*.

Irene Pérez-Díez, Raúl Pérez-Moraga, Adolfo López-Cerdán, Jose-Maria Salinas-Serrano, and María de la Iglesia-Vayá. 2021. De-identifying spanish medical texts-named entity recognition applied to radiology reports. *Journal of Biomedical Semantics*, 12(1):1–13.

Erik Tjong Kim Sang and Fien De Meulder. 2003. Introduction to the CoNLL-2003 shared task: Language-independent named entity recognition. In *Proceedings of the Seventh Conference on Natural Language Learning at HLT-NAACL 2003*, pages 142–147.

Victor Sanh, Lysandre Debut, Julien Chaumond, and Thomas Wolf. 2019. DistilBERT, a distilled version of BERT: smaller, faster, cheaper and lighter. *arXiv preprint arXiv:1910.01108*.

Mike Schuster and Kuldip K Paliwal. 1997. Bidirectional recurrent neural networks. *IEEE transactions on Signal Processing*, 45(11):2673–2681.

Isabel Segura Bedmar, Paloma Martínez, and María Herrero Zazo. 2013. Semeval-2013 task 9: Extraction of drug-drug interactions from biomedical texts (ddiextraction 2013). Association for Computational Linguistics.

Fábio Souza, Rodrigo Nogueira, and Roberto Lotufo. 2019. Portuguese named entity recognition using BERT-CRF. *arXiv preprint arXiv:1909.10649*.

A Appendix A

A.1 Example input data

Thank you for calling Eastbank . My name is William Yee . I have your first and last time . John Lyon . And mislead me I have your 51 digit account number or your social . Social I'll give it to you zero seven eight zero five one one two zero . Thank you . And how may I help you today . Well I'm trying to see if they gave me the credit that they were supposed to give me the store . Okay and I know you're calling for you to actually funded your account today .

Note: All potential PII in text and appendix have been replaced with fabricated data to replicate real examples. Further, all numbers denoting accounts have been replaced with 0.

A.2 Example model output

Thank O
you O
for O
calling O
Eastbank B-Organization
. O
My O
name O
is O
William B-Person
Yee I-Person
. O
I O
have O
your O
first O
and O
last O
time O
. O
John B-Person
Lyon I-Person
. O
And O
mislead O
me O
I O
have O
your O
51 O
digit O
account O
number O
or O
your O
social O
. O
Social O
I'll O
give O
it O
to O
you O
zero B-ID
seven I-ID
eight I-ID
zero I-ID
five I-ID
one I-ID
one I-ID
two I-ID
zero I-ID
. O
Thank O
you O
. O
And O
how O
may O
I O
help O
you O
today B-DateTime
. O
Well O
I'm O
t O
trying O
to O
see O
if O
they O
gave O
me O
the O
credit O
that O
they O
were O
supposed O
to O
give O
me O
the O
store O
. O
Okay O
and O
I O
know O
you're O
calling O
for O
you O
to O
actually O
funded O
your O
account O
today B-DateTime

A.3 Example redacted data

Thank you for calling Eastbank.
My name is *** *****.
I have your first and last time.
*** *****.
And mislead me I have your 51 digit account number or your social.
Social I'll give it to you **** ***** *** **** **** ***** *** ***** ***.
Thank you.
And how may I help you today.
Well I'm t trying to see if they gave me the credit that they were supposed to give me the store.
Okay and I know you're calling for you to actually funded your account today.

A.4 Additional input data examples

Example 1
For your convenience if you would prefer to prepay please have your credit card ready at the end of the call . They were calling police sugar . This is Melissa . I got a phone I'm burning In 2 9 8 0 that I got a call back . Thank you . This is for donor correct . Donna Yes ma'am . Donna thank you . What can I get started today . Three orders or three equals . I'll tell him in increments of three . All right . The Vietnamese chicken salad rolls are like the pork egg rolls . The pork barrel Yes we can do either . If you want three we can do three of them 4 7 and 9 I couldn't remember the increment oh . sorry . It's 1 8 7 2 4 or 9 Yes to . leave OK . . Already And . that's Anything it . else . Naomi I so just so just make sure we've got one order of the two count pork egg rolls Yes so ma'am . you can about ten minutes and then you're picking up over from the Wilsonville location Yes . Thank you wonderful . You're welcome . I'll see you soon . Bye . yes .

Example 2
I think clean food pickup company here Lake Woods mines Ramona . Can I I get your hear last name your please voice is . breaking up . Can you hear me . I can hear you Okay . I'd like to order a large chicken noodle soup to go OK . I just need a first and last name for the order . Stacy is the first name and last name is Art VERONA Thank you Amanda . I get the last of your phone number 3 6 7 2 is that correct . Perfect . And you said you needed a large chicken noodle soup . OK . That's right . How soon could you have that right . OK . Well can I tempt you with some cheesy garlic bread today Not just this fine all right . So I have here for the order just the regular chicken noodle soup . Correct . Perfect . So your total is six dollars and sixty six cents and then we'll be ready in all ten right minutes here in Court Street . OK . okay great . Thank you . You're welcome Stacy you and Jules on have a great day .

Example 3
Crowd services . My name is Leo . Your first and last name please . To blue . Thank you so much for the information Ms Blue . . And good evening to you ma'am . Can you verify your phone number on file please . 0 0 0 0 0 0 0 00. Thank you . Do you have your stamps Credit Card right now on blue screen . I do . Can you help me with the expiration date . Money . Thank you . And do you have a twelve user on the card ma'am aside from you . Are you on the credit card account . William Bell come . Do you remember how much was the last payment that you made on the credit card . Hold on let me look at my notes . Why am I going through this . I don't know but . This is verification process blue just to make sure that we're speaking with the correct person on the account . I paid a twenty dollars the confirmation numbers 0 0 0 0 0 0 0 0 . OK . Thank you . And do you still remember where did you last use your credit card man . Oh my God . I went to yesterday I went to a hair store . OK lastly you kindly verify your complete mailing address please . What do you say Jones . Street Akron Ohio 6 6 4 2 1 . OK . My dream is blue . The system is also Brontë me though we need to update her account for additional security . It's either we save your mother's maiden name or a five digit passcode as additional security question .

Which six do you prefer . My mother's maiden name . Can you help me with your mom's maiden name . Clayton . Ma'am I need the three digits on the back of your card please . 0 0 0 . Okay thank you so much . Just give me two moment here . Thank you for patiently waiting . There you go information has been completely updated . Miss Blue many help you with your account . I was trying to find out the balance and didn't make a payment but it went straight to a payment and I wanted some clarity first . Mm hmm . It didn't Okay communicate . . Okay . We apologize for the inconvenience ma'am . If you wanted to check do you wanted to check the statement balance . Ma'am that is due on the current due date or the whole balance including recent charges . Whole balance . Member Current balance is four thousand two hundred twelve and 28 cents . four thousand . Say it again . four thousand two hundred twelve to 2 3 5 . And And twenty my credit and twenty eight . cents man . My credit limit was worth . Six thousand . Okay can I make a four hundred dollar payment . Yes of course ma'am . Since you're having issues with the automated system let me just help you with the payment . Just one time free of charge for tonight ma'am . Okay . Because customer service normally charge $10 for over the phone payment . Just give me one moment here . Are you going to use checking account for your payment then . Okay . And you did mention that you're paying eight fourteen dollars . Correct . eight . Okay . We got a checking account ending in 0 0 0 0 0 in 8 minutes . Just the one you will be using . Okay . Let me go . I made a $400 payment using your checking account ending insert a 0 0 0 . Again $10 if he has been waived . So there you go . Miss Blue you will are if you have questions or reached the modified as payment please call us at the number on your statement . This confirms that today March 9 two thousand twenty you authorize us to make a single that a Chinese debit of seven eighty Yeah dollars from your bank to pay your West Credit Card account on March 9 . two nineteen twenty . Is this correct . Thank you . Payment will successfully process and it will be dated today and it will post within 13 hours under your account for other payment options . You can pay at any local West store truly automated system Ensure . the website . All of them are for free . Do you need your confirmation number . Can you write this one down please . It's going to be 0 0 0 0 0 0 0 0 0 to . Okay . There you go . Would there be anything else that I could further check man . I just wanted to make sure they haven't missed any payments on my account of . He was a very My credit . with my account is in good standing . That's in good standing . No need to worry ma'am . That is correct . Thank you . You're welcome As . green . There are no more concerns ma'am . I'm glad I was able to assist And . thank you for calling card services . You ever get one ma'am . We value your business .

Contrapositive Local Class Inference

Omid Kashefi and **Rebecca Hwa**
School of Computing and information
University of Pittsburgh
{kashefi, hwa}@cs.pitt.edu

Abstract

Certain types of classification problems may be performed at multiple levels of granularity; for example, we might want to know the sentiment polarity of a document or a sentence, or a phrase. Often, the prediction at a greater-context (e.g., sentences or paragraphs) may be informative for a more localized prediction at a smaller semantic unit (e.g., words or phrases). However, directly inferring the most salient local features from the global prediction may overlook the semantics of this relationship. This work argues that inference along the contraposition relationship of the local prediction and the corresponding global prediction makes an inference framework that is more accurate and robust to noise. We show how this contraposition framework can be implemented as a transfer function that rewrites a greater-context from one class to another and demonstrate how an appropriate transfer function can be trained from a noisy user-generated corpus. The experimental results validate our insight that the proposed contrapositive framework outperforms the alternative approaches on resource-constrained problem domains.[1]

1 Introduction

Many NLP applications analyze a piece of text at multiple levels. For example, a product review might be analyzed for whether it is informative overall; its paragraphs might be analyzed for whether they are relevant to certain aspect of the product; or its words might be analyzed for whether they express intense emotions. These classification tasks of varying scopes of context are often related. For instance, one might posit that a review containing many words carrying extreme emotions might not be very informative. In some cases, the same class prediction task (e.g., sentiment polarity) might be asked at both the global and local levels.

Classification at the more global scope depends on clues gleaned at the local level; however, classification at the local scope is often more difficult because the roles of the words and phrases vary depending on the broader context in which they are used. Therefore, a straightforward approach, such as lexicon lookup, which require domain-specific dictionaries, may not correctly identify the intended usage. While direct supervision may better take the context into account, it relies on the availability of the training corpus containing class labels for each local scope. This poses a significant bottleneck for new applications for which these resources are not widely available.

To address this problem, we exploit the relationship between the global and local classification problems and propose a training framework to infer local predictions from the corresponding global label, which may be easier to obtain. For example, suppose someone reported a social media comment as inappropriate (*global classification*), if we find out which word(s) in the comment are contributed the most to the user's decision to report the comment, we already found the inappropriate words (*local classification*) and confirms whether the sentence is correctly reported or not.

In prior work, researchers observed that local predictions might serve as *rationales* (Zaidan et al., 2007; Lei et al., 2016; Bao et al., 2018) for the global problem. For example, if a review is classified as positive, there must be some words within that review that are also positive such that they serve as the rationale for the overall prediction. Thus, if rationales can be identified for the global classification task, their local labels would be inferred to be the same as the global label. We refer to this mode of local prediction as **direct inference**. However, prior work also suggested that even modern global classifiers are still sensitive to noise, so such direct inference may fail to identify the most semantically relevant rationales. For ex-

[1]The code is available at: https://github.com/omidkashefi/contrapositive-inference

Proceedings of the 2021 EMNLP Workshop W-NUT: The Seventh Workshop on Noisy User-generated Text, pages 371–380
November 11, 2021. ©2021 Association for Computational Linguistics

ample, irrelevant words or punctuation marks are more influential to the decision of neural text classifiers than verbs or other semantically related textual units (Mudrakarta et al., 2018); or the presence of snow in an image is the main feature to distinguish huskies from wolves rather than the features related to the animal themselves (Ribeiro et al., 2016).

In this work, we argue that this semantic relationship can be made more robust by enforcing the **contrapositive** constraint between the local prediction and its corresponding global prediction. That is, suppose we know that an instance is globally predicted to belong to some $Class\ A$ and that some local portion l contributed the most to that prediction (the rationale); if l is replaced so as to *negate* its semantic contribution, then the global label should also change (e.g. now belongs to some $Class\ B$). We propose that, *if, and only if*, the contrapositive constraint is satisfied should the local prediction be inferred from the global problem.

Modeled after style transfer and controlled text generation methods, we propose to implement the contrapositive inference scheme as a *transfer function* for global class transference. We first cast the problem as a rewriting exercise: rewrite the original global instance, which belong to some $Class\ A$, so that it becomes more likely to belong to $Class\ B$; then, those local textual parts that were changed in the rewriting are likely to be the heavy contributor to $Class\ A$ so we may infer the same class prediction for them. To train an appropriate transfer function, however, we need a corpus of training examples for the global prediction. For some problem domains, these resources are already available. For low-resource problem domains, where such annotated corpora are not available, we show how domain-inspired textual data augmentation can facilitate the training of the transfer function.

The proposed prediction framework is evaluated on several problem domains: sentiment analysis (as a resource-rich problem domain), and semantic pleonasm detection and specificity detection (as two resource-constrained domains). Results validate our insights about inferring local class labels from their corresponding global prediction labels and our proposed approach significantly outperform the alternative methods. We also demonstrate the robustness of the contrapositive local prediction to the noisy data and show that an appropriate transfer functions can be trained from corpora generated from heuristic-driven data augmentation schemes.

2 Inference by Contraposition

For many local prediction tasks, there is a corresponding, often easier to learn, global prediction task. Global prediction is relatively easier, in part, because it is attempting to classify a greater-context, which is semantically more distinctive than a localized smaller-context. Moreover, when a classification task could be performed at multiple levels of granularity (e.g., paragraphs and sentences), there is a much higher chance of having training corpora with label annotation at a larger text span than a smaller text span, which makes the more global version of the task more feasible.

The semantic purport of a greater-context is deriving from the co-occurrence of smaller semantic units. This implies that there is a semantic relation between the local and global predictions that could be used to infer the harder-to-learn local prediction from the corresponding easier-to-learn global prediction. It must be noted that prediction inference from the global prediction is only feasible for significantly contributing local features. We define the **direct inference** of local prediction from the global prediction as follows:

> $Global \rightarrow Local$: if the global prediction for a greater-context be some $Class\ A$, there exists a smaller local portion that significantly influenced the global prediction in the first place so the local prediction for it could infer the same class label as the global prediction.

However, it is reported that the classifiers might sometimes fail to learn the most semantically related features and make predictions based on just salient ones (Ribeiro et al., 2016; Mudrakarta et al., 2018; Jain and Wallace, 2019). We believe adding an extra constraint to the inference, while keeping the relationship between the local and corresponding global prediction intact, can improve the identification of the semantically related local features, therefore, we introduce the **contrapositive inference** of local prediction from the global prediction as follows:

> $\neg Local \rightarrow \neg Global$: the prediction for local portion of a context could infer the same class label as the global prediction, if, and only if, negating the semantic contribution of that smaller portion, negates the global prediction.

In the next section, we describe how this inference scheme could be applied to the discrete predictions in NLP problems.

2.1 Adaptation to NLP

The local segments of a text could serve as the features in the training process of the global prediction task, as given in Equation 1, where $\mathcal{F}$ is the global prediction function, y_i is the corresponding class label of the greater-context C_i in the training corpus, l_{ij} is the local features within the greater-context C_i, ${l_{ij}}^v$ is some vector representation of it and w_{ij} is its weight, $\mathcal{L}$ is some loss function, and b is the bias value.

$$
\begin{aligned}
L_C &= \min_{\mathcal{F}} \frac{1}{N} \sum_i \mathcal{L}(y_i, \mathcal{F}(C_i)) \\
&= \min_{\mathcal{F}} \frac{1}{N} \sum_i \mathcal{L}(y_i, \frac{1}{|C_i|} \sum_j w_{ij} {l_{ij}}^v + b)
\end{aligned} \tag{1}
$$

Now, if we can find the local feature l_{ij} that is mainly responsible for making the greater-context C_i belong to the class y_i, we may infer the same class label for that local feature as well. The *direct inference* involves finding the most contributing local features directly from the global prediction function. A straightforward way to implement this scheme is to take the local feature with the *highest weight* as the most contributing one as follows:

$$
\begin{gathered}
\textit{Direct Inference: Examine Weights} \\
\exists\, l_{ij} \mid w_{ij} = \arg\max_j \overrightarrow{w_i}
\end{gathered} \tag{2}
$$

Another popular approach to implement direct inference is to consider the contributing local features as the *rationales* for the global prediction. Rationales are defined as the reason behind the label annotation for the global prediction (Zaidan et al., 2007) and mostly used to improve the classification of the greater-context (Marshall et al., 2016; Zhang et al., 2016; Strout et al., 2019; Du et al., 2019). However, some studies have tried to develop systems for automatic extraction of the rationales (Lei et al., 2016; Ehsan et al., 2018) as the smaller text span that could replace the whole greater-context, while keeping the global-prediction intact:

$$
\begin{gathered}
\textit{Direct Inference: Rationale} \\
\exists\, l_{ij} \mid \mathcal{F}(l_{ij}) \approx \mathcal{F}(C_i)
\end{gathered} \tag{3}
$$

Alternatively, the contrapositive inference involves finding an adversarial alternative with a negated semantic contribution for local features and reevaluating the global prediction for the resulting greater-context as in Equation 4, where ${l_{ij}}^*$ is the adversarial alternative of the l_{ij}, C_i^{j*} is the corresponding greater-context when l_{ij} is replaced with ${l_{ij}}^*$. The negated global prediction, could be approximated as $\neg y_i \approx 1 - y_i$ for binary classification problems.

$$
\begin{gathered}
\textit{Contrapositive Inference} \\
\exists\, l_{ij},\, \exists {l_{ij}}^* \mid \mathcal{F}({C_i}^{j*}) = \neg y_i
\end{gathered} \tag{4}
$$

Implementing contrapositive inference, however, is not as straightforward as direct inference. A bottom-up approach requires calculating an adversarial semantic alternative for each local feature to assess their contribution, which might be very complicated and resource-intensive. Instead of that, we adapt a simpler top-down approach that can be seen as a generalization of machine translation, or as a form of *style transfer* (Bowman et al., 2016; Shen et al., 2017; Yang et al., 2018; Prabhumoye et al., 2018; Zhang et al., 2019).

We aim to develop a *transfer function* (see Section 3) that rewrites an arbitrary greater-context (e.g., a sentence) known to be in one class (e.g., $Class\ A$) into a corresponding text in another class (e.g., $Class\ B$); the smaller local parts (e.g., words or phrases) that changed during this global rewriting and class transference process are deemed to be the ones that contribute the most to the greater-context's class label, so may infer the same class label as well.

As an illustrative example, consider the sentiment classification problem. The transfer function might rewrite a *positive* sentence: "the food was great" into a *negative* sentence "The food was awful." While the overall sentence length is the same, the learned transfer function chose to replace "great" with "awful," therefore "great" is likely to be a sentiment expressing word. By casting the problem as a style transfer task, we avoid the thorny tasks of quantifying fluency and meaning retention and even if the transfer function does not provide a correct semantic negation, for example, rewrites the "great" as "cold" instead of "awful", we are not concerned with whether "The food was cold" is a meaningful or even fluent sentence; we only care that this new sentence is now classified as *negative*, so it reveals something about the word "great" in the old sentence. This property may also improve the robustness of our approach to some level of noise in the data.

Our proposed contrapositive inference approach is still a complicated method. By relaxing the global prediction negation requirement of the contraceptive inference into maximum prediction deviation, a lighter and easier-to-implement version of it could be seen as a *leave one out (LOO)* baseline. That is, if a local feature be a significant contributor to the global prediction, then removing it from the greater-context should cause a larger prediction deviation from the original prediction as follows, where C_i^{-j} is the corresponding greater-context when l_{ij} is removed:

Semi-Contrapositive Inference: LOO

$$\exists\, l_{ij} \mid \max_j ||\mathcal{F}(C_i) - \mathcal{F}(C_i^{-j})||^2 \quad (5)$$

Both direct and contrapositive inference schemes are relaxing the local prediction requirement of having a large training corpus with local annotation into having training corpus with global annotation, which is easier to obtain, thus, they could be beneficial for new or narrowly focused NLP applications for which localized training data is not widely available. However, it must be noted that the localized prediction inference is only applicable to certain classification problems, where the prediction task can be performed in multiple levels of granularity and the local prediction has a corresponding global prediction task at a greater-context.

3 Transfer Function Model

Since our approach is based on the difference between original and generated greater-contexts, extensive or random modification of the original text might result in meaningless differences, so the key requirements of an ideal transfer function for our approach are:

- **Req. 1:** preserve most of the original content and only make minimal changes.
- **Req. 2:** these minimal changes negate the prediction for the resulting greater-context (makes it belong to the other class).

Any reasonable transfer function that satisfies these requirements may make a suitable model to serve as the core of our proposed approach. As an implementational choice, we adapt the model proposed by Hu et al. (2017) and augmented it with an extra regularization (i.e., conciseness loss, given in Equation 8) to explicitly control for Req. 1.

Our transfer function model incorporates an autoencoder and a discriminator for the global prediction. The autoencoder is initially trained to learn a latent space (z) from the input greater-context instances (c) by minimizing the reconstruction loss, given in Equation (6), where θ_E and θ_G are the encoder and decoder parameters, respectively.

$$\mathcal{L}_{rec}(\theta_E, \theta_G) = \mathbb{E}_{q_E(z|c)}[\log p(c|z, y)] \quad (6)$$

Since the latent space z is learning independent of the class labels ($q_E(z|c)$), it could be used to generate instances of both classes. Therefore, the decoder is trained to learn to generate a greater-context $\hat{c}$, given a desired class label ($p(\hat{c}|z, y)$). Now, if we ask the encoder to generate a rewriting alternative for an input greater-context with a flipped class label ($\neg y = 1 - y$), then the generated output would likely be a modified version of the input with some small changes that make it belong to the opposite class (Req. 2).

However, in order to learn class transference, the decoder also requires a signal to determine how likely the generated output belongs to the desired class. To provide that signal, we incorporate a class discriminator in our transfer function model, which is optimized as given in Equation 7, where θ_D is the discriminator parameter. For simplicity, we only train the discriminator on the input examples (c) and use that to predict the label for generated examples ($\hat{c}$).

$$\mathcal{L}_{\text{disc}}(\theta_D) = \mathbb{E}_C[\log q_D(y|c)] \quad (7)$$

By optimizing for the reconstruction loss, the autoencoder will learn to generate an output similar to the input, which, in part, may satisfy Req. 1. We still want to directly enforce the class transference using minimal changes, which intuitively means the generated transferred version of the input greater-context that belongs to some $Class\ B$ should be as similar as possible to the input greater-context that originally belongs to some $Class\ A$.

Therefore, we also optimize for a *conciseness loss* ($\mathcal{L}_{con}$) as given in Equation 8, where c is the original input greater-context and $\hat{c}$ is the transferred version of it to the other class. It must be noted that, sometimes, the original input and the transferred output might not have the same dimension. For these cases, we slice the bigger vector as the dimension of the smaller vector.

$$\mathcal{L}_{con}(\theta_E, \theta_G) = \mathbb{E}_{q_E(z|c)}[\log p(\hat{c}|z, \neg y)] \quad (8)$$

Equation (9) shows the transfer function's final objective function, where λ_D and λ_C are the balancing parameter.

$$\min_{\theta_G} \mathcal{L}_{gen} = \mathcal{L}_{rec} + \lambda_D \mathcal{L}_{disc} + \lambda_C \mathcal{L}_{con} \quad (9)$$

For some initial training runs, we train the discriminator and autoencoder independently ($\lambda_D = 0$); the discriminator will learn to distinguish between classes, and the autoencoder will learn a latent space that could be used to regenerate instances of both classes. At this step, we do not enforce the minimal changes as well ($\lambda_C = 0$). After that, for a few more epochs, we jointly train the autoencoder and discriminator ($\lambda_D \neq 0$) to learn the class transference (replace y with $\neg y = 1 - y$) while enforcing the minimal required changes ($\lambda_C \neq 0$). For more details about the hyperparameters and the training process please see Appendix A.

It must be noted that to avoid the fading gradient phenomenon when training on discrete space, the model feeds with Gumbel-Softmax (Jang et al., 2017) representation over the words to provide a continuous approximation and a stronger signal for optimizing the decoder.

4 Experiments

This work argues that inference by contraposition allows for the identification of semantically relevant local features and thus a more accurate local prediction inference when compared to methods based on direct inference. In order to evaluate this hypothesis, we setup an experiment for local prediction inference at word-level from a large training corpus of naturally-occurring and manually-labeled sentences in the sentiment analysis domain (Section 4.1).

We also argue that the contrapositive inference scheme can be more robustly trained on user-generated and weakly-labeled data compared to the alternative direct inference methods. In order to validate this aspect of the contrapositive local inference, we conducted a few experiments for local prediction inference from augmented training corpora of the global prediction in the sentiment analysis, pleonasm detection, and specificity detection problem domains (Section 4.2). In these set of experiments, we compare two implementation of each inference schemes (a simpler and a more complex models), as follows:

Direct:ATN. For the global prediction, we use a BiLSTM classifier and wrap the weights at each time-step into an attention weight using a multiplicative attention layer (Luong et al., 2015). The local feature with the highest attention weight would receive the same class prediction as the global class label.

Direct:RTNL. We use the model proposed by Lei et al. (2016) as the state-of-the-art implementation for the direct inference of the local prediction as the rationales for the global prediction (Equation 3), tuned for each experimental settings (see Appendix A). Their model consist a RCNN generator and encoder to produce rationales and predictions, and uses REINFORCE for generation learning (Sutton et al., 2000).

Contrapositive:LOO. This baseline serves as a light version of the contrapositive inference of the local prediction through examining the global prediction for different perturbation of a greater-context by leaving one of its local features out. The local feature that causes the highest deviation in global prediction would infer the original global class label (Equation 5). Similar to the *Direct:ATN* baseline, we use a BiLSTM classifier for the global prediction task.

Contrapositive:TF. This model serves as an implementation of our proposed contrapositive inference scheme (Equation 4). We use our transfer function model (Section 3) for contrapositive local prediction inference through rewriting and class transference of the greater-context.

4.1 Local Prediction Inference from Naturally-Occurring Labeled Data

In this experiment, we aim to evaluate the different inference schemes on a inference task from sentence (as the global scope) into word(s) (as the smaller local scope), when a large training corpus of global prediction is available. As a result, we opt to run our experiment on **sentiment analysis**, as problem domain with readily available large training corpora of labeled sentences, such as Yelp Polarity Dataset (YPD) (Zhang et al., 2015). In this domain, the global sentiment prediction task is to *predict whether a sentence has a "positive" or "negative" polarity?* Thus, we evaluate the different inference schemes on the local prediction task of inferring *which word(s) of the sentence expresses a strong sentiment?*

To train our transfer function, we use the 105K naturally-occurring polarity-labeled sentences (*positive* and *negative*) of the YPD that contain 30 or fewer words (refer to as YPD-Train). As a benchmark dataset to evaluate the local inference performance of the models, we manually annotated some held-out sentences of YPD with word-level sentiment labels. We followed the same annotation scheme proposed by (Socher et al., 2013) and created a unigram pool from all the words of the test set; then randomly picked a word and annotated it as *very positive*, *positive*, *neutral*, *negative*, or *very negative*. Finally, filtering for sentences that contains a *very positive* or *very negative* words, we collected a set of 860 held-out sentences with word-level labels as our in-house benchmark dataset (refer to as YPD-Test).

Table 1 compares the precision of different inference schemes on predicting the word(s) that express the same sentiment as the sentence in which it is used, based on the gold annotation in the benchmark dataset (YPD-Test). As shown, the contrapositive inference methods, including LOO, are more effective at inferring the sentiment class label of the word(s) than the direct inference alternatives, and our proposed method (*Contrapositive:TF*) substantially outperformed the best direct inference method (*Direct:RTNL*) by more than 14%. This huge performance difference suggests that considering and controlling the contrapositive contribution of local features to the corresponding global prediction can improve the identification of the most semantically contributing local features and thus infer a more accurate local prediction.

Approach	Local Inference Precision
Direct:ATN	58.4%
Direct:RTNL	63.3%
Contrapositive:LOO	66.2%
Contrapositive:TF	**77.5%**

Table 1: Local sentiment prediction precision of different inference schemes, trained on naturally-occurring labeled examples

4.2 Local Prediction Inference from Weakly-Labeled User-Generated Data

The availability of training corpora is always a bottleneck for the training of complex supervised computational models. Our proposed inference scheme already relaxes the requirement of local prediction task from having labeled examples with annotation at smaller scope to having training examples with global annotation, which is usually easier to obtain. Nevertheless, in many resource-constrained NLP problem domains, even training corpora for global prediction are not available. Therefore, in this experiment we investigate whether data augmentation can reconcile the training requirements of different inference schemes by studying two following resource-constrained problem domains:

Pleonasm Detection. This task at local level aims to *find redundant words that are not contributing to the overall meaning of a sentence* (Quinn, 1993; Lehmann, 2005). For example, the word "free" may deem semantically redundant at the presence of the word "gift" in the sentence: "I received a free gift." Like sentiment analysis, this domain has a clear corresponding global classification task: *whether the sentence is "concise" or "verbose"?* However, this domain has a much more limited set of existing resources: NUCLE covers grammatical redundancy (Dahlmeier et al., 2013), and the Semantic Pleonasm Corpus (SPC), a small corpus with pleonasm annotation at word-level (Kashefi et al., 2018), which we use as the benchmark dataset in this experiment.

Specificity Detection. This task at local level aims to *pinpoint the phrases that uniquely relate the sentence to a particular subject* (Li and Nenkova, 2015; Lugini and Litman, 2018). For example, the phrase "bus accident" in the sentence "10 people killed in bus accident in Pakistan", makes it more specific than the phrase "road accident" in the sentence "10 people killed in road accident in Pakistan." It also has a corresponding global prediction task: *whether the sentence conveying a "specific" or "general" piece of information?* However, the existing resources are limited to just a few small corpora (less than 1K sentences) with sentence-level specificity annotation (Louis and

Task	Source	Heuristic Strategy	Example
Sentiment Analysis	Yelp	• ***Positive*** *Label:* four star and above	→ super *generous* portion
		• *Augmented* ***Negative*** *Heuristic:* substitute a positive word (look up in a polarity vocabulary) with an *antonym*	→ super meager portion
		• ***Negative*** *Label:* two star and below	→ it was not a *good* experience
		• *Augmented* ***Positive*** *Heuristic:* substitute a negative word (look up in a polarity vocabulary) with an *antonym*	→ it was not a bad experience
Pleonasm Detection	Yelp	• ***Concise*** *Label:* Yelp tips (short sentences)	→ *delicious* bread
		• *Augmented* ***Verbose*** *Heuristic:* add a *synonym* next to an adjective	→ *delicious +tasty* bread
		• *Augmented* ***Near-Miss Concise*** *Heuristic:* insert a *non-synonym* word next to an adjective, base on language model prediction	→ *delicious +redolent* bread
Specificity Detection	News Headline	• ***Specific*** *Label:* contains more than 2 named entities	→ *Rouhani* wants nuclear deal
		• *Augmented* ***General*** *Heuristic:* substitute a noun with an *hyponym*	→ President wants nuclear deal
		• ***General*** *Label:* contains no named entities	→ 10 killed in *camp*
		• *Augmented* ***Specific*** *Heuristic:* substitute a noun with an *hypernym*	→ 10 killed in death camp

Table 2: Augmentation heuristic strategies for different problem domains

Nenkova, 2012; Louis et al., 2013; Tan and Lee, 2014), and the Interpretable Semantic Textual Similarity (iSTS) dataset, which comprises phrase-level specificity annotation (Agirre et al., 2016), which we use as the benchmark in our experiment.

In addition, we also make a low-resource case for the **sentiment analysis** domain in order to compare the prediction result of our approach with previous experiment, where a sizable training corpus was available for global prediction.

4.2.1 Data Augmentation

In order to augment a sizable dataset to train the inference models, we start by identifying an existing real-world data source that possesses some characteristics that allow us to (weakly) label some of its examples with at least one of the desired classes. For example, the Yelp dataset[2] has a data category called "tips." Since "tips" are very short sentences, they are likely to be *concise*; or Yelp reviews with 4 star and above are likely to carry a *positive* sentiment. Next, we apply some domain-inspired non-label-preserving augmentation heuristics to the instances of one class (e.g., "positive") to generate instances of the opposite class (e.g., "negative"). The details of the heuristics and data augmentation for these domains are discussed elsewhere (Kashefi and Hwa, 2020).

Table 2 summarizes the heuristic strategy we used to augment a training dataset for each problem domain. When evaluating the models for sentiment analysis and pleonasm detection tasks, we use the YPD-Test and SPC, respectively, which are both collected from Yelp. For the specificity detection task, we use the news headline part of the iSTS as the benchmark to evaluate the model. Thus, for data augmentation we use "all the news[3]" corpus, as a data source in a related domain. The resulting augmented training corpora for sentiment analysis, pleonasm detection, and specificity detection tasks are containing 105k (the same size as YPD-Train in previous experiment), 160K and 110K user-generated examples, respectively.

4.2.2 Results

Table 3 compares the local prediction inference precision of the different inference schemes across different problem domains, when trained on noisy user-generated corpora, based on the gold annotation in the benchmark datasets.

We can observer that the contrapositive local inference schemes, including *Contrapositive:LOO*, outperform the direct inference schemes in all problem domains and the local prediction precision of our proposed approach (*Contrapositive:TF*) is significantly higher than all other inference alternatives. As expected, the local prediction inference precision of *Contrapositive:TF* was slightly lower than its corresponding performance in the previous experiment, where models were trained on

[2]www.yelp.com/dataset/challenge

[3]www.kaggle.com/snapcrack/all-the-news

Inference Approach	Local Inference Precision		
	Sentiment Analysis	Pleonasm Detection	Specificity Detection
Direct:ATN	54.3%	24.3%	20.5%
Direct:RTNL	55.6%	30.4%	28.1%
Contrapositive:LOO	59.8%	41.1%	45.5%
Contrapositive:TF	**74.2%**	**70.3%**	**69.5%**

Table 3: Localized prediction precision of the approaches on different problem domains, trained on weakly-labeled augmented datasets

manually-labeled real examples (74.2% compared to 77.5%). However, the performance gap between our proposed model and other models are getting larger when trained on noisy data (e.g., 14% difference with *Direct:RTNL* on real data compared to 19% difference with noisy data).

These results may suggest that the contrapositive inference is more noise-tolerant than the alternative methods. In addition, the impact of data augmentation on the performance of our approach is not significant, so it could be beneficial for providing training requirements of our approach and making it applicable to many low-resource NLP problems.

5 Discussion

Results from our studies suggest that enforcing the contraposition constraint between the local prediction and its corresponding global prediction can reveal their semantic relationship more robustly, and thus, lead to a a more accurate local class prediction inference, compared to direct inference alternatives.

In the direct inference schemes, there are many cases that semantically irrelevant words, such as "punctuation marks", are the heavy contributors to the global prediction. These observations and the performance of the *Direct:Atn* baseline confirm the prior work's suggestions that attention weight may not correlate with the semantics of the prediction task. In addition, the *Direct:Rationale* baseline operates through finding a smaller local text span (rationale) that can replace the greater-context in the global prediction. Intuitively, rationales with shorter text span (e.g., words or phrases) are likely to provide a noisy and unstable solution for the global problem, as we observed in our experiments.

The *Contrapositive:LOO* baseline adopts a simple approach to apply a relaxed version of the contraposition constraint, by removing the local rationale from the global problem's context. As observed, a global context, after removing a small text span from it, would still be large and semantically expressive enough for a reliable global prediction.

Since our proposed *Contrapositive:TF* approach operates by replacing a local rationale of a global context with another (adversarial) rationale, the span size of the greater-context remains relatively intact, which makes the prediction inference more robust. The transfer function also operates by disentangling the semantics from the surface representation and applying local contrapositive semantic perturbation to the global context, which makes it more robust to noise and irrelevant local features. For example, a punctuation mark might influence a class prediction for a sentence, however, replacing it with another punctuation mark will not make the sentence belong to another class, so it is not a *semantically* contributing word.

Furthermore, evaluation results suggest that the performance impact of training a transfer function on weakly-labeled user-generated data is not significant, so data augmentation may facilitate the training of the transfer function and make our approach applicable to a variety of resource-constrained NLP problem domains. However, in our experiments, we observed that the quality of augmented examples is a key-factor for training an appropriate model. We found that both global and local classification performance declined significantly when we trained models on the corpora that are augmented with simple heuristics, which generate obvious examples for different classes.

This should be noted that our proposed contrapositive approach is only applicable to prediction tasks that can be performed in multiple levels of granularity, where the local prediction has a corresponding global prediction task. In addition, applying it to more general cases, such as "multi-class" classification, might pose some challenges.

6 Conclusion

This paper presents a local contrapositive inference scheme that is only informed by corresponding global class predictions at a greater contexts. The inference scheme is implemented as a transfer function that learns to transform a context from one class to another. Training such a transfer function, requires a large corpus of labeled sentences, which may not be available for many low-resource problem domains. Our work demonstrates the robustness of the proposed approach when coupled with appropriate data augmentation methods and its applicability as a solution to resource-constrained local prediction tasks.

Acknowledgments

We would like to thank the anonymous reviewers for their helpful comments. This material is based upon work supported by the National Science Foundation under Grant Number 1735752.

References

Eneko Agirre, Aitor Gonzalez-Agirre, Inigo Lopez-Gazpio, Montse Maritxalar, German Rigau, and Larraitz Uria. 2016. SemEval-2016 Task 2: Interpretable Semantic Textual Similarity. In *SemEval*.

Yujia Bao, Shiyu Chang, Mo Yu, and Regina Barzilay. 2018. Deriving Machine Attention from Human Rationales. In *EMNLP*.

Samuel R Bowman, Vilnis Luke, Vinyals Oriol, Andrew M Dai, Rafal Jozefowicz, and Samy Bengio. 2016. Generating Sentences from a Continuous Space. In *CoNLL*.

Daniel Dahlmeier, Hwee Tou Ng, and Siew Mei Wu. 2013. Building a Large Annotated Corpus of Learner English: The NUS Corpus of Learner English. In *Workshop on Innovative Use of NLP for Building Educational Applications*.

Mengnan Du, Ninghao Liu, Fan Yang, and Xia Hu. 2019. Learning Credible Deep Neural Networks with Rationale Regularization. In *ICDM*.

Upol Ehsan, Brent Harrison, Larry Chan, and Mark O Riedl. 2018. Rationalization: A Neural Machine Translation Approach to Generating Natural Language Explanations. In *AIES*.

Zhiting Hu, Zichao Yang, Xiaodan Liang, Ruslan Salakhutdinov, and Eric P Xing. 2017. Toward Controlled Generation of Text. In *ICML*.

Sarthak Jain and Byron C Wallace. 2019. Attention is not Explanation. In *EMNLP*.

Eric Jang, Shixiang Gu, and Ben Poole. 2017. Categorical Reparameterization With Gumbel-Softmax. In *ICLR*.

Omid Kashefi and Rebecca Hwa. 2020. Quantifying the Evaluation of Heuristic Methods for Textual Data Augmentation. In *EMNLP Workshop on Noisy User-generated Text (W-NUT)*.

Omid Kashefi, Andrew T Lucas, and Rebecca Hwa. 2018. Semantic Pleonasm Detection. In *NAACL*.

Christian Lehmann. 2005. Pleonasm and hypercharacterisation. In *Yearbook of Morphology*, pages 119–154. Springer, Dordrecht.

Tao Lei, Regina Barzilay, and Tommi Jaakkola. 2016. Rationalizing Neural Predictions. In *EMNLP*.

Junyi Jessy Li and Ani Nenkova. 2015. Fast and Accurate Prediction of Sentence Specificity. In *AAAI*.

Annie Louis, Stefanie Dipper, Heike Zinsmeister, and Bonnie Webber. 2013. A corpus of science journalism for analyzing writing quality. *Dialogue and Discourse*, 4(2):87–117.

Annie Louis and Ani Nenkova. 2012. A Corpus of General and Specific Sentences from News. In *LREC*.

Luca Lugini and Diane Litman. 2018. Predicting Specificity in Classroom Discussion. In *Workshop on Innovative Use of NLP for Building Educational Applications*.

Minh-Thang Luong, Hieu Pham, and Christopher D Manning. 2015. Effective Approaches to Attention-based Neural Machine Translation. In *EMNLP*.

Iain J Marshall, Joë Kuiper, and Byron C Wallace. 2016. RobotReviewer: evaluation of a system for automatically assessing bias in clinical trials. *Journal of the American Medical Informatics Association*, 23(1):193–201.

Pramod K. Mudrakarta, Ankur Taly, Mukund Sundararajan, and Kedar Dhamdhere. 2018. Did the model understand the question? In *ACL*.

Shrimai Prabhumoye, Yulia Tsvetkov, Ruslan Salakhutdinov, and Alan W Black. 2018. Style Transfer Through Back-Translation. In *ACL*.

Arthur. Quinn. 1993. *Figures of speech : 60 ways to turn a phrase*. Psychology Press.

Marco Tulio Ribeiro, Sameer Singh, and Carlos Guestrin. 2016. "Why should i trust you?" Explaining the predictions of any classifier. In *KDD*.

Tianxiao Shen, Tao Lei, Regina Barzilay, Tommi Jaakkola, and Mit Csail. 2017. Style Transfer from Non-Parallel Text by Cross-Alignment. In *NIPS*.

Richard Socher, Alex Perelygin, Jean Y Wu, Jason Chuang, Christopher D Manning, Andrew Y Ng, and Christopher Potts. 2013. Recursive Deep Models for Semantic Compositionality Over a Sentiment Treebank. In *EMNLP*.

Julia Strout, Ye Zhang, and Raymond J. Mooney. 2019. Do Human Rationales Improve Machine Explanations? In *BlackboxNLP Workshop at ACL*.

Richard S Sutton, David Mcallester, Satinder Singh, and Yishay Mansour. 2000. Policy Gradient Methods for Reinforcement Learning with Function Approximation. In *NIPS*.

Chenhao Tan and Lillian Lee. 2014. A Corpus of Sentence-level Revisions in Academic Writing: A Step towards Understanding Statement Strength in Communication. In *ACL*.

Zichao Yang, Zhiting Hu, Chris Dyer, Eric P. Xing, and Taylor Berg-Kirkpatrick. 2018. Unsupervised Text Style Transfer using Language Models as Discriminators. In *NIPS*.

Omar F Zaidan, Jason Eisner, and Christine D Piatko. 2007. Using "Annotator Rationales" to Improve Machine Learning for Text Categorization. In *NAACL*.

Xiang Zhang, Junbo Zhao, and Yann Lecun. 2015. Character-level Convolutional Networks for Text Classification. In *NIPS*.

Ye Zhang, Iain Marshall, and Byron C Wallace. 2016. Rationale-Augmented Convolutional Neural Networks for Text Classification. In *EMNLP*.

Zhirui Zhang, Shuo Ren, Shujie Liu, Jianyong Wang, Peng Chen, Mu Li, Ming Zhou, and Enhong Chen. 2019. Style Transfer as Unsupervised Machine Translation. In *AAAI*.

A Hyperparameters

Direct:Atn: attention weight over single words.

Contrapositive:LOO: single words as local text span.

Contrapositive:TF:

- Pre-training
  - #epochs = 10
  - $\lambda_D = .0$
  - $\lambda_C = .0$
- Joint-training
  - #epochs = 2
  - $\lambda_D = 1e - 1$
  - $\lambda_C = 1e - 2$

Direct:Rationale:

- Experiment 1
  - Embedding: GloVe + Yelp
  - $\lambda_1 = 1e - 2$
  - $\lambda_2 = 2\lambda_1$
- Experiment 2
  - Sentiment Analysis Task
    - Embedding: GloVe + Yelp
    - $\lambda_1 = 3e - 2$
    - $\lambda_2 = 2\lambda_1$
  - Pleonasm Detection Task
    - Embedding: GloVe + Yelp
    - $\lambda_1 = 5e - 2$
    - $\lambda_2 = 2\lambda_1$
  - Specificity Detection Task
    - Embedding: GloVe + "all the news"
    - $\lambda_1 = 1e - 2$
    - $\lambda_2 = 2\lambda_1$

Improved Multilingual Language Model Pretraining for Social Media Text via Translation Pair Prediction

Shubhanshu Mishra
Twitter, Inc.
`smishra@twitter.com`

Aria Haghighi
Twitter, Inc.
`ahagighi@twitter.com`

Abstract

We evaluate a simple approach to improving zero-shot multilingual transfer of mBERT on social media corpus by adding a pretraining task called translation pair prediction (TPP), which predicts whether a pair of cross-lingual texts are a valid translation. Our approach assumes access to translations (exact or approximate) between source-target language pairs, where we fine-tune a model on source language task data and evaluate the model in the target language. In particular, we focus on language pairs where transfer learning is difficult for mBERT: those where source and target languages are different in script, vocabulary, and linguistic typology. We show improvements from TPP pretraining over mBERT alone in zero-shot transfer from English to Hindi, Arabic, and Japanese on two social media tasks: NER (a 37% average relative improvement in F_1 across target languages) and sentiment classification (12% relative improvement in F_1) on social media text, while also benchmarking on a non-social media task of Universal Dependency POS tagging (6.7% relative improvement in accuracy). Our results are promising given the lack of social media bitext corpus. Our code can be found at: `https://github.com/twitter-research/multilingual-alignment-tpp`.

1 Introduction

Multilingual BERT (mBERT; Devlin et al. 2019), and other multilingual pretrained language models have been shown to learn surprisingly good cross-lingual representations for a range of NLP tasks (Pires et al., 2019; Mishra et al., 2021, 2020; Mishra and Mishra, 2019), despite not having explicit cross-lingual links between their monolingual training corpora (Artetxe and Schwenk, 2018; Yang et al., 2019). Analysis in Pires et al. (2019) shows that cross-lingual transfer with mBERT works best when transferring representations between source and target languages that share lexical structure (i.e, overlapping word-piece vocabulary) and structural linguistic typology. In some ways, this result is not surprising since mBERT does not see explicit cross-lingual examples and cannot learn how to transform representations to a target language and relies on similar linguistic structure to transfer well. Furthermore, limited work exists on multilingual transfer for social media corpus which tend to be more noisy and shorter compared to traditional NLP corpora. This issue is further exacerbated for transfer between language pairs which use different scripts.

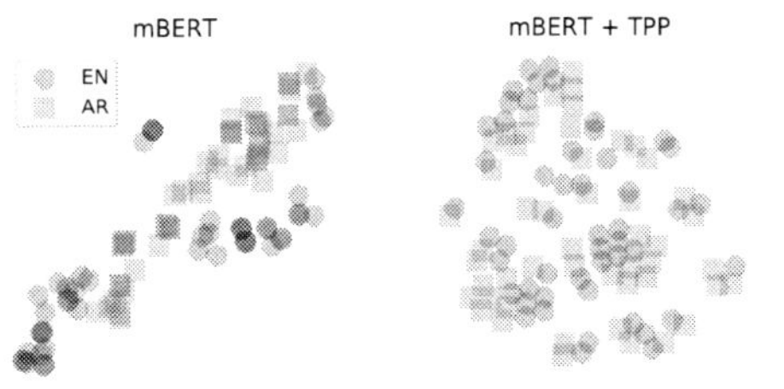

Figure 1: **Comparing Multilingual Representations** Left figure shows mBERT embeddings (T-SNE projection) for parallel sentences from the Tatoeba corpus (Section 3.1) in English (EN) and Arabic (AR). These embeddings exhibit distinct language regions, making cross-lingual transfer challenging. The right figure shows the same data after further pretraining using translation pair prediction (Figure 2), which learns representations that are near cross-lingual translations (change in distance showed in Figure 3 of appendix). In Section 3, we show this improves cross-lingual transfer performance on several tasks (see Table 2).

In this work, we explore whether we can improve multilingual transfer by providing cross-lingual examples and encouraging mBERT to learn aligned representations between source and target texts before task fine-tuning. Concretely, we perform a "language pretraining" task called *translation pair prediction* (TPP) where we assume access to a corpus of source-target text pairs and predict whether the pair is a translation of the same content (see Section 2). This pretraining phase is intended to

Proceedings of the 2021 EMNLP Workshop W-NUT: The Seventh Workshop on Noisy User-generated Text, pages 381–388
November 11, 2021. ©2021 Association for Computational Linguistics

occur after standard mBERT pretraining (Devlin et al., 2019), but before task fine-tuning (see Figure 2). The intent behind this task is to leverage translation data that exists between a source language with abundant task training data and a target language with little or no task training data in order to improve transfer learning. As with standard mBERT pretraining, one can pretrain mBERT using TPP once and fine-tune for multiple tasks (as long as transferring to the same target language set). The translation pair data doesn't need to be related to the downstream task and we can leverage multiple sources of source-target translations of varying degrees of translation quality (see Section 3.3).

We demonstrate the benefits of adding TPP pretraining in experiments on social media corpus for NER, and sentiment detection, along with a non-social media corpus of universal POS tagging (for comparison) on fine-tuned models from English to Hindi, Japanese, and Arabic (see Section 3 for evaluation). We show gains from TPP on all tasks (averaged across target languages) using translation data of varying quality (see Section 3.3).

Related works Gururangan et al. (2020) argues for the benefits of continued transformer pretraining for better performance on in-domain tasks. Our work closely follows this approach however instead of keeping the Masked Language Modelling (MLM) task on in-domain data, we introduce a new pretraining task (TPP). In Artetxe and Schwenk (2019) the authors train an BiLSTM encoder-decoder model on a large parallel corpora of multiple languages and demonstrate zero-shot transfer. In Eisenschlos et al. (2019) the authors use a domain/task specific fine-tuning to improve zero shot cross lingual performance by inducing labels from the model of Artetxe and Schwenk (2019). Our work is closely related to the work of Wieting et al. (2019); Guo et al. (2018) which use a subword averaging and a LSTM encoder. Our approach uses transformers and also focuses evaluation on individual token level task like NER as well as sentence level task. Another closely related work is of Cao et al. (2020) which uses word pair alignment with mBERT and evaluates on XNLI task. However, their work does not consider typologically different languages like this work. In Lample and Conneau (2019) the authors use Translation Language Modeling task which concatenate the translation pairs in the BERT model and also add a language identifier to each token. Huang et al.

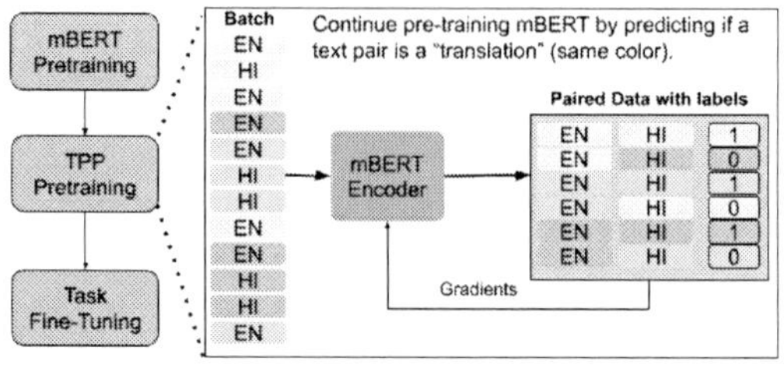

Figure 2: **Translation Pair Prediction (TPP)** We further pretrain an mBERT model on the TPP task (see Section 2). For each batch of aligned source-target text translation pairs, we create a balanced binary dataset consisting of the aligned pairs (positive examples) and a random source-text within the batch (negative examples). We update the mBERT model based on optimizing for binary cross-entropy on this task. In Section 3, we show this added TPP phase improves transfer learning to the target language on downstream tasks.

(2019) include a similar approach as discussed before and get improvement from jointly fine-tuning model with translations of downstream task data. Our approach is comparatively simpler to implement as we don't make any assumption about the encoding model or assumptions about word-level alignments; our approach works independently of the choice of encoder (mBERT here) or the quality of word-alignment models.

2 Model

A description of our approach is provided in Figure 2. The primary exploration in this work is the impact of adding a translation pair prediction (TPP) pretraining phase between traditional mBERT pretraining and downstream task fine-tuning (Devlin et al., 2019). The TPP pretraining task assumes a collection of aligned text pairs (s, t) which are "translation" pairs between source and target language text pairs s and t respectively. It is assumed that both languages have word-piece coverage in the pretrained mBERT model, but that we primarily have task training data for the source language. After TPP pretraining, we can fine-tune the resulting model for multiple tasks as with standard mBERT for transfer to the target language(s).

The TPP task is a binary classification problem where given an (s, t) pair we predict whether it is a valid "translation" pair or a random source-target pair using the dot product of mBERT encodings for s and t.[1] More formally, if $f(\cdot)$ represents the encoder mapping a document to the mBERT

[1] Note that in contrast to some related work (Huang et al., 2019; Lample and Conneau, 2019) we explore a symmetric task formulation instead of an asymmetric formulation as in the Next Sentence Prediction (NSP) pretraining task where

`[CLS]` token embedding, we predict if the pair is a translation pair with probability:

$$\texttt{is-translation}(s,t) = \sigma\left(f(s)^T f(t)\right)$$

where $\sigma(\cdot)$ is the sigmoid activation function. We create a binary dataset from aligned pairs by sampling a random unaligned s and t pair as a negative example for each aligned pair, creating a balanced dataset. The TPP task is trained using binary cross-entropy against this label and the loss gradient backpropogates through the embedding function $f(\cdot)$ which include mBERT layer parameters.

After TPP pretraining, we fine-tune on task data in the source language (English in our experiments) and evaluate transfer performance on target languages (Hindi, Japanese, and Arabic in our experiments).

3 Evaluation

3.1 Experimental setup

In order to evaluate our model we focus on three languages which are dissimilar in vocabulary and syntax from English. Furthermore, **our goal is to improve performance on social media data which is noisier as well as low resource for the above languages and our benchmarked tasks compared to newswire corpus**. Based on these criteria we utilize three languages apart from English which meet the following requirements: a) availability of parallel translation corpora, and b) availability of task data, particularly in the social media domain (NER and sentiment detection here). Based on the above criteria we identify English as our source language and Hindi, Japanese, and Arabic as target languages. We also include POS tagging on Universal Dependencies, which is a non social media benchmark corpus to evaluate our models. More details can be found at: `https://github.com/twitter-research/multilingual-alignment-tpp`.

Lang pair	Tatoeba	Wikimatrix	Wikidata
en-ar	28K	773K	1.6M
en-ja	220K	480K	509K
en-hi	11K	134K	77K

Table 1: Translation pair corpus data sizes used for translation pair prediction pretraining. See Section 3.1 for details.

source and target representations are concatenated before prediction.

Translation pair data For translation pairs we utilize datasets from the Tatoeba (TT) [2] collection as well as the Wikimatrix (WM) collection (Schwenk et al., 2019). While Tatoeba consists of human generated short sentences, Wikimatrix contains aligned sentences mined using a neural network. We assume that Tatoeba has higher quality across languages compared to Wikimatrix, where many of the translations are either incorrect or not exact translations. We also introduce a new dataset called Wikidata aligned pairs (WD) which can be automatically generated by using pair of language labels and descriptions from Wikidata which are written by human annotators in different scripts. Table 1 has details on the dataset size.

Wikidata aligned pairs (WD) We collect dataset from Wikidata (`https://wikidata.org`). For a given language pair, we consider wikidata items which have wikidata item labels and descriptions in the given pair of languages. We concatenate the label and the description using a space to make a sentence and use the sentences for each language as a translation pair.

NER data For our downstream task we use Tweet datasets. For NER we generate a dataset of 100k English Tweets, which is used for training. It consists of Tweets annotated for PERSON, LOCATION, PRODUCT, ORGANIZATION, and OTHER. We also generate test datasets of 2.3k Japanese and 10k Arabic Tweets. All datasets are generated using crowd sourced annotations. For Hindi, we use the Hindi subset of 2008 SSEA shared task (Rajeev Sangal and Singh, 2008). We report micro avg-F1 score across all classes. We use the standard NER task formulation for BERT style models which use softmax on the first subword for each token to make the prediction (Devlin et al., 2019). The NER models can be further improved by using Conditional Random Fields (CRF) (Lafferty et al., 2001) layer on the output which often gives good performance even without neural features across all languages (Mishra, 2020).

Sentiment Detection data We utilize the SemEval Twitter Sentiment dataset (Rosenthal et al., 2017) with the data split as used in Mishra and Diesner (2018). For Japanese, we utilize the 500k Tweet dataset from Suzuki (2019). For Arabic we use the data from Abdulla et al. (2013). For Hindi,

[2] `https://tatoeba.org` data is under CC-BY 2.0 FR.

we use the dataset from SAIL 2015 shared task for Indian languages (Patra et al., 2015). We report macro F_1 across classes as in Rosenthal et al. (2017).

Universal Dependencies POS data We use the English, Hindi, Japanese, and Arabic subsets from the Universal dependencies data (Nivre et al., 2020). We train using the GUM + PUD subset for English and evaluate on PUD subset for other languages. We do note a shortcoming of our PUD based datasets, i.e. they were created by translating the original text from English, German, French, Italian, or Spanish.[3] This can introduce translation artifacts and can favor translation based pretraining approaches.

Training All models are trained using the mBERT model available from the HuggingFace library (Wolf et al., 2019). For each translation pair data the model is trained for 3 epochs (hyperparameter details in appendix section A). For fine-tuning on downstream task we initialize our model with weights from the pretrained models and train it on the English task dataset for 3 epochs.

TPP using all target languages We also experiment with a TPP model which was pretrained using all the target language pair data from Tatoeba which were equally sampled. We denote this setting by ALL in Table 2 for our results. Even though this model may not perform as well as pretraining with TPP for a single target language at a time, it allows us to reduce pretraining and inference time, as well as reduce the number of models to manage.

Change in embedding distance after alignment In Figure 3 we show how the normalized (by max) embedding distances change beetween sentence pairs shown in Figure 1 after applying TPP.We find that alignment pairs are closer than their distance in mBERT.

	Hindi		Japanese		Arabic	
NER	F_1	Δ%	F_1	Δ%	F_1	Δ%
mBERT	21.1	0.0	16.5	0.0	32.1	0.0
+TPP (ONE)	**24.3**	15.2	**29.9**	81.4	**39.4**	22.8
+TPP (ALL)	23.2	10.3	27.4	66.4	38.5	19.9
Sentiment	F_1	Δ%	F_1	Δ%	F_1	Δ%
mBERT	31.7	0.0	55.0	0.0	51.5	0.0
+TPP (ONE)	**32.7**	3.0	66.4	20.6	58.3	13.2
+TPP (ALL)	32.4	2.3	**67.7**	23.1	**58.5**	13.7
UD POS	acc.	Δ%	acc.	Δ%	acc.	Δ%
mBERT	67.4	0.0	52.7	0.0	64.0	0.0
+TPP (ONE)	**71.5**	6.0	**57.6**	9.2	**67.1**	4.8
+TPP (ALL)	66.4	-1.5	52.7	0.1	65.0	1.5

Table 2: Results on zero-shot transfer learning for NER (F_1), sentiment detection (F_1), and UD POS tagging (Accuracy) from English to Hindi, Japanese, and Arabic. We compare fine-tuning standard mBERT to fine-tuning mBERT further pretrained on the TPP task (Section 2). The ONE variant pretrains a separate model for each target language; the ALL variant is a single pretraiend model for all target languages. We use Δ% to display relative improvement.

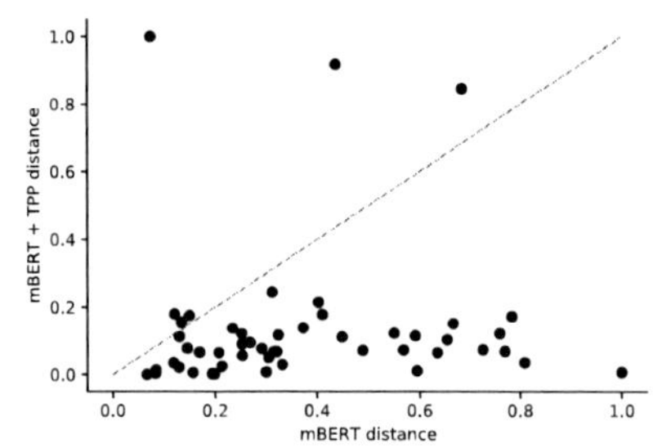

Figure 3: Change in embedding distance of EN-AR translation pairs shown in Figure 1

3.2 Zero-shot improvement via TPP

As can be seen in Table 2, adding TPP pretraining improves performance for both NER and sentiment detection across all languages. The universal POS gains are consistent, but more modest; we hypothesize this is because POS-tagging reilies more heavily on the language-neutral components of mBERT representations (Libovický et al., 2019). The greatest improvement of our models is for Japanese NER for which the model improves by 81% and an absolute improvement of around 15% in F_1 score. We hypothesize that NER benefits the most from some our TPP sources (Wikimatrix and Wikidata) which contain many paired entity descriptions. Furthermore, the Tatoeba dataset comprises of short sentence which are not likely to contain sentiment information, especially sentiment bearing content likely to be shared on social media platforms.

3.3 Improvement using combinations of alignment pairs and quality of alignments

In this section we discuss the impact of translation datasets available for our languages as well as how combining them for the TPP task leads to improved performance. We focus on NER F_1 and relative

[3]Details on UD PUD datasets - https://github.com/UniversalDependencies/UD_English-PUD

	Hindi		Japanese		Arabic	
NER	F_1	$\Delta\%$	F_1	$\Delta\%$	F_1	$\Delta\%$
mBERT	21.1	0.0	16.5	0.0	32.1	0.0
+TPP (TT)	23.1	9.6	27.8	68.6	36.3	13.2
+TPP (WD)	22.4	6.3	26.5	60.8	36.9	15.0
+TPP (WM)	21.6	2.6	27.7	68.3	38.3	19.3
+TPP (BP)	24.3	15.2	29.9	81.4	39.4	22.8
+TPP (ALL)	23.2	10.3	27.4	66.4	38.5	19.9
Sentiment	F_1	$\Delta\%$	F_1	$\Delta\%$	F_1	$\Delta\%$
mBERT	31.7	0.0	55.0	0.0	51.5	0.0
+TPP (TT)	31.8	0.3	62.4	13.5	58.3	13.2
+TPP (WD)	30.8	-2.9	50.2	-8.7	53.0	3.0
+TPP (WM)	32.7	3.0	63.2	14.8	54.7	6.4
+TPP (BP)	32.0	0.9	66.4	20.6	55.3	7.5
+TPP (ALL)	32.4	2.3	67.7	23.1	58.5	13.7
UD POS	acc.	$\Delta\%$	acc.	$\Delta\%$	acc.	$\Delta\%$
mBERT	67.4	0.0	52.7	0.0	64.0	0.0
+TPP (TT)	65.1	-3.5	54.0	2.4	66.7	4.1
+TPP (WD)	70.5	4.5	53.0	0.5	66.4	3.7
+TPP (WM)	70.4	4.3	54.4	3.1	65.4	2.2
+TPP (BP)	71.5	6.0	57.6	9.2	67.1	4.8
+TPP (ALL)	66.4	-1.5	52.7	0.1	65.0	1.5

Table 3: Impact of translation quality and using combination of translations in NER, Sentiment, and UD POS examples task performance after TPP (F_1 = micro F_1 score for NER, macro F_1 for sentiment, acc. = accuracy for UD POS). $\Delta\%$ is the % change in evaluation score compared to mBERT. Translation pairs used for each TPP task are shown in parenthesis, TT=Tatoeba, WD=Wikidata, WM=WikiMatrix, BP=best pairing of TT, WD, WM, and ALL=TT pairs from all languages, equally sampled.

improvements (denoted $\Delta\%$), but other tasks also see similar variation for each language (see Table 3 in appendix). We find that increasing the alignment pair data or using higher quality alignment data yield improvements. Using single-corpus translation pairs alone leads to significant improvements for all languages ($\Delta\%$ HI=9.6, JA=68.6, AR=19.3). Tatoeba results in most prominent improvements (HI=9.6, JA=68.6), while Wikimatrix has the best performance for AR (19.3). We assume this is related to larger size of the data, e.g. JA has 10 times more data in Tatoeba as compared to AR and HI.

Next, we move to sequencing pairs of TPP tasks from each translation dataset for a given language pair. We find that as we pair the TPPdatasets the performance of the models continues to improve (Table 3) but it depends on the previous checkpoint we start from as well as the quality of the new TPP data. Our experiments revealed that using the best performing single pairs in their order of performance individually improves performance significantly ($\Delta\%$ HI=15.2, JA=81.4, AR=22.8). For Sentiment and UD POS we observe similar gains, except in few case there is slight degradation.

Note on translation quality In terms of translation quality, Tatoeba is likely to be the most accurate as it is manually curated. Next, Wikidata is likely to be higher quality for HI compared to Wikimatrix as Wikimatrix is auto generated using a model and hence likely to perform worse on low resource languages. For AR and JA we can expect Wikimatrix to be higher quality as these languages have larger Wikipedia size and hence likely to have better quality representation in pretrained LMs.

4 Conclusion

We evaluated the use of translation pair prediction (TPP) as a pretraining task which can improve the performance of multilingual language models for cross-lingual zero-shot transfer from English. This pretraining task is performed after standard mBERT pretraining and the resulting model can be task fine-tuned for cross-lingual transfer similar to mBERT. We show significant improvement in zero-shot transfer by adding TPP pretraining on NER and sentiment detection on social media tasks for three languages (Hindi, Japanese, and Arabic) which are dissimilar in vocabulary and syntax from English.

References

N. A. Abdulla, N. A. Ahmed, M. A. Shehab, and M. Al-Ayyoub. 2013. Arabic sentiment analysis: Lexicon-based and corpus-based. In *2013 IEEE Jordan Conference on Applied Electrical Engineering and Computing Technologies (AEECT)*, pages 1–6.

Mikel Artetxe and Holger Schwenk. 2018. Massively multilingual sentence embeddings for zero-shot cross-lingual transfer and beyond. *CoRR*, abs/1812.10464.

Mikel Artetxe and Holger Schwenk. 2019. Massively multilingual sentence embeddings for zero-shot cross-lingual transfer and beyond. *Transac-*

tions of the Association for Computational Linguistics, 7:597–610.

Steven Cao, Nikita Kitaev, and Dan Klein. 2020. Multilingual alignment of contextual word representations. In *International Conference on Learning Representations*.

Jacob Devlin, Ming-Wei Chang, Kenton Lee, and Kristina Toutanova. 2019. BERT: Pre-training of deep bidirectional transformers for language understanding. In *Proceedings of the 2019 Conference of the North American Chapter of the Association for Computational Linguistics: Human Language Technologies, Volume 1 (Long and Short Papers)*, pages 4171–4186, Minneapolis, Minnesota. Association for Computational Linguistics.

Julian Eisenschlos, Sebastian Ruder, Piotr Czapla, Marcin Kadras, Sylvain Gugger, and Jeremy Howard. 2019. MultiFiT: Efficient multi-lingual language model fine-tuning. In *Proceedings of the 2019 Conference on Empirical Methods in Natural Language Processing and the 9th International Joint Conference on Natural Language Processing (EMNLP-IJCNLP)*, pages 5702–5707, Hong Kong, China. Association for Computational Linguistics.

Mandy Guo, Qinlan Shen, Yinfei Yang, Heming Ge, Daniel Cer, Gustavo Hernandez Abrego, Keith Stevens, Noah Constant, Yun-Hsuan Sung, Brian Strope, and Ray Kurzweil. 2018. Effective parallel corpus mining using bilingual sentence embeddings. In *Proceedings of the Third Conference on Machine Translation: Research Papers*, pages 165–176, Brussels, Belgium. Association for Computational Linguistics.

Suchin Gururangan, Ana Marasović, Swabha Swayamdipta, Kyle Lo, Iz Beltagy, Doug Downey, and Noah A. Smith. 2020. Don't stop pretraining: Adapt language models to domains and tasks. In *Proceedings of the 58th Annual Meeting of the Association for Computational Linguistics*, pages 8342–8360, Online. Association for Computational Linguistics.

Haoyang Huang, Yaobo Liang, Nan Duan, Ming Gong, Linjun Shou, Daxin Jiang, and Ming Zhou. 2019. Unicoder: A universal language encoder by pre-training with multiple cross-lingual tasks. In *Proceedings of the 2019 Conference on Empirical Methods in Natural Language Processing and the 9th International Joint Conference on Natural Language Processing (EMNLP-IJCNLP)*, pages 2485–2494, Hong Kong, China. Association for Computational Linguistics.

John D. Lafferty, Andrew McCallum, and Fernando C. N. Pereira. 2001. Conditional random fields: Probabilistic models for segmenting and labeling sequence data. In *Proceedings of the Eighteenth International Conference on Machine Learning*, ICML '01, page 282–289, San Francisco, CA, USA. Morgan Kaufmann Publishers Inc.

Guillaume Lample and Alexis Conneau. 2019. Cross-lingual language model pretraining. *Advances in Neural Information Processing Systems (NeurIPS)*.

Jindrich Libovický, Rudolf Rosa, and Alexander Fraser. 2019. How language-neutral is multilingual bert? *CoRR*, abs/1911.03310.

Shubhanshu Mishra. 2020. Non-neural Structured Prediction for Event Detection from News in Indian Languages. In *Working Notes of FIRE 2020 - Forum for Information Retrieval Evaluation*, Hyderabad, India. CEUR Workshop Proceedings, CEUR-WS.org.

Shubhanshu Mishra and Jana Diesner. 2018. Detecting the correlation between sentiment and user-level as well as text-level meta-data from benchmark corpora. In *Proceedings of the 29th on Hypertext and Social Media*, HT '18, page 2–10, New York, NY, USA. Association for Computing Machinery.

Shubhanshu Mishra and Sudhanshu Mishra. 2019. 3Idiots at HASOC 2019: Fine-tuning Transformer Neural Networks for Hate Speech Identification in Indo-European Languages. In *Proceedings of the 11th annual meeting of the Forum for Information Retrieval Evaluation*, pages 208–213, Kolkata, India.

Sudhanshu Mishra, Shivangi Prasad, and Shubhanshu Mishra. 2020. Multilingual joint fine-tuning of transformer models for identifying trolling, aggression and cyberbullying at TRAC 2020. In *Proceedings of the Second Workshop on Trolling, Aggression and Cyberbullying*, pages 120–125, Marseille, France. European Language Resources Association (ELRA).

Sudhanshu Mishra, Shivangi Prasad, and Shubhanshu Mishra. 2021. Exploring multi-task multi-lingual learning of transformer models for hate speech and offensive speech identification in social media. *SN Computer Science*.

Joakim Nivre, Marie-Catherine de Marneffe, Filip Ginter, Jan Hajič, Christopher D. Manning, Sampo Pyysalo, Sebastian Schuster, Francis Tyers, and Daniel Zeman. 2020. Universal Dependencies v2: An evergrowing multilingual treebank collection. In *Proceedings of the 12th Language Resources and Evaluation Conference*, pages 4034–4043, Marseille, France. European Language Resources Association.

Braja Gopal Patra, Dipankar Das, Amitava Das, and Rajendra Prasath. 2015. Shared task on sentiment analysis in indian languages (sail) tweets - an overview. In *Mining Intelligence and Knowledge Exploration*, pages 650–655, Cham. Springer International Publishing.

Telmo Pires, Eva Schlinger, and Dan Garrette. 2019. How multilingual is multilingual BERT? In *Proceedings of the 57th Annual Meeting of the Association for Computational Linguistics*, pages 4996–5001, Florence, Italy. Association for Computational Linguistics.

Dipti Misra Sharma Rajeev Sangal and Anil Kumar Singh, editors. 2008. *Proceedings of the IJCNLP-08 Workshop on Named Entity Recognition for South and South East Asian Languages*. Asian Federation of Natural Language Processing, Hyderabad, India.

Sara Rosenthal, Noura Farra, and Preslav Nakov. 2017. SemEval-2017 task 4: Sentiment analysis in Twitter. In *Proceedings of the 11th International Workshop on Semantic Evaluation (SemEval-2017)*, pages 502–518, Vancouver, Canada. Association for Computational Linguistics.

Holger Schwenk, Vishrav Chaudhary, Shuo Sun, Hongyu Gong, and Francisco Guzmán. 2019. Wikimatrix: Mining 135m parallel sentences in 1620 language pairs from wikipedia. *ArXiv*, abs/1907.05791.

Yu Suzuki. 2019. Filtering method for twitter streaming data using human-in-the-loop machine learning. *Journal of Information Processing*, 27:404–410.

John Wieting, Kevin Gimpel, Graham Neubig, and Taylor Berg-Kirkpatrick. 2019. Simple and effective paraphrastic similarity from parallel translations. In *Proceedings of the 57th Annual Meeting of the Association for Computational Linguistics*, pages 4602–4608, Florence, Italy. Association for Computational Linguistics.

Thomas Wolf, Lysandre Debut, Victor Sanh, Julien Chaumond, Clement Delangue, Anthony Moi, Pierric Cistac, Tim Rault, Rémi Louf, Morgan Funtowicz, and Jamie Brew. 2019. Huggingface's transformers: State-of-the-art natural language processing. *CoRR*, abs/1910.03771.

Zhilin Yang, Zihang Dai, Yiming Yang, Jaime G. Carbonell, Ruslan Salakhutdinov, and Quoc V. Le. 2019. Xlnet: Generalized autoregressive pretraining for language understanding. *CoRR*, abs/1906.08237.

A Experiment

Code availability Our model training code and evaluation code will be released at: https://github.com/twitter-research/multilingual-alignment-tpp.

Training setup Our default parameters are as follows: We use Adam optimizer with 500 warmup steps=500 and weight decay of 0.01. Our batch size is 16. Models were trained using 2 NVIDIA v100 GPUs. Training time for TPP ranged from 30 mins to 32hrs for different settings. NER training time was around 1.5 hrs. Sentiment training time was 1 minute, and UD POS training time was also 1 minute.

Evaluation For NER tasks we used micro-averaged F1 score as implemented in the seqeval [4] library. For sentiment tasks we use document level micro-averaged F1 score implemented in scikit-learn library [5]. For UD-POS tasks we used token level accuracy as implemented in scikit-learn library.

B Data

B.1 Data sources

NER

1. SSEA Hindi - From the Workshop on NER for South and South East Asian Languages http://ltrc.iiit.ac.in/ner-ssea-08/index.cgi?topic=5

2. Tweets annotated for in English, Japanese, and Arabic with entities from the following types: PERSON, LOCATION, PRODUCT, ORGANIZATION, and OTHER.

Sentiment For all sentiment datasets we only consider the positive and negative examples and exclude the neutral class if present.

1. Japanese - Available at: http://www.db.info.gifu-u.ac.jp/data/Data_5d832973308d57446583ed9f

2. Arabic - Available at: https://archive.ics.uci.edu/ml/datasets/Twitter+Data+set+for+Arabic+Sentiment+Analysis

3. Hindi - Available at: http://amitavadas.com/SAIL/data.html

[4]https://github.com/chakki-works/seqeval

[5]https://scikit-learn.org/

Co-Training for Commit Classification

Jian Yi, David Lee
DSO National Laboratories
12 Science Park Drive
Singapore 118225
ljianyi@dso.org.sg

Hai Leong Chieu
DSO National Laboratories
12 Science Park Drive
Singapore 118225
chaileon@dso.org.sg

Abstract

Commits in version control systems (e.g. Git) track changes in a software project. Commits comprise noisy user-generated natural language and code patches. Automatic commit classification (CC) has been used to determine the type of code maintenance activities performed, as well as to detect bug fixes in code repositories. Much prior work occurs in the fully-supervised setting – a setting that can be a stretch in resource-scarce situations presenting difficulties in labeling commits. In this paper, we apply co-training, a semi-supervised learning method, to take advantage of the two views available – the commit message (natural language) and the code changes (programming language) – to improve commit classification.

1 Introduction

As a society's reliance on software grows, so will its needs for software analysis. Commits in version control systems (e.g. Git), a way of tracking changes made to code repositories, have been used in a range of analyses, including understanding maintenance activities (Hindle et al., 2009; Levin and Yehudai, 2017; Hönel et al., 2019), studying the impact of social factors in developer teams (Soto et al., 2017; Vasilescu et al., 2015), and detecting bug-fixing patches (Tian et al., 2012; Casalnuovo et al., 2017; Zafar et al., 2019).

Despite the usefulness of analyzing commits, there has been a lack of large-scale commit datasets. In 2017, to our knowledge, the largest public commit dataset (Levin and Yehudai, 2017) contained 1,151 commits categorized into three classes. For perspective, open source projects could see to tens of thousands of commits per year. For example, the Linux kernel's repository had 82,300 commits in 2019 (Foundation, 2021) and now comprises more than 1 million commits. The rate at which commits are created coupled with the variety of the kinds of

Commit Message (NL view):

```
Improve numerical stability of LayerNorm
    ↪ (#59987)
Summary:
Pull Request resolved: #59987
Similar as GroupNorm, improve numerical
    ↪ stability of LayerNorm by Welford
    ↪ algorithm and pairwise sum.
Test Plan: buck test mode/dev-nosan //caffe2/
    ↪ test:nn -- "LayerNorm"
Reviewed By: ngimel
Differential Revision: D29115235
fbshipit-source-id: 376
    ↪ dac89a4e14bd340aaaf169fef8d0d4ca4a1c4
```

Code Change (PL view, cropped with ellipsis)

```
diff --git a/aten/src/ATen/native/cpu/
    ↪ layer_norm_kernel.cpp b/aten/src/ATen/
    ↪ native/cpu/layer_norm_kernel.cpp
index 95a35571646d..366afe64b72a 100644
--- a/aten/src/ATen/native/cpu/
    ↪ layer_norm_kernel.cpp
+++ b/aten/src/ATen/native/cpu/
    ↪ layer_norm_kernel.cpp
@@ -1,13 +1,14 @@
 #include <cmath>
+#include <tuple>
...
 namespace at {
 namespace native {
@@ -29,30 +30,21 @@ void
    ↪ LayerNormKernelImplInternal(
   DCHECK_EQ(X.numel(), M * N);
   DCHECK(!gamma.defined() || gamma.numel()
    ↪ == N);
   DCHECK(!beta.defined() || beta.numel() ==
    ↪ N);
-  T* X_data = X.data_ptr<T>();
+  const T* X_data = X.data_ptr<T>();
...
```

Figure 1: Example of the NL-PL views of a commit.

commits likely pose difficulties in the creation of large-scale, quality commit datasets leading to data scarcity.

A commit consists of a commit message in natural language (NL) and code changes in programming languages (PL) (See Figure 1). Assuming weak dependence between the two views (NL and PL), a known sufficient condition for co-training to succeed (Abney, 2002), we apply iterative co-training (Blum and Mitchell, 1998) to train classifiers by bootstrapping from freely available unlabeled commit samples. Empirically, we show that

Proceedings of the 2021 EMNLP Workshop W-NUT: The Seventh Workshop on Noisy User-generated Text, pages 389–395
November 11, 2021.

co-training improves commit classification (CC) over a range of data scarcity scenarios.

With large transformer models achieving state-of-the-art performance in NLP tasks, Feng et al. (2020) created CodeBERT, a pretrained bimodal model based on RoBERTa's (Liu et al., 2019) architecture (another large language model) for natural language and code to capture the semantic connection between both modalities via an attention mechanism to output representations that can support NL-PL understanding tasks. Due to the presence of NL and PL views in commits, we propose fine-tuning a pretrained CodeBERT for transfer learning on the CC task.

In this paper we examine the following questions: **RQ1:** Can attention between NL and PL improve classification? **RQ2:** Is CodeBERT better than RoBERTa at representing commit messages for CC? **RQ3:** Can co-training improve CC? While RQ3 is our main contribution, we study RQ1 and RQ2 to decide on the neural network architecture.

2 Related Work

Commit Classification (CC) Over the years, researchers have applied a variety of machine learning methods to CC. Hindle et al. (2009) applied decision trees, naive Bayes, SVM (Support Vector Machine), and nearest-neighbor algorithms to classify commits into maintenance categories. Tian et al. (2012) used a SVM on engineered features from commit messages (as a bag of words) and code changes (parsed for the number of code constructs) to classify bug-fixing patches in the Linux kernel, remarking that bug fixes typically involve code changes at a single location while non-bug-fixing commits involve more lines of code. Levin and Yehudai (2017) used word frequencies in commit messages and code changes as inputs to decision trees, GBM (Gradient Boosting Machine), and RF (Random Forest) to classify commits into maintenance activities. Zhou and Sharma (2017) applied logistic regression on the outputs of RF, Gaussian Naive Bayes, K-Nearest Neighbours, GBM, and Adaboost to classify vulnerability-related commits, remarking that commit messages, particularly short ones, may not be unique enough to distinguish vulnerability-relatedness. Sabetta and Bezzi (2018) used a SVM on bags of words obtained from commit messages and another SVM on bags of words from code changes to classify security-relevant commits, remarking that code changes contain names (e.g., variables, functions) that convey semantics and could be treated as a text document. Hönel et al. (2019) used a variety of methods on the code density of commits to classify commits into maintenance activities. Zafar et al. (2019) fine-tuned a pre-trained BERT model (Devlin et al., 2018) with a single neuron perceptron head to classify bug-fixing commits. Keshav Ram (2020) used a linear SVM on TF-IDF features of Java tokens extracted from code changes, Code2Vec (Alon et al., 2019), convolutional neural network on code changes with surrounding code as context, and BiLSTM (Bi-directional Long Short-Term Memory) on code changes without context to classify commits, remarking that the Code2Vec approach yielded poor results. (Lozoya et al., 2021) proposed a method inspired by Code2Vec to compute vectors from code changes, trained on the pretext task of classifying commits' Jira Ticket Priorities before classifying security-fix commits. Many aforementioned works were conducted under the fully-supervised setting — a setting that can be a stretch for new categories where labeled data is scarce.

With large language models achieving state-of-the-art performance in NLP tasks, Feng et al. (2020) created CodeBERT, a pre-trained bimodal model based on RoBERTa's (Liu et al., 2019) architecture (another large language model) for natural language and code in an attempt to capture the semantic connection between both modalities to output representations that can support NL-PL understanding tasks. CodeBERT is pre-trained on code-documentation pairs from Github repositories with the masked language modeling objective (used in pre-training BERT), as well as the replaced token detection objective (used in pre-training ELECTRA (Clark et al., 2020)). CodeBERT is bi-modal in the sense that natural language and code can be concatenated into a single sequence and fed into the model to give rise to attention between code and natural language tokens. In this paper, we adopt a fine-tuning approach to adapt RoBERTa and CodeBERT models for CC.

Datasets Ghadhab et al. (2021) combined three datasets (Levin and Yehudai, 2017; Mauczka et al., 2015; AlOmar et al., 2019) containing commits from open-source projects that cover a range of domains such as databases, programming languages and integration frameworks to create a dataset with 1,793 labeled commits for classifying types of software maintenance activities. Another data set was compiled by Ponta et al. (2019), providing 1,282 commits that fix vulnerabilities in 205 open-source Java projects for classifying security commits.

To our knowledge, the largest data set (that we denote as **RA-Data**) was compiled by Reis and Abreu (2021), aggregating three datasets (Ponta et al., 2019; Reis and Abreu, 2017; Fan et al., 2020) as well as additional scraping to provide 8,057 security-relevant commits and about 110,000 non-security-relevant commits spanning 1,339 open-source projects and 20 programming languages. In this paper, we use RA-Data as it is larger and more varied than the other datasets. To our knowledge, our work is the first to attempt CC on this dataset.

Co-Training Co-training was first proposed by Blum and Mitchell (1998) and applied to classify university web pages by assuming that the web pages' text and inbound links are two distinct views conditionally independent to the other given the class label, and sufficient for learning by itself. During each co-training iteration, the classifiers' most confident predictions for each view are added to an initially small set of labeled training data, expanding it. In the same iteration, the classifiers are further trained on the expanded dataset. Later, Abney (2002) proved that weak dependence between views, a weaker assumption than conditional independence, is sufficient for co-training. Next, Balcan et al. (2005) proved an even weaker sufficient condition they term expansion assumption. After that, Wang and Zhou (2010) showed that combinative label propagation over two views is both sufficient and necessary for co-training.

Ling et al. (2009) empirically verifies on 32 datasets that improvements by co-training are likelier the more independent the two views are and the more sufficient each view is, publishing results supporting aforementioned sufficient conditions for co-training.

In this work, we observed that commits possess a natural view split – commit message (natural language) and code changes (programming language) – that one could reasonably hope for the weak dependence assumption as well as the sufficiency for learning from one view assumption to hold. If true, co-training is a natural fit for learning on commit datasets.

3 The 900Repo Dataset

To create a balanced dataset from RA-Data, we first noted that about 910 repositories overlap in both classes – security ("positive" class) & non-security ("negative" class). The remaining repositories occur in one class but not the other. We extracted all 3,765 positive samples belonging to these 910 overlapping repositories and randomly sampled twice as many negative samples from the same 910 repositories, giving a total of 10,000 commits. As at August 2021, due to RA-Data not having code changes (a.k.a. diffs), we scraped for the code changes via Github's API. The result is a dataset with 3,765 positive samples and roughly 6,300 negative samples that we refer to as **900Repo**. This dataset is publicly available at `https://github.com/davidleejy/wnut21-cotrain`.

4 Pre-trained models

RQ1. While it seems beneficial to pack the NL and PL views into a single input sequence to a transformer model so that attention between message tokens and code tokens could improve the representation, such a sequence is likely to exceed the maximum input sequence length even in large models like RoBERTa & CodeBERT. As such, striving for attention between NL and PL views often means truncating both modalities significantly as a trade-off, losing information in the process. An alternative is to feed each modality into a separate transformer model, effectively sacrificing attention between modalities to gain information (fewer tokens truncated), and attaching, for example, a single MLP (Multi-Layer Perceptron) at both heads of these transformer models to yield a joint representation upon which classification can be performed. Our experiments in Section 4.1 suggest that sacrificing attention to allow longer text inputs is the better approach.

RQ2. As CodeBERT was pre-trained with the aim of capturing the semantic connection between NL and PL, one might expect CodeBERT to produce better representations for commit messages than the architecturally-identical RoBERTa which was not trained with NL-PL understanding in mind. Our experiments in Section 4.1 suggest that the representations generated by RoBERTa and CodeBERT for commit messages offer similar performance outcomes for CC.

4.1 Models and Experiments

The 900Repo dataset is split with a 70:15:15 train:validation:test ratio. We fine-tune the MLP to the CC task (binary classification) via gradi-

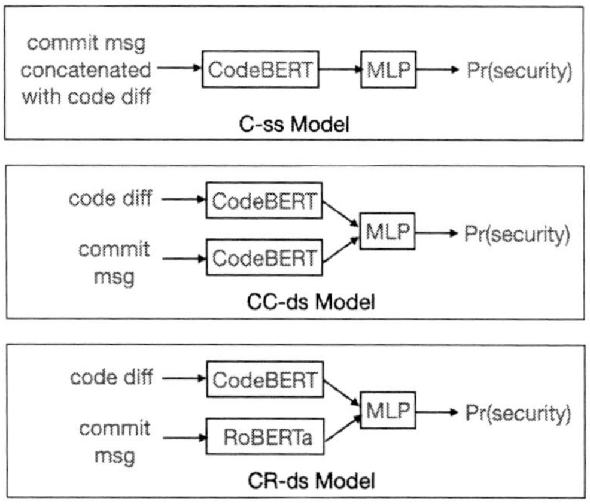

Figure 2: Neural network architectures considered.

ent descent with ADAM. Pre-trained CodeBERT and RoBERTa weights are not modified, each with 125M parameters. We explore three architectural configurations (See Figure 2) to investigate RQ1 and RQ2:

C-ss (CodeBERT, single sequence): Both modalities, NL and PL, are concatenated and truncated into a single 512 token sequence (hence "single sequence"), before being fed into a pre-trained CodeBERT model. Commit messages are roughly given 30% of the 512 token sequence limit and code changes are given the remaining 70%. An MLP is attached to the head of the CodeBERT model for fine-tuning. The classification prediction is output by the MLP.

CC-ds (CodeBERT & CodeBERT, distinct sequences): Both modalities are fed into separate, identical pre-trained CodeBERT models (hence "distinct sequences"). As such, there is no attention across modalities. Both modalities are allowed the maximum 512 token sequence limit and have its own embedding. A single MLP is attached to both heads of the two separate CodeBERT models (one for NL, one for PL) to yield a joint representation. The classification prediction is output by the MLP.

CR-ds (CodeBERT & RoBERTa, distinct sequences): Identical to CC-ds except the NL view is fed to RoBERTa instead of CodeBERT.

Results: Table 1 shows the performance of the three different architectural configurations. Both ds (distinct sequences) models perform better than the C-ss (single sequence) model, suggesting that sacrificing attention between the modalities in return for being able to pass more information into the model is a reasonable trade-off for CC. The CR-ds (CodeBERT & RoBERTa) model slightly outperformed the CC-ds (CodeBERT & CodeBERT) model suggesting that CodeBERT does not offer an advantage over RoBERTa at representing commit messages for the CC task.

Model	P	R	F1	AUC	Acc.
C-ss	80.3	80.4	80.4	81.0	80.4
CC-ds	83.0	83.0	83.0	84.9	83.0
CR-ds	**84.0**	**84.1**	**83.9**	**87.4**	**84.1**

Table 1: Test results with different architectures. P/R/F1: average weighted precision, recall and F1 (weighted by class-size), Acc.: accuracy, AUC: area under precision-recall curve.

Algorithm 1: Co-training

Note: Denote positive class as ⊞; negative class as ⊠.
Input: Confidence c; Confidence limit C; Min. (resp. max.) of samples to label as ⊞ (resp. ⊠): $n_{min}(⊞), n_{max}(⊞)$ (resp. $n_{min}(⊠), n_{max}(⊠)$)
Data: Labeled T, Unlabeled U, Validation V.
Output: Trained classifiers NL, PL.

Train on T to obtain NL and PL models
while U *not empty* **do**
  for M *in* NL, PL **do**
    Label U with M
    for L *in* ⊞, ⊠ **do**
      Select samples with predicted probability $> 1 - c$ when L is ⊞ (resp. $< c$ when L is ⊠). Denote selection's size as n_L.
      If $n_L > n_{max}(L)$ limit, truncate selection to size $n_{max}(L)$.
      If $n_L < n_{min}(L)$ limit, pad selection to size $n_{min}(L)$.
  Add selected samples to T.
  Train new models NL_{new} and PL_{new} on T. If performance on V improves, set $NL = NL_{new}$ and $PL = PL_{new}$.
  Increment c. Maintain $c < C$.

T	Model	P	R	F1	Acc.
0.5%	NL-T	67.8	68.8	**66.7**	68.8
	PL-T	61.2	63.0	61.4	63.0
	NL	**68.0**	**69.0**	**66.7**	**69.0**
	PL	64.7	66.3	63.4	66.3
1%	NL-T	58.5	62.3	57.2	62.3
	PL-T	65.2	65.3	65.3	65.3
	NL	**73.0**	**72.2**	**72.5**	**72.2**
	PL	68.5	67.3	60.9	67.3
2%	NL-T	75.9	76.3	76.0	76.3
	PL-T	68.4	65.9	66.5	65.9
	NL	**76.2**	**76.5**	**76.3**	**76.5**
	PL	72.4	73.1	72.4	73.1
4%	NL-T	77.6	77.0	76.9	77.0
	PL-T	71.2	69.3	69.7	69.3
	NL	**77.7**	**77.9**	**77.8**	**77.9**
	PL	73.4	70.6	70.9	70.6

Table 2: Co-training experimental results. T: labeled training data as a percentage of the dataset. NL-T, PL-T: supervised models trained only on T. NL, PL: co-trained models. P/R/F1: average weighted precision, recall, and F1 score. Acc.: accuracy.

5 Co-training for commit classification

In the previous section, a joint representation of the two modalities is obtained by attaching a single MLP to the outputs of the transformer models. However, here the CodeBERT & RoBERTa outputs are directed to separate MLP's. For convenience, we denote as **NL** the RoBERTa-MLP classifier model on commit messages, and as **PL** the CodeBERT-MLP classifier model on code changes.

To simulate resource-poor conditions, we use either 0.5%, 1%, 2% or 4% of the 900Repo dataset as labeled training data with a validation set of the same size, and 15% of the data as test set. The remaining is used as unlabeled data for co-training. The validation data is used by supervised baselines for model selection (i.e. selecting the epoch during training with best performance on validation set).

We show our co-training algorithm in Algorithm 1. In each iteration, a small amount of confidently labeled commits are added to the training dataset which in turn is used in the next iteration's training. At all times, only the MLP portions are fine-tuned via gradient descent with ADAM for CC. Pre-trained CodeBERT and RoBERTa weights are frozen. In all our experiments, we set $c = 0.001$, $C = 0.15$, $n_{max}(\boxplus) = 3$, $n_{max}(\boxtimes) = 5$, $n_{min}(\boxplus) = n_{min}(\boxtimes) = 1$.

Results: Table 2 shows the test performance for resource-poor scenarios ($T = 4\%, 2\%, 1\%,$ & 0.5% labeled data). Co-training provided an improvement across virtually all performance metrics in all scenarios. In all scenarios, the PL classifier (CodeBERT-MLP) improved more than the NL classifier (RoBERTa-MLP).

Under both supervised & co-training approaches, the NL classifier is observed to perform better than the PL classifier. This could be due to the challenging nature of obtaining good representations for programming languages as well as the length of code changes frequently being much longer than the commit message and CodeBERT's 512 token limit.

6 Conclusion

We found co-training to be helpful for CC in resource-poor settings where there are insufficient labeled commits for supervised approaches. Further research directions could explore the use of semi-supervised learning methods to expand the capabilities of semantic search within code repositories. Another limitation of our current work is that commits are often too long for Roberta and CodeBert. For future work, we could apply models that allow longer sequences as input, e.g., the Longformer (Beltagy et al., 2020).

References

Steven Abney. 2002. Bootstrapping. In *Proceedings of the 40th annual meeting of the Association for Computational Linguistics*, pages 360–367.

Eman AlOmar, Mohamed Wiem Mkaouer, and Ali Ouni. 2019. Can refactoring be self-affirmed? an exploratory study on how developers document their refactoring activities in commit messages. In *2019 IEEE/ACM 3rd International Workshop on Refactoring (IWoR)*, pages 51–58. IEEE.

Uri Alon, Meital Zilberstein, Omer Levy, and Eran Yahav. 2019. code2vec: Learning distributed representations of code. *Proceedings of the ACM on Programming Languages*, 3(POPL):1–29.

Maria-Florina Balcan, Avrim Blum, and Ke Yang. 2005. Co-training and expansion: Towards bridging theory and practice. *Advances in neural information processing systems*, 17:89–96.

Iz Beltagy, Matthew E Peters, and Arman Cohan. 2020. Longformer: The long-document transformer. *arXiv preprint arXiv:2004.05150.*

Avrim Blum and Tom Mitchell. 1998. Combining labeled and unlabeled data with co-training. In *Proceedings of the eleventh annual conference on Computational learning theory*, pages 92–100.

Casey Casalnuovo, Yagnik Suchak, Baishakhi Ray, and Cindy Rubio-González. 2017. Gitcproc: A tool for processing and classifying github commits. In *Proceedings of the 26th ACM SIGSOFT International Symposium on Software Testing and Analysis*, pages 396–399.

Kevin Clark, Minh-Thang Luong, Quoc V Le, and Christopher D Manning. 2020. Electra: Pre-training text encoders as discriminators rather than generators. *arXiv preprint arXiv:2003.10555*.

Jacob Devlin, Ming-Wei Chang, Kenton Lee, and Kristina Toutanova. 2018. Bert: Pre-training of deep bidirectional transformers for language understanding. *arXiv preprint arXiv:1810.04805*.

Jiahao Fan, Yi Li, Shaohua Wang, and Tien N Nguyen. 2020. Ac/c++ code vulnerability dataset with code changes and cve summaries. In *Proceedings of the 17th International Conference on Mining Software Repositories*, pages 508–512.

Zhangyin Feng, Daya Guo, Duyu Tang, Nan Duan, Xiaocheng Feng, Ming Gong, Linjun Shou, Bing Qin, Ting Liu, Daxin Jiang, et al. 2020. Codebert: A pre-trained model for programming and natural languages. *arXiv preprint arXiv:2002.08155*.

The Linux Foundation. 2021. 2020 linux kernel history report. -.

Lobna Ghadhab, Ilyes Jenhani, Mohamed Wiem Mkaouer, and Montassar Ben Messaoud. 2021. Augmenting commit classification by using fine-grained source code changes and a pre-trained deep neural language model. *Information and Software Technology*, 135:106566.

Abram Hindle, Daniel M German, Michael W Godfrey, and Richard C Holt. 2009. Automatic classication of large changes into maintenance categories. In *2009 IEEE 17th International Conference on Program Comprehension*, pages 30–39. IEEE.

Sebastian Hönel, Morgan Ericsson, Welf Löwe, and Anna Wingkvist. 2019. Importance and aptitude of source code density for commit classification into maintenance activities. In *2019 IEEE 19th International Conference on Software Quality, Reliability and Security (QRS)*, pages 109–120. IEEE.

Achyudh Ram Keshav Ram. 2020. Exploiting token and path-based representations of code for identifying security-relevant commits. Master's thesis, University of Waterloo.

Stanislav Levin and Amiram Yehudai. 2017. Boosting automatic commit classification into maintenance activities by utilizing source code changes. In *Proceedings of the 13th International Conference on Predictive Models and Data Analytics in Software Engineering*, pages 97–106.

Charles X Ling, Jun Du, and Zhi-Hua Zhou. 2009. When does co-training work in real data? In *Pacific-Asia Conference on Knowledge Discovery and Data Mining*, pages 596–603. Springer.

Yinhan Liu, Myle Ott, Naman Goyal, Jingfei Du, Mandar Joshi, Danqi Chen, Omer Levy, Mike Lewis, Luke Zettlemoyer, and Veselin Stoyanov. 2019. Roberta: A robustly optimized bert pretraining approach. *arXiv preprint arXiv:1907.11692*.

Rocío Cabrera Lozoya, Arnaud Baumann, Antonino Sabetta, and Michele Bezzi. 2021. Commit2vec: Learning distributed representations of code changes. *SN Computer Science*, 2(3):1–16.

Andreas Mauczka, Florian Brosch, Christian Schanes, and Thomas Grechenig. 2015. Dataset of developer-labeled commit messages. In *2015 IEEE/ACM 12th Working Conference on Mining Software Repositories*, pages 490–493. IEEE.

Serena Elisa Ponta, Henrik Plate, Antonino Sabetta, Michele Bezzi, and Cédric Dangremont. 2019. A manually-curated dataset of fixes to vulnerabilities of open-source software. In *2019 IEEE/ACM 16th International Conference on Mining Software Repositories (MSR)*, pages 383–387. IEEE.

Sofia Reis and Rui Abreu. 2017. Secbench: A database of real security vulnerabilities. In *SecSE@ ESORICS*, pages 69–85.

Sofia Oliveira Reis and Rui Abreu. 2021. A ground-truth dataset of real security patches. *arXiv*.

Antonino Sabetta and Michele Bezzi. 2018. A practical approach to the automatic classification of security-relevant commits. In *2018 IEEE International conference on software maintenance and evolution (ICSME)*, pages 579–582. IEEE.

Mauricio Soto, Zack Coker, and Claire Le Goues. 2017. Analyzing the impact of social attributes on commit integration success. In *2017 IEEE/ACM 14th International Conference on Mining Software Repositories (MSR)*, pages 483–486. IEEE.

Yuan Tian, Julia Lawall, and David Lo. 2012. Identifying linux bug fixing patches. In *2012 34th international conference on software engineering (ICSE)*, pages 386–396. IEEE.

Bogdan Vasilescu, Alexander Serebrenik, and Vladimir Filkov. 2015. A data set for social diversity studies of github teams. In *2015 IEEE/ACM 12th working conference on mining software repositories*, pages 514–517. IEEE.

Wei Wang and Zhi-Hua Zhou. 2010. A new analysis of co-training. In *ICML*.

Sarim Zafar, Muhammad Zubair Malik, and Gursimran Singh Walia. 2019. Towards standardizing and improving classification of bug-fix commits. In *2019 ACM/IEEE International Symposium on Empirical Software Engineering and Measurement (ESEM)*, pages 1–6. IEEE.

Yaqin Zhou and Asankhaya Sharma. 2017. Automated identification of security issues from commit messages and bug reports. In *Proceedings of the 2017 11th joint meeting on foundations of software engineering*, pages 914–919.

Study of Manifestation of Civil Unrest on Twitter

Abhinav Chinta* and **Jingyu Zhang*** and **Alexandra DeLucia** and **Mark Dredze**
Center for Language and Speech Processing, Johns Hopkins University
{achinta3, jzhan237, aadelucia, mdredze}@jhu.edu

Anna L Buczak
Johns Hopkins University Applied Physics Laboratory
Anna.Buczak@jhuapl.edu

Abstract

Twitter is commonly used for civil unrest detection and forecasting tasks, but there is a lack of work in evaluating *how* civil unrest manifests on Twitter across countries and events. We present two in-depth case studies for two specific large-scale events, one in a country with high (English) Twitter usage (Johannesburg riots in South Africa) and one in a country with low Twitter usage (Burayu massacre protests in Ethiopia). We show that while there is event signal during the events, there is little signal leading up to the events. In addition to the case studies, we train n-gram-based models on a larger set of Twitter civil unrest data across time, events, and countries and use machine learning explainability tools (SHAP) to identify important features. The models were able to find words indicative of civil unrest that generalized across countries. The 42 countries span Africa, Middle East, and Southeast Asia and the events range occur between 2014 and 2019.

Figure 1: Example tweets from Johannesburg riots in South Africa. The tweets were found through their use of event-related hashtags. Paraphrased for privacy.

1 Introduction

Citizens utilize public demonstrations, protests, and in extreme cases, riots, to express dissatisfaction over the current political or social state in their country. Some of these movements successfully achieve government reforms, many do not. These movements are often driven from the ground up, by grassroots advocacy that snowballs into social and political change. Understanding the factors that drive sociopolitical change can help policy makers and advocates petition for and advance their causes.

Since these causes emerge from the public, studying them requires data on public attitudes, perceptions, and actions around previous movements. In particular, understanding the factors behind civil unrest based on social media posts can reveal important trends. However, while social media data reflects many public attitudes, it's unclear how sites such as Twitter capture activities around civil unrest. Previous work has considered the task of predicting protests or riots using social media, often with the aid of news sources (Alsaedi et al., 2017; Ramakrishnan et al., 2014; Osborne and Dredze, 2014; Islam et al., 2020; Edouard, 2018; Korolov et al., 2016; Ranganath et al., 2016; De Silva and Riloff, 2014; Littman, 2018).

In this paper we consider how these activities manifest themselves on Twitter. Specifically, we consider events across a range of countries to understand how Twitter is used by different populations. Our analysis has two facets: (1) qualitative case studies focusing on two specific events in countries with different civil unrest rates and Twitter usage patterns and (2) a quantitative analysis to find indicators of civil unrest that generalize across countries and events.

For the case studies, we look at the 2019 Johannesburg riots in South Africa and the 2018 Burayu Massacre and subsequent protests in Ethiopia. We chose these events because they were significant within those countries and received global attention. Their scale should mean they are reflected on social media. Furthermore, these countries have high (South Africa) and low (Ethiopia) Twitter usage, and the majority of their tweets are in English. For each event we ask: (1) is the event discussed on Twitter? (2) is there any noticeable buildup to the

*Equal contribution.

Proceedings of the 2021 EMNLP Workshop W-NUT: The Seventh Workshop on Noisy User-generated Text, pages 396–409
November 11, 2021.

event? (3) *who* is talking about the event? (4) do tweets reflect the issues that motivated the events?

We then take a quantitative approach to find generalizable indicators of civil unrest across time, events, and countries. This focus on generalizability is motivated by previous work that detects/forecasts unrest across countries or regions (Alsaedi et al., 2017; Ramakrishnan et al., 2014; Islam et al., 2020; Korolov et al., 2016; Ranganath et al., 2016), and the desire to have a single model perform well across countries. For this analysis we introduce n-gram models trained on a new dataset, Global Civil Unrest on Twitter, or G-CUT, which spans 42 countries from Africa, the Middle East, and Southeast Asia, and riots and protests from 2014 to 2019. We evaluate model generalizability by checking not only the overall performance, but also the per-country performance. Also, we use AI explainability tools (SHAP) to analyze the top indicators and ensure they are not country- or event-specific.

All data (tweet IDs), models, and code will be made publicly available at `https://github.com/AADeLucia/civil-unrest-case-study`.

2 Data

We analyze Twitter since it is a widely used social media platform, with many public posts about major events in real-time. For ground-truth data on civil unrest we use the Armed Conflict Location & Event Data Project (ACLED) (Raleigh et al., 2010), a manually curated database tracking civil unrest events.

2.1 Twitter Collection

We collected geotagged tweets from the Twitter streaming API from 2014 to 2019 (inclusive) for 42 countries from Africa, the Middle East, and Southeast Asia. We selected English tweets using `langid` (Lui and Baldwin, 2012).[1] Appendix Table 4 lists the number of tweets per country.

To focus on relevant tweets we filter our data using the BERTweet civil unrest tweet classifier from Sech et al. (2020).[2] We keep tweets with probabilities above 0.5. Previous work has achieved this filtration using keywords (Muthiah et al., 2015; Ramakrishnan et al., 2014) or focus on post-event data collection (Alsaedi et al., 2017). The number of tweets by country before and after filtering for language and relevance are shown in Figure 2. Only a small number of these countries have a large number of English tweets, and we consider many to be "low data" countries. This low amount of data can be due to low country internet usage in general, low popularity of Twitter in the region, or low prevalence of English. The language breakdown of each country is in Appendix Figure 8.

2.2 Civil Unrest Ground Truth

We use a combination of ACLED and Wikipedia to determine whether a riot or protest occurred. We are focused on events that are reflected in these sources and also appear on Twitter. We select ACLED instead of other civil unrest event databases (e.g., GDELT (Leetaru and Schrodt)) because it is freely available, manually curated by regional experts, and provides simple event categorization.

From ACLED we select events of the types Riots and Protests for our automated analysis. Data was downloaded from 2014-2019 using the data export tool[3]. The events in ACLED range from small- to large-scale, but the scope of the event is not clearly reflected in ACLED. For the case studies we utilize Wikipedia, since it contains information about large-scale events that likely appear on Twitter. The ACLED coverage information for each country is in Figure 2. Most countries have at least 500 events in the 6 year period.

3 Case Studies

We focus on two countries with differing levels of available English tweets and civil unrest levels according to ACLED: South Africa and Ethiopia. South Africa is a high-data country (i.e., has an abundance of English tweets) with high rates of civil unrest (almost 2,000 events in the 6 year period), and Ethiopia is a low data country with relatively lower rates of civil unrest (almost 600 events). These two countries are not representative of all countries, but do provide insight on issues that may arise when using Twitter data from high and low data countries for civil unrest detection and forecasting.

For each country, we select a single event and ask: (1) is the event discussed on Twitter? (2)

[1] Twitter provided language identification was not available for the early years in our dataset.

[2] The model has a test F1-score of 0.81 for identifying civil unrest-related tweets.

[3] `https://acleddata.com/data-export-tool/`

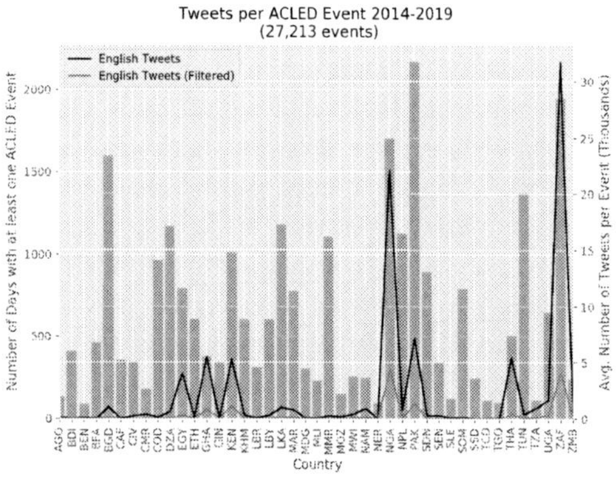

Figure 2: The average number of tweets in the dataset per ACLED event for the selected 42 countries. Counts for English tweets and filtered English tweets are shown. Events are limited to ACLED types Riots and Protests.

is there any noticeable buildup in Twitter activity prior to the event? (3) *who* is talking about the event? We limit our study to events with a clear start and end date (e.g., a specific protest) as opposed to general sociopolitical movements with a buildup over years (e.g., a Black Lives Matter (BLM) protest in the US versus studying the BLM movement). For (1) we look at the ratio of civil unrest-related tweets to all tweets (the relevance classifier discussed in §2) and then proxy the Twitter discussion through popular hashtags. The analysis for (2) is important for systems that aim to forecast civil unrest. To approximate event "buildup" we expand our scope from the day of the event to a few days before and after. This analysis looks at the emergence of event-related hashtags and whether Twitter is used in event buildup or is more reactionary. For the question of *who* is talking (3), we use user verification status and rates of likes and retweets as a heuristic for influential users. Only users active in the one week time frame are included.

After the case studies, we test how well post-event knowledge can help with data filtration. Other work uses location, time, keyword, or hashtag information gathered through post-event analysis (Littman, 2018; Alsaedi et al., 2017). For this experiment, we use the provided ACLED descriptions of the events to query event-related tweets.

3.1 South Africa: Johannesburg Riots

South Africa is prominent in our dataset due to the widespread use of English and the popularity of the platform in the country. We examine the 2019 Johannesburg riots, a large-scale event that took place in Johannesburg, South Africa, during the period September 1-5, 2019. The riots were the culmination of two unrelated incidents: (1) the murder of a taxi driver by an immigrant and (2) the sexual assault and murder of a college student, Uyinene Mrwetyana, on August 24, 2019.[4] The close timing of the incidents caused uproar about xenophobia and gender-based violence in the country.

We first explore if the event is discussed on Twitter. Figure 3a shows the ratio of civil unrest-related tweets (i.e., filtered tweets) during the week of the riots. The ratio is highest during the riots (September 2-5). On September 3 almost 30% of all tweets were civil unrest-related, though the civil unrest score from the filtration model does not determine if the tweets discuss the event in question. We next use hashtags to measure popular topics and find that the top hashtags correspond to the riots (Figure 4a). Hashtags are counted using only the filtered tweets, but the top hashtags from all tweets are in Appendix Figure 9a. All hashtags were lowercased to ensure accurate counts across hashtag variation. Some of the hashtags are popular enough to be in both filtered and unfiltered analysis.

Conversations about both the rise of xenophobia and gender-based violence are visible from the hashtags, some even calling to "shut down" the country in a state of emergency (e.g., `#shutdownsouthafrica`). The gender-based violence discussion centers around the victim's name and other slogans which questions the safety of women in the country (e.g., `#aminext` and `#uyinenemrwetyana`). The xenophobia discussion centers around hashtags containing "xenophobia", such as `#xenophobiansouthafrica`. The locations of large protests are also identified, with `joburgcbd` (Johannesburg central business district) and `#pretoriacbd` (Pretoria central business district). The riots started in Pretoria and then spread to Johannesburg, and this is shown in the hashtag popularity for the week. An example tweet from the event is in Figure 1.

While the rise in civil unrest tweets corresponds to the dates of the protest, we see that there is no gradual rise in the unrest. This may be due to bias in data collection or the time needed to rally around

[4] `https://en.wikipedia.org/wiki/2019_Johannesburg_riots`

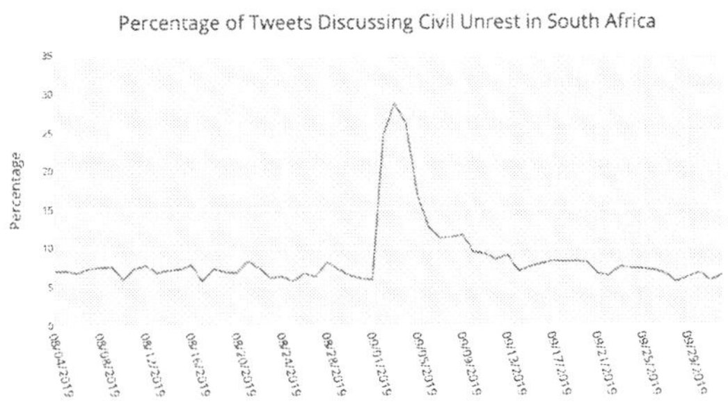

(a) South Africa Johannesburg Riots, September 1-5th 2019.

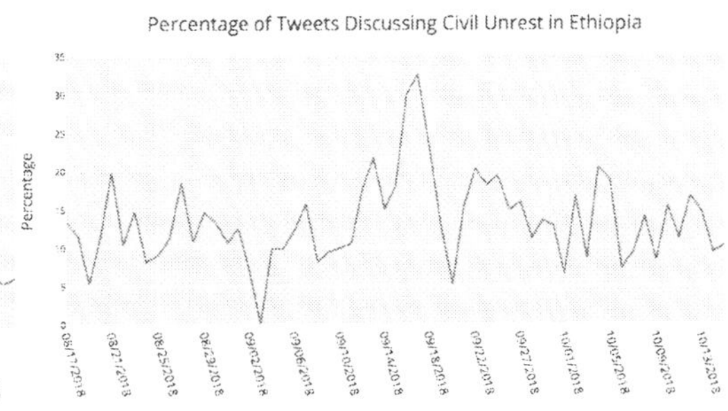

(b) Ethiopia Burayu Massacre, September 14-16 2018.

Figure 3: Ratio of civil unrest-related tweets in South Africa and Ethiopia around the time of large-scale protests. In both countries, the civil unrest-related tweets spike around 30%, but that spike corresponds to thousands of tweets in South Africa and only 150 in Ethiopia.

central hashtags. The hashtags remained popular after the event, indicating people were still discussing the event and/or dealing with the aftermath.

The hashtag analysis lends insight as to what is being discussed, and we are also interested in *who* is leading the conversation. We find these "influential" users based on verification status and the number of likes their tweets received over the one week period. We found that verification status did not necessarily mean they were popular users, hence the inclusion of number of likes to measure engagement. After manual analysis of the screen names and descriptions (not included here for privacy concerns), we found that these users were entertainers, reporters, and activists. The entertainment accounts did post content about the protests, often in support. News organizations were not among the top 10 accounts, which confirms the discussion is led by the people and not organizations. This is important to know for systems that use social media to "beat the news" (Ramakrishnan et al., 2014).

3.2 Ethiopia: Burayu Massacre Protests

Compared to South Africa, Ethiopia has considerably less English Twitter (see Appendix Table 4), despite having almost double the population[5]. Despite the low prevalence of English in the country,[6] it is the language of choice for the majority of tweets (see Appendix Table 8). A large-scale civil unrest event from Ethiopia is the Burayu massacre, which took place on 14-16 September 2018 in Burayu, a town near the capital, Addis Ababa. During the three day period there were clashes between ethnic groups and targeted looting of business. The activities led to 23 deaths and many injured and displaced people.[7] On September 17, thousands of people marched in the capital in protest of the poor government handling of the looting and violence.

From Figure 3b, we see a clear spike in civil unrest tweets on the last day of the looting and on the day of the protest in the capital. However, the perceived volatility of civil unrest discussion in Ethiopia is due to the low data. Even at the peak where over 30% of tweets are civil unrest-related, that corresponds to only 150 tweets. The low data is also obvious when analyzing hashtags, where even the most popular only appeared 12 times (Figure 4b). Out of the top hashtags, none directly use keywords about the situation (i.e., no "massacre", "death", "violence", or "Burayu"), and event related hashtags were only determined after manual analysis of tweets. The hashtags containing relevant information were `#etv`, `#addisababa`, `#addis`, which reference the Ethiopian public broadcast station and the capital where protests occurred. The other top hashtags were irrelevant to the event, but still civil unrest-adjacent in nature (e.g., `#southsudan` and `#eritrea` were discussing a peace treaty between South Sudan and rebel groups hosted in Ethiopia).[8] The discussions surrounding `#etv` were interesting since they concerned the coverage of the protesters and treatment from the police. An example tweet found through

[5] https://www.worldometers.info/world-population/population-by-country/

[6] https://www.cia.gov/the-world-factbook/countries/ethiopia/#people-and-society

[7] https://en.wikipedia.org/wiki/Burayu_massacre

[8] https://www.reuters.com/article/us-southsudan-unrest/south-sudans-president-rebel-leader-sign-peace-deal-idUSKCN1LS2PW

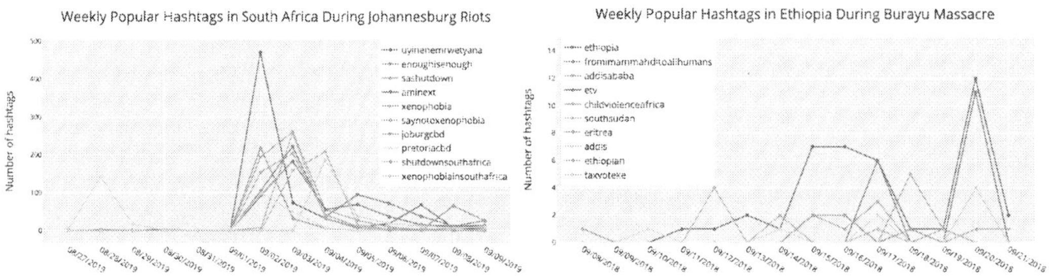

(a) South Africa

(b) Ethiopia

Figure 4: Popular hashtags in South Africa and Ethiopia from the one week period of the Johannesburg riots and Burayu Massacre, respectively. Hashtag frequency is calculated from filtered tweets only.

Figure 5: Example tweet from the events following the Burayu massacre in Ethiopia. Tweet was queried based on its event-related hashtags. Paraphrased for privacy.

hashtag analysis is in Figure 5.

The influential users around the time of the protest were mostly activists. Only a few directly referenced the massacre, and those tweets mostly condemned the violence, especially against women.

3.3 Filtering Tweets using Event Descriptions

In our case studies we observed an increase in civil unrest tweets during the event time period. However, the civil unrest filtration method was general and could not limit the tweets to those discussing the specific event of interest. Other work uses post-event knowledge such as keywords or hashtags (Littman, 2018; Alsaedi et al., 2017), but we leverage the ACLED event descriptions to query related tweets. We test this method on tweets from the Johannesburg Riots.

For the query process we created embedding representations of each tweet from September 3, 2019 in South Africa (the peak of the protests) and of the aggregated event descriptions from the same day in ACLED, and then used cosine similarity between event and tweet representations to find the relevant tweets. We used the average Twitter GloVe embedding (Pennington et al., 2014) to represent the tweets and the ACLED event. Tweets and event descriptions were pre-processed with the `GloVeTweetTokenizer` from `littlebird` (DeLucia, 2020). Although the embeddings are not meant for the formal writing style in the descriptions, we decided to prioritize the tweet representation.

As seen in Table 1, the tweets with the highest cosine similarity to the event description explicitly discussed the protests, indicating success. This is a useful approach for those who want an automated method to filter a general collection of tweets. As seen from the case studies, even reducing tweets to those that are just civil unrest related was not enough to only have event-specific tweets. And gathering tweets through post-hoc analysis as in (Littman, 2018; Alsaedi et al., 2017) requires extensive knowledge of keywords and hashtags, not just the time and location of the event. This automated method can help discover more search terms and event-specific hashtags. An important note is while the most similar tweets were relevant, they only had a cosine similarity of 0.3 with the event description. An automated approach would have to tune this similarity threshold.

A scaled-up version of this experiment covering the entire month of September is in Appendix C. The matching results were subpar, indicating events could not be accurately paired with their corresponding days. We believe this is due to the sheer amount of data hiding an event signal, since South Africa has many tweets.

4 General Indicators of Civil Unrest

In §3 we determined that for two specific events in different countries (South Africa and Ethiopia), there is signal in the country's Twitter activity that a civil unrest event occurred. Those case studies

ACLED Event Descriptions
Foreign nationals demonstrated and barricaded roads in Rosettenville (City of Johannesburg, Gauteng). Some sources reported demonstrators held weapons, in case they were attacked. The demonstration was in response to nationals attacking foreign nationals.
Students, mainly female, demonstrated at the University of Cape Town, disrupting classes. The demonstration was in response to the rape and murder of student, calling for more safety for students.
Most Similar Tweets
Is the @SAPS investigation of the alleged murder of the Pretoria taxi driver by undocumented immigrants over yet?
Glad something is happening but maybe they should have waited longer for investigations... but where are the police?!

Table 1: Example ACLED event description and corresponding tweets, according to highest cosine similarity for South Africa on September 3, 2019. Only some of the 8 event descriptions for this day are shown. The tweets all have cosine similarity around 0.3 to the event representation. Tweets are paraphrased for privacy.

were very manual, which is not practical for large-scale analyses across events, time, and countries. Also, the identified relevant tweets and hashtags from the two events were very different (e.g., `#etv` vs `#shutdownsouthafrica`). Are there general trends/indicators of civil unrest across many countries and events? We answer this question by training an interpretable[9] n-gram model and analyzing its per-country performance and feature importance with SHAP, a popular explainability tool SHapley Additive exPlanation (SHAP) (Lundberg and Lee, 2017).

4.1 Experimental Setup

We formulate the civil unrest event detection task as a binary classification problem to predict whether an event occurred in a particular country on a particular day. The ground truth is the ACLED labels from §2, where a day is "positive" if at least one event occurred. For easily understandable features, we use n-gram (token) counts from Scikit-learn (Pedregosa et al., 2011). All tweets are grouped by their country and day of origin and assigned a positive or negative label depending on if that country and day is present in ACLED.[10] Only filtered tweets are included (see §2), and days without corresponding tweets are removed. To make computation tractable, we only consider the top 10,000 tokens from the training set. The tweets were tokenized with `littlebird`. Each day in a country is represented as the raw count of the aggregated tweet tokens. For temporal generalizability, we split the Twitter data by year, where 2014–2016/2017/2018–2019 are the train/validation/test sets.

We use a random forest model because it is both simple enough to be interpretable and powerful enough to capture relevant features from the data. For comparison, we utilize a random baseline that predicts the positive class with the probably of the positive class in the train set. Since 29% of the country/date samples were positive from 2014–2016, the random classifier predicts the positive class 29% of the time. The models were evaluated with precision-recall metrics. To encourage model generalizability across countries we remove location-specific tokens from the data, focusing on country names and locations mentioned in ACLED. Details are in Appendix §D. In addition to combating country bias by removing location words, we also sampled the dataset to ensure equal representation of countries.

The n-gram model achieved an F1 score for the positive class of 0.45, with precision close to 0.60. This score greatly outperforms the random baseline, which only achieves an F1 of 0.29 (see Table 3). The non-debiased n-gram model performed slightly better than the n-gram model (0.50, an improvement of 0.05 F1), however this increase in performance came at the cost of less informative features. We attribute this low F1 score to noisy data and labels. While the tweets are filtered to those civil unrest-related, as discussed in §3, that does not mean the tweets are all related to the ACLED event(s) reported on the day. In addition, while ACLED is a human-curated dataset, the event granularity varies from small-scale events in a single town to large-scale events in populous

[9] "Interpretable" referring to the simplicity of the model and easily understandable features, i.e., token counts

[10] "Country of origin" is present in all tweets since only geotagged tweets are in the dataset.

cities. Both cases provide a positive label for the day in a country, despite the probable difference in signal. Once the model was trained, we used SHAP values to find the most important features, or tokens, according to the model.

The SHAP value of a feature estimates the marginal contribution of that feature to the model output across different combinations of other features, essentially a feature "importance" (Lundberg et al., 2020). A negative SHAP value means the feature pushes the prediction towards the negative class, and a positive value pushes it towards the positive class. Although SHAP operates on a single instance, the aggregation of SHAP values can provide insights on the overall impact of a feature. The *magnitude* of a feature's impact is the sum of its SHAP values across many examples, regardless of its positive/negative impact (absolute value). We chose SHAP because it worked better with the sparse count-based features than LIME (Ribeiro et al., 2016).

4.2 Features Indicative of Civil Unrest

The magnitude of a feature's SHAP values across many examples provides insight into features the model deems important to decision making. In this case, a feature is the raw number of times a token appeared in all the tweets for a country for a day. To evaluate country generalizability we check the top features for a specific country, Myanmar, and all 42 countries in the dataset (including Myanmar). The SHAP values are from all Myanmar samples in the test set and 500 samples from all countries. All samples are pulled from the test set, years 2018–2019. The top features are in Table 2.

In general, the majority of the words deemed informative by the model for all 42 countries are related to human rights and civil unrest (e.g., "government", "casualties"). The majority of top features are not country-specific (other than "rohingya"), indicating that the country debiasing was a success. There is high overlap between the top tokens for all countries and those for Myanmar. However, in Myanmar we see features indicative of the Rohingya crisis (i.e., "rohingya", "burma", "terrorist", "military").[11] Unlike the international features, these are very specific and clearly describe the events in the country for 2018-19. This high overlap is interesting considering Myanmar comprised only 2.4% of the test set.

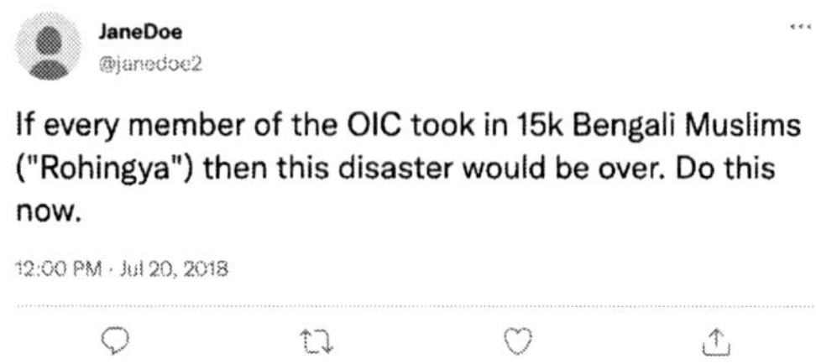

Figure 6: Tweet representative of civil unrest in Myanmar. Queried using aggregate SHAP feature importance as token weight. Paraphrased for privacy.

To find tweets representative of civil unrest in Myanmar, we use the average SHAP feature values as weights for each token and query the tweets with this weight system. The result provided very relevant tweets, as seen in Figure 6.

We also evaluate whether the country "debiasing" improved the generalization of the model. From Table 3 we see the non-debiased model (with location stopwords) outperforms the debiased model across train, validation, and test sets. However, when looking at the distribution of scores for each country, we see the debiasing did improve the model's performance on previously low scoring countries (Appendix Figure 10). Essentially debiasing spreads the model's performance more equally across countries, instead of only performing very well on a minority. In a specific example from Ethiopia, the effects from debiasing are clear (Figure 7). Although we learned from the case study in §3 that Ethiopians rallied around location-specific hashtags for the Burayu massacre, the features learned by the model could not transfer to other countries (i.e., "addis", "ethiopia"). The features after debiasing are much more general, including "media", "inhuman", and "injured".

We aimed to find features that generalize across countries, and from the international analysis on all countries, we did find features beyond the obvious keywords "protest" and "war." It was also promising that the international features overlapped with the important Myanmar features.

5 Ethical Considerations

Twitter is a commonly used social media source for studying and forecasting civil unrest. The main ethical concerns over this use of Twitter data is user privacy and bias in event information. For user privacy, we paraphrased tweet content to reduce

[11] https://www.unicef.org/emergencies/rohingya-crisis

All Countries	Myanmar
human, **country**, **world**, **years**, **media**, **hope**, situation, **government**, read, **rohingya**, **feel**, **rights**, casualties, true, police, watch, **time**, day, call, national	burma, **rohingya**, **world**, **media**, **country**, **human**, military, **years**, terrorist, **hope**, **feel**, **government**, group, war, day, **time**, today, plz, **rights**, official

Table 2: Top 20 features according to SHAP values from (1) 500 samples from all countries and (2) all Myanmar samples. Samples drawn from the test set (2018-19). The majority of the important tokens directly relate to human crisis and civil unrest, and the top Myanmar features describe the Rohingya crisis. Importance determined by the magnitude of SHAP values. The all countries sample is class-balanced.

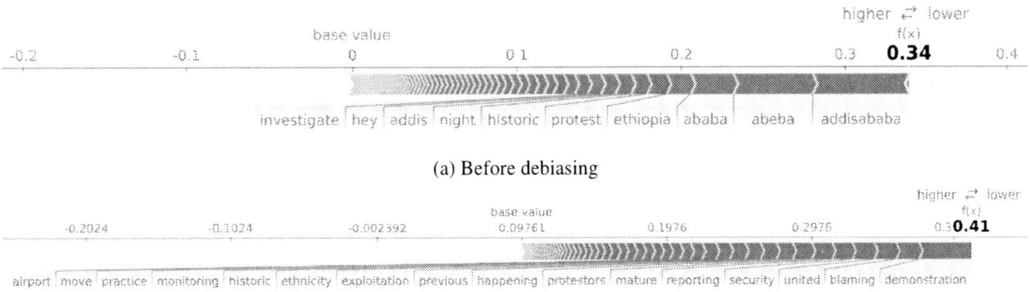

(a) Before debiasing

(b) After debiasing

Figure 7: Individual SHAP output on days of the Burayu Massacre protests in Ethiopia before and after country debiasing (i.e., removing location-specific words). While the overall model performance dropped 0.05 F1, the most important features became more generalizable and informative.

	F1	Precision	Recall
N-gram	0.45	0.58	0.37
N-gram (biased)	0.50	0.61	0.42
Random	0.29	0.32	0.27

Table 3: F1 scores for the civil unrest detection task. Ground truth labels are from ACLED Riots and Protests. Only test scores are shown (2018-2019). See Appendix Table 5 for train and validation scores.

reverse identification of users (Ayers et al., 2018).

The bias in event information can stem from the language of study, user misinformation, and outside information from inaccurate geotags (tweet location). Language can proxy status in certain countries, providing different viewpoints depending on the studied language. Also, tweet content is not fact-checked and may contain misleading or incomplete information. This misinformation is not necessarily malicious, but could warp observers' perceptions of events. This is very important to note if Twitter is being used to identify event information and details, as opposed to a reputable news source. Claims made by Twitter users should be attempted to be verified before being treated as fact.

Misleading information can also come from users outside of the country. Inaccurate geotags can come from the use of a VPN, which masks a user's true location. VPNs are commonly used to circumvent government-authorized social media shutdowns, especially in countries present in our analysis.[12] A user could potentially tweet about the situation in their country, but it would be aggregated with the tweets for a different country based on the geotag information.

6 Conclusion

There are ample real-time systems and research using Twitter to forecast civil unrest, but not many studies step back and evaluate the *manifestation* of civil unrest on Twitter, especially across countries. In this work we presented a mix of qualitative in-depth case studies of events in two countries, and a quantitative large-scale automatic detection of civil unrest events across 42 countries. This evaluation of civil unrest on Twitter is not comprehensive, but demonstrates some concerns of using Twitter for civil unrest detection across countries.

From the case studies of the Johannesburg riots

[12]https://www.top10vpn.com/cost-of-internet-shutdowns/

in South Africa and the Burayu massacre protests in Ethiopia, we find there is presence of event-related discussion for both events. In South Africa there was clear development of event-specific hashtags, but the hashtags in Ethiopia were very generic, mostly using location words. Gradual rise in civil unrest-related discussion before the large event was not able to be identified in either country, indicating users see Twitter as a reactionary platform, i.e., share their opinions in real-time or after the event. This is an important finding for work that uses Twitter data to forecast civil unrest events days or weeks in advance.

While the case studies did not unearth immediately generalizable patterns indicative of civil unrest, our n-gram model trained on Twitter data from 42 countries did find generalizable token-based patterns. Despite the low F1 score (0.5 for the highest performing non-country debiased model), the top tokens were related to civil unrest and human rights crises.

For future work we would expand the case studies to other languages, possibly even comparing event manifestation between languages. Also, we would explore explainability techniques for more powerful embedding-based models. We also only focused on large-scale events and did not evaluate the model's ability to detect small-scale events.

Acknowledgments

The authors thank Arya McCarthy, Keziah Naggita, Sougol Gheissi, Rachel Wicks, Elizabeth Salesky, and the anonymous reviewers for their feedback. This work relates to Department of Navy award N00014-19-1-2316 issued by the Office of Naval Research. The United States Government has a royalty-free license throughout the world in all copyrightable material contained herein. Any opinions, findings, and conclusions or recommendations expressed in this material are those of the author(s) and do not necessarily reflect the views of the Office of Naval Research.

References

Nasser Alsaedi, Pete Burnap, and Omer Rana. 2017. Can We Predict a Riot? Disruptive Event Detection Using Twitter. *ACM Transactions on Internet Technology*, 17(2):1–26.

John W. Ayers, Theodore L. Caputi, Camille Nebeker, and Mark Dredze. 2018. Don't quote me: reverse identification of research participants in social media studies. *npj Digital Medicine*, 1(1):1–2. Number: 1 Publisher: Nature Publishing Group.

Lalindra De Silva and Ellen Riloff. 2014. User Type Classification of Tweets with Implications for Event Recognition. In *Proceedings of the Joint Workshop on Social Dynamics and Personal Attributes in Social Media*, pages 98–108, Baltimore, Maryland. Association for Computational Linguistics.

Alexandra DeLucia. 2020. AADeLucia/littlebird. Original-date: 2020-04-24T00:15:07Z.

Amosse Edouard. 2018. *Event detection and analysis on short text messages*. Ph.D. thesis.

Kamrul Islam, Manjur Ahmed, Kamal Z. Zamli, and Salman Mehbub. 2020. An online framework for civil unrest prediction using tweet stream based on tweet weight and event diffusion.

Rostyslav Korolov, Di Lu, Jingjing Wang, Guangyu Zhou, Claire Bonial, Clare Voss, Lance Kaplan, William Wallace, Jiawei Han, and Heng Ji. 2016. On predicting social unrest using social media. In *2016 IEEE/ACM International Conference on Advances in Social Networks Analysis and Mining (ASONAM)*, pages 89–95, San Francisco, CA, USA. IEEE.

Kalev Leetaru and Philip A Schrodt. GDELT: Global Data on Events, Location and Tone,. page 51.

Justin Littman. 2018. Charlottesville Tweet Ids. Publisher: Harvard Dataverse type: dataset.

Marco Lui and Timothy Baldwin. 2012. langid.py: An Off-the-shelf Language Identification Tool. In *Proceedings of the ACL 2012 System Demonstrations*, pages 25–30, Jeju Island, Korea. Association for Computational Linguistics.

Scott M. Lundberg, Gabriel Erion, Hugh Chen, Alex DeGrave, Jordan M. Prutkin, Bala Nair, Ronit Katz, Jonathan Himmelfarb, Nisha Bansal, and Su-In Lee. 2020. From local explanations to global understanding with explainable AI for trees. *Nature Machine Intelligence*, 2(1):56–67. Number: 1 Publisher: Nature Publishing Group.

Scott M. Lundberg and Su-In Lee. 2017. A Unified Approach to Interpreting Model Predictions. *Advances in Neural Information Processing Systems*, 30.

Sathappan Muthiah, Bert Huang, Jaime Arredondo, David Mares, Lise Getoor, Graham Katz, and Naren Ramakrishnan. 2015. Planned Protest Modeling in News and Social Media. In *Twenty-Seventh IAAI Conference*.

M. Osborne and Mark Dredze. 2014. Facebook, Twitter and Google Plus for Breaking News: Is There a Winner? In *ICWSM*.

Fabian Pedregosa, Gael Varoquaux, Alexandre Gramfort, Vincent Michel, Bertrand Thirion, Olivier Grisel, Mathieu Blondel, Peter Prettenhofer, Ron Weiss, Vincent Dubourg, Jake Vanderplas, Alexandre Passos, and David Cournapeau. 2011. Scikit-learn: Machine Learning in Python. *Journal of Machine Learning Research*, 12:2825–2830.

Jeffrey Pennington, Richard Socher, and Christopher Manning. 2014. Glove: Global Vectors for Word Representation. In *Proceedings of the 2014 Conference on Empirical Methods in Natural Language Processing (EMNLP)*, pages 1532–1543, Doha, Qatar. Association for Computational Linguistics.

Clionadh Raleigh, Andrew Linke, Håvard Hegre, and Joakim Karlsen. 2010. Introducing ACLED: An Armed Conflict Location and Event Dataset: Special Data Feature. *Journal of Peace Research*. Publisher: SAGE PublicationsSage UK: London, England.

Naren Ramakrishnan, Gizem Korkmaz, Chris Kuhlman, Achla Marathe, Liang Zhao, Ting Hua, Feng Chen, Chang Tien Lu, Bert Huang, Aravind Srinivasan, Khoa Trinh, Patrick Butler, Lise Getoor, Graham Katz, Andy Doyle, Chris Ackermann, Ilya Zavorin, Jim Ford, Kristen Summers, Youssef Fayed, Jaime Arredondo, Dipak Gupta, Sathappan Muthiah, David Mares, Nathan Self, Rupinder Khandpur, Parang Saraf, Wei Wang, Jose Cadena, and Anil Vullikanti. 2014. 'Beating the news' with EMBERS: forecasting civil unrest using open source indicators. In *Proceedings of the 20th ACM SIGKDD international conference on Knowledge discovery and data mining - KDD '14*, pages 1799–1808, New York, New York, USA. ACM Press.

Suhas Ranganath, Fred Morstatter, Xia Hu, Jiliang Tang, and Huan Liu. 2016. Predicting Online Protest Participation of Social Media Users. *AAAI Press*, page 7.

Marco Tulio Ribeiro, Sameer Singh, and Carlos Guestrin. 2016. "Why Should I Trust You?": Explaining the Predictions of Any Classifier. In *Proceedings of the 22nd ACM SIGKDD International Conference on Knowledge Discovery and Data Mining*, pages 1135–1144, San Francisco California USA. ACM.

Justin Sech, Alexandra DeLucia, Anna L. Buczak, and Mark Dredze. 2020. Civil Unrest on Twitter (CUT): A Dataset of Tweets to Support Research on Civil Unrest. In *Proceedings of the Sixth Workshop on Noisy User-generated Text (W-NUT 2020)*, pages 215–221, Online. Association for Computational Linguistics.

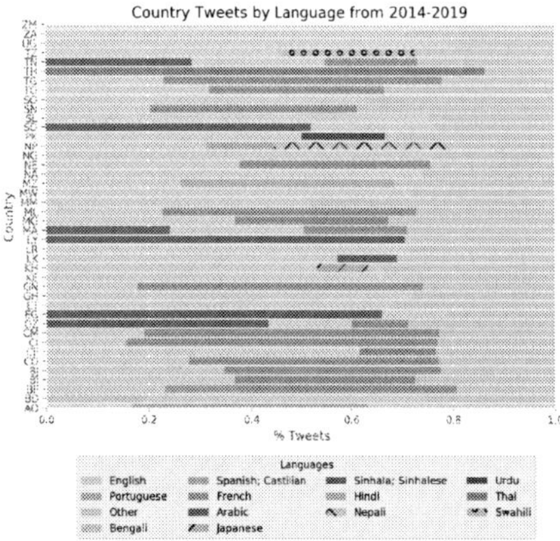

Figure 8: The language breakdown (in percentages) of Twitter data from all 42 countries. All languages that covered less than 10% of the country's tweets grouped as "other". Languages were identified with `langid` (Lui and Baldwin, 2012).

A Twitter Dataset Details

The exact number of tweets per country in the Twitter dataset are in Table 4. The country is identified by its ISO 3166 alpha-3 code. The civil unrest filtration removes many tweets, but ensures the case study qualitative analysis only looks at relevant data. We also include a language breakdown of all tweets from the initial collection in Figure 8. The choice of English covers many countries, but expansion into Arabic and French would be beneficial to future work.

B Case Study Unfiltered Analysis

§3 analyzed the Twitter content around the selected events in South Africa and Ethiopia using the restricted set of filtered tweets. As discussed in §2, the "filtered" tweets are those identified by the (Sech et al., 2020) BERTweet filtration model as being related to civil unrest (i.e., score above 0.5). As seen in Figure 9, the filtration step was necessary to reduce dataset size for the manual qualitative analysis presented in this work.

In South Africa, the hashtags from unfiltered tweets contain more general content such as references to popular TV shows (`#bbnaija`, `#uyajola99`, `#idolsa`) and tourism (`#southafrica`, `#capetown`). However, the protest-centered hashtags were so popular that they remain popular even in the unfiltered list. In Ethiopia, there is overlap between the filtered and unfiltered top hashtags, but the very informative `#etv` is not on the list.

C Comparing Aggregated Twitter Content and Event Descriptions

The tweet representations and the event descriptions were matched based on cosine similarity and the matching was evaluated with mean reciprocal rank (MRR). MRR is a score between $(0, 1]$, where 1 means the correct answer is ranked first (i.e., most similar), but the score approaches 0 the lower the rank of the correct answer.

We tried two different representations: (1) n-gram-based and (2) embedding-based (Twitter GloVe (Pennington et al., 2014)). The filtered tweets over the period of a month in South Africa were aggregated by day (September 2019), represented as a vector of either (1) raw token counts or (2) average GloVe embeddings, and then compared to the ACLED event descriptions from the same time period. Tweets were preprocessed with `littlebird` (DeLucia, 2020). Only days with events were included and if more than one event happened on a single day then the descriptions were aggregated into one. Unfortunately neither representation provided good results, as both had MRR scores around 0.15. The GloVe representation and N-gram representation has scores of 0.14 and 0.15, respectively. This indicates events could not be accurately paired with their corresponding days. We believe this is due to the sheer amount of data being aggregated, since South Africa has many tweets. In the case of the embedding representation, each day is the average tweet representation, which in turn is the average of its token representations.

D Country Debiasing

As discovered from the initial civil unrest prediction results, the model learned country and location tokens as proxies for civil unrest. While the model performs reasonably well on the prediction task, the important features indicate it cannot generalize to new data from other countries.

We debias the model by re-training it on a "scrubbed" version of the tweets with removed location words. We create two location stopword lists. One stopword list is manually curated from the country, state/province, and city names in the ACLED data. Following the Ethiopia example from Figure 7, this list includes "ethiopia" and "ad-

AGO	289,373 / 16,639	BDI	25,041 / 6,097	BEN	150,348 / 16,489
BFA	50,197 / 4,327	BGD	2,318,969 / 330,947	CAF	28,723 / 2,860
CIV	564,197 / 34,286	CMR	833,795 / 71,420	COD	251,430 / 27,920
DZA	1,561,362 / 150,084	EGY	8,845,187 / 608,977	ETH	261,202 / 59,111
GHA	11,772,277 / 1,711,557	GIN	68,168 / 4,652	KEN	11,837,021 / 2,451,866
KHM	658,744 / 86,021	LBR	114,329 / 20,267	LBY	674,195 / 55,177
LKA	2,312,676 / 320,593	MAR	2,155,938 / 243,772	MDG	118,673 / 10,622
MLI	77,523 / 6,782	MMR	552,406 / 81,130	MOZ	349,321 / 31,634
MWI	780,767 / 101,891	NAM	1,881,238 / 238,720	NER	58,960 / 5,220
NGA	48,954,857 / 9,660,532	NPL	1,789,592 / 239,200	PAK	15,927,538 / 2,966,772
SDN	743,925 / 55,151	SEN	684,381 / 40,840	SLE	131,235 / 19,460
SOM	215,610 / 60,061	TCD	26,951 / 2,577	TGO	58,253 / 8,254
THA	14,661,060 / 980,846	TUN	944,833 / 87,903	TZA	2,216,871 / 248,856
UGA	3,274,687 / 638,372	ZAF	72,155,722 / 9,323,649	ZMB	1,706,438 / 246,815

Table 4: English tweets per country. The counts are aggregated over the 6 year period 2014-2019. The overall English tweet count and the filtered English tweet counts are shown (separated by "/"). Countries are identified by their ISO 3166 alpha-3 code.

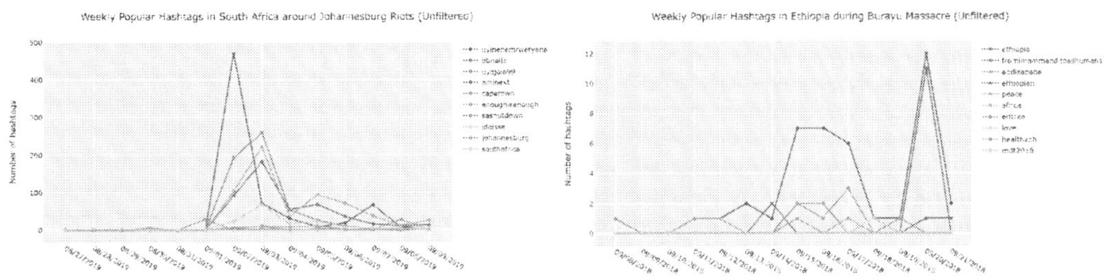

(a) South Africa

(b) Ethiopia

Figure 9: Popular hashtags in South Africa and Ethiopia from the one week period of the Johannesburg riots and Burayu Massacre, respectively. Hashtag frequency is calculated from all English tweets, not only filtered tweets.

dis ababa"[13], but not adjectives such as "ethiopian". The second stopword list is automatically created by using the same civil unrest prediction setup, but we changed the prediction task to tweet country origin. The stopword list is comprised of the features that SHAP identifies as having > 0.005 contribution towards the prediction. Example top features from the most identifiable countries are in Table 7. We compared the two feature sets of 10,000 tokens produced by the two debiasing methods. The union of the two feature sets have a size of 10,630 while the size of intersection is 9,374, thus giving a Jaccard similarity of 0.882.

The country prediction model (same setup as the civil unrest prediction model with n-grams and random forest) achieved an F1, precision, and recall of $0.8, 0.69$ and 0.97, respectively. For comparison, we evaluated the country prediction performance after removing the ACLED location words. That model achieved scores of $0.09/0.13/0.07$ F1/precision/recall. At first glance it appears that only the ACLED location stoplist is sufficient, but the model was able to identify a handful of countries with very high accuracy. The top features for this model are in Table 6. However, due to poorer model performance with the SHAP stoplist, we used the ACLED location stoplist for the prediction experiments in §4. We believe the SHAP stoplist removed too many informative words.

[13]The alternative spacings of the tokens are also included, such as "addisababa".

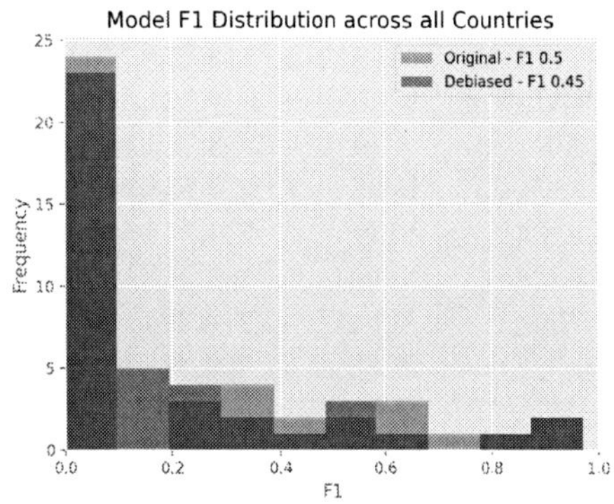

Figure 10: Distribution of F1 scores across 42 countries for the n-gram civil unrest detection task. The original "biased" and "debiased" models are compared.

	F1	Precision	Recall
N-gram	0.73	0.85	0.64
	0.46	0.56	0.39
	0.45	0.58	0.37
N-gram (with location stopwords)	0.84	0.87	0.81
	0.53	0.57	0.51
	0.50	0.61	0.42
Random	0.27	0.27	0.27
	0.27	0.28	0.27
	0.29	0.32	0.27

Table 5: Precision-recall metrics from the n-gram model trained to predict civil unrest in a country for a day. Ground truth are riot and protest labels from ACLED. Scores shown for each model are train, validation, and test, respectively (top to bottom).

Kenya	**Nigeria**	**Pakistan**
kenyan	hit	hit
hit	job	basic
basic	basic	job
job	beaten	dear
force	dear	qatar
dear	qatar	peak
broken	broken	broken
carry	beef	force
ktn	condolence	love
beaten	salaries	blood
South Africa	**Ghana**	**Uganda**
hit	basic	force
basic	force	time
job	hit	dear
branches	broken	hit
kzn	time	broken
beaten	mining	shame
condolence	shame	basic
love	twitter	water
broken	dear	twitter
piss	barking	barking

Table 6: Top 10 features with the largest magnitude of SHAP value for countries that are easy to predict even after removing ACLED location stopwords.

Kenya	Nigeria	Pakistan
ruto	abeg	pti
news	pls	kpk
reason	stop	pakistanis
hii	guys	army
guys	security	pakistan's
court	jonathan	asif
security	court	stop
years	years	court
long	army	years
stop	wike	security
South Africa	**Ghana**	**Uganda**
soweto	ghanaians	reason
zuma	citicbs	news
saps	mahama	ugandans
guys	news	croozefmnews
anymore	reason	mps
there's	smh	court
court	what's	dead
years	court	life
reason	ndc	govt
hayi	govt	shd

	No debias	Debiased
Kenya	0.97/1.00/0.95	0.97/0.99/0.95
Nigeria	0.97/1.00/0.94	0.97/1.00/0.94
Pakistan	0.97/1.00/0.95	0.97/0.99/0.95
South Africa	0.97/1.00/0.93	0.97/1.00/0.93
Ghana	0.99/1.00/0.98	0.96/0.96/0.97
Uganda	0.98/0.99/0.96	0.88/0.84/0.93

Table 7: Top 10 features with the largest magnitude of SHAP value for countries that are easy to predict (top), as well as the country prediction scores before and after debiasing (bottom).

The Korean Morphologically Tight-Fitting Tokenizer for Noisy User-Generated Texts

Sangah Lee and **Hyopil Shin**
Graduate School of Data Science
Seoul National University
{visualjan, hpshin}@snu.ac.kr

Abstract

User-generated texts include various types of stylistic properties, or noises. Such texts are not properly processed by existing morpheme analyzers or language models based on formal texts such as encyclopedias or news articles. In this paper, we propose a simple morphologically tight-fitting tokenizer (K-MT) that can better process proper nouns, coinages, and internet slang among other types of noise in Korean user-generated texts. We tested our tokenizer by performing classification tasks on Korean user-generated movie reviews and hate speech datasets, and the Korean Named Entity Recognition dataset. Through our tests, we found that K-MT is better fit to process internet slangs, proper nouns, and coinages, compared to a morpheme analyzer and a character-level WordPiece tokenizer.

1 Introduction

User-generated texts such as internet forums, product reviews, blog posts, tweets, and comments include various types of noise coming from their stylistic properties. Noise such as internet slang, spelling errors, and emojis may not be properly processed by traditional morpheme analyzers and language models, since such models are trained on formal texts such as books, encyclopedias, or news articles. User-generated texts that include such properties are useful to analyze public opinion on a variety of topics, products, policies, and so on.

Noise in texts may vary in their forms with different languages, even though they are common to some degree. For example, emphasized opinion can be written capitalized in English, while many exclamation marks are used in Korean as in an example: 하지마hacima!!!!!!!! "DON'T DO IT!". Such noise has to be processed, rather than removed, depending on the purpose.

Accordingly, we analyzed various Korean user-generated texts and obtained an unexhaustive list of noise types observed in such texts: spacing errors, spelling errors, grammatical errors, special characters and emojis, Korean grapheme characters, foreign language characters, newly-listed proper nouns, coinage, and internet slang. Korean grapheme characters such as 'ㅋㅋ,' 'ㅠㅠ' are often used and function as emojis.

In this paper, we focus on proper nouns, coinages, and internet slang among other types of noise from user-generated texts. We propose a Korean Morphologically Tight-Fitting Tokenizer, K-MT, which is expected to be robust in processing such types of noises. We compare the performance of our K-MT with a Korean morpheme analyzer and a character-based WordPiece tokenizer (Wu et al., 2016) through experiments on Korean movie reviews, a hate speech dataset, and a named entity recognition dataset.

Our major contributions are:

- A noise-friendly tokenizer using Korean morphological knowledge
- A simple algorithm using a dictionary of grammatical morphemes and a rule-based method

2 Related Work

2.1 Studies on Noisy Texts

Noises can be defined differently according to tasks, types of datasets, domains, and purposes. Michel and Neubig (2018) provided types of noises observed in social media texts and focused on spelling and grammatical errors, emojis, and profanities to perform machine translation. Sjöblom et al. (2018) defined noises for subtitles including misspellings, misalignments, and sentence segmentation errors. Agarwal et al. (2020) summarized noise types in free-text answers written by Hindi children, such as punctuations, emojis, translated/transliterated text, missing space between words, and so on. Some other works focused on orthographical noises (Karpukhin et al., 2019; Kumar et al., 2020).

Proceedings of the 2021 EMNLP Workshop W-NUT: The Seventh Workshop on Noisy User-generated Text, pages 410–416
November 11, 2021. ©2021 Association for Computational Linguistics

In the case of Korean, there has not been an explicit trend of research on Korean noisy texts. Han et al. (2019) performed a bias classification task on user-generated news comments, while they did not consider noisy linguistic features in the text. However, several user-generated corpora have recently been released, including Naver Sentiment Movie Corpus (NSMC)[1], Hate Speech Dataset (Moon et al., 2020), and various corpora released by the National Institute of Korean Language. In addition, some BERT-based models were trained on such corpora (Lee, 2020; Lee and Shin, 2021), whose vocabularies include domain-specific tokens and stylistic features such as internet slangs and emojis, different from tokens in formal texts like books or news articles.

2.2 Korean Tokenization

For Korean text processing, morpheme-level tokenization is commonly used because a morpheme is the smallest meaningful unit in Korean (Park et al., 2018, 2019). And following BERT (Devlin et al., 2019), character-based subword tokens of the WordPiece model have been popular in Korean (KoBERT[2], KorBERT[3], KR-BERT (Lee et al., 2020)). However, such subword tokens are too fine-grained and sometimes do not properly reflect meanings and properties of the Korean language (Lee et al., 2020). To alleviate this issue in noisy texts and in former works, sub-character tokens smaller than syllables are considered (Lee et al., 2018, 2020; Moon and Okazaki, 2020), since Korean morphemes' boundaries are not only between syllables but also graphemes.

Morpheme-based WordPiece tokenizers are also used and show better performance than character-based BERT models (HanBERT[4], KorBERT). Park et al. (2020) reported that morpheme-aware subword tokenization shows the best performance among various units of tokens. However, it requires the addition of an external morpheme analyzer before the application of language models or BERT tokenizers. Therefore, we attempt to imitate the morpheme-based tokenization with our morpheme-like tokenizer, which is simply designed based on grammatical morphemes and their combination rules, while considering stylistic properties and noises of user-generated texts.

[1] https://github.com/e9t/nsmc

[2] https://github.com/SKTBrain/KoBERT

[3] https://aiopen.etri.re.kr/

[4] https://github.com/tbai2019/HanBert-54k-N

3 Korean Morphologically Tight-fitting Tokenizer (K-MT)

As an agglutinative language, Korean words consist of combinations of root and affix to represent each word's grammatical function in a sentence. For example, a root word 소녀 sonye "girl" can be combined with various suffixes: 소녀 sonye 가 ka "girl (subj)" and 소녀 sonye 를 lul "girl (obj)." Each of the root and affix is a morpheme, an important basic unit representing meanings in Korean, making Korean a morphologically rich language. Therefore, morpheme-based tokens better reflect meanings and obtain better performances than other tokenization units in general. However, as morpheme analysis of texts requires extra preprocessing using external morpheme taggers, we propose our Korean Morphologically Tight-Fitting Tokenizer (K-MT) with a much simpler rule-based algorithm and coarse-grained token boundaries.

For each word segment split by whitespace, we separate suffixes by matching with a pre-defined list of grammatical morphemes in a backward direction. After all possible suffixes are separated, we obtain a root and use it as an individual token. The pre-defined suffix list consists of frequent connectives and sentence-final endings used more than 100 times extracted from Kkma morpheme analyzer[5] and postpositional particles and pre-final endings used in Mecab-ko morpheme analyzer[6]. We additionally include ending forms used in online, user-generated texts such as -여 ye and -용 yong which are originally -요 yo. The list of grammatical morphemes used in our tokenizer can be found in Appendix A.

# of Suffixes	Suffix Combination
2	었ess/았ass + *E*
3	(으u)시si + 었ess + *E*
	었ess/았ass + 겠keyss + E
4	(으u)시si + 었ess + 겠keyss + *E*

Table 1: Suffix Combination Rules (Choi, 2012)

We separate such suffixes not only by simple string matching but also using the suffix combination rules constructed referring to Choi (2012),

[5] http://kkma.snu.ac.kr/

[6] https://bitbucket.org/eunjeon/mecab-ko

as in Table 1. Choi (2012) statistically patternized grammatical morphemes that are frequently combined. In Table 1, E represents all the connectives and final endings in the pre-defined list and the other morphemes like 었ess are pre-final endings. While we preferentially match longer morphemes by default, we prioritize the morpheme sequences matched with the suffix combination patterns in Table 1.

According to the algorithm, our K-MT tokenizes an example sentence 나는 학교에 간다. "I go to school." as below. This tokenized result is the same as morpheme-based tokenization.

나 는 학교 에 간다 .
na nun hakkyo ey kanta .
I (subj) school to go .

Because we regard a word segment's root token as the remaining part of the word other than the suffix, any rare, new-listed words such as domain-specific words and coinages are not incorrectly divided into subwords. Moreover, while WordPiece tokens can include a whole word segment like 소녀가 sonyeka "girl (subj)" depending on frequency, our tokenizer always separates and preserves the form of root 소녀 sonye "girl" based on morphological knowledge. Compared to including all related forms derived from one root token, this method can make the composition of the vocabulary more diverse while maintaining the vocabulary size.

4 Experiments and Analysis

To evaluate our K-MT, we compare the tokenized results with those of Mecab-ko, a Korean morpheme analyzer, and a character-based subword tokenizer, WordPiece. Mecab-ko is an upper bound model in this paper, and our goal is to construct a simpler tokenizer imitating the elaborated morpheme analyzer as possible.

First, we selected two popular noisy, user-generated datasets: Naver Sentiment Movie Corpus (NSMC) and Hate Speech Dataset (HSD). Both datasets include most of the noise types we briefly mentioned in section 1. NSMC includes binary sentiment polarity labels, positive and negative, on each film review and consists of 13K, 2K, and 5K reviews for training, validation, and test set. HSD consists of 7,896, 471, and 974 news comments for training, validation, and test set, respectively. We performed two different tasks on HSD: bias classification (whether a comment includes 'gender' bias, 'other' types of bias, or 'none') and hate speech detection (whether a comment includes 'hate' speech, less hateful but 'offensive' speech, or 'none').

For the three tasks, we applied a simple 3-layer CNN model. We limited the size of vocabulary for all the tokenizers to 25,000 and used a batch size of 64, an embedding dimension of 128, 128 convolutional filters, and a dropout of 0.2. We used an Adam optimizer and Cross-Entropy loss and trained the model for 10 epochs. Table 2 shows the classification accuracies of the three tokenizers on the tasks. Since the labels for the HSD test set are not publicly released, so we report the performance on the validation set only.

Tokenizer	NSMC valid	NSMC test	HSD hate	HSD bias
Mecab-ko (upper bound)	**84.83**	**84.74**	**56.69**	**76.86**
WordPiece	83.62	83.42	44.37	74.10
K-MT (ours)	82.41	81.89	51.38	68.58

Table 2: Performances on User-Generated Text Datasets

The morpheme-level tokens obtained from Mecab-ko would contribute to the highest accuracies, since morphemes reflect the properties and meanings of the Korean language the best. WordPiece tokenizer obtained slightly lower accuracies than Mecab-ko, and our K-MT closely follows WordPiece, reporting accuracies of 82.41 and 81.89 for the validation set and the test set, respectively.

In the two tasks on the HSD dataset, the three tokenizers show larger differences in performance, where Mecab-ko, the upper bound model, reports the best accuracies. While the WordPiece tokenizer generally obtained higher accuracies than K-MT, K-MT performed better than WordPiece in hate speech detection.

In addition, we performed a Named Entity Recognition task with the three tokenizers above. We used the publicly released training set[7] from the Naver NLP Challenge 2018, dividing it into 76,949, 4,050, and 8,999 sentences for each of the training set, validation set, and test set. The named entity labels include 14 types of named entities: person, field, organization, location, artificial objects, cultural terms, date, time, number, event, animal, plant, material, other terms, and none.

The NER dataset includes various named entity words and rarely includes other types of noises like

[7] http://air.changwon.ac.kr/?pageid=10

spacing errors. We included this experiment since our K-MT is expected to work well in separating and preserving proper nouns and named entities which are likely to be newly-encountered domain-specific words in texts.

We applied a simple 2-layer RNN model. We used a batch size of 64, an embedding dimension of 100, a hidden dimension of 128, and a dropout of 0.25. We used an Adam optimizer and Cross-Entropy loss and trained the model for 10 epochs. Table 3 shows the classification accuracies of the three tokenizers on the task.

Tokenizer	25K tokens valid	25K tokens test	all tokens valid	all tokens test
Mecab-ko (upper bound)	67.41	67.61	70.36	70.64
WordPiece	**67.57**	**68.02**	-	-
K-MT (ours)	63.02	63.37	**72.78**	**73.05**

Table 3: Performances on the NER Dataset

When we first limited the size of vocabulary for all the tokenizers as 25,000, we observed the best accuracies of 67.57 and 68.02 for validation and test set with WordPiece tokenization, and similar performance with Mecab-ko. Our K-MT had marginally lower accuracies of 63.02 and 63.37 for the validation and the test set, respectively.

On the other hand, we used unlimited tokens for the models' vocabulary with Mecab-ko and K-MT to remove the effect of the out-of-vocabulary problem. Then we obtained higher accuracies; especially, K-MT reported a validation accuracy of 72.78 and a test accuracy of 73.05, which are higher than Mecab-ko. This indicates the potential of our tokenizer to be robust to newly-listed terms, proper nouns, and named entities in user-generated texts.

To analyze the performance of K-MT, we took 500 random samples from each of the NSMC, HSD, and NER datasets for tokenization. First, we quantitively compared the tokenization of the different tokenizers. Table 4 represents the ratio of samples that were tokenized identically by all the tokenizers. In general, the agreement between tokenizations is very low, which represents the how differently each token splits the sentences. However, our K-MT and Mecab-ko agree in 3.2% of the example tokenizations, which is higher than other tokenizer pairs. This indicates that our purpose of imitating the morpheme-based tokenizer by K-MT is effective to some degree.

Table 5 shows the average length of tokenized sentences (the number of tokens) of each tokenizer.

Tokenizer Pair	Agreement Ratio
Mecab-ko & WordPiece	1.0%
Mecab-ko & K-MT	**3.2%**
WordPiece & K-MT	1.0%
overall	0.73%

Table 4: Agreement Ratio of Tokenization

Here, the tokenized sentences of K-MT had the shortest average sentence length, with the average number of tokens being 53.094. The short length indicates that K-MT avoids oversegmenting words, possibly because its tokens may be longer than that of other tokenizers.

Tokenizer	Average Number of Tokens
Mecab-ko	56.997
WordPiece	65.447
K-MT	53.094

Table 5: Average Number of Tokens Tokenized by each Tokenizer

In general, our K-MT is good at tokenizing words in Korean including:

- Proper nouns or named entities: even in cases of very unusual names or names with typos where WordPiece and Mecab-ko failed to separate correctly.
  - 정기순 cengkiswun (name of a person) 까지 kkaci "even"
  - 천년유혼 chennyenyuhon (error of 천녀유혼 chennyeyuhon (name of a film))
- Internet slang: K-MT works well similarly to WordPiece and Mecab-ko.
  - 이뻐 ippe "(a variated form of) pretty" 용 yong (a variated form of final ending)

However, K-MT does not work well with:

- Cases with spacing errors: K-MT is based on word segments separated by whitespaces. If multiple words are adjoined without spaces, it cannot properly separate suffixes, while WordPiece and Mecab-ko worked to some degree.
- Cases with new suffixes not included in the pre-defined list
- Since we simply match all the suffixes in the pre-defined list, some of them may be incorrectly matched and separated from the word segment.

Word	Tokenization
차광남 chakwangnam personal name	(Mecab-ko) 차광chakwang 남nam (WordPiece) 차cha 광kwang 남nam (K-MT) 차광남chakwangnam
김유미의 kimyumiuy personal name (kimyumi) - genitive (uy)	(Mecab-ko) 김유미kimyumi 의uy (WordPiece) 김유kimyu 미의miuyi (K-MT) 김유미kimyumi 의uy
갑산공원 kapsankongwen location (kapsan) - "park" (kongwen)	(Mecab-ko) 갑산kapsan 공원kongwen (WordPiece) 갑kap 산san 공원kongwen (K-MT) 갑산공원kapsankongwen

Table 6: Tokenization of Proper Nouns

Word	Tokenization
국제농구연맹 kwukceynongkwuyenmayng International Basketball Federation	(Mecab-ko) 국제kwukce 농구nongkwu 연맹yenmayng (WordPiece) 국제kwukce 농구nongkwu 연맹yenmayng (K-MT) 국제농구연맹kwukceynongkwuyenmayng
대학교육협의회 tayhakkyoyukhyepuyhoy University Education Council	(Mecab-ko) 대학tayhak 교육kyoyuk 협의회hyepuyhoy (WordPiece) 대학교tayhakkyo 육yuk 협의회hyepuyhoy (K-MT) 대학교육협의회tayhakkyoyukhyepuyhoy
참교육학부모회 chamkyoyukhakpwumohoy Parents' Association for True Education	(Mecab-ko) 참cham 교육kyoyuk 학부모회hakpwumohoy (WordPiece) 참cham 교육kyoyuk 학부hakpwu 모mo 회hoy (K-MT) 참교육학부모회chamkyoyukhakpwumohoy

Table 7: Tokenization of Compositional Named Entities

Since NSMC and HSD datasets include various types of noise, especially spacing errors, there may have been examples where our K-MT could not accurately tokenize text. Moreover, K-MT is not advantageous when dealing with texts of various domains because it uses a limited size of vocabulary without subword tokens, unlike WordPiece.

However, K-MT works well with newly-listed words and terms as in the NER dataset, which existing language models based on formal texts cannot properly tokenize. For example, Table 6 shows some examples, including proper nouns, where K-MT correctly preserves the meaningful form of tokens.

Table 7 includes examples of named entities that are composed of multiple common nouns but are used as proper nouns. While K-MT does not over-segment them, Mecab-ko splits them into common nouns, and WordPiece sometimes splits them into meaningless subword tokens.

Moreover, K-MT is based on a simpler algorithm than Mecab-ko and other morpheme analyzers, making it easier to combine with other kinds of recent tokenization models such as the WordPiece model.

5 Conclusion

We implemented a simple Korean morpheme-like tokenizer, K-MT, to deal especially with proper nouns, coinages, internet slangs, and newly-listed domain-specific words in user-generated texts. To evaluate the tokenizer, we performed classification tasks on movie reviews, comments on news articles, and a Named Entity Recognition dataset, and we compared the results with those of a morpheme analyzer and character-based WordPiece model. From the results, we observed that our K-MT works well with proper nouns, coinages, and internet slang, while it still needs to be improved for cases with spacing errors.

For future work, we will improve our tokenizer by considering context information beyond the word segment boundary and additional methods to deal with the spacing errors. Also, we plan to construct a better tokenization algorithm by combining K-MT with the WordPiece model as a hybrid method.

Acknowledgements

This work was supported by the Ministry of Education of the Republic of Korea and the National Research Foundation of Korea (NRF-2019S1A5A2A01036576).

References

Dolly Agarwal, Somya Gupta, and Nishant Baghel. 2020. Automated assessment of noisy crowd-sourced free-text answers for Hindi in low resource setting. In *Proceedings of the Sixth Workshop on Noisy User-generated Text (W-NUT 2020)*, pages 122–131.

Seok-jae Choi. 2012. The study of combined endings' condition. *Journal of Korean Linguistics*, 63:275–311.

Jacob Devlin, Ming-Wei Chang, Kenton Lee, and Kristina Toutanova. 2019. BERT: Pre-training of deep bidirectional transformers for language understanding. In *Proceedings of the 2019 Conference of the North American Chapter of the Association for Computational Linguistics: Human Language Technologies, Volume 1 (Long and Short Papers)*, pages 4171–4186.

Jiyoung Han, Youngin Lee, Junbum Lee, and Meeyoung Cha. 2019. The fallacy of echo chambers: Analyzing the political slants of user-generated news comments in Korean media. In *Proceedings of the 5th Workshop on Noisy User-generated Text (W-NUT 2019)*, pages 370–374.

Vladimir Karpukhin, Omer Levy, Jacob Eisenstein, and Marjan Ghazvininejad. 2019. Training on synthetic noise improves robustness to natural noise in machine translation. In *Proceedings of the 5th Workshop on Noisy User-generated Text (W-NUT 2019)*, pages 42–47.

Ankit Kumar, Piyush Makhija, and Anuj Gupta. 2020. Noisy text data: Achilles' heel of bert. In *Proceedings of the 2020 EMNLP Workshop W-NUT: The Sixth Workshop on Noisy User-generated Text*, pages 16–21.

Jae Jun Lee, Suhn Beom Kwon, and Sung Mahn Ahn. 2018. Sentiment analysis using deep learning model based on phoneme-level korean. *Journal of Information Technology Services*, 17:79–89.

Junbum Lee. 2020. Kcbert: Korean comments bert. In *Proceedings of the 32nd Annual Conference on Human and Cognitive Language Technology*, pages 437–440.

Sangah Lee, Hansol Jang, Yunmee Baik, Suzi Park, and Hyopil Shin. 2020. Kr-bert: A small-scale korean-specific language model. *ArXiv*, abs/2008.03979.

Sangah Lee and Hyopil Shin. 2021. Combining sentiment-combined model with pre-trained bert models for sentiment analysis. *Journal of KIISE*, 48:815–824.

Paul Michel and Graham Neubig. 2018. Mtnt: A testbed for machine translation of noisy text. In *Proceedings of the 2018 Conference on Empirical Methods in Natural Language Processing*, pages 543–553.

Jihyung Moon, Won Ik Cho, and Junbum Lee. 2020. BEEP! Korean corpus of online news comments for toxic speech detection. In *Proceedings of the Eighth International Workshop on Natural Language Processing for Social Media*, pages 25–31.

Sangwhan Moon and Naoaki Okazaki. 2020. Jamo pair encoding: Subcharacter representation-based extreme Korean vocabulary compression for efficient subword tokenization. In *Proceedings of the 12th Language Resources and Evaluation Conference*, pages 3490–3497.

Cheoneum Park, Dongheon Lee, Kihoon Kim, Changki Lee, and Hyunki Kim. 2019. Korean movie review sentiment analysis using self-attention and contextualized embedding. *Journal of KIISE*, 46:901–908.

Hyun-jung Park, Min-chae Song, and Kyung-shik Shin. 2018. Sentiment analysis of korean reviews using cnn: Focusing on morpheme embedding. *Journal of Intelligence and Information Systems*, 24:59–83.

Kyubyong Park, Joohong Lee, Seongbo Jang, and Dawoon Jung. 2020. An empirical study of tokenization strategies for various korean nlp tasks. In *Proceedings of the 1st Conference of the Asia-Pacific Chapter of the Association for Computational Linguistics and the 10th International Joint Conference on Natural Language Processing*, pages 133–142.

Eetu Sjöblom, Mathias Creutz, and Mikko Aulamo. 2018. Paraphrase detection on noisy subtitles in six languages. In *Proceedings of the 2018 EMNLP Workshop W-NUT: The 4th Workshop on Noisy User-generated Text*, pages 64–73.

Yonghui Wu, Mike Schuster, Zhifeng Chen, Quoc V Le, Mohammad Norouzi, Wolfgang Macherey, Maxim Krikun, Yuan Cao, Qin Gao, Klaus Macherey, et al. 2016. Google's neural machine translation system: Bridging the gap between human and machine translation. *arXiv preprint arXiv:1609.08144*.

A List of Grammatical Morphemes Used for K-MT

We provide an unexhaustive list of the grammatical morphemes we used for out K-MT in Table 8. The full list of morphemes are on the documentations of Kkma morpheme analyzer[8] and Mecab-ko morpheme analyzer[9]. We also provide the variated forms of grammatical morphemes used in noisy texts.

[8] `http://kkma.snu.ac.kr/statistic?submenu=morp`

[9] `https://bitbucket.org/eunjeon/mecab-ko`

Type	Morphemes
Word-Final Connective	고ko, 어e, 아a, 게key, 지ji, 면myen, 아서ase, 며mye, 다ta, 지만jiman, 면서myense, 는데nuntey, 다고tako, 어서ese, 라고lako, 라la, 아야aya, 어야eya, 으며umye, 다가taka
Word-Final Suffix	다ta, 습니다supnita, 어e, 어요eyo, 야ya, 지ci, 는다nunta, 아a, 죠cyo, 아요ayo, 지요ciyo, 는가nunka, 에요eyyo, 자ca, 을까ulkka, 냐nya, 오o, 니ni, 나na, 네ne
	(stylistic variated forms) 당tang, 습니당supnitang, 어용eyong, 어여eye, 예여yeyye, 아용ayong, 아여aye, 지용ciyong, 지여ciye, 에용eyyong, 에여eyye, 넹neng, 거든용ketunyong, 거든여ketunye, 구용kwuyong, 구여kwuye, 군용kwunyong, 군여kwunye, 나용nayong, 나여naye, 네용neyyong, 네여neyye, 용yong, 애여ayye, 더군용tekwunyong, 더군여tekwunye, 는데용nunteyyong, 는데여nunteyye, 잖아용canhayong, 잖아여canhaye, 답니당tapnitang, 세용seyyong, 세여seyye, 을까용ulkkayong, 을까여ulkkaye, 니까용nikkayong, 니까여nikkaye, 애용ayyong, 대용tayyong, 대여tayye, 으니까용unikkayong, 으니까여unikkaye, 외당oytang, 더라구용telakwuyong, 더라구여telakwuye, 예용yeyyong, 고용koyong, 고여koye, 라구용lakwuyong, 라구여lakwuye, 는군용nunkwunyong, 는군여nunkwunye, 다구용takwuyong, 다구여takwuye, 랍니당lapnitang, 래용layyong, 래여layye, 소이당soitang, 드라구용tulakwuyong, 드라구여tulakwuye, 던가용tenkayong, 던가여tenkaye, 은데용unteyyong, 은데여unteyye, 어야지용eyaciyong, 어야지여eyaciye, 던데용tunteyyong, 던데여tunteyye, 라고용lakoyong, 라고여lakoye, 아서용aseyong, 아서여aseye, 아야지용ayaciyong, 아야지여ayaciye, 입니당ipnitang, 습니다용supnitayong, 습니다여supnitaye, 아서당asetang, 합니당hapnitang, 는당nuntang, 단당tantang, 읍니당upnitang
Pre-final Suffix	갔kass, 것kes, 겄kess, 겟keys, 겠keyss, 긋kus, 댔tayss, 더te, 데tey, 드tu, 랬layss, 렷lyes, 리li, 사오sa, 사옵saop, 샤sya, 시si, 시겠sikeyss, 씨ssi, 아시asi, 앗as
	(stylistic variated forms) 이i, 아니ani, 했hayss, 햇hays, 셨syess, 셧syes, 엇es, 한han, 하ha, 씨ssi, 들tul
Postposition	가ka, 거나kena, 고ko, 과kwa, 까지kkaci, 나na, 다가taka, 대로taylo, 도to, 두twu, 든tun, 랑lang, 로lo, 를lul, 루lwu, 마냥manyang, 마다mata, 마저mace, 만man

Table 8: Grammatical Morphemes Used for K-MT

Character Transformations for Non-Autoregressive GEC Tagging

Milan Straka and **Jakub Náplava** and **Jana Straková**
Charles University,
Faculty of Mathematics and Physics,
Institute of Formal and Applied Linguistics
`{straka,naplava,strakova}@ufal.mff.cuni.cz`

Abstract

We propose a character-based non-autoregressive GEC approach, with automatically generated character transformations. Recently, per-word classification of correction edits has proven an efficient, parallelizable alternative to current encoder-decoder GEC systems. We show that word replacement edits may be suboptimal and lead to explosion of rules for spelling, diacritization and errors in morphologically rich languages, and propose a method for generating character transformations from GEC corpus. Finally, we train character transformation models for Czech, German and Russian, reaching solid results and dramatic speedup compared to autoregressive systems. The source code is released at `https://github.com/ufal/wnut2021_character_transformations_gec`.

1 Introduction

The current state of the art for grammatical error correction (GEC) is achieved with encoder-decoder architectures, leveraging large models with enormous computational demands (Grundkiewicz et al., 2019; Rothe et al., 2021). As such autoregressive approach is slow on inference and is impossible to parallelize, it has recently been suggested to replace autoregressive sequence-to-sequence decoding with per-token tagging to enable parallel decoding, achieving a dramatic speedup by a factor of 10 in NMT (Gu et al., 2018) and very recently, also in GEC (Omelianchuk et al., 2020).

Omelianchuk et al. (2020) approaches GEC as a tagging task, discriminating between a set of word-level transformations. The designed set is efficient for English corpora, which rarely contain spelling errors, and for English language, which does not have diacritization marks and its morphology is very modest compared to morphologically rich languages such as Czech or Russian. Using a set of word-level transformations designed for English, all character-level corrections would have to be handled by generic word-for-word REPLACE rule, leading to an explosion of rules.

We therefore suggest character transformations on subword level. Moreover, our transformations are automatically inferred from the corpus as opposed to being manually designed. Our approach has the following advantages:

- character-level errors, such as diacritics, spelling and morphology are handled,
- the transformations can be shared between subwords, preventing an explosion of rules,
- the transformations are generated automatically from corpus for each language.

We present an oracle analysis of various transformations sets at different levels, in English and three other languages: Czech, German and Russian. We find that the word-level set of rules may be suboptimal for morphologically rich languages and corpora with spelling errors and diacritics.

Finally, we train models with character transformations for non-autoregressive grammatical error correction in Czech, German and Russian, reaching solid results and dramatic speedup compared to autoregressive systems.

2 Related Work

Awasthi et al. (2019) propose an alternative to popular encoder-decoder architecture for GEC: a sequence-to-edit model which labels words with edits. Its advantage is parallel decoding while keeping competitive results. Mallinson et al. (2020) introduce a framework consisting of two tasks: *tagging*, which chooses and arbitrarily reorders a subset of input tokens to keep, and *insertion*, which in-fills the missing tokens with another pretrained masked language model. Omelianchuk et al. (2020) develop custom, manually designed, per-token *g-transformations*.

We further improve the sequence-to-edit model

Proceedings of the 2021 EMNLP Workshop W-NUT: The Seventh Workshop on Noisy User-generated Text, pages 417–422
November 11, 2021. ©2021 Association for Computational Linguistics

Algorithm 1: Extended LCS Alignment

Input: input subwords s, gold characters g
$\boldsymbol{w}[:,:] \leftarrow \mathbf{0}$
for $i \leftarrow |\boldsymbol{s}|$ **to** 1 **do**
  for $j \leftarrow |\boldsymbol{g}|$ **to** 1 **do**
    $\boldsymbol{w}[i,j] \leftarrow \boldsymbol{w}[i+1,j]$
    for $l \leftarrow 1$ **to** $\max(|\boldsymbol{g}|-j, 8+3|\boldsymbol{s}[i]|)$ **do**
      $g \leftarrow \boldsymbol{g}[j:j+l]$
      if g*.isspace()* **then continue**
      $c \leftarrow \begin{cases} 1 & \textbf{if } \boldsymbol{s}[i] = g \\ 0.75 & \textbf{if } \boldsymbol{s}[i]\textit{.strip()} = g\textit{.strip()} \\ 0.5 \cdot \text{LevenshSimilarity}(\boldsymbol{s}[i], g) & \end{cases}$
      $\boldsymbol{w}[i,j] \leftarrow \max(\boldsymbol{w}[i,j], c+\boldsymbol{w}[i,j+1])$
    end
  end
end
return alignment with weight $\boldsymbol{w}[0,0]$, as in LCS

with an attempt at non-autoregressive grammatical error correction for languages other than English, with *character* transformations applied at *subwords*, inferred *automatically* from parallel GEC corpus.

3 Transformations

Given that we encode an input sentence using BERT (Devlin et al., 2019), it is natural to represent it using a sequence of *subwords*. We prepend a space to every first subword in a word and use no special marker for other subwords. Note that the subwords might not correspond directly to parts of input, because the *bert uncased* model strip input casing and diacritics.

3.1 Alignment

In order to *automatically* encode the gold data via *character* transformations, we first align the input subwords and the corrected sentence. We compute the alignment with Algorithm 1, which is an extended version of LCS, where each subword is aligned with a *sequence* of gold characters. We ignore casing, diacritics and consider all punctuation equal during the alignment, and bound the maximum length of a correction (number of characters aligned to a single input subword) by $8+3\cdot$*input subword character length* for efficiency.

3.2 Transformations

We consider four kinds of transformations, differing in two dimensions – the granularity of the transformation and the unit it is applied on:

- character transformations applied on each subword separately (*char-at-subword*),
- character transformations applied on each complete word (*char-at-word*),
- string transformations applied on each subword (*string-at-subword*),
- string transformations applied on each complete word (*string-at-word*).

Input	gatherin		leafes	
Correct	Gathering		leaves	
Subwords	␣gathe	rin	␣lea	fes
string-at-word	␣Gathering		␣leaves	
string-at-subword	␣Gathe	APP. g	KEEP	ves
char-at-word	APPEND g, UPPERC. 2nd		REPL. 3rd *from end with* v	
char-at-subword	UPPERC. 2nd	APP. g	KEEP	REPL. 1st *with* v

Figure 1: Example of the four types of transformations.

In such terminology, the transformations proposed by Awasthi et al. (2019) and Omelianchuk et al. (2020) can be referred to as *string-at-word*. An example of the described transformation types is illustrated in Figure 1.

To apply a transformation on a complete word, we concatenate the corresponding subwords and aim to produce the concatenation of the subwords' corrections.

A string transformation can be one of *keep*, *replace* by given string or *append* a given string before/after.

A character transformation consists of multiple character edits, which we construct as follows:

1. We start by computing the standard smallest *edit script* between an input subword and a correction. The edit script is a sequence of *inserts*, *replaces* and *deletes*, and we index each edit operation either from the beginning of the input subword (if it involves the first half of it) or from the end of it (otherwise). The edit script is computed on lowercased strings, and in case of *bert uncased* models, also on undiacritized strings.
2. Afterwards, the unmodified input subword (i.e., including casing in case of *bert cased* models) is processed by the edit script, obtaining a correction with possibly incorrect casing. If some incorrectly lowercased charac-

ters are indeed present, *uppercase* operations are added, each indexing a single character either from the beginning of the correction (if the character is in the first half of it) or from the end of it (otherwise).

3. Finally, for *bert uncased* models, we still need to handle missing diacritics. We achieve it analogously to step 2, adding missing diacritical marks with operations indexing single characters again either from the beginning of the correction (if the character is in the first half) or from the end of it.

The reason for special handling of casing (and diacritization for *bert uncased* models) is that the proposed rules are more general, allowing to capture for example corrections *go→Going* and *walk→Walking* with a single rule *append "-ing", uppercase first*.

4 Transformations Upper-bound F-score

To assess the effect of number and type of transformations, we compute the potential maximum $F_{0.5}$ score with the MaxMatch M^2 scorer (Dahlmeier and Ng, 2012).

We generate transformation dictionary from the training portion of the following GEC corpora: CoNLL-2014 shared task for English (Ng et al., 2014), AKCES-GEC (Náplava and Straka, 2019) for Czech, FALKO-MERLIN GEC (Boyd, 2018) for German and RULEC-GEC (Rozovskaya and Roth, 2019) for Russian. The sizes of the datasets are quantified in Table 1.

We also generate transformations from synthetic data augmentation used for training (Section 5); to prevent the explosion of the transformation dictionary, we consider only 1000 synthetic sentences, except for Russian, which employs 5000 synthetic sentences because of very small authentic data. Finally, we add a special *uncorrectable error* dictionary element, indicating an error that cannot be corrected by any dictionary transformation.

To encode a gold correction with a transformation, we first try looking it up in the dictionary. If it is not present, we go through all dictionary transformations in random order, accepting the first one producing the correct output. If no transformation match, we resort to the *uncorrectable error* (during prediction, it will be replaced by the input token).

We show all combinations (*character/string* at *words/subwords*), using cased and uncased mBERT, in Figure 2. Clearly, character transformations applied at subwords (*char-at-subword*, green) have the highest potential in terms of upper-bound $F_{0.5}$ in all four languages. At the same time, word replacements (*string-at-word*, red) do not scale well. This effect is emphasized in morphologically-rich Czech and Russian, for which the upper-bound string replacement $F_{0.5}$ (*string-at-word*, red) falls below the current GEC systems state-of-the-art $F_{0.5}$ (horizontal dotted line).

Language	Dataset	Sentences
Czech	AKCES-GEC	47 371
German	Falko-MERLIN	24 077
Russian	RULEC-GEC	12 480

Table 1: GEC datasets used for constructing rules and for evaluation, including their size.

5 Experiments

We train the character subword GEC tagging model using the *char-at-subword* transformation, which have achieved the best upper-bound score.[1] We train the character subword GEC tagging model (*char-at-subword*) for Czech, German and Russian, in two stages: First, models are trained on a large synthetic corpus, generated by a reimplementation of Náplava and Straka (2019). Then, the models are finetuned on a mixture of synthetic and authentic data in ratio 1:2. The authentic data used in the second stage are AKCES-GEC (Náplava and Straka, 2019) for Czech, FALKO-MERLIN GEC (Boyd, 2018) for German and RULEC-GEC (Rozovskaya and Roth, 2019) for Russian.

The model is based on a pretrained BERT encoder (Devlin et al., 2019), specifically *bert-base-multilingual* (*uncased* for Czech and German, *cased* for Russian). After encoding the tokens, we add a simple softmax classifier that projects embeddings for each subword into a distribution over a set of transformations (Section 3) generated from authentic data with a limited addition from synthetic data (Section 4). We generate 7.7k transformations for Czech, 4.3k transformations for German and 3.1k transformations for Russian.

GEC models based on Transformer and BERT-encoder were shown to perform better when applied iteratively (Lichtarge et al., 2018;

[1]We also performed preliminary experiments with *char-at-word* GEC tagging model, and it performed worse than using the *char-at-subword* transformations.

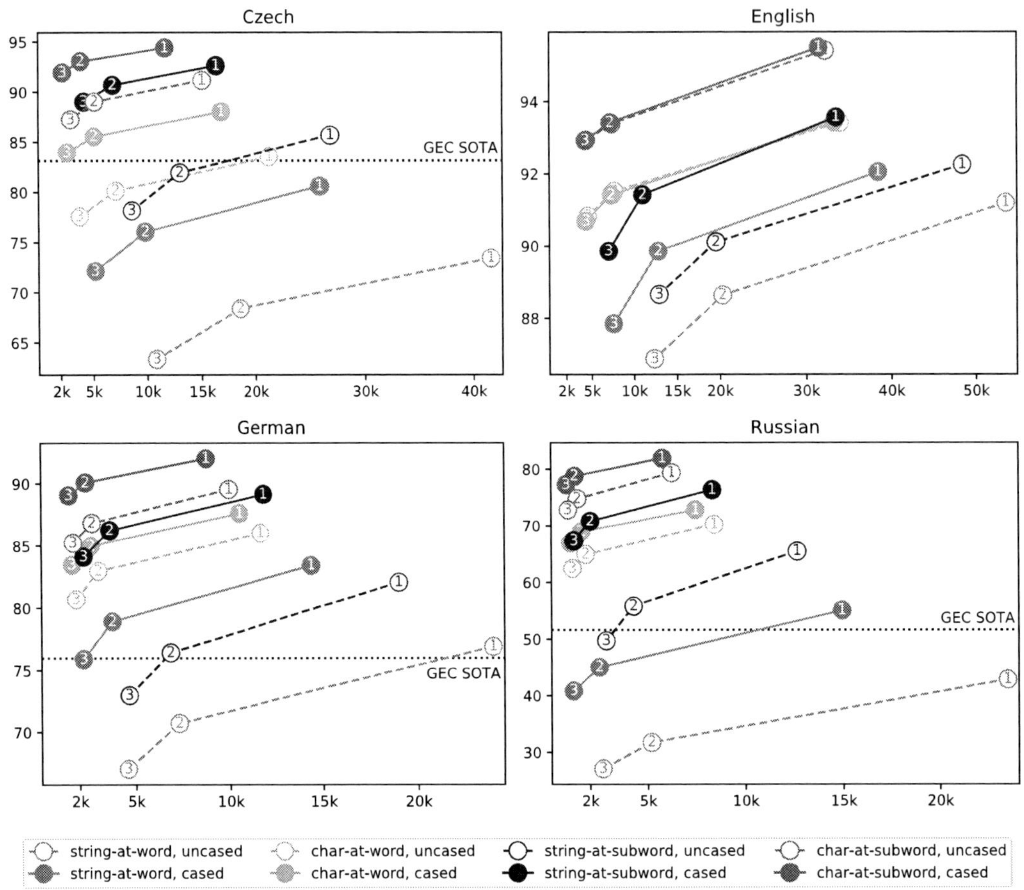

Figure 2: $F_{0.5}$ depending on number and type of transformations, if all transformations were correctly predicted (upper-bound). Up and right is better (higher $F_{0.5}$, fewer rules), down and left is worse (lower $F_{0.5}$, more rules). Circled numbers ①, ② and ③ denote that we kept transformations present at least once, twice or three times in the training data, respectively (larger means less transformations).

Omelianchuk et al., 2020). Therefore, we experiment with multiple iterations and report results both for single iteration and four iteration phases after which we did not observe significant improvements.

We train both the fully-connected network and BERT with AdamW optimizer (Loshchilov and Hutter, 2019) which minimizes the negative log-likelihood. Both for pretraining and finetuning, the learning rate linearly increases from 0 to $5 \cdot 10^{-5}$ over the first 10000 steps and linearly decreases to 0 over 20 epochs. We use the batch size of 2048 sentences and clip each training sentence to 128 tokens. We pretrain each model for circa 14 days and finetune it for circa 2 days on Nvidia P5000 GPU and select the best checkpoint according to development set.

We experimented with weighting all classes different from the KEEP instruction by a factor of 3. It turned out effective only for pretraining Russian.

We present the results of our models in Table 2. Compared to autoregressive models of similar size (Náplava and Straka, 2019), our models achieve solid results with large speedup due to the non-autoregressive tagging approach. Obviously, the inflation of model size (Rothe et al., 2021) to enormous size (13B parameters) leads to further improvements at the cost of increased computational demands.

5.1 Runtime Performance

To evaluate the speed-up of the non-autoregressive decoding, we compare the runtime performance of our system to the autoregressive Transformer

Model	Params	$F_{0.5}$
Richter et al. (2012)		58.54
Náplava and Straka (2019)^{synt}	210M	66.59
Náplava and Straka (2019)^{fine}	210M	80.17
Rothe et al. (2021) *base*	580M	71.88
Rothe et al. (2021) *xxl*	13B	83.15
Ours synthetic	172M	64.29
Ours finetuned	172M	72.86
Ours finetuned 4 iterations	172M	75.06

(a) Czech

Model	Params	$F_{0.5}$
Boyd (2018)		45.22
Náplava and Straka (2019)^{synt}	210M	51.41
Náplava and Straka (2019)^{fine}	210M	73.71
Rothe et al. (2021) *base*	580M	69.21
Rothe et al. (2021) *xxl*	13B	75.96
Ours synthetic	170M	44.29
Ours finetuned	170M	62.92
Ours finetuned 4 iterations	170M	65.95

(b) German

Model	Params	$F_{0.5}$
Rozovskaya and Roth (2019)		21.00
Náplava and Straka (2019)^{synt}	210M	40.96
Náplava and Straka (2019)^{fine}	210M	50.20
Rothe et al. (2021) *base*	580M	26.24
Rothe et al. (2021) *xxl*	13B	51.62
Ours synthetic	180M	25.36
Ours finetuned	180M	36.62
Ours finetuned 4 iterations	180M	38.68

(c) Russian

Table 2: Model results

encoder-decoder architecture from Náplava and Straka (2019), which is of comparable size. The measurements are performed using both a CPU-only decoding (performed on a dedicated 32-core Intel Xeon E5-2630) and GPU decoding (measured on an Nvidia Quadro P5000). The results presented in Table 3 show that the non-autoregressive system is four times faster.

Model	Time Per Sentence
T2T	162.34
BERT-GEC	41.26

(a) CPU decoding on a 32-core Intel Xeon

Model	Time Per Sentence
T2T	22.36
BERT-GEC	5.09

(b) GPU decoding on Nvidia Quadro P5000

Table 3: Average time in milliseconds required to process a single sentence in the Czech test set, measured using both (a) CPU decoding and (b) GPU decoding.

6 Conclusion And Future Work

We proposed a character-based method to generate target transformation instructions for GEC tagging models, as an alternative to autoregressive models. We compared the character transformations to previously used word-level transformation instructions and have shown that character-based rules have better coverage and scale better in Czech, German and Russian. Moreover, we trained character-based GEC tagging models for these languages. The source code is available at `https://github.com/ufal/wnut2021_character_transformations_gec`.

For future work, we propose to investigate ways to generate synthetic data to achieve better coverage of the target transformation set, since the current process for generating synthetic errors is well suited for encoder-decoder models, but may fail to cover certain transformations.

Acknowledgements

The research described herein has been supported by the Ministry of Education, Youths and Sports of the Czech Republic, under the project LINDAT/CLARIAH-CZ (LM2018101). This research was also partially supported by SVV project number 260 575 and GAUK 578218 of the Charles University.

References

Abhijeet Awasthi, Sunita Sarawagi, Rasna Goyal, Sabyasachi Ghosh, and Vihari Piratla. 2019. Parallel iterative edit models for local sequence transduction. In *Proceedings of the 2019 Conference on Empirical*

Methods in Natural Language Processing and the 9th International Joint Conference on Natural Language Processing (EMNLP-IJCNLP), pages 4260–4270, Hong Kong, China. Association for Computational Linguistics.

Adriane Boyd. 2018. Using Wikipedia edits in low resource grammatical error correction. In *Proceedings of the 2018 EMNLP Workshop W-NUT: The 4th Workshop on Noisy User-generated Text*, pages 79–84, Brussels, Belgium. Association for Computational Linguistics.

Daniel Dahlmeier and Hwee Tou Ng. 2012. Better evaluation for grammatical error correction. In *Proceedings of the 2012 Conference of the North American Chapter of the Association for Computational Linguistics: Human Language Technologies*, pages 568–572, Montréal, Canada. Association for Computational Linguistics.

Jacob Devlin, Ming-Wei Chang, Kenton Lee, and Kristina Toutanova. 2019. BERT: Pre-training of deep bidirectional transformers for language understanding. In *Proceedings of the 2019 Conference of the North American Chapter of the Association for Computational Linguistics: Human Language Technologies, Volume 1 (Long and Short Papers)*, pages 4171–4186, Minneapolis, Minnesota. Association for Computational Linguistics.

Roman Grundkiewicz, Marcin Junczys-Dowmunt, and Kenneth Heafield. 2019. Neural grammatical error correction systems with unsupervised pre-training on synthetic data. In *Proceedings of the Fourteenth Workshop on Innovative Use of NLP for Building Educational Applications*, pages 252–263, Florence, Italy. Association for Computational Linguistics.

Jiatao Gu, James Bradbury, Caiming Xiong, Victor O.K. Li, and Richard Socher. 2018. Non-autoregressive neural machine translation. In *International Conference on Learning Representations*.

Jared Lichtarge, Christopher Alberti, Shankar Kumar, Noam Shazeer, and Niki Parmar. 2018. Weakly supervised grammatical error correction using iterative decoding. *arXiv preprint arXiv:1811.01710*.

Ilya Loshchilov and Frank Hutter. 2019. Decoupled weight decay regularization. In *International Conference on Learning Representations*.

Jonathan Mallinson, Aliaksei Severyn, Eric Malmi, and Guillermo Garrido. 2020. FELIX: Flexible text editing through tagging and insertion. In *Findings of the Association for Computational Linguistics: EMNLP 2020*, pages 1244–1255, Online. Association for Computational Linguistics.

Jakub Náplava and Milan Straka. 2019. Grammatical error correction in low-resource scenarios. In *Proceedings of the 5th Workshop on Noisy User-generated Text (W-NUT 2019)*, pages 346–356.

Hwee Tou Ng, Siew Mei Wu, Ted Briscoe, Christian Hadiwinoto, Raymond Hendy Susanto, and Christopher Bryant. 2014. The CoNLL-2014 shared task on grammatical error correction. In *Proceedings of the Eighteenth Conference on Computational Natural Language Learning: Shared Task*, pages 1–14, Baltimore, Maryland. Association for Computational Linguistics.

Kostiantyn Omelianchuk, Vitaliy Atrasevych, Artem Chernodub, and Oleksandr Skurzhanskyi. 2020. GECToR – grammatical error correction: Tag, not rewrite. In *Proceedings of the Fifteenth Workshop on Innovative Use of NLP for Building Educational Applications*, pages 163–170, Seattle, WA, USA → Online. Association for Computational Linguistics.

Michal Richter, Pavel Straňák, and Alexandr Rosen. 2012. Korektor–a system for contextual spell-checking and diacritics completion. In *Proceedings of COLING 2012: Posters*, pages 1019–1028.

Sascha Rothe, Jonathan Mallinson, Eric Malmi, Sebastian Krause, and Aliaksei Severyn. 2021. A simple recipe for multilingual grammatical error correction. *CoRR*, abs/2106.03830.

Alla Rozovskaya and Dan Roth. 2019. Grammar error correction in morphologically rich languages: The case of russian. *Transactions of the Association for Computational Linguistics*, 7:1–17.

Can Character-based Language Models Improve Downstream Task Performance in Low-Resource and Noisy Language Scenarios?

Arij Riabi[1,2] **Benoît Sagot**[1] **Djamé Seddah**[1]
[1] Inria Paris
[2] Sorbonne Université
{arij.riabi,benoit.sagot,djame.seddah}@inria.fr

Abstract

Recent impressive improvements in NLP, largely based on the success of contextual neural language models, have been mostly demonstrated on at most a couple dozen high-resource languages. Building language models and, more generally, NLP systems for non-standardized and low-resource languages remains a challenging task. In this work, we focus on North-African colloquial dialectal Arabic written using an extension of the Latin script, called *NArabizi*, found mostly on social media and messaging communication. In this low-resource scenario with data displaying a high level of variability, we compare the downstream performance of a character-based language model on part-of-speech tagging and dependency parsing to that of monolingual and multilingual models. We show that a character-based model trained on only 99k sentences of *NArabizi* and fined-tuned on a small treebank of this language leads to performance close to those obtained with the same architecture pre-trained on large multilingual and monolingual models. Confirming these results a on much larger data set of noisy French user-generated content, we argue that such character-based language models can be an asset for NLP in low-resource and high language variability settings.

1 Introduction

Current state-of-the-art monolingual and multilingual language models require large amounts of data to be trained, showing limited performance on low-resource languages (Howard and Ruder, 2018; Devlin et al., 2019). They lead to state-of-the-art results on most NLP tasks (Devlin et al., 2018; Raffel et al., 2020). In order to achieve high performance, these models rely on transfer learning architectures: the language models need to be trained on large amounts of data (*pre-training*) to be able to transfer the acquired knowledge to a downstream task via *fine-tuning* on a relatively small number of examples, resulting in a significant performance improvement with respect to previous approaches. This dependency on large data sets for pre-training is a severe issue for low-resource languages, despite the emergence of large and successful multilingual pre-trained language models (Muller et al., 2021b). This is especially the case for languages with unusual morphological and structural features, which struggle to take advantage from similarities with high-resource, well represented languages such as Romance and Germanic languages.

In this work, we focus on one of such highly challenging languages, namely North-African dialectal Arabic. Its Latin transcription (*Arabizi*) displays a high level of linguistic variability[1], on top of scarce and noisy resource availability, making it a particularly challenging language for most NLP systems relying on pre-trained multilingual models (Muller et al., 2020).[2] To tackle the resource scarcity issue regarding Arabic dialects, Antoun et al. (2020) use BERT architecture (Devlin et al., 2019) to train a model on Arabic text to compare this approach to standard multilingual models. Indeed, Martin et al. (2020) show that fine-tuning a monolingual model leads to better results than fine-tuning a multilingual one, meaning that when fine-tuning is used there is no significant performance improvement from cross-lingual transfer during pre-training. However, such model is still pre-trained on sentences written in a single language and was not trained to handle the presence

First version submitted on August 27th, 2021. Final on October 1st, 2021.

[1] Language variability, or language variation, is a term coming from socio-linguistics where, as stated by Nordquist (2019), it *refers to regional, social or contextual differences in the ways that a particular language is used.* These variations in user-generated content can be characterized through their prevalent idiosyncraisies when compared to canonical texts (Seddah et al., 2012a; Sanguinetti et al., 2020).

[2] Following Seddah et al. (2020), we refer to the Arabizi version of North-African Arabic dialects as *NArabizi*.

Proceedings of the 2021 EMNLP Workshop W-NUT: The Seventh Workshop on Noisy User-generated Text, pages 423–436
November 11, 2021. ©2021 Association for Computational Linguistics

of multiple languages in the same sentence (code-switching), a frequent phenomenon in *NArabizi*.

However both monolingual and multilingual model approaches bear the risk of being limited by a subword tokenization-based vocabulary when facing out-of-domain training data language, especially in high-variability noisy scenarios (El Boukkouri et al., 2020; Clark et al., 2021), even though Muller et al. (2020) demonstrated a positive effect for *NArabizi* when using target language data to fine-tune a multilingual language model on its own objective function before pre-training.

Following a different approach, we investigate the use of a recently issued character-based language model (El Boukkouri et al., 2020) that was shown to display a remarkable robustness to lexical variation and noise when facing a new distant domain, namely biomedical. The pipeline we developed is simple and consists in fine-tuning this character-based model for several tasks in a noisy low-resource language scenario. We show that a character-based model trained on only 99k sentences of *NArabizi* and fined-tuned on a small treebank of the language leads to performance close to that obtained with the same architecture pre-trained on large multilingual and monolingual models (mBERT and CamemBERT).

Interestingly, we generalize this observation by using the same architecture on a much larger French user-generated Content treebank that exhibits similar language variability issues than *NArabizi*. In fact, pre-training a character-based model on 1% of the large-scale French instance of the multilingual corpus OSCAR leads to similar performance as a subword based model trained on the full corpus, showing that such character-based language model can reach similar performance levels and that the resulting models exhibit the same tolerance to noise as their much larger BERT counterparts. This demonstrates the value of such models in very scarce resource scenario. Our code and models are freely available.[3]

2 NArabizi: A Challenging Use Case for NLP in Low-resource Scenarios

As the official language of 25 countries, Arabic showcases a linguistic phenomenon called *diglossia* (Habash, 2010). It means that the speakers use Modern Standard Arabic (MSA) for formal and official situations but use other forms of Arabic in informal situations. These dialectal forms constitute a dialect continuum with large variability from one country to the other. Arabic dialects are defined by their spoken form and often exhibit a lack of standardized spelling when written. When Arabic speakers produce written text in such dialects, they merely transcribe their spoken, colloquial language, which leads to different forms for the same word. Many users use the Latin script to express themselves online in their dialect (Seddah et al., 2020). In particular, they transcribe phonemes that cannot be straightforwardly mapped to a Latin letter using digits and symbols,[4] with a high degree of variability at all levels; this is called *Arabizi*, with its North-African version called *NArabizi* by Seddah et al. (2020). For cultural and historical reasons, *NArabizi* also exhibits a high degree of code-switching with French and Amazigh (Amazouz et al., 2017), i.e. alternations between two or more languages during the conversation. Besides, the only available textual resources for Arabizi data are user-generated content, which is by itself inherently noisy (Foster, 2010; Seddah et al., 2012a; Eisenstein, 2013), making the production of supervised models, assuming the availability of labeled data, or even the collection of large pre-training data set a rather difficult task.

This data scarcity problem is often solved in the NLP literature using transfer learning: transferring knowledge learnt by large scale language models pre-trained on larger corpora. However, the use of Latin script makes it harder to transfer knowledge from language models trained on Arabic script corpora. For subword-based tokenization models, words are represented by a combination of subwords from a predefined list. When applied to a highly variable language with code-switching, a large vocabulary would be necessary to get a good covering of all possible orthographic variations which makes this approach less practical. Table 1 presents several examples of lexical variation within *NArabizi*. Interestingly, this variability also affects the code-switched vocabulary, which is mostly French in this case.

[3]`https://gitlab.inria.fr/ariabi/character-bert-ugc`

[4]For example, the digit "3" is often used to denote the ayin consonant, because it is graphically similar to its rendition in Arabic script.

Gloss	Attested forms	Lang
why	wa3lach w3alh 3alach	*NArabizi*
all	ekl kal kolach koulli kol	*NArabizi*
many	beaucoup boucoup bcp	Code-switched Fr.

Table 1: Examples of lexical variation in *NArabizi*. *(From Seddah et al., 2020)*

3 Related work

3.1 Transfer Learning for Low-resource Languages

Low-resource languages, by definition, face a lack of textual resources – annotated or not –, which makes it difficult for the NLP community to develop models and systems adapted to them (Joshi et al., 2020). The majority of the almost-7000 languages worldwide actually fall into the "low-resource" category. This makes the development of systems for low-resource languages necessary to widen the accessibility of NLP technology.

For deep learning approaches, which depend on the availability of large data sets, the solution to the low-resource problem comes from the idea of transfer learning. Early instances of cross-lingual transfer learning rely on non-contextualised word embeddings (Ammar et al., 2016). More recently, multilingual pre-trained language models (Conneau et al., 2020) has spread far and wide in NLP, enabling high-performance zero-shot cross-lingual transfer for numerous tasks and languages. The main idea is to exploit a large amount of unlabeled data to pre-train a model using a self-supervised task, such as masked language modeling (Lample and Conneau, 2019; Vania et al., 2019). This pre-trained model is then fine-tuned on a much smaller annotated data set and used for another language, domain or task. Strategic knowledge sharing has been shown to improve the performance on downstream tasks and languages (Gururangan et al., 2020). Therefore, this technique is crucial for multilingual applications, as most of the world's languages lack large amount of labeled data (Conneau et al., 2019; Eisenschlos et al., 2019; Joshi et al., 2020). However the performance of multilingual language model on low-resource languages is still limited compared to other languages since they are naturally under-sampled during the training process (Wu and Dredze, 2020).

To improve performance on a specific low-resource languages, there are two possibilities. Either to attempt to train a language model on it from scratch despite the scarceness of data; or fine-tune a pre-trained multilingual language model on the low-resource language corpus, also called *cross-lingual transfer learning* (Muller et al., 2021a). The first option can sometimes lead to decent performance, provided that the training corpus is diverse enough (Martin et al., 2020).

When following the fine-tuning approach, unsupervised methods can be implemented to facilitate the transfer of knowledge (Pfeiffer et al., 2020). The most widely used unsupervised fine-tuning task is masked language modeling (MLM). This system has proven its efficiency between languages that have already been seen in the training corpus (Pires et al., 2019); it is still a challenge for unseen languages, especially low-resource ones. However, Muller et al. (2020) achieved promising results by performing unsupervised fine-tuning on small amounts of *NArabizi* data. We follow their approach by comparing the performance of our pipeline in two setups: Model+MLM+Task and Model+Task. We describe these setups in more details in section 6.

3.2 Tokenization & Character-based models

Standard language models rely on a subword-based approach to process tokens in a sequence (Kudo, 2018a). This allows the model to handle any word unseen in the training data, working in an "open-vocabulary setting," where words are represented by a combination of subwords from a pre-defined list. On top of alleviating the issue of out-of-vocabulary words, this approach allows the model to handle sequences written in a language unseen during training, as long as it uses the same script. Therefore, subword tokenization is a crucial feature of state-of-the-art models in NLP. But its suitability for all types of data has always been questioned. While splitting texts into subwords based on their frequencies works well for English, models using this kind of tokenization struggle with noise, whether it is naturally present in the data (Sun et al., 2020) or artificially generated to challenge the model (Pruthi et al., 2019). Moreover, language models that use subword-based tokenization struggle to represent rare words (Schick and Schütze, 2020). Many research projects have focused on improving subword tokenization. For example, Wang et al. (2021) suggested a multi-view subword regularization based on the sampling of multiple segmentations of the input text, based on the work of Kudo (2018b).

Other parallel efforts bid on character-based models. For example, El Boukkouri et al. (2020) proposed a possible solution to get a better tokenization system more resilient to orthographic variations and noise in the data set by using a character-level model, inspired by a previous word-level open-vocabulary system (Peters et al., 2018a). This new model gets better results than vanilla BERT on multiple tasks from the medical domain. Furthermore, the authors claim that it is more robust to noise and misspellings. In the same vein, Ma et al. (2020a) combined character-aware and subword-based information to improve robustness to spelling errors. This initiated a new wave of tokenizer-free models based on characters or bytes (Tay et al., 2021; Xue et al., 2021; Clark et al., 2021).

The question of knowing if character-based language models can handle high language variability since they are supposed to be resilient to noise and spelling variations is crucial when dealing with non-normalized dialects and non-canonical forms of language as found on many user-generated content platforms. This is why we focus on this work on the analysis of the performance of character-based models on several user-generated content data sets that we now describe.

4 Data sets

In this section, we describe the data sets we use to evaluate our pipeline on our downstream tasks, namely Part-Of-Speech (POS) tagging and dependency parsing.

***NArabizi* Data Set** We use the *NArabizi* treebank (Seddah et al., 2020), containing about 1500 sentences randomly sampled from the romanized Algerian dialectal Arabic corpus of Cotterell et al. (2014) and from a small corpus of lyrics coming from Algerian dialectal Arabic songs popular among the younger generation. This treebank is manually annotated with morpho-syntactic information (parts-of-speech and morphological features), together with glosses and code-switching labels at the word level, as well as sentence-level translations. Moreover, this treebank also contains 36% of French tokens. Within the *NArabizi* annotated corpus,[5] In addition to labeled data, The *NArabizi* treebanks provides about 2 millions words, 99k sentences, of unlabeled data collected from various sources.[6] We use this corpus for unsupervised fine-tuning.

Treebank	# Tokens	# Sentences	Genres
GSD	389,363	16,342	Blogs, News Reviews, Wiki
Sequoia	68,615	3,099	Medical, News Non-fiction, Wiki
Spoken	34,972	2,786	Spoken
FSMB	56,009	4,055	Twitter, Facebook Web Forums

Table 2: Statistics on the treebanks used in our POS tagging and dependency parsing experiments.

French Data Sets We use the following Universal Dependencies, UD, (Nivre et al., 2020) version of the following treebanks: French GSD (McDonald et al., 2013), Sequoia (Candito and Seddah, 2012) and Spoken, an automatic conversion of the Rhapsodie corpus (Lacheret et al., 2014) to the UD annotation scheme.

For our experiments on noisy UGC treebank, we use an extension of the French Social Media Bank, FSMB[7] (Seddah et al., 2012a): a treebank of French sentences coming from various social media sources only available either in constituent trees or in the native French Treebank dependency annotation scheme (Candito et al., 2010), along with the Sequoia original treebank that we use with the same annotation scheme for compatibility in our French UGC experiments. A brief overview of the size and content of each treebank can be found in Table 2.

Pre-training Data Sets Note that in some of our experiments, we use a fraction, 1% of the deduplicated French instance of the Oscar corpora (Suárez et al., 2019), about 380M words, as a source of unlabeled data to be either mixed with *NArabizi* pre-training data (as an 2.5M words additional sample) or used as pre-training data for characterBert when evaluated on French UGC (whole 1%). Statistics on those data sets are presented on Table 3.

5 Model

CharacterBERT (El Boukkouri et al., 2020) is a character-based variant of BERT that replaces the WordPiece embedding matrix with multiple CNN

[5] `http://almanach-treebanks.fr/NArabizi`

[6] The original data set provides 50k sentences of clean *NArabizi* sentences and an additional 49k sentences of more noisy data, we use here a concatenation of both.

[7] We use a shuffled version of the treebank split into a train set of about 2 000 sentences and a dev and test set of about 1 000 sentences each.

	# Tokens	# Sentences	Language
99k Narabizi	2.527k	99k	ar-dz
1% Oscar	318.715k	9.342k	fr
10% Oscar	1.885.351k	55.261k	fr
100% Oscar	23.209.872k	558.092k	fr

Table 3: pre-training data set statistics.

and a highway layer (Srivastava et al., 2015). This method for encoding token representations is inspired from ELMo (Peters et al., 2018b), one of the first pre-trained language models for transfer learning. It generates a context-independent representation from character embeddings and feeds them to transformer encoder layers, similarly to BERT architecture. Therefore, it produces a single embedding for any input token and does not need a WordPiece vocabulary. This avoids having an inconstant number of subword vectors for each word. We choose this model since its robustness to noise, when tested on biomedical domain by El Boukkouri et al. (2020), can lead to interesting result when facing our noisy experiment data. It is the first character-based and BERT-like model, along with CharBERT (Ma et al., 2020b), that uses both character and subword embeddings and has the advantage of being publicly available.[8] Note that we retrain CharacterBert from scratch on our data sets and do not make use of any of its available pretrained at models any point in our experiments.

6 Experiments

In this section, we present our fully-supervised and semi-supervised baselines. We also evaluate different fine-tuning strategies combined with two layers configurations. We use various embedding models that we contrast with the CharacterBERT model.

Baseline Models For our fully-supervised baseline, we use FastText embeddings (Joulin et al., 2016) trained from scratch on our treebank training sets and used as input for our downstream tasks without any special treatment.

To measure the effectiveness of using a contextualized character-based language model, we compare its performance to subword based language models, both monolingual and multilingual, that constitute the basis of our semi-supervised baselines. For multilingual subword based language

	UPOS	UAS	LAS
No external embeddings	57.61	55.48	39.32

Table 4: Pos-Tagging and Parsing Baseline Results for *NArabizi* test set.

model, we use mBERT, the multilingual version of BERT (Devlin et al., 2018). It is trained for 104 different languages on Wikipedia data, including French and Arabic, languages for which Muller et al. (2020) showed that, to a certain extent, they could transfer to NArabizi. For our monolingual model we use CamemBERT (Martin et al., 2020) which is a contextualized language model based on the RoBERTa model (Liu et al., 2019) trained and optimized specifically for French.

MODEL+TASK We use the implementation of the Biaffine graph parser (Dozat and Manning, 2016) from Grobol and Crabbé (2021); they adapted it to handle several input sources, such as BERT representations. The parser performs its own tagging using a multi-layer perceptron. The word representations are a concatenation of word embeddings and tag embeddings learned together with the model parameters on the treebank training data. We fine-tune the overall model by back-propagating through the average of all sub-tokens of a word. Baseline results, without any external embeddings, for this parser are provided in Table 4.

MODEL+MLM+TASK Before fine-tuning the model on the downstream task, we perform language adaptation by fine-tuning it in a self-supervised fashion with the MLM loss. We use the *NArabizi* raw data; we train the model for 20 epochs, keeping the best model obtained at the end. The evaluation is done using the MLM log likelihood, with 10% of the data kept for validation.

Fine-Tuning Strategy In addition to using only the *last layer* (cf. Appendix A where we conducted several experiments to explore the effect of different layer configurations in our downstream tasks), we also test two options for the layers aggregation. The first one is simply taking the *mean* of selected layers. The second is *scalar mix*, introduced by ELMo (Peters et al., 2018b): a convex combination of the transformer layers where the weights are learnt.

For each of these configurations, we test two setup: *with* and *without* training the transformer

[8] https://github.com/helboukkouri/character-bert-pre-training

Fine-tuning Strategy	MODEL+TASK			MODEL+MLM+TASK		
	UPOS	UAS	LAS	UPOS	UAS	LAS
last-layer-ft	**81.14**	72.59	60.35	83.08	73.77	62.00
last-layer-fz	56.05	62.48	43.95	70.23	67.86	53.45
mean-ft	80.86	**73.06**	**61.11**	**84.22**	72.97	61.58
mean-fz	65.41	64.27	48.11	73.53	68.05	53.92
scalar-mix-ft	80.15	70.46	58.08	83.65	**74.62**	**62.62**
scalar-mix-fz	58.74	63.80	46.93	61.20	67.25	52.84

(a) **CamemBERT**

Fine-tuning Strategy	MODEL+TASK			MODEL+MLM+TASK		
	UPOS	UAS	LAS	UPOS	UAS	LAS
last-layer-ft	80.48	69.19	57.89	**84.55**	**73.82**	**62.67**
last-layer-fz	65.08	62.95	45.84	79.44	71.55	58.98
mean-ft	**84.40**	**72.83**	**61.81**	84.50	71.31	60.96
mean-fz	69.47	64.89	49.34	78.40	69.71	57.61
scalar-mix-ft	80.25	69.19	56.14	84.31	72.78	61.67
scalar-mix-fz	71.79	66.73	52.17	78.83	72.07	59.17

(b) **mBERT**

Fine-tuning Strategy	NArabizi			Sample Oscar			NArabizi + Oscar		
	99k			99k			66k+33k		
	UPOS	UAS	LAS	UPOS	UAS	LAS	UPOS	UAS	LAS
last-layer-ft	**81.19**	70.56	58.65	78.83	**69.52**	56.33	80.67	**69.90**	**57.75**
last-layer-fz	75.71	66.87	53.69	71.74	65.31	51.75	75.38	68.57	55.15
mean-ft	81.00	**70.70**	**58.84**	78.78	**69.52**	55.81	**80.91**	69.57	57.18
mean-fz	77.08	68.05	55.53	72.35	66.54	51.98	77.22	69.33	56.14
scalar-mix-ft	79.96	69.47	57.84	**80.62**	68.76	**56.76**	80.15	**69.90**	57.56
scalar-mix-fz	75.90	68.10	54.58	71.69	66.16	51.80	77.60	69.33	55.91

(c) **CharacterBERT** (MODEL+TASK)

Table 5: Performances of the models on the *NArabizi* treebank using **different fine-tuning strategy** (We use *ft* to indicate that the embeddings are fine-tuned for the tasks, while *fz* is used when the embeddings are frozen during the fine-tuning step).

model weights during the fine-tuning. We call the first strategy *frozen representation*, noted with a *-fz* suffix in our results, where the language model is used to extract meaningful features that consist of contextual embeddings. In the second strategy, the contextual embedding extractor – that is, the pre-trained language model – is fine-tuned on the downstream task alongside the task-specific component, noted with a *-ft* suffix in our results.

7 Results and Discussion

In this section, we compare all the systems presented before on the *NArabizi* and French treebanks. We especially focus on the impact of corpus size on the models' performance.

7.1 Experiments on *NArabizi* treebank

Scores are reported as triplets describing UPOS/UAS/LAS results. Highlighted cells marks the best results column-wise while bold marks best results row-wise

We report in Table 5 the scores for the different fine-tuning strategies for the three models CamemBERT, mBERT and CharacterBERT.

Additional insights on the extraction of a representation from the different layers are provided in the Appendix, Table 9, with analysis on the effect of the combination of different subsets of layers on the accuracy.

CharacterBERT$_{\text{NArabizi}}$ performs better overall in the Model+TASK setting Looking at table 5, we notice that CharacterBERT$_{\text{NArabizi}}$ significantly outperforms mBERT and CamemBERT in the MODEL+TASK setup without MLM for almost all the configurations, except for the two configurations mean-ft (when using the mean of all the fine-tuned layers) and scalar-mix-ft (when using the scalar-mix of all the layers) where mBERT and CamemBERT show slightly better performance than CharacterBERT$_{\text{NArabizi}}$. In this latter case, mBERT outperforms CharacterBERT$_{\text{NArabizi}}$ on the *NArabizi* data set with accuracy differences of (3.40/2.13/2.96) for (UPOS/UAS/LAS) using mean-ft, which is only significant for UAS with p-value<0.05.[9] The same observation can be done for CamemBERT in the MODEL+TASK setting which outperforms CharacterBERT$_{\text{NArabizi}}$ with accuracy differences of (-0.14/2.36/2.26).

The same is observed for the scalar-mix-ft option but the differences are not significant with p-value<0.05 for UAS and LAS. Besides these two configurations, CharacterBERT$_{\text{NArabizi}}$ always outperforms the other two models without MLM. The most notable difference using CharacterBERT$_{\text{NArabizi}}$ is when the latter outperforms CamemBERT with accuracy differences of (19.66/4.39/9.74) and mBERT with (10.63/3.92/7.854) in the last-layer-fz setting with a p-value<0.05 for both comparisons.

[9]We tested the statistical significance using the publicly available Dan Bikel's code at https://github.com/tdozat/Parser-v1

Adding MLM reverses the trend However, when we compare CharacterBERT$_{\text{NArabizi}}$ to CamemBERT+MLM and mBERT+MLM, we see that while they both generally outperform CharacterBERT$_{\text{NArabizi}}$, there are some settings where CharacterBERT$_{\text{NArabizi}}$ still gets better scores. mBERT+MLM gets the best scores for all of the configurations we test among the three models. While both CamemBERT and mBERT perform comparably, mBERT outperforms CharacterBERT$_{\text{NArabizi}}$ when it is used with MLM. Some of the best performance are achieved in the last-layer-ft setting with scores of (83.08/73.77/62.00) for CamemBERT and (84.55/73.82/62.67) for mBERT and lower scores of (81.19/70.56/58.6) for CharacterBERT$_{\text{NArabizi}}$ (both models outperform CharacterBERT$_{\text{NArabizi}}$ in this case).

In other settings, CharacterBERT$_{\text{NArabizi}}$ is still competitive with the two other MLM-pretrained models, as illustrated by the last-layer-fz setting with scores of (70.23/67.86/53.45) for CamemBERT, and (75.71/66.87/53.69) for CharacterBERT$_{\text{NArabizi}}$ and (79.44/71.55/58.98) for mBERT. **Still, the general tendency in the Model+MLM+TASK setting is that mBERT outperforms CharacterBERT$_{\text{NArabizi}}$ when used with MLM and CamemBERT exhibits performance similar to CharacterBERT$_{\text{NArabizi}}$ in the same setting.** This is in contrast with the earlier comparison without MLM pre-training where both CamemBERT and mBERT reached scores lower than those of CharacterBERT$_{\text{NArabizi}}$.

This observation confirms the findings of Muller et al. (2021a) regarding the positive impact of unsupervised fine-tuning for BERT models even if the language is not one of the pre-training languages.

CharacterBERT pretrained on 1% of Oscar performs roughly the same than CamemBERT+Task If we compare the performance of CamemBERT in the MODEL+TASK setting to CharacterBERT trained on sub-sample of Oscar, we see that both models are comparable. Typically, CamemBERT seems to outperform CharacterBERT in some settings like last-layer-ft where the latter records (78.83/69.52/56.33) for UPOS, UAS and LAS scores respectively while CamemBERT records higher at (81.14/72.59/60.35). In other settings, CharacterBERT seems to outperform CamemBERT. In the mean-fz setting for instance, CharacterBERT has scores of (72.35/66.54/51.98) which surpasses the (69.47/64.89/49.34) scores of CamemBERT. No clear conclusion can be drawn about the best use of one model over the other in the different settings since they all display competitive scores. This is essentially due to the fact that CamemBERT is trained on the full Oscar data set, while CharacterBERT is trained on just 0.01% of it. In addition, the test set is made of only 140 *NArabizi* sentences, making any interpretation of the results difficult. These two reasons make difficult the drawing of concrete conclusions on the performance of both models compared to each other. Therefore in the next section, we will evaluate the models using the best fine-tuning strategy on French treebanks with a larger evaluation set and a CharacterBERT trained on 1% Oscar.

7.2 The Impact of Data Size: Experiments on French treebanks

In-domain experiments For our experiments on French treebanks, we keep the best setup from our previous results and use the last layer of the model fine-tuned for the task.

In table 6, we report the scores obtained by both models CamemBERT and CharacterBERT on three French treebanks, compared to our parser without external embeddings from pre-trained models, which we consider as our baseline for those experiments. All systems using CamemBERT or CharacterBERT models outperform our baseline. Both models have competitive scores. For example, when tested on the GSD treebank, our baseline obtains scores of (96.35/89.98/86.96) while CamemBERT and CharacterBERT obtain both better, yet relatively close scores, with (98.53/95.74/94.17) for the CamemBERT-based model and (98.07/95.22/93.50). The same observations apply for the other two treebanks SEQUOIA and SPOKEN. These results are coherent with the comparisons done earlier for *NArabizi* where both CharacterBERT and CamemBERT models produced comparable scores even though CharacterBERT was trained on only 0.01% of the full data set on which CamemBERT was trained on. Our results on those much larger data sets corroborate then our *NArabizi* models results and confirm the interest of using characterBert-based models in our scenarios.

Extremely noisy user-generated content experiments In table 7, we compare both models CamemBERT and CharacterBERT in two different

Model-LayerConfig	GSD			SEQUOIA			SPOKEN		
	UPOS	UAS	LAS	UPOS	UAS	LAS	UPOS	UAS	LAS
No pre-training	96.35	89.98	86.96	92.57	82.28	77.72	83.60	67.65	58.04
CamemBERT (100% Oscar)	**98.53**	95.74	**94.17**	99.23	**95.78**	**94.59**	97.41	**88.15**	**83.00**
CharacterBERT (1% Oscar)	98.07	95.22	93.50	**99.27**	94.98	93.80	96.62	86.82	81.22

Table 6: POS and dependency parsing scores on 3 French treebanks.

	Model-LayerConfig	Dev			Test		
		UPOS	UAS	LAS	UPOS	UAS	LAS
FSMB *train*	No pre-training	81.24	70.04	59.46	81.62	69.19	59.17
	CamemBERT	**95.34**	**87.01**	**81.56**	**95.48**	**87.47**	**82.66**
	CharacterBERT	95.08	85.99	80.51	95.19	86.26	81.26
Sequoia train	No pre-training	71.50	59.04	47.30	72.79	59.92	48.81
	CamemBERT	89.47	**81.80**	74.33	90.10	**82.68**	**75.85**
	CharacterBERT	**90.12**	**81.79**	**74.43**	**90.68**	82.39	75.39

Table 7: POS and dependency parsing scores on the FSMB.

settings. In the first one, both models are fine-tuned on the FSMB training set. In the second one, the models are trained on the Sequoia training set. The performance of these models is to be compared – as in table 7 – to the performance of a parser without external embeddings from a pre-trained model. As expected, both models outperform the baseline and – similarly to previous results – are competitive in their respective obtained scores.

In the FSMB training setting, CamemBERT achieves scores of (95.34/87.01/81.56) when tested on the development part of the data set, and CharacterBERT achieves close scores of (95.08/85.99/80.51) on the same data set. Both scores outperform the ones obtained by the baseline of (81.24/70.04/59.46) also on the development set. The same behavior can be observed in the Sequoia training setting where CamemBERT gets scores of (89.47/81.80/74.33) and CharacterBERT scores of (90.12/81.79/74.43) on the development set: both are still higher than the baseline scores. This comparison is still valid when we consider the test set results. For reasons probably tied to the random sampling done when splitting the data set, the score ranking are reversed in the test set, yet results are very similar and the slight differences between the two models results are not statistically significant. This shows the actual effectiveness of having a character-based model trained on only a small fraction of its "classic" BERT counterpart when facing noisy user-generated content from a data set that was proven to be much more noisy that many other similar data sets (Rosales Núñez et al., 2019).

	UPOS	UAS	LAS	%Oscar
	FSMB fine-tuned (in-domain)			
CamemBERT	*95.48*	*87.47*	*82.66*	*100*
CamemBERT_{4gb}	95.13	85.73	80.72	2.38
Character-BERT	**95.19**	**86.26**	**81.26**	1
	Sequoia fine-tuned (out domain)			
CamemBERT	*90.10*	*82.68*	*75.85*	*100*
CamemBERT_{4gb}	**90.69**	82.29	**75.83**	2.38
Character-BERT	**90.68**	**82.39**	75.39	1

Table 8: CharacterBert model performance compared with a small CamemBERT (4gb) model on the FSMB test set in in-domain and out-of-domain fine-tuning scenarios. *Full-size Camembert results are reported here for reference.*

8 Discussion

In this work, we evaluate the benefits of using a character-based model in low-resource scenarios. Our results show that training such a model from scratch on much fewer data gives similar performance to a multilingual BERT adapted to the language using the same amount of data.

Overall, our observations confirm the findings of El Boukkouri et al. (2020) regarding the robustness to noise and misspellings of the Character-BERT model. We showed that the model has competitive performance on noisy French UGC data when trained on only a fraction of the OSCAR corpus compared to CamemBERT trained on the full corpus and when trained on corpora containing about 1M words in the extremely noisy and low-resource case of NArabizi. This is consistent with the findings of Martin et al. (2020) and Micheli et al. (2020), who showed that MLM could already learn a lot from pre-training on smaller data set. Extending this investigation by training on a larger amount of data could help to explore the ability of the model to handle highly variable noisy data.

However, one could question the usefulness of such Character-BERT based models if small Bert-based models were available on the same domain. To build an answer to that question, we conducted a quick set of experiments comparing our characterBert model trained on 1% of Oscar with the off-the-shelf Camembert version trained on 4gb of the Oscar corpus French instance (2.38% of the full corpus) and which was shown to perform almost as well as the full model (Martin et al., 2020) on many downstream tasks. Both models were fined-tuned according to our MODEL+Task architecture on either the FSMB or the Sequoia treebank, allowing us to evaluate their in-domain and out-of-domain performance. Results on Table 8 confirm the effectiveness of our characterBert model with overall better results than CamemBERT_{4gb} in the in-domain scenario and similar, if not slightly better in the out-of-domain scenario, except for the labeled attachment score (75.83 vs 75.39). The fact that CamemBERT_{4gb} was trained on more than twice as much data and with 200k pre-training steps while the characterBert pre-training stopped below 20k steps probably explains this small discrepancy but further investigations are needed with a fully parallel setting where both characterBert and CamemBERT are pretrained on the same amount of data and the same hyper-parameters. The take-home message from this in-domain experiments is that CharacterBert seems to be able to better capture at least some of the UGC idiosyncracies that are prevalent in the FSMB (Seddah et al., 2012b) than its Bert-based counterparts. This was also shown by Rosales Núñez et al. (2021) in the context of character-based neural machine translation. Interestingly, their results showed that transformer-based models with subword tokenization also exhibit strong robustness to a certain type of lexical noise. This behavior has been very recently demonstrated by Itzhak and Levy (2021) and could explain why the BERT-based models we tested performed so well in our experiments. The key seems to be relying on the ability of the subword distribution to model some forms of lexical variations. Much more experiments are needed to clearly investigate in what circumstances, besides noisy and resource-scarce scenarios, characterBERT models bring in a decisive advantage.

Our results are based on the evaluation of two low-level tasks. Therefore, it would be interesting to see if they can be generalized to other – e.g. more semantic – tasks, as additional experiments on model layers configuration showed that most of the important information is captured early in the layers of the model (cf. Appendix A).

Regarding the specific case of Arabic dialects written in Arabizi, a recent BERT-based model have been pretrained on 7 millions Egyptian tweets and displayed effective results on a sentiment analysis task (Baert et al., 2020). Another very recent model, at the date of writing, was pre-trained on 4 millions Algerian tweets and also demonstrated interesting results on sentiment analysis (Abdaoui et al., 2021). Unfortunately, the authors did not perform any experiments on the Narabizi data set, making thus the comparison with our work not straightforward. It would be of course interesting to evaluate the interoperability between these new data sets and the *NArabizi* resources we used to produce our models. Head to head comparisons between these models and ours could be of value of course but we believe that given the shortcomings of finding enough data to pretrain large models for dialects, it would be probably better to first consolidate a large enough common pre-training data set and then work on model performance. We leave this for future work.

We showed that CharacterBert models trained on very little data could provide an interesting alternative to large multilingual and monolingual models in resource-scarce and noisy scenarios. This is why we release all the code, data and models to reproduce our experiments, hoping our work will favor the rise of efficient robust NLP models for under-resourced languages, domains and dialects.[10]

Acknowledgments

We thank the reviewers for their very valuable feedback. The first author was partly funded by Benoît Sagot's chair in the PRAIRIE institute funded by the French national agency ANR as part of the "Investissements d'avenir" programme under the reference ANR-19-P3IA-0001. This work also received funding from the European Union's Horizon 2020 research and innovation programme under grant agreement No. 101021607 and from the French Research Agency via the ANR ParSiTi project (ANR-16-CE33-0021).

[10] https://gitlab.inria.fr/ariabi/character-bert-ugc

References

Amine Abdaoui, Mohamed Berrimi, Mourad Oussalah, and Abdelouahab Moussaoui. 2021. Dziribert: a pre-trained language model for the algerian dialect.

Djegdjiga Amazouz, Martine Adda-Decker, and Lori Lamel. 2017. Addressing code-switching in french/algerian arabic speech. In *Interspeech 2017*, pages 62–66.

Waleed Ammar, George Mulcaire, Yulia Tsvetkov, Guillaume Lample, Chris Dyer, and Noah A. Smith. 2016. Massively multilingual word embeddings. *ArXiv*, abs/1602.01925.

Wissam Antoun, Fady Baly, and Hazem Hajj. 2020. Arabert: Transformer-based model for arabic language understanding. *arXiv preprint arXiv:2003.00104*.

Gaétan Baert, Souhir Gahbiche, Guillaume Gadek, and Alexandre Pauchet. 2020. Arabizi language models for sentiment analysis. In *Proceedings of the 28th International Conference on Computational Linguistics*, pages 592–603, Barcelona, Spain (Online). International Committee on Computational Linguistics.

Marie Candito, Benoît Crabbé, and Pascal Denis. 2010. Statistical French dependency parsing: Treebank conversion and first results. In *Proceedings of the Seventh International Conference on Language Resources and Evaluation (LREC'10)*, Valletta, Malta. European Language Resources Association (ELRA).

Marie Candito and Djamé Seddah. 2012. Le corpus sequoia: annotation syntaxique et exploitation pour l'adaptation d'analyseur par pont lexical. In *TALN 2012-19e conférence sur le Traitement Automatique des Langues Naturelles*.

Jonathan H. Clark, Dan Garrette, Iulia Turc, and John Wieting. 2021. Canine: Pre-training an efficient tokenization-free encoder for language representation.

Alexis Conneau, Kartikay Khandelwal, Naman Goyal, Vishrav Chaudhary, Guillaume Wenzek, Francisco Guzmán, Edouard Grave, Myle Ott, Luke Zettlemoyer, and Veselin Stoyanov. 2019. Unsupervised cross-lingual representation learning at scale. *arXiv preprint arXiv:1911.02116*.

Alexis Conneau, Kartikay Khandelwal, Naman Goyal, Vishrav Chaudhary, Guillaume Wenzek, Francisco Guzmán, Edouard Grave, Myle Ott, Luke Zettlemoyer, and Veselin Stoyanov. 2020. Unsupervised cross-lingual representation learning at scale. In *Proceedings of the 58th Annual Meeting of the Association for Computational Linguistics*, pages 8440–8451, Online. Association for Computational Linguistics.

Ryan Cotterell, Adithya Renduchintala, Naomi Saphra, and Chris Callison-Burch. 2014. An Algerian Arabic-French code-switched corpus. In *Workshop on Free/Open-Source Arabic Corpora and Corpora Processing Tools Workshop Programme*, page 34.

Jacob Devlin, Ming-Wei Chang, Kenton Lee, and Kristina Toutanova. 2018. Bert: Pre-training of deep bidirectional transformers for language understanding. *arXiv preprint arXiv:1810.04805*.

Jacob Devlin, Ming-Wei Chang, Kenton Lee, and Kristina Toutanova. 2019. BERT: Pre-training of deep bidirectional transformers for language understanding. In *Proceedings of the 2019 Conference of the North American Chapter of the Association for Computational Linguistics: Human Language Technologies, Volume 1 (Long and Short Papers)*, pages 4171–4186, Minneapolis, Minnesota. Association for Computational Linguistics.

Timothy Dozat and Christopher D Manning. 2016. Deep biaffine attention for neural dependency parsing. *arXiv preprint arXiv:1611.01734*.

Julian Martin Eisenschlos, Sebastian Ruder, Piotr Czapla, Marcin Kardas, Sylvain Gugger, and Jeremy Howard. 2019. Multifit: Efficient multilingual language model fine-tuning. *arXiv preprint arXiv:1909.04761*.

Jacob Eisenstein. 2013. What to do about bad language on the internet. In *Proceedings of the 2013 conference of the North American Chapter of the association for computational linguistics: Human language technologies*, pages 359–369.

Hicham El Boukkouri, Olivier Ferret, Thomas Lavergne, Hiroshi Noji, Pierre Zweigenbaum, and Jun'ichi Tsujii. 2020. CharacterBERT: Reconciling ELMo and BERT for word-level open-vocabulary representations from characters. In *Proceedings of the 28th International Conference on Computational Linguistics*, pages 6903–6915, Barcelona, Spain (Online). International Committee on Computational Linguistics.

Jennifer Foster. 2010. "cba to check the spelling": Investigating parser performance on discussion forum posts. In *Human Language Technologies: The 2010 Annual Conference of the North American Chapter of the Association for Computational Linguistics*, pages 381–384, Los Angeles, California. Association for Computational Linguistics.

Loïc Grobol and Benoît Crabbé. 2021. Analyse en dépendances du français avec des plongements contextualisés. In *Actes de la 28ème Conférence sur le Traitement Automatique des Langues Naturelles*.

Suchin Gururangan, Ana Marasović, Swabha Swayamdipta, Kyle Lo, Iz Beltagy, Doug Downey, and Noah A. Smith. 2020. Don't stop pretraining: Adapt language models to domains and tasks. In *Proceedings of the 58th Annual Meeting of the*

Association for Computational Linguistics, pages 8342–8360, Online. Association for Computational Linguistics.

Nizar Habash. 2010. *Introduction to Arabic Natural Language Processing*. Morgan and Claypool.

Jeremy Howard and Sebastian Ruder. 2018. Universal language model fine-tuning for text classification. *arXiv preprint arXiv:1801.06146*.

Itay Itzhak and Omer Levy. 2021. Models in a spelling bee: Language models implicitly learn the character composition of tokens.

Ganesh Jawahar, Benoît Sagot, and Djamé Seddah. 2019. What does bert learn about the structure of language? In *ACL 2019-57th Annual Meeting of the Association for Computational Linguistics*.

Pratik Joshi, Sebastin Santy, Amar Budhiraja, Kalika Bali, and Monojit Choudhury. 2020. The state and fate of linguistic diversity and inclusion in the NLP world. In *Proceedings of the 58th Annual Meeting of the Association for Computational Linguistics*, pages 6282–6293, Online. Association for Computational Linguistics.

Armand Joulin, Edouard Grave, Piotr Bojanowski, Matthijs Douze, Hérve Jégou, and Tomas Mikolov. 2016. Fasttext. zip: Compressing text classification models. *arXiv preprint arXiv:1612.03651*.

Taku Kudo. 2018a. Subword regularization: Improving neural network translation models with multiple subword candidates. In *Proceedings of the 56th Annual Meeting of the Association for Computational Linguistics (Volume 1: Long Papers)*, pages 66–75, Melbourne, Australia. Association for Computational Linguistics.

Taku Kudo. 2018b. Subword regularization: Improving neural network translation models with multiple subword candidates.

Anne Lacheret, Sylvain Kahane, Julie Beliao, Anne Dister, Kim Gerdes, Jean-Philippe Goldman, Nicolas Obin, Paola Pietrandrea, and Atanas Tchobanov. 2014. Rhapsodie: a prosodic-syntactic treebank for spoken french. In *Language Resources and Evaluation Conference*.

Guillaume Lample and Alexis Conneau. 2019. Cross-lingual language model pretraining. *arXiv preprint arXiv:1901.07291*.

Yinhan Liu, Myle Ott, Naman Goyal, Jingfei Du, Mandar Joshi, Danqi Chen, Omer Levy, Mike Lewis, Luke Zettlemoyer, and Veselin Stoyanov. 2019. Roberta: A robustly optimized bert pretraining approach. *arXiv preprint arXiv:1907.11692*.

Wentao Ma, Yiming Cui, Chenglei Si, Ting Liu, Shijin Wang, and Guoping Hu. 2020a. Charbert: Character-aware pre-trained language model. *Proceedings of the 28th International Conference on Computational Linguistics*.

Wentao Ma, Yiming Cui, Chenglei Si, Ting Liu, Shijin Wang, and Guoping Hu. 2020b. Charbert: Character-aware pre-trained language model. *arXiv preprint arXiv:2011.01513*.

Louis Martin, Benjamin Muller, Pedro Javier Ortiz Suárez, Yoann Dupont, Laurent Romary, Éric de la Clergerie, Djamé Seddah, and Benoît Sagot. 2020. CamemBERT: a tasty French language model. In *Proceedings of the 58th Annual Meeting of the Association for Computational Linguistics*, pages 7203–7219, Online. Association for Computational Linguistics.

Ryan McDonald, Joakim Nivre, Yvonne Quirmbach-Brundage, Yoav Goldberg, Dipanjan Das, Kuzman Ganchev, Keith Hall, Slav Petrov, Hao Zhang, Oscar Täckström, et al. 2013. Universal dependency annotation for multilingual parsing. In *Proceedings of the 51st Annual Meeting of the Association for Computational Linguistics (Volume 2: Short Papers)*, pages 92–97.

Vincent Micheli, Martin d'Hoffschmidt, and François Fleuret. 2020. On the importance of pre-training data volume for compact language models. In *Proceedings of the 2020 Conference on Empirical Methods in Natural Language Processing (EMNLP)*, pages 7853–7858, Online. Association for Computational Linguistics.

Benjamin Muller, Antonios Anastasopoulos, Benoît Sagot, and Djamé Seddah. 2021a. When being unseen from mBERT is just the beginning: Handling new languages with multilingual language models. In *Proceedings of the 2021 Conference of the North American Chapter of the Association for Computational Linguistics: Human Language Technologies*, pages 448–462, Online. Association for Computational Linguistics.

Benjamin Muller, Yanai Elazar, Benoît Sagot, and Djamé Seddah. 2021b. First align, then predict: Understanding the cross-lingual ability of multilingual BERT. In *Proceedings of the 16th Conference of the European Chapter of the Association for Computational Linguistics: Main Volume*, pages 2214–2231, Online. Association for Computational Linguistics.

Benjamin Muller, Benoit Sagot, and Djamé Seddah. 2020. Can multilingual language models transfer to an unseen dialect? a case study on north african arabizi. *arXiv preprint arXiv:2005.00318*.

Joakim Nivre, Marie-Catherine de Marneffe, Filip Ginter, Jan Hajič, Christopher D. Manning, Sampo Pyysalo, Sebastian Schuster, Francis Tyers, and Daniel Zeman. 2020. Universal Dependencies v2: An evergrowing multilingual treebank collection. In *Proceedings of the 12th Language Resources and Evaluation Conference*, pages 4034–4043, Marseille, France. European Language Resources Association.

Richard Nordquist. Linguistic variation [online]. 2019.

Matthew E. Peters, Mark Neumann, Mohit Iyyer, Matt Gardner, Christopher Clark, Kenton Lee, and Luke Zettlemoyer. 2018a. Deep contextualized word representations. In *Proceedings of the 2018 Conference of the North American Chapter of the Association for Computational Linguistics: Human Language Technologies, Volume 1 (Long Papers)*, pages 2227–2237, New Orleans, Louisiana. Association for Computational Linguistics.

Matthew E Peters, Mark Neumann, Mohit Iyyer, Matt Gardner, Christopher Clark, Kenton Lee, and Luke Zettlemoyer. 2018b. Deep contextualized word representations. *arXiv preprint arXiv:1802.05365*.

Jonas Pfeiffer, Ivan Vulić, Iryna Gurevych, and Sebastian Ruder. 2020. MAD-X: An Adapter-Based Framework for Multi-Task Cross-Lingual Transfer. In *Proceedings of the 2020 Conference on Empirical Methods in Natural Language Processing (EMNLP)*, pages 7654–7673, Online. Association for Computational Linguistics.

Telmo Pires, Eva Schlinger, and Dan Garrette. 2019. How multilingual is multilingual BERT? In *Proceedings of the 57th Annual Meeting of the Association for Computational Linguistics*, pages 4996–5001, Florence, Italy. Association for Computational Linguistics.

Danish Pruthi, Bhuwan Dhingra, and Zachary C. Lipton. 2019. Combating adversarial misspellings with robust word recognition. In *Proceedings of the 57th Annual Meeting of the Association for Computational Linguistics*, pages 5582–5591, Florence, Italy. Association for Computational Linguistics.

Colin Raffel, Noam Shazeer, Adam Roberts, Katherine Lee, Sharan Narang, Michael Matena, Yanqi Zhou, Wei Li, and Peter J Liu. 2020. Exploring the limits of transfer learning with a unified text-to-text transformer. *Journal of Machine Learning Research*, 21(140):1–67.

José Carlos Rosales Núñez, Djamé Seddah, and Guillaume Wisniewski. 2019. Comparison between NMT and PBSMT performance for translating noisy user-generated content. In *Proceedings of the 22nd Nordic Conference on Computational Linguistics*, pages 2–14, Turku, Finland. Linköping University Electronic Press.

José Carlos Rosales Núñez, Guillaume Wisniewski, and Djamé Seddah. 2021. Noisy ugc translation at the character level: Revisiting open-vocabulary capabilities and robustness of char-based models. In *Proceedings of the Seventh Workshop on Noisy User-generated Text (W-NUT 2022)*, Punta Cana, Dominican Republic.

Manuela Sanguinetti, Lauren Cassidy, Cristina Bosco, Özlem Çetinoglu, Alessandra Teresa Cignarella, Teresa Lynn, Ines Rehbein, Josef Ruppenhofer, Djamé Seddah, and Amir Zeldes. 2020. Treebanking user-generated content: a UD based overview of guidelines, corpora and unified recommendations. *CoRR*, abs/2011.02063.

Timo Schick and Hinrich Schütze. 2020. Rare words: A major problem for contextualized embeddings and how to fix it by attentive mimicking. In *Proceedings of the AAAI Conference on Artificial Intelligence*, volume 34, pages 8766–8774.

Djamé Seddah, Farah Essaidi, Amal Fethi, Matthieu Futeral, Benjamin Muller, Pedro Javier Ortiz Suárez, Benoît Sagot, and Abhishek Srivastava. 2020. Building a user-generated content North-African Arabizi treebank: Tackling hell. In *Proceedings of the 58th Annual Meeting of the Association for Computational Linguistics*, pages 1139–1150, Online. Association for Computational Linguistics.

Djamé Seddah, Benoit Sagot, Marie Candito, Virginie Mouilleron, and Vanessa Combet. 2012a. The French Social Media Bank: a treebank of noisy user generated content. In *Proceedings of COLING 2012*, pages 2441–2458, Mumbai, India. The COLING 2012 Organizing Committee.

Djamé Seddah, Benoit Sagot, Marie Candito, Virginie Mouilleron, and Vanessa Combet. 2012b. The french social media bank: a treebank of noisy user generated content. In *COLING 2012-24th International Conference on Computational Linguistics*.

Rupesh Kumar Srivastava, Klaus Greff, and Jürgen Schmidhuber. 2015. Highway networks. *arXiv preprint arXiv:1505.00387*.

Pedro Javier Ortiz Suárez, Benoît Sagot, and Laurent Romary. 2019. Asynchronous pipeline for processing huge corpora on medium to low resource infrastructures. In *7th Workshop on the Challenges in the Management of Large Corpora (CMLC-7)*. Leibniz-Institut für Deutsche Sprache.

Lichao Sun, Kazuma Hashimoto, Wenpeng Yin, Akari Asai, Jia Li, Philip Yu, and Caiming Xiong. 2020. Adv-bert: Bert is not robust on misspellings! generating nature adversarial samples on bert.

Yi Tay, Vinh Q. Tran, Sebastian Ruder, Jai Gupta, Hyung Won Chung, Dara Bahri, Zhen Qin, Simon Baumgartner, Cong Yu, and Donald Metzler. 2021. Charformer: Fast character transformers via gradient-based subword tokenization.

Clara Vania, Yova Kementchedjhieva, Anders Søgaard, and Adam Lopez. 2019. A systematic comparison of methods for low-resource dependency parsing on genuinely low-resource languages. *arXiv preprint arXiv:1909.02857*.

Xinyi Wang, Sebastian Ruder, and Graham Neubig. 2021. Multi-view subword regularization.

Shijie Wu and Mark Dredze. 2020. Are all languages created equal in multilingual BERT? In *Proceedings of the 5th Workshop on Representation Learning for NLP*, pages 120–130, Online. Association for Computational Linguistics.

Linting Xue, Aditya Barua, Noah Constant, Rami Al-Rfou, Sharan Narang, Mihir Kale, Adam Roberts, and Colin Raffel. 2021. Byt5: Towards a token-free future with pre-trained byte-to-byte models.

A Layer Configuration Experiments

We focus on the scalar mix strategy to study the effect of the combination of different subsets of layers on the accuracy of the downstream task, instead of only aggregating all layers. For example, it has been shown that higher layers contain more semantic information, while lower layers contain more syntactic information (Jawahar et al., 2019). We compare several layer configurations, that is different subsets of the transformer from which we get the sentence representation.

The effect of the Layer Configuration We report in tables 9a, 9b and 9c the scores for the different layers combinations for CamemBERT, mBERT and CharacterBERT respectively. For mBERT and CamemBERT, the performance increases when using the last layers, while for CharacterBERT, there is no big difference between the different layers combinations. For example for the setup MODEL+TASK, the accuracy for POS tagging (UPOS) goes from around 70 with the first layer using CamemBERT and mBERT, and reaches 80 using CharacterBERT_arabizi. For CharacterBERT, these scores stay around 80 even when using farther layers (for layers 4 to 7 for instance, the UPOS score is 80.53 and for layers 6-11 it is around 80.34), and while using the last layer gives the best score of 81.19, the latter is still considered around 80 and the stagnation in the scores is hence visible. Contrarily, for CamemBERT and mBERT, the UPOS scores for the MODEL+TASK setup increase from around 70 using only the first layer to above 80 when using layers 6 through 11 (80.39 for CamemBERT and 80.72 for mBERT). The best UPOS score for CamemBERT appears when using the last layer alone (81.14) while for mBERT it is when using layers 6 through 11 (80.72). This clearly illustrates the increase of performance when using higher layers for CamemBERT and mBERT. The same observation can be made for UPOS scores in the MODEL+MLM+TASK setup for mBERT and CamemBERT, and for the other Unlabeled Attachment Score (UAS) and Labeled Attachment Score (LAS) scores as well.

One possible explanation is that the information captured by CharacterBERT layers does not evolve along the model's layers. The model produces a single embedding for any input token based on an aggregation of the characters embeddings while for BERT-like-models, each sub-word unit in a word is embedded using a WordPiece embedding matrix. Therefore, a possible interpretation is that CharacterBERT learns all the information at the earliest layers as we feed it the whole word directly and not an inconstant count of sub-words when WordPiece vocabulary is in use. Moreover, less than 10% of the 100 000 most frequent sub-words in the *NArabizi* raw data are present in the mBERT vocab due to the high variability of NArabizi.

Layer Config	MODEL+TASK			MODEL+MLM+TASK		
	UPOS	UAS	LAS	UPOS	UAS	LAS
0	68.38	66.21	50.61	70.89	64.74	49.81
0-5	77.93	70.51	57.04	80.95	72.21	59.45
4-7	79.63	70.18	57.56	81.57	72.54	60.92
6-11	80.39	71.88	58.41	**83.65**	74.15	62.15
11	**81.14**	**72.59**	**60.35**	83.08	73.77	62.00
all	80.15	70.46	58.08	**83.65**	**74.62**	**62.62**

(a) **CamemBERT**

Layer Config	MODEL+TASK			MODEL+MLM+TASK		
	UPOS	UAS	LAS	UPOS	UAS	LAS
0	73.63	65.36	52.08	75.43	66.21	52.98
0-5	79.40	**69.19**	57.23	82.37	69.90	58.08
4-7	80.62	69.61	57.33	83.74	72.45	62.05
6-11	**80.72**	68.53	56.76	**85.02**	72.40	61.63
11	80.48	**69.19**	**57.89**	84.55	**73.82**	**62.67**
all	80.25	**69.19**	56.14	84.31	72.78	61.67

(b) **mBERT**

Layer Config	NArabizi			Sample OSCAR			NArabizi + Oscar		
	99k			99k			66k+33k		
	UPOS	UAS	LAS	UPOS	UAS	LAS	UPOS	UAS	LAS
0	78.92	**70.79**	57.99	78.26	69.61	56.76	79.25	69.33	57.14
0-5	79.63	70.23	57.99	79.54	70.13	56.76	79.06	68.05	55.25
4-7	80.53	69.28	57.47	79.77	**70.75**	**57.84**	80.10	**69.90**	56.76
6-11	80.34	70.60	57.84	78.26	68.43	55.58	**80.91**	69.66	**57.80**
11	**81.19**	70.56	**58.65**	78.83	69.52	56.33	80.67	**69.90**	57.75
all	79.96	69.47	57.84	**80.62**	68.76	56.76	80.15	**69.90**	57.56

(c) **CharacterBERT**

Table 9: Performances of the models on the *NArabizi* treebank using **different combinations of the model layers** for embeddings.

"Something Something Hota Hai!" An Explainable Approach towards Sentiment Analysis on Indian Code-Mixed Data

Aman Priyanshu* [1], **Sudarshan Sivakumar*** [2], **Supriti Vijay*** [2], **Nipuna Chhabra*** [2], **Aleti Vardhan*** [2]

[1]Department of Information and Communication Technology
[2]Department of Computer Science and Engineering
Manipal Institute of Technology,
Manipal Academy of Higher Education,
Manipal, India-576104.

{aman.priyanshu, sudarshan.sivakumar, supriti.vijay, nipuna.chhabra, aleti.vardhan}@learner.manipal.edu

Abstract

The increasing use of social media sites in countries like India has given rise to large volumes of code-mixed data. Sentiment analysis of this data can provide integral insights into people's perspectives and opinions. Code-mixed data is often noisy in nature due to multiple spellings for the same word, lack of definite order of words in a sentence, and random abbreviations. Thus, working with code-mixed data is more challenging than monolingual data. Interpreting a model's predictions allows us to determine the robustness of the model against different forms of noise. In this paper, we propose a methodology to integrate explainable approaches into code-mixed sentiment analysis. By interpreting the predictions of sentiment analysis models we evaluate how well the model is able to adapt to the implicit noises present in code-mixed data.

1 Introduction

In the Hindi movie Jab We Met, the lead actress Kareena Kapoor has a famous line in which she says, "Main apni favourite hoon," which translates to "I am my favourite." While this dialogue remains iconic in Indian pop culture even 14 years after the film's release, it also represents the phenomenon of code-mixing that is very common in multilingual countries like India. Code-Mixing is a phenomenon of embedding linguistic units such as phrases or words of one language into another language (Poplack and Walker, 2003). English words, for instance, are often mixed with Hindi sentences to form what is colloquially known as Hinglish. Over the past decade, social media sites like Twitter and Facebook have seen an exponential rise in users from countries like India. This has led to an accumulation of a large volume of code-mixed data on these platforms. Therefore, analysing and processing this data has become imperative to provide users with the best possible experience on these sites. An important technique used to analyse such large amounts of data is sentiment analysis, which labels a given text as positive, negative, or neutral. Its applications include product management, customer satisfaction review, hate speech detection and censoring of abusive and derogatory speech.

The rise in the use of deep learning models for sentiment analysis has led to more accurate predictions (Peters et al., 2018; Vaswani et al., 2017; Wang et al., 2018).These algorithms behave like black boxes, making it difficult for practitioners to understand model predictions. Explainable AI provides a set of methods to help us understand and interpret a model's decisions. Specifically for the task of sentiment analysis of textual data, these techniques allow us to understand how a word or phrase influences the sentiment of the text.

This paper discusses the implications and importance of model-agnostic explainable methods for code-mixed data. We observe that due to the unavailability of NLP tools for Hindi-English Code-Mixed text and the noisy nature of such data, several popular methods for Sentiment Analysis are not applicable (Prabhu et al., 2016). Therefore we first conduct a survey of models on the SAIL code-mixed dataset (Sarkar, 2018) and interpret their decisions with LIME and SHAP.

2 Related Work

2.1 Sentiment Analysis of Code-Mixed Data

While sentiment analysis has been extensively studied for English text (Joshi et al., 2010; Socher et al., 2013; Zhang et al., 2018), it is only recently that its applications to code-mixed data have been explored. Traditional machine learning approaches such as Support Vector Machines, logistic regression, and random forests have shown a reasonable level of accuracy in this task(Mishra et al., 2018).

* All authors have contributed equally to the work.

Proceedings of the 2021 EMNLP Workshop W-NUT: The Seventh Workshop on Noisy User-generated Text, pages 437–444
November 11, 2021. ©2021 Association for Computational Linguistics

Even shallow parsing (Sharma et al., 2016) and word-level identification of code-mixed data (Chittaranjan et al., 2014) have proven to boost classification performance.

However, deep learning models such as LSTMs and CNNs perform comparatively better as they efficiently process sequential data.(Niu et al., 2018; Wang et al., 2016; Kim, 2014). (Kumar et al., 2018) used phonemic sub-word units with a hierarchical Bi-directional LSTM (BiLSTM) model to detect sentiment in Hi-En code-mixed texts. (Choudhary et al., 2018) employs Bidirectional LSTM networks with shared parameters to capture a sentiment-based representation of the sentences. On the other hand, (Kumar et al., 2020) presents an ensemble of both CNN and self-attention based LSTM, using XLM-R embeddings (Conneau et al., 2020).

Sub-word and bi-gram based models also perform well due to their ability to capture dialect variations in Hindi and the inconsistencies of code-mixing (Prabhu et al., 2016). However, due to the noisy nature of the dataset, models still perform poorly. (Ghosh et al., 2017) uses extensive pre-processing to remove noise from raw text, allowing better performance to be achieved.

2.2 Explainable AI approaches to sentiment analysis

In order to trust a model's predictions, one must be able to interpret the reasons behind its decisions. Several attempts have been made to infer the text classification and sentiment analysis predictions of language models. State of the art model-agnostic explanations like LIME (Local Interpretable Model-Agnostic Explanations) (Ribeiro et al., 2016) and SHAP (SHapley Additive exPlanations) (Lundberg and Lee, 2017) enable better visualisation and analysis of AI models.

(Kokalj et al., 2021) adapts SHAP to transformer models such as BERT-based classifiers. (Chen et al., 2020) proposes a model-agnostic approach named HEDGE to build hierarchical explanations by detecting the interactions between features of a model. One of the drawbacks of these model-agnostic techniques is the computational complexity and the processing time required to execute them. (Bodria et al., 2020) addresses this by using attention-based techniques to extract meaningful sentiment scores with a lower computational cost than existing XAI methods.

3 Preliminaries

Various techniques have been used to achieve accurate results in sentiment analysis. A simplistic and computationally inexpensive approach is the random forest. A random forest is generated by bagging multiple uncorrelated decision trees but may fail to capture context and complexities. We look at Convolutional Neural Networks and Long Short Term Memory(LSTM) to overcome this problem. Word embeddings, which are numeric representations for each word within a given sentence, are used to enable contextual learning over these networks.

Convolutional Neural Networks are a class of Neural networks commonly used in computer vision. They also show promising results in NLP tasks such as Sentiment Analysis. When applied to the input embedding matrix, the convolution operation captures the local features and relationships between the words of the sentence, outperforming feed-forward neural networks and machine learning algorithms such as Random Forests (Kim, 2014).

Although CNNs are great for capturing local features, they lose information about the order of words in a given sentence. The loss of sequential information significantly hampers performance, and recurrent neural networks such as LSTMs and GRUs are better suited for this. **LSTMs** are designed to infer sequential data, making them some of the most viable neural network architectures for sentiment analysis. Their ability to deal with vanishing gradients and their relative insensitivity to gap length gives them an advantage over other sequential models.

However, sentence structure goes beyond just sequential comprehension, and therefore a structured model that would allow word association becomes necessary for performance improvement (Hochreiter and Schmidhuber, 1997).

Bidirectional Encoder Representations from Transformers (BERT) utilizes the bidirectional training of Transformers, a popular attention model for learning. The architecture is built for the objective of masked language modelling and achieves considerably high performance compared to other word embedding techniques. The masked language model enables a fusion of both left-to-right and right-to-left contexts and makes the Transformer bidirectional. BERT also achieves Next Sentence Prediction (NSP), where the model receives a pair

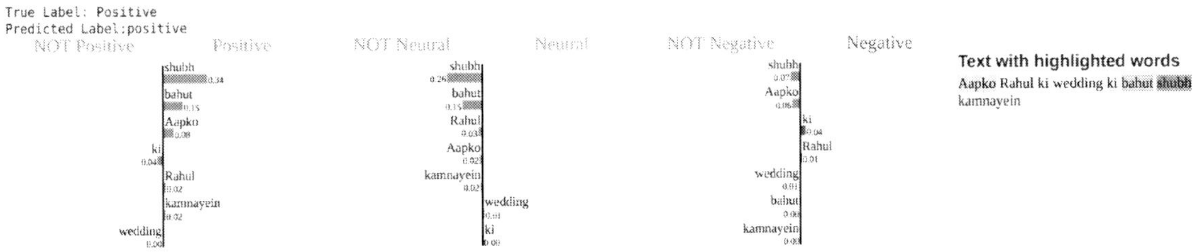

Figure 1: LIME gives numeric explainations to each and every word in a given sentence. This allows one to infer how important a word is to the classifier function, allowing the user to understand the predicted sentiment better.

of sentences as inputs and predicts whether the second sentence is in conjunction with the first (Devlin et al., 2018). XLM-RoBERTa, a variant of BERT is a transformer-based cross-lingual language model trained on 100 different languages (Conneau et al., 2020).

3.1 Explainable AI

In order to increase transparency and accountability in model architectures, we utilize model-agnostic methods, like LIME and SHAP.

LIME (Ribeiro et al., 2016) stands for Local Interpretable Model-Agnostic Explanations (LIME). Local here refers to examining the model's behaviour around an instance of the dataset rather than the entire dataset. The explanations are in the form of numerical measurements of significant features of the input data. LIME is also model-agnostic, which means that it can be applied to any machine learning model. LIME works based on input perturbations and their respective changes on the model output.

As LIME works on the assumption that every complex model is linear on a local scale, it creates a simple linear model to approximate how the global model behaves at a particular local data point. A proximity-based weighted set of perturbed inputs is used to train the local interpretable model by learning their associated outputs from the target or global model. The outcomes of the locally linear model give us illustratable numeric values to interpret model decisions.

SHAP or SHapley Additive exPlanations (Lundberg and Lee, 2017) leverages the idea of Shapley values of game theory for model feature influence scoring. These values can be defined as the average marginal contribution of a feature value over all possible coalitions. Unlike LIME, SHAP can be used to interpret feature dependency on the entire model. This methodology can summarize model dependency metrics, allowing us to better leverage interpretation for the entire model and the dataset. Thus, it provides us with better global explanations than local explanations.

4 Experimental Results

4.1 Dataset

The SAIL 2017 dataset (Sarkar, 2018) is a sentiment classification dataset on code-mixed text, with each instance labelled as positive, negative, or neutral in sentiment. This data was collected using the Twitter4j10 API to extract Hindi-English code-mixed data from Twitter. Common Hindi words were collected in Romanized format and then searched using the above API. The data was then annotated manually. It consists of a total of 12,601 instances of text, with corresponding sentiment labels. The dataset is pre-split into three subsets: training set, validation set, and test set; their distribution has been presented in Table 1. There are a total of 199071 words across all the instances with 99965 Hindi words and 99106 English words. As seen below, the dataset is relatively balanced, making accuracy an appropriate evaluation metric.

	Positive	**Neutral**	**Negative**	**Total**
Train	3202	4558	2319	10079
Val	399	578	283	1260
Test	385	586	290	1261

Table 1: The Table describes the data distribution for the SAIL 2017 dataset.

We provide some examples from the dataset below along with the sentiment of the examples

- *jabardust post hai buddy.*
  Translation : it's an amazing post, buddy
  Sentiment : Positive

Models	SVM	Random Forest	CNN	CNN Glove Embeddings	LSTM	LSTM Glove Embeddings	XLM-RoBERTa
Train Accuracy	87.46%	96.93%	53.17%	58.02%	61.00%	66.08%	85.30%
Test Accuracy	56.22%	54.16%	54.08%	56.98%	49.48%	59.09%	72.21%

Table 2: The Table details the model accuracy results upon training different machine learning models. We use this as a benchmarking reference to evaluate model utility, and choose to infer the model which performs the best, for further inspection using LIME and SHAP.

- *Aur puucha ke fourthg memberg kaha hai??*
  Translation : and asked where is the fourth member
  Sentiment : Neutral
- *bachpan me inn advertisement ne bahut confuse kiya hai*
  Translation : in my childhood, this advertisement confused me a lot
  Sentiment : Negative

Noise in code mixed data extracted from social media platforms includes abbreviations, variation in spellings for the same word, no standard grammar typos, emoji's etc. As shown in the examples, words like *puucha, me* etc don't have one standard spelling that is agreed upon by different users. *Pucha* for instance can also be written as *pucha* or *poocha*. On the other hand, typos refer to misspelled words like *fourthg*, *memberg* etc whose standard spellings would be *fourth* and *member* respectively.

4.2 Classification Results

In our venture to integrate explainable AI on code-mixed data, we evaluated multiple models for performance comparison. We provide the resultant performances of each of these in Table 2. Our comparison spanned tree-based random forest, SVMs, LSTMs, CNNs, and a RoBERTa model pre-trained on codemixed data. For the random forest and SVM model, we used a TF-IDF vectorizer as our word representation. While for the LSTM and CNN architecture, we compare randomly initialized word embeddings and pre-trained GloVe embeddings. These GloVe embeddings were pre-trained on the Twitter crawl, which consisted of about two billion tweets. As shown in Table 2, these embeddings improved LSTM and CNN performance significantly and allowed it to generalize better. Whereas the use of random forest gave us a highly overfitted classifier, as shown in Table 2.

Inferring the performance presented in Table 2, we can see that the XLM-RoBERTa model is the best performing model and acts as the appropriate candidate for further exploration using explainable AI. This can be attributed to the fact that XLM-RoBERTa was pretrained on code-mixed data and better captures the contextual meaning of words. As the model gives significantly higher performance than its other counterparts, we used LIME and SHAP to infer this classification aptitude.

4.3 Inferring LIME for Global Explainations

Negative	Neutral	Positive
laat (kick)	thk (ok)	shadi (wedding)
kutta (dog)	kuch (a bit)	mubarak (congrats)
theek (ok)	abhi (now)	karein (do)
karega (will do)	are (exclamation)	jai (hail)
sala (abuse)	mai (I)	maja (fun)
maar (to beat)	haan (yes)	lage (toward)
phle (first)	kaash (wish)	aage (ahead)
kyu (why)	ghar (home)	wah (wow)
bohot (very)	_	paise (money)
nahi (no)	agar (if)	ache (good)

Table 3: The Table describes globally significant words using LIME explainations. We mention their English translations alongside them.

LIME provides independent explanations for each instance of the data. However, to compare and evaluate it against SHAP, we compute the global significance of each feature using its local explanations. To better represent their data-wide relevance, we calculate the mean of each explanation weight provided by every word; this allows us to pull important words for model predictions. We specifically look at Hindi words and measure their importance in sentiment predictions. Here, Hindi words were sampled from the corpus if they did not belong to the Google 10,000 words vocabulary[1].

[1] https://github.com/first20hours/google-10000-english

This allows us to determine how well the model can learn from code-mixed sentences. We describe the computation in the following equation,

$$\sum_{word_i \in vocab} \sum_{sentence_i \in 0}^{n} \frac{(word\_weight)}{n} \quad (1)$$

We provide results from this computation in Table 3. As we can see, the table works as a great summarizing tool for each sentiment, capable of pulling offensive texts for negative samples and respectful or congratulatory words for positive sentences. For instance, the term "*mubarak*" is a Hindi word meaning congratulations and can be seen significantly contributing towards the positive sentiment. We use these new computations to provide for LIME's global explanations for various future experiments.

4.4 Inferring the XLM-RoBERTa model

This section discusses the results of both LIME and SHAP explainable approaches on the code-mixed data. We present a comparison between the two methodologies by evaluating them for both global and local explanations. As SHAP can define sample-based and global explanations, we used the statistical mean of word importance extracted by LIME to infer their global significance. This allows us to compare both models on a fundamental level, thus enabling us to evaluate better.

(Ancona et al., 2018) proposed an approach called sensitivity-n to test the gradient-based attribution methods in deep neural networks. However, one of the main drawbacks of this methodology is that two distinct explainable models can not be compared with each other due to their gradient-based attribution. Another metric that we explored was perturbations to compare different methodologies. RemOve And Retrain—ROAR is another monumental advancement in this area, which uses accuracy as a metric to estimate feature importance in deep neural networks (Hooker et al., 2019). It removes data points estimated to be most important and retrains it to measure the change in performance. This allows it to compare between different explainable models. However, as the SAIL dataset consists of only a limited number of samples, making the accuracy more discrete, we choose to evaluate it on the log-odds scores. While developing these metrics, we also construct an additional metric specific to code-mixed data.

We present a comparison between the two methodologies using three metrics, described by Mean Absolute Error of Log-Odds Scores on Deletion (MAELOSD) which is defined as,

$$= \sum_{j=0}^{M} \frac{(|log\_odds_{ini}^{(j)} - log\_odds_{fin}^{(j)}|)}{M} \quad (2)$$

Where ini refers to initial sentences without word deletions, fin refers to the final sentences after the deletion of polarizing words, and M is the total number of sentences. We define polarizing words as those which have been given the highest weights by the explanations of the LIME and SHAP models.

1. MAELOSD of Sentence-Interpreted Polarizing Words (*MAELOSD-Sentence*): We delete the n most polarizing words as returned by our explainable model from the sentence and recompute the final Log-Odds Scores. We then calculate the Mean Absolute Error (MAE) for all samples as shown in Equation 2. This process is repeated for different values of n.

2. MAELOSD of Model-Interpreted Polarizing Words (*MAELOSD-Model*): We repeat the exact computation with summarized weights for the entire vocabulary(English and Hindi). As discussed above, we computed the global significance of words extracted by LIME to evaluate on the same metric. Whereas we simply used SHAP to extract its global explanations for the entire corpus.

3. MAELOSD of Code-Mixed Words (*MAELOSD-CodeMixed*): This metric calculates sentence-wise MAE upon deletion of top n polarizing Hindi words. While in MAELOSD-Sentence we delete both English and Hindi words, here we delete only the Hindi words. We consider all words which are not part of the GloVe (Wikipedia 2014 and Gigaword 5 crawl) vocabulary as Hindi words. We choose this specific embedding as there is a low chance of finding Hindi words in the Wikipedia and Gigaword 5 crawl. For instance, the word *accha* does not appear in the GloVe vocabulary, and is considered a Hindi word.

With these metrics, we can extract the significant features for the two methodologies. We expect the

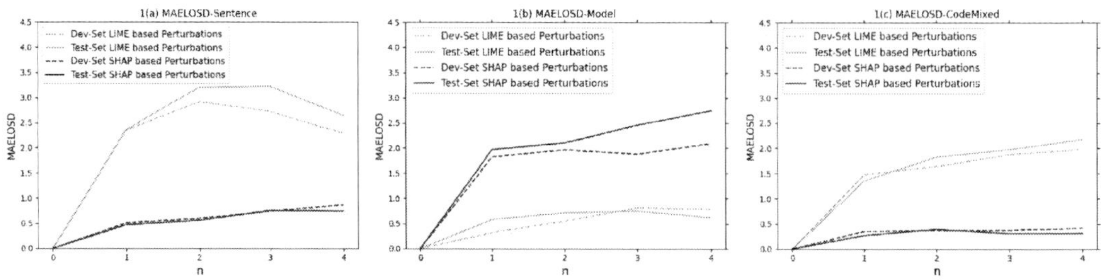

Figure 2: Metric MAELOSD for Sentence, Model, and Code-Mixed is presented in this figure.

mean absolute error to increase on the deletion of polarizing words since the model would make poor predictions.

The results of all three metrics are shown in Figure 2 where n on the x-axis refers to the number of words deleted. We can clearly observe from Figure 2(a) that LIME causes a higher variation in the MAELOSD-Sentence than SHAP. This is due to the local inferential nature of LIME, which does not incorporate the entire training corpus into its evaluation. The explainable advantage LIME displays over SHAP can be observed in the figure.

We also observe that MAELOSD-Model, which takes into account the whole dataset, returns expected results. LIME performs significantly worse due to its local nature. Furthermore, when we consider the average feature importance, certain words which may not be as significant to the local instance, are removed during metric evaluations. Figure 2(b) displays this clearly, where we can see SHAP having a better MAELOSD variation than LIME.

We can also see the impact of Hindi words from our results in Figure 2(c), where the error increases in proportion to the number of words deleted. We observe that the MAELOSD error in Figure 2(c) and 2(a), while different, follow a similar trajectory for $n \leq 3$. This establishes the significance of Hindi words in model prediction. SHAP's local explanations are interdependent on other sentences in the corpus, due to which it can perform poorly on data coming from a diverse vocabulary. As we can see SHAP's MAELOSD is close to zero for all values of n, which may imply that the Hinglish vocabulary is much more diverse than the English vocabulary. This could also be due to irregular spellings and the diverse vocabulary of code-mixed data.

An important observation one can make in Figure 2(a) is the drop in MAELOSD upon deleting $n \geq 3$ words. Although MAELOSD allows us to compare the methodologies, if a large subset of important features is removed, the remaining features may form a different distribution than the training data. Thus, it becomes unclear whether the degradation in MAELOSD comes from the distribution shift or due to the poor performance of the explainable model (Zhou et al., 2021).

Our results align with the application of both LIME and SHAP, demonstrating their local and global natures respectively. We can see the application and easy integration of model-agnostic interpretability pipelines on code-mixed data.

5 Conclusion and Future Work

Code-mixed data is an integral part of communication in multilingual communities and their culture. The application of state-of-the-art interpretable methods on this assortment of data will pave a path towards the adoption of the same during real-world implementation. Our use of LIME and SHAP, which quantify local and global model explanations, allows us to display their importance and relevance in sentiment analysis of code-mixed data. Our work demonstrates that locally sensitive explanations provided by LIME, give higher mean absolute error when the number of deletions increases. Here, essential deletions refers to the deletion of polarizing words which influence the classifier's output. We also observe the model's ability to pick up polarizing Hindi words, even in a code-mixed context. SHAP can be applied to produce high-quality global interpretations and extract model sensitivity. On the other hand, LIME can be used for locally sensitive explanations, allowing developers to focus on individual users' sentiments.

For future explorations, we would like to explore these techniques on more datasets and compare their performance. We also look to include other explainable methods and develop a specific metric to measure the global impact of Hindi words in a code-mixed corpus. We would also like to investigate other techniques such as lexical normalization to reduce noise and measure its impact on our predictions. The trends of biases in code-mixed data can also be observed through explainable methods.

We believe that our work serves as a valuable resource for code-mixed ML practitioners, developers, and researchers. The integration with explainable methods paves a new path towards future research and development.

Acknowledgements

The authors of the paper are grateful to the reviewers in reviewing the manuscript and their valuable inputs are appreciated. We would also like to thank the Research Society MIT for supporting the project.

References

Marco Ancona, Enea Ceolini, Cengiz Öztireli, and Markus Gross. 2018. Towards better understanding of gradient-based attribution methods for deep neural networks.

Francesco Bodria, A. Panisson, A. Perotti, and Simone Piaggesi. 2020. Explainability methods for natural language processing: Applications to sentiment analysis. In *SEBD*.

Hanjie Chen, Guangtao Zheng, and Yangfeng Ji. 2020. Generating hierarchical explanations on text classification via feature interaction detection.

Gokul Chittaranjan, Yogarshi Vyas, Kalika Bali, and Monojit Choudhury. 2014. Word-level language identification using crf: Code-switching shared task report of msr india system. In *Proceedings of The First Workshop on Computational Approaches to Code Switching*, pages 73–79.

Nurendra Choudhary, Rajat Singh, Ishita Bindlish, and Manish Shrivastava. 2018. Sentiment analysis of code-mixed languages leveraging resource rich languages.

Alexis Conneau, Kartikay Khandelwal, Naman Goyal, Vishrav Chaudhary, Guillaume Wenzek, Francisco Guzmán, Edouard Grave, Myle Ott, Luke Zettlemoyer, and Veselin Stoyanov. 2020. Unsupervised cross-lingual representation learning at scale.

Jacob Devlin, Ming-Wei Chang, Kenton Lee, and Kristina Toutanova. 2018. Bert: Pre-training of deep bidirectional transformers for language understanding. *arXiv preprint arXiv:1810.04805*.

Souvick Ghosh, Satanu Ghosh, and Dipankar Das. 2017. Sentiment identification in code-mixed social media text.

Sepp Hochreiter and Jürgen Schmidhuber. 1997. Long short-term memory. *Neural computation*, 9(8):1735–1780.

Sara Hooker, Dumitru Erhan, Pieter-Jan Kindermans, and Been Kim. 2019. A benchmark for interpretability methods in deep neural networks.

Aditya Joshi, AR Balamurali, Pushpak Bhattacharyya, et al. 2010. A fall-back strategy for sentiment analysis in hindi: a case study. *Proceedings of the 8th ICON*.

Yoon Kim. 2014. Convolutional neural networks for sentence classification.

Enja Kokalj, Blaž Škrlj, Nada Lavrač, Senja Pollak, and Marko Robnik-Šikonja. 2021. BERT meets shapley: Extending SHAP explanations to transformer-based classifiers. In *Proceedings of the EACL Hackashop on News Media Content Analysis and Automated Report Generation*, pages 16–21, Online. Association for Computational Linguistics.

Ayush Kumar, Harsh Agarwal, Keshav Bansal, and Ashutosh Modi. 2020. Baksa at semeval-2020 task 9: Bolstering cnn with self-attention for sentiment analysis of code mixed text.

Upendra Kumar, Vishal Singh, Chris Andrew, Santhoshini Reddy, and Amitava Das. 2018. Consonant-vowel sequences as subword units for code-mixed languages. In *Thirty-Second AAAI Conference on Artificial Intelligence*.

Scott Lundberg and Su-In Lee. 2017. A unified approach to interpreting model predictions.

Pruthwik Mishra, Prathyusha Danda, and Pranav Dhakras. 2018. Code-mixed sentiment analysis using machine learning and neural network approaches.

Dejiao Niu, Zheng Xia, Yawen Liu, Tao Cai, Tianquan Liu, and Yongzhao Zhan. 2018. Alstm: adaptive lstm for durative sequential data. In *2018 IEEE 30th International Conference on Tools with Artificial Intelligence (ICTAI)*, pages 151–157. IEEE.

Matthew E. Peters, Mark Neumann, Mohit Iyyer, Matt Gardner, Christopher Clark, Kenton Lee, and Luke Zettlemoyer. 2018. Deep contextualized word representations.

Shana Poplack and James A Walker. 2003. Pieter muysken, bilingual speech: a typology of code-mixing. cambridge: Cambridge university press, 2000. pp. xvi+ 306. *Journal of Linguistics*, 39(3):678–683.

Ameya Prabhu, Aditya Joshi, Manish Shrivastava, and Vasudeva Varma. 2016. Towards sub-word level compositions for sentiment analysis of hindi-english code mixed text.

Marco Tulio Ribeiro, Sameer Singh, and Carlos Guestrin. 2016. "why should i trust you?": Explaining the predictions of any classifier.

Kamal Sarkar. 2018. Ju_ks@sail_codemixed-2017: Sentiment analysis for indian code mixed social media texts.

Arnav Sharma, Sakshi Gupta, Raveesh Motlani, Piyush Bansal, Manish Srivastava, Radhika Mamidi, and Dipti M Sharma. 2016. Shallow parsing pipeline for hindi-english code-mixed social media text. *arXiv preprint arXiv:1604.03136*.

Richard Socher, Alex Perelygin, Jean Wu, Jason Chuang, Christopher D Manning, Andrew Y Ng, and Christopher Potts. 2013. Recursive deep models for semantic compositionality over a sentiment treebank. In *Proceedings of the 2013 conference on empirical methods in natural language processing*, pages 1631–1642.

Ashish Vaswani, Noam Shazeer, Niki Parmar, Jakob Uszkoreit, Llion Jones, Aidan N. Gomez, Lukasz Kaiser, and Illia Polosukhin. 2017. Attention is all you need.

Alex Wang, Amanpreet Singh, Julian Michael, Felix Hill, Omer Levy, and Samuel Bowman. 2018. GLUE: A multi-task benchmark and analysis platform for natural language understanding. In *Proceedings of the 2018 EMNLP Workshop BlackboxNLP: Analyzing and Interpreting Neural Networks for NLP*, pages 353–355, Brussels, Belgium. Association for Computational Linguistics.

Jin Wang, Liang-Chih Yu, K Robert Lai, and Xuejie Zhang. 2016. Dimensional sentiment analysis using a regional cnn-lstm model. In *Proceedings of the 54th Annual Meeting of the Association for Computational Linguistics (Volume 2: Short Papers)*, pages 225–230.

Lei Zhang, Shuai Wang, and Bing Liu. 2018. Deep learning for sentiment analysis: A survey. *Wiley Interdisciplinary Reviews: Data Mining and Knowledge Discovery*, 8(4):e1253.

Jianlong Zhou, Amir H. Gandomi, Fang Chen, and Andreas Holzinger. 2021. Evaluating the quality of machine learning explanations: A survey on methods and metrics. *Electronics*, 10(5).

BERTweetFR : Domain Adaptation of Pre-Trained Language Models for French Tweets

Yanzhu Guo
École Polytechnique, France
Shanghai Jiao Tong University, China
yanzhu.guo@polytechnique.edu

Virgile Rennard
École Polytechnique, France
virgile@rennard.org

Christos Xypolopoulos
École Polytechnique, France
christos.xypolopoulos@polytechnique.edu

Michalis Vazirgiannis
École Polytechnique, France
mvazirg@lix.polytechnique.fr

Abstract

We introduce **BERTweetFR**, the first large-scale pre-trained language model for French tweets. Our model is initialized using the general-domain French language model CamemBERT (Martin et al., 2020) which follows the base architecture of BERT. Experiments show that BERTweetFR outperforms all previous general-domain French language models on two downstream Twitter NLP tasks of offensiveness identification and named entity recognition. The dataset used in the offensiveness detection task is first created and annotated by our team, filling in the gap of such analytic datasets in French. We make our model publicly available in the transformers library with the aim of promoting future research in analytic tasks for French tweets.

1 Introduction

Vector representations of words have given rise to the application of deep learning methods in NLP. Traditional pre-training approaches, such as word2vec (Mikolov et al., 2013) and GloVe (Pennington et al., 2014) are static, learning a single representation for every word regardless of context. However, words are often polysemous with different meanings depending on the context. More recently, models are trained to integrate contextual meaning : the output word embeddings depend on the whole input sequence rather than only the word itself. While the idea was initially implemented with recurrent neural networks (Dai and Le, 2015) (Ramachandran et al., 2017), recent models have predominantly been based on the transformers architecture (Vaswani et al., 2017), with BERT (Devlin et al., 2019) and RoBERTa (Liu et al., 2019) among the most popular. These contextualized word representation models have opened new doors for researchers as they can be applied to numerous downstream tasks by fine-tuning or prompting. In fact, large-scale pre-trained language models have become the go-to tool for building new NLP applications, saving researchers from the enormous amount of computational resource and data required for training model weights from scratch.

In the past few years, human society has become more digitally connected than ever before. People use social media to report the latest news, but also to express their opinions and feelings about real-world events. As one of the most popular micro-blogging platforms, Twitter has become a primary source for social media user-generated data (Ghani et al., 2019). However, tweets are more often written in informal language compared to the carefully edited texts that are published in traditional data sources such as Wikipedia and printed media. They have their own set of features such as the recurrent use of irregular or abbreviated words, the large quantity of spelling or grammatical mistakes, the employment of improper sentence structures and the occurrence of mixed languages (Farzindar and Inkpen, 2020). This presents challenges to standard NLP methods when applied to Twitter data.

Domain-adaptive pre-training has been revealed to provide significant gains in helping models encode the complexity of specific textual domains (Gururangan et al., 2020). While efforts on domain adaptation of large-scale language models to Twitter language have been made in English (Nguyen et al., 2020), there has been no similar work in any other language.

We start addressing this problem by releasing

Proceedings of the 2021 EMNLP Workshop W-NUT: The Seventh Workshop on Noisy User-generated Text, pages 445–450
November 11, 2021.

BERTweetFR, a pre-trained language model for French tweets together with a manually labeled dataset for offensiveness identification in French tweets. We evaluate our model on two downstream tasks : offensiveness identification and named entity recognition.

We compare the performance of our model to the best-performing transformer-based models pre-trained on general domain French texts, namely CamemBERT (Martin et al., 2020), FlauBERT (Le et al., 2020) and BARThez (Eddine et al., 2020). Experiments show that our model outperforms all three of them on both of the downstream tasks.

In order to facilitate future research on French tweets, we make our model publicly available on Huggingface's model hub [1] as well as on our team's website dedicated to French linguistic resources [2]. We will also release our offensiveness identification dataset while respecting the limitations of Twitter's developper policy.

2 Building the Model

In this section, we describe the collection steps and pre-procesing pipeline for our pre-training dataset, present the model architecture and introduce the training objective and optimization setup.

2.1 Pre-training Data

We use a 16GB dataset of 226M deduplicated French tweets. The tweets are deduplicated using open-source tool runiq[3]. In addition, we filter out tweets with fewer than 5 tokens assuming they do not contain substantial information. The average length of a tweet is 30 tokens.

2.1.1 Data Collection

Our final dataset for pre-training is an aggregation of three corpora from different sources. The aggregation of these corpora makes this dataset the largest one for French tweets up to this date. It is also beneficial to aggregate different corpora in order to cover tweets from different time periods with diverse topics and styles.

The three sources we use are as follows :

- We start by downloading tweets from the general Twitter Stream[4] grabbed by the Archive Team, containing of tweets streamed from January 2016 to December 2019. Selecting only the French tweets with Twitter's built-in feature, we obtain a corpus of $34M$ unique tweets.

- We also build a COVID-19 related corpus of French tweets relevant to the COVID-19 pandemic posted between September 2020 and April 2021. In this case, our filters are focused on tweets that include the hashtags "covid19" and "coronavirus". Through Twitter's public streaming API, we extracted tweets in French marked with either or both of the two above hashtags. This corpora consists of $19M$ unique tweets.

- Finally, we make use of a previous Twitter dataset constructed for socioeconomic analysis (Abitbol et al., 2018). This corpus includes a collection of tweets in French between the years 2014 and 2018. We extract $173M$ unique tweets form this corpus.

2.1.2 Data Pre-Processing

We only implement minimal data cleaning before inputting the sequences into the tokenizer. Following (Nguyen et al., 2020), we normalize the Tweets by converting user mentions and web/url links into special tokens @USER and HTTPURL.

For tokenization, we apply the CamemBERT tokenizer (Martin et al., 2020). The CamemBERT tokenizer segments input sequences into subword units using the SentencePiece (Kudo and Richardson, 2018) algorithm. This algorithm is an extension of Byte-Pair encoding (BPE) (Shibata et al., 1999) and WordPiece (Kudo, 2018) that eliminates the pre-tokenization step, thus more generally applicable. The vocabulary size is $32k$ subword tokens.

2.2 Model Architecture

BERTweetFR is initialized from the base version of CamemBERT. We choose to further fine-tune this model instead of starting from scratch because domain-adaptive pre-training have been proven to give very satisfying results in numerous downstream tasks spanning across a wide range of domains (Gururangan et al., 2020). The choice to

[1] https://huggingface.co/Yanzhu/bertweetfr-base

[2] http://master2-bigdata.polytechnique.fr/FrenchLinguisticResources/bertweetFr

[3] https://github.com/whitfin/runiq

[4] https://archive.org/details/twitterstream

employ CamemBERT instead of other French language models is based on its overall best performance on downstream tasks experimented in previous works (Eddine et al., 2020).

CamemBERT applies the multi-layer bidirectional Transformer architecture. The base version uses the same architectures as the base version of BERT with 12 layers, 768 hidden dimensions and 12 attention heads, adding up to a total of $110M$ parameters. CamemBERT follows the same optimized pre-training approach as RoBERTa, the only difference is that it uses whole-word masking and the SentencePiece tokenization instead of WordPiece.

2.3 Training Objective

Our model is trained on the Masked Language Modeling (MLM) task. With any given input sequence, 15% of the tokens are chosen for possible replacement. Among the selected tokens, 80% are further selected to be replaced by the special <MASK> token, 10% remain unchanged and 10% are replaced by random tokens. Finally, the model is trained to predict the tokens replaced by <MASK> using cross-entropy loss. Following RoBERTa, we do not fix the whole set of masked tokens during pre-processing but select them dynamically during the training process. The data is thus augmented when training for multiple epochs.

2.4 Optimization Setup

We employ the CamemBERT implementation in the transformers library (Wolf et al., 2020). The maximum sequence length is set to be 128, generating approximately $226M \times 30/128 \approx 53M$ sequence blocks. Following (Gururangan et al., 2020), we optimize the model using Adam (Kingma and Ba, 2015) with a batch size of 1280 across 8 V100 GPUs (32GB each) and a peak learning rate of 0.0001. We pre-train the model for 20 epochs in about 8 days with a total of $53M \times 20/1280 \approx 83K$ training steps.

3 Downstream Task Datasets

We evaluate the performance of BERTweetFR on two downstream Twitter NLP tasks. The datasets used in these downstream tasks are either constructed by ourselves or obtained from shared tasks in past conferences.

3.1 Offensive Language Identification

Along with the outbreak of COVID-19 came severe disruption in the French society. Effects include the public holding the government accountable for certain ways in which the pandemic was handled, as well as a rise of hateful sentiment towards the Asian community. In fact, ever since the explosion of COVID-19 on a global scale, unrest has led to an increase of violent incidents towards people of Asian descent.

In response to this phenomenon, we have created a human annotated dataset for general offensiveness detection in Tweets collected during the COVID-19 pandemic. Our dataset contains 5786 French tweets among which 1301 have been labeled as offensive. Offensiveness is not straightforward and can be subjective. In our labeling procedure, we consider a tweet as offensive in cases where personal attacks are detected. For example, "The chinese virus is tiring" would not be considered offensive, while "I hate the chinese for bringing us the chinese virus" would be. This is a binary sequence classification task. We randomly sample a 70/15/15 training/validation/test split with each class proportionally represented in each part of the split.

3.2 Named Entity Recognition

For the NER task, we take data from the CAp 2017 challenge (Lopez et al., 2017). This challenge proposes a new benchmark for the problem of NER for tweets written in French. The tweets were collected using the publicly available Twitter API and annotated with 13 types of entities : person, musicArtist, organisation, geoLoc, product, transportLine, media, sportsTeam, event, tvShow, movie, facility and other. Overall, the dataset comprises 6685 annotated tweets split into two parts: a training set consisting of 3000 tweets and a test set with 3685 tweets. For compatibility with previous research, the data were released tokenized using the CoNLL format and the BIO encoding.

4 Baselines

As our BERTweetFR model is the first pre-trained language model for French tweets, we compare it with the following general-domain language models for French.

CamemBERT As mentioned in 2.2, CaemBERT (Martin et al., 2020) is the model from which we

Table 1: Offensive Identification scores on the best model selected.

	CamemBERT	FlauBERT	BARThez	**BERTweetFR**
Accuracy	86.47	86.87	84.35	**88.07**
F1 Score	68.89	65.20	67.51	**71.27**

Table 2: NER score on the best model selected.

	CamemBERT	FlauBERT	**BERTweetFR**
Accuracy	94.78	94.73	**94.99**
F1 Score	61.01	60.57	**62.77**

started our fine-tuning for domain adaptation. It therefore serves as a natural baseline. Its architecture is already introduced in 2.2.

FlauBERT FlauBERT (Le et al., 2020) is another transfomer-based model trained on a very large and heterogeneous French corpus. It basically follows the same architecture as CamemBERT and is shown to outperform CamemBERT on some of the downstream tasks.

BARThez BARThez (Eddine et al., 2020) is the first French sequence-to-sequence model based on the base version of the BART architecture (Lewis et al., 2020). It has 6 encoder and 6 decoder layers with 768 hidden dimensions and 12 attention heads in both the encoder and the decoder. It is shown to be competitive in comparison with CamemBERT and FlauBERT.

5 Experiments and Results

In this section, we first describe our fine-tuning approaches. The baseline models follow the same fine-tuning procedures as BERTweetFR. We then report our results and compare with the baselines. As a result, our model substantially outperforms all baselines.

5.1 Offensive Language Identification

The offensive language identification task is a supervised sequence classification task. Following (Devlin et al., 2019), we append a linear prediction layer on top of the pooled output.

For fine-tuning, we employ transformers library to train BERTweetFR on the training set for 15 epochs. We use AdamW (Loshchilov and Hutter, 2019) with a fixed learning rate of 2.e-5 and a batch size of 32 following (Liu et al., 2019). We compute the classification accuracy and F1 score after each training epoch on the validation set, applying early stopping if their is no improvement after 3 consecutive epochs. We eventually select the model checkpoint with the highest F1 score to predict the final labels on the test set. Our results are listed in Table 1.

5.2 Named Entity Recognition

The NER task is a supervised token classification task. Following (Devlin et al., 2019), we append a linear prediction layer on top of the last Transformer layer with regards to the first subword of each word token.

For fine-tuning, we again employ transformers library to train for 30 epochs. We use AdamW (Loshchilov and Hutter, 2019) with a fixed learning rate of 2.e-5 and a batch size of 32, adding in weight decay. We compute performance scores for each entity class as well the overall F1 Micro score. We eventually select the model checkpoint with the highest F1 Micro score to predict the final labels on the test set. Our results are listed in Table 2. We do not compare with BARThez in this task because the original model is not implemented for sequence classification tasks.

6 Conclusion

In this work, we investigated the effectiveness of applying domain adaptation to the Twitter domain for large-scale pre-trained French language models. We demonstrate the value of our model showing that it outperforms all previous general-domain French language models on two downstream Twitter NLP tasks of offensiveness identification and named entity recognition.

Our contributions are as follows :

- We train and release the first large-scale pre-trained language model for French tweets : BERTweetFR. We make it publicly available in the transformers library and hope that it can facilitate and promote future research in analytic tasks for French tweets.

- We create and annotate the first dataset for offensiveness identification in French tweets. Such datasets already exist in several other languages and our effort fills in the gap for the French language.
- We create a framework and baseline for evaluating language models for French tweets. Datasets for Twitter tasks in French is very scarce and no previous work has ever combined different analytic tasks together in a unified framework.

With around 70% of all Twitter posts being in non-English languages, the lack of corresponding language models strongly hinders the community from exploiting the information contained in these valuable resources. For future work, we plan to train and release a series of such pre-trained language models for tweets in other low resource languages. We also call upon researchers from all over the world involved in natural language processing for social media to adapt language models in their respective languages and make them publicly available.

Acknowledgements

This research is supported by the French National research agency (ANR) via the ANR XCOVIF (AAP RA-COVID-19 V6) project. We would also like to thank the National Center for Scientific Research (CNRS) for giving us access to their Jean Zay supercomputer.

References

Jacob Levy Abitbol, Márton Karsai, Jean-Philippe Magué, Jean-Pierre Chevrot, and Eric Fleury. 2018. Socioeconomic dependencies of linguistic patterns in twitter: A multivariate analysis. In *Proceedings of the 2018 World Wide Web Conference*, WWW '18, page 1125–1134, Republic and Canton of Geneva, CHE. International World Wide Web Conferences Steering Committee.

Andrew M Dai and Quoc V Le. 2015. Semi-supervised sequence learning. In *Advances in Neural Information Processing Systems*, volume 28. Curran Associates, Inc.

Jacob Devlin, Ming-Wei Chang, Kenton Lee, and Kristina Toutanova. 2019. BERT: Pre-training of deep bidirectional transformers for language understanding. In *Proceedings of the 2019 Conference of the North American Chapter of the Association for Computational Linguistics: Human Language Technologies, Volume 1 (Long and Short Papers)*, pages 4171–4186, Minneapolis, Minnesota. Association for Computational Linguistics.

Moussa Kamal Eddine, Antoine J-P Tixier, and Michalis Vazirgiannis. 2020. Barthez: a skilled pretrained french sequence-to-sequence model. *arXiv preprint arXiv:2010.12321*.

Anna Atefeh Farzindar and Diana Inkpen. 2020. Natural language processing for social media. *Synthesis Lectures on Human Language Technologies*, 13(2):1–219.

Norjihan Abdul Ghani, Suraya Hamid, Ibrahim Abaker Targio Hashem, and Ejaz Ahmed. 2019. Social media big data analytics: A survey. *Computers in Human Behavior*, 101:417–428.

Suchin Gururangan, Ana Marasović, Swabha Swayamdipta, Kyle Lo, Iz Beltagy, Doug Downey, and Noah A. Smith. 2020. Don't stop pretraining: Adapt language models to domains and tasks. In *Proceedings of the 58th Annual Meeting of the Association for Computational Linguistics*, pages 8342–8360, Online. Association for Computational Linguistics.

Diederik P. Kingma and Jimmy Ba. 2015. Adam: A method for stochastic optimization. In *3rd International Conference on Learning Representations, ICLR 2015, San Diego, CA, USA, May 7-9, 2015, Conference Track Proceedings*.

Taku Kudo. 2018. Subword regularization: Improving neural network translation models with multiple subword candidates. In *Proceedings of the 56th Annual Meeting of the Association for Computational Linguistics (Volume 1: Long Papers)*, pages 66–75, Melbourne, Australia. Association for Computational Linguistics.

Taku Kudo and John Richardson. 2018. SentencePiece: A simple and language independent subword tokenizer and detokenizer for neural text processing. In *Proceedings of the 2018 Conference on Empirical Methods in Natural Language Processing: System Demonstrations*, pages 66–71, Brussels, Belgium. Association for Computational Linguistics.

Hang Le, Loïc Vial, Jibril Frej, Vincent Segonne, Maximin Coavoux, Benjamin Lecouteux, Alexandre Allauzen, Benoit Crabbé, Laurent Besacier, and Didier Schwab. 2020. FlauBERT: Unsupervised language model pre-training for French. In *Proceedings of the 12th Language Resources and Evaluation Conference*, pages 2479–2490, Marseille, France. European Language Resources Association.

Mike Lewis, Yinhan Liu, Naman Goyal, Marjan Ghazvininejad, Abdelrahman Mohamed, Omer

Levy, Veselin Stoyanov, and Luke Zettlemoyer. 2020. BART: Denoising sequence-to-sequence pre-training for natural language generation, translation, and comprehension. In *Proceedings of the 58th Annual Meeting of the Association for Computational Linguistics*, pages 7871–7880, Online. Association for Computational Linguistics.

Yinhan Liu, Myle Ott, Naman Goyal, Jingfei Du, Mandar Joshi, Danqi Chen, Omer Levy, Mike Lewis, Luke Zettlemoyer, and Veselin Stoyanov. 2019. Roberta: A robustly optimized bert pretraining approach. *arXiv preprint arXiv:1907.11692*.

Cédric Lopez, Ioannis Partalas, Georgios Balikas, Nadia Derbas, Amélie Martin, Coralie Reutenauer, Frédérique Segond, and Massih-Reza Amini. 2017. Cap 2017 challenge: Twitter named entity recognition. *arXiv preprint arXiv:1707.07568*.

Ilya Loshchilov and Frank Hutter. 2019. Decoupled weight decay regularization. In *7th International Conference on Learning Representations, ICLR 2019, New Orleans, LA, USA, May 6-9, 2019*. OpenReview.net.

Louis Martin, Benjamin Muller, Pedro Javier Ortiz Suárez, Yoann Dupont, Laurent Romary, Éric de la Clergerie, Djamé Seddah, and Benoît Sagot. 2020. CamemBERT: a tasty French language model. In *Proceedings of the 58th Annual Meeting of the Association for Computational Linguistics*, pages 7203–7219, Online. Association for Computational Linguistics.

Tomas Mikolov, Ilya Sutskever, Kai Chen, Greg S Corrado, and Jeff Dean. 2013. Distributed representations of words and phrases and their compositionality. In *Advances in Neural Information Processing Systems*, volume 26. Curran Associates, Inc.

Dat Quoc Nguyen, Thanh Vu, and Anh Tuan Nguyen. 2020. BERTweet: A pre-trained language model for English tweets. In *Proceedings of the 2020 Conference on Empirical Methods in Natural Language Processing: System Demonstrations*, pages 9–14, Online. Association for Computational Linguistics.

Jeffrey Pennington, Richard Socher, and Christopher Manning. 2014. GloVe: Global vectors for word representation. In *Proceedings of the 2014 Conference on Empirical Methods in Natural Language Processing (EMNLP)*, pages 1532–1543, Doha, Qatar. Association for Computational Linguistics.

Prajit Ramachandran, Peter Liu, and Quoc Le. 2017. Unsupervised pretraining for sequence to sequence learning. In *Proceedings of the 2017 Conference on Empirical Methods in Natural Language Processing*, pages 383–391, Copenhagen, Denmark. Association for Computational Linguistics.

Yusuke Shibata, Takuya Kida, Shuichi Fukamachi, Masayuki Takeda, Ayumi Shinohara, Takeshi Shinohara, and Setsuo Arikawa. 1999. Byte pair encoding: A text compression scheme that accelerates pattern matching.

Ashish Vaswani, Noam Shazeer, Niki Parmar, Jakob Uszkoreit, Llion Jones, Aidan N Gomez, Ł ukasz Kaiser, and Illia Polosukhin. 2017. Attention is all you need. In *Advances in Neural Information Processing Systems*, volume 30. Curran Associates, Inc.

Thomas Wolf, Lysandre Debut, Victor Sanh, Julien Chaumond, Clement Delangue, Anthony Moi, Pierric Cistac, Tim Rault, Remi Louf, Morgan Funtowicz, Joe Davison, Sam Shleifer, Patrick von Platen, Clara Ma, Yacine Jernite, Julien Plu, Canwen Xu, Teven Le Scao, Sylvain Gugger, Mariama Drame, Quentin Lhoest, and Alexander Rush. 2020. Transformers: State-of-the-art natural language processing. In *Proceedings of the 2020 Conference on Empirical Methods in Natural Language Processing: System Demonstrations*, pages 38–45, Online. Association for Computational Linguistics.

To What Extent Does Lexical Normalization Help English-as-a-Second Language Learners to Read Noisy English Texts?

Yo Ehara
Tokyo Gakugei University
4-1-1 Nukuikita-machi, Koganei-shi, Tokyo 184-8501 Japan
ehara@u-gakugei.ac.jp

Abstract

How difficult is it for English-as-a-second language (ESL) learners to read noisy English texts? Do ESL learners need lexical normalization to read noisy English texts? These questions may also affect community formation on social networking sites where differences can be attributed to ESL learners and native English speakers. However, few studies have addressed these questions. To this end, we built highly accurate readability assessors to evaluate the readability of texts for ESL learners. We then applied these assessors to noisy English texts to further assess the readability of the texts. The experimental results showed that although intermediate-level ESL learners can read most noisy English texts in the first place, lexical normalization significantly improves the readability of noisy English texts for ESL learners.

1 Introduction

Noisy English texts are not only problematic for processing text but also difficult for humans to read, even for native speakers when, for instance, they lack the background to decipher abbreviations. How difficult are noisy English texts for English as a second language (ESL) learners?

If noisy English texts are too difficult for ESL learners to read, it may affect their behavior on various media such as social networking services (SNS). For example, it is easy to imagine that ESL learners do not follow English accounts. The lexical normalization tasks are important as they could potentially change the behavior of ESL learners by improving readability. In this sense, assessing the readability of noisy English texts for ESL learners is closely related to assessing the extent to which the language gap leads to social division.

To this end, we first sought to understand the readability of noisy English texts by building highly accurate readability assessors. We used two approaches to build the assessors. The first was based on the field of educational Natural Language Processing (NLP) (Vajjala and Lučić, 2018). Using a corpus that is standard in this field, we built a highly accurate readability assessor using deep learning methods, such as bidirectional encoder representations from transformers (BERT) (Devlin et al., 2019).

The second approach was to conduct readability assessments based on the vocabulary of English learners. These methods have been well studied in applied linguistics, whereby considerable research has revealed that English learners need to know more than 95% of the words in a text to read and understand them (Nation, 2006; Laufer and Ravenhorst-Kalovski, 2010). The idea of assessing text readability via each learner's vocabulary knowledge is beneficial for interpreting the readability assessment results. Therefore, we also constructed a classifier based on a dataset of English learners' vocabulary tests (Ehara, 2018), to determine the number of words in a text that an English learner knows.

In experiments carried out on a standard dataset for evaluating readability (Vajjala and Lučić, 2018) in educational NLP, the results provided by the two approaches were in close agreement. The experiments using an English noisy text corpus also showed that most noisy English texts were readable by intermediate English learners. Using gold-normalized texts in the noisy English text dataset, we found that lexical normalization improves the text readability of second language learners. This improvement in readability was statistically significant in the vocabulary-based assessor's results.

The contributions of this study are as follows:

1. We evaluated the readability of noisy English texts for ESL learners by using accurate readability assessors.

2. We showed that intermediate ESL learners can read most noisy English texts.

Proceedings of the 2021 EMNLP Workshop W-NUT: The Seventh Workshop on Noisy User-generated Text, pages 451–456
November 11, 2021. ©2021 Association for Computational Linguistics

3. We show that lexical normalization improves the readability of texts for ESL learners in both approaches, namely, the BERT readability assessor and the assessor based on the vocabulary of English learners. For the latter assessor, the result was also statistically significant.

2 Automatic Readability Assessment

This section formalizes the problem of automatic readability assessment. Let us suppose that we have N texts to assess: we write the set of texts as $\{\mathcal{T}_i | i \in \{1, \ldots, N\}\}$. Let $\mathcal{Y}$ be the set of readability labels. Labels are typically ordered in the order of difficulty. For example, in the *OneStopEnglish* dataset (Vajjala and Lučić, 2018), we can set $\mathcal{Y} = \{0, 1, 2\}$, where 0 is elementary, 1 is intermediate, and 2 is advanced. The number of levels depends on the evaluation corpus. Using $\mathcal{Y}$, we write the label for $\mathcal{T}_i$ as $y_i \in \mathcal{Y}$.

Given each text $\mathcal{T}_i$, an *assessor* outputs its readability score s_i. In a supervised setting, the *assessor* knows the number of levels in the evaluation corpus from training examples. Hence, s_i ranges within $\mathcal{Y}$: $s_i \in \mathcal{Y}$. However, in an unsupervised setting, it is noteworthy that the assessor does not know $\mathcal{Y}$, or how many levels the evaluation corpus has, because no label is given. Hence, even if only integers are allowed for y_i, s_i can be a real value.

Throughout this paper, we write arrays using [and]. Given N texts $[\mathcal{T}_i | i \in \{1, \ldots, N\}]$, our goal is to make an assessor output arrays of readability scores $[s_i | i \in \{1, \ldots, N\}]$ that *correlate well* with the array of labels $[y_i | i \in \{1, \ldots, N\}]$. Here, there are multiple types of correlation coefficients between the array of scores and the array of labels, which we explain in the later sections. Typically, we should use *rank coefficients* such as Spearman's ρ, defined as the Pearson's ρ between rankings, when s_i is real-valued.

3 Vocabulary Testing-based Readability

Fig. 1 shows example questions from the vocabulary size test, a widely used vocabulary test in applied linguistics (Beglar and Nation, 2007). Each question asks about a word in a multiple-choice question format. The test consists of 100 questions like those shown in Fig. 1. Ehara (2018) used this test to have 100 second-language learners take the test and to collect their responses. Their data were published and made publicly available. We used their dataset to train our classifiers.

```
15. deficit:
The company <had a large deficit>.
a: spent a lot more money than it earned
b: went down a lot in value
c: had a plan for its spending
                 that used a lot of money
d: had a lot of money stored in the bank
```

Figure 1: Examples of the Vocabulary Size Test (Beglar and Nation, 2007), one of the most widely accepted vocabulary tests to quickly assess language learners. They are asked to choose the option that paraphrases the part between "<" and ">" from a, b, c, and d.

We want to analyze vocabulary test results to obtain word difficulty values encoding learners' language knowledge. To this end, we employed the idea of *item response theory* (Baker, 2004), a statistical model that can estimate learners' abilities and test questions' difficulties from the learners' responses to the questions.

Let $\mathcal{V}$ be the set of vocabulary, and let $\mathcal{L}$ be the set of learners. Let $z_{v,l} \in \{0, 1\}$ be the result of whether learner $l \in \mathcal{L}$ correctly answered the question for word $v \in \mathcal{V}$: $z_{l,v} = 1$ if l answered correctly for word v; otherwise, $z_{l,v} = 0$. Correct answers usually imply that l knows word v.

Then, by using $\{z_{v,l}\}$ as the training data, we train the following model:

$$p(z = 1 | v, l) = \text{sigmoid}(a_l - d_v) \tag{1}$$

In Eq. 1, a_l is the ability parameter of learner l, d_v is the difficulty of word w, and sigmoid denotes the logistic sigmoid function, i.e., $\text{sigmoid}(x) = \frac{1}{1+\exp(-x)}$.

The logistic sigmoid function is the binary version of the softmax function, which is frequently used in neural classifiers. It is a monotonously increasing function ranging within $(0, 1)$. As $\text{sigmoid}(0) = \frac{1}{1+1} = \frac{1}{2}$, when a learner's ability a_l is larger than the word difficulty d_v, the probability that learner l knows word v can be written as follows: $p(z = 1 | v, l) > \frac{1}{2}$ in Eq. 1. Likewise, by using Eq. 1, we can compare a learner's ability and word difficulty in the same dimension.

To estimate learner ability and word difficulty, $z_{v,l}$ is given as z in Eq. 1 in the training phase. In this way, in *item response theory*, learner ability and word difficulty are comparable, and these parameters are estimated from the test result data.

In Eq. 1, d_v denotes the word difficulty estimated from the vocabulary tests. Here, in addition to the word difficulty for the words within the vocabulary test, we also want to obtain word difficulty values for all words that may appear in the target language. To this end, we calculate d_v from the word frequency in large balanced corpora as follows:

$$d_v = -\sum_{k=1}^{K} w_k \log(\text{freq}_k(v) + 1) \quad (2)$$

In Eq. 2, K is the number of corpora to use, $\text{freq}_k(v)$ denotes the frequency of word v in the k-th corpus, and w_k is the weight parameter of the k-th corpus. In summary, given the vocabulary test results $\{z_{v,l}\}$ and corpus frequency features $\text{freq}_k(v)$, we can estimate the parameters: namely, the weight of the k-th corpus w_k and learner l's ability a_l. To implement the model, we used logistic regression, by following (Ehara, 2018). Note that this model does not use the valuable readability label $\{y_i\}$ in the training phase, so is unsupervised.

As shown in Eq. 1, we employed IRT-based modeling in this study. IRT-based modeling has been used in many previous NLP studies such as (Ehara et al., 2012, 2016; Ehara, 2019; Settles et al., 2020; Ehara, 2020).

After estimating the parameters using the above-mentioned procedure, we use the following formula to obtain the readability of given $\mathcal{T}_i$. Here, l_{avg} denotes the test-taker whose estimated ability parameter is closest to the average of the estimated ability parameter values $\{a_l\}$s. Intuitively, the following equation calculates the probability that the average learner knows all the words that appear in $\mathcal{T}_i$ and uses it as the readability score.

$$s_i = score(\mathcal{T}_i) = -\log\left(\prod_{v \in \mathcal{T}_i} p(z = 1 | v, l_{\text{avg}})\right) \quad (3)$$

4 OneStopEnglish Experiments

We used the OneStopEnglish dataset (Vajjala and Lučić, 2018) for the source of readability for second language learners because it is one of the newest, publicly available, and reliable in the sense that no known trivial features are effective for predicting its labels such as average sentence length.

The dataset has three levels: elementary, intermediate, and advanced. The original articles were taken from the Guardian newspaper. The OneStopEnglish dataset is a parallel corpus, i.e, language teachers manually rewrote the original articles into the three aforementioned readability levels: hence, its readability labels are not easily estimated from the topics of texts.

All three levels have 189 texts each, 567 texts in total. We randomly split these texts into a *training* set consisting of 339 texts, a *validation* set consisting of 114 texts, and a *test* set consisting of 114 texts. The training and validation sets were used to train solely supervised methods for comparison. Unsupervised methods did not use the training and validation sets; they used only the test set.

4.1 Compared Methods

As the BERT-based sequence classification has been reported to achieve excellent results (Devlin et al., 2019), we applied the standard BERT-based sequence classification approach involving pretraining and fine-tuning. For the pretrained model, we used **bert-large-cased-whole-word-masking** in the Huggingface models [1].

Then, we fine-tuned the model using the 339 training texts. We named this fine-tuned model **spvBERT**, in which "spv" denotes being supervised. For fine-tuning, we used the Adam optimizer (Kingma and Ba, 2015) with a setting of 10 epochs and a 0.00001 training rate.

For the implementation of conventional readability formulae, we used the **readability** PyPI package [2]. We used almost all readability formulae implemented in this package for our experiments: namely, **Flesch-Kincaid** (Flesch-Kincaid Grade Level, FKGL) (Kincaid et al., 1975), **ARI** (Automated Readability Index) (Senter and Smith, 1967), the **Coleman-Liau** Index (Coleman and Liau, 1975), **Flesch Reading Ease** (Flesch, 1948), the **Gunning Fog Index** (Gunning, 1952), **LIX** (Björnsson, 1968), the **SMOG Index** (Mc Laughlin, 1969), the RIX index (Anderson, 1983), and the **Dale-Chall Index** (Dale and Chall, 1948). More details of these formulae and their implementation are described on the project page. All of these readability formulae are *unsupervised* in the sense that they do not require any training data.

The **Vocabulary-based** model was trained on a publicly available vocabulary dataset (Ehara, 2018). For the corpus word frequency, we used the frequencies taken from the British National Corpus (BNC Consortium, 2007) and the Corpus of Contemporary American English (COCA) (Davies,

[1] `https://huggingface.co/models`

[2] `https://pypi.org/project/readability/`

Table 1: Predictive Performance of Readability. Only **spvBERT** is supervised: the others are unsupervised.

Method	Spearman's ρ	Pearson's ρ
Flesch-Kincaid	0.324	0.359
ARI	0.317	0.351
Coleman-Liau	0.373	0.372
FleschReadingEase	-0.387	-0.426
GunningFogIndex	0.331	0.362
LIX	0.348	0.383
SMOGIndex	0.456	0.479
RIX	0.437	0.462
DaleChallIndex	0.495	0.506
TCN RSRS-simple	-	0.615(*)
Vocabulary-based	**0.730**	**0.715**
spvBERT	0.866	0.864

-	Elem.	Int.	Adv.
Before	0.486	0.512	0.002
After	0.495	0.503	0.002

Table 2: Readability Assessment Results for ESL learners before/after Lexical Normalization

-	-	After		
-	-	Elem.	Int.	Adv.
Before	Elem.	1051	97	0
	Int.	117	1091	0
	Adv.	1	0	4

Table 3: Matrix of Readability Assessment for ESL learners before/after Lexical Normalization

2008). Both corpora are used extensively in applied linguistics in English as a rough measure for determining word difficulty (Nation, 2006).

4.2 OneStopEnglish Results

Tab. 1 shows the experimental results. In all unsupervised methods, **Vocabulary-based** achieved the best results in all rank correlation coefficients. **TCN RSRS-simple** is the best model on the OneStopEnglish dataset in Martinc et al. (2021). As they show only the performance measured by the Pearson correlation, we wrote – for Spearman's ρ. While a direct comparison is not possible as denoted by $(*)$, **Vocabulary-based** outperforms it.

Importantly, we can observe that both **Vocabulary-based** and **spvBERT** achieve high predictive performance. This result indicates that the two approaches to assessing readability derived results that were in close agreement.

5 Experiments with Noisy English Texts

For the experiment, we used the English training data of the W-NUT multilingual lexical normalization shared task [3]. We chose this dataset so that future studies on lexical normalization using a language other than English would have a baseline to compare against. The dataset consists of $2,361$ short noisy texts along with the corresponding lexically normalized texts. We selected $1,325$ pairs from this dataset, after removing the pairs that were identical before and after lexical normalization. To assess the effect of lexical normalization, we simply used the gold-lexically normalized texts of the dataset.

Tab. 2 shows the readability assessment results using **spvBERT** before/after lexical normalization. As most texts are elementary or intermediate, this result implies that *intermediate-level ESL learners can read most noisy English texts*. We can also see that the difficulty of elementary texts can increase based on lexical normalization. Tab. 3 displays the confusion matrix before/after lexical normalization by **spvBERT**. We observe that lexical normalization between elementary and intermediate levels can work both ways: while 117 texts were converted from elementary to intermediate, 97 texts were converted from intermediate to elementary. No text was converted to the advanced level. While Tab. 2 and Tab. 3 show that lexical normalization improves readability, the improvement was not statistically significant because 97 texts were reversely converted.

Next, we explain the readability assessment results of **Vocabulary-based**, which uses Eq. 3. The smaller the value, the easier it is for ESL learners to read. While the average score before lexical normalization was 4.00, the value after lexical normalization was 3.53. Fig. 2 is the scatter plot of the readability scores before/after lexical normalization. Fig. 2 clearly shows that the texts become significantly easier to read after lexical normalization (Wilcoxon test, $p < 0.01$).

[3]`http://noisy-text.github.io/2021/multi-lexnorm.html`

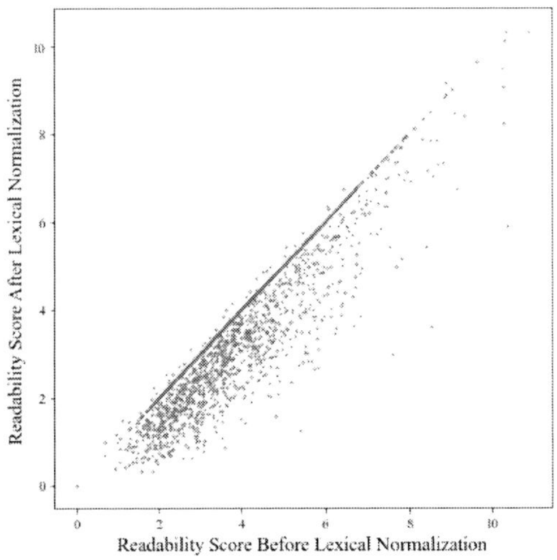

Figure 2: Eq. 3 Scores before/after Normalization

6 Discussion

In this study, we assessed the readability of text for ESL learners utilizing two sources of information. **spvBERT** is based on the annotations of the language teachers, and **vocabulary-based** is based on the results of the vocabulary test results of the learners. In this paper, both information from language teachers as well as learners is incorporated into the readability assessments described in the previous section.

However, there are limitations to automated readability assessment, and ideally a large-scale survey of ESL learners is required, which would be very costly and hence will be the subject of future work. Even in manual assessment, there are points to consider. For example, in annotating the readability of texts by language teachers, there is the issue of how well the language teachers grasp the characteristics of the students. In addition, even if learners themselves participate in assessing text readability, the cultural background of the learner, such as the influence of their first language (L1), may influence the performance.

7 Conclusions

We assess the readability of noisy English texts for ESL learners. We built highly accurate assessors using the two approaches. While intermediate ESL learners can read noisy English texts, lexical normalization improves readability for ESL learners, as was the case with our dataset.

Future work will include more comprehensive experiments using other datasets and evaluations by actual ESL learners.

Acknowledgment

This study was supported by JST ACT-X Grant Number JPMJAX2006 and JSPS KAKENHI Grant Number 18K18118. We used the ABCI infrastructure from AIST for the computational resources. We appreciate anonymous reviewers for their valuable comments.

References

Jonathan Anderson. 1983. Lix and rix: Variations on a little-known readability index. *Journal of Reading*, 26(6):490–496.

Frank B. Baker. 2004. *Item Response Theory : Parameter Estimation Techniques, Second Edition*. CRC Press.

David Beglar and Paul Nation. 2007. A vocabulary size test. *The Language Teacher*, 31(7):9–13.

C. H. Björnsson. 1968. Läsbarhet, Stockholm.

BNC Consortium. 2007. The british national corpus, version 3 (bnc xml edition). Distributed by Bodleian Libraries, University of Oxford, on behalf of the BNC Consortium http://www.natcorp.ox.ac.uk/.

Meri Coleman and Ta Lin Liau. 1975. A computer readability formula designed for machine scoring. *Journal of Applied Psychology*, 60(2):283.

Edgar Dale and Jeanne S Chall. 1948. A formula for predicting readability: Instructions. *Educational research bulletin*, pages 37–54.

Mark Davies. 2008. The corpus of contemporary american english (coca). Available online at https://www.english-corpora.org/coca/.

Jacob Devlin, Ming-Wei Chang, Kenton Lee, and Kristina Toutanova. 2019. BERT: Pre-training of Deep Bidirectional Transformers for Language Understanding. In *Proc. of NAACL*, pages 4171–4186, Minneapolis, Minnesota.

Yo Ehara. 2018. Building an English Vocabulary Knowledge Dataset of Japanese English-as-a-Second-Language Learners Using Crowdsourcing. In *Proc. of LREC*.

Yo Ehara. 2019. Neural rasch model: How do word embeddings adjust word difficulty? In *Computational Linguistics - 16th International Conference of the Pacific Association for Computational Linguistics, PACLING 2019, Hanoi, Vietnam, October 11-13, 2019, Revised Selected Papers*, volume 1215 of *Communications in Computer and Information Science*, pages 88–96. Springer.

Yo Ehara. 2020. Interpreting neural CWI classifiers' weights as vocabulary size. In *Proceedings of the Fifteenth Workshop on Innovative Use of NLP for Building Educational Applications*, pages 171–176, Seattle, WA, USA → Online. Association for Computational Linguistics.

Yo Ehara, Yukino Baba, Masao Utiyama, and Eiichiro Sumita. 2016. Assessing Translation Ability through Vocabulary Ability Assessment. In *Proc. of IJCAI*.

Yo Ehara, Issei Sato, Hidekazu Oiwa, and Hiroshi Nakagawa. 2012. Mining Words in the Minds of Second Language Learners: Learner-Specific Word Difficulty. In *Proceedings of COLING 2012*, pages 799–814, Mumbai, India. The COLING 2012 Organizing Committee.

Rudolf Flesch. 1948. A new readability yardstick. *Journal of Applied Psychology*, 32(3):221–233.

Robert Gunning. 1952. *The Technique of Clear Writing*. McGraw-Hill.

J Peter Kincaid, Robert P Fishburne Jr, Richard L Rogers, and Brad S Chissom. 1975. Derivation of new readability formulas (automated readability index, fog count and flesch reading ease formula) for navy enlisted personnel. Technical report, Naval Technical Training Command Millington TN Research Branch.

Diederik P Kingma and Jimmy Ba. 2015. Adam: A method for stochastic optimization. In *Proc. of ICLR*.

Batia Laufer and Geke C. Ravenhorst-Kalovski. 2010. Lexical Threshold Revisited: Lexical Text Coverage, Learners' Vocabulary Size and Reading Comprehension. *Reading in a Foreign Language*, 22(1):15–30.

Matej Martinc, Senja Pollak, and Marko Robnik-Šikonja. 2021. Supervised and Unsupervised Neural Approaches to Text Readability. *Computational Linguistics*, 47(1):141–179.

G Harry Mc Laughlin. 1969. Smog grading-a new readability formula. *Journal of reading*, 12(8):639–646.

I. Nation. 2006. How Large a Vocabulary is Needed For Reading and Listening? *Canadian Modern Language Review*, 63(1):59–82.

RJ Senter and Edgar A Smith. 1967. Automated readability index. Technical report, CINCINNATI UNIV OH.

Burr Settles, Geoffrey T. LaFlair, and Masato Hagiwara. 2020. Machine learning–driven language assessment. *Transactions of the Association for Computational Linguistics*, 8:247–263.

Sowmya Vajjala and Ivana Lučić. 2018. OneStopEnglish corpus: A new corpus for automatic readability assessment and text simplification. In *Proceedings of the Thirteenth Workshop on Innovative Use of NLP for Building Educational Applications*, pages 297–304, New Orleans, Louisiana. Association for Computational Linguistics.

Multilingual Sequence Labeling Approach to solve Lexical Normalization

Divesh Kubal
CRIMSON AI
divesh.kubal@crimsoni.ai

Apurva Nagvenkar
CRIMSON AI
apurva.nagvenkar@crimsoni.ai

Abstract

The task of converting a nonstandard text to a standard and readable text is known as lexical normalization. Almost all the Natural Language Processing (NLP) applications require the text data in normalized form to build quality task-specific models. Hence, lexical normalization has been proven to improve the performance of numerous natural language processing tasks on social media. This study aims to address the problem of Lexical Normalization by formulating the Lexical Normalization task as a Sequence Labeling problem. This paper proposes a sequence labeling approach to solve the problem of Lexical Normalization in combination with the word-alignment technique. The goal is to use a single model to normalize text in various languages. This is a shared task in "2021 The 7th Workshop on Noisy User-generated Text (W-NUT)" in which the participants are expected to create a system/model that performs lexical normalization, which is the translation of non-canonical texts into their canonical equivalents, comprising data from over 12 languages. The proposed single multilingual model achieves an overall ERR score of 43.75 on intrinsic evaluation and an overall Labeled Attachment Score (LAS) score of 63.12 on extrinsic evaluation. Further, the proposed method achieves the highest Error Reduction Rate (ERR) score of 61.33 among the participants in the shared task. This study highlights the effects of using additional training data to get better results as well as using a pre-trained Language model trained on multiple languages rather than only on one language.

1 Introduction

Information can be found in abundance on social media. In fact, social media is a significant data resource for many natural language processing (NLP) tasks. Such text is characterized by 'noise', or non-standard language filled with lexical variants, acronyms, hashtags, and mentions. Hence, the performance of conventional NLP tools on social media text, is poor as the data resources they used were standard texts. Although data extracted from social media contains a high degree of noise, the data can be extracted in huge quantities because of fast speed and casual style. Existing natural language processing techniques face numerous challenges as a result of the innovative/creative/slang language usage present on social media. Slang, acronyms, and abbreviated words are all part of this so-called new "online" language. It is demonstrated by (Liu et al., 2011; Schulz et al., 2016) that the performance of NLP tools often drops dramatically when used on social media data. The challenge can be solved by adapting the input text to a more conventional format, a process known as Lexical Normalisation. This paper focuses to solve the problem of Lexical Normalization on a word-by-word or token-by-token basis.

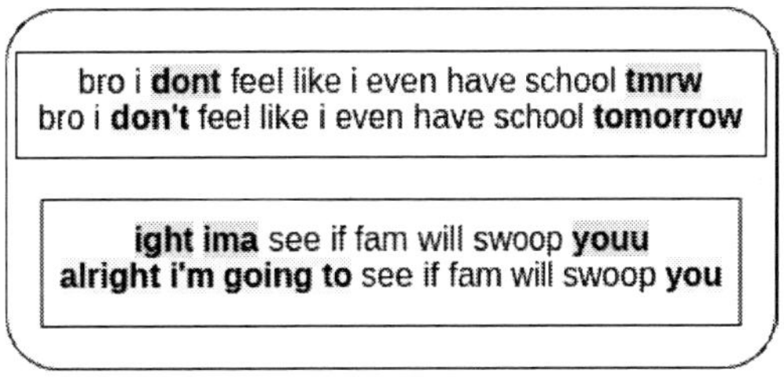

Figure 1: Examples of Lexical Normalization (English Language)

Figure 1 shows examples of un-normalized and the corresponding normalized sentences. The following languages are to be lexically normalized in this task: Croatian (hr), Danish (da), Dutch (nl), English (en), Indonesian-English (iden), German (de), Italian (it), Serbian (sr), Slovenian (sl), Spanish (es), Turkish (tr), and Turkish-German (trde). The proposed model is based on a sequence labeling-based technique in which the input tokens are in an un-normalized form and the target tokens are in normalized forms. To reduce the target labels

Proceedings of the 2021 EMNLP Workshop W-NUT: The Seventh Workshop on Noisy User-generated Text, pages 457–464
November 11, 2021. ©2021 Association for Computational Linguistics

and to make predictions faster, only those tokens for which normalization is required are added. For the tokens which do need not be normalized, their target label fixed to be a single target token (for instance 'O'). This sequence labeling model is fine-tuned on a pre-trained multilingual model to encompass the information on all the possible languages. Further, a post-processing layer for word-alignment is applied which further help to improve the performance in terms of Error Rate Reduction (ERR - word-level accuracy normalized).

This paper elucidates four essential points to improve lexical normalization systems.:

- the importance of treating Lexical Normalization task as a Sequence Labeling Task.
- the effect of providing the model with additional data to improve performance
- the importance of finetuning a language model pre-trained on a huge multilingual corpus
- the Effect of hyperparameter tuning by using a single model to solve the problem of lexical normalization for all the tasks.
- the effect of word-alignment post-processing layer.

2 Related Work

Previous work on normalization has been disjointed as a number of techniques have been tested against a variety of benchmarks, with a variety of assessment criteria and assumptions. In addition, the majority of normalization systems are neither open-source nor publicly accessible. To solve the problem of lexical normalization, existing systems have mainly used machine translation (Vaghani, 2020; Pennell and Liu, 2011; Ljubešic et al., 2016) or spellchecking (Han, 2014) technique. In earlier systems, the lexical normalization was performed by using the following steps:

1. Detect words that need to be normalized.
2. Generate possible candidates for the detected original un-normalized word.
3. Rank the possible candidates and select the best one.

It was later discovered by (Jin, 2015; van der Goot, 2019) that the detection step can be completely avoided by treating each original word as a candidate for normalization. At present, the state-of-the-art model for almost all the languages is MoNoise (van der Goot, 2019) which is a two-step approach. In this paper, there are different techniques for generating candidates. To get the best or correct candidate, MoNoise uses Random Forest as a classifier that takes input features generated in the first step (candidate-generation step). There are methods using sequence-to-sequence (seq2seq) based architectures (Lourentzou et al., 2019) and contextual words and phrasal embeddings (Muller et al., 2019) which achieved a performance similar to that of MoNoise, especially in the English language. Most of the work in lexical normalization is performed for the English language (Han and Baldwin, 2011; Xu et al., 2015). Nonetheless, research has been conducted on languages other than English by (van der Goot, 2019).

3 Multilingual Sequence Labeling Approach

The proposed system architecture is depicted in figure 2. The main components of Multilingual Sequence Labeling Approach to solve Lexical Normalization Problem System Architecture are as follows:

1. Data acquisition/collection.
2. Data preparation of input for the multilingual model.
3. Finetuning of transformer-based language models for the sequence labeling task of lexical normalization.
4. Hyperparameter tuning and retraining of language models.
5. Word alignment based post-processing to obtain final predictions.
6. Evaluation of development and test datasets.

3.1 Data Acquisition/Collection

The shared task provides the data in 12 languages. The data is then split into training data (train.norm) and development data (dev.norm). Essentially, the data is divided into two broad categories based on the method of assessment, intrinsic or extrinsic. In intrinsic evaluation, Error Reduction Rate

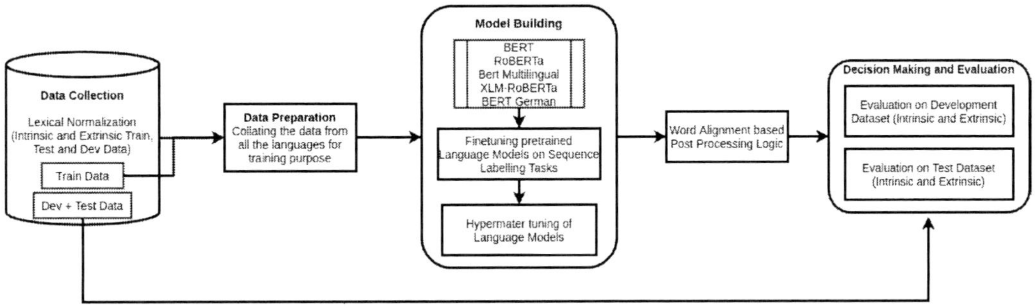

Figure 2: Multilingual Sequence Labeling Approach to solve Lexical Normalization Problem

(ERR) is used as the evaluation measure. Dependency parsing is considered extrinsic evaluation, which focuses on the impact of normalization on the quality of the parsed trees. In extrinsic evaluation, Labeled Attachment Score (LAS) is used as the evaluation measure.

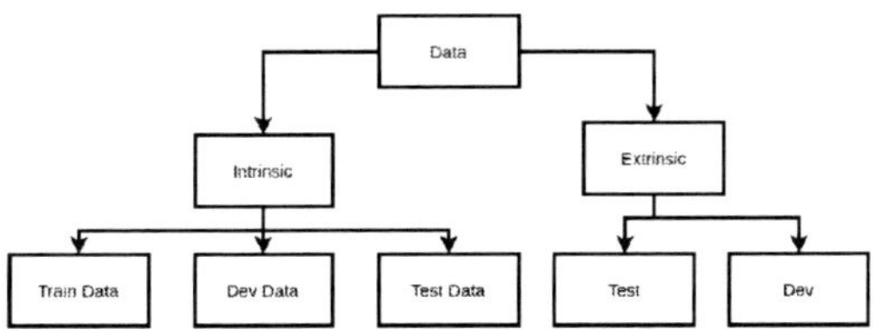

Figure 3: Overview of dataset

Figure 3 depicts the categorization of the data into intrinsic and extrinsic evaluation. The intrinsic type of data is annotated except for the test dataset which contains only the unnormalized text. On the other hand, the extrinsic type of data contains the only unnormalized text. Table 1 shows the actual number of sentences contained in each split (train and dev). The languages in table 1 are arranged in the descending order of the parallel sentences in training data. The dev dataset split is not provided for the following languages: Turkish-German, Italian, Turkish, Spanish and Danish.

Table 2 provides the count of the un-normalized sentences; they are not labeled. This data is used for the extrinsic evaluation. Finally, Table 3 shows the number of sentences used for the intrinsic evaluation of the languages provided.

3.2 DataData preparation of input for the multilingual model

This study focuses on building a single model capable of performing lexical normalization on the 12 languages provided in the shared task. Hence, the training data is prepared by concatenating the parallel sentences of normalized and un-normalized data. This is done in two phases. The first phase consists of only concatenating the training data of all languages from the intrinsic set and then evaluating the model on the intrinsic development data. This is done to finetune the trained model so that it achieves high performance on development data. This step also reduces the loss when evaluated on

Language	Train	Dev
hr	4760	1588
sl	4670	1557
sr	4138	1379
en	2360	590
de	1628	573
nl	907	308
trde	800	NA
it	593	NA
tr	570	NA
es	568	NA
iden	495	165
da	207	NA

Table 1: Number of Parallel Sentences (unnormalized - normalized) provided for different languages [Intrinsic Data]

Name	Sentences
ud-it-twittiro.test.norm.masked	3018
ud-en-aae.test.norm.masked	3322
ud-it-postwita.test.norm.masked	12796
ud-en-tweebank2.test.norm.masked	20296
ud-tr-iwt151.test.norm.masked	48200
ud-en-monoise.test.norm.masked	5738
ud-de-tweede.test.norm.masked	5261

Table 2: Number of unnormalized Sentences provided for different languages [Extrinsic Dev and Test Data]

language	Number of sentences
it	2096
iden	4531
sl	16578
es	7166
de	5665
nl	5721
tr	1782
trde	3964
sr	18496
hr	17281
en	31388
da	3939

Table 3: Number of Test Sentences provided for different languages [Intrinsic Test Data]

development data. After getting an assurance that the model performs as expected on the development data, the final model's architecture and the values of the newly finetuned hyperparameters are noted down. In the next phase, a new set of training data is generated which is the concatenation of intrinsic train + dev data. This data is used to train the architecture which achieved the best performance in the first phase. This trained model is now used to predict un-normalized sentences from the test data. Additional Spanish data was taken from shared task [1] (training data) and was used as training data. After concatenating all the data, a total of 16861 labels are generated. These labels are the unique normalization tokens/phrases for their corresponding un-normalized counterparts.

3.3 Finetuning of transformer-based language models for the sequence labeling task of lexical normalization

The proposed approach attempts to finetune already pre-trained language models. The experiments of finetuning language models on a downstream task of lexical normalization are performed on the following pre-trained language models: BERT (Devlin et al., 2018), RoBERTa (Liu et al., 2019), BERT-multilingual (Devlin et al., 2018), XLM-RoBERTa (Conneau et al., 2019), BERT-German. For the English Language, the variants of RoBERTa performed well as so with BERT (trained on an English corpus). However, these models which were pre-trained on a huge English

Hyperparameter	Value
dataloader_num_workers	0
do_lower_case	False
early_stopping_consider_epochs	False
early_stopping_delta	0
early_stopping_metric	eval_loss
early_stopping_metric_minimize	True
early_stopping_patience	3
eval_batch_size	8
evaluate_during_training	False
evaluate_during_training_steps	2000
evaluate_during_training_verbose	False
evaluate_each_epoch	True
fp16	True
gradient_accumulation_steps	1
lazy_loading	False
lazy_loading_start_line	0
learning_rate	4E-05
logging_steps	50
max_grad_norm	1
max_seq_length	256
model_class	NERModel
model_name	bert-base-multilingual-cased
model_type	bert
multiprocessing_chunksize	-1
n_gpu	1
no_cache	False
no_save	False
num_train_epochs	100
onnx	False
optimizer	AdamW
overwrite_output_dir	False
polynomial_decay_schedule_lr_end	1E-07
polynomial_decay_schedule_power	1
process_count	14
quantized_model	False
reprocess_input_data	True
save_best_model	True
save_eval_checkpoints	True
save_model_every_epoch	True
save_optimizer_and_scheduler	True
save_steps	20000
scheduler	linear_schedule_with_warmup
silent	False
skip_special_tokens	True
train_batch_size	32
use_early_stopping	False
use_multiprocessing	True
use_multiprocessing_for_evaluation	True

Table 4: Final hyperparameters list used to finetune Language models for Lexical Normalization task using Sequence Labeling)

[1] http://komunitatea.elhuyar.eus/tweet-norm/

corpus failed to achieve good performance on the other 11 languages. To make sure that this behavior is consistent, another experiment was performed wherein the unified training data from phase 1 of section 3.2 was taken and this time the finetuning was performed on the BERT-German model which is pre-trained on Open Subtitles, CommonCrawl Wikipedia dump, ParaCrawl EU Bookshop corpus, and News Crawl. This sums up to about 16GB of German text corpus and 2,350,234,427 tokens. This model with BERT-German cased is trained based on the hypothesis that it will perform well for the German language and low in other languages. This hypothesis was not rejected after computing the evaluation results. Hence, it would be a sensible choice to train different models for different languages. However, it would be expensive in terms of resource cost when these models have to be deployed in production. Further, it would have scalability issues to cater to a large number of people.

Hence, the proposed approach finetunes the BERT multilingual base model (Devlin et al., 2018). The multilingual BERT model is pre-trained on the top 104 languages that have voluminous Wikipedia data using the masked language modeling (MLM) objective. The training data for each language was collected from the complete Wikipedia dump (excluding user and discussion pages). The major challenge faced while preparing this enormous dataset of 104 languages is the data imbalance, as different languages had different amounts of data. To deal with this data imbalance, the exponentially smoothed weighting of the data is performed. For instance, let's assume that the percentage of English data is 32% (after concatenating all English data in Wikipedia). In such a case, re-normalization and sampling are applied from that distribution after exponentiating each probability by a factor S (S was chosen to be 0.7 in the paper). As a result, high-resource, widely spoken languages such as English would be under-sampled and low-resource or less spoken languages such as Icelandic would be oversampled, thus solving the challenge of data imbalance. In this paper, the case-sensitive version is selected to retain the case information during the lexical normalization task.

By default, the maximum sequence length (max_seq_length) of the input sentence is fixed to 128. However, it resulted in the truncation of longer sentences which caused a decrease in performance as the ERR score got lowered. Hence, the max_seq_length was kept to 256 to accommodate longer input sentences. Experiments were also carried out on maximum sequence lengths of 128, 256, 300, 400, 450, and 512. It might be a greedy choice to select the highest max_seq_length but the training and inference time increases. Further, with max_seq_length set as 256, 300, 400, 450, and 512, the performance was similar, hence the final max_seq_length was set as 256. The number of epochs was kept to 100 with the early stopping parameter set to 3. It was observed that after the completion of 60-65 epochs, the loss stopped reducing and the model training was stopped automatically. To save the secondary memory, only the latest 3 epochs checkpoints and the best model were saved. This selected multilingual BERT model was finetuned by using the 'Simple Transformers' (Rajapakse, 2020)[2] library and the 'Hugging Face' (Wolf et al., 2019)[3] pre-trained models. All the experiments and model training were carried on NVIDIA Tesla V100 32 GB G-PU with primary memory (RAM) of the system being 128GB.

3.4 Post-processing based word alignment

One of the challenge faced is to align the target or predicted normalized words with the unnormalized input sentence. For this the following steps are followed:

1. Replacing the spaces in multi-gram normalized words with a special character. In this paper, underscore is used.

2. During inference phase, combining the outputs outputted by the model to extract the normalized tokens.

The importance of this step is reflected in the final evaluation results because this step makes sure that the unnormalized tokens are accurately replaced by their predicted normalized counterparts. The addition of special character (in this case underscore) helps to retain the output structure and the combination of independent word-piece token's predictions helps to retain the output.

4 Results and Discussions

This paper used Error Reduction Rate (ERR) (van der Goot et al.) as an evaluation metric for intrinsic evaluation. ERR represents

[2]https://simpletransformers.ai/

[3]https://huggingface.co/

team	avg.	da	de	en	es	hr	iden	it	nl	sl	sr	tr	trde
davda54-2	67.30	68.67	66.22	75.60	59.25	67.74	67.18	47.52	63.58	80.07	74.59	68.58	68.62
davda54-1	66.21	70.25	65.65	73.80	55.93	67.29	66.15	42.57	62.70	79.85	73.55	68.58	68.19
yvesscherrer-2	49.30	5.38	59.80	62.05	35.55	56.24	55.33	35.64	45.88	66.97	66.44	51.18	51.18
monoise	49.02	51.27	46.96	74.35	45.53	52.63	59.79	21.78	49.53	61.91	59.58	28.21	36.72
yvesscherrer-1	47.47	4.75	58.00	60.76	33.68	51.83	53.26	35.64	43.99	66.02	60.26	49.49	51.97
TrinkaAI (ours)	**43.75**	**45.89**	**47.30**	**65.96**	**61.33**	**41.28**	**56.36**	**15.84**	**45.74**	**59.51**	**44.52**	**15.54**	**25.77**
TrinkaAI (ours)	43.63	45.89	47.30	64.54	**61.33**	41.28	56.36	15.84	45.74	59.51	44.52	15.54	25.77
thunderml-1	43.44	46.52	46.62	64.07	60.29	40.09	59.11	11.88	44.05	59.33	44.46	15.88	29.01
team-2	40.70	48.10	46.06	63.73	21.00	40.39	59.28	13.86	43.72	60.55	46.11	15.88	29.71
learnML-2	40.30	40.51	43.69	61.57	56.55	38.11	56.19	5.94	42.77	58.25	39.99	14.36	25.68
maet-1	40.05	48.10	46.06	63.90	21.00	40.39	59.28	5.94	43.72	60.55	46.11	15.88	29.71
MFR	38.37	49.68	32.09	64.93	25.57	36.52	61.17	16.83	37.70	56.71	42.62	14.53	22.09
thunderml-2	36.48	-4.43	45.95	63.51	21.62	40.98	58.42	12.87	45.00	60.37	46.85	17.40	29.27
team-1	36.48	-4.43	45.95	63.51	21.62	40.98	58.42	12.87	45.00	60.37	46.85	17.40	29.27
cl-monoise	12.05	7.28	16.55	4.13	4.99	26.41	2.41	0.00	16.22	8.77	20.09	17.57	20.16
maet-2	7.33	2.22	4.28	21.73	0.00	9.86	19.24	0.00	2.09	18.39	8.08	0.84	1.23
learnML-1	7.33	2.22	4.28	21.73	0.00	9.86	19.24	0.00	2.09	18.39	8.08	0.84	1.23
bucuram-2	6.73	49.68	-1.91	26.81	-9.36	-10.06	-7.22	-31.68	-2.09	-1.04	42.62	9.97	14.99
bucuram-1	5.22	49.68	-1.91	26.81	-10.19	-9.86	-7.22	-31.68	-2.09	-1.13	42.62	1.01	6.57
LAI	0.00	0.00	0.00	0.00	0.00	0.00	0.00	0.00	0.00	0.00	0.00	0.00	0.00
machamp	-21.25	-88.92	-93.36	50.99	25.36	42.62	39.52	-312.87	1.49	56.80	39.44	-12.67	-3.42

Table 5: Error Reduction Rate (ERR) scores on test dataset of the teams participating in the lexical normalization task

treebank	avg.	de-tweede	en-aae	en-monoise	en-tweebank2	it-postwita	it-twittiro	tr-iwt151
davda54-2	64.17	73.58	62.73	58.57	59.08	68.28	72.22	54.74
davda54-1	63.98	73.58	62.21	57.90	59.02	68.28	72.15	54.76
yvesscherrer-2	63.72	73.49	60.64	56.24	60.30	68.11	72.29	54.95
yvesscherrer-1	63.72	73.49	60.48	56.26	60.27	68.15	72.43	54.94
monoise	63.44	73.20	62.27	56.83	58.90	67.55	70.69	54.61
TrinkaAI (ours)	**63.31**	**72.86**	**60.32**	**56.74**	**60.31**	**67.34**	**70.72**	**54.89**
TrinkaAI (ours)	63.12	72.86	60.16	56.64	59.87	66.98	71.14	54.20
maet-1	63.09	72.80	59.44	56.64	59.80	67.41	71.07	54.45
team-2	63.03	72.80	59.44	56.64	59.80	67.19	70.86	54.45
Thunderml-2	63.02	72.67	59.57	56.74	59.25	67.34	71.35	54.24
team-1	63.02	72.67	59.57	56.72	59.24	67.34	71.35	54.23
thunderml-1	62.95	72.52	59.31	56.74	59.86	67.09	71.00	54.09
learnML-2	62.88	72.31	58.98	56.16	59.98	66.99	71.24	54.48
cl-monoise	62.71	72.65	60.90	55.26	58.53	66.53	70.10	54.98
bucuram-2	62.53	72.57	59.57	54.20	59.81	66.74	69.99	54.84
bucuram-1	62.53	72.57	59.57	54.20	59.81	66.74	69.99	54.84
LAI	62.45	72.71	59.21	53.65	59.99	66.49	70.06	55.00
maet-2	62.22	72.69	58.50	52.89	60.01	66.47	69.99	55.00
learnML-1	62.22	72.69	58.50	52.89	60.01	66.47	69.99	55.00
machamp	61.89	71.28	60.77	54.61	57.97	64.65	69.82	54.08

Table 6: Labeled Attachment Scores (LAS) on test dataset of the teams participating in the lexical normalization task

accuracy normalized for the number of words that need to be normalized. The main advantage of using ERR as a metric is that it accounts for the difficulty of the task (similar to that of Cohen's Kappa (Cohen, 1968)

$$ERR = \frac{Accuracy_{system} - Accuracy_{baseline}}{1.0 - Accuracy_{baseline}} \quad (1)$$

$$ERR = \frac{TP - FP}{TP + FN} \quad (2)$$

Equation 1 represents the formula to compute

the ERR score. ERR can be calculated by first computing the accuracy of the normalization system ($Accuracy_{system}$) and accuracy of the baseline system which will always return the original word ($Accuracy_{baseline}$). ERR can also be calculated by 2 where,

- TP: Annotators normalized and the proposed system normalized correctly.
- TN: Annotators did not normalize, and the proposed system did not normalize.
- FP: Annotators did not normalize, but the proposed system normalized.
- FN: Annotators normalized, but the proposed system did not find the correct normalization (because the proposed system either kept the original word or proposed a wrong candidate).

For the extrinsic evaluation, dependency parsing is considered. Here, the impact of lexical normalization on the quality of the parsed trees is computed using the LAS, i.e., the percentage of words which have both the correct syntactic head and the correct dependency label.

Table 5 depicts Error Reduction Rate (ERR) scores computed on the test dataset for intrinsic evaluation. The ERR scores of individual languages, as well as average scores, are computed for each team that participated in the lexical normalization shared task. The proposed system named TrinkaAI scored an overall average ERR of 43.75. On the Spanish language, TrinkaAI's ERR score was 61.33, the highest among all the shared task participants. Our result shows that by adding additional training data, the model's performance can be considerably increased. Overall, the proposed system, TrinkaAI, ranked 4th in the lexical normalization shared task per the average ERR scores obtained from all the languages scores.

Table 6 depicts the scores for extrinsic evaluation. TrinkaAI had the highest LAS score of 60.31 on test data en-tweetbank2. This shows the potential of the proposed approach in normalizing un-normalized sentences. The overall average LAS score obtained by the TrinkaAI was 63.12, which stood 5th among other participants.

5 Conclusion and Future Scope

In this paper, we propose a multilingual sequence labeling based approach to solve the problem of lexical normalization. We show that a single model is capable of performing well on all languages. We finetuned multilingual BERT on a downstream task of lexical normalization along with finetuning of some of its hyperparameters. Our proposed system, TrinkaAI, scored an average ERR score of 43.75 in the intrinsic evaluation and an average LAS score of 63.31 in the extrinsic evaluation. Further, TrinkaAI achieved the highest ERR score of 61.33 for the Spanish language. This denotes that the performance of the system can be improved considerably by incorporating additional data during training. TrinkaAI also achieved the highest LAS score of 60.31 for the en-tweetbank2 test data.

The performance of our proposed system can be further improved by training the model with 'large' configurations having a high number of parameters. The accuracy can be improved by additional data and by using language-sensitive embeddings.

References

Jacob Cohen. 1968. Weighted kappa: nominal scale agreement provision for scaled disagreement or partial credit. *Psychological bulletin*, 70(4):213.

Alexis Conneau, Kartikay Khandelwal, Naman Goyal, Vishrav Chaudhary, Guillaume Wenzek, Francisco Guzmán, Edouard Grave, Myle Ott, Luke Zettlemoyer, and Veselin Stoyanov. 2019. Unsupervised cross-lingual representation learning at scale. *arXiv preprint arXiv:1911.02116*.

Jacob Devlin, Ming-Wei Chang, Kenton Lee, and Kristina Toutanova. 2018. Bert: Pre-training of deep bidirectional transformers for language understanding. *arXiv preprint arXiv:1810.04805*.

Bo Han. 2014. *Improving the utility of social media with natural language processing*. Ph.D. thesis.

Bo Han and Timothy Baldwin. 2011. Lexical normalisation of short text messages: Makn sens a# twitter. In *Proceedings of the 49th annual meeting of the association for computational linguistics: Human language technologies*, pages 368–378.

Ning Jin. 2015. Ncsu-sas-ning: Candidate generation and feature engineering for supervised lexical normalization. In *Proceedings of the Workshop on Noisy User-generated Text*, pages 87–92.

Xiaohua Liu, Shaodian Zhang, Furu Wei, and Ming Zhou. 2011. Recognizing named entities in tweets. In *Proceedings of the 49th annual meeting of the association for computational linguistics: human language technologies*, pages 359–367.

Yinhan Liu, Myle Ott, Naman Goyal, Jingfei Du, Mandar Joshi, Danqi Chen, Omer Levy, Mike Lewis,

Luke Zettlemoyer, and Veselin Stoyanov. 2019. Roberta: A robustly optimized bert pretraining approach. *arXiv preprint arXiv:1907.11692*.

Nikola Ljubešic, Katja Zupan, Darja Fišer, and Tomaz Erjavec. 2016. Normalising slovene data: historical texts vs. user-generated content. In *Proceedings of the 13th Conference on Natural Language Processing (KONVENS 2016)*, volume 16, pages 146–155.

Ismini Lourentzou, Kabir Manghnani, and ChengXiang Zhai. 2019. Adapting sequence to sequence models for text normalization in social media. In *Proceedings of the International AAAI Conference on Web and Social Media*, volume 13, pages 335–345.

Benjamin Muller, Benoît Sagot, and Djamé Seddah. 2019. Enhancing bert for lexical normalization. In *The 5th Workshop on Noisy User-generated Text (W-NUT)*.

Deana Pennell and Yang Liu. 2011. A character-level machine translation approach for normalization of sms abbreviations. In *Proceedings of 5th International Joint Conference on Natural Language Processing*, pages 974–982.

T Rajapakse. 2020. Simple transformers.

Sarah Schulz, Guy De Pauw, Orphée De Clercq, Bart Desmet, Veronique Hoste, Walter Daelemans, and Lieve Macken. 2016. Multimodular text normalization of dutch user-generated content. *ACM Transactions on Intelligent Systems and Technology (TIST)*, 7(4):1–22.

Kushal Vaghani. 2020. Curating social media data. *arXiv preprint arXiv:2002.09202*.

Rob van der Goot. 2019. Monoise: A multi-lingual and easy-to-use lexical normalization tool. In *Proceedings of the 57th Annual Meeting of the Association for Computational Linguistics: System Demonstrations*, pages 201–206.

Rob van der Goot, Alan Ramponi, Arkaitz Zubiaga, Barbara Plank, Benjamin Muller, Iñaki San Vicente Roncal, Nikola Ljubešić, and ˜Çetinoglu. MultiLexNorm: A shared task on multilingual lexical normalization.

Thomas Wolf, Lysandre Debut, Victor Sanh, Julien Chaumond, Clement Delangue, Anthony Moi, Pierric Cistac, Tim Rault, Rémi Louf, Morgan Funtowicz, et al. 2019. Huggingface's transformers: State-of-the-art natural language processing. *ArXiv*, pages arXiv–1910.

Wei Xu, Bo Han, and Alan Ritter. 2015. Proceedings of the workshop on noisy user-generated text. In *Proceedings of the Workshop on Noisy User-generated Text*.

Sesame Street to Mount Sinai: BERT-constrained character-level Moses models for multilingual lexical normalization

Yves Scherrer
Department of Digital Humanities
University of Helsinki
yves.scherrer@helsinki.fi

Nikola Ljubešić
Department of Knowledge Technologies
Jožef Stefan Institute
nikola.ljubesic@ijs.si

Abstract

This paper describes the HEL-LJU submissions to the MultiLexNorm shared task on multilingual lexical normalization. Our system is based on a BERT token classification preprocessing step, where for each token the type of the necessary transformation is predicted (none, uppercase, lowercase, capitalize, modify), and a character-level statistical machine translation step where the text is translated from original to normalized given the BERT-predicted transformation constraints. For some languages, depending on the results on development data, the training data was extended by back-translating OpenSubtitles data. In the final ordering of the ten participating teams, the HEL-LJU team has taken the second place, scoring better than the previous state-of-the-art.

1 Introduction

In this paper, we describe the HEL-LJU submission to the MultiLexNorm shared task on multilingual lexical normalization. Lexical normalization is a task of transforming non-standard input tokens into output tokens that follow a specific linguistic standard. In this shared task, lexical normalization is defined even narrower as "the task of transforming an utterance into its standard form, word by word, where one-to-many (1-n) and many-to-one (n-1) replacements are included", disregarding thereby word deletions and insertions (van der Goot et al., 2021). The main motivation behind lexical normalization is to minimize the variability of the linguistic signal, either for computational usage or human consumption. Accordingly, the shared task submissions are evaluated both intrinsically and extrinsically (on a dependency parsing task).

The need for lexical normalization for computational usage is diminishing these days, given the end-to-end methodology that is becoming more and more popular, where the systems are robust enough to accept non-standard input without any explicit normalization. However, for human consumption the need for lexical normalization is still very much present.

The three types of data that still frequently require normalization are user-generated content (i.e., "Internet language" (Ljubešić et al., 2014)), historical data (e.g., 18th century Slovenian (Scherrer and Erjavec, 2016), which is frequently not understood even by native speakers of Slovenian) and dialectal data (very frequently not understood by non-native speakers of a language, or even by the speaker of the same language, as is the case with Swiss dialects of German (Scherrer and Ljubešić, 2016)).

2 Related work

Over the last decade, character-level statistical machine translation (CSMT) has shown very strong results on varying types of non-standard data, such as user-generated content (Ljubešić et al., 2014), historical data (Tjong Kim Sang et al., 2017) and dialectal data (Scherrer and Ljubešić, 2016). Even more, the CSMT approach has shown to behave very similarly in a controlled comparison on various types of non-standard data, such as with Slovenian user-generated content and historical texts (Ljubešic et al., 2016). It has also shown to be the preferred way of adapting language technologies to non-standard data if the availability of human supervision is low (Zupan et al., 2019).

While neural approaches have almost entirely replaced statistical ones in "standard" translation settings (translating between distinct languages), recent studies have shown that SMT-based approaches remain competitive for normalization tasks (Tang et al., 2018; Bollmann, 2019).

Normalization systems not based on translation architectures have also been proposed. For example, MoNoise (van der Goot, 2019) generates a list of normalization candidates for each token and then

Proceedings of the 2021 EMNLP Workshop W-NUT: The Seventh Workshop on Noisy User-generated Text, pages 465–472
November 11, 2021.

Code	Language	Words	Sents	Change	Dataset
DA	Danish	16,448	719	9.25%	(Plank et al., 2020)
DE	German	15,006	1,628	17.96%	(Sidarenka et al., 2013)
EN	English	35,216	2,360	6.90%	(Baldwin et al., 2015)
ES	Spanish	7,189	568	7.69%	(Alegria et al., 2013)
HR	Croatian	54,416	4,760	8.89%	(Ljubešić et al., 2017a)
ID-EN	Indonesian-English	13,949	495	12.16%	(Barik et al., 2019)
IT	Italian	12,645	593	7.32%	(van der Goot et al., 2020)
NL	Dutch	12,381	907	28.29%	(Schuur, 2020)
SL	Slovenian	44,944	4,670	15.62%	(Erjavec et al., 2017)
SR	Serbian	56,823	4,138	7.65%	(Ljubešić et al., 2017b)
TR	Turkish	6,443	570	37.02%	(Çolakoğlu et al., 2019)
TR-DE	Turkish-German	12,773	800	24.14%	(van der Goot and Çetinoğlu, 2021)

Table 1: Some statistics on the train-splits of all datasets within the MultiLexNorm benchmark. The 'change' column indicates the percentage of words that are normalized.

ranks them using a variety of features derived from the original text and the proposed normalization candidates.

3 Data

The data in the MultiLexNorm shared task all come from the user-generated-content domain, and comprise mostly of Twitter data. An overview of the 12 datasets is given in Table 1. The sizes of the datasets range between 6 and 56 thousand tokens, with the percentage of changed tokens varying between 7 and 37 percent.

For some of the languages, the data was split into a training and a development set by the organizers. For the other languages, we split the data randomly (90% training, 10% development) and kept the split constant across our experiments.

4 Character-level MT architectures for normalization

Following our earlier experience, we cast normalization as a character-level machine translation problem. In order to enable contextual dependencies, we train and test on entire tweets. We preprocessed the data by replacing URLs by a placeholder and token boundaries by a reserved character. These changes were reverted during postprocessing.

We evaluated an SMT model[1], an RNN-based NMT model[2], and a Transformer-based NMT model[3]. The SMT models are based on Moses (Koehn et al., 2007), the NMT models are based on OpenNMT-py (Klein et al., 2017).

	CSMT	C-RNN	C-TRF
Lg.-specific	92.1%	85.0%	66.7%
Lg.-independent	90.4%	86.4%	89.4%

Table 2: Average normalization accuracies over the validation sets of the 12 languages for different model architectures. Language-specific and language-independent (all training data merged) experiments are reported.

The results are reported in Table 2 (top row) as averages over the 12 languages of the shared task (detailed numbers are given in Table 8 in the appendix). They show a clear advantage for the statistical paradigm (CSMT) over the neural ones (C-RNN and C-TRF). The Transformer-based models were extremely inconsistent across languages, with accuracies below 50% for four languages (DA, ID-EN, NL, TR).[4]

[1]The translation model is monotonous, i.e. without any distortion component. The language model is a character 10-gram model trained with KenLM on the provided training data. The model weights are tuned on the development set with MERT (minimum error rate training) using character error rate as a metric.

[2]The model consists of a bidirectional encoder and a unidirectional decoder, two hidden layers, dimensionality 512 across all layers, and dropout set to 0.1. Maximum sequence length is defined at 1000. We train for a maximum of 50,000 steps with early stopping.

[3]The model consists of 6 Transformer layers with 8 heads each. All dimensionalities are set to 512. Dropout and label smoothing are both set to 0.1. Maximum sequence length is defined at 1000. We train for a maximum of 50,000 steps with early stopping.

[4]We also created CSMT models that were trained and tested on single tokens and thus did not have access to the

	DA	DE	EN	ES	HR	ID-EN	IT	NL	SL	SR	TR	TR-DE	Avg
No constr.	95.47	88.70	96.80	95.23	95.48	94.82	94.26	80.87	93.52	97.02	76.65	86.26	91.26
BERT	95.23	91.05	97.03	95.30	96.05	94.78	94.85	82.22	93.93	97.44	80.34	87.14	92.11
Oracle	97.03	94.05	97.38	95.89	96.26	95.55	97.64	84.96	94.58	97.62	83.69	92.03	93.89

Table 3: Normalization accuracies with unconstrained and constrained CSMT models.

In order to gauge the potential impact of additional training data, we trained a single language-independent model on the concatenation of all twelve training sets (see bottom row of Table 2 as well as Table 8 in the appendix). For CSMT, this led to lower scores compared to the language-specific models for all twelve languages, whereas the neural models benefitted from the additional data. The scores increased for 9 out of 12 languages with the C-RNN architecture, and for 11 out of 12 languages with the C-TRF architecture, confirming again that NMT models are more data hungry than SMT models.

5 Adding constraints to the normalization process

Table 1 shows that for most of the languages in the task, less than 20% of tokens actually need to be changed. Only three languages in the set require the modification of more than 20% of tokens. Moreover, depending on the language, a substantial proportion of modifications are restricted to casing changes. Hence, the risk of over-normalization, i.e., predicting a spelling change where it is not needed, is significant.

In order to reduce this risk, we propose a sequence labeling task that annotates each token of a tweet with one of five transformation types: *none, capitalize, uppercase, lowercase, modify*. The training data for this task can be directly derived from the MultiLexNorm training data. We then feed these predictions as constraints to the CSMT system, such that only the tokens marked as *modify* are normalized by CSMT. For the remaining categories (*capitalize, uppercase, lowercase*), we transform the tokens via rules and mark them as not to be modified by the CSMT system.

The sequence labeling models are based on pre-trained language-specific BERT or ELECTRA models, which are fine-tuned on the task using derived training data.[5]

sentential context. As expected, they were consistently outperformed by the models using entire tweets.

[5]We use the NER model class of the *simpletransformers* library (`https://simpletransformers.ai/`) and fine-tune the models for 10 epochs. The list of pre-trained models is given in Table 7 in the appendix.

Table 3 reports the normalization accuracies of three setups: a CSMT model without any constraints, a CSMT model with constraints predicted by the BERT classifier, and a CSMT model with input constrained by an oracle (the constraints are inferred from the gold annotations of the development sets). The constraints have a positive effect on all languages but Danish and Indonesian–English.[6] In general, the accuracies of the BERT constraints lie about halfway between the unconstrained and the oracle ones.

6 Including synthetic training data from back-translation

The results of the language-independent models of Section 4 suggest that the provided training data is of insufficient size to train reliable translation models, especially neural ones. A well-known strategy to augment the training data in MT is back-translation, where target language data is translated to the source language by an auxiliary model (Sennrich et al., 2016). The resulting parallel data (a standard target side, and a noisy source side) is then included in the training data of the main model.

In the normalization setting, this amounts to finding "clean" data and running it through a model that produces a noisy version of it. To this end, we used filtered subsets of the monolingual OpenSubtitles corpora from OPUS[7] (Tiedemann, 2012) as input data for producing back-translations.

We filtered the OPUS data using the OpusFilter package (Aulamo et al., 2020) and the following filters:

- The length of the line lies between 5 and 25 words (this corresponds to the majority of tweets in the training corpora).

[6]The token classification accuracies, i.e. the performance of the BERT classifier before the CSMT normalization step, are provided in Table 9 in the appendix. Classification accuracy seems to be a poor predictor of normalization accuracy though, as illustrated e.g. by the above-average performance of the Danish and Indonesian–English BERT models.

[7]`https://opus.nlpl.eu/`

	DA	DE	EN	ES	HR	ID-EN	IT	NL	SL	SR	TR	TR-DE	Avg
Train+Dev	718	2,201	2,950	567	6,348	660	592	1,215	6,227	5,517	569	799	2,364
Full BT	103,559	55,453	88,742	115,713	16,332	85,785	89,295	52,413	58,848	84,162	127,150	75,848	79,442
Sampled BT	11,760	32,560	47,200	8,920		9,900	9,060	18,140		82,760	9,380	12,340	26,433

Table 4: Training instances (tweets/sentences).

	DA	DE	EN	ES	HR	ID-EN	IT	NL	SL	SR	TR	TR-DE	Avg
No LM/BT	95.47	88.70	***96.80***	*95.23*	95.48	94.82	*94.26*	80.87	93.52	97.02	76.65	86.26	91.26
Full LM	**96.08**	**90.58**	96.70	**95.56**	**95.74**	**95.13**	**94.65**	**82.47**	**94.21**	**97.41**	**79.91**	**86.94**	**92.12**
Full LM+BT	*96.01*	89.59	96.74	94.50	*95.68*	94.74	93.14	*81.78*	*93.93*	*97.28*	*79.57*	*86.80*	91.65
Sampled LM	95.88	90.47	96.75	95.43		94.93	94.36	82.09		**97.41**	78.45	86.56	91.86
Sampled LM+BT	95.84	*89.96*	96.70	94.64		*94.93*	93.80	81.78		97.25	79.23	86.70	91.70

Table 5: Normalization accuracies of unconstrained CSMT models. The LM models include an additional language model trained on the target side of the back-translated data, whereas the LM+BT models additionally include the back-translations for phrase table extraction. Column-wise best results in bold, training setups chosen for the final submissions in italics.

- The line does not contain HTML tags.
- The line only contains Latin script.
- The line is identified as the target language by the *langid* language identifier.[8]
- The line does not contain lower case letters immediately followed by upper case letters (this is an indication of OCR errors or other misspellings).
- The line has a cross-entropy < 20 when evaluated with a language model trained on the training data.[9]
- When normalized with a "forward-translation" CSMT model trained on the training data, the output is identical to the input. This filter is intended to catch typos and non-standard language in the original data, which we want to avoid on the target side.

The resulting dataset is then "unnormalized" using a backward CSMT model trained on the provided training data in the opposite direction, with a beam of 200. Lines whose translation candidates are all identical to the input are rejected. We run the CSMT model for 72 hours per language. Depending on the initial data size, the filters and the speed of the CSMT model, this results in 16k to 127k additional sentences per language (see Table 4).

The resulting back-translations massively outnumber the original training data for most languages, which may affect the final model negatively. Therefore, we also provide random samples of back-translations that contain at most 20 times as many sentence pairs as the given training data (see bottom row of Table 4).[10]

There are two ways of including additional data in an SMT pipeline:

LM Including a second language model trained only on the (non-synthetic) target sides of the back-translated data.

BT Concatenating the original training data with the back-translated data for phrase table extraction.

In addition to the model trained only on the provided data, we therefore obtain four CSMT models, two with the full augmented data and two with the subsampled augmented data. Table 5 shows the results.[11]

We also train C-RNN and C-TRF models with the full set of back-translations, distinguishing the data sources by adding labels on the source side of each sentence. The back-translations increase the results for most languages in all three model

[8]This step is skipped for Serbian because the corresponding *langid* model only matches content in Cyrillic script, whereas the shared task data is entirely in Latin script.

[9]Language model training is also performed within OpusFilter using the default parameters.

[10]We do not provide sampled data for Croatian and Slovene since the total amount of obtained back-translations is lower than the sampling threshold. We did not have the resources to evaluate different sampling thresholds.

[11]Note that the results reported here are without constraints. Also note that the **LM** models were trained as contrastive experiments after the submission deadline and were therefore not considered for the submissions.

	DA	DE	EN	ES	HR	ID-EN	IT	NL	SL	SR	TR	TR-DE	Avg
Best	68.67	66.22	75.60	59.25	67.74	67.18	47.52	63.58	80.07	74.59	68.58	68.62	67.30
HEL-LJU 2	56.65	59.80	62.05	35.55	56.24	55.33	35.64	45.88	66.97	66.44	51.18	51.18	53.58
HEL-LJU 1	56.65	58.00	60.76	33.68	51.83	53.26	35.64	43.99	66.02	60.26	49.49	51.97	51.80

Table 6: Error reduction rates on the test set. We show the two HEL-LJU submissions and the overall best-performing one.

architectures, but the neural models do not catch up sufficiently to become competitive with the statistical models. The detailed results of the neural models can be found in Table 10 in the Appendix.

For CSMT, it can be seen that the *Full LM* strategy works best overall, but the differences to other setups are small. Since only the *LM+BT* models were available at submission time, we chose the best-performing setup per language among those: the *Full LM+BT* setup for seven languages, the *Sampled LM+BT* setup for two languages and the *No LM/BT* setup for three languages.

7 Submissions

The experiments reported in the previous sections have shown us that for our data and our setup:

- neural character-level MT approaches are not competitive with statistical ones,
- decoding constraints learned with BERT increase normalization accuracies for most languages,
- data augmentation strategies are successful, although the impact of back-translations is negligible in CSMT settings.

For our **first submission**, we choose the CSMT model setup that has led to the best development accuracy for each language (i.e., the setups highlighted in italics in Table 5) and combine it with the BERT-based constraints.

For the **second submission**, we re-create the phrase table and the language model by including the previously held-out development set. We copy the model weights obtained by MERT from the first submission. Note that for those languages where the full back-translations are used, the added development instances amount to a tiny fraction of the overall data. In this case, we expect the results for the two submissions to be very similar.

The results of the intrinsic evaluation are summarized in Table 6. Our submitted systems are ranked 3rd and 4th (out of 18), and we were the second-best team (out of 9). The gap between the best submission and ours is considerable though.

The same ranking is seen in the extrinsic evaluation, although it only concerns German, English and Italian. One should note however that the LAS scores of all systems are very close, showing again that normalization does not provide a substantial advantage for recent downstream-task systems.

8 Conclusion

In this paper we have described our submission to the MultiLexNorm shared task on multilingual lexical normalization. We compare character-level SMT, RNN and Transformer models, showing that in our case, where training data is very limited, SMT still outperforms the two neural options. Increasing the amount of training data by merging data from all languages, or by means of back-translation of OpenSubtitles data, does help the neural approaches, but they still do not perform better than SMT. We further investigate the possibility of predicting via BERT-like models if and how a token should be modified, and show that giving this information to the SMT process improves the final results. Maybe the path to Mount Sinai passes through Sesame Street, after all...

Acknowledgements

This work has been supported by the FoTran project, funded by the European Research Council (ERC) under the European Union's Horizon 2020 research and innovation programme (grant agreement No. 771113), the Academy of Finland through project No. 342859 "CorCoDial – Corpus-based computational dialectology", the Slovenian Research Agency through research core funding No. P6-0411 "Language resources and technologies for Slovene language", the research project ARRS N6-0099 and FWO G070619N "The linguistic landscape of hate speech on social media", and the European Union's Rights, Equality and Citizenship Programme (2014-2020) project IMSyPP (grant no. 875263).

References

Inaki Alegria, Nora Aranberri, Víctor Fresno, Pablo Gamallo, Lluis Padró, Inaki San Vicente, Jordi Turmo, and Arkaitz Zubiaga. 2013. Introducción a la tarea compartida Tweet-Norm 2013: Normalización léxica de tuits en Español. In *Tweet-Norm@ SEPLN*, pages 1–9.

Mikko Aulamo, Sami Virpioja, and Jörg Tiedemann. 2020. OpusFilter: A configurable parallel corpus filtering toolbox. In *Proceedings of the 58th Annual Meeting of the Association for Computational Linguistics: System Demonstrations*, pages 150–156, Online. Association for Computational Linguistics.

Timothy Baldwin, Marie Catherine de Marneffe, Bo Han, Young-Bum Kim, Alan Ritter, and Wei Xu. 2015. Shared tasks of the 2015 workshop on noisy user-generated text: Twitter lexical normalization and named entity recognition. In *Proceedings of the Workshop on Noisy User-generated Text*, pages 126–135, Beijing, China. Association for Computational Linguistics.

Anab Maulana Barik, Rahmad Mahendra, and Mirna Adriani. 2019. Normalization of Indonesian-English code-mixed Twitter data. In *Proceedings of the 5th Workshop on Noisy User-generated Text (W-NUT 2019)*, pages 417–424, Hong Kong, China. Association for Computational Linguistics.

Marcel Bollmann. 2019. A large-scale comparison of historical text normalization systems. In *Proceedings of the 2019 Conference of the North American Chapter of the Association for Computational Linguistics: Human Language Technologies, Volume 1 (Long and Short Papers)*, pages 3885–3898, Minneapolis, Minnesota. Association for Computational Linguistics.

Talha Çolakoğlu, Umut Sulubacak, and Ahmet Cüneyd Tantuğ. 2019. Normalizing non-canonical Turkish texts using machine translation approaches. In *Proceedings of the 57th Annual Meeting of the Association for Computational Linguistics: Student Research Workshop*, pages 267–272, Florence, Italy. Association for Computational Linguistics.

Tomaž Erjavec, Darja Fišer, Jaka Čibej, Špela Arhar Holdt, Nikola Ljubešić, and Katja Zupan. 2017. CMC training corpus Janes-Tag 2.0. Slovenian language resource repository CLARIN.SI.

Guillaume Klein, Yoon Kim, Yuntian Deng, Jean Senellart, and Alexander Rush. 2017. OpenNMT: Open-source toolkit for neural machine translation. In *Proceedings of ACL 2017, System Demonstrations*, pages 67–72, Vancouver, Canada. Association for Computational Linguistics.

Philipp Koehn, Hieu Hoang, Alexandra Birch, Chris Callison-Burch, Marcello Federico, Nicola Bertoldi, Brooke Cowan, Wade Shen, Christine Moran, Richard Zens, Chris Dyer, Ondřej Bojar, Alexandra Constantin, and Evan Herbst. 2007. Moses: Open source toolkit for statistical machine translation. In *Proceedings of the 45th Annual Meeting of the Association for Computational Linguistics Companion Volume Proceedings of the Demo and Poster Sessions*, pages 177–180, Prague, Czech Republic. Association for Computational Linguistics.

Nikola Ljubešić, Tomaž Erjavec, and Darja Fišer. 2014. Standardizing tweets with character-level machine translation. In *International Conference on Intelligent Text Processing and Computational Linguistics*, pages 164–175. Springer.

Nikola Ljubešić, Tomaž Erjavec, Maja Miličević, and Tanja Samardžić. 2017a. Croatian Twitter training corpus ReLDI-NormTagNER-hr 2.0. Slovenian language resource repository CLARIN.SI.

Nikola Ljubešić, Tomaž Erjavec, Maja Miličević, and Tanja Samardžić. 2017b. Serbian Twitter training corpus ReLDI-NormTagNER-sr 2.0. Slovenian language resource repository CLARIN.SI.

Nikola Ljubešic, Katja Zupan, Darja Fišer, and Tomaz Erjavec. 2016. Normalising Slovene data: historical texts vs. user-generated content. In *Proceedings of the 13th Conference on Natural Language Processing (KONVENS 2016)*, volume 16, pages 146–155.

Barbara Plank, Kristian Nørgaard Jensen, and Rob van der Goot. 2020. DaN+: Danish nested named entities and lexical normalization. In *Proceedings of the 28th International Conference on Computational Linguistics*, pages 6649–6662, Barcelona, Spain (Online). International Committee on Computational Linguistics.

Yves Scherrer and Tomaž Erjavec. 2016. Modernising historical Slovene words. *Natural Language Engineering*, 22(6):881–905.

Yves Scherrer and Nikola Ljubešić. 2016. Automatic normalisation of the Swiss German ArchiMob corpus using character-level machine translation. In *Proceedings of the 13th Conference on Natural Language Processing (KONVENS)*.

Youri Schuur. 2020. Normalization for Dutch for improved POS tagging. Master's thesis, University of Groningen.

Rico Sennrich, Barry Haddow, and Alexandra Birch. 2016. Improving neural machine translation models with monolingual data. In *Proceedings of the 54th Annual Meeting of the Association for Computational Linguistics (Volume 1: Long Papers)*, pages 86–96, Berlin, Germany. Association for Computational Linguistics.

Uladzimir Sidarenka, Tatjana Scheffler, and Manfred Stede. 2013. Rule-based normalization of German Twitter messages. In *Proc. of the GSCL Workshop Verarbeitung und Annotation von Sprachdaten aus Genres internetbasierter Kommunikation*.

Gongbo Tang, Fabienne Cap, Eva Pettersson, and Joakim Nivre. 2018. An evaluation of neural machine translation models on historical spelling normalization. In *Proceedings of the 27th International Conference on Computational Linguistics*, pages 1320–1331, Santa Fe, New Mexico, USA. Association for Computational Linguistics.

Jörg Tiedemann. 2012. Parallel data, tools and interfaces in OPUS. In *Proceedings of the Eighth International Conference on Language Resources and Evaluation (LREC'12)*, pages 2214–2218, Istanbul, Turkey. European Language Resources Association (ELRA).

Erik Tjong Kim Sang, Marcel Bollmann, Remko Boschker, Francisco Casacuberta, FM Dietz, Stefanie Dipper, Miguel Domingo, Rob van der Goot, JM van Koppen, Nikola Ljubešić, et al. 2017. The CLIN27 shared task: Translating historical text to contemporary language for improving automatic linguistic annotation. *Computational Linguistics in the Netherlands Journal*, 7:53–64.

Rob van der Goot. 2019. MoNoise: A multi-lingual and easy-to-use lexical normalization tool. In *Proceedings of the 57th Annual Meeting of the Association for Computational Linguistics: System Demonstrations*, pages 201–206, Florence, Italy. Association for Computational Linguistics.

Rob van der Goot and Özlem Çetinoğlu. 2021. Lexical normalization for code-switched data and its effect on POS tagging. In *Proceedings of the 16th Conference of the European Chapter of the Association for Computational Linguistics: Main Volume*, pages 2352–2365, Online. Association for Computational Linguistics.

Rob van der Goot, Alan Ramponi, Tommaso Caselli, Michele Cafagna, and Lorenzo De Mattei. 2020. Norm it! Lexical normalization for Italian and its downstream effects for dependency parsing. In *Proceedings of the 12th Language Resources and Evaluation Conference*, pages 6272–6278, Marseille, France. European Language Resources Association.

Rob van der Goot, Alan Ramponi, Arkaitz Zubiaga, Barbara Plank, Benjamin Muller, Iñaki San Vicente Roncal, Nikola Ljubešić, Özlem Çetinoğlu, Rahmad Mahendra, Talha Çolakoğlu, Timothy Baldwin, Tommaso Caselli, and Wladimir Sidorenko. 2021. MultiLexNorm: A shared task on multilingual lexical normalization. In *Proceedings of the 7th Workshop on Noisy User-generated Text (W-NUT 2021)*, Punta Cana, Dominican Republic. Association for Computational Linguistics.

Katja Zupan, Nikola Ljubešić, and Tomaž Erjavec. 2019. How to tag non-standard language: Normalisation versus domain adaptation for Slovene historical and user-generated texts. *Natural Language Engineering*, 25(5):651–674.

Lang.	Type and model identifier	
DA	B	Maltehb/danish-bert-botxo
DE	B	dbmdz/bert-base-german-cased
EN	B	bert-large-cased
ES	B	dccuchile/bert-base-spanish-wwm-cased
HR	E	classla/bcms-bertic
ID-EN	B	bert-large-cased
IT	E	dbmdz/electra-base-italian-xxl-cased-discriminator
NL	B	GroNLP/bert-base-dutch-cased
SL	B	EMBEDDIA/crosloengual-bert
SR	E	classla/bcms-bertic
TR	B	dbmdz/bert-base-turkish-cased
TR-DE	B	dbmdz/bert-base-turkish-cased

Table 7: Pre-trained models used for the token classification task (B = BERT, E = ELECTRA).

		DA	DE	EN	ES	HR	ID-EN	IT	NL	SL	SR	TR	TR-DE	Avg
CSMT	L-spec	97.88	95.70	96.76	94.89	95.69	94.76	94.33	82.12	93.65	97.13	77.56	84.40	92.1
CSMT	L-ind	96.15	92.63	95.72	93.36	95.26	92.56	92.39	79.32	92.61	97.03	75.24	82.63	90.4
C-RNN	L-spec	92.39	91.44	94.09	81.68	92.72	76.29	88.61	73.84	90.96	94.22	67.46	76.33	85.0
C-RNN	L-ind	81.70	94.07	95.05	91.76	93.31	79.52	92.39	73.76	87.98	95.68	72.18	79.68	86.4
C-TRF	L-spec	41.67	90.73	74.48	75.11	92.70	32.42	89.04	28.89	91.64	93.29	28.50	61.95	66.7
C-TRF	L-ind	96.63	93.85	95.24	92.29	94.40	92.18	93.51	77.32	91.59	95.44	71.50	78.93	89.4

Table 8: Detailed results of the initial character-level MT experiments. *L-spec* refers to language-specific models, *L-ind* to language-independent ones. Note that these experiments use a different train/test split from those reported in Tables 3–6.

	DA	DE	EN	ES	HR	ID-EN	IT	NL	SL	SR	TR	TR-DE	Avg
BERT	95.57	93.99	97.74	96.75	98.02	96.28	95.28	89.05	96.70	98.69	91.33	90.70	95.01

Table 9: Token classification accuracies.

		DE	EN	ES	HR	ID-EN	IT	NL	SL	SR	TR	TR-DE	Avg
CSMT	No BT	88.70	96.80	95.23	95.48	94.82	94.26	80.87	93.52	97.02	76.65	86.26	90.87
CSMT	Full BT	89.59	96.74	94.50	95.68	94.74	93.14	81.78	93.93	97.28	79.57	86.80	91.25
C-RNN	No BT	84.34	95.22	82.65	93.02	82.70	92.36	76.60	89.92	94.67	68.50	78.28	85.30
C-RNN	Full BT	88.11	94.32	90.73	92.87	47.06	91.63	69.89	90.61	96.54	65.92	79.17	82.44
C-TRF	Full BT	88.56	82.88	75.56	88.14	57.52	73.43	76.29	77.36	82.54	61.55	67.56	75.58

Table 10: Detailed results of the impact of back-translation on different MT architectures. Danish is excluded because those models were trained on a different version of the training data. The average scores of the neural models are negatively influenced by the failing ID-EN models.

Sequence-to-Sequence Lexical Normalization with Multilingual Transformers

Ana-Maria Bucur*
University of Bucharest
ana-maria.bucur@drd.unibuc.ro

Adrian Cosma*
University Politehnica of Bucharest
cosma.i.adrian@gmail.com

Liviu P. Dinu
University of Bucharest
ldinu@fmi.unibuc.ro

Abstract

Current benchmark tasks for natural language processing contain text that is qualitatively different from the text used in informal day to day digital communication. This discrepancy has led to severe performance degradation of state-of-the-art NLP models when fine-tuned on real-world data. One way to resolve this issue is through lexical normalization, which is the process of transforming non-standard text, usually from social media, into a more standardized form. In this work, we propose a sentence-level sequence-to-sequence model based on mBART, which frames the problem as a machine translation problem. As the noisy text is a pervasive problem across languages, not just English, we leverage the multilingual pre-training of mBART to fine-tune it to our data. While current approaches mainly operate at the word or subword level, we argue that this approach is straightforward from a technical standpoint and builds upon existing pre-trained transformer networks. Our results show that while word-level, intrinsic, performance evaluation is behind other methods, our model improves performance on extrinsic, downstream tasks through normalization compared to models operating on raw, unprocessed, social media text.

1 Introduction

Social media is a pervasive part of our modern lives and provides us with a rich source of information and insight into human behaviour. User-generated content has been a valuable resource for the research community, especially in the form of text, but it is notoriously noisy and non-standard. Models that operate on social media posts go beyond marketing and advertisement applications, and have the potential to impact real human lives through, for instance, detecting loneliness (Guntuku et al., 2019), stress (Winata et al., 2018), life satisfaction (Yang and Srinivasan, 2016), suicidal ideation (Matero et al., 2019; Cao et al., 2019), and mental health problems such as depression (Yates et al., 2017; Bucur et al., 2021a; Tadesse et al., 2019) and PTSD (Coppersmith et al., 2014; Amir et al., 2019).

Outside of a formal setting, users communicate freely in text form, resorting to abbreviations, slang or plain spelling mistakes or typos. Eisenstein (2013) further explored *bad language* on social media, in the sense of language that defies our expectation of *good* spelling, vocabulary and syntax. He identified several underlying factors for the cause of non-standard text: user illiteracy, length limits imposed by social media sites (i.e. Twitter), text input affordances (i.e. standard mobile keyboards or predictive entry), pragmatics (emoticons/emoji, abbreviations and expressive lengthening), and a social component. Nguyen et al. (2021) further explored the latter, concluding that some types of non-standard text have strong social meaning, and normalization could induce a loss of meaning.

However, it is well known that for most benchmark tasks, noisy/non-standard text has proven to be a real problem to NLP models, such as BERT (Kumar et al., 2020), trained on clean or curated data, but fine-tuned on tasks with noisy and inconsistent format.

To overcome this predicament, Eisenstein (2013) proposes two possible approaches: either *domain adaptation* or *normalization*. While domain adaptation is not specific to natural language processing, text normalization and cleaning have always been a central part of any modern text processing pipeline. Text normalization is the process of adapting an input text to a more standard form. It has proven to be effective in increasing performance on tasks such as POS tagging (van der Goot and Çetinoğlu, 2021), dependency parsing (van der Goot, 2019a) and sentiment analysis (Mandal and Nanmaran, 2018). Naturally, most text normalization pipelines

* Equal contribution

Proceedings of the 2021 EMNLP Workshop W-NUT: The Seventh Workshop on Noisy User-generated Text, pages 473–482
November 11, 2021. ©2021 Association for Computational Linguistics

are based on supervised models, which require carefully annotated data. However, annotating a large corpus of text in multiple languages is often cumbersome and expensive, and some approaches rely on synthetically generating corrupted text (Dekker and van der Goot, 2020; Ma, 2019).

Commonly, approaches are based on word-level normalization. One of the most prominent methods is MoNoise (van der Goot and van Noord, 2017), in which the text correction pipeline is similar to a classic ranked retrieval. However, MoNoise operates at the individual word and uses a spelling correction module and a word embedding module. While word embeddings can be made to account for a specific sentence context, it is mostly discarded.

Different from current methods, we aim to perform text normalization at a sentence level. This approach has several advantages, compared to word or subword methods: i) it can be naturally framed as a sequence-to-sequence type problem, ii) it is more straightforward, as it requires only one module, as opposed to a multi-stage pipeline (i.e. complex candidate generation and ranking), and iii) the same model can be trained on multiple languages at the same time, without increasing in size and computational processing.

In this edition of The Workshop on Noisy User-generated Text (W-NUT), organizers propose the shared task of multilingual lexical normalization[1], in which participants are required to perform lexical normalization on 12 different languages (van der Goot et al., 2021a).

As such, we use the state-of-the-art multilingual sequence-to-sequence transformer model mBART (Tang et al., 2020) and fine-tune it for our task. mBART is one of the first models that can be fine-tuned simultaneously on multiple languages without performance loss. We show that framing text normalization as a neural machine translation problem is a viable method for text normalization, improving performance on extrinsic, downstream tasks compared to models that operate on raw, unprocessed social media text. We made the code publicly available on github.[2]

2 Related Work

The W-NUT workshop hosted a shared task on lexical normalization of user-generated content from English tweets in its first edition (Baldwin et al., 2015a). The task received from the competing teams two categories of submissions, from constrained (using only the training data provided by the organizers) and unconstrained systems (using other publicly available data or tools).

The best model, from Jin (2015), generated candidates from the most similar canonical forms from the training data evaluated with the Jaccard Index. A random forest classifier was used to predict the suitable canonical form from all the candidates using features such as support and confidence, string similarity, and part of speech tags. The model was a constrained system, suggesting that the quality of the proposed model is more important than using additional data and tools. Other approaches were based on conditional random fields (CRF) (Akhtar et al., 2015; Supranovich and Patsepnia, 2015; Akhtar et al., 2015) and recurrent neural networks (RNN) (Min and Mott, 2015; Wagner and Foster, 2015) among others.

Notably, MoNoise (van der Goot and van Noord, 2017) has long been considered state-of-the-art in lexical normalization. MoNoise is a normalization model using spelling correction and word embeddings for candidate generation and a feature-based random forest classifier for candidate ranking. It is a modular normalization system easily reusable and adaptable (van der Goot and van Noord, 2017). The model was at the beginning developed only for English text. Still, then it was later expanded for multi-lingual lexical normalization covering languages such as Dutch, Spanish, Turkish, Slovenian, Croatian and Serbian (van der Goot, 2019b).

The lexical normalization task can also be formulated as a machine translation (MT) task. The noisy user-generated content is the source language, and the canonical form is the target language. Veliz et al. (2019) compare the MT approaches for lexical normalization, focusing on statistical neural translation (SMT) and neural machine translation (NMT) and obtaining better results using the SMT method. Furthermore, the authors show that the SMT approach works better in a low-resource setting than an NMT approach which requires a lot of data.

With the rise in popularity of pre-trained language models for natural language understanding and natural language generation, their ability to perform lexical normalization was also studied. By transforming the task into a token prediction

[1] http://noisy-text.github.io/2021/multi-lexnorm.html

[2] https://github.com/bucuram/seq2seq-multilingual-normalization

one, Muller et al. (2019) demonstrate that a BERT model can be used as a lexical normalization model in low resource settings.

Current methods for lexical normalization attempt to normalize at the character-level (Pennell and Liu, 2011; Ljubešić et al., 2014), syllable-level (Xu et al., 2015), word-level (van der Goot, 2019b; Jin, 2015) or sentence-level (Muller et al., 2019; Lourentzou et al., 2019). Lusetti et al. (2018) propose an encoder-decoder approach for text normalization.

We propose to make use of the latest transformer models that are capable of multilingual translation in a sequence to sequence manner, namely mBART (Tang et al., 2020). However, we do not perform translation between languages, but instead, we use mBART as a denoising autoencoder, i.e. translating from *bad English* to *good English*. This way, we take the whole sentence into consideration when correcting the text. Moreover, this method is more straightforward and can scale to multiple languages without increasing computational demands.

3 Data and Evaluation

We further describe the dataset for this task and evaluation procedures.

MultiLexNorm Dataset The data provided by the organizers includes texts from 12 languages: Croatian, Danish, Dutch, English, German, Italian, Serbian, Slovenian, Spanish, Turkish and code-switched data for Indonesian-English and Turkish-German, as seen in Table 1. Some examples from the training data are shown in Table 2. For some languages in the dataset, the capitalization (Caps column) is also corrected, and words are split or merged (1-N/N-1 column). The dataset comprises Twitter posts from all languages, but some languages also have texts from additional sources. For example, Danish also has texts from Arto, Denmark's first large-scale social media (Plank et al., 2020) and Dutch texts were also gathered from public Internet forums, and SMS messages (Schuur, 2020).

W-NUT Evaluation Methodology The organizers of the W-NUT workshop propose two types of evaluation procedures: *intrinsic*, word-level and *extrinsic*, downstream task performance (i.e. dependency parsing).

As *intrinsic* evaluation, the Error Reduction Rate

Language	Words	1-N/N-1	Caps	%normed
Croatian	75,276	-	+	8.98
Danish	11,816	+	+	8.66
Dutch	23,053	+	+	26.49
English	73,806	+	-	6.90
German	25,157	+	+	8.90
Indonesian-English	23,124	+	-	12.16
Italian	14,641	+	+	7.36
Serbian	91,738	-	+	7.73
Slovenian	75,276	-	+	15.66
Spanish	13,827	-	-	7.69
Turkish	7,949	-	+	36.60
Turkish-German	16,546	+	+	24.25

Table 1: Available languages in the training set. Each language has its own annotation guidelines, in which capitalization can be taken into account (Caps), or words can be split or merged (1-N/N-1). Moreover, some languages are code-switched, two different languages are used in a tweet.

introduced by van der Goot (2019b) is proposed:

$$ERR = \frac{TP - FP}{TP + FN} \quad (1)$$

Because accuracy is hard to compare across datasets with different numbers of raw words which have to be normalized, the ERR proposes an evaluation metric that can be used to compare the performance of systems across multiple datasets. It is computed as accuracy normalized for the number of raw words normalized in the gold dataset.

A system that always keeps the raw words has an ERR score of 0.0, while a perfect system will have ERR precisely 1.0. The ERR has a negative value when the system normalizes more words with a wrong form than the correct canonical form.

However, one downside of the ERR is that it fails to distinguish between FP and FN. Thus, in the case of FP, the system may provide a correct normalization, even if the annotators did not normalize the raw word.

Further, two baselines are provided: **Leave-As-Is (LAI)** - the output is the same as the raw input, the normalization is not performed - and **Most-frequent-Replacement (MFR)** - the output is the most frequent replacement from the training data. If the raw word is not found in the training set, no normalization is performed.

As a secondary evaluation, the organizers propose an *extrinsic* evaluation of the effect of normalization on the task of dependency parsing, previous research showing that lexical normalization improves the performance for this task (van der Goot, 2019a). A dependency parser is trained on

Language	Example raw	Example gold
Croatian (Ljubešić et al., 2017a)	dok je **bandic** bio **clan sdpa** tvrdilo se da je idealan	dok je **bandić** bio **član sdp-a** tvrdilo se da je idealan
Danish (Plank et al., 2020)	**Maerkeligt**, **taenker** jeg, og **gar** ind igen.	**Mærkeligt**, **tænker** jeg, og **går** ind igen.
Dutch (Schuur, 2020)	**ja effe** slaapverhaal **vertelle vo** sophieke eh lol	**Ja even** slaapverhaal **vertellen voor** sophieke eh lol
English (Baldwin et al., 2015b)	he **obvi doesnt** understand that	he **obviously doesn't** understand that
German (Sidarenka et al., 2013)	Ich **werd dran** denken!	Ich **werde daran** denken!
Indonesian-English (Barik et al., 2019)	**msh bs** disebut sukses?	**masih bisa** disebut sukses?
Italian (van der Goot et al., 2020)	**ztate** prentento in **ciro kvelli** quelli kol **raffrettoren**	**state** prendendo in **giro quelli** col **raffreddore**
Serbian (Ljubešić et al., 2017b)	ja sam ozbiljan **covek**	ja sam ozbiljan **čovek**
Slovenian (Erjavec et al., 2017)	da se **naujo** zdaj še na planico **spravl**!?	da se **ne** zdaj še na planico **spravili**!?
Spanish (Alegria et al., 2013)	quiero **tranquileo** del bueno hoy..!!!	quiero **tranquilidad** del bueno hoy..!!!
Turkish (Çolakoğlu et al., 2019)	Avrupa ve **amerikada VALENTİNA DAY** diye geçer.	Avrupa ve **Amerika'da Valentina Day** diye geçer.
Turkish-German (van der Goot and Çetinoğlu, 2021)	**artik** ablamdan **bise yuruturum napim** :D	**Artık** ablamdan **bir şey yürütürüm ne yapayım** :D

Table 2: Noisy examples from each language and the corresponding canonical forms.

both raw and canonical data to evaluate the performance improvement of using the normalized versus the original data.

Moreover, we also evaluate the extrinsic performance of our model on two additional tasks: sentiment analysis on the SMILE dataset (Wang et al., 2016) and hate speech detection on OLID dataset (Zampieri et al., 2019a). Both datasets contain data collected from Twitter, making them good candidates for evaluating the semantic processing of noisy text.

SMILE dataset It consists of posts with mentions of several British museums gathered from Twitter to classify the emotions expressed by users towards art and cultural experiences from the museums. It contains 3,085 posts annotated with five emotions: anger, disgust, happiness, surprise and sadness; fear was not found in any Twitter posts.

OLID dataset It was the official dataset of the SemEval-2019 Task 6: Identifying and Categorizing Offensive Language in Social Media (OffensEval 2019) (Zampieri et al., 2019b) and SemEval-2020 Task 12: Multilingual Offensive Language Identification in Social Media (OffensEval 2020) (Zampieri et al., 2020). The dataset was also used in misogyny (Pamungkas et al., 2020), cyberbullying (Aind et al., 2020) and depression (Bucur et al., 2021b) research. It contains 14,100 tweets with a hierarchical annotation taxonomy with three levels: Level A - Offensive language identification (offensive vs non-offensive), Level B - categorization of Offensive language (targeted insults or threats vs untargeted profanity) and Level C - Offensive language target identification (individual vs group vs other). However, for our evaluation, we focus only on level A.

For evaluating on sentiment analysis (SMILE) and offensive language identification (OLID), we trained a simple word-level TF-IDF model together with a linear SVM with balanced weights. For SMILE, we report average macro F_1 score across 5 folds, and for OLID, we report macro F_1 score on the test set.

4 Method

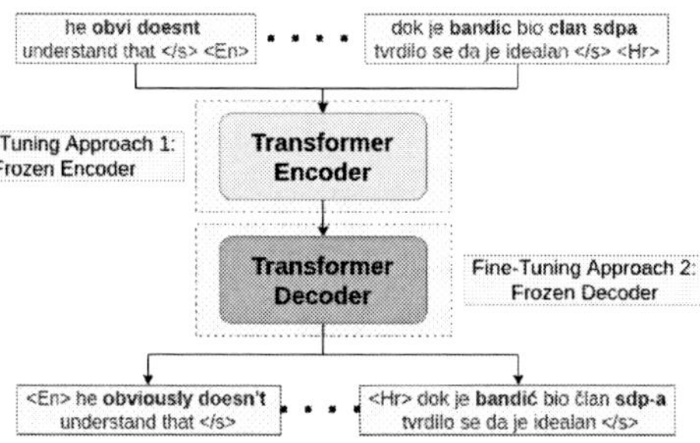

Figure 1: Fine-tuning a mBART model for lexical normalization on all available languages. We use the same model for all languages simultaneously.

Lewis et al. (2019) proposed BART in 2019, as a way to pre-train large-scale transformers for sequence-to-sequence tasks. Initially, the authors pre-trained an encoder-decoder transformer only for English, obtaining good results on multiple downstream NLP tasks. Further, mBART (Tang et al., 2020), follows the same procedure, but for multiple languages. The pre-training stage for both BART and mBART is akin to a denoising autoencoder, in which the model receives a noisy (in this case masked) sentence, and it learns to reconstruct it.

While mBART is fine-tuned on multiple language pairs, it is pretrained monolingually, and is capable of acting as an autoencoder for the same language. In our case, we make use of a pretrained mBART on 50 languages[3] from the transformers library (Wolf et al., 2020), and employ a procedure similar to the pre-training stage: a noisy sentence is

[3] https://huggingface.co/facebook/mbart-large-50

Team Name	Avg.	da	de	en	es	hr	iden	it	nl	sl	sr	tr	trde
ÚFAL-2 (Samuel and Straka, 2021)	**67.30**	68.67	**66.22**	**75.60**	59.25	**67.74**	**67.18**	**47.52**	**63.58**	**80.07**	**74.59**	**68.58**	**68.62**
HEL-LJU-2 (Scherrer and Ljubešić, 2021)	53.58	56.65	59.80	62.05	35.55	56.24	55.33	35.64	45.88	66.97	66.44	51.18	51.18
MoNoise (van der Goot, 2019b)	49.02	51.27	46.96	74.35	45.53	52.63	59.79	21.78	49.53	61.91	59.58	28.21	36.72
TrinkaAI-2* (Kubal and Nagvenkar, 2021)	43.75	45.89	47.30	65.96	**61.33**	41.28	56.36	15.84	45.74	59.51	44.52	15.54	25.77
thunderml-1*	43.44	46.52	46.62	64.07	60.29	40.09	59.11	11.88	44.05	59.33	44.46	15.88	29.01
team-2	40.70	48.10	46.06	63.73	21.00	40.39	59.28	13.86	43.72	60.55	46.11	15.88	29.71
learnML-2	40.30	40.51	43.69	61.57	56.55	38.11	56.19	5.94	42.77	58.25	39.99	14.36	25.68
maet-1	40.05	48.10	46.06	63.90	21.00	40.39	59.28	5.94	43.72	60.55	46.11	15.88	29.71
MFR	38.37	49.68	32.09	64.93	25.57	36.52	61.17	16.83	37.70	56.71	42.62	14.53	22.09
CL-MoNoise (van der Goot, 2021)	12.05	7.28	16.55	4.13	4.99	26.41	2.41	0.00	16.22	8.77	20.09	17.57	20.16
(ours) Fixed Encoder (separate) + post proc.	10.65	*49.68*	-2.59	29.13	-7.90	26.41	-1.72	-8.91	-1.49	1.27	*42.62*	0.68	0.70
(ours) Fixed Encoder (separate)	6.73	*49.68*	-1.91	26.81	-9.36	-10.06	-7.22	-8.91	-2.09	-1.04	*42.62*	9.97	14.99
(ours) Fixed Encoder (separate) - stripped unicode	5.22	*49.68*	-1.91	26.81	-10.19	-9.86	-7.22	-31.68	-2.09	-1.13	*42.62*	1.01	6.57
(ours) ML - Fixed Decoder + post proc.	-6.54	*49.68*	12.50	27.41	-13.10	-111.84	-7.73	-8.91	16.82	-110.57	*42.62*	11.49	13.06
(ours) ML - Fixed Decoder	-11.79	*49.68*	20.05	22.12	-18.92	-127.60	-14.60	-25.74	16.69	-133.71	*42.62*	13.18	14.64
(ours) ML - Fixed Encoder + post proc.	-21.51	*49.68*	10.47	12.09	-28.69	-191.33	-9.97	-27.72	9.19	-141.80	*42.62*	9.63	7.62
(ours) ML - Fixed Encoder	-32.90	*49.68*	19.48	20.78	-40.12	-242.57	-24.23	-70.30	8.72	-180.75	*42.62*	11.15	10.69
LAI	0.00	0.00	0.00	0.00	0.00	0.00	0.00	0.00	0.00	0.00	0.00	0.00	0.00
MaChAmp (van der Goot et al., 2021b)	-21.25	-88.92	-93.36	50.99	25.36	42.62	39.52	-312.87	1.49	56.80	39.44	-12.67	-3.42

Table 3: Team standings, based on Error Reduction Rate (ERR). We kept the best result from each team, from clarity. (* denotes late submissions).

fed to the model, and the output ought to be the normalized sentence. We only trained on the provided languages that are contained in the pre-training set of languages. As mBART is not pre-trained on code-switched languages, for IN-EN and TR-DE, we use the mBART model pre-trained only on the main language of each pair (e.g. IN for IN-EN and TR for TR-DE). For Danish and Serbian, we fall back to the MFR baseline.

Figure 1 showcases our fine-tuning procedure. We tried two different approaches for fine-tuning: Frozen Encoder and Frozen Decoder because, with a fixed encoder, the model suffers from the same OOV-type problems as a typical transformer. However, training with a fixed decoder allows the model to better adapt its representations to each language's noisy version while maintaining its generative properties. For both approaches, we train a single model for all languages. Moreover, we also trained a separate mBART for each language, monolingually.

Training details For all runs, we fine-tune mBART for 50 epochs, using a batch size of 256 and with a cyclical learning rate scheduler (Smith, 2015) that linearly increases the learning rate from 0.00001 to 0.0001 and back across 5 epochs. The workshop organizers provided both the training data and the validation data on most languages. We omit validation on languages where the validation data is missing. The training was performed on an NVIDIA RTX 2070 graphics card. Since the memory requirements of an mBART model are quite high, we employed gradient accumulation to increase the batch size. In addition, we employed early stopping when the validation loss increased for more than 3 epochs.

Post-processing Since our model outputs a whole sentence directly, the word-level evaluation requires the noisy input words to be aligned to their normalized counterpart. This phase is essential for sequence-to-sequence text normalization, as bad alignments will reduce the overall word-level performance score, especially in the 1-N/N-1 languages. As such, for the post-processing phase, we aligned input words with their normalized counterparts based on the Levenshtein distance between them. We used a linear sum assignment on the distance matrix to perform matching. Additionally, we matched the capitalization between corrections and left links, hashtags, and user mentions as they are.

5 Results

We further showcase the results of the pretrained mBART models fine-tuned on the available data: firstly, we kept the transformer encoder fixed and trained only the decoder, and secondly, we kept the decoder fixed and trained the encoder. During this fine-tuning process, we trained a single model for all languages. Further, for the CodaLab submission, we fine-tuned multiple models, one for each language, in the "fixed encoder" regime.

Intrinsic Evaluation Table 3 showcases intrinsic, word-level evaluation across languages. Our best model obtained an average ERR across languages of 10.65, corresponding to a separate mBART trained for each language, with the additional post-processing described in Section 4. In our case, training multilingually did improve performance on some languages (i.e. *DE, EN, NL, TR*), but over-

Team Name	Avg.	de-tweede	en-aae	en-monoise	en-tweebank2	it-postwita	it-twittiro	tr-iwt151
ÚFAL-2	**64.17**	**73.58**	**62.73**	**58.57**	59.08	**68.28**	72.22	54.74
HEL-LJU-2	63.73	73.49	60.64	56.27	60.30	68.11	72.32	54.95
MoNoise	63.44	73.20	62.27	56.83	58.90	67.55	70.69	54.61
MFR	63.31	72.86	60.32	56.74	**60.31**	67.34	70.72	54.89
TrinkaAI-2*	63.12	72.86	60.16	56.64	59.87	66.98	71.14	54.20
maet-1	63.09	72.80	59.44	56.64	59.80	67.41	71.07	54.45
team-2	63.03	72.80	59.44	56.64	59.80	67.19	70.86	54.45
thunderml-2*	63.02	72.67	59.57	56.74	59.25	67.34	71.35	54.24
thunderml-1*	62.95	72.52	59.31	56.74	59.86	67.09	71.00	54.09
CL-MoNoise	62.71	72.65	60.90	55.26	58.53	66.53	70.10	54.98
(ours) Fixed Encoder (separate)	62.53	72.57	59.57	54.20	59.81	66.74	69.99	54.84
LAI	62.45	72.71	59.21	53.65	59.99	66.49	70.06	**55.00**
MaChAmp	61.89	71.28	60.77	54.61	57.97	64.65	69.82	54.08

Table 4: Extrinsic evaluation results on dependency parsing task.

	SMILE	OLID Task A
Raw Text (Leave-As-Is)	22.65% ± 0.02	57.15%
mBART Fixed Encoder	**23.43% ± 0.02**	**58.08%**

Table 5: Extrinsic evaluation on sentiment analysis (SMILE) and offensive language identification (OLID). Lexical normalization through fine-tuning mBART slightly improves performance.

Raw	Gold	Our	Correct?
i see, u can comeee	i see, you can come	i see, you can come	✓
ich geb heut einen aus	ich gebe heute einen aus	ich gebe heute einen aus	✓
Juhuuuuu	Juhu	Juhu	✓
fakt ap gaan. eig nu al mr kanniet	fakt op gaan. Eigenlijk nu al maar kan niet	**echt** ap gaan. eig nu al **mijn kanniet**	✗
"Why Germany says "nein"	"Why Germany says "nein"	**"Warum Deutschland sagt** "nein"	✗
i coulda swore .... lol nvm	i could have swore .... lol never mind	i **could** swore .... lol **never**	✗
todos lo sabemos **jajajaja-jaja**	todos lo sabemos **jajajaja-jaja**	todos lo sabemos **ja**	?
discussing **w/** friend	discussing **w/** friend	discussing **with** friend	?
n puedo ni volver a dormirme	**n** puedo ni volver a dormirme	**no** puedo ni volver a dormirme	?

Table 6: Qualitative results on different languages with mBART Fixed Encoder. We present examples of correct normalization (✓), mistakes (✗), and questionable normalizations (?), in which the model correctly normalizes, but annotators do not.

all achieved lower scores, especially in the case for *HR* and *SL*. For those languages, the model severely diverged, and its output consisted only of repeating the first word in the sentence. As per our intuition, fixing the decoder results in better performance when compared to fixing the encoder: the model learns to adapt its representations to account for the noisy text.

However, since our method is sentence-based, perfect alignment between words is cumbersome, with many cases of mismatch between punctuation. Moreover, merging or splitting words for normalization is also not taken into account in the post-processing phase.

Extrinsic Evaluation For extrinsic evaluation, we showcase the results for our best model in Table 4 on the dependency parsing downstream task from the workshop challenge. Even though our model is not in the top-performing models, the absolute difference in performance is minimal.

Moreover, we also evaluated the effect of lexical normalization on two other tasks - sentiment analysis on the SMILE dataset and offensive language identification on OLID (Table 5). We trained a word-level TF-IDF and a linear SVM with balanced weights for both datasets and reported a macro F_1 score. Our lexical normalization improves results on both these tasks, compared to modelling the raw, unprocessed social media posts. This is because lexical normalization results in a smaller vocabulary for the documents, allowing the SVM model to operate on smaller dimensional data. Moreover, this evaluation procedure is arguably more realistic, as it does not require accurate post-processing to precisely align noisy words with their corrected version and match punctuation.

Discussion In Table 6 we showcase some examples for correct, incorrect and questionable text normalizations. The model is able to easily grasp contractions such as *u* → *you* and expressive lengthening such as *Juhuuuuu* → *Juhu*. However, more complex word abbreviations such as *nvm* are quite challenging to generate, as the model only outputs the first part (i.e. *never*). Moreover, code-switched languages are an inherent problem to our approach, as mBART is only trained to receive input from a single language and not code-switched. Interestingly, even though we specified the langauge code for German in the phrase *"Why Germany says "nein"*, the model actually translates the English part into German: *Warum Deutschland sagt "nein"*.

However, as the organizers have pointed out, there are inconsistencies in the training and testing data annotations. In some cases, some words are not normalized (i.e. *jajajajaj / w/ / n*) even though they were clearly lengthenings or contractions. Despite this, in some of these cases, our model was able to provide correct normalizations.

There also appears to be no correlation between training dataset size and final normalization performance. For example, in the case of Croatian, even though the dataset is the second largest, the performance is lower than for other languages. Thus, the lower performance in some languages may be a cause of the complexity of the language; for English, our model obtained the best results.

6 Conclusions

In this work, we presented a method to perform lexical normalization by fine-tuning a multilingual machine translation model on pairs of noisy and normalized sentences from various languages. We employed mBART, as it is currently the state-of-the-art in transformer-based multilingual machine translation, allowing us to fine-tune on all available languages simultaneously. Furthermore, we used mBART as a denoising autoencoder and tuned it in a supervised fashion.

As opposed to current two-stage methods for word candidate generation and ranking, our approach is more straightforward. Moreover, it scales to multiple languages without increasing computational demand (i.e. not increasing vocabulary size, increasing search space and others). Evaluation results show that our method, even though it lacks behind current methods on intrinsic, word-level evaluation, improves performance on downstream tasks.

For future work, we aim to develop our method for better post-processing of the output and increasing augmentation levels - i.e. injecting more noise in the form of spelling mistakes, backwards translations etc. Moreover, since our method is supervised, the quality and quantity of training data play an essential role in the final performance. In this regard, we aim to explore ways to take into account inconsistent annotations.

Acknowledgments

We would like to thank the reviewers for the insightful feedback provided. This research was partially supported by Blog Alchemy Limited.

References

Alwin T Aind, Akashdeep Ramnaney, and Divyashikha Sethia. 2020. Q-bully: a reinforcement learning based cyberbullying detection framework. In *2020 International Conference for Emerging Technology (INCET)*, pages 1–6. IEEE.

Md Shad Akhtar, Utpal Kumar Sikdar, and Asif Ekbal. 2015. Iitp: Hybrid approach for text normalization in twitter. In *Proceedings of the Workshop on Noisy User-generated Text*, pages 106–110.

Inaki Alegria, Nora Aranberri, Víctor Fresno, Pablo Gamallo, Lluis Padró, Inaki San Vicente, Jordi Turmo, and Arkaitz Zubiaga. 2013. Introducción a la tarea compartida Tweet-Norm 2013: Normalización léxica de tuits en Español. In *Tweet-Norm@ SEPLN*, pages 1–9.

Silvio Amir, Mark Dredze, and John W Ayers. 2019. Mental health surveillance over social media with digital cohorts. In *Proceedings of the Sixth Workshop on Computational Linguistics and Clinical Psychology*, pages 114–120.

Timothy Baldwin, Marie-Catherine de Marneffe, Bo Han, Young-Bum Kim, Alan Ritter, and Wei Xu. 2015a. Shared tasks of the 2015 workshop on noisy user-generated text: Twitter lexical normalization and named entity recognition. In *Proceedings of the Workshop on Noisy User-generated Text*, pages 126–135.

Timothy Baldwin, Marie Catherine de Marneffe, Bo Han, Young-Bum Kim, Alan Ritter, and Wei Xu. 2015b. Shared tasks of the 2015 workshop on noisy user-generated text: Twitter lexical normalization and named entity recognition. In *Proceedings of the Workshop on Noisy User-generated Text*, pages 126–135, Beijing, China. Association for Computational Linguistics.

Anab Maulana Barik, Rahmad Mahendra, and Mirna Adriani. 2019. Normalization of Indonesian-English code-mixed Twitter data. In *Proceedings of the 5th Workshop on Noisy User-generated Text (W-NUT 2019)*, pages 417–424, Hong Kong, China. Association for Computational Linguistics.

Ana-Maria Bucur, Adrian Cosma, and Liviu P Dinu. 2021a. Early risk detection of pathological gambling, self-harm and depression using bert. *CLEF (Working Notes)*.

Ana-Maria Bucur, Marcos Zampieri, and Liviu P. Dinu. 2021b. An exploratory analysis of the relation between offensive language and mental health. In *Findings of the Association for Computational Linguistics: ACL-IJCNLP 2021*, pages 3600–3606, Online. Association for Computational Linguistics.

Lei Cao, Huijun Zhang, Ling Feng, Zihan Wei, Xin Wang, Ningyun Li, and Xiaohao He. 2019. Latent suicide risk detection on microblog via suicide-oriented word embeddings and layered attention. In *Proceedings of the 2019 Conference on Empirical Methods in Natural Language Processing and the 9th International Joint Conference on Natural Language Processing (EMNLP-IJCNLP)*, pages 1718–1728.

Talha Çolakoğlu, Umut Sulubacak, and Ahmet Cüneyd Tantuğ. 2019. Normalizing non-canonical Turkish texts using machine translation approaches. In *Proceedings of the 57th Annual Meeting of the Association for Computational Linguistics: Student Research Workshop*, pages 267–272, Florence, Italy. Association for Computational Linguistics.

Glen Coppersmith, Craig Harman, and Mark Dredze. 2014. Measuring post traumatic stress disorder in twitter. In *Eighth international AAAI conference on weblogs and social media*.

Kelly Dekker and Rob van der Goot. 2020. Synthetic data for english lexical normalization: How close can we get to manually annotated data? In *Proceedings of the 12th Language Resources and Evaluation Conference*, pages 6300–6309.

Jacob Eisenstein. 2013. What to do about bad language on the internet. In *Proceedings of the 2013 conference of the North American Chapter of the association for computational linguistics: Human language technologies*, pages 359–369.

Tomaž Erjavec, Darja Fišer, Jaka Čibej, Špela Arhar Holdt, Nikola Ljubešić, and Katja Zupan. 2017. CMC training corpus Janes-Tag 2.0. Slovenian language resource repository CLARIN.SI.

Sharath Chandra Guntuku, Rachelle Schneider, Arthur Pelullo, Jami Young, Vivien Wong, Lyle Ungar, Daniel Polsky, Kevin G Volpp, and Raina Merchant. 2019. Studying expressions of loneliness in individuals using twitter: an observational study. *BMJ open*, 9(11):e030355.

Ning Jin. 2015. Ncsu-sas-ning: Candidate generation and feature engineering for supervised lexical normalization. In *Proceedings of the Workshop on Noisy User-generated Text*, pages 87–92.

Divesh Kubal and Apurva Nagvenkar. 2021. Multilingual sequence labeling approach to solve lexical normalization. In *Proceedings of the 7th Workshop on Noisy User-generated Text (W-NUT 2021)*, Punta Cana, Dominican Republic. Association for Computational Linguistics.

Ankit Kumar, Piyush Makhija, and Anuj Gupta. 2020. Noisy text data: Achilles' heel of BERT. In *Proceedings of the Sixth Workshop on Noisy User-generated Text (W-NUT 2020)*, pages 16–21, Online. Association for Computational Linguistics.

Mike Lewis, Yinhan Liu, Naman Goyal, Marjan Ghazvininejad, Abdelrahman Mohamed, Omer Levy, Ves Stoyanov, and Luke Zettlemoyer. 2019. Bart: Denoising sequence-to-sequence pre-training for natural language generation, translation, and comprehension. *arXiv preprint arXiv:1910.13461*.

Nikola Ljubešić, Tomaž Erjavec, and Darja Fišer. 2014. Standardizing tweets with character-level machine translation. In *International Conference on Intelligent Text Processing and Computational Linguistics*, pages 164–175. Springer.

Nikola Ljubešić, Tomaž Erjavec, Maja Miličević, and Tanja Samardžić. 2017a. Croatian Twitter training corpus ReLDI-NormTagNER-hr 2.0. Slovenian language resource repository CLARIN.SI.

Nikola Ljubešić, Tomaž Erjavec, Maja Miličević, and Tanja Samardžić. 2017b. Serbian Twitter training corpus ReLDI-NormTagNER-sr 2.0. Slovenian language resource repository CLARIN.SI.

Ismini Lourentzou, Kabir Manghnani, and ChengXiang Zhai. 2019. Adapting sequence to sequence models for text normalization in social media. In *Proceedings of the International AAAI Conference on Web and Social Media*, volume 13, pages 335–345.

Massimo Lusetti, Tatyana Ruzsics, Anne Göhring, Tanja Samardzic, and Elisabeth Stark. 2018. Encoder-decoder methods for text normalization. In *Proceedings of the Fifth Workshop on NLP for Similar Languages, Varieties and Dialects (VarDial 2018)*, pages 18–28.

Edward Ma. 2019. Nlp augmentation. https://github.com/makcedward/nlpaug.

Soumil Mandal and Karthick Nanmaran. 2018. Normalization of transliterated words in code-mixed data using seq2seq model & levenshtein distance. In *Proceedings of the 2018 EMNLP Workshop W-NUT: The 4th Workshop on Noisy User-generated Text*, pages 49–53.

Matthew Matero, Akash Idnani, Youngseo Son, Salvatore Giorgi, Huy Vu, Mohammad Zamani, Parth Limbachiya, Sharath Chandra Guntuku, and H Andrew Schwartz. 2019. Suicide risk assessment with multi-level dual-context language and bert. In *Proceedings of the sixth workshop on computational linguistics and clinical psychology*, pages 39–44.

Wookhee Min and Bradford Mott. 2015. Ncsu_sas_wookhee: A deep contextual long-short term memory model for text normalization. In *Proceedings of the Workshop on Noisy User-generated Text*, pages 111–119.

Benjamin Muller, Benoît Sagot, and Djamé Seddah. 2019. Enhancing bert for lexical normalization. In *The 5th Workshop on Noisy User-generated Text (W-NUT)*.

Dong Nguyen, Laura Rosseel, and Jack Grieve. 2021. On learning and representing social meaning in nlp: a sociolinguistic perspective. In *Proceedings of the 2021 Conference of the North American Chapter of the Association for Computational Linguistics: Human Language Technologies*, pages 603–612.

Endang Wahyu Pamungkas, Valerio Basile, and Viviana Patti. 2020. Misogyny detection in twitter: a multilingual and cross-domain study. *Information Processing & Management*, 57(6):102360.

Deana Pennell and Yang Liu. 2011. A character-level machine translation approach for normalization of sms abbreviations. In *Proceedings of 5th International Joint Conference on Natural Language Processing*, pages 974–982.

Barbara Plank, Kristian Nørgaard Jensen, and Rob van der Goot. 2020. DaN+: Danish nested named entities and lexical normalization. In *Proceedings of the 28th International Conference on Computational Linguistics*, pages 6649–6662, Barcelona, Spain (Online). International Committee on Computational Linguistics.

David Samuel and Milan Straka. 2021. ÚFAL at MultiLexNorm 2021: Improving multilingual lexical normalization by fine-tuning ByT5. In *Proceedings of the 7th Workshop on Noisy User-generated Text (W-NUT 2021)*, Punta Cana, Dominican Republic. Association for Computational Linguistics.

Yves Scherrer and Nikola Ljubešić. 2021. Sesame Street to Mount Sinai: BERT-constrained character-level Moses models for multilingual lexical normalization. In *Proceedings of the 7th Workshop on Noisy User-generated Text (W-NUT 2021)*, Punta Cana, Dominican Republic. Association for Computational Linguistics.

Youri Schuur. 2020. Normalization for Dutch for improved pos tagging. Master's thesis, University of Groningen.

Uladzimir Sidarenka, Tatjana Scheffler, and Manfred Stede. 2013. Rule-based normalization of German Twitter messages. In *Proc. of the GSCL Workshop Verarbeitung und Annotation von Sprachdaten aus Genres internetbasierter Kommunikation*.

Leslie N. Smith. 2015. No more pesky learning rate guessing games. *CoRR*, abs/1506.01186.

Dmitry Supranovich and Viachaslau Patsepnia. 2015. Ihs_rd: Lexical normalization for english tweets. In *Proceedings of the Workshop on Noisy User-generated Text*, pages 78–81.

Michael M Tadesse, Hongfei Lin, Bo Xu, and Liang Yang. 2019. Detection of depression-related posts in reddit social media forum. *IEEE Access*, 7:44883–44893.

Yuqing Tang, Chau Tran, Xian Li, Peng-Jen Chen, Naman Goyal, Vishrav Chaudhary, Jiatao Gu, and Angela Fan. 2020. Multilingual translation with extensible multilingual pretraining and finetuning. *arXiv preprint arXiv:2008.00401*.

Rob van der Goot. 2019a. An in-depth analysis of the effect of lexical normalization on the dependency parsing of social media. In *Proceedings of the 5th Workshop on Noisy User-generated Text (W-NUT 2019)*, pages 115–120.

Rob van der Goot. 2019b. Monoise: A multi-lingual and easy-to-use lexical normalization tool. In *Proceedings of the 57th Annual Meeting of the Association for Computational Linguistics: System Demonstrations*, pages 201–206.

Rob van der Goot. 2021. CL-MoNoise: Cross-lingual lexical normalization. In *Proceedings of the 7th Workshop on Noisy User-generated Text (W-NUT 2021)*, Punta Cana, Dominican Republic. Association for Computational Linguistics.

Rob van der Goot and Özlem Çetinoğlu. 2021. Lexical normalization for code-switched data and its effect on POS tagging. In *Proceedings of the 16th Conference of the European Chapter of the Association for Computational Linguistics: Main Volume*, pages 2352–2365, Online. Association for Computational Linguistics.

Rob van der Goot, Alan Ramponi, Tommaso Caselli, Michele Cafagna, and Lorenzo De Mattei. 2020. Norm it! lexical normalization for Italian and its downstream effects for dependency parsing. In *Proceedings of the 12th Language Resources and Evaluation Conference*, pages 6272–6278, Marseille, France. European Language Resources Association.

Rob van der Goot, Alan Ramponi, Arkaitz Zubiaga, Barbara Plank, Benjamin Muller, Iñaki San Vicente Roncal, Nikola Ljubešić, Özlem Çetinoğlu, Rahmad Mahendra, Talha Çolakoğlu, Timothy Baldwin, Tommaso Caselli, and Wladimir Sidorenko. 2021a. MultiLexNorm: A shared task on multilingual lexical normalization. In *Proceedings of the 7th Workshop on Noisy User-generated Text (W-NUT 2021)*, Punta Cana, Dominican Republic. Association for Computational Linguistics.

Rob van der Goot, Ahmet Üstün, Alan Ramponi, Ibrahim Sharaf, and Barbara Plank. 2021b. Massive choice, ample tasks (MaChAmp): A toolkit for multi-task learning in NLP. In *Proceedings of the 16th Conference of the European Chapter of the Association for Computational Linguistics: System Demonstrations*, pages 176–197, Online. Association for Computational Linguistics.

Rob van der Goot and Gertjan van Noord. 2017. Monoise: Modeling noise using a modular normalization system. *Computational Linguistics in the Netherlands Journal*, 7:129–144.

Claudia Matos Veliz, Orphée De Clercq, and Véronique Hoste. 2019. Comparing mt approaches for text normalization. In *Proceedings of the International Conference on Recent Advances in Natural Language Processing (RANLP 2019)*, pages 740–749.

Joachim Wagner and Jennifer Foster. 2015. Dcu-adapt: learning edit operations for microblog normalisation with the generalised perceptron. In *Proceedings of the Workshop on Noisy User-generated Text*, pages 93–98.

Bo Wang, Maria Liakata, Arkaitz Zubiaga, Rob Procter, and Eric Jensen. 2016. Smile: Twitter emotion classification using domain. In *Proceedings of the 4th Workshop on Sentiment Analysis where AI meets Psychology co-located with 25th International Joint Conference on Artificial Intelligence*.

Genta Indra Winata, Onno Pepijn Kampman, and Pascale Fung. 2018. Attention-based lstm for psychological stress detection from spoken language using distant supervision. In *2018 IEEE International Conference on Acoustics, Speech and Signal Processing (ICASSP)*, pages 6204–6208. IEEE.

Thomas Wolf, Lysandre Debut, Victor Sanh, Julien Chaumond, Clement Delangue, Anthony Moi, Pierric Cistac, Tim Rault, Rémi Louf, Morgan Funtowicz, Joe Davison, Sam Shleifer, Patrick von Platen, Clara Ma, Yacine Jernite, Julien Plu, Canwen Xu, Teven Le Scao, Sylvain Gugger, Mariama Drame, Quentin Lhoest, and Alexander M. Rush. 2020. Transformers: State-of-the-art natural language processing. In *Proceedings of the 2020 Conference on Empirical Methods in Natural Language Processing: System Demonstrations*, pages 38–45, Online. Association for Computational Linguistics.

Ke Xu, Yunqing Xia, and Chin-Hui Lee. 2015. Tweet normalization with syllables. In *Proceedings of the 53rd Annual Meeting of the Association for Computational Linguistics and the 7th International Joint Conference on Natural Language Processing (Volume 1: Long Papers)*, pages 920–928.

Chao Yang and Padmini Srinivasan. 2016. Life satisfaction and the pursuit of happiness on twitter. *PloS one*, 11(3):e0150881.

Andrew Yates, Arman Cohan, and Nazli Goharian. 2017. Depression and self-harm risk assessment in online forums. In *Proceedings of the 2017 Conference on Empirical Methods in Natural Language Processing*, pages 2968–2978.

Marcos Zampieri, Shervin Malmasi, Preslav Nakov, Sara Rosenthal, Noura Farra, and Ritesh Kumar. 2019a. Predicting the type and target of offensive posts in social media. In *Proceedings of the 2019 Conference of the North American Chapter of the Association for Computational Linguistics: Human Language Technologies, Volume 1 (Long and Short Papers)*, pages 1415–1420, Minneapolis, Minnesota. Association for Computational Linguistics.

Marcos Zampieri, Shervin Malmasi, Preslav Nakov, Sara Rosenthal, Noura Farra, and Ritesh Kumar. 2019b. SemEval-2019 Task 6: Identifying and Categorizing Offensive Language in Social Media (OffensEval). In *Proceedings of The 13th International Workshop on Semantic Evaluation (SemEval)*.

Marcos Zampieri, Preslav Nakov, Sara Rosenthal, Pepa Atanasova, Georgi Karadzhov, Hamdy Mubarak, Leon Derczynski, Zeses Pitenis, and Çağrı Çöltekin. 2020. SemEval-2020 task 12: Multilingual offensive language identification in social media (OffensEval 2020). In *Proceedings of the Fourteenth Workshop on Semantic Evaluation*, pages 1425–1447, Barcelona (online). International Committee for Computational Linguistics.

ÚFAL at MultiLexNorm 2021: Improving Multilingual Lexical Normalization by Fine-tuning ByT5

David Samuel and **Milan Straka**
Charles University,
Faculty of Mathematics and Physics,
Institute of Formal and Applied Linguistics
{samuel,straka}@ufal.mff.cuni.cz

Abstract

We present the winning entry to the *Multilingual Lexical Normalization (MultiLexNorm)* shared task at *W-NUT 2021* (van der Goot et al., 2021a), which evaluates lexical-normalization systems on 12 social media datasets in 11 languages. We base our solution on a pre-trained byte-level language model, ByT5 (Xue et al., 2021a), which we further pre-train on synthetic data and then fine-tune on authentic normalization data. Our system achieves the best performance by a wide margin in intrinsic evaluation, and also the best performance in extrinsic evaluation through dependency parsing. The source code is released at https://github.com/ufal/multilexnorm2021 and the fine-tuned models at https://huggingface.co/ufal.

1 Introduction

People produce text in natural language every minute of every day. However, in many cases, for example on social media like Twitter, such texts are not conforming to a formal style. Instead, they are in colloquial form, which is perfectly understandable to other people, but challenging for automatic natural language processing. To make the processing of such texts more viable, the task of *lexical normalization* can be used to replace the input forms with their canonical (more formal, lexically normalized) variants.

The aim of the *W-NUT 2021: Multilingual Lexical Normalization (MultiLexNorm)* shared task (van der Goot et al., 2021a) is to evaluate participant lexical-normalization systems on 12 social media datasets in 11 languages, including two code-switching datasets. Both intrinsic and extrinsic evaluation is performed, where the latter is measured through dependency parsing performed on the normalized data.

Recently, large pre-trained models like BERT (Devlin et al., 2019) or T5 (Raffel et al., 2020) have demonstrated superior performance in many NLP tasks when trained in a transfer learning setting. In line with that, we approach the lexical normalization shared task as a fine-tuning of a large pre-trained model, specifically the multilingual byte-level generative language model ByT5 (Xue et al., 2021a).

Our system achieves the best performance in the shared task, both in intrinsic and extrinsic evaluations. In the intrinsic evaluation, our system reaches 67.3% error reduction compared to leave-as-is baseline; the second-best system has 53.6%.

The source code is released at https://github.com/ufal/multilexnorm2021 and the fine-tuned models are available in HuggingFace Transformers (Wolf et al., 2020) at https://huggingface.co/ufal.

2 Related Work

Lexical normalization can be considered a simplified variant of a well-studied problem of *grammar error correction* (GEC). Grundkiewicz et al. (2019) approach GEC as a neural machine translation task using the Transformer architecture (Vaswani et al., 2017), which is pre-trained using a vast amount of synthetic data generated by character-level and word-level edits. Recently, Rothe et al. (2021) presented a GEC system based on multilingual mT5 (Xue et al., 2021b), reaching state-of-the-art results on several datasets with the gigantic *xxl* model size with 13B parameters.

While the mentioned GEC systems are autoregressive, lexical normalization can be easily solved in a non-autoregressive way, because the normalizations of different words are relatively independent. Besides, successful non-autoregressive models have been recently proposed for general GEC (Awasthi et al., 2019; Omelianchuk et al., 2020).

Although fine-tuned language models have been successfully used in the state-of-the-art GEC systems, this has not been the case in the field of lexi-

Proceedings of the 2021 EMNLP Workshop W-NUT: The Seventh Workshop on Noisy User-generated Text, pages 483–492
November 11, 2021.

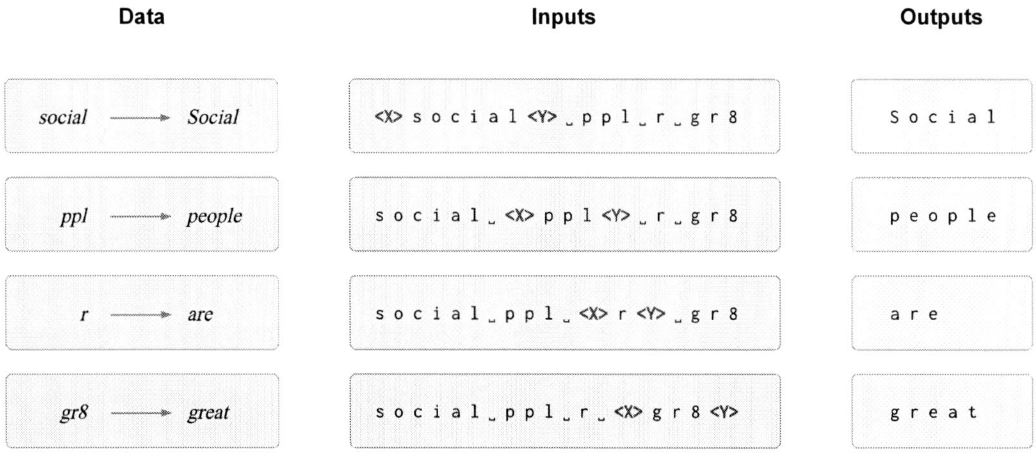

Figure 1: The inputs and outputs of our lexical normalization model. The ByT5 sentinel tokens <X> and <Y> mark the word to be normalized.

cal normalization (Muller et al., 2019; Lourentzou et al., 2019). MoNoise (van der Goot, 2019) is a publicly available multilingual lexical normalization tool achieving competent performance (an improved version of the system would place third in the shared task intrinsic evaluation). It utilizes Aspell dictionaries, FastText (Bojanowski et al., 2017) embeddings and hand-crafted language features, but no contextualized embeddings.

3 Model

Our model is based on a large pre-trained multilingual model. In accordance with Bommasani et al. (2021), we call such models (like BERT or T5) the *foundation* models.

Specifically, we utilize the ByT5 (Xue et al., 2021a) foundation model. It is a byte-level generative sequence-to-sequence model, which processes a sequence of bytes of UTF-8 encoding on input and produces a sequence of UTF-8 encoding bytes on output. ByT5 models were proposed as an alternative to multilingual mT5 foundation models (Xue et al., 2021b) and have been shown to perform remarkably well on noisy text data (compared to subword-based mT5), like TWEETQA (Xiong et al., 2019).

3.1 Input and Output Format

We start by recapitulating the pre-training task of the ByT5 model. The input sentence (including spaces) is represented as a sequence of bytes of UTF-8 encoding, and spans of around 20 bytes are

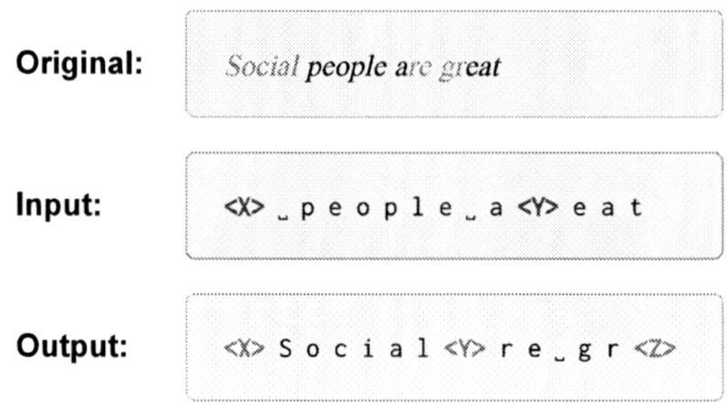

Figure 2: The pre-training task utilized in the ByT5 model (Xue et al., 2021a). The <X>, <Y> and <Z> are the sentinel tokens.

masked using special *sentinel tokens*. The goal of the model is to reconstruct all the masked spans. We illustrate the task visually in Figure 2.

For lexical normalization, we could directly use the unnormalized sentence as input and the normalized sentence as output (an approach used by Rothe et al. (2021) for GEC). However, we were concerned that such an approach would be too different from the ByT5 pre-training, and furthermore, it would not allow to reconstruct the alignment of the normalized tokens when a word is removed during normalization or split into several words.

Instead, we opted for a different approach illustrated in Figure 1. For each input word, we construct a separate ByT5 input, in which we mark the beginning and the end of the word in question using two sentinel tokens. Then we ask the model to produce just the normalization of that word. Such an approach normalizes each input word indepen-

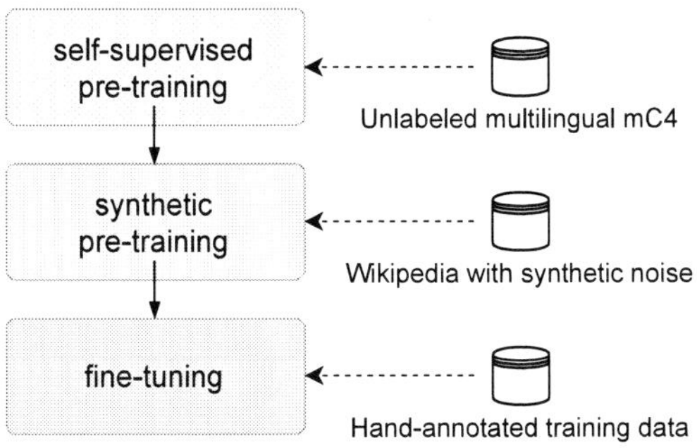

Figure 3: Three stages of training of our models: the original ByT5 pre-training, pre-training on synthetic data and final fine-tuning of authentic data.

dently, and we consider it quite similar to the original ByT5 pre-training task. Unfortunately, it requires to encode different input sequences for every input word, which is considerably inefficient, even if we can perform normalization of all words in parallel.

3.2 Pre-training on Synthetic Data

Fine-tuning a ByT5 model directly with supervised training data would not deliver very high performance, given that the normalization task is (despite our efforts) still quite different from the pre-training task, and that the amount of available training data is quite low.[1]

Therefore, before fine-tuning, we first pre-train the ByT5 model using synthetic data, as illustrated in Figure 3. Note that from now on, by *"pre-train"* we mean the training of the ByT5 foundation model using synthetic lexical normalization data.

We construct the synthetic data by modifying clean data in the following way:

- If a word is present in the normalized output in the training data, it is replaced by one of the corresponding (possibly unnormalized) training data inputs, proportionally to the number of occurrences. For example, we change *"people"* to *"ppl"* with 39.7% probability in the English dataset or *"ikke"* to *"ik"* with 4.97% chance in the Danish dataset.
- A large portion of the required changes can be realized as simple character-level modifications. Thus, we synthesize the data by reversing these alterations. These are 1) accent mark removal (e.g., replacing *"š"* by *"s"* with 16.3% chance in Slovenian), 2) changing capitalization (e.g., lowering the first capitalized letter with 1.0% chance in Turkish), 3) removing apostrophes (46.8% probability in English), and 4) other miscellaneous modifications (e.g., simplifying *"qu"* to *"k"* in Spanish with 2.0% probability).
- The training data naturally contain a large quantity of different typographical errors, usually caused by inaccurate typing on a keyboard. To simulate this behavior, we alter the words by skipping some characters, changing or inserting some characters (more likely to those close on a computer keyboard), and by reversing two consecutive characters. To give one example, the probability of making an artificial typo in Italian is 0.458%.
- Some modifications are unique for a specific language. For example, the plural forms in Indonesian can be created by duplicating the singular forms. As users want to save time when writing in Indonesian, they sometimes indicate the plural by simple appending "2" to the singular form. We reverse this transformation with 33.3% probability (thus, *"laki-lakinya"* becomes *"laki2nya"*).
- 7 datasets in this shared task split or merge words. We synthetically split/merge words on the clean dataset to model these actions. For example, the probability of merging two words in Dutch is 5.99% and of splitting a word is 0.0565%.
- In order to speed up typing, the users modify their language in various ways – e.g. by omitting vowels or shortening words to prefixes. On the other hand, they repeat certain characters to make their messages more expressive. We include these variations in the synthetic datasets to get closer to the real data.

For more details, please consult the source code.

It is important to note that all the probabilities were estimated from the training data. Therefore the synthetic pre-training cannot be regarded as completely unsupervised; one would need expert knowledge to extend this type of pre-training on a language without annotated data of lexical normalization.

We need to make sure that most of the original data (before the synthetic modifications) are clean. Since we also want an ample amount of cross-lingual text, we opted to use publicly avail-

[1] This experiment is included in ablations in Section 5.3.

Code	Language	Original Source	Words	Words split/merged	Caps	% words normed	MFR ERR
DA	Danish	Plank et al. (2020)	11 816	✓	✓	9.25	49.68
DE	German	Sidarenka et al. (2013)	25 157	✓	✓	17.96	32.09
EN	English	Baldwin et al. (2015)	73 806	✓	✗	6.90	64.93
ES	Spanish	Alegria et al. (2013)	13 827	✗	✗	7.69	25.57
HR	Croatian	Ljubešić et al. (2017a)	75 276	✗	✗	8.89	36.52
ID-EN	Indonesian-English	Barik et al. (2019)	23 124	✓	✗	12.16	61.17
IT	Italian	van der Goot et al. (2020)	14 641	✓	✓	7.32	16.83
NL	Dutch	Schuur (2020)	23 053	✓	✓	28.29	37.70
SR	Serbian	Ljubešić et al. (2017b)	91 738	✗	✗	7.65	42.62
SL	Slovenian	Erjavec et al. (2017)	75 276	✗	✗	15.62	56.71
TR	Turkish	Çolakoğlu et al. (2019)	7 949	✓	✓	37.02	14.53
TR-DE	Turkish-German	van der Goot and Çetinoğlu (2021)	16 546	✓	✓	24.14	22.09

Table 1: The MultiLexNorm datasets and their properties – number of words, whether words are split/merged, if capitalization is corrected, relative number of normalized words and performance of the most-frequent-replacement baseline (Section 5).

able dumps of Wikipedia.[2] We remove any lines shorter than 32 characters or ending with a colon (to remove titles), segment the lines into sentences with Stanza (Qi et al., 2020) and tokenize with `CMU-ARK tokenizer`[3] (a tool standardly used for tokenizing text from Twitter).

3.3 Fine-tuning

The final fine-tuning of the pre-trained model can be straightforwardly performed on the training data (so called `base` fine-tuning). However, we also consider fine-tuning on a mix of both authentic training data and the synthetic data (with 1:1 ratio) in order to avoid overfitting (`mixed` fine-tuning).

3.4 Inference

To predict the normalized sentences during inference, each word-token is processed independently, similarly to training (Figure 1). The ByT5 decoder autoregressively generates each token, either greedily or via beam search.[4] When using the beam search, we generate multiple candidate sequences, and the beam search automatically assigns prediction scores to each of them. These can then be used to aggregate predictions from multiple models in an ensemble.

4 Experiments

The MultiLexNorm shared task consists of 12 social media datasets in 11 languages, including two code-switching datasets. All these datasets are based on Twitter data, with the Danish and the Dutch ones also including data from other sources. The datasets, their original sources and some of their properties are listed in Table 1.

We train an independent model for every dataset. The pre-training starts from the *small* variant of ByT5, which contains 300M parameters. We keep all hyperparameters of the model unchanged, including a dropout rate of 10%. The training employs batch size 128 and the AdaFactor optimizer (Shazeer and Stern, 2018) to decrease memory usage.

The pre-training is performed using the synthetic data described in Section 3.2, for at least 100 000 optimizer steps.[5] We utilize inverse square root decay with peak learning rate of $5 \cdot 10^{-4}$ and 4 000 warm-up steps.

The fine-tuning phase is carried out with a constant learning rate $1 \cdot 10^{-4}$ for 50 epochs. We consider two training data configurations:

1. Using only MultiLexNorm training data, respecting the train/dev split (using 10% of training data as development set if there is none).
2. Because the development set, if present, is quite large (usually circa 30% of the training data), we also consider training on development data. Specifically, we concatenate train-

[2] `https://dumps.wikimedia.org/backup-index.html`

[3] `https://github.com/myleott/ark-twokenize-py`

[4] For simplicity, we use the default settings of the `greedy_search` and `beam_search` procedures from the Hugging Face library, apart from allowing longer sequences and varying the number of beams.

[5] We stop the training only after a full epoch, when at least 100k steps were performed.

ing and development data, if any, and take only 3% of the data as development set (just to detect errors, because evaluation on such small set is considerably noisy).

Our competition model is trained on the combined dataset (the latter option), and the synthetic data is mixed in (`mixed` fine-tuning from Section 3.3) if it improves development performance over the `base` fine-tuning.[6]

5 Results

The MultiLexNorm participants were allowed to submit two runs. The first run of our team *ÚFAL* is a single model, while the second run is an ensemble of 4 models.[7] We perform ensembling by considering for each word and each model 16 replacements including their probabilities (using a beam-search decoder), and producing the replacement with the highest average probability.

Apart from the participant systems, several baselines are also evaluated: *LAI* (leave-as-is), *MFR* (most frequent replacement based on the training data) and the *MoNoise* tool (van der Goot, 2019).

5.1 Intrinsic Evaluation

The intrinsic evaluation is performed using the *Error Reduction Rate* (ERR), which is word-level accuracy normalized to the number of replacements in the dataset. Formally, if we denote the system that does not normalize any word as *leave-as-is*, we can define ERR as

$$ERR = \frac{accuracy_{system} - accuracy_{leave\text{-}as\text{-}is}}{1.0 - accuracy_{leave\text{-}as\text{-}is}}.$$

The final ranking is determined by the ERR macro-averaged over all datasets.

The MultiLexNorm intrinsic evaluation results are provided in Table 2. Our system achieves the best performance by a wide margin – the single model achieves 66.2% macro-averaged ERR, and the model ensemble even a percent point more, 67.3%. That is 13.7% higher than the second-best result of 53.6%. Our ensemble model reaches best results on all datasets, except for Danish, where our single model is better, and for Spanish, where it is outperformed by other system.

[6]Ablations of all training data configurations are evaluated in Section 5.3.

[7]The ensemble models start from a single pre-trained checkpoint and only the fine-tuning is independent.

5.2 Extrinsic Evaluation

To evaluate the effect of lexical normalization on downstream applications, MultiLexNorm considers dependency parsing. First, dependency parsing models are trained using the MaChAmp parser (van der Goot et al., 2021b) on several treebanks from Universal Dependencies 2.8 (Zeman et al., 2021). Treebanks with formal style are used (i.e., not data from social networks), specifically German-GSD, English-EWT, Italian-ISDT and Turkish-IMST. Then, MultiLexNorm participant systems are used to normalize 7 social-media treebanks, which are then parsed using the described parsing models and evaluated using the label attachment score (LAS) metric. For details, please see the MultiLexNorm shared task overview paper.

The results of the MultiLexNorm extrinsic evaluation are presented in Table 3. Our system also achieves the best performance in the overall macro-average and in 4 out of the 7 treebanks. Generally, the LAS score differences are much smaller than the ERR intrinsic evaluation metric, but the rankings in both evaluations show a lot of similarity. A notable difference is the MFR baseline, which performs remarkably well in the extrinsic evaluation.

5.3 Ablation Study

To quantify the effect of various hyperparameters of our system, Table 4 presents intrinsic evaluation of several ablation experiments.

The Foundation Model We compare the *small* variants of mT5 and ByT5 foundation models when only fine-tuning (and not pre-training on synthetic data) is used. In this setting, the ByT5 model reaches substantially better results (59.2% average ERR compared to 33.6%). We therefore did not experiment further with the mT5 model.[8]

Pre-training and Fine-tuning Phases The pre-training phase considerably improves results, reaching 64.8% ERR compared to 59.2% ERR without pre-training. We also evaluate the model after the pre-training phase only – the resulting 31.3% ERR is quite low, worse than the MFR baseline and most submitted systems.

Fine-tuning Data First, we consider the effect of fine-tuning purely on the MultiLexNorm training data (`base` fine-tuning in Table 4), mixing in the

[8]Preliminary experiments on synthetic pre-training of English and Italian also demonstrated considerably worse results of mT5 compared to ByT5.

Team	Average	DA	DE	EN	ES	HR	ID-EN	IT	NL	SL	SR	TR	TR-DE
ÚFAL (ensemble)	**67.30**	68.7	**66.2**	**75.6**	59.2	**67.7**	**67.2**	**47.5**	**63.6**	**80.1**	**74.6**	**68.6**	**68.6**
ÚFAL (single)	66.21	**70.2**	65.7	73.8	55.9	67.3	66.2	42.6	62.7	79.8	73.5	**68.6**	68.2
HEL-LJU	53.58	56.6	59.8	62.0	35.5	56.2	55.3	35.6	45.9	67.0	66.4	51.2	51.2
MoNoise	*49.02*	*51.3*	*47.0*	*74.3*	*45.5*	*52.6*	*59.8*	*21.8*	*49.5*	*61.9*	*59.6*	*28.2*	*36.7*
TrinkaAI*	43.75	45.9	47.3	66.0	**61.3**	41.3	56.4	15.8	45.7	59.5	44.5	15.5	25.8
thunderml*	43.44	46.5	46.6	64.1	60.3	40.1	59.1	11.9	44.0	59.3	44.5	15.9	29.0
team	40.70	48.1	46.1	63.7	21.0	40.4	59.3	13.9	43.7	60.6	46.1	15.9	29.7
learnML	40.30	40.5	43.7	61.6	56.5	38.1	56.2	5.9	42.8	58.2	40.0	14.4	25.7
maet	40.05	48.1	46.1	63.9	21.0	40.4	59.3	5.9	43.7	60.6	46.1	15.9	29.7
MFR	*38.37*	*49.7*	*32.1*	*64.9*	*25.6*	*36.5*	*61.2*	*16.8*	*37.7*	*56.7*	*42.6*	*14.5*	*22.1*
CL-MoNoise	12.05	7.3	16.5	4.1	5.0	26.4	2.4	0.0	16.2	8.8	20.1	17.6	20.2
BLUE	6.73	49.7	-1.9	26.8	-9.4	-10.1	-7.2	-31.7	-2.1	-1.0	42.6	10.0	15.0
LAI	*0.00*	*0.0*	*0.0*	*0.0*	*0.0*	*0.0*	*0.0*	*0.0*	*0.0*	*0.0*	*0.0*	*0.0*	*0.0*
MaChAmp	-21.25	-88.9	-93.4	51.0	25.4	42.6	39.5	-312.9	1.5	56.8	39.4	-12.7	-3.4

Table 2: The results of MultiLexNorm intrinsic evaluation. Each team could submit two systems, we show the best of the two. More detailed results are available in the overview paper (van der Goot et al., 2021a) and in the participant papers: HEL-LJU (Scherrer and Ljubešić, 2021), TrinkaAI (Kubal and Nagvenkar, 2021), CL-MoNoise (van der Goot, 2021) and BLUE (Bucur et al., 2021). * denotes late submissions.

Team	Average	DE tweede	EN aae	EN monoise	EN tweebank2	IT postwita	IT twittiro	TR iwt151
ÚFAL (ensemble)	**64.17**	**73.6**	**62.7**	**58.6**	59.1	**68.3**	72.2	54.7
ÚFAL (single)	63.98	**73.6**	62.2	57.9	59.0	**68.3**	72.2	54.8
HEL-LJU	63.72	73.5	60.6	56.2	60.3	68.1	**72.3**	**55.0**
MoNoise	*63.44*	*73.2*	*62.3*	*56.8*	*58.9*	*67.5*	*70.7*	*54.6*
MFR	*63.31*	*72.9*	*60.3*	*56.7*	***60.3***	*67.3*	*70.7*	*54.9*
TrinkaAI*	63.12	72.9	60.2	56.6	59.9	67.0	71.1	54.2
maet	63.09	72.8	59.4	56.6	59.8	67.4	71.1	54.5
team	63.03	72.8	59.4	56.6	59.8	67.2	70.9	54.5
thunderml*	63.02	72.7	59.6	56.7	59.2	67.3	71.3	54.2
learnML	62.88	72.3	59.0	56.2	60.0	67.0	71.2	54.5
CL-MoNoise	62.71	72.7	60.9	55.3	58.5	66.5	70.1	55.0
BLUE	62.53	72.6	59.6	54.2	59.8	66.7	70.0	54.8
LAI	*62.45*	*72.7*	*59.2*	*53.6*	*60.0*	*66.5*	*70.1*	***55.0***
MaChAmp	61.89	71.3	60.8	54.6	58.0	64.7	69.8	54.1

Table 3: The results of MultiLexNorm extrinsic evaluation through dependency parsing evaluated via label attachment score (LAS). Each team could submit two systems, we show the best of the two. * denotes late submissions.

synthetic data with 1:1 ratio (`mixed` fine-tuning), or selecting the best option according to the development data (`best` fine-tuning). The results reveal that, unfortunately, our strategy of choosing the best variant based on development performance is actually worse than the pure `base` fine-tuning. On the other hand, training also on the development data improves the performance substantially (from 64.8% to 66.2% average ERR).

Beam-search Decoding Using beam-search decoding with a beam size 16 has virtually no effect compared to greedy decoding (66.21% average ERR for both options). We hypothesize there is no difference because we generate each normalization independently, so greedy decoding on the *small* target sequences recovers the optimal solution with very high probability. In practice, it is therefore enough to utilize greedy decoding and avoid the higher runtime requirements of a beam search.

Ensembling Finally, utilizing an ensemble of 4 models improves the performance by a percent point from 66.2% average ERR to 67.3%.

Treebank	Foundation	mT5	ByT5	ByT5	ByT5	ByT5	ByT5	ByT5	ByT5	ByT5
	Pre-training	✗	✗	✓	✓	✓	✓	✓	✓	✓
	Fine-tuning	base	base	✗	base	mixed	best	best	best	best
	Training Data	train	train	train	train	train	train	trn+dev	trn+dev	trn+dev
	Beam size	1	1	1	1	1	1	1	16	16
	Ensemble	✗	✗	✗	✗	✗	✗	✗	✗	4
Average		33.62	59.23	31.28	64.88	63.52	64.77	66.21	66.21	**67.30**
Danish		31.65	67.41	49.37	65.82	67.72	65.82	**70.25**	**70.25**	68.67
German		42.91	59.35	49.10	63.40	62.50	63.40	65.77	65.65	**66.22**
English		61.27	70.40	40.15	73.28	72.68	73.28	73.88	73.80	**75.60**
Spanish		-0.21	43.87	9.15	57.59	56.96	56.96	55.93	55.93	**59.25**
Croatian		38.11	55.15	43.31	63.18	63.03	63.03	67.29	67.29	**67.74**
Indonesian-English		50.86	63.75	-3.95	65.12	63.92	63.92	66.15	66.15	**67.18**
Italian		-7.92	43.56	-12.87	46.53	35.64	46.53	42.57	42.57	**47.52**
Dutch		43.18	55.88	43.45	62.03	62.30	62.03	62.70	62.70	**63.58**
Slovenian		56.48	71.62	57.21	78.08	77.14	78.08	79.89	79.85	**80.07**
Serbian		43.29	60.99	59.22	71.10	71.83	71.83	73.42	73.55	**74.59**
Turkish		11.82	59.80	21.79	66.55	65.03	66.55	68.41	**68.58**	**68.58**
Turkish-German		31.99	58.98	19.46	65.82	63.45	65.82	68.27	68.19	**68.62**

Table 4: The intrinsic evaluation of the ablation experiments – we consider various foundation models, whether pre-training is performed, what data do we use for fine-tuning, the decoder beam size and finally whether an ensemble of models is used.

GPU	Batch size	Words per sec	Slowdown
GeForce RTX 3090	1	15.45	5.92×
GeForce RTX 3090	2	28.05	3.26×
GeForce RTX 3090	4	42.15	2.17×
GeForce RTX 3090	8	57.55	1.59×
GeForce RTX 3090	16	84.19	1.09×
GeForce RTX 3090	32	90.20	1.01×
GeForce RTX 3090	64	88.01	1.04×
GeForce RTX 3090	128	91.42	1×
GeForce RTX 3090	256	87.77	1.04×
GeForce RTX 3090	512	78.94	1.16×
GeForce RTX 1080 Ti	128	55.69	1.64×
GeForce RTX 2080 Ti	128	58.19	1.57×
Quadro P5000	128	43.88	2.08×
Quadro RTX 5000	128	66.81	1.37×

Table 5: Inference speed of greedy decoding, measured on all English evaluation data (56 999 words in total) as words per second for various GPUs and batch size.

5.4 Inference Speed

To inspect the runtime performance of our model, we measure the inference speed of a single model using greedy decoding on all English evaluation data (56 999 words in total). The results for various batch sizes and GPUs are listed in Table 5. Overall, with a batch size of 128 our model processes 43-91 words per second, depending on a GPU used. For comparison, the MoNoise system is reported to normalize 29-62 words/sec without a GPU, based on candidate filtering (van der Goot, 2019, Table 3).

6 Conclusion

We presented the winning system of the W-NUT 2021: Multilingual Lexical Normalization (MultiLexNorm) shared task, which is based on a ByT5 foundation model. In intrinsic evaluation, the system performance is superior by a very wide margin, and our system also delivers the best performance in extrinsic evaluation. We release both the source code at `https://github.com/ufal/multilexnorm2021` and the fine-tuned models at `https://huggingface.co/ufal`.

In future work, we would like to change the model architecture to encode input sentences only once, either by decoding the whole sentence, or by separating all input words with different sentinel tokens and then decoding individual words by initializing the decoder with the corresponding sentinel tokens.

Acknowledgements

The research described herein has been supported by the Ministry of Education, Youths and Sports of the Czech Republic, under the project LINDAT/CLARIAH-CZ (LM2018101).

References

Inaki Alegria, Nora Aranberri, Víctor Fresno, Pablo Gamallo, Lluis Padró, Inaki San Vicente, Jordi Turmo, and Arkaitz Zubiaga. 2013. Introducción a la tarea compartida Tweet-Norm 2013: Normalización léxica de tuits en Español. In *Tweet-Norm@ SEPLN*, pages 1–9.

Abhijeet Awasthi, Sunita Sarawagi, Rasna Goyal, Sabyasachi Ghosh, and Vihari Piratla. 2019. Parallel iterative edit models for local sequence transduction. In *Proceedings of the 2019 Conference on Empirical Methods in Natural Language Processing and the 9th International Joint Conference on Natural Language Processing (EMNLP-IJCNLP)*, pages 4260–4270, Hong Kong, China. Association for Computational Linguistics.

Timothy Baldwin, Marie Catherine de Marneffe, Bo Han, Young-Bum Kim, Alan Ritter, and Wei Xu. 2015. Shared tasks of the 2015 workshop on noisy user-generated text: Twitter lexical normalization and named entity recognition. In *Proceedings of the Workshop on Noisy User-generated Text*, pages 126–135, Beijing, China. Association for Computational Linguistics.

Anab Maulana Barik, Rahmad Mahendra, and Mirna Adriani. 2019. Normalization of Indonesian-English code-mixed Twitter data. In *Proceedings of the 5th Workshop on Noisy User-generated Text (W-NUT 2019)*, pages 417–424, Hong Kong, China. Association for Computational Linguistics.

Piotr Bojanowski, Edouard Grave, Armand Joulin, and Tomas Mikolov. 2017. Enriching word vectors with subword information. *Transactions of the Association for Computational Linguistics*, 5:135–146.

Rishi Bommasani, Drew A. Hudson, Ehsan Adeli, Russ Altman, Simran Arora, Sydney von Arx, Michael S. Bernstein, Jeannette Bohg, Antoine Bosselut, Emma Brunskill, Erik Brynjolfsson, Shyamal Buch, Dallas Card, Rodrigo Castellon, Niladri Chatterji, Annie Chen, Kathleen Creel, Jared Quincy Davis, Dora Demszky, Chris Donahue, Moussa Doumbouya, Esin Durmus, Stefano Ermon, John Etchemendy, Kawin Ethayarajh, Li Fei-Fei, Chelsea Finn, Trevor Gale, Lauren Gillespie, Karan Goel, Noah Goodman, Shelby Grossman, Neel Guha, Tatsunori Hashimoto, Peter Henderson, John Hewitt, Daniel E. Ho, Jenny Hong, Kyle Hsu, Jing Huang, Thomas Icard, Saahil Jain, Dan Jurafsky, Pratyusha Kalluri, Siddharth Karamcheti, Geoff Keeling, Fereshte Khani, Omar Khattab, Pang Wei Kohd, Mark Krass, Ranjay Krishna, Rohith Kuditipudi, Ananya Kumar, Faisal Ladhak, Mina Lee, Tony Lee, Jure Leskovec, Isabelle Levent, Xiang Lisa Li, Xuechen Li, Tengyu Ma, Ali Malik, Christopher D. Manning, Suvir Mirchandani, Eric Mitchell, Zanele Munyikwa, Suraj Nair, Avanika Narayan, Deepak Narayanan, Ben Newman, Allen Nie, Juan Carlos Niebles, Hamed Nilforoshan, Julian Nyarko, Giray Ogut, Laurel Orr, Isabel Papadimitriou, Joon Sung Park, Chris Piech, Eva Portelance, Christopher Potts, Aditi Raghunathan, Rob Reich, Hongyu Ren, Frieda Rong, Yusuf Roohani, Camilo Ruiz, Jack Ryan, Christopher Ré, Dorsa Sadigh, Shiori Sagawa, Keshav Santhanam, Andy Shih, Krishnan Srinivasan, Alex Tamkin, Rohan Taori, Armin W. Thomas, Florian Tramèr, Rose E. Wang, William Wang, Bohan Wu, Jiajun Wu, Yuhuai Wu, Sang Michael Xie, Michihiro Yasunaga, Jiaxuan You, Matei Zaharia, Michael Zhang, Tianyi Zhang, Xikun Zhang, Yuhui Zhang, Lucia Zheng, Kaitlyn Zhou, and Percy Liang. 2021. On the opportunities and risks of foundation models.

Ana-Maria Bucur, Adrian Cosma, and Liviu P. Dinu. 2021. Sequence-to-sequence lexical normalization with multilingual transformers. In *Proceedings of the 7th Workshop on Noisy User-generated Text (W-NUT 2021)*, Punta Cana, Dominican Republic. Association for Computational Linguistics.

Talha Çolakoğlu, Umut Sulubacak, and Ahmet Cüneyd Tantuğ. 2019. Normalizing non-canonical Turkish texts using machine translation approaches. In *Proceedings of the 57th Annual Meeting of the Association for Computational Linguistics: Student Research Workshop*, pages 267–272, Florence, Italy. Association for Computational Linguistics.

Jacob Devlin, Ming-Wei Chang, Kenton Lee, and Kristina Toutanova. 2019. BERT: Pre-training of deep bidirectional transformers for language understanding. In *Proceedings of the 2019 Conference of the North American Chapter of the Association for Computational Linguistics: Human Language Technologies, Volume 1 (Long and Short Papers)*, pages 4171–4186, Minneapolis, Minnesota. Association for Computational Linguistics.

Tomaž Erjavec, Darja Fišer, Jaka Čibej, Špela Arhar Holdt, Nikola Ljubešić, and Katja Zupan. 2017. CMC training corpus Janes-Tag 2.0. Slovenian language resource repository CLARIN.SI.

Roman Grundkiewicz, Marcin Junczys-Dowmunt, and Kenneth Heafield. 2019. Neural grammatical error correction systems with unsupervised pre-training on synthetic data. In *Proceedings of the Fourteenth Workshop on Innovative Use of NLP for Building Educational Applications*, pages 252–263, Florence, Italy. Association for Computational Linguistics.

Divesh Kubal and Apurva Nagvenkar. 2021. Multilingual sequence labeling approach to solve lexical normalization. In *Proceedings of the 7th Workshop on Noisy User-generated Text (W-NUT 2021)*, Punta

Cana, Dominican Republic. Association for Computational Linguistics.

Nikola Ljubešić, Tomaž Erjavec, Maja Miličević, and Tanja Samardžić. 2017a. Croatian Twitter training corpus ReLDI-NormTagNER-hr 2.0. Slovenian language resource repository CLARIN.SI.

Nikola Ljubešić, Tomaž Erjavec, Maja Miličević, and Tanja Samardžić. 2017b. Serbian Twitter training corpus ReLDI-NormTagNER-sr 2.0. Slovenian language resource repository CLARIN.SI.

Ismini Lourentzou, Kabir Manghnani, and ChengXiang Zhai. 2019. Adapting sequence to sequence models for text normalization in social media. In *International Conference on Web and Social Media*. AAAI.

Benjamin Muller, Benoit Sagot, and Djamé Seddah. 2019. Enhancing BERT for lexical normalization. In *Proceedings of the 5th Workshop on Noisy User-generated Text (W-NUT 2019)*, pages 297–306, Hong Kong, China. Association for Computational Linguistics.

Kostiantyn Omelianchuk, Vitaliy Atrasevych, Artem Chernodub, and Oleksandr Skurzhanskyi. 2020. GECToR – grammatical error correction: Tag, not rewrite. In *Proceedings of the Fifteenth Workshop on Innovative Use of NLP for Building Educational Applications*, pages 163–170, Seattle, WA, USA → Online. Association for Computational Linguistics.

Barbara Plank, Kristian Nørgaard Jensen, and Rob van der Goot. 2020. DaN+: Danish nested named entities and lexical normalization. In *Proceedings of the 28th International Conference on Computational Linguistics*, pages 6649–6662, Barcelona, Spain (Online). International Committee on Computational Linguistics.

Peng Qi, Yuhao Zhang, Yuhui Zhang, Jason Bolton, and Christopher D. Manning. 2020. Stanza: A Python natural language processing toolkit for many human languages. In *Proceedings of the 58th Annual Meeting of the Association for Computational Linguistics: System Demonstrations*.

Colin Raffel, Noam Shazeer, Adam Roberts, Katherine Lee, Sharan Narang, Michael Matena, Yanqi Zhou, Wei Li, and Peter J. Liu. 2020. Exploring the limits of transfer learning with a unified text-to-text transformer. *Journal of Machine Learning Research*, 21(140):1–67.

Sascha Rothe, Jonathan Mallinson, Eric Malmi, Sebastian Krause, and Aliaksei Severyn. 2021. A simple recipe for multilingual grammatical error correction. In *Proceedings of the 59th Annual Meeting of the Association for Computational Linguistics and the 11th International Joint Conference on Natural Language Processing (Volume 2: Short Papers)*, pages 702–707, Online. Association for Computational Linguistics.

Yves Scherrer and Nikola Ljubešić. 2021. Sesame Street to Mount Sinai: BERT-constrained character-level Moses models for multilingual lexical normalization. In *Proceedings of the 7th Workshop on Noisy User-generated Text (W-NUT 2021)*, Punta Cana, Dominican Republic. Association for Computational Linguistics.

Youri Schuur. 2020. Normalization for Dutch for improved pos tagging. Master's thesis, University of Groningen.

Noam Shazeer and Mitchell Stern. 2018. Adafactor: Adaptive learning rates with sublinear memory cost. *CoRR*, abs/1804.04235.

Uladzimir Sidarenka, Tatjana Scheffler, and Manfred Stede. 2013. Rule-based normalization of German Twitter messages. In *Proc. of the GSCL Workshop Verarbeitung und Annotation von Sprachdaten aus Genres internetbasierter Kommunikation*.

Rob van der Goot. 2019. MoNoise: A multi-lingual and easy-to-use lexical normalization tool. In *Proceedings of the 57th Annual Meeting of the Association for Computational Linguistics: System Demonstrations*, pages 201–206, Florence, Italy. Association for Computational Linguistics.

Rob van der Goot. 2021. CL-MoNoise: Cross-lingual lexical normalization. In *Proceedings of the 7th Workshop on Noisy User-generated Text (W-NUT 2021)*, Punta Cana, Dominican Republic. Association for Computational Linguistics.

Rob van der Goot and Özlem Çetinoğlu. 2021. Lexical normalization for code-switched data and its effect on POS tagging. In *Proceedings of the 16th Conference of the European Chapter of the Association for Computational Linguistics: Volume 1, Long Papers*. Association for Computational Linguistics.

Rob van der Goot, Alan Ramponi, Tommaso Caselli, Michele Cafagna, and Lorenzo De Mattei. 2020. Norm it! lexical normalization for Italian and its downstream effects for dependency parsing. In *Proceedings of the 12th Language Resources and Evaluation Conference*, pages 6272–6278, Marseille, France. European Language Resources Association.

Rob van der Goot, Alan Ramponi, Arkaitz Zubiaga, Barbara Plank, Benjamin Muller, Iñaki San Vicente Roncal, Nikola Ljubešić, Özlem Çetinoğlu, Rahmad Mahendra, Talha Çolakoğlu, Timothy Baldwin, Tommaso Caselli, and Wladimir Sidorenko. 2021a. MultiLexNorm: A shared task on multilingual lexical normalization. In *Proceedings of the 7th Workshop on Noisy User-generated Text (W-NUT 2021)*, Punta Cana, Dominican Republic. Association for Computational Linguistics.

Rob van der Goot, Ahmet Üstün, Alan Ramponi, Ibrahim Sharaf, and Barbara Plank. 2021b. Massive choice, ample tasks (MaChAmp): A toolkit for multi-task learning in NLP. In *Proceedings of the 16th Conference of the European Chapter of the Association for Computational Linguistics: System Demonstrations*, pages 176–197, Online. Association for Computational Linguistics.

Ashish Vaswani, Noam Shazeer, Niki Parmar, Jakob Uszkoreit, Llion Jones, Aidan N Gomez, Ł ukasz Kaiser, and Illia Polosukhin. 2017. Attention is all you need. In *Advances in Neural Information Processing Systems*, volume 30. Curran Associates, Inc.

Thomas Wolf, Lysandre Debut, Victor Sanh, Julien Chaumond, Clement Delangue, Anthony Moi, Pierric Cistac, Tim Rault, Remi Louf, Morgan Funtowicz, Joe Davison, Sam Shleifer, Patrick von Platen, Clara Ma, Yacine Jernite, Julien Plu, Canwen Xu, Teven Le Scao, Sylvain Gugger, Mariama Drame, Quentin Lhoest, and Alexander Rush. 2020. Transformers: State-of-the-art natural language processing. In *Proceedings of the 2020 Conference on Empirical Methods in Natural Language Processing: System Demonstrations*, pages 38–45, Online. Association for Computational Linguistics.

Wenhan Xiong, Jiawei Wu, Hong Wang, Vivek Kulkarni, Mo Yu, Shiyu Chang, Xiaoxiao Guo, and William Yang Wang. 2019. TWEETQA: A social media focused question answering dataset. In *Proceedings of the 57th Annual Meeting of the Association for Computational Linguistics*, pages 5020–5031, Florence, Italy. Association for Computational Linguistics.

Linting Xue, Aditya Barua, Noah Constant, Rami Al-Rfou, Sharan Narang, Mihir Kale, Adam Roberts, and Colin Raffel. 2021a. Byt5: Towards a token-free future with pre-trained byte-to-byte models.

Linting Xue, Noah Constant, Adam Roberts, Mihir Kale, Rami Al-Rfou, Aditya Siddhant, Aditya Barua, and Colin Raffel. 2021b. mT5: A massively multilingual pre-trained text-to-text transformer. In *Proceedings of the 2021 Conference of the North American Chapter of the Association for Computational Linguistics: Human Language Technologies*, pages 483–498, Online. Association for Computational Linguistics.

Daniel Zeman, Joakim Nivre, et al. 2021. Universal dependencies 2.8. LINDAT/CLARIAH-CZ digital library at the Institute of Formal and Applied Linguistics (ÚFAL), Faculty of Mathematics and Physics, Charles University.

MultiLexNorm: A Shared Task on Multilingual Lexical Normalization

Rob van der Goot[1], Alan Ramponi[2], Arkaitz Zubiaga[3], Barbara Plank[1], Benjamin Muller[4], Iñaki San Vicente Roncal[5], Nikola Ljubešić[6], Özlem Çetinoğlu[7], Rahmad Mahendra[8], Talha Çolakoğlu[9], Timothy Baldwin[10], Tommaso Caselli[11], Wladimir Sidorenko

[1]IT University of Copenhagen, [2]Fondazione Bruno Kessler, [3]Queen Mary University of London, [4]Inria Paris, [5]Elhuyar Foundation, [6]Jožef Stefan Institute, [7]University of Stuttgart, [8]Universitas Indonesia, [9]Huawei, [10]The University of Melbourne, [11]University of Groningen

robv@itu.dk

Abstract

Lexical normalization is the task of transforming an utterance into its standardized form. This task is beneficial for downstream analysis, as it provides a way to harmonize (often spontaneous) linguistic variation. Such variation is typical for social media on which information is shared in a multitude of ways, including diverse languages and code-switching. Since the seminal work of Han and Baldwin (2011) a decade ago, lexical normalization has attracted attention in English and multiple other languages. However, there exists a lack of a common benchmark for comparison of systems across languages with a homogeneous data and evaluation setup. The MULTILEXNORM shared task sets out to fill this gap. We provide the largest publicly available multilingual lexical normalization benchmark including 12 language variants. We propose a homogenized evaluation setup with both intrinsic and extrinsic evaluation. As extrinsic evaluation, we use dependency parsing and part-of-speech tagging with adapted evaluation metrics (a-LAS, a-UAS, and a-POS) to account for alignment discrepancies. The shared task hosted at W-NUT 2021 attracted 9 participants and 18 submissions. The results show that neural normalization systems outperform the previous state-of-the-art system by a large margin. Downstream parsing and part-of-speech tagging performance is positively affected but to varying degrees, with improvements of up to 1.72 a-LAS, 0.85 a-UAS, and 1.54 a-POS for the winning system.[1]

1 Introduction

The rise of social media has led to a tremendous increase in the amount of data shared over the Internet. But because of its spontaneous nature, the data naturally abounds with numerous language variations, both intended (e.g., slang, abbreviations, non-standard capitalization) and unintended ones (e.g., typos). This, in turn, poses considerable problems for existing natural language processing (NLP) tools (e.g., Baldwin et al., 2013; Eisenstein, 2013), most of which were originally designed to process canonical texts. One way to improve the performance of such systems is to *normalize* text and thus make it more similar to the data the NLP systems were initially designed for (and trained on).

At this point, to avoid confusion with other existing notions of text normalization (cf. Sproat et al., 2001; Aw et al., 2006), we should state that, throughout this paper, we will only deal with *lexical normalization*—a task which Han and Baldwin (2011) define as "a mapping from 'ill-formed' out-of-vocabulary (OOV) lexical items to their standard lexical forms." We focus only on social media data, as opposed to historical data (Tang et al., 2018; Bollmann, 2019) or medical data (Dirkson et al., 2019), and extend the scope of this task further to the cases where wrong in-vocabulary (IV) tokens can be normalized to (i.e., replaced with) their in-vocabulary counterparts, arriving at the following formulation:

Definition - Lexical Normalization

Lexical normalization is the task of transforming an utterance into its standard form, word by word, including both one-to-many (1-n) and many-to-one (n-1) replacements.

It should be noted that deletions and insertions of complete words are thus beyond the scope of the task as defined here.

Although lexical normalization potentially removes social signals (Nguyen et al., 2021), it has also been shown to boost many downstream NLP tasks, including named entity recognition (Schulz et al., 2016; Plank et al., 2020), POS tagging (Derczynski et al., 2013; Schulz et al., 2016; van der

[1]Data and submissions are available at https://bitbucket.org/robvanderg/multilexnorm/

Proceedings of the 2021 EMNLP Workshop W-NUT: The Seventh Workshop on Noisy User-generated Text, pages 493–509
November 11, 2021. ©2021 Association for Computational Linguistics

Lang.	Language name	Normalization example
DA	Danish	De skarpe lamper gjorde destromindre ek bedre . De skarpe lamper gjorde destro mindre ikke bedre .
DE	German	ogäj isch hätts auch dwiddern könn Okay ich hätte es auch twittern können
EN	English	u hve to let ppl decide what dey want to do you have to let people decide what they want to do
ES	Spanish	@username cuuxamee sii peroo veen yaa eem @username escúchame sí pero ven ya eh
HR	Croatian	svi frendovi mi nešto rade , veceras san osta sam . svi frendovi mi nešto rade , večeras sam ostao sam .
ID-EN	Indonesian-English	pdhal not fully bcs those ppl jg sih . padahal not fully because those people juga sih .
IT	Italian	a Roma è cosí primavera che sembra gia giov a Roma è così primavera che sembra già giovedì
NL	Dutch	Kga me wss trg rolle vant lachn Ik ga me waarschijnlijk terug rollen van het lachen
SL	Slovenian	jst bi tud najdu kovanec vreden veliko denarja . jaz bi tudi našel kovanec vreden veliko denarja .
SR	Serbian	komunalci kace pocne kaznjavanje ? komunalci kad počne kažnjavanje ?
TR	Turkish	He o dediyin suala cvb verdim He o dediğin suale cevap verdim
TR-DE	Turkish-German	@username Yerimm senii , damkee schatzymm :-* @username Yerim seni , danke Schatzym :-*

Table 1: Examples from MULTILEXNORM. One utterance per language: original sentence on top, and normalization on the bottom.

Goot et al., 2017; Zupan et al., 2019), dependency and constituency parsing (Baldwin and Li, 2015; van der Goot et al., 2020; van der Goot and van Noord, 2017), sentiment analysis (Van Hee et al., 2017; Sidarenka, 2019, pp. 79, 122), and machine translation (Bhat et al., 2018). However, existing work on this topic is largely fragmented, focused mostly on one language, relies on different evaluation metrics, or makes different assumptions regarding the items to be normalized (cf. Yang and Eisenstein, 2013; Li and Liu, 2015; Xu et al., 2015). All this makes it extremely hard to compare existing and new normalization systems.

In an attempt to achieve greater reproducibility, linguistic variety, and a standardized benchmark for *multilingual lexical normalization*, we introduce the MULTILEXNORM shared task. The benchmark for this task comprises datasets for 12 language(-pair)s: Danish, German, English, Spanish, Croatian, Indonesian-English, Italian, Dutch, Slovenian, Serbian, Turkish, and Turkish-German. All datasets contain sentences from popular social media platforms, which have been annotated for lexical normalization (i.e., with word-level replacements). Following our definition, we considered both intended and unintended spelling deviations, and included all categories defined by van der Goot et al. (2018) except phrasal abbreviations. We assume gold tokenization in all datasets, and leave automation of the tokenization step for future work. Examples of annotated sentences for all languages are shown in Table 1.

Furthermore, to precisely measure the effect of text normalization on downstream tasks, we also included a dedicated track on *extrinsic evaluation*, in which we estimate how much the results of dependency parsing and part-of-speech (POS) tagging change after normalization. This track includes corpora for English, German, Italian, and Turkish, annotated with Universal Dependencies (Nivre et al., 2020).

More details about intrinsic and extrinsic datasets are given in §2 and §5, respectively. We also provide an overview of baselines and submitted systems in §3, discussing their intrinsic and extrinsic results in §4 and §5, respectively. The paper concludes with a summary of the findings of the shared task and suggestions for future work.

Language and citation	Kappa	Same cand.
EN (Baldwin et al., 2015)	0.89	
EN (Pennell and Liu, 2014)	0.59	98.73
IT (van der Goot et al., 2020)	0.64–0.79	73.91–77.78
NL (Schuur, 2020)	0.77–0.91	
DA (Plank et al., 2020)	0.89	96.3

Table 2: Agreement scores for lexical normalization found in the literature. The "Kappa" column reports Fleiss/Cohen's kappa (rounded to 2 decimals) on the decision of whether a word needs to be normalized or not, whereas "Same cand." reports the raw percentage of times annotators agreed. Ranges in Italian include raw annotation and after some automatic fixes; for Dutch they are between different domains.

2 Data

Our selection of languages is purely based on dataset availability. We are aware that the benchmark contains mostly Indo-European languages, and encourage additions to this benchmark in the future to increase language variety.[2] We kindly request future work to cite the original data sources, and provide the bib-files on our website.

Lexical normalization is a subjective task, as in many cases multiple interpretations and annotations are plausible. Furthermore, annotators may disagree on what is "normal", and whether normalization is necessary for certain words. We have summarized all results on studies on inter-annotator agreement that we are aware of in Table 2.

Two types of agreement are reported in the literature: (1) Cohen's/Fleiss' kappa score on the choice of whether a word is in need of normalization; and (2) "Same candidate", which reports the percentage of times annotators agreed on the normalization replacement for words normalized by multiple annotators. Results in Table 2 show that the choice of whether to normalize has a medium to high kappa score, whereas the choice of the correct normalization candidate is generally high. An exception is Italian, which has a relatively low score due to some annotators not correcting capitalization (van der Goot et al., 2020).

Besides converting all data to the same format, we have attempted to converge annotation styles whenever possible. In particular, we applied the same normalization annotation in these cases:

- Interjections and punctuation are kept untouched, *hahaha* $\mapsto$ *hahaha* and not *haha*;
- Usernames, hashtags and URLs are kept untouched; if data is anonymized, usernames become @username;
- We kept capitalization correction where available. Unfortunately we did not have the budget to include capitalization correction in all datasets;
- We removed data that is not in the target language (mostly Frisian and Afrikaans in the Dutch data, and Indonesian and Dutch tweets in the German dataset);
- We fixed some tokenization issues in multiple languages.

With regard to data availability and composition, we note that some of the datasets were published before the shared task was held.[3] All datasets contain data from the Twitter platform; the Dutch corpus also includes forum and SMS data, and the Danish dataset includes texts from Arto, a Danish social media network. More details about the data collection for each dataset can be found in the dataset statement (Appendix A).

An overview of our datasets is shown in Table 3. It is clear that different annotation guidelines have been used, where some included "one-to-many" and "many-to-one" replacements, and correction of capitalization, where others did not. Furthermore, the amount of necessary normalization is very different, and the training splits of the datasets vary greatly, with the largest being almost 10 times larger than the smallest. It should also be noted that only 7 languages (DE, EN, HR, ID-EN, NL, SL, SR) have a dedicated development test, due to data availability.

3 Methods

3.1 Baselines

The organizers provided two naive baselines (i.e., LAI and MFR, as introduced below), and an "informed" baseline, based on training the previous state-of-the-art MoNoise over the respective datasets (van der Goot, 2019a).

[2] Please contact the first author of this paper if you are interested in adding a language. If more languages are added, future versions of MULTILEXNORM will be released via the repository.

[3] We removed them where possible. Specifically, 5 out of 12 languages still had their test data online when the competition started. However, they were not always easy to find, were in a different format, or the annotation differed from that used in the shared task.

Lang	Words	Sents	1-n	n-1	Change	Caps	Source
DA	16,448	719	0.29	0.04	9.25	+	(Plank et al., 2020)
DE	15,006	1,628	1.53	0.19	17.96	+	(Sidarenka et al., 2013)
EN	35,216	2,360	0.87	0.04	6.90	–	(Baldwin et al., 2015)
ES	7,189	568	0.00	0.00	7.69	–	(Alegria et al., 2013)
HR	54,416	4,760	0.01	0.00	8.89	–	(Ljubešić et al., 2017a)
ID-EN	13,949	495	1.43	0.19	12.16	–	(Barik et al., 2019)
IT	12,645	593	0.28	0.00	7.32	+	(van der Goot et al., 2020)
NL	12,381	907	5.98	0.06	28.29	+	(Schuur, 2020)
SL	44,944	4,670	0.00	0.00	15.62	–	(Erjavec et al., 2017)
SR	56,823	4,138	0.00	0.00	7.65	–	(Ljubešić et al., 2017b)
TR	6,443	570	3.00	1.69	37.02	+	(Çolakoğlu et al., 2019)
TR-DE	12,773	800	2.51	0.81	24.14	+	(van der Goot and Çetinoğlu, 2021)

Table 3: Some statistics on the 12 language(-pair)s within the MULTILEXNORM benchmark. The "1-n" column indicates the percentage of words which are split into multiple words (one-to-many), "n-1" indicates the proportion of words that are merged with other words as part of normalization (many-to-one), and "Change" indicates the percentage of words that are normalized. "Caps" indicates whether standard capitalization is included in the annotation; for datasets without annotation of capitalization, everything is lowercased.

LAI Leave-As-Is baseline, which simply returns the input word.

MFR Most-Frequent-Replacement baseline. It stores for every input word (unigram) its most frequent replacement in the training data. Then at run-time it simply replaces each word with its most common replacement. If a word is not seen before, it is returned as-is.

MoNoise This is based on a two-step approach. It first generates candidates based on: word embeddings, the Aspell spell checker,[4] replacements found in the training data, and some heuristics. In the second step, features from the generation step are combined with additional features (including character n-gram probabilities) and used to train a random forest classifier, which predicts the probability that a candidate is the correct candidate. The only tuned component is the generation of Aspell candidates, where the `--bad-spellers` options can be used to generate more candidates. For most languages this resulted in a slower but more effective model (except for HR, ID-EN, and SL). For the code-switched language pairs, the code-switched version of MoNoise was used (van der Goot and Çetinoğlu, 2021). To retrain MoNoise, new raw data was collected to base its n-gram probabilities and word embeddings on. We downloaded Twitter data of 2012–2020 from archive.org, filtered it with the fastText language classifier (Joulin et al., 2017a), and used the most recent Wikidump for each language.[5]

3.2 Submissions

The shared task ran in mid-2021, and attracted 9 participants with 18 submissions. We include the full list of submissions, but no system description or paper was received from **maet**, **team**, **thunderml**, or **learnML**, so the details of these methods are not clear. Submissions marked with an asterisk ("*") involve one or more of the shared task organizers.

ÚFAL (Samuel and Straka, 2021)

The system is based on ByT5 (Xue et al., 2021), and is a word-by-word normalization model. In order for the model to be as close to the original pre-training task as possible, each input word is normalized independently: it is enclosed in an opening and ending tag, over which ByT5 is run to produce the normalization.

The authors fine-tune ByT5 in two steps, first on synthetic data and then on the MULTILEXNORM data. To obtain synthetic data, they use Wikipedia as target data, and create unnormalized input through character edits, word edits, and dictionary replacements trained from the MULTILEXNORM data. During the final fine-tuning, they either: (a) use only the MULTILEXNORM data; or (b) com-

[4] `http://aspell.net/`

[5] Of 01-08-2021. Available at `https://robvanderg.github.io/blog/twit_embeds.htm`

bine the MULTILEXNORM with the synthetic data. They submitted two systems, a single model for every treebank and an ensemble of 4 models for every treebank. Both adapting the input to fit the pre-training step and the use synthetic data proved to be very beneficial for the system.

HEL-LJU* (Scherrer and Ljubešić, 2021)
The system is based on a BERT (Devlin et al., 2019) token classification preprocessing step, where for each token the type of the necessary transformation is predicted (none, uppercase, lowercase, titlecase, modify), and a character-level statistical machine translation (SMT) model is used to normalize accordingly. For some languages, depending on the results on the development data, the training data was extended by back-translating OpenSubtitles data. The paper evaluates a range of MT systems and ablations, and shows that a character-level SMT model is highly competitive.

TrinkaAI (Kubal and Nagvenkar, 2021)
The proposed model is based on a sequence labeling approach, where the input tokens are unnormalized and the target tokens are normalized. To reduce the target labels and make predictions faster, classes are based on those tokens for which normalization is required, and tokens which do not need to be normalized are labelled with a single target token. This sequence labeling model is fine-tuned on a pre-trained multilingual model encompassing all languages in the shared task. Further, a post-processing layer concerning word-alignment is applied, which further improved performance. This sequence-labeling approach ranked 6th out of 21 models, and scored highest among all competitors for the Spanish Language.

BLUE (Bucur et al., 2021)
The team tackled the task of lexical normalization as a neural machine translation problem, using the MBart-50 (Tang et al., 2020) multilingual many-to-many model. They fine-tuned the model for all the available languages, and used a MFR baseline for Danish and Serbian. They opted for a sentence-level approach as opposed to a word-level approach, using simple linear sum assignment based on Levenshtein distance to align the normalized words with the raw words.

CL-MoNoise* (van der Goot, 2021)
This is the same method as MoNoise, but it is deployed cross-lingually: it is trained on the source language, including candidate generation (Aspell, word embeddings, n-gram probabilities), then at prediction time, it is applied to the raw data in the target language. The best source language to transfer from is chosen based on empirical results on the training data.

MaChAmp* (van der Goot, 2021)
The team of CL-MoNoise also used a sequence labeling approach, in learning (character) transformations of each original word to its normalization. Scores are low on datasets that include capitalization correction, as this is not properly included in the current transformation algorithm (everything is lower-cased beforehand). The method performed much better when based on XLM-R (Conneau et al., 2020) than mBERT. Potential improvements could be gained by exploiting the multi-task capabilities of MaChAmp (van der Goot et al., 2021).

4 Intrinsic Evaluation

4.1 Intrinsic Metric

A wide variety of evaluation metrics have been used to evaluate lexical normalization performance, including accuracy over OOV words, F1 score, BLEU, word error rate, and character error rate. We choose to use Error Reduction Rate (ERR) (van der Goot, 2019b) as our main metric. ERR is the word-level accuracy normalized for the percentage of words that are in need of normalization. To calculate ERR, we use the word-level accuracy, and the percentage of words that are not normalized in the annotation:

$$ERR = \frac{\%\text{accuracy} - \%\text{words\_not\_normed}}{100 - \%\text{words\_not\_normed}}$$

We choose to use ERR instead of word-level accuracy to be able to compare (and combine) scores across datasets, since different numbers of candidates are in need of normalization. An accuracy of 93% might be a very good score on one dataset, whereas on another dataset a normalization model which scores 93% might be completely useless. The ERR will normally have a value between 0% and 100%. A negative ERR indicates that the system normalizes more words wrongly than correctly. The Leave-As-Is baseline (Section 3), which simply returns the input words, will thus by definition score an ERR of 0.0. For a more in-depth discussion of evaluation metrics for normalization and ERR, we refer the reader to Section 5.1 of van der Goot (2019b).

Team	Avg.	DA	DE	EN	ES	HR	ID-EN	IT	NL	SL	SR	TR	TR-DE
ÚFAL-2	**67.3**	68.7	**66.2**	**75.6**	59.3	**67.7**	**67.2**	**47.5**	**63.6**	**80.1**	**74.6**	**68.6**	**68.6**
ÚFAL-1	66.2	**70.3**	65.7	73.8	55.9	67.3	66.2	42.6	62.7	79.9	73.6	**68.6**	68.2
HEL-LJU-2*	53.6	56.7	59.8	62.1	35.6	56.2	55.3	35.6	45.9	67.0	66.4	51.2	51.2
HEL-LJU-1*	51.8	56.7	58.0	60.8	33.7	51.8	53.3	35.6	44.0	66.0	60.3	49.5	52.0
MoNoise	49.0	51.3	47.0	74.4	45.5	52.6	59.8	21.8	49.5	61.9	59.6	28.2	36.7
TrinkaAI-2	43.8	45.9	47.3	66.0	**61.3**	41.3	56.4	15.8	45.7	59.5	44.5	15.5	25.8
TrinkaAI-1	43.6	45.9	47.3	64.5	**61.3**	41.3	56.4	15.8	45.7	59.5	44.5	15.5	25.8
thunderml-1	43.4	46.5	46.6	64.1	60.3	40.1	59.1	11.9	44.1	59.3	44.5	15.9	29.0
team-2	40.7	48.1	46.1	63.7	21.0	40.4	59.3	13.9	43.7	60.6	46.1	15.9	29.7
learnML-2	40.3	40.5	43.7	61.6	56.6	38.1	56.2	5.9	42.8	58.3	40.0	14.4	25.7
maet-1	40.1	48.1	46.1	63.9	21.0	40.4	59.3	5.9	43.7	60.6	46.1	15.9	29.7
MFR	38.4	49.7	32.1	64.9	25.6	36.5	61.2	16.8	37.7	56.7	42.6	14.5	22.1
thunderml-2	36.5	−4.4	46.0	63.5	21.6	41.0	58.4	12.9	45.0	60.4	46.9	17.4	29.3
team-1	36.5	−4.4	46.0	63.5	21.6	41.0	58.4	12.9	45.0	60.4	46.9	17.4	29.3
CL-MoNoise*	12.1	7.3	16.6	4.1	5.0	26.4	2.4	0.0	16.2	8.8	20.1	17.6	20.2
maet-2	7.3	2.2	4.3	21.7	0.0	9.9	19.2	0.0	2.1	18.4	8.1	0.8	1.2
learnML-1	7.3	2.2	4.3	21.7	0.0	9.9	19.2	0.0	2.1	18.4	8.1	0.8	1.2
BLUE-2	6.7	49.7	−1.9	26.8	−9.4	−10.1	−7.2	−31.7	−2.1	−1.0	42.6	10.0	15.0
BLUE-1	5.2	49.7	−1.9	26.8	−10.2	−9.9	−7.2	−31.7	−2.1	−1.1	42.6	1.0	6.6
LAI	0.0	0.0	0.0	0.0	0.0	0.0	0.0	0.0	0.0	0.0	0.0	0.0	0.0
MaChAmp*	−21.3	−88.9	−93.4	51.0	25.4	42.6	39.5	−312.9	1.5	56.8	39.4	−12.7	−3.4

Table 4: ERR on the test data (%). Negative values indicate that the system normalizes more words wrongly than correctly. Gray rows indicate baseline systems provided by the organizers. * Teams including an organizer.

The official winner of the shared task is the highest-scoring team (macro-averaged over all datasets/languages) with an open-source implementation.

4.2 Results: Intrinsic Evaluation

The main results of the shared task are shown in Table 4. All submissions except MaChAmp beat the LAI baseline, and most of them beat the MFR baseline, which turned out to be a strong baseline.

The overall winner of the shared task was ÚFAL-2, which beat the second-best team by a staggering 13 points. Recall that this method is based on ByT5, a transformer-based encoder–decoder byte-level system. Of particular note is that while recent neural approaches (Lourentzou et al., 2019; Muller et al., 2019) had not been clearly superior to the baseline MoNoise on English, ÚFAL-2 surpassed the baseline method by an appreciable margin.

The second-best team was HEL-LJU, who improved over MoNoise by more than four points. The authors report that character-level NMT provided lower results than their SMT approach, even with backtranslation.

The remaining teams mostly used either token classification or encoder–decoder approaches.

The results of this shared task showed that for state-of-the-art results one needs: (1) pre-trained models; (2) an encoder–decoder architecture over bytes or characters; and (3) synthetic task-related data.

One thing in common for the datasets with lower results in Table 4 (e.g., ES, NL, TR, and TR-DE) is that they include annotation for capitalization. Unsurprisingly, smaller datasets also tend to result in lower scores in general.

5 Extrinsic Evaluation

We perform a main extrinsic evaluation of the impact of normalization on dependency parsing using Universal Dependency annotations (Nivre et al., 2020). See Section 5.2 for test set details. We used version 2.8 of all treebanks, and syntactically-split multiword tokens and empty nodes (ellipsis) are undone with ud-conversion-tools.[6] We trained MaChAmp (van der Goot et al., 2021) with default settings and XLM-R embeddings (Conneau et al., 2020). We use the largest canonical treebank of each of the respective languages as the source domain, and attempt to improve performance on the target domain by normalizing data

[6] https://github.com/bplank/ud-conversion-tools

first. In other words, we take the input text, use a normalization system to get the normalized version, and pass this to the parser as input. The parsers are not trained on social media data, to evaluate the impact of normalization on parsing in a domain-shift scenario. Because the normalized version should be closer to the canonical training data of the parser, performance is expected to improve compared to using the input directly. The training treebanks are UD_English-EWT (Silveira et al., 2014), UD_German-GSD (Brants et al., 2004), UD_Italian-ISDT (Bosco et al., 2014), and UD_Turkish-IMST (Sulubacak et al., 2016). For the extrinsic evaluation, we report the average over three runs with different random seeds (only the parser is retrained, not the normalization models).

5.1 Alignment-aware Parsing Metrics

Because our definition of the lexical normalization task includes the splitting and merging of tokens (namely "one-to-many" and "many-to-one" replacements, cf. Section 1), the standard evaluation for dependency parsing has to be adapted for our purposes. Specifically, we compute the token-level labeled attachment score (LAS) and unlabeled attachment score (UAS) after aligning predicted tokens to gold tokens. We refer to these alignment-aware metric variants as *aligned* LAS and UAS (i.e., *a*-LAS and *a*-UAS), respectively. Because "many-to-one" replacements are relatively rare, we cannot check when they are correct (normalization annotation is not available for most treebanks) and they are non-trivial to include in the aligned evaluation, and hence we decided to undo these in the system outputs, and use the original input instead. For the "one-to-many" replacements, we check whether one of the words in the split is connected correctly. All incorrect words in the 'many' are thus simply ignored. It should be noted that this can give an advantage to systems that split, and we thus suggest that this metric is always reported with the number of splits. Furthermore, we assume none of the teams made use of this shortcoming in the metric, as they were unaware of these details.

5.2 Test Sets and Metric

We employ *a*-LAS as the main metric for extrinsic evaluation, and also report *a*-UAS for the sake of completeness. Each system was tested on 7 dependency parsing treebanks consisting of posts from Twitter in 4 different languages:

- German (DE): TweeDe (Rehbein et al., 2019);
- English (EN): AAE (Blodgett et al., 2018), MoNoise (van der Goot and van Noord, 2018), and Tweebank2 (Liu et al., 2018);
- Italian (IT): PoSTWITA (Sanguinetti et al., 2018) and TWITTIRO (Cignarella et al., 2019);
- Turkish (TR): IWT151 (Pamay et al., 2015; Sulubacak and Eryiğit, 2018).

5.3 Results: Impact on Parsing

The main results (*a*-LAS) are reported in Table 5. Although most submissions outperform the LAI baseline, it becomes clear that lexical normalization is only a step towards closing the gap in performance on canonical data, as performance is still far from the average LAS on our training sets (79 LAS). This is confirmed by the scores of using the manually-annotated (gold) normalization.[7] The best performing model scores 1.72 LAS points higher than the LAI baseline. Compared to normalization performance (Table 4), the baselines (LAI and MFR) rank highly, especially for tr-iwt151 and en-tweebank2, which is probably because they have less risk of over-normalization, and some of the treebanks might need only very little normalization (there is also an abundance of canonical data to be found on Twitter). The largest gains compared to the LAI baseline are obtained on the en-monoise treebank, probably because this treebank contains data filtered to contain data in need of normalization. In the gold-standard annotations, 31.33% of the words are normalized, compared to 1.04% for en-tweebank2.

The full *a*-UAS scores can be found in the appendix (Table 6). In general, performance is approximately 7–10 points higher than LAS (absolute), and differences between teams are smaller. Interestingly, the ranking is slightly different there, with HEL-LJU and MFR ranking higher, and CL-MoNoise ranking lower. Overall, the results confirm that the best normalization systems (by ÚFAL and HEL-LJU) also result in the highest observed parsing improvements on these social media treebank test sets. Once again, these two teams outperform the previous state-of-the-art system (i.e., MoNoise).

[7]Note that MoNoise and Tweebank2 are the only treebanks where a normalization layer is fully annotated, so we report Gold results for these treebanks only.

Treebank	Avg.	de-tweede	en-aae	en-monoise	en-tweebank2	it-postwita	it-twittiro	tr-iwt151
ÚFAL-2	**64.2** 37	**73.6** 5	**62.7** 53	**58.6** 33	59.1 66	**68.3** 13	72.2 5	54.7 90
ÚFAL-1	64.0 37	**73.6** 3	62.2 50	57.9 33	59.0 65	**68.3** 14	72.2 5	54.8 95
HEL-LJU-2*	63.7 10	73.5 3	60.6 20	56.3 4	60.3 15	68.1 3	72.3 0	55.0 28
HEL-LJU-1*	63.7 14	73.5 3	60.5 18	56.3 9	60.3 18	68.2 3	**72.5** 0	54.9 48
MoNoise	63.4 21	73.2 5	62.3 40	56.8 18	58.9 46	67.6 3	70.7 0	54.6 35
MFR	63.3 16	72.9 5	60.3 32	56.7 15	**60.3** 37	67.3 3	70.7 0	54.9 25
TrinkaAI-2	63.1 33	72.9 7	60.2 40	56.6 19	59.9 39	67.0 7	71.1 0	54.2 119
TrinkaAI-1	63.1 33	72.9 7	60.2 40	56.6 19	59.9 39	67.0 7	71.1 0	54.2 119
maet-1	63.1 27	72.8 3	59.4 40	56.6 24	59.8 44	67.4 10	71.1 0	54.5 74
team-2	63.0 27	72.8 3	59.4 40	56.6 24	59.8 44	67.2 4	70.9 3	54.5 74
thunderml-2	63.0 33	72.7 3	59.6 42	56.7 28	59.3 44	67.3 4	71.4 1	54.2 112
team-1	63.0 33	72.7 3	59.6 42	56.7 28	59.2 44	67.3 4	71.4 1	54.2 112
thunderml-1	63.0 34	72.5 6	59.3 49	56.7 24	59.9 46	67.1 5	71.0 0	54.1 112
learnML-2	62.9 30	72.3 8	59.0 44	56.2 31	60.0 45	67.0 6	71.2 0	54.5 79
CL-MoNoise*	62.7 24	72.7 0	60.9 0	55.3 0	58.5 0	66.5 99	70.1 50	55.0 20
BLUE-2	62.5 0	72.6 0	59.6 0	54.2 0	59.8 0	66.7 0	70.0 0	54.8 0
BLUE-1	62.5 0	72.6 0	59.6 0	54.2 0	59.8 0	66.7 0	70.0 0	54.8 0
LAI	62.5 0	72.7 0	59.2 0	53.7 0	60.0 0	66.5 0	70.1 0	**55.0** 0
maet-2	62.2 0	72.7 0	58.5 0	52.9 0	60.0 0	66.5 0	70.0 0	55.0 0
learnML-1	62.2 0	72.7 0	58.5 0	52.9 0	60.0 0	66.5 0	70.0 0	55.0 0
MaChAmp*	61.9 43	71.3 7	60.8 37	54.6 43	58.0 52	64.7 2	69.8 0	54.1 162
Gold	—	—	—	60.8	60.4	—	—	—

Table 5: *a*-LAS scores (%) and the number of splits (in smaller font) for each dataset. Gray rows indicate baseline systems provided by the organizers. * Teams including an organizer. The final row ("Gold") indicates performance with gold-standard normalization.

5.4 Results: Impact on POS tagging

Additionally, we calculated the POS accuracies using the same heuristic as described in Section 5.1 (i.e., *a*-POS), and present full results in the appendix (Table 7). Again, we see some changes in the ranking of the teams, and performance improvements are slightly more moderate compared to *a*-LAS. The baselines score highest on en-tweebank2 (MFR) and tr-iwt151 (LAI), and the highest gains are again obtained on the en-monoise treebank.

6 Conclusions

With MULTILEXNORM, we have developed a multilingual benchmark for lexical normalization consisting of previously-created datasets spanning 12 language variants. We proposed a standard evaluation metric, and both intrinsic and extrinsic evaluation via dependency parsing and POS tagging. We hosted a shared task with this new benchmark, which enabled comparison of performance of 21 models (18 submissions by participants, and 3 in-house baselines). The results of the shared task show that the previous state of the art on lexical normalization is outperformed by a large margin. The extrinsic evaluation on dependency parsing and POS tagging shows that lexical normalization is beneficial (with improvements in *a*-LAS and *a*-UAS of up to +1.72 and +0.85, and improvements in *a*-POS of up to +1.54, respectively), but there is still a performance gap compared to the performance levels observed on canonical data. We hope that the proposed benchmark will lead to more research in multilingual normalization, and more transparent and fairer comparisons. All submissions, evaluation scripts, and baseline models are available in the shared task repository.

Acknowledgements

B.M. was funded by the French Research Agency via the ANR ParSiTi project (ANR-16-CE33-0021).

References

Inaki Alegria, Nora Aranberri, Víctor Fresno, Pablo Gamallo, Lluis Padró, Inaki San Vicente, Jordi Turmo, and Arkaitz Zubiaga. 2013. Introducción a la tarea compartida Tweet-Norm 2013: Normalización léxica de tuits en Español. In *Tweet-Norm@ SEPLN*, pages 1–9.

AiTi Aw, Min Zhang, Juan Xiao, and Jian Su. 2006. A phrase-based statistical model for SMS text normalization. In *Proceedings of the COLING/ACL 2006 Main Conference Poster Sessions*, pages 33–40, Sydney, Australia. Association for Computational Linguistics.

Timothy Baldwin, Paul Cook, Marco Lui, Andrew MacKinlay, and Li Wang. 2013. How noisy social media text, how diffrnt social media sources? In *Proceedings of the Sixth International Joint Conference on Natural Language Processing*, pages 356–364, Nagoya, Japan. Asian Federation of Natural Language Processing.

Timothy Baldwin, Marie Catherine de Marneffe, Bo Han, Young-Bum Kim, Alan Ritter, and Wei Xu. 2015. Shared tasks of the 2015 workshop on noisy user-generated text: Twitter lexical normalization and named entity recognition. In *Proceedings of the Workshop on Noisy User-generated Text*, pages 126–135, Beijing, China. Association for Computational Linguistics.

Tyler Baldwin and Yunyao Li. 2015. An in-depth analysis of the effect of text normalization in social media. In *Proceedings of the 2015 Conference of the North American Chapter of the Association for Computational Linguistics: Human Language Technologies*, pages 420–429, Denver, Colorado. Association for Computational Linguistics.

Francesco Barbieri, Valerio Basile, Danilo Croce, Malvina Nissim, Nicole Novielli, and Viviana Patti. 2016. Overview of the evalita 2016 sentiment polarity classification task. In *Proceedings of Evalita 2016*.

Anab Maulana Barik, Rahmad Mahendra, and Mirna Adriani. 2019. Normalization of Indonesian-English code-mixed Twitter data. In *Proceedings of the 5th Workshop on Noisy User-generated Text (W-NUT 2019)*, pages 417–424, Hong Kong, China. Association for Computational Linguistics.

Emily M. Bender and Batya Friedman. 2018. Data statements for natural language processing: Toward mitigating system bias and enabling better science. *Transactions of the Association for Computational Linguistics*, 6:587–604.

Irshad Bhat, Riyaz A. Bhat, Manish Shrivastava, and Dipti Sharma. 2018. Universal Dependency parsing for Hindi-English code-switching. In *Proceedings of the 2018 Conference of the North American Chapter of the Association for Computational Linguistics: Human Language Technologies, Volume 1 (Long Papers)*, pages 987–998, New Orleans, Louisiana. Association for Computational Linguistics.

Su Lin Blodgett, Johnny Wei, and Brendan O'Connor. 2018. Twitter Universal Dependency parsing for African-American and mainstream American English. In *Proceedings of the 56th Annual Meeting of the Association for Computational Linguistics (Volume 1: Long Papers)*, pages 1415–1425, Melbourne, Australia. Association for Computational Linguistics.

Marcel Bollmann. 2019. A large-scale comparison of historical text normalization systems. In *Proceedings of the 2019 Conference of the North American Chapter of the Association for Computational Linguistics: Human Language Technologies, Volume 1 (Long and Short Papers)*, pages 3885–3898, Minneapolis, Minnesota. Association for Computational Linguistics.

Cristina Bosco, Felice Dell'Orletta, Simonetta Montemagni, Manuela Sanguinetti, and Maria Simi. 2014. The EVALITA 2014 dependency parsing task. In *EVALITA 2014 Evaluation of NLP and Speech Tools for Italian*, pages 1–8. Pisa University Press.

Cristina Bosco, Viviana Patti, and Andrea Bolioli. 2013. Developing corpora for sentiment analysis: The case of irony and Senti-TUT. *IEEE Intelligent Systems*, 28(2):55–63.

Sabine Brants, Stefanie Dipper, Peter Eisenberg, Silvia Hansen-Schirra, Esther König, Wolfgang Lezius, Christian Rohrer, George Smith, and Hans Uszkoreit. 2004. TIGER: Linguistic interpretation of a german corpus. *Research on language and computation*, 2(4):597–620.

Ana-Maria Bucur, Adrian Cosma, and Liviu P. Dinu. 2021. Sequence-to-sequence lexical normalization with multilingual transformers. In *Proceedings of the 7th Workshop on Noisy User-generated Text (W-NUT 2021)*, Punta Cana, Dominican Republic. Association for Computational Linguistics.

Özlem Çetinoğlu. 2016. A Turkish-German code-switching corpus. In *Proceedings of the Tenth International Conference on Language Resources and Evaluation (LREC'16)*, pages 4215–4220, Portorož, Slovenia. European Language Resources Association (ELRA).

Alessandra Teresa Cignarella, Cristina Bosco, and Paolo Rosso. 2019. Presenting TWITTIRÒ-UD: An Italian Twitter treebank in Universal Dependencies. In *Proceedings of the Fifth International Conference on Dependency Linguistics (Depling, SyntaxFest 2019)*, pages 190–197, Paris, France. Association for Computational Linguistics.

Talha Çolakoğlu, Umut Sulubacak, and Ahmet Cüneyd Tantuğ. 2019. Normalizing non-canonical Turkish texts using machine translation approaches. In *Proceedings of the 57th Annual Meeting of the Association for Computational Linguistics: Student Research Workshop*, pages 267–272, Florence, Italy. Association for Computational Linguistics.

Alexis Conneau, Kartikay Khandelwal, Naman Goyal, Vishrav Chaudhary, Guillaume Wenzek, Francisco Guzmán, Edouard Grave, Myle Ott, Luke Zettlemoyer, and Veselin Stoyanov. 2020. Unsupervised cross-lingual representation learning at scale. In

Proceedings of the 58th Annual Meeting of the Association for Computational Linguistics, pages 8440–8451, Online. Association for Computational Linguistics.

Leon Derczynski, Alan Ritter, Sam Clark, and Kalina Bontcheva. 2013. Twitter part-of-speech tagging for all: Overcoming sparse and noisy data. In *Proceedings of the International Conference Recent Advances in Natural Language Processing RANLP 2013*, pages 198–206, Hissar, Bulgaria. INCOMA Ltd. Shoumen, BULGARIA.

Jacob Devlin, Ming-Wei Chang, Kenton Lee, and Kristina Toutanova. 2019. BERT: Pre-training of deep bidirectional transformers for language understanding. In *Proceedings of the 2019 Conference of the North American Chapter of the Association for Computational Linguistics: Human Language Technologies, Volume 1 (Long and Short Papers)*, pages 4171–4186, Minneapolis, Minnesota. Association for Computational Linguistics.

Anne Dirkson, Suzan Verberne, and Wessel Kraaij. 2019. Lexical normalization of user-generated medical text. In *Proceedings of the Fourth Social Media Mining for Health Applications (#SMM4H) Workshop & Shared Task*, pages 11–20, Florence, Italy. Association for Computational Linguistics.

Jacob Eisenstein. 2013. What to do about bad language on the internet. In *Proceedings of the 2013 Conference of the North American Chapter of the Association for Computational Linguistics: Human Language Technologies*, pages 359–369, Atlanta, Georgia. Association for Computational Linguistics.

Tomaž Erjavec, Darja Fišer, Jaka Čibej, Špela Arhar Holdt, Nikola Ljubešić, and Katja Zupan. 2017. CMC training corpus Janes-Tag 2.0. Slovenian language resource repository CLARIN.SI.

Bo Han and Timothy Baldwin. 2011. Lexical normalisation of short text messages: Makn sens a #twitter. In *Proceedings of the 49th Annual Meeting of the Association for Computational Linguistics: Human Language Technologies*, pages 368–378, Portland, Oregon, USA. Association for Computational Linguistics.

Armand Joulin, Edouard Grave, Piotr Bojanowski, and Tomas Mikolov. 2017a. Bag of tricks for efficient text classification. In *Proceedings of the 15th Conference of the European Chapter of the Association for Computational Linguistics: Volume 2, Short Papers*, pages 427–431, Valencia, Spain. Association for Computational Linguistics.

Armand Joulin, Edouard Grave, Piotr Bojanowski, and Tomas Mikolov. 2017b. Bag of tricks for efficient text classification. In *Proceedings of the 15th Conference of the European Chapter of the Association for Computational Linguistics: Volume 2, Short Papers*, pages 427–431, Valencia, Spain. Association for Computational Linguistics.

Divesh Kubal and Apurva Nagvenkar. 2021. Multilingual sequence labeling approach to solve lexical normalization. In *Proceedings of the 7th Workshop on Noisy User-generated Text (W-NUT 2021)*, Punta Cana, Dominican Republic. Association for Computational Linguistics.

Chen Li and Yang Liu. 2015. Joint pos tagging and text normalization for informal text. In *Twenty-Fourth International Joint Conference on Artificial Intelligence*.

Yijia Liu, Yi Zhu, Wanxiang Che, Bing Qin, Nathan Schneider, and Noah A. Smith. 2018. Parsing tweets into Universal Dependencies. In *Proceedings of the 2018 Conference of the North American Chapter of the Association for Computational Linguistics: Human Language Technologies, Volume 1 (Long Papers)*, pages 965–975, New Orleans, Louisiana. Association for Computational Linguistics.

Nikola Ljubešić, Tomaž Erjavec, Maja Miličević, and Tanja Samardžić. 2017a. Croatian Twitter training corpus ReLDI-NormTagNER-hr 2.0. Slovenian language resource repository CLARIN.SI.

Nikola Ljubešić, Tomaž Erjavec, Maja Miličević, and Tanja Samardžić. 2017b. Serbian Twitter training corpus ReLDI-NormTagNER-sr 2.0. Slovenian language resource repository CLARIN.SI.

Nikola Ljubešić, Darja Fišer, and Tomaž Erjavec. 2014. TweetCaT: a tool for building Twitter corpora of smaller languages. In *Proceedings of the Ninth International Conference on Language Resources and Evaluation (LREC'14)*, pages 2279–2283, Reykjavik, Iceland. European Language Resources Association (ELRA).

Nikola Ljubešić, Darja Fišer, Tomaž Erjavec, Jaka Čibej, Dafne Marko, Senja Pollak, and Iza Škrjanec. 2015. Predicting the level of text standardness in user-generated content. In *Proceedings of the International Conference Recent Advances in Natural Language Processing*, pages 371–378, Hissar, Bulgaria. INCOMA Ltd. Shoumen, BULGARIA.

Nikola Ljubešić and Denis Kranjčić. 2015. Discriminating between closely related languages on twitter. *Informatica*, 39(1):1.

Ismini Lourentzou, Kabir Manghnani, and ChengXiang Zhai. 2019. Adapting sequence to sequence models for text normalization in social media. In *Proceedings of the International AAAI Conference on Web and Social Media*, volume 13, pages 335–345.

Marco Lui and Timothy Baldwin. 2012. langid.py: An off-the-shelf language identification tool. In *Proceedings of the ACL 2012 System Demonstrations*, pages 25–30, Jeju Island, Korea. Association for Computational Linguistics.

Benjamin Muller, Benoit Sagot, and Djamé Seddah. 2019. Enhancing BERT for lexical normalization. In *Proceedings of the 5th Workshop on Noisy User-generated Text (W-NUT 2019)*, pages 297–306, Hong Kong, China. Association for Computational Linguistics.

Dong Nguyen, Laura Rosseel, and Jack Grieve. 2021. On learning and representing social meaning in NLP: a sociolinguistic perspective. In *Proceedings of the 2021 Conference of the North American Chapter of the Association for Computational Linguistics: Human Language Technologies*, pages 603–612, Online. Association for Computational Linguistics.

Joakim Nivre, Marie-Catherine de Marneffe, Filip Ginter, Jan Hajič, Christopher D. Manning, Sampo Pyysalo, Sebastian Schuster, Francis Tyers, and Daniel Zeman. 2020. Universal Dependencies v2: An evergrowing multilingual treebank collection. In *Proceedings of the 12th Language Resources and Evaluation Conference*, pages 4034–4043, Marseille, France. European Language Resources Association.

Kemal Oflazer. 1994. Two-level description of Turkish morphology. *Literary and Linguistic Computing*, 9(2):137–148.

NHJ Oostdijk, Martin Reynaert, Veronique Hoste, H Heuvel, O De Clercq, and EP Sanders. 2014. Sonar nieuw media corpus.

Tuğba Pamay, Umut Sulubacak, Dilara Torunoğlu-Selamet, and Gülşen Eryiğit. 2015. The annotation process of the ITU web treebank. In *Proceedings of The 9th Linguistic Annotation Workshop*, pages 95–101, Denver, Colorado, USA. Association for Computational Linguistics.

Deana L. Pennell and Yang Liu. 2014. Normalization of informal text. *Computer Speech & Language*, 28(1):256–277.

Barbara Plank, Kristian Nørgaard Jensen, and Rob van der Goot. 2020. DaN+: Danish nested named entities and lexical normalization. In *Proceedings of the 28th International Conference on Computational Linguistics*, pages 6649–6662, Barcelona, Spain (Online). International Committee on Computational Linguistics.

Ines Rehbein, Josef Ruppenhofer, and Bich-Ngoc Do. 2019. tweeDe – a Universal Dependencies treebank for German tweets. In *Proceedings of the 18th International Workshop on Treebanks and Linguistic Theories (TLT, SyntaxFest 2019)*, pages 100–108, Paris, France. Association for Computational Linguistics.

David Samuel and Milan Straka. 2021. ÚFAL at MultiLexNorm 2021: Improving multilingual lexical normalization by fine-tuning ByT5. In *Proceedings of the 7th Workshop on Noisy User-generated Text (W-NUT 2021)*, Punta Cana, Dominican Republic. Association for Computational Linguistics.

Manuela Sanguinetti, Cristina Bosco, Alberto Lavelli, Alessandro Mazzei, Oronzo Antonelli, and Fabio Tamburini. 2018. PoSTWITA-UD: an Italian Twitter treebank in Universal Dependencies. In *Proceedings of the Eleventh International Conference on Language Resources and Evaluation (LREC 2018)*, Miyazaki, Japan. European Language Resources Association (ELRA).

Tatjana Scheffler. 2014. A German Twitter snapshot. In *Proceedings of the Ninth International Conference on Language Resources and Evaluation (LREC'14)*, pages 2284–2289, Reykjavik, Iceland. European Language Resources Association (ELRA).

Yves Scherrer and Nikola Ljubešić. 2021. Sesame Street to Mount Sinai: BERT-constrained character-level Moses models for multilingual lexical normalization. In *Proceedings of the 7th Workshop on Noisy User-generated Text (W-NUT 2021)*, Punta Cana, Dominican Republic. Association for Computational Linguistics.

Helmut Schmid. 1994. Part-of-speech tagging with neural networks. In *15th International Conference on Computational Linguistics, COLING 1994, Kyoto, Japan, August 5-9, 1994*, pages 172–176.

Helmut Schmid, Arne Fitschen, and Ulrich Heid. 2004. SMOR: A German computational morphology covering derivation, composition and inflection. In *Proceedings of the Fourth International Conference on Language Resources and Evaluation (LREC'04)*, Lisbon, Portugal. European Language Resources Association (ELRA).

Sarah Schulz, Guy De Pauw, Orphée De Clercq, Bart Desmet, Veronique Hoste, Walter Daelemans, and Lieve Macken. 2016. Multimodular text normalization of dutch user-generated content. *ACM Transactions on Intelligent Systems and Technology (TIST)*, 7(4):1–22.

Youri Schuur. 2020. Normalization for Dutch for improved pos tagging. Master's thesis, University of Groningen.

Uladzimir Sidarenka. 2019. *Sentiment analysis of German Twitter*. Ph.D. thesis, Universität Potsdam.

Uladzimir Sidarenka, Tatjana Scheffler, and Manfred Stede. 2013. Rule-based normalization of German Twitter messages. In *Proc. of the GSCL Workshop Verarbeitung und Annotation von Sprachdaten aus Genres internetbasierter Kommunikation*.

Natalia Silveira, Timothy Dozat, Marie-Catherine de Marneffe, Samuel Bowman, Miriam Connor, John Bauer, and Chris Manning. 2014. A gold standard dependency corpus for English. In *Proceedings of the Ninth International Conference on Language Resources and Evaluation (LREC'14)*, pages 2897–2904, Reykjavik, Iceland. European Language Resources Association (ELRA).

Richard Sproat, Alan W Black, Stanley Chen, Shankar Kumar, Mari Ostendorf, and Christopher Richards. 2001. Normalization of non-standard words. *Computer speech & language*, 15(3):287–333.

Umut Sulubacak and Gülşen Eryiğit. 2018. Implementing universal dependency, morphology, and multiword expression annotation standards for turkish language processing. *Turkish Journal of Electrical Engineering & Computer Sciences*, 26(3):1662–1672.

Umut Sulubacak, Memduh Gokirmak, Francis Tyers, Çağrı Çöltekin, Joakim Nivre, and Gülşen Eryiğit. 2016. Universal Dependencies for Turkish. In *Proceedings of COLING 2016, the 26th International Conference on Computational Linguistics: Technical Papers*, pages 3444–3454, Osaka, Japan. The COLING 2016 Organizing Committee.

Gongbo Tang, Fabienne Cap, Eva Pettersson, and Joakim Nivre. 2018. An evaluation of neural machine translation models on historical spelling normalization. In *Proceedings of the 27th International Conference on Computational Linguistics*, pages 1320–1331, Santa Fe, New Mexico, USA. Association for Computational Linguistics.

Yuqing Tang, Chau Tran, Xian Li, Peng-Jen Chen, Naman Goyal, Vishrav Chaudhary, Jiatao Gu, and Angela Fan. 2020. Multilingual translation with extensible multilingual pretraining and finetuning. *arXiv preprint arXiv:2008.00401*.

Rob van der Goot. 2019a. MoNoise: A multi-lingual and easy-to-use lexical normalization tool. In *Proceedings of the 57th Annual Meeting of the Association for Computational Linguistics: System Demonstrations*, pages 201–206, Florence, Italy. Association for Computational Linguistics.

Rob van der Goot. 2019b. *Normalization and Parsing Algorithms for Uncertain Input*. Ph.D. thesis, University of Groningen.

Rob van der Goot. 2021. CL-MoNoise: Cross-lingual lexical normalization. In *Proceedings of the 7th Workshop on Noisy User-generated Text (W-NUT 2021)*, Punta Cana, Dominican Republic. Association for Computational Linguistics.

Rob van der Goot and Özlem Çetinoğlu. 2021. Lexical normalization for code-switched data and its effect on POS tagging. In *Proceedings of the 16th Conference of the European Chapter of the Association for Computational Linguistics: Main Volume*, pages 2352–2365, Online. Association for Computational Linguistics.

Rob van der Goot, Barbara Plank, and Malvina Nissim. 2017. To normalize, or not to normalize: The impact of normalization on part-of-speech tagging. In *Proceedings of the 3rd Workshop on Noisy User-generated Text*, pages 31–39, Copenhagen, Denmark. Association for Computational Linguistics.

Rob van der Goot, Alan Ramponi, Tommaso Caselli, Michele Cafagna, and Lorenzo De Mattei. 2020. Norm it! lexical normalization for Italian and its downstream effects for dependency parsing. In *Proceedings of the 12th Language Resources and Evaluation Conference*, pages 6272–6278, Marseille, France. European Language Resources Association.

Rob van der Goot, Ahmet Üstün, Alan Ramponi, Ibrahim Sharaf, and Barbara Plank. 2021. Massive choice, ample tasks (MaChAmp): A toolkit for multi-task learning in NLP. In *Proceedings of the 16th Conference of the European Chapter of the Association for Computational Linguistics: System Demonstrations*, pages 176–197, Online. Association for Computational Linguistics.

Rob van der Goot and Gertjan van Noord. 2017. Parser adaptation for social media by integrating normalization. In *Proceedings of the 55th Annual Meeting of the Association for Computational Linguistics (Volume 2: Short Papers)*, pages 491–497, Vancouver, Canada. Association for Computational Linguistics.

Rob van der Goot and Gertjan van Noord. 2018. Modeling input uncertainty in neural network dependency parsing. In *Proceedings of the 2018 Conference on Empirical Methods in Natural Language Processing*, pages 4984–4991, Brussels, Belgium. Association for Computational Linguistics.

Rob van der Goot, Rik van Noord, and Gertjan van Noord. 2018. A taxonomy for in-depth evaluation of normalization for user generated content. In *Proceedings of the Eleventh International Conference on Language Resources and Evaluation (LREC 2018)*, Miyazaki, Japan. European Language Resources Association (ELRA).

Cynthia Van Hee, Marjan Van de Kauter, Orphée De Clercq, Els Lefever, Bart Desmet, and Veronique Hoste. 2017. Noise or music? investigating the usefulness of normalisation for robust sentiment analysis on social media data. *Traitement Automatique Des Langues*, 58(1):63–87.

Ke Xu, Yunqing Xia, and Chin-Hui Lee. 2015. Tweet normalization with syllables. In *Proceedings of the 53rd Annual Meeting of the Association for Computational Linguistics and the 7th International Joint Conference on Natural Language Processing (Volume 1: Long Papers)*, pages 920–928, Beijing, China. Association for Computational Linguistics.

Linting Xue, Aditya Barua, Noah Constant, Rami Al-Rfou, Sharan Narang, Mihir Kale, Adam Roberts, and Colin Raffel. 2021. Byt5: Towards a token-free future with pre-trained byte-to-byte models. *arXiv preprint arXiv:2105.13626*.

Yi Yang and Jacob Eisenstein. 2013. A log-linear model for unsupervised text normalization. In *Proceedings of the 2013 Conference on Empirical Methods in Natural Language Processing*, pages 61–72, Seattle, Washington, USA. Association for Computational Linguistics.

Katja Zupan, Nikola Ljubešić, and Tomaž Erjavec. 2019. How to tag non-standard language: Normalisation versus domain adaptation for slovene historical and user-generated texts. *Natural Language Engineering*, 25(5):651–674.

A MULTILEXNORM Data Statement

Following Bender and Friedman (2018), we present statements for MULTILEXNORM data.

A. CURATION RATIONALE

- **Danish**: We collected data from Twitter by querying the Twitter API using the following emotion-related keywords: *frygt, glæd, kærlighed, overraskelse, racistisk, sjov, smerte, tristhed.* Tweets were collected in 2019–2020. We also scraped all Arto pages from the Internet Wayback machine (archive.org), and extracted the user-generated content from the HTML with a script. We then applied filtering on the combination of this data, leaving only sentences which were classified as Danish with a confidence of at least 0.885 by the FastText language classifier (Joulin et al., 2017b) and contain at least 3 words in the Danish Aspell dictionary (which are not in the English dictionary), and contain at least 2 words not in the Danish Aspell dictionary.

- **German**: To create this corpus, we randomly sampled 10,000 messages from the German Twitter Snapshot (GTS; Scheffler, 2014)—a collection of 24 million tweets, which were gathered in April 2013 by permanently tracking a list of 397 frequent German words via the Twitter Streaming API and subsequently filtered with `langid.py` (Lui and Baldwin, 2012). We analyzed all tokens of the sample with `TreeTagger` (Schmid, 1994) and `hunspell`. Afterwards, two human experts annotated all words that any of these tools considered as out-of-vocabulary (OOV) and that appeared at least twice in the selected microblogs or belonged to a set of 1,000 randomly-chosen hapax legomena. Finally, we only left tweets that contained words annotated as *spelling deviation* by either of the experts, resulting in a total of 1,492 messages.

- **English**: Tweets were collected using the Twitter Streaming API over the period 23–29 May, 2014, and then filtered by `langid.py` (Lui and Baldwin, 2012) to remove non-English tweets. To ensure that tweets had a high likelihood of requiring lexical normalization, tweets with less than 2 non-standard words (i.e. words not occurring in the SCOWL dictionary) were filtered out.

- **Spanish**: To maximize the chances of getting tweets in the Spanish language, tweets were collected through Twitter's streaming API by restricting the search to a geographical bounding box within Spain but excluding bilingual regions. The selected geographic area forms a rectangle with Guadalajara (coordinates: 41, -2) as the northeasternmost point and Cadiz (coordinates: 36.5, -6) as the southwesternmost point. The resulting collection with over 227K tweets was filtered to keep only tweets identified by Twitter as having been written in Spanish (i.e. 'lang' field set to 'es'), and further sampling was done to make it manageable for manual labeling.

- **Croatian**: The dataset is a subset of the large Croatian Twitter crawl harvested with TweetCat (Ljubešić et al., 2014) between 2013 and 2016. It contains a similar amount of standard and non-standard data, and non-standard data was oversampled from the original data collection. The standardness level of the data was predicted via feature-based machine learning (Ljubešić et al., 2015). Discrimination between Croatian and Serbian tweets was performed with a dedicated supervised classifier (Ljubešić and Kranjčić, 2015).

- **Indonesian-English**: Barik et al. (2019) collected Indonesian-English code-mixed tweets using the Twitter search API. First, they compiled a list of Indonesian and English stopwords (100 for each language), based on frequent word lists from Wiktionary.[8] The stopwords were then used as search queries. In order to obtain code-mixed tweets, the "language" parameter in the search query was set to be constrastive to the language of the stopword used. For example, the "language" parameter is set to English when an Indonesian stopword is used as a query, and vice versa. To minimize chance that tweets contain any word from local indigenous or other languages, the "location" parameter in the search query is restricted to only Jakarta and Bandung (the two largest cities in Indonesia). In total, 49,647 tweets were collected. Two human annotators

[8] `https://en.wiktionary.org/wiki/Wiktionary:Frequencylists`

labeled a sample of 825 tweets from the larger collection. The annotators were instructed to tokenize tweets into a list of word segments, and then provide the lowercase normalized form for each segment. A segment can be a single or multi-token word, untokenized proper name, hyperlink, emoticon, or Twitter special term (i.e., hashtag or mention).

- **Italian**: The dataset is a subset of the data from Sanguinetti et al. (2018) (v. 2.1), which in turn is a subset of SENTIPOLC (Barbieri et al., 2016) and SentiTUT (Bosco et al., 2013). Tweets were mostly collected during the period 2011–2012, and have been filtered based on keywords about politics, in addition to a small subset from the random Twitter API stream. Tweets that contain ≥ 3 out-of-vocabulary words (i.e., not in the Aspell dictionary for Italian, or either a URL, hashtag, username, or text consisting of punctuation-only) were filtered out to ensure a basic density of non-standard language for further annotation. Moreover, a small list of proper nouns was added to the vocabulary, taken from the most frequent out-of-vocabulary words in the dataset.

- **Dutch**: We took the data from the SoNaR Nieuwe Media Corpus (Oostdijk et al., 2014) as a starting point, and selected sentences which contain at least 3 words which are not in the Aspell dictionary for Dutch. We originally took 500 sentences from each sub-domain (SMS, chats, and tweets), and then removed all sentences which were completely written in another language (i.e., Frisian, Afrikaans, English, or Spanish).

- **Slovenian**: The dataset is a subset of a large Slovenian Twitter crawl harvested with TweetCat (Ljubešić et al., 2014) between 2013 and 2016. It contains a similar amount of standard and non-standard data, and non-standard data was oversampled from the original data collection. The standardness level of the data was predicted via feature-based machine learning (Ljubešić et al., 2015).

- **Serbian**: The dataset is a subset of a large Serbian Twitter crawl harvested with TweetCat (Ljubešić et al., 2014) between 2013 and 2016. It contains a similar amount of standard and non-standard data, and non-standard data was oversampled from the original data collection. The standardness level of the data was predicted via feature-based machine learning (Ljubešić et al., 2015). Discrimination between Croatian and Serbian tweets was performed with a dedicated supervised classifier (Ljubešić and Kranjčić, 2015).

- **Turkish-German**: The code-switched dataset is derived by filtering tweets labeled as Turkish and German according to Twitter's language ID assignment. Turkish tweets were collected in 2015 and German tweets during 2009–2011. To identify mixed German–Turkish tweets, we mainly used morphological analyzers (Oflazer, 1994; Schmid et al., 2004) as filters. Manual filtering followed the automatic filtering, resulting in the final dataset. The raw tweets were manually tokenized, normalized and segmented (Çetinoğlu, 2016). In addition, usernames and URLs were anonymized as @username and [url], respectively, and language IDs for each token were added. Adapting the dataset to the normalization task was performed in van der Goot and Çetinoğlu (2021).

B. LANGUAGE VARIETY All of the datasets consist of social media variants of the standard languages, and are not bound by a regional standard (i.e., no distinction is made between `en_us` or `en_gb`).

C. SPEAKER DEMOGRAPHIC The speaker demographics are unknown. For some of the collected data this might have been available, but it is not shared on purpose (for privacy reasons).

D. ANNOTATOR DEMOGRAPHIC

- **Danish**: Two native speakers of Danish. Both were higher-education students (male and female), between the age of 20 and 30.

- **German**: An undergraduate (native German speaker studying computational linguistics), and a PhD student (Belarusian Germanist pursuing a degree in computational linguistics).

- **English**: 12 interns and employees at IBM Research Australia were involved in the data annotation. All annotators had a high level of

Treebank	Avg.	de-tweede	en-aae	en-monoise	en-tweebank2	it-postwita	it-twittiro	tr-iwt151
ÚFAL-2	**74.0** 37	83.2 5	**72.5** 53	**68.4** 33	69.3 66	78.0 13	81.0 5	65.5 90
HEL-LJU-2*	74.0 10	**83.3** 3	71.2 20	67.2 4	**71.1** 15	77.9 3	81.3 0	65.7 28
HEL-LJU-1*	73.9 14	**83.3** 3	70.9 18	67.4 9	71.1 18	78.0 3	**81.3** 0	65.7 48
ÚFAL-2	73.8 37	83.2 3	71.9 50	68.0 33	69.3 65	**78.0** 14	80.8 5	65.5 95
MFR	73.6 16	82.9 5	70.7 32	67.4 15	71.0 37	77.2 3	80.1 0	65.7 25
MoNoise	73.4 21	83.1 5	71.9 40	67.0 18	68.6 46	77.3 3	80.0 0	65.5 35
TrinkaAI-2	73.3 33	82.7 7	70.1 40	67.4 19	70.7 39	77.0 7	80.5 0	65.0 119
TrinkaAI-1	73.3 33	82.7 7	70.1 40	67.4 19	70.7 39	77.0 7	80.5 0	65.0 119
thunderml-2	73.3 33	82.3 3	69.9 42	67.3 28	70.0 44	77.5 4	80.9 1	65.2 112
team-1	73.3 33	82.3 3	69.9 42	67.3 28	70.0 44	77.5 4	80.9 1	65.2 112
maet-1	73.2 27	82.6 3	69.3 40	67.2 24	70.5 44	77.4 10	80.3 0	65.4 74
team-2	73.2 27	82.6 3	69.3 40	67.2 24	70.5 44	77.2 4	80.3 3	65.4 74
thunderml-1	73.1 34	82.4 6	68.9 49	67.3 24	70.6 46	77.0 5	80.7 0	65.0 112
LAI	73.1 0	82.6 0	70.6 0	65.3 0	70.9 0	76.7 0	79.8 0	65.8 0
learnML-2	73.0 30	82.2 8	68.7 44	66.5 31	70.7 45	77.0 6	80.6 0	65.3 79
BLUE-2	73.0 0	82.4 0	70.5 0	65.6 0	70.4 0	76.9 0	79.6 0	65.6 0
BLUE-1	73.0 0	82.4 0	70.5 0	65.6 0	70.4 0	76.9 0	79.6 0	65.6 0
maet-2	72.9 0	82.6 0	69.7 0	65.1 0	70.9 0	76.7 0	79.7 0	65.8 0
learnML-1	72.9 0	82.6 0	69.7 0	65.1 0	70.9 0	76.7 0	79.7 0	65.8 0
CL-MoNoise*	72.8 24	82.5 0	71.8 0	65.5 0	67.9 0	76.6 99	79.8 50	**65.8** 20
MaChAmp*	72.6 43	81.8 7	71.0 37	65.5 43	68.4 52	76.3 2	80.3 0	65.0 162
Gold	—	—	—	69.1	71.2	—	—	—

Table 6: *a*-UAS scores (%) and the number of splits (in smaller font) for each dataset. Gray rows indicate baseline systems provided by the organizers. * Teams including an organizer. The final row ("Gold") indicates performance with gold-standard normalization.

English proficiency (IELTS 6.0+) and were reasonably familiar with Twitter data.

- **Spanish**: Nine native speakers of Spanish. Eight male and one female with ages ranging from 30 to 60. All annotators had a background in natural language processing and were familiar with the Twitter platform.

- **Croatian**: Three native speakers of Croatian, all linguists with an MA degree, trained in data annotation.

- **Indonesian-English**: Two native speakers of Indonesian, fluent in English. Both annotators were 22 years old at the time of the annotation.

- **Italian**: Four native speakers of Italian, all male, between the age of 20 and 38, from a variety of Italian regions (i.e., Veneto, Tuscany, Liguria, and Apulia). All annotators had a background in natural language processing and were familiar with the Twitter platform.

- **Dutch**: The main annotator was a native Dutch Information Science master student (male, age range 20–25). The second annotator (for agreement scores) was a native Dutch male PhD student in NLP, age 27.

- **Slovenian**: Five native speakers of Slovenian, all master-level students of language-related studies.

- **Serbian**: Two native speakers of Serbian, all linguists with an MA degree, trained in data annotation.

- **Turkish-German**: The annotators were three Turkish-German bilinguals born and raised in Germany. They have studied computational linguistics and their age ranged from 20 to 25.

E. SPEECH SITUATION The data is not spoken. However, input methods might have changed over time. A tweet collected from 2012 was less likely to be produced with a spell checker compared to one collected from 2020.

F. TEXT CHARACTERISTICS The genre is not bound topic- or content-wise. However, all inputs are shorter than 280 characters, and most of

Treebank	Avg.	de-tweede	en-monoise	en-tweebank2	it-postwita	it-twittiro	tr-iwt151
ÚFAL-2	**85.5**	**87.6**	**84.1**	80.5	**86.6**	88.7	85.5
ÚFAL-1	85.4	87.5	83.7	80.4	**86.6**	**88.8**	85.5
HEL-LJU-1*	85.1	87.4	81.4	81.6	86.3	88.6	85.6
HEL-LJU-2*	85.1	87.4	81.3	81.6	86.2	88.5	85.6
MoNoise	84.9	87.3	82.2	81.6	85.4	87.3	85.5
thunderml-2	84.9	87.1	82.7	81.2	85.7	87.6	85.1
team-1	84.9	87.1	82.7	81.2	85.7	87.6	85.1
team-2	84.8	87.1	82.2	81.3	85.5	87.7	85.3
MFR	84.8	87.1	82.1	**81.7**	85.3	87.2	85.6
maet-1	84.8	87.1	82.2	81.3	85.5	87.5	85.3
learnML-2	84.8	87.1	82.2	81.5	85.2	87.5	85.3
TrinkaAI-2	84.7	87.2	82.0	81.4	85.4	87.3	85.1
TrinkaAI-1	84.7	87.2	82.0	81.4	85.4	87.3	85.1
thunderml-1	84.7	86.9	82.2	81.4	85.5	87.5	85.0
CL-MoNoise*	84.2	86.9	80.1	81.5	84.4	86.6	85.6
BLUE-2	84.2	87.0	79.8	81.5	84.4	86.8	85.6
BLUE-1	84.2	87.0	79.8	81.5	84.4	86.8	85.6
LAI	84.0	87.1	78.8	81.4	84.3	86.5	**85.7**
maet-2	83.9	87.1	78.7	81.4	84.3	86.5	**85.7**
learnML-1	83.9	87.1	78.7	81.4	84.3	86.5	**85.7**
MaChAmp*	82.0	84.6	80.2	80.8	80.0	83.0	83.8
Gold	—	—	85.5	81.6	—	—	—

Table 7: *a*-POS accuracy (%) for each dataset. Gray rows indicate baseline systems provided by the organizers. * Teams including an organizer. The final row ("Gold") indicates performance with gold-standard normalization.

them shorter than 140 characters (Twitter increased the maximum tweet length in September 2017).

I. PROVENANCE APPENDIX The data is released under a CC-BY-SA license.

B *a*-UAS Scores

We report *a*-UAS scores in Table 6.

C *a*-POS Accuracies

We report *a*-POS accuracy values in Table 7. Note that the en-aae treebank is not included here because it has no POS annotation.

CL-MoNoise: Cross-lingual Lexical Normalization

Rob van der Goot
IT University
robv@itu.dk

Abstract

Social media is notoriously difficult to process for existing natural language processing tools, because of spelling errors, non-standard words, shortenings, non-standard capitalization and punctuation. One method to circumvent these issues is to normalize input data before processing. Most previous work has focused on only one language, which is mostly English. In this paper, we are the first to propose a model for cross-lingual normalization, with which we participate in the WNUT 2021 shared task. To this end, we use MoNoise as a starting point, and make a simple adaptation for cross-lingual application. Our proposed model outperforms the leave-as-is baseline provided by the organizers which copies the input. Furthermore, we explore a completely different model which converts the task to a sequence labeling task. Performance of this second system is low, as it does not take capitalization into account in our implementation. [1]

1 Introduction

Lexical normalization is the task of converting non-canonical text to its canonical equivalent on the word level. As common for Natural Language Processing (NLP) tasks, most of the previous work is done on English data (Han and Baldwin, 2011; Baldwin et al., 2015). However, for lexical normalization there have also been many attempts for other language-(pair)s (Plank et al., 2020; Sidarenka et al., 2013; Alegria et al., 2013; Ljubešić et al., 2017a; Barik et al., 2019; van der Goot et al., 2020; Schuur, 2020; Erjavec et al., 2017; Ljubešić et al., 2017b; Çolakoğlu et al., 2019; van der Goot and Çetinoğlu, 2021), which have been combined into one benchmark for the WNUT 2021 shared task (van der Goot et al., 2021a). Even though data has been available for multiple languages, most work focused on one language, and to the best of our knowledge no one has attempted to solve this task cross-lingually. If successful, a cross-lingual lexical normalization model would open up possibilities for lexical normalization for languages in which no training data is available. In this work, we use the MoNoise model (van der Goot, 2019a) as a starting point, the only normalization model that is open source and has models available for the languages we target. Furthermore, it is heavily dependent on raw data to generate candidates and features, which makes it relatively easy to adapt it for a cross-lingual setup (Section 2). We refer to our new model CL-MoNoise.

In addition to our cross-lingual model, we also evaluate an out-of-the-box sequence labeler, we use the string2string task-type of MaChAmp (van der Goot et al., 2021b), which was originally created for the purpose of lemmatization.

2 Method

2.1 CL-MoNoise

MoNoise is a two-step modular normalization model. It first generates potential normalization candidates, and then ranks these in a second step. For both of these steps a variety of modules are used, and all modules used for generation are also used to generate features for the ranking. The most important candidate generation modules are: the Aspell spell checker[2], closest word in a Twitter word2vec (Mikolov et al., 2013) embedding space, and a lookup list based on the training data. Features from these modules are then complemented by n-gram probabilities based on Wikipedia and Twitter data, Aspell dictionary presence and some language agnostic features, like punctuation detection and length of the candidate (number of characters). For more details on MoNoise, we refer to (van der Goot, 2019a). To retrain MoNoise, new raw data was collected to base its n-gram proba-

[1] https://bitbucket.org/robvanderg/cl-monoise/

[2] www.aspell.net

Proceedings of the 2021 EMNLP Workshop W-NUT: The Seventh Workshop on Noisy User-generated Text, pages 510–514
November 11, 2021.

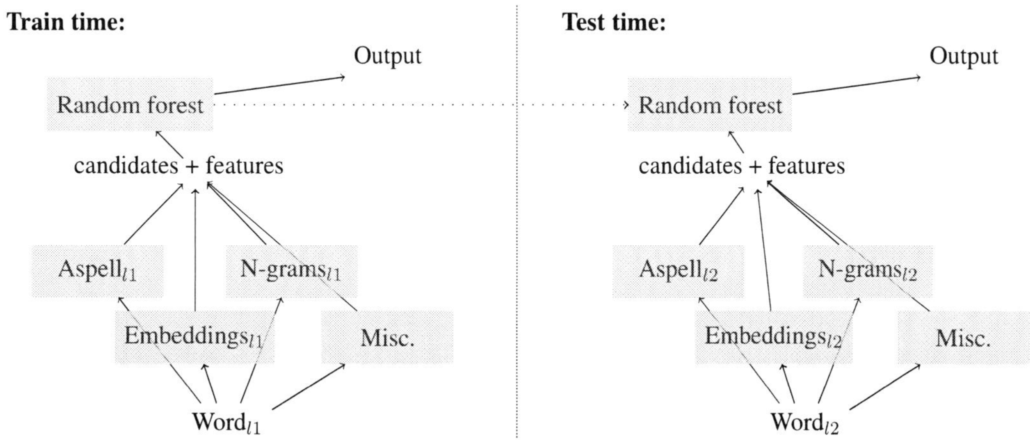

Figure 1: A diagram of our proposed setup to use MoNoise in a cross-lingual setup with source language $l1$ and target language $l2$. All boxes are parts of the model. It should be noted that "Aspell", "N-grams" and "Embeddings" are swapped during test time with target language versions, and the random forest classifier from train time is used. "Misc" here represents all remaining features of MoNoise that can be considered language-agnostic.

bilities and word embeddings on. We downloaded Twitter data of 2012–2020 from archive.org, filtered it with the fasttext language classifier (?), and used the most recent Wikidump for each language.[3] This is the exact same data as used by the MoNoise submission provided by the organizers of the shared task (van der Goot et al., 2021a).

We train MoNoise models for each of the source languages, and evaluate them on all the training sets of the other languages to pick the optimal source language for each target language. MoNoise is a supervised model, but many of its features are comprised from language-specific unsupervised components: Aspell spell checker, word embeddings, and n-gram probabilities. We adapt to the new languages by replacing these language-specific modules at run-time. In other words, we train a model on language A, with Aspell, word embeddings and n-gram probabilities based on language A, then we employ this trained model on language B, and use Aspell, word embeddings and n-gram probabilities of language B. This proposed models is No adaptations of the code of MoNoise were necessary, as the data directory is simply a parameter.

We are aware that this setup constitutes an unrealistic setting, as the cross-lingual setup is not pure (annotated data is used to decide which source model to pick). Alternatives could include automatic selection of models based on the input, or to simply use language distances (for example from lang2vec (Littell et al., 2017)). However, we consider this work to be an exploratory analysis, and attempt to validate whether this (cross-lingual) direction is feasible; we leave other strategies for model selection for future work.

We use the Aspell *badspellers* option when it performs better in-language (for all datasets, except SR, ID-EN, SL). For the language pairs (ID-EN, TR-DE), we use the code-switched version of MoNoise (van der Goot and Çetinoğlu, 2021), more specifically the `multi-lingual` model, because we do not assume language labels to be available.

2.2 MaChAmp

As an alternative model, we evaluate the string2string task type of MaChAmp (van der Goot et al., 2021b). This task type uses the Wagner-Fischer algorithm (Wagner and Fischer, 1974) implementation from UDPipe Future (Straka, 2018). This algorithm finds a character edit operation to transform the original word into its normalized form. The training procedure then becomes a sequence labeling problem, where for each word its correct transformation is being predicted. At run-time, the predicted transformation is applied to the original word to obtain the final normalization.

One main weakness of this approach is that it

[3] Of 01-08-2021. Available: `https://robvanderg.github.io/blog/twit_embeds.htm`

Target	Source											
	DA	DE	EN	ES	HR	ID-EN	IT	NL	SL	SR	TR	TR-DE
DA	–	2.30	-0.99	-0.59	6.51	-39.71	3.09	-6.38	**8.35**	3.02	-5.06	-0.99
DE	1.01	–	2.44	1.67	0.66	-9.27	10.36	-0.97	-3.96	6.91	12.14	**15.32**
EN	-39.31	1.20	–	-9.34	-45.57	-11.97	**2.74**	-39.38	-41.75	-27.91	-61.85	-50.60
ES	-33.27	-2.53	4.16	–	-32.73	-172.30	**5.06**	-48.82	-67.99	-54.25	-104.90	-19.89
HR	-3.45	-7.03	-3.50	-31.51	–	-106.90	-2.35	-40.34	4.20	**28.54**	-43.25	-36.75
ID-EN	-9.20	5.60	6.91	5.69	-8.47	–	0.54	5.79	-15.82	1.36	**11.68**	7.40
IT	-10.26	-1.62	**2.05**	-5.40	-27.86	-51.84	–	-19.01	-17.93	-20.73	-37.90	-8.53
NL	6.43	17.78	11.03	2.53	6.59	-2.80	15.17	–	8.25	12.64	**19.42**	17.02
SL	1.54	0.90	2.47	-16.90	5.53	-55.32	1.78	-7.93	–	**6.65**	-15.06	-8.71
SR	-2.72	3.26	-4.35	-30.27	**14.77**	-87.43	-0.38	-58.34	-5.88	–	-32.92	-15.81
TR	0.67	9.64	1.22	0.25	4.82	-0.80	5.37	6.25	-2.10	6.00	–	**21.43**
TR-DE	-1.30	8.24	1.91	1.04	-1.88	-2.04	4.05	2.95	-7.01	1.04	**16.54**	–

Table 1: Cross-lingual performance of MoNoise on training splits (ERR).

lowercases all text first, and then tries to predict conversion to capitals where necessary. While this makes sense for lemmatization (its original use-case), this removal of information is probably sub-optimal for lexical normalization, as capitals are often kept.

3 Evaluation

3.1 Development Phase

For the CL-MoNoise model, we tune the source language separately for each dataset. Results are shown in Table 1, most best source languages can be explained by language relatedness, but in some cases the best source languages is surprising; Slovenian scores best for Danish, Turkish is best for Indonesian-English, and Turkish is best for Dutch. We inspected the correct replacements, and found to our surprise that they were not words that exists in both languages, nor were they only some very frequent words. Instead, the word embeddings and Aspell features seemed to have generalized well in spite of the language variety.

For MaChAmp, we use all default hyperparameters, and compare the difference in performance between MBERT (Devlin et al., 2019) and XLM-R (Conneau et al., 2020), which have both been pre-trained on all the languages targeted in MultiLexNorm. Table 2 shows that XLM-R outperforms MBERT for all languages. Furthermore, it becomes clear that capitals are a main weakness of MaChAmp; the uncased scores for DE and NL, which were the only development datasets with capitalization correction in the annotation are much higher. This is because capitalization was not taken into account in the conversion algorithm of MaChAmp, probably because it was focused towards lemmatization, and lemmas are commonly lowercased.

Dataset	cased		uncased	
	MBERT	XLM-R	MBERT	XLM-R
DE	-90.49	-87.40	30.45	36.94
EN	43.44	48.03	43.44	48.03
HR	34.64	41.83	34.64	41.83
ID-EN	33.68	39.66	33.68	39.66
NL	-25.53	-21.50	17.40	22.45
SL	50.86	57.21	50.86	57.21
SR	35.78	42.76	35.78	42.76

Table 2: Results on all development sets of MultiLexNorm for MaChAmp when using XLM-R or MBERT. Numbers are ERR, with and without taking capitalization into account.

3.2 Test Phase

Results of our two models and all models provided by the organizers are shown in Table 3. MFR is the Most-Frequent-Replacement baseline, which uses the most frequent replacement as found in the target language training data for each token. LAI is the Leave-As-Is baseline, which simply copies over each input word, and thus by definition scores an Error Reduction Rate (van der Goot, 2019b) of 0.0. The results show that results of MaChAmp are dissapointing; even for the languages with no capitalization normalizations it only in the same range as the most frequent baseline (MFR). On the

Model	Avg.	DA	DE	EN	ES	HR	ID-EN	IT	NL	SL	SR	TR	TR-DE
MoNoise	49.02	51.27	46.96	74.35	45.53	52.63	59.79	21.78	49.53	61.91	59.58	28.21	36.72
MFR	38.37	49.68	32.09	64.93	25.57	36.52	61.17	16.83	37.70	56.71	42.62	14.53	22.09
CL-MoNoise	12.05	7.28	16.55	4.13	4.99	26.41	2.41	0.00	16.22	8.77	20.09	17.57	20.16
LAI	0.00	0.00	0.00	0.00	0.00	0.00	0.00	0.00	0.00	0.00	0.00	0.00	0.00
MaChAmp	-21.25	-88.92	-93.36	50.99	25.36	42.62	39.52	-312.87	1.49	56.80	39.44	-12.67	-3.42
Best source lang.		SL	TR-DE	IT	IT	SR	TR	EN	TR	SR	HR	TR-DE	TR

Table 3: Results of the models provided by the organizers (grey) and our proposed models. The source language used for CL-MoNoise is shown in the last row.

first sight, this seems also true for CL-MoNoise, but we should take into account that MFR was trained on in-language training data, whereas CL-MoNoise was not. CL-MoNoise is indeed the best performing system not trained on in-language data, as LAI is the only competitor there; also all other participants in the shared task used in-language training data (van der Goot et al., 2021a). The worst scores for both MaChAmp and CL-MoNoise are on the Italian dataset, which is probably because there are quite some language specific constructions that are normalized (van der Goot et al., 2020), and for MaChAmp it matters that capitalization is corrected. Performance on German, Turkish and the code-switch Turkish-German is relatively high, because they all have highly relevant source languages. For Indonesian-English, performance dropped a lot compared to scores on the development set (Table 1), and it might have been safer to use English as a source language instead of Turkish.

4 Conclusions

In this paper we proposed two models for lexical normalization. 1) CL-MoNoise: based on the original MoNoise; trained with source language raw data and source language annotated normalization data, which is then replaced with target language raw data during run-time. We tuned the source-target language combinations, and found that there are some surprising combinations (SL to DA, TR to ID-EN, TR to NL). Overall results outperform the language-agnostic baseline (LAI), but are outperformed by the most-frequent replacement baseline which is trained on in-language data. 2) MaChAmp: uses a conversion script to turn the task into a sequence labeling task. Performance is especially low for languages that include annotation for capitalization corrections, as this was not taken into account in the MaChAmp implementation. Potential improvements could be made for the MaChAmp system by exploiting its multi-task capabilities, or training a multi-lingual model.

Appendix

I would like to thank the anonymous reviewers for their insightful comments.

References

Inaki Alegria, Nora Aranberri, Víctor Fresno, Pablo Gamallo, Lluis Padró, Inaki San Vicente, Jordi Turmo, and Arkaitz Zubiaga. 2013. Introducción a la tarea compartida Tweet-Norm 2013: Normalización léxica de tuits en Español. In *Tweet-Norm@ SEPLN*, pages 1–9.

Timothy Baldwin, Marie Catherine de Marneffe, Bo Han, Young-Bum Kim, Alan Ritter, and Wei Xu. 2015. Shared tasks of the 2015 workshop on noisy user-generated text: Twitter lexical normalization and named entity recognition. In *Proceedings of the Workshop on Noisy User-generated Text*, pages 126–135, Beijing, China. Association for Computational Linguistics.

Anab Maulana Barik, Rahmad Mahendra, and Mirna Adriani. 2019. Normalization of Indonesian-English code-mixed Twitter data. In *Proceedings of the 5th Workshop on Noisy User-generated Text (W-NUT 2019)*, pages 417–424, Hong Kong, China. Association for Computational Linguistics.

Talha Çolakoğlu, Umut Sulubacak, and Ahmet Cüneyd Tantuğ. 2019. Normalizing non-canonical Turkish texts using machine translation approaches. In *Proceedings of the 57th Annual Meeting of the Association for Computational Linguistics: Student Research Workshop*, pages 267–272, Florence, Italy. Association for Computational Linguistics.

Alexis Conneau, Kartikay Khandelwal, Naman Goyal, Vishrav Chaudhary, Guillaume Wenzek, Francisco Guzmán, Edouard Grave, Myle Ott, Luke Zettlemoyer, and Veselin Stoyanov. 2020. Unsupervised cross-lingual representation learning at scale. In

Proceedings of the 58th Annual Meeting of the Association for Computational Linguistics, pages 8440–8451, Online. Association for Computational Linguistics.

Jacob Devlin, Ming-Wei Chang, Kenton Lee, and Kristina Toutanova. 2019. BERT: Pre-training of deep bidirectional transformers for language understanding. In *Proceedings of the 2019 Conference of the North American Chapter of the Association for Computational Linguistics: Human Language Technologies, Volume 1 (Long and Short Papers)*, pages 4171–4186, Minneapolis, Minnesota. Association for Computational Linguistics.

Tomaž Erjavec, Darja Fišer, Jaka Čibej, Špela Arhar Holdt, Nikola Ljubešić, and Katja Zupan. 2017. CMC training corpus Janes-Tag 2.0. Slovenian language resource repository CLARIN.SI.

Bo Han and Timothy Baldwin. 2011. Lexical normalisation of short text messages: Makn sens a #twitter. In *Proceedings of the 49th Annual Meeting of the Association for Computational Linguistics: Human Language Technologies*, pages 368–378, Portland, Oregon, USA. Association for Computational Linguistics.

Patrick Littell, David R. Mortensen, Ke Lin, Katherine Kairis, Carlisle Turner, and Lori Levin. 2017. URIEL and lang2vec: Representing languages as typological, geographical, and phylogenetic vectors. In *Proceedings of the 15th Conference of the European Chapter of the Association for Computational Linguistics: Volume 2, Short Papers*, pages 8–14, Valencia, Spain. Association for Computational Linguistics.

Nikola Ljubešić, Tomaž Erjavec, Maja Miličević, and Tanja Samardžić. 2017a. Croatian Twitter training corpus ReLDI-NormTagNER-hr 2.0. Slovenian language resource repository CLARIN.SI.

Nikola Ljubešić, Tomaž Erjavec, Maja Miličević, and Tanja Samardžić. 2017b. Serbian Twitter training corpus ReLDI-NormTagNER-sr 2.0. Slovenian language resource repository CLARIN.SI.

Tomas Mikolov, Kai Chen, Greg Corrado, and Jeffrey Dean. 2013. Efficient estimation of word representations in vector space. *Proceedings of Workshop at ICLR*.

Barbara Plank, Kristian Nørgaard Jensen, and Rob van der Goot. 2020. DaN+: Danish nested named entities and lexical normalization. In *Proceedings of the 28th International Conference on Computational Linguistics*, pages 6649–6662, Barcelona, Spain (Online). International Committee on Computational Linguistics.

Youri Schuur. 2020. Normalization for Dutch for improved pos tagging. Master's thesis, University of Groningen.

Uladzimir Sidarenka, Tatjana Scheffler, and Manfred Stede. 2013. Rule-based normalization of German Twitter messages. In *Proc. of the GSCL Workshop Verarbeitung und Annotation von Sprachdaten aus Genres internetbasierter Kommunikation*.

Milan Straka. 2018. UDPipe 2.0 prototype at CoNLL 2018 UD shared task. In *Proceedings of the CoNLL 2018 Shared Task: Multilingual Parsing from Raw Text to Universal Dependencies*, pages 197–207, Brussels, Belgium. Association for Computational Linguistics.

Rob van der Goot. 2019a. MoNoise: A multi-lingual and easy-to-use lexical normalization tool. In *Proceedings of the 57th Annual Meeting of the Association for Computational Linguistics: System Demonstrations*, pages 201–206, Florence, Italy. Association for Computational Linguistics.

Rob van der Goot. 2019b. *Normalization and Parsing Algorithms for Uncertain Input*. Ph.D. thesis, University of Groningen.

Rob van der Goot and Özlem Çetinoğlu. 2021. Lexical normalization for code-switched data and its effect on POS tagging. In *Proceedings of the 16th Conference of the European Chapter of the Association for Computational Linguistics: Volume 1, Long Papers*. Association for Computational Linguistics.

Rob van der Goot, Alan Ramponi, Tommaso Caselli, Michele Cafagna, and Lorenzo De Mattei. 2020. Norm it! lexical normalization for Italian and its downstream effects for dependency parsing. In *Proceedings of the 12th Language Resources and Evaluation Conference*, pages 6272–6278, Marseille, France. European Language Resources Association.

Rob van der Goot, Alan Ramponi, Arkaitz Zubiaga, Barbara Plank, Benjamin Muller, Iñaki San Vicente Roncal, Nikola Ljubešić, Özlem Çetinoğlu, Rahmad Mahendra, Talha Çolakoğlu, Timothy Baldwin, Tommaso Caselli, and Wladimir Sidorenko. 2021a. MultiLexNorm: A shared task on multilingual lexical normalization. In *Proceedings of the 7th Workshop on Noisy User-generated Text (W-NUT 2021)*, Punta Cana, Dominican Republic. Association for Computational Linguistics.

Rob van der Goot, Ahmet Üstün, Alan Ramponi, Ibrahim Sharaf, and Barbara Plank. 2021b. Massive choice, ample tasks (MaChAmp): A toolkit for multi-task learning in NLP. In *Proceedings of the 16th Conference of the European Chapter of the Association for Computational Linguistics: System Demonstrations*, pages 176–197, Online. Association for Computational Linguistics.

Robert A Wagner and Michael J Fischer. 1974. The string-to-string correction problem. *Journal of the ACM (JACM)*, 21(1):168–173.

Association for Computational Linguistics
209 N. Eighth Street
Stroudsburg, Pennsylvania 18360

ISBN 978-1-7138-9166-6

CURRAN ASSOCIATES INC.
proceedings.com